Welcome

Thanks for opening this book! If you wish, it will change your life by turning you into a computer expert quickly. If you've been an expert already, it will turn you into a *better* expert. It's the only book that explains all important computer topics well.

Here's the only reason why this book is good: I've been foolish enough to spend 27 years improving it! This 27th edition is a major improvement over the 26th; it contains the changes readers worldwide requested.

This book gives you what you want.

> Unlike a "Dummies" book (which is written for dummies and keeps them dumb) and a "standard textbook" (which is shoved at overworked college students and makes them snore louder), this book throws you into the action fast, makes you competent, and then makes you wise. It explains how to buy a computer, then how to use it (covering all popular operating systems and application programs), then how to reprogram it to change its soul, then how to launch your career.

Every major computer magazine has praised this book for being "the best". It's not perfect, but it's better than any other.

> If you're a computer expert already, you might notice a few sentences that have become outdated. I apologize. Documenting the entire computer industry is as tough as catching a greased pig: whenever I think I've finally caught the truth, the computer industry bolts ahead into a strange new direction. That's why this project never ends: finishing this edition means it's time to start writing the next, and then the next, in endless frustration! If you have suggestions for the next edition, please tell me.

I wish this book didn't have to exist.

> I wish computer companies would create pleasant hardware and software, accompanied by pleasant manuals. Until that happens, scribes like me are doomed to spending our lives explaining the computer industry's mistakes.

Phone me

This is the only available book whose author is foolish enough to give you his home phone number: it's **603-666-6644**. It's easy to memorize: after dialing New Hampshire's area code (603), **press the six key several times (66666) then 44**. Call whenever you have a question about computers — or life! I'll help you, free, even if your question is weird or personal.

This free consulting service has saved readers many kilohours and kilobucks. Readers have smuggled copies of this book worldwide, so each month I get phone calls from all over the world, as *thousands* of new budding gurus phone me for help.

Call day or night, 24 hours: I'm usually in, and I sleep just lightly.

Let's get started!

> Welcome to your new computer. I'll be your computer tutor.
> Hands on keyboard! Eyes up front! Press those keys! Do not grunt!
> When you get a bit confused, snatch this book and come peruse.
> If you want to learn some more, call 666-6644.

This book's become too huge to read over the phone. If you ask me a question answered in the book, I'll tell you which pages reveal the answer. After you've read, phone me with any further questions.

> For advice about which computer to buy, read the *newest* edition of the book, then phone me. For help curing an ill computer, call me when *your phone is next to the computer*. For help running a program, phone me when you're at the computer and *have the program's official manual*.
> To handle hundreds of calls per day while I'm in the middle of managing my staff and creating new editions, I try to keep the average call to 7 minutes. **Begin by saying your name, city, how you got my number ("from the 27th edition"), and a one-sentence summary of your question.** Then we'll chat — unless I'm in the middle of another call or meeting, in which case I'll call you back, free!

Come visit

Whenever you visit New Hampshire, you can drop in and use my free computer library. Drop in anytime: day or night! But **in case I'm having an orgy with my 30 computers, please phone first** to pick a time when we're cooled down.

> I'm in New Hampshire and also cyberspace, where you can visit my secret fun site (**secretfun.com**) and torture me with e-mail to **russ@secretfun.com**.

Mail the coupon

Mail us the coupon on this book's last page. It puts you on our mailing list, which gets you FREE info on our many wild services. You also get discounts on extra copies of this book.

Love your librarian

These details will help your librarian fill in the file cards and not get fired.

Title:	The Secret Guide to Computers, 27th edition for 2001
So-called author:	Russ Walter (also known as "Russy-poo")
Publisher:	the same servant as the author
Physical address:	bedroom at 196 Tiffany Lane, Manchester NH 03104-4782
Mental address:	www.secretfun.com or get personal with russ@secretfun.com
Copywrong:	end of 2000 (October) by Russ Walter
International Standard Book Number (ISBN):	0-939151-27-8
Library of Congress:	pending; earlier edition was 89-51851, QA 76 .W3

Elfish fun

I wrote this book myself, but over the years I've been helped by many elves and associated critters.

Sorcerer's apprentices:	Len Pallazola	Kira Barnum	Maura Cabral
Friendly ghosts:	Yvonne Bohemier	Linda Gardner	Cathy Carlson
Meadow sprites:	Irene Vassos	Richard Grant	
Wandering minstrels:	Larry Mancini	Jeff Lowe	
Singing Chinese Madonnas:	Donna Walter	Donna Liao	
Artistes bizarre:	Cindy Best	Susan Goldenberg	
Bubbly brights:	Anthony Kind	Nancy Kafka	
Babbling Brooklines:	Lisbeth Shaw	Michael Krigsman	
Gigantic alien brains:	Roy Krantz	Adam Green	
Wonder women:	Ruth Spingarn	Lili Timmons	
Queens of bygone days:	Priscilla Grogan	Julianne Wattles	
Brothers grin:	Dan Walter	Jim Walter	
Printer devils:	John Pow	Banta	
Art collectors:	Dover	Formatt	
Gnome (and is an island unto himself):	Russy-poo		

Introductory junk

My editor told me to put this stuff in. You don't have to read it.

Dedication I dedicate this book to the computer, without whom I'd be unemployed.

What this book will do for you It'll make you even richer than the author! Alas, he's broke.

Prerequisite This book was written for idiots. To see whether you can get through the math, take this test: count to ten but (here's the catch!) without looking at your fingers.

Acknowledgment I'd like to thank:

> my many friends (whose names I've gladly forgotten)
> my students (who naturally aren't my friends)
> my word processor (which has a mind of its own)
> all others who helped make this book impossible

Apology Any original ideas in this book are errors.

Disclaimer The author denies any knowledge of the scintillating illegal activities he depicts.

Copyright Our copyright policy is simple: hey, copying is all right! Make as many copies as you like, and don't pay us a cent. Just follow the "free reprint" instructions on page 9.

Forward …because it's too late to turn back.

What's in this book

The Secret Guide to Computers is the world's only *complete* computer tutorial. It covers *everything* important about computers! It explains how to **buy**, **operate**, **apply**, and **program** computers.

Feast your eyes on the massive table of contents, splashed across the next page. It's divided into five columns:

> The first column, "Buyer's guide", covers how to **buy** a computer.
>
> The second column covers how to **operate** a computer (by using "Operating systems" and "Word processing").
>
> The third column cover how to **apply** a computer (by using "Communication" and "Tricky applications").
>
> The fourth column, "Programming", covers how to **program** a computer (to make that mean machine do whatever you wish).
>
> The last column, "Endnotes", reveals secrets I was afraid to tell earlier.

Let's look more closely....

Buyer's guide

The Guide begins by explaining computer technology, computer jargon, and how to buy a great computer cheaply.

It analyzes each of the computer's parts (the **chips**, **disks**, **screens**, **printers**, **other hardware**, and **software**) and tells you the best way to buy a complete computer system. It explains how to buy the most common kind of computers (**IBM-compatibles**), the fascinating competitors from **Apple**, and **alternative computers** that are wildly different.

The Guide makes specific recommendations about which brands to buy and where to buy them. It delves into each manufacturer's goodies and not-so-goodies. It reveals the nasty details that salespeople try to hide. It turns you into a German nun, who knows the difference between what's blessed and what's wurst.

Operating systems

After getting a computer, you operate it by typing commands on its keyboard or wiggling its mouse. The Guide explains the popular operating systems: **Windows 95, 98, & Me** (used for most new computers), **Windows 3.1 & 3.11** (for older computers), **MS-DOS** (for all IBM-compatible computers), and the **Mac system** (for the Apple Macintosh).

Word processing

The most popular thing to do with a computer is to make it replace your typewriter. That's called "word processing". The word-processing chapter explains how to use the best word-processing programs: **Microsoft Word** (which performs the fanciest tricks and is the standard for most businesses), **Microsoft Works** (which is easier to learn and costs less), **WordPerfect** (similar to Microsoft Word but costs less, causes fewer hassles, and is especially popular in law firms), and **Q&A Write** (which is so simple that it doesn't even require you to learn Windows).

Communication

Computers form their own society: they chat with computers in other rooms, other cities, and other countries! The most popular way to let your computer chat with far-away computers is to use a worldwide network called "the **Internet**." The Guide demystifies that (so you become an "Internut"), then reveals how to make your computer send a **fax** and chat with nearby computers that form **local-area networks**.

Tricky applications

The Guide explores even the trickiest applications. You learn how to handle **spreadsheets** (tables of numbers) by using Excel, Quattro Pro, and Works; **databases** (computerized file cards) by using Microsoft Access and simpler systems (FileMaker Pro, Works, and Q&A File); then go wild with **graphics**, **desktop publishing**, **multimedia**; **accounting**, **personal programs** (everything from lovemaking to therapy!), **games** (seductive fun!), and **artificial intelligence** (so the computer seems to become human).

Programming

Our world is split into three classes of people:

> *avoiders* (who fear and loathe computers and avoid them)
> *users* (who use computers but don't really understand them)
> *programmers* (who understand computers and can teach them new tricks)

The Guide elevates your mind to the heights of class 3: it turns you into a sophisticated programmer.

Since the Guide's explanation of "BASIC" expands your understanding of computers so dramatically, don't wait! Start reading it the same day you start "Spreadsheets" — as if you were taking two courses simultaneously.

To program the computer, you feed it instructions written in a *computer language*. The Guide explains all the popular computer languages.

> The programming section begins with the easiest popular language (**BASIC**) in all 3 popular versions: GWBASIC, QBASIC, and Visual BASIC. Then it explains **PASCAL** (the language that forces you to organize your mind), **C & C++** (the most popular languages among experts, who've used them to create all the popular programs for word processing, communication, spreadsheets, and databases), **JAVA** (for programming the Internet), **DBASE** (the fanciest language for handling databases), and **LOGO** (used by kids in elementary school to make turtles dance across the computer's screen).
>
> In the "good old days", when programmers were treated like gods, the most popular computer languages were **FORTRAN** (for scientists) and **COBOL** (for businesses). Though they're called "the languages for old fogies" now, many big computers still thrive on them — and so do many careers! The Guide covers a semester's course in each.

A gigantic chapter analyzes 23 **strange tongues** and divides those computer languages into three categories.

> *mainstream languages*: FORTRAN, ALGOL, COBOL, BASIC, PL/I, PASCAL, MODULA, C, ADA, DBASE, EASY
> *radical languages*: LISP, SNOBOL, APL, LOGO, FORTH, PILOT
> *specialized languages*: APT, DYNAMO, GPSS, RPG, SPSS, PROLOG

The chapter tutors you in all of them. It even includes a multilingual dictionary that helps you translate programs to different computer languages.

To top it all off, you learn how to program by using the most common **assembler** for the IBM PC and translate your programs to the Macintosh and other computers.

Endnotes

I hate to admit it, but occasionally computers break! They'll break less often if you follow my tricks for **maintenance**; but if you get unlucky, the chapter on **repairs** explains how to fix them. The Guide even explains how to cure a computer that's ill from **viruses**.

We members of the computer industry all have skeletons in our closet. The Guide digs up **our past** and counsels you about how to improve your career and **your future**.

You also get an explanation of **numerical analysis**, an **index** to the entire Guide, and **coupons** for getting more goodies! Wow!

Table of contents

Praised by reviewers

If you like this book, you're not alone.

Praised by computer magazines

All the famous computer magazines call Russ Walter "Boston's computer guru" and praise him for giving free consulting even in the middle of the night. Here's how they evaluate The Secret Guide to Computers....

PC World: "Russ Walter is a PC pioneer, a trailblazer, the user's champion. Nobody does a more thorough, practical, and entertaining job of teaching PC technology. His incomparable Guide receives nothing but praise for its scope, wit, and enormous practicality. It offers a generous compendium of industry gossip, buying advice, and detailed, foolproof tutorials. It's a wonderful bargain."

Byte: "The Guide is amazing. If you need to understand computers and haven't had much luck at it, or have to teach other people about computers, or just want to read a good book about computers, get the Guide."

Computer Currents: "Your computer literacy quotient will always come up short unless you know something about Russ Walter. He's a folk hero. He knows virtually everything about personal computers and makes learning about computers fun. If you've given up in disgust and dismay at reading other computer books, get the Guide. It should be next to every PC in the country. PC vendors would do themselves and their customers a big favor by packing a copy of the Guide with every computer that goes out the door. The Guide deserves the very highest recommendation."

PC Magazine: "The Guide explains the computer industry, hardware, languages, operating systems, and applications in a knowledgeable and amusing fashion. It includes Russ Walter's unbiased view of the successes and failures of various companies, replete with inside gossip. By working your way through it, you'll know more than many who make their living with PCs. Whether novice or expert, you'll learn from the Guide and have a good time doing so. No other computer book is a better value."

Abacus: "Alternative-culture Walter provides the best current treatment of programming languages. It's irreverent, reminiscent of the underground books of the 1960's. It's simple to read, fast-paced, surprisingly complete, full of locker-room computer gossip, and loaded with examples."

Infoworld: "Russ Walter is recognized and respected in many parts of the country as a knowledgeable and effective instructor. His Guide is readable, outrageous, and includes a wealth of information."

Mac User: "It's an everything-under-one-roof computer technology guide."

Computerworld: "The Guide by unconventional computer guru Russ Walter is informative and entertaining."

Computer Shopper: "The Guide covers the entire spectrum. It's incredibly informative and amusing."

Home Office Computing: "Russ Walter is a computer missionary who's a success story."

Classroom Computer Learning: "Russ Walter's courses are intensive and inexpensive."

Compute: "Russ Walter is an industry leader."

Praised by the classics
Earlier editions of the Guide were praised by all the classic computer magazines.

Popular Computing: "Russ Walter is king of the East Coast computer cognoscenti. His Guide is the biggest bargain in computer tutorials in our hemisphere. If CBS ever decides to replace Andy Rooney with a '60 Minutes' computer pundit, they'd need to look no further than Russ Walter. His wry Walterian observations enliven nearly every page of his book. His Guide is the first collection of computer writings that one might dare call literature."

Personal Computing: "The Guide is bulging with information. You'll enjoy it. Russ Walter's approach to text-writing sets a new style that other authors might do well to follow. It's readable, instructive, and downright entertaining. If more college texts were written in the Russ Walter style, more college students would reach their commencement day."

Creative Computing: "The Guide is fascinating, easy to understand, an excellent book at a ridiculously low price. We especially endorse it."

Cider Press: "The Guide should be given to all beginners with the purchase of their computers."

Softalk: "The Guide fires well-deserved salvos at many sacred cows. It's long been a cult hit."

Computer Bargain Info: "The Guide is widely acclaimed by experts as brilliant."

Eighty Micro: "Theatrical, madcap Russ is a cult hero."

Interface Age: "The Guide is a best buy."

Enter: "It's the best book about computer languages."

Microcomputing: "Plan ahead; get in on the Secret now."

Praised by mass-market magazines
Mass-market magazines call the Guide amazing.

Scientific American: "The Guide is irresistible. Every instruction leads to a useful result. Walter's candor shines; he makes clear the faults and foibles others ignore or cast in vague hints. The effect is that of a private conversation with a well-informed talkative friend who knows the inside story. The text reads like the patter of a talented midnight disc jockey; it's flip, self-deprecatory, randy, and good-humored. His useful frank content and coherent style are unique. First-rate advice on what and how to buy are part of the rich mix. No room holding a small computer and an adult learning to use it is well equipped without the Guide."

The Whole Earth Catalog in its "Coevolution Quarterly": "The personal-computer subculture was noted for its fierce honesty in its early years. The Guide is one of the few intro books to carry on that tradition, and the only introductory survey of equipment that's kept up to date. Russ Walter jokes, bitches, enthuses, condemns, and charms. The book tells the bald truth in comprehensible language."

Omni: "Guru Russ Walter sympathizes deeply with people facing a system crash at midnight, so he broadcasts his home phone number and answers calls by the light of his computers, cursors winking. He's considered an excellent teacher. His Guide is utterly comprehensive."

Changing Times: "Russ Walter is a computer whiz whose mission is to educate people about computers. Like a doctor, he lets strangers call him in the middle of the night for help with diagnosing a sick computer. His Guide covers everything you ever wanted to know."

Esquire: "The handy Guide contains lots of fact and opinion untainted by bias."

Barron's: "Russ Walter is an expert who answers questions for free and has been inundated by calls."

Praised by computer clubs

Computer clubs call the Guide the best computer book, in their newsletters, newspapers, and magazines.

Boston Computer Society: "The Guide is cleverly graduated, outrageous, and funny. Russ Walter turns computerese into plain speaking, while making you giggle. He's years ahead of the pack that claims to have ways of instructing computer novices. His unique mix of zany humor and step-by-step instruction avoids the mistakes of manuals that attempt to follow his lead."

Connecticut Computer Society: "Russ Walter's books have been used by insiders for years. He's special as a teacher because of three factors: his comprehensive knowledge of many computers and their languages, operating system, and applications; his ability to break complicated processes into the smallest components; and his humor. A valuable feature of the Guide is his candid comments about various computers and software. He's one of the few people able to review languages, machines, and software, all in a humorous, clear manner, with the whole endeavor set off by his sense of industry perspective, history, and culture. If you're ever struck with a computer problem, give Russ a call."

New England Computer Society: "Russ Walter is considered one of the few true computer gurus. His Guide is the world's best tutorial. It's the single best present anyone could receive who cares to know more about computers without going crazy."

New York's "NYPC": "The Guide is the perfect text for anyone beginning to learn about computers because it contains real info in readable form about a range of subjects otherwise requiring a whole reference library. It's even better for the experienced computer user, since it also contains many, many advanced concepts that one person could hardly remember. But one person apparently remembered them all: Russ Walter. He's a fountain of computer knowledge and can even explain it in words of one syllable. His Guide reads like a novel: you can read simply for fun. It's recommended to anyone from rank beginner to seasoned power user."

Sacramento (California) PC Users Group: "The Guide is the best collection of computer help ever written. It includes just about everything you'd want to know about computers. You'll find answers for all the questions you thought of and some you didn't think of. No holds barred, Walter even tells you who in the industry made the mistakes and rotten computers, and who seemed to succeed in spite of themselves. The Guide is fascinating. It's recommended for anyone even slightly interested in computers."

Praised by librarians

Librarians call the Guide the best computer book ever written.

School Library Journal: "The Guide is a gold mine of information. It's crystal clear, while at the same time Walter delivers a laugh a paragraph along with a lot of excellent info. It's accessible even to kids, who will love its loony humor. Buy it; you'll like it."

Wilson Library Bulletin: "The Guide is distinguished by its blend of clarity, organization, and humor. It cuts through the techno-haze. It packs more simple, fresh explication per page than anything else available."

Praised around the world

The Guide is praised by newspapers around the world.

Australia's "Sydney Morning Herald": "The Guide is the best computer intro published anywhere in the world. It gives a total overview of personal computers. It's stimulating, educational, provocative, and a damn good read."

The Australian: "The Guide's coverage of programming is intelligent, urbane, extremely funny, and full of great ideas."

England's "Manchester Guardian": "Russ Walter is a welcome relief. The internationally renowned computer guru tries to keep computerdom's honesty alive. His Guide is an extraordinary source of information."

Silicon Valley's "Times Tribune": "The Guide invites you to throw aside all rules of conventional texts and plunge into the computer world entirely naked and unafraid. This book makes learning not only fun, but hilarious, inspiring, and addicting."

Dallas Times Herald: "Easily the best beginners' book seen, it's not just for beginners. Its strength is how simple it makes everything, without sacrificing what matters."

Detroit News: "Russ Walter is a legendary teacher. His fiercely honest Guide packs an incredible amount of info. It's the only book that includes everything. He gives you all the dirt about the companies and their hardware, evaluates their business practices, and exposes problems they try to hide. Phone him. You'll always get a truthful answer."

Chicago Tribune: "The Guide is the best computer book. It's a cornucopia of computer delights written by Russ Walter, a great altruist and dreamer."

Kentucky's "Louisville Courier": "Walter's Guide will teach you more computer fundamentals than the thick books in the average bookstore. The Guide gives his no-bull insights. He not only discusses computer mail-order sources, which most books avoid; he names the bad guys. The Guide's biggest appeal is its humor, wit, and personality."

Philadelphia Inquirer: "Russ Walter is the Ann Landers for computer klutzes, a high-tech hero. His wacky, massive Guide is filled with his folksy wit."

New York Times: "The computer-obsessed will revel in Walter's Guide. He covers just about every subject in the microcomputer universe. It's unlikely you have a question his book doesn't answer."

Wall Street Journal: "Russ Walter is a computer expert, a guru who doesn't mind phone calls. He brings religious-like fervor to the digital world. His students are grateful. His Guide gets good reviews. He's influential."

Connecticut's "Hartford Courant": "If you plan to buy a personal computer, the best gift to give yourself is the Guide. It's crammed with info. It became an instant success as one of the few microcomputer books that was not only understandable and inexpensive but also witty — a combination still too rare today."

Boston Globe: "Russ Walter is a unique resource, important to beginning and advanced users. His Guide is practical, down-to-earth, and easy to read."

Boston Phoenix: "Russ Walter has achieved international cult status. He knows his stuff, and his comprehensive Guide is a great deal."

Fan mail

From our readers, we've received *thousands* of letters and phone calls, praising us. Here are some recent examples.

Intoxicated

Our books make readers go nuts.

Get high "I'm high! Not on marijuana, crack, or cocaine, but on what I did at my computer with BASIC and your Guide." (Beverly, Massachusetts)

Strange laughs "I enjoy the Guide *immensely*! My fellow workers think I'm strange because of all my laughing while reading it. Whenever I feel tired or bored, I pick up the Guide. It's very refreshing!" (Acton, Massachusetts)

Poo-poo "I finished the book at 2:30 AM and had to sit down and send you a big THANK-YOU-poo. A poet I am not, crazy I was not, until I started 18 months ago with this computer and then came *poo* who sealed my lot." (Hinesville, Georgia)

Computer dreams "Wow — I loved your book. My husband says I talk about computers in my sleep." (Los Altos Hills, California)

Bedtime story "The book's next to the bed, where my wife and I can see who grabs it first. The loser must find something else to do, which often causes serious degradation of reading comprehension." (Danville, New Hampshire)

Love in Paris "If you ever come to Paris, give me a call. I'll be more than happy to meet the guy I admire most in the computer industry." (Paris)

Sex "Great book. Better than sex." (Worcester, Massachusetts)

Devil "This book is great. It moves like the fastest Mac, soars with the eagles, and dances with the devil." (Chicago)

God "I'm a Russy groupie now! You are God! Your book lets me put it all together." (San Diego)

National TV "Great! When are you going on national TV? America needs you!" (Berkeley, California)

National debt "I think you do a fabulous job with computers! You should be in Washington & organize our country, and maybe we could be debt-free." (Tavares, Florida)

Beginners

Even beginners can master the Guide.

Godsend "You're a godsend. You saved me from being bamboozled by the local computer store." (Boston)

Saint "You should be canonized for bringing clarity and humor to a field often incomprehensible and dull." (Houston)

Companion to the lonely "Your book's a nice companion when I'm alone, because it talks. It answers more questions than I can ask." (Carson, California)

Computer disease "I was scared to go near a computer. I thought I might catch something. Now I can't wait." (Paterson, New Jersey)

Face-off "I used to be an idiot. Now I can stare my computer in the face. Thanks." (San Antonio, Texas)

Amaze the professor "I *love* the Guide! I've read it before taking a BASIC course, and I'm amazing my professor with my secret skills!" (Olney, Illinois)

Walking encyclopedia "Your Guide really helps. I work with a great programmer who's like a walking computer encyclopedia. Now I know what he's saying!" (San Leandro, California)

Muscle in "So many computer experts speak a language all their own. They look down on us and consider us to be outsiders trying to muscle our way into their world. Thanks for helping the outsiders." (New Iberia, Lousiana)

Facing fear "Thank you! I'm 42, married to a computer guru, with two daughters who've been in front of a computer since first grade. *Finally*, I feel that I can face my fear and that I'm not alone." (Malvern, Pennsylvania)

Granny's clammy "I'm a 58-year-old grandma. My daughter gave me an IBM PC. After weeks of frustration I got your Guide. Now I'm happy as a clam at high tide, eager to learn more & more. Wow!" (Seattle)

Moment of discovery "After retiring, I searched for something to stimulate my mind. I bought a computer and tried to unravel its mysteries. The more I studied big books bought from computer stores, the more confused I became. Then I stumbled across the Guide. At that precise moment I discovered the beautiful, crazy, wild world of the computer! Thanks." (Tewksbury, Massachusetts)

Bury the Book of Songs "This is the microcomputer book that should be buried in a time capsule for future archaeologists. By reading it, I've made my computer sing. My wife recognizes the melodies and wants to read the book." (Park Forest, Illinois)

Experts

Experts love the Guide.

PC Week reporter "I write for *PC Week* and think the Guide is the *best* book of its kind. I'm sending a copy to my little brother, who's a budding byte-head." (Boston)

Editor at Lotus "Thanks *so* much for sending the Guide. It's great! Seems I'm the only one here in my office at Lotus who hadn't heard about it. You've got quite a following. Again, thanks!" (Cambridge, Massachusetts)

Math professor "I'm a math professor. The Guide's the best way in the universe to keep up to date with computers. People don't have to read anything else — it's *all* there." (New York City)

Diehard mainframer "It is really neat! I've been a mainframe computer consultant for many years, and when your book came yesterday I couldn't put it down." (Cleveland Heights, Ohio)

Refreshed programmers "I passed the Guide around my team of mainframe programmers, and most of them bought. It's so refreshing, after the parched dryness of IBM-ese, to find a book in English!" (Union, New Jersey)

Research center "Our research center uses and misuses gigabytes of computers. The Guide will improve our use/misuse ratio." (Naperville, Illinois)

Careers

The Guide's propelled many careers.

Land a first job "Last month, I bought your Guide. I've never seen so much info, packed so densely, in so entertaining a read. I was just offered a computer job, thanks to a presentation based on your Guide. I'm very, very, very happy I bought your book." (San Francisco)

Land a top job "Thanks to the Guide, I got an excellent job guiding the selection of computers in a department of over 250 users!" (New York City)

Found Wall Street "Eight years ago, I took your intro programming course. Now I run the computer department of a Wall Street brokerage firm. I'm responsible for 30 people and millions of dollars of computer equipment. The Guide's always been my foremost reference. Thank you for the key to wonderful new worlds." (Long Beach, New York)

Consultant's dream "Inspired by your book, your love for computers, and your burning desire to show the world that computers are fun and easily accessible, I entered the computer field. Now I'm a computer consultant. Your ideas come from the heart. Thanks for following your dream." (Skokie, Illinois)

Kid who grew up "Years ago, I saw you sell books while wearing a wizard's cap. I bought a book and was as impressed as a 16-year-old could be. Now I've earned B.A.'s in Computer Science and English, and I'm contemplating teaching computers to high school students. I can think of no better way to plan a course outline than around your Guide." (Pennington, New Jersey)

Better late than never

Readers wish they'd found the Guide sooner.

1 year "I learned more from the Guide than from a year in the computer industry." (Redwood City, California)

5 years "I've fumbled for 5 years with computers and many books, all with short-lived flashes of enthusiasm, until I found your Guide. It's the first book that showed a light at the end of the tunnel, even for one as dull-brained as I." (Boise)

17 years "Though in a computer company for 17 years, I didn't learn anything about computers until I began reading the Guide. I love it! I always thought computer people were generically boring, but your book's changed my mind." (Hopkinton, Massachusetts)

Prince Charming arrives "Where have you been all my life? I wish I'd heard of your Guide long ago. I'd have made far fewer mistakes if it had been here alongside my computer." (White Stone, Virginia)

Hack a Mac "Great book. I'm 14 and always wanted to hack. Thanks to your Guide, I laughed myself to death and look forward to gutting my Mac. Yours is the friendliest, funniest book on computers I've seen. I'm finally going to teach my parents BASIC. If I'd started out with the Guide, I'd have saved five years of fooling around in the dark." (Northport, Alabama)

Pass-alongs

Readers pass the Guide to their friends.

Round the office "Send 150 books. I passed my Guide around the office, and just about everyone who saw it wants copies." (Middleburg Heights, Ohio)

Coordinating the coordinators "Your book is amazing! I'm telling the other 50 PC coordinators in my company to be sure they're in on the secret. Bless you for your magnanimous philosophy!" (Morristown, New Jersey)

Hide your secrets "I thought the Guide marvelous and proudly displayed it on my desk. A friend from South Africa saw it and said our friendship depended on letting her take it home with her. What could I do? You've gone international. I'm ordering another copy. Should I hide the book this time?" (Cinnaminson, New Jersey)

Cries and anger "I made the mistake of letting several friends borrow my copy of the Guide. Each time I tried getting it back, it was a battle. (I hate to see grown people cry.) I promised to order them copies of their own. I delayed several months, and now I've got an angry mob outside my door. While you process my order, I'll try pacifying them by reading aloud." (Winston-Salem, North Carolina)

Round the house "Dad bought your Guide to help him understand my computer. It's become the most widely read book in our house. We love it!" (Boca Raton, Florida)

Squabble with Dad "I love the Guide. Dad & I squabble over our only copy. Send a second so I can finish the Guide in peace." (New York City)

Change my brother "The Guide changed my computer scorn & fear to interest. Send my brother a copy, to effect the same transformation." (New York City)

Selling clones "I took the Guide to a meeting and used your words as a reason why the group should buy an IBM PC clone instead of the other computer they were looking at. It worked." (Sparks, Nevada)

Make your guru giggle "I showed the Guide to my guru. Between laughs, chuckles, and guffaws, he agreed to use it to teach his high-school computer class. He even admitted he'd learned something, and that's the most unheard of thing I ever heard of." (Arivaca, Arizona)

Smarter sales reps "Our company just released its first software product, and our sales reps are panic-stricken. I'm giving them the Guide to increase their computer background. Thanks for a super book." (Pittsburgh)

Advancing secretary "I'm ordering an extra copy for my secretary, to start her on the path to a higher paying and better regarded position." (Belleville, Illinois)

Compared with other publishers

The Guide's better than any other book.

Better than 10 "I learned more from your Guide than from a total of 10 books read previously." (Honolulu)

No big bucks "Your book is great! Its crazy style really keeps the pages turning. I appreciate someone who doesn't try to make big bucks off someone trying to learn. Thanks." (Vancouver, Washington)

Rip-off "If you can break even at your book's low price, lots of guys are ripping us off." (Choctaw, Oklahoma)

Who are we?

This section reveals who we are — even if you'd rather not know.

Interview with Russ

In this interview, Russ answers the most popular questions about this book and what's behind it.

Why did you write the Secret Guide? I saw my students spending too much effort taking notes, so I made up my own notes to hand them. Over the years, my notes got longer, so this 27th edition totals 639 pages. Each time I develop a new edition, I try to make it the kind of book I wish I had when *I* was a student.

What does the Guide cover? Everything. Every computer topic is touched on, and the most important topics are covered in depth.

Who reads the Guide? All sorts. Kids read it because it's easy; computer professionals read it because it contains lots of secret tidbits you can't find anywhere else.

Why do you charge so little? I'm not trying to make a profit. I'm just trying to make people happy — by charging as little as possible, while still covering my expenses. Instead of "charging as much as the market will bear", I try to "charge so little that the public will cheer".

Do you really answer the phone 24 hours a day? When do you sleep? When folks call in the middle of the night, I wake up, answer their questions, then go back to bed. I'm near the phone 85% of the time. If you get no answer, I'm out on a brief errand, so please call again. If you get an answering machine, I'm out on a longer project: just leave your number and I'll call you back at my expense, even if it's long distance.

Why do you give phone help free? Are you a masochist, a saint, or a nut? I give the free help for three reasons: I like to be a nice guy; it keeps me in touch with my readers, who suggest how to improve the Guide further; and the happy callers tell their friends about me, so I don't have to spend money on advertising.

At computer shows, do you really appear as a witch? I wear a witch's black hat and red kimono over a monk's habit and roller skates, while my white gloves caress an African spear. Why? Because it's fun!

Did you write the whole Guide yourself? I wrote the first 22 editions myself. I was helped by many suggestions from my readers, friends, and staff, who also contributed some examples and phrases.

The 23rd edition included some paragraphs written by my research assistant, Len Pallazola, and edited by me. His paragraphs appeared mainly in sections about the Internet, Novell networks, Doom, Visual BASIC, viruses, the jargon dictionary, and the vendor directory. In later editions, I replaced some of those paragraphs with my own improvements.

What's your background? I got degrees in math and education from Dartmouth and Harvard, taught at several colleges (Wellesley, Wesleyan, and Northeastern), and was a founding editor of *Personal Computing* magazine. But most of my expertise comes from spending long hours every day reading computer books and magazines, discussing computer questions on the phone, and analyzing the philosophy underlying the computer industry.

About the so-called author

Since the author is so lifeless, we can keep his bio mercifully short.

Birth of a notion The author, Russy-poo, was conceived in 1946. So was the modern ("stored-program") computer.

Nine months later, Russy-poo was hatched. The modern computer took a few years longer, so Russ got a head start. But the computer quickly caught up. Ever since, they've been racing against each other, to see who's smartest.

The race is close, because Russ and the computer have so much in common. Folks say the computer "acts human" and say Russ's personality is "as a dead as a computer".

Junior Jews Russ resembles a computer in many ways. For example, both are Jewish.

The father of the modern computer was John von Neumann, a Jew of German descent. After living in Hungary, he fled the Nazis and became a famous U.S. mathematician.

The father of Russy-poo Walter was Henry Walter, a German Jew who fled the Nazis and became a famous U.S. dental salesman. To dentists, he sold teeth, dental chairs, and balloons to amuse the kids while their mouths were mauled.

The race for brains To try beating the computer, Russ got his bachelor's degree in math from Dartmouth in yummy '69 and sadly stayed a bachelor for many years (unless you count the computer he got married to).

After Dartmouth, he got an M.A.T. in math education from Harvard. Since he went to Harvard, you know he's a genius. Like most genii, he achieved the high honor of being a junior-high teacher.

After his classes showered him with the Paper Airplane Award, he moved on to teach at an exclusive private school for girls who were very exclusive. ("Exclusive" means everyone can come except you.)

After teaching every grade from 2 through 12 (he taught the 2nd-grade girls how to run the computer, and the 12th graders less intellectual things), he fled reality by joining Wesleyan University's math Ph.D. program in Connecticut's Middletown (the middle of Nowhere), where after 18 months of highbrow hoopla he was seduced by a computer to whom he's now happily married.

Married life After the wedding, Russ moved with his electrifying wife to Northeastern University in Boston (home of the bean and the cod), where he did a hilarious job of teaching in the naughty Department of "Graphic Science". After quitting Northeastern and also editorship of Personal Computing, he spends his time now happily losing money by publishing this book.

Since his wife was lonely, he bought her 40 computers to keep her company, with names such as "Anita Atari", "Aphrodite the Apple", "Baby Blue Burping Bonnie", "Coco the Incredible Clown", "Jack the Shack", "Kooky Casio", "Slick Vic", and "Terrible Tina with her Texas Instruments". He hid them in a van and drove them around the country, where they performed orgies and did a strip tease, to show students a thing or two about computer anatomy.

Banned in Boston, Russ and his groupies moved north, to Somerville. In 1998, when Somerville became an overpriced slumville, they moved further north, to New Hampshire, which dubs itself "the granite state", since Russ has rocks in his head.

That year, Russ became a bigamist: though still married to a computer, he also married a human. Russ is strange, but his human wife is even stranger — a young philosopher from China. The couple is called "Russy-poo old and Pu-pu egg-foo young."

Russs's body

Russs's body Here are Russ's stats, from head to toe:

> **head** in the clouds, **hair** departing, **brow** beaten
> **eyes** glazed, **lashes** 40, **nose** to the grindstone
> **mouth** off, **smile** bionic, **tongue** bitten, **teeth** remembered
> **cheeks** in a royal flush, **chin** up, **shoulders** burdened
> **wrists** watched, **hands** some, **thumbs** up
> **heart** all, **back** got everyone on it, **ass** unintentionally, **buns** toasted
> **knees** knocked, **heeled** well, **arches** gothic, **toes** stepped on

He wears a stuffed shirt, slick slacks, and sacramental socks — very holy!

Russs's résumé We told Russ to write this book because when he handed us the following résumé, we knew he was the kind of author that publishers dream about: nuts enough to work for free!

> **Age:** too. **Sex:** yes! **Race:** rat. **Religion:** Reformed Nerd.
> **Address:** wear pants instead. **State:** distressed.
> **Father:** time. **Mother:** earth. **Spouse:** Brussels.
> **Occupation:** vegetable. **Career goal:** play dead.
> **Hobbies:** sleeping and crying. **Sports:** dodging tomatoes.
> **Greatest pleasure:** hiding under the sink. **Favorite food:** thought.
> **Humor:** less.

About the company

What company? C'mon over, bring milk and cookies, and then we'll have some helluva company!

Come visit our Home Office, in Russ's home. It includes our Production Department, near or in Russ's bed. Russ gave birth to this book himself; nobody else would dare!

Special services

We do everything possible to make you happy....

Discounts We give you a 20% discount for buying 2 copies of this book, 40% for 4 copies, and 60% for 60 copies (so you pay just $6.60 per copy). Use the coupon on the back page.

Bulk orders If you give us a prepaid order for least 640 books, we typically give you an even *bigger* discount: *more* than 60%! Phone 603-666-6644 and ask about "bulk orders". Discounts and terms depend on how many books you want, where you want us to ship them, how you plan to distribute them, how many we have in stock, and your track record with us.

Use your past You're reading the 27th edition. To compute your discount, we count how many copies of the 27th edition you've ordered from us *so far*. For example, if you previously ordered 30 copies of the 27th edition and order 30 more, we say "Oh, you're up to 60 copies now!" and give you a 60% discount on the second order.

If you got a discount on the 25th or 26th edition because you bought many copies, we'll give you the same discount on the 27th edition even if you're buying just one copy.

To get a discount based on past orders, mail us the coupon on the back page. Next to your name, write your phone number and say, "I'm taking a discount because of past orders."

Free reprints You may copy this book free. Copy as many pages as you like, make lots of copies, and don't pay us a cent!

Just **phone Russ first** (at 603-666-6644) and say which pages you're going to copy. **Put this notice at the beginning of your reprint:**

Then **send us a copy** of your reprint.

You may give — or sell — the reprints to anybody. Go distribute them on paper, on disk, or electronically by phone. The Guide's being distributed by thousands of teachers, consultants, and stores and translated to other languages. Join those folks! Add your own comments, call yourself a co-author, and become famous! It's free!

Books on disks Instead of books printed on paper, you can request books printed on disks. For example, if you're ordering 4 books, you can scribble this note on the coupon: "Send 3 on paper and 1 on disk."

We'll send 1.44M disks in Microsoft Word 7 format. They'll help you write your *own* book and develop material to put on a computerized bulletin board or Internet Web site.

If you get books on disk, get at least one book on paper since the disks do *not* contain our headlines, graphics, special symbols, special fonts, and printer drivers.

Internet We're on the Internet! Visit our Secret Fun site, **www.secretfun.com**. It reveals the newest secrets about *The Secret Guide to Computers*, contains links to other secret fun Internet sites, and lets you send us e-mail. Or just go ahead and send e-mail directly to **russ@secretfun.com**.

Many friends have created other Internet Web sites about Russ Walter and *The Secret Guide to Computers*.

> To find those sites, look at the links on **www.secretfun.com**, or use a search engine such as www.go.com to search for "Russ Walter". For example, you can read earlier editions of *The Secret Guide to Computers*, free, at **webpixie.com/secret** and **computercraft.com/docs/secretguide.html**; you can buy paper copies of *The Secret Guide to Computers* from online bookstores such as **amazon.com**, **barnesandnoble.com**, **fatbrain.com**, and **web2u.com**.

Preserved classics You're reading the 27th edition. We've also reprinted earlier editions, which include extra details about the famous old computers and software that became classics.

For example, we offer these editions:

> the 26th edition for $6
> the 25th edition for $5
> the 24th edition for $4
> the 23rd edition for $3
> the 11th edition's volume 1 for 30¢

Those insanely low prices are ideal for schools on tight budgets and for low-cost gifts to your friends. For details about those famous classic editions, ask us to send the free "classics memo and order form".

Blitz courses Russ gives his "blitz" course all over the world. Offered several times a year, it turns you into a complete computer expert in an intensive weekend.

Saturday (from 9AM to 9PM) covers the first four chapters: buyer's guide, operating systems, word processing, and communication. Sunday (9AM to 5PM) covers the other three: tricky applications, programming, and endnotes.

The entire 20-hour course costs just $50. That's just $2.50 per hour! To pay even less per person, form a group with your friends. For details, phone or use the back page's coupon.

Strange stuff We're developing future editions, videotapes, and *The Secret Guide to Tricky Living*. Get on our mailing list by using the coupon on the back page. Russ answers questions about life — everything from sex to skunks. Phone 603-666-6644 anytime!

What's a "computer"?

Up until 1940, computers were people. Dictionaries said a "computer" was "a person who computes". For example, astronomers hired many computers, who computed the positions of the stars. People who computed were called "computers"; machines that computed were called "calculators".

After 1940, human computers were gradually replaced by gigantic machines, called "electronic computers". Today the word "computer" means "a *machine* that computes". This book explains how to buy and use such machines.

During the 1950's, people began to realize that electronic computers can do *more* than compute. Today's computers spend hardly any time doing numerical computations; they spend most of their time thinking about words and ideas instead. Calling such wonderful machines "computers" is misleading; they ought to be called "thinkers" instead! The French call them "ordinateurs", which means "organizers" and more accurately describes what the machines do than our old-fashioned word "computers".

If an alien would visit our planet and see how our computers act, the alien might deduce:

> A "computer" is "a machine that thinks".

But if the alien comes from a strange colony of uptight chatterboxes called "lawyers", the alien would analyze further and say more precisely:

> A "computer" is "any machine that can seem to do useful thinking".

That's the definition I'll use in this book!

Since today's computers spend most of their time dealing with words & ideas — and very *little* time dealing with numbers — you need to know just a *little* math to understand computers. If you know 5.2 is more than 5 and less than 6, you know more than enough math to master this book and get hired as a computer expert! Becoming a computer expert is easier than becoming an auto mechanic, and you don't get greasy!

Kinds of computers

Computers come in all shapes and sizes.

Three computer sizes

Computers come in three general sizes: big, small, and teeny-weeny.

If the computer is big,	it's called a **maxicomputer** (or **mainframe**).
If the computer is small,	it's called a **minicomputer**.
If the computer is teeny-weeny,	it's called a **microcomputer**.

How big must a computer be for folks to call it a *maxi*computer? Opinions differ, but here are some guidelines:

Typically, a maxicomputer fills a whole room;
a minicomputer fits in a corner of a room;
a microcomputer can fit on a desk.

Typically, a microcomputer costs between $1 and $10,000;
a minicomputer costs between $10,000 and $300,000;
a maxicomputer costs between $300,000 and $20,000,000.

If a new computer understands the same commands as an old computer, the new computer is labeled the same as the old computer, regardless of its price.

For example, if somebody invents a new computer that understands the same commands as an old minicomputer, the new computer is called a "minicomputer" too, even if it costs less than $10,000 or more than $300,000. If it costs less than $10,000, it's called a **low-end minicomputer** (and probably runs slowly); if it costs more than $300,000, it's called a **high-end minicomputer** or **supermini** (and probably runs fast).

Companies began selling maxicomputers in the 1950's, minicomputers in the 1960's, and microcomputers in the 1970's. Now you can buy all three sizes.

Microcomputers are more affordable than bigger computers and therefore more popular. Most computers are microcomputers. **Over 99.9% of all computers sold are microcomputers.**

This book emphasizes microcomputers — because they're the most popular, most affordable, and most modern — but analyzes big old computers too!

If a computer is big, you can call it either a "**maxicomputer**" or a "**mainframe**". Nowadays, the two terms are synonyms. Most computerists still say "**mainframe**", which is an old-fashioned term; but I'll say "**maxicomputer**", which is easier to understand.

The typical microcomputer is used by just one person at a time and is therefore called a **personal computer** (or **PC**). The typical maxicomputer or minicomputer handles several people simultaneously and is therefore called a **multi-user system**. But a special kind of minicomputer acts as a **graphics/engineering workstation** instead: it's used to produce graphics that are extra big, extra high-quality, and extra fast, for beautiful artwork, Hollywood special effects, ads, magazines, and "artist renderings" of creations by architects and engineers. Like microcomputers, graphics/engineering workstations are considered modern and nifty.

If you work in a company that bought an older minicomputer or maxicomputer years ago, and you're still stuck using that outdated overpriced unreliable awkward junk, the polite way to describe your situation is to say that you're using a **legacy system**, because the computer you're using is a legacy handed down from the employees who preceded you. Yes, a **legacy system** is an outdated maxicomputer or minicomputer. It makes employees complain, "We're stuck with this legacy system. We wish we had new, nifty microcomputers or graphics/engineering workstations instead!"

Networks

Instead of buying a single big computer, the typical big company buys many little computers and wires them together, to form a **network**.

> If the network's computers are all in the same office building, the network is called a **local-area network (LAN)**.
>
> If the computers are farther apart, the network is called a **wide-area network (WAN)**.

Each computer in the network is called a **node**.

A special person, called the **network supervisor**, manages the network, by controlling the network's main computer, called the **server**. Ordinary folks (called **users**) sit at the network's lesser computers (called **workstations**), which all are wired to the server.

In a typical network, the workstations are all personal computers. The server is a souped-up microcomputer or minicomputer or maxicomputer.

Companies who make "maxicomputers" and "minicomputers" feel nervous about using those terms, which are less modern and less cool than "microcomputers", so they typically advertise their computers as being "powerful servers" instead.

The most famous wide-area network is the **Internet**. It began in the 1950's as a small network that let a few universities communicate with each other. During the 1990's, the Internet expanded dramatically, so now it includes many millions of personal computers all over the world. If you buy a personal computer and attach it to the Internet by phone, you can share info with other folks all over the world.

IBM

The main computer manufacturer is **IBM**, which stands for **International Business Machines Corporation**.

> Too often, it's also stood for "Incredibly Boring Machines", "Inertia Breeds Mediocrity", "International Big Mother", "Imperialism By Marketing", "Idolized By Management", "Incompetents Become Managers", "Intolerant of Beards & Mustaches", "It Baffles Me", "It's a Big Mess", and "It's Better Manually". But those negative comments apply just to IBM's past: in the 1990's IBM switched; it became open-minded and friendly.

The company got its name because its most famous leader, Tom Watson, had previously been vice-president of **National Cash Register (NCR)**; he decided to one-up NCR by developing a company that would be *more* than national (**International**) and sell *more* than just cash registers (*all* kinds of **Business Machines**).

IBM makes maxicomputers, minicomputers, and microcomputers.

Maxicomputers

The first maxicomputer that was mass-produced was the **Univac 1**, built in 1951 by the **Remington Rand** company, which is now part of **Unisys**.

IBM Most of today's maxicomputers are souped-up versions of the **IBM System/360**, which IBM announced in 1964. IBM called it the "360" because it was the first IBM computer that could accomplish the "full circle" of computer applications, instead of just science applications or business applications. In 1970, IBM invented a souped-up version (called the **IBM System/370**) and then further improvements.

IBM's newest maxicomputer is the **IBM System/390**. It understands the same commands as the IBM 360 and 370 but obeys the commands faster and understands extra commands. The newest version of the IBM System/390 is called the **Generation 6 (G6)**.

Since IBM's first popular maxicomputers were colored blue, IBM is nicknamed "Big Blue".

IBM's competitors IBM sells more maxicomputers than all IBM's competitors combined.

> During the 1960's, maxicomputers were made by eight companies, called "IBM and the Seven Dwarfs". The dwarfs were **Burroughs**, **Univac**, **NCR** (which stood for National Cash Register), **Control Data**, **Honeywell** (whose original factory was next to a well), **RCA** (which stood for "Radio Corporation of America"), and **General Electric**.
>
> In 1970, General Electric sold its computer division to Honeywell. In 1971, RCA's computer division shut down. That left just five dwarfs, whose initials spelled the word BUNCH. Cynics said that maxicomputers were made by "IBM and the BUNCH".
>
> IBM's top engineer (Gene Amdahl) and Control Data's top engineer (Seymour Cray) both quit and started their own computer companies, called **Amdahl** and **Cray**.
>
> During the 1980's and 1990's, each company in the BUNCH disintegrated: Burroughs merged with Univac to form **Unisys**; NCR was bought by **AT&T** (but then split away from AT&T and became independent again); Control Data stopped building computers; and Honeywell sold its computer division to a French company, **Bull**.
>
> Since maxicomputers are big and old-fashioned, they're called **dinosaurs** — and so are the folks who use them. When maxicomputer manufacturers merge, to form bigger conglomerate companies, the merger is called **dinosaur mating**.
>
> While the BUNCH was disintegrating, a Japanese company (**Hitachi**) started building maxicomputers that imitate IBM's.

Minicomputers

The first minicomputer that was mass-produced was the **PDP-8**, built in 1965 by **Digital Equipment Corporation (DEC)**. In 1970, DEC invented a fancier minicomputer, called the **PDP-11**. For many years, the PDP-8 and PDP-11 remained the world's most popular minicomputers. Eventually, DEC replaced them with the **Vax** (a souped-up PDP-11), then a further improvement (called the **Alpha**).

DEC's been headquartered in Massachusetts. Other popular minicomputer specialists — also in Massachusetts — have been **Data General (DG)**, **Prime**, and **Wang**; but Prime and Wang have stopped building minicomputers.

In 1998, DEC became part of **Compaq**, which mainly builds microcomputers instead.

Now the most exciting companies building minicomputers are Californian: **Silicon Graphics Incorporated (SGI)**, **Hewlett-Packard (HP)**, and **Sun** (which was started by Stanford University students and stands for "Stanford University Network"). Sun's minicomputers are also used as Internet servers.

Most companies that make maxicomputers also make minicomputers. For example, IBM makes two minicomputers:

> The **Advanced System 400 (AS/400)** handles corporate accounting.
> The **Real-time System 6000 (RS/6000)** handles science and the Internet.

Microcomputers

The first microcomputer that was mass-produced was the **Altair**, built in 1975 by **Micro Instrumentation and Telemetry Systems (MITS)**, which is now part of **Pertec**. It's no longer made.

Apple The most inspiring microcomputers are made by **Apple**.

Apple's first computer was called the **Apple 1**. Then came improved versions (called the **Apple 2**, the **2+**, the **2e**, the **2c**, the **2c+**, and the **2GS**), which are called the **Apple 2 family**.

Apple has stopped making them. Now Apple sells instead a much fancier, totally different kind of microcomputer, called the **Macintosh** (or **Mac**). Of all computers built today, the Mac is the easiest to learn how to use. The most popular kind of Mac is called the **Internet Mac (iMac)**.

IBM IBM's most influential microcomputer was the **IBM Personal Computer (IBM PC)**, invented in 1981. In 1983, IBM invented a slightly improved version, called the **IBM PC eXTended (IBM PC XT)**. In 1984, IBM invented a much faster version, called the **IBM PC with Advanced Technology (IBM PC AT)**.

In 1987, IBM stopped making all those microcomputers and instead began making a new series of microcomputers, called the **Personal System 2 (PS/2)**.

> The PS/2 computers ran the same programs as the IBM PC but displayed prettier graphics and included "slicker" technology. But PS/2 computers were overpriced. In 1990, IBM began selling **PS/1 computers**, which resembled PS/2 computers but cost less. In 1992, IBM began selling **Valuepoint computers**, which cost even less. In 1993, IBM began selling **Ambra computers**, which cost even less.

IBM has stopped selling all those microcomputers. Now IBM's most popular microcomputer is the **Aptiva**, which is faster and has better graphics and sound. IBM also sells the **Thinkpad** (which is smaller) and the **IBM PC 300** (for businesses having local-area networks).

Popular clones Many companies make microcomputers that imitate IBM's. Those imitations are called **compatibles** or **clones**. Cynics call them **clowns**. They run the same programs as IBM's microcomputers but cost even less.

The most popular IBM clones are manufactured by **Compaq**, **Hewlett-Packard**, **Dell**, and **Gateway**. Of those four clone makers, Compaq charges the most, Gateway charges the least, and the others charge in-between.

How sold? Apple, Compaq, and Hewlett-Packard sell mainly through stores. (For example, you can buy them at discount stores such as **Staples**, **Office Depot**, **Costco**, **Sam's Club**, **Best Buy**, **Circuit City**, **Comp USA**, **Micro Center**, **Fry's Electronics**, and **J&R Computer World**.) Dell and Gateway computers are sold mainly by mail-order. IBM sells mainly to large corporations.

Cheaper clones Apple, IBM, Compaq, Hewlett-Packard, Dell, and Gateway are big manufacturers. To pay less, buy from smaller manufacturers instead, who advertise in computer magazines such as **Computer Shopper**.

For example, consider buying from **NuTrend** (at 888-842-6678), which is a division of **ABS**. A bargain hunter's paradise, NuTrend and ABS charge much less than famous brands.

Wild ducks Instead of buying from the leaders (Apple and IBM) and followers (who build clones), some folks bought cheaper computers made by wild-duck companies who dared to be different. The most popular wild-duck companies were **Commodore**, **Atari**, and **Tandy**.

Commodore made wild-duck computers such as the **Commodore 64**, the **Commodore 128**, the **Pet**, the **Vic**, and the **Amiga**. (The Amiga was particularly good at handling animated color graphics and videotapes.) Atari made **the Atari 800**, the **Atari XE**, and the **Atari ST**. (The Atari ST was particularly good at handling music.) Tandy's Radio Shack (TRS) made the **TRS-80** and the **Radio Shack Color Computer**.

> Wild-duck computers are no longer actively marketed. Commodore went bankrupt, Atari is barely alive, and Tandy switched to selling computers made by IBM and Compaq. But many Americans still own the *millions* of wild-duck computers sold during the early 1980's, before IBM PC clones became so popular and cheap. Those old wild-duck computers — abandoned by their owners, imprisoned forever in the darkness of American closets, and unable to re-emerge into the mainstream of American life — are the forgotten hostages of IBM clone wars. Now you can buy wild-duck computers for under $20 in the used-computer marketplace: try garage sales and flea markets.

Who uses what? The typical business uses an IBM PC (or an XT, AT, PS/2, PS/1, Valuepoint, Ambra, Aptiva, or clone). So does the typical college and high school. Some businesses and colleges use Macs. The Macs are particularly popular among artists, musicians, and advertising agencies. Some video artists (who create cartoons, weather maps, and other graphics for TV) still use the Amiga, though most video artists have switched to Macs. Some elementary schools still use Apple 2 computers, though most have switched to Macs or IBM clones. Wild-duck computers appeal to hobbyists seeking cheap thrills.

> Of all the general-purpose computers sold today **in the world**,
>
> 8% are personal computers built by IBM,
>
> 14% are clones by Compaq,
> 10% are clones by Dell,
> 8% are clones by Hewlett-Packard,
> 4% are clones by Gateway,
> 50% are clones built by a wide variety of other manufacturers,
>
> 4% are Macs (built by Apple),
>
> and the remaining 2% are weird (maxicomputers, minicomputers, wild ducks).

Since percentages bob up and down by 2% each month, I've rounded all those percentages to the nearest 2%.

Here's a summary:

> Of all the general-purpose computers sold today in the world,
> 94% are IBM-compatible personal computers (built by IBM and cloners),
> 4% are Macs,
> 2% are weird (maxicomputers, minicomputers, wild ducks).

In the USA, Dell is stronger and IBM is weaker:

> Of all the general-purpose computers sold today **in the USA**,
>
> 6% are personal computers built by IBM,
>
> 16% are clones by Compaq,
> 16% are clones by Dell,
> 10% are clones by Hewlett-Packard,
> 10% are clones by Gateway,
> 34% are clones built by a wide variety of other manufacturers,
>
> 6% are Macs (built by Apple),
>
> and the remaining 2% are weird (maxicomputers, minicomputers, wild ducks).

More people buy clones than IBM's originals. In fact, Compaq sells more computers than IBM. Dell also sells more computers than IBM. Yes, IBM is now ranks just third in number of computers sold! But IBM still makes the biggest profits, because IBM supplements its microcomputer sales by also selling minicomputers and expensive maxicomputers and doing lots of consulting.

Standard computers

Computers come in all shapes and sizes, but during the 1990's a new standard arose. Now most computers being sold meet this standard — and cost about $1,000. **A standard computer includes the following parts....**

The main part is a box called the **system unit**. If the system unit is tall, it's called a **tower**; if the system unit is wide instead, it's called a **desktop unit**.

> The typical tower is about 17 inches tall (and just 8 inches wide).
> The typical desktop unit is about 17 inches wide (and just 6 inches tall).
>
> Since a tower (17"×8") is slightly bigger than a desktop unit (17"×6"), a tower costs slightly more (and can contain more goodies).
>
> Regardless of whether you buy a tower or a desktop unit, the distance from the front to back is 16½ inches.

If you buy a desktop unit, put it on your desk. If you buy a tower instead, erect it on the floor *under* your desk, next to one of the desk's legs. Men are particularly proud of their towering erections next to the legs.

Eight cables come out the system unit's rear:

> One of those cables is called the **power cord**. It goes to the electrical outlet socket in the room's wall (or to a power strip connected to that outlet). That cable feeds power to the computer.
>
> One cable goes to the **keyboard**, which looks like a typewriter's keyboard. To send a message to the computer, type the message on the keyboard. A standard computer keyboard contains 104 keys, which let you type all the letters of the alphabet, all the digits, all the punctuation symbols, and other symbols too. Some of the keys are for editing: they help you edit what you typed.
>
> One cable goes to the **monitor**, which looks like a TV set: it contains a screen that shows the words you typed, the computer's answers, and pictures.
>
> One cable goes to the **mouse**, which is a small box about the size of a pack of cigarettes. If you slide the mouse across your desk, an arrow moves across your monitor's screen. So to move the screen's arrow, slide the mouse! To manipulate an object on the monitor's screen, slide the mouse until the screen's arrow moves to that object; then press the mouse's left button.
>
> One cable goes to the **printer**, which is a box that prints on paper.
>
> One cable goes to **stereo speakers**, so the computer can produce sound effects, play music, sing, and talk to you!
>
> The final two cables are **phone cords**. One of them goes to your telephone; the other goes to the telephone jack in your room's wall. By using those cables, the computer can make phone calls: it can phone other computers (such as computers that are on the Internet), chat with them, make love to them, and control *your* phone calls too!

Altogether, the standard computer includes:

> the system unit
>
> a keyboard, monitor, mouse, printer, speakers,
> and cables from all those components to the system unit
>
> power cords from wall (or power strip) to the system unit, monitor, and printer
>
> phone cords from the system unit to the phone and to the wall's phone jack

Advertised price When you buy a computer, the advertised price includes most of those items: it typically includes the system unit, computer keyboard, mouse, and pair of stereo speakers. But **the printer is NOT included in the advertised price: it costs extra.**

Does the advertised price include the monitor? To find out, read the ad carefully!

> If you're lucky, the ad says "**monitor included**". If the ad says "**monitor optional**" instead, the monitor is *not* included in the advertised price: the monitor costs extra.
>
> Fortunately, in ads from mail-order companies, the monitor is typically "included" in the advertised price. Unfortunately, in ads from local stores, the monitor is typically *not* included in the advertised price; the monitor is "optional" and costs extra.
>
> So if a mail-order company and a local store each advertise a computer for $1000, the mail-order company is probably offering a better deal, since the mail-order price probably includes the monitor, while the local store's price does not.

Extras If your computer is extra-fancy, three extra cables come out of the system unit's rear:

> A cable goes to a **microphone (mike)**, which lets you feed sounds into the computer. If you talk and sing into the mike, the computer can make digital recordings of your speech and performance, analyze them, and react accordingly!
>
> A cable goes to a **scanner**, which is a box that you can shove a sheet of paper into; the scanner reads what's on the paper and tells the computer what the paper said. If you rip an article out of a newspaper and feed it into the scanner, the scanner will transmit the newspaper's article to the computer, so the computer can analyze what's in the newspaper's article and become a smarter computer! If you feed a photo into the scanner, the scanner will transmit the photo to the computer, and the photo will appear on the computer's screen.
>
> If your computer is part of a local-area network, an **Ethernet cable** goes to other computers that are part of the network.

Summary You've learned that in a standard computer system, the main box is called the **system unit**. The other devices that sit nearby the system unit are called the **external peripherals**: they include the keyboard, monitor, mouse, printer, speakers, and — if your system is fancy — a microphone and scanner. Cables run from the external peripherals to the system unit's rear.

Setup Setting up the computer is easy! Just plug the cables into the components, and you're done!

Choose a safe environment During the summer, protect the computer's parts from overheating.

> Keep the computer cool! Turn it off when the room temperature rises over 93° — unless you buy a fan that creates a strong breeze, or you turn the computer off within 90 minutes to let it cool down. Pull down the window shade closest to the computer, to prevent sunlight from beating directly onto the computer.

During the winter, turn the computer off when the room temperature is below 50°.

> If the computer sat overnight in a cold, unheated car or office, don't use the computer until it warms up and any dewdrops in it evaporate.

Make sure your computer gets enough electricity.

> Check which outlets in your house or office attach to which fuses, to make sure the computer's not on the same circuit as an electric heater, refrigerator, air conditioner, or other major appliance that consumes enough electricity to dim the lights.

Portable computers

Instead of buying a standard computer (tower or desktop), you can buy a **portable computer**, which is easier to carry. To be called **portable**, the computer must weigh less than 32 pounds. That weight must include all parts except the printer. The computer must be small enough to be carried with one hand. (To make it easy to carry with one hand, the computer typically has a handle.)

To describe portable computers more precisely, 5 terms have been invented: **luggable**, **laptop**, **notebook**, **subnotebook**, and **pocket**. Careless beginners use those 5 terms interchangeably and call *all* portable computers "laptops" or "notebooks"; but **careful experts define the terms as follows:**

> A **luggable computer** is about the size of a portable sewing machine or bulging briefcase. Carrying it is not pleasant, but you can lug it if you have a strong arm. The typical luggable computer weighs about 20 pounds, but any weight between 16 and 32 pounds is considered "luggable".
>
> A **laptop computer** is smaller. It's small enough to fit in your lap. The typical laptop computer weighs about 14 pounds, but any weight between 8 and 16 pounds is considered "laptop".
>
> A **notebook computer** is even smaller. It's about the size of a student's 3-ring-binder notebook holding a ream of paper. It's about 11 inches wide, 9 inches from front to back, and 2 inches thick. The typical notebook computer weighs about 7 pounds, but any weight between 4 and 8 pounds is considered "notebook".
>
> A **subnotebook computer** is even smaller. The typical subnotebook computer weighs about 3½ pounds, but any weight between 2 and 4 pounds is considered "subnotebook".
>
> A **pocket computer** is the smallest kind of portable computer. It's small enough to fit in your pocket. It looks like a pocket calculator but includes keys you can press for typing all the letters of the alphabet. It weighs less than 2 pounds.

Of those 5 kinds of portable computers, the most popular is "notebook". Now over 90% of all portable computers being sold are notebook computers.

Luggable, and laptop computers are too big and heavy to carry pleasantly. Subnotebook and pocket computers are too tiny and cramped: their screens are too tiny to read pleasantly and their keyboards are too tiny to type on easily. Notebook computers are just the right size!

Here are more details about notebook computers:

> The most popular notebook computers are made by **Compaq** and **Toshiba**. Other famous notebook computers are made by **IBM** and **Apple**. Companies such as **Sager** and **Hyperdata** sell notebook computers that are better deals: they include more equipment per dollar. Most notebook computers cost between $1000 and $4000.
>
> The typical notebook computer opens to reveal two parts. The bottom part (1 inch high) contains the main system-unit circuitry with a built-in keyboard, built-in pair of stereo speakers, built-in **touchpad** (a square pad you rub with your finger instead of using a mouse), and built-in battery. The top part unfolds to become a screen (made of the same materials used in screens of pocket calculators and digital wristwatches).
>
> The notebook computer can get power from its built-in battery; but if you plug the computer into a wall's electrical outlet, the computer will use the wall's power instead while the battery recharges.

Here are more details about pocket computers:

> A pocket computer is also called a **hand-held computer** or **palmtop computer**.
>
> The typical pocket computer comes with programs that help you jot notes, store phone numbers, and keep track of appointments and to-do lists. That kind of pocket computer is called a **personal digital assistant (PDA)**.
>
> The fanciest pocket computer is the **Newton**, developed by a research team from **Apple** and **Sharp**. It comes with many nifty programs that make it a PDA. Instead of including a keyboard, it includes a tablet you write on with a pen; the computer tries to read your scribbled handwriting — but often makes mistakes!
>
> A similar pocket computer is the **Palm Pilot**, made by the **U.S. Robotics** division of **3Com**. It's more popular than the Newton and more popular than all other pocket computers, because it's easy to use and reliable. The professional version costs $249; version 3 costs $329.
>
> Pocket computers that are more traditional and use a keyboard are made by **Sharp**, **Casio**, Hewlett-**Packard**, **Poquet**, **Atari**, and **Radio Shack**. Most cost between $70 and $600.

Unfortunately, portable computers (such as notebook computers) are all ridiculously expensive. Portable cuteness costs a *lot!* A portable computer costs about twice as much as a desktop computer having similar computational abilities. Buy a portable computer just if you insist on taking a computer with you when traveling — and you're rich enough to pay for it.

Hidden computers

A **hidden computer** (or **embedded computer**) hides inside another device.

> For example, a computer hides inside your digital watch. Other computers hide inside your pocket calculator, your Nintendo video-game machine, your microwave oven, and your car's dashboard.

Since such a computer dedicates its entire life to performing just one task (such as "telling the time"), it's also called a **dedicated computer**. Most such computers cost under $10.

Prices drop

On average, computer prices drop 3% per month. That price decline's been in effect ever since the 1940's, and there's no sign of it stopping.

Suppose for a particular computer item the average price charged by dealers is $100. Next month, that item's average price will probably drop 3%, to $97. After *two* months, its average price will have dropped about 3% again, so its price will be 97% of $97, which is $94.09.

Here's how the math works out:

> On the average, computer prices drop about 3% per month,
> 30% per year,
> 50% every two years,
> 90% every six years,
> 99% every twelve years.

Therefore:

> If a computer item's average price is $100 today, it will probably be $97 next month,
> $70 a year from now,
> $50 two years from now,
> $10 six years from now,
> $1 twelve years from now.

The typical computer system costs between $1000 and $2000. Here's what the math looks like for a $2000 system:

> If a computer system costs you $2000 today, it will probably cost you
> $1940 if you buy a month from now,
> $1400 if you buy a year from now,
> $1000 if you buy 2 years from now,
> $200 if you buy 6 years from now,
> $20 if you buy 12 years from now.

Does that mean computer stores will be selling lots of computers for $20 twelve years from now? No! Instead, computer stores will *still* be selling computers for about $2000, but those $2000 systems-of-the-future will be much fancier than the systems sold today. By comparison, today's systems will look primitive — much too primitive to run the programs-of-the-future — so they'll be sold off as old, quaint, primitive junk in flea markets and garage sales.

Find that hard to believe? To become a believer in rapidly dropping prices, just try this experiment: walk into a flea market or garage sale today, and you'll see computer systems selling for $20 that sold for $2000 twelve years ago!

So the longer you wait to buy a computer, the less you'll pay. But the longer you wait, the longer you'll be deprived of having a computer, and the further behind you'll be in computerizing your life and turning yourself into a computer expert.

Don't wait. Begin your new computerized life now!

System's parts

Let's look more closely at the parts of a complete system.

Three main parts

A computer includes three main parts:

> The part that *thinks* is called the **processor** (because it processes info).
>
> The part that *remembers* the computer's thoughts is called the **memory**.
>
> The part that *communicates* those thoughts is called the **in/out system**, because it passes info into and out of the computer.

When you buy a computer, make sure the price includes all three parts!

Each part is important. A computer without memory is as useless as a person who says "I had a great idea, but I can't remember it." A computer without an in/out system is as useless as a person who says, "I had a great idea, and I even remember it, but I won't tell you."

I/O The computer part that communicates — the in/out system — is also called the **input/output system** (or **I/O system**). It consists of many **I/O devices**. The most popular I/O devices to buy are a keyboard, monitor, mouse, printer, and speakers.

> When you buy a computer, check whether the price includes all those I/O devices. If you get them all and they work well, you can join the many excited computerists who sing every day, "I/O, I/O, now off to work I go!"
>
> Two of those devices — the keyboard and mouse — let you put info into the computer. They're called the **input devices**. The other devices — the monitor, printer, and speakers — let the computer spit out the answers and are called the **output devices**.

System unit If your computer is standard, cables run from all those I/O devices to the system unit's rear. Inside the system unit lurks circuitry that helps those I/O devices work. The system unit also includes the **processor** (which thinks) and the **memory** (which remembers).

Inside the system unit

The system unit is a magical box that you'll probably never need to open. But someday, you'll get curious about what's inside.

Here's how to peek inside the system unit of a standard computer (tower or desktop):

> Make sure the computer's turned off.
>
> Remove the screws from the 4 corners of the system unit's back wall. Notice how big those screws are. Remove any other screws of that size from the back wall's edges.
>
> Then remove the system unit's cover. (If the unit's a *tower*, pull the cover back slightly, then lift it. If the unit's a *desktop*, slide the cover forward — or if it refuses, try sliding the cover back — then lift it slightly. *If the cover doesn't quite come off*, jiggle it slightly, and also double-check whether you've removed all the screws holding it in place.)
>
> Finally, peek into the system unit and admire the goodies within! To be safe, avoid touching them.

Inside the system unit, you see several green plastic boards, called **circuit boards** (because they have electric circuits on them). On each circuit board, you see many black rectangular objects, called **chips**: each chip contains a miniature electronic circuit inside!

Motherboard The biggest circuit board is called the **motherboard** (or, more briefly, **mobo**). It's about the size of sheet of paper (8½" × 11"). In a desktop unit, the motherboard lies flat on the bottom; in a tower, the motherboard is vertical, attached to the tower's right edge.

On the motherboard, the biggest chip is the one that does most of the thinking. That chip is called the **central processing unit (CPU)**. It's also called the **microprocessor**. A standard computer uses a brand of microprocessor called a **Pentium**, manufactured by an intelligent California company called **Intel**.

Yes, in a microcomputer, most of the thinking is done by a single chip, called the microprocessor.

> In older, bigger computers, the thinking is done by a gigantic collection of chips working together, instead of a single microprocessor chip. That collection is called the **processor**. The term **microprocessor** was invented by folks amazed that a processor could be made small enough to fit on a single chip.

Expansion cards Besides the motherboard, the system unit contains smaller circuit boards (called **expansion cards**) that snap into slots in the motherboard.

> The most important expansion card is the **video card**. It manages the monitor and attaches to the cable that comes from the monitor.
>
> Another expansion card is the **sound card**. It manages the pair of stereo speakers and attaches to the cable that comes from them.
>
> Another expansion card is the **multi-I/O card**. It manages the printer and mouse and attaches to the cables that come from them.
>
> Another expansion card is the **modem** (pronounced "mode em"). It manages phone signals and attaches to cables that come from the phone and the phone jack.

The keyboard does *not* have its own expansion card. Instead, the keyboard's cable plugs directly into the motherboard.

Memory The three most popular kinds of memory are **ROM chips**, **RAM chips**, and **disks**.

ROM chips remember info *permanently*.

> Even if you turn off the computer's power, ROM chips continue to remember what they've been told. The most important ROM chips are on the motherboard.

RAM chips remember info *temporarily*.

> They're electronic scratchpads that the CPU uses to store temporary reminders. For example, they remember what problem the computer's working on at the moment. They get erased when you switch to a different computer problem or turn the computer off.
>
> In an old computer, most RAM chips are on the motherboard, where the RAM chips are arranged in rows, 8 or 9 RAM chips per row. In a new computer, the RAM chips are instead on tiny expansion cards, which snap into tiny slots on the motherboard: each tiny RAM cards is called a **single in-line memory module (SIMM)** and holds 3, 8, or 9 RAM chips.

Disks work slower than ROM chips and RAM chips but can hold more info. Like ROM chips, disks can remember info *permanently*: unplugging the computer does *not* erase the disks. To use a disk, you must put it into a **disk drive**, which reads what's on the disk. In a standard computer, the system unit includes 3 disk drives, to handle 3 kinds of disks:

> A **CD-ROM disk** looks like a Compact Disk (CD) that music comes on, but a CD-ROM disk contain computer data instead of just music.
>
> A **floppy disk** is made of flimsy material but comes encased is a sturdy square jacket, which is typically 3½ inches on each side (though older disks come in 5¼-inch jackets instead). You can insert the floppy disk (including its jacket) into the floppy-disk drive. You can also remove the floppy disk (including its jacket) from the drive.
>
> The typical **hard disk** is made of hard material, hides in the hard-disk drive permanently, and never comes out, so you never see it.

Each of those three types has its own advantages:

> CD-ROM and floppy disks can be removed from their drives.
> The typical hard disk cannot.
>
> You can edit info if it's on a hard disk or floppy disk,
> but not if it's on a typical CD-ROM disk.
>
> The typical hard disk can hold lots of info.
> The typical CD-ROM disk holds less.
> A floppy disk holds even less.

Power supply The **power cord** comes from your office's wall and goes into the back of the system unit. Look inside the system unit, at the back wall, where the power cord goes in. There you see, inside the system unit, a big metal box, called the **power supply**.

If you look in a *tower*, the power supply is usually at the top of the back wall.

If you stand in front of a *desktop* computer and look down into it, so you see an aerial view, the power supply is usually in the back right corner.

The power supply is an **AC/DC transformer**: it converts the alternating current (coming from your office's wall) to the direct current that your computer requires.

The 3 wares

Computer equipment is called **hardware** because it's built from wires, screws, and other parts you can buy in hardware & electronics stores. Hardware includes the CPU, memory, I/O, cables, and power supply.

The info that the computer deals with is called **software**, because you can't feel it: it flows through the computer's circuits as coded pulses of electricity.

The computer can handle two kinds of software: **data** (lists of names, addresses, numbers, words, and facts) and **programs** (lists of instructions that tell the computer what to do).

To feed the computer some software (data and programs), you can type the software on the keyboard, or insert ROM chips or disks containing the software, or let the computer receive the software from another computer (by running wires between the computers or letting the computers chat with each other by phone).

If you feed the computer wrong software — wrong facts or wrong instructions — the computer will print wrong answers. Wrong stuff is called **garbage**. If you feed the computer some garbage, the computer spits out garbage answers.

So if a computer prints wrong answers, the computer might not be broken; it might just have been fed wrong data or programs. If you think the computer's broken and tell a technician to fix it, the technician might reply, "Hey, the computer's fine! Don't blame the computer! It's *your* fault for feeding it garbage! If you put garbage in, you get garbage out!" That's called the principle of **garbage in, garbage out** (which is abbreviated **GIGO**, pronounced "guy go"). The technician will say, "it's just a case of GIGO".

The person sitting at the computer is called the **liveware**, **operator**, **user**, or **meathead** — because the person's head is made of meat instead of wires.

The term **meathead** was first shouted publicly by that TV character from New York: Archie Bunker. The term **liveware** was invented in 1982 by Garry Trudeau, creator of the Doonesbury cartoons.

For a complete **computer system**, you need all 3 wares: the hardware (equipment), software (info), and liveware (people).

Beware of the 3 wares! You can spend lots to buy hardware (and repair it), buy software (and improve it), and hire people to help you (and train them). Make sure you've budgeted for all 3 wares!

Congratulations! Now you know the three ways that buying a computer can suck up your money. Yes, buying a computer can really suck.

Computers are like drugs: you begin by spending very little on them but soon get so excited by the experience — and so hooked — that you wind up spending more and more to feed your habit.

Your first computer experience seems innocent: you spend just a little money for a cute little computer. You turn the computer on, tell it to play a game, and suddenly the computer's screen shows dazzling superhuman colors that swirl hypnotically before you. You say "Wow, look at all those colors!" and feel a supernatural high.

But after two months of freaking out with your new computer, the high wears off and you wonder, "What can I buy that's new, exciting, and gives me an even bigger high?" So you buy more stuff to attach to your computer. Now you're in really deep, financially and spiritually. You're hooked. You've become addicted to computers. Each month you return to your favorite computer store to search for an even bigger high — and spend more money.

Look at me. I'm a typical computer junkie. I've already bought 40 computers, and I'm still going. Somebody help me! My computers have taken over my home. Whenever I try to go to sleep, I see those computers staring at me, their lights winking, tempting me to spend a few more hours in naughty fun, even if the sun's already beginning to rise.

Computerists use the same lingo as druggies. For example, to buy a computer, you go to a **dealer**; and when you finally start using your computer, you're called a **user**.

As you get in deeper, searching for greater highs, you squander even more money on computer equipment, called **hardware**. You stay up late (playing computer games or removing errors), so next morning you come into work bleary-eyed. Your boss soon suspects your computer habit, realizes you're not giving full attention to your job, and fires you.

Jobless while your computer bills mount ever higher, you soon run out of money to spend on computers but still urge to spend more! To support your habit, you write or buy programs and try to resell them to friends. That makes you a pusher. You turn your friends into addicts too, and you all join the ever-increasing subculture of computer junkies.

Here's the only difference between drugs and computers: if you're into drugs, people call you a "washout"; but if you're into computers, people say you have a "wonderful career" — and they're right!

As a computer pusher, you can make lots of dough; but to do it successfully, you must do it in style: instead of calling yourself a "pusher", call yourself a **computer consultant**. Yes, a computer consultant is a person who gives computer advice to other victims — and pushes them into buying more computers!

A computer consultant who gives free computer help seems kind is a wolf in sheep's clothing. The truth is revealed in these lines of Tom Lehrer's song, "The Old Dope Peddler":

He gives the kids free samples
Because he knows full well
That today's young innocent faces
Will be tomorrow's clientele.

Your marriage

The computer will fascinate you. It'll seduce you to spend more and more time with it. You'll fall in love with it.

You'll start buying it presents. You'll buy it exotic foods (expensive programs to munch on). You'll buy it new clothes (dress it in a pretty little cloth cover, to keep the dust off). You'll adorn it with expensive jewels (a printer and extra disks).

Then the computer will demand you give it more. While you're enjoying an exciting orgy with your computer and think it's the most joyous thing that ever happened to you, suddenly the computer will demand you buy it more memory. It'll refuse to continue the orgy until you agree to its demand. And you'll agree — eagerly!

The computer's a demanding lover. You'll feel married to it.

Marrying a computer is much groovier than marrying a person: computers are good at "getting it on" (they make you feel all electric and tingly) and they never argue (they're always ready to "do it", except when they "have a headache").

I wanted to call this book "The *Sexual* Guide to Computers" and put a photo of my computer wife and me on the cover; but some communities still prohibit mixed marriages. That cover would be banned in Boston, which (alas!) is where I've lived. So I had to play cool and say "Secret" Guide to Computers. But here's the real secret: this book's about sex.

If you get married to a computer but you're already married to a human, your human spouse will call you a "bigamist" and feel jealous of the computer. Your marriage to that human can deteriorate and end in divorce.

Several women got divorced because they took my computer course. Their husbands had two complaints:

> "You spend most of your time with the computer instead of with me. When you *do* spend time with me, all you want to talk about is the computer."

To prevent such marital problems, coax your spouse to play a game on the computer. Your spouse will get hooked on the game, become as addicted to the computer as you, enjoy blabbing about the computer with you, and encourage you spend money on your habit. Sociologists call that **technological progress**.

Why buy a computer?

The average American has three goals: to make money, have fun, and "become a better person". Making money is called **business**; having fun is called **pleasure**; and becoming a better person is called **personal development**. The computer will help you do all three: it'll improve your business, increase your pleasure, and help you grow into a better person.

Nowadays, computers are bought by men, women, and children of all ages.

The *traditional* computer buyer's a male who comes out at noon:

> During lunch hour, he walks into a computer store and says he wants to computerize his business: do his accounting and handle his mailing list. The computer store's salesperson talks him into also wanting a word-processing program, to help handle business correspondence.
>
> After visiting one or two other computer stores, he buys a computer. Though the computer costs a lot, the salesperson reminds him that the IRS gives a tax break for buying it since it's a "business expense".
>
> He brings it home but feels guilty about having spent so much. How will he convince his wife that the purchase was wise?
>
> Suppose his wife's an old-fashioned mom who cooks. He tries to convince her that the computer will help her cook....
>
> "It will help you store your recipes, darling," he coos.
>
> "No thanks," she replies. "When I find a recipe in the newspaper, I don't want to spend 20 minutes typing the goddam entire recipe into the computer. I'd rather just clip it out of the newspaper and — presto! — tape it to a file card. My manual system is faster than a computerized one!"
>
> He tries again. "You could use the computer to store your phone numbers. When you want to find a phone number, the computer will tell you instantly."
>
> She retorts, "No thanks. To make a phone call, I don't want to have to turn the computer on, request the phone-number program, wait for the computer to ask whose number I'm interested in, type in the jerk's entire name, then wait for the computer to respond. Instead of doing all that, it's quicker to just open my little black phone book, flip to the page where the number is, and dial my friend. Try again, lover-boy!"
>
> "Well, darling, you could use the computer to remind you of birthdays and appointments."
>
> "You must be crazy! I remember them quite well without a computer. I scribble a note on my calendar, which serves fine and costs just $10 instead of $1000. I understand how a disorganized bird-brain, like you, might need a computer to survive; but since I'm better organized, I don't need to rely on mechanical help."
>
> Though admitting the computer does *not* fulfill any real need in the home, he lusts to buy a computer anyway — for the thrill of it — and looks for an excuse to justify the cost. **The computer's a solution looking for a problem.**

Women buy computers too:

> Apple ran a TV ad showing Dick Cavett in a kitchen, as he interviews a woman who bought a computer. "You're using it to store your recipes?" he asks. "No!" she retorts, "I'm using it to chart stocks!"

If you buy a computer, the idea of "using the computer to run your business" and "using the computer to store recipes" are just excuses. **Here are the REAL reasons why people buy computers....**

> **Teenager:** "Computers are a blast: sci-fi come true! Programming computers is the next best thing to becoming an astronaut!"
>
> **Parent:** "Computers are taking over! My kids must learn to master computers, to survive! If I buy my kids a computer, they'll explore it (instead of sex & drugs), wonder how it's programmed, become programmers, get straight A's in school, become computer consultants, and make lots of dough, so they can support me in my old age and I can brag about them to my neighbors."
>
> **Grandparent:** "I want to be part of the 20th century. The whole world's becoming computerized, and I don't want my grandkids to think I'm 'out of it.' I want to taste this new excitement. I wouldn't blow money on this stuff myself, but my kids are giving me a computer so the grandkids can send me mail and photos electronically, using the Internet. Those grandkids are so cute! Computers are so much fun!"
>
> **Kindergartner:** "Grandma, I wanna computer for my birthday! And if you don't buy it, they say I'll never go to Harvard."
>
> **Social climber:** "Damn! Now that big cars and cell phones are passé, the computer's the only status symbol left. I'm sick of being intimidated by neighbors and bosses spouting computer jargon, and I'm tired of the guys at the bar bragging about how big their computers are. I'm gonna learn that mumbo-jumbo myself so I can get back at those pompous asses and intimidate *them*!"
>
> **Worried worker:** "My company is computerizing. If I don't master computers, they might master *me* and steal my job! If I learn enough about computers, I can keep my job. I can even get promoted, then quit and become a rich computer consultant!"
>
> **Middle-aged:** "My life's become boring. I need a fresh new hobby — a computer! It would be fun and help my business. I could fondle that cute toy even after my company retires me. Hey, I could start my *own* business, advertise on the Internet, and become internationally famous!"
>
> **Adventurer:** "The computer's a challenge. If I can master it, I know I'm not as stupid as people say!"
>
> **Wanting what's due:** "I've worked hard all my life; I *deserve* a computer! I'm gonna get my hands on that mean machine, force it to obey all my commands, and make it my personal slave."
>
> **Subversive:** "If Big Brother has Big Blue watching me, I'll turn my computer into Big Mama and scramble their waves!"
>
> **Doctor:** "Playing with the computer's anatomy is like playing God. Besides, the computer could make my patients pay their bills!"
>
> **English teacher:** "My students get so hooked on computer games! I'm gonna find out why, then sneakily make computers channel the kids' excitement toward a higher good: poetry!"
>
> **Social-studies teacher:** "The Internet is amazing! So much info is being published there about current events and our history & future! I've gotta show it to my students, so they become part of what this world is about! Then they can do research by using the Internet, publish their *own* papers on the Internet, and become internationally famous! I'll become the teacher that makes our school famous, and I'll become famous myself!"

Will your computer fulfill all those dreams? This Guide will help you find out!

Hassles

When you buy a new computer for your business, you'll have lots of hassles.

Repairs Since a complete computer system includes so many parts (CPU, RAM, keyboard, disk drives, printer, software, etc.), *at least one* of them won't work properly, and you'll need to fix it. Since the manufacturer or store will provide free repairs during the first year, you'll lose nothing but your temper.

Manuals You won't completely understand the manuals for your hardware and software, so you'll ask your friends and me for help. You can also try getting help from the manufacturers and dealers; but if your question's long-winded, their answers will be curt.

If the dealer who sold you the computer is honest, he'll say, "I don't know how to run all the hardware and software I sold you. To learn how, read the manuals. No, I haven't read them myself, because they're too long-winded, complicated, and vague. If you don't like the manuals, take our courses, which are expensive and won't teach you as much as you need but at least will make you feel you're making *some* progress."

Most dealers are not that candid.

Programs If you try writing your own programs, you'll discover Murphy's law: no matter how long you think a program will take to write, it will take you longer. If you're wiser and try to buy a finished program from somebody else, you'll find the program works worse than advertised, its manual is missing or unintelligible, and you'll need to modify the program to meet your personal needs.

Data entry If you figure out how to use the program, your next torture is to type the data you want the program to process. The typing is sheer drudgery, but you must do it.

Worthwhile? Those headaches are just the *beginning* of what can become an extended nightmare. Buying a computer starts by being exciting but quickly becomes nerve-racking.

Eventually, you'll get past that nerve-racking transition stage and become thrilled.

That painful transition is worth the effort if you plan to use the computer a lot. But if you plan to use a computer just occasionally, you might be better off not buying a computer at all: continue doing your work manually.

Promises Salespeople wanting you to buy fancy hardware or software say "it will be great", but computer stuff never turns out as good as promised.

For example, there's the tale of the woman who was married three times but remained a virgin. Her first husband, on his wedding night, discovered he was impotent; her second husband, on *his* wedding night, decided he was gay; and her third husband was a computer salesman who spent the whole night saying how great it was going to be.

Moral: computer salesmen make great promises but don't deliver.

There's also the story of how a programmer died and came to the gates of Heaven, guarded by St. Peter, who let the programmer choose between Heaven and Hell. The programmer peeked at Heaven and saw angels singing boring songs. He peeked at Hell and saw wild orgies, so he chose Hell. Suddenly the wild orgies vanished, and he was dragged to a chamber of eternal torture. When he asked "What happened to the wild orgies?", the devil replied "Oh, that was just the demo."

Moral: many wild technologies are enticing; but when you try actually experiencing them, you have a devil of a time!

To keep up-to-date about computers, read newspapers and magazines. They contain the latest computer news, criticize hardware and software, advise you on what to buy, and include ads for the newest products, services, and discount dealers.

Some ads and articles use technical computer jargon, which you'll understand by reading this book.

How to get periodicals

Visit your local computer stores, bookstores, and newspaper stands, and buy a copy of each newspaper and magazine that interests you.

If you live near Boston, you'll find many computer magazines in the kiosks in the middle of Harvard Square (at **Out of Town News** and **Nini's Corner**) and at a chain of convenience stores called **White Hen Pantry**. Two computer-store chains (**Comp USA** and **Micro Center**) sell computer magazines at discounted prices.

After reading the periodicals you bought — or borrowed from your local library — subscribe to the ones you like best.

Most periodicals come with a coupon that gives you a "special" discount off the subscription price "for new subscribers, if you hurry". Don't bother hurrying: the same discount is offered to practically everybody every year. And next year, when you renew, you'll be offered the same "special" discount, "for our loyal readers, if you hurry".

Shortly after buying a one-year subscription, you'll receive a dishonest letter from the publisher warning that your subscription will "run out soon" and that "if you renew now, you'll get a special discount". Don't believe the letter; "run out soon" usually means "run out eight months from now", and "if you renew now" means "if you renew sometime within the eight months, or even later". Feel free to wait.

How to read reviews

Many computer periodicals review the newest hardware and software. Don't take the reviews too seriously: the typical review is written by just one person and reflects just that individual's opinion.

Some reviewers are too easy: they heap praise and say everything is "excellent". Other reviewers are too demanding: they say everything is "terrible". If one product gets a rave review, and a competing product gets a scathing review, the reason might be the difference between reviewers rather than the difference between products.

Giant conglomerates

Most computer magazines and newspapers are published by two giant conglomerates: **Ziff-Davis** and **IDG**.

Ziff-Davis is a gigantic publisher in Manhattan. By the 1970's Ziff-Davis was publishing magazines about many hobbies. In 1982, when computers became a popular hobby, Ziff-Davis bought several computer-magazine publishers, so it's become a conglomerate of hobby-magazine and computer-magazine publishers. Ziff-Davis is usually called **ZD** or just **Ziff**. It's based in Manhattan. It was bought by a Japanese company called **Softbank**, which then resold it to a group of American investors.

IDG (based in Framingham, Massachusetts) began publishing **Computerworld** in 1967. Later it bought up and published many other computer periodicals around the world. Now IDG publishes 270 computer periodicals in 75 countries.

Ziff and IDG have declared war on each other. For example, IDG refuses to publish articles by columnists who submit articles to Ziff. Each computer columnist must choose between either being a **Ziffer** or an **IDG'er**.

Mostly monthly

Most computer magazines are published monthly and let you buy individual issues (for under $5) or an annual subscription (for about $25).

General computer magazines

Here are the 7 best computer magazines for the general public:

Magazine	Publisher	Price	Pages	1 year	2 yrs.	Editorial office	Toll free
Computer Shopper	Ziff-Davis	$3.99	350	12 issues, $25	$45	NY 212-503-3900	800-274-6384
PC World	IDG	$5.99	250	12 issues, $22	$44	CA 415-243-0500	800-825-7595
PC Magazine	Ziff-Davis	$4.99	250	22 issues, $35	$60	NY 212-503-5255	800-289-0429
Smart Computing	Sandhills	$4.95	100	12 issues, $29	$48	NE 402-477-8900	800-733-3809
Family PC	Ziff-Davis	$3.99	150	12 issues, $12	$12	MA 413-582-9200	800-413-9749
Maximum PC	Imagine	$7.99	100	12 issues, $12	$24	CA 415-468-4684	800-274-3421
Computer Currents	IDG	$5	50	12 issues, $20	$40	CA 510-547-6800	800-365-7773

I've put the most important (Computer Shopper) at the top of the list, and listed the others in order of importance. That list shows each periodical's name, publisher, price (for a single issue), number of pages (rounded to the nearest 50), how many issues are printed per year, price of a 1-year subscription (using the discount card that's in the magazine), price of a 2-year subscription, editorial office's state and phone number, and any toll-free number for ordering a subscription.

To be fully aware of what's happening with computers, get all 7 of those magazines. If you can't afford all 7, start at the list's top and work your way down.

Topping the list is **Computer Shopper**.

It's bigger than any other computer magazine. Though not as huge as it was during the mid-1990's, each issue still contains at least 350 pages.

It's the only magazine where the most aggressive discount dealers advertise. It's where you'll find the lowest prices. That's why people buy it: to look at the ads. It's also the only magazine that includes an ad-product index, where you can look up any product (such as "laser printers by Hewlett-Packard") and find the page numbers of all ads offering that product.

Browsing through Computer Shopper, you might see an ad bragging that a product was declared "Computer Shopper Best Buy of the Year". That praise sounds impressive — until you realize that the judges were "all the magazine subscribers who sent in postcards", and the award just means the subscribers admired the ad's low price and didn't necessarily try or even see the product!

Subscribers receive Computer Shopper about the 15th day of the preceding month: for example, they receive the February issue on about January 15th. You won't find it in stores until about 2 weeks after that: for example, you won't find the February issue in stores until the last few days of January.

Computer Shopper used to be independent but was bought by Ziff-Davis (which in turn was bought by Softbank).

PC World is the best-balanced magazine. It's smaller than Computer Shopper and more carefully edited.

Of all the computer magazines, PC World does the best job of surveying readers to find out which computer brands are the most reliable and which computer companies are most helpful when answering phone calls. PC World publishes the survey results twice a year.

PC World is the only computer magazine that has an active consumer-complaint department. It publishes complaints about rip-offs and bad service. It also plays consumer advocate and gets the baddies to change their ways and give refunds to customers.

Even if you buy just one issue of PC World, you can learn a lot from it, since each issue includes an updated list of the best brands of desktop computers, notebook computers, printers, video cards, and modems, with detailed ratings.

Each issue of **PC Magazine** concentrates on a few topics and covers them more thoroughly than any other magazine. For example, a PC Magazine article about printers will compare more printers than any other magazine.

Since the typical PC Magazine article is thorough and long, just a few articles appear in each issue. But a 1-year subscription gets you lots of issues: 22 of them (1 issue in July, 1 in August, and 2 in each other month).

PC Magazine tends to recommend computer equipment that's expensive, since PC Magazine assumes its typical reader is willing to spend $4,000 on a computer system. I wish the magazine would try to help readers whose income is lower.

I can't imagine anybody reading a complete issue of PC Magazine from cover to cover. Do you really want to read so many details about *every* printer? PC Magazine is like an encyclopedia: you're not supposed to read it all, but you're glad to know it's all there.

PC Magazine is historic: it was the first magazine about the IBM PC and clones. At first, it was independent. When Ziff-Davis bought it, most of the staff quit and started PC World for Ziff-Davis's competitor, IDG. Then Ziff-Davis hired a new staff, which was excellent. But eventually, PC Magazine's top editors left to start newer magazines.

Of all the magazines, the easiest to read is **Smart Computing**.

Since it's easy, it was called "PC Novice"; but in 1997 changed its name to "Smart Computing" to emphasize that it helps *everybody* who wants to become smarter, not just beginners.

Each article is superbly crafted to explain even the most difficult topics simply. If you want to understand how computers work, this is the magazine to get. Unlike other computer magazines, this magazine emphasizes "how computers work" rather than "which brands to buy". This magazine is the shortest — but sweetest!

All other computer magazines are published in California or on the East Coast, but Smart Computing is published in Nebraska instead. Maybe that's why its writing is straightforward instead of strung out.

Robin Raskin left PC Magazine and is now editor-in-chief of the best new magazine, **Family PC**.

It's published by Ziff-Davis working with Disney. Like other Disney productions, it's easy to understand, charming, and family-oriented.

It contains the most accurate appraisals of which computer equipment & programs are the easiest & most pleasant for ordinary folks to use.

If you buy a 1-year subscription ($12), the second year is free!

Maximum PC is the most youthful, exciting, and irreverent computer magazine. It emphasizes computer games and other high-tech wow. Subscriptions cost just $12 per year. A single issue is expensive ($7.99) because it includes a CD-ROM disk.

Like a newspaper, **Computer Currents** is printed on extra-wide pages of newsprint paper. At first glance, it looks like a thin version of Computer Shopper. Like Computer Shopper, its main importance is its ads.

It's printed in 8 local editions: San Francisco, Los Angeles, Chicago, Dallas, Austin, Houston, Atlanta, and Boston. Each edition has its own ads from local dealers and its own local news. If you live near one of those cities, Computer Currents is the best way to find out about local computer dealers and events.

Each issue also includes some articles of national importance. The articles have a delightfully relaxed, chatty style and stay short enough to be to-the-point.

Of all computer magazines, Computer Currents has the most devilish back page: it contains satire by the world's best computer satirist (Lincoln Spector) and a cartoon by the world's best computer cartoonist (Rich Tennant). They'll make you laugh, especially after you've immersed yourself in computer culture long enough to understand what they're satirizing.

In the San Francisco area, Computer Currents is distributed free at newsstands. In most other parts of the country, you must buy a subscription.

Specialized magazines

Here are the best magazines about the **Internet**:

Magazine	Publisher	Price	Pages	1 year	2 yrs.	Editorial office	Toll free
Yahoo Internet Life	Ziff-Davis	$2.99	100	12 issues, $20	$40	NY 212-503-4790	
Net Guide	CMP	$3.95	200	12 issues, $15	$30	NY 516-562-5000	800-829-0421

Yahoo Internet Life is the most fun; **Net Guide** covers topics that are more serious.

Here are the best magazines about Apple's **Mac computers**:

Magazine	Publisher	Price	Pages	1 year	2 yrs.	Editorial office	Toll free
Macworld	Mac Pub'ing	$7.99	200	12 issues, $35	$50	CA 415-243-0505	800-627-2247
Mac Addict	Imagine	$7.99	150+CD	12 issues, $30	$60	CA 415-468-4869	

The two serious Mac magazines used to be IDG's **Macworld** and Ziff's **Mac User**, but in 1997 those magazines merged into a combo called **Macworld**, It's published by a company called **Mac Publishing**, owned by IDG and Ziff working together. **Mac Addict** is wackier and costs more because it comes with a CD.

Computer newsweeklies

Here are the 4 best sources of weekly news about computers:

Newsweekly	Publisher	Price	Pages	1 year	Editorial office	Toll free
Industry Standard	IDG	$3.95	200	48 issues, $50 or $0	CA 415-733-5400	800-395-1977
Computerworld	IDG	$5	100	51 issues, $58 or $0	MA 508-879-0700	800-669-1002
E Week	Ziff-Davis	$3.95	100	51 issues, $195 or $0	MA 617-393-3700	800-451-1032
Infoworld	IDG	$3.95	100	51 issues, $160 or $0	CA 415-572-7341	

Each is published weekly (except the week after Christmas and The Industry Standard's extra holidays). **The Industry Standard** is a weekly magazine that's easy to read and emphasizes Internet business; the other three are newspapers that discuss computers more generally and are tougher to digest. **E Week** (which used to be called **PC Week**) emphasizes the IBM PC and clones; **Infoworld** emphasizes networking PC's together; **Computerworld** emphasizes bigger systems and management/social issues.

They're intended for computerists who buy lots of computers. To subscribe, you complete application forms asking how many computer purchases you make or influence yearly. If you answer acceptably, you get the newspapers free; otherwise, you must pay a lot.

That method of distribution — "specialists get it free, idiots pay through the nose" — is called **controlled circulation**. It assures advertisers that the readers are either influential or rich. Alas, it widens the gap between the "haves" and the "have-nots": if you're a low-income novice, this policy is guaranteed to "keep you in your place", unless you're lucky enough to find those magazines in your local library.

Examine the back page

In many computer magazines and newspapers, the most fascinating writing occurs on the back page.

For example, the best humorists are Lincoln Spector (on the back page of Computer Currents), Rich Tennant (whose cartoons grace the back page of Computer Currents, PC Magazine, and Computerworld), and Carl Steadman (on the back page of The Industry Standard). The best rumor-mongerer is **Spencer F. Katt** (who's a cartoon cat on the back page of PC Week).

Daily newspapers

For today's news about computers, read the business section of your town's daily newspaper, or read national newspapers such as **USA Today**, **The Wall Street Journal**, and **The New York Times**.

Every Thursday is computer day. That's when **The New York Times** publishes its Circuits section (which is section E), and that's when **The Wall Street Journal** runs Walter Mossberg's computer column (on the first page of the Marketplace section).

Discount dealers

In computer magazines and newspapers, many ads offering big discounts. And if you buy from a dealer who isn't in your state, the dealer won't charge you sales tax.

Discount dealers change prices every month. Instead of asking them for catalogs (which might be out of date), examine their most recent ads. Then phone to confirm the prices. Usually, prices go down every month, but sometimes they rise.

Before buying, ask whether the product's in stock, how long the dealer will take to fill your order, and how it will be shipped. Ask what the dealer charges for shipping: many dealers overcharge! Ask whether there's a surcharge for using a credit card. Since products are improved often, make sure the dealer is selling you the *newest* version.

If the product you get is defective, the dealer or manufacturer will fix or replace it. But if the product is merely "disappointing" or doesn't do what you expected or isn't compatible with the rest of your computer system, tough luck!

Many discount dealers say "all sales are final." Other dealers let you return computers but not printers, monitors, or software. Some dealers let you return products but charge you a "restocking fee", which can be up to 25% of the purchase price!

So before you buy, ask questions about the product's abilities to make sure it will do what you expect. Tell the dealer what hardware and software you own, and ask the dealer whether the product's compatible with your system.

The typical product comes in a cardboard box. On the back of the box (or on some other side), you'll usually see a list of the **system requirements**. That's a list of what hardware and software you must already own to make that product work with *your* computer.

Use your credit card

Pay by credit card rather than a check. If you pay by credit card and have an unresolved complaint about what you bought, Federal laws say that the credit-card company can't bill you! Moreover, if the mail-order company takes your money, spends it, and then goes bankrupt before shipping your goods, the credit-card company gets stuck, not you!

The nicest credit cards (such as Citibank's) double the manufacturer's warranty, so a "one-year warranty" becomes a *two*-year warranty! Does *your* credit card give you that warranty extension? Ask your bank!

What's missing?

When buying computer equipment, find out what the advertised price does *not* include.

For example, the advertised price for a "complete computer system" might not include the screen. Ask! In a typical printer ad, the price does *not* include the cable that goes from the printer to your computer.

Read the fine print

When reading an ad, make sure you read the fine print at the bottom of the ad. It contains many disclaimers, which admit that the deal isn't quite as good as the rest of the ad implies.

> In the middle of an ad, next to an exciting price or feature or warranty, you'll often see an asterisk (*). The asterisk means: "for details, read the fine print at the bottom of the ad". That fine print contains disclaimers that will disappoint you. In long multi-page ads, the fine print is often buried at the bottom of just *one* of the ad's pages, far away from the page where the asterisk appeared, in the hope that you won't notice the fine print.
>
> So if you see what looks like a great deal, but the deal has an asterisk next to it, the asterisk means "the deal is not really as great as we imply".

Many computer ads contain this fine print:

"Monitor optional" means this price does *not* include a monitor. The monitor costs extra, even though the ad shows a photo of a computer with a monitor.

"Upgrade price" means you get this price just if you already own an older version of this stuff.

"With system purchase" means you get this price just if you're stupid enough to also buy an overpriced full computer system at the same time.

"Reflects cash discount" means you get this price just if you're stupid enough to pay cash instead of using a credit card. (By paying cash, you can't complain to a credit-card company if you get ripped you off.) If you use a credit card, the seller will charge you about 3% above the advertised price.

"Includes rebate" means you must pay more, then request a rebate from the manufacturer. (You'll probably never get that rebate, since you'll forget to ask for the rebate form, or you'll forget to mail the rebate form to the manufacturer, or the rebate form will have already expired, or you'll lose the receipt or code number you must mail with the rebate form to get the rebate, or you can't mail the receipt because you already used it to apply for a rebate on a second item you bought simultaneously, or the manufacturer loses your paperwork or is a jerk who waits many months to send the rebate or goes bankrupt.)

"Manufacturer's warranty" means that if the stuff breaks, don't ask the seller for help. Phone the original manufacturer instead (who'll probably ignore you).

"Factory serviced" means another customer bought this stuff, didn't like it, and returned it to the factory, which examined it and thinks it's good enough to resell (after jiggling it a bit), so now *you're* getting stuck with this lemon.

"For in-stock items" means that although the seller promised to ship immediately, the seller won't if you order stuff that's not yet in the warehouse.

"25% restocking fee" means that if you return the stuff, you won't get your money back. Instead, the seller will keep 25% of your money (as a restocking fee) and return just 75% to you.

Mail-order dealers

Back in the 1980's, two big mail-order dealers set the tone for the rest of the discount industry. Those dealers were **Telemart** and **PC Connection**.

When **Telemart** went bankrupt in 1993, its assets were sold to **Computer Discount Warehouse (CDW)**, which has continued Telemart's tradition of low prices and wide selection. Phone CDW in Illinois at 800-500-4CDW (for Mac goodies) or 800-454-4CDW (for IBM-compatible goodies).

PC Connection has the best reputation for service because it processes orders fast, charges little for shipping, handles hassle orders promptly and generously, and gives technical help on a toll-free 800 number.

> PC Connection is in the tiny town of Marlow, New Hampshire. It began in a barn, then expanded to fill the inn across the street.
>
> PC Connection has two divisions: IBM and Mac.
>
> The IBM division advertises in *PC World* (phone 800-800-0003 or 603-446-0003) and *PC Magazine* (phone 800-800-0004 or 603-446-0004). The Mac division calls itself **Mac Connection** in *Macworld* (phone 800-800-3333 or 603-446-3333). You can use the 800 numbers even if you're in Alaska, Hawaii, Puerto Rico, Virgin Islands, and Canada.
>
> Each division works round-the-clock, 24 hours daily. Your order's shipped immediately, even if you've paid by check. (Checks are cleared in less than a day.) Your order's shipped by Airborne overnight express so it reaches you the next day; if you order between 12:01AM and 3:15AM Eastern Time, you'll usually receive your order the *same* day (because the company built a warehouse next to Airborne's airport in Ohio).
>
> The IBM division is nice, the Mac division is even nicer! The IBM division's toll-free number is usually busy; the Mac division's toll-free number usually gets you a sales rep immediately. The IBM division offers fairly low prices (but not as low as other discount dealers); the Mac division offers rock-bottom prices, lower than almost any other Mac dealer.
>
> The computer isn't quite as nice as before. For shipping, the company used to charge $5 or less, even if your order was huge, but now charges more. The company used to give a money-back guarantee but now gives no refunds for returned computers & printers and charges a 15% restocking fee for all other items.

The competitor that PC Connection fears the most is New Jersey's **Micro Warehouse**, which offers a greater variety of hardware and software. But Micro Warehouse gives less technical help and sometimes has delays in shipping.

> Like PC Connection, Micro Warehouse has two divisions. For the IBM division, phone 800-367-7080 or 732-905-5245. For the Mac division (which is called **Mac Warehouse**), phone 800-255-6227 or 732-367-0440.
>
> Micro Warehouse bought several competitors, such as **USA Flex** and **Network Express**. To reach "USA Flex" or "Network Express", call Micro Warehouse.

Another competitor is Washington State's **Multiple Zones**.

> Like Micro Warehouse, it offers low prices on IBM and Mac goodies. Its IBM division, **PC Zone**, is at 800-258-2088. The Mac division, **Mac Zone**, is at 800-248-0800. For international calls to either division, phone 425-883-3088.

A big discount dealer called **Insight** used to advertise in *Computer Shopper* magazine but now advertises electronically instead, using the Internet. Insight is in Arizona at 800-INSIGHT or 602-902-1176.

Egghead Discount Software was a chain of stores giving discounts on software for the IBM PC and Mac. In February 1998, Egghead closed all its stores and now sells just by mail-order.

> Phone Egghead's headquarters in Washington State at 800-EGGHEAD. Egghead charges less than other mail-order dealers. Egghead's service has been poor, but now Egghead is trying to improve.
>
> Egghead has acquired a discount dealer called **Surplus Direct**, which sells old versions of excellent IBM-compatible software at very low prices: often $19.95! Phone Surplus Direct in Oregon at 800-753-7877 or 541-387-6000.
>
> Even if you want the newest software, your best bet's often to buy an old version from Surplus Direct and then use that purchase as an excuse to get the special "upgrade price" on the new version. The old version's price plus the upgrade price is usually less than the price of buying the new version directly.

Stores

If you need hardware or software fast and can't wait for mail-order dealers to ship, go to the local computer stores that advertise in the business section of your local newspaper.

To encourage a store to give you a discount, mention low prices from competitors and agree to buy many items at once. Say that if you don't get a discount, you'll shop elsewhere. Many stores do **price-matching**: they'll match the price of any other local store, though not the prices of mail-order dealers. Some stores let salespeople give 10% discounts, which are subtracted from the salesperson's commission.

IBM and Apple give educational discounts to schools, teachers, and some college students. To find out whether *you* can get educational discounts, ask your school's administrators and your town's computer stores.

For low prices, visit a chain of huge superstores called **Comp USA**.

> It began in Dallas in 1984, when it was called **Soft Warehouse** and sold software by mail-order. It opened its first retail store in 1985. It opened a bigger store — a **superstore** — in 1988. In 1991 it changed its name to **Comp USA**, because it was also selling computer hardware. It became a big chain of superstores.
>
> In 1996, it bought a mail-order company called **PCs Compleat**. In 1996, it bought a competing chain of superstores, called **Computer City**, which had been secretly owned by Tandy's Radio Shack.
>
> Now Comp USA is a chain of about 200 superstores in 42 states. For example, its New York City store is at 420 5th Ave., 212-764-6224.
>
> To find the Comp USA store nearest *you*, phone 800-Comp-USA. Phone day or night, 24 hours, and use that number to order computer goodies or a free catalog.
>
> For **software and Hewlett-Packard printers**, Comp USA charges less than most other stores and mail-order dealers. For other printers and accessories, Comp USA's prices aren't as aggressive: you'll pay less at a competing superstore chain called **Staples** (which sells computers and also **general office supplies**). But Comp USA offers a greater variety of computer products than Staples, and Comp USA's salespeople are more knowledgeable and helpful.
>
> Unfortunately, Comp USA handles repairs slowly (you must wait about a week), and Comp USA's prices for most hardware are slightly above other discounters. To get an IBM clone cheaply, buy elsewhere. But Comp USA is the only big chain of stores where you can still buy a **Mac**.

Another computer-superstore chain is **Micro Center**.

> It has 18 superstores (in Massachusetts, New York, Pennsylvania, Ohio, Virginia, Georgia, Illinois, Minnesota, Kansas, Colorado, Texas, and California).
>
> It's the most pleasant place to browse, since the staff is friendly and the selection is huge: the typical Micro Center store contains 45,000 square feet displaying 36,000 products. A gigantic room is devoted to books, a gigantic room is devoted to Macs, a gigantic room is devoted to I/O devices (such as printers and scanners), etc. To find the store nearest you, phone 800-743-7537.
>
> Micro Center's salespeople are usually more knowledgeable than Comp USA's and make customers happier.

In cities where chains compete against each other, Comp USA lowers prices to undercut competitors.

> Comp USA puts up signs comparing prices and showing how much you save by shopping at Comp USA instead of Micro Center. But Micro Center still has the lowest prices on certain items, especially blank disks, computer magazines, and old editions of books.

In California's Silicon Valley, visit a chain of superstores called **Fry's Electronics**, which has been a local favorite for many years. In New York City, visit a superstore called **J&R Computer World**, which is near Wall Street (15 Park Row, New York City NY 10038, 800-221-8180 or 212-238-9000).

Bagel boys

Three discount dealers in New York City are called the **bagel boys** because most of their employees resemble me: Jewish men who enjoy eating bagels. (Yum!) Many of their employees are Hassidic Jews, an ultra-traditional sect who wear black suits, black coats, black hats, and beards. For the Jewish Sabbath, they close on Friday afternoon, stay shut on Saturday, and reopen on Sunday.

Those dealers sold cameras and other photography equipment, then started selling computer hardware also, plus a little software. They offer especially low prices on **printers, monitors, modems, and notebook computers**.

Here's how to reach them:

S&W Computers & Electronics, 31 W. 21st St.	800-874-1235	212-463-8330
Tri State Computer, 650 6th Ave. (at 20th St.)	800-433-5199	212-633-2530
Harmony Computers, 1801 Flatbush Ave. Br'klyn	800-441-1144	718-692-3232

If you phone Tri State computer, ask for David Rohinsky at extension 223. He'll treat you extra-nice.

Those three stores accept both walk-ins and mail-order. They've all advertised in *Computer Shopper* and *The New York Times*, though lately they've reduced their advertising.

Since they offer rock-bottom prices and deliver fast, I often buy there. But they have these drawbacks:

> Their tech-support staffs are too small. You'll get faster repairs elsewhere.
>
> They often buy overstocked items from other dealers and resell them; but since those items have changed hands, the manufacturer's "limited warranty" on those items is no longer valid.
>
> Though reputable now, their past was murky. In 1994, the biggest software company (Microsoft) sued Harmony for distributing software improperly. During the 1980's, Tri State advertised printers at low prices but honored those prices just if you overpaid for the printer's cable. Most of those companies removed supplies & programs from the boxes of printers & computers they sold and charged extra to put the goodies back in.

Computer shows

Another way to find low prices is at a computer show. The lowest prices are at small shows called **flea markets** or **swap meets**.

Many vendors at shows offer discounts, especially during the show's last three hours. When you buy at a show, jot down the vendor's name, address, and phone number, in case the goods don't work.

Beware: many vendors at those shows are like gypsies, traveling from show to show and hard to reach if you have a complaint. Many sell computers containing illegal copies of software that was never paid for and whose instruction manuals are missing. Make sure any software you buy comes with an official instruction manual (published by the company that invented the software), not just a book from a bookstore.

Used computers

Instead of buying a new computer, you can save money by getting a used one.

The oldest source of used microcomputers is **The Boston Computer Exchange** (**BoCoEx** or **BCE**), begun in 1982; phone 800-262-6399 or 617-625-7722. Another used-computer broker is Atlanta's **American Computer Exchange** (**AmCoEx**) at 800-786-0717 or 404-250-0050.

New computers cheap

On page 72, I'll explain the *best* way to buy a complete new IBM clone cheaply.

CHIPS

Chip technology

The **system unit** is the box containing the CPU and other goodies (such as the speaker, power supply, and memory). If you unscrew that box and pry it open to see the circuitry inside, you'll see a green plastic board, on which is printed an electrical wiring diagram.

Since the diagram's printed in copper (instead of ink), the diagram conducts electricity; so it isn't just a diagram of an electrical circuit; it *is* an electrical circuit!

The green plastic board — including the circuit printed on it — is called a **printed-circuit board (PC board)**. Each wire that's stamped onto the PC board is called a **trace**.

The typical computer contains several PC boards.

Motherboard & babies

In your computer, the largest and most important PC board is called the **motherboard** (or, more briefly, **mobo**). It lies flat on the bottom of the system unit.

The other PC boards are smaller. Those little baby boards (about the size of a postcard) are called **PC cards**.

The typical motherboard has several **slots** on it. Into each slot, you can put a PC card.

PCMCIA cards

If you buy a modern notebook computer, you'll see the case's right-hand wall has a special slot in it. You can shove a card into that slot without opening the notebook's case.

The kind of card that fits into that special slot is small and thin — the size of a credit card. That kind of card was invented by the **Personal-Computer Memory-Card International Assocation (PCMCIA)** and therefore called a **PCMCIA card**. That slot is called a **PCMCIA slot**.

People have trouble remembering what "PCMCIA" stands for. Cynics say it stands for "People Can't Memorize Computer Industry Acronyms". Since "PCMCIA" also stands for "Politically Correct Members of the CIA", computerists pronounce "PCMCIA" in two breaths: they say "PCM", then pause, then say "CIA".

Some PCMCIA cards are *very* thin. Other PCMCIA cards are slightly thicker, so they can hold extra circuitry. A PCMCIA card and its slot are called **Type 1** if their thickness is 3.3 millimeters, **Type 2** if 5 millimeters, **Type 3** if 10.5 millimeters, **Type 4** if 18 millimeters.

Caterpillars

On each PC board, you'll see black rectangles. If you look closely at a black rectangle, you'll see it has tiny legs, so it looks like a black caterpillar. (Though farmers think it looks like a "black caterpillar", city folks think it looks more like a "yucky roach". Kids call it just "a black thingy with legs".)

The "caterpillars" come in many sizes. In a typical computer, the shortest caterpillars are three-quarters of an inch long and have 7 pairs of legs; the longest are two inches long and have 20 pairs of legs.

Though each black caterpillar has legs, it doesn't move. It's permanently mounted on the PC board.

Each leg is made of tin and called a **pin**.

Sadistic hobbyists play a game where they yank the caterpillars from a PC board and throw the caterpillars across the room. That game's called "tin-pin bowling".

Hidden inside the caterpillar is a metal square, called a **chip**, which is very tiny. The typical chip is just an eighth of an inch long, an eighth of an inch wide, and a hundredth of an inch thick! On that tiny metal chip are etched *thousands* of microscopic electronic circuits! Since all those circuits are on the chip, the chip's called an **integrated circuit (IC)**.

Four purposes

Each chip serves a purpose. If the chip's purpose is to "think", it's called a **processor chip**. If the chip's purpose is to "remember" information, it's called a **memory chip**. If the chip's purpose is to help devices communicate with each other, it's called an **interface chip**. If the chip's purpose is to act as a slave and helper to other chips, it's called a **support chip**.

So a chip is either a processor chip or a memory chip or an interface chip or a support chip — or it's a combination chip that accomplishes *several* purposes.

How chips are designed

To design a chip, the manufacturer hires an artist, who draws on paper a big sketch of what circuits are to be put onto the chip. It helps if the artist also has a degree in engineering — and knows how to use another computer to help draw all the lines.

After the big sketch is drawn, it is photographed.

Have you ever photographed your friend and asked the photography store for an "enlargement"? To produce a chip, the chip's manufacturer does the opposite: it photographs the sketch but produces a "reduction" to just an eighth of an inch on each side! Whereas a photo of your friend is made on treated paper, the tiny photo of the chip's circuitry consists of metal and semiconductors on treated silicon so the photo's an actual working circuit! That photographic process is called **photolithography** (or **photolith**).

Many copies of that photo are made on a large silicon wafer. Then a cookie cutter slices the wafer into hundreds of chips. Each chip is put into its own caterpillar.

The caterpillar's purpose is just to hide and protect the chip inside it; the caterpillar's just a strange-looking package containing the chip. Since the caterpillar's a package that has two rows of legs, it's called a **dual in-line package (DIP)**. That DIP's only purpose is to house the chip.

Computer hobbyists are always talking about chips & DIPs. That's why computer hobbyists, at parties, serve chips & dips. And that's why computer hobbyists are called "dipchips".

Buying chips

If you ask a computer dealer to sell you a chip, the dealer also gives you the chip's DIP (the entire caterpillar). Since you've asked for a chip but also received a DIP, you might get confused and think that the caterpillar (the DIP) is the chip. But that caterpillar's *not* the chip; the chip hides inside the caterpillar.

The typical caterpillar-and-chip costs $3. You might pay somewhat more or somewhat less, depending on how fancy the chip's circuitry is.

If the circuits in a chip are defective, it's called a "buffalo chip". Folks who dislike that tacky term say "potato chip" or "chocolate chip" instead, like this: "Hey, the computer's not working! It must be made of chocolate chips!"

You can get chips from these famous mail-order chip suppliers:

Chip supplier	Address	Phone
JDR Microdevices	1850 S. 10th St., San Jose CA 95112	800-538-5000 or 408-494-1400
Jameco	1355 Shoreway Rd., Belmont CA 94002	800-831-4242 or 650-592-8097
ACP	1310 E. Edinger, Santa Ana CA 92705	800-FONE-ACP

The following chip suppliers are newer and often charge less:

Chip supplier	Address	Phone
Spartan Technologies	1500 E. Higgins Rd. #A, Elk Grove Village IL 60007	888-393-0340 or 847-364-9900
Memory Man	PO Box 11227, New Orleans LA 70181	800-MEGABYTE or 504-818-2717
Chip Merchant	9541 Ridgehaven Ct., San Diego CA 92123	800-426-6375 or 619-268-4774
A+ Memory Express	15140 Valley Blvd., City of Industry CA 91744	800-877-8188 or 818-333-6389

How chips chat

The chip inside the caterpillar acts as the caterpillar's brain. The caterpillar also contains a "nervous system", made of thin wires that run from the brain (the chip) to the legs (the pins). The wires in the caterpillar's nervous system are very thin: each wire's diameter is about half of a thousandth of an inch.

If one caterpillar wants to send electrical signals to another caterpillar, the signals go from the first caterpillar's brain (chip) through the caterpillar's nervous system to its legs (pins). Each pin is attached to a trace (wire) on the PC board. The signals travel through those traces, which carry the signals across the PC board until the signals reach the second caterpillar's pins. Then the signals travel through the second caterpillar's nervous system to that caterpillar's brain (chip).

__Binary code__ To communicate with each other, the caterpillars use a secret code. Each code is a series of 1's and 0's. For example, the code for the letter A is 01000001; the code for the letter B is 01000010; the code for the number 5 is 101; the code for the number 6 is 110.

That's called the **binary code**, because each digit in the code has just *two* possibilities: it's either a 1 or a 0. In the code, each 1 or 0 is called a **binary digit**.

A **binary digit** is called a **bit**. So in the computer, each **bit** is a 1 or a 0.

When a caterpillar wants to send a message to another caterpillar, it sends the message in binary code. To send a 1, the caterpillar sends a high voltage through the wires; to send a 0, the caterpillar sends little or no voltage through the wires.

So to send the number 5, whose code number is 101, the caterpillar sends a high voltage (1), then a low voltage (0), then a high voltage (1). To send those three bits (1, 0, and then 1), the caterpillar can send them in sequence through the same leg (pin); or for faster transmission, the caterpillar can send them through three pins simultaneously: the first pin sends 1, while the next pin sends 0 and the third pin sends 1.

The speed at which bits are sent is measured in **bits per second (bps)**.

Bipolar versus MOS

Chips can be manufactured in two ways:

The old way's called **bipolar**.

The new way's called **metal-oxide semiconductor** (**MOS**, which is pronounced "moss"). It's more popular because it costs less, consumes less electricity, and can hold more circuitry inside the chip.

Microcomputers use just MOS. Minicomputers and maxicomputers use mainly MOS chips but also contain a few bipolar chips, because bipolar chips have one (and only one) advantage over MOS chips: bipolar chips work faster.

The most popular kind of MOS is called **negative-channel MOS**. (It's also called **n-channel MOS** or **NMOS**, which is pronounced "en moss".) The main alternative, called **complementary MOS** (or **CMOS**, pronounced "sea moss"), consumes even less electricity but can't hold as much circuitry inside the chip. CMOS chips are used in simple-minded battery-operated computers (such as digital watches, pocket calculators, pocket computers, and notebook computers) and in some parts of larger computers.

The part of the computer that thinks ("the brain") is called the **processor** (or **central processing unit** or **CPU**).

In a maxicomputer or minicomputer, the processor consists of several chips, which are **processor chips**.

In a microcomputer, the processor is so small that it consists of just a single chip, called a **microprocessor**. It sits on the motherboard. Yes, in a typical microcomputer, the part that does all the thinking is just a tiny square of metal, less than ¼" on each side!

Intel's designs

In the IBM PC and clones, the microprocessor uses a design invented by **Intel**. I'll explain Intel's microprocessors now (and discuss competitors later).

In the original IBM PC (and in the IBM PC XT), the microprocessor was the **Intel 8088**. IBM computers (and clones) containing that chip are called **XT-class computers**.

Later, Intel invented an improved version, called the **Intel 80286**. Since "80286" is too long a number for us humans to remember, most of us just call it the **Intel 286**. Since IBM used it in the IBM PC AT computer, all computers using that chip are called **AT-class computers**.

After inventing the Intel 286, Intel invented a further improvement (called the **Intel 386**), then an even further improvement (called the **Intel 486**).

In 1993, Intel began selling an even further improvement, which ought to be called a **586**; but Intel calls it the **Pentium** instead, so Intel can trademark the name and prevent companies from copying it. It's the first computer chip that sounds like a breakfast cereal: "Hey, kids, to put zip into your life, try Penti-yumms. They build strong bodies, 5 ways!"

While inventing the Pentium, Intel gave it this secret code-name: **"P5"**. Many folks still call that chip the P5.

So altogether, IBM microcomputers and clones come in five popular classes:

Chip	Invented	Transistors on chip
8088	1979	29,000 transistors
286	1982	134,000 transistors
386	1985	275,000 transistors
486	1989	1,200,000 transistors
Pentium (P5)	1993	3,100,000 transistors

Some programs run okay on any chip; but many *modern* programs require a 386, 486, or Pentium and won't run on an 8088 or 286.

To run modern programs FAST and use all the modern features, you need a Pentium. Most computers built today contain a Pentium.

The 8088, 286, 386, and 486 chips are found just in pocket computers, used computers, and old computers that liquidators try to unload. Many homes and offices still have old 8088 computers, bought many years ago. Folks who still use those ancient computers restrict themselves to running very old-fashioned programs.

Megahertz

In an army, when soldiers march, they're kept in step by a drill sergeant who yells out, rhythmically, "Hup, two, three, four! Hup, two, three, four! Hup, two, three, four!"

Like a soldier, the microprocessor takes the next step in obeying your program just when instructed by the computer's "drill sergeant", which is called the **computer clock**. The clock rhythmically sends out a pulse of electricity; each time the clock sends out a pulse, the microprocessor does one more step in obeying your program.

The clock sends out *millions* of pulses every second, so the microprocessor accomplishes *millions* of steps in your program every second!

Each pulse is called a **clock cycle**. The clock's speed is measured in **cycles per seconds**.

A "cycle per second" is called a **hertz (Hz)**, in honor of the German physicist Heinrich Hertz. A "million cycles per second" is called a **megahertz (MHz)**.

When Intel invented the Pentium chip in 1993, the Pentium's clock did 60 million cycles per second. That's 60 megahertz! Intel also invented a faster Pentium, at 66 megahertz, then even faster Pentiums at 75, 90, 100, 120, 133, 150, 166, 200, 233, 266, 300, 333, 350, 400, 450, 500, 550, 600, 650, 667, 700, 733, 750, 800, 850, 866, and 933 megahertz. For example, a 200-megahertz Pentium thinks twice as fast as a 100-megahertz Pentium.

A 60-megahertz Pentium is called a **Pentium-60**. A 200-megahertz Pentium is called a **Pentium-200**.

Slower than a Pentium

The Pentium is an amazing chip: while it thinks about one part of your program, it simultaneously starts getting the next part of your program ready for processing. That chip's ability to do several things simultaneously is called **parallel processing**.

The Pentium is smarter than earlier chips (the 8088, 286, 386, and 486): the Pentium can perform more tasks simultaneously; it performs more parallel processing.

Earlier chips seem slower: too often during a clock cycle in earlier chips, part of the chip "does nothing" while waiting for the other part of the chip to catch up. Those earlier chips therefore accomplish less useful work during a clock cycle than a Pentium.

> During a clock cycle, a 486 accomplishes half as much useful work as a Pentium. We say the 486's **usefulness factor** is ½.
>
> During a clock cycle, a 386 accomplishes a quarter as much useful work as a Pentium, so the 386's usefulness factor is ¼. A 286's usefulness factor is $\frac{1}{5}$. An 8088's usefulness factor is $\frac{1}{20}$.

You've seen that those early chips accomplish less useful work during a clock cycle than a Pentium. Moreover, they accomplish fewer clock cycles per second than a Pentium; they have fewer megahertz:

Chip	Megahertz	Usefulness
Intel 8088	4.77, 7.18	$\frac{1}{20}$
Intel 286	6, 8, 10, 12	$\frac{1}{5}$
Intel 386	16, 20, 25, 33	$\frac{1}{4}$
Intel 486	20, 25, 33, 50, 66, 75, 100	$\frac{1}{2}$
Pentium	60, 66, 75, 90, 100, 120, 133, 150, 166, 200, 233, 266, 300, 333, 350, 400, 450, 500, 550, 600, 650, 667, 700, 733, 750, 800, 850, 866, 933, 1000	1

For example, suppose you buy an Intel 486 going at 100-megahertz. Since it suffers from a usefulness factor of ½, it accomplishes just ½ as much useful work per cycle as a 100-megahertz Pentium, so it acts about as fast as a 50-megahertz Pentium. A 20-megahertz 386, which suffers from a usefulness factor of ¼, acts about as fast as a 5-megahertz Pentium. A 10-megahertz 286, which suffers from a usefulness factor of $\frac{1}{5}$, acts about as fast as a 2-megahertz Pentium.

The slowest chip is a 4.77-megahertz 8088. Since it suffers from a usefulness factor of $\frac{1}{20}$, it acts about as fast as a 0.2385-megahertz Pentium. That's 4193 times slower than the fastest Pentium, which goes at 1000 megahertz. Yes, the fastest IBM-compatible computers think over 4000 times faster than the slowest ones! That's progress!

The "usefulness factor" is just an approximate average. During a cycle, for example, a 486 accomplishes about ½ as much useful work as a Pentium, *on the average*; but on certain tasks a 486 accomplishes *more* than "½ as much", and on other tasks it accomplishes less.

Variant chips

The Intel 8088 comes in two versions. One version (called simply the "8088") goes slightly slower than the other version (called the **8086**).

The Intel 386 comes in two versions. One version (called the **386SX**) goes slightly slower than the other version (called the **386DX**).

The Intel 486 comes in two versions. One version (called the **486SX**) goes slower than the other version (called the **486DX**). Moreover, the 486DX comes in three varieties: the original 486DX, the **486DX2**, and the **486DX4**.

Intel's invented six versions of the Pentium:

> The **Pentium classic** is the oldest and slowest kind of Pentium. Invented in 1993, it's the kind of Pentium found in most computers built from 1993 through 1996.
>
> The **Pentium MMX** is slightly faster. Invented in January 1997, it's the kind of Pentium found in most computers built in 1997. It runs most programs about 15% faster than a Pentium classic; for example, a 200-megahertz Pentium MMX runs programs about 15% faster than a 200-megahertz Pentium classic. That's because the Pentium MMX is designed slightly better than a Pentium classic and contains twice as much **internal level-1 cache memory** (an extremely fast form of memory that holds a copy of what's coming from other memory). It's called **MMX** because it also understands 57 extra instructions (called **MultiMedia eXtensions**), which can theoretically increase the speed of multimedia (video & sound) dramatically; but no important programs have been invented yet to make good use of those 57 extra instructions. Those 57 extra instructions just duplicate some of the intelligence found on fancy video-&-sound cards anyway. Intel's official name for this chip is **"Pentium with MMX Technology"**, but most folks say just **"Pentium MMX"**.
>
> The **Pentium 2** is even faster. Invented in May 1997, it became popular when Intel dropped the price in 1998. It runs most programs about 30% faster than a Pentium MMX. Like the Pentium MMX, it understands the 57 multimedia instructions. Intel's official name for this chips is **"Pentium II"**; but to avoid Roman numerals I'll write **"Pentium 2"**.
>
> The Pentium 2 replaces an old 1995 expensive version, called the **Pentium Pro**, which ran some programs fast but ran other programs slowly (even slower than a Pentium classic!) and lacked MMX. The Pentium Pro was nicknamed the **686** or **P6**; the Pentium 2 now inherits those same nicknames.
>
> To help folks who can't afford a real Pentium 2, Intel began selling a cheaper version, called the **Pentium Celeron**, in 1998. It's slower.
>
> In February 1999, Intel invented a speeded-up Pentium 2, called the **Pentium 3**. Using a technique called **Single-Instruction Multiple-Data (SIMD)**, it understands 70 extra instructions, called **Streaming SIMD Extensions (SSE)**, which few programs use yet.

Here's how many megahertz are available:

Intel chip	Megahertz
8088	4.77, 7.18
8086	8, 10
286	6, 8, 10, 12
386SX	16, 20, 25, 33
386DX	16, 20, 25, 33
486SX	20, 25, 33
486DX	25, 33, 50
486DX2	50, 66
486DX4	75, 100
Pentium classic	60, 66, 75, 90, 100, 120, 133, 150, 166, 200
Pentium Pro	150, 166, 180, 200
Pentium MMX	166, 200, 233
Pentium Celeron	266, 300, 333, 366, 400, 433, 466, 500, 533, 566, 600, 633, 667, 700
Pentium 2	233, 266, 300, 333, 350, 400, 450
Pentium 3	450, 500, 533, 550, 600, 650, 667, 700, 733, 750, 800, 850, 866, 933, 1000

Here are some prices:

Intel chip	Megahertz	Price
486DX2	66	$10
Pentium classic	133	$22
Pentium classic	166	$31
Pentium MMX	233	$43
Pentium Celeron	400	$79
Pentium Celeron	466	$83
Pentium Celeron	533	$96
Pentium Celeron	566	$104
Pentium Celeron	600	$109
Pentium Celeron	633	$143
Pentium Celeron	667	$182
Pentium 3	733	$219
Pentium 3	800	$277
Pentium 3	850	$435
Pentium 3	866	$452
Pentium 3	933	$656
Pentium 3	1000	$990

That chart shows the price charged by discount dealers (such as Spartan Technologies, Memory Man, and The Chip Merchant) for a single chip when this book went to press in August 2000. By the time you read this, prices might be lower, since Intel drops prices frequently (about every 2 months). If you buy 1000 chips at a time directly from Intel, you pay even less.

Imitations

Intel's competitors have imitated Intel's chips. Some of the imitations go faster than Intel's originals!

Intel chip	The most popular imitations, and their speeds
8088	The V20 chip, made by NEC, imitates the 8088 but goes faster: 10 megahertz.
8086	The V30 chip, made by NEC, imitates the 8086 and goes fast: 10 megahertz.
286	Imitations made by Harris come in 16-megahertz and 20-megahertz versions.
386SX&DX	Imitations made by AMD (Advanced Micro Devices) come in 40-megahertz versions.
486SX&DX	AMD's imitations of the 486 are excellent and come in 66-megahertz, 80-megahertz, 100-megahertz, and 120-megahertz versions. Cyrix and IBM make awful 486 imitations that go *much slower* than Intel's originals and ought to be called "386½" instead of "486". Cyrix's imitation of the 486SX is called the 486SLC; Cyrix's imitation of the 486DX is called the 486DLC. IBM's imitation of the 486DX is called the Blue Lightning (BL).
Pentium classic	Imitations are made by AMD and Cyrix. They work much slower than Intel's Pentium and should be called "486½" instead. For example, a 133-megahertz AMD 586 goes about as fast as an 80-megahertz Pentium would go.

Pentium Pro	Cyrix makes an imitation named the 686, but it's slow: cynics call it the "586½".
Pentium 2	AMD makes an imitation called the K6 and also makes an improved K6, called the K6-2. Both versions are slightly slower than a Pentium 2 but much faster than a Pentium MMX. Their prices are ridiculously low. For a K6-2, discount dealers (such as Spartan Technologies and Memory Man) charge just $63 for 533 MHz, $75 for 550 MHz. The K6-2 is an amazing bargain! Its decent speed and ridiculously low price makes it the best value of chips made today. Cyrix's imitations (the 6x86MX and the M2) are both disappointing.
Pentium Celeron	AMD makes an imitation called the Duron. Discount dealers (such as Spartan Technologies and Memory Man) charge just $72 for 600 MHz, $87 for 650 MHz, $109 for 700 MHz.
Pentium 3	AMD makes an imitation whose official name is Athlon and whose nickname is K7. Discount dealers (such as Spartan Technologies and Memory Man) charge just $157 for 700 MHz, $170 for 750 MHz, $196 for 800 MHz, $259 for 850 MHz, $295 for 900 MHz, $384 for 950 MHz, $514 for 1000 MHz, $749 for 1100 MHz.

Half-assed systems

While a chip is waiting for you to tell it what to do, the chip accomplishes nothing useful during the wait: it just mumbles to itself.

To make full use of a fast Pentium, make sure you know what commands to give the computer. To help the chip reach its full potential, buy lots of RAM, big disk drives, and a quick printer. Otherwise, the Pentium will act as idiotic as if it's in the army: it will just "hurry up and then wait" for other parts of the system to catch up and tell it what to do next.

A mind is a terrible thing to waste! To avoid wasting the computer's mind (the CPU), make sure the other computer parts are good enough to match the CPU and keep it from waiting.

If you get suckered into buying a computer that has a fast Pentium chip but insufficient RAM, insufficient disk drives, and a slow printer, you've bought a computer that's just half-fast; it's half-assed.

Total cost

When you buy a microcomputer, its advertised price includes a microprocessor, motherboard, and other goodies. Pay for the microprocessor separately just if you're inventing your own computer, buying parts for a broken computer, or upgrading your computer by switching to a faster microprocessor & motherboard.

Though the microprocessor is cheap, the computer containing it can cost thousands of dollars. That's because the microprocessor is just a tiny part of the computer. In addition to the microprocessor, you want memory chips, interface chips, support chips, PC boards (to put the chips on), I/O devices (a keyboard, screen, printer, speaker, and mouse), disks, and software.

Discount dealers, used-computer stores, and garage sales get you IBM clones for these prices:

Chip	Complete computer
8088 or 8086	$50
286	$100
386	$200
486	$300
Pentium	$800

Those prices include nearly everything you need (such as the CPU, memory chips, disks, keyboard, and a screen displaying many colors) but do *not* include a printer or software. Those prices are approximate; the exact price you pay depends on the CPU's speed (how many megahertz) and on the other components' speed, quality, and size.

Notice that a 286 computer costs $100, which is $50 more than an 8086 computer. That's because a 286 computer includes a better CPU chip and also comes with a better keyboard, better screen, better memory chips, and better disks.

Math coprocessor

Each Pentium chip includes **math coprocessor circuitry**, which handles advanced math fast. That circuitry can multiply & divide long numbers & decimals; it can also compute square roots, logarithms, and trigonometry.

Primitive chips — the 8088, 8086, 286, 386SX, 386DX, and 486SX — do *not* include such circuitry.

> To make a primitive chip do advanced math, you must feed the chip a program that teaches the chip how to break the advanced problem down into a series of simpler problems. That program runs slowly — nearly 100 times slower than if a math coprocessor were present!
>
> You'll be *very* annoyed at the slowness if you're a scientist trying to do advanced math — or an artist trying to rotate a picture, since the computer computes the rotated image's new coordinates by using trigonometry. For example, if you draw a 3-D picture of a house and then ask the computer to show how the house looks from a different angle, you need a math coprocessor to avoid a long delay.
>
> But if you use the computer just as a souped-up typewriter (to record and edit your writing) or as an electronic filing cabinet (to record names and addresses on a mailing list), you'll never notice the lack of a math coprocessor, since you're not doing advanced math.

Each **486DX** chip (and 486DX2 and 486DX4) includes math-coprocessor circuitry; the **486SX** does not. So **here's the only difference between a 486DX and a 486SX: the 486SX lacks math-coprocessor circuitry.**

> Intel invented the 486DX, then later invented the 486SX by using this manufacturing technique: Intel took each 486DX whose math coprocessor was faulty and called it a 486SX. So a 486SX was just a defective 486DX.
>
> If you buy a 486SX today, you get a 486DX whose math coprocessor is either defective or missing.

If your CPU lacks math-coprocessor circuitry (because your CPU is an 8088, 8086, 286, 386, or 486SX), here's how to do math quickly: buy a supplementary chip, called a **math coprocessor chip**. Put it next to the CPU chip on the motherboard. It contains the math-coprocessor circuitry that the CPU lacks.

CPU	Which math coprocessor to buy
8088, 8086	Intel 8087
286	Intel 287
386SX	Intel 387SX
386DX	Intel 387DX
486SX	Intel 487SX

Chart of details

Here are more details about how Intel's chips differ from each other:

Chip	Internal accum.	External data path	Address	MMX	SSE	Math copr.	Internal MHz	External Mhz
8088	16-bit	8-bit	20-bit	no	no	no	4.77, 7.18	same as internal
8086	16-bit	16-bit	20-bit	no	no	no	8, 10	same as internal
286	16-bit	16-bit	24-bit	no	no	no	6, 8, 10, 12	same as internal
386SX	32-bit	16-bit	24-bit	no	no	no	16, 20, 25, 33	same as internal
386DX	32-bit	32-bit	32-bit	no	no	no	20, 25, 33	same as internal
486SX	32-bit	32-bit	32-bit	no	no	no	25, 33	same as internal
486DX	32-bit	32-bit	32-bit	no	no	yes	25, 33, 50	same as internal
486DX2	32-bit	32-bit	32-bit	no	no	yes	50, 66	one-half of internal
486DX4	32-bit	32-bit	32-bit	no	no	yes	75, 100	one-third of internal
Pentium classic	64-bit	64-bit	32-bit	no	no	yes	75	50
Pentium classic	64-bit	64-bit	32-bit	no	no	yes	60, 90, 120, 150	60
Pentium classic	64-bit	64-bit	32-bit	no	no	yes	66, 100, 133, 166, 200	66
Pentium MMX	64-bit	64-bit	32-bit	yes	no	yes	166, 200, 233	66
Pentium Pro	86-bit	86-bit	36-bit	no	no	yes	150, 180	60
Pentium Pro	86-bit	86-bit	36-bit	no	no	yes	166, 200	66
Pentium Celeron	86-bit	86-bit	36-bit	yes	no	yes	266,300,333,366,400,433,466,500	66
Pentium 2	86-bit	86-bit	36-bit	yes	no	yes	233, 266, 300, 333	66
Pentium 2	86-bit	86-bit	36-bit	yes	no	yes	350, 400, 450	100
Pentium 3	86-bit	86-bit	36-bit	yes	yes	yes	450,500,550,600,650,667,700, 733,750,800,850,866,933	100

Here are more details about what the chart means....

Internal accumulator
Each chip contains **registers**. Each register can hold a binary code number (such as 01000001).

The chip's main register is called the **accumulator**.

> If the accumulator is wide enough to hold 32 bits (such as 10000110111001111110010101010101), the accumulator is called **32-bit**; the chip is said to **contain a 32-bit accumulator** and be **32-bit internally**.
>
> If the accumulator is narrower and holds just 16 bits, the accumulator is called **16-bit**. In that case, the chip can handle code numbers that are 16 bits long but *not* code numbers that are 32 bits long. If you try to feed that chip a 32-bit code number, the chip won't understand it.
>
> **The typical program uses just 16-bit instructions.** (Instead of using a 32-bit instruction, it uses a pair of 16-bit instructions.)
>
> But **a few fancy programs use 32-bit instructions**. To run those 32-bit programs, you must buy a chip that's 32-bit internally. The chart shows that to run the fanciest programs (32-bit), you must buy at least a 386SX.

External data path
The column marked "**external data path**" tells how many of the chip's pins transmit data.

> As you can see from the chart, the 386SX is "32-bit internal, 16-bit external". That means the 386SX contains a 32-bit accumulator but has just 16 data pins. To transmit the accumulator's 32 bits, the chip sends out 16 of the bits (on the 16 data pins), then sends out the next 16 bits by using those same pins.
>
> That technique of using just a few pins to transmit many bits is called **multiplexing**. Computerists say the 386SX is "a 32-bit chip **multiplexed** onto 16 pins"; they say **the 386SX is a multiplexed 386DX**. That's why the 386SX is slightly slower than the 386DX: to transmit the 32 bits, the 386SX must send out two bursts of 16 bits, whereas the 386DX can send out a single burst of 32 bits all at once!
>
> Notice that the 386SX is just as smart as the 386DX — it understands the same 32-bit codes — but it transmits them more slowly (as 2 bursts of 16, instead of 1 burst of 32). So **the 386SX is smart but a slow communicator** — like Einstein with his mouth full and trying to talk through a narrow drinking straw.
>
> **The 8088 is a multiplexed 8086.** Like the 8086, the 8088 thinks about 16 bits; but the 8088 must send them out in two 8-bit bursts.

Address
The computer's main memory (which consists of RAM chips and ROM chips) is like a city: each location in it has an **address**. If the main memory is large enough to hold lots of info, it has lots of addresses.

A city has addresses such as "231 17th Street, Apartment 501". In the computer's main memory, each address is a binary code number instead, such as 01000101010111101010.

For an 8088 or 8086, each address must be brief: just 20 bits long. An 8088 or 8086 therefore can't handle a big main memory — and can't handle big programs.

A 286 can handle longer addresses (24-bit) so it can handle the big main memory required by modern big programs. To run modern big programs, you must buy at least a 286.

> Though 24-bit addresses are long enough to handle all popular programs sold today, the chart shows that the fanciest chips permit even bigger addresses (32-bit or 36-bit), to prepare for the bigger programs of the far future — and to handle computers that are networked together and share a gigantic big RAM.

External megahertz

If a chip is simple (an 8088, 8086, 286, 386SX, 386DX, 486SX, or 486DX), it communicates at the same speed as it thinks. For example, a chip that thinks at 20 megahertz communicates at 20 megahertz.

The laws of physics make it difficult & expensive to manufacture a motherboard that communicates faster than 66 megahertz. The typical CPU chip thinking faster than 66 megahertz therefore slows down when communicating with the other chips on the motherboard.

> For example, suppose you buy a Pentium 2 chip that's advertised as being "333-megahertz". That means the chip performs 333 million cycles per second while thinking; but when the chip wants to transmit its answers (or questions) to other chips on the motherboard, the chip performs the transmission at just 66 megahertz. So the chip thinks quickly but talks slowly — like a lawyer smart enough to talk slowly to a stupid jury.
>
> The chart shows that most Pentium chips communicate at 50, 60, or 66 megahertz. Just the fastest Pentium 2 chips (the Pentium 2-350, Pentium 2-400, and Pentium 2-450) and Pentium 3 chips communicate at 100 megahertz.
>
> A **486DX2** chip communicates half as fast as it thinks. For example, a 50-megahertz 486DX2 chip communicates at 25-megahertz. That chip is said to be **50 megahertz internally, 25 megahertz externally**. Since that chip thinks twice as fast as it communicates, it's called a **clock-doubled chip**.
>
> A **486DX4** chip communicates a third as fast as it thinks. For example, a 75-megahertz 486DX4 chip communicates at 25-megahertz. Since that chip thinks three times as fast as it communicates, it's called a **clock-tripled chip**. Since the chip is clock-tripled, it *ought* to be called a "486DX3"; but Intel calls it a "486DX4" instead because Intel wants to pretend it's better than "486DX3" chips manufactured by IBM.

Motorola

Intel's biggest competitor is **Motorola**. It manufactures the **6809E microprocessor**, the **68000** (which is faster and understands advanced commands), several souped-up versions of the 68000, and the **Power PC**:

Chip	Price	Computers that use it
6809E	$3	Radio Shack Color Computer
68000	$9	Mac, Mac Plus, Mac SE, Mac Classic, Amiga (500, 600, 1000, 2000), Atari ST
68020	$45	Mac LC, old Mac 2, Amiga 1200
68030	lots	Mac (SE/30, Classic 2, LC 2, LC 3), new Mac 2, Amiga 2500 & 3000
68040	lots	Mac Centris, Mac Quadra, and Amiga 4000
Power PC	lots	Power Mac, iMac

Motorola's microprocessors are *not* Intel clones. They use different commands than Intel and require different software.

When fed the proper software, they work as fast as Intel's microprocessors:

Motorola's 6809E	is about as fast as Intel's 8080 (which was the predecessor to the 8088)
Motorola's 68000	is about as fast as Intel's 8086
Motorola's 68020	is about as fast as Intel's 286
Motorola's 68030	is about as fast as Intel's 386
Motorola's 68040	is about as fast as Intel's 486
Motorola's Power PC	is about as fast as Intel's Pentium

What's the Power PC?

Motorola's fastest microprocessor, the **Power PC**, was invented by a team of researchers from three companies (Motorola, Apple, and IBM), all working together. That's why it's called the **love-triangle chip**. It was invented to prevent Intel from monopolizing the microcomputer marketplace.

> The first version of the Power PC, called the **Power PC 601**, was manufactured just by IBM. Later versions (the **Power PC 603, 604,** and **604e**) are manufactured by both Motorola and IBM.

The Power PC is used in Apple's newest Mac computers, such as the **Power Mac** and the **iMac**.

Intel emulation

Suppose your computer's microprocessor is made by Motorola, but somebody gives you software written for Intel microprocessors instead. You can run that software on your computer if you feed your computer an **Intel emulator** (software that makes Motorola microprocessors imitate Intel's). But Intel emulator software runs slowly. To accomplish tasks faster, buy software that runs directly on Motorola microprocessors without needing an Intel emulator.

Math coprocessor

Want a Motorola math coprocessor?

> For the 6809E CPU, no math coprocessor is available. For the 68000 or 68020, buy **the 68881 math coprocessor** ($49). For the 68030, buy the **68882 math coprocessor** ($69). The 68040 comes in two versions: the standard version (called the **68RC040**) includes math-coprocessor circuitry; the stripped-down version (called the **68LC040**) does not. The Power PC includes math-coprocessor circuitry. In Motorola & Mac jargon, a math coprocessors is called a **floating-point unit (FPU)**.

Primitive computers

Primitive old microcomputers contain microprocessors invented by **Zilog** and **MOS Technology**. They're *not* Intel clones.

Zilog, which was owned by Exxon, made the **Z-80A microprocessor**, which was super-cheap: just $2! It's in many obsolete computers, such as the Radio Shack TRS-80 models 1 & 2 & 3 & 4 & 12, the Kaypro 2 & 4 & 10, the Epson QX-10 & Geneva, the Timex-Sinclair 1000 & 1500, and the Coleco Adam.

The **6502 microprocessor** was invented by **MOS Technology**, which became part of Commodore. It was also manufactured by other chip makers, and you could get souped-up versions that understood extra commands and went faster.

Chip	Price	Computers that use it
6502	$2	Apple 2 & 2+ & old 2e, Atari 800
65C02	$7	Apple 2c & 2c+ & new 2e
6510	$15	Commodore 64 & 128 & Vic
65C816	$17	Apple 2GS

The 65C02 and the 65C816 are made of CMOS; that's why their names contain the letter C. The other chips in that table are traditional: they're made of NMOS.

How many pins?

A cheap microprocessor (such as an 8088, 8086, Z-80, 6502, or 6809E) comes in a DIP (caterpillar) that has 40 pins (20 pairs of pins).

Fancier chips have more pins.

> For example, the Motorola 68000 comes in a DIP that has 64 pins.
>
> If a chip is even fancier (such as the 68-pin Intel 286 or the 132-pin Intel 386DX), it requires too many pins to fit in a DIP. Instead of coming in a DIP, the chip usually comes in a **pin grid array (PGA)**, which is a square having many pins underneath it, as if it were a square porcupine lying on its back.

Memory chips

Although the CPU (the computer's brain) can think, it can't remember anything. It can't even remember what problem it was working on!

Besides buying a CPU, you must also buy **memory chips**, which remember what problem the CPU was working on. To find out what the problem was, the CPU looks at the memory chips frequently — about a million times every second!

The part of the computer's main circuitry that contains the memory chips is called the **main memory**.

The typical memory chip comes in a DIP that has 8 pairs of legs (16 pins). In a typical microcomputer, the motherboard contains lots of memory chips.

If you buy extra memory chips (so that your computer can remember extra information), and the extra memory chips don't all fit on the motherboard, you must buy an extra PC card to mount them on; that extra card is called a **memory card**. If the memory card comes in a cute little cartridge that you can pop into and out of the computer easily, it's called a **memory cartridge**.

Warning: if you buy a memory chip or card or cartridge, and want to pop it into the computer, turn off the computer's power first. If you forget, and accidentally leave the power on while you're inserting (or removing) the memory, you might wreck your computer!

You need two kinds of memory chips: **RAM** and **ROM**. The **RAM** chips remember information temporarily; the **ROM** chips remember information permanently. Let's begin by looking at RAM chips.

RAM

If a chip remembers information just temporarily, it's called a **random-access memory chip (RAM chip)**.

When you buy RAM chips, they contain no information yet; you tell the CPU what information to put into them. Later, you can make the CPU erase that information and insert new information instead. The RAM chips hold information just temporarily: when you turn the computer's power off, the RAM chips are automatically erased.

Whenever the CPU tries to solve a problem, the CPU stores the problem in the RAM chips, temporarily. There it also stores all instructions on how to solve the problem; the instructions are called the **program**.

If you buy more RAM chips, the CPU can handle longer problems and programs. If the computer doesn't have enough RAM chips to hold the entire problem or program, you must split the problem or program into several shorter ones instead, and tell the CPU to work on each of the short ones temporarily.

How RAM is measured A **character** is any symbol you can type on the keyboard, such as a letter or digit or punctuation mark or blank space. For example, the word HAT consists of 3 characters; the phrase Mr. Poe consists of 7 characters (M, R, the period, the space, P, O, and E). The phrase LOVE 2 KISS U consists of 13 characters.

Instead of saying "character", hungry programmers say **byte**. So LOVE 2 KISS U consists of 13 bytes. If, in the RAM, you store LOVE 2 KISS U, that phrase occupies 13 bytes of the RAM.

RAM chips are manufactured by a process that involves doubling. The most popular unit of RAM is "2 bytes times 2 times 2 times 2 times 2 times 2 times 2 times 2 times 2 times 2", which is 1024 bytes, which is called a **kilobyte**. So **the definition of a kilobyte is "1024 bytes"**.

Although a kilobyte is exactly 1024 bytes, the following approximations are useful.

> A kilobyte is about a thousand bytes. It's about how many characters you see on the screen of a TV computer. It's about *half* as many characters as you see on the screen of an 80-column monitor. It's about a *quarter* as many characters as you get on a typewritten page (assuming the page is single-spaced with one-inch margins and elite type).

The abbreviation for *kilobyte* is **K**. For example, if a salesperson says the computer has a "64K RAM", the salesperson means the main circuitry includes enough RAM chips to hold 64 kilobytes of information, which is slightly over 64,000 bytes.

A **megabyte** is 1024 kilobytes. Since a kilobyte is 1024 bytes, **a megabyte is "1024 times 1024" bytes, which is 1,048,576 bytes altogether**, which is slightly more than a million bytes. It's about how much you can fit in a 250-page book (assuming the book has single-spaced typewritten pages). The abbreviation for *megabyte* is **meg** or **M**.

A **gigabyte** (pronounced "gig a bite") is 1024 megabytes. It's slightly more than a billion bytes.

A **terabyte** is 1024 gigabytes. It's slightly more than a trillion bytes.

In honor of the words "kilobyte", "megabyte", "gigabyte", and "terabyte", many programmers name their puppies Killer Byte, Make a Byte, Giggle Byte, and Terror Byte.

Rows of RAM chips In a primitive microcomputer (such as the Commodore 64), the RAM is a row of eight NMOS chips on the motherboard. That row of chips holds 64K altogether. So it holds 64 kilobytes, which is slightly more than 64 thousand bytes (since a kilobyte is slightly more than a thousand bytes).

> That row of chips is called a **64K chip set**. Each chip in that set is called a "64K chip", but remember that you need a whole row of those 64K chips to produce a 64K RAM.
>
> Mail-order discount dealers charge 50¢ for a 64K chip. So to get 64K of RAM, you need a 64K chip set, which is a row of eight 64K chips, which costs "8 times 50¢", which is $4.
>
> The most popular style of 64K chip is the **TI 4164**. Although that style was invented by Texas Instruments, other manufacturers have copied it.

If your computer is slightly fancier (such as the Apple 2c), it has *two* rows of 64K chips. Since each row is a 64K RAM, the two rows together total 128K.

If your computer is even fancier, it has *many* rows of 64K chips.

> For example, your computer might have four rows of 64K chips. Since each row is a 64K RAM, the four rows together total 256K.

64K chips didn't become popular until 1982. If your computer was built before then, it probably contains inferior chips: instead of containing a row of 64K chips, it contains a row of 16K chips or 4K chips.

During the 1980's, computer engineers invented 256K and 1M chips. The most popular style of 256K chip is called the **41256**, which you can get from discount dealers for $2. A 1M chip costs $4.

If your computer has very little RAM, you can try to enlarge the RAM, by adding extra rows of RAM chips to the motherboard. But if the motherboard's already full, you must buy an extra PC card to put the extra chips on. That extra PC card is called a **RAM memory card**.

Parity chip The IBM PC and some clones contain an extra chip in each row, so that each row contains 9 chips instead of 8.

The row's ninth chip is called the **parity chip**. It double-checks the work done by the other 8 chips, to make sure they're all working correctly!

So for an IBM PC or one of those clones, you must buy 9 chips to fill a row.

Strips of RAM chips If your computer is ultra-modern and you want to insert an extra row of RAM chips, you do *not* have to insert 8 or 9 separate chips into the motherboard. Instead, you can buy a strip (tiny memory card) that contains all 8 or 9 chips and just pop the whole strip into the computer's motherboard, in one blow.

If the strip is typical, it contains a single row of chips, pops into one of the motherboard's slots, and is called a **Single In-line Memory Module (SIMM)**.

If the strip is fancy, it contains *two* rows of chips (one row on each side of the strip) and is called a **Dual In-line Memory Module (DIMM)**.

If the strip is old-fashioned and weird, it pops into a series of pinholes instead of a slot and is called a **Single In-line Pin Package (SIPP)**.

Here's what SIMMs and DIMMs cost:

$3 for a SIMM	that holds	1 megabyte
$6 for a SIMM	that holds	4 megabytes
$8 for a SIMM	that holds	8 megabytes
$24 for a DIMM	that holds	16 megabytes
$36 for a DIMM	that holds	32 megabytes
$68 for a DIMM	that holds	64 megabytes
$129 for a DIMM	that holds	128 megabytes

You can get those prices from discount dealers, such as:

Company	Phone
Spartan Technologies	888-373-0340, 847-364-9900
A+ Memory Express	800-877-8188, 818-333-6389
Memory Man	800-MEGABYTE, 504-818-2717

SIPPs cost $5 more than SIMMs.

Some computers use SIMMs containing a set of just 2, 3, or 4 chips. That set of special chips imitates 8 or 9 normal chips.

In old-fashioned computers, each SIMM fits into a motherboard slot by using 30 big pins. In computers that are more modern, each SIMM uses 72 big pins instead. The typical DIMM uses 168 big pins.

A **nanosecond** is a billionth of a second.

The typical SIMM contains chips that are fast: they retrieve info in 60 nanoseconds. Old-fashioned SIMMs contain slower chips, requiring 70 or 80 nanoseconds.

Newer SIMMs include circuitry called **Extended Data Out (EDO)**, which transfers data from the SIMM to the CPU faster.

The typical DIMM uses an even faster technology, called **Synchronous Dynamic RAM (SDRAM)**, which requires just 10 nanoseconds.

If you want to buy an extra SIMM or DIMM to put in your computer, make sure you buy the same kind as the others that are already in your computer. Make sure the extra SIMM or DIMM has the same number of pins (30, 72, or 168?), the same number of chips on it (2, 3, 4, 8, 9, or more?), operates at the same number of nanoseconds (10, 60, 70, or 80?), and uses the same technology (standard, EDO, or SDRAM?).

Let your memory grow In a typical computer, the RAM contains *several* rows of chips, so that the total RAM contains *several* megabytes.

Here's how much RAM you typically get altogether:

Computer's price	Typical quantity of RAM	
$25-$50	64K (64 kilobytes,	65,536 bytes)
$50-$75	128K (128 kilobytes,	131,072 bytes)
$75-$100	256K (256 kilobytes,	262,144 bytes)
$100-$125	512K (512 kilobytes,	524,288 bytes)
$125-$150	1M (1 megabyte,	1,048,576 bytes)
$150-$200	2M (2 megabytes,	2,097,152 bytes)
$200-$300	4M (4 megabytes,	4,194,304 bytes)
$300-$400	8M (8 megabytes,	8,388,608 bytes)
$400-$500	16M (16 megabytes,	16,777,216 bytes)
$500-$700	32M (32 megabytes,	33,554,432 bytes)
$700-$1,400	64M (64 megabytes,	67,108,864 bytes)
$1,400-$4,000	128M (128 megabytes,	134,217,728 bytes)

Mac The original Mac (nicknamed the **Slim Mac**) included 128K of RAM. Then came a version nicknamed the **Fat Mac**, which included 512K. Next came an improvement called the **Mac Plus**, which included 1M.

Those Macs are obsolete. All Macs sold today come with at least 64M, which is what you need to run modern Mac software.

Classic computers The **Commodore 64** computer got its name because it contained 64K of RAM. Then Commodore invented an improved version, the **Commodore 128**, which contained 128K of RAM.

The **Laser 128** imitates the Apple 2c. Each comes with 128K of RAM.

IBM The original IBM PC came with just 16K of RAM, but you could add extra RAM to it. Here's how much RAM the typical IBM PC or clone contains now:

CPU	Typical quantity of main RAM
8088	512K or 640K
286	640K or 1M
386	2M or 4M
486	4M or 8M
Pentium	16M, 32M, 64M, or 128M

To run modern IBM PC software, you need at least 16M of main RAM. To run the FANCY modern IBM PC software WELL, you need at least 32M. Get at least 32M!

For computers having lots of RAM, here's how it's divvied up:

The first 640K of main RAM is called the **base memory** (or **conventional memory**). That's the part of the RAM that the computer can handle easily and fast.

The next 384K is called **upper memory**. It's relatively unimportant, since most programs don't know how to use it.

Those two parts (the conventional memory and the upper memory) consume a total of 640K+384K, which is 1024K, which is one megabyte.

The rest of the main RAM (beyond that first megabyte) is typically called the **extended** memory. The first 64K of extended memory is called the **high memory area (HMA)** because it's just slightly higher than the base memory and upper memory. (The rest of extended memory should be called "even higher memory", but nobody does.)

NMOS RAM versus CMOS Most RAM chips are NMOS. The prices I quoted you were for NMOS.

If your computer operates on batteries, it uses CMOS instead, which consumes less electricity than NMOS.

Unfortunately, CMOS chips cost more than NMOS. For example, a 64K chip costs 50¢ if made of NMOS, but costs $4 if CMOS.

Dynamic versus static A RAM chip is either **dynamic** or **static**.

If it's **dynamic**, it stores data for just 2 milliseconds. After the 2 milliseconds, the electrical charges that represent the data dissipate and become too weak to detect.

When you buy a PC board containing dynamic RAM chips, the PC board also includes a **refresh circuit**. The refresh circuit automatically reads the data from the dynamic RAM chips, then rewrites the data onto the chips before 2 milliseconds go by. Every 2 milliseconds, the refresh circuit reads the data from the chips and rewrites the data, so that the data stays refreshed.

If a chip is **static** instead of dynamic, the electrical charge never dissipates, so you don't need a refresh circuit. (But you must still keep the power turned on.)

In the past, computer designers used just static RAM because they feared dynamic RAM's refresh circuit wouldn't work. But today, refresh circuits are reliable, and the most popular kind of RAM is dynamic NMOS.

Dynamic RAM is called **DRAM** (pronounced "dee ram"). Static RAM is called **SRAM** (pronounced "ess ram").

Static NMOS is still available. CMOS and bipolar are always static.

Bipolar cache

In a maxicomputer, minicomputer, or modern microcomputer, the RAM is divided into two sections. One section is huge, contains many rows of NMOS chips, and is called the **main RAM**. The other section is tiny, contains just a few bipolar chips, and is called the **cache** (which is pronounced "cash").

The cache's bipolar chips work much faster than the main RAM's NMOS chips.

In most IBM clones containing a 486DX or Pentium, the NMOS chips retrieve information in 60 or 70 nanoseconds, and the bipolar chips take 15 or 20 nanoseconds.

The typical bipolar chip holds 32 kilobytes and costs $5. That's a lot to pay for just "32 kilobytes", which is $\frac{1}{32}$ of a megabyte! Yes, bipolar chips are pricey!

The typical computer contains a few bipolar cache chips.

> In the typical IBM clone containing a Pentium,
> the main RAM holds 16M or 32M or 64M or 128M,
> but the cache holds just ½ M (which is 512K).

So the bipolar cache is memory that's super-fast, small, and pricey.

In the bipolar cache, the computer keeps a copy of the main RAM's info that you've been using recently, so the CPU can grab that info again super-quickly.

ROM

If a chip remembers information permanently, it's called a **read-only memory chip (ROM chip)**, because you can read the information but can't change it. The ROM chip contains permanent, eternal truths and facts put there by the manufacturer, and it remembers that info forever, even if you turn off the power.

Here's the difference between RAM and ROM:

> **RAM chips** remember, temporarily, info supplied by you.
> **ROM chips** remember, forever, info supplied by the manufacturer.

The typical computer includes many RAM chips (arranged in rows) but just a *few* ROM chips (typically 6).

What kind of info is in ROM?

In your computer, one of the ROM chips contains instructions that tell the CPU what to do first when you turn the power on. Those instructions are called the **ROM bootstrap**, because they help the computer system start itself going and "pull itself up by its own bootstraps".

In the typical microcomputer, that ROM chip also contains instructions that help the CPU transfer information from the keyboard to the screen and printer. Those instructions are called the **ROM operating system** or the **ROM basic input-output system (ROM BIOS)**.

In the typical microcomputer, one of the ROM chips tells the computer how to make each character on the screen out of dots. That chip is called the **character generator**.

In famous old microcomputers, several ROM chips contain definitions of fundamental English words, which are called **BASIC** words.

> For example, those ROM chips contain the definitions of BASIC words such as PRINT, INPUT, IF, and THEN. Those BASIC definitions in the ROM are called the **ROM BASIC interpreter**.

Commodore 64

For example, let's look inside a primitive computer: the Commodore 64. It contains just four ROM chips:

> The first chip contains 8K, for the ROM bootstrap and ROM BIOS. The second contains Commodore's 8K ROM BASIC. The third contains Commodore's 4K character generator. The fourth contains ¼K that tells the computer how to make the screen produce pretty colors.

IBM

In the typical IBM PC or clone, the motherboard contains a **ROM BIOS chip**.

> That chip contains the ROM BIOS and also the ROM bootstrap. If your computer is manufactured by IBM, that chip is designed by IBM; if your computer is a clone, that chip is an imitation designed by a company such as **Phoenix**. Such a chip designed by Phoenix is called a **Phoenix ROM BIOS chip**. Other companies that design ROM BIOS chips for clones are **Quadtel** (which was recently bought by Phoenix), **Award** (which was recently bought by Phoenix), and **American Megatrends Incorporated (AMI)** (which remains independent).

On a special PC card (called a **video display card**), you'll find a ROM chip containing the character generator.

If your computer is old and built by IBM, some chips on the motherboard contain the ROM BASIC interpreter. If your computer is new or a clone, all of BASIC comes on a disk instead of in ROM chips.

> Altogether, the original IBM PC contained six ROM chips: the ROM BIOS chip, the character generator, and four ROM BASIC interpreter chips. Each of those six chips contained 8K, so that the computer's ROM totaled 48K. On newer computers from IBM and clones, the total is slightly different.

Extra ROM chips

Some microcomputers include extra ROM chips that tell the computer how to handle specific applications, such as word processing and accounting.

ROM cartridges

If your computer attaches to a TV and is old-fashioned (such as a Commodore Vic, Commodore 64, Commodore 128, Atari 800, Atari 800XL, or Radio Shack Color Computer), you can pop **ROM cartridges** into the computer. A **ROM cartridge** is a cartridge containing a PC card full of ROM chips. Etched into those ROM chips is a program.

> The typical ROM cartridge contains a program that plays a video game, such as Space Invaders or Pac Man or computer chess. You can also buy ROM cartridges that contain programs for word processing, music, art, or tutoring you. Each ROM cartridge costs about $30.

How ROM chips are made

The info in a ROM chip is said to be **burned into** the chip. To burn in the info, the manufacturer can use two methods.

One method is to burn the info into the ROM chip while the chip's being made. A ROM chip produced by that method is called a **custom ROM chip**.

An alternate method is to make a ROM chip that contains no info but can be fed info later. Such a ROM chip is called a **programmable ROM chip (PROM)**. To feed it info later, you attach it to a device called a **PROM burner**, which copies info from a RAM to the PROM. Info burned into the PROM can't be erased, unless the PROM's a special kind: **an erasable PROM (EPROM)**.

> To erase a typical EPROM, shine an intense ultraviolet light at it for 20 minutes. That's called an **ultraviolet-erasable PROM (UV-EPROM)**.
> A fancier kind of EPROM can be erased quickly by sending it a 25-volt shock for a tenth of a second. That's called an electrically erasable PROM (EEPROM) or electrically alterable PROM (EAPROM).
> After you erase an EPROM, you can feed it new info.
> If you're a manufacturer designing a new computer, begin by using an erasable PROM (EPROM), so you can make changes easily. When you decide not to make any more changes, switch to a non-erasable PROM, which costs less to manufacture. If your computer becomes so popular that you need to manufacture over 10,000 copies of the ROM, switch to a custom ROM, which costs more to design and "tool up for" but costs less to make copies of.

DISKS

Fundamentals

Memory comes in three popular forms: RAM chips, ROM chips, and disks. You already learned about RAM chips and ROM chips. Let's examine disks. A computer disk is round, like a phonograph record.

Three kinds

You can buy three popular kinds of computer disks:

> A **floppy disk** is made of flimsy material. It's permanently encased in a sturdy, square dust jacket.
> A **hard disk** is made of firmer material. It typically hides in your computer permanently, unseen.
> A **CD-ROM** is a compact disk. It's the same kind of CD compact disk that plays music.

Each kind has its own advantages and disadvantages.

Floppy disks are the cheapest (under 50¢ per disk) and the easiest to mail to your friends: just stick the floppy disk in an envelope, perhaps with some padding. Unfortunately, floppy disks work the most slowly, and they hold the least data: the typical floppy disk holds about 1 megabyte, while the typical hard disk or CD-ROM can hold *many hundreds* of megabytes.

Hard disks work the fastest — over 20 times faster than the other kinds! But hard disks are also the most expensive. Moreover, they typically can't be removed from your computer and therefore can't be mailed to your friends.

CD-ROMs are the best value: CD-ROM disks cost less than 1¢ per megabyte to manufacture. But they have a frustrating limitation: the information on CD-ROM disks can*not* be edited.

Since each kind of disk has its own advantages and disadvantages, you'll want to buy all three kinds.

Spelling

Computer experts argue about spelling. Some experts write "**disk**", others write "**disc**".

Most manufacturers write "**disk**" when referring to floppy disks or hard disks, but write "**disc**" when referring to CD-ROMs. That inconsistency annoys me.

To be more consistent, I'll always write "**disk**", even when referring to CD-ROMs. Most computer magazines (such as *PC Magazine* and *PC World*) feel the same way I do: they always write "**disk**". The growing tendency is to always write "**disk**".

For hard disks, IBM used to write "**disc**" but now writes "**disk**".

Floppy disks

A **floppy disk** (or **diskette**) is round but comes permanently sealed in a square **dust jacket**. (Don't try to remove the floppy disk from its square jacket.)

The floppy disk is as thin and flimsy as a sheet of paper but is protected by the sturdy, square jacket that encases it.

Three standard sizes

Floppy disks come in three standard sizes:

> The most popular size is called a **3½-inch** floppy disk, because it comes in a square jacket that's about 3½ inches on each side. (Actually, each side of the jacket is slightly *more* than 3½ inches, and the disk's diameter is slightly *less*.)
>
> An older size, used mainly on older computers, is called **5¼-inch**. It comes in square jacket that's exactly 5¼ inches on each side.
>
> An even older size, **8-inch**, is used just on ancient computers that are no longer built.

Those three sizes have nicknames:

> An 8-inch floppy disk is called a **large floppy**.
> A 5¼-inch floppy disk is called a **minifloppy**.
> A 3½-inch floppy disk is called a **microfloppy**.

Here's their history:

> **8-inch** floppies were invented in the **early 1970's** by **IBM**.
>
> **5¼-inch** floppies were invented in the **late 1970's** by **Shugart Associates**, which later became part of Xerox.
>
> **3½-inch** floppies were invented in the **1980's** by **Sony**. They've become the most popular size because they're the smallest, cutest, and sturdiest. They're small enough to fit in the pocket of your shirt, cute enough to impress your friends, and sturdy enough to survive when you fall on your face. They're also easy to mail, since they're small enough to fit in a standard white business envelope and sturdy enough to survive the U.S. Postal System. Yup, nice things come in small packages!

Jacket colors

The jacket of a 5¼-inch or 8-inch floppy disk is usually black. The jacket of a 3½-inch floppy disk is usually black, blue, white, or beige (very light grayish brown). If you pay a surcharge, you can get jackets that have wilder colors.

Magnetized iron

The round disk (which hides inside the square jacket) is coated with rust, so it looks brown. Since the rust is made of iron, which can be magnetized, the disk stores magnetic signals. The pattern of magnetic signals is a code representing your data.

Drives

To use a floppy disk, you must buy a **floppy-disk drive**, which is a computerized record player.

If the drive is **external**, it's a box sitting near the computer. If the drive is **internal**, it's built into the middle of the computer.

The drive has a slit in its front side. To use the drive, push the disk (including its jacket) into the slit.

When pushing the sheathed treasure into the box's slit, don't shove too hard. Oooh! Please be gentle!

When you push your disk into the slit, don't push the disk in backwards or upside-down! **Here's how to push the disk in correctly:**

First, notice that the disk's jacket has a label on it and also has a big oval cutout. (If the disk is 3½-inch, the cutout is covered by a metal slider.) Insert the disk so that **the oval cutout goes into the drive before the label does.** If the drive's slit is horizontal, make sure the label is on the *top* side of the jacket; if the drive is vertical, make sure the label is on the *left* side of the jacket.

After putting the disk into the slit, close the latch to cover the slit. (If the disk is 3½-inch, there is no latch.) Since the slit and latch act as a **door**, closing the latch is called **closing the door.**

As soon as you close the door, the disk drive automatically positions the disk onto the turntable that's hidden inside the drive. The turntable's called the **spindle**. It can spin the disk quickly.

Like a record player, the disk drive contains an arm with a "needle" on it. The needle is called the **read-write head**, because it can read what's on the disk and also write new information onto the disk.

Here's how to write new info onto the disk:

By using the computer's keyboard or mouse, command the computer to use the disk. Then type the info you want to transfer to the disk.

To transfer the info to the disk, the computer lowers the read-write head onto the disk. An electrical charge passes through the head. The charge creates an electromagnetic field, which magnetizes the iron on the disk's surface. Each iron particle has its own north and south pole; the patterns formed by the north and south poles are a code that stands for the information you're storing.

Tracks As the disk spins, the head remains stationary, so that the head draws a circle on the spinning disk's surface. The circle's called a **track**.

To draw the circle, the head doesn't use ink; instead, it uses a pattern of magnetic pulses. Since your eye can't see magnetism, your eye can't see the circle; but it's there!

When you start using a blank disk, the arm puts the head near the disk's outer rim, so that the head's track (circle) is almost as wide as the disk. That track's called **track 0**.

Then the arm lifts the head, moves the head slightly closer to the virgin disk's center, and puts the head back down onto the disk again. The head draws another circular track on the disk, but this new circular track is slightly smaller than the previous one. It's called **track 1**.

Then the head draws track 2, then track 3, then track 4, and so on, until the head gets near the center of the disk, and draws the last circular track (which is smaller than the other tracks).

To organize the info on a track, the computer divides the track into **sectors**. Each "sector" is an arc of the circle.

Single-sided versus double-sided drives A modern disk drive has two read-write heads. One head uses the disk's top surface, while the other head uses the disk's bottom, so that the drive can use both sides of the disk simultaneously. That's called a **double-sided disk drive**. The drive puts information onto the disk by first using track 0 of the main side, then track 0 of the flip side, then track 1 of the main side, then track 1 of the flip side, etc.

If a disk drive is *not* modern — if it's ancient and primitive — it has just *one* read-write head, which uses just one side of the disk. The flip side of the disk is unused. That kind of drive is called a **single-sided disk drive**. Which side of the disk does the drive use? Though some drives use the side that has the label, other drives (by other manufacturers) use the side *opposite* the label instead.

Double-sided is also called **DS** and **2-sided** and **2S**. **Single-sided** is also called **SS** and **1-sided** and **1S**.

Capacity How many kilobytes can you fit on a floppy disk? The answer depends on which kind of drive you have.

The most popular kind of drive is called a **3½-inch high-density floppy drive**. Here's how it works:

It holds a 3½-inch floppy disk. It writes on both sides of the disk simultaneously, since it's a double-sided disk drive. It writes 80 tracks on each side. It divides each track into 18 sectors. Each sector holds "512 bytes", which is half a kilobyte, ½K.

Since the disk has 2 sides, 80 tracks per side, 18 sectors per track, and ½K per sector, the disk's total capacity is "2 times 80 times 18 times ½K", which is 1440K. So altogether, the disk holds 1440K. That's called **1.44M** (where an **M** is defined as being 1000K). That's why a 3½-inch high-density floppy drive is also called a **1.44M drive**. The kind of disk you put into it is called a **1.44M floppy disk** (or a **3½-inch high-density floppy disk**). Since the disk holds 1.44M (which is 1440K), and since a K is 1024 bytes, the disk holds "1440 times 1024" bytes, which is 1,474,560 bytes altogether. That's a lot of bytes!

Although the disk holds 1440K, some of those K are used for "bureaucratic overhead" (such as holding a directory that reminds the computer which data is where on your disk). A Mac uses just 1 sector (½K) for bureaucratic overhead. An IBM-compatible computer uses 33 sectors (16½K) for bureaucratic overhead, leaving just 1423½K (1,457,664 bytes) for your data.

When you buy a blank disk to put in a 1.44M drive, make sure the disk is the right kind. Make sure the disk is 3½-inch; and to get full use of what the drive can accomplish, make sure the disk is high-density! The abbreviation for "high-density" is **HD**. A high-density 3½-inch disk has the letters **HD** stamped in white on its jacket; but the H overlaps the D, so it looks like this: **HD**. Also, a high-density 3½-inch disk has an extra square hole cut through its jacket.

Old computers use inferior floppy drives, whose capacities are *below* 1.44M.

A capacity below 150K	is called **single-density (SD)**.
A capacity above 150M but below 1M	is called **double-density (DD)**.
A capacity above 1M	is called **high-density (HD)**.

Anything below high-density is called **low-density**.

Although the jacket of a high-density 3½-inch disk has "HD" stamped on it and an extra hole punched through it, the jackets of other kinds of disks often lack any distinguishing marks. Too bad!

Popular IBM-compatible drives

For IBM-compatible computers, four kinds of floppy drives have been popular:

IBM drive's name	Capacity	Details
5¼-inch double-density	360K	40 tracks per side, 9 sectors per track
5¼-inch high-density	1200K (which is 1.2M)	80 tracks per side, 15 sectors per track
3½-inch double-density	720K	80 tracks per side, 9 sectors per track
3½-inch high-density	1440K (which is 1.44M)	80 tracks per side, 18 sectors per track

Each of those IBM-compatible drives is double-sided and has ½K per sector. They're manufactured by companies such as **NEC**, **Teac**, **Chinon**, **Epson**, and **Alps**. The fanciest drives (3½-inch high-density) used to be expensive, but now you can buy them for just $29 from mail-order discount dealers (such as **USA Flex** at 444 Scott Dr., Bloomingdale IL 60108, phone 800-723-2261 or 708-582-6206).

Mac drives

For Mac computers, three kinds of floppy drives have been popular:

Mac drive's name	Capacity	Details
1-sided double-density	400K	1 side, 8-12 sectors per track
2-sided double-density	800K	2 sides, 8-12 sectors per track
high-density	1440K (which is 1.44M)	2 sides, 18 sectors per track

Each Mac drive is 3½-inch and has 80 tracks per side, ½K per sector. The Mac's high-density drive is called the **Mac Superdrive**.

On a disk, the inner tracks have smaller diameters than the outer tracks. Most drives squeeze as many sectors onto an inner track as onto an outer track, but the Mac double-density drives puts fewer sectors onto the inner tracks and put extra sectors onto the outer tracks. Specifically, the outer 16 tracks are divided into 12 sectors, the next 16 tracks into 11 sectors, the next 16 into 10, the next 16 into 9, and the inner 16 into 8.

Ancient computers

For ancient computers, many kinds of floppy drives were invented:

Computer	Drive capacity	Details
Apple 2 family	140K	5¼", 1 side, 35 tracks, 16 sectors, ¼K per sector
Tandy Color Computer	157½K	5¼", 1 side, 35 tracks, 18 sectors, ¼K per sector
Tandy Models 3, 4, 4P	180K	5¼", 1 side, 40 tracks, 18 sectors, ¼K per sector
Tandy Model 4D	360K	5¼", 2 sides, 40 tracks, 18 sectors, ¼K per sector
Commodore 64	170¾K	5¼", 1 side, 35 tracks, 17-21 sectors, ¼K per sector
Commodore Amiga	880K	3½", 2 sides, 80 tracks, 11 sectors, ½K per sector

For the Commodore 64, the 17 outer tracks are divided into 21 sectors, the next 7 tracks into 19 sectors, the next 6 tracks into 18 sectors, and the inner 5 tracks into 17 sectors.

Speed

In the disk drive, the disk spins quickly. The exact speed depends on what size disk the drive uses.

Low-density 5¼-inch disks revolve 5 times per second. That makes 300 revolutions per minute, 300 rpm. 8-inch disks and high-density 5¼-inch disks revolve faster: 6 times per second (360 rpm). 3½-inch disks revolve even faster: between 6½ and 10 times per second.

Buying disks

When you buy a floppy disk, make sure its size matches the size of the drive. For example, a 3½-inch disk will *not* work in a 5¼-inch drive.

If you buy a blank 3½-inch floppy disk, you can stick it into any normal 3½-inch drive, regardless of who manufactured the drive and who manufactured the computer. But after you've put info onto the disk, that info is understandable only to *your* kind of computer. For example, an Apple 2c cannot understand what an IBM PC writes.

When you go into a computer store to buy a disk that contains software, tell the salesperson which kind of computer you have, so that the salesperson can give you a disk containing info understandable to *your* computer.

If your drive is single-density or double-density, it can*not* handle high-density disks at all.

Here are peculiarities about 5¼-inch drives and disks:

If your drive is 5¼-inch and high-density, it can *read* single-density and double-density disks, but it might have trouble writing new information onto them. So when buying blank disks for your 5¼-inch high-density drive to write on, avoid buying single-density or double-density disks.

The three crummy kinds of 5¼-inch floppy disks (single-sided single-density, single-sided double-density, and double-sided double-density) are all manufactured by the same process as each other. The only difference is the manufacturer's "guarantee": a double-sided double-density disk is "guaranteed" to work on both sides and hold lots of data; a single-sided or single-density disk is not. Even if you buy a disk that has a poor guarantee (just "single-sided single-density"), it typically works fine even if you use both sides and store lots of data. The only difference is that the manufacturer hasn't bothered testing the second side and hasn't bothered testing double-density data. During the 1970's and 1980's, single-sided single-density disks were significantly cheaper than double-sided double-density, but now the prices are about the same.

Formatting the disk

Before you can use a blank floppy disk, its surface must be **formatted** (divided into tracks and sectors). Buy a disk that's been formatted already, or buy an unformatted disk and format it yourself (by typing a command on your computer's keyboard or by using the mouse).

After the disk's been formatted, you can store whatever information you wish onto the disk. Do *not* tell the drive to format that disk again. If you accidentally make the drive format the same disk again, the drive will create new tracks and sectors on the disk, and erase the old tracks and sectors, and therefore erase all your old data!

Name brands

The most famous manufacturers of floppy disks are **Verbatim** and **Maxell**. But instead of buying those brands, buy **generic** floppy disks instead. The generics cost less and typically work just as well.

Discount dealers

To get the lowest prices on generic floppy disks, contact **MEI Micro Center** (1100 Steelwood Rd., Columbus OH 43212, 800-634-3478) or **Diskettes Unlimited** (6206 Long Dr., Houston TX 77087, 800-DOG-DISK).

For example, here are the prices from MEI Micro Center for double-sided disks:

Kind of disk	100disks 1000
5¼-in. double-density, unformatted	$19+$1.20 $160+$12
5¼-in. high-density, unformatted	$26+$1.20 $210+$12
3½-in. high-density, formatted	$28+$2.40 $250+$24

Add up the prices of what you want, then add the handling charge ($3.25). For example, for 100 of the best disks (3½-inch high-density, formatted), MEI charges you $28 (for the disks) + $2.40 (shipping) + $3.25 (handling), which is $33.65. That's about 34¢ per disk. For 1000 of the best disks, MEI charges you $250 + $24 + $3.25, which is $277.25, which comes to about 28¢ per disk. Diskettes Unlimited charges even less but might give you slightly lower quality; for details, phone them.

What's a disk worth?

Although you can buy a blank floppy disk for under 50¢, a disk containing info costs much more. The price depends on how valuable the info is. A disk that explains to the computer how to play a game costs about $25. A disk teaching the computer how to handle a general business task (such as accounting, filing, or correspondence) usually costs about $100.

A disk containing intimate, personal data about your business's customers, suppliers, employees, and methods is worth even more — perhaps *thousands* of dollars! To compute how much it's worth to you, imagine that you've lost it, or that it fell into the wrong hands!

Protect your disks

Most parts of a computer system are sturdy: even if you bang on the keyboard and rap your fist against the screen, you probably won't do any harm. Only one part of a computer system is delicate: that part is the disk. Unfortunately, the magnetic signals on your disk are easy to destroy.

One way to accidentally destroy them is to put your disk near a magnet; so **keep your disks away from magnets!** For example, keep your disk away from paper clips that have been in a magnetized paper-clip holder. Keep your disk away from speakers (such as the speakers in your stereo, TV, and phone), because all speakers contain magnets. Keep your disk away from electric motors, because motors generate an electromagnetic field. So to be safe, keep your disk at least *6 inches* away from paper clips, stereos, TV's, phones, and motors.

Keep your disk away from heat, because heat destroys the disk's magnetism and "melts" your data. So don't leave your disk in the hot sun; don't leave it on a sunny windowsill; don't leave it in the back of your car on a hot day. If your disk drive or computer feels hot, quickly lower the temperature, by getting an air conditioner or at least a fan.

3½-inch floppy disks come in strong jackets, but 5¼-inch and 8-inch floppy disks come in jackets that are too weak and thin to protect disks from pressure. **Don't squeeze your disk.** Don't put it under a heavy object, such as a paperweight or a book. If you want to write a note on the disk's jacket, don't use a ball-point pen (which crushes the disk); use a soft felt-tip pen

instead.

Keep the disk away from dust. For example, don't smoke cigarettes near the disk, because the smoke becomes dust that lands on the disk and wrecks the data.

Keep the disk dry. If you must transport a disk during a rainstorm, put the disk in a plastic bag. Never drink coffee or soda near the disk: your drink might spill.

To handle the disk, **touch just the disk's jacket, not the brown disk itself**. Holes in the jacket let you see the brown disk inside; don't put your fingers in the holes.

Power surges in ancient computers

If your computer's an IBM clone or by Apple, skip ahead to the next topic ("Write-protect notch").

If your computer is made by Commodore or Radio Shack and is so ancient that it's *not* an IBM PC clone, be careful: flipping the power switch on your ancient computer creates an electrical surge that wrecks the disk. On such a computer, don't flip the power switch when the drive contains a disk. Flip the power switch just when the drive's *empty*.

To turn such a computer on, make sure the drive's *empty*, then flip the power switch on. After the power's come on, insert the disk.

Before turning such a computer off, remove the disk from the drive. When the drive's *empty*, turn off the power.

Write-protect notch

When you buy a blank 5¼-inch or 8-inch floppy disk, the disk comes in a square black jacket. Since the jacket's square, it has four sides; but one of the sides has a notch cut into it. You can cover the notch, by sticking a plastic **tab** over it. The tab has a gummed back, so you can stick it on the disk easily and cover the notch. You get the tab free when you buy the disk.

(For a 3½-inch disk, the notch is different: it's a square hole near the jacket's corner but not on the jacket's edge. To cover it, you use a black slider instead of a tab. On old Apple Mac disks, the slider was red instead of black.)

Whenever you ask the computer to change the info on the disk, the drive checks whether you've covered the notch.

For a 5¼-inch disk, the normal situation is for the notch to be uncovered. For a 3½-inch or 8-inch disk, the normal situation is for the notch to be covered.

If the situation's normal, the computer will obey your command: it will change the info on the disk as you wish. But **if the situation's abnormal (because the notch is covered when it should be uncovered, or is uncovered when it should be covered), the computer will refuse to change the disk's info**.

Suppose your disk contains valuable info, and you're afraid some idiot will accidentally erase or alter that info. To prevent such an accident, make the situation abnormal (by changing whether the notch is covered), so that the computer will refuse to change the disk's info. It will refuse to erase the disk; it will refuse to add new info to the disk; it will refuse to alter the disk; it will refuse to write onto the disk. The disk is protected from being changed; it's protected from being written on. The disk is **write-protected** (or **locked**).

Since the tab affects whether the disk is write-protected, the tab is called a **write-protect tab**, and the notch is called a **write-protect notch**.

When you buy a disk that already contains info, the disk usually comes write-protected, to protect you from accidentally erasing the info. So if you buy a 5¼-inch floppy disk that already contains info, it might come with a write-protect tab already covering the notch, to write-protect the disk.

Instead of creating a notch and then covering it with a tab, some manufacturers save money by getting special disks that have no notch. The computer treats a notchless disk the same way as a disk whose notch is covered.

Backup Even if you handle your disk very carefully, eventually something will go wrong, and some of the info on your disk will get wrecked accidentally.

To prepare for that inevitable calamity, tell the computer to copy all info from the disk onto a blank disk, so that the blank disk becomes an exact copy of the original. Store the copy far away from the original: store it in another room, or — better yet — another building, or — better yet — another city.

The copy is called a **backup**. Use the backup disk when the original disk gets wrecked.

Making a backup disk is like buying an insurance policy: it protects you against disasters.

When you buy a floppy that already contains software, try copying the floppy before you begin using it.

> If you're lucky, the computer will make the backup copy without any hassles. If you're unlucky, the software company has put instructions on the floppy that make the computer *refuse* to copy the disk, because the company fears that you'll illegally give copies to all your friends for free. A floppy that the computer refuses to copy, and which is therefore protected against illegal copying, is called **copy-protected**. A floppy that you *can* copy is called **copyable** (or **unprotected**).

Drive cleaners Don't bother trying to clean the heads of your floppy drive. The heads don't collect much dirt anyway, since the floppy disk's jacket has a cloth liner that traps most dirt. If your disk ever starts to act unreliable, clean the heads if you wish, but the culprit is more likely a **misaligned** head, a brownout, overheating, defective software, or a mistyped command.

Super-capacity floppies

A standard floppy disk holds up to 1.44M. **Super-capacity** floppy disks can hold even more.

Zip The most popular super-capacity floppy disk is the **Zip disk**. Slightly bigger than a 3½-inch floppy disk, it's **4-inch**. It **holds 100M**, which is 70 times as much as a 1.44M floppy!

Zip disks cost $13 each if you buy 2, $12 each if you buy 6, $11 each if you buy 10, $10 each if you buy 20.

To use Zip disks, you must buy a **Zip drive**. It reads just Zip disks and costs $89. (That price includes one blank Zip disk.)

The Zip drive is made by **Iomega**. Zip disks are available from many manufacturers, such as **Iomega** and **Sony**. You can buy Zip drives and disks at your local computer store.

Zip 250 You can buy a **Zip 250 disk**, which resembles a Zip disk but **holds 250M** instead of 100M. Zip 250 disks cost $18 for 1, $17 each if you buy 4. To use them, you must buy a **Zip 250 drive**, which can also handle traditional Zip disks and costs $187.

LS-120 A pleasant alternative is the **laser servo 120M disk (LS-120 disk)**. Like a 1.44M disk, an LS-120 disk is 3½-inch, but it holds more (120M).

LS-120 disks cost $14 each if you buy 3, $12 each if you buy 5, $10 each if you buy 10. LS-120 disks made by **Imation** are called **SuperDisks**.

To use LS-120 disks, you must buy an **LS-120 drive**. It reads LS-120 disks and 1.44M disks. It costs $100. It's faster than a Zip drive. You can buy LS-120 drives made by **Imation** and **O.R. Technology**.

PD The final step up is the **Panasonic disk (PD)**. It's 5-inch and **holds 650M**. It **costs $34**, but you can pay just $30 each by getting 10 at a time.

To use PD disks, you must buy a **PD drive**. It reads PD disks and CD-ROM disks. It costs $349. You can buy PD drives made by **Panasonic**, **Toray**, and **Micro Solutions**.

Hard disks

Hard disks are better than floppy disks in three ways:

> **Hard disks are sturdier than floppies.**
> Hard disks are hard and firm; they don't flop or jiggle.
> They're more reliable than floppies.
>
> **Hard drives hold more information than floppy drives.**
> The typical floppy drive holds 1.44 megabytes.
> The typical hard drive holds 20 gigabytes (which is about 20,000 megabytes).
>
> **Hard drives work faster than floppies.**
> The typical floppy disk rotates between 5 and 10 times per second.
> The typical hard disk rotates between 90 and 167 times per second.

Hard drives cost more than floppy drives. The typical floppy drive costs $29; the typical hard drive costs about $240.

Unfortunately, the typical hard disk can't be removed from its drive: the hard disk is **non-removable**, stuck inside its drive permanently. (Hard disks that are **removable** are rare.)

Since the typical hard disk is stuck forever inside its drive, in one fixed place, it's called a **fixed disk**.

Though the typical floppy-disk drive holds just one disk at a time, the typical hard-disk drive holds a whole **stack** of disks and handles all the stack's disks simultaneously, by using many arms and read-write heads.

> For example, a 20-gigabyte hard drive holds a non-removable stack of disks, and the entire stack totals 20 gigabytes. Each disk in the stack is called a **platter**. If your hard drive is the rare kind that holds a *removable* stack of disks, the stack comes in a **cartridge** or **pack** that you can remove from the hard drive.

Back in 1977, the typical hard disk had a 14-inch diameter and was removable. The hard-disk drive was a big cabinet, the size of a top-loading washing machine; it cost about $30,000 and held 100 megabytes. It required a minicomputer or mainframe.

Hard disks, drives, and prices have all shrunk since then! Now the typical hard disk has a diameter of just 3½ inches. The typical hard drive is just 1 inch tall, costs about $160, and holds 20,000 megabytes. It fits in a desktop microcomputer.

Some notebook computers use tiny hard disks whose diameter is just 2½ inches.

IBM drive letters

The typical IBM-compatible computer has both a floppy drive and a hard drive. The floppy drive is called **drive A**; the hard drive is called **drive C**.

> If the computer has *two* floppy drives,
> the main floppy drive is called **drive A**; the other floppy drive is called **drive B**.
>
> If the computer has *two* hard drives,
> the main hard drive is called **drive C**; the other hard drive is called **drive D**.

Copy from floppy to hard & back

When you buy a program, it usually comes on a floppy disk or a CD-ROM disk. If it comes on a floppy disk, put that floppy disk into the floppy drive, then copy the program from the floppy disk to the hard disk. (To copy the program onto an IBM-compatible hard disk, type the word "copy" or "install" or "setup" or use your mouse. To find out which to do and when, follow the instructions in the manual that came with the program.)

Then use just the copy on the hard disk (which is sturdier, holds more info, and works faster than the floppy disk).

Like floppy disks, hard disks are coated with magnetized iron. Floppy disks and hard disks are both called **magnetic disks**. Like floppy disks, hard disks are in constant danger of losing their magnetic signals — and your data!

Protect yourself! Every day, take any new info that's on your hard disk and copy it onto a pile of floppy disks, so those floppy disks contain a **backup copy** of what was new on your hard disk.

To avoid giant disasters, avoid creating giant files. If you're writing a book and want to store it on your hard disk, split the book into chapters, and make each chapter a separate file, so if you accidentally say "delete" you'll lose just one chapter instead of your entire masterpiece.

How the head works

In a floppy drive, the read-write head (the "needle") touches the spinning floppy disk. But in a *hard* drive, the read-write head does *not* touch the spinning hard disk; instead, it hovers over the disk.

> The distance from the read-write head to the hard disk is a tiny fraction of an inch, and small enough so that the read-write head can detect the disk's magnetism and alter it.
>
> Since the head doesn't actually touch the disk, there isn't any friction, so the head and the disk don't suffer from any wear-and-tear. A hard-disk system therefore lasts longer than a floppy-disk system and is more reliable.

Winchester drives In all modern hard drives, the head acts as a miniature airplane: it **flies** above the disk.

> It flies at a very low altitude: a tiny fraction of an inch. The only thing keeping the head off the rotating disk is a tiny cushion of air — a breeze caused by the disk's motion.
>
> When you unplug the drive, the disk stops rotating, so the breeze stops, and the head comes to rest on a **landing strip**, which is like a miniature airport.
>
> Such a drive is called a **flying-head drive**. It's also called a **Winchester drive**, because "Winchester" was IBM's secret code-name for that technology when IBM was inventing it.
>
> The head flies at an altitude that's extremely low — about a ten-thousandth of an inch! That's even smaller than the width of a particle of dust or cigarette smoke! So if any dust or smoke lands onto the disk, the head will smash against it, and you'll have a major disaster.
>
> To prevent such a disaster, the entire Winchester drive is sealed airtight, to prevent any dust or smoke from entering the drive and getting onto the disk. Since the drive is sealed, you can't remove the disks (unless you buy an extremely expensive Winchester drive that has a flexible seal).

Speed

Here's how the computer retrieves data from the drive.

First, the drive's head moves to the correct track.

> The time that the head spends moving is called the **seek time**. Since that time depends on how far the head is from the correct track, it depends on where the correct track is *and where the head is moving from*.
>
> According to calculus, on the average the head must move across a third of the tracks to reach the correct track. That's why the time to traverse a third of the tracks is called the **average seek time**.
>
> A **millisecond (ms)** is a thousandth of a second. In a typical hard drive, the average seek time is 10 milliseconds. (In the fastest hard drives, the average seek time is 7½ milliseconds; in the slowest hard drives made today, the average seek time is 14 milliseconds; in older hard drives that are no longer made, the average seek time was 28 milliseconds.)

After the head reaches the correct track, it must wait for the disk to rotate, until the correct sector reaches the head.

> That rotation time is called the **latency**. On the average, the head must wait for half a revolution; so the **average latency time** is a half-revolution. The typical hard drive rotates 90 times per second, so a half-revolution takes half of a 90th of a second, so it's a 180th of a second, so it's about .006 seconds, which is 6 milliseconds.
>
> If you add the average seek time to the average latency time, you get the total **average access time**. So for a typical hard drive, the average access time = 10 milliseconds seek + 6 milliseconds latency = 16 milliseconds.
>
> During the last few years, hard drive manufacturers have become dishonest: they say the "average access time" is 10 milliseconds, when they should actually say the "average seek time" is 10 milliseconds.

After the head finally reaches the correct sector, you must wait for the head to read the data. If the data consumes *several* sectors, you must wait for the head to read all those sectors.

Manufacturers

Most hard drives for microcomputers are manufactured by three American companies: **Seagate Technology (ST)**, **Quantum**, and **Western Digital**.

> **Seagate** was the first of those companies to make hard drives for microcomputers, and it set the standard that the other companies had to follow. New Seagate drives work fine, though Seagate's older models were often noisy and unreliable.
>
> **Quantum** became famous by manufacturing the hard drives that Apple buys to put in Mac computers. Quantum also builds drives for IBM PC clones. Quantum drives are excellent.
>
> **Western Digital** has invented hard drives that cost less. They're popular in cheap clones and discount computer stores.

Conner was the first company to invent hard drives tiny enough to fit in a laptop or notebook computer.

> Seagate ignored the laptop/notebook market too long, and Conner's popularity zoomed up fast. Conner became the fastest-growing company in the history of American industry! But then Conner's competitors caught up and Conner's popularity sunk back down. In Febuary 1996, Seagate bought Conner.

Other popular manufacturers of hard drives are America's **Maxtor** & **Micropolis**, Japan's **NEC** & **Fujitsu**, and Korea's **Samsung**.

When buying a hard drive, you might also need to buy a **hard-drive controller**.

How many sectors?

How many sectors do you get on a track?

> Back in the 1980's, the typical hard-drive controller for IBM-compatible computers put 17 sectors on each track. That scheme was called the **Seagate Technology 506 with Modified Frequency Modulation (ST506 MFM)**.
>
> An improved scheme, which squeezed 26 sectors onto each track, was called the **ST506 with Run Length Limited (ST506 RLL)**. A further improvement, which squeezed 34 sectors onto each track, was called the **Enhanced Small Device Interface (ESDI)**.
>
> Squeezing extra sectors onto each track increases the drive's **capacity** (total number of megabytes) and also the **transfer rate** (the number of sectors that the head reads per rotation or per second).
>
> All those schemes — MFM, RLL, and ESDI — have become obsolete.

Now the most popular scheme is called **Integrated Drive Electronics (IDE)**. Like ESDI, it squeezes 34 sectors onto each track; but it uses special tricks to transfer data faster.

> The original version of IDE was limited to small drives: up to 528M.
>
> A new, improved version, called **Enhanced IDE (EIDE)**, can handle bigger drives. It also goes faster: it transfers 16.6 megabytes per second. Enhanced IDE was invented by Western Digital and is also used by Conner and Maxtor. Seagate invented competing methods (called **Fast ATA-2** and **Fast ATA-3**), which also transfer 16.6 megabytes per second; they're used by Seagate, Quantum, Fujitsu, and Samsung.
>
> Those technologies (Enhanced IDE, Fast ATA-2, and Fast ATA-3) have all being replaced by **Ultra**, which transfers twice as fast: 33.3 megabytes per second! The Ultra version of EIDE is called **Ultra IDE**; the Ultra version of Fast ATA is called **Ultra ATA**.
>
> An extra-fast Ultra ATA has been invented. Called **Ultra ATA-66**, it transfers 66.6 megeabytes per second instead of 33.3. You can buy Ultra ATA-66 drives holding up to 76.8 gigabytes.

A totally different fast scheme is the **Small Computer System Interface** (or **SCSI**, which is pronounced "scuzzy").

> The newest, fastest version of SCSI, called **Ultra 160 SCSI**, transfers 160 megabytes per second.

During the 1980's and early 1990's, SCSI was used on most Mac hard drives and the biggest IBM-compatible hard drives, because IDE drives were too slow and held just a few megabytes. But during the late 1990's, IDE drives became dramatically faster, bigger and cheaper, so SCSI drives have become unpopular.

Discounts on drives

You can buy hard drives cheaply from these discount dealers:

Dirt Cheap Drives
usually lowest prices; ships just to USA
open weekdays 8AM-8PM, Saturday 9AM-3PM, Central Time
3716 Timber Drive, Dickinson TX 77539
phone 800-473-0960 or 281-534-4140

Megahaus
low prices; ships to USA & Canada
open weekdays 8AM-8PM, Saturday 9AM-3PM, Central Time
2201 Pine Drive, Dickinson TX 77539
phone 800-786-1185 or 281-534-3919

Insight (and its division called Hard Drives International)
slightly higher prices; ships to all countries
open always (every day & night, round-the-clock, 24 hours)
1912 W. Fourth St., Tempe AZ 85281
phone 800-INSIGHT or 602-902-1176

IBM-compatible drives Modern, popular IBM-compatible hard drives are Ultra ATA (or Ultra ATA-66), hold 20 or 30 gigabytes, and cost **about $5 per gigabyte**, so:

A 20-gigabyte drive costs about $100.
A 30-gigabyte drive costs about $150.

Besides buying the hard drive, you must also buy a card to put in the computer's slot (unless your computer contains such a card already). For example, here are the prices charged by Dirt Cheap Drives for Ultra ATA (and Ultra ATA-2) drives:

Capacity	Rotation	Cache	Brand	Model number		Price
10.2 G	5400 rpm	½ M	Seagate	ST3	10212 A	$79
15.3 G	5400 rpm	½ M	Maxtor	M3	1536 U2	$85
20.4 G	5400 rpm	½ M	Seagate	ST3	20423 A	$89
30.7 G	5400 rpm	½ M	Maxtor	M3	3073 U4	$129
30.7 G	7200 rpm	2 M	IBM	07N	3929	$179
40 G	7200 rpm	2 M	Maxtor	M5	4098 U8	$235
46.1 G	7200 rpm	2 M	IBM	07N	3931	$269
61.4 G	7200 rpm	2 M	IBM	07N	3933	$454
76.8 G	7200 rpm	2 M	IBM	07N	3935	$555

In that chart, "G" means "gigabytes". (When discussing hard drives, a "gigabyte" is defined to mean "1000 megabytes".)

For Western Digital drives, the model number is 10 times the number of gigs.
For Maxtor drives, the model number's main part is 100 times the number of gigs.
For Quantum drives, the model number is 1000 times the number of gigs.
For Seagate drives, the model number's main part is 1000 times the number of gigs.

A cable runs from the drive to a card, which fits into an IBM AT slot. The card costs extra:

For Ultra ATA-66 drives, get an **Ultra ATA-66 controller card**, which costs $35. For Ultra 160 SCSI drives, get an **Ultra 160 SCSI controller card** instead, which costs $159.

The drive's **cache** (or **buffer**) is RAM chips holding copies of the sectors you used recently — so if you want to look at those sectors again, you can read from the RAM chips (which are fast) instead of waiting for the disk to spin (which is slow).

Those were the prices when this book went to press in September 2000. By the time you read this book, prices might be even lower.

During the last 10 years, hard-drive prices have dropped — and hard-drive capacities have grown — dramatically! Here's what size hard drive you could get for about $100, $200, $300, and $1000 each year:

Year	$100	$200	$300	$1000
1991		.04 G (= 40 M)	.08 G (= 80 M)	.34 G (= 340 M)
1992		.05 G (= 50 M)	.09 G (= 90 M)	.34 G (= 340 M)
1993		.13 G (= 130 M)	.25 G (= 250 M)	1.0 G
1994		.34 G (= 340 M)	.42 G (= 420 M)	1.8 G
1995		.85 G (= 850 M)	1.2 G	4.2 G
1996		1.2 G	2.1 G	4.2 G
1997	1.2 G	3.5 G	5.2 G	9.0 G
1998	2.5 G	8.6 G	12.7 G	
1999	6.4 G	13.0 G	20.4 G	
2000	20.4 G	30.7 G	46.1 G	

Mac drives The price of a Mac hard drive depends on whether the drive is **internal** (fits inside the Mac) or **external** (comes in a separate box that you put next to the Mac). Internal drives are cheaper; but if your Mac is small or filled up, you must buy an external drive instead.

For an external 20.4-gigabyte hard drive that attaches to the iMac's USB port, Megahaus charges $195.

Buy a big drive Back in the 1980's, a 40-megabyte drive was considered "big", and it was the most popular size to buy. In the 1990's, a 40-megabyte drive is considered too small, because the major programs consume about 40 megabytes *each*. Ten major programs consume a total of about 400 megabytes — plus about 40 megabytes more for Windows itself.

Buy at least a 10-gigabyte drive. A 10-gigabyte drive costs just *slightly* more than a 5-gigabyte drive and will last you for many years. You're buying peace of mind!

It's much cheaper to buy a 10-gigabyte-megabyte drive now than to buy a 5-gigabyte-megabyte drive now and another 5-gigabyte-megabyte drive later.

Another reason for buying a 10-gigabyte drive is that it will act faster than a 5-gigabyte drive.

For example, suppose you want to store 5 gigabytes of info, and you're debating whether to buy a 5-gigabyte drive or an 10-gigabyte drive. Suppose each drive is advertised as having a 10-millisecond seek time. The 10-gigabyte drive will nevertheless act faster. Here's why....

Suppose you buy the 10-gigabyte drive and use just the first 5 gigabytes of it. Since you're using just the first half of the drive, the head needs to move just half as far as usual; so over the 5-gigabyte part that you're using, the effective average seek time is just half as much as usual: it's 5 milliseconds!

Removable hard disks Instead of buying a super-capacity floppy drive (such as a Zip drive, Zip 250 drive, LS-120 drive, or PD drive), consider buying a hard drive called the **Orb**, manufactured by **Castlewood**. It costs $175 and includes a 2.2-gigabyte hard disk that's removable. You can buy extra 2.2-gigabyte hard disks for just $29 each. Such a hard disk holds *much* more than a super-capacity floppy disk; it's a better deal. Get those prices from discount dealers such as Dirt Cheap Drives.

RAID

If you need more than 25 gigabytes, attach several hard drives together, and make the drives all act simultaneously. The group of drives is called a **drive array** and acts as one huge drive. That technique is called **RAID** (which originally stood for **Redundant Array of Inexpensive Disks** but now stands for **Redundant Array of Independent Disks**).

Here are the most popular versions of RAID:

RAID level 0, called **data striping**, is the fastest. It divides each long file into several **stripes**. A stripe's first part is put onto drive 1, second part onto drive 2, third part onto drive 3, etc., simultaneously, so that the stripe spans across all the drives. Each drive therefore has to handle just *part* of each stripe and just *part* of each file and finishes faster.

RAID level 1, called **data mirroring**, is the safest. It uses just two drives. It puts each file onto drive 1 and simultaneously puts a backup copy of the file onto drive 2, so that drive 2 always contains an exact copy of what's on drive 1. That way, if drive 1 ever fails, the computer can get the info from drive 2.

RAID level 3, called **shared data parity**, is more sophisticated: it's a clever compromise between RAID level 0 and RAID level 1. Like RAID level 0, it divides each long file into stripes, puts a stripe's first part onto drive 1, second part onto drive 2, third part onto drive 3, etc.; but onto the final drive it puts **parity info** instead, which is info that the computer uses to double-check the accuracy of the other drives.

RAID level 5, called **distributed data parity**, is the most sophisticated. It resembles RAID level 3; but instead of putting all the parity info onto the *last* disk, it puts the first stripe's parity info onto the *first* disk, the second stripe's parity info onto the *second* disk, etc., so that the parity info is distributed among *all* the disks, to prevent the last disk from getting overworked and bogging down the whole system.

CD-ROMs

Instead of buying a program on a floppy disk, you can buy a program on the same kind of **compact disk (CD)** that holds music.

> A CD that holds music is called a **music CD** (or **audio CD**).
>
> A CD that holds computer data instead is called a **computer CD** (or **data CD**). Since the computer data on it cannot be erased, a computer-data CD is also called a **CD read-only memory (CD-ROM)**.

To make your computer read the CD-ROM disk, put the disk into a **CD-ROM drive**, which is a souped-up version of the kind of CD player that plays music.

Like an ordinary CD player, a CD-ROM drive uses just **optics**. No magnetism is involved. The drive just shines a laser beam at the shiny disk and notices, from the reflection, which indentations (**pits**) are on the disk. The pattern of pits is a code that represents the data. So a CD-ROM drive is an example of an **optical disk drive**.

To put the disk into the drive, press a button on the drive. That makes the drive stick its tongue out at you! The tongue is called a **tray**. Put the disk onto the tray, so that the disk's label is face-up. (If the drive is old-fashioned, you must put the disk into a **caddy** first; but the most modern drives are **caddyless**.) Then push the tray back into the drive. Finally, use the keyboard or mouse to give a command that makes the computer taste what you've put on its tongue.

IBM drive letters

Here's how a modern IBM-compatible computer assigns the drives:

> Drive A is a 3½-inch floppy drive (1.44M).
> Drive B is a 5¼-inch floppy drive (1.2M).
> Drive C is a hard drive (about 4G).
> Drive D is typically a CD-ROM drive.

But if your computer has *two* hard drives, here's what happens: the first hard drive is C, the second hard drive is D, and the CD-ROM drive is the next letter (E).

If you bought just *one* hard drive but plan to buy a second hard drive later, you can leave "drive D" empty and make the CD-ROM drive be E.

Size

CD-ROM disks come in two sizes:

> The standard size has a diameter of 12 centimeters (which is about 5 inches) and holds 650 megabytes.
> The miniature size has a diameter of 8 centimeters (which is about 3 inches) and holds 180 megabytes.

Your CD-ROM drive can handle *both* sizes of CD-ROM disks. Each CD-ROM disk is single-sided: all the data is on the disk's *bottom* side — the side that doesn't have a label.

On a standard-size CD-ROM disk, there are 2 billion pits. They're all arranged into a single spiral (like the groove on a phonograph record). If you were to unravel the spiral, to make it a straight line, it would be 3 miles long!

On a CD, each "song" is called a **track**; it can hold music or computer data. Each "song" (track) can be as long or as short as you wish.

The standard-size CD can hold 99 tracks, totaling an hour of music (for an audio CD) or 650 megabytes (for a CD-ROM disk).

Yes, a standard-size CD-ROM disk holds 650 megabytes, which is a lot!

> It's about 450 times as much as a high-density 1.44M floppy.
> It's about 1800 times as much as a 360K floppy.

Since a CD-ROM disk holds so much, a single CD-ROM can hold a whole library (including encyclopedias, dictionaries, other reference materials, famous novels, programs, artwork, music, and videos). It's the ideal way to distribute massive quantities of information! Moreover, a CD-ROM disk costs just $1.50 to manufacture (once you've bought the appropriate CD-ROM-making equipment, which costs several thousand dollars).

CD-ROM disks store info differently than floppy & hard disks:

> On a CD, each track is part of a spiral.
> On a floppy disk or hard disk, each track is a circle.
>
> On a CD, different tracks have different lengths and hold a different number of bytes.
> On a typical floppy disk or hard disk, all tracks have the same number of bytes as each other.

Speed

When buying a CD-ROM drive, the most important factor to consider is the drive's speed.

Transfer rate The speed at which the drive spins is called the **transfer rate**. The higher, the better!

On the first CD-ROM drives that were invented, the transfer rate was the same speed as music CD's: 150 kilobytes per second.

> Then came drives that could spin twice as fast: 300 kilobytes/second. That's called **double speed** or **2X**.
> Then came drives that could spin thrice as fast: 450 kilobytes/second. That's called **triple speed** or **3X**.
> Then came drives that spun four times as fast: 600 kilobytes/second. That's called **quad speed** or **4X**.

Then came 4½X drives, then **6X**, then **8X**, then **10X**, then **12X**. During the summer of 1997, most drives sold were 12X, which transfers 1800 kilobytes/second.

Then came drives that were even faster. For example, you could buy a drive called **24X/12X** (or **24X maximum** or **24X max**), whose outer tracks are read at a maximum speed of 24X, though the inner tracks are read at just 12X.

Now you can buy drives that go even faster: **72X max!**

Seek time The average time it takes for the head to move to the correct track is called the **average seek time**.

The lower the average seek time, the better!

> Under 100 milliseconds is great.
> 100-200 milliseconds is okay.
> Over 200 milliseconds is terrible.

Buying a drive

Here are the cheapest good drives:

Transfer rate	Seek	Buffer	Brand	Model	Price
48X max	65 ms	¼M	Mitsumi	CRMCFX 48X	$53
62X max	90 ms	2M	Kenwood	UCR 420	$109
72X max	100 ms	2M	Kenwood	UCR 421	$125

Each of those drives is IDE. You can get those prices from these discount dealers:

Dirt Cheap Drives, 3716 Timber Drive, Dickinson TX 77539
phone 800-473-0960 or 281-534-4140

Megahaus, 2201 Pine Dr., Dickinson TX 77539
phone 800-786-1185 or 281-534-3919

Tri State Computer, 650 6th Ave. (at 20th St.), New York NY 10011
phone 800-433-5199 or 212-633-2530

Those prices are for just the bare drive; add $30 for an installation kit.

If you already own a CD-ROM drive that's at least 2X, don't bother replacing it by a faster one. Faster drives make most CD-ROM program run just *slightly* faster, since most CD-ROM programs are still designed under the assumption each CD-ROM drive is just 2X.

External drives Those prices are for **internal drives**, which fit inside the computer's system unit. If your system unit is filled up and doesn't have any room left to insert an internal drive, you must buy an **external drive** instead, which sits outside the system unit and costs about $30 more.

Multimedia kits If you buy a CD-ROM drive, you'll also want a **sound card**, a pair of **stereo speakers**, and a few sample CD-ROM disks (so you can admire all that equipment you bought). That combo — a CD-ROM drive, sound card, pair of speakers, and sample CD-ROM disks — is called a **multimedia kit**.

The most popular 24X-max multimedia kit is the **Sound Blaster Discovery AWE64 24X**, made by **Creative Labs**. You can get it for just $139 from discount dealers such as Harmony.

Tough installation

Warning: **CD-ROM drives (and multimedia kits) are extremely difficult to install correctly** because they tend to conflict with other hardware and software. Even if you follow the instructions in the setup manual, the stuff typically doesn't work.

If you try to get help by phoning the company that made the multimedia kit (such as Creative Labs), you almost always get a busy signal. Even if you finally get through to a technician, the technician can't help you much, since the technician doesn't know enough details about the other hardware and software your computer contains.

Most consumers give up in disgust, return the stuff to the store, and pay the store about $70 to do the installation.

Some stores offer "free" installation — but do so by advertising a higher price for the CD-ROM drive.

When you buy a new computer, you can ask the salesperson to include a multimedia kit and install it. A computer that includes an installed multimedia kit is called a **multimedia computer system**.

Caring for your CD-ROM disks
A CD-ROM disk's main enemy is dirt.

When you buy a CD-ROM disk, it comes in a clear square box, called the **jewel box**. To use the CD-ROM disk, remove it from the jewel box and put the disk into the drive. When you finish using the disk, put it back into the jewel box, which keeps the dust off the disk.

When putting the CD-ROM disk into or out of a drive, don't put your fingers on the disk's surface: instead, **hold the disk by its edge**, so your greasy fingerprints don't get on the disk's surface.

Once a month, gently **wipe any dust** off the CD-ROM disk's bottom surface (where the data is). While wiping, be gentle and don't get your greasy fingerprints on the disk. Start in the middle and wipe toward the outer edge.

For example, my assistant and I were getting lots of error messages when using a sample CD-ROM disk we bought from Microsoft. I was going to phone Microsoft to complain, but my assistant asked, "What about dust?" I flipped the CD-ROM disk over and sure enough, a big ball of dust was on the disk's bottom side, where the data is recorded. I wiped it off. That CD-ROM disk has worked perfectly ever since.

I was so embarrassed! If my assistant hadn't reminded me to wipe the dust off, I'd have wasted hours of Microsoft's time hunting uselessly for a high-tech reason my CD-ROM disk wasn't working.

Don't put any fluids on the disk. The fluids that clean phonograph records will *wreck* CD-ROM disks.

If you want to write on the disk, **use a felt-tipped pen** (not a ballpoint or pencil). Don't stick any labels on the disk.

The typical CD-ROM disk will last about 12 years. Then the aluminum on its surface will start to oxidize (corrode), and the CD will become unreadable.

CD-R

You can create your own CD's, in the privacy of your home, if you buy a **CD-Recordable drive (CD-R drive)**.

The cheapest popular CD-R drive is made by **Mitsumi**. It costs less than $195. That price is for a complete kit that includes the drive, the software, and 1 sample blank disk. Unfortunately, like most CD-R drives, it writes onto the CD slowly (at a speed of 2X) and reads from the CD slowly (8X). It also requires you to buy blank **CD-R disks**, which cost $1.20 each if you buy 5, $1.10 each if you buy 20, $1 each if you buy 50, 89¢ each if you buy 100. All those prices are from a discount dealer, **Dirt Cheap Drives** (800-473-0960).

Although a CD-R drive can write onto a disk, it can*not* erase or edit what you wrote. For more flexibility, you can buy a **CD-ReWritable drive (CD-RW drive)**, which can write onto a blank CD and then edit what you wrote.

CD-RW drives cost slightly more than CD-R drives. The cheapest CD-RW drive is made by **Teac**. It costs $199. That price is for a complete kit that includes the drive, the software, and 2 sample blank disk. The drive writes 4X and reads 32X. It uses blank **CD-RW disks**, which cost $1.60 each if you buy 5, $1.10 each if you buy 20, $1.04 each if you buy 100. It can also act as a plain CD-R drive (using plain CD-R disks), and it can read ordinary CD-ROM disks. All those prices are from Dirt Cheap Drives.

DVD

In 1997, the electronics industry began selling an improved kind of CD, called a **Digital Versatile Disk (DVD)**. It looks like a standard-size CD but holds more info.

Unlike a standard CD, which holds just an hour of music or 650M of data, a standard DVD can hold a 2-hour movie (including the video and sound) or 4.7G of data. Since it can hold a movie, some movie lovers call it a "Digital Video Disk", but it's more versatile than just that!

A DVD can be recorded on just the bottom side (like a CD) or on both sides. (To use the second side, you must remove the disk from the drive and flip the disk upside down, like you'd flip a phonograph record.) A dual-sided DVD can therefore hold 9.4G of data.

An improved technology, called **dual-layer DVD**, puts nearly *two* layers of data on each side, so you get 8.5G per side, 17G total.

A DVD that contains computer data (instead of a movie or music) is called a **DVD-ROM disk**. To use it, put it in a **DVD-ROM drive**, which costs just $105. At that price, you get a drive that can read computer data but not Hollywood movies. To watch Hollywood movies, you'll also need a **Moving Picture Expert Group's version 2 decoder card (MPEG-2 decoder card)**, which costs $99.

Every DVD-ROM drive can read DVD-ROM disks and also standard CD-ROM disks. Unfortunately, just *modern* DVD-ROM drives can also read CD-R and CD-RW disks.

To create your *own* DVDs in your own home, you can buy a **DVD-Recordable drive (DVD-R drive)**, which is expensive. To create *and edit* your own DVDs, you must buy a **DVD-RAM drive**, which costs even more: $279. For a blank DVD-RAM disk holding 5.2G, you pay $37 for 1, $35 each if you buy 5, $33 each if you buy 10.

SCREENS

What's a screen?

The computer's **screen** is an ordinary TV (the same kind you watch Bill Cosby on) or *resembles* a TV. The screen shows what you typed on the keyboard and also shows the computer's responses.

The computer's screen is also called the **display**.

Monitors

A **computer monitor** resembles a TV but produces a sharper picture and costs more.

Like a TV, the typical computer monitor contains a picture tube. The tube in a TV or monitor is called a **cathode-ray tube (CRT)**.

Stand-alone versus built-in

The monitor can be either **stand-alone** or **built-in**.

If your computer is standard, it uses a **stand-alone monitor**, which looks like a TV but has no antenna and no dial for selecting channels: the only channel you get is "computer". Before buying a computer that uses a stand-alone monitor, ask whether the computer's price includes the monitor: the monitor might cost extra. The monitor's price includes a cable that runs from the monitor to the computer's system unit.

Some non-standard computers use a **built-in monitor**, which is a screen that's permanently screwed into the front or top of the computer's system unit. That makes the system unit heavy and big so it's difficult for a thief to lift, hide, and steal. Built-in monitors are particularly popular in public schools in high-crime areas. Most other organizations prefer stand-alone monitors, which are easier to move (to a more convenient place on your desk or a more convenient room) and which are easier to replace (if you need repairs or you want to switch to a fancier monitor).

Colors

When buying a TV, you ask for either "color" or "black-and-white". Similarly, when buying a computer monitor, ask for either **color** or **monochrome**. A color monitor displays all colors of the rainbow; a monochrome monitor displays just black-and-light.

Four kinds of monochrome monitors are common:

A	**paper-white monitor**	displays black and white.
An	**amber monitor**	displays black and yellow.
A	**green-screen monitor**	displays black and light green.
A	**gray-scale monitor**	displays many shades of gray.

A color TV costs more than black-and-white. Similarly, a color monitor (that displays all the colors of the rainbow) costs more than a monochrome monitor:

Most monochrome monitors cost between $80 and $100.
Most color monitors cost between $100 and $800.

If your computer system is standard, its monitor is color. Monochrome monitors are outdated.

On the monitor's screen, the picture shown is made of thousands of tiny dots. Each tiny dot is called a **picture's element (pixel)**.

In a standard color monitor, each pixel is made of three phosphors: one kind glows **red** if hit by an electron; another kind turns **green**, another kind turns **blue**. That kind of monitor is called a **red-green-blue monitor (RGB monitor)**.

Inside the monitor, three **guns** can shoot beams of electrons at the phosphors. The **red gun** can shoot electrons at the red phosphors (to make them glow red); the **green gun** can shoot at the green phosphors (to make them glow green); the **blue gun** can shoot at the red phosphors (to make them glow blue).

> To make a pixel turn **red**, the computer tells the monitor's red gun to shoot at that pixel's red phosphor, so the pixel's phosphor glows red. To make a pixel turn **green**, the computer makes the monitor's green gun shoot at the pixel's green phosphor. **Blue** is similar.
>
> To make a pixel be very bright, the computer makes the monitor's three guns all fire at the same pixel, so the pixel's red, green, and blue phosphors all glow simultaneously. That makes the pixel be very bright —a hot **white** flash.
>
> To make a pixel be **black**, the computer makes *none* of the guns fire at the pixel.
>
> To make the pixel be **cyan (greenish blue)**, the computer makes the green and blue guns fire simultaneously at the pixel. To make the pixel be **magenta (purplish red)**, the computer makes the red and blue guns fire. To make the pixel be **yellow**, the computer makes the red and green guns fire (which produces a color that's brighter and lighter than red or green alone).

That's how to produce 8 colors: red, green, blue, white, black, cyan, magenta, and yellow.

Although a primitive RGB monitor produces just 8 colors, a better RGB monitor can produce extra colors by varying the strength of the electron beams. For example, instead of the red gun being either "on" or "off", it can be "completely on", "partly on", or "off".

Here are the names for the different levels of RGB monitors:

> A **primitive RGB monitor** can produce **8 colors**. Its cable to the computer includes a red-gun wire, a green-gun wire, and a blue-gun wire. Each wire's current has 2 choices (on or off), so the total number of color choices is "2 times 2 times 2", which is 8.
>
> A **Computer Graphics Adapter monitor (CGA monitor)** can produce **16 colors**. Its cable to the computer includes a red-gun wire, a green-gun wire, a blue-gun wire, and an intensity wire. Each wire's current has 2 choices (on or off), so the total number of choices is "2 times 2 times 2 times 2", which is 16.
>
> An **Enhanced Graphics Adapter monitor (EGA monitor)** can produce **64 colors**. Its cable to the computer includes 2 red-gun wires (generating a total of 4 levels of red-gun intensity), 2 green-gun wires, and 2 blue-gun wires, so the total number of choices is "4 times 4 times 4", which is 64.
>
> A **Video Graphics Array monitor (VGA monitor)** can produce **over 16 million colors**. Its cable to the computer includes 1 red-gun wire, 1 green-gun wire, and 1 blue-gun wire, and each wire can handle 256 levels of intensity, so the total number of choices is "256 times 256 times 256", which is 16,777,216.

VGA has become the standard. Primitive RGB, CGA, and EGA monitors are obsolete.

For a VGA monitor, the cable to the computer includes 1 red-gun wire, 1 green-gun wire, 1 blue-gun wire, and several other wires to help administer the signals. Altogether, the VGA cable contains 15 wires.

CGA and EGA cables each contain just 9 wires. If you see a monitor whose cable contains just 9 wires, the monitor is either CGA or EGA. It's therefore obsolete.

Size

The typical VGA color monitor's screen is **17-inch (17")**. That means the distance from the picture tube's top left corner to the picture tube's bottom right corner is 17 inches, measured diagonally.

Although the picture tube's diagonal size is 17-inch, you see just 16 inches, because 1 inch is hidden behind the plastic that makes up the monitor's case.

Most monitors are made by companies whose US headquarters are in California. Consumers complained to California's attorney general that such a monitor shouldn't be called "17-inch", since just 16 inches are viewable. California now requires all ads for "17-inch" monitors to include a comment, in parentheses, saying that the **viewable image size (vis)** is just 16 inches, so the ad looks like this:

> 17" monitor (16" vis)

Instead of buying a 17-inch monitor, you can buy a bigger one (19-inch or 21-inch) or a smaller one (15-inch or 14-inch). In each case, the viewable image size is about an inch less than the size of the tube.

Here's what VGA color monitors cost:

Size	Price
14" (13" vis)	$119
15" (14" vis)	$125
17" (16" vis)	$189
19" (18" vis)	$315
21" (20" vis)	$739

Those are the prices charged by discount dealers such as **Harmony** (phone 800-870-1663 or 718-692-3232) and **Treasure Chest** (phone 800-677-9781).

A 14" monitor (13" vis) is adequate for most people and most software, but few companies still offer 14" monitors. 15" shows the same info as 14" but slightly magnified, so you can read "the fine print" on the screen more easily. 17", 19", and 21" monitors are a pleasure; they're especially helpful if you're trying to create fine graphics (or ads) or many side-by-side columns (as in a newspaper, magazine, newsletter, textbook, or big table of numbers) or you have poor eyesight (or you're sharing the computer with somebody who has poor eyesight).

Resolution

Each position on the screen is called a **pixel**. The pixels are arranged in rows and columns, to form a grid. In a primitive VGA monitor, the screen is wide enough to hold 640 columns of pixels, and the screen is tall enough to hold 480 rows of pixels, so altogether the number of pixels in the grid is "640 times 480", which is written "640×480", which is pronounced "640 by 480". That's called the screen's **resolution**.

If you buy a big VGA monitor (such as 21-inch), the screen is big enough to hold *lots* of pixels. You can use such a screen in two ways: you can make the screen either show lots of tiny pixels or show a smaller number of fat pixels.

Here's how many pixels the typical screen can display:

> If screen is 14" (13" viewable), it handles 640×480 well, 800×600 poorly.
> If screen is 15" (14" viewable), it handles 800×600 well, 1024×768 poorly.
> If screen is 17" (16" viewable), it handles 1024×768 well, 1280×1024 poorly.
> If screen is 19" (18" viewable), it handles 1280×1024 well, 1600×1200 poorly.
> If screen is 21" (20" viewable), it handles 1600×1200 well, 1800×1440 poorly.

Those resolutions have nicknames:

Resolution	Nickname	Alternative nicknames
640×480	**minimal VGA**	
800×600	**super VGA (SVGA)**	**VGA Plus**
1024×768	**eXtended GA (XGA)**	**nice SVGA** or **Ultra VGA (UVGA)**
1280×1024	**Super XGA (SXGA)**	
1600×1200	**Ultra XGA (UXGA)**	

Refresh rate

Here's how the red gun works:

> It aims at the first pixel on the screen, decides how many electrons to fire at that pixel's red phosphor (depending on how red you want the pixel to be), and fires those electrons. Those electrons excite the first pixel's red phosphor and make the phosphor glow the appropriate amount. Then the red gun does the same thing for the screen's second pixel, then the third pixel, etc.
>
> While the gun is dealing with later pixels, the gun is ignoring the first pixel's red phosphor, whose glow starts to fade. When the red gun finishes handling the last pixel, that gun hurries back to the first pixel and gives its red phosphor another shot of electrons, to refresh the phosphor's glow.

If the gun doesn't get back to the first pixel soon enough, that pixel's glow will have faded too much, and your eye will notice the fading and consider it an annoying flicker.

To avoid annoying flicker, the gun must get back to the phosphor fast, in less than an 85th of a second. That means it must refresh the phosphor at least 85 times per second. Instead of saying "the gun must refresh the phosphor at least 85 times per second," engineers say "the **vertical refresh rate** must be at least **85 hertz (85 Hz)**."

If the vertical refresh rate is less than 85 hertz, your eye might detect some flicker, which will annoy you. The flicker will be noticeable mainly if you look at the screen out of the corner of your eye, since your eye's peripheral vision is most sensitive to flicker.

> 85 hertz is excellent, flicker-free.
> 75 hertz is rather good. It's acceptable to most folks, annoying to some.
> 60 hertz is rather bad. It's annoying to everybody but still usable.
> Below 60 hertz is terrible, unusable.

The typical cheap 17" monitor can show 1024×768 resolution well (at 85 hertz) but shows 1280×1024 resolution poorly (at 60 hertz). The ad for such a monitor typically begins by bragging that it can display 1280×1024 but then admits it handles that resolution poorly and should be used at just 1024×768; it says:

> 1280×1024 @ 60Hz, 1024×768 @ 85Hz

Trinitron

In a traditional picture tube, each pixel is a trio of phosphor dots (red, green, and blue), arranged as three points of a triangle. That technique is called a **dot-trio shadow mask**.

Sony invented a more expensive kind of picture tube, called the **Trinitron**, using a technique called **aperture grille**: each pixel is a trio of vertical stripes (red, green, and blue), arranged side-by-side, like fence posts. That technique produces brighter colors and straighter vertical lines. But it makes diagonal lines look too bumpy; and if your eyesight is good, you'll notice an annoying grid of thin horizontal wires, which hold the vertical phosphors in place.

Dot pitch

The distance from a red phosphor to the closest nearest red phosphor is called the **dot pitch**. On a standard monitor, the dot pitch is **.28 millimeters (.28mm)**.

The smaller the dot pitch, the better. The best monitors have a dot pitch of .26, .25, .24, .23, .22, or .21.

Terrible monitors have a dot pitch of .31, .39, .42, or .51. Their screens are too blurry to let you read small characters.

On a Sony Trinitron monitor, the dot pitch is usually .25.

Flat screen

In a typical monitor, the picture tube's surface is curved. If you pay slightly extra, you can buy a **flat-screen monitor** instead, whose picture tube's surface is flat. It has two advantages:

> It displays horizontal and vertical lines more accurately (without curving).
> It reflects light from fewer angles (so you see fewer annoying reflections).

Where to put the monitor

According to researchers such as the government's **National Institute of Occupational Safety and Health (NIOSH)**, here's where you should put the monitor so you'll be comfortable while you're working at the computer....

Put the monitor slightly lower than your eyes, so you look *down* at the monitor (instead of looking up, which would strain your neck). When you're looking at the center of the monitor's screen, you should be looking down slightly (at an angle that's 15 degrees below horizontal).

Put the monitor a moderate distance from your face. NIOSH recommended that the distance from your eyes to the center of the monitor's screen be 17 inches; but that recommendation was made several years ago, when the typical monitor screen was just 12-inch. Now screens are bigger, so you need to sit farther from the screen to see the whole screen: a distance of 23 inches feels good to me.

Keep the room rather dark, to avoid having light reflected off the monitor's surface. **Put the monitor perpendicular to any light source**, so no light source shines directly onto the monitor's screen (which would create an annoying reflection) and no light source shines directly onto the monitor's back (since such a light source would also be shining into your eyes and create an annoying glare).

Video terminals

A **video-display terminal (VDT)** is a monitor that has an attached keyboard and communicates with a big computer.

If 200 people are using a maxicomputer simultaneously, just one of them is sitting at the maxicomputer's main console. The other 199 people typically sit at 199 video-display terminals (or 199 personal computers), which are in different rooms or even different cities.

TV sets

If your computer is old and primitive (such as an Apple 2 or Radio Shack Color Computer or Commodore 64 or Commodore VIC or Atari 800), you can attach it to an ordinary TV set instead of to a monitor. Here's how to attach such a computer to a TV set:

> Look at your TV's antenna. Wires run from the antenna to two screws, which are on the back of the TV. Loosen those two screws, to detach the antenna from the TV. Instead of attaching the antenna's wires to those two screws, attach the antenna's wires to a **switch box** (which is included in the price of such a computer), and then attach the switchbox to the two screws on the back of the TV, so the switchbox sits between the antenna and the TV. Finally, run an **RCA cord** from the switchbox to the back of the computer.
>
> The switch box has a switch on it. If you move the switch toward the antenna, you have a normal TV, so you can watch Bill Cosby. If you move the switch toward the computer's RCA cord, your TV's controlled by the computer so the computer can write messages on your TV screen.
>
> By moving the switch, you can make your TV act either normal or computerized. Your family will argue about which way to move the switch.
>
> That switch box is the same kind used by video-game machines. When you buy a TV computer, the salesperson gives you the switch box and RCA cord, free!
>
> To use the computer, flip the computer's switch to channel 3 or 4, then turn your TV's dial to the same channel.
>
> To get a sharp picture on your TV screen, *avoid* the channel used by your local TV station. For example, if you live in Boston, CBS hogs channel 4, so *avoid* channel 4; put your computer and TV on channel 3 instead.
>
> Though most computers (such as Commodore and Radio Shack) use channels 3 and 4, some computers (such as Atari) use channels 2 and 3 instead. Some other computers use channels 10 and 33 and 34 instead.
>
> If the image on your TV screen looks *fuzzy* — so that you can barely read the computer's writing — adjust the TV's "fine tuning" knob.

Besides writing messages on your TV's screen, the computer can also draw its own *pictures* on the TV. If your TV has color, you'll see the pictures in color.

When you watch Bill Cosby on TV, his face's size depends on the size of your TV's screen. If your TV's screen is tiny (less than 12 inches), his face looks small; if your TV's screen is 25 inches, his face looks bigger; and if you have a projection TV with a gigantic 60-inch screen, his face looks gigantic. The same is true for the messages & pictures that the computer sends to the TV: the bigger the TV's screen, the more magnified the computer's messages & pictures.

The computer can make the TV screen show words, numbers, and formulas. Those words, numbers, and formulas are made of **characters**: each character is a letter of the alphabet, a digit, or any other symbol you can type.

The ideal TV computer would make the TV display 25 lines of info, with each line of info containing 40 characters, so the total number of characters you see on the screen simultaneously is "25 times 40", which is 1000.

But most TV computers are less than perfect: they display slightly *fewer* than 25 lines of info and slightly *fewer* than 40 characters per line, so the total number of characters you see on the TV screen simultaneously is slightly less than 1000.

Liquid crystals

If your computer is tiny, it comes with a tiny screen, called a **liquid-crystal display (LCD)**. That's the kind of screen you see on digital watches, pocket calculators, pocket computers, subnotebook computers, notebook computers, and laptop computers.

Those computers use LCD screens instead of traditional picture tubes because LCD screens consume less electricity, weigh less, and are less bulky. Since an LCD screen uses little electricity, it can run on batteries. A traditional picture tube can*not* run on batteries. If your computer system runs on batteries, its screen is an LCD.

Desktop and tower computers use traditional picture tubes, for these reasons:

> Big picture tubes cost less than big LCD screens.
>
> The image on the typical LCD screen has poor contrast and resolution and responds too slowly to computer commands.

Kinds of LCD screens

A traditional LCD screen displays black characters on a white background. The screen consists of thousands of tiny crystals. Each crystal is normally white, but temporarily changes to black when an electrical charge passes through it. Newer LCD screens can display colors.

The main manufacturer of LCD screens is **Sharp**. Sharp's LCD screens are used in many brands of computers.

A notebook computer's price depends mainly on what kind of LCD screen it includes. Most folks buy color LCD screens, though blank-and-white monochrome LCD screens are cheaper. For color LCD screens, the old-fashioned kind is called **passive**; the next step up is **dual-scan passive**, which is brighter and works faster; the next step up is **high-performance addressing (HPA)**; the most expensive is **active-matrix**, which is the brightest and works the fastest.

> Passive is also called **super-twist nematic (STN)**.
> Dual-scan passive is called **double-layer STN (DSTN)**.
> Active-matrix is called **thin-film transistor (TFT)**.

Most folks buy color screens that are active-matrix (which is the best type) or dual-scan passive (which costs $100 less).

LCD monitors

The typical LCD screen is built into a small computer (such as a notebook computer). A different way to get an LCD screen is to buy an **LCD monitor**, which acts as a monitor but includes an LCD screen instead of a CRT. You can attach the LCD monitor to a desktop or tower computer.

An LCD monitor is convenient because it consumes less desk space than a CRT. Unfortunately, an LCD monitor is very expensive (over $1,000).

LCD plates

An **LCD plate** (or **LCD overhead-projection panel**) is a special LCD screen that you put on an overhead projector, which projects the LCD's image onto the wall of your office or classroom or auditorium, so that the image becomes several feet across.

The nicest low-cost LCD plate is the **Sharp QA-75**. It can display many shades of gray. It sells for about $1500. It attaches to the IBM PC, and you can buy a cable to connect it to a Mac.

PRINTERS

Fundamentals

A computer usually displays its answers on a screen. If you want the computer to copy the answers onto paper, attach the computer to a **printer**, which is a device that prints on paper.

The typical printer looks like a typewriter but lacks a keyboard. To feed information to the printer, you type on the *computer's* keyboard. The computer transmits your request through a cable of wires running from the back of the computer to the back of the printer.

A computer's advertised price usually does *not* include a printer and cable. The cable costs about $8; the typical printer costs several hundred dollars.

Printers are more annoying than screens. Printers are noisier, slower, cost more, consume more electricity, need repairs more often, and require you to buy paper and ink. But you'll want a printer anyway, to copy the computer's answers onto paper that you can give your computerless friends. Another reason to get a printer is that a sheet of paper is bigger than a screen and lets you see more information at once.

Printer dealers

To get a printer cheaply, phone these mail-order discount dealers:

Tri State Computer
650 6th Ave. (at 20th St.)
New York NY 10011
800-433-5199 or 212-633-2530

Harmony Computers & Electronics
1801 Flatbush Ave.
Brooklyn NY 11210
800-441-1144 or 718-692-3232

Micro Warehouse
444 Scott Dr.
Bloomingdale, IL 60108
800-551-3146 or 908-905-5245

Micro Warehouse offers the greatest variety of printers but charges more than the other companies. To get special attention, ask Tri State for **David Rohinsky at extension 223** and tell him you're reading *The Secret Guide to Computers*.

To get low prices locally, walk into chains of discount superstores, such as **Comp USA** (which sells all kinds of computer equipment) and **Staples** (which sells all kinds of office supplies and some computer equipment).

Three kinds of printers

Three kinds of printers are popular.

A **dot-matrix printer** looks like a typewriter but has no keyboard. Like a typewriter, it smashes an inked ribbon against the paper. Like a typewriter, it's cheap: it typically costs about $150.

An **ink-jet printer** looks like a dot-matrix printer; but instead of containing a ribbon, it contains tiny hoses that squirt ink at the paper. It prints more beautifully than a dot-matrix printer and costs more. It typically costs about $200.

A **laser printer** looks like a photocopier. Like a photocopier, it contains a rotating drum and inky toner. It prints even more beautifully than the other two kinds of printers. Like a photocopier, it's expensive: it typically costs about $400.

Special requirements

As you progress from a dot-matrix printer to an ink-jet printer to a laser printer, the quality tends to go up, and so does the price. But here are exceptions....

Color If you need to print in color (instead of just black-and-white), get an ink-jet printer. The typical ink-jet printer can print in color beautifully. (Dot-matrix printers produce colors too crudely and slowly. Laser printers produce just black-and-white, except for ridiculously expensive laser printers that produce color and cost about $4,000.)

Mailing labels Although you can print mailing labels on all three kinds of printers, the *easiest* way to print mailing labels is on a dot-matrix printer.

Multi-part forms If you want to print on a multipart form (using carbon paper or carbonless NCR paper), you must buy a dot-matrix printer.

Old accounting software Some old accounting software requires that you buy a dot-matrix printer. It also requires that the printer be an expensive kind that can handle extra-wide paper.

Cost of consumables

After you've bought the printer and used it for a while, the **ink** supply will run out, so you must buy more ink.

In the typical **dot-matrix printer**, the inked ribbon costs about $5 and lasts about 1000 pages, so it costs about a half a penny per page. That's cheap!

In the typical **ink-jet printer**, the ink cartridge costs about $20 and lasts about 500 pages, so it costs about 4 cents per page. That's expensive!

In the typical **laser printer**, the toner cartridge costs about $80 and lasts about 4000 pages, so it costs about 2 cents per page. That's expensive, but not as expensive as the ink in an ink-jet printer.

Those prices assume you're printing black text. If you're printing graphics or color, the cost per page goes up drastically. For example, full-color graphics on an ink-jet printer cost about 50 cents per page.

For all three kinds of printers, you must also pay for the **paper**, which costs about 1 cent per sheet if you buy a small quantity (such as a 500 sheets), or a half a cent per sheet if you buy a large quantity (such as 5000 sheets). For low prices on paper, go to Staples.

You must also pay for the **electricity** to run the printer; but the electricity's cost is negligible (much less than a penny per page) if you turn the printer off when you're not printing.

Warning: if you leave a laser printer on even when not printing, its total yearly electric cost can get high, since the laser printer contains a big electric heater. (You might even notice the lights in your room go dim when the heater kicks on.)

Daisy-wheel printers

Although the most popular kinds of printers are dot-matrix, ink-jet, and laser, some folks still use an older kind of printer, called a **daisy-wheel printer**. It's cute! Here's how it works....

Like a typewriter and a dot-matrix printer, a daisy-wheel printer smashes an inked ribbon against paper. To do that, the daisy-wheel printer contains a device called a **daisy wheel**, which is an artificial daisy flower made of plastic or metal. On each of the daisy's petals is embossed a character: a letter, a digit, or a symbol. For example, one petal has the letter A embossed on it; another petal has B; another petal has C; etc.

Notice that each character is **embossed**. (The word "embossed" is like "engraved", but an "embossed" character is raised *up* from the surface instead of etched into the surface.)

To print the letter C, the printer spins the daisy wheel until the C petal is in front of the inked ribbon. Then a hammer bangs the C petal against the ribbon, which in turn hits the paper, so that an inked C appears on the paper.

Boldface The printer can print each character extra-dark or regular. To print a character extra-dark, the printer prints the character, moves to the right just 120th of an inch, and then reprints the character. Since the second printing is *almost* in the same place as the original character, the character looks darkened and slightly fatter. Those darkened, fattened characters are called **boldfaced**.

Different wheels You can remove the daisy wheel from the printer and insert a different daisy wheel instead. Each daisy wheel contains a different **font**. For example, one daisy wheel contains italics; a different daisy wheel contains Greek symbols used by scientists.

The printer holds just one daisy wheel at a time. To switch to italics in the middle of your printing, you must stop the printer, switch daisy wheels (a tedious activity that requires your own manual labor!), and then press a button for the printer to resume printing.

Manufacturers The most famous daisy-wheel printer manufacturer was **Diablo**, founded by Mr. Lee in California. He sold the company to Xerox, then founded a second daisy-wheel printer company, **Qume** (pronounced "kyoom"), which he sold to ITT. In 1988 he bought Qume back. Other companies (such as **Brother** and **Juki**) invented imitations that claimed to be **Diablo & Qume compatible**.

Variants of the daisy wheel Over the years, many variants of the daisy wheel have been invented.

For example, **Nippon Electric Company (NEC)** invented a "wilted" daisy wheel, whose petals are bent. The wilted daisy wheel is called a **thimble**. Computerists like it because it spins faster than a traditional daisy and also produces a sharper image. It's used just in NEC's **Spinwriter** and **Elf** printers.

Another variation of the daisy wheel is the plastic **golf ball**, which has characters embossed all over it. IBM calls it a **Selectric typing element**. IBM uses it in typewriters, typesetting machines, and printers. It produces better-looking characters than daisy wheels or thimbles. Since it spins too slowly and needs too many repairs, IBM is discontinuing it.

Gigantic printers used by maxicomputers and minicomputers have characters embossed on **bands**, **chains**, and **drums** instead of daisies. Those printers are fast and cost many thousands of dollars.

Look closer

Now let's take a closer look at each of the three popular kinds of printers: dot-matrix, ink-jet, and laser....

Dot-matrix printers

A **dot-matrix printer** resembles a daisy-wheel printer; but instead of containing a daisy wheel, it contains a few **guns**, as if it were a super-cowboy whose belt contains several holsters.

Each gun shoots a pin at the inked ribbon. When the pin's tip hits the ribbon and smashes the ribbon against the paper, a dot of ink appears on the paper. Then the pin retracts back into the gun that fired it.

Since each gun has its own pin, the number of guns is the same as the number of pins.

9-pin printers

If the printer is of average quality, it has 9 guns — and therefore 9 pins. It's called a **9-pin printer**. The 9 guns are stacked on top of each other, in a column that's called the **print head**. If all the guns fire simultaneously, the pins smash against the ribbon simultaneously, so the paper shows 9 dots in a vertical column. The dots are very close to each other, so that the column of dots looks like a single vertical line. If just *some* of the 9 pins press against the ribbon, you get fewer than 9 dots, so you see just *part* of a vertical line.

To print a character, the print head's 9 guns print part of a vertical line; then the print head moves to the right and prints part of another vertical line, then moves to the right again and prints part of another vertical line, etc. Each character is made of parts of vertical lines — and each part is made of dots.

The pattern of dots that makes up a character is called the **dot matrix**. That's why such a printer's called a **9-pin dot-matrix printer**.

Inside the printer is a ROM chip that holds the definition of each character. For example, the ROM's definition of "M" says which pins to fire to produce the letter "M". To use the ROM chip, the printer contains its own CPU chip and its own RAM.

When microcomputers first became popular, most dot-matrix printers for them were built by a New Hampshire company, **Centronics**. In 1980, Japanese companies took over the marketplace. Centronics went bankrupt. The two Japanese companies that dominate the industry now are **Epson** and **Panasonic**.

Epson Epson became popular because it was the first company to develop a disposable print head — so that when the print head wears out, you can throw it away and pop in a new one yourself, without needing a repairman. Also, Epson was the first company to develop a low-cost dot-matrix impact printer whose dots look "clean and crisp" instead of looking like "fuzzy blobs". Epson was the main reason why Centronics went bankrupt.

Epson is part of a Japanese conglomerate called the **Seiko Group**, which became famous by timing the athletes in the 1964 Tokyo Olympics. To time them accurately, the Seiko Group invented a quartz clock attached to an electronic printer. Later, the quartz clock was miniaturized and marketed to consumers as the "Seiko watch", which became the best-selling watch in the whole world. The electronic printer, or "E.P.", led to a better printer, called the "son of E.P.", or "EP's son". That's how the Epson division was founded and got its name!

Epson's first 9-pin printer was the **MX-80**. Then came an improvement, called the **FX-80**. Those printers are obsolete; they've been replaced by Epson's newest 9-pin wonders, the **FX-880** (which costs $250) and the **FX-1180** (which can handle extra-wide paper and costs $380). Epson's cheapest and slowest 9-pin printer is the **LX-300+** ($190). You can get those prices from discount dealers (such as Tri State).

Panasonic For a 9-pin printer, I recommend buying the **Panasonic 1150** instead, because it prints more beautifully and costs just $149 from discount dealers such as Harmony. Too bad it can't handle extra-wide paper!

Other Japanese Besides Epson and Panasonic, four other Japanese companies are also popular: **NEC**, **Oki**, **Citizen**, and **Star**.

Compatibility Printers from all six of those Japanese companies are intended mainly for the IBM PC, though they work with Apple 2 and Commodore computers also.

Apple The most popular printers for the Mac were the **Imagewriter** and the **Imagewriter 2**. They were designed by Apple to print exact copies of the Mac's screen. They even print copies of the screen's wild fonts and graphics. Apple stopped selling them.

7-pin printers

Although the average dot-matrix printer uses 9 pins, some older printers use just 7 pins instead of 9. Unfortunately, 7-pin printers can't print letters that dip below the line (g, j, p, q, and y) and can't underline. Some 7-pin printers print just capitals; other 7-pin printers "cheat" by raising the letters g, j, p, q, and y slightly.

24-pin printers

Although 9 pins are enough to print English, they're *not* enough to print advanced Japanese, which requires 24 pins instead.

Manufacturers The first company to popularize 24-pin printers was **Toshiba**. Its printers printed Japanese — and English — beautifully. 24-pin Toshiba printers became popular in America, because they print English characters more beautifully than 9-pin printers.

Epson and all the other Japanese printer companies have copied Toshiba. Here are the cheapest wonderful 24-pin printers:

> The **Epson Action Printer 3250** has a black ribbon and costs $150.
> The **Panasonic 2130** has a black ribbon and costs $169 ($199 minus $30 rebate).
> The **Panasonic 2135** has a multicolor ribbon and costs $239.
> The **Epson LQ-570e** is sturdier, easier to operate, has a black ribbon, and costs $240.

You can get those prices from Tri State and Harmony. While supplies last, Tri State has an even better deal: get a refurbished Epson LQ-570+ for just $160! Phone Tri State at 800-433-5199 or 212-633-2530.

The cheapest 24-pin printer that handles wide paper is the **Epson LQ-2080** ($400).

24-pin printers print more beautifully than 9-pin printers but print slower, are less rugged, and don't bang hard enough to print multiple copies on thick multi-part forms.

Pin arrangement In a typical, cheap 24-pin printer (such as the Epson Action Printer 3250), the even-numbered pins are slightly to the right of the odd-numbered pins, so you see two columns of pins. After firing the even-numbered pins, the print head moves to the right and fires the odd-numbered pins, whose dots on paper overlap the dots from the even-numbered pins. The overlap insures that the vertical column of up to 24 dots has no unwanted gaps.

In fancier 24-pin printers (such as the Panasonic 2130 & 2135), the 24 pins are arranged as a diamond instead of two columns, so that the sound of firing pins is staggered: when you print a vertical line you hear a quiet hum instead of two bangs.

Beyond 24 pins

The fastest dot-matrix printers use multiple print heads, so that they can print several characters simultaneously.

Why the daisies died

During the 1970's, daisy-wheel printers were popular, but they've died out. Computerists have switched to dot-matrix printers instead, for the following reasons.

The mechanism that spins the daisy is expensive, slow, and frequently needs repairs.

Dot-matrix printers can easily print graphics by making the pictures out of little dots. Daisy wheels cannot.

Although the first dot-matrix printers had just 7 pins and printed ugly characters, the newest 9-pin and 24-pin printers from Epson and Panasonic print prettier characters than the average daisy wheel. Moreover, you can make the typical 9-pin printer imitate an 18-pin printer by doing **2-pass printing**, in which the printer prints a line of text, jerks the paper up very slightly, and then prints the line again so the new dots fill the gaps between the old dots.

If you have a daisy-wheel printer and want to change to a different font (such as italics), you must spend your time manually switching daisy wheels. If you have a dot-matrix printer instead, just tell the printer which font you want (by pressing a button on the printer or on your computer's keyboard), and the printer will automatically switch to different patterns of dots to produce the different font, since the printer's ROM contains the definitions of *many* fonts. To make a daisy-wheel printer print so many fonts, you must buy several dozen daisy wheels, costing a total of several hundred dollars.

So daisy-wheel printers died because of competition from dot-matrix printers — and from ink-jet and laser printers, which print even more beautifully! Let's examine those super-beautiful printers now....

Ink-jet printers

An **ink-jet printer** resembles a dot-matrix printer but contains hoses instead of guns. The hoses (called **nozzles**) squirt ink at the paper. There are no pins or ribbons.

> When you use an ink-jet printer, you hear the splash of ink squirting the paper. That splash is quieter than the bang produced when a dot-matrix printer's pins smash a ribbon. If you like quiet, you'll love ink-jet printers!

Most ink-jet printers can print in color. They mix together the three primary ink colors (red, blue, and yellow) to form all the colors of the rainbow.

The most popular ink-jet printers are made by **Hewlett-Packard (HP)**. Recently, **Epson** and **Canon** have started making ink-jet printers also.

The ink-jet printers from all three of those companies are excellent. Each company makes a wide variety of ink-jet printers, at prices ranging from about $100 to about $1000. Here are some general tendencies:

> HP's printers produce the best-quality black. Canon's produce the worst.
> HP's printers produce the prettiest colors. Canon's produce the ugliest.
> Epson's printers produce the finest color details. Canon's produce the crudest.
> HP's printers are the best at avoiding paper jams. Epson's are the worst.
> HP's printers are the fastest. Epson's are the slowest.
> HP's printers cost the most. Canon's cost the least.

Each manufacturer has its own brand names:

> HP's ink-jet printers are called **Desk Jets**. Canon's ink-jet printers are called **Bubble Jets**. Epson's ink-jet printers are called **Styluses**.
> Most printers are designed for the IBM PC. Most printers can be attached to a Mac also. Special Mac-only models are also available: HP's Mac-only models are called **Desk Writers**; Canon's Mac-only models, called **Stylewriters**, were marketed by Apple.

How does the ink get out of the nozzle and onto the paper?

> In ink-jet printers by HP and Canon, a bubble of ink in the nozzle gets heated and becomes hot enough to burst and splash onto the paper. Epson's ink-jet printers use a different technique, in which the nozzle suddenly constricts and forces the ink out.

When using an ink-jet printer, try different brands of paper.

> Some brands of paper absorb ink better. If you choose the wrong brand, the ink will **wick** (spread out erratically through the strands of the paper's fiber). Start by trying cheap copier paper, then explore alternatives. The paper brand you buy makes a much bigger difference with ink-jet printers than with dot-matrix or laser printers. Canon's printers are the best at tolerating paper differences, but Canon's ink is water-based and smears slightly if the paper or envelope gets wet (from rain or a sweaty thumb).

HP, Canon, and Epson are being attacked by three aggressive competitors (**Xerox**, **Brother**, and **Lexmark**), which sometimes offer better deals.

You can buy from discount dealers:

> **Tri State** tends to have the lowest prices on **HP and Brother printers**.
> **Harmony** has lowest prices on **Epson, Canon, Xerox, and Lexmark printers**.
> **PC Connection** has the **most informative catalog**.

Ink-jet printers are divided into several categories....

Dual-cartridge color

The most popular category is **dual-cartridge color**. If you buy an ink-jet printer in this category, you can insert two ink cartridges simultaneously, side by side.

One cartridge contains black ink. The other cartridge contains the color trio (red, blue, and yellow). The computer mixes together all 4 (black, red, blue, and yellow) to form all possible colors. That method is called the **4-color process**.

Epson's newest such printer is the **Stylus Color 777**, which costs just $89 from Harmony.

> It prints precisely: the resolution is 2880 dots per inch vertically, 720 dots per inch horizontally, and the dots are squirted onto the paper neatly, without splatter. It prints fast: up to 8 pages per minute for black, 6 pages per minute for color. Those high speeds are obtained just while printing text in low resolution (360 dots per inch). To print a color photo in high resolution takes 1½ minutes for 4"×6", 3 minutes for 8"×10". It comes with a 1-year warranty. The cartridges are long-lasting: they'll print 600 pages of black text, 300 pages of color text; before the ink runs out and you must insert new cartridges. The black print head contains 144 nozzles; the color print head contains 144 nozzles (48 per color).

To compete against Epson, Canon offers several competitors. Canon's cheapest is the **Bubble Jet Color 2100 (BJC-2100)**.

> It lists for $100, but you get a $50 rebate, bringing the final cost down to just $50! That gets you 720×360 dpi, 5 ppm black, 2 ppm color, 1-year warranty. The price includes a cartridge containing all 4 colors. An all-black cartridge costs extra and is needed to achieve the "5 ppm black" speed.

HP offers these:

HP Printer	Speed	Color resolution	Price
Desk Jet 840C	8 ppm black, 3 ppm color	600×1200	$149
Desk Jet 930C	9 ppm black, 7½ ppm color	2400×1200	$190
Desk Jet 950C	11 ppm black, 8½ ppm color	2400×1200	$280

Each can produce 600×600 black. Though HP's black and color resolutions have low numbers, HP's color looks good because HP's printers can make each dot be several sizes. That chart shows price charged by Tri State.

Single-cartridge color

A cheaper category is **single-cartridge color**. This category lets you insert either a black cartridge or a color cartridge, but you cannot insert both cartridges simultaneously.

If you try to print black while the color cartridge is in, the computer tries to imitate "black" by printing red, blue, and yellow on top of each other. That produces a "mud" instead of a true black, and it's also very slow. If you try to make such a printer reproduce a photograph, the image produced looks slightly "muddy", "washed-out", with poor contrast.

But the price is deliciously low! The main such printer has been Canon's **BJC-1000**. Here's why it costs little:

> It comes in a box that includes one color cartridge (to get you started) but no black cartridge (which costs extra). The printer produces just 720×360 black, 360×360 color. The printer is very slow: just 4 ppm black, 0.6 ppm color. Its black print head contains just 64 nozzles; it color print head contains just 48 nozzles (16 per color).

It's been selling for $75, sometimes minus a $30 rebate (bringing the final cost down to $45), but it's being discontinued in favor of the BJC-2100, which costs just slightly more and is much better.

Lexmark's **Z-12 Color Jetprinter** is a single-cartridge color printer that's better than the BJC-1000.

> You can order it directly from Lexmark for $50 (plus tax and shipping) at Lexmark's Internet Web site (www.lexmark.com). Like the BJC-1000, its price includes a color cartridge but no black cartridge (which costs extra). Lexmark claims "1200 dpi" and "6 ppm black, 3 ppm color". Lexmark also includes discount coupons so you can get good software cheap.

Special printers

The following printers have unusual abilities, for use by unusual folks.

Portable You can buy these portable ink-jet printers, which are tiny and weigh little: Brother's **MP-21C** ($240, 2 pounds), Canon's **BJC-80** ($190, 4 pounds), and Canon's **BJC-50** ($305, 2 pounds, prints slower and more crudely than the BJC-80 but has the advantage of weighing less). They all work slowly, print less beautifully than desktop printers, and can't handle big stacks of paper.

> Instead of buying a portable printer, consider buying Canon's BJC-1000. At 4.8 pounds, it weighs just *slightly* more than a portable printer and tends to work faster, print more beautifully, handle paper better, and cost less!

Wide-carriage Most ink-jet printers handle just normal-width paper, which is 8½ inches wide. Canon, Epson, and HP all make expensive ink-jet printers that To print colors on wider paper, get Canon's **BJC-4550** ($269, 11"-by-17" paper) or Epson's **Stylus 1520** ($449, 17"-by-22").

4-cartridge color Suppose you're printing a picture that contains lots of red but not much blue or yellow. When you use up all the red ink in a tricolor cartridge, you must throw the whole cartridge away, even though blue and yellow ink remain in the cartridge. What a waste! Canon's **BJC-3000** prevents such waste.

> It uses 4 separate cartridges (a black cartridge, a red cartridge, a blue cartridge, and a yellow cartridge), so when the red ink runs out you can discard the red cartridge without having to discard any blue or yellow ink. It prints 9ppm black, 4ppm color. It costs just $99. Unfortunately, its cartridges are rather expensive.

Laser printers

A **laser printer**, like an office photocopier, contains a drum and uses toner made of ink. The printer shines a laser beam at the drum, which picks up the toner and deposits it on the paper.

Laserjet 5

For the IBM PC, the most popular laser printers are made by Hewlett-Packard (HP), whose laser printers are called **Laserjets**. After inventing its first Laserjet, HP invented a better version (the **Laserjet 2**), then an even better version (the **Laserjet 3**), then an even better version (the **Laserjet 4**).

Finally, in 1996, HP invented a truly great version: the **Laserjet 5**. I used it to print this book. It's terrific!

> It can print 12 pages per minute (12 **ppm**). It can print 600 dots per inch (600 **dpi**); and it uses a trick called **Resolution Enhancement Technology (RET)**, which can shift each dot slightly left or right and make each dot slightly larger or smaller.
>
> Its ROM contains the definitions of 45 fonts. Each of those fonts is **scalable**: you can make the characters as big or tiny as you wish. You also get a disk containing the definitions of 65 additional scalable fonts: put that disk into your computer, copy those font definitions to your computer's hard disk, then tell your computer to copy those font definitions to the printer's RAM. So altogether, the printer can handle two kinds of fonts: the 45 **internal fonts** that were inside the printer originally, and **soft fonts** that are copied into the printer's RAM from the computer's disks.
>
> The printer contains 4 megabytes of RAM, so it can handle lots of soft fonts and graphics on the same page. Moreover, the printer uses a trick called **data compression**, which compresses the data so that twice as much data can fit in the RAM (as if the RAM were 8 megabytes).

Discount dealers have sold it for $988.

Cheaper Laserjets

For folks who can't afford a Laserjet 5 at $988, HP invented a cheap **Personal version** (called the **Laserjet 5P**) and an even cheaper **Lower-cost version** (called the **Laserjet 5L**).

Afterwards, HP invented an improved 5P (called the **6P**, sold by discounters for $709) and an improved 5L (called the **6L**, sold by discounters for $379).

Newer Laserjets

HP has stopped selling all those Laserjets (the Laserjet 1, 2, 3, 4, 5, 5P, 5L, 6P, and 6L). Now HP sells these newer Laserjets instead:

Laser printer	Resolution	Black	Color	RAM	Paper	Printer codes	Price
Laserjet 1100xi	600dpi+RET	8ppm	no	2M+compr'n	8½"×14"	PCL 5e	$400-$30
Laserjet 2100xi	1200dpi+RET	10ppm	no	4M+compr'n	8½"×14"	PCL 6	$660
Laserjet 2100M	1200dpi+RET	10ppm	no	8M+compr'n	8½"×14"	PCL 6, PS 2	$740
Laserjet 4050	1200dpi+RET	17ppm	no	8M+compr'n	8½"×14"	PCL 6, PS 2	$1070-$100
Laserjet 5000	1200dpi+RET	16ppm	no	4M+compr'n	11"×17"	PCL 6, PS 2	$1400
Laserjet 8000	1200dpi+RET	24ppm	no	16M+compr'n	11"×17"	PCL 6, PS 2	$2050
Laserjet 8100	1200dpi+RET	32ppm	no	16M+compr'n	11"×17"	PCL 6, PS 2	$2500
Color Laserjet 4500	600dpi+RET	16ppm	4ppm	32M+compr'n	8½"×14"	PCL 5c, PS 2	$2400
Color Laserjet 8550	600dpi+RET	24ppm	6ppm	32M+compr'n	12"×18½"	PCL E5c,PS 3	$4858

You can get those prices from discount dealers such as Tri State. In that chart, here's what the "Printer codes" column means....

> When your computer wants to give the printer an instruction (such as "draw a diagonal line across the paper" or "make that scalable font bigger"), the computer sends the printer a code.
>
> HP's Laserjets understand a code called **Printer Control Language (PCL)**, invented by HP. The newest versions of PCL are **PCL 5e** (which is plain), **PCL 5c** (which can handle colors), **PCL Enhanced 5c** (which can handle colors faster), and **PCL 6** (which can handle 1200 dpi). They're understood by the new Laserjets. Older Laserjets understand just older versions of PCL and can't perform as many tricks.
>
> Most IBM-compatible laser printers (such as the ones by Epson, Panasonic, and Sharp) understand PCL, so that they imitate HP's laser printers, run the same software as HP's laser printers, and are **HP-compatible**. But most of them understand just *old* versions of PCL and can't perform as many tricks as HP's newest Laserjets.
>
> Some laser printers understand a different code, called **PostScript (PS)**, invented by a company called **Adobe**.
>
> Back in the 1980's, when PCL was still very primitive, Postscript was more advanced than PCL. The fanciest laser printers from HP's competitors used Postscript. The very fanciest laser printers were bilingual: they understood both PCL and Postscript.
>
> Now that PCL has improved, it's about as good as Postscript. PCL printers cost less to manufacture than Postscript printers.

In Postscript, each command that the computer sends the printer is written by using English words. Unfortunately, those words are long and consume lots of bytes. In PCL, each command is written as a brief series of code numbers instead. Since PCL commands consume fewer bytes than Postscript commands, the computer can transmit PCL commands to the printer faster than Postscript commands, and PCL commands can fit in less RAM.

Some Apple Mac programs require a Postscript printer. Some big printing companies that run printing presses require Postscript.

HP's competitors

HP has many competitors.

NEC's printers tend to go faster.
Lexmark's printers tend to go faster and print more dpi (to produce finer text and photographs).
Printers from **Panasonic**, **Brother**, and **Okidata** tend to cost less; they're bargains.
Printers from **Kyocera** cost less to run, because their toner (ink) cartridges last longer and cost less per page.

But I recommend buying from HP, because people who own HP Laserjets are *very* happy, including me! HP Laserjets are more reliable than other brands, need repairs less often than other brands, cause fewer software headaches than other brands, cost just *slightly* more than other brands, and let you buy more toner from your local store more easily. The only exception to my "buy HP" advice is HP's Color Laserjets, which always get worse ratings than **Magicolor** laser printers, which are made by **QMS**. But you shouldn't buy a color laser printer anyway: color laser printers are too expensive; and they're much slower than black-only laser printers, even when printing just black! To get color, buy a nice, cheap color inkjet printer instead!

Apple used to make a Mac-compatible laser printer called the **Laserwriter**. Apple stopped making it. If you have a Mac, Apple recommends that you buy any laser printer that can handle Postscript. For example, buy the **HP Laserjet 2100M**: it's the Mac-compatible version of the HP Laserjet 2100; it can handle the IBM PC and also the Mac.

Print engines

Each monochrome HP laser printer contains a photocopier print engine manufactured by Canon. In fact, each monochrome HP laser printer is just a modified Canon photocopier!

In many of QMS's color laser printers, the print engine is made by Hitachi. Lexmark, Panasonic, Brother, and Okidata make their own print engines.

Older Laserjets

Many offices still use older Laserjets. Here's how famous old Laserjets compare with modern ones:

Printer	Resolution	RAM	Speed	Variants
Laserjet 2	300dpi	½M	8 ppm	2P is 4ppm
Laserjet 3	300dpi+RET	1M	8 ppm	3P is 4ppm and ½M
Laserjet 4	600dpi+RET	2M+com'n	8 ppm	4P is 4ppm, 4 Plus is 12ppm, 4L is 4ppm&1M&300dpi
Laserjet 5	600dp +RET	2M+com'n	12 ppm	5P is 6ppm, 6P is 8ppm, 5L is 4ppm&1M, 6L is 6ppm&1M

Under $300

HP's cheapest laser printer is the Laserjet 1100xi, which costs $400-$30=$370.

Can't afford $370? Then get a **refurbished Laserjet 6L** from Harmony for **$289**.

To pay even less, get a new **OkiPage 8W** (600 dpi, no RET, 8ppm) from Tri State for **$229**. That printer gives you 600 dpi (but no RET) and 8 ppm. It's cheap because it contains very little RAM (it uses the RAM that's in the *computer* instead) and it contains fewer moving parts since it contains a **light-emitting diode array (LED array)** instead of a traditional laser.

Printer technology

Now let's plunge into the technical details of printer technology!

Impact versus non-impact

A printer that smashes an inked ribbon against the paper is called an **impact printer**. The most popular kind of impact printer is the dot-matrix printer. Other impact printers use daisy wheels, thimbles, golf balls, bands, chains, and drums. They all make lots of noise, though manufacturers have tried to make the noise acceptable by putting the printers in **noise-reducing enclosures** and by modifying the timing of the smashes.

A printer that does *not* smash an inked ribbon is called a **non-impact printer**. Non-impact printers are all quiet! The most popular non-impact printers are ink-jet printers and laser printers. Other non-impact printers are **thermal printers** (whose hot pins scorch the paper), and **thermal-transfer printers** (which melt hot colored wax onto the paper).

Each has its own disadvantages. Thermal printers require special "scorchable" paper. Thermal-transfer printers require expensive ribbons made of colored wax.

Resolution

If a printer creates characters out of dots, the quality of the printing depends on how fine the dots are — the "number of dots per inch", which is called the **print resolution**.

9-pin printers usually print 72 dots per inch vertically. That's called **draft quality**, because it's good enough for rough drafts but not for final copy. It's also called **business quality**, because it's good enough for sending memos to your coworkers and accountant.

If you make a 9-pin printer do 2 passes, it prints 144 dots per inch. That's called **correspondence quality**, because it's good enough for sending pleasant letters to your friends. It's also called **near-letter-quality (NLQ)**, because it looks nearly as good as the letters produced on a typewriter. The typical 9-pin printer has a switch you can flip, to choose either 1-pass draft quality (which is fast) or 2-pass correspondence quality (which is slower but prettier).

A 24-pin printer prints 180 dots per inch. That's called **letter quality (LQ)**, because it looks as good as the letters printed by a typical typewriter or daisy-wheel printer. It's good enough for writing letters to people you're trying to impress.

A standard laser printer prints 300 dots per inch. That's called **desktop-publishing quality**, because it's good enough for printing newsletters. It's also called **near-typeset-quality**, because it looks nearly as good as a typesetting machine.

A standard typesetting machine prints 1200 or 2400 dots per inch. Those are the resolutions used for printing America's popular magazines, newspapers, and books.

HP's Laserjet 2P Plus, 3, 3P, and 4L all print 300 dots per inch; but the 3, 3P, and 4L produce prettier output than the 2P Plus by using this trick: they can print each dot at 5 different sizes (ranging from "normal" to "extra tiny") and nudge each dot slightly to the right or left. HP's Laserjet 4 and 4P print 600 dots per inch.

Ink-jet printers by Canon and Epson usually print 360 dots per inch. HP's ink-jet printers usually print 300 dots per inch.

Character size

To measure a character's size, you must measure both its width and its height.

Width Like an old-fashioned typewriter, a traditional printer makes each character a tenth of an inch wide. That's called "10 characters per inch" or **10 cpi** or **10-pitch** or **pica** (pronounced "pike uh").

Some printers make all the characters narrower so you get 12 characters per inch. That's called **12 cpi** or **12-pitch** or **elite**.

The typical dot-matrix impact printer lets you choose practically any width you wish. For example, the Epson LQ-850 can print 5, 6, 7½, 8 1/3, 10, 12, 15, $16^2/_3$, and 20 cpi. The widest sizes (5, 6, 7½, and $8^1/_3$ cpi) are called **double-width**, because they're twice as wide as 10, 12, 15, and $16^2/_3$ cpi. The narrowest sizes ($16^2/_3$ and 20 cpi) are called **condensed** or **compressed**; they're 60% as wide as 10 and 12 cpi.

Some printers make each character a different width, so that a "W" is very wide and an "i" is narrow; that's called **proportional spacing**. It looks much nicer than uniform spacing (such as 10 cpi or 12 cpi). The typical modern printer lets you choose either proportional spacing or uniform spacing. Uniform spacing is usually called **monospacing**.

Height The typical sheet of paper is 11 inches tall. If you put one-inch margins at the top and bottom, you're left with 9 inches to print on.

After printing a line of type, the typical typewriter or printer jerks up the paper a sixth of an inch, then prints the next line. As a result, you get 6 lines of type per inch, so the entire sheet of paper shows "9 times 6" lines of type, which is 54 lines.

The fanciest printers, such as laser printers, can make characters extra-tall or extra-short. The character's height is measured in **points**. Each **point** is $1/_{72}$ of an inch. A character that's an inch tall is therefore called "72 points tall". A character that's half an inch tall is 36 points tall.

Like a typewriter, a printer normally makes characters 10 points tall. (More precisely, it makes the top of a capital "Y" 10 points higher than the bottom of a small "y".) It also leaves a 2-point gap above the top of the "Y", to separate it from the characters on the previous line. That 2-point gap is called the **leading** (pronounced "ledding"). That technique is called "10-point type with 2-point leading". Since the type plus the leading totals 12 points, it's also called "10-point type on 12" (or "10 on 12" or "10/12").

Fonts

You can make a capital T in two ways. The simple way is draw a horizontal bar and a vertical bar, like this: T. The fancy way is to add **serifs** at the ends of the bars, like this: T. A character such as T, which is without serifs, is called **sans serif**, because "sans" is the French word for "without".

Monospaced fonts The most popular monospaced fonts are **Courier** (which has serifs) and **Letter Gothic** (which is sans serif). Letter Gothic was invented by IBM in 1956 for typewriters. Courier was invented for typewriters also.

Proportionally-spaced fonts The most popular proportionally spaced fonts are **Times Roman** (which has serifs) and **Helvetica** (which is sans serif). Times Roman was invented by *The Times* newspaper of London in 1931. Helvetica was invented by Max Miedinger of Switzerland in 1954. (The name "Helvetica" comes from "Helvetia", the Latin name for Switzerland.)

Samples Here are samples from the laser printer that printed this book (an HP Laserjet 5 printer):

```
This is Courier. It's 12 points high and 10 cpi.
This is Courier Bold. This is Courier Italic.
This is Courier Bold Italic.

This is Letter Gothic. It's 12 points high and 12 cpi.
This is Letter Gothic Bold. This is Letter Gothic Italic.
This is Letter Gothic Bold Italic.
```

This is 8-point Times Roman. It's very tiny, but sometimes nice things come in small packages.
This is 9-point Times Roman, 10-point Times Roman, 11-point Times Roman,
12-point Times Roman, 13-point Times Roman,
14-point Times Roman, **14-point Times Roman Bold,**
14-point Times Roman Italic, ***and Times Roman Bold Italic.***

This is 8-point Helvetica. It's very tiny, but sometimes nice things come in small packages.
This is 9-point Helvetica, 10-point Helvetica, 11-point Helvetica,
12-point Helvetica, 13-point Helvetica,
14-point Helvetica, **14-point Helvetica Bold,**
14-point Helvetica Italic, ***and Helvetica Bold Italic.***

This is 14-point Coronet. It's a kind of script. Capitals are tall, most other letters tiny.
This is 14-point Marigold. Notice that the capital letters are surprisingly short.

This is 10-point Omega, **Omega Bold,** *Omega Italic,* ***and Omega Bold Italic.***
10-point Garamond, **Garamond Bold,** *Garamond Italic,* ***Garamond Bold Italic.***
10-point Antique Olive, **Antique Olive Bold,** *Antique Olive Italic.*
This is 10-point Albertus, **and this is 10-point Albertus Extra Bold.**

This is 10-point Univers, **Univers Bold,** *Univers Italic,* ***Univers Bold Italic,***
Univers Condensed, **Univers Condensed Bold,** *Univers Condensed Italic,* ***Univers Cond. Bold Italic.***

```
This is Line Printer. It comes in just one size: 8½-point. It's 16.67 cpi.
```

Here are samples from a 24-pin dot-matrix printer, the Epson LQ-570:

```
This is Epson's 10-cpi Courier.    This is 15-cpi Courier.
This is Epson's 10-cpi Prestige.   This is 15-cpi Prestige.
This is Epson's 10-cpi OCR-B.      This is 15-cpi OCR-B.
This is Epson's 10-cpi Orator-S.   This is 15-cpi Orator-S.
This is Epson's 10-cpi Script.     This is 15-cpi Script.
This is Epson's 10-cpi Script C.   This is 15-cpi Script C.

This is Epson's version of Times Roman. It's proportional.
This is Epson's version of Helvetica. It's proportional.
```

Here are samples from an ink-jet printer, the Canon BJ-200e. In these samples, the Canon is pretending it's the Epson LQ-570. The Canon's imitative printing looks better than Epson's original, since Canon's printer is an ink-jet instead of a dot-matrix. Look at how pretty Canon's printing is:

```
This is Epson's 10-cpi Courier.    This is 15-cpi Courier.
This is Epson's 10-cpi Prestige.   This is 15-cpi Prestige.
This is Epson's 10-cpi Orator-S.   This is 15-cpi Orator-S.
This is Epson's 10-cpi Script.     This is 15-cpi Script.

This is Epson's version of Times Roman. It's proportional.
This is Epson's version of Helvetica. It's proportional.
```

Canon doesn't imitate Epson's OCR-B or Script C.

Paper

Laser printers and most ink-jet printers accept a stack of ordinary copier paper. You put that paper into the printer's **paper tray**, which is also called the **paper bin** and also called the **cut-sheet paper feeder**.

Dot-matrix printers Though some dot-matrix printers handle stacks of ordinary copier paper, most dot-matrix printers handle paper differently. Here's how....

To pull paper into the printer, dot-matrix printers can use two methods.

The simplest method is to imitate a typewriter: use a rubber roller that grabs the paper by friction. That method's called **friction feed**. Unfortunately, friction is unreliable: the paper will slip slightly, especially when you get near the bottom of the sheet.

A more reliable method is to use paper that has holes in the margins. The printer has **feeder pins** that fit in the holes and pull the paper up through the printer very accurately. That method, which is called **pin feed**, has just one disadvantage: you must buy paper having holes in the margins.

If your printer uses pin feed and is fancy, it has a clamp that helps the pins stay in the holes. The clamp (with its pins) is called a **tractor**. You get a tractor at each margin. A printer that has tractors is said to have **tractor feed**. Usually the tractors are **movable**, so that you can move the right-hand tractor closer to the left-hand tractor, to handle narrower paper or mailing labels.

A **dual-feed** printer can feed the paper *both* ways — by friction and by pins — because it has a rubber roller and also has sets of pins. The printer has a lever to the left of the roller and pins: if you pull the lever one way, the paper will pass by the roller, for friction feed; if you pull the lever the other way, the paper will pass by the pins, for pin feed.

Most dot-matrix printers have dual feed with movable tractors.

Paper that has holes in it is called **pin-feed paper** (or **tractor-feed paper**).

Like a long tablecloth folded up and stored in your closet, pin-feed paper comes in a long, continuous sheet that's folded. Since it comes folded but can later be unfolded ("fanned out"), it's also called **fanfold paper**. It's perforated so you can rip it into individual sheets after the printer finishes printing on it. If the paper's fancy, its margin is perforated too, so that after the printing is done you can rip off the margin, including its ugly holes, and you're left with what looks like ordinary typing paper.

The fanciest perforated paper is called **micro-perf**. Its perforation is so fine that when you rip along the perforation, the edge is almost smooth.

Paper width Most printers can use ordinary typing paper or copier paper. Such paper is 8½ inches wide. On each line of that paper, you can squeeze 85 characters at 10 cpi, or 170 characters at 20 cpi, if you have no margins.

Pin-feed paper is usually an inch wider (9½ inches wide), so that the margins are wide enough to include the holes.

Some printers can handle pin-feed paper that's extra-wide (15 inches). Those **wide-carriage printers** typically cost about $130 more than standard-width printers.

Speed

The typical printer's advertisement brags about the printer's speed by measuring it in **characters per second (cps)** or **lines per minute (lpm)** or **pages per minute (ppm)**. But those measurements are misleading.

Dot-matrix and ink-jet printers For example, Epson advertised its LQ-850 dot-matrix printer as "264 cps", but it achieved that speed only when making the characters small (12 cpi) and ugly (draft quality). To print characters that were large (10 cpi) and pretty (letter quality), the speed dropped to 73 cps.

Panasonic advertised its KX-P1091 dot-matrix printer as "192 cps", but it achieved that speed only if you threw an internal switch that made the characters even uglier than usual!

For dot-matrix and ink-jet printers, the advertised speed ignores how long the printer takes to jerk up the paper. For example the typical "80-cps" printer will print 80 characters within a second but then take an extra second to jerk up the paper to the next line, so at the end of two seconds you still see just 80 characters on the paper.

Daisy-wheel printers To get an amazingly high cps rating, one daisy-wheel manufacturer fed its printer a document consisting of just one character repeated many times, so the daisy never had to rotate!

Laser printers To justify a claim of "8 pages per minute", Apple salesmen noticed that their Laserwriter 2 NT printer takes a minute to produce 8 *extra* copies of a page. They ignored the wait of *several minutes* for the *first* copy!

Like Apple, most other laser-printer manufacturers say "8 pages per minute" when they should really say: "$\frac{1}{8}$ of a minute per additional copy of the same page".

Keep your eyes open Don't trust any ads about speed! To discover a printer's true speed, hold a stopwatch while the printer prints many kinds of documents (involving small characters, big characters, short lines, long lines, draft quality, letter quality, and graphics).

Interfacing

A cable of wires runs from the printer to the computer. The cable costs about $8 and is *not* included in the printer's advertised price: the cable costs extra.

One end of the cable plugs into a socket at the back of the printer. The other end of the cable plugs into a socket at the back of the computer. The socket at the back of the computer is called the computer's **printer port**.

If you open your computer, you'll discover which part of the computer's circuitry the printer port is attached to. In a typical computer, the printer port is attached to the motherboard; but in some computers (such as the original IBM PC), the printer port is attached to a small PC card instead, called a **printer interface card**, which might not be included in the computer's advertised price.

When the computer wants the printer to print some data, the computer sends the data to the printer port; then the data flows through the cable to the printer.

Serial versus parallel The cable contains many wires. Some of them are never used: they're in the cable just in case a computer expert someday figures out a reason to use them. Some of the wires in the cable transmit information about scheduling: they let the computer and printer argue about when to send the data. If the computer's port is **serial**, just one of the wires transmits the data itself; if the computer's port is **parallel**, eight wires transmit the data simultaneously.

Parallel ports are more popular than serial ports, because parallel ports transmit data faster, are more modern, and are easier to learn how to use. Unfortunately, parallel ports handle only short distances: if the printer is far away from the computer, you must use a serial port instead.

When you buy a printer, make sure the printer matches the computer's port. If your computer's port is parallel, you must buy a parallel printer; if your computer's port is serial, you must buy a serial printer instead.

If your computer has *two* printer ports — one parallel, one serial — you can attach the computer to either type of printer; but I recommend that you choose a printer that's parallel, because parallel printers cost less, and because many word-processing programs require that the printer be parallel.

Standard cables The typical parallel printer expects you to use a cable containing 36 wires. Just 8 of the wires transmit the data; the remaining wires can be used for other purposes. That 36-wire scheme is called the **industry-standard Centronics-compatible parallel interface**.

The typical serial printer expects you to use a cable containing just 25 wires. Of the 25 wires, just 1 transmits data from the computer to the printer; the remaining wires can be used for other purposes. That 25-wire scheme is called the **recommended standard 232C serial interface (RS-232C serial interface)**.

Weird cables If your computer is an IBM PC or clone, you'll get a surprise when you try attaching it to a parallel printer (which expects 36 wires): your computer's parallel port contains just 25 wires instead of 36! To attach the computer's 25-wire parallel port to a 36-wire parallel printer, computer stores sell a weird cable that has 25 wires on one end and 36 wires on the other. It's called an **IBM printer cable**. If it's fancy enough to handle transmissions in both directions, it's called a **bidirectional IBM printer cable**. If it's even fancier and can handle transmissions *quickly* in both directions, it's called an **IEEE 1284 cable**.

If your computer is small, cute, and old (such as the Apple 2c, 2GS, Commodore 64, Radio Shack Color Computer, or old Mac), you'll get a surprise when you try attaching it to a standard serial printer (which expects 25 wires): your computer's serial port contains fewer than 10 wires! You must buy a weird cable that has 25 wires on one end and fewer on the other.

To attach a printer to an iMac, you must buy a **Universal Serial Bus cable (USB cable)**.

OTHER HARDWARE

Keyboards

The usual way to communicate with the computer is to type messages on the computer's **keyboard**.

In 1981, IBM invented a keyboard containing **83 keys**. That keyboard is called the **XT keyboard**, because it was used on the original IBM PC and the IBM PC XT.
In 1986, IBM began selling a fancier keyboard, containing **101 keys**. It's called the **AT keyboard**, because it was used on the IBM PC AT.
In 1995, Microsoft began selling an even fancier keyboard, containing **104 keys**. It's called the **Windows keyboard**, because it contains extra keys for Windows.

Now **"104 keys" has become the standard**. Microsoft, IBM, and competitors all sell keyboards containing 104 keys.

The 104 keys are arranged like this:

The keyboard can print all the letters of the alphabet (from A to Z), all the digits (from 0 to 9), and these symbols:

Symbol	Official name	Nicknames used by computer enthusiasts
.	period	dot, decimal point, point, full stop
,	comma	cedilla
:	colon	dots, double stop
;	semicolon	semi
!	exclamation point	bang, shriek
?	question mark	ques, query, what, huh, wildchar
"	quotation mark	quote, double quote, dieresis, rabbit ears
'	apostrophe	single quote, acute accent, prime
`	grave accent	left single quote, open single quote, open quote, backquote
^	circumflex	caret, hat
~	tilde	squiggle, twiddle, not
=	equals	is, gets, takes
+	plus	add
-	minus	dash, hyphen
_	underline	underscore, under
*	asterisk	star, splat, wildcard
&	ampersand	amper, amp, and, pretzel
@	at sign	at, whorl, strudel
$	dollar sign	dollar, buck, string
#	number sign	pound sign, pound, tic-tac-toe
%	percent sign	percent, grapes
/	slash	forward slash, rising slash, slant, stroke
\	backslash	reverse slash, falling slash, backwhack
|	vertical line	vertical bar, bar, pipe, enlarged colon
( )	parentheses	open parenthesis & close parenthesis, left paren & right paren
[ ]	brackets	open bracket & close bracket, square brackets
{ }	braces	curly brackets, curly braces, squiggly braces, left tit & right tit
<>	brockets	angle brackets, less than & greater than, from & to, suck & blow

For example, the symbol * is officially called an "asterisk". More briefly, it's called a "star". It's also called a "splat", since it looks like a squashed bug. In some programs, an asterisk means "match anything", as in a card game where the Joker's a "wildcard" that matches any other card.

In the diagram, I wrote the words "Shift", "Backspace", "LeftTab", "Tab", "Enter", "Windows", and "Menu" on some keys;. To help people who don't read English, keyboard manufacturers usually put symbols on those keys.

> The Shift key shows a fat arrow pointing up.
> The Backspace key shows an arrow pointing left.
> The Tab key shows arrows crashing into walls.
> The Enter key shows an arrow that's bent (going down and then left).
> The Menu key shows a diagonal arrow pointing up at a menu.
> The Windows keys shows a flying window (having 4 curved windowpanes).

Stare at *your* computer's keyboard and find these keys:

Key	Where to find it
Tab	the Tab key is left of the Q key
Backspace	if 101 or 104 keys, the Backspace key is left of the Insert key
	if just 83 keys, the Backspace key is left of the NumLock key
Shift	if 101 or 104 keys, the Shift keys are above the Ctrl keys
	if just 83 keys, the Shift keys are above Alt and CapsLock
Enter	if 101 or 104 keys, the Enter key is above the right-hand Shift key
	if just 83 keys, the Enter key is above the PrtSc key
Windows	if 104 keys, the Windows keys are next to the Alt keys
	if 83 or 101 keys, the Windows keys are missing
Menu	if 104 keys, the Menu key is next to the right-hand Ctrl key
	if 83 or 101 keys, the Menu key is missing

The keyboard contains special keys that help you do special activities (such as moving around the screen while you type):

Key	Usual purpose
↑	move up, to the line above
↓	move down, to the line below
←	move left, to the previous character
→	move right, to the next character
Home	move back to the beginning
End	move ahead to the end
Page Up	move back to the previous page
Page Down	move ahead to the next page
Tab	hop to the next field or far to the right
Enter	finish a command or paragraph
Pause	pause until you press the Enter key
PrintScreen	copy from the screen onto paper or onto the computer's clipboard
Shift	capitalize a letter
CapsLock	change whether all letters are automatically capitalized
NumLock	change whether keys on keyboard's right side produce numbers
ScrollLock	change how text moves up & down
Insert	change whether to insert extra characters in the middle of the text
Delete	delete the current character
Backspace	delete the previous character
Esc	escape from a mistake
Windows	show you the Windows-start menu
Menu	show you a short-cut menu
F1	get help from the computer
F2, F3, etc.	do special activities
Ctrl	do special activities
Alt	do special activities

The CapsLock, NumLock, ScrollLock, and Insert keys are called **toggle keys**: they create special effects, which end when you press the toggle key again.

SHIFT key

If a key has two symbols on it, the key normally uses the bottom symbol. To type the top symbol instead, press the key *while holding down the SHIFT key*.

Number keys

To type a number easily, use the keys in the top row of the keyboard's main section. (For example, to type 4, press the key that has a 4 and a dollar sign.)

To keep your life simple, do *not* press the number keys on the right side of the keyboard. Those keys produce numbers just if the NumLock key is pressed beforehand, by you or the computer.

If the NumLock key was pressed to produce numbers, and you want to *stop* making the right-hand keys produce numbers, tap the NumLock key again.

Missing keys

If your keyboard has 101 keys instead of 104, your keyboard is missing the Menu key and the two Windows keys. Those 3 keys are unimportant, since most folks prefer to use a mouse instead of tapping those keys. If you wish, you can substitute other keys instead:

> Instead of tapping the Menu key,
> tap the F10 key while holding down the Shift key.
>
> Instead of tapping a Windows key,
> tap the Esc key while holding down the Ctrl key.

If your keyboard has just 83 keys, you suffer:

> Your keyboard is missing the Menu key and the two Windows keys
>
> Your keyboard is missing the F11 and F12 keys. The F1 through F10 keys are arranged in two columns down the keyboard's left edge, instead of being spread out across the keyboard's top.
>
> Your keyboard is missing the second Ctrl key, the second Alt key, the second Enter key, and the second / key.
>
> Your keyboard is missing the Pause key. (Instead, you must tap the NumLock key while holding down the Ctrl key.)
>
> The PrintScreen key is labeled "PrtSc" and works just while holding down the Shift key. (If you don't hold down the Shift key, the PrtSc key acts as the second * key.)
>
> Your keyboard is missing the 4 arrow keys and these 6 editing keys: Insert, Delete, Home, End, PageUp, and PageDown. (To perform those functions, you must press number keys after you've turned off the NumLock.)

83-key keyboards work just with outdated computers. If you're using an 83-key keyboard, that's proof your computer is outdated! Buy a new computer system!

Kinds of keyboards

When buying a keyboard, you have many choices. You can buy an **XT** keyboard (83 keys), **AT** keyboard (101 keys), **augmented AT** keyboard (101 keys plus an extra copy of the backslash key), or **Windows** keyboard (101 keys plus 3 special keys that help run software called "Windows 95"). You can buy a **standard-size** keyboard (with a ledge above the top row, for placing your pencil or notes), **compact** keyboard (which has no ledge and consumes less desk space), **foldable** keyboard (which folds in half, as if you're closing a book, so it consumes half as much desk space when not in use), or **split** keyboard (whose left third is separated from the rest, so you can have the comfort of typing while your forearms are parallel to each other). You can buy a **tactile** keyboard (which gives you helpful feedback by making a click whenever you hit a key), **silent** keyboard (which helps your neighbors by not making clicks), or **spill-resistant** keyboard (which is silent and also doesn't mind having coffee or soda spilled on it).

The best split keyboard is the one made by **Addison** because it's tactile, requires little pressure, and costs just $50 at Staples discount stores.

Phone **Janesway** at 800-431-1348 or 914-699-6710. At extension 2230, ask Joel Hudesman for the best spill-resistant keyboards ($30) and foldable keyboards ($70). Get free shipping by saying you've read *The Secret Guide to Computers*.

Graphics-input devices

If you feed the computer a picture (such as a photograph, drawing, or diagram), the computer will analyze the picture and even help you improve it. To feed the computer a picture of an object, you can use four methods....

Method 1: point a traditional **video camera** (or camcorder) at the object, while the camera is wired to the computer.

Method 2: take picture of the object by using a **digital camera**, which contains a disk or RAM chips that record the image; then transfer the image to a computer.

Method 3: draw on paper, which you then feed to an **optical scanner** wired to the computer. Of the optical scanners that cost under $150, the best are Microtek's **X6** (which handles colors the best) and Visioneer's **One Touch** (which is much easier to use and reads words the best but handles colors less accurately).

Method 4: draw the picture by using a pen wired to the computer. The computerized pen can be a **light pen**, **touch screen**, **graphics tablet**, **mouse**, **trackball**, or **joystick**.

Light pens

A **light pen** is a computerized pen that you point at the screen of your TV or monitor. To draw, you move the pen across the screen.

Light pens are cheap: prices begin at $20. But light pens are less reliable, less convenient, and less popular than other graphics-input devices.

Touch screens

A **touch screen** is a special overlay that covers the screen and lets you draw with your finger instead of with a light pen.

Graphics tablets

A **graphics tablet** is a computerized board that lies flat on your desk. To draw, you move either a pen or your finger across the board. Modern notebook computers include a tiny graphics tablet (called a **touchpad** or **glidepad**), stroked with your finger and built into the keyboard (in front of the SPACE bar).

Mice

A **mouse** is a computerized box that's about as big as a pack of cigarettes. To draw, you slide the mouse across your desk, as if it were a fat pen.

When you slide the typical mouse, a ball in its belly rolls on the table. The computer senses how many times the ball rotated and in what direction.

The mouse was invented at Xerox's **Palo Alto Research Center (PARC)**. The first company to provide mice to the general public was **Apple**, which provided a free mouse with every Lisa and Mac computer. Now a free mouse comes with each IBM PC and clone, too.

The nicest mouse for the IBM PC is the **Microsoft Mouse**.

Its first version was boring.

Then came an improved version, nicknamed **"The Dove Bar"** because it was shaped like a bar of Dove soap. It felt great in your hand; but trying to draw a picture by using that mouse — or *any* mouse — was as clumsy as drawing with a bar of soap.

Then came a further improvement, nicknamed **"The Dog's Paw"** because it was shaped like a dog's lower leg: it was long with an asymmetrical bump (paw) at the end. It felt even better than The Dove Bar, if your hand was big enough to hold it.

The next improvement, nicknamed **"The Wheel Mouse"**, looked like The Dog's Paw but added a wheel you could rotate with your fingers.

The newest version, nicknamed **"The Sneaker"** and officially called the **Intellimouse Pro**, resembles the Wheel Mouse but its left side is taller, like the raised arch of a fancy sneaker. It costs $65.

Mice from no-name manufacturers cost under $10. Microsoft made a cheap mouse too, called the **Home Mouse**, in the shape of a home, with the mouse's cord coming out of the chimney. Microsoft's newest cheap mouse is called the **Basic Mouse**; at $16, it's small enough to be used by kids, lefties, and short people.

Trackballs

A **trackball** is a box that has a ball sticking out the top of it. To draw, just put your fingers on the ball and rotate it. Some notebook computers have a trackball built into the keyboard.

Technologically, a trackball's the same as a typical mouse: each is a box containing a ball. For a trackball, the ball sticks *up* from the box and you finger it directly; for a mouse, the ball hides *underneath* and gets rotated when you move the box. The mouse feels more natural (somewhat like gripping a pen) but requires lots of desk space (so you can move the box).

The trackball was invented first. The mouse came later and has become more popular — except on notebook computers, which use trackballs and touchpads to save space.

Joysticks

A **joystick** is a box with a stick coming out of its top. To draw, you move the stick in any direction (left, right, forward, back, or diagonally) as if you were the pilot of a small airplane.

Speakers

To produce sounds, the typical computer uses a **speaker** (similar to the speakers in your stereo system, but smaller).

The speaker is typically inside the system unit. Some computers use the speaker in your TV or monitor instead. The newest computers come with a pair of **external stereo speakers**, which sit outside the system unit and produce louder sounds. The fanciest new computers come with *three* external stereo speakers: the third speaker is called the **subwoofer** and produces a big, loud, booming bass.

Aesthetic computers, such as the Mac, can make speakers play nice music. IBM's first PC was a boring business computer that produced just harsh beeps, but IBM's newest computers let you produce sounds as good as a Mac by inserting a **sound card** (such as the **Sound Blaster**).

Fancy computers speak words by including circuitry called a **speech synthesizer**.

The newest computers come with a **microphone**. By using the microphone, you can make the computer record sounds. For example, you can make the computer record the sound of your voice and imitate it, so the computer sounds just like you!

Modems

You can connect your computer to a telephone line so your computer can chat with other computers around the world! Here's how....

To let your computer chat with a computer that's far away, attach each computer to telephone lines by using a "special device" that turns computer signals into telephone signals, and turns telephone signals back into computer signals.

Turning a computer signal into a telephone signal is called **modulating the signal**. Turning a telephone signal back into a computer signal is called **demodulating the signal**. Since the "special device" can modulate and also demodulate signals, the device is called a **modulator/demodulator** (or **modem**, which is pronounced "mode em").

Acoustic versus direct-connect

You can buy two kinds of modems.

The old-fashioned kind is a black box that has big ears on top, so that it can listen to the telephone. Because of its big ears, it's called a **Mickey Mouse modem** or an **acoustic coupler**. It usually costs $120.

The newer kind of modem plugs directly into the phone system, as if it were an answering machine. It doesn't have any ears: it has telephone wires instead. It's called a **direct-connect modem**. It usually costs under $100, and it's cheaper and more reliable than a Mickey Mouse modem. It's more popular than a Mickey Mouse modem because it's better than a Mickey Mouse modem in every way, except that you can't attach it to pay phones or to phones in hotel rooms.

Kinds of direct-connect modems

A direct-connect modem can be either **external** or **internal**. If it's **external**, it's a box that sits next to your computer. If it's **internal**, it's a printed-circuit card that hides inside your computer. Regardless of whether it's external or internal, a wire runs from it to the phone system.

Internal modems are more popular than external ones, because external modems cost more and require that you buy a cable to run from the modem to the computer. But external modems have the advantage of being easier to control, since they give you push-buttons and blinking lights.

Most computers include internal modems at no extra charge.

Most direct-connect modems have fancy features, such as **auto-dial** (which means the modem can memorize the other computer's phone number and dial it for you) and **auto-answer** (which means the modem automatically answers the phone whenever the other computer calls). A direct-connect modem having many such fancy features is called **smart**. Nearly all modems sold today are smart.

10 bits per character

To transmit a character, the modem usually transmits a 10-bit number, like this: 1001011101.

> The first bit (which is always a 1) is called the **start bit**; it means "hey, wake up, and get ready to receive the data I'm going to send you". The last bit (which is always a 1) is called the **stop bit**; it means "hey, I'm done, you can go back to sleep until I send you more data". The eight middle bits (such as 00101110) are usually called the **data bits**: they're a code that represents 1 byte of information (1 character). So to transmit 1 character, the modem transmits 10 bits.

Speed

A traditional modem transmits **2400 bits per second (2400 bps)**. That speed is also called **2400 baud**. Since 10 bits make a character, that kind of modem transmits 240 characters per second. That speed is reasonably fast: it's about as fast as the average person can read.

Faster modems can transmit **9600 bits per second** (which is 9600 bps, 9600 baud, 960 characters per second). That's faster than you can read, but it's appropriate for transmitting documents that you want to *skim*, programs that you want to *run*, and graphics.

Even faster modems can transmit **14400 bits per second**. Since 1000 bits is called a **kilobit**, 14400 bits per second is called **14.4 kilobits per second** (or 14.4 **kbps** or 14.4 **kilobaud**).

All those modems are obsolete. Now the most common speed for transmitting data is **28.8 kilobits per second** (which is 28.8 kbps, 28.8 kilobaud).

Most modems sold today can go even faster, **33.6 kilobits per second**, but most people using them still transmit at just 28.8 kilobits per second to be compatible with friends using older modems.

Slowing down A few computerists still use ancient, primitive modems transmitting just 1200 bits per second (1200 baud) or 300 bits per second.

If you buy a fast modem, you can tell it to go slower. For example, if you buy a 33.6-kilobaud modem, you can tell it to go at eight popular speeds: super-fast (33.6 kilobaud), fast (28.8 kilobaud), medium-fast 14.4 kilobaud), medium (9600 baud), medium-slow (2400 baud), slow (1200 baud), and super-slow (300 baud).

To communicate with a friend's computer, your modem must go at the same speed as your friend's. For example, if you buy a 33.6-kilobaud modem but your friend has just a 300-baud modem, your modem's software will detect the slowness of your friend's modem and automatically **downshift** (slow down) to 300 baud.

56-kilobaud modems The newest modems claim to go even faster, about **56 kilobits per second** (56 kbps, 56 kilobaud), but those claims are misleading!

> The government's **Federal Communications Commission (FCC)** restricts phone transmissions to 53 kilobaud, to prevent phone switches from overheating. In most communities, the phone companies can't handle transmissions faster than 45 kilobaud reliably. So if you buy a 56-kilobaud modem, it will probably be restricted to about 45 kilobaud.
>
> In 25% of all communities, the phone system is so poor that a 56-kilobaud modem won't go any faster than a 33.6-kilobaud modem.
>
> Moreover, so-called "56-kilobaud modems" go faster than 33.6 kilobaud just when you're *using the Internet* (not when you're communicating directly with friends), and just when you're *receiving* (not sending) Internet data, and just when you're receiving the data from an Internet service provider that uses the same type of 56-kilobaud modem as yours.
>
> One type of 56-kilobaud modem, called **x2**, was invented by **U.S. Robotics**, which makes modems and is now a division of **3Com**. The other type, called **k56flex**, was invented by modem-chip-maker **Rockwell** and AT&T-spinoff **Lucent**. The two types are not compatible with each other. A third type, called **V.90**, has been developed. Most modem makers promised that if you bought an x2 or k56flex modem, you'd get a free upgrade to V.90.

Standards

Standards for modem communication have been invented by **AT&T** and the **International Telecommunications Union (ITU)**. Here's what they call their standards:

Speed	ITU standard	AT&T standard
300 bps	V.21	Bell 103
1200 bps	V.22	Bell 212a
2400 bps	V.22bis	
9600 bps	V.32	
14400 bps	V.32bis	
19200 bps	V.32terbo	
28800 bps	V.34 (or V.fast)	
56600 bps	V.90	

For example, if you see an ad for a **V.22-compatible modem** or a **Bell 212a modem**, the ad is trying to sell you a 1200 bps modem.

Though the ITU speaks English, it used to speak French and have a French name (the **Comité Consultatif International Télégraphique et Téléphonique**, or **CCITT**).

Notice that the second version of V.22 is called **V.22bis**, because **bis** is a French word that means "2nd version". Notice that the third version of V.32 is called **V.32terbo**, because **terbo** is an international word that combines the French "ter" (which means 3) with the English word "turbo" (which means "fast"). Those confusing terms made folks complain that "CCITT" stood for "Committee for Confusing International Telecommunications Terms".

Fax

You can send messages from your computer to fax machines around the world, if you buy a **fax/modem**, which is a modem that can also send faxes. If the fax/modem is fancy, it can also *receive* faxes and print them on your printer.

The typical modern fax/modem can transmit modem data (to other computers) at 33.6 kilobaud but transmits faxes (to fax machines) at just 14.4 kilobaud. It's called a **33.6/14.4-kilobaud fax/modem**. (Most ads list the modem speed first, then the fax speed, because the modem speed is more important.)

A few years ago, the most common kind of fax/modem was a slow kind that sends modem data at 2400 baud, faxes at 9600 baud. It's called a **2400/9600-baud fax/modem**. More briefly, it's called a **2496 fax/modem**. Yes, every 2496 fax/modem can *send* faxes at 9600 baud; but the cheapest 2496 fax/modems *receive* faxes at just 4800 baud — or can't receive faxes at all!

Brands

The most famous modems were made by **Hayes**, which charged high prices. Now many companies make cheaper modems that imitate Hayes' and are called **Hayes-compatible**. Nearly all modems sold today are Hayes-compatible.

For example, high-quality Hayes-compatible modems have been built by **Everex** and **Practical Peripherals**. To avoid competition from those companies, Hayes sued Everex and bought Practical Peripherals. So Everex had to pay Hayes a royalty (and eventually stopped selling modems), and Practical Peripherals became owned by Hayes.

Now the most popular Hayes-compatible modems are the ones made by the **U.S. Robotics** division of **3Com**. An internal U.S. Robotics 56 kilobaud fax/modem costs just $59. A popular alternative is **Diamond**, whose 56-kilobaud fax/modem sells for just $40. Even cheaper is **Conexant** (a division of **Rockwell**), whose 56-kilobaud fax/modem sells for just $20! You can get those prices from discount dealers such as **PC Connection** (800-800-5555), **Tri State Computer** (800-433-5199 or 212-633-2530) and **Harmony** (800-870-1663 or 718-692-3232). Those prices are after rebates.

COM1 versus COM2

A modem is an example of a **serial device**. You might own another serial device also, such as a serial mouse or a serial printer.

The IBM PC can handle two serial devices simultaneously. The first serial device is called **communication device #1 (COM1)**. The second serial device is called **COM2**.

If you add a modem to your IBM PC or clone, you must decide whether to call the modem COM1 or COM2.

Most hardware and software assume the modem is COM2. To avoid headaches, make the modem be COM2. Here's how.

If the modem is external, run its cable to your computer's COM2 port. (If your computer doesn't have a COM2 port yet, buy a **serial interface card** containing it.)

If the modem is internal, make sure the switch or jumper on the modem is set to the COM2 position; and make sure no other hardware in your computer system is called COM2. For example, if your computer contains a serial interface card having a COM2 port on it, you must **disable** the serial interface card's COM2 port (by moving a jumper or switch on it).

Avoid using COM3 or COM4, since the computer has trouble handling COM3 and COM4 reliably. (COM3 often conflicts with COM1, and COM4 often conflicts with COM2.)

Like a disk, a magnetic tape consists of magnetized rust. Just as you put a disk into a disk drive, you put a tape into a **tape drive**.

Tape drives are slower than disk drives. To skip from the disk's beginning to the disk's end, the disk drive's arm simply hops from the outermost track to the innermost track. But to skip from the beginning of a tape to the end of a tape, you must wait for the tape drive to wind the entire tape.

Cassettes for primitive computers

The cheapest kind of tape drive is an audio cassette tape recorder — the same kind you use for listening to music, at the beach or in your car.

Radio Shack You can attach that kind of tape recorder to an old Radio Shack computer (such as the Radio Shack TRS-80 model 1, 3, or 4 or the Radio Shack Color Computer).

Wires run from the tape recorder to the computer, and the computer sings a song into the tape recorder; the song is a code that represents the data.

Unfortunately, audio cassette tape recorders aren't very reliable.

If you're using one of those old Radio Shack computers, you can improve the reliability somewhat by getting Radio Shack's own tape recorder, which is specially designed to work well with computers and automatically controls the tape's volume. But since a tape recorder is so much slower than a disk drive, I recommend that you *not* buy Radio Shack's tape recorder, and instead keep saving your pennies until you can afford a disk drive.

Commodore & Atari Old computers by Commodore and Atari (such as the Commodore Vic, Commodore 64, Commodore 128, and Atari 800) do *not* attach to ordinary audio cassette tape recorders; you must buy special cassette tape recorders sold by Commodore and Atari or — better yet —buy a disk drive instead, if you can afford it.

Coleco The Adam computer, manufactured by Coleco, comes with a built-in cassette tape recorder, at no extra charge.

That tape recorder is high-speed and requires specially lubricated tapes, sold by Coleco. Since it handles just tapes that contain computer information and can*not* play ordinary musical tapes, it's called a **digital cassette tape drive** instead of an audio cassette recorder. But though Coleco's tape recorder handles computer data rather well and is called "high-speed", it's slower than a disk drive.

Modern microcomputers

Most people who buy modern computers (such as the Mac, Commodore Amiga, IBM PC, and clones) buy disk drives and don't bother using tapes at all.

If you buy a hard disk, how do you make a backup copy of that hard disk, and where do you put the backup? You could put the backup copy onto a second hard disk or onto a pile of about 50 floppy disks. Another possibility is to put the backup copy onto a special super-fast digital cassette tape drive that holds super-long cassette tapes that can contain backups.

Colorado The most popular such tape drives have been the **Jumbo 120**, the **Jumbo 250**, and the **Jumbo 350**, all built by **Colorado Memory Systems** (which used to be an independent company but is now owned by Hewlett-Packard). Those Jumbo drives work with the IBM PC and clones.

The Jumbo 120 can back up a 120-megabyte hard disk by taking the hard disk's data, compressing it into a shorthand notation, and then storing the compressed data on a 60-megabyte tape. Because of that scheme, the Jumbo 120 is called a **60/120M tape drive**.

The **Jumbo 250** can back up a 250-megabyte hard disk by compressing the hard disk's data onto a 120-megabyte tape.

The **Jumbo 350** can back up a 350-megabyte hard disk by compressing the hard disk's data onto a 170-megabyte tape. The drive costs $69. The tapes cost $17 each (in quantity 5).

Here are the newest drives from Colorado:

Drive	Capacity	Prices
T1000	0.8G (=800M)	$99 drive, $26 tape
T3000	3.2G	$139 drive, $30 tape
5-gig	5G	$169 drive, $35 tape
8-gig	8G	$219 drive, $34 tape

For example, the T1000 drive backs up an 800M hard disk by compressing the hard disk's data onto a 400M tape.

Ditto Instead of buying a Colorado tape drive, you can pay less by getting a different brand, called a **Ditto** drive, manufactured by **Iomega**.

Drive	Price
2G version	$109 for the drive, $20 for the tape
7G version	$169 for the drive, $30 for the tape.
10G version	$249 for the drive, just $26 for the tape

Where to buy You can get Colorado and Ditto drives at those low prices from a New York City discount dealer called **Harmony** (800-441-1144 or 718-692-3232).

Internal versus external All those tape-drive prices are for drives that are **internal**: they go *inside* your computer. External versions cost extra.

Alternatives Instead of buying a tape drive, the typical computerist uses a pile of floppy disks or super-floppy disks or buys a second hard drive.

Big reels for big computers

Maxicomputers and minicomputers use big reels of tape for three purposes: to backup big disks, to send data by mail, and to store the **archives** (old files that are used rarely if ever).

The reel's diameter is 10½ inches. If you unwind the tape, you'll find the tape is half an inch wide and almost half a *mile* long! The exact length is 2400 feet.

To use a reel of tape, you put the reel into a **reel-to-reel tape drive**, which typically costs about $5000 and writes 1600 bytes per inch, so that the entire tape holds 43 megabytes. Super-fancy drives, used only on the largest maxicomputers, squeeze 6250 bytes onto every inch (instead of 1600), so that they squeeze 171 megabytes onto a single reel of tape.

IBM's fanciest drive not only writes 6250 bytes per inch but also does the writing amazingly quickly. It moves the tape at 200 inches per second, so that it transfers about 1.2 megabytes per second.

Cases

The motherboard and other main circuitry are enclosed in a box. The box and the circuitry inside it are called the **system unit**. The box itself — without its contents — is called the **case**.

Interference

The computer thinks at about the same speed (number of cycles per second) as radio & TV waves. If you put your computer next to a radio or TV, the computer's electromagnetic "thought waves" cause static on the radio or TV. To decrease that interference, move the computer away from the radio or TV (or change the position of the radio or TV's antenna).

The **Federal Communications Commission (FCC)** prohibits you from owning any device (such as a computer) that interferes with your neighbors' radio and TV.

> The FCC requires all computers to pass the **FCC class A non-interference test**. Any computer used in a *residential* area must also pass the **FCC class B non-interference test**, which is harder to pass than the class A test.
>
> To help the computer pass the class A and class B tests, manufacturers line the insides of cases with metal that breaks up the electromagnetic waves.
>
> When you buy a computer, ask whether it's **FCC class B approved**. If it's not — if it's just FCC class A approved — you cannot legally use it in a residential area.

Surge suppressors

Instead of plugging your computer into the wall, you can plug it into a **surge suppressor**, which is a special extension cord that protects your computer against surges in electrical power.

Unless you live in a neighborhood or building that has extremely poor electricity, don't bother buying a surge suppressor. The typical computer has some surge protection built into it *already*.

> If you're worried about thunderstorms sending surges to your computer, just unplug your computer during storms! If your air conditioner or electric heater consumes too much electricity and causes a brownout (so your computer acts unreliably), use a plain extension cord to plug your computer into a different outlet, so that the computer's not on the same circuit as the power-hungry appliance.
>
> During the summer, most computer errors are caused by temperatures over 95°, *not* by power surges.

SOFTWARE

Kinds of software

The information stored in the computer is called **software**. Most software stays in RAM temporarily and is erased from RAM when you no longer need it. But *some* software stays in the computer's circuits *permanently*: it hides in the ROM and is called **firmware**.

To feed firmware to the computer, stick extra ROM chips into the main circuitry. To feed other kinds of software to the computer, use the keyboard, disk, or tape: type the information on the keyboard, or insert a disk or tape containing the information.

You can feed the computer four kinds of software: an **operating system**, a **language**, **application programs**, and **data**. Let's look at them....

Operating systems

An **operating system** is a set of instructions that explains to the CPU how to handle the keyboard, the screen, the printer, and the disk drive.

The operating system is divided into two parts.

The fundamental part is in the ROM chips provided by the manufacturer. The advanced part is on a disk and called the **disk operating system** (or **DOS**, which is pronounced "doss"). So to use the operating system's advanced part, you must make sure the computer contains a disk (floppy or hard) containing DOS.

Different computers use different operating systems:

Mac computers use the **Mac Operating System (Mac OS)**. Apple 2 computers use **Apple DOS** or **Pro DOS**. Radio Shack's TRS-80 computers use **TRSDOS** (pronounced "triss doss"). DEC's Vax minicomputers use an operating system called the **Virtual Memory System (VMS)**. Ancient microcomputers use the **Control Program for Microcomputers (CP/M)**. IBM maxicomputers use the **Multiple Virtual Storage (MVS)** system or the **Virtual Machine with Conversational Monitor System (VM with CMS)**.

IBM PC and clones

Most of IBM's personal computers (such as the IBM PC, IBM PC XT, IBM PC AT, IBM PS/1, and IBM PS/2) use an operating system called **PC-DOS**. Clones use a variant called **MicroSoft DOS** (which is abbreviated as **MS-DOS**, which is pronounced "em ess doss").

Instead of buying MS-DOS (or PC-DOS), you can buy a newer operating system called **Windows 95**, invented in 1995 by Microsoft. Since Windows 95 is a complete operating system, you can buy and use it without buying MS-DOS.

In 1998, Microsoft invented **Windows 98**, which is even better than Windows 95.
In 2000, Microsoft invented **Windows Millennium Edition (Windows Me)**, which is even better.

Some computers still use an ancient Windows version, called **Windows 3.1**, which is *not* a complete operating system; instead, it's a *supplement* to MS-DOS.

Before using Windows 3.1, you must put MS-DOS (or PC-DOS) into your computer. Having MS-DOS supplemented by Windows 3.1 is *almost* as nice as having Windows 95. A supplement (such as Windows 3.1) that modernizes an ugly operating system (such as MS-DOS) and hides the system's ugliness is called an **operating-system shell**.

Each of those Windows versions is intended to run on a single computer. To run a **network** of computers, you can buy a special network version, called **Windows New Technology (Windows NT)**, or its further improvement (called **Windows 2000**).

PC-DOS, MS-DOS, Windows 3.1, Windows 95, Windows 98, Windows Me, Windows NT, and Windows 2000 are all called **operating environments**.

Unix

AT&T's Bell Laboratories invented an operating system called **Unix**. It's pronounced "you nicks", so it sounds like "eunuchs", which are castrated men. (Be careful! A female computer manager who seems to be saying "get me eunuchs" probably wants an operating system, not castrated men.) "Unix" is an abbreviation for "UNICS", which stands for "UNified Information and Computing System".

The original version of Unix was limited to DEC minicomputers used by just one person at a time. Newer versions of Unix can handle *any* manufacturer's maxi, mini, or micro, even when shared by lots of people at a time.

A Finnish programmer named **Linus Torvalds** (whose first name is pronounced "lee nuss") invented a Unix imitation called "**Linus Unix**" or **Linux** (pronounced "lee nucks"). It's free! It runs on 386, 486, and Pentium computers and also on Atari and Commodore Amiga computers. The most popular way to get it is to buy a **distribution** (which includes Linux plus extras), published by **Mandrake** or **Corel** or **Red Hat**. (Mandrake's is the cheapest; Corel's is the easiest for beginners; Red Hat's is the hardest but does the best job of setting up a network.)

Though many programmers adore Unix, it won't outsell Windows, since Unix is harder to learn and had its main features stolen by new versions of MS-DOS & Windows. But Unix networks are more reliable than Window networks and form the basis of the Internet.

Languages that humans normally speak — such as English, Spanish, French, Russian, and Chinese — are called **natural languages**. They're too complicated for computers to understand.

To communicate with computers, programmers use **computer languages** instead. The most popular computer languages are **BASIC**, **C++**, **JAVA**, **COBOL**, **PASCAL**, **LOGO**, and **DBASE**. Each is a tiny *part* of English — a part small enough for the computer to master. To teach the computer one of those tiny languages, you feed the computer a ROM or disk containing definitions of that tiny language's words.

The typical microcomputer's ROM chips contain part of BASIC and part of the operating system. To use the computer fully, you must insert a disk containing the rest of BASIC and DOS.

Different people prefer different languages. Most students prefer LOGO in elementary school, BASIC in middle school, PASCAL in high school, and C++ in college. To do accounting, most business executives prefer DBASE (or an updated version of it) on microcomputers, COBOL on maxicomputers. To create animated ads on the Internet, the best language is JAVA.

Although those seven languages are the most popular, many others have been invented. Five old languages still in use are **FORTRAN**, **RPG**, **LISP**, **PL/I**, and **SPSS**. Five new languages are **FORTH**, **PILOT**, **PROLOG**, **ADA**, and **MODULA**.

The Secret Guide to Computers tutors you in *all* those languages and more, so you become a virtuoso!

The computer will do whatever you wish — if you tell it how. To tell the computer how to do what you wish, you feed it a **program**, which is a list of instructions, written in BASIC or in some other computer language.

To feed the computer a program, type the program on the keyboard, or buy a disk containing the program and put that disk into the drive. But before buying the disk, make sure it will work with *your* computer. For example, if the disk says "for MS-DOS computers", it will work with an IBM PC but not with an Apple.

A person who invents a program is called a **programmer**. Becoming a programmer is easy: you can become a programmer in just a few minutes! Becoming a *good* programmer takes longer.

You can buy two kinds of programs. The most popular kind is called an **application program**: it handles a specific application, such as payroll or psychotherapy or chess. The other kind of program is called a **system program**: it creates a system that just helps programmers write more programs!

Main applications

An old-fashioned office contains a typewriter, filing cabinet, and calculator. A modern office contains a computer instead.

To make the computer replace your typewriter, buy a **word-processing program**. To replace your filing cabinet, buy a **database program**. To replace your calculator, buy a **spreadsheet program**. Each program typically comes on a set of disks.

Why computerize? To save time! A word-processing program lets you edit mistakes faster than a typewriter. A database program lets you find info faster than thumbing through file cards. A spreadsheet program lets you revise numbers and totals faster than rekeying them on a calculator.

But even the most modern computerized offices still contain typewriters, filing cabinets, and calculators. Those pre-computer relics aren't used much, but they're still used *occasionally*, to accomplish tiny tasks for which a computer would be overkill.

A typewriter is more practical than a computer, if what you're typing is short (a paragraph or less), or if you're typing answers onto a form somebody mailed you. A filing cabinet is more practical than a computer, if you're filing fewer than 100 items, or if you're filing documents that were mailed to you and that would take too long to retype into the computer. A calculator is more practical than a computer if you're manipulating fewer than 10 numbers or writing numbers onto a pre-printed form.

But for *most* tasks, the computer is far superior to pre-computer relics. Here are the details.

Word processing A word-processing program helps you write memos, letters, reports, and books. It also helps you edit what you wrote.

As you type on the keyboard, the screen shows what you typed. By pressing buttons, you can edit what's on the screen and copy it onto paper and onto a disk.

The most popular word-processing programs are **WordPerfect** and **Microsoft Word**. Each runs on the IBM PC and the Mac.

During the late 1980's and early 1990's, most IBM PC users preferred WordPerfect, and most Mac users preferred Microsoft Word. During the 1990's, Microsoft Word's IBM version improved dramatically but Mac version did not. Now preferences are reversed:

Businesses using the IBM PC had preferred WordPerfect but now are switching to Microsoft Word. Businesses using Macs had preferred Microsoft Word but now are switching to WordPerfect.

Though WordPerfect and Microsoft Word are popular among experts, they're complex. Many simpler word-processing programs have been invented for beginners.

Spreadsheets A spreadsheet program handles tables of numbers. For example, it can handle your budget, inventory, general ledger, baseball statistics, and student test scores.

As you type the numbers, the computer puts them onto the screen in neat columns. You can tell the program to compute the totals, subtotals, and percentages and put them on the screen also.

The computer lets you revise the numbers. Whenever you revise a number, the computer instantaneously recalculates all the totals, subtotals, and percentages and shows them on the screen, faster than your eye can blink!

When the numbers on the screen finally appeal to you (for example, your budget finally balances), press a button that makes the printer print onto paper the entire table of numbers, including even the totals, subtotals, and percentages. Pressing another button makes the computer copy the table onto a disk. The most popular spreadsheet programs can also graph the data.

Spreadsheet programs can become weapons that mesmerize people into believing everything you say — even if what you're saying is wrong.

> For example, suppose you want to submit a budget. If you scribble the budget on a scrap of paper, nobody will take you seriously; but if you put your data into a spreadsheet program that spits out beautifully aligned columns with totals, subtotals, percentages, bar charts, and pie charts, your audience will assume your budget's carefully thought out and applaud it, even though it's just a pretty presentation of the same crude guesses you'd have scribbled on paper.

The most famous spreadsheet program is **Lotus 1-2-3**, which runs on the IBM PC. For a fancier spreadsheet program, get a competitor called **Quattro Pro**.

The fanciest spreadsheet program of all is **Excel**, invented by Microsoft. It requires either a modern IBM PC (containing Microsoft Windows) or a Mac.

The typical spreadsheet program expects the entire spreadsheet to fit in the computer's RAM. If your spreadsheet contains too many rows and columns to fit in RAM, your spreadsheet program will slow down — or, if it's old-fashioned, stop working altogether! You'll want to buy more RAM — or switch to using a database program instead, since database programs handle disks better than spreadsheet programs.

Databases A database program helps you manipulate long lists of data, such as names, addresses, phone numbers, birthdays, comments about folks you know (your friends, customers, suppliers, employees, students, and teachers), past-due bills, and any other data you wish!

As you type the list of data, the computer automatically copies it onto a disk. The computer lets you edit that data and insert extra data in the middle of the list. The program makes the printer print the data in any order you wish: alphabetical order, ZIP-code order, chronological order, or however else you please.

The program can search through all that data and find, in just a few seconds, the data that's unusual. For example, it can find everybody whose birthday is *today*, or everybody who's blond and under 18, or everybody who lives out-of-state and has owed you more than $30 for over a year.

The best easy-to-use database program is **Q&A** (which stands for "Questions & Answers"). It also includes an easy-to-use word processor.

> Q&A is published by **Symantec** and available for just $139 (plus $7 shipping) by phoning **Professional Computer Technology Associates** at 215-598-8440.
> Q&A requires an IBM PC or clone. The DOS version of Q&A works well, even if you have Windows. Never buy "Q&A for Windows", which is a totally different product and terrible!
> To computerize your business cheaply and pleasantly, get an IBM PC clone and the DOS version of Q&A. If your business is typical, Q&A is the only applications program you'll ever need, since Q&A includes a top-notch database system and an easy-to-understand word processor.

Though this book discusses hundreds of application programs, I use just two of them daily: Q&A and Microsoft Word. I use Q&A to run my book business, course business, accounting, and life. To type this book, I could have used Q&A but decided to use Microsoft Word instead, because Microsoft Word lets me perform extra word-processing tricks that make the book look pretty.

So Q&A and Microsoft Word are the only two application programs I need. Maybe you'll discover they're the only application programs *you* need!

If you have a Mac, you can't run Q&A. Instead, get

Filemaker Pro. It's an easy-to-use program that performs *almost* as many database tricks as Q&A but lacks a word processor. Discount dealers sell it for $177. Filemaker Pro is also available for IBM PC computers using Windows.

If you need different database tricks than Q&A performs, get Filemaker Pro or **Alpha** or **Approach** or **Microsoft Access** (which is harder) or **Paradox** (which is even harder) or invent your *own* database program (by using a programming language called **DBASE** or an imitation called **FOXPRO**).

> The typical business makes the mistake of buying a fancy database programming language (such as DBASE) and hiring a consultant to write fancy database programs. Six months later, the business complains that it's paid the consultant $2000 in fees and the consultant's program *still* doesn't work. The business would have been better off using Q&A, which is so easy it doesn't need a consultant.

Compulsive perfectionism

The most successful business programs are the ones that make work become fun, by turning the work into a video game. That's why word processing programs and spreadsheet programs are so successful — they let you move letters and numbers around the screen, edit the errors by "zapping" them, and let you press a button that makes the screen explode with totals, subtotals, counts, and other information.

Sometimes, word processing can be *too* much fun. Since it's so much fun to edit on a word processor, people using word processors edit more thoroughly than people using typewriters or pens. Word processing fosters **compulsive perfectionism**.

Word-processed documents wind up better-written than non-electronic documents but take longer to finish. According to a survey by Colorado State, people using word processors take about 30% longer to generate memos than people using pens, and the word-processed memos are needlessly long.

Graphics

The first easy-to-use graphics program was **Mac Paint**, developed by Apple Computer Incorporated for the Mac. It lets you use the Mac's mouse to draw pictures on the screen, copy them onto paper, and perform special effects. It's fun. It's the program that made the Mac popular.

Mac paint has been replaced by dozens of fancier programs that run on the Mac, IBM PC, and all other popular computers.

Architects and engineers draw blueprints by using a program for **computer-aided design (CAD)**.

If you're giving a talk at a business meeting, you can illuminate your talk by creating a slide show. Each slide contains a summary of your advice, with pictures, photos, and graphs. The computer can help you create those slides, if you get a **presentation program**. The best presentation-graphics programs are Microsoft's **PowerPoint** and Lotus's **Freelance**.

Desktop publishing

A program that lets you combine graphics with text — to create posters, ads, and newsletters — is called a **page-layout program** or **desktop-publishing program**.

The fanciest desktop publishing programs are **Pagemaker**, **Frame Maker**, **Quark XPress**, and **Ventura Publisher**. Each runs on the IBM PC and Mac. They let you easily create headlines and multiple columns with graphics. They're complex and expensive.

For the IBM PC, you have a simpler, cheaper alternative: **Microsoft Publisher**. Discount dealers sell it for just $70. It asks you questions about what you want to create; then it creates a mock-up of what you desire. Just edit the mock-up (by changing its words and pictures to the ones you want), and you're done!

Office suites

Instead of buying a word-processing program, a spreadsheet program, and other programs separately, you can buy an **office suite**, which includes them all!

The best and most popular office suite is **Microsoft Office**. The newest version, called **Microsoft Office 2000** (because it was invented shortly before the year 2000), comes in five editions:

> The **small-business edition** is the most popular. It includes a word-processing program (Microsoft Word), spreadsheet program (Excel), desktop-publishing program (Microsoft Publisher), and Small Business Tools. Discount dealers charge $438 normally, but just $230 if you already own a competing product (or Microsoft Works), just $190 (after rebate) if you already own an earlier version.
>
> The **standard edition** is priced the same. It includes a presentation program (Power Point) instead of a desktop-publishing program, and it omits Small Business Tools. It appeals just to companies that use Power Point.
>
> The **professional edition** resembles the small-business edition but also includes the presentation program (PowerPoint) and a database program (Microsoft Access). It costs $528 normally, $330 as a competitive upgrade, $290 as a version upgrade.
>
> The **premium edition** resembles the professional edition but also includes a drawing program (Photo Draw) and a program that lets you create your own pages to put on the Internet (Front Page). This is the edition that most computer experts buy. It costs $698 normally, $430 as a competitive upgrade, $380 as a version upgrade. For $20 extra, you also get an Intellimouse Pro.
>
> The **developer edition** resembles the premium edition but also includes Developer Tools that let you create your own programs. It costs $900 normally, $605 as a competitive upgrade, $555 as a version upgrade.

Microsoft Office 2000's main competitor is Corel's **WordPerfect Office 2000**, which costs less and comes in three editions:

> The **standard edition** includes a word-processing program (WordPerfect), spreadsheet program (Quattro Pro), and presentation program (Corel Presentations), and Internet page-creation program (Trellix). It costs $280 normally, $100 as an upgrade.
>
> The **voice-powered edition** resembles the standard edition but also includes a program that lets you dictate into a microphone (Dragon Naturally Speaking). It costs $300 normally, $137 as an upgrade.
>
> The **professional edition** resembles the voice-powered edition but also includes a database program (Paradox). It costs $337 normally, $180 as an upgrade.

Another competitor is Lotus's **Smart Suite Millennium Edition 9.5**, which is the most amazing bargain — it includes the most software per dollar:

> It includes a word-processing program (Word Pro), spreadsheet program (Lotus 1-2-3), database program (Approach), presentation program (Freelance), and dictation program (Via Voice). You get all that for just $300 normally, $100 as a upgrade.

Integrated programs

Instead of buying an office suite, you can pay less by getting a cute little program, called an **integrated program**, which does a little bit of everything!

The best integrated programs are **Q&A**, **Microsoft Works**, and **Apple Works**. Here's how they compare.

> **Q&A** is the best at handling databases. Q&A's main weakness is that it does *not* handle spreadsheets at all. Get the DOS version, since the Windows version is terrible.
>
> **Microsoft Works** is the best at handling word processing and spreadsheets. Its Windows version is good; its DOS and Mac versions are not. It costs $50. **Here's a trick: buy Microsoft Works to get the competitive-upgrade price on Microsoft Office!** Or get the Microsoft Works Suite, which costs $100 and also includes Microsoft Word, Microsoft Money (a checkbook-balancing program), and Encarta (a computerized encyclopedia).
>
> **Apple Works** is the best at handling desktop publishing. It comes free with all new Macs. You can also buy versions of it for Windows and the Apple 2. It's published by Apple, which used to call it **Claris Works**.

PFS First Choice was an excellent integrated program for DOS but is no longer marketed. IBM clones built by Tandy came with an integrated program called **Deskmate**.

Creative applications

You can buy programs that teach you new skills, produce music, play games, and perform wild tricks.

Vertical software

Software that can be used by a *wide variety* of businesses is called **horizontal software**. Programs for word processing, spreadsheets, and databases are all examples of horizontal software.

Software targeted to a specific industry is called **vertical software**. Programs specifically for doctors, lawyers, and real-estate management are all examples of vertical software.

> Vertical software is expensive because it can't be mass-marketed to the general public and isn't available from discount dealers. The typical vertical-market program costs about $2000, whereas the typical horizontal-market program costs about $200 from discount dealers.
>
> Until the price of vertical software declines, use horizontal software instead. With just a few hours of effort, you can customize horizontal software to fit your own specific needs.

Viruses

Some nasty programmers have invented **computer viruses**, which are programs that purposely damage your other programs and sneakily copy themselves onto every disk that you use. To avoid catching a virus, make sure all software entering your computer comes from reputable, safe sources. On pages 592-599, I'll explain the different kinds of viruses and how to eradicate them.

Data

If you buy a simple, old program, it comes on a floppy disk. Here's how to use that **program disk**, if you have just one floppy disk drive and no hard drive:

> First, put the program disk into the drive, and press some buttons (or type a word) that makes the computer look at the disk. (To find out which buttons to press, read the manual that came with the program.)
>
> When the computer finishes looking at the disk, remove the disk from the drive.
>
> Insert a second disk, called the **data disk**. At first, the data disk contains no information; it's blank. Put your fingers on the keyboard and type the **data** that you want the computer to manipulate. The computer will display your data on the screen and copy it onto the data disk.
>
> At night, before you go to bed, hide the data disk (which contains all the personal data you fed the computer) to protect it from any accidents and from any competitors, vandals, toddlers, pets, and goblins that go bump in the night.

Two floppy drives

If your computer has *two* floppy disk drives, put the program disk in the main drive ("drive A") and the data disk in the other drive ("drive B").

Hard drive

If your computer has one floppy disk drive plus one hard disk drive, put the program disk in the floppy disk drive, copy its program onto the hard disk, then use just the hard disk. The hard disk holds the program and data.

CD-ROM drive

If the program comes on a CD-ROM disk and your computer has a CD-ROM drive, put the program disk into the CD-ROM drive. Then copy its program onto the hard disk.

The CD-ROM disk that contains the program might also contain lots of music, video, and other data. If the data is too big to fit on the hard disk, you must keep the CD-ROM disk in the drive while running the program, so the computer can access whatever part of the CD-ROM's data is needed at the moment.

Software companies

Will your computer be pleasant to use? The answer depends mainly on which software you buy. Software companies will influence your life more than any hardware manufacturer.

The 14 dominant software companies are **Microsoft**, **Novell**, **Corel**, **Lotus**, **Borland**, **Symantec**, **Oracle**, **Computer Associates**, **Intuit**, **Adobe**, **Autodesk**, **The Learning Company**, **Electronic Arts**, and **Netscape**. Here's why....

Microsoft

The most important software company is **Microsoft**, which takes in about 24 billion dollars of revenue per year. It makes the most popular operating system (which are **MS-DOS** and **Windows**). The company's main founder, Bill Gates, became a billionaire when he was 30 years old and appeared on the cover of Time Magazine. On October 28, 1995, Bill celebrated his 40th birthday — and was worth 14.7 billion dollars. At the beginning of 1997, he was worth 24 billion dollars; seven months later, at the end of July, he was worth 40 billion dollars. Two years later, in mid-1999, he was worth 100 billion dollars. He doesn't have that much cash in his pocket, of course: most of his billions are invested in Microsoft stock. He's the richest person in the world, just because he owns 15% of Microsoft, whose stock is overpriced.

> 100 billion dollars is a lot of money! For example, even if you earn 100 million dollars per year, you'll need to work 1000 years to get what Bill has. Programmers often measure their salaries in **microbills**, where a **microbill** is defined as being a millionth of Bill Gates' worth, so a microbill is currently $100,000. Bill plans to donate 95% of his wealth before he dies; he's begun by giving a large grant to libraries. Bill's 100 billion dollars is enough to give $360 to each American, or $16 to each person on the planet. His 100 billion dollar bills, if laid end-to-end, would stretch to the moon and back, 20 times.

Microsoft is the most diversified software company: besides selling operating systems, it also sells a word-processing program (**Microsoft Word**), a spreadsheet program (**Excel**), a desktop-publishing program (**Microsoft Publisher**), database programs (**Access** and **Fox Pro**), an integrated program (**Microsoft Works**), a computerized encyclopedia (**Encarta**), programming languages (Microsoft BASIC, PASCAL, C, and others),and a wide variety of other software. It's the main software publisher for the IBM PC and Mac. It also wrote the versions of BASIC used by the Apple 2 family, Commodore Amiga, Commodore 64, and Radio Shack TRS-80.

Microsoft continually develops new products because of pressure from competitors. For example, Microsoft was forced to improve Microsoft Word because of competition from WordPerfect and improve Microsoft C because of competition from Borland's C. Those continual pressures to improve keep Microsoft a vibrant, dynamically changing company.

Novell & Corel

Novell makes **Netware** & **Intranetware**, which are programs letting you wire computers together so the computers can communicate with each other.

In 1994, Novell bought **WordPerfect Corporation**, which made the most popular word-processing program, WordPerfect. Novell's purchase was natural, since both companies were in Utah. WordPerfect Corporation sold out to Novell because WordPerfect Corporation was having financial trouble, since many customers were switching to Microsoft Word, which has been improving dramatically.

Novell also bought a product called **Quattro Pro**, which was invented by a company called **Borland**. Borland sold that product to Novell because Borland was having financial trouble competing against Microsoft.

Novell's founder, Ray Noorda, has quit. Novell's next head, Robert Frankenberg, tried to make the company smaller and more manageable, so in 1996 he sold WordPerfect and Quattro Pro to a Canadian company, **Corel**, which is famous for inventing a graphics program called **Corel Draw**.

Novell takes in about 1¼ billion dollars per year. Corel takes in about ¼ of a billion dollars per year. Novell owns 7% of Corel.

Lotus

Lotus made the most popular spreadsheet program (which was **1-2-3**). For too many years, Lotus sat on its laurels, and customers gradually began to switch to competitors such as Microsoft Excel and Quattro Pro. We expected Lotus to die.

But during the 1990's, Lotus displayed good taste and made wise moves: it dramatically improved 1-2-3; it bought a company called **Samna**, which made the nicest word-processing program (**Ami Pro**), so Ami Pro became a Lotus product; it began selling an easy-to-use presentation-graphics program, **Freelance**; and it began selling a product called **Notes**, which helps people send electronic mail to each other and edit each other's documents.

In 1995, IBM bought Lotus, so now Lotus is part of IBM, which takes in about 87 billion dollars per year.

Borland

Borland was started by Philippe Kahn, who grew up in France.

> To study math, he went to a university in Zurich, Switzerland, where he got curious about computers and decided to take a computer class.
>
> The university offered two introductory classes: one explained how to program using a language called **PL/I**, the other explained **PASCAL**. Since PASCAL was brand new then, nobody had heard of it, so 200 students signed up for PL/I and just 5 students signed up for PASCAL. Philippe signed up for PASCAL because he hated big classes. His professor was PASCAL's inventor, Niklaus Wirth.
>
> In 1983, Philippe went to California and started a computer company. Since he was an illegal alien, he tried to pretend he was thoroughly American and named his company **Borland**, in honor of the land that produced astronaut Frank Borman. His first product was **Turbo PASCAL**, which he had created back in Europe with the help of two friends.
>
> Most other versions of PASCAL were selling for hundreds of dollars. Philippe read a book saying people buy mail-order items on impulse only if priced under $50, so he charged $49.95. The book and Philippe were right: at $49.95, Turbo PASCAL became a smashing success.
>
> Later, Philippe improved Turbo PASCAL and raised its price to $149.95. He also bought other software publishers and merged them into Borland, so Borland became huge.
>
> Philippe occasionally experimented with dropping prices. For example, he dropped the price of Borland's spreadsheet program, **Quattro Pro**, to just $49.95, even though Quattro Pro was in some ways better than 1-2-3, which Lotus was selling for about $300. Microsoft's head, Bill Gates, said that the competitor that worried him the most was Borland, because he feared Philippe would pull another publicity stunt and drop prices below $50 again, forcing Microsoft to do the same.
>
> During the 1980's, Borland bought two companies that invented wonderful database programs: **Reflex** and **Paradox**. Borland eventually stopped selling Reflex, but Paradox lives on.
>
> Paradox's main competitor was **DBASE**, published by a company called **Ashton-Tate**. Philippe decided to win the competition against Ashton-Tate the easy way: he *bought* Ashton-Tate, so now Borland publishes both Paradox and DBASE. Philippe said he bought Ashton-Tate mainly to get his hands on Ashton-Tate's mailing list, so he could sell DBASE users on the idea of converting to Paradox.
>
> But Philippe paid too much for Ashton-Tate, whose products, employees, and mailing lists were all becoming stale. Since Ashton-Tate was bigger than Borland, Philippe had to borrow lots of money to buy Ashton-Tate, and he had trouble paying it back. Buying Ashton-Tate was his biggest mistake.

By 1994, he was having trouble competing against Microsoft's rapidly improving products and trouble repaying the money he'd borrowed to finance the takeover of Ashton-Tate. Financially strapped, he sold Novell his crown jewel, Quattro Pro, gave Novell the right to make a million copies of Paradox.

Novell's founder, Ray Noorda, said candidly he wasn't thrilled by Quattro Pro but wanted to buy it anyway, just as an excuse to give Philippe some money, so Philippe could stay in business and scare Microsoft, so Bill Gates would devote his energy to fighting Philippe instead of fighting Novell.

In 1995, Philippe stepped down from being the head of Borland. Now Philippe spends most of his time running a new start-up company, called **Starfish Software**.

Borland is now a division of **Inprise**, which takes in about $1/6$ of a billion dollars per year. Microsoft owns 10% of Inprise.

Why fight?

The heads of computer companies still act like a bunch of tussling toddlers. I'm waiting for their mama to say, "Boys, boys, will you please stop fighting, shake hands, and make up!"

If Israel can make peace with the PLO and Jordan, why can't Bill Gates make peace with his competitors? Answer: they're all greedy — and Bill is brash. (For example, during an interview with CBS's Connie Chung, he walked out when she mispronounced "DOS" and asked a pointed question about a competitor.)

But Bill's actually somewhat glad at his competitors' successes, since Microsoft *needs* to have enough successful competitors to prevent the Justice Department from declaring that Microsoft's too big a monopoly. By letting several competitors invent new ideas and bring them all to market, we consumers get to choose for ourselves which ideas are best — and vote on them with our dollars — rather than kowtow to a single dictator.

Symantec

My favorite database program, **Q&A**, is published by **Symantec**.

Like Lotus, Symantec shows good taste in acquisitions: it bought two companies making good versions of the C programming language (**Lightspeed** and **Zortech**) and also bought two companies making **DOS utility programs** that fix DOS's weaknesses (**Peter Norton Software** and **Central Point Software**). Now Symantec takes in about ¾ of a billion dollars per year.

Symantec tries hard to improve all those acquired products, but I wish it would improve Q&A instead! I'm sad to see Q&A, the world's best database program, be neglected and fall into obsolescence.

Specialized companies

Oracle and **Computer Associates (CA)** make software that runs on computers of all sizes: maxicomputers, minicomputers, and microcomputers.

Oracle's software handles databases. Oracle takes in 10 billion dollars per year. Oracle was founded by Larry Ellison, who still runs the company. Since he owns 24% of Oracle's stock, he's a multibillionaire, nearly as rich as Bill Gates, and yes, he's still single!

CA's software handles accounting (such as bill-paying, bill-collecting, inventory, and payroll). CA is run by a Chinese immigrant on Long Island, New York: Charles Wang (pronounced "wong", not "wang"). Try saying this sentence fast: "wong" is right, "wang" is wrong. CA's software is so boring that consumers don't know it exists, but Computer Associates takes in 6 billion dollars per year.

Intuit makes programs that handle accounting on microcomputers. Intuit's programs are cheap: under $100.

Intuit's most popular accounting programs are **Quicken** (which tracks expenses and balances your checkbook), **Quickbooks** (which handles all major business accounting), and **Turbo Tax** (which helps you fill in your 1040 income-tax form for the IRS). Turbo Tax used to be published by a company called **Chipsoft**, but Intuit bought Chipsoft in 1994.

In 1995, Microsoft tried to buy Intuit — and Intuit agreed — but Microsoft changed its mind when the Justice Department accused Microsoft of becoming too big a monopoly.

Intuit takes in 1 billion dollars per year.

Adobe makes **Postscript** software (used in many laser printers). In 1994, Adobe bought **Aldus** (the company that invented the first desktop-publishing program, **Pagemaker**). Adobe takes in 1 billion dollars per year.

Autodesk publishes **Autocad**, which is the fanciest program for handling computer-aided design (CAD). Autodesk takes in $5/6$ of a billion dollars per year.

Softkey, **Spinnaker Software**, **Broderbund**, and **The Learning Company** all published cheap programs, priced between $2 and $50 each. Those four companies merged: the combo, called **The Learning Company**, is now owned by the **Mattel** toy company.

Like Broderbund, **Electronic Arts** makes excellent educational games and low-cost tools for budding young artists and musicians. It also makes video games for Sony's Playstation.

Netscape makes **Netscape Navigator**, which can help your computer communicate with the Internet. In 1999, Netscape became part of **America OnLine**.

Buying software

You'll want four kinds of software: an operating system (which teaches the CPU how to handle the keyboard, screen, printer, and disks); a computer language (such as BASIC); application programs (such as a word-processing program, a spreadsheet program, and a database program); and data.

When shopping for a computer, beware: its advertised price usually does *not* include all four kinds of software. Ask the seller which software is included and how much the other software costs.

The typical fancy program (such as a word-processing program, database program, or spreadsheet program) has a **list price** of $495. That's also called the **manufacturer's suggested retail price (MSRP)**. If you buy the program directly from the software's publisher, that's the price you'll pay. (You'll also pay about $7 for shipping & handling. If the publisher has a sales office in your state, you'll also be charged for sales tax, even if you're phoning the manufacturer's out-of-state headquarters.)

That list price is made ridiculously high as a marketing ploy, to give you the impression that the program is fancy.

But if you walk into a typical computer store, you will *not* pay $495 for the program. Instead, you'll pay $299. That's called the **street price** because it's the price you see when you walk down the street and peek in the windows of computer stores. (You'll also pay sales tax.)

Instead of charging $299, mail-order dealers charge slightly less: $279. That's called the **mail-order price**. (You'll also pay about $7 for shipping & handling, but you won't pay tax if the mail-order company is out-of-state.) Another way to get that kind of price is to visit a discount computer superstore such as Comp USA.

Version upgrades

If you already own an older version of the program, you can switch to the new version cheaply, by asking for the **version upgrade**, which costs just $99. You can order the version upgrade at your local computer store, or from mail-order dealers, or directly from the program's publisher. The most aggressive dealers (such as Comp USA) charge slightly less: $95.

To qualify for the version upgrade, you must *prove* that you already own an older version of the program. You can do that in several ways:

If you're ordering directly from the program's publisher, the program's publisher will check its records to verify that you had sent in your registration card for the previous version. If you're ordering at a local computer store, bring in the official instruction manual that came with the old version: the store will rip out the manual's first page (the title page) and mail it to the publisher. If you lost that manual, you can instead give the store Disk 1 of the old version's set of disks. The store needs the *original* title page or disk; copies are not accepted. If you're ordering from a mail-order dealer, send the dealer the title page by mail or fax.

Some manufacturers (such as Microsoft) use a simpler way to qualify you for the version upgrade: when you install the new version, it automatically searches your computer's hard disk for the old version and refuses to run if the old version is missing.

If you bought the old version shortly before the new version came out, you can get the new version free! Just phone the publisher and ask for the **free version upgrade**.

Here's how you prove you bought the old version shortly before the new version came out (where "shortly before" is usually defined as meaning "within 60 days"): mail either your dated sales slip or a "free version-upgrade certificate" that came in the old version's box. Though the upgrade is "free", you must pay an exorbitant charge for shipping and handling ($10 for just the disks, $30 for disks plus manuals).

Competitive upgrades

If you don't own an older version of the program, you can't get the version-upgrade price. Here's the best you can do: if you already own a competing program (such as a different brand of word processor that competes against the word processor you're trying to buy), ask for the **competitive-upgrade price**. It's usually $129, which is just slightly higher than the version-upgrade price. Get it from your local store, mail-order dealer, or directly from the publisher.

To prove you qualify for the competitive-upgrade price, provide the title page or Disk 1 of the competing program (or have Microsoft's software automatically scan for such programs).

Copying software

If you buy a program, you should make backup copies of the disks. Use the backup copies in case the original disks get damaged.

You're *not* allowed to give copies of the disks to your friends. That's against the law! If your friends want to use the program, they must buy it from the software publisher or a dealer, so that the programmer receives royalties.

If you give copies to your friends and become a lawbreaker, you're called a **pirate**; making the copies is called **piracy**; the copies are called **pirated software** or **hot software**. Don't be a pirate! Don't distribute hot software!

Some software publishers use tricks that make the computer refuse to copy the program. Those tricks are called **copy protection**; the software is **copy protected**. But even if the software publisher doesn't use such tricks, it's still against the law to make copies of the program for other people, since the program is still copy*righted*.

If your friends want to try a program before buying it, don't give them a copy of the program! Instead, tell your friends to visit you and use the program while they sit at your computer. That's legal, and it also lets you help your friends figure out how to use the software.

If you buy a version upgrade, you're *not* allowed to give the older version to a friend to use on a different computer.

You must destroy the older version — or keep it just for emergencies, in case the newer version stops working.

Demo disks

Besides sitting at a friend's computer, another way to "try before you buy" is to phone the program's publisher and ask for a free **demo disk**.

Although some demo disks are just useless animated ads, the best publishers

provide useful demo disks (called **trial-size versions**) that closely imitate the full versions. For example, the typical trial-size version of a word-processing program has nearly all the features of the full version, but it refuses to print memos that are more than a page long and refuses to copy your writing onto a disk.

Trial-size versions are nicknamed **crippled software**, because each trial-size version has one or two abilities cut off. Playing with crippled software is a great way to give yourself a free education!

Freeware

Software that you're allowed to copy and use freely is called **freeware**. For example, most demo disks and trial-size versions are freeware.

Most software invented by schools, government agencies, and computer clubs is freeware. Ask!

Shareware

Shareware is software that comes with a plea: although the author lets you copy the software and try it, you're encouraged to mail the author a contribution if you like what you tried.

The suggested contribution, typically $25, is called a **registration fee**. It makes you a **registered user** and puts you on the author's mailing list, so the author can mail you a printed manual and newer versions of the software.

Though most shareware authors merely "ask" for contributions, other shareware authors "demand" that you send a contribution if you use the software for longer than a month. Software for which a contribution is "demanded" is called **guiltware** — because if you don't send the contribution, the author says you're guilty of breaking the law.

To get shareware, copy it from a friend. If none of your friends own the shareware you want, buy the disks from a computer club or store for about $5 per disk; but remember that the $5 pays for just the disk, not the registration fee (which you're honor-bound to mail in if you extensively use the program).

Beta versions

After inventing a program, its publisher must **test** it, to make sure it works on many kinds of computer equipment and in many situations. At first, the publisher's employees test the program on their own computers: that's called **alpha testing**. Next, the publishing company lets *outsiders* try the still-not-quite-perfected program: that's called **beta testing**.

The outsiders who try it are called **beta testers**; the version being tested by outsiders is called a **beta version**. Beta versions are sometimes distributed for free or at a reduced price; but if you use a beta version, don't rely on it, since it hasn't been perfected yet.

Special deals

If your office wants many employees to use a program, ask the publisher for a **site license**, which permits your company to make copies for all employees in the office. Typically the employees are *not* allowed to take the copies home: the copies must all be used at the same site.

If you're in a school and trying to teach kids how to use a program, ask the publisher for a trial-size version or **academic version** or **educational site license**.

If you own two computers and want to put the same program on both, you must typically buy two copies of the program. For example, if you want to put Windows 98 on two computers, you must buy two copies of Windows 98 (to avoid piracy), unless both computers are on the same site and you have a site license. Microsoft and some other major software publishers permit this exception, called the **portable-computer rule**:

If you're sitting at a computer, and you're the main person who uses that computer (so no other human uses it more than you), you're allowed to copy application programs from that computer to a portable computer (so you can work while you're traveling and take your work from office to home and to client sites); but just *you* are allowed to run that program on your portable computer (not other colleagues, not other family members, not friends). This rule lets you copy just application programs (such as Microsoft Word), not operating systems (such as Windows 98), not programming languages (such as C). Moreover, the application programs must have been purchased normally (not site-licensed).

IBM technologies

The most popular microcomputers are made by IBM and imitators.

How IBM arose

IBM bases its entire marketing strategy on one word: react. IBM never creates a new kind of computer; instead, IBM watches its competitors' products, notices which ones sell well, and then designs a product that meets the same needs better.

Even IBM's own name is a reaction.

> IBM was started by Tom Watson. He'd been a salesman for National Cash Register (NCR) but was fired, so he took over a competing company (CTR) and vowed to make it even bigger than National Cash Register. To be bigger than "National", he called his company "International"; to be bigger than a "Cash Register" company, he bragged that his company would sell all kinds of "Business Machines". That's how the name "International Business Machine Corp." — IBM — was hatched. IBM quickly outgrew NCR.

IBM sold lots of business machines, especially to the U.S. Census Bureau. But in 1951, Remington Rand Corp. (which later merged with Sperry) developed the Univac computer and convinced the Census to use it instead of IBM's non-computerized equipment. To react, IBM quickly invented its own computers, which were more practical than the Univac. IBM quickly became the #1 computer company — and Sperry's Univac dropped to #2.

All of IBM's early computers were big. IBM ignored the whole concept of microcomputers for many years. IBM's first microcomputers, the IBM 5100 and IBM System 23, weren't taken seriously — not even by IBM.

IBM PC

When many IBM customers began buying Apple 2 microcomputers to do Visicalc spreadsheets, IBM reacted by developing an improved microcomputer, called the **IBM Personal Computer (IBM PC)**, which did everything that Apple 2 computers could do, but better.

To invent the IBM PC, IBM created three secret research teams who competed against each other. The winner was the research team headed by Philip "Don" Estridge in Boca Raton, Florida. His team examined everything created by the other microcomputer companies (Apple, Radio Shack, Commodore, etc.) and combined their best ideas, to produce a relatively low-cost computer better than all competitors.

Don's team developed the IBM PC secretly. IBM didn't announce it to the public until August 12, 1981.

The IBM PC was a smashing success: IBM quickly became the #1 microcomputer company — and Apple dropped to #2.

The IBM PC became the best-selling microcomputer for business. More high-quality business programs became available for the IBM PC than for any other microcomputer. It became the standard against which all other microcomputers were compared. Even today, to use the best business programs you must buy an IBM PC or clone.

The IBM PC consists of three parts: a **system unit** (which contains most of the circuitry), a **keyboard**, and a **monitor**. Cables run from the keyboard and monitor to the system unit.

Keyboard The IBM PC's keyboard contains 83 keys:

> 26 keys contain the letters of the alphabet.
> 10 keys (in the top row) contain the digits.
> 10 keys (on the keyboard's right side) form a numeric keypad. It contains the digits rearranged to imitate a calculator.
> 13 keys contain symbols for math and punctuation.
> 14 keys give you control. They let you edit your mistakes, create blank spaces and capitals, etc.
> 10 function keys (labeled F1, F2, F3, F4, F5, F6, F7, F8, F9, and F10) can be programmed to mean whatever you wish!

The keyboard was designed by Don Estridge personally.

> To fit all those keys on the small keyboard, he had to make the ENTER and SHIFT keys smaller than typists liked. Above the top row of keys, he put a shelf to hold pencils; to make room for that shelf, he had to put the 10 function keys at the left side of the keyboard, even though it would have been more natural to put the F1 key near the 1 key, the F2 key near the 2 key, etc.

System unit The IBM PC's system unit contains a 63½-watt **power supply** (which transforms AC current to DC) and a **motherboard**. On the motherboard, IBM puts the CPU, RAM chips, ROM chips, and support chips.

The motherboard also includes 5 slots that hold printed-circuit cards. The motherboard's 62 wires that run to and through the slots are called the **bus**. 8 of those wires carry data; the other 54 wires are "bureaucratic overhead" that helps control the flow. Since just eight wires carry data, the bus is called an **8-bit data bus**, its slots are called **8-bit slots**, and the printed-circuit cards that you put into the slots are called **8-bit cards**.

The CPU, which is on the motherboard, is an Intel 8088 running at a speed of 4.77 million cycles per second (4.77 **megahertz**).

In the original IBM PC, the motherboard could hold 4 rows of 16K RAM chips. 1 row of chips was included in the base price; the other 3 rows of chips cost extra. If you paid the extra cost and got all 4 rows of chips, you had a total of 64K.

Later, IBM improved the motherboard, so that it uses 64K chips instead of 16K chips. The 4 rows of 64K chips produce a grand total of 256K.

To expand beyond 256K, you must buy a **memory card**, which contains sockets for holding extra RAM chips.

The motherboard contains five 8K ROM chips. One of them contains the BIOS; the other four contain BASIC.

The motherboard includes a hookup to your home's cassette tape recorder, to make the tape recorder imitate a slow disk drive.

> For faster speed, you must buy a disk drive (which costs extra), and a controller card to connect the disk drive to. The original IBM PC was limited to two 5¼-inch disk drives, and each disk held just 160K. Later, IBM improved the disk system, so that each disk could hold 360K. (To make the improvement, IBM switched to *double*-sided disks and divided each track into 9 sectors instead of 8.)

Monitor The IBM PC's base price doesn't include a monitor — or even a video card to attach the monitor to.

When IBM announced the IBM PC, it announced two kinds of video cards. One kind, the **Monochrome Display Adapter (MDA)**, attaches to a TTL monochrome monitor. The other kind, the **Color/Graphics Adapter (CGA)**, attaches to an RGB color monitor instead.

Each of those cards gives you a hidden bonus. Hiding on the MDA card is a printer port, so you can attach a printer. Hiding on the CGA card is an RCA jack, so you can attach a composite color monitor or a TV switch box.

Why the IBM PC became popular

To invent the IBM PC, IBM combined all the best ideas that other computer companies had invented previously. IBM did it all legally: IBM found the best hardware and software companies and paid them manufacturing fees and royalties. IBM listened well: IBM put into the IBM PC all the inexpensive features that business users were begging computer companies to provide.

IBM had originally planned to charge a high price for the IBM PC; but in August 1981, a week before IBM announced the IBM PC to the world, IBM's top management decided to slash the prices by 25%. So the IBM PC was not only nice but also priced 25% less than the rumor mill had expected. Customers were thrilled and bought IBM PC's quickly.

At first, very few programs were available for it, but IBM turned that liability into a virtue: IBM ran ads telling programmers that since IBM hadn't written enough programs for the PC, programmers could get rich by writing their own. Because of those ads, many programmers bought the PC and wrote thousands of programs for it. All those programs eventually increased the computer's popularity even further.

IBM PC XT & clones

In March 1983, IBM announced the **IBM PC eXTended (IBM PC XT)**.

It resembles the IBM PC but includes a larger power supply (135 watts instead of 63½) and more expansion slots (8 instead of 5). The larger power supply lets the XT handle a hard disk.

When IBM began selling the XT, IBM included a floppy disk drive, a 10-megabyte 85-millisecond hard disk, and serial port in the base price, but IBM later made them optional.

Many companies sell XT clones. The typical XT clone is better than the original XT in several ways....

Keyboard Most clones have extra-large RETURN and SHIFT keys, so your fingers can hit those keys more easily.

Power supply In most clones, the power supply is extra-large (150 watts instead of 135).

CPU Instead of using an 8088 CPU, most clones use an 8088-1 CPU, which thinks twice as fast (10 megahertz instead of 4.77). Clones using that double-speed CPU are called **turbo XT clones**.

Memory DOS easily handles 640K of RAM and a 30-megabyte hard disk. (To go beyond those limits, you must use tricks.) The typical clone attains those limits: its motherboard contains 640K of RAM, and its hard disk holds 30 megabytes. IBM's XT disk holds just a third as much. Moreover, the typical clone's hard disk is faster: its average seek time is 65 milliseconds instead of 85.

Monitor A company called **Hercules** invented a video card that improves on IBM's MDA card.

> Like the MDA card, the Hercules card produces pretty characters on a TTL monochrome monitor and includes a parallel printer port. The Hercules card has this advantage: it can generate graphics.
>
> Several companies make video cards imitating the Hercules card. Those imitations are called **Hercules-compatible graphics cards**.
>
> The typical XT clone includes a TTL monochrome monitor attached to a Hercules-compatible graphics card.

IBM PC AT & clones

In August 1984, IBM announced the **IBM PC with Advanced Technology (IBM PC AT)**. It runs several times as fast as the XT because it contains a faster CPU and disk drives. Other companies have developed AT clones that go even faster.

CPU The CPU is an Intel 80286, which beats the 8088 by performing more cycles per second and also processing about 3 times as much information per cycle.

> In IBM's original version of the AT, the 80286 CPU performed 6 million cycles per second (6 megahertz). In 1986, IBM switched to a faster 80286 that runs at 8 megahertz. Clones go even faster: 12 megahertz!

Bus The bus is 16-bit. That bus is called the **AT bus** or the **Industry Standard Architecture bus (ISA bus)**. Into its 16-bit slots, you can put 16-bit cards or old XT-style 8-bit cards.

Hard drives The AT handles faster hard drives than the XT.

> IBM's original hard drive for the AT had a 40-millisecond average seek time and held 20 megabytes. That drive, built for IBM by a company called **CMI**, was unreliable. IBM eventually switched to a different supplier, and CMI went bankrupt.
>
> Most clones contain reliable drives that go faster (28 milliseconds) and hold more (40 megabytes and beyond).

Floppy drives The AT's floppy drive squeezes 1.2 megabytes onto high-density 5¼-inch floppy disks. That drive can also read the 360K disks created by XT computers, but it can*not* reliably create a 360K disk to send to an XT computer.

> The typical computerist puts *two* floppy drives into the AT. The first drive deals mainly with 1.2 megabyte disks. The other drive is an XT-style 360K drive, which sits in the AT just to communicate to XT computers.

Keyboard The AT's original keyboard had 84 keys. Typists liked it better than the PC and XT keyboards, because it had bigger ENTER and SHIFT keys.

In January 1986, IBM switched to a bigger keyboard having 101 keys. Its function keys (F1, F2, etc.) were in the top row (near the pencil ledge) instead of at the left.

Main power supply The AT's main power supply is 192 watts. Clones use power supplies that are 200 watts.

SETUP When you first buy an AT, you (or your dealer) must run the **SETUP program**, which comes on a disk or in a ROM chip.

> The SETUP program makes the AT ask you how much RAM you bought, which monitor and disk drives you bought, and whether you bought a math coprocessor. The AT copies your answers into a CMOS RAM chip, powered by a battery sitting in a holder just left of the main power supply.
>
> Even when you turn off the computer's main power switch, the CMOS RAM chip keeps remembering your answers — until its battery runs out after 4 years (or 1 year in some clones). Then the computer displays the wrong date and time and won't let you use the hard disk — until you run the SETUP program again, preferably with a fresh battery.

Improved graphics & PS/2

In September 1984, IBM announced an improved color video system. It consists of a video card called the **Enhanced Graphics Adapter (EGA)** and a compatible color monitor (called an **EGA monitor**).

> You can put an EGA card into the IBM PC, IBM PC XT, or IBM PC AT. The EGA system is better than CGA, because EGA can display more colors and finer resolution (more dots per inch), and EGA obeys the computer's commands faster.

At the same time, IBM announced an even fancier video system, called the **Professional Graphics Controller (PGC)**, but it was too expensive to be popular.

On April 2, 1987, IBM announced a whole new series of computers, called the **Personal System 2 (PS/2)**, which runs the same programs as the PC but adds better graphics. Soon afterwards, IBM stopped making its old classic computers (the IBM PC, IBM PC XT, and IBM PC AT).

The classic computers used 5¼-inch floppy disks. The PS/2 computers use 3½-inch floppy disks instead, which take up less space on your desk, are sturdier, hold more bytes per square inch, and consume less electricity.

Different models The cheapest PS/2 computer is the **PS/2 model 25**; the most expensive is the **PS/2 model 95**. Other models are in between.

By June 1991, IBM had invented these desktop models—

Model	CPU	Bus	Video	Floppy
25, 30	8086	XT	MCGA	720K
25/286, 30/286	286	AT	VGA	1440K
50, 50Z	286	MCA	VGA	1440K
35, 40	386SX	AT	VGA	1440K
55	386SX	MCA	VGA	1440K
57	386SX	MCA	VGA	2880K
70	386DX	MCA	VGA	1440K
90	486	MCA	XGA	1440K

and these tower models—

Model 60 is a tower version of model 50.
Model 65 is a tower version of model 55.
Model 80 is a tower version of model 70.
Model 95 is a tower version of model 90.

and these portable models:

Model L40 is a notebook version of model 40.
Model P70 is a luggable version of model 70.
Model P75 is a luggable version of model 90.

Floppy drive In models containing an 8086 CPU, the 3½-inch floppy drive is **double-density (DD)**, so it puts 720K on a disk. In most other models, the 3½-inch floppy drive is **high-density (HD)**, so it puts 1440K on a disk. The model 57 contains an experimental 3½-inch floppy drive that's **extra-high density (ED)**, so it puts 2880K on a disk.

Bus The models containing an 8086 CPU use the same 8-bit bus as the old IBM PC and IBM PC XT. All other under-50 models use the IBM PC AT 16-bit bus.

Models 50 and up contain a new style of bus, called the **Micro Channel**, using a technology called **Micro Channel Architecture (MCA)**.

The Micro Channel transmits data faster than the old bus. It includes 16-bit and 32-bit slots. Unfortunately, the Micro Channel's 16-bit slots are a different size than the 16-bit slots in the IBM PC AT; you cannot put an IBM PC, XT, or AT card into a Micro Channel slot.

IBM holds a patent on the Micro Channel bus.

Clone companies that copy the Micro Channel bus pay IBM a licensing fee. Other clone companies use the AT bus (ISA bus) instead, or a new 32-bit version of it (the **Extended ISA bus**, which is called the **EISA bus**, pronounced "ees uh bus"), or an even faster 32-bit version (the **Video Electronics Standards Association local bus**, called the **VESA local bus** or **VL bus**), or the fastest version (the **Peripheral Component Interconnect bus**, called the **PCI bus** and used mainly in computers containing a Pentium CPU).

MCGA The models containing an 8086 CPU also contain a chip called the **Multi-Color Graphics Array (MCGA)**, which produces nice graphics.

The MCGA lets you create your own color by mixing an amount of red from 0 to 63, an amount of green from 0 to 63, and an amount of blue from 0 to 63; so altogether, the number of possible colors you can create is "64 times 64 times 64", which is 262,144.

After you create your favorite colors, the computer will let you display 256 of them on the screen simultaneously. You position those colors on the screen by using a coordinate system that permits an X value from 0 to 319 and a Y value from 0 to 199.

If you're willing to use just 2 colors instead of 256, the computer will let you do higher-resolution drawing, in which the X value goes from 0 to 639 (so you have 640 choices) and the Y value goes from 0 to 479 (so you have 480 choices). That's called **640-by-480 resolution**.

VGA The models containing a 286 or 386 CPU contain a fancier graphics chip, called the **Video Graphics Array (VGA)**. Its 256-color mode is the same as MCGA's, but its high-resolution mode permits 16 colors instead of 2.

IBM's competitors sell clones whose graphics are even better than VGA:

Besides giving you VGA's high resolution of 640-by-480, they give you an even higher resolution of 800-by-600 and an even higher resolution of 1024-by-768.

Instead of giving you 262,144 colors, the fanciest clones give you 16,777,216 colors (by letting the red, green, and blue each range up to 255 instead of 63).

Since 16,777,216 colors are even more than the human eye can distinguish, clones that have 16,777,216 colors are said to have **true color**. They're also said to have **24-bit color** (because to distinguish among 16,777,216 colors, the computer must store each color as a 24-bit number).

If you buy a clone containing one of those souped-up VGA systems, make sure the VGA card contains at least 512K of video RAM instead of just 256K. You need that extra RAM to get lots of colors at the super-high resolutions:

Video RAM	How many colors you can see simultaneously
256K	256 colors at 640×400; 16 colors at 800×600; 2 colors at 1280×1024
512K	256 colors at 640×480; 16 colors at 1024×768; 2 colors at 1280×1024
1M	16,777,216 colors at 640×480; 65,536 at 800×600; 256 at 1024×768; 16 at 1280×1024
2M	16,777,216 colors at 800×600; 65,536 at 1024×768; 256 at 1280×1024

Make sure the VGA card is 16-bit instead of 8-bit, so it can accept 16 bits of information at once. Then it can handle all those colors and dots *quickly!*

Since VGA is so wonderful, practically everybody who buys an IBM clone orders VGA.

VGA's popularity led VGA monitors and cards to be mass-produced on gigantic assembly lines, which dropped VGA's price even lower than EGA's. Since VGA is now cheaper and better than EGA, nobody buys EGA monitors or cards anymore (except people repairing old EGA systems).

XGA The PS/2 models having a 486 CPU contain a fancy graphics chip called the **eXtended Graphics Array (XGA)**. It resembles 1024-by-768 VGA.

Price The price of each PS/2 depends on how much RAM you buy, what size hard disk you buy, and what kind of monitor you buy. (If you can't afford a color monitor, buy a **gray-scale monitor** that shows shades of gray instead. The shades of gray crudely imitate the color graphics you'd get from MCGA, VGA, or XGA.)

If somebody offers you a "complete PS/2 system" cheaply, check whether that "complete" price includes the monitor. Usually it doesn't!

Cheaper than PS/2

The PS/2 computers were too expensive. In 1990, IBM invented a cheaper series of computers, called the **PS/1**. In 1992, IBM invented an even cheaper series, called the **PS/Valuepoint**.

In 1993, IBM invented an even cheaper series called the **Ambra**, which IBM sold just by mail to compete against mail-order clone companies.

The IBM division that produced and sold the Ambra was understaffed, confused, and mismanaged: shipments were delayed and unpredictable, many Ambras were defective, and customers had difficulty getting IBM's Ambra division to send a repairman. Though the Ambra division advertised heavily, it was so badly managed and got such a bad reputation that it lost money. In 1994, IBM shut the division down.

In 1994, IBM began selling a nicer series, called the **Aptiva**.

IBM's flops

Some of your friends might still own IBM's other microcomputers, which were less successful.

IBM's **PC Junior** was intended for schoolkids. It had pretty graphics and a low price; but its add-ons were too expensive, its keyboard was awkward, and its circuitry differed enough from the original PC so the Junior refused to run some of the PC's programs.

IBM's **PC Portable** was a luggable inspired by Compaq but didn't include enough expansion slots.

After IBM invented the 8-megahertz AT, IBM had too many 6-megahertz and XT parts left in its warehouse. To use up those old parts, IBM created the **XT/286**, which contained a 6-megahertz AT CPU attached to an XT disk drive. The XT/286 was as unpopular as its parts.

Don's demise

Though Don Estridge became popular for inventing the IBM PC and XT, his next two projects disappointed IBM: the PC Junior didn't sell well, and the AT's CMI hard drive was unreliable.

His bosses kicked him out of the Boca Raton research office and hid him in an obscure part of the company. A few months later, when he flew on a Delta jet, the jet crashed and killed him.

How clones are priced

Instead of buying from IBM, save money! Buy a clone instead!

Here's how most clones are priced. (I'll show you the prices that were in effect when this book went to press in August 2000. Prices drop about 3% per month, 30% per year.)

$900 gets you a "standard" clone. That's the cheapest kind of modern clone.

If you pay *more* than $900, you get a clone that's fancier — a powerful "muscle machine" that will impress your friends. They'll be impressed by how much money you spent. (If you pay *much* more than $900, they might also be impressed by how stupid you were to overspend.)

If you pay *less* than $900, you get a clone that's old-fashioned. If you pay *slightly* less than $900, the clone will still run most programs fine, though your friends will laugh at you for buying such a puny, quaint computer. If you pay *much* less than $900, the clone will probably have some difficulty running modern programs. But hey, if you can't afford $900, a substandard clone is better than no computer at all! If you buy a substandard clone, your next task is to figure out which software it can handle well; then buy just that kind of software.

Here are the details. (I've rounded all prices to the nearest $25.)

CPU

The standard clone's CPU is a Pentium Celeron, running at a speed of 600 megahertz. It's fast enough to perform most tasks quickly. To get an even faster Pentium, you must pay a surcharge:

CPU			Surcharge
Pentium Celeron at	600 megahertz		$0
Pentium Celeron at	633 megahertz		$25
Pentium Celeron at	677 megahertz		$75
Pentium 3	at	733 megahertz	$100
Pentium 3	at	800 megahertz	$175
Pentium 3	at	850 megahertz	$325
Pentium 3	at	866 megahertz	$350
Pentium 3	at	933 megahertz	$550
Pentium 3	at	1000 megahertz	$875

Those faster CPUs are just *slightly* faster than a 600-megahertz Celeron and are overpriced. Don't buy them until Intel lowers their prices. For now, get just a 600-megahertz Celeron.

If you're willing to accept slower Celeron, at 500 megahertz, deduct $25.

To save money, buy an AMD K6-2 or AMD Duron (which are as good as a Pentium Celeron but cost less) or an AMD Athlon (which is as good as a Pentium 3 but costs less).

RAM

The standard clone's RAM is 64M. If you want 128M instead, add $50.

Though 64M is usually enough, 128M helps some programs run faster.

If you're willing to accept just 32M (which is substandard), deduct $25. But some Windows programs (such as Internet Explorer 5.5) are **memory hogs** that expect you to have at least 64M. If you have just 32M, the memory-hog programs will still run, but slowly.

Hard drive

The standard clone's hard drive is 10 gigabytes (10G). If you want a bigger hard drive, you must pay a surcharge:

Hard drive	Surcharge
10 gigabytes	$0
20 gigabytes	$25
30 gigabytes	$75
40 gigabytes	$125

Though 10 gigabytes is enough to run today's software, I recommend getting at least 20 gigabytes, since programmers have recently been inventing bigger software. Software size is increasing dramatically! A 20-gigabyte drive costs about $25 more than a 10-gigabyte drive; that $25 is a worthwhile insurance policy against future increases in software size.

Video

The standard clone includes a 17-inch color monitor. Add $125 for 19-inch, $550 for 21-inch. Deduct $75 for 15-inch, $100 for 14-inch. Though 15-inch is adequate, you should get at least 17-inch, which is much more pleasant, more common, required by some programs for standard operation, and worth the $75 difference.

The standard video card has 8M of RAM on it. Add $50 if 16M, $100 if 32M. Deduct $25 if 4M.

Other hardware

The standard clone's CD-ROM drive is 48X max. Add $75 if the drive can also handle DVD. Deduct $50 if the drive is missing.

The standard clone includes a sound card and a pair of stereo speakers. The sound card should be able to do **wave-table** synthesis (which means it can produce extra-realistic sounds by creating tables of sound waves), or else deduct $25. Add $50 if you also get a **subwoofer** (a third speaker, which gives you a richer bass). If you get no sound card and no speakers, deduct $100.

The standard clone's modem has an advertised speed of 56 kilobaud and can also handle faxes. Deduct $50 if you get no modem.

The standard clone includes a **keyboard**, **mouse**, and **3½-inch floppy drive**. Add $75 if it also includes a **Zip drive** (or **LS-120 drive** or tape drive).

The standard clone comes in a **tower case**. Deduct $25 if the case is a **desktop** instead of a desktop. The tower case is more common and has two advantages: it can hold extra cards (but you probably won't buy any!) and it can sit on the floor (so your desk is uncluttered and your monitor sits low enough to be seen without craning your neck up).

Software

The standard clone includes Windows 98 or Windows ME. Deduct $100 if you get no Windows or no Windows manual.

The standard clone comes with a **checkbook-balancing program**, such as Quicken or Microsoft Money (or deduct $25). It comes with a CD-ROM disk containing an **encyclopedia**, such as Compton's Encyclopedia or Grolier's Encyclopedia or Microsoft Encarta (or deduct $25).

The standard clone comes with an **integrated program** (such as **Microsoft Works**). Add $25 if you get a **suite** instead (such as **Microsoft Works Suite** or **Lotus Smart Suite** or **Corel WordPerfect Office**). Add $125 if you get **Microsoft Office Small Business Edition** instead. Deduct $25 if you get no integrated program and no suite.

Those prices are what big clone makers add in for software that comes with the computer. If instead you buy the software separately later, you'll pay much more!

Guarantees

The standard clone comes with a **30-day money-back guarantee**, a **1-year warranty**, and **lifetime toll-free tech support for hardware & software**.

Add $50 if the warranty is 3-year instead of 1-year. Deduct $25 if the warranty is 3-month instead of 1-year.

Deduct $75 if the company is run by jerks. Here are signs that the company is run by jerks: the money-back guarantee is missing or shorter than 30 days (or you get charged a "restocking fee" for returning the computer), or the warranty is less than 1-year, or the advertised price applies just if you pay cash instead of using a credit card, or the tech-support phone number is not toll-free or requires you to pay a fee for software questions or is limited to 1 year or is usually busy or is unanswered or routes you to a person who says to leave your phone number but doesn't return your call.

Kinds of clones

You've seen that a **standard clone** costs just $900. But an **upscale clone** includes extras that raise the total cost to $1125; a **fancy clone** raises the total cost to $1725; a **luxury clone** raises the total cost to $1850; and a **downscale clone** lowers the total cost to $625. Here's how:

Feature	Standard clone	Upscale clone		Fancy clone		Luxury clone		Downscale clone	
CPU	Celeron 600MHz	Celeron 633MHz	($25 extra)	Pentium 3 733MHz	($100 extra)	Pentium 3 800MHz	($175 extra)	Celeron 500MHz	($25 less)
RAM	64M	128M	($50 extra)	128M	($50 extra)	128M	($50 extra)	32M	($25 less)
hard drive	10 gigabytes	20 gigabytes	($25 extra)	30 gigabytes	($75 extra)	40 gigabytes	($125 extra)	10 gigabytes	
video	17-inch, 8M	17-inch, 32M	($100 extra)	19-inch, 32M	($225 extra)	19-inch, 32M	($225 extra)	15-inch, 4M	($100 less)
CD-ROM drive	48X max	48X max		DVD	($75 extra)	DVD	($75 extra)	48X max	
Zip drive	none	none		one	($75 extra)	one	($75 extra)	none	
sound	wave-table	wave-table		wave-table subwoofer	($50 extra)	wave-table subwoofer	($50 extra)	wave-table	
fax/modem	56 kilobaud	56 kilobaud		56 kilobaud		56 kilobaud		56 kilobaud	
case	tower	tower		tower		tower		desktop	($25 less)
applications	chbk,ency,integ	chbk,ency,suite	($25 extra)	chbk,ency,MS Office	($125 extra)	chbk,ency,MS Office	($125 extra)	none	($75 less)
warranty	1-year	1-year		3-year	($50 extra)	3-year	($50 extra)	3-month	($25 less)
TOTAL	**$900**	$900 + $225 extra = **$1125**		$900 + $825 extra = **$1725**		$900 + $950 extra = **$1850**		$900 - $275 = **$625**	

Those prices do *not* include a printer, which is priced separately.

Which kind to buy Though a **standard clone** is adequate, a **fancy clone** is much nicer and will give you a happy thrill. It's the kind of clone most computer experts recommend.

If a fancy clone is beyond your budget but you'd like something better than just "standard", buy an **upscale clone**, which is a compromise. It will give you the pleasure of being uppity, better than standard.

A **luxury clone** is what computer experts lust for, but spending so much money is foolish. To get a taste of luxury without being a fool, buy a fancy clone but soup it up by adding whichever luxurious element excites you the most. For example, if you're mainly lusting for a 40-gigabyte hard drive, go ahead: buy a fancy clone but with a 40-gigabyte hard drive instead of 30-gigabyte.

If you're on a very tight budget and can't afford even a standard clone, buy a **downscale clone**. It will still run most programs okay. Just be aware that within 2 years, you'll have an urge to soup it up, and making the alterations will cost you more (in labor charges, etc.) than if you buy a standard clone all at once.

Notebooks are pricey

The first rule about buying a notebook (or laptop) computer is: don't buy one unless you must! Try buying a desktop computer instead!

Though notebook computers are portable and cute, you pay a *lot* for portable cuteness.

For example, suppose you want to buy this kind of modest computer: a 500 MHz Celeron (or AMD K6-2) with 64-megabyte RAM, 10-gigabyte hard drive, floppy drive, color screen, mouse (or touchpad), CD-ROM drive, sound, 56K modem, and Windows (98 or ME). You can get a desktop computer fitting that description, from the most aggressive discount dealers, for about $700; to get a *notebook* computer fitting that description, you must pay about $1100 instead.

If you can afford $1100, should you buy a notebook computer? No! Here's what $1100 gets you:

$1100 notebook	$1100 desktop
AMD K6-2 at 500 MHz	AMD Duron at 700 MHz
64-megabyte RAM	128-megabyte RAM
6-gigabyte hard drive	20-gigabyte hard drive
13" 800×600 screen	17"/16" 1280×1024 screen
24X CD-ROM drive	DVD drive
stereo sound	stereo sound + subwoofer
56K modem & Windows	56K modem & Windows

Desktop computers give you much more equipment per dollar than notebook computers. So don't buy a notebook unless you *must*.

If you need to use a computer in two locations, don't buy a notebook: buy two desktop computers instead! Buying two desktop computers costs about the same as buying one notebook. Or buy a desktop computer that's light enough to carry to your car easily.

Buy a notebook computer just if you need to travel often to many locations or if you're a student or researcher needing to take notes in a lecture or library.

When buying a notebook computer, the price depends mainly on what kind of screen you get. Most folks buy color screens, though black-and-white monochrome screens are cheaper. For color screens, the old-fashioned kind is called **passive**; the next step up is **dual-scan passive**, which is brighter and works faster; the most expensive is **active-matrix**, which is even brighter and works even faster. Passive is also called **STN**; dual-scan passive is called **DSTN**; active-matrix is called **TFT**.

Most folks buy color screens that are **active-matrix** (which is the best type) or **dual-scan passive** (which costs $100 less). To help folks who are debating between those two types, some Compaq notebooks use a compromise called **high-performance addressing (HPA)**.

Famous clones

I'd like to tell you about a company that makes reliable, powerful IBM clones, charges you very little, and is a pleasure to call if you ever need technical help.

That's what I'd *like* to tell you, but I haven't found such a company yet! If you find one, let me know!

> Each day, I falsely think I've finally found my hero company. I tell the name of the hero-company-du-jour to folks like you who call me for advice. But like O.J. Simpson, my hoped-for hero gets quickly accused by my customers of doubly murdering them in some way. How depressing! Can't any company do things right? I've been writing this book for over 25 years and have yet to find a company I still feel proud about. I'm disgusted.

Hero companies rise but then fall because they suffer through the following business cycle:

> When the company begins, it's new and unknown, so it tries hard to get attention for itself by offering low prices. It also tries to help its customers by offering good service.
>
> When news spreads about how the company offers low prices and good service, the company gets deluged with more customers than it can handle — and it's also stuck answering phone calls from old customers who still need help but aren't buying anything new.
>
> To eliminate the overload, the company must either accept fewer customers (by raising prices — or by lowering them slower than the rest of the industry), or offer less service per customer (by refusing to hire enough staff to handle all the questions), or hire extra staff (who are usually less talented than the company's founders but nevertheless expect high pay). In any of those cases, the company becomes less pleasant and heroism is relegated to history. The company becomes just one more inconsequential player in the vast scheme of computer life.

This chapter portrays the players. Warning: these portraits are anatomically correct — they show which companies are pricks.

The computer industry's a soap opera in which consumers face new personal horrors daily. I wrote this in September 2000, but you can get the newest breathtaking episode of the computer industry's drama, *How the Screw-You Turns*, by phoning me anytime. I'll tell you the newest dirt about wannabe and were-to-be hero companies.

So before buying a computer, **phone me at 603-666-6644** to get my new advice free. Tell me your needs, and I'll try to recommend the best vendor for *you*. Before phoning me, become a knowledgeable consumer by reading this chapter.

ABS & NuTrend

Of all the major reputable computer manufacturers, **ABS** charges the least!

You can buy from ABS headquarters or from its **NuTrend Computer** division, which charges even less. Here's what NuTrend charged when this book went to press in September 2000:

CPU type	MHz	RAM	Hard drive	Video	CD	Stereo speakers	Price
AMD K6-2	500	64M	10 gigabytes	15" 8M	52X	2 speakers	$719
AMD K6-2	533	64M	10 gigabytes	15" 8M	52X	2 speakers	$729
AMD K6-2	533	64M	10 gigabytes	17" 8M	52X	2 speakers	$778
AMD Duron	600	128M	20 gigabytes	17" 32M	DVD	2 speakers + subwoofer	$979
AMD Duron	650	128M	20 gigabytes	17" 32M	DVD	2 speakers + subwoofer	$989
AMD Duron	700	128M	20 gigabytes	17" 32M	DVD	2 speakers + subwoofer	$999
AMD Athlon	700	128M	20 gigabytes	17" 32M	DVD	2 speakers + subwoofer	$1099
AMD Athlon	750	128M	20 gigabytes	17" 32M	DVD	2 speakers + subwoofer	$1119
AMD Athlon	750	128M	20 gigabytes	19" 32M	DVD	2 speakers + subwoofer	$1249
AMD Athlon	800	128M	20 gigabytes	19" 32M	DVD	2 speakers + subwoofer	$1269
AMD Athlon	800	128M	30 gigabytes	19" 32M	DVD	2 speakers + subwoofer	$1359
AMD Athlon	800	128M	30 gigabytes	19" 32M	DVD	4 speakers + subwoofer	$1389
AMD Athlon	800	128M	40 gigabytes	19" 32M	DVD	4 speakers + subwoofer	$1619
AMD Athlon	850	128M	40 gigabytes	19" 32M	DVD	4 speakers + subwoofer	$1679
AMD Athlon	950	128M	40 gigabytes	19" 32M	DVD	4 speakers + subwoofer	$1789
AMD Athlon	1000	128M	40 gigabytes	19" 32M	DVD	4 speakers + subwoofer	$1899

For example, the chart's bottom line says:

NuTrend will sell you a computer system in which the CPU is fast (an AMD Athlon running at a speed of 1000 megahertz, which is 1 gigahertz), the RAM is big (128 megabytes), the hard drive is big (40 gigabytes), the monitor's screen contains a 19-inch tube (measured diagonally), the video card contains 32 megabytes of RAM, the CD-ROM drive can also handle DVD, and the 4 normal speakers are supplemented by a 5th speaker (subwoofer) to produce a booming bass. The total price is just $1899.

Each NuTrend system comes in a tower case. The motherboard includes a PCI bus. You also get a 56K V.90 fax/modem, a wave-table sound card, 1.44M floppy drive, mouse, 104-key keyboard, microphone, Windows Me, WordPerfect Office 2000, and a CD containing Grolier's encyclopedia.

Lower prices NuTrend will probably charge you even less. For example, if you order by using NuTrend's Internet Web site, you'll often get a lower price than advertised in magazines. Prices drop every month. For example, when this book went to press at the end of September 2000, NuTrend was in the process of dropping some prices by an additional $300. If you buy on certain days, NuTrend offers a $75 rebate; NuTrend will send you an e-mail telling you when the rebates are, if you get on NuTrend's mailing list. After you buy a NuTrend computer, NuTrend will give you a $20 rebate for every friend whom you convince to buy a NuTrend computer.

Software deals NuTrend sells software at low prices.. For example, it sells Microsoft Works Suite for $89, Microsoft Office Small Business Edition for $199, and Corel Draw 9 for $99. Those prices are for full versions of the software, bought with your computer.

A few years ago, I bought a computer myself from NuTrend. I'm satisfied because the machine works okay and costs little. I've had these minor frustrations....

The hard drive is slow: it's from a good manufacturer, Quantum, but it's Quantum's cheapest model. The image on the screen is slightly fuzzy: the monitor is from a good manufacturer, Optiquest, but it's Optiquest's cheapest model. The mouse card was screwed in crooked, so the mouse's cord wouldn't fit into it until I opened the computer and readjusted the card. The computer has two "power on" switches, whose relationship to each other is confusing. The diagram showing beginners how to plug the components into the back of the computer didn't match the way the computer actually looked. The Windows "guided tour" tutorial wouldn't run, until I reinstalled the software. The salesman lied about software: he said Lotus Smart Suite 97 is the newest version, but it's not. WordPerfect Suite 8 came on a CD-ROM with no manual.

ABS and NuTrend are near Los Angeles. They're next door to each other. Here's how to reach them:

ABS Computer Technologies
9997 Rose Hills Road
Whittier CA 90601
main phone & sales: 800-876-8088 or 562-695-8823
tech support questions: 800-865-2471
Internet Web site: www.buyabs.com

NuTrend Computer
9999 Rose Hills Road
Whittier CA 90601
main phone & sales: 888-482-6678 or 562-692-4462
tech support questions: 888-525-5181
Internet Web site: www.nutrend.com

Services When you order, you must wait a week for NuTrend to build your computer, then wait another week for UPS to ship it to you by ground, which costs $75 if you're in New England, less if you're closer to California.

In the past, ABS didn't use enough packing material.

Customers often complained that the cable to the floppy drive fell out during shipping. They had to open the computer and push the cable into the back of the drive again. When they asked ABS about the problem, the technician seemed to say "It's a Peking problem"; but he was trying to say "It's a packing problem" with a Chinese accent. (Customers complain they can't understand the accents of ABS's technicians.)

But the computer I received recently from NuTrend was packed fine.

Founded in 1981 and run by Fred Chang, ABS has been a member of the Better Business Bureau. The Bureau has reported many unresolved complaints about ABS, such as delays in getting refunds, but some ABS customers have good luck and tell me they're happy.

For answers to tech-support questions, phone 800-865-2471. ABS used to be bad at answering that phone: customers told me they typically got put on hold for 20 minutes, then disconnected. But in 1999, I and my readers and the editors of Computer Shopper magazine all got through to ABS and NuTrend tech support *immediately*, indicating that ABS and NuTrend offered better tech support "big-name brands". Unfortunately, in the year 2000, tech support got worse: expect a 20-minute delay before talking to a human.

ABS gives you a 30-day money-back guarantee, a 3-year warranty, and free phone help forever (lifetime), toll-free.

Women used to complain to me that ABS employees assume all women are stupid. Examples:

When a woman asked a question about Windows 95, the ABS staff brushed her off by saying, "It's not our job to explain Windows 95."

When an Alaska woman who runs a computer company bought 5 ABS computers and then tried asking a question, the ABS staff tried to brush her off by saying, "Why don't you ask your husband?" She replied, "Because I know more about computers than he does. He's a fisherman."

But I haven't heard such complaints lately. Maybe ABS has improved?

Emachines

Emachines is the only major company that advertises computers for under $500 and lets you buy them in stores.

History Here's how the Emachines company began…

Radio Shack is owned by Tandy, which also used to own a chain of discount computer superstores called **Computer City**. Tandy eventually gave up trying to run Computer City and sold that chain to Comp USA. Computer City's president (Stephen Dukker) was dismayed at becoming a Comp USA vice-president, so he quit and started his own company, **Emachines**, which invents cheap computer systems (under $500) and sells them to retail stores such as Comp USA.

He started Emachines in September 1998, using money invested by two Korean companies: **Trigem** (which makes Emachine's computers) and **Korea Data Systems (KDS)** (which makes Emachine's monitors).

He was wildly successful. Nine months later, in June 1999, his company become the third-biggest seller of desktop&tower computers in computer stores: just Compaq and Hewlett-Packard sell more desktop&tower computers than he. In the next month, July 1999, he shipped his 1 millionth computer. In September 2000, he shipped his 3 millionth computer.

Prices Here are Emachine's prices:

CPU	MHz	RAM	Hard drive	CD	Price
Celeron	566	32M	7.5 gigs	40X	$474-$75=$399
Celeron	633	64M	20 gigs	DVD	$674-$75=$599
Celeron	633	64M	20 gigs	48X + CD-RW	$774-$75=$699
Celeron	700	64M	30 gigs	48X + DVD + CD-RW	$874-$75=$799

In that chart, the "minus $75" means you get a $75 rebate. Each price includes a keyboard, mouse, pair of speakers, 56K fax/modem, and Windows Me.

The prices do *not* include a monitor. (You can get a 14-inch monitor for about $100 from a variety of sources.) There is no video card: the video circuitry uses part of the main RAM.

You get a 1-year warranty. (Add $89 if you want a 3-year warranty instead.)

Where to buy You can buy Emachines from computer stores (Comp USA and Micro Center), electronics stores (Circuit City, Best Buy, Fry's, J&R, and BrandsMart), office-supply stores (Staples and Office Depot), department stores (Sears), warehouse stores (Costco and BJ's), mail-order computer dealers (Micro Warehouse and Tiger Direct), general mail-order catalogues (Damark, and Fingerhut), and many other places also!

His *con*tribution to the world of cheap computers is: *dis*tribution!

$400 rebate He offers an extra $400 rebate if you sign a 3-year contract to use Compuserve as your Internet service provider, at a cost of $21.95 per month, so the contract costs you a total of "36 months times $21.95", which is $790.20. So for the cheapest Emachines computer, the price is "$474 minus a $75 rebate minus a $400 Compuserve rebate", making the final price be about $0.

Stores advertise it as being a "free computer", neglecting to mention that the price does not include a monitor and requires you to sign a $790.20 Compuserve contract. That kind of advertising was popular in November 1999, when many Emachines were sold; but in the year 2000, many state governments declared those ads "misleading" and banned them.

Micro Center

The first major company to sell good computers for under $500 was **Micro Electronics Incorporated (MEI)**, which runs a chain of stores called **Micro Center**. It manufactures a computer called the **PowerSpec** and has sold it for just $399! The $399 version is no longer available, but Micro Center will sell you a fancier version for a price that's still low:

CPU	MHz	RAM	Hard drive	Video RAM	CD	Price
Celeron	633	64M	20 gigs	4M	48X	$649
Pentium 3	667	64M	30 gigs	4M	48X	$799
Pentium 3	733	128M	30 gigs	4M	48X	$949
Pentium 3	800	128M	45 gigs	32M	48X + CD-RW	$1399
Pentium 3	933	128M	45 gigs	32M	48X + CD-RW	$1899

Each price includes a keyboard, mouse, pair of speakers, Windows, and the Microsoft Works Suite. Those prices do not include a monitor.

Those were Micro Center's list prices as of September 2000. Prices continually drop, and Micro Center often has a special "sale price".

You can buy PowerSpec computers at a Micro Center superstore (a pleasant place to shop!) or mail-order (800-382-2390).

Gateway

Gateway was the first company to sell lots of computers by mail. Here's how Gateway became mail-order king.

How Gateway arose Gateway began because of cows:

In the 1800's, George Waitt began a cattle company. According to legend, he got his first herd by grabbing cattle that jumped off barges into the Missouri River on the way to the stockyards.

His cattle business passed to his descendants and eventually into the hands of his great-grandson, Norm, who built the Waitt Cattle Company into one of the biggest cattle firms in the Midwest. The company is on the Missouri River, in Iowa's Sioux City, which is where Iowa meets South Dakota and Nebraska.

Norm's sons — Norm Junior and Ted — preferred computers to cows, so on September 5th, 1985, they started the "Gateway 2000" company in their dad's office. They told him computers are easier to ship than cows, since computers can take a long journey without needing to be fed and without making a mess in their boxes.

22-year-old Ted was the engineer and called himself "president"; Norm Junior was the businessman and called himself "vice president". Their main investor was their grandma, who secured a $10,000 loan. They hired just one employee: Mike Hammond.

At first, they sold just parts for the Texas Instruments Professional Computer. Soon they began building their own computers. By the end of 1985, they'd sold 50 systems, for which customers paid a total of $100,000.

Gateway grew rapidly:

Year	Computers sold	Revenue	Employees
1985	50 computers	$100,000	2
1986	300 computers	$1,000,000	4
1987	500 computers	$1,500,000	8
1988	4,000 computers	$11,700,000	33
1989	25,000 computers	$70,500,000	176
1990	100,000 computers	$275,500,000	600
1991	225,000 computers	$626,700,000	1,300
1992	even more computers!	$1,100,000,000	1,876
1993	even more computers!	$1,700,000,000	3,500
1994	even more computers!	$2,700,000,000	4,500
1995	1,338,000 computers	$3,700,000,000	9,300
1996	1,909,000 computers	$5,000,000,000	9,700
1997	2,580,000 computers	$6,300,000,000	13,300
1998	even more computers!	$7,500,000,000	19,300
1999	even more computers!	$8,600,000,000	21,000

For each year, that chart shows how many computers were sold during the year, the total numbers of dollars that customers paid for them and for add-ons, and how many employees Gateway had at the year's end.

Here are highlights from the history of Ted Waitt and his employees during those years:

In 1986, they moved to a bigger office in the Sioux City Livestock Exchange Building.

In 1988, Ted began a national marketing campaign by designing his own ads and running them in *Computer Shopper* magazine. His most famous ad showed a gigantic two-page photo of his family's cattle farm and the headline, "Computers from Iowa?" The computer industry was stunned — cowed — by the ad's huge size and the low prices it offered for IBM clones. In the ad, Ted emphasized that Gateway was run by hard-working, honest Midwesterners who gave honest value. (At that time, most clones came from California or Texas; but Californians had a reputation for being "flaky", and Texans had a reputation for being "lawless"). Though cynics called Gateway "the cow computer", it was a success. In September, the company moved a few miles south to a larger plant in Sergeant Bluff, Iowa. Gateway's operations there began with 28 employees.

In the summer of 1989, Gateway grew to 150 employees, so Gateway began building a bigger plant. To get tax breaks and business grants, Gateway built it upriver at North Sioux City, South Dakota, and moved there in January 1990.

In 1990, Gateway became more professional. In 1989, the "instruction manual" was 2 pages; in 1990, it was 2 books. In 1989, the "tech support staff" (which answers technical questions from customers) consisted of just 1 person, and you had to wait 2 days for him to return your call; in 1990, the tech support staff included 35 people, and you could get through in 2 minutes. Gateway also switched to superior hard drives and monitors. In 1990, customers paid Gateway 275½ million dollars, generating a net profit of $25 million.

By early 1992, Gateway was selling nearly 2,000 computers per day and had 1,300 employees, including over 100 salespeople and 200 tech-support specialists to answer technical questions. Not bad, for a company whose president was just 30! Since Gateway was owned by just Norm Junior and Ted, those two boys became quite rich!

In March 1993, Gateway hired its 2000th employee. In April 1993, Gateway sold its one millionth computer. In December 1993, Gateway went public, so now you can buy Gateway stock and own part of that dreamy company, which by May 1995 had become so big that it answered over 12,000 tech-support calls in one day.

On September 5th, 1995, Gateway's 6000 employees celebrated the company's 10th anniversary.

Now Ted owns 44% of Gateway's stock; Norm owns 8%.

Though Gateway's become huge and has offices worldwide (in France, Germany, Ireland, Australia, and soon Japan), it's still headquartered in North Sioux City, a small behind-the-times town that got its first 4-way stop sign in 1992, first McDonald's hamburger joint in 1994, and doesn't have any traffic lights yet.

Gateway gets along well with its neighbors: in fact, two former mayors of Sioux City have become Gateway employees!

Gateway's become a rapidly growing cash cow: moo-lah, moo-lah! But Gateway hasn't lost its sense of humor. When you buy a Gateway computer, it comes in a box painted to look like a dairy cow: white with black spots.

Ben & Jerry's Ice Cream sued Gateway for copying the idea of putting cow spots on packages. Meanwhile, Gateway sued a shareware distributor called **Tucows** for using spotted cows to sell computer products. Those suits have been settled.

On January 1, 2000, Ted Waitt decided to semi-retire: he turned the day-to-day operation of Gateway over to Jeff Weitzen, who had joined Gateway 2 years earlier after working at AT&T for 18 years. So now Jeffrey is Gateway's President and Chief Executive Officer (CEO), though Ted is still Chairman of Gateway's Board of Directors.

Gateway's ads Each Gateway ad begins with gigantic photographs.

In early ads, the photos showed individuals in beautiful landscapes. Later ads showed hordes of Gateway employees dressed as Robin Hood's men in Sherwood Forest, top-hatted performers in Vegas cabarets, teenagers in a nostalgic 1950's diner bathed in neon glow, or movie directors applauding a ship full of pirates.

The eye-popping photos, which seem to have nothing to do with computers, grab your attention. (Gateway's diner ad includes the only photo I've ever seen that makes meat loaf look romantic!) Then you get headlines and florid prose that try to relate the scene to Gateway's computers. Finally, after all that multi-page image-building nonsense, you get to the ad's finale, which reveals Gateway's great technical specifications (specs), great service policies, and low prices.

That way of building an ad — fluff followed by stuff — has worked wonders for Gateway! Idiots admire the photos, techies admire the specs, and everybody buys!

Gateway was the first big mail-order manufacturer to give honest pricing: the advertised price includes everything except shipping. The price even includes a color monitor. And since all components are high-quality, a Gateway system's a *dream* system. With dreamy ads and a low price, how can you *not* buy?

How to reach Gateway Gateway ships worldwide.

If you're in the USA,	phone Gateway at 800-LAD-2000.
If you're in Canada,	phone Gateway at 800-846-3609.
If you're in Puerto Rico,	phone Gateway at 800-846-3613.
If you're in Mexico,	phone Gateway at 95-888-888-0074.
From anywhere in the world,	phone Gateway at 605-232-2000.
Internet Web site:	www.gateway.com

Gateway's sales department is open weekdays 7AM-10PM, Saturday 9AM-4PM, Central Time. Gateway is closed on Sunday.

If you wish to write, address your mail to Gateway 2000, 610 Gateway Drive, PO Box 2000, North Sioux City SD 57049-2000.

Price list Gateway has advertised these prices:

CPU	MHz	RAM	Hard drive	Video	CD	Stereo speakers	Extras	Price
Celeron	633	64M	7.5 gigabytes	15" 4M	48X	2 speakers		$799
Celeron	733	64M	7.5 gigabytes	17" 4M	48X	2 speakers		$999
Athlon	800	64M	15 gigabytes	17" 16M	48X	2 speakers	printer, camera	$1299
Athlon	900	64M	30 gigabytes	17" 32M	DVD	2 speakers + subwoofer	printer, camera	$1599
Athlon	1000	128M	30 gigabytes	17" 32M	DVD	2 speakers + subwoofer	printer, camera	$1999
Athlon	1100	128M	45 gigabytes	19" 64M	DVD	2 speakers + subwoofer	printer, camera	$2499

For example, the chart's bottom line says:

Gateway will sell you a computer system in which the CPU is fast (an Athlon running at a speed of 1100 megahertz, which is 1.1 gigahertz), the RAM is big (128 megabytes), the hard drive is big (45 gigabytes), the monitor's screen contains a 19-inch tube (measured diagonally), the video card contains 64 megabytes of RAM, the CD-ROM drive can also handle DVD, and the 2 stereo speakers are supplemented by a third speaker (subwoofer) to produce a booming bass. The price includes an inkjet printer and a handheld digital camera, but don't get excited: the inkjet printer is slow, and the handheld camera produces just low-resolution pictures, 640-by-480. The total price is $2499.

Each of those Gateway systems includes a tower case, PCI bus, a 56.6-kilobaud fax/modem card (using x2 chips), a wave-table sound card, a 1.44M floppy drive, a mouse, Windows Me, and 1 year of free Internet access from America Online (AOL).

The price also includes the Microsoft Works Suite. Add $129 if you want Microsoft Office Small Business Edition instead.

Prices drop Gateway advertised those prices in September 2000. By the time you read this book, Gateway's advertised prices might be even lower.

When you phone Gateway to check a price, Gateway's salespeople often quote you a *lower* price than advertised. That's because Gateway's prices drop often, and the ads aren't as up-to-date as what the salespeople say. Moreover, Gateway likes to fool competitors by pretending to have high prices while actually offering prices so low you can't say no, so competitors can't figure out why everybody's buying from Gateway.

Gateway usually drops its prices during the last week of each month. **If you order from Gateway's Internet Web site instead of by phone, Gateway often deducts $50.**

Shipping If you order a computer, you must typically wait 3 weeks to receive it because Gateway is swamped with orders and won't ship until about 3 weeks after you order. Then Gateway will ship the computer by 2-day air and charge you $95 for shipping.

Customers complain that $95 is too much for shipping, so Gateway's begun offering another choice: for just $50, Gateway will ship by UPS ground instead, which takes about a week.

Tax Like most mail-order companies, Gateway used to charge sales tax just to customers who were in Gateway's state (South Dakota). Recently, Gateway's been forced to charge tax to customers in California, New York, Florida, Massachusetts, Kentucky, and many other states — about 30 states altogether! When you phone Gateway, ask the salesperson whether *you* must pay tax.

Support Gateway's warranty used to be just 1 year, but now Gateway gives a 3-year warranty on the entire system. Gateway also gives you a 30-day money-back guarantee, lifetime toll-free tech support, 3-year on-site service (from Dow Jones, if you're within 100 miles of a Dow Jones service center), and free shipping of replacement parts by overnight air.

If you have a problem and want to speak to a technician, phone Gateway's technical-support department at 800-846-2301. Gateway advertises "24-hour technical support", but that's just for helpful recorded messages: live humans are usually available just weekdays 6AM-midnight, Saturday 9AM-2PM, Central Time.

Delays Up through 1992, Gateway's popularity grew rapidly, and Gateway got more customers than its staff could handle.

> Customers complained about getting busy signals, shipping delays, and incompetent tech-support staff. The delays got worse and worse, until they reached a crisis point in January 1993. By then, many of Gateway's former customers got disgusted, switched to other vendors instead, and complained to me and other journalists. *Infoworld*, *The Wall Street Journal*, and I wrote articles saying how bad Gateway had become.
>
> That was enough of a "kick in the pants" to make Gateway clean up its act. After January 1993, Gateway gradually improved the quantity and quality of its staff. By August 1993 Gateway's service and support had become no worse than the industry average.
>
> But in September 1993, Gateway started to get overloaded again; and by Christmas 1993, Gateway was so overloaded that customers began to complain. By January 1994, Gateway was back in a full-blown crisis again — just like the year before! Throughout the first half of 1994, Gateway's delays were intolerable: 5 weeks to get a computer, and next-to-impossible to get through to the technical-service department.
>
> Then Gateway improved again. Shipping delays dropped from 5 weeks back down to 2 weeks. Gateway added more technicians to its staff and in November 1994 built a new, expanded service department in Kansas City, Missouri. By the summer of 1995, Gateway's technical support had improved so much that the computer magazines were saying Gateway's technical support was actually *good!*
>
> When Windows 95 came out on August 24, 1995, Gateway suddenly got swamped with questions about it, and Gateway became overloaded. Callers to Gateway's technical-support number were greeted with a recorded message that began, "Due to the large number of Windows 95 calls...."

Now Gateway's catching up, and delays in getting through to technical support are decreasing. But I expect the tech-support staff at Gateway, like the rest of the computer industry, will continue to be overloaded each December & January (when Americans try to understand & fix the computers received for Christmas) and underloaded each July & August (when Americans think about the beach instead of computers).

Every January, newspapers print articles about how awful Gateway is; then Gateway apologizes; then by August everybody praises Gateway for being wonderful; and then the following January everybody wants to sue Gateway again.

Aren't business cycles fun?

Premium Service If you pay a $99 bribe, Gateway gives you priority over other customers: you get a special 800 number to phone for faster technical support, and you get 3 years of on-site service instead of just 1 year. Gateway calls this **Premium Service**.

Stores Gateway used to sell just by mail but recently has set up **Gateway Country** showrooms in many cities. Each showroom is full of Gateway computers and decorated with cow spots. The showrooms also offer courses, but not much tech support. Some of the Gateway Country showrooms are inside **Office Max** office-supply superstores.

Keyboard Some Gateway computers come with the **AnyKey keyboard**, which is manufactured by **Maxiswitch** and completely programmable: you can program any key to do any function. For example, if you don't like the SHIFT key's location, you can program a different key to act as the SHIFT key.

Unfortunately, that feature is *too* fancy: many beginners accidentally hit the **Remap key**, which then remaps all the other keys so no key works as expected! Beginners have trouble finding the instructions that explain how to reset the keyboard to act normally again.

Worry no more! Here are the instructions for how to make your AnyKey keyboard act normal again:

> While holding down the Ctrl and Alt keys, tap the **Suspend Macro key**. That procedure will probably make your keyboard act normal again.
>
> If that procedure *doesn't* make your keyboard act normal yet, the Ctrl and Alt keys are themselves screwed up! Fix them by doing this: press the Remap key once, then the Ctrl key twice, then the Alt key twice, then the Remap key once. Then try the procedure again: while holding down the Ctrl and Alt keys, tap the Suspend Macro key.

Notebooks Gateway sells notebook computers, but the prices are too high (starting at $1399) and the warranty is short (just 1 year).

Gateway versus NuTrend Gateway charges more than NuTrend but sometimes provides better service and free Internet access. NuTrend gives you more hardware per dollar and charges tax just to California.

Packard Bell

Packard Bell was the first company to successfully sell cheap IBM clones through department stores. In November 1999, Packard Bell went out of business, but its influence lives on. Here are the details.

Packard Bell marketed mainly to average Americans in the early 1990's, when Americans were starting to get curious about computers but didn't understand them and didn't want to spend much. Since the average American avoided computer stores and feared buying a computer by mail-order, Packard Bell sold cheap clones through chains of discount department stores (such as Sears, Walmart, Sam's Club, Lechmere, Price/Costco, Staples, and Office Max). Department stores had been afraid to sell computers, because the stores didn't want to deal with repairs; but Packard Bell told the stores, "Don't worry: if the computer breaks, *we'll* fix it, and we'll handle all tech support." So the department stores tried selling Packard Bell computers. They were priced about $1000 (which at that time was much cheaper than other brands). They were popular because they were cheap, available in department stores, and included 15 easy-to-use programs, loaded already on the hard disk, for immediate access. The programs included games, tutorials, educational experiences, and simple productivity tools (such as Microsoft Works, which included a word processor, database, spreadsheet, etc.).

To keep the advertised price low, Packard Bell typically included a poor monitor (.39mm dot pitch, interlaced) or didn't include any monitor at all. Also Packard Bell provided programs on the hard disk but *not* on floppy disks: if you accidentally erased the hard disk, you lost the programs!

During the early 1990's, getting a Packard Bell computer repaired was tough. I wrote this comment in the 1990 edition of *The Secret Guide to Computers*:

> Warning: getting a Packard Bell computer repaired is tough. Dealers complain that Packard Bell doesn't provide replacement parts; customers complain that dealers say to phone Packard Bell, which rarely answers the phone. When it *does* answer, it says to leave your phone number for a call back. Then it either neglects to call you or tells you to phone a service company that tells you to get lost.

By 1993, Packard Bell improved slightly, but then Packard Bell's phone-support center got wrecked by the earthquake in Northridge & Los Angeles in January 1994. Customers who called after that got just circuit-busy messages.

In July 1994, Packard Bell moved its support center to Utah, which has fewer earthquakes. The support center was in the town of Magna, a suburb of Salt Lake City. But if you tried phoning Packard Bell's support center, you still usually got a recorded message saying that all lines were busy and you should try writing a letter or sending electronic mail instead. But sending "electronic mail" was difficult when your computer was broken!

In 1996, Packard Bell began requiring most callers to call a 900 number instead for software help.

In spite of its questionable repair record, Packard Bell grew rapidly and became one of the biggest computer companies in the USA. That's because Packard Bell had the right formula:

> good distribution (you can find Packard Bell computers at most department stores across the USA), good price (cheaper than IBM, Compaq, and other famous brands), good easy-to-use programs (though they're the cheap kind that don't cost Packard Bell much), repairs handled directly by Packard Bell (so the department stores don't need any computer technicians on their staff), and a good-sounding name ("Packard Bell")

The name "Packard Bell" sounded good because it reminded consumers of the Bell Telephone companies, and consumers thought "Packard Bell" might be related to "Pacific Bell" or some other well-respected phone company — perhaps a merger between Hewlett-Packard and Ma Bell? To encourage that misconception, Packard Bell's slogan was "America grew up listening to us."

But actually, Packard Bell began as an independent company that never had anything to do with phone companies. Back in the 1950's, some radios were built by a company called "Packard Bell". In 1986, an Israeli tank driver (Mr. Beny Alagem) came to the United States, started a computer company, and bought the name "Packard Bell" from the radio company for $100,000 to make his new computer company sound related to a phone company. Some states required him to sell his "Packard Bell computers" with a disclaimer warning consumers that Packard Bell computers are "not affiliated with any Bell System entity".

In surveys of customer satisfaction done by *PC Magazine* and *PC World*, customers who bought Packard Bell computers were much less happy than customers who bought other brands. Though the typical Packard Bell computer worked okay, if you *did* need a repair you'd get *very* frustrated trying to reach Packard Bell's tech-support center.

But a *few* Packard Bell customers were *thrilled* with tech support! That's because they bought their Packard Bell computers from computer stores instead of department stores, and the computer stores were willing to fix computers immediately without waiting for the customers to phone Packard Bell.

Eventually, Packard Bell became more traditional:

> Packard Bell switched to a better monitor (.28mm dot pitch, non-interlaced), though it was typically "not included" in the advertised price. Fewer programs were included. Packard Bell provided 2 disks (1 floppy disk plus 1 CD-ROM disk) that contained copies of what was on the hard disk.

Packard Bell's competitors eventually copied Packard Bell's good features and avoided Packard Bell's bad features, so consumers switched to those nicer companies and avoided Packard Bell. Finally, in 1998, Packard Bell ran into financial difficulties and couldn't pay its suppliers. To bail itself out, it sold its stock to a Japanese company, **Nippon Electric Company (NEC)**, so Packard Bell became owned by NEC and was called **NEC Packard Bell**. But in November 1999, NEC finally gave up trying to run Packard Bell and shut Packard Bell down.

Compaq

The first company that made high-quality IBM clones was **Compaq**. (Before Compaq, the only IBM clones available were crummy.)

Now **Compaq sells more computers than any other manufacturer**. Yes, it sells more computers than IBM, Gateway, Dell, Packard Bell, and the rest of the gang.

Compaq is based in Houston, Texas. You can reach Compaq by phoning 800-at-Compaq or viewing Compaq's Internet Web site, www.compaq.com.

How Compaq began

It all began on a napkin. Sitting in a restaurant, two engineers drew on a napkin their picture of what the ideal IBM clone would look like. Instead of being a desktop computer, it would be a luggable having a 9-inch built-in screen and a handle, the whole computer system being small enough so you could pick it up with one hand. Then they built it! Since it was compact, they called it the **Compaq Portable Computer** and called the company **Compaq Computer Corporation**.

They began selling it in 1983, helped by venture-capital funding from Ben Rosen. They charged about the same for it as IBM charged for the IBM PC.

They sold it just to dealers who'd been approved by IBM to sell the IBM PC. That way, they knew all their dealers were reliable — and they competed directly against IBM, in the same stores.

They succeeded fantastically. That first year, sales totaled 100 million dollars.

In 1984, they inserted a hard drive into the computer and called that souped-up luggable the **Compaq Plus**. They also built a desktop computer called the **Deskpro**. Like Compaq's portable computers, the Deskpro was priced about the same as IBM's computers, was sold just through IBM dealers, and was built well — a marvel of engineering, better than IBM's.

Later, Compaq expanded: it built IBM clones in many sizes, from towers down to subnotebooks. Compaq computers have gotten the highest praise — and ridiculously high prices. On many technological issues, Compaq has been the first company to innovate: for example, when Intel invented the 386 chip, the first company to use it was Compaq, not IBM.

New leadership

Compaq was founded by Rod Canion. Under his leadership, Compaq developed a reputation for high quality and high prices. Engineers said that Compaq's computers were **overdesigned**: they were built more sturdily than necessary for average use and were therefore too expensive.

Worried about Compaq's high prices, some Compaq employees went on a secret mission, without telling Rod: they sneaked into a computer show, pretended they weren't from Compaq, pretended they were starting a new computer company, and tried to buy computer parts from Compaq's suppliers. Compaq's suppliers offered them lower prices than the suppliers were offering Compaq — because Compaq had developed a reputation as an overly fussy company to do business with.

The secret missionaries went back to Compaq and reported their findings to the board of directors, who were becoming upset at Compaq's astronomically high prices; so in 1991 the board fired Rod and replaced him with a cost cutter, Eckhard Pfeiffer (from Germany).

He lowered Compaq's prices, so Compaq became affordable, and he gave up the idea that Compaq should have super-high quality. He began selling through a greater variety of dealers and through mail-order.

The low-price wide-distribution strategy worked well. More people bought Compaq computers. Sales zoomed, though Compaq's "quality reputation" declined.

Yes, Compaq started to imitate Packard Bell: Compaq lowered its prices and its service!

In February 1995, Compaq started this nasty new service policy:

> If you phone Compaq for help, Compaq's staff asks for your credit-card number first, then listens to your questions. Unless your difficulties are caused by a mistake made by Compaq Corporation, you're charged $35 per question.

Eventually, Compaq dropped that nasty policy: tech-support calls are now free during the "initial period" (1 year on hardware questions, 3 months on software questions, longer if your Compaq was expensive): call 800-ok-Compaq, day or night (24 hours).

> After the "initial period" is over, help costs $19.95 per question, billed to your credit card when you call 800-ok-Compaq. (If your question has a short answer, you can pay less by calling 900-RED-HELP instead, which charges $2 per minute, $20 maximum.)

Eventually, Compaq started having financial difficulties, because Eckhard Pfeiffer made Compaq buy Digital Equipment Corporation and also because Compaq was having trouble competing against IBM clones priced under $700; so the board of directors fired him.

Now Compaq is run by Michael Capellas, a low-key friendly computer technician that everybody likes. He's trying to create computers that are low-cost but exciting. Though he's the Chief Executive Officer (CEO), the Chairman of the Board is still Ben Rosen (the venture capitalist who funded the founder).

Bargain notebooks

In July 2000, I had to buy a notebook computer for my stepdaughter. Since I'm supposed to be a "computer expert", I dutifully looked at all the ads in computer magazines and talked to my friends in the computer industry, trying to find the best deal. I thought the best deal would be some sort of mail-order company; but the best deal on a notebook computer turned out to be from Compaq!

I bought a **Compaq Presario 1200-XL118**. Here's why it was a great deal....

> Its list price was $1199. The box included a $100 rebate coupon from Compaq, bringing the effective price down to $1099. Circuit City was having a "$100 off" sale that week, bringing the effective price down to $999. Instead of buying at Circuit City, I bought it at Staples, which has a price-matching policy and was also supposed to have a huge extra rebate for good customers that month, though I later discovered that Staples' "extra rebate" is just for office supplies, not computers. (I hate misleading advertising — don't you?)
>
> I chose that model because it contains everything a normal person needs, at a low price. It includes an adequate CPU chip (AMD K6-2 at 500 megahertz), an adequate RAM (64 megabytes), an adequate hard drive (6 gigabytes), an adequate screen (13-inch color 800-by-600 HPA), an adequate CD-ROM drive (24X max), a good pointing device (a Touchpad), a good pair of stereo speakers (built into the keyboard), the other hardware you expect (a 56K fax/modem, a 3½-inch floppy drive, a NiMH battery, an AC/DC adapter, and a phone cord), and good software (Windows, Microsoft Works, Microsoft Word, the Encarta encyclopedia, and anti-virus software). It includes many connectors so you can attach many other devices: you get a parallel printer port (so you can attach a printer), a traditional 9-pin serial port, a **Universal Serial Bus port (USB port)**, a **PS/2 port** (so you can attach a mouse or external keyboard), a video port (so you can attach an external monitor), a headphone jack (so you can attach a headphone or big speaker), a microphone jack (so you can attach a microphone), and a Type 3 PCMCIA card slot.

Now Compaq sells an improved version, the **Compaq Presario 1200-XL119**, for the same price ($1199) but including more RAM (96M instead of 64M).

Compaq also sells a variant, called the **Compaq Presario 12XL300**, for $1299. Its CPU is faster (a 600-megahertz Celeron instead of a 500-megahertz K6-2), though its hard drive is slightly smaller (5 gigabytes instead of 6) and its RAM is still 64M.

Compaq's prices do *not* include a carrying case.

Refurbished computers

Compaq is more honest than most competitors about returned parts. If a customer returns computer equipment and Compaq determines that the equipment works okay, Compaq resells that equipment to other customers, but just in computers marked "refurbished". (Other manufacturers, such as Packard Bell, have been dishonest: they've pretended refurbished computers were "new".)

To save money, consider buying a refurbished Compaq computer from the **Compaq Factory Outlet Store** (10251 N. Freeway, Houston TX 77037, 888-202-4368, 281-927-6700, www.compaqfactoryoutlet.com). But be careful: refurbished computers often contain outdated versions of Windows, outdated versions of other software, no rebate coupons. The warranty is just 90 days and is weakened by a bizarre clause that says: if Compaq can't fix your computer, Compaq can choose to give you your money back, minus a 15% restocking fee.

If you see the Factory Outlet Store's ad for a refurbished computer at an amazingly low price and ask the store about it, the store will usually say, "Sorry, that one is sold out."

Beware Although I bought a Compaq notebook, I still avoid buying Compaq desktops, for several reasons:

Compaq's advertised price doesn't include the monitor. For many Compaq systems, the monitor is very expensive, since Compaq's monitor includes the speakers. If you try to save money by getting a generic monitor instead of a Compaq monitor, you have no speakers and hear no sounds.

Compaq's modem and sound card are often combined — so if you try fiddling with the hardware or software for one of those two devices, the other device stops working.

Compaq's warranty period and free-technical-support period are usually shorter than for mail-order companies. When you buy a Compaq, the salesperson will try to talk you into spending about $200 extra for an extended warranty, because that overpriced extended warranty is where the store makes its profit. The extended warranty, sold to you for $200, costs the store just $50, because the third-party repair company doing the warranty work knows the warranty contains clauses that make the warranty useless in most situations. The warranty does not cover software, does not cover damage, does not cover tech support, does not cover explaining how to use the computer, does not cover services (such as "trying to recover the info from your hard disk before we reformat it"), does not cover computers that have been altered, and does not cover year 1, which is the year when you're most likely to need help.

Bargain notebooks

To buy a good notebook computer at a ridiculously low price, look at Compaq's under-$1300 offerings, which I discussed earlier. For fancier computers, at higher prices, explore these mail-order alternatives:

Sager (18005 Cortney Ct., Industry CA 91748, 800-669-1624, 818-964-8682, www.sagernotebook.com)
BSI (9440 Telstar Ave. #4, El Monte CA 91731, 800-872-4547, 818-442-0020, www.bsicomputer.com)
HyperData (809 S. Lemon Ave., Walnut CA 91789, 800-786-3343, 909-368-2960, www.hyperdatadirect.com)

All three companies became famous by advertising in *Computer Shopper* magazine. Sager still advertises there, but BSI & Hyperdata now advertise just on the Internet.

Though Sager still advertises in *Computer Shopper*, Sager offers slightly lower prices on its Internet Web site. Here's what they were when this book went to press in September 2000:

CPU	MHz	RAM	Hard drive	Screen	CD-ROM	Price
AMD K6-2	450	64M	6 gigabytes	13.3"	24X	$999
Pentium 3	700	64M	12 gigabytes	13.3"	DVD	$1875
Pentium 3	700	128M	12 gigabytes	14.1"	DVD	$2045
Pentium 3	800	128M	20 gigabytes	14.1"	DVD	$2195

Each screen is the best kind (color, active-matrix, 1024-by-768). Each computer includes the best kind of pointing device (a Touchpad), the best kind of battery (lithium-ion) a 56K fax/modem, stereo speakers (built into the keyboard), a 3½-inch floppy drive, lots of ports, and Windows, and comes with a free carrying case.

Dell

Though Compaq was the first company to make good IBM clones, its clones were expensive. The first company that sold fast IBM clones *cheaply* was **PC's Limited**, founded in 1984 by a 19-year-old kid, Michael Dell. He operated out of the bedroom of his condo apartment, near the University of Texas in Austin.

At first, his prices were low — and so were his quality and service.

Many of the computers he shipped didn't work: they were **dead on arrival (DOA)**. When his customers tried to return the defective computer equipment to him for repair or a refund, his company ignored the customer altogether. By 1986, many upset customers considered him a con artist and wrote bitter letters about him to computer magazines. He responded by saying that his multi-million-dollar company was growing faster than expected and couldn't keep up with the demand for after-sale service. (Hmm… sounds like Gateway!)

In 1987, Dell raised his quality and service — and his prices. In 1988, he changed the company's name to **Dell Computer Corporation**.

Now he charges almost as much as IBM and Compaq.

His quality and service have become top-notch. They've set the standard for the rest of the computer industry. In speed and quality contests, his computers often beat IBM and Compaq.

In 1997 Dell officially became the top dog in the computer-quality wars: according to *PC World* magazine's surveys of its readers, **Dell computers are more reliable than any other brand, and Dell's tech-support staff does the best job of fixing any problems promptly**. Dell has retained that title ever since.

Dell's ads bashed Compaq for having higher prices than Dell and worse policies about getting repairs — since Dell offered on-site service and Compaq doesn't.

For example, in 1991 Dell ran an ad calling Dell's notebook computer a "road warrior" and Compaq's a "road worrier". It showed the Dell screen saying, "With next day on-site service in 50 states, nothing's going to stop you." It showed the Compaq screen saying, "Just pray you don't need any service while you're on the road, or you're dead meat."

His ads were misleading. His prices were much lower than Compaq's *list* price but just *slightly* less than the discount price at which Compaq computers were normally sold. Though Compaq didn't provide free on-site service, you could sometimes get your Compaq repaired fast by driving to a nearby Compaq dealer.

Like IBM and Compaq, Dell has dropped its prices, though they're still higher than Gateway's. Dell tried selling through discount-store chains but gave up and decided to return to selling just by mail. Though Compaq is king of retail sales, Dell has become king of mail-order sales. Now Dell sells more computers by mail-order than Gateway and all other companies.

Dell computers used to come with this guarantee: if Dell doesn't answer your tech-support call within 5 minutes, Dell will give you $25! Dell doesn't make that guarantee anymore.

Dell gives lifetime toll-free technical support for hardware questions and usually answers its phones promptly. Unfortunately, Dell has reduced DOS & Windows technical support from "lifetime" to "30 days".

To get a free Dell catalog or chat with a Dell sales rep, phone 800-BUY-DELL.

Micron

Micron is one of America's biggest manufacturers of RAM chips. Recently, Micron began selling complete computer systems also.

Its computers come with lots of RAM (since the RAM chips cost Micron nearly nothing) and run fast. According to surveys of computer users by PC World, Micron's computers are extremely reliable. Micron used to be excellent at answering tech-support calls and resolving problems immediately, but at the end of 1995 Micron's tech-support staff started becoming overloaded. To reduce the overload, in February 1996 Micron started a new nasty policy: tech-support about software is now restricted to just 30 days. Micron's prices are high, like prices from Dell.

Micron bought a competitor called **Zeos** and phased out the Zeos name. Micron's in Idaho at 800-700-0591 or 208-893-8970.

Hewlett-Packard

Hewlett-Packard (HP) has sold minicomputers, printers, scanners, calculators, and other electronic devices for many years. HP equipment is always excellent but pricey. In 1995, HP began manufacturing an IBM clone called the **Pavilion**. You can buy it at your local computer store. It's popular because it costs less than Compaq's desktop computers and HP's service is slightly better than Compaq's.

Quantex

For many years, I recommended **Quantex** computers, because Quantex computers were high-quality but priced low. Of all the quality-oriented computer companies, Quantex charged the least. Occasionally, Quantex offered poor technical support, but in most months the technical support was fine.

That changed in January 2000, when many people who worked for Quantex technical-support department quit, to work for another company that paid higher. Also, though Quantex offered wonderfully fancy computers for about $2000, Quantex wasn't creative enough in developing computers priced at $1000, which was the price most consumers were starting to demand.

Quantex and its sister companies (**CyberMax**, **Pionex**, **Micro Professionals**, and **Computer Sales Professional's PC Professional**) were all secretly owned by **Fountain**, which was based in New Jersey and Taiwan. In August 2000, Fountain went chapter-11 bankrupt. Quantex is still in business, but barely, and it hardly ever answers phone calls anymore. Stay away from Quantex until it gets its act together again, if ever.

Industrial nuts

To get the lowest computer prices, many people have been phoning a secret group of amazing companies advertising in *Computer Shopper*. The group is called **the industrial nuts** because the employees are industrious, the prices are nutty, and the location is these two Los Angeles suburbs: "City of Industry" and "Walnut". The owners and employees seem mostly Chinese.

Recently, most of those companies shut down, but the following are still in business:

Company	Phone	Address	City	State	ZIP
ProStar Computers	800-243-5654, 626-854-3428	1128 Coiner Ct.	City of Industry	CA	91748
Sager	800-669-1624, 626-964-8682	18005 Cortney Ct.	City of Industry	CA	91748
Syscon Technology	888-538-8828, 626-854-1151	18343 Gale Ave.	City of Industry	CA	91748
Tempest Micro	800-818-5163, 909-595-0550	18760 East Amar Rd. #188	Walnut	CA	91789
Hyperdata Tech.	800-786-3343, 909-468-2960	809 South Lemon Ave.	Walnut	CA	91789

ProStar, Sager, and HyperData sell notebook computers.

Syscon advertises low prices for tower computers; but the prices are misleading, since they don't include a legal copy of Windows, for which Syscon charges $90 extra.

These 20 industrial nuts have gone out of business:

All Computer, Altus, A+ Computer, Bit Computer, Comtrade, Cornell Computer Systems, CS Source, Cyberex, Digitron, EDO Micro, Enpower, Multiwave, Nimble, PC Channel, Premio, Professional Technologies, Quanson, Royal, Wonderex, Zenon

Syscon is in the same building that Zenon was in and is probably owned by the same folks.

Cleveland commandos

In 1997, *Computer Shopper* was deluged with ads from a horde of companies in Cleveland and its suburbs. Those companies offered low prices, nearly as low as the industrial nuts. Recently, most of those companies shut down, but the following are still in business:

Company	Phone	Address	City	State	ZIP
Adamant Computers	800-284-2257, 216-595-1211	4572 Renaissance Pkwy.	Cleveland	OH	44128
Micro Pro	800-442-6786, 216-661-7218	5400 Brookpark Rd.	Cleveland	OH	44129
A2Z Computers	800-983-8889, 216-442-8889	701 Beta Dr. #19	Cleveland	OH	44143
Americomp	800-217-2667, 440-498-9620	5380-E Naiman Parkway	Solon	OH	44139

Those companies have advertised under alternative names:

Company	Alternative names
Micro Pro	Micro Pulse, Magic PC
A2Z Computers	First Compuchoice, Computer King
Americomp	American Computech, Microvision

Those alternative names are no longer used.

These 15 commandos have dived to their death and gone out of business:

American Micro, Amp Tech, Artcomp, ABC Computers, Cyberspace Computers, Digit Micro, Legend Micro, Micro X, Micronix, New Age Micro, Odyssey Technology, PC Importers, Quickline Micro, Starquest, Unicent

Alternatives

Here are other choices to consider....

Acer is a consortium of Taiwanese computer companies.

> It has 20 factories, sells computers in 90 countries, and has annual sales of about 3 billion dollars. Acer computers are particularly popular in Southeast Asia and Latin America. Acer makes "Acer computers" and "Acros computers". They've been sold mainly through computer stores and department stores, but recently Acer gave up trying to sell through department stores. Acer supplies parts for other brands of computers. Acer also sells by mail-order at 800-230-ACER, but Acer's prices aren't low enough to compete against mail-order companies.

AST is a big computer manufacturer in Irvine, California.

> "AST" stands for the names of its founders, "Albert, Safi, and Tom". Albert and Tom have left AST, which is now headed by Safi. (Computer-trivia question: what's Safi's last name, and how do you spell it? Answer: Qureshey.) AST builds fine computers, sold through computer stores and priced below computers from IBM & Compaq, though above mail-order. In 1993, Tandy (which owns Radio Shack) stopped building computers and sold its factories to AST. For a while, AST manufactured all Tandy and Radio Shack computers and also Dell's notebook computers. But recently, Radio Shack and Dell have switched from AST to other suppliers. AST's finances are shaky.

Monorail manufactured a wonderful computer that was the ideal compromise between being a desktop computer and a laptop computer.

> It was small (almost as small as a laptop computer) but cost much less than any laptop or notebook. It was the ideal computer for somebody living in a cramped apartment and living on a cramped budget. Though small and cheap, the computer was full-featured, so you could get your work done and use the Internet, too.
>
> Unlike other computers, which are boring white or beige, Monorail's computer was sexy black. It consisted of three parts: a mouse (which was black), a keyboard (which was also black), and a thin black box (which was 15 inches wide, 11 inches high, and just 3¼ inches thick). The black box's front was a notebook-style computer screen (dual-scan passive color), but the black box also contained the rest of the computer: CPU, RAM, hard drive, floppy drive, CD-ROM drive, stereo speakers, microphone, and fax/modem! Even though the black box contained all those goodies, notebook-computer technology let the box be just 3¼ inches thick.
>
> The price was just $799 for the standard version. I bought a souped-up version myself, and it's been the most trouble-free computer I've ever owned. Though slightly too large to fit in my lap, it fits in a big lady's handbag, which makes it easy to carry. The price was low because the computer includes no battery: you plug the computer directly into your room's electrical socket.

Unfortunately, when the price of traditional notebook computers dropped, Monorail decided to stop competing. Now Monorail makes just boring computers, like everybody else.

Midwest Micro still makes desktop & tower computers but has stopped making notebook computers. Its ads imitate Gateway's, but its service and support aren't quite as good. Midwest Micro is owned by a modem manufacturer called **Infotel**.

VTech is a Hong Kong company that made wonderful low-cost computers under its own label and the **Expotech** label. In earlier editions, I recommended them.

> VTech sold the Expotech label to a company called **Telecom**, which sold "Expotech" computers built by VTech, then sold "Expotech" computers built by competitors. If you have an Expotech computer, you can get repairs by calling the **Expo Direct** division of **Motherboards Direct** at 800-705-6342, where the sales manager is Tim Lilly, who worked at VTech and Telecom.

Bargain-brand computers are sold by discount department stores at low prices. Those computers cost so little because they're crummy. Check the specs! Here's another reason why those computers cost so little: when you ask the dealer for help, the dealer will typically say "I don't know. Phone the manufacturer." But you'll find that the manufacturer's phone number is usually busy. Before buying a computer, try this experiment: ask the dealer what phone number to call for repairs or technical assistance, then try phoning that number and see whether anybody answers!

Local heroes? In many towns, entrepreneurs sell computers for ridiculously low prices in computer shows and tiny stores. Before buying, check the computer's technical specifications and the dealer's reputation. If the dealer offers you software, make sure the dealer also gives you an official manual from the software's publisher, with a warranty/registration card; otherwise, the software might be an illegal hot copy.

A used computer whose CPU is slow (a 286) typically costs about $100. That price includes even the hard disk and monitor. Buy it from a friend, relative, or neighbor moving up to a fancier computer.

For further advice, phone me anytime at 603-666-6644.

APPLE

Apple's influence

What's the most important computer company? IBM? Microsoft?

No! The most important computer company is actually **Apple**. That's the company that's had the greatest influence on how we deal with computers today.

Apple was the first computer manufacturer to popularize these ideas successfully:

> screens showing colors (instead of just black-and-white)
>
> 3½-inch floppy disks (instead of 5¼-inch, which are flimsy and less reliable)
> CD-ROM disks (instead of just floppy disks, which hold less data)
>
> using a mouse (instead of just the keyboard's arrow keys and TAB keys)
> using pictures (called **icons**) instead of just words
> pull-down menus (coming down from a menu bar, which is at the screen's top)
>
> laser printers (instead of just dot-matrix printers, which print in an ugly way)
> desktop publishing (instead of word processing, which can't handle beauty)
> pretty fonts (instead of typewriter-style fonts, which are monospaced and ugly)
> paint & draw programs (so you can create graphics easily, without math)

Apple didn't *invent* any of those ideas, but Apple was the first company to *popularize* them, make people *want* them, and thereby change our idea of what a computer should do.

> 3½-inch disks were invented by Sony. The first mouse was invented by the Stanford Research Institute. The first good mouse software was invented by Xerox. The first personal laser printers were invented by Hewlett-Packard. The first modern desktop-publishing program was invented by a software company, Aldus. But it was Apple's further product development and marketing that made those products *desirable*.

Though just 4% of the computers sold today are made by Apple, we all owe a big debt to Apple for how that company improved our world.

Here's how Apple arose and changed our lives....

Original Apple

The original Apple computer was invented by Steve Wozniak, who was an engineer at Hewlett-Packard. In 1975, he offered the plans to his boss at Hewlett-Packard, but his boss said Steve's computer didn't fit into Hewlett-Packard's marketing plan. His boss suggested that Steve start his own company. Steve did.

He worked with his friend, Steve Jobs. Steve Wozniak was the engineer; Steve Jobs was the businessman. Both were young: Steve Wozniak was 22; Steve Jobs was 19. Both were college drop-outs. They'd worked together before: when high-school students, they'd built and sold **blue boxes** (boxes that people attached to telephones to illegally make long-distance calls free). Steve & Steve had sold 200 blue boxes at $80 each, giving them a total of $16,000 in illegal money.

To begin Apple Computer Company, Steve & Steve invested just $1300, which they got by selling a used Volkswagen Micro Bus and a used calculator.

They built the first Apple computer in their garage. They sold it by word of mouth, then later by ads. The advertised price was just $666.60.

Like all computers of that era, the first Apple computer was primitive: it had *none* of the features for which Apple is now famous. (No color, no 3½-inch floppy disks, no CD-ROM disks, no mouse, no icons, no pull-down menus, no laser printers, no desktop publishing, no pretty fonts, no paint & draw programs.)

Apple 2

The original Apple computer looked pathetic. But in 1977, Steve & Steve invented a slicker version, called the **Apple 2**. Unlike the original Apple, the Apple 2 included a keyboard and displayed graphics in color. It cost $970.

The Apple 2 became a smashing success, because it was the first computer for under $1000 that could display colors on a TV. It was the *only* such computer for many years, until Commodore finally invented the Vic, which was even cheaper (under $300).

At first, folks used the Apple 2 just to play games and didn't take it seriously. But two surprise events changed the world's feelings about Apple.

MECC

The first surprise was that the Minnesota state government decided to buy lots of Apple 2 computers, put them in Minnesota schools, and write programs for them. That state agency, called the **Minnesota Educational Computing Consortium (MECC)**, then distributed the programs free to other schools across America.

Soon, schools across America discovered that personal computers could be useful in education. Since the only good educational programs came from Minnesota and required Apples, schools across America bought Apples — and then wrote more programs for the Apples they'd bought. Apple became the "standard" computer for education — just because of the chain reaction that started with a chance event in Minnesota. The chain reaction spread fast, as teachers fell in love with the Apple's color graphics.

Visicalc

The next surprise was that a graduate student at the Harvard Business School and his friend at M.I.T. got together and wrote the first spreadsheet program, called **Visicalc**. They wrote it for the Apple 2 computer, because it was the only low-cost computer that had a reliable disk operating system.

(Commodore's computers didn't have disks yet, and Radio Shack's disk operating system was buggy until the following year. Apple's success was due to Steve Wozniak's brilliance: he invented a disk-controller card that was amazingly cheap and reliable.)

The Visicalc spreadsheet program was so wonderful that accountants and business managers all over the country bought it — and therefore had to buy Apple computers to run it on.

> Visicalc was more nifty than any accounting program that had been invented on even the largest IBM maxicomputers. Visicalc proved that little Apples could be more convenient than even the most gigantic IBM.
>
> Eventually, Visicalc became available for other computers; but at first, Visicalc required an Apple, and Visicalc's success led to the success of Apple.
>
> In a typical large corporation, the corporate accountant wanted to buy an Apple with Visicalc. Since the corporation's data-processing director liked big computers and refused to buy microcomputers, the accountant who wanted Visicalc resorted to an old business trick: he lied. He pretended to spend $2000 for "typewriters" but bought an Apple instead. He snuck it into the company and plopped it on his desk. That happened all across America, so all large corporations had thousands of Apples sitting on the desks of accountants and managers but disguised as "typewriters" or "word processors".
>
> Yes, Apple computers infiltrated American corporations by subversion. It was an underground movement that annoyed IBM so much that IBM eventually decided to invent a personal computer of its own.

Apple 2+

In 1979, Apple Computer Corporation began shipping an improved Apple 2, called the **Apple 2+**.

Its main improvement was that its ROM chips contained a better version of BASIC, called **Applesoft BASIC**, which could handle decimals. (The version of BASIC in the old Apple 2's ROM chips handled just integers.)

Another improvement was how the RESET key acted.

> On the old Apple 2, pressing the RESET key would abort a program, so the program would stop running. Too many consumers pressed the RESET key accidentally and got upset. On the Apple 2+, pressing the RESET key aborted a program just if you simultaneously held down the CONTROL key.

Slots

In the Apple 2+ and its predecessors, the motherboard contained eight slots, numbered from 0 to 7. Each slot could hold a printed-circuit card.

> Slot 0 was for a **memory card** (containing extra RAM).
> Slot 1 was for a **printer card** (containing a parallel printer port).
> Slot 2 was for an **internal modem** (for attaching to a phone).
> Slot 3 was for an **80-column card** (to make the screen display 80 characters per line instead of 40).
> Slot 6 was for a **disk controller**.
> Cards in slots 4, 5, and 7 were more exotic.

Apple 2e

In 1983, Apple began shipping a further improvement, called the **Apple 2 extended, expanded, enhanced (Apple 2e)**. Most programs written for the Apple 1, 2, and 2+ also ran on the Apple 2e.

Keyboard To improve on the Apple 2+ keyboard (which contained just 52 keys), the Apple 2e keyboard contained 11 extra keys, making a total of 63. The extra keys helped you type lowercase letters, type special symbols, edit your writing, and control your programs.

For example, the Apple 2e keyboard contained all four arrow keys (↑, ↓, ←, and →), so you could easily move around the screen in all four directions. (The ↑ and ↓ keys were missing from the Apple 2+ keyboard.)

The Apple 2e keyboard contained a DELETE key, so you could easily delete an error from the middle of your writing. (The DELETE key was missing from the Apple 2+ keyboard.)

Slot 0 Unlike its predecessors, the Apple 2e omitted slot 0, because the Apple 2e didn't need a RAM card: the Apple 2e's motherboard already contained lots of RAM (64K).

Slot 3A The Apple 2e contained an extra slot, called **slot 3A**. It resembled slot 3 but held a more modern kind of video card that came in two versions: the plain version let your Apple display 80 characters per line; the fancy version did the same but also included a row of 64K RAM chips, so that your Apple contains 128K of RAM altogether.

Apple 2e versus IBM clones The Apple 2e was invented in 1983 — the same year as the IBM XT. Which was better?

An Apple 2e was generally worse than an IBM XT or an IBM XT clone. For example, the Apple 2e system had less RAM (128K instead of 640K), fewer keys on the keyboard (63 instead of 83), inferior disk drives (writing just 140K on the disk instead of 360K), and a crippled version of BASIC (understanding just 114 words instead of 178).

Though worse than an IBM XT, the Apple 2e became quite popular in 1983, because **more educational programs and games were available for the Apple 2e than for any other computer**. That's because the Apple 2e still ran thousands of programs that were invented years earlier for its predecessors: the Apple 1, 2, and 2+. Fewer educational programs and games were being written for the IBM XT and clones, because the IBM XT cost more than schools and kids could afford. Although the IBM XT became the standard computer for business, the Apple 2e became the standard computer for schools and kids.

Apple 2c

In 1984, Apple created a shrunken Apple 2e called the **Apple 2 compact (Apple 2c)**. Besides being smaller and lighter than the Apple 2e, it cost less. It also consumed less electricity.

But advanced hobbyists spurned the 2c — and stayed with the 2e instead — because the 2c didn't have any slots for adding cards; it wasn't expandable.

> The typical consumer didn't need extra cards anyway, since the 2c's motherboard included everything a beginner wanted: 128K of RAM, 80-character-per-line video circuitry, a disk controller, and two serial ports. You could run cables from the back of the 2c to a serial printer, modem, second disk drive, and joystick.

When the 2c first came out, its ROM was fancier than the 2e's, so that the 2c could handle BASIC and a mouse better than the 2e. But in February 1985, Apple began putting the fancy ROM chips in the 2e also, so that every new 2e handles BASIC and a mouse as well as the 2c.

Apple 2c+ Apple invented an improved Apple 2c, called the **Apple 2c+**, whose disk drive was 3½-inch instead of 5¼-inch. Apple's 3½-inch drive was technologically superior to Apple's 5¼-inch drive; but unfortunately, most educational software still came on 5¼-inch disks and was not available on 3½-inch disks yet.

Apple 2GS

In 1986, Apple created an improved version of the Apple 2e and called it the **Apple 2 with amazing graphics & sound (Apple 2GS)**.

> Its graphics were fairly good (better than EGA, though not as good as VGA). Its musical abilities were amazing. They arose from Apple's **Ensoniq chip**, which could produce 32 musical voices simultaneously!
>
> The computer contained an extra-fast CPU (the 65816), 128k of ROM, 256K of general-purpose RAM, and 64K of RAM for the sound synthesizer.
>
> To run the popular 2GS programs, you needed add an extra 256K of RAM, to bring the total RAM up to 512K. Many folks went further and bought 1M of RAM.
>
> Discount dealers sold the 2GS with 1M RAM for $800. That price did *not* include a monitor or any disk drives. To run the popular programs well, you had to buy a *color* monitor and *two* disk drives.

Apple 2 family

All those computers resembled each other, so that most programs written for the Apple 2 also worked on the Apple 2+, 2e, 2c, 2c+, and 2GS.

Apple has stopped marketing all those computers, but you can still buy them as "used computers" from your neighbors.

Clones

Instead of buying computers built by Apple, some folks bought imitations, such as the **Pineapple**, the **Orange**, the **Pear**, and the **Franklin**. Such imitations were popular in the United States, Hong Kong, and especially the Soviet Union. Apple sued most of those companies (because they illegally copied Apple's ROM) and made them stop building clones.

Laser 128 Apple permitted one clone to remain: the **Laser 128**, because that clone's designer imitated the functions of Apple's ROM without exactly copying it.

> The Laser 128 imitated the Apple 2c. Like the Apple 2c, the Laser 128 included 128K of RAM, a disk drive, and a serial port. In three ways, it was *better* than an Apple 2c: it included a parallel printer port (so you could attach a greater variety of printers), a numeric keypad (so you could enter data into spreadsheets more easily), and a slot (so you could add an Apple 2e expansion card). It ran most Apple 2c programs perfectly. (Just 5% of the popular Apple 2c programs were incompatible with the Laser 128.)
>
> A souped-up version, called the **Laser 128EX**, went three times as fast.
>
> The Laser 128 and 128EX were built by the **Laser Computer** division of **VTech**, the same company that made IBM clones.

Apple 3

Back in 1980, shortly after the Apple 2+ was invented, Apple began selling the **Apple 3**. It was much fancier than the Apple 2+. Unfortunately, it was ridiculously expensive (it listed for $4995, plus a monitor and hard drive), it couldn't run some of the Apple 2+ software, and the first ones off the assembly line were defective. Few people bought it.

When the IBM PC came out and consumers realized the PC was better and cheaper than the Apple 3, interest in the Apple 3 vanished. Apple gave up trying to sell the Apple 3 but incorporated the Apple 3's best features into later, cheaper Apples: the Apple 2e and the Apple 2GS.

Lisa

Back in 1963, when Steve & Steve were just kids in elementary school, Doug Engelbart invented the world's first computer mouse. He was at the Stanford Research Institute. During the 1970's, researchers at **Xerox's Palo Alto Research Center (Xerox PARC)** used his mouse as the basis of a fancy computer system, called the **Alto**. Xerox considered the Alto too big and expensive to sell well but invited the world to see it.

In 1979, Apple employees nudged Steve Jobs to go to Xerox and see the Alto. Steve was impressed by the Alto and decided to invent a smaller, cheaper version, which he called the **Lisa**, because that was his daughter's name.

The Lisa changed the computer world forever. Before the Lisa, personal computers were awkward to use. The Lisa was the first affordable personal computer that made good use of a **mouse**, **icons**, **horizontal menus**, and **pull-down menus**.

> The Lisa's screen displayed cute little drawings, called **icons**. Some of the icons stood for activities. To make the Lisa perform an activity, you looked on the screen for the activity's icon. (For example, to make the computer delete a file, you began by looking for a picture of a garbage can.) When you pointed at the icon by using a mouse, and clicked the mouse's button, the Lisa performed the icon's activity.
>
> The Lisa also used **horizontal menus** and **pull-down menus**. (A horizontal menu is a list of topics printed across the top line of the screen. If you choose one of those general topics by using the mouse, a column of more specific choices appears underneath that topic; that column of specific activities is called a **pull-down menu**. You then look at the pull-down menu, find the specific activity you're interested in, click at it by using the mouse, and the computer immediately starts performing that activity.)
>
> Pointing at icons, horizontal menus, and pull-down menus is much easier to learn than using the kinds of computer systems other manufacturers had developed before. It's also fun! Yes, the Lisa was the first computer whose business programs were truly fun to run. And because it was so easy to learn to use, customers could start using it without reading the manuals. Everybody praised the Lisa and called it a new breakthrough in software technology.

Though the Lisa was "affordable", it was affordable by just the rich: it cost nearly $10,000. For the Lisa, Apple invented some special business programs that were fun and easy to use; but the Lisa could *not* run Apple 2 programs, since the Lisa had a completely different CPU.

> Independent programmers had difficulty developing their *own* programs for the Lisa, since Apple didn't supply enough programming tools. Apple never invented a version of BASIC, delayed introducing a version of PASCAL, and didn't make detailed manuals available to the average programmer. And though icons and pull-down menus are easy to use, they're difficult for programmers to invent.

Apple gradually lowered the Lisa's price.

Macs

In January 1984, Apple introduced the **Macintosh (Mac)**, which was a stripped-down Lisa. Like the original Lisa, the Mac uses a mouse, icons, horizontal menus, and pull-down menus. The Mac's price is low enough to make it popular.

The Mac is even more fun and easy than the Lisa! It appeals to beginners scared of computers. Advanced computerists like it also, because it feels ultra-modern, handles graphics quickly, and passes data from one program to another simply.

The original version of the Mac ran too slowly, but the newest versions run faster. They're priced nearly as low as IBM clones.

Since the Mac's so easy to use and priced nearly as low as IBM clones, many people have bought it. Lots of software's been developed for it — much more than for the Lisa.

To run Mac software well, you must buy a Mac. Since popular Mac software does *not* run well on the Lisa, Apple has stopped selling the Lisa and stopped selling a compromise called the **Mac XL**.

The first Macs

Apple began selling the Mac for $2495. The Mac's original version consisted of three parts: the mouse, the keyboard, and the system unit.

> The system unit contained a 9-inch black-and-white screen (whose resolution was 512 by 384), a 3½-inch floppy disk drive, and a motherboard. On the motherboard sat an 8-megahertz **68000** CPU, two ROM chips (containing most of the operating system and many routines for drawing graphics), rows of RAM chips, a disk controller, and two serial ports (for attaching a printer and a modem).

That Mac was called the **original 128K Mac** because it includes 128K of RAM (plus 64K of ROM).

Then Apple invented an improvement called the **512K Mac** because it included 512K of RAM. (It used two rows of 256K chips instead of two rows of 64K chips.) Apple wanted to call it the "Big Mac" but feared that customers would think it was a hamburger.

In January 1986, Apple began selling a new, improved Mac, called the **Mac Plus**. It surpassed the 512K Mac in several ways:

> It contains a bigger RAM (1 megabyte instead of 512K), a bigger ROM (128K instead of 64K), a better disk drive (double-sided instead of single-sided), a bigger keyboard (which contains extra keys), and a port that let you add a hard-disk drive more easily. The improved ROM, RAM, disk drive, keyboard, and port all served the same goal: they provided hardware and software tricks that let Mac programs run faster.

Like the 128K and 512K Macs, the Mac Plus included one floppy drive.

Mac SE

In 1987, Apple introduced an even fancier Mac, called the **Mac SE**. It ran software 15% faster than the Mac Plus because it contains a cleverer ROM (256K instead of 128K) and fancier support chips. It was also more **expandable**: it let you insert extra circuitry more easily. The keyboard cost extra: you could buy the **standard keyboard** (which had 81 keys) or the **extended keyboard** (which had 105 keys and cost more).

Mac 2

When Apple introduced the Mac SE, Apple also introduced a luxury model, called the **Mac 2**. It contains a faster CPU (a 16-megahertz **68020**) and 6 slots for inserting printed-circuit cards.

Instead of sticking you with a 9-inch black-and-white monitor, it let you use any kind of monitor you wish: you could choose big or small; you could choose black-and-white or gray-scale or color. The monitor cost extra; so did the keyboard (standard or extended) and video card (which you put into a slot and attached the monitor to).

Since the Mac 2 let you choose your own monitor, the Mac 2 was called a **modular Mac**. When buying a modular Mac, remember that the monitor costs extra!

Performas vs. Quadras

In 1990, Apple stopped selling all the Macs that I've mentioned so far — the 128K Mac, 512K Mac, Mac Plus, Mac SE, and Mac 2. Apple switched to Macs that are more modern.

> Apple's first great modern Mac came in 1991. It was called the **Quadra**. It contained a **68040** CPU. It was called the **Quadra** because of the "4" in "68040". The **Quadra** was intended for folks smart enough to know that "quadra" is the Latin word for "4". It was intended to be sold by expert salespeople to expert customers.
>
> In 1992, Apple invented a "simplified Quadra", called the **Performa**, for beginners. It was intended to be sold by idiotic salespeople to idiotic customers, who think the word "performer" should be pronounced "performa".

Then customers could choose between the Performa (for beginners) and the Quadra (which was still available, for experts).

> Performa computers were sold mainly by idiots in office-supply stores (such as Staples & Office Max). Quadra computers were sold just by computer experts from computer stores (such as Comp USA).
>
> A Performa's price included lots of software — especially games and tutorials for beginners. A Quadra's price included very little software. You bought your own — or invented it yourself!
>
> For help with a Performa computer, you phoned "babysitters" at Apple's headquarters (800-sos-Apple). To repair a Quadra, you phoned the computer technicians at the computer store where you bought it.
>
> A Performa's price was simple: it included a keyboard, monitor, & fax/modem; no surcharges or choices! For a Quadra, you had to decide which keyboard, monitor, and fax/modem you wanted; they cost extra.

Though Performas were idiotic, they were the best values: you got more hardware and software per dollar when you bought a Performa than when you bought a Quadra. The Quadras were just for annoyingly fussy nerds who insisted on customizing the computers, making their own decisions about which keyboard, monitor, and fax/modem to use.

At first, the rule was simple: Quadras were sold just at computer stores; Performas were sold just at general stores. At the end of 1994, Apple began letting computer stores sell *both* kinds of computers (Quadras and Performas), to handle both kinds of customers (experts and idiots). Non-computer stores (such as Staples) were still restricted to selling to idiots: they sold just Performas, no Quadras.

Performas came in several varieties: you could choose a normal CPU (a **68030**), a faster CPU (a **68040**), or an even faster CPU (a **Power PC chip**).

Power Macs

After watching the Performa-versus-Quadra war, Apple decided on a compromise: all new Macs include a keyboard (Performa won that battle!), but you can typically choose your own monitor (Quadra won that battle!).

In 1994, Apple began selling powerful Macs, called **Power Macs**. Each contains a fast CPU chip, called the **Power PC**.

The newest kind of Power Mac is the **Power Mac G4**, invented in August 1999. In July 2000 it improved slightly, so its base price of $1599 includes:

```
mouse, keyboard, DVD drive, tower case (graphite gray front, silver gray sides, clear handles)
16M video RAM
400-megahertz CPU (add $600 for a pair of 450-megahertz, $900 for a pair of 500-megahertz)
64M RAM (add $150 for 128M, $450 for 256M, $750 for 384M, $1050 for 512M, $1650 for 768M)
20G hard drive (add $150 for 30G, $250 for 40G)
56K fax/modem (or else subtract $50)
```

That price does *not* include a monitor. For a 17-inch monitor (having a 16-inch viewable image size), Apple charges $499.

The price does *not* include a floppy-disk drive. To handle floppy disks, most Mac buyers pay $135 for a SuperDisk Drive (which can handle traditional 3½-inch 1.4-megabyte floppy disks and also 120-megabyte LS-120 SuperDisks).

Your total starting cost is therefore $1599 (for the base system) + $499 (for a 17-inch monitor) + $135 (for a SuperDisk Drive), which adds up to $2233. (You'll also want to add a printer.)

You can buy directly from Apple (at **800-MY-APPLE**) or from your local Apple dealer. Many dealers offer rebates and include extra RAM.

iMac

In August 1998, Apple began selling simplified Macs, to help beginners use the Internet. Each simplified Mac is called an **Internet Mac (iMac)**.

The original version cost $1299:

```
It was a 38-pound sort-of-luggable Mac that included a built-in 15-inch monitor, 24X CD-ROM drive,
56K fax/modem, stereo speakers, 4-gigabyte hard drive, 2-megabyte video RAM, fast CPU (a PowerPC
G3 chip running at 233-megahertz), and a 32-megabyte main RAM. The price also included a keyboard
and mouse.
```

Afterwards, Apple switched to better versions and also dropped the price:

Month invented	CPU	Main RAM	Hard drive	Video RAM	What it cost
August 1998	233 MHz	32M	4 gigabytes	2M	$1299
January 1999	266 MHz	32M	6 gigabytes	6M	$1199
April 1999	333 MHz	32M	6 gigabytes	6M	$1199
October 1999	350 MHz	64M	6 gigabytes	8M	$999
September 2000	350 MHz	64M	7 gigabytes	8M	$799

The iMac looks out-of-this-world!

```
It looks like an airplane's nose cone — or an ostrich egg from outer space. It's translucent — which
means you can almost see through it, like trying to look through a frosted shower-stall door to see the
sexy woman inside. Intriguing! Every reviewer who's seen the iMac loves it, and so do Apple's
customers. I bought one myself. It's great!
```

Instead of being old-fashioned white or beige, the iMac comes in eye-popping colors.

```
The 233MHz iMac is a blue-green aqua called Bondi blue, to honor the ocean waters of Bondi beach
(which is near Sidney, Australia). The 266MHz and 333MHz iMacs come in five fruit colors instead:
choose blueberry, strawberry, grape, lime, or tangerine. The 350 MHz iMac comes in blueberry
for the October 1999 model, indigo blue for the September 2000 model.
   Apple has been praised by designers for making the world more colorful, a rebellion from the old drab
world of white, beige, and black. (Inspired by that praise, Apple changed the Power Mac's color too, from
white to blue!)
```

To publicize the iMac, Apple invented many hip slogans, such as "I think, therefore iMac."

The iMac is a good deal, if you're satisfied with its small screen (15-inch instead of 17-inch). If you need a bigger screen, get a standard Power Mac instead.

The iMac's price does *not* include a floppy-disk drive.

```
To handle floppy disks, most iMac buyers pay $135 for a SuperDisk Drive (which can handle traditional
3½-inch 1.4-megabyte floppy disks and also 120-megabyte LS-120 SuperDisks). That brings the total
cost to $799+$135, which is $934.
```

The original iMac's mouse was circular, so it looked like a hockey puck or yo-yo. It was cute but confused beginners who couldn't tell which way to turn it. The September 2000 iMac's mouse is oblong and more practical; it's called the **Apple Pro Mouse**.

Your iMac normally comes with a "1-year warranty", which says Apple will fix the hardware if it breaks during the first year. Your iMac normally comes with just "3 months of tech support", which means Apple will give you free help about hardware and the operating system for just 3 months.

```
If you buy Apple's support contract, called AppleCare, which costs $149, your warranty and tech
support are extended, so they last for 3 years. AppleCare covers just Apple's hardware and the operating
system: it does not cover other hardware and software. I recommend you do not buy AppleCare: instead,
pay consultants and repair shops when necessary.
```

iMac DV

In October 1999, Apple invented a souped-up iMac, fancy enough to edit movies made with a digital video camera. That iMac was called the **iMac Digital Video (iMac DV)**. At the same time, Apple invented an even fancier iMac, called the **iMac DV Special Edition (iMac DV SE)**. Here are the specs:

Name	CPU	Main RAM	Drive	Color	What it cost
iMac DV	400 MHz	64M	10 gigabytes	5 fruits	$1299
iMac DV SE	400 MHz	128M	13 gigabytes	graphite gray	$1499

Each includes an 8M video RAM, a DVD drive (instead of a CD-ROM drive), **iMovie** (a movie-editing program) and two **FireWire ports** (so you can attach your Mac to two high-speed devices, such as digital video cameras).

In July 2000, Apple switched to these improved versions:

Name	CPU	Main RAM	Drive	Color	Price
iMac DV	400 MHz	64M	10 gigabytes	indigo blue or ruby red	$999
iMac DV+	450 MHz	128M	20 gigabytes	indigo blue, ruby red, or sage green	$1299
iMac DV SE	500 MHz	128M	30 gigabytes	graphite gray or snow white	$1499

The $999 version includes a CD-ROM drive; the other versions include DVD.

If you want a new iMac DV but don't have $999 in your pocket, no problem!

Apple offers loans for a new iMac DV: no down payment, no payments for 4 months, after which you pay about $24 per month for about 5½ years, bringing your total cost to about $1600.

PowerBooks

Back in 1991, Apple began selling notebook computers, called **PowerBooks**. In 1997, Apple began selling an improved version, called the **PowerBook G3**.

The newest Powerbook is the **PowerBook G3**. It includes a built-in keyboard, touchpad (which Apple calls a "trackpad"), 56K modem, and lithium battery. It comes in three versions.

The cheapest version, which is inspired by the iMac and called the **iBook**, costs just $1599. It comes in two colors: choose **blueberry** or **tangerine**. It includes a good screen (12.1-inch 800-by-600 active-matrix color with 4M video RAM), 300-megahertz CPU, 64M RAM, 6G hard drive, and 24X CD-ROM drive.

The next version, the **iBook Special Edition**, goes slightly faster (333 megahertz), comes in a more businesslike color (graphite gray), and costs $200 more ($1799). It's just for rich assholes who are willing to blow $200 for a slight increase in speed and a hoity-toity color.

The fanciest, most traditional version, costs $2499. It's black. It includes a fancy screen (14.1-inch 1024-by-768 active-matrix color with 8M video RAM), DVD drive, 400-megahertz CPU (add $500 for 500-megahertz), 64M main RAM (add $200 for 128M, $400 for 192M, and $600 for 256M), and 6G hard drive (add $300 for 12G, $600 for 18G). It's just for the super-rich who demand the ultimate power.

Since no floppy drive is included, add $135 for a SuperDisk Drive.

Clones

In 1995, Apple's executives began letting other companies make clones of Macs.

Those companies paid Apple a licensing fee. The most successful of those companies was **Power Computing**, whose clones run much faster than Apple's originals! Clones were also made by **Radius**, **Motorola**, and **Umax**.

But in 1997, Apple had a change of heart and withdrew the licenses of all the clone makers except **Umax**. Apple restricted Umax to making just clones that are "junk" (priced under $1000).

Should you buy a Mac?

When the Mac first came out, computer experts loved it and praised it for being easier than an IBM PC.

Then Microsoft invented **Windows**, which made the IBM PC resemble a Mac.

The first version of Windows was terrible, much worse than a Mac. Nobody took that version of Windows seriously. But over the years, Microsoft gradually improved Windows.

When **Windows 3.0** came out, it was good enough to be useable. Though still not as nice as a Mac, it became popular because it ran on IBM PC clones, which cost much less than Macs.

When **Windows 3.1** came out, some folks even *liked* it.

When **Windows 95** came out in 1995, the Mac became doomed. Most critics agreed that Windows 95 was *better* than a Mac. **Windows 98** was a further improvement. Moreover, an IBM PC running Windows 98 costs *less* than a Mac.

Now it's *Apple's* turn to play catch-up. I wish Apple well!

Apple faces a new problem: since practically everybody has switched to buying IBM clones (with Windows 98) instead of Macs, most programmers aren't bothering to write Mac programs anymore.

If you buy a Mac, you'll be stuck running old program versions, written years ago. Those versions aren't as pleasant as new programs. As a result, the Mac has actually become *harder* to use than an IBM clone!

The big exception to Mac's downfall is the graphics-art community.

Years ago, before Windows became good, folks in the graphics-arts community (such as ad agencies, newspapers, magazines, artists, and companies running printing presses) standardized on using Macs. They still use Macs.

Some universities standardized on Macs because Apple Computer Inc. gave those universities a discount. As the discounts expire, I expect most of those universities will shift to buying IBM clones instead.

After being founded by **Steve Wozniak** and **Steve Jobs**, Apple's leadership changed.

Steve Wozniak got in an airplane crash that hurt his head and gave him amnesia, so he left the company and enrolled in college under a fake name ("Rocky Clark"). After he graduated, he returned to Apple Computer Company quietly. Steve Jobs managed the company.

Though Apple was successful, Steve Jobs' strategies upset some computerists.

For example, Apple's ads claimed that the Apple was the first personal computer (it was *not* the first!); Apple launched a big campaign to make businessmen buy Apple PASCAL (though Apple PASCAL didn't help the average businessman at all); Apple prohibited its dealers from displaying games (though Apple later relented); and Apple prohibited authorized dealers from selling Apples by mail order.

Apple Computer Inc. donated computers to schools for three reasons: to be nice, get a tax write-off, and lure schools into buying Apples (to be compatible with the Apples that the schools received free). But if Apple were *really* nice, it would have lowered prices to let low-income consumers afford them. Apple sold just to the "chic", not the poor.

Steve & Steve both left Apple and went separate ways.

Apple's next head was **John Sculley**, a marketer who used to be a vice-president of Pepsi. He made Pepsi the #2 soft drink (just behind Coke) and kept Apple the #2 microcomputer company (just behind IBM).

In 1993, he had Apple invent and sell a palmtop computer called the **Newton**. Instead of containing a keyboard, it contained a tablet you could write on with a pen. The computer tried to read your handwritten words. But the computer couldn't read handwriting accurately enough. Apple's board of directors ousted him for spending too much effort on the Newton and not enough on Apple's mainstream products.

Apple's next head was **Michael Spindler**, an efficient German who dropped Apple's costs and prices. But in 1995, Apple's profits plunged for three reasons:

Microsoft began selling Windows 95 (which let IBM clones become nearly as pleasant as Macs).

Intel dramatically dropped prices on the Pentium chips used in IBM clones.

Spindler predicted incorrectly which Macs would sell well, so Apple got stuck with unsold inventory of some models, parts shortages for others.

In January 1996, Apple's board of directors fired him and replaced him with **Gil Amelio**. To cut costs, he fired lots of employees. Then the board fired him.

Now **Steve Jobs** is back in charge. He's popular.

ALTERNATIVE COMPUTERS

Commodore

Commodore, a computer company, is called "the house that Jack built" because it was started by Jack Tramiel.

How Commodore began

Jack began his career by being in the wrong place at the wrong time: he was a Jew in Poland during World War 2. He was thrown into the Auschwitz concentration camp, where he learned to view life as a war to survive. When he escaped from the camp, he moved to Canada and started an aggressive, ruthless company called **Commodore**, whose motto to survive was, "Business is war!".

At first, Commodore just repaired typewriters; but it grew fast and started manufacturing pocket calculators.

War of the chips

In Commodore's calculators, the CPU was a microprocessor chip manufactured by **MOS Technology**, a company with a troubled past:

> Back in 1974, the most popular microprocessors were the Intel 8080 and the Motorola 6800. But one of the 6800's inventors, a guy named Chuck Peddle, quit Motorola in 1975 and started a new company with his friends. That start-up company, **MOS Technology**, began manufacturing the 6501 microprocessor, which resembled Motorola's 6800.
>
> When Motorola threatened to sue, MOS Technology stopped making the 6501 and switched to the 6502, which Chuck Peddle designed differently enough to avoid a suit. That 6502 chip became very popular and was used in many devices, including Commodore's calculators. **Commodore was one of MOS Technology's biggest customers.**
>
> Though the 6502 was legal, **Motorola sued MOS Technology** for its illegal predecessor, the 6501. The suit dragged through the courts for two years and cost MOS Technology many thousands of dollars in lawyers' fees. Finally, in 1977, Motorola won $200,000. The lawyer fees and $200,000 put MOS Technology in financial trouble.

MOS Technology wanted to be bought by some company having lots of cash. Commodore, rich by then, bought it.

Just before that sale, Canada's tax laws changed. To duck taxes, Commodore moved its headquarters (in theory) to the Bahamas. That's how MOS Technology became part of "Commodore Limited", a Bahamas company, and how Commodore found itself running a company that made chips. Commodore had entered the computer business.

Dealing with competitors

At MOS Technology, Chuck Peddle had sold a 6502 chip to Steve Wozniak for $25. Steve used the chip to create the Apple computer. When Commodore saw Apple computers becoming popular in California, Commodore offered to buy the Apple Computer Company — and almost succeeded. Apple wanted $15,000 more than Commodore offered, so the deal never came off. If Commodore would have offered just $15,000 more, Apple would today be part of Commodore!

After failed negotiations with Apple, Commodore hired Chuck Peddle to design a "Commodore computer", which Commodore hoped to sell through Radio Shack's stores. Radio Shack said, "Great idea! Finish designing your computer, and tell us more." Commodore finished designing it and showed it to Radio Shack. Radio Shack said, "Your argument for selling low-cost computers was so convincing, we decided to build our own. Thanks for the idea." That's how Radio Shack got the idea of manufacturing computers!

Pet

Rebuffed by Apple and Radio Shack, Jack Tramiel decided to fight back by building a computer better and cheaper than anything Apple and Radio Shack had. Commodore called its new computer the **Pet**, because Commodore's marketing director was the guy who invented the Pet Rock. He reckoned that if folks were stupid enough to buy a Pet Rock, they'd really love a Pet computer! He was right: folks loved the idea of a Pet Computer. Sales skyrocketed.

Commodore told the press that "Pet" was an abbreviation for "Personal Electronic Transactor". Actually, Commodore invented "Pet" first and later made up what it stood for.

Commodore announced the Pet in 1977 and said its $495 price would include *everything*: the CPU, RAM, ROM, keyboard, monitor, and tape recorder. The ROM would have a good version of BASIC. The screen would display capital letters, lower-case letters, punctuation, math symbols, and many weirder symbols also (such as hearts, diamonds, clubs, spades, curves, circles, and rectangles).

Other microcomputer manufacturers were scared because Commodore's price was far below everybody else's, Commodore's computer offered more features, and Commodore was rich enough to spend more on ads & marketing than all other manufacturers combined.

Many computer magazines called the Pet "the birth of a new generation" in personal computers. The Pet's designer, Chuck Peddle, was treated to many interviews.

Disappointments Commodore raised its price from $495 to $595 before taking orders. To order the Pet, the customer had to send $595, plus shipping charges, then wait for Commodore to deliver. Many folks mailed Commodore the money and waited long, but Commodore didn't ship. Folks got impatient. Computer stores that had advertised the Pet got worried: customers who'd prepaid complained to the stores, but the stores couldn't get Commodore to ship.

Meanwhile, Radio Shack entered the market with its TRS-80 model 1 priced at $599 — about the same price as Commodore's Pet. **Radio Shack was kinder than Commodore:**

> **Radio Shack asked customers for just a 10% deposit.** Commodore required payment in full.
>
> **Radio Shack didn't charge for shipping.** Commodore did.
>
> **Radio Shack set up repair centers throughout the USA.** Commodore's only repair center was in California.
>
> **Radio Shack delivered computers fast.** Commodore still wasn't delivering! Finally, Commodore admitted that the $595 Pet would *not* be delivered anytime soon! Commodore would deliver instead a $795 version that included 4K of extra RAM. So if you already sent $595 to Commodore and wanted a computer soon, you'd have to send an extra $200. That was a rip-off, since 4K of extra RAM was *not* worth an extra $200; but customers were so desperate that they sent the $200 anyway.
>
> **Radio Shack shipped its computers on a first-come, first-served basis;** if you ordered a Radio Shack computer, Radio Shack gave you an accurate estimate of when you'd receive it. Commodore gave preferential treatment to its "friends"; if you ordered a computer from Commodore, you hadn't the faintest idea of when it would arrive, since you didn't know how many "friends" were on Commodore's list.
>
> **Radio Shack's computer came with a 232-page manual that was cheery and easy.** Commodore's computer came with just 10 loose pages that were incomplete and hard to understand.

After announcing a low-cost printer, Commodore changed its mind and decided to sell just an expensive printer. Commodore announced a low-cost disk drive but then reneged and decided to sell just an expensive unit containing two disk drives. Those lies lowered public confidence in Commodore.

At first, the Pet was the world's best-selling computer; but all those disappointments made its popularity drop to #3, below Radio Shack (#1) and Apple (#2).

Commodore developed a souped-up Pet, called the **Commodore Business Machine (CBM)**, but it wasn't enough to let Commodore rise above the number 3 spot. As Commodore's fortunes dipped, Chuck Peddle and his friends quit. Apple hired them but treated them as second-class citizens, so they returned to Commodore.

The problem with RAM

Commodore came out with several Pet versions, each containing a different quantity of RAM. If you bought a cheap version and wanted to increase its RAM, Commodore refused to install extra RAM: instead, Commodore insisted you buy a whole new Pet.

Some customers tried buying extra RAM from chip dealers and installing the chips themselves. To stop those tinkerers, Commodore began cutting a hole in the PC board where the extra RAM chips would go. Commodore was an asshole.

The problem with tape

Commodore changed the Pet's tape-handling system. The new system was incompatible with the old: tapes created for the old Pet wouldn't work on the new Pet. Commodore didn't tell customers of the change. Customers who wrote programs for old Pets and then bought additional Pets discovered that their programs didn't work on the new Pets. They thought their new Pets were broken.

When Commodore secretly changed the tape system, companies selling tapes of Pet computer programs received angry letters from customers who bought the tapes and couldn't make them work on their new Pets. The customers though the companies were crooks; the companies thought the customers were lying. Eventually, folks realized the real culprit was Commodore, who'd changed the Pet secretly.

When the companies discovered that Commodore had changed the Pet without providing a label to distinguish new Pets from old, the companies realized they'd have to give each customer two copies of each program, so the customer could try both versions. That's when many companies gave up trying to sell Pet tapes. They sold tapes for Apple and Radio Shack computers instead. Commodore programs became rare.

Vic

Jack's experience at Auschwitz made him scared of Nazis and the Japanese. He feared that the Japanese would invade the USA by flooding America with cheap Japanese computers to put Commodore and other American companies out of business. And he noticed that Commodore's share of the computer market was already sinking.

Paranoid, in April 1980 he called his engineers together and screamed at them, "The Japanese are coming! The Japanese are coming! So we'll become the Japanese!" He laid out his bold plan: Commodore would build the world's first under-$300 computer to display colors on an ordinary TV and produce three-part harmony through the TV's speaker. At that time, the only under-$300 computer was Sinclair's ZX-80, which was black-and-white and crummy.

Commodore's engineers replied, "Build a color computer cheaply? Impossible!" Jack replied, "Do it!" Commodore's engineers finally managed to do it.

MOS Technology, owned by Commodore, had already invented the amazing **Video Interface Chip (Vic)**, which could handle the entire process of sending computer output to the TV screen. Since that chip was cheap, Commodore decided to use it in the under-$300 computer. Unfortunately, it put just 22 characters per line on the screen. (By contrast, the Pet had 40 characters per line, and most computers today have 80 characters per line.) So the under-$300 computer would display just 22 characters per line.

Naming the computer

Since the new computer was feminine and foxy, Commodore wanted to call it the "Vixen". But Commodore discovered that a "Vixen" computer couldn't sell in Germany, because "Vixen" sounds like the German word "Wichsen", which is obscene.

Commodore hastily changed the name to Vic and ran TV ads for the "Vic" computer. But that got Commodore into even worse trouble, since "Vic" sounds like the German word "Ficke", which is even *more* obscene!

Commodore kept calling it the "Vic" in the USA but called it the "VC" computer in Germany and pretended "VC" stood for "Volks Computer".

Price

Commodore began shipping the Vic in 1981 at $299.95. Over the years, the price gradually dropped to $55.

Ads

To sell the Vic, Commodore tried three kinds of ads.

The first featured TV star William Shatner, who played Captain Kirk in Star Trek. The ad emphasized how the Vic was wonderful, amazing, out of this world, fun! But then people started thinking of the Vic as just a sci-fi toy.

To combat the "toy" image, Commodore changed to a second kind of ad, which said the Vic was as cheap as a video-game machine but more educational for your kids. When Texas Instruments began making similar claims, Commodore changed to a third kind of ad, which revealed that Commodore's disk drives, printers, and phone hookups cost much less than Texas Instruments'.

Popularity

The Vic's low price, fun colors, and effective ads made it become popular fast in the USA, England, Germany, and Japan. Commodore quickly sold over a million Vics! **The Vic became the world's best-selling computer!**

Commodore 64

In 1982, Commodore began selling an improved Vic, called the **Commodore 64** because it included 64K of RAM. (The original Vic had just 5K.) The Commodore 64 also improved on the Vic by displaying 40 characters per line (instead of just 22) and including 20K of ROM (instead of just 16K).

Price

The Commodore 64's price went through 4 phases.

In phase 1, $599.95 was the recommended list price, and Commodore tried to force all dealers to charge that. If a dealer advertised a discount, Commodore refused to send that dealer any more computers. (Commodore's policy was an example of **price fixing**, which is illegal.)

In phase 2, Commodore allowed discounts. Dealers charged just $350. Moreover, Commodore mailed a $100 rebate to anybody trading in another computer or a video-game machine. Bargain-hunters bought the cheap Timex Sinclair 1000 computer just to trade in for a Commodore 64. A New York dealer, "Crazy Eddy", sold junky video-game machines for $10 just so his customers could mail them to Commodore for the $100 rebate. Commodore donated most of the trade-ins to charities for a tax write-off but kept some Timex Sinclair 1000's for use as doorstops.

In phase 3, Commodore stopped the rebate but offered a lower price: discount dealers charged just $148.

In phase 4, the Commodore made an improved version, the **Commodore 64C**, which discounters sold for just $119. It came with a copy of the **Geos** operating system, which made it resemble a Mac; and its keyboard contained extra keys.

Why so cheap? Here's why the Commodore 64 cost so much less than an Apple 2c or IBM PC.

The Commodore 64's advertised price did *not* include a disk drive or monitor. Moreover, **Commodore's disk drives and monitors were terrible:**

Commodore's original disk drive, the Model 1541, needed repairs often (because its head went out of alignment), ran slowly (because its cable to the computer contained just one wire to transmit data, instead of several wires in parallel), and put few bytes on the disk (just single-sided single-density).

Commodore's original color monitor, the Model 1702, produced a blurry image (because the monitor was composite instead of RGB). Since the image was *not* sharp enough to display 80 characters per line clearly, most Commodore 64 software displayed just 40 characters per line. IBM PC software displayed 80 instead. Another problem with Commodore's video was that the M looked too much like N, and the B looked like 8.

Eventually, Commodore developed an improved monitor (the **1802**) and improved disk drives (the **1541C** and **1541-2**).

The Commodore 64 had a weaker BASIC than the Apple 2 and IBM PC. It didn't even include a command to let you draw a diagonal line across the screen.

The Commodore 64's printer port was non-standard: it worked just with strange printers manufactured by Commodore, unless you bought a special adapter.

Popularity Because the Commodore 64 was cheap, Commodore sold over a million of them.

Many programmers who wrote programs for Apple computers rewrote their programs to also work on the Commodore 64. Soon the Commodore 64 ran nearly as many popular programs as the Apple 2c.

The Commodore 64's price, even after adding the price of a disk drive and a monitor, still totaled less than the price of an Apple 2e, Apple 2c, IBM PC, or IBM PC Junior. The Commodore 64 was a fantastically good value! It also contained a fancy music synthesizer chip that produced a wide variety of musical tone qualities: when it played music, it sounded much better than an Apple 2e or 2c or IBM.

Jack jumps ship

After the Commodore 64 became successful, Jack Tramiel wanted to hire his sons to help run Commodore; but Commodore's other major shareholders refused to deal with Jack's sons, so Jack quit. He sold his 2 million shares of Commodore stock, at $40 per share, netting himself 80 million dollars in cash.

New computers

After Jack quit, Commodore tried selling two new computers — the **Commodore 16** and **Commodore Plus 4** — but they had serious flaws. Then Commodore invented two great computers: the **Commodore 128** and **Amiga**.

The **Commodore 128** ran all the Commodore 64 software and also included a better version of BASIC, better keyboard, and better video. To go with it, Commodore invented a better RGB monitor (**Model 1902**) and better disk drive (**Model 1571**). Later, Commodore invented the **Commodore 128D** computer, which included a built-in disk drive.

The **Amiga** is even newer and fancier. It contains three special chips that produce fast animated graphics in beautiful shades of color. Like the Mac, it uses a mouse and pull-down menus.

The Amiga's first version was called the **Amiga 1000**. Later, Commodore replaced it by newer versions: the Amiga 500, 600, 1200, 2000, 3000, and 4000.

Amigas are used mainly by video professionals and by others interested in animated graphics. On TV, weathermen use Amigas to show the weather moving across the weather map.

Aside from graphics, not enough good software is available for Amigas. The Amigas are not compatible with the Commodore 64 or Mac. The Amiga 2000 can be made to imitate an IBM PC but costs more than most IBM clones.

Bankruptcy

In 1994, Commodore filed for bankruptcy. What was left of Commodore was purchased by **Escom**, which then sold Amiga Technologies to **Visual Information Services Corp. (Viscorp)**, which sold it to **Gateway**, which has abandoned the technology.

Tandy

Tandy, which owns Radio Shack, has been around for many years.

Thanks to Tandy

Radio Shack helped the computer industry in many ways:

Radio Shack was the first big chain of stores to sell computers nationally. It was the first chain to reach rural areas.

Radio Shack invented the first low-cost assembled computer. That was the TRS-80 model 1, which cost $599, including the monitor.

Radio Shack was the first company to keep computer prices low without skimping on quality.

Radio Shack sold the first notebook computer. That was the Tandy 100, invented by Tandy with help from Microsoft and a Japanese manufacturer, Kyocera.

Radio Shack sold the first pocket computers. They were manufactured for Tandy by Sharp and Casio.

Radio Shack invented the first cheap computer having fancy graphics commands. That was the Color Computer, whose BASIC was designed by Microsoft as a "rough draft" for the fancier BASIC in the IBM PC.

But when the IBM PC came out and became the standard American computer, Americans became conservative and wanted to buy just traditional IBM PC's and clones. Tandy had difficulty figuring out how to be profitably innovative. Tandy tried building IBM clones innovatively, but in 1993 gave up: it stopped manufacturing computers and sold all its factories to another computer company, **AST**. Afterwards, Tandy sold computers built by AST, then switched to selling computers built by IBM. Now Tandy sells computers built by Compaq instead.

Nicknames

Tandy's computers are often called "TRS" computers. The "TRS" stands for "Tandy's Radio Shack". Cynics add the letters A and H, and call them "TRASH" computers, so Tandy's customers are called "trash collectors". On the other hand, Apple lovers are called "worms", "pie people", "fruits", and "suffering from Appleplexy"; IBM lovers are called "blue bloods" (because old IBM computers were blue); Commodore lovers are called "boat people", "swabbies", and "deck ducks"; and kids who play with Atari computers are called "Atari-eyed dreamers & screamers".

How Tandy began

The Tandy Leather Company was begun by Charles Tandy. Later, he acquired Radio Shack, which had been a Boston-based chain of discount electronics stores.

Under his leadership from his Fort Worth headquarters, Tandy/Radio Shack succeeded and grew 30% per year, fueled by the CB radio craze that was sweeping America. When the market for CB radios declined, he began looking for a new product to sell, to continue his 30% growth.

Commodore was inventing a computer and tried to convince Tandy's staff to sell it. Don French, a Tandy salesman whose hobby was building computers, told Charles Tandy that Radio Shack should start selling computers.

Instead of buying computers from Commodore, Radio Shack hired Steve Leininger to design a Radio Shack computer and **keep the cost as low as possible:**

Steve wanted his computer to handle lower-case letters instead of just capitals. But since attaching the lower-case chip would have added 10¢ to the cost, management rejected lower case: **Radio Shack's computer handled just capitals.** (In those days, lower-case letters weren't considered important. Later, when customers began demanding lower-case letters, Radio Shack regretted not spending the extra dime. Customers were spending $50 to rip open the Radio Shack and rearrange the chips to get lower-case.)

The monitor was a modified black-and-white TV built for Radio Shack by RCA. RCA told Radio Shack that the standard color for the TV's case was "Mercedes silver"; any other color would cost extra. Radio Shack accepted Mercedes silver and painted the rest of the computer to match the TV. When you use a Radio Shack computer, you're supposed to feel as if you're driving a Mercedes; but since Mercedes silver looked like gray, Radio Shack became nicknamed "the great gray monster". Californians preferred Apples, whose beige matched their living-room decors. (Later, in 1982, Radio Shack wised up and switched from "Mercedes silver" to white.)

Radio Shack's original computer listed for just $599 and consisted of four devices: a keyboard (in which hid the CPU, ROM, & RAM), a monitor (built for Radio Shack by RCA), a cheap Radio Shack tape recorder, and an AC/DC transformer. Wires ran between those devices, so that the whole system looked like an octopus. Radio Shack wanted to put the AC/DC transformer *inside* the keyboard, to make the computer system consist of three boxes instead of four; but that *internal* transformer would have delayed approval from Underwriters Laboratories for 6 months, and Radio Shack couldn't wait that long.

Radio Shack named its computer the **TRS-80** because it was by Tandy's Radio Shack and contained a Z-80 CPU.

To announce the computer, Radio Shack called a press conference to take place in August 1977 on a Monday morning on the front steps of the New York Stock Exchange. But when Radio Shack's leaders stood on those steps and were surrounded by reporters, a guy ran up and yelled that a bomb went off two blocks away. The reporters ran off to the bomb site, and Radio Shack couldn't announce its computer!

Radio Shack rushed to find a new place to announce the computer. Radio Shack heard that the Boston Computer Society was going to run a computer show that week — Wednesday through Friday. So Radio Shack's management drove to Boston, got a booth at the show, announced its computer there — and was shocked to discover that the whole show and Boston Computer Society were run by Jonathan Rotenberg, a 14-year-old kid!

That intro was successful: people liked and bought Radio Shack's new computer. The base price was $599. For a complete business system (including two disk drives and a printer), Radio Shack charged $2600, while Radio Shack's competitors charged over $4500.

Problems with DOS Radio Shack hired Randy Cook to write the DOS. My friend Dick Miller tried DOS version 1.0 and noticed it didn't work; it didn't even boot! He told Radio Shack, which told Randy Cook, who fixed the problem and wrote version 1.1. Dick noticed it worked better but still had a big flaw: it didn't tell you how much disk space was left and — even worse — as soon as the disk was filled it would self-destruct! Then came version 1.2, which worked better but not perfectly.

Since Radio Shack's DOS was still buggy, Visicalc's inventors put Visicalc onto the Apple instead of the TRS-80. Apple became known as the "Visicalc machine", and many accountants began buying Apples instead of TRS-80's.

Meanwhile, a Colorado company named Apparat invented its own improvements to Radio Shack's DOS. Apparat showed its improvements to Dick, who liked them and recommended calling them "NEWDOS". Many folks bought NEWDOS and formed NEWDOS colonies.

Dealing with the public In 1977, when Radio Shack began selling the TRS-80, customers didn't understand what computers were.

At a Radio Shack show, I saw a police chief buy a TRS-80. While carrying it out of the room, he called back over his shoulder, "By the way, how do you program it?" He expected a one-sentence answer.

Radio Shack provided a toll-free 800 number for customers to call in case they had any questions. Many customers called because they were confused. For example, many customers had this gripe: "I put my mouth next to the tape recorder and yelled TWO PLUS TWO, but it didn't say FOUR!"

Radio Shack's first version of BASIC provided just three error messages: WHAT (which means "I don't know what you're talking about"), HOW (which means "I don't know how to handle a number that big") and SORRY (which means "I'm sorry I can't do that — you didn't buy enough RAM yet"). Those error messages confused beginners. For example, this conversation occurred between a Radio Shack customer and a Radio Shack technician who answered the 800 number (Chris Daly)....

Chris: "What's your problem?"
Customer: "I plugged in the video, then the tape recorder, then…"
Chris: "Yes, sir, but what's the problem?"
Customer: "It doesn't work."
Chris: "How do you *know* it doesn't work?"
Customer: "It says READY."
Chris: "What's wrong with that? It's *supposed* to say READY."
Customer: "It isn't ready."
Chris: "How do you *know* it isn't ready?"
Customer: "I asked it 'Where's my wife Martha?', and it just said WHAT."

Other Z-80 computers After the TRS-80, Tandy invented improved versions: the TRS-80 Models 2, 3, 4, 4D, 4P, 12, 16, & 16B, and the Tandy 6000. Like the Model 1, they contained a Z-80 CPU and included a monochrome monitor.

Coco To compete against the Commodore 64, Tandy invented the **Color Computer**, nicknamed the **Coco**.

Like the Commodore 64, the Coco could attach to either a monitor or an ordinary TV, and it could store programs on either a disk or an ordinary cassette tape (the same kind of tape that you listen to music on).

Tandy began selling the Coco in 1980 — the year before IBM began selling the PC. Microsoft invented the Coco's BASIC ROM and also invented the IBM PC's. The Coco's BASIC ROM was Microsoft's rough draft of the ROM that went into the IBM PC. The Coco acted as "an IBM PC that wasn't quite right yet". In the Coco's BASIC, the commands for handling graphics & music were similar to the IBM PC's but more awkward. Folks who couldn't afford an IBM PC but wanted to learn to program it bought the Coco.

The original Coco was called the **Coco 1**. Then came improved versions (the **Coco 2** and **Coco 3**) and a cheap, tiny version (the **Micro Coco**).

Pocket computers Tandy sold 8 different pocket computers, numbered **PC-1** through **PC-8**. They fit in your pocket, ran on batteries, and included LCD screens.

Notebook computers In 1983, Tandy, Epson, and NEC all tried to sell cheap notebook computers. Just Tandy's became popular, because it was the cheapest ($499) and the easiest to learn how to use. It was called the **Model 100**.

Later Tandy sold an improved version, the **Model 102**, which included more RAM (32K), weighed less (just 3 pounds), and listed for $599. It including a nice keyboard, a screen displaying eight 40-character lines, a 32K ROM (containing BASIC, a word-processing program, some filing programs, and a telecommunications program), and 300-baud modem (for attaching to a phone, after you bought a $19.95 cable). It was 8½ inches by 12 inches and just 1½ inches thick. Reporters used it to take notes and phone them to the newspaper.

Popularity

Tandy's 7000 Radio Shack stores penetrated every major city and also remote rural areas, where few other computer stores compete.

Tandy offered "solid value". Tandy kept its quality high and its prices below IBM's and Apple's (though not as low as generic clones). Tandy's computers and prices were aimed at middle-America consumers, not business executives (who buy from IBM) or bargain-hunting hobbyists (who buy mail-order).

Tandy's computers were built reliably. Tandy's assembly line checked them thoroughly before shipping to Tandy's stores. If a Tandy computer needed repair during the warranty period, the customer could just bring it to the local Radio Shack store, which would fix it free even if the customer bought it from a different store. If the warranty expired, Radio Shack charged very little for the labor of fixing it.

Bad attitude

During the 1970's, Tandy's headquarters provided toll-free numbers that customers could call for technical help. Later, Tandy switched to numbers that were not toll-free. Recently, Tandy's become even worse, by refusing to answer any questions unless the customer buys a support contract. Tandy's claim to offer better support than mail-order companies is Texas bull.

During the 1980's, Tandy established a dress code for its computer centers: employees who met the public had to don blue or gray suits, blue or white shirts, no beards, and no moustaches. Tandy fired a center manager for refusing to shave his beard. Wasn't the personal-computing revolution supposed to give us tools to express our *individuality*?

Recently, Tandy shut down all its computer centers. At regular Radio Shack stores, beards are permitted.

Atari

Of all the major computer manufacturers, Atari has been the most creative — and the strangest!

Atari is in the USA's strangest state: California. Even Atari's name is strange: "Atari" is a Japanese war cry that means "beware!"

Video games

In 1972, Atari invented the world's first popular video game, **Pong**. Next, Atari invented the game called **Asteroids**, then dozens of other games. Atari's games were placed in arcades and bars. To play the games, you had to insert quarters. In 1975, Atari invented a machine that could play Pong on your home's TV.

In 1976, Atari gave up its independence and was bought by Warner Communications (the gigantic company that owned Warner Brothers movies & cartoons, Warner Cable TV, and DC Comics).

In 1977, Atari invented the **Video Computer System (VCS)**, a machine playing many games on your home TV. Each game came as a ROM cartridge. Later, Nintendo and Sega invented machines that were similar but fancier.

Early personal computers

In 1979, Atari began selling complete personal computers. Atari's first two computers were the **Atari 400** (cheap!) and the **Atari 800** (which had a nicer keyboard). They were far ahead of their time. Of all the microcomputers being sold, Atari's had the best graphics, best music, and best way of editing programs. Compared to Atari, the Apples looked pitiful! Yet Atari charged *less* than Apple!

But **Atari made two mistakes:**

> The first mistake was that **Atari didn't hire Bill Gates to write its version of BASIC**. Instead, it hired the same jerk who invented Apple's DOS. Like Apple's DOS, Atari's BASIC looks simple but can't handle serious business problems.
>
> The second mistake was **Atari's belief that personal computers would be used mainly for games**. Atari didn't realize that personal computers would be used mainly for work. Atari developed spectacular games but not enough software to handle work such as word processing, accounting, and filing.

Atari developed some slightly improved computers (the **600 XL**, **800 XL**, and **1200 XL**) but still lost lots of money.

Jack attack

Atari got bought by Jack Tramiel, who'd headed Commodore. Here's why:

> When Jack quit being the head of Commodore, he sold his Commodore stock for 80 million dollars. He used some of that cash to take his wife on a trip around the world.
>
> When they reached Japan, the heads of Japanese computer companies said, "Jack, we're glad you quit Commodore, because now we can enter the American computer market without having to fight you."
>
> That comment scared Jack. He didn't want to let the Japanese invade the U.S. computer market. So he started a second computer company, Tramiel Associates, just to stop the Japanese invasion.
>
> Tramiel Associates bought Atari from Warner. Since Jack was rich and Atari was nearly worthless (having accumulated lots of debt), Jack managed to buy all of Atari at 4PM one afternoon by using his Visa card. Now Jack and his sons run Atari.

Jack replaced Atari's computers by two new computers (the **65 XE** and the **130 XE**), which ran the same software as Atari's earlier computers but cost less. Then in 1985, he began selling the **Atari 520ST**, which was cheap imitation of Apple's Macintosh computer, and therefore nicknamed the "Jackintosh". It used the **Gem operating system**, invented by **Digital Research** for the Atari and the IBM PC. Gem made the 520 ST look like a Mac but did *not* run Mac software: you had to buy software specially modified to work on the 520 ST.

When the 520 ST first came out, its prices were about half as much as the Mac and Amiga so that, by comparison, the Mac and Amiga looked overpriced. To fight back, Apple lowered the Mac's price, and Commodore lowered the Amiga's. But the 520 ST remained the cheapest of the bunch.

When Apple announced the Mac Plus, which contained 1 megabyte of RAM, Atari retaliated with the **1040 ST**, which contained 1 megabyte also. Then Atari announced a 2-megabyte version (the **Mega-2**) and 4-meg version (the **Mega-4**).

Atari's had difficulty competing in the USA, but Atari computers remained popular in Europe for a while. Eventually, Atari's fortunes declined. Finally, in 1996, Atari died: it got merged into another company, **JTS**, which makes disk drives.

OPERATING SYSTEMS

Background

To begin operating a computer, you find its power switch, turn it on, and then what?

What do you type? What do you do? How will the computer respond?

The answers to those questions depend on which **operating system** your computer uses.

Most IBM clones use an operating system called **MS-DOS**, supplemented by **Windows** (which lets you more easily use a mouse). Mac computers use a different operating system instead, called the **Mac System**. This book explains how to use all three: MS-DOS, Windows, and the Mac System.

Other kinds of computers use different operating systems instead.

Three kinds of user interface

How do you give commands to the computer? The answer depends on what kind of **user interface** the operating system uses. Three kinds of user interface have been invented.

Command-driven In a **command-driven** interface, you give commands to the computer by **typing the commands on the keyboard**.

For example, MS-DOS uses a command-driven interface. To command MS-DOS to copy a file, you sit at the keyboard, type the word "copy", then type the details about which file you want to copy and which disk you want to copy it to. To command MS-DOS to erase a file so the file is deleted, you type the word "erase" or "del", then type the name of the file you want to delete.

Menu-driven In a **menu-driven** interface, you act as if you were in a restaurant and ordering food from a menu: you give orders to the computer by **choosing your order from a menu that appears on the screen**.

For example, Pro DOS (an operating system used on some Apple 2 computers) has a menu-driven interface. When you start using Pro DOS, the screen shows a menu that begins like this:

```
1.  Copy files
2.  Delete files
```

If you want to copy a file, press the "1" key on the keyboard. If you want to delete a file instead, press the "2" key. Afterwards, the computer lets you choose *which* file to copy or delete.

Icon-driven In an **icon-driven** interface, the screen shows lots of cute little pictures; each little picture is called an **icon**. To give orders to the computer, you **point at one of the icons by using a mouse**, then use the mouse to make the icon move or disappear or turn black or otherwise change appearance.

For example, the Mac's operating system (which is called the Mac System) has an icon-driven interface. When you turn the Mac on, the screen gets filled with lots of little icons.

If you want to copy a file from the Mac's hard disk to a floppy disk, just use the mouse! Point at the icon (picture) that represents the file, then drag the file's icon to the floppy disk's icon. Dragging the file's icon to the floppy's icon makes the computer drag the file itself to the floppy itself.

One of the icons on the screen is a picture of a trash can. To delete a file, drag the file's icon to the trash-can icon. When you finish, the trash can will bulge, which means the file's been deleted, thrown away.

Multiuser systems

Our country is run by monsters! Big monster computers run our government, banks, insurance companies, utility companies, airlines, and railroads. To handle so many people and tasks simultaneously, those computers use advanced operating systems. Here's how they arose:

Back in the 1950's, the only kind of operating system was **single-user**: it handled just one person at a time. If two people wanted to use the computer, the second person had to stand in line behind the first person until the first finished.

The first improvement over single-user operating systems was **batch processing**. In a batch-processing system, the second person didn't have to stand in line to use the computer. Instead, he fed his program onto the computer's disk (or other kind of memory) and walked away. The computer ran it automatically when the first person's program finished. That procedure was called **batch processing** because the computer could store a whole batch of programs on the disk and run them in order.

While running your program, the CPU often waits for computer devices to catch up. For example, if your program makes the printer print, the CPU waits for the printer to finish. While the CPU waits for the printer (or another slow device), you should let the CPU temporarily work on the next guy's program. That's called **multiprogramming**, because the CPU switches its attention among several programs.

In a simple multiprogramming system, the CPU follows this strategy: it begins working on the first guy's program; but when that program makes the CPU wait for a slow device, the CPU starts working on the second program. When the second program makes the CPU wait also, the CPU switches its attention to the third program, etc. But the first program always has top priority: as soon as that first program can continue (because the printer finished), the CPU resumes work on that program and puts all other programs on hold.

Suppose one guy's program requires an hour of computer time, but another guy's program requires just one minute. If the guy with the hour-long program is mean and insists on going first, the other guy must wait an hour to run the one-minute program. An improved operating system can "psyche out" the situation and help the second guy without waiting for the first guy to finish. Here's how the operating system works....

A **jiffy** is a sixtieth of a second. During the first jiffy, the CPU works on the first guy's program. During the next jiffy, the CPU works on the second guy's program. During the third jiffy, the CPU works on a third guy's program, and so on, until each program has received a jiffy. Then, like a card dealer, the CPU "deals" a second jiffy to each program, then deals a third jiffy, etc. If one of the programs requires little CPU time, it will finish after being dealt just a few jiffies and "drop out" of the game, without waiting for all the other players to finish.

In that scheme, each jiffy is called a **time slice**. Since the computer deals time slices as if dealing to a circle of card players, the technique's called **round-robin time-slicing**.

To make that technique practical, attach the computer to many terminals, so each guy has his own terminal. The CPU goes round and round, switching its attention from terminal to terminal every jiffy.

If you sit at a terminal, a few jiffies later the CPU gets to your terminal, gives you its full attention for a jiffy, then ignores you for several jiffies while it handles the other users, then comes back to you again. Since jiffies are quick, you don't notice that the CPU ignores you for several jiffies.

That technique's an example of **timesharing**, which is defined as "an operating system creating the *illusion* that the CPU gives you its full attention continuously".

In that system, if your program needs to use the printer, the CPU sends some data out to the printer but then *immediately* moves on to the next person, without waiting for the printer to catch up, and without giving you a full jiffy of attention. After the CPU's given the other people their jiffies, the computer returns to you again and checks whether the printer has finished your job yet.

While the CPU works on a particular guy, the **state** of that guy's program is stored in the CPU and RAM. When that guy's jiffy ends, the CPU typically copies that guy's state onto the disk, then copies the next guy's state from disk to the CPU and RAM. So every time the CPU switches from one guy to the next, the CPU must typically do lots of disk I/O (unless the CPU's RAM is large enough to hold both guy's programs simultaneously). Such disk I/O is "bureaucratic overhead" consuming lots of time. To reduce that overhead, switch guys less often. Here's how to make the CPU switch guys less often but still switch fast enough to maintain each guy's illusion of getting continuous attention.

Suppose a guy's a "CPU hog": he's running a program that won't finish for several hours. Instead of giving him many short time slices, the CPU should act more efficiently by totally ignoring him for several hours (which will make everybody else in the computer room cheer!) and then give him a solid block of time toward the end of those hours. He'll never know the difference: his job will finish at the same time as it would otherwise. And the CPU will waste less time in bureaucratic overhead, since it won't have to switch attention to and from him so often.

To determine who's the hog, the CPU counts how many jiffies and how much RAM each guy's been using. If a guy's count is high, he's been acting hoggish and will probably continue to hog, so the CPU ignores him until later when he's given a solid block of time. If that block is *too* long, the other guys will be ignored too long and think the CPU broke; so that solid block should be just a few seconds. If he doesn't finish within a few seconds, give him another block later.

The Decsystem-20 and other great timesharing systems have used that strategy.

Now you know how to make many people share a single CPU efficiently. But since the CPU chip in an IBM PC costs just a few dollars, why bother sharing it? Why not simply give each guy his own CPU? Today many companies are abandoning maxicomputers that have fancy timesharing operating systems and are replacing them by a collection of IBM PC clones, each of which handles just one person at a time. That's called **distributed processing**: tying together many little CPU's instead of forcing everybody to share one big CPU.

Prepare to operate

Here's how to start using an IBM-compatible computer. (If you're using a Mac instead, skip ahead to page 150.)

If you ever have difficulty following my instructions, **phone me anytime for free help at 603-666-6644**.

Unpack the computer
When you buy a computer system, it typically comes in three cardboard boxes. Open them, and put the contents on your desk.

One box contains the monitor.
One box contains the printer.
One box contains the computer's main part (**system unit**), keyboard, mouse, speakers, and disks. Each box also contains power cords, cables, and instruction manuals.

Here are exceptions:
If you bought a portable computer (notebook or laptop), there is no monitor.
If you didn't buy a printer, the printer box is missing.
If you bought a tower computer, put it on the floor instead of on your desk.
Your computer might have no mouse or no speakers.

Into the back of the system unit, plug the cables that come from the monitor, printer, keyboard, mouse and speakers. Into your wall's electrical socket (or power strip), plug the power cords that come from the monitor, printer, speakers, and system unit. (On some computers, the cabling is different.)

Empty the floppy drives
At the front of the system unit, you'll see one or two slots. (In most computers, the slots are horizontal.) You can put floppy disks into those slots. Those slots are called the **floppy drives**.

Exception: if your computer is a notebook or laptop, the floppy drives might be in the computer's right side instead of in the front.

Remove any disks from the floppy drives, so that the floppy drives are empty and you can start fresh.

Turn on the computer
Flick the computer's power switch to the ON position. Can't find the power switch? Here are some hints:

The power switch is on or near the system unit's *right* side. If you don't find the switch on the right side, check the right part of the front side or the right part of the back side. On traditional computers, the power switch is red. It might say "1" instead of "ON" and "0" instead of "OFF". On some computers (such as Quantex's), the power "switch" is actually a pushbutton on the front, near the right. Some computers (such as NuTrend's) have a 1-0 power switch (on the back) plus a power button (on the front): adjust both.

Turn on the screen
Turn on the computer's screen (monitor).

After a few seconds, the screen will display some messages. (If you don't see the messages clearly, make sure the cable from the screen to the system unit is plugged in tightly, and adjust the screen's contrast and brightness knobs.)

Examine the keyboard
Test your powers of observation by staring at the keyboard. Try to find the following keys (but don't press them yet)....

Find the **ENTER key**. That's the big key on the right side of the keyboard's main section. It has a bent arrow on it. It's also called the **RETURN key**. Pressing it makes the computer read what you typed and proceed.

Find the **BACKSPACE key**. It's above the ENTER key and to the right of the + key. It has a left-arrow on it. You press it when you want to erase a mistake.

Find the key that has the letter A on it. When you press the A key, you'll be typing a small "a".

Near the keyboard's bottom left corner, find the **SHIFT key**. It has an up-arrow on it. Under the ENTER key, you'll see another SHIFT key. Press either SHIFT key when you want to capitalize a letter. For example, to type a capital A, hold down a SHIFT key; and while you keep holding down the SHIFT key, tap the A key.

Find the key that looks like this:

```
!
1
```

It's near the keyboard's top left corner. That's the **1 key**. You press it when you want to type the number 1. Press the keys to its right when you want to type the numbers 2, 3, 4, 5, 6, 7, 8, 9, and 0. If you press the 1 key while holding down a SHIFT key, you'll be typing an exclamation point (!). Here's the rule: if a key shows two symbols (such as ! and 1), and you want to type the top symbol (!), you must typically hold down a SHIFT key.

Find the key that has the letter U on it. To the right of that key, you'll see the letters I and O. Don't confuse the letter I with the number 1; don't confuse the letter O with the number 0.

In the keyboard's bottom row, find the wide key that has nothing written on it. That's the **SPACE bar**. Press it whenever you want to leave a blank space.

Which operating system?
To find out which operating system you're using. Look at your screen.

If the screen's bottom left corner says "Start", you're probably using Windows 95 or 98: turn to page 95.
If the screen says "Program Manager", you're probably using Windows 3.1 or 3.11: turn to page 108.
If the screen says "C:\>", you're probably using just MS-DOS: turn to page 114.

If the screen says something else, ask your dealer which operating system you got, then turn to the appropriate page.

WINDOWS 95, 98, & ME

Starting

Microsoft has improved Windows.

In 1995, Microsoft invented **Windows 95**.	
In 1998, Microsoft invented **Windows 98**.	
In 1999, Microsoft invented **Windows 98 Second Edition (Windows 98 SE)**.	
In 2000, Microsoft invented **Windows Millennium Edition (Windows Me)**.	

Windows 98 SE and Windows Me are both very similar to Windows 98. The differences are miniscule. That's why Microsoft charges just $60 to upgrade from Windows 98 to Windows Me. Most industry experts laugh at "Windows Me" and say the upgrade is worth even less than that.

Why did Microsoft's chairman, Bill Gates, call it "Windows Me"? Cynics say **Windows Me** stands for "I should have called it **Windows** 98 Third Edition, but I called it Windows Me so you'll give more money to **Me**."

Make sure your computer has enough RAM:

Windows 3.1	requires	1M of RAM to run at all,	8M to run well.
Windows 95	requires	4M of RAM to run at all,	16M to run well.
Windows 98&SE	require	16M of RAM to run at all,	32M to run well.
Windows Me	requires	32M of RAM to run at all,	64M to run well.

Windows Me price

Windows Me lists for $209. When you buy a new computer, Windows Me is usually included by the computer's manufacturer at no extra charge.

If your computer has Windows 95, you can upgrade to Windows Me for $109. If your computer has Windows 98 or Windows 98SE, you can upgrade to Windows Me for just $60.

Those prices are from Microsoft; add shipping and tax. Some discount dealers charge $10 less.

What's in this chapter

This chapter explains Windows 95 and 98. **If you're using Windows 98 SE or Windows Me, follow my instructions for Windows 98**, which is similar.

Alternative chapters

If you plan to keep using an ancient version of Windows (such as Windows 3.0, Windows 3.1, or Windows 3.11), turn to the next chapter instead, which is called "Windows 3.1 & 3.11". If you're not using Windows at all — if you're using just MS-DOS or a Mac — turn to the MS-DOS or Mac chapters.

Turn on

When your computer contains Windows 98 (or 98 SE or 95 or Me), here's how to start using it.

If you have a printer, make sure a cable runs from it to the computer.

Turn on the computer, without any disks in the floppy drives; then immediately turn on the printer. (For details, read "Prepare to operate" on page 94. For free help, phone me anytime at 603-666-6644.)

The computer says "Microsoft Windows 98" (or "Microsoft Windows 95" or something similar).

If the computer says "Add New Hardware Wizard" (for example, because it detected that you attached a new printer), press the ENTER key several times (typically 5 times), until the computer stops saying "Add New Hardware Wizard".

Eventually, the screen's bottom left corner says "Start".

Position the mouse

Look at the computer's mouse. The mouse's **tail** is a cable that runs from the mouse to the computer. The area where the tail meets the mouse is called the mouse's **ass**.

The mouse's underside — its belly — has a hole in it, and a ball in the hole.

Put the mouse on your desk and directly in front of your right arm. Make the mouse lie flat (so its ball rubs against the desk). **Make the mouse face you** so you don't see its ass.

Move the arrow

Move the mouse across your desk. As you move the mouse, remember to keep it flat and facing you.

On the screen, you'll see an arrow, which is called the **mouse pointer**. As you move the mouse, the arrow moves also. If you move the mouse to the left, the arrow moves to the left. If you move the mouse to the right, the arrow moves to the right. If you move the mouse toward you, the arrow moves down. If you move the mouse away from you, the arrow moves up.

Practice moving the arrow by moving the mouse. Remember to keep the mouse facing you at all times.

If you want to move the arrow far and your desk is small, move the mouse until it reaches the desk's edge; then lift the mouse off the desk, lay the mouse gently on the middle of the desk, and rub the mouse across the desk in the same direction as before.

Click on Start

The most important part of the arrow is its tip, which is called the **hot spot**. Move the arrow so its hot spot (tip) is in the middle of the word "Start". When you do that, you're **pointing at** the word "Start".

On the top of the mouse, you'll see 2 or 3 rectangular buttons you can press. **The main button is the one on the left.** Tapping it is called **clicking**. So to **click**, tap the left button.

While you're pointing at the word "Start", click (by tapping the left button). That's called **clicking "Start"**.

When you click "Start", Windows 98 shows you this **Start menu**:

(Windows 95 omits "Windows Update" and "Favorites".)

Shut Down

On that Start menu, the bottom choice says "Shut Down". **Whenever you finish using Windows 98 (or 95), click "Shut Down"** (by pointing at "Shut Down" and then tapping the left mouse button).

Practice that now! Click "Shut Down".

In Windows 98, the computer asks, "What do you want the computer to do?" (In Windows 95, the computer asks instead, "Are you sure?")

Press the ENTER key. Wait while the computer tidies the info on your hard disk.

Then, if your computer is modern, it will turn its own power off.. If your computer is older, the computer will say "It's now safe to turn off your computer" and wait for *you* to turn it off.

Accessories menu

Make the Start menu appear on the screen.

In that menu, notice that the word "Programs" has the symbol " ▶ " next to it. That symbol means that if you choose "Programs" from the Start menu, you'll see *another* menu.

Try it: point at the word "Programs". Windows 98 shows you this **Programs menu**:

```
Accessories            ▶
Internet Explorer      ▶
Online Services        ▶
StartUp                ▶
MS-DOS Prompt
Windows Explorer
```

(Windows 95 sometimes omits "Internet Explorer", and it says "Microsoft Exchange" and "The Microsoft Network" instead of "Online Services".) If you bought extra programs, the menu mentions them too.

From that menu, choose "Accessories", by pointing at it. Windows 98 shows you this **Accessories menu**:

```
Communications   ▶
Entertainment    ▶
Games            ▶
System Tools     ▶
Calculator
Imaging
Notepad
Paint
WordPad
```

(Windows 95 says "Multimedia" instead of "Entertainment", says "Fax" and "HyperTerminal" and "Phone Dialer" instead of "Communications", and omits "Imaging".)

Calculator

The accessories menu includes a "Calculator". To use the calculator, get the accessories menu onto the screen (by clicking "Start" then "Programs" then "Accessories") and then click "Calculator". You'll see the **Calculator window**, containing a picture of a pocket calculator.

How to calculate

To compute 42+5, click the calculator's 4 key (by using the mouse to point at the 4 key and then clicking), then click 2, then +, then 5, then =. The calculator will show the answer, 47.

Instead of using the mouse, you can do that calculation a different way, by using the computer's keyboard. Try it! On the computer's keyboard, tap the 4 key, then the 2 key, then (while holding down the SHIFT key) the + key, then 5, then =. The calculator will show 47.

Try fancier calculations, by pressing these calculator buttons:

Button	Meaning
+	plus
-	minus
*	times
/	divided by
=	total
.	decimal point
C	clear
Backspace	backspace

If you're using Windows 95 (instead of 98), the backspace button is labeled "Back" (instead of "Backspace").

Standard versus scientific

You can choose two kinds of calculators. A **standard calculator** is small and cute: it does just arithmetic. A **scientific calculator** is big and imposing: it includes extra buttons, so you can do advanced math.

The first time you (or your colleagues) ask for the calculator, the computer shows a standard calculator (small and cute). If you want the calculator to be scientific instead, choose **Scientific** from the **View menu**. (To do that, click the word "View", then click the word "Scientific".) Then you'll see extra buttons, such as these:

Button	Meaning
x^2	squared
x^3	cubed
n!	factorial
pi	pi (which is 3.141592653589793238462643383832795)

If you click the 7 button and then say "**squared**" (by pressing the x^2 button), the computer will multiply 7 by itself and say 49 (which is called "7 squared"). If you click the 7 button and then say "**cubed**" (by pressing the x^3 button), the computer will do "7 times 7 times 7" and say 343 (which is called "7 cubed"). If you click the 7 button and then say "**factorial**" (by pressing the n! button), the computer will multiply together all the numbers up to 7 (1 times 2 times 3 times 4 times 5 times 6 times 7) and say 5040 (which is called "7 factorial").

> If you're using Windows 98 and click the **pi** button, the computer will say 3.1415926535897932384626433832795.
>
> If you're using Windows 95, the pi button is capitalized (so it's labeled "**PI**") and it's less accurate: it says PI is 3.14159265359.

The scientific calculator also contains buttons that help you handle big exponents, logarithms, trigonometry, statistics, hexadecimal numbers, and assembly-language programming. I'll explain the mathematical concepts behind those buttons later, on page 388 (exponents), 389 (logarithms), 402 (trigonometry), 565 (hexadecimal numbers), and 575 (assembly-language programming). If you're adventurous, just go push buttons and see what happens: no matter which button you press, the computer won't blow up!

After making the calculator be scientific, you can make it become standard again by choosing **Standard** from the View menu.

Close

In the Calculator window's top right corner, a square button has an X on it. That's called the **X button** (or the **close button**).

When you finish using the Calculator window, click that button. It **closes** the Calculator window, so the Calculator window disappears.

WordPad

When you buy Windows 95 or 98, you get a word-processing program free! That word-processing program is called **WordPad**. It's one of the Windows accessories. To use it, get the accessories menu onto the screen (by clicking "Start" then "Programs" then "Accessories") and then click "WordPad". You'll see the **WordPad window**.

In the window's top right corner, you see the X button. Next to the X button is the **resize button**. Clicking the resize button changes the window's size.

Try clicking the resize button: see the window's size change! Try clicking the resize button *again*: see the window's size change *again*!

If the window is small, clicking the resize button makes the window become huge so it consumes the whole screen. If the window is huge and consumes the whole screen, clicking the resize button makes the window become small.

If the window consumes the whole screen, the window is said to be **maximized**. If the window is smaller, the window is said to be **restored** to a small size.

Click the resize button if necessary, so that the WordPad window consumes the whole screen (and is maximized).

Now that the WordPad window consumes the whole screen, you can easily do word processing: you can easily type words and sentences. Try it! Type whatever sentences you wish to make up. For example, try typing a memo to your friends, or a story, or a poem. Be creative! Whatever you type is called a **document**.

Use the keyboard

Read the section called "Examine the keyboard", which is on page 94. Here are more hints that will help you type....

Capitals To capitalize a letter of the alphabet, type that letter while holding down the **SHIFT key**. (One SHIFT key is next to the Z key; the other SHIFT key is next to the ? key. Each SHIFT key has an up-arrow on it.)

To capitalize a whole passage, tap the **CAPS LOCK key**, then type the passage. The computer will automatically capitalize the passage as you type it. When you finish typing the passage, tap the CAPS LOCK key again: that tells the computer to stop capitalizing.

BACKSPACE key If you make a mistake, press the **BACKSPACE key**. That makes the computer erase the last character you typed. (The BACKSPACE key is in the top right corner of the keyboard's main section. It's to the right of the + key, and it has a left-arrow on it.)

To erase the last *two* characters you typed, press the BACKSPACE key *twice*.

Word wrap If you're typing near the screen's right edge, and you type a word that's too long to fit on the screen, the computer will automatically move the word to the line below. Moving the word to the line below is called **word wrap**.

ENTER key When you finish a paragraph, press the **ENTER key**. That makes the computer move to the line underneath so you can start typing the next paragraph.

If you want to double-space between the paragraphs, press the ENTER key *twice*.

TAB key If you want to indent a line (such as the first line of a paragraph), begin the line by pressing the **TAB key**. The computer will indent the line a half inch.

Nudge a phrase To move a phrase toward the right, press the TAB key several times before typing the phrase. To move a phrase down, press the ENTER key several times before typing the phrase.

Alt symbols You can type these alternative symbols:

128 Ç	144 É	160 á	225 ß
129 ü	145 æ	161 í	
130 é	146 Æ	162 ó	227 ¶
131 â	147 ô	163 ú	
132 ä	148 ö	164 ñ	230 µ
133 à	149 ò	165 Ñ	
134 å	150 û	166 ª	241 ±
135 ç	151 ù	167 º	
136 ê	152 ÿ	168 ¿	246 ÷
137 ë	153 Ö		
138 è	154 Ü	170 ¬	248 °
139 ï	155 ¢	171 ½	249 •
140 î	156 £	172 ¼	250 ·
141 ì	157 ¥	173 ¡	
142 Ä	158 P	174 «	
143 Å	159 ƒ	175 »	253 ²

For example, here's how to type the symbol ñ, whose code number is 164. Hold down the Alt key; and while you keep holding down the Alt key, type 164 *by using the numeric keypad* (the number keys on the far right side of the keyboard). When you finish typing 164, lift your finger from the Alt key, and you'll see ñ on your screen! Try it!

Windows copied that chart from DOS. But Windows goes beyond DOS by letting you also use this fancier chart:

		0192 À	0224 à
	0161 ¡	0193 Á	0225 á
0130 ,	0162 ¢	0194 Â	0226 â
0131 ƒ	0163 £	0195 Ã	0227 ã
0132 „	0164 ¤	0196 Ä	0228 ä
0133 …	0165 ¥	0197 Å	0229 å
0134 †	0166 ¦	0198 Æ	0230 æ
0135 ‡	0167 §	0199 Ç	0231 ç
0136 ˆ	0168 ¨	0200 È	0232 è
0137 ‰	0169 ©	0201 É	0233 é
0138 Š	0170 ª	0202 Ê	0234 ê
0139 ‹	0171 «	0203 Ë	0235 ë
0140 Œ	0172 ¬	0204 Ì	0236 ì
	0173 -	0205 Í	0237 í
	0174 ®	0206 Î	0238 î
	0175 ¯	0207 Ï	0239 ï
	0176 °	0208 Ð	0240 ð
0145 Ÿ	0177 ±	0209 Ñ	0241 ñ
0146 '	0178 ²	0210 Ò	0242 ò
0147 ¡	0179 ³	0211 Ó	0243 ó
0148 "	0180 ´	0212 Ô	0244 ô
0149 •	0181 µ	0213 Õ	0245 õ
0150 –	0182 ¶	0214 Ö	0246 ö
0151 —	0183 ·	0215 ×	0247 ÷
0152 ~	0184 ¸	0216 Ø	0248 ø
0153 ™	0185 ¹	0217 Ù	0249 ù
0154 š	0186 º	0218 Ú	0250 ú
0155 ›	0187 »	0219 Û	0251 û
0156 œ	0188 ¼	0220 Ü	0252 ü
	0189 ½	0221 Ý	0253 ý
	0190 ¾	0222 Þ	0254 þ
0159 Ÿ	0191 ¿	0223 ß	0255 ÿ

For example, here's how to type the symbol ã, whose code number is 0227: while holding down the Alt key, type 0227 on the numeric keypad.

Scroll arrows

If your document contains too many lines to fit on the screen, the screen will show just *part* of the document, accompanied by two arrows at the screen's right edge: a **scroll-up arrow** (▲) and a **scroll-down arrow** (▼).

To see a higher part of your document, click the scroll-up arrow (▲).
To see a lower part of your document, click the scroll-down arrow (▼).

Insert characters

To insert extra characters anywhere in your document, click where you want the extra characters to appear (by moving the mouse's pointer there and then pressing the mouse's button). Then type the extra characters.

For example, suppose you typed the word "fat" and want to change it to "fault". Click between the "a" and the "t", then type "ul".

(When you're using Windows, notice that you click *between* letters, not *on* letters.)

As you type the extra characters, the screen's other characters move out of the way to make room for the extra characters.

While you're inserting the extra characters, you can erase nearby mistakes by pressing the BACKSPACE key or DELETE key. The BACKSPACE key erases the character that's *before* the mouse's pointer. The DELETE key erases the character that's *after* the mouse's pointer.

Split a paragraph

Here's how to split a long paragraph in half, to form two short paragraphs.

Decide which word should begin the second short paragraph. Click the left edge of that word's first letter.

Press the BACKSPACE key (to erase the space before that word), then press the ENTER key. Now you've split the long paragraph in two!

If you want to double-space between the two short paragraphs, press the ENTER key again. If you want to indent the second paragraph, press the TAB key.

Combine paragraphs

After typing two paragraphs, here's how to combine them, to form a single paragraph that's longer.

Click at the end of the first paragraph. Press the DELETE key several times, to delete unwanted ENTERs and TABs. Now you've combined the two paragraphs into one!

Then press the SPACE bar (to insert a space between the two sentences).

Movement keys

To move to different parts of your document, you can use your mouse. To move faster, press these keys instead:

Key you press	Where the pointer will move
right-arrow	right to the next character
left-arrow	left to the previous character
down-arrow	down to the line below
up-arrow	up to the line above
END	right to the end of the line
HOME	left to beginning of the line
PAGE DOWN	down to the next screenful
PAGE UP	up to the previous screenful

Here's what happens if you press the movement keys while holding down the Ctrl key:

Keys you press	Where the pointer will move
Ctrl with right-arrow	right (to the next word or punctuation symbol)
Ctrl with left-arrow	left (to the beginning of a word or punctuation)
Ctrl with down-arrow	down to the next paragraph
Ctrl with up-arrow	up to the beginning of a paragraph
Ctrl with PAGE DOWN	down to the end of the screen's last word
Ctrl with PAGE UP	up to the beginning of the screen's first word
Ctrl with END	down to the end of the document
Ctrl with HOME	up to the beginning of the document

Buttons

Near the top of the screen, you see these buttons:

Here is each button's name:

If you forget a button's name, try this trick: point at the button (by using the mouse but *without* clicking), then wait a second. Underneath the button, you'll see the button's name; and at the screen's bottom left corner, you'll see a short explanation of what the button does.

To use a button, press it by clicking it with the mouse. Here are the details….

Underline Here's how to underline a phrase (like this). Push in the **Underline button** (which says U̲ on it) by clicking it. Then type the phrase you want underlined. Then pop the Underline button back out (by clicking it again).

Bold Here's how to make a phrase be bold (**like this**). Push in the **Bold button** (which says **B** on it) by clicking it. Then type the phrase you want emboldened. Then pop the Bold button back out (by clicking it again).

Here's how to make a phrase be bold and underlined (**like this**). Push in the Bold and Underline buttons (by clicking them both). Then type the phrase. Then pop those buttons back out (by clicking them again).

Italic Here's how to italicize a phrase (*like this*). Push in the **Italic button** (which says *I* on it) by clicking it. Then type the phrase you want italicized. Then pop the Italic button back out (by clicking it again).

Color Here's how to change a phrase's color. Click the **Color button**. You'll see a list of 15 colors (plus "White" and "Automatic"). Click the color you want. Then type the phrase you want colorized. Then click the Color button again and click "Black".

Alignment While typing a line, you can click one of these **alignment buttons**: **Center**, **Align Left**, or **Align Right**.

Clicking the **Center button** makes the line be centered,

like this line

Clicking the **Align Right button** makes the line be at the right margin,

like this line

Clicking the **Align Left button** makes the line be at the left margin,

like this line

Clicking one of those buttons affects not just the line you're typing but also all other lines in the same paragraph. When you click one of those buttons, you're pushing the button in; that button pops back out when you push a different alignment button instead.

When you start typing a new document, the computer assumes you want the document to be aligned left, so the computer pushes the Align Left button in. If you want a different alignment, push a different alignment button instead.

Clicking an alignment button affects the entire paragraph you're typing, but the paragraphs you typed earlier remain unaffected. To change the alignment of a paragraph you typed earlier, click in the middle of that paragraph and then click the alignment button you wish.

When you start typing a new paragraph, the computer gives the new paragraph the same alignment as the paragraph above, unless you say differently (by pressing one of the alignment buttons).

Here's how to create a centered title. Press the ENTER key twice (to leave a big blank space above the title). Then press the Center button (so the title will be centered) and the Bold button (so the title will be bold), type the words you want to be in the title, and press the ENTER key afterwards. Congratulations: you've created a centered title! Next, make the paragraph underneath the title be normal: make that paragraph be uncentered (click the Align Left button) and make it be unbolded (click the Bold button, so the Bold button pops back out).

Bullets While you're typing a paragraph, you can push in the **Bullets button** (by clicking it). That makes the computer indent the entire paragraph and also put a bullet (the symbol •) to the left of the paragraph's first line. That's called a **bulleted paragraph**.

After you've typed a bulleted paragraph, any new paragraphs you type underneath will be bulleted also — until you request an *un*bulleted paragraph (by popping the Bullet button back out).

Font Size

Left of the Bold button, the screen also shows a box containing the number 10. That's called the **Font Size box**. The 10 in it means the characters you're typing are **10 points** high.

If you change that number to 20, the characters will be twice as high (and also twice as wide). To change the number to 20, click in the Font Size box, then type 20 and press ENTER. Try it! Any new characters you type afterwards will be the size you chose. (Characters typed earlier don't change size.)

You can make the font size be 10 or 20 or any other size you like. For best results, pick a number from 8 to 72. (If you pick a number smaller than 8 or bigger than 72, the result is ugly.) The number can end in .5; for example, you can pick 8 or 8.5 or 9 or 9.5 or 10.

Font

At the screen's left edge, you see a box saying "Times New Roman". That's called the **Font box**. Next to that box is the symbol ▾; click it.

You'll see the **Font menu**, which is a list of fonts in alphabetical order. (To see the rest of the list, press the up-arrow or down-arrow keys.)

Click whichever font you want. To avoid hassles, choose a font that has a "TT" in front of it. (The "TT" means it's a **True Type font**. For most purposes the best fonts are:

> TT Times New Roman (which is the best for most paragraphs and looks like this)
> TT Arial (which is the best for most headlines & footnotes and looks like this)
> TT Courier New (which is the best for tables of numbers)

Delete all

Here's how to delete the entire document, so you can start over. While holding down the Ctrl key, press the A key (which means "all"). All of the document turns black. Then press the DELETE key. All of the document disappears, so you can start over!

Select

Here's how to change a phrase you typed previously.

Point at the phrase's beginning. Then hold down the mouse's left button; and while you keep holding down that button, move to the phrase's end.

(Moving the mouse while holding down the left button is called **dragging**. You're **dragging** from the phrase's beginning to the phrase's end.)

The phrase that you dragged across turns black. Turning the phrase black is called **selecting the phrase**.

Then say what to do to the phrase. For example, choose one of these activities:

> To underline the phrase, push in the Underline button.
> To make the phrase be bold, push in the Bold button.
> To italicize the phrase, push in the Italic button.
> To prevent the phrase from being underlined, bold, or italicized, pop those buttons back out.
> To change how the phrase's paragraphs are aligned, click one of the alignment buttons.
> To change the phrase's point size, click the Font Size box then type the size and press ENTER.
> To change the phrase's font, choose the font you want from the Font menu.
> To delete the phrase, press the DELETE key.
> To replace the phrase, just type whatever words you want the phrase to become.

To move a phrase to a new location, just "select the phrase, and then drag from the phrase's middle to the new location." Here are the details:

> First, select the phrase you want to move, so the phrase turns black. Then take your finger off the mouse's button. Move the mouse's pointer to the phrase's middle (so you see an arrow). Finally, hold down the mouse's button; and while you keep holding down the mouse's button, drag to wherever you want the phrase to move. (Drag anywhere you wish in the document, or drag to the end of the document. The computer won't let you drag past the document's end.) At the end of the drag, lift your finger from the mouse's button; then the phrase moves where you wished!

Extra buttons

Near the screen's top left corner, you see these extra buttons:

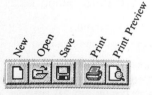

Here's how to use them….

Save Here's how to **save** the document (copy it onto the hard disk). Click the **Save button**. Then invent a name for the document. The name can be short (such as "Joe") or long (such as "Stupidest Memo of 1999"). At the end of the name, press the ENTER key. Then the computer will copy the document onto the disk.

If you change your mind afterwards, edit the document some more: when you finish that editing, save it by clicking the Save button again. If you're typing a long document, click the Save button about every 10 minutes, so that if an accident happens you'll lose at most 10 minutes of work.

Print To print the document onto paper, click the **Print button**.

Print Preview If you're wondering what a page will look like but don't want to waste a sheet of paper to find out, click the **Print Preview button**. The computer will show you a **mock-up** of what the entire page will look like: **you'll see the entire page, shrunk to fit on the screen**, so the characters on the page appear very tiny. Those characters are too tiny to read, but you'll see the page's overall appearance: how much of the page is filled up, which parts of the page are blank, and whether the info on the page is centered. When you finish admiring that mock-up, click the word "Close".

Finishing When you finish working on a document, you can click the **New button** or the **Open button**. If you click the **New button** and then press ENTER, the computer will let you start typing a new document. If instead you click the **Open button**, the computer will show you a list of the documents you saved earlier; click the document you want, then press ENTER, which makes the computer put the document onto the screen and let you edit it.

When you finish using WordPad, click the X button (at the screen's top right corner). That closes the WordPad window, so the WordPad window disappears.

Before the computer obeys the New button, Open button, or X button, the computer checks whether you saved your document. If you didn't save your document, the computer asks, "Save changes?" If you click "Yes", the computer copies your document's most recent version to the hard disk; if you click "No" instead, the computer ignores and forgets your most recent editing.

Time

While you're using Windows 95 or 98, the screen's bottom right corner is a box that shows the time, like this:

10:45PM

If you move the mouse's arrow there, the date will flash on the screen briefly.

Double-click

To get more details about the time and date, **double-click** that time box. To double-click the box, move the arrow to the box, then tap the mouse's left button twice *quickly*, so the taps are less than .4 seconds apart.

While tapping the left button twice, make sure the mouse remains still. Don't let the mouse jiggle, not even a smidgin! While double-clicking, your desk should be like Christmas Eve, where "not a creature is stirring, not even a mouse".

Double-clicking is also called **opening**. Double-clicking the time box is called "**opening** the time box".

Double-clicking the time box makes the computer show you a calendar for the entire month, with today's date highlighted in blue. You'll also see the face of a traditional clock, with an hour hand, minute hand, and second hand that all move. You'll see the time zone, such as "Eastern Daylight Time".

Reset

If the calendar, clock, or time zone are wrong, here's how to reset them.

To change the year, click the ▲ (or ▼) symbol that's next to the year. To change the month, click the ▼ symbol that's next to the month, then click the correct month. To change the date, click the correct date.

To change the time, click the part of the time that you want to change (the hours, minutes, seconds, or AM/PM), then click the ▲ or ▼ symbol nearby. To change the time zone, click "Time Zone", then press the keyboard's right-arrow key (or left-arrow key) several times, until your time zone is chosen, then click "Date & Time". To see immediately the results of changing the time or the time zone, click "Apply".

Finish

When you finish using that clock/calendar window, click "OK".

Paint

To paint pictures, get the accessories menu onto the screen (by clicking "Start" then "Programs" then "Accessories") and then click "Paint". You'll see the **Paint window**.

Make sure the Paint window consumes the whole screen. (If it doesn't consume the whole screen yet, maximize the window by clicking the resize button, which is next to the X button.)

Move the mouse pointer to the screen's middle. Then drag (move the mouse while holding down the mouse's left button). As you drag, you'll be drawing a squiggle.

For example, try drawing a smile:

> To do that, put the mouse pointer where you want the smile to begin (at the smile's top left corner), then depress the mouse's left button while you draw the smile. When you finish drawing the smile, lift the mouse's button. Then draw the rest of the face!

When you draw, you're normally drawing in black. At the screen's bottom, you see 28 **colors**: red, yellow, green, etc. To draw in one of those colors instead of in black, click the color you want.

Near the screen's top left corner, you see these buttons:

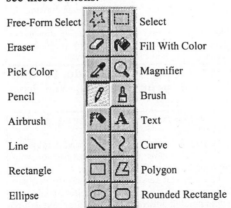

Free-Form Select		Select
Eraser		Fill With Color
Pick Color		Magnifier
Pencil		Brush
Airbrush		Text
Line		Curve
Rectangle		Polygon
Ellipse		Rounded Rectangle

To use a button, push it in by clicking it. When you start using Paint, the computer assumes you want to use the Pencil, so it pushes the **Pencil button** in. If you want to use a different tool, click a different button instead. Let's start with the most popular choices....

Brush

To draw a fatter squiggle, click the **Brush button**. Then put the mouse pointer in the screen's middle, where you want the squiggle to begin, and drag! Try it now!

Eraser

To erase a mistake, click the **Eraser button**. Then drag across the part of your drawing you want to erase. The part you drag across will become white.

Airbrush

To vandalize your drawing by using a can of spray paint, click the **Airbrush button**. Then put the mouse pointer where you want to begin spraying, and drag!

Line

To draw a line that's exactly straight, click the **Line button**. Then put the mouse pointer where you want the line to begin, and drag to where you want the line to end.

If you hold down the SHIFT key while doing that dragging, you'll force the line to be **perfectly simple** (perfectly vertical, perfectly horizontal, or at a perfect 45-degree angle).

Ctrl key

While holding down the Ctrl key, you can tap the Z, S, P, N, or O key. Here are the details:

> If you make a mistake, **zap** the mistake by press Ctrl with Z. That makes the computer zap (undo) your last action. To zap your last *two* actions, press Ctrl with Z *twice*. To zap your last *three* actions, press Ctrl with Z *three times*. "Three times" is the limit of what you can zap: you cannot zap the last four actions.
>
> To **save** your painting (copy it onto the hard disk), press Ctrl with S. Then type whatever name you want the painting to have, and press ENTER. Afterwards, if you edit your document further, save that editing by pressing Ctrl with S again.
>
> To **print** your painting onto paper, press Ctrl with P. Then press ENTER. If your printer can't print colors, it will substitute shades of gray.
>
> To start working on a **new** painting, press Ctrl with N.
>
> To **open** a painting (use a painting that you saved earlier), press Ctrl with the letter O. The computer will show you a list of the paintings you saved earler; click the painting you want, then press ENTER, which makes the computer put the painting onto the screen and let you edit it.

X button

When you finish using Paint, click the X button (at the screen's top right corner). That closes the Paint window, so the Paint window disappears.

Did you save?

Before the computer obeys Ctrl N, Ctrl O, or the X button, the computer checks whether you saved your painting. If you didn't save your painting, the computer asks, "Save changes?"

> If you click "Yes", the computer copies your painting's most recent version to the hard disk.

> If you click "No" instead, the computer ignores and forgets your most recent drawing efforts.

Advanced buttons

You've learned how to use the easy buttons (pencil, brush, eraser, airbrush, and line). Here's how to use the other buttons, which are more advanced.

Rectangle To draw a rectangle whose sides are exactly straight, click the **Rectangle button**. Then put the mouse pointer where you want the rectangle's top left corner to be, and drag to where you want the rectangle's opposite corner.

If you hold down the SHIFT key while doing that dragging, you'll force the rectangle to be a perfect **square**.

Rectangle variants Instead of clicking the Rectangle button, try clicking these variants:

If you click **Rounded Rectangle** instead of Rectangle, you'll force the rectangle's corners to be rounded (instead of sharp 90-degree angles). If you hold down the SHIFT key while dragging out the rounded rectangle, you'll create a **rounded square**.

If you click **Ellipse** instead of Rectangle, you'll force the rectangle's corners to be *very* rounded, so the rectangle looks like an ellipse (oval). If you hold down the SHIFT key while dragging out the ellipse, you'll create a perfect **circle**.

If you click **Text** instead of Rectangle, the rectangle will temporarily have dashed lines instead of solid lines. After creating that dashed rectangle, type whatever words you want inside the rectangle. Then click outside the rectangle. The dashed lines will disappear, so you won't see a rectangle, but you'll still see the words you typed.

Polygon To draw a polygon (a shape that has many straight sides and corners), click the **Polygon button**. Then put the mouse pointer where you want the polygon's first corner to be, and drag to where you want the second corner. Click where you want the third corner, click where you want the fourth corner, click where you want the fifth corner, etc.

At the last corner, double-click instead of click. The double-clicking makes the computer complete the polygon: it makes the computer draw the final side back to the first corner.

Curve To draw a curve, click the **Curve button**. Then put the mouse pointer where you want the curve to begin, and drag to where you want the curve to end. Then take your finger off the mouse's button.

You temporarily see a straight line. To turn that line into a curve, bend the line's middle, by pointing at the line's middle and dragging that midpoint in the direction you want to bend it. (While doing that dragging, try wiggling the mouse in all four directions, until the line bends close to the way you want.) Then take your finger off the mouse's button.

To bend the line more, and even create a second bend (arc) in the line,

drag again. (You get just two chances to bend the line.)

Fill With Color After you've drawn a closed shape (a rectangle, square, rounded rectangle, rounded square, ellipse, circle, or polygon, or "a squiggle that forms a loop so it ends where it started"), here's how to fill in the shape's interior (middle), so the interior becomes colored instead of white:

Click the **Fill With Color button**, then click your favorite color (from the 28 choices at the screen's bottom), then click in the shape's interior.

If you click outside the shape instead of inside, you'll be coloring the shape's exterior.

Pick Color In the middle of your drawing, if you see a color that you've used and like, here's how to use it again:

Click the **Pick Color button**. Click in the middle of your drawing, where your favorite color is. Then draw some more shapes; they'll be in the color you picked.

Select Here's how to alter part of your drawing.

First, say which part of your drawing to alter, by using one of these methods....

Method 1: click the **Select button**. Draw a dashed rectangle around that part of your drawing: to do that, put the mouse pointer where you want the rectangle's top left corner to be, and drag to where you want the rectangle's opposite corner.

Method 2: click the **Free-Form Select button**. Draw a loop around that part of your drawing: to do that, put the mouse pointer where you want the loop to begin, and drag until you've drawn the loop. (The loop will temporarily turn into a rectangle, but don't let that bother you.)

Then say what to do to that part of your drawing. You have these choices:

To **delete** that part of your drawing, press the DELETE key.

To **move** that part of your drawing, point at the rectangle's middle and drag that part of your drawing to wherever you want.

To **copy** that part of your drawing (so that part appears *twice*), point at the rectangle's middle and, while holding down the Ctrl key, drag that part of your drawing to wherever you want the second copy to be.

To **rotate** that part of your drawing, press Ctrl with R, then click "Flip vertical" (to flip that part upside-down) or "Flip horizontal" (to see a mirror image of that part) or "Rotate by angle" (to stand that part on its end). Click "OK".

To **invert** the colors in that part of your drawing, press Ctrl with I. In Windows 98, that makes black becomes white, white becomes black, yellow becomes blue, blue becomes yellow, green becomes purple, purple becomes green, red becomes greenish blue, and greenish blue becomes red. (In Windows 95, the color changes make less sense.)

To **widen** that part of your drawing, press Ctrl with W. (If you're using Windows 95 instead of 98, then double-click in the first % box.) Type 200 (to make that part of your drawing twice as wide) or 300 (to make that part three times as wide) or whatever other percentage you wish. Click "OK".

While you're using Windows 95 or 98, the screen's top left corner usually shows an **icon** (little picture) entitled "My Computer".

Right-click My Computer

To discover secrets about your computer, **right-click** the "My Computer" icon. (That means click it by using the rightmost button instead of the left button.)

You'll see a **shortcut menu**. The menu's bottom choice is "Properties". Click the word "Properties" (by using the left mouse button).

You'll see a message about your computer's properties. For example, on one of my computers the message says —

```
System:
   Microsoft Windows 95
   4.00.950a

Registered to:
   Russ Walter
   The Secret Guide to Computers
   32295-OEM-0005556-34353

Computer:
   Quantex Microsystems, Inc.
   Pentium(r)
   16.0MB RAM
```

That means I'm using just Windows 95 (not Windows 98), I'm using version 4.00.950a (which is newer and better than version 4.00.950 but not as new as version 4.00.950 B), the computer is registered to me & my company, the computer was manufactured by Quantex Microsystems, the computer's CPU chip is a Pentium (which is a registered trademark of Intel), and the computer contains 16 megabytes of RAM chips.

On one of my newer computers, the message says —

```
System:
   Microsoft Windows 98
   4.10.1998

Registered to:
   User
   ...
   24498-OEM-0070275-56731

Computer:
   AuthenticAMD
   AMD-K6(tm) 3D processor
   Intel MMX(TM) Technology
   64.0MB RAM
```

That means I'm using Windows 98, I haven't registered the computer yet, the computer's CPU chip is manufactured by AMD instead of by Intel but uses Intel's MMX technology, and the computer contains 64 megabytes of RAM chips.

What message does *your* computer show? When you finish admiring the message, click "OK".

Windows 98's custom style

If you're using Windows 98 (instead of 95), you should do this:

> Click "Start" then "Settings" then "Folder Options".
> Click "Classic style" then "Apply".
> Click "Custom" then "Settings" then "For all folders with HTML content".
> Click "OK" then "Close".

That procedure gives your computer the **best custom style**, so you can follow the instructions in this chapter and in Microsoft's manuals and tutorials.

Your computer and your copy of Windows 98 probably came with that procedure done already, but do it again to be sure. **If you're sharing the computer with friends, ask their permission before doing the procedure.**

Double-click My Computer

To see different secrets about your computer, double-click the My Computer icon. You'll see the **My Computer window**.

That window contains an icon for each disk drive. For example, if your computer has a floppy drive called "A:", a hard drive called "C:", and a CD-ROM drive called "D:", you'll see a "Floppy A:" icon, a "C:" icon, and a "D:" icon.

The window also contains a Printers icon and a Control Panel icon. It might also contain a Dial-Up Networking icon. (If you're using Windows 98, it also contains a Scheduled Tasks icon.)

Manipulate your hard disk

To find out about your hard disk, click the "C:" icon, which is in the My Computer window. Then the My Computer window changes:

> If you're using Windows 95, the bottom right corner of the My Computer window will tell you how much of the disk's capacity is still unused (free).
>
> If you're using Windows 98, the left part of the My Computer window is a pie chart showing the disk's total capacity, how much of it is used up, and how much of it is still unused (free).

To find out *more* about your hard disk, *right*-click the "C:" icon (so you see a shortcut menu), then choose "Properties" from that menu (by clicking "Properties"). You'll see a *fancy* pie chart showing the disk's total capacity, how much of it is used up, and how much of it is still unused (free). When you finish admiring that chart, click "OK".

If you *double*-click the "C:" icon, you'll see the **C window**, which lists files that are on the hard disk. Make sure the C window consumes the whole screen. (If it doesn't consume the whole screen yet, maximize the C window by clicking the resize button, which is next to the X button.) If the hard disk contains more files than can fit on the screen, view the remaining files by pressing the ▾ and ▴ buttons, which are at the screen's right edge.

For each file, you see the file's name and a tiny picture (**icon**) representing the file.

> If the file's a **document**, its icon looks like a **notepad** (or else **a page whose top right corner is bent**).
>
> If the file's an **application program**, its icon looks like a **window**.
>
> If the file's a **folder** containing other files, its icon looks like a **yellow manila folder**. If you double-click that icon, a new window shows you what files are in the folder. (When you finish admiring the new window, close it by clicking its X button.)

If you click a file's icon, here's what happens:

> If the file's a document or program, the screen's bottom shows you how many bytes are in the file.
>
> If you're using Windows 98, the screen's left shows you the file's MS-DOS name, the file's type ("Document" or "Application" or "Folder"), the date when the file was last modified, and (if the file's a document or application) the file's size (rounded).

Double-clicking a program's icon will make the computer try to run the program; don't do that unless you've read instructions about how to run the program successfully! *Double*-clicking a document's icon will make the computer try to use that document: the computer will try to run the program that created the document, but sometimes the computer can't correctly deduce which program created the document.

View menu While you're viewing icons, you can change their appearance by clicking the word "View", which gives a **View menu**. From that menu, choose either **Large Icons** (to make the icons as large & lovely as when you bought the computer), **Small Icons** (to make the icons small, so you fit more of them on the screen), **List** (to make the icons small and organized so you begin by reading down the left column), or **Details** (to make each icon small and accompanied by a comment showing the file's size and the date when the file was last modified). Usually you'll be happiest if you choose "List".

New folder To create a new folder, click "File" (which is at the screen's top left corner), so you see the File menu. From that menu, choose "New", then click "Folder".

A new folder will appear. Type a name for it (and press ENTER).

Close the C window When you finish examining the files that are on hard disk C, close the C window by clicking its X button.

Manipulate floppy disks

To analyze a floppy disk that contains info, put the floppy disk into drive A. Then double-click the "Floppy A:" icon, which is in the My Computer Window. You'll see the **A window**, which lists the files that are on the floppy disk.

Make sure the A window consumes the whole screen. (If it doesn't consume the whole screen yet, maximize the A window by clicking the resize button, which is next to the X button.)

If the floppy disk contains more files than can fit on the screen, view the remaining files by pressing the ▾ and ▴ buttons, which are at the screen's right edge.

For each file, you see the file's name and an icon representing the file. When you finish examining them, close the A window by clicking its X button.

Format a floppy disk If you buy a new floppy disk that doesn't contain any info yet, that disk must be formatted. Probably the disk's been formatted for you by the disk's manufacturer; but if the disk hasn't been formatted yet, you must format it yourself. Warning: formatting a disk erases any info that was on the disk.

To format a floppy disk, put the disk into drive A. In the My Computer window, right-click the "Floppy A:" icon. Left-click "Format", then "Start", then "Close", then "Close" again.

Duplicate a floppy disk If you have a 3½-inch 1.44M floppy disk that contains info, and you have a 3½-inch 1.44M floppy disk that's blank, here's how to copy all info from the first disk to the second so the second becomes an exact duplicate of the first.

Put the first disk (which contains info) into drive A. In the My Computer window, right-click the "Floppy A:" icon. Click "Copy Disk" and press ENTER. When the computer tells you, put the blank disk into drive A (after removing the other disk) and press ENTER. The computer will say "Copy completed successfully". Click "Close".

Close

When you finish using the My Computer window, close it by clicking its X button.

File's shortcut menu

When you turn on the computer, Windows 95 and 98 make the screen show the Start button, the My Computer icon, the Recycle Bin icon, and several other icons.

Suppose you've created a document by using WordPad or Paint.

> In Windows 95, your document's icon is probably on the screen already.
>
> Windows 98 makes your screen show a folder called "My Documents"; your document's icon is buried in that folder.

If you're interested in a file, make that file's icon appear on the screen. If the file you're interested in doesn't have an icon on the screen yet, here's how to make the icon appear. If the icon is in a folder that's on the screen (such as Windows 98's "My Documents" folder), double-click the folder's icon. If the icon is *not* in a folder on screen, do this:

> Double-click the My Computer Icon. Then double-clicking the "C:" icon (if the file's on the hard disk) or the "Floppy A:" icon (if the file's on a floppy disk in drive A). Then you see icons for many files and folders. If you still don't see the file's icon but the file's in a folder, make the file's icon appear by double-clicking the folder's icon.

Once the file's icon is on the screen, right-click on the file's icon. You'll see the file's shortcut menu, which offers these choices:

> Open
> Send To
> Cut
> Copy
> Rename
> Properties

(For some kinds of files, the shortcut menu offers extra choices also.)

Here's what each choice means....

Properties

If you choose "Properties", the computer tells you the file's name, the folder it's in, the file's size, the file's MS-DOS name, the date when the file was last modified, the date when the file was last used (accessed), and other info about the file. When you finish admiring that info, click "OK".

Rename

If you choose "Rename", the computer lets you change the file's name. Type a new name (and press ENTER).

Shortcut Instead of right-clicking the file's icon and then choosing Rename, you can left-click the file's icon and then left-click the file's name.

Open

If you choose "Open", the computer opens the file, so it does the same thing as if you double-clicked the file's icon:

> If the file's a folder,   the computer opens the folder and shows what's inside.
> If the file's a program,   the computer runs the program.
> If the file's a document, the computer uses the document (by running the program that created the document).

Send To

If you choose "Send To" and the file's on the hard disk, the computer lets you send a copy of the file to a floppy disk. After choosing "Send To", put the floppy disk into drive A. Then click the "Floppy A" icon.

Exception: on some computers (such as the Windows 95 computer I bought from Quantex), "Floppy A" is not one of the choices. To fix that error and make "Floppy A" become one of the choices, do this:

> Close all windows (by clicking their X buttons). Double-click the My Computer icon, then the "C:" icon, then the Windows icon, then the SendTo icon. From the File menu, choose New, then Shortcut. Put a floppy disk into drive A. On the keyboard, type "a:" (and then press the ENTER key twice). Close all windows (by clicking their X buttons).

Copy

If you choose "Copy", the computer lets you copy the file anywhere you wish!

After choosing "Copy", right-click where you want the copy of the file to appear. For example, you can:

> right-click on a blank place next to the file (so the copy's icon will appear next to the original's icon),
> or right-click on a folder's icon (so the copy will be inserted into that folder),
> or open a new window & right-click on a blank place in that window,
> or right-click on a blank place that's not in any window.

Then click "Paste". The copy will appear.

Each copy takes up space on the disk. For example, if the original file is 1 megabyte long, the copy will be 1 megabyte long also, so the original file plus its copy will consume a total of 2 megabytes.

Paste Shortcut If you click "Paste Shortcut" instead of "Paste", the copy will not consume a megabyte; it will consume just a few bytes telling the computer to refer to the original file for details. In that case, the copy is called a **shortcut**. The shortcut's icon has a bent arrow on it, to emphasize that the shortcut just points back to the original file.

If a file's icon is hard to get to (because the file's in a folder that's in another folder that's in another folder), create a shortcut to it by doing this:

> Right-click the file's icon, then choose "Copy", then close all windows (by clicking their X boxes).
>
> Right-click on a blank place in the middle of the screen, then click "Paste Shortcut". A shortcut to the file's icon will appear where you clicked.

To access the file, just double-click the shortcut's icon.

Copy from floppy disk to hard disk Here's how to copy a file from a floppy disk to your hard disk.

Put the floppy disk into drive A. In the My Computer window, double-click the "3½ Floppy (A:)" icon. Right-click the icon of the file you want to copy. Click "Copy".

Close the "Floppy A:" window (by clicking its X box). Double-click the "C:" icon.

Which of the hard disk's folders do you want to copy the file to? Either right-click that folder's icon, or right-click on a blank place in that folder's window.

Then click "Paste".

Cut

If you choose "Cut", the computer lets you make the file vanish from its current location and reappear in a new location. After choosing "Cut", right-click at the place where you want the file to reappear, then click "Paste".

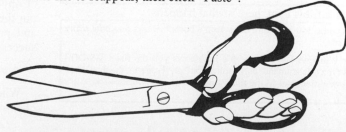

Deleting files

Here's how to delete a file: click its icon, then press the DELETE key, then the ENTER key.

Try it!

Go ahead: try that procedure! To be safe, delete a file that's unimportant, such as a short, junky document you created by using WordPad or Paint.

While you're in the middle of using WordPad, here's the easiest way to delete a WordPad document:

> Click the Open button, so you see a list of WordPad documents and their icons.
> Click the document you want to delete.
> Press the DELETE key, then the ENTER key.

While you're in the middle of using Paint, here's the easiest way to delete a painting you created:

> Press Ctrl with O, so you see a list of paintings you created and their icons.
> Click the painting you want to delete.
> Press the DELETE key, then the ENTER key.

Deleted immediately?

If you use say to delete a file from a *floppy* disk, the computer deletes the file immediately. But if you try to delete a file from the *hard* disk instead, the computer does *not* delete the file immediately; instead, the computer moves the file to the **Recycle Bin**, which holds hard-disk files you said to delete.

Peek in the Recycle Bin

To discover what's in the Recycle Bin, double-click the **Recycle Bin icon**. (It's at the screen's left edge.) You'll see the **Recycle Bin window**, which shows a list of files you said to delete. (If you don't see a file list, the Recycle Bin is empty.)

To see lots of info about the files in the Recycle Bin, make sure the Recycle Bin window is maximized (so it consumes the whole screen), and make sure you're seeing the Details view (by clicking "View" then "Details").

To see even more details about a certain file, right-click the file's icon and then click "Properties". When you finish admiring the details, click "OK".

Restore or delete? If you change your mind and do *not* want to delete a certain file, right-click the file's icon and then click "Restore". That makes the computer pull the file out of the Recycle Bin and put the file back to its original location on the hard disk.

If, on the other hand, you really *do* want to delete a certain file, click the file's icon and then press the DELETE key; then press ENTER. The file will disappear.

To delete *all* files from the Recycle Bin, click "File" and then "Empty Recycle Bin"; then press the ENTER key. Everything in the Recycle Bin will disappear.

Close When you finish admiring the Recycle Bin window, click its X box.

Avoid the Recycle Bin

You've learned that to delete a file, the usual procedure is to click the file's icon, then tap the DELETE key, then tap the ENTER key. If the file was on the hard disk, that procedure moves the file into the Recycle Bin.

Notice that the procedure involves tapping the DELETE key. If, while you're tapping the DELETE key, you hold down the SHIFT key, the computer deletes the file immediately instead of moving it to the Recycle Bin.

Tricks

These tricks will make you a pro.

System tools

To improve the way your computer acts do this: double-click the My Computer icon, then right-click the "C:" icon, then click "Properties", then click "Tools".

ScanDisk To make sure your hard disk contains no errors, click "Check Now".

Then click either "Standard" or "Thorough". If you click "Standard", the computer will give your hard disk a standard checkup, which takes about a minute. If you click "Thorough", the computer will give your hard disk a more thorough checkup, which takes about an hour. (Those times are just approximate. The exact times depend on how fast your computer & hard drive are and how much info's on your hard disk.)

After clicking "Standard" or "Thorough", press ENTER. The computer will check your drive for errors, by using a program called **ScanDisk**.

If the computer says "ScanDisk found data in lost file fragments", click "Discard" and then "OK".

When the computer finishes checking your drive, it will say "ScanDisk Results". (If you're lucky and there are no errors, the computer will also say "ScanDisk did not find any errors on this drive.") The computer will also tell you how many bytes are on the disk. When you finish reading those messages, press ENTER twice.

Defrag To make your hard disk run faster, click "Defragment Now". If the computer gives you a choice between "Start", "Select Drive", "Advanced", and "Exit", click "Start".

That makes the computer rearrange the info on your hard disk to let the computer access it faster. For example, if one of your hard disk's files is **fragmented** (split into several fragments that are scattered across the disk), the computer will try to **defragment (defrag)** the file to make it consist of a single big chunk that the computer can access faster.

When the computer finishes rearranging your hard disk's files, the computer will say "Defragmentation of drive C is complete." Press ENTER.

Close When you finish using the system tools, close the window by clicking its X box. Then close the My Computer window by clicking its X box also.

Start menu

When you click the Start button (at the screen's bottom left corner), Windows 98 shows you this **Start menu**:

```
Windows Update
Programs       ▶
Favorites      ▶
Documents      ▶
Settings       ▶
Find           ▶
Help
Run
Shut Down
```

You've already learned about "Programs" and "Shut Down".

Two of the choices — "Windows Update" and "Favorites" — deal with the Internet. Windows 95 omits those choices. I'll explain the Internet on pages 208-230.

Let's examine the other choices....

Documents If you choose "Documents", the computer shows you the **Document menu**, which is a list of the last 15 documents you used. (If your computer is new and you haven't used 15 documents yet, the list is shorter.)

> Windows 95 shows the list in alphabetical order (from A to Z).
> Windows 98 shows the list in chronological order (from oldest to newest).

To use one of those documents, click it. Then the computer runs the program that created the document, and the computer lets you use the document. When you finish using the document, close its window (by clicking its X box).

Suppose you delete one of those 15 documents (by double-clicking My Computer, then double-clicking "C:", then clicking the document's icon, then pressing the DELETE key; or by double-clicking Windows 98's My Documents folder, then clicking the document's icon, then pressing the DELETE key). Even though you've deleted the document, it remains mentioned in the Document menu. So although the Document menu lists the last 15 documents you mentioned, those 15 documents don't necessarily still exist!

Find To use a file that's on your hard disk, the traditional method is to double-click the My Computer icon, then double-click the "C:", then double-click any folders that the file is in (until the file's icon appears), then double-click the file's icon. To use that procedure, you must double-click many times (especially if the file is buried in a folder that's in another folder that's in other folders), and that procedure works just if you already know which folders the file is in. Such hunting for your buried treasure can be hard work!

Here's a faster way to unearth the file....

From the Start menu, choose "Find". Then click "Files or Folders". You'll see the **Find Files window**.

Then type the file's name — or whatever part of the name you can remember. For example, if you want to search for a file that might be called "Lovers" or "My Love" or "To My Lovely", just type "Love".

At the end of your typing, do *not* press ENTER yet; instead, examine the Look In box.

> If the Look In box contains "C:", the computer will look through your entire hard disk; if the Look In box contains "My Documents" instead, the computer will look through just the My Documents folder. If you don't like what's in the Look In box, change it by clicking its down-arrow and then click the choice you wish.

When the Look In box contains what you wish, press ENTER.

The computer will search your entire hard drive for any files having that name. It will show you a list of all such files. To see the list fully, maximize the Find Files window by clicking its resize button (which is next to the X button), so the window consumes the whole screen.

If no file in that list interests you, close the window by clicking the X box.

If one of those files *does* interest you, double-click it. Then the computer will start using it.

> If the file's a program, the computer will run the program.
> If the file's a document, the computer will run the program that created it.
> If the file's a folder, the computer will show you what's in the folder.

Run Here's a faster way to tell the computer to run WordPad: from the Start menu, choose "Run"; then type "wordpad" and press ENTER.

To run Paint instead of WordPad, type "mspaint" instead of "wordpad". To run the Calculator, type "calc" instead.

When you buy a program, it typically comes on a disk (a floppy disk or a CD-ROM disk). The instructions for copying it onto your hard disk might say to run a program called "install" or "setup". To obey such instructions, do this:

> Put the floppy disk or CD-ROM disk into your disk drive. Choose "Run" from the Start menu.
> If the program came on a floppy disk, type "a:install" or "a:setup" (whichever they said to type). If the program came on a CD-ROM disk and your CD-ROM drive is called "D:", type "d:install" or "d:setup" (whichever they said). If the program came on a CD-ROM disk and your CD-ROM drive is called "E:", type "e:install" or "e:setup" (whichever they said).
> At the end of your typing, press ENTER.

Settings To change the way your computer acts, do this: from the Start menu, choose "Settings", then click "Control Panel". You'll see the **Control Panel window**. For Windows 98, that window contains these 23 icons:

> 32bit ODBC, Accessibility Options, Add New Hardware, Add/Remove Programs, Date/Time, Desktop Themes, Display, Fonts, Game Controllers, Internet, Keyboard, Modems, Mouse, Multimedia, Network, Passwords, Power Management, Printers, Regional Settings, Sounds, System, Telephony, Users

(Windows 95 says Power instead of Power Management, says Joystick instead of Game Controllers, omits 4 icons (32bit ODBC, Desktop Themes, Telephony, and Users) but adds Mail-and-Fax.)

For your first experiment, double-click the **Mouse** icon.

> You'll see the **Mouse Properties window**. To modify the mouse's motion, click "Motion". Then if you put a ✓ in the "Show pointer trails" box (by clicking it), you'll see a trail of mouse pointers whenever you move the mouse. To make the trail be long and obvious, make sure the slider is dragged toward the right, to the "Long" position.
> The long trail helps you notice the mouse pointer more easily. It's useful when you're giving a presentation to a group of people and want to make sure they always notice where the mouse is moving. It's also useful if you're on a laptop computer whose screen is "passive matrix", which is too slow to show mouse motions well.
> If you change your mind, stop the trails by clicking the "Show pointer trails" box again, so the check mark disappears.
> When you finish experimenting with pointer trails, close the Mouse Properties window by clicking "OK".

You can experiment by double-clicking any of the other icons in the Control Panel window, but be careful! If you tell the computer to use hardware you don't own, Windows will stop working! Before changing a setting, make a note to yourself of what the setting was, so you can get back to it! Be especially cautious about playing with the Display icon, since if you make a wrong choice your screen will be unreadable!

When you finish playing with the Control Panel window, close it by clicking its X box.

If you're using Windows 98 (instead of 95), try this experiment:

> From the Start menu, choose "Settings" then "Folder Options". Click "Web style", then press ENTER.
> Then your computer will act quite differently. Each major icon's name is underlined. To open a major icon, click it just once (instead of double-clicking). To select a major icon, just put the mouse's pointer on it and wait a second, *without* clicking: the icon will darken and be selected. When dealing with major icons, each window usually maximizes itself and makes all other windows close. When you finish using a window, either click its X button (which closes that window) or else click its Back button (which is near the window's top left corner and closes that window and shows you the previous window).
> When you finish experimenting with those features, return the computer back to normal by following the procedure on page 102, in the section called "Windows 98's custom style".

Help For further help in learning how to use Windows 95 or 98, choose "Help" from the Start menu. Then click either "Contents" or "Index".

> **If you choose "Contents",** the computer shows a list of the *major* topics. Click the topic you want help about; if you then see a list of subtopics, click the subtopic you want help about. If you're using Windows 95 instead of 98, you must *double*-click instead of click.
>
> **If you choose "Index",** the computer tries to show an alphabetical index of *all* topics about Windows 95 (or 98). You see just the index's beginning; to see the index section about the topic you wish, type the first few letters of the topic's name. When you see your desired topic, double-click it.

When you finish using help, close the help window by clicking its X box. (If you don't see an X box, click "Exit" and then click "Exit Tour".)

Play a music CD

Before 1980, music came on records or tapes. Nowadays, music comes on compact discs instead. If you've gone to a music store and bought a compact disc containing music, you can shove that disk into your computer's CD-ROM drive while Windows is running. The computer will play the compact disc as background music, while you continue your work.

Volume To adjust the music's volume, turn the **volume knob**, which is typically on the front of the right speaker. (For some old systems, the volume knob is on the computer's back wall instead, below where the speaker's cable enters the computer.)

On some systems, the screen's bottom right corner shows a **Volume icon** (which looks like a blaring loudspeaker and is next to the time). If you click that icon, you'll see a slider. Using the mouse, drag the slider up (to raise the volume) or down (to lower it).

CD Player button While the music plays, a **CD Player button** appears at the screen's bottom next to the Start button. On that button, you see which track (song) you're playing and how many minutes & seconds of that track have elapsed.

To control the music, click the CD Player button. You'll see the **CD Player window**. In that window, click the ‖ button to pause in the middle of a song, ■ to stop back at the beginning of track 1, ▶ to resume playing, ▶▶| to skip ahead to the next track, |◀◀ to hop back to the beginning of the current track. Hold down the ▶▶ button awhile to go fast-forward, ◀◀ to reverse. Click ▲ to eject the disk from the drive (so you can insert a different disk instead). When you tire of listening to your CD collection, click eject (▲) and click the window's X button.

Taskbar

At the screen's bottom, you see a gray bar, called the **taskbar**.

> It's about half an inch tall, and it's very wide: it runs across the screen, from the screen's bottom left corner to the bottom right corner. The taskbar includes the "Start" button (at the screen's bottom left corner), the time box (at the screen's bottom right corner), and everything between them.

When you're running a task (program), the taskbar usually shows a button for that task. For example, while you're running WordPad, you see a WordPad button on the taskbar. While you're running Paint, you see a Paint button on the taskbar.

Try this experiment:

> Start running WordPad (by clicking Start then Programs then Accessories then WordPad). Now the taskbar includes a WordPad button. Since WordPad is a word-processing program, type a few words, so you've created a short document on your screen.

> While WordPad is still on your screen, start running Paint (by clicking Start then Programs then Accessories then Paint). Now the taskbar includes a WordPad button and a Paint button, because WordPad and Paint are both running simultaneously: they're both in the computer's RAM memory chips. Paint is blocking your view of WordPad, but WordPad is still running also.
>
> To see WordPad better, click WordPad's button on the toolbar. Then you'll see WordPad clearly, and WordPad will block your view of Paint.
>
> Here's the rule: clicking WordPad's button lets you see WordPad better; clicking Paint's button lets you see Paint better. Both programs are in RAM simultaneously, until you close them (by clicking their X buttons).
>
> You can run *several* program simultaneously (for example, you can run WordPad, Paint, and Calculator all simultaneously, so you see all their buttons on the taskbar simultaneously). But if you try to run many programs simultaneously, the computer is likely to get confused and fail (especially if you bought too little RAM or you're using an old version of Windows 95 or your computer's been on for many hours in a row). To avoid headaches, run no more than two major programs at a time.

Clipboard

You can copy data from one document to another, even if the documents were created by different programs, and even if one "document" is a drawing and the other "document" contains mostly words. (For example, you can copy data that's a drawing, from Paint to WordPad.) Here's how:

> Get onto the screen the data you want to copy.
> Select that data, by dragging across it. (If that data is in Paint, click Paint's Select button before dragging.)
> Say "**copy**" by pressing **Ctrl with C**. That secretly copies the data to the **Clipboard** (a file you can't see).
>
> Get onto the screen the document you want to copy the data to.
> In that document, click where you want the data to be inserted.
> Say "**Velcro**" by pressing **Ctrl with V**. That sticks the Clipboard's data into the document.
>
> (If you're sticking the data into a WordPad document, the computer sticks it where you requested. If you're sticking the data into a Paint document, the computer insists on sticking it at the painting's top left corner; then drag the data where you want it.)

Keyboard

A traditional keyboard contains 101 keys. If your keyboard is designed especially for Windows 95 and 98, it contains 3 extra keys near the SPACE bar, so you get 104 keys altogether.

Two of those extra keys are the **Windows keys**: each shows a flying window. **If you press either of the Windows keys, the Start menu appears**. So pressing either of those has the same effect as if your mouse clicked the Start button. You can press *either* of the Windows keys: those two keys serve the same purpose as each other, except that one is nearer your left hand, the other is nearer your right. Your keyboard has two SHIFT keys, two Ctrl keys, two Alt keys, and two Windows keys.

The other extra key, called the **menu key**, shows an arrow pointing at a menu. **If you press the menu key, a shortcut menu appears.** For example, if you click an icon and then press the menu key, that icon's shortcut menu appears.

Property window Here are 4 ways to make an icon's property window appear....

Right-click method:	right-click the icon (so the icon's shortcut menu appears), then click "Properties"
Menu-key method:	click the icon, press the menu key (so the icon's shortcut menu appears), then either click "Properties" or press the R key (which is the code for "Properties")
Alt-double method:	while holding down the Alt key, double-click the icon
Alt-enter method:	click the icon; then while holding down the Alt key, tap the ENTER key

Use whichever method you wish! My favorites are the right-click method (which feels the most natural) and the Alt-double method (which is usually the fastest).

Alt F4 Try this experiment: while holding down the Alt key, tap the F4 key.

> If a window is open, that makes the computer click the window's X box, so the window closes. (If *two* windows are open, here's how to close both: while holding down the Alt key, tap the F4 key twice. If *several* windows are open, here's how to close them all: while holding down the Alt and SHIFT keys, tap the F4 key.)
>
> If no windows are open, Alt with F4 makes the computer choose Shut Down from the Start menu.

Problem: someday your mouse stops working (because the mouse is broken or the computer gets too confused to handle the mouse). To get out of that mess, press Alt F4 several times (to close your windows and shut down the computer). Then try again to turn the computer on.

Dig deeper

> While using Windows 95, 98, or Me, you can give **MS-DOS commands**. Details are on pages 114-149.
> To make Windows 95, 98, and Me run better, **clean your software**. Details are on pages 575-578.
> Windows 95, 98, and Me handle your **modem** (page 205), the **Internet**, (pages 206-230) and **faxes** (page 231).

WINDOWS 3.1 & 3.11

Starting

Though most new computers come with Windows 98, most companies still have old computers using old versions of Windows, such as **Windows 3.1** and **Windows 3.11**.

This chapter explains Windows 3.1. Most of this chapter's explanation also applies to Windows 3.11, which is similar but slightly fancier. If you're using Windows 3.0, do yourself a favor: switch to Windows 3.1, 3.11, 95, or 98.

Prepare for Windows

Before putting Windows 3.1 or 3.11 into your computer, you must buy MS-DOS (version 3.1 or higher), a hard drive, and other good hardware:

Windows requires a fast CPU: a 286, 386, 486, or Pentium. The *advanced* parts of Windows require a 386, 486, or Pentium.

Windows 3.1 (or 3.11) requires at least 1M of RAM. To run Windows fast and without hassles, you need 4M. Some Windows programs require 8M.

Windows requires a graphics video card: Hercules, CGA, EGA, or VGA. To run Windows pleasantly, get a VGA card and VGA color monitor; otherwise, the screen's display is crude and slow.

Since Windows comes on high-density floppy disks, get a high-density floppy drive! Otherwise, you must mail the high-density floppy disks back to Microsoft and exchange them for low-density floppy disks.

Buy a mouse! Without a mouse, you must use awkward keystrokes that are hard to remember.

This chapter assumes you've bought enough software and hardware to run Windows well: MS-DOS 3.1 or higher, a hard drive, a 386 or 486 or Pentium, 4M of RAM, a VGA color monitor, a high-density floppy drive, and a mouse.

Cost Windows 3.11 lists for $150. Discount dealers sell it for $89. If you already have Windows 1, 2, or 3, you can upgrade to Windows 3.11 for just $49. It usually comes on 3½-inch high-density floppies; if you don't have a 3½-inch drive, buy a 5¼-inch version instead.

Installation procedure
Here's how to copy Windows 3.1 to the hard disk.

Turn on the computer without any floppy in drive A. Windows 3.1 comes on a set of floppy disks; you get six 3½-inch disks or seven 5¼-inch disks. When you see the C prompt, put Windows Disk 1 into drive A and type "a:".

The computer will display an A prompt. Type "setup". The computer will say "Windows Setup", then pause, then say "Welcome to Setup". Press ENTER twice.

The computer will say, "Please insert Disk 2." Insert it into drive A and press ENTER. (If you're using 5¼-inch disks, the computer will then say, "Please insert Disk 3." Insert it and press ENTER.)

The computer will say, "Please type your full name." Type your name. (At the end of your name, if your copy of Windows is owned by your company, press TAB and then type your company's name.) At the end of all your typing, press ENTER twice.

When the computer tells you, insert additional disks and press ENTER.

After you've inserted Disk 6 and pressed ENTER, the computer will say "Select a printer". You'll see an alphabetized list of printers. Tap the down-arrow key several times, until *your* printer appears on the screen and is blue. Press ENTER twice. (If you're using 5¼-inch disks, the computer will then say, "Please insert Disk 7." Insert it and press ENTER.)

The computer will look for programs on your hard disk. If the computer pauses at a program and waits for your response, tap the down-arrow key several times until the program's name is blue, then press ENTER.

On the screen, you'll see buttons labeled "Run Tutorial" and "Skip Tutorial". Choose "Skip Tutorial" by pressing the S key.

The computer will say, "Windows is now set up." Press D.

You'll see a C prompt, like this:
`C:\WINDOWS>`
Turn off the computer, so you can start fresh.

Run Windows

Here's how to start using Windows 3.1 (or 3.11).

Turn on the computer, without any disks in the floppy drives. (For details, read "Prepare to operate" on page 94. For free help, phone me anytime at 603-666-6644.)

If the computer says —

`C:\>`

type "win" so the screen looks like this:

`C:\>win`

At the end of typing "win", press the ENTER key.

Program Manager window

A box containing information is called a **window**. You see this window:

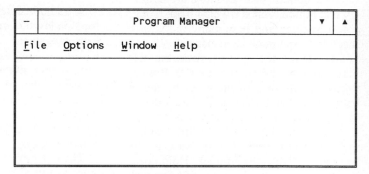

On the window's top line, you see the window's **title**: "Program Manager". That tells you the window is called the **Program Manager window**.

In the middle of that big window, you might see a small window, such as the **Main window**:

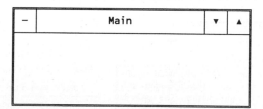

If you see the Main window (or another small window), do this: while holding down the Ctrl key, tap the F4 key. That makes the small window disappear, so the only window on the screen is the Program Manager window.

Position the mouse & move the arrow
Read about these topics on page 96.

Choose from a menu
The most important part of the arrow is its tip, which is called the **hot spot**.

For an experiment, move the arrow so its hot spot (tip) is in the middle of the word "File". When you do that, you're **pointing at** the word "File".

On the top of the mouse, you'll see 2 or 3 rectangular buttons you can press. **The main button is the one on the left.** That's the only button Windows uses. Tapping it is called **clicking**. So to **click**, tap the left button.

While you're pointing at the word "File", click (by tapping the left button). That's called **clicking "File"**.

When you click "File", you'll see this **File menu**:

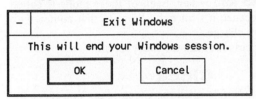

```
New...
Open
Move...
Copy...
Delete
Properties...
Run...
Exit Windows...
```

In that menu, the bottom choice is "Exit Windows". If you choose "Exit Windows", the computer will stop using Windows.

Try it! Click "Exit Windows" (by moving the arrow there and then tapping the left button). You'll see this window:

```
┌─┬──────────────────────────────┐
│-│         Exit Windows         │
├─┴──────────────────────────────┤
│  This will end your Windows session. │
│   ┌──────────┐   ┌──────────┐  │
│   │    OK    │   │  Cancel  │  │
│   └──────────┘   └──────────┘  │
└────────────────────────────────┘
```

If you want to exit from Windows, click "OK" (by moving the arrow there and then clicking). If you do *not* want to exit from Windows, click "Cancel" instead.

That whole procedure for exiting from Windows can be summarized in one sentence:

Choose "Exit Windows" from the File menu, then click OK.

After you've exited from Windows, the screen will turn completely black. Then the computer will say:

C:\>

That symbol, which is called the "C prompt", means you can safely turn off the computer. Then if you wish, turn off the computer!

Try that procedure! Notice it involves these three steps....

Step 1: choose from a menu bar
The first step is to choose "File" from this menu:

```
┌────────────────────────────────────┐
│  File   Options   Window   Help     │
└────────────────────────────────────┘
```

That menu's in a horizontal box. The box is called a **menu bar**.

To choose a word (such as "File") from a menu bar, you can use three methods:

Mouse method: by using the mouse, click the word you want.

Arrow-key method: move to the menu (by tapping the Alt key), move to the word you want (by pressing the right-arrow key several times, if necessary), then press ENTER.

Underlined-letter method: move to the menu (by tapping the Alt key), then type the word's underlined letter (for example, type the F in "File").

The mouse method is the simplest. Use the other methods if your mouse is broken or missing or makes your flesh crawl.

Step 2: choose from a pull-down menu
After you choose "File", this menu appears underneath "File":

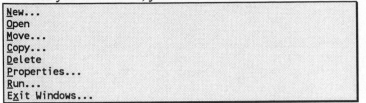

```
┌────────────────┐
│ New...         │
│ Open           │
│ Move...        │
│ Copy...        │
│ Delete         │
│ Properties...  │
│ Run...         │
│ Exit Windows...│
└────────────────┘
```

That menu is a vertical list that "falls down" from the word "File". It's called a **pull-down menu**.

To choose a command (such as "Exit Windows") from a pull-down menu, you can use the same three methods:

Mouse method: by using the mouse, click the command you want.

Arrow-key method: move to the command you want (by pressing the down-arrow key several times), then press ENTER.

Underlined-letter method: type the underlined letter (for example, type the x in "Exit Windows").

Step 3: choose from a dialog box
After you choose "Exit Windows", this window appears:

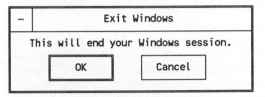

```
┌─┬──────────────────────────────┐
│-│         Exit Windows         │
├─┴──────────────────────────────┤
│  This will end your Windows session. │
│   ┌──────────┐   ┌──────────┐  │
│   │    OK    │   │  Cancel  │  │
│   └──────────┘   └──────────┘  │
└────────────────────────────────┘
```

That window warns that you're about to exit from Windows and asks you whether you're sure. If you're sure you want to exit from Windows, click "OK"; otherwise, click "Cancel".

Since that window lets the computer chat with you about your intentions, it's called a **dialog box**. (According to English teachers, it ought to be called a "dialogue box", but computer nerds refuse to type the "ue".)

In the dialog box, each major choice (such as "OK" and "Cancel") is called a **button**. Each button looks like a rectangle. Usually the "OK" button is **highlighted** (its sides are made of doubled or thickened lines).

To communicate with the computer, press one of the buttons. To press a button, you can use two methods:

Mouse method: by using the mouse, click the button you want.

ENTER method: to press the highlighted button (which is usually "OK"), press ENTER; to press a different button instead, move to it (by pressing the TAB key several times) so the button is highlighted, then press ENTER.

Here's a short cut: to press the "Cancel" button, just press the Esc key (which means "Escape and Cancel").

Three dots Notice that the bottom of the File menu says "Exit Windows...". The three dots (...) tell you that if you choose that command, you'll encounter a dialog box.

Resize a window
You can make a window be three sizes: **maximum**, **normal**, or **minimum**.

A **maximum** window consumes the whole screen.
A **normal** window fills about half the screen.
A **minimum** window is shrunk so it's a tiny picture, called an **icon**.

The symbol for maximum is ▲ (a triangle pointing up).
The symbol for minimum is ▼ (a triangle pointing down).
The symbol for normal is ↕ (a pair of balanced triangles).

If a window is normal, its top right corner contains the symbols ▼ and ▲ . Using your mouse, click ▼ to make the window become minimum; click ▲ to make the window become maximum.

If a window is maximum, its top right corner contains the symbols for minimum and normal. Click one of those symbols to make the window change size.

If a window is minimum, it's just a tiny picture — an icon. Try clicking that icon. Then you'll see a menu. From the menu, choose **Maximize** (to make the window become maximum) or **Restore** (to make the window become whatever size it was previously).

Try it! Make the Program Manager's window become maximum, minimum, and normal again.

Drag

To **drag** an object, point at it (by using the mouse), then hold down the mouse's left button, and while you keep that button down, move the mouse.

For example, try this experiment. Make the Program Manager's window be minimum, so it's just an icon. Point at the icon (by using the mouse), then hold down the mouse's left button, and while you keep that button down, move the mouse. As you move the mouse, the icon moves. You can drag the icon anywhere on the screen! Try it! Here's the rule: if a window is minimum (so it's just an icon), and you want to move it to a different part of the screen, drag it.

Here's another experiment to try. Make the Program Manager's window be normal, so it fills about half the screen. At the top of that window, you'll see the words "Program Manager". Those words are called the window's **title**. Point at that title ("Program Manager"), then drag it to a different part of the screen (by holding down the mouse's button as you move the mouse). As you drag the title, you'll also be automatically dragging the entire window. Here's the rule: **to move a normal window, drag its title**.

A normal window is a rectangle. To change its width, drag its right-hand edge. To change its height, drag its bottom edge. To change its width and height simultaneously, drag its bottom right corner.

Try it! Make the Program Manager be a normal window, then change its width and height by dragging its edges and bottom right corner.

Scroll arrows

Here's another series of experiments to try.

Make the Program Manager be a maximum window, so it consumes the whole screen. Inside that big window, you'll see five icons (little pictures), called **Accessories**, **Games**, **StartUp**, **Applications**, and **Main**. If somebody else was using the computer, you might see some extra icons.

Make the Program Manager be a normal window (so it fills about half the screen). You'll probably still see those icons in the Program Manager window.

Make the Program Manager's window be smaller, by dragging its edges or bottom right corner. Make the window too small to hold all the icons, so you see just *some* of the icons. Instead of seeing everything that belongs in the Window, you see just a **partial view**.

When you see a partial view, you see arrows near the window's corners. By clicking the arrows, you can shift your view. To see icons farther to the right, click the right-arrow. (To see icons even *farther* to the right, click the right-arrow again. To see icons *very* far to the right, click the right-arrow repeatedly — or point at the right-arrow and then hold down the mouse's left button awhile.) To see icons farther to the left, click the left-arrow; to see icons that are higher, click the up-arrow; to see icons that are lower, click the down-arrow.

Try it! Click those arrows! They're called **scroll arrows**.

Make the Program Manager window be rather large, so it consumes most of the screen but not the top quarter of the screen. In that window, look for the **Accessories** icon. (If you don't see that icon, adjust the window by using the scroll arrows.)

Double-click the Accessories icon. To double-click the icon, move the arrow to the icon, then tap the mouse's left button twice *quickly*, so the two taps are less than .4 seconds apart.

While tapping the left button twice, make sure the mouse remains still. Don't let the mouse jiggle, not even a smidgin! While double-clicking, your desk should be like Christmas Eve, where "not a creature is stirring, not even a mouse".

You'll see the **Accessories window**. In that window, you'll see 13 icons: **Write**, **Paintbrush**, **Terminal**, **Notepad**, **Recorder**, **Cardfile**, **Calendar**, **Calculator**, **Clock**, **Object Packager**, **Character Map**, **Media Player**, and **Sound Recorder**. Each of those icons is called an **accessory**, because it's an extra "jewel" that comes with Windows at no extra charge.

The following accessories are the most useful.

Clock

To use the Clock, double-click the Clock icon. You'll see the **Clock window**, with a picture of a clock in it.

You can choose two kinds of clocks. An **analog clock** has an hour hand, minute hand, and second hand. A **digital clock** has no hands: it shows just digits.

The first time you (or your colleagues) ask for the clock, Windows 3.1 shows a digital clock. To switch from digital to analog, choose **Analog** from the **Settings menu**. (To do that, click the word "Settings", then click the word "Analog".) To switch back to a digital clock, choose **Digital** from the Settings menu.

The clock normally shows the correct time. (If the clock's time is wrong, here's how to reset it: exit from Windows, then give the "time" command from the DOS prompt.)

The clock also shows the date.

The clock keeps on ticking — silently. If you want to put yourself into a trance, watch the analog clock's second hand move. (It's better than counting sheep.)

If you want the clock to be larger, maximize its window by clicking ▲. Then the clock will fill the whole screen. That's how to turn your entire $2,000 computer into a $2 clock! But hey, it's a *high-tech* clock! To freak out your friends, hide the keyboard and system unit under the desk, so your friends see just the screen displaying the analog clock.

If you want the clock to be tiny, minimize its window by clicking ▼. Then the clock will be a tiny icon. Even though it's tiny, it still runs! Though it's too tiny to show the seconds, it still shows the correct hour and minutes.

Close When you finish using the clock, **close** it. Here's how.

Make the Clock window be normal or maximum. In the Clock window's top left corner, you'll see a square containing a horizontal bar:

-

That square is called the **control box**. When you finish using the Clock window, double-click the control box. That makes the Clock window disappear.

Calculator

To use the Calculator, double-click the Calculator icon. You'll see the **Calculator window**, containing a picture of a pocket calculator.

How to calculate Read about this topic on page 97.

Warning: if your version of Windows was created before 1995, the computer has trouble subtracting numbers that end in ".01". For example, if you compute 2.01 minus 2, the correct answer is .01, but the computer mistakenly says 0 instead.

Standard versus scientific Read about this topic on page 97.

Close When you finish using the calculator, double-click its control box.

Write

When you buy Windows, you get a word-processing program free! That word-processing program is called **Write**. It's one of the Windows accessories.

To use Write, double-click the Write icon. You'll see the **Write window**. Maximize it by clicking ▲.

Now you can do word processing: you can type words and sentences simply. Try it! Type whatever sentences you wish to make up. For example, try typing a memo to your friends, or a story, or a poem. Be creative! Whatever you type is called a **document**.

While you're typing, you see the symbol ¤. That symbol appears at the end of what you've typed; that symbol marks the end of your document.

Use the keyboard Read about this topic on page 98.

Scroll through documents If your document contains too many lines to fit on the screen, the screen will show just *part* of the document. To see the rest of the document, click the scroll arrows.

Insert characters Read about this topic on page 99.

Split a paragraph Read about this topic on page 99.

Combine paragraphs Read about this topic on page 99.

Movement keys To move to different parts of your document, you can use your mouse. To move faster, press these keys instead:

Key you press	Where the pointer will move
right-arrow	right to the next character
left-arrow	left to the previous character
down-arrow	down to the line below
up-arrow	up to the line above
END	right to the end of the line
HOME	left to the beginning of the line
PAGE DOWN	down to the next screenful
PAGE UP	up to the previous screenful
Ctrl with right-arrow	right (to the next word or punctuation symbol)
Ctrl with left-arrow	left (to the beginning of a word or punctuation)
Ctrl with PAGE DOWN	down to the screen's bottom line
Ctrl with PAGE UP	up to the screen's top line
Ctrl with END	down to the end of the document
Ctrl with HOME	up to the beginning of the document

Menu bar While you're using Write, the top of the screen shows this menu bar:

File	Edit	Find	Character	Paragraph	Document	Help

Let's use that menu bar....

Underline Here's how to underline a phrase (like this). Choose **Underline** from the **Character menu**. Type the phrase. Then choose **Regular** from the Character menu.

Bold Here's how to make a phrase be bold (like this). Choose **Bold** from the Character menu. Type the phrase. Then choose Regular from the Character menu.

Here's how to make a phrase be bold and underlined (like this). Choose Bold from the Character menu. Choose Underline from the Character menu. Type the phrase. Then choose Regular from the Character menu.

Italics Here's how to italicize a phrase (*like this*). Choose **Italics** from the Character menu. Type the phrase. Then choose Regular from the Character menu. (That technique works only if your printer can italicize.)

Select text Here's how to dramatically change a phrase you typed.

Point at the phrase's beginning, then drag to the phrase's end (while holding down the mouse's left button). The whole phrase turns black. Turning the phrase black is called **selecting the phrase**.

Then say what to do to the phrase. For example, choose one of these activities:

To underline the phrase, choose Underline from the Character menu.
To make the phrase be bold, choose Bold from the Character menu.
To italicize the phrase, choose Italics from the Character menu.
To delete the phrase, press the DELETE key.
To replace the phrase, just type whatever words you want the phrase to become.

To copy the phrase (so it appears twice), do this:
while holding down the Alt key, click where you want the copy to appear.

To move the phrase (so it appears just in the new location), do this:
while holding down the Alt and SHIFT keys, click where you want the phrase to appear.

Other ways to select The usual way to select a phrase is to point at the phrase's beginning, then drag to the phrase's end. But sometimes other methods are faster! To select a phrase, choose one of these methods:

Method 1: point at the phrase's beginning, then drag to the phrase's end.
Method 2: click the phrase's beginning; then while holding down the SHIFT key, click the phrase's end.

Method 3: by using your keyboard's movement keys (such as the up-arrow, down-arrow, left-arrow, and right-arrow keys), move to the phrase's beginning; then while holding down the SHIFT key, use the movement keys to move to the phrase's end.

Method 4: to select just one word, double-click in the middle of it.
Method 5: to select a sentence, click in the middle of the sentence while holding down the Ctrl key.

Method 6: to select a whole line, click the screen's left edge, left of the line.
Method 7: to select a whole paragraph, double-click the screen's left edge, left of the paragraph.
Method 8: to select the whole document, click the screen's left edge while holding down the Ctrl key.

Center Here's how to center a title. Choose **Centered** from the **Paragraph menu**. Type the title. At the end of the title, press ENTER. Then choose **Normal** from the Paragraph menu.

Here's how to center a title you typed previously: click anywhere in the title, then choose Center from the Paragraph menu. Here's how to *uncenter* a title you typed previously: click anywhere in the title, then choose Normal from the Paragraph menu.

Save To copy the document onto the disk, choose **Save** from the **File menu**.

Then invent a name for your document. The name must be short: no more than 8 letters. For example, the name can be "jennifer" or "al". Type the name you wish and press ENTER.

That makes the computer copy the document onto the hard disk. For example, if you named the document "jennifer", the computer will put in your hard disk's WINDOWS subdirectory a file called "JENNIFER.WRI", which means "JENNIFER created by the WRIte program".

Afterwards, if you change your mind and want to do more editing, go ahead! Edit the document some more. When you finish that editing, save it by choosing Save from the File menu again.

Print To copy the document onto paper, choose **Print** from the File menu, then press ENTER.

Finish When you finish working on a document, choose **New**, **Open**, or **Exit** from the File menu.

If you choose **New**, the computer will let you start typing a new document. If you choose **Open** and then double-click the name of an old document, the computer will put that document onto the screen and let you edit it. If you choose **Exit**, the computer will stop using Write and let you use a different accessory instead.

Before the computer obeys New, Open, or Exit, it checks whether you saved your document. If you didn't save your document, the computer asks, "Save current changes?" If you click "Yes", the computer copies your document's most recent version to the hard disk; if you click "No" instead, the computer ignores and forgets your most recent editing.

Paintbrush

When you buy Windows, you get a paint program free! That program, called **Paintbrush**, lets you paint pictures. It's one of the Windows accessories.

To use Paintbrush, double-click the Paintbrush icon. You'll see the **Paintbrush window**. Maximize it by clicking ▲.

Move the mouse pointer to the screen's middle. Then drag (move the mouse while holding down the mouse's left button). As you drag, you'll be drawing a squiggle.

For example, try drawing a smile. To do that, put the mouse pointer where you want the smile to begin (at the smile's top left corner), then depress the mouse's left button while you draw the smile. When you finish drawing the smile, lift the mouse's button. Then draw the rest of the face!

Colors When you draw, you're normally drawing in black.

At the screen's bottom, you'll see 28 colors: red, yellow, green, etc. To draw in one of those colors instead of in black, click the color you want.

Line Here's how to draw a line that's perfectly straight.

At the left side of the screen, you'll see many icons. One of the icons is a diagonal line. Click it. Put the mouse pointer in the screen's middle, where you want the line to begin, and drag to where you want the line to end.

When you finish drawing lines and want **to draw squiggles instead, click the brush icon** (which is above the line icon).

Rectangle Here's how to draw a rectangle whose sides are perfectly straight.

At the left side of the screen, you'll see two icons that are rectangles. Click the left rectangle.

Put the mouse pointer in the screen's middle, where you want the rectangle's top left corner to be. Drag to where you want the rectangle's opposite corner.

Spray Here's how to vandalize your own drawing, by using a can of spray paint!

At the left side of the screen, you'll see an icon that's a can of spray paint. Click it. Put the mouse in the screen's middle, where you want to begin spraying, and drag!

Erase To erase a mistake, click the simple eraser icon, which is *above the brush icon*.

Then drag across the part of your drawing that you want to erase. The part you drag across will become white.

Thickness At the screen's bottom left corner, you'll see eight horizontal lines, ranging from "thin" to "thick". Click the thickness you want.

For example, if you click the thickest line, everything you draw will be very thick. Your squiggles, lines, and rectangles will all be very thick — as if you were using a brush that's very thick and wide. The eraser will be thick and wide too, and so will the nozzle on the can of spray paint.

Save To copy your drawing onto the disk, choose **Save** from the **File menu**.

Then invent a name for your document. The name must be short: no more than 8 letters. For example, the name can be "jennifer" or "al". Type the name you wish and press ENTER.

That makes the computer copy the document onto the hard disk. For example, if you named the document "jennifer", the computer will put in your hard disk's WINDOWS subdirectory a file called "JENNIFER.BMP", which means "JENNIFER the Bit MaP". (A **bit map** is a picture made of many itty-bitty dots.)

Afterwards, if you change your mind and want to improve the drawing, go ahead! When you finish making improvements, save them by choosing Save from the File menu again.

Print To copy the drawing onto paper, choose **Print** from the File menu, then press ENTER.

Unfortunately, the typical printer can't print colors. It prints black-and-white instead.

Instead of printing a dark color (such as blue), the printer will print black. Instead of printing a light color (such as yellow), the printer will print white.

Finish When you finish fiddling with a drawing, choose **New**, **Open**, or **Exit** from the File menu.

If you choose **New**, the computer will let you start a new drawing. If you choose **Open** and then double-click the name of an old drawing, the computer will put that drawing onto the screen. If you choose **Exit**, the computer will exit from Paintbrush so you can use a different accessory instead.

If you say New, Open, or Exit without saving your drawing, the computer asks, "Save current changes?" If you click "Yes", the computer copies your drawing to the hard disk; if you click "No" instead, the computer ignores and forgets your recent drawing efforts.

Close

When you finish using the accessories, close the Accessories window by double-clicking its control box.

Main window

Make the Program Manager window be normal.

In that window, you'll see the **Main** icon. Double-click it.

You'll see the **Main window**, which contains 8 icons: **File Manager**, **Control Panel**, **Print Manager**, **Clipboard Viewer**, **MS-DOS Prompt**, **Windows Setup**, **PIF Editor**, and **Read Me**.

Here's how to use the icons that are popular.

File Manager

To manipulate the files on your hard disk, double-click the File Manager icon.

You'll see the **File Manager window** and the **Directory Tree window**.

In the Directory Tree window, you'll see the names of your hard disk's subdirectories. The names are in alphabetical order.

By using your keyboard's up-arrow and down-arrow keys, move the cursor to the subdirectory that interests you. (For example, try moving the cursor to the WINDOWS subdirectory.) Then press ENTER.

You'll see the names of your files in the subdirectory. The names are in alphabetical order. Move the cursor to the file that interests you (by using the mouse).

For example, try moving the cursor to a file you invented, such as JENNIFER.WRI.

Then say what to do to the file. Choose one of these activities:

To delete the file, press the DELETE key. Then press ENTER twice.

To peek at the file, press ENTER. When you finish peeking at the file, double-click the file's close box.

To rename the file, choose **Rename** from the **File menu**. Then type the new name you're inventing (such as JENNY.WRI). Make sure you type the correct three-letter ending: for example, type ".WRI" at the end of a Write document's name; type ".BMP" at the end of a Paintbrush drawing's name. After typing the three-letter ending, press ENTER.

When you finish using the File Manager, choose **Exit** from the File menu.

Control Panel

To change how Windows acts, double-click the Control Panel icon.

You'll see the **Control Panel window**, which contains 12 icons: **Color**, **Fonts**, **Ports**, **Mouse**, **Desktop**, **Keyboard**, **Printers**, **International**, **Date/Time**, **386 Enhanced**, **Drivers**, and **Sound**. (The 386 Enhanced icon appears just if you have a 386 or 486 or Pentium, and you have at least 2 megabytes of RAM.)

Here's how to use icons that are popular.

Date/Time To reset the date and time without leaving Windows, double-click the Date/Time icon.

The computer will say what it thinks the date and time are. If the computer is wrong, click the part of the date or time you want to change.

To the right of where you clicked, you'll see an up-arrow and a down-arrow. To make the date or time later, click the up-arrow; to make the date or time earlier, click the down-arrow.

When the date and time look correct, click "OK".

Color To change the screen's colors, double-click the Color icon. You'll see the **Color window**. Near that window's top-right corner, you'll see an arrow pointing down at a hyphen. Click that arrow.

You'll see this list of color schemes:

```
Windows Default
Arizona
Black Leather Jacket
Bordeaux
Cinnamon
Designer
Emerald City
Fluorescent
Hotdog Stand
LCD Default Screen Settings
LCD Reversed - Dark
Mahogany
Monochrome
Ocean
Pastel
Patchwork
Plasma PS
Rugby
The Blue
Tweed
Valentine
Wingtips
```

Press your keyboard's HOME key (to make sure you're at the top of the list). Tap your keyboard's down-arrow key several times, until you reach your favorite color scheme. Then press ENTER. All the screen's colors will change and become your favorites!

Printers If you bought a font cartridge for your laser printer, tell the computer which font cartridge you bought. To do that, double-click the Printers icon.

You'll see the **Printers window**.

Click the word "Setup". At the screen's bottom left corner, you'll see a list of font cartridges. (To see the bottom of the list, click the scroll arrow next to it.) Click the cartridge you bought. Click "OK". Click "Close".

Close When you finish using the Control Panel window, close it by double-clicking its control box.

Close

When you finish using the Main window, close it by double-clicking its control box.

Dig deeper

To make Windows 3.1 & 3.11 run better, **clean your software**. I explain how on pages 579-580; but to understand them, read the MS-DOS chapter first. Here it is....

Get into DOS

If you have an IBM-compatible computer, it understands MS-DOS commands — even if your computer comes with Windows. This chapter explains how to give MS-DOS commands.

MS-DOS commands are worth learning because they give you total control over your computer. They solve the difficulties caused when Windows acts strangely or conks out — which happens often!

MS-DOS commands are trustworthy: when you give an MS-DOS command, you know exactly what will happen. When you give a Windows command, you can't be sure of the consequences: Windows is flaky and full of unfortunate surprises. Technicians repairing computers rely on MS-DOS. Also, MS-DOS runs well and fast even on old, decrepit, or broken computers, whereas Windows usually runs slowly or erratically or not-at-all.

Versions

MS-DOS comes in many versions. Versions for the IBM PC are called **PC-DOS**. Versions for clones built by Compaq are called **Compaq DOS**.

Get the MS-DOS version intended for *your* computer. Get it from the dealer who sold you the computer. If you use the wrong version of DOS — for example, if you try using PC-DOS on a Compaq computer, or using Compaq DOS on a different brand of clone — the computer might gripe (especially when you try programming in BASIC) or give you the wrong time or do something else weird.

Here's how Microsoft and IBM gradually improved PC-DOS (which is the IBM PC version of MS-DOS).

The original version of PC-DOS was called **version 1**. Then came an improvement called version 1.1. Then came versions 2, 2.1, 3, 3.1, 3.2, and 3.3.

Version 1 handled just the original IBM PC and its 5¼-inch floppy disks. That version wrote on just one side of each disk and put 8 sectors on each track, so that each disk held 160K. **Version 1.1** could write on *both* sides of each disk, so that each disk held 320K.

Version 2 could also handle the IBM PC XT and its 10-megabyte hard disk. That version also squeezed more data onto each floppy disk: onto each track, it put 9 sectors instead of 8, so the floppy disk held 360K instead of 320K. **Version 2.1** could also handle the IBM PC Junior.

Version 3 could also handle the IBM PC AT, its 20-megabyte and 30-megabyte hard disks, and its high-density 5¼-inch floppy disks (which held 1.2 megabytes instead of 360K). **Version 3.1** could also handle networks. **Version 3.2** could also handle the IBM PC Convertible and its 3½-inch 720K floppies. **Version 3.3** could also handle the IBM PS/2 and its 3½-inch 1.44 megabyte floppies.

Other early versions of MS-DOS (such as Compaq DOS) were numbered similarly to PC-DOS. For example, Compaq DOS version 3.31 resembled PC-DOS version 3.3 but let you more easily handle hard disks bigger than 30 megabytes.

In July 1988, Microsoft and IBM began selling **version 4**. Like Compaq DOS version 3.31, it let you handle huge hard disks easily. But alas, version 4 consumed too much RAM and was incompatible with some older programs.

In June 1991, Microsoft and IBM began selling **version 5**, which fixed DOS 4's problems and included many exciting new commands. In 1993 they began selling **version 6**, which was even fancier.

Afterwards, Microsoft and IBM parted company and competed against each other. IBM invented and sold **version 6.1**, without involvement from Microsoft. Then Microsoft fought back by inventing and selling **version 6.2**. Then IBM retaliated with **version 6.3** and **version 7**.

Then Microsoft invented **Windows 95**, which includes a DOS version I'll call **DOS 95**. (Microsoft sometimes calls it "DOS 7", but I'll say "DOS 95" to avoid confusion with IBM's DOS 7.) Finally, Microsoft invented Windows 98, which includes **DOS 98**.

Headaches Some DOS versions give you headaches.
Versions 1.0 and 1.1 can't handle hard disks at all.
Versions 2.0 and 2.1 have difficulty handling hard disks bigger than 16 megabytes. Here's why:

> When you first use a hard disk, DOS is supposed to search for bad sectors on the hard disk, draw a **map** of where those bad sectors are, and remember to avoid those bad sectors. Versions 2.0 and 2.1 search for bad sectors throughout the first 16 megabytes *but don't bother to map the bad sectors on the rest of a big hard disk*. Those versions of DOS seems fine at first; but when you finally fill more than 16 megabytes of your disk, the computer eventually encounters bad sectors it didn't map, gets upset, and refuses to run your programs.

Versions 3.0 and 3.2 make lots of errors. Avoid them.
Versions before 3.2 can't handle 3½-inch floppies. **Version 3.2** handles 3½-inch floppies, but just if they're double-density instead of high-density.
Version 4 consumes too much RAM.
Versions 6.1, 6.3, and 7 are weird, since they're the only versions that Microsoft didn't help design. They're the only versions that don't accept standard Microsoft commands.
Versions 3.3, 5, 6.2, 95, and 98 work fine. That's why they're the most popular versions! **Version 6.0** works acceptably just if you avoid using its three fanciest routines (**Double Space**, **Smart Drive**, and **Mem Maker**), which are disastrously unreliable. **Version 6.2** includes improved versions of those routines. **Version 95** is version 6.2 modified to be compatible with Windows 95. **Version 98** is version 95 modified to be compatible with Windows 98.

A company called **Stac Electronics** sued Microsoft for putting Stac's ideas into Double Space. In 1994, Stac won the suit. The judge ordered Microsoft to pay Stac and stop selling versions 6.0 and 6.2, so Microsoft came out with **version 6.21** (which omits Double Space) and **version 6.22** (which includes a Double Space clone called **Drive Space**). When Stac complained that Microsoft wasn't removing all remaining copies of versions 6 and 6.2 from shelves quickly enough, Microsoft squashed the problem by paying Stac even more and buying 15% of the Stac company itself. So now Microsoft is a Stac shareholder, and the two companies are buddies.

DR DOS Instead of buying MS-DOS, you can buy an imitation called **DR DOS** (or **Novell DOS**). It's made by a company called **Digital Research (DR)**, which is now owned by **Novell**. Though DR DOS resembles MS-DOS, I prefer MS-DOS because it includes BASIC and is more compatible with Windows and other software.

Which version I'll emphasize I'll emphasize how to use DOS 6.2. My explanation of DOS 6.2 applies to all its variants (DOS 6.20, 6.21, and 6.22).

I'll also explain how other DOS versions differ from 6.2.

To keep this chapter mercifully short, I'll assume your computer is normal. For example, I'll assume you're using a reasonably new version of DOS (version 2 or higher), you're not using IBM's weird versions (6.1 and 6.3), and you're not using DR-DOS or Novell DOS.

I'll assume your computer has a hard drive. (If your computer does *not* have a hard drive, read the 15th edition. To get that edition, phone me at 603-666-6644.)

Modern versus classic DOS versions 5, 6, 6.2, 95, and 98 are similar to each other. I'll refer to them as **modern DOS**. Earlier DOS versions (2, 2.1, 2.2, 3, 3.1, 3.2, 3.3, and 4) are called **classic DOS**.

Notice that in the computer industry, the word "classic" is a euphemism that means "old, obsolete, and decrepit". Go ahead: follow that tradition! Next time you meet a person who's old, obsolete, and decrepit, say "You're a classic!"

Cost

The best way to get DOS is from the dealer who sold you the computer. Most dealers include DOS in the computer's price, but other dealers charge for DOS separately.

DOS 98 DOS 98 is part of Windows 98. The only way to get DOS 98 is to get Windows 98. Most computers come with Windows 98 (and hence DOS 98).

DOS 95 DOS 95 is part of Windows 95. The only way to get DOS 95 is to get Windows 95.

Piracy If you buy two computers, you must buy two copies of DOS (or of Windows 95 or 98). It's illegal to buy just one DOS and copy it to the other computer. That's called **illegal copying**; it's **piracy**.

Some dealers illegally copy DOS onto the computer's hard disk without paying Microsoft or IBM. Recently, Microsoft has been requiring every dealer who copies DOS onto a hard disk to give the customer an official **Microsoft certificate of authenticity** with a hologram sticker on it. The certificate comes from Microsoft and proves the DOS was paid for.

Usually, the certificate comes with an official Microsoft manual (not just a book from a bookstore!) and an official set of DOS floppy disks (on which are pasted official Microsoft labels that are printed, not handwritten!). But the manual and floppies are optional, and some dealers are too cheap to provide them. Windows 95 and 98 often come on a CD-ROM disk instead of floppy disks.

If you get neither a manual nor floppies nor a CD-ROM, your dealer (or the dealer's supplier) is a crook or an ass.

How to upgrade If you own an old version of DOS, you can switch to MS-DOS 6.22 by getting the **MS-DOS 6.22 upgrade** for about $50. Switching is simple if you have a high-density 3½-inch floppy drive and already own a version numbered *above* 2.1.

If you already have Windows 95, you have DOS 95; if you already have Windows 98, you have DOS 98. Since those versions of DOS are better than DOS 6.22, do *not* switch to DOS 6.22!

If you own MS-DOS 6.0, you can switch to MS-DOS 6.22 for under $10 by getting the **MS-DOS 6.22 Step Up** disk (which is 3½-inch high-density). That disk works just if you already own MS-DOS 6.0 (or 6.20 or 6.21). It does *not* work if you own an older DOS and does *not* work if you own DOS 6.1, 6.3, or 7 (which are the weird versions by IBM). Since it costs

little and it improves DOS just slightly, it does *not* come with a certificate, hologram, or manual.

List of commands & equations

To use DOS, you put your fingers on the keyboard and type a DOS command or equation. The popular DOS commands & equations are explained on these pages:

Command	What the computer will do	Page
a:	make drive A be the current drive	121
attrib +r mary	make MARY be a read-only file	144
b:	make drive B be the current drive	121
backup c:mary a:	copy MARY to a set of floppies in drive A	147
c:	make drive C be the current drive	121
cd sarah	make SARAH be the current directory	121
chkdsk	check the disk for bytes and errors	122
cls	clear the screen, so it becomes blank	117
copy con mary	copy from keyboard to a file called MARY	126
date	show the date, and let it be changed	117
defrag	rearrange files so they're not fragmented	141
del mary	delete a file called MARY from the disk	128
deltree sarah	delete the SARAH folder & everything in it	128
dir	show a directory of all files	118
dir sarah	show a directory of all the files in SARAH	120
dir sarah /s	show the SARAH directory & subdirectories	143
diskcopy a: b:	make disk B be an exact copy of disk A	125
do music	do the MUSIC program in MUSIC folder	149
echo off	stop displaying DOS commands	130
echo wow	show the word "wow" on the screen	117
edit mary	edit file called MARY, using modern editor	128
edlin mary	edit file called MARY, using an old editor	129
fdisk	partition the hard disk into C, D, E, etc.	138
format a:	format the disk in drive A	124
format a: /s	format disk in drive A & make it bootable	138
ftp ftp.gis.net	use Unix to send files to Internet provider GIS	230
help	list all the DOS commands & explain them	144
intersvr	be the server in an Interlnk network	234
Lh doskey	load the doskey driver into upper memory	136
Lh mode LPT1 retry=b	wait for printer to respond, even if long wait	136
Lh mouse	load the mouse driver into upper memory	136
Lh mscdex /d:mscd000	load CD-ROM driver into upper memory	136
md sarah	make a new directory, called SARAH	126
mem	show how big the RAM memory is	140
more<mary	show a file called MARY, a page at a time	144
move mary a:	move MARY to drive A, and delete from C	128
msav	run the MicroSoft Anti-Virus program	142
msbackup	copy from the hard disk to a set of floppies	146
msd	make MicroSoftDiagnostics analyze computer	140
path c:\dos	whenever a program not found, search c:\dos	135
print mary	copy a file called MARY onto paper	143
prompt pg	make prompt be "C:\>" instead of "C>"	135
rd sarah	remove directory SARAH from the disk	128
rem written by Joey	ignore this remark & skip ahead to next line	144
ren mary lambchop	rename MARY; change to LAMBCHOP	128
restore a: c: /s	copy all backed-up files to the hard disk	147
scandisk	scan the disk for errors and fix them	141
set temp=c:\temp	define "temp" to mean "c:\temp"	135
share /L:500 /f:5100	check if programs interfere with each other	137
subst a: b:\	when told to use drive A, will use B instead	148
sys a:	copy the DOS system files to drive A	138
time	show the time, and let it be changed	117
type mary	show, on the screen, what's in the MARY file	127
undelete	try to retrieve any files accidentally deleted	144
unformat a:	try to unformat the disk in drive A	124
ver	say which version of DOS is being used	117
win	start running Windows	137
xcopy a: b: /s	copy all files and subdirectories from A to B	145

Equation	Meaning	Page
buffers=40	handle 40 sectors at once	133
device=dos\emm386.exe ram d=64	use expanded RAM	133
device=dos\himem.sys /testmem:off	use extended RAM	132
device=dos\interlnk.exe	be client in Interlnk network	234
devicehigh=dos\setver.exe	handle old software	134
devicehigh=toshiba.sys /d:mscd000	use CD-ROM drive	134
dos=high,umb	use high & upper RAM	133
files=50	handle 50 files at once	133
lastdrive=f	accept drives A through F	134
stacks=0,0	create no stacks	133

Get to the standard C prompt

Here's how to start using DOS.

I'll assume DOS is already on your hard disk. If you've been using Windows (version 3.1, 3.11, 95, 98, or any other popular version), congratulations: DOS is already on your hard disk! Even if you don't have Windows, DOS is probably on your hard disk anyway, since nearly all computers that have hard disks are sold with DOS already on the hard disk.

Turn on the computer, without any disks in the floppy drives. (For details, read "Prepare to operate" on page 94. For free help, phone me anytime at 603-666-6644.)

Your next goal is to make this symbol appear at the screen's bottom:

```
C:\>
```

That symbol is called the **standard C prompt**. Notice that it consists of 4 characters: a **capital C**, a **colon**, a **backslash**, and a **greater sign**.

<u>Using Windows 95 or 98?</u> Here's the best way to make the standard C prompt appear if you're using Windows 95 or 98:

Make sure the screen's bottom left corner says "Start". Then using your mouse, click the word "Start", then the word "Programs", then "MS-DOS Prompt". The computer will say "C:\WINDOWS". Then on the keyboard, type "cd \" (and press the ENTER key). The computer will say "C:\>". Then try this experiment: while holding down the Alt key, tap the ENTER key once or twice, until the screen's appearance pleases you.

<u>Using Windows 3.11 or earlier?</u> Here's the best way to make the standard C prompt appear if you're using Windows 3.1 or 3.11 (or any earlier version of Windows):

If your screen's bottom line already says "C:\>", you're done! Otherwise, do the following.... Make sure the screen's top line says "Program Manager". Then using your mouse, click the word "File" (near the screen's top right corner), then the word "Exit", then the word "OK". The computer will probably say "C:\>". If the computer says something else instead (such as "C:\WINDOWS"), make it say "C:\>" by doing this: type "cd \" (and press the ENTER key).

<u>Not using Windows?</u> Here's the best way to make the standard C prompt appear if you not using Windows:

The screen's bottom line probably says "C:\>" already. If not, here's what to do....

If the bottom message says "C:\DOS>" or "C:\WINDOWS>" or "C:\MENU>" or "C:\WP>" or something similar, type "cd \" (then press the ENTER key).

If the bottom message says "C>", type "prompt pg" (then press the ENTER key).

If the bottom message says "D>" or "E>" or "F>" or begins with "D:" or "E:" or "F:", type "c:" (then press the ENTER key).

If the bottom message says "Enter new date (mm-dd-yy)", press the ENTER key twice.

If the screen's top line says "MS-DOS Shell" or "Start Programs", press the F3 key.

If the screen shows a list of choices, choose "Exit to DOS".

If the screen says "A>" or "A:\>" or "Non-System disk or disk error" or "1LIST", you probably have disks stuck in the floppy drives (or else your hard disk lacks DOS or is defective or missing). Remove any disks from the floppy drives. Then turn the computer off, wait until the computer is quiet, then try turning the computer back on.

After doing one of those actions, check whether the screen says "C:\>". If it does *not* say "C:\>" yet, look through that list of actions again, and keep trying until you finally see "C:\>".

<u>Use those methods</u> This chapter assumes you made the standard C prompt appear by using one of those methods. Though Microsoft keeps inventing alternative methods to make the standard C prompt appear, the alternative methods consume more RAM or omit some DOS drivers, and so DOS commands and programs don't work as well. To avoid disappointments, use just the *best* methods of making the standard C prompt appear, which I listed above!

How to shut down

When you finish using the computer, here's the safest way to shut the computer down, so you don't lose any data.

First, make the computer display the standard C prompt, so the screen's bottom message is this:

```
C:\>
```

If you're using Windows 95 or 98, do this:

Type the word "exit" (and press ENTER). Then click "Start" then "Shut Down", then press the ENTER key, then wait until the computer says "It's now safe to turn off your computer".

If you're *not* using Windows 95 or 98, wait 10 seconds.

The purpose of that wait is to let the DOS 6.0 version of the SMARTDRIVE caching program finish editing your hard disk. While it edits, you'll hear some clicking sounds. If you're sure you're not using that caching program or a similar program, you don't need to wait. If you're using a different version of SMARTDRIVE — such as the version that comes with DOS 5 or DOS 6.2 or Windows — you don't need to wait.

Remove any floppy disks from the drives. If your screen is a monitor, turn it off. Then turn off the computer.

Simple commands

After the C prompt (which is "C:\>"), the computer waits for you to type a **DOS command**. When typing a DOS command, remember these principles:

> Type the command after the C prompt. Remember that the C prompt is typed by the computer, not by you.
>
> To capitalize a letter, or type a character that's on the top part of a key, hold down the SHIFT key; and while you keep holding down the SHIFT key, tap the key that has the character you want.
>
> If you type a command incorrectly, press the BACKSPACE key, which is above the ENTER key and has a left-arrow on it.
>
> When you finish typing a command, press the ENTER key. That key makes the computer read what you typed.

Start by trying these simple DOS commands....

Version (ver)

After the C prompt you can type "ver", like this:

```
C:\>ver
```

(When you finish typing that command, remember to press the ENTER key.)

The "ver" command makes the computer tell you which VERsion of MS-DOS you're using. For example, if you're using MS-DOS Version 6.2, the computer will say:

```
MS-DOS Version 6.20
```

If you're using MS-DOS Version 95 (which is part of Windows 95), the computer will say:

```
Windows 95
```

If you're using MS-DOS Version 98 (which is part of Windows 98), the computer will say:

```
Windows 98
```

Echo

The computer's your obedient slave: it will say whatever you wish!

For example, here's how to make the computer say "wow". After the C prompt, type "echo wow", like this:

```
C:\>echo wow
```

(To type the space after the word *echo*, press the **SPACE bar**, which is the long horizontal bar at the bottom of the keyboard.) Remember to press the ENTER key at the end of that command. Then the computer will say:

```
wow
```

If you want the computer to say it loves you, type this:

```
C:\>echo I love you
```

(To capitalize the letter I, hold down the SHIFT key; and while you keep holding down the SHIFT key, tap the I key.) That command makes the computer say:

```
I love you
```

If you want the computer to say it likes strawberry ice cream, type this:

```
C:\>echo I like strawberry ice cream
```

Then the computer will say:

```
I like strawberry ice cream
```

Be creative! Make the computer say something wild!

Notice that the echo command makes the computer act like a canyon: whatever you say into the computer, the echo command makes the computer echo back.

Clear screen (cls)

Suppose you make the computer say "I love you" (and other things that are even wilder), and then your boss walks by. You might be embarrassed to let your boss see your love messages. Here's how to hide all the screen's messages.

After the C prompt, type "cls", like this:

```
C:\>cls
```

The "cls" command makes the computer CLear the Screen, so all messages on the screen are erased and the screen becomes blank. The only thing that will remain on the screen is —

```
C:\>
```

so that you can give another command.

Date

The computer has a built-in calendar. To use it, type "date" after the C prompt like this:

```
C:\>date
```

That makes the computer tell you the date. For example, if today is Wednesday, March 24, 1999, the computer should say:

```
Current date is Wed 03-24-1999
```

To remember the date, the computer uses its built-in digital clock/calendar. If the clock/calendar's battery has run down or is missing, the computer will say a wrong date.

Confirming the date After the computer says what it thinks the date is, it says:

```
Enter new date (mm-dd-yy):
```

If the computer's date seems correct, press the ENTER key.

If you notice that the computer's date is wrong, remind the computer of the correct date. For example, if the correct date is March 24, 1999, type "3-24-99" then press ENTER at the end of that date. (Do *not* type "Wednesday" or "Wed"; the computer will figure that out automatically.)

Time

To find out what time it is, type "time" after the C prompt like this:

```
C:\>time
```

That makes the computer tell you the time.

For example, if the time is 2.71 seconds after 1:45AM, the computer will say:

```
Current time is  1:45:02.71a
```

The "a" means "AM". (If your DOS is classic, it will omit the "a".)

If the time is 2.71 seconds after 1:45PM, the computer will say:

```
Current time is  1:45:02.71p
```

The "p" means "PM". (If your DOS is classic, it will omit the "p", use a 24-hour clock, and say "13:45:02.71".)

To remember the time, the computer uses its built-in digital clock. The computer will say a wrong time if the clock's battery has run down or is missing, or the clock's thinking has been interrupted by other computer activities, or your town has switched to daylight savings time, or you've taken the computer on an airplane to a different time zone.

Confirming the time

Confirming the time After the computer says what it thinks the time is, it says:

```
Enter new time:
```

If the computer's time seems correct, press the ENTER key.

If you notice that the computer's time is wrong, remind the computer of the correct time. For example, if the correct time is exactly 1:45PM, type "1:45p" (for modern DOS) or "13:45" (for classic DOS); then press ENTER at the end of that time.

Directory (dir)

After the C prompt you can type "dir", like this:

```
C:\>dir
```

That "dir" command makes the computer show you a directory of the files that are stored on the hard disk.

If you're using DOS 6.2, the directory looks like this:

```
DOS           <DIR>        06-01-94    3:53a
TEMP          <DIR>        06-01-94    4:20a
WINDOWS       <DIR>        06-02-94    3:10a
WP            <DIR>        06-19-94    6:24p
QA            <DIR>        06-04-94    5:48p
MSOFFICE      <DIR>        11-24-94   10:10p
BACKUP        <DIR>        06-09-94    4:06p
COMMAND  COM         54,619 09-30-93    6:20a
CONFIG   SYS            182 06-28-95   11:12p
AUTOEXEC BAT            166 06-29-95   12:39a
DO       BAT             44 06-09-95   11:18p
```

(On your computer, the directory might look slightly different, depending on what your hard disk contains and which version of DOS you're using. For example, if your DOS is earlier than version 6.2, it's too stupid to put commas in big numbers such as 54,619.)

In that sample directory, one line says:

```
COMMAND  COM         54,619 09-30-93    6:20a
```

That line says the hard disk has a file whose name is "COMMAND.COM"; that file contains 54,619 bytes and was last updated on September 30, 1993, at 6:20AM.

The next line says the disk also has a file named "CONFIG.SYS", which contains 182 bytes and was last updated on June 28, 1994 at 11:12PM. The lines underneath say that the disk also has a file called "AUTOEXEC.BAT" and a file called "DO.BAT".

Extensions Notice that a file's name (such as "AUTOEXEC.BAT") consists of up to 8 characters (such as "AUTOEXEC"), then a period, then an **extension** of up to 3 characters (such as "BAT"). The period separates the main part of the filename from the extension.

In the directory that the computer prints on your screen, each line shows a file's name and extension but doesn't bother showing the period.

The period is called a **dot**. So if you're chatting with another computer expert about "AUTOEXEC.BAT", pronounce it "AUTOEXEC dot BAT".

The computer can handle many different types of files. Each type has a different extension:

Extension	What the file contains
.BAT	a **BAT**ch of DOS commands
.COM	a short program that's been **COM**piled
.EXE	a fancy program that you can **EXE**cute
.BAS	a program written by using **BAS**IC
.PRG	a **PR**o**G**ram written by using DBASE or FOXPRO
.SYS	list of hardware you bought & how you want **SYS**tem to operate
.386	info that's useful just if your CPU is a **386** (or 486 or Pentium)
.TXT	Te**XT** that you can read
.HLP	messages that He**LP** you learn how to use a program you bought
.DOC	**DOC**ument written by a word processor such as Microsoft Word
.OLD	an **OLD**, outdated version, being kept just in case of emergency
.BAK	a **BA**c**K**up version, being kept just in case of emergency
.DAT	**DAT**a
.TMP	Te**MP**orary data, which the computer will use and then erase
.INI	data to **INI**tialize a program, so the program starts properly
.DBF	a **D**ata**B**ase **F**ile that contains data used by DBASE or FOXPRO
.DTF	a **D**a**T**abase **F**ile that contains data used by Q&A
.IDX	an **I**n**D**e**X** to a database file
.XLS	an **EX**ce**L** **S**preadsheet, created by using the Excel program
.WK1	a **W**or**K**sheet created by using the **1**-2-3 spreadsheet program
.WQ1	a **W**orksheet created by using **Q**uattro (which imitates **1**-2-3)

Folders The sample directory's top line says:

```
DOS           <DIR>        06-01-94    3:53a
```

That line says the hard disk has a file named "DOS". The <DIR> means that the file is actually a **directory folder** that contains other files! That folder was created on June 1, 1994 at 3:53AM; many items have been put in that folder since then.

The next line says:

```
TEMP          <DIR>        06-01-94    4:20a
```

That means the hard disk has a folder named "TEMP", created on June 1, 1994 at 4:20AM.

The lines underneath say that the hard disk also has folders named "WINDOWS", "WP", "QA", "MSOFFICE", and "BACKUP".

Summary statistics When the computer finishes printing the directory, it prints summary statistics:

```
        11 file(s)        55,011 bytes
                      21,426,176 bytes free
```

That means the directory contains 11 files. (7 of them are folders, such as DOS and WINDOWS. The other 4 are simple files, such as COMMAND.COM and CONFIG.SYS.)

The simple files consume 55,011 bytes altogether. The hard disk uses other bytes to store the folders and any files that are in the folders.

(If your DOS is classic, it doesn't bother to say "55,011 bytes".)

Besides the simple files, folders, and files in folders, the hard disk also contains these 6 special items: 2 **hidden files** (called "IO.SYS" and "MSDOS.SYS"), 2 copies of the **file allocation table (FAT)**, the **boot record**, and the directory itself.

The "21,426,176 bytes free" means that over 21 million bytes on the hard disk are still unused. (On *your* computer, the number of bytes free might be different.)

Pausing When you type "dir", the computer tries to show you a directory of the files that are stored on the hard disk. If your hard disk has more files than can fit on the screen, the list of files moves up the screen too quickly for you to read.

Here's how to see the directory more easily....

Instead of typing "dir", type "dir /p", like this:

```
C:\>dir /p
```

That means "directory pausing". When you give that command, the computer starts printing the directory on the screen; but when the screen becomes full, the computer pauses and says:

```
Press any key to continue
```

While the computer pauses, read the part of the directory that's on the screen. When you finish reading that part, strike a key (such as the ENTER key). Then the computer will print the rest of the directory, pausing at the end of each screenful (page).

So "dir /p" means "directory, pausing at the end of each page" (or "directory paged").

Wide If you type "dir /w", you'll see a directory that's wide and leaves out the details; the computer will print:

```
[DOS]          [TEMP]           [WINDOWS]       [WP]         [QA]
[MSOFFICE]     [BACKUP]         COMMAND.COM     CONFIG.SYS   AUTOEXEC.BAT
DO.BAT
```

What's a switch?
A **switch** is a comment that begins with a **slash**. You've already learned about two switches: "/p" and "/w".

To type the slash, make sure you press the **forward slash** key, which says "/" on it. Do *not* press the key that says "\", which is a **backslash**.

If you wish, you can put a blank space before the slash. The blank space is optional. For example, you can say either "dir /p" or "dir/p".

You can combine switches. For example, if you want the directory to pause and also be wide, say "dir /p/w".

The computer doesn't care which switch you type first: typing "dir /p/w" does the same thing as typing "dir /w/p".

Fancy switches (in modern DOS)
If your DOS is classic, skip ahead to the next section, entitled "Attributes". Modern DOS understands these fancy switches....

Order. You can put the letter O after dir, like this: "dir /o". That shows you the directory in alphabetical order: the computer lists the folders from A to Z, then lists the other files from A to Z, like this:

```
BACKUP        <DIR>          06-09-94    4:06p
DOS           <DIR>          06-01-94    3:53a
MSOFFICE      <DIR>          11-24-94   10:10p
QA            <DIR>          06-04-94    5:48p
TEMP          <DIR>          06-01-94    4:20a
WINDOWS       <DIR>          06-02-94    3:10a
WP            <DIR>          06-19-94    6:24p
AUTOEXEC BAT            166  06-29-95   12:39a
COMMAND  COM         54,619  09-30-93    6:20a
CONFIG   SYS            182  06-28-95   11:12p
DO       BAT             44  06-09-95   11:18p
```

If you want to see the directory in *chronological* order (from the oldest date to the newest date), say "dir /od" (which means "DIRrectory in Order of Date"). If you want to see the directory in order of size, say "dir /os"; that makes the computer display the folders first, then display the other files in order of size, from the smallest number of bytes to the largest.

If you want to see the directory alphabetized by extension (so that all the .BAT files come before the .COM files), say "dir /oe" (which means "DIRectory in Order of Extension"). Better yet, say "dir /oen" (which means "DIRectory in Order of Extension and Name"), so that all the .BAT files come before the .COM files, and all the .BAT files are in alphabetical order.

At the end of any of those commands, you can put "/p" to make the computer pause at the end of each screenful.

Lowercase. You can put the letter L after dir, like this: "dir /l". That shows you the directory in lowercase letters instead of capitals, so you see this:

```
dos           <DIR>          06-01-94    3:53a
temp          <DIR>          06-01-94    4:20a
windows       <DIR>          06-02-94    3:10a
wp            <DIR>          06-19-94    6:24p
qa            <DIR>          06-04-94    5:48p
msoffice      <DIR>          11-24-94   10:10p
backup        <DIR>          06-09-94    4:06p
command   com        54,619  09-30-93    6:20a
config    sys           182  06-28-95   11:12p
autoexec  bat           166  06-29-95   12:39a
do        bat            44  06-09-95   11:18p
```

That L switch was invented because most people can read lowercase words faster than capitalized words.

Brief. You can say "dir /b". That makes the computer print the directory briefly, without bothering to print each file's length, time, and date, and without bothering to print summary statistics. The computer will print just:

```
DOS
TEMP
WINDOWS
WP
QA
MSOFFICE
BACKUP
COMMAND.COM
CONFIG.SYS
AUTOEXEC.BAT
DO.BAT
```

The computer will print it very fast — instantly!

The computer doesn't understand "dir /b/w". If you say "dir /b/w", the computer ignores the /w and does just "dir /b".

Attributes Some files have special qualities, called **attributes**.

For example, your hard disk contains two special files, called "**IO.SYS**" and "**MSDOS.SYS**". Those files contain the fundamentals of DOS and must never be erased! To prevent you from accidentally erasing them, the computer **hides** them from you, so you don't even know they're there! When you say "dir", the computer is sneaky and purposely avoids mentioning those two files!

Modern DOS lets you say "dir /a", which makes the computer show a directory of All files, including even the files that are hidden! If you say "dir /a/p", the computer will pause at the end of each screenful.

Modern DOS also lets you say "dir /ah", which makes the computer show a directory of All the Hidden files but not the other files. For example, if you say "dir /ah" using DOS 6.2, the typical computer will say:

```
IO      SYS     40,566  09-30-93   6:20a
MSDOS   SYS     38,138  09-30-93   6:20a
```

The computer might say you also have a hidden file called "**386SPART.PAR**", which is huge: typically about 20,000,000 bytes! It's called the **permanent swap file** and helps Windows run faster.

If you're using PC-DOS instead of generic MS-DOS (because your computer's built by IBM instead of being a generic clone), the "IO.SYS" and "MSDOS.SYS" files are named "IBMBIO.COM" and "IBMDOS.COM" instead.

Modern DOS lets you see the names of all your folders (directories). Just say "dir /ad". That makes the computer show a directory of All Directories. The computer will say:

```
DOS         <DIR>       06-01-94   3:53a
TEMP        <DIR>       06-01-94   4:20a
WINDOWS     <DIR>       06-02-94   3:10a
WP          <DIR>       06-19-94   6:24p
QA          <DIR>       06-04-94   5:48p
MSOFFICE    <DIR>       11-24-94  10:10p
BACKUP      <DIR>       06-09-94   4:06p
```

What's in a folder? To find out what's in a folder, say "dir" then the folder's name. For example, to find out what's in the DOS folder, say "dir dos", like this:

```
C:\>dir dos
```

You can put a switch at the end of that command:

```
C:\>dir dos /p
```

To find out what's in the WINDOWS folder, say "dir windows". (That command works just if you have a WINDOWS folder. If you do *not* have a WINDOWS folder, the computer gripes by saying "File not found".)

Saying "dir dos" shows you the files that are in the DOS folder. That list of files is called the **DOS directory**. Saying "dir windows" shows you the files that are in the Windows folder; that list of files is called the **Windows directory**. Saying just "dir" shows you the files that are *not* in folders; that list of files is called the **main directory** (or **root directory**).

So to see the root directory, just type "dir" after the standard C prompt, like this:

```
C:\>dir
```

The other directories (such as the DOS directory and the Windows directory) are called **subdirectories**.

Just one file To find info about one file, say "dir" then the file's name. For example, to find info about "COMMAND.COM", say "dir command.com". The computer will print:

```
COMMAND  COM    54,619  09-30-93   6:20a
```

Versions of COMMAND.COM To tell which version of COMMAND.COM you have, use this chart:

COMMAND.COM version	Size	Date	Time
COMMAND.COM in MS-DOS 5	47,845 bytes	04-09-91	5:00a
COMMAND.COM in MS-DOS 6	52,925 bytes	03-10-93	6:00a
COMMAND.COM in MS-DOS 6.20	54,619 bytes	09-30-93	6:20a
COMMAND.COM in MS-DOS 6.21	54,619 bytes	02-13-94	6:21a
COMMAND.COM in MS-DOS 6.22	54,645 bytes	05-31-94	6:22a
COMMAND.COM in MS-DOS 95	92,870 bytes	07-11-95	9:50a
COMMAND.COM in MS-DOS 95A	92,870 bytes	01-16-96	4:53a
COMMAND.COM in MS-DOS 95B	93,812 bytes	08-24-96	11:11a
COMMAND.COM in MS-DOS 98	93,880 bytes	05-11-98	8:01p

For the versions in the top part of the chart, notice that the version number is the same as the time: MS-DOS 5 was invented at 5am, MS-DOS 6 was invented at 6am, MS-DOS 6.20 was invented at 6:20am, and MS-DOS 95 (in Windows 95) was invented at 9:50am. So either Microsoft programmers did all their work early in the morning, or else Microsoft lied about the time.

Most computerists believe that Microsoft lied about the time — not just the time when COMMAND.COM was invented, but also the time when future products will come out. As Microsoft programmers say, "Time is reprogrammable."

What if your COMMAND.COM does *not* say 5am, 6am, 6:20am, 6:21am, 6:22am, or 9:50am, or your COMMAND.COM has a different date or size than listed in that chart? Then you're probably using an older version (such as version 4, which was timed at 12am), or a newer version, or a variant version (such as IBM PC-DOS), or a version that's been infected by a virus.

Try this experiment: examine your DOS directory by saying "dir dos /p". (If you're using DOS 95 or 98, say "dir windows\command /p" instead.) You'll notice that most of your DOS files have the same date and time as your COMMAND.COM.

Wildcards The symbol "*" is called an **asterisk** or a **star**. To type it, tap the 8 key while holding down the SHIFT key.

Try this experiment: type "dir *.bat". (That command is pronounced "dir star dot bat".) That makes the computer print an abridged directory, showing information about just the files whose names end in ".bat". The computer will print:

```
AUTOEXEC BAT       106  06-29-95   12:39a
DO       BAT        44  06-09-95   11:18p
```

The symbol "*" means "anything". That's why saying "dir *.bat" makes the computer show a directory of anything that ends in ".bat".

To see a directory of files whose names *begin* with d, say "dir d*". The computer will print:

```
DOS         <DIR>       06-01-94   3:53a
DO       BAT        44  06-09-95   11:18p
```

A symbol (such as "*") that "matches anything" is called a **wildcard**.

Different drives Your computer's main floppy drive is called **drive A**. If your computer has *two* floppy drives, the second floppy drive is called **drive B**. In most computers, drive A is on *top* of drive B or to the *left* of drive B.

The main part of your computer's main hard drive is called **drive C**. If your computer has more than one hard drive, or its hard drive is **partitioned** into several parts, or you have a CD-ROM drive, or your computer is wired to other computers on a computer network, those additional disk surfaces are called **drive D**, **drive E**, **drive F**, etc.

To practice using drive A, try this experiment....

> **Step 1: find drive A.** It's the main floppy drive. If your computer has *two* floppy drives, drive A is probably on *top* of drive B or to the *left* of drive B.
>
> **Step 2: notice drive A's size.** Take a ruler and measure the slot in drive A. If the slot is 5¼ inches long, drive A is called 5¼-inch. If the slot is 3½ inches long, drive A is called 3½-inch.
>
> **Step 3: grab a floppy disk.** Pick a disk the same size as drive A. (For example, if drive A is 5¼-inch, pick a disk that's 5¼-inch.) Pick a disk that contains information already. (For example, pick a floppy disk that contains DOS or Windows or Word Perfect or a game or some other program or data.)
>
> **Step 4: put that disk into drive A.** If the drive's slot is horizontal, make sure the disk's label is on TOP of the disk; if the slot is vertical, make sure the disk's label is on the disk's LEFT side. If the disk is 5¼-inch, it has a big oval cutout; if the disk is 3½-inch, it has a chrome metal slider; make sure that cutout or slider goes into the drive BEFORE the label does. If the disk is 5¼-inch, close the drive's door, as follows: if the slot is horizontal, pull the door latch down; if the slot is vertical, pull the door latch to the right.
>
> **Step 5: type "dir a:".** You can type "dir a:" after the standard C prompt, so your screen looks like this:
> ```
> C:\>dir a:
> ```
> To type the colon ":", make sure you hold down the SHIFT key.

If you're lucky, the computer will print a directory that lists the files on drive A's disk.

If you're *unlucky*, the computer will gripe by saying "Not ready reading drive A" or "General failure reading drive A". Then the computer will ask:
```
Abort, Retry, Fail?
```
To respond, choose Abort (by pressing the A key). Then the computer will say "C:\>" again. Try again to do the five steps properly. (Make sure you don't insert the disk backwards or upside-down. If you're using a 5¼-inch disk, make sure you close the door. If you're still having trouble, try using a different floppy disk or the other floppy drive.)

Once you've mastered the art of typing "dir a:", be bold: experiment! For example, try typing switches (such as "dir a: /p") or wildcards (such as "dir a:*.bat" or "dir a:w*"). Try putting other floppy disks into drive A, and find out what's on them (by typing "dir a:" again).

If you have a drive B, put a floppy disk into it and find out what's on that disk by typing "dir b:".

Change drive (a: or b: or c:)

When the computer is waiting for you to type a DOS command, the computer normally prints this prompt:
```
C:\>
```
That's called the **standard C prompt**. It means the computer is thinking about drive C.

A prompt Here's how to change the prompt, so the computer will think about drive A instead of drive C. In drive A put a floppy that contains info, then say "a:", so your screen looks like this:
```
C:\>a:
```
When you press ENTER at the end of that line, the computer changes the prompt to this:
```
A:\>
```
That's called the **A prompt**. It means that the computer is thinking about drive A.

After the A prompt, try saying "dir", so your screen looks like this:
```
A:\>dir
```
Because of the A prompt, that "dir" makes the computer print a directory of drive A (instead of drive C).

When you finish using the floppy in drive A and want to use the hard disk again, make the computer return to a standard C prompt. Here's how. After the A prompt, type "c:", so your screen looks like this:
```
A:\>c:
```

When you press ENTER at the end of that line, the computer will change the prompt back to this:
```
C:\>
```
The drive the computer thinks about is called the **current drive** (or **default drive**). If the computer says "C:\>", the default drive is C; if the computer says "A:\>", the default drive is A.

So to make A become the default drive, say "a:" (and press ENTER). To make C become the default drive again, say "c:" (and press ENTER).

B prompt If you have a drive B, try this experiment: in drive B put a floppy that contains info, then say "b:" (and press ENTER). The computer changes the prompt to this:
```
B:\>
```
Then if you type "dir", the computer will print a directory of drive B. To return to a C prompt, type "c:" (and press ENTER).

Change directory (cd)

One of the folders on your hard disk is called DOS. To find out what's in that folder, you can say "dir dos" after the C prompt, like this:
```
C:\>dir dos
```
Here's another way to find out what's in the DOS folder. Say "cd dos". (The "cd" means "change directory".) That makes the computer think about the DOS folder. The computer changes the prompt to this:
```
C:\DOS>
```
That means the computer is thinking about drive C's DOS folder. If you type "dir" after that prompt, the computer will print a directory of the files in drive C's DOS folder.

When you finish using the DOS folder, you should **return to the standard C prompt by saying "cd \"**. (Make sure you type a backslash \, not a forward slash /.) Then the computer will print a standard C prompt again:
```
C:\>
```
Suppose your hard disk contains a WINDOWS folder. Here's how to explore what's in that folder....

First, make sure the screen shows a standard C prompt: "C:\>". Then say "cd windows". That makes the computer think about the WINDOWS folder, so the computer changes the prompt to this:
```
C:\WINDOWS>
```
To find out what's in that WINDOWS folder, say "dir /p", which makes the computer print a directory of the files in the WINDOWS folder.

You get a surprise: one of the files in the WINDOWS folder is another folder, called SYSTEM. Yes, SYSTEM is a folder that's inside the WINDOWS folder.

To find out what's in the SYSTEM folder, say "cd system" after the prompt, so your screen looks like this:
```
C:\WINDOWS>cd system
```
That makes the computer think about the SYSTEM folder inside the WINDOWS folder, so the computer changes the prompt to this:
```
C:\WINDOWS\SYSTEM>
```
Then if you say "dir", the computer will print a directory of the files in the WINDOWS SYSTEM folder.

Parents When a folder is inside another folder, the situation resembles a pregnant woman: the inner folder is called the **child**; the outer folder is called the **mommy** (or **parent**). For example, the SYSTEM folder is the child of the WINDOWS folder.

When you finish using the SYSTEM folder, you have a choice. **If you say "cd ..", those two periods make computer return to the mommy folder** (WINDOWS) and say:

```
C:\WINDOWS>
```

If instead you say "cd \", the backslash makes the computer return to the root directory and say:

```
C:\>
```

Saying "cd .." is therefore called "returning to mommy". Saying "cd \" is called "returning to your roots". Whenever you feel lost and scared, return to mommy or your roots!

Pointer files

Socrates warned, "Know thyself." Freud warned, "Be prepared to tell me about your mother."

To obey their warnings, each folder contains a Socrates file and a Freud file. The Socrates file, called ".", reminds the folder of what files are in the folder. The Freud file, called "..", reminds the folder of who the folder's mother is, so the computer will know what to do when you type "cd ..".

That's why, when you're in the middle of a folder and say "dir", the first two files you see in the directory are called "." and "..". They're called **pointer files** because they point to the folder's inner self and mommy.

Short cut

Suppose the computer says:

```
C:\DOS>
```

That means the computer is thinking about the DOS folder. To make the computer think about the WINDOWS SYSTEM folder instead, you can use two methods.

The normal method is to say "cd \" (which makes the computer leave the DOS folder and return to the standard C prompt), then say "cd windows", then say "cd system".

The shorter method is to combine all those cd commands into this single command: "cd \windows\system". In that command, make sure you type the backslashes.

Backslash versus forward slash

Don't confuse the backslash (\) with a forward slash (/).

Type a backslash (\) when you're discussing folders, such as "cd \windows\system".
Type a forward slash (/) when you're giving switches, such as "dir /p" or "dir /w".

External commands

So far, you've learned 7 major commands: ver, echo, cls, date, time, dir, and cd. How does the computer understand them?

When you turn on the computer, the computer automatically runs a program called "COMMAND.COM", which teaches the computer how to react to those commands. Since the definitions of those commands are stored inside COMMAND.COM, those commands are called **internal commands**.

Now you're going to learn 3 fancy commands whose definitions are too long to fit in COMMAND.COM. The 3 fancy commands are "format" (which puts a format onto a disk), "diskcopy" (which makes a copy of a disk), and "chkdsk" (which checks your disk). Don't type them until I fully explain how to use them.

The definition of "format" is in a file called "FORMAT.COM". The definition of "diskcopy" is in a file called "DISKCOPY.COM". The definition of "chkdsk" is in a file that classic DOS calls "CHKDSK.COM" but modern DOS calls "CHKDSK.EXE".

Since the definitions of "format", "diskcopy", and "chkdsk" lie outside of COMMAND.COM, those 3 commands are called **external commands**.

When you give one of those external commands, the computer tries to obey the command by running the FORMAT.COM program, DISKCOPY.COM program, CHKDSK.COM program, or CHKDSK.EXE program.

If your computer is set up normally, those programs are in drive C's DOS folder. In that case, if you say —

```
C:\>dir dos /p
```

you'll see that the DOS directory includes FORMAT.COM, DISKCOPY.COM, and CHKDSK.EXE (or CHKDSK.COM).

But alas, your computer might be set up *ab*normally. Those programs might be in the root directory instead of in a DOS subdirectory. Those programs might be in a subdirectory which, instead of being called "DOS", is called "BIN" or "UTIL". Those programs might be on a drive D instead of C.

If you're using DOS 95 (which is part of Windows 95) or DOS 98 (which is part of Windows 98), those programs are typically on drive C in a subdirectory called "WINDOWS\COMMAND".

Where are those programs in *your* computer? Find out now! Say —

```
C:\>dir dos /p
```

If you see that the DOS directory includes FORMAT.COM, DISKCOPY.COM, and CHKDSK.EXE (or CHKDSK.COM), you're lucky. If you're unlucky, explore other directories (by saying " dir /p" or "dir bin /p" or "dir util /p" or "dir d: /p" or "dir a: /p" or "dir windows\command /p"), until you find the directory that contains those external DOS programs.

Check disk (chkdsk)

To check your computer's disk and RAM, type "chkdsk". Try it now!

If your computer is set up properly, it has a feature called **path to DOS**, so you can type "chkdsk" after any prompt, so your screen looks like this —

```
C:\>chkdsk
```

or like this —

```
C:\DOS>chkdsk
```

or like this —

```
C:\WINDOWS>chkdsk
```

or even like this —

```
C:\WINDOWS\SYSTEM>chkdsk
```

Then the computer will print a message saying how many bytes are in your hard drive and your RAM.

Example For example, when I say "chkdsk" on my old computer, the computer prints this message:

```
  212,058,112 bytes total disk space
       81,920 bytes in 2 hidden files
      389,120 bytes in 85 directories
  190,115,840 bytes in 3,324 user files
       45,056 bytes in bad sectors
   21,426,176 bytes available on disk

        4,096 bytes in each allocation unit
       51,772 total allocation units on disk
        5,231 available allocation units on disk

      655,360 total bytes memory
      634,464 bytes free
```

The top line says the hard disk is big enough to hold 212,058,112 bytes altogether. That's about 212 million bytes. Since a million bytes is about the same as a megabyte, that's about 200 megabytes.

The next line says 81,920 bytes are in the 2 hidden files (IO.SYS and MSDOS.SYS).

The next line says the disk contains 85 folders (subdirectories). For each folder, the computer must store the folder's name and a list of which files are in the folder. Altogether, those 85 folder names and 85 folder lists consume 389,120 bytes.

The disk contains 3,324 user files. (Those are the files that aren't hidden and aren't names of folders.) Some of those files are in the root directory and can be seen when you type "dir"; the rest of those files are buried in folders. Altogether, those 3,324 user files consume 190,115,840 bytes.

It's difficult to manufacture a flawless hard disk. Most hard disks contain some unreliable areas, which are called **bad sectors**. According to the "chkdsk" command, my computer knows that 45,056 bytes on the hard disk's surface are in bad sectors. Since the computer *knows* that those sectors are bad, the computer won't put any data there, and those bad sectors won't do any harm.

The typical hard drive contains fewer than 200,000 bytes in bad sectors. The typical floppy disk has no bad sectors at all.

(If your hard disk contains *more* than 200,000 bytes in bad sectors, or the number of bytes in bad sectors increases rapidly each month, return the disk to your dealer for repair or replacement. If a floppy disk contains any bad sectors at all, buy a different floppy disk instead, since nearby sectors might be partly unreliable, and discount dealers sell new floppy disks for less than $1.)

Although the top line says my hard disk is big enough to hold about 212 million bytes, the lines below show that most of those bytes are used for the 2 hidden files, the 85 folders, the 3,324 user files, and bad sectors. Just 21,426,176 bytes remain unused; they're available for any additional files we want to put on the disk.

Each file consists of several **clusters** on the disk's surface. The next line says that each cluster (allocation unit) consists of 4,096 bytes (which is 4 kilobytes). The next lines say that altogether the disk holds 51,772 clusters, of which 5,231 remain unused.

The bottom two lines discuss the RAM chips, not the hard disk. They say that the RAM chips contain 655,360 bytes (640 kilobytes) of conventional memory. Some of those bytes are used by DOS itself; 634,464 bytes remain unused; they're available for any program we wish to run.

Actually, I bought more RAM chips — 4 megabytes altogether! But just 640K of them are used for conventional memory. The rest of them are used for extended and expanded memory, which the "chkdsk" command doesn't analyze.

Even if you buy many megabytes of RAM, the largest RAM quantity that the "chkdsk" command will ever mention is 655,360 bytes, because 655,360 bytes is the largest size that *conventional* RAM can be.

Bad command When you say "chkdsk", the computer might say:

```
Bad command or file name
```

That means the computer can't find the CHKDSK program. To solve that problem, examine your spelling: maybe you spelled "chkdsk" incorrectly?

If you spelled "chkdsk" correctly, maybe your computer is set up incorrectly. To handle such a computer, remind the computer that the "chkdsk" command is in the DOS subdirectory (by typing "\dos\chkdsk" instead of just "chkdsk").

If you don't have a DOS subdirectory but instead have a subdirectory called BIN, try typing "\bin\chkdsk". If instead you have a subdirectory called UTIL, try typing "\util\chkdsk".

Different drives If you say "chkdsk" after the C prompt, the computer will check the disk in drive C.

To check the disk in drive A, say "chkdsk a:". To check disk B, say "chkdsk b:".

Lost chains If you accidentally turn off the computer while the computer is in the middle of thinking about a file, the computer might get confused and forget the file's name and which folder the file belongs to. Such a file, whose identity has been lost, is called a **lost chain**.

When you say "chkdsk", the computer checks whether your disk contains any lost chains. If the computer notices a lost chain, the computer will say "errors" and might ask:

```
Convert lost chains to files?
```

To reply, press the N key.

Fix (in every DOS except 95&98) If you say "chkdsk" and the computer notices errors on your disk (such as lost chains), the computer tells you about the errors but doesn't fix them.

To fix the errors, say "chkdsk" again but put "/f" at the end of the command, like this:

```
C:\>chkdsk /f
```

The "/f" makes the computer fix minor errors (such as lost chains).

That command works fine in every DOS except DOS 95&98 (which are part of modern Windows, which has its own way of fixing errors). If you're using DOS 6.2, the computer says:

```
Instead of using CHKDSK /F, try using SCANDISK.
Do you still want to run CHKDSK /F (Y/N)?
```

To reply, press Y then ENTER.

If the computer asks "Convert lost chains to files?", press the N key. Then the computer will get rid of the "lost chains" problem by erasing those chains.

(Almost always, the chains contain fragments of old junk that you want erased. If you press Y instead of N, the computer will turn those chains into files instead of erasing them. The files will be named "FILE0000.CHK", "FILE0001.CHK", "FILE0002.CHK", etc.)

If you want to check the disk in drive A and fix it, say "chkdsk a: /f".

Format (in every DOS) & unformat (in modern DOS)

Suppose you buy a blank floppy disk. Before you can use that disk, it must be **formatted**.

You can buy disks that have been formatted. If your disk has *not* been formatted yet, you must format it yourself; here's how.

Follow 9 steps To avoid difficulties when formatting, follow these 9 steps....

Step 1: make sure the disk is blank and a virgin, never used before. Take the disk out of a new, unopened box of blank disks. Do *not* use a disk that already contains info!

Step 2: make sure the disk is the same size as the drive you plan to put it in. If the drive's slot is 5¼ inches long, make sure the disk is 5¼-inch. If the drive's slot is 3½ inches long, make sure the disk is 3½-inch.

Step 3: make sure the disk is the same density as the drive. If the drive is high-density, make sure the disk is high-density. If the drive is double-density, make sure the disk is double-density. Here's how:

To find out the density of the drive, ask your dealer (or read the ads and manuals that came with the computer). A 5¼-inch drive holds 360K if double-density, 1.2M if high-density. A 3½-inch drive holds 720K if double-density, 1.44M if high-density. In a typical 8088 computer, the drives are double-density. In a typical 386, 486, or Pentium computer, the drives are high-density. In a typical 286 computer, drive A is high-density; drive B is either a double-density 5¼-inch or a high-density 3½-inch.

To find out the density of the disk, read the disk's label and the box the disk came in. "HD" means high-density; "DD" means double-density. The typical high-density 3½-inch disk has "HD" stamped on it and has square cutouts in *two* of the disk's corners (instead of just one corner). The typical double-density 5¼-inch disk is made of magnetic material that's brownish-gray (instead of charcoal gray) and has its central hole reinforced by a Mylar ring.

Step 4: temporarily empty the drives. Remove any disks from the floppy drives.

Step 5: get the standard prompt onto the screen. Make the computer say "C:\>".

Step 6: say "format a:" or "format b:" (and press ENTER at the end of that line). If you're planning to put the blank disk into drive A, say "format a:". If you're planning to put the blank disk into drive B, say "format b:". Be sure to say "format a:" or "format b:" rather than just "format". Then if you're lucky, the computer will say:

```
Insert new diskette
and press ENTER when ready
```

(If instead the computer says "Bad command or file name", remind the computer which folder FORMAT.COM is in. For example, if FORMAT.COM is in a folder called DOS, say "\dos\format a:"; if FORMAT.COM is in a folder called BIN, say "\bin\format a:".)

Step 7: put the blank disk into the drive. If you said "format a:", put the blank disk into drive A. If you said "format b:", put the blank disk into drive B. If the disk is 5¼-inch, close the drive's door.

Step 8: press the ENTER key. If you're lucky, the computer will say "Formatting" and will format the blank disk.

The formatting takes about a minute. During that time, the computer divides the disk's surface into tracks and sectors, checks the disk's surface for flaws, and puts these 4 items onto the disk: the **boot record**, the **directory**, and 2 copies of the **file allocation table (FAT)**. When the formatting is finished, the computer will say "Format complete".

(If the computer gripes, try again to do steps 1-8 correctly!)

Step 9: answer questions. If you're using modern DOS or DOS 4, the computer will ask:

```
Volume label (11 characters, ENTER for none)?
```

Then you can invent a name for the disk. Keep the name short: no more than 11 characters. Type the name, then press ENTER. (If you're too lazy to invent a name, press ENTER without typing a name.) Then in the future, whenever you ask the computer to print the disk's directory, the computer will automatically print the disk's name at the top of the directory.

At the end of the whole formatting procedure, the computer will ask:

```
Format another (Y/N)?
```

If you want to format another blank disk, press the Y key (which means "Yes"); otherwise, press the N key (which means "No"). Then press ENTER.

Mistakes When giving the format command, what happens if you make a mistake?

Make sure the disk you're formatting was blank. If it wasn't blank, the computer will automatically *make* it blank, by destroying the information on it!

Make sure you say which drive to format. To format the disk in drive A, say "format a:". To format the disk in drive B, say "format b:".

If you forget to say "a:" or "b:" after the word "format", the computer gets nasty. Modern DOS and DOS 4 make the computer print this gripe:

```
Required parameter missing
```

DOS 3.2 & 3.3 make the computer print this gripe instead:

```
Drive letter must be specified
```

If you're using an even older version of DOS, the computer won't gripe. Instead, it will format whatever disk is in the default drive, which might not be the drive you intended! For example, if the default drive is C, the computer will format drive C's hard disk, and so it will erase the information on your hard disk!

Format the whole box If you buy a box of unformatted blank disks, format all the disks in the box immediately. Avoid giving the format command again — until you buy your next box of unformatted blank disks.

Unformat (modern DOS but not 95&98) Suppose you accidentally format a disk that contained some important files. When the formatting is done, the files seem to be gone.

If you're using DOS 5, 6, or 6.2, you can get the files back! Just tell the computer to **unformat** the disk. For example, to unformat the disk in drive A, say "unformat a:". The computer will say, "Press ENTER when ready." Press ENTER. The computer will ask, "Are you sure?" Press Y. Then the computer will unformat the disk. Afterwards, if you say "dir a:", you'll see that the files are still there!

Unconditional format (modern DOS) Modern DOS lets you say "/u" at the end of the format command, like this: **"format a: /u"**. That formats the disk faster, so you don't have to wait long for the formatting to finish. The "/u" also reduces the chance that the computer will gripe at you. To make modern DOS to format a disk, I usually say "/u".

The only disadvantage of saying "format a: /u" is that the disk cannot be unformatted. The "/u" tells the computer to format **unconditionally** and not waste time worrying about whether you'll change your mind and want to unformat. Saying "/u" means you're confident and demand quick results.

Quick format (in modern DOS) Suppose a disk in drive A has been formatted and contains files, but you no longer need those files. To erase all the files on the disk, you can just reformat the disk by again saying "format a:".

Unfortunately, saying "format a:" makes you wait about a minute, while the computer erases the files and divides the disk's surface into tracks and sectors again.

Modern DOS lets you reformat faster by saying "**format a: /q/u**". The "/q" tells the computer to reformat *quickly*, by erasing the files but not bothering to redivide the disk's surface into tracks and sectors; the computer will reuse the tracks and sectors. The "/u" tells the computer to reformat *unconditionally*, without preparing for the possibility of an unformat. The computer accomplishes "format a: /q/u" in just a few seconds.

Double-density format (DOS 3 & up)

Suppose you buy a double-density disk. If you want to format it, the most reliable way is to use a double-density drive. If you lack a double-density drive, try formatting the double-density disk in a high-density drive, helped by one of the trick format commands listed below. These trick format commands work well if the disk is 3½-inch. If the disk is 5¼-inch, these tricks are less reliable, but you're welcome to try them anyway!

Here are the tricks for trying to format a double-density disk in high-density drive A....

Modern DOS and DOS 4 let you do this:

> If the disk is 3½-inch, say "format a: /f:720", which means format for 720K.
> If the disk is 5¼-inch, say "format a: /f:360", which means format for 360K.

To make modern DOS finish the format faster and with less chance of griping, put "/u" at the command's end:

> If the disk is 3½-inch, say "format a: /f:720 /u".
> If the disk is 5¼-inch, say "format a: /f:360 /u".

DOS 3.3 doesn't understand "/f:". Do this instead:

> If disk is 3½-inch, say "format a: /n:9". The "/n:9" means 9 sectors per track.
> If disk is 5¼-inch, say "format a: /4". The "/4" means 40 tracks.

Those are the commands to format a double-density disk in a high-density drive.

DOS 3, 3.1, and 3.2 can't handle high-density 3½-inch drives but use the same command as DOS 3.3 for handling high-density 5¼-inch drives. DOS 1, 1.1, 2, and 2.1 can't handle high-density drives at all.

Diskcopy

To copy a floppy disk, give the "diskcopy" command. It copies info from one floppy disk (called the **source**) to a blank floppy (called the **target**). It copies the entire disk, so that at the end of the process the target disk will become an exact clone of the source disk.

Follow 7 steps To avoid difficulties when copying disks, follow these 7 steps....

Step 1: choose a source disk. Decide which disk you want to copy. It must be a *floppy* disk, since the "diskcopy" command copies just floppy disks, not hard disks.

Step 2: choose a target disk. It should be blank and a virgin, never used before. It must be the same type of disk as the source disk: specifically, it must be floppy, and it must be the same size and density as the source disk. For example, if the source disk is 5¼-inch, the target disk must be 5¼-inch (not 3½-inch); if the source disk is double-density, the target disk must be double-density (not high-density).

Step 3: temporarily empty the drives. Remove any disks from the floppy drives.

Step 4: get the standard prompt onto the screen. Make the computer say "C:\>".

Step 5: say "diskcopy a: b:" or "diskcopy a: a:" or "diskcopy b: b:" (and press ENTER at end of that line). If the source disk can be read by both drives A and B, say "diskcopy a: b:". If the source disk can be read by drive A but not B, say "diskcopy a: a:". If the source disk can be read by

drive B but not A, say "diskcopy b: b:".

Confused? Use this chart:

Source disk	Drive A	Drive B	What to type
1.44M	1.44M	1.44M	diskcopy a: b:
1.44M	1.44M	not 1.44M	diskcopy a: a:
1.44M	not 1.44M	1.44M	diskcopy b: b:
1.2M	1.2M	1.2M	diskcopy a: b:
1.2M	1.2M	not 1.2M	diskcopy a: a:
1.2M	not 1.2M	1.2M	diskcopy b: b:
360K	5¼-inch	5¼-inch	diskcopy a: b:
360K	5¼-inch	not 5¼-inch	diskcopy a: a:
360K	not 5¼-inch	5¼-inch	diskcopy b: b:
720K	3½-inch	3½-inch	diskcopy a: b:
720K	3½-inch	not 3½-inch	diskcopy a: a:
720K	not 3½-inch	3½-inch	diskcopy b: b:

Then if you're lucky, the computer will say, "Insert SOURCE disk".

(If instead the computer says "Bad command or file name", remind the computer which folder DISKCOPY.COM is in. For example, if DISKCOPY.COM is in a folder called DOS, give a command such as "\dos\diskcopy a: b:".)

Step 6: insert the appropriate disks and press ENTER. Here are the details....

What you said	What to do now
diskcopy a: b:	Put the source disk into drive A.
	Put the target disk into drive B.
	Press ENTER.
	Wait until the computer asks "Copy another"?
diskcopy a: a:	Put the source disk into drive A.
	Press ENTER.
	When computer says so, put target disk in drive A.
	Press ENTER.
	When computer says so, put source disk into drive A.
	Press ENTER.
	Continue swapping the source and target disks,
	until the computer asks "Copy another"?
diskcopy b: b:	Put the source disk into drive B.
	Press ENTER.
	When computer says so, put target disk into drive B.
	Press ENTER.
	When computer says so, put source disk into drive B.
	Press ENTER.
	Continue swapping the source and target disks,
	until the computer asks "Copy another"?

During this step, the computer copies info from the source disk to the RAM chips, and then from the RAM chips to the target disk. If the target disk wasn't formatted previously, the computer formats it automatically while doing this step.

Step 7: press Y or N. If you want to copy another disk, press the Y key (which means "Yes"); otherwise, press the N key (which means "No").

Copy DOS You should make copies of your DOS disks and any other important software you bought, by saying "diskcopy a: b:" (or "diskcopy a: a:"). Then use the copies. Store the original disks in a safe place — so that if a copy ever gets damaged, you can go back to the original.

Copy protection Although the "diskcopy" command usually works, sometimes it doesn't! The computer might *refuse* to copy a disk!

That happens if the disk's programs were written by programmers who fear you'll give copies of the disk to all your friends without paying royalties. Those programmers alter the disk, to prevent "diskcopy" from working.

A disk altered to prevent the "diskcopy" command from working is said to be a **copy-protected disk**.

Edit your disks

Here's how to edit the info on your disks.

Make directory (md)

Let's create a new folder on your hard disk.

First, get a standard C prompt, so your screen looks like this:

```
C:\>
```

Then invent a name for your folder. The name can be up to 8 characters long, such as SARAH or TONY or JUNK or POETRY or FIDDLING. Type "md" then the name.

For example, **to Make a Directory called SARAH, say "md sarah"** after the C prompt, like this:

```
C:\>md sarah
```

At the end of that line, press the ENTER key. The computer will pause briefly, while it creates a SARAH directory. (If the computer says "Directory already exists" or "Unable to create directory", your disk *already* contained something called SARAH, and you must pick a different name instead.)

Then the computer will say "C:\>" again, so you can give another DOS command.

To prove that the SARAH directory was created, say "dir sarah". The computer will show that SARAH contains two files: Socrates (.) and Freud (..).

Go ahead! Create a folder named SARAH and other folders!

Cd Suppose you've created a SARAH folder. If you wish, you can go into the SARAH folder by saying "cd sarah", which means "Change Directory to SARAH". That makes the computer say:

```
C:\SARAH>
```

Then if you say "dir", the computer will show you the SARAH directory's two files. To return to the root directory, say "cd \".

Copy

The Jewish religion prohibits Orthodox Jews from eating ham. That's why Mary had a little lamb:

```
Mary had a little lamb,
'Cause Jewish girls can't eat no ham.
If Mary were a Hindu now,
Mary couldn't eat no cow.
Religions all are fine and dandy,
Even my dentist's, which says "No candy!"
But Ma's religion makes me shiver.
That's why mine says "Ma, no liver!"
```

Copy from console Here's how to put that poem onto your hard disk and call it MARY.

First, type "copy con mary" after the C prompt, like this:

```
C:\>copy con mary
```

(If your hard disk *already* contains a file named MARY, DOS 6.2 and 95 make the computer ask, "Overwrite MARY?" To reply, press the Y key then ENTER.)

Underneath that typing, type the poem. (If you don't like that poem, make up your own! If you're a slow typist, make up a poem that's shorter to type, or type just the first two lines.)

Underneath your poem, press the F6 key and then the ENTER key. The computer will automatically copy your poem onto the hard disk and call it MARY.

To prove that your computer put the poem onto the disk, look at the hard disk's directory, by typing "dir /p". You'll see that one of the files in the directory is MARY.

Your computer's **console** consists of the keyboard and screen. Saying "copy con mary" tells the computer that you want to copy from the console (keyboard and screen) to a disk file named MARY.

Copy to console Suppose your disk contains a file called MARY. To find out what's in MARY, say "copy mary con". That makes the computer copy MARY from the disk to your console's screen. For example, if MARY was a poem, the poem will appear on your screen.

Filenames You can give a file any short name you wish, such as MARY or LAMBCHOP. **Keep the filename short: you can't make it longer than 8 characters.**

At the end of the filename, you can put a period and a 3-character **extension**.

For example, you can name a file "LAMBCHOP.YUM". In that example, the "LAMBCHOP" is called the **filename**; the "YUM" is called the **extension**.

Copy to floppy After you've created a file named MARY on your hard disk, you can copy MARY to a floppy disk. Here's how.

If drive A contains a formatted floppy disk, **you can copy MARY to drive A's disk by saying "copy mary a:".** Try it!

(If the computer gripes by saying "Write protect error", your floppy disk is a special kind that can't be written on. To reply, press the A key, which means "Abort", then try using a different floppy disk instead.)

To prove that MARY's been copied to drive A, make the computer print the directory of drive A, by saying "dir a:".

To copy MARY from the hard drive to drive B, say "copy mary b:".

Suppose you've put MARY on a floppy disk in drive A and want to copy MARY from that floppy disk to a disk in drive B. Make the computer say "A:\>", then say "copy mary b:".

Suppose MARY's on a floppy disk in drive A and you want to copy MARY to another floppy disk, but you don't have a drive B. Even though you don't have a drive B, you can say "copy mary b:". The computer will pretend your single floppy drive is both A and B; the computer will tell you when to remove disk A from the drive and insert disk B instead.

Copy to folder Suppose MARY is on a floppy disk in drive A, and your hard disk contains a folder called SARAH. Here's how to copy MARY to the SARAH folder. At the standard C prompt, say "copy a:mary sarah", so your screen looks like this:

```
C:\>copy a:mary sarah
```

That tells the computer to copy drive A's MARY to the SARAH folder. (When giving that command, do *not* put a space after the "a:".)

Here's another way to copy drive A's MARY file to the hard disk's SARAH folder. First, get into the SARAH folder by saying "cd sarah". That makes the computer say:

```
C:\SARAH>
```

Then tell the computer to copy drive A's MARY by saying "copy a:mary", so your screen looks like this:

```
C:\SARAH>copy a:mary
```

(When giving that command, do *not* put a space after the "a:".)

Many ways to copy

Here's a list of the many ways to copy a file.

Goal	What to say		
copy from the keyboard to a hard-disk file called MARY	`C:\>copy con mary`		
copy MARY from the hard disk to your screen	`C:\>copy mary con`		
copy MARY from the hard disk to drive A	`C:\>copy mary a:`		
copy MARY from the hard disk to drive B	`C:\>copy mary b:`		
copy MARY from drive A to drive B	`A:\>copy mary b:`		
copy MARY from drive A (to the hard disk)	`C:\>copy a:mary`		
copy MARY from drive A to the hard disk's SARAH folder	`C:\>copy a:mary sarah`	or say	`C:\SARAH>copy a:mary`
copy everything from drive A to the hard disk's SARAH folder	`C:\>copy a:*.* sarah`	or say	`C:\SARAH>copy a:*.*`
copy everything from the SARAH folder to drive A	`C:\>copy sarah a:`	or say	`C:\SARAH>copy *.* a:`
copy MARY from the SARAH folder to drive A	`C:\>copy sarah\mary a:`	or say	`C:\SARAH>copy mary a:`
copy everything from the SARAH folder to the TONY folder	`C:\>copy sarah tony`	or say	`C:\SARAH>copy *.* \tony`
copy MARY from the SARAH folder to the TONY folder	`C:\>copy sarah\mary tony`	or say	`C:\SARAH>copy mary \tony`
make a copy of MARY, but call the copy "SUE"	`C:\>copy mary sue`		

Copy entire floppy to another floppy

Suppose drive A's floppy disk contains important info, and you want to copy all that info to another disk.

If possible, use the "diskcopy" command, by saying "diskcopy a: b:" or "diskcopy a: a:". That makes an exact copy of the entire disk. Unfortunately, the "diskcopy" command can't handle hard disks, and it requires that the target disk be exactly the same size and density as the source disk.

An alternative way to copy all files from drive A to drive B is to say:

```
A:\>copy *.* b:
```

That tells the computer to copy files from drive A to drive B. But that "copy" command does *not* copy the hidden files (IO.SYS and MSDOS.SYS), does *not* copy folders, and does *not* copy any files buried in folders. It copies just the visible simple files listed in the root directory. And before giving that "copy" command you must make sure drive B's disk has been formatted.

Copy entire floppy to the hard disk

To copy all files from drive A to the *hard* disk, you can use several methods.

One method is to **make a hard-disk folder**, such as SARAH, by saying:

```
C:\>md sarah
```

Then copy files from drive A to that folder by saying:

```
C:\>copy a:*.* sarah
```

That copies just the simple files that are visible in drive A's root directory.

When giving that command, make sure you mention a hard-disk folder such as SARAH. Do *not* just say "copy a:*.*" without mentioning SARAH. If you make the mistake of saying just "copy a:*.*", the computer will copy drive A's files to your hard directory's *root* directory, where they'll destroy any hard disk files that have similar names.

For example, if drive A contains a file called "AUTOEXEC.BAT" and you make the mistake of saying "copy a:*.*", that file will be copied to your hard disk's root directory and destroy the AUTOEXEC.BAT file that was on your hard disk previously. Then your hard disk won't work properly, and you'll phone me with tears in your eyes about how you wrecked your hard disk.

Spare yourself the agony: remember to **never say just "copy a:*.*"**. Instead, always mention a folder, such as "copy a:*.* sarah".

When you buy a program, you usually get an instruction manual and a set of floppy disks. Read the instruction manual — especially the part entitled "Getting started" or "Installation". It tells you the programmer's opinion of the best way to copy the floppy disks onto your hard disk.

Instead of having you create a folder such as SARAH and then having you say "copy a:*.* sarah", the instruction manual usually tells you to put the first floppy disk into drive A and then type "a:install" or "a:setup". When you type that command, the computer starts running a program called "INSTALL.EXE" or "SETUP.EXE" on the first floppy disk. That program automatically creates a folder on your hard disk and copies files to that folder from the floppy disk. Then the program makes the computer tell you to insert the other floppy disks, and the program automatically copies files from those disks to your hard disk's folder.

During that process, the program asks you questions about what kind of computer equipment you bought and what your desires are. The program copies just the files that are relevant to your needs and desires; it also edits those files to meet your needs more closely.

Type

Suppose you've put on your hard disk a file called MARY containing a poem. To see the poem on your screen, you can tell the computer to copy MARY to the console's screen, by saying "copy mary con". An even easier way to copy MARY to the screen is to say just "type mary".

Experiment! See what's in your hard disk's "AUTOEXEC.BAT" file by saying "type autoexec.bat", like this:

```
C:\>type autoexec.bat
```

See what's in your hard disk's "CONFIG.SYS" file by saying:

```
C:\>type config.sys
```

Which files are ASCII MARY, AUTOEXEC.BAT, and CONFIG.SYS all contain words and numbers that you can read on the screen. Other files are weirder. For example, if you say "type command.com", you'll see strange symbols instead of words and numbers.

Files such as MARY, AUTOEXEC.BAT, and CONFIG.SYS, which all contain words and numbers you can read, are called **ASCII files** (pronounced "ass key files"). The COMMAND.COM file contains special symbols and is therefore *not* an ASCII file.

If somebody says, "Give me an ASCII file", that person wants to be given a floppy disk that contains an ASCII file, which is a file that the person can read by giving the "type" command.

Files that end in .BAT are always ASCII files. Files ending in .COM and .EXE are never ASCII files. Files ending in .TXT are usually ASCII files.

Congratulations! You've learned all the essentials of DOS! If you're in a rush, you may skip ahead to other chapters. If you keep reading here, you'll become a DOS *expert!*

Rename (ren)

Suppose a file is named MARY. To change that file's name to LAMBCHOP, say "rename mary lambchop".

Before giving that command, make sure the computer has given you the right prompt. For example, if MARY is on drive A, change the name to LAMBCHOP by saying:

```
A:\>rename mary lambchop
```

If MARY is in the hard drive's SARAH folder, change the name MARY to LAMBCHOP by saying:

```
C:\SARAH>rename mary lambchop
```

Instead of typing the word "rename", you can type just "ren", like this: "ren mary lambchop".

By saying "rename" (or "ren"), you can rename a simple file (such as MARY), but you cannot rename a folder. For example, if you have a folder named SARAH, you cannot change SARAH to TONY by saying "rename".

Delete (del)

Suppose a file is named MARY. To delete that file from the disk, say "del mary".

Before giving that command, make sure the computer has given you the right prompt. For example, if MARY is on drive A, delete MARY by saying:

```
A:\>del mary
```

If MARY is in the hard drive's SARAH folder, delete MARY by saying:

```
C:\SARAH>del mary
```

Delete all files To delete *all* files from the SARAH folder, say:

```
C:\>del sarah
```

The computer will ask, "Are you sure?" To reply, press the Y key (which means Yes) and then ENTER.

Then the computer will delete all files from the SARAH folder — except for Socrates (.), Freud (..), any hidden files, and any folders that are inside the SARAH folder.

To delete all files from drive A, say:

```
A:\>del *.*
```

When the computer asks "Are you sure?", press Y then ENTER. Then the computer will delete all files from drive A — except for hidden files and folders.

Move (in DOS 6 & up)

DOS 6, 6.2, and 95 let you say "move". The word "move" serves two purposes....

Purpose 1: move a file For example, suppose MARY is a file on the hard disk, and you want to move MARY to drive A. Just say:

```
C:\>move mary a:
```

That copies MARY from the hard disk to drive A and then deletes MARY from the hard disk.

Saying "move mary a:" has the same effect as saying "copy mary a:" and then "del mary". So "move" means "make a copy and then destroy the original".

Purpose 2: rename a folder If SARAH is a folder and you want to change its name to TONY, say "move sarah tony", like this:

```
C:\>move sarah tony
```

Remove directory (rd)

Suppose your hard disk contains a folder named SARAH. Here's how to remove that folder from the hard disk.

First, delete all files from the SARAH folder by saying:

```
C:\>del sarah
```

When the computer asks "Are you sure?", press the Y key and then ENTER.

Now the SARAH folder should be empty. Finally, get rid of the SARAH folder itself, by saying Remove the Directory SARAH:

```
C:\>rd sarah
```

If you're lucky, the computer will respond by saying just:

```
C:\>
```

That means the SARAH folder has been removed. If you're *un*lucky, the computer will gripe by saying:

```
Invalid path, not directory,
or directory not empty
C:\>
```

That means the SARAH folder can't be removed yet, because the SARAH folder isn't empty yet: it contains other folders or hidden files. Get rid of the folders inside it, then try again to say "rd sarah".

Deltree (in DOS 6 & up)

If you want to delete a folder named SARAH, you can use this shortcut in DOS 6, 6.2, and 95: just say "deltree sarah", like this....

```
C:\>deltree sarah
```

The computer will ask whether you're sure; press Y then ENTER. Then the computer will delete all the files in the SARAH folder, delete any folders in the SARAH folder, and remove the SARAH folder itself. So the computer automatically does "del sarah" and "rd sarah" and does the same for any folders in SARAH.

Saying "deltree sarah" is nifty, because it automatically makes the computer perform a series of "del" and "rd" commands for you.

The "deltree sarah" means "delete the tree of SARAH". It makes the computer delete the SARAH folder and also any files or folders that have been sprouting in SARAH.

Edit (in modern DOS)

To edit a file easily, give the "edit" command. To give that command, you must buy modern DOS.

(If you're using a classic DOS instead, skip ahead to the next section, which explains how to give the "edlin" command instead.)

Before giving the "edit" command, decide which file you want to edit. (For example, suppose you want to edit a file you created called "MARY".)

Make the computer give you the correct prompt. (For example, if MARY is in your hard disk's root directory, make the computer say "C:\>". If MARY is in your hard disk's SARAH folder, make the computer say "C:\SARAH>". If MARY is in drive B, make the computer say "B:\>".)

After that prompt, say "edit mary".

If you're lucky, the screen's bottom line will say "MS-DOS Editor", the screen's top line will say "File", and the screen's second line will say "MARY". (If instead the computer gripes, make sure your DOS folder contains EDIT.COM, EDIT.HLP, and QBASIC.EXE.)

In the middle of the screen, you'll see all of MARY's lines:

```
Mary had a little lamb,
'Cause Jewish girls can't eat no ham.
If Mary were a Hindu now,
Mary couldn't eat no cow.
Religions all are fine and dandy,
Even my dentist's, which says "No candy!"
But Ma's religion makes me shiver.
That's why mine says "Ma, no liver!"
```

NUM LOCK key In your keyboard's upper-right corner, you might see a light marked "Num Lock". If that light is glowing, turn it off by pressing the **NUM LOCK key** underneath it.

Cursor On your screen, the first character (the M) is underlined. The underline blinks. That blinking underline is called the **cursor**.

To move that cursor to the right, press the key that has a right-arrow on it. You can move the cursor in all four directions, by pressing the right-arrow, left-arrow, down-arrow, and up-arrow keys. Each of those keys automatically repeats: so to move the cursor to the right *several* characters, just keep your finger on the right-arrow key a while.

(If pressing the arrow keys makes you see numbers instead of a moving cursor, press the NUM LOCK key.)

To move the cursor all the way left, to the line's beginning, press the **HOME key**. To move the cursor far right, to the line's end, just past the line's last word, press the **END key**.

Insert a character Here's how to insert extra characters anywhere in your document. Move the cursor to where you want the extra characters to begin. Then type the characters you want to insert. To make room for characters you're inserting, other characters on that line will automatically move to the right.

Insert a line To insert an extra line in your document, move the cursor to the screen's left edge, where you want the extra line to begin.

Press the ENTER key. You'll see a blank line. To make room for it, other lines automatically moved down.

Leave the new line blank, or type there whatever characters you wish!

Delete a character To delete the character you just typed, press the **BACKSPACE key** (which is above the ENTER key and has a left-arrow on it).

To delete a character you typed long ago, move the cursor to that character, then press the **DELETE key** (which says "Delete" or "Del" on it). To delete a passage typed long ago, move the cursor to the passage's beginning, then tap the DELETE key several times (or hold down the DELETE key a while), until the passage disappears.

Delete a line To delete an entire line, put the cursor anywhere in that line. Then, while holding down the Ctrl key, tap the Y key (which means "**Yank the line**"). The entire line will disappear.

Use that same technique to eliminate a blank line: put the cursor at the blank line, then press Ctrl with Y.

Move a line To move a line far up or far down, first delete the line from its old position (by moving the cursor to that line, then pressing Ctrl with Y), so the line temporarily disappears.

Where do you want to move the line? Put the cursor at the screen's left edge, just under where you want the line to reappear.

Then do this: while holding down the SHIFT key, tap the INSERT key. The line will magically reappear there! To make room for it, other lines will automatically move down.

Exit When you finish editing the file, tap 4 keys:

```
Tap the Alt key (which means "Menu").
Tap the F key (which means "File").
Tap the X key (which means "eXit").
Tap the ENTER key (which means "Yes").
```

That makes the computer exit from the editor. You see a DOS prompt (such as "C:\>"), so you can give another DOS command.

Make a big boo-boo? If you make a big mistake and wish you hadn't tried to edit MARY, tap 4 keys:

```
Tap the Alt key (which means "Menu").
Tap the F key (which means "File").
Tap the X key (which means "eXit").
Tap the N key (which means "No").
```

That makes the computer ignore all the editing you've done, so that MARY returns to its original state. MARY returns to the state it was in before you started using the editor.

You see a DOS prompt (such as "C:\>"), so you can give another DOS command.

Edlin (in early DOS versions)

If your DOS is classic, edit a file by giving the "edlin" command. (If your DOS is modern, don't bother reading this; skip ahead to the next topic, "Batch Files".)

Here's how to give the "edlin" command.

First, decide which file you want to edit. (For example, suppose you want to edit a file you created called "MARY".)

Next, make the computer give you the correct prompt. (For example, if MARY is in your hard disk's root directory, make the computer say "C:\>". If MARY is in your hard disk's SARAH folder, make the computer say "C:\SARAH>". If MARY is in drive B, make the computer say "B:\>".)

After that prompt, say "edlin mary".

If you're lucky, the computer will say:

```
End of input file
```

(If instead the computer says "Bad command or file name", your computer is set up incorrectly and can't find the EDLIN.COM program. In that case, remind the computer where the EDLIN.COM program is. For example, if the EDLIN.COM program is in your hard disk's DOS folder, say "c:\dos\edlin mary". If the EDLIN.COM program is in drive A, say "a:edlin mary".)

Then the computer will print an asterisk:

```
*
```

After the asterisk, you can type any edlin command.

List For your first edlin command, type "1L" after the asterisk, so your screen looks like this:

```
*1L
```

That makes the computer print a List of MARY's lines, starting at line 1. The computer automatically numbers the lines, so you see this:

```
1:*Mary had a little lamb,
2: 'Cause Jewish girls can't eat no ham.
3: If Mary were a Hindu now,
4: Mary couldn't eat no cow.
5: Religions all are fine and dandy,
6: Even my dentist's, which says "No candy!"
7: But Ma's religion makes me shiver.
8: That's why mine says "Ma, no liver!"
```

Underneath, the computer prints another asterisk, so you can give another edlin command.

Edit If you want to edit line 5, type "5" (and then press ENTER).

The computer will print a copy of line 5, so you see this:

```
    5:*Religions all are fine and dandy,
```

Underneath, retype that line however you want it. For example, try typing "Religions can be wonderful and fancy,". To save time, instead of retyping the word "Religions" (which is unchanged), just press the right-arrow key 9 times (since "Religions" has 9 characters).

When you finish retyping the line, press ENTER at the end of it.

Delete If you want to Delete line 6, type "6D" after the asterisk. That makes the computer delete line 6 and renumber all the lines that came underneath it.

Then look at the new version of MARY, by typing "1L" again.

Insert Here's how to insert extra lines and make them become lines 3 and 4, so that the old lines 3 and 4 become 5 and 6.

Type "3I" after the asterisk. The computer will say:

```
    3:*
```

Then type whatever words you want to be in the new line 3.

When you press the ENTER key at the end of that line, the computer will say:

```
    4:*
```

Then type whatever words you want to be in the new line 4.

When you press the ENTER key at the end of that line, the computer will say:

```
    5:*
```

If you don't want to type a new line 5, say Cancel, by tapping the C key *while holding down the Ctrl key.*

Then look at the new version of MARY, by typing 1L again.

Exit When you finish editing MARY, type "E" after the asterisk. That makes the computer End the editing and Exit from edlin. You see a DOS prompt (such as "C:\>"), so you can give another DOS command.

When exiting from edlin, the computer puts *two* versions of MARY onto the disk. The new, edited version is named "MARY". The previous version is on the disk also, but its name has been changed to "MARY.BAK".

Make a big boo-boo? If you make a big mistake and wish you hadn't tried to edit MARY, type "Q" after the asterisk. That tells the computer to Quit.

The computer asks "Abort edit?" Press Y and then ENTER.

That makes the computer ignore all the editing you've done, so that MARY returns to its original state. MARY returns to the state it was in before you started using edlin.

You see a DOS prompt (such as "C:\>"), so you can give another DOS command.

Optional capitals When giving an edlin command, you do *not* have to capitalize. For example, to delete line 6 you can type "6d" instead of "6D".

You can invent your own command and make it stand for a list of other commands.

For example, let's invent a command called "status" that makes the computer display a wide directory and also remind you of which DOS version you're using. To invent that "status" command, just create a file called "STATUS.BAT", which contains two lines, "dir /w" and "ver".

To create that STATUS.BAT file, type this —

```
C:\>copy con status.bat
dir /w
ver
```

then press the F6 key and then the ENTER key.

Afterwards, whenever you type the word "status", like this —

```
C:\>status
```

the computer will look at the file "STATUS.BAT" and obey the commands you stored there: the computer will automatically do "dir /w" and then "ver".

A file that's a list of commands is called a **batch file**. The file "STATUS.BAT" is a batch file, because it's a list of two commands ("dir /w" and "ver"). The name of every batch file must end in ".BAT", which stands for "batch".

Echo off

While the computer performs a batch file, the computer prints little messages reminding you of what it's doing. For example, while the computer performs the "ver" command in "STATUS.BAT", the computer prints the word "ver" on your screen. Each such message is called an **echo**.

If you don't want to see such messages, say "echo off" at the beginning of your batch file, like this:

```
A>copy con status.bat
echo off
dir /w
ver
```

Clear screen (cls)

Another command you can put at the beginning of your batch file is "cls". That makes the computer begin by erasing the screen, so you don't see any distractions.

Put "cls" just under "echo off", so that the computer even erases the words "echo off" from the screen. Here's what the batch file looks like now:

```
C:\>copy con status.bat
echo off
cls
dir /w
ver
```

Echo

Let's define "chick", so that if you say —

```
C:\>chick
```

the computer will recite this chicken riddle:

```
Why did the chicken cross the road?
To escape from Colonel Sanders!
```

To define "chick", type this —

```
C:\>copy con chick.bat
echo off
cls
echo Why did the chicken cross the road?
echo To escape from Colonel Sanders!
```

then press F6 and ENTER.

Replaceable parameter (%1)

You can define "greet", so that if you say —

```
C:\>greet Peter
```

the computer will say:

```
What will Peter do today?
Will Peter work, or will Peter play?
Peter needs a holiday.
Welcome, Peter! Hip, hip, hooray!
```

If you say —

```
C:\>greet Suzie
```

the computer will say:

```
What will Suzie do today?
Will Suzie work, or will Suzie play?
Suzie needs a holiday.
Welcome, Suzie! Hip, hip, hooray!
```

If you say —

```
C:\>greet Godzilla
```

the computer will say:

```
What will Godzilla do today?
Will Godzilla work, or will Godzilla play?
Godzilla needs a holiday.
Welcome, Godzilla! Hip, hip, hooray!
```

To define "greet", type this —

```
C:\>copy con greet.bat
echo off
cls
echo What will %1 do today?
echo Will %1 work, or will %1 play?
echo %1 needs a holiday.
echo Welcome, %1! Hip, hip, hooray!
```

then press F6 and ENTER. Make sure you type the "%1" in that batch file.

Afterwards, when you say "greet Peter" or "greet Suzie" or "greet Godzilla", the computer will print a greeting to Peter or Suzie or Godzilla, by automatically substituting the person's name for "%1". Try it!

@Echo off (in DOS 3.3 & up)

So far, you've learned two sophisticated ways to begin a batch file.

One way is to begin by saying:

```
echo off
```

That prevents the computer from printing echo messages. Unfortunately, that method still leaves the words "echo off" on your screen.

The second way is to begin by saying:

```
echo off
cls
```

That flashes the words "echo off" on your screen, then immediately erases those words (because "cls" erases the screen). Unfortunately, "cls" erases all previous commands from the screen also; that prevents you from browsing at the screen to see what you had done previously.

The *most* sophisticated way to begin a batch file is to begin by saying:

```
@echo off
```

without saying "cls". (To type the symbol "@", tap the 2 key while holding down the SHIFT key.) The symbol "@" prevents the words "echo off" from appearing on your screen but still lets you see all previous screen activity.

The "@echo off" command is understood just by DOS 3.3, DOS 4, and modern DOS.

When you turn the computer on, it goes through a procedure called **booting**. Here's what the computer does while it's booting.

POST

First, the computer plays doctor and gives itself a checkup, to make sure all its innards are working okay. That's called the **power-on self test (POST)**.

Code numbers If the IBM PC detects an illness, it prints a code number telling you where the illness is:

Code number	Which part of the computer is ill
0	main power supply (or other fundamentals)
1	motherboard (or the battery for the date & time)
2	RAM chips
3	keyboard
4	monochrome monitor (or its video card)
5	CGA color monitor (or its video card)
6	floppy-disk drive (or its controller)
7	math coprocessor chip (8087 or 80287 chip)
9	LPT1 parallel port (to attach the printer to)
11	COM1 serial port (to attach a modem or mouse)
12	COM2 serial port (to attach a modem or mouse)
13	joystick (or other device attached to game port)
14	printer
17	hard disk (or its drive or controller)
24	EGA or VGA color monitor (or its video card)
30	network card
48	internal modem
70	BIOS chips
86	mouse
89	MIDI adapter (for attaching a music-synthesizer keyboard)

After printing the code number, it prints a two-digit number, which is usually 01. For example, the computer usually prints 301 if the keyboard is broken (or not plugged into the system unit, or plugged in loosely, or has an XT-AT switch in the wrong position). The computer usually prints 1701 if the hard disk is broken (or the hard disk's controller is broken or the hard disk's cable to the controller is loose).

Although the IBM PC prints those code numbers, modern clones print English words instead. For example, if a modern clone detects that the keyboard is broken, the clone says "Keyboard error" or "Keyboard failure" or "No scancode from keyboard" or some similar message.

Experiment! Turn off your computer, unplug its keyboard, turn the computer back on, and see how *your* computer gripes! (Then turn the computer off again, and plug the keyboard back in.)

RAM test To test the RAM chips, the computer puts data into them, then reads the chips to see if the data remains.

During that process, the typical computer will tell you how much RAM you have. For example, if you have 640K of RAM, the screen will show the computer counting up to 640K.

If your computer is old-fashioned, you'll see it count up to 640K *twice*. The first time it counts to 640K, it puts data into the RAM chips; the second time it counts to 640K, it reads the chips to see whether the data's still there. For that kind of computer, if you trust the RAM chips and don't want to wait for the computer to test them, press the SPACE bar in the middle of the test. That interrupts the RAM test and makes the computer move on to the next activity.

During the RAM test, the original IBM PC shows no numbers on the screen at all. That computer leaves you in the dark until the RAM test is done.

Beeps At the end of the entire POST testing, the computer gives a short beep, which tells you the testing's done.

If you ever hear a *long* beep, or a *series* of several beeps, the computer's trying to send you an alarm. Look at the messages on the screen for details! If you hear the alarm but don't see any messages on the screen, the cause is usually a faulty electrical current: the power cord (that goes from the computer to the wall) is loose, or your town's electric company isn't generating enough volts, or an appliance in your building (such as an electric heater or refrigerator) is stealing too much electricity, or the power supply inside your computer is bad, or your motherboard is very defective.

If you hear the short beep that means the POST test is done, and you don't hear any alarms, but your screen is totally dark, the problem is probably just your screen. Make sure the screen is turned on (so its power light glows); make sure the screen's contrast and brightness knobs are turned up; make sure the cable that runs from the screen to the computer is plugged in tight; and make sure one of your colleagues didn't attach the wrong screen to the wrong computer!

Boot drive

After finishing the power-on self test, the computer decides which disk drive will be the **boot drive**.

To decide, the computer begins by checking whether drive A contains a formatted disk. If it *does* contain a formatted disk, it becomes the boot drive (so that later the computer will eventually print "A>" or "A:\>" on your screen).

If drive A does *not* contain a formatted disk (or the drive's door is accidentally open), the computer looks for drive C. If the computer finds drive C (because you bought a hard disk and formatted the main part of it), drive C becomes the boot drive (so that later the computer will eventually print "C>" or "C:\>" on your screen).

If drive A doesn't contain a formatted disk but you don't have a drive C either, here's what happens. If your computer's built by IBM, the computer prints "IBM Personal Computer BASIC" on your screen and lets you write programs in BASIC. If your computer's a clone instead, it waits for you to insert a formatted disk into drive A.

Hidden system files

Next, the computer searches in the boot drive's root directory for two hidden system files.

MS-DOS calls them "IO.SYS" and "MSDOS.SYS". PC-DOS calls them "IBMIO.COM" and "IBMDOS.COM".

No system files? If the computer doesn't find the hidden system files, the computer gripes:

```
Non-System disk or disk error
Replace and press any key to continue
```

To reply, put in drive A a disk containing those files (or make drive A be empty and hope that drive C contains those files). Then press ENTER. Again the computer will choose a boot drive and search for hidden system files.

CONFIG.SYS

Next, the computer looks in the boot drive's root directory for a file called "CONFIG.SYS". It tells the computer how to manage hardware intelligently — how to CONFIGure your SYStem. If the computer does *not* find CONFIG.SYS, the computer does *not* gripe; instead, the computer just manages hardware stupidly.

The CONFIG.SYS file consists of a list of equations.

For DOS 3.3, CONFIG.SYS should usually be this list of equations:

```
stacks=0,0
buffers=15
files=30
```

For DOS 6.2, CONFIG.SYS should usually be this list —

```
device=dos\himem.sys /testmem:off
device=dos\emm386.exe ram d=64
dos=high,umb
stacks=0,0
buffers=40
files=50
devicehigh=mtmcdas.sys /d:mscd000 /p:320
```

except that you must modify the bottom equation to match the kind of CD-ROM drive you have.

For DOS 95&98, CONFIG.SYS should usually be this list:

```
device=windows\himem.sys /testmem:off
device=windows\emm386.exe ram d=64
dos=high,umb
```

That's what CONFIG.SYS should look like on typical computers — but *your* computer might not be typical! To find out what CONFIG.SYS is on your computer, say:

```
C:\>type config.sys
```

Let's examine those equations more closely....

HIMEM.SYS On many computers, CONFIG.SYS's top equation says:

```
device=dos\himem.sys /testmem:off
```

That equation makes the computer to look in your DOS folder for a program called **HIMEM.SYS** and run that program. The HIMEM.SYS program teaches the computer how to manage the **high memory**, which is also called **extended RAM**; it's the RAM beyond the first megabyte.

At the end of that equation, the "/testmem:off" says to skip a second test of that memory (since testing the memory once is enough).

What's the *best* way to write the HIMEM.SYS equation? That depends on which DOS you have:

DOS version	What to say
95 or 98	device=windows\himem.sys /testmem:off
6.2	device=dos\himem.sys /testmem:off
6	device=dos\himem.sys
5, with Windows	device=windows\himem.sys
5, without Windows	device=dos\himem.sys
before 5, with Windows	device=windows\himem.sys
before 5, without Windows	omit the equation

Omit the equation if your computer is so primitive that it has less than 1M of RAM or its CPU is *slower* than a 286.

Here's why:

The HIMEM.SYS program comes with modern DOS and with Windows. If you have neither modern DOS nor Windows, you can't use HIMEM.SYS.

Since HIMEM.SYS's purpose is to manipulate RAM beyond the first megabyte, omit HIMEM.SYS equation if you have just 1 megabyte. If your CPU is an 8088 or 8086, it can't handle extended memory, and therefore can't use HIMEM.SYS, so omit the HIMEM.SYS equation.

Modern DOS's HIMEM.SYS is usually in the DOS directory (so say "dos\himem.sys"); but if you're using Windows 95 or if your version of Windows is much newer than your version of DOS, say "windows\himem.sys" instead.

The DOS 6.2, 95, and 98 versions of HIMEM.SYS retest the RAM unless you say "/testmem:off".

A program that teaches the computer how to manage extra hardware is called a **device driver**. For example, HIMEM.SYS is a device driver. To use a device driver easily, mention it in a CONFIG.SYS equation that begins by saying "device=".

EMM386.EXE On many computers, CONFIG.SYS's second equation says:

```
device=dos\emm386.exe ram d=64
```

That equation tells the computer to run a device driver, in your DOS folder, called **EMM386.EXE**. That device driver manages **upper memory** and also turns some extended RAM into **expanded RAM** (which is the kind of RAM required by old-fashioned programs). That program is called EMM386.EXE because it's an **E**xpanded **M**emory **M**anager that runs on any computer whose CPU is at least a **386**. It runs if your CPU is a 386, 486, or Pentium.

What's the *best* way to write the EMM386.EXE equation? That depends on which DOS you have:

DOS version	What to say
95 or 98	device=windows\emm386.exe ram d=64
6 or 6.2, with sound card	device=dos\emm386.exe ram d=64
6 or 6.2, without sound card	device=dos\emm386.exe ram
5, with Windows	device=windows\emm386.exe 256 ram
5, without Windows	device=dos\emm386.exe 256 ram
before 5, with Windows	device=windows\emm386.exe 256 ram
before 5, without Windows	omit the equation

Omit the equation if your computer is so primitive that its CPU is *slower* than a 386.

Here's why:

> The EMM386.EXE program comes with modern DOS and with Windows. It works just if your CPU is at least a 386 and your CONFIG.SYS file contains a HIMEM.SYS equation. You must use a version of EMM386.EXE that's compatible with HIMEM.SYS: if you said "dos\himem.sys", you must say "dos\emm386.exe"; if you said "windows\himem.sys", you must say "windows\emm386.exe". The EMM386.EXE program reserves at most 32K of RAM for **direct memory access (DMA)**, unless you say "d=64", which reserves 64K instead; so say "d=64" if you have a sound card (or any other device requiring more than 32K of DMA).

Windows programs use **extended RAM**. Big, old DOS programs (such as the DOS versions of Word Perfect, Lotus 1-2-3, and Flight Simulator) use **expanded RAM** instead.

If your version of EMM386.EXE is new (version 6, 6.2, 95, or 98), it automatically figures out how much expanded RAM is best for each program.

If your version of EMM386.EXE is old (version 5 or earlier), you must tell the computer *how much* expanded RAM to create, by mentioning a number such as 256 (which tells the computer to create 256K of expanded RAM). In the chart above, the lines saying "256 ram" tell the computer to turn 256K of extended RAM into expanded RAM, to help big, old DOS programs run. If you're not using any big, old DOS programs, omit the "256 ram" and say "noems" instead (which tells the computer you want "NO Expanded Memory System"). If you're using *mainly* big, old DOS programs wanting expanded memory, you can make those programs run better by picking a bigger number such as "512 ram" or "1024 ram" or even "2048 ram"; but if you make the number *too* big, your other programs (such as Windows programs) will run worse, and the computer might also complain you don't have enough RAM to accomplish your goals.

DOS On many computers, CONFIG.SYS's third equation says:

```
dos=high,umb
```

That equation moves some software out of the base RAM and puts that software elsewhere instead, so the base RAM has more space left for other programs. That equation is an abbreviation for this pair of equations:

Equation	Meaning
dos=high	move buffers & part of DOS to the high memory area
dos=umb	move utility programs to the upper memory area

What's the *best* way to write the "dos=" line? That depends on which DOS you have:

DOS version	What to say
95 or 98	dos=high,umb
5, 6, or 6.2, with at least a 386 CPU	dos=high,umb
5, 6, or 6.2, with a 286 CPU and at least 1M	dos=high
5, 6, or 6.2, with less than a 286 or less than 1M	omit the equation
before 5	omit the equation

Here's why:

> The computer understands "dos=" just if your DOS is modern and CONFIG.SYS contains a HIMEM.SYS equation. The computer understands "umb" just if CONFIG.SYS contains an EMM386.EXE equation.

Stacks In DOS 3.3, 4, 5, 6, and 6.2, CONFIG.SYS's fourth equation should say:

```
stacks=0,0
```

That tells the computer that your software takes care of interruptions well, so there are no stacks of unexplained interrupts, and the computer doesn't need to reserve any RAM for them.

Some dealers make the mistake of saying "stacks=9,256" instead. That forces the computer to build 9 stacks of 256K bytes. Those stacks will probably never be used: they just waste RAM! I've never seen a computer where saying "stacks=9,256" is helpful. Say "stacks=0,0" instead.

In DOS 95&98, saying "stacks=0,0" doesn't make much difference, so you just omit that line altogether. In DOS 3.2 and earlier, omit the stacks equation, since those earlier DOS's don't understand stacks.

Buffers On many computers, CONFIG.SYS's next equation says:

```
buffers=40
```

That makes the computer reserve enough RAM to hold copies of 40 of the disk's sectors. That speeds up the computer since the computer can look at those RAM copies faster than waiting for the disk to spin to the correct sector.

Each buffer consumes ½K of RAM. The 40 buffers therefore consume 20K of RAM.

If your DOS is classic, or your RAM is smaller than 1M, or you're using a program called SMARTDRV (which I don't recommend), you can't afford to devote 20K of RAM to buffers, so ask for *fewer* than 40 buffers: say "buffers=15".

In DOS 95&98, omit the buffers equation. DOS 95&98 automatically give you 30 buffers, which is the right quantity for DOS 95&98.

Files On many computers, CONFIG.SYS's next equation says:

```
files=50
```

That makes the computer reserve enough RAM to hold 50 filenames, so the computer can manipulate 50 files simultaneously.

Most programs manipulate just a *few* files simultaneously. For those programs, saying "files=30" is fine. But some programs try to manipulate *more* than 30 files simultaneously and require you to say "files=50" or even "files=60" or even "files=99".

If you wish, start by saying "files=30" and then see whether any of your fancy programs complain; if they complain, switch to a higher number.

If your DOS is fancy, your programs are probably fancy too, so you'll want to manipulate more files simultaneously. Here's a good rule of thumb:

> For DOS 5, 6, or 6.2, say "files=50".
> For any earlier DOS, say "files=30" (to consume less RAM).
> For DOS 95&98, omit the equation. (DOS 95&98 automatically give you 60 files.)

CD-ROM DOS 95&98 automatically teach the computer how to use a CD-ROM drive.

If you have a CD-ROM drive but your DOS is *not* 95 or 98, give an equation that teaches the computer how to use a CD-ROM drive. The equation begins by saying "devicehigh=" and mentions a CD-ROM driver.

> If the CD-ROM drive is manufactured by Toshiba,
> its driver program is usually called TOSHIBA.SYS.
> The equation looks like this: "devicehigh=toshiba.sys /d:mscd000".
>
> If the CD-ROM drive is manufactured by Sony,
> its driver program is usually called SLCD.SYS.
> The equation looks like this: "devicehigh=slcd.sys /d:mscd000 /b:300 /m:p".
>
> If the CD-ROM drive is manufactured by Mitsumi,
> its driver program is usually called MTMCDAS.SYS.
> The equation looks like this: "devicehigh=mtmcdas.sys /d:mscd000 /p:320".

On *your* computer, the equation might be slightly different, to make *your* particular CD-ROM drive be compatible with *your* computer. If your CD-ROM drive works fine, so does your CONFIG.SYS's CD-ROM equation: leave it the way your manufacturer gave it to you!

Notice that **the equation should say "devicehigh=" instead of "device=". The "high" makes the computer put the driver program into upper memory instead of base RAM, so the base RAM is free for other purposes.**

Your own CONFIG.SYS

If your drive C's root directory doesn't contain a CONFIG.SYS file yet, create one! For example, you can create a CONFIG.SYS file for DOS 6.2 by typing this —

```
C:\>copy con config.sys
device=dos\himem.sys /testmem:off
device=dos\emm386.exe ram d=64
dos=high,umb
stacks=0,0
buffers=40
files=50
devicehigh=mtmcdas.sys /d:mscd000 /p:320
```

and then pressing the F6 key and then ENTER. But remember that you must modify those equations to handle your computer's peculiarities, as I suggested when I explained each equation.

If your drive C's root directory contains a CONFIG.SYS file *already*, you can edit it by saying "edit config.sys" (in modern DOS) or "edlin config.sys" (in classic DOS). But **before you perform surgery on your CONFIG.SYS file, copy it onto a floppy disk** (by saying "copy config.sys a:"), so that if you make a mistake you can return to what you had before.

The computer examines the CONFIG.SYS equations just when the computer is booting. If you edit CONFIG.SYS or create a new CONFIG.SYS, **the computer won't obey the new CONFIG.SYS equations until the next time you boot the computer.**

If your dealer or colleague has put many strange lines into your CONFIG.SYS file, do *not* erase them until you find out why they're there. Most of those lines are probably time-wasting junk put there by bloated Microsoft DOS installation routines and should be erased, but *some* of those lines might be essential. Be especially cautious about erasing any lines saying "device=" or "devicehigh=".

When in doubt, leave your CONFIG.SYS alone. Better safe than sorry! Follow the advice of the world's best repairman: "If it ain't broke, don't fix it."

Hints

If you're ambitious and try to "improve" a CONFIG.SYS file, here are some hints.

Say "devicehigh" instead of "device", except for the lines about HIMEM.SYS and EMM386. For "devicehigh" to work, CONFIG.SYS must mention "umb".

When you switch to a newer version of DOS, some old software might gripe about the switch and say "incorrect DOS version". To stop the gripe, buy newer software or add this equation to the bottom of CONFIG.SYS:

Your new DOS version	What to say
95 or 98	devicehigh=windows\setver.exe
5, 6, or 6.2	devicehigh=dos\setver.exe

That equation makes your new DOS pretend to be an older version, so your old commands still work.

Most computers have a drive A (which is the main floppy drive), maybe a drive B (an extra floppy drive), a drive C (the main hard drive), and maybe drives D & E. The computer assumes the last drive is E or earlier. To force the computer to accept a drive F, say **"lastdrive=f"**. To force the computer to accept drives F and G, say **"lastdrive=g"**. To force the computer to accept drives F, G, and H, say "lastdrive=h". To force the computer to accept *all* drive letters (up through Z), say "lastdrive=z". If you don't need any drive letters past E, you can save some RAM by removing any "lastdrive" equation.

If CONFIG.SYS contains equations mentioning **"smartdrv"** or **"fastopen"**, their purpose is to help the computer get information from the disk faster; but if you have an IDE drive (or any other drive with a built-in disk cache), your drive is fast enough already! You should usually remove any mention of "fastopen" (which conflicts with commands such as "defrag") and "smartdrv" (which consumes too much RAM, can conflict with telecommunications programs, and can cause inconsistent writing to the disk).

To avoid conflicts, the letters **"emm"** must appear in CONFIG.SYS just once. For example, if your CONFIG.SYS mentions "emm386.exe", it must *not* mention "emm386.sys" or anything about **"qemm"** or **"nemm"**.

You can remove any equation about **"fcbs"**, since its only purpose is to help run ancient programs that nobody uses anymore anyway. Even if you remove the fcbs equation, the computer will automatically do "fcbs=4" anyway, which lets the computer simultaneously use 4 file control blocks (FCBs).

Remove any equation saying **"break=on"**, since that equation slows your computer down. The purpose of "break=on" is to let you interrupt the computer more easily; but once you learn how to control the computer correctly, you won't want to interrupt it anyway!

If you remove an equation saying **"shell"**, you must copy COMMAND.COM from the DOS folder to the root directory by saying —

```
C:\>copy dos\command.com
```

and if you're using DOS version 4 (or 4.01) you must also say:

```
C:\>copy dos\share.exe
```

If your computer's a Leading Edge Model D, make sure CONFIG.SYS contains an equation saying **"device=clkdvr.sys"** and the root directory contains Leading Edge's CLKDVR.SYS program, which teaches your computer how to give the correct date and time.

For free help, phone me anytime at 603-666-6644.

COMMAND.COM

After the computer deals with the issue of CONFIG.SYS, the computer looks in the boot drive for a program called "COMMAND.COM". (The computer looks in the root directory, unless CONFIG.SYS contained a "shell=" equation telling the computer to look in the DOS folder instead.)

If the computer doesn't find COMMAND.COM, the computer gripes:

```
Bad or missing Command Interpreter
```

If the computer *does* find COMMAND.COM, the computer runs the COMMAND.COM program, which teaches the computer how to react to internal commands (such as ver, echo, cls, date, time, dir, cd, md, copy, type, rename, ren, del, and rd).

AUTOEXEC.BAT

Next, the computer looks in the boot drive's root directory for a batch file called "AUTOEXEC.BAT". The computer AUTOmatically EXECutes any commands in that file.

For DOS 3.3, AUTOEXEC.BAT should usually be this list of commands:

```
@echo off
prompt $p$g
```

For DOS 6.2, AUTOEXEC.BAT should look like this —

```
@echo off
path c:\dos;c:\windows
set temp=c:\temp
set blaster=a220 i7 d1 t4
set sound=c:\sgnxpro
Lh mouse
Lh doskey
Lh mscdex /d:mscd000 /m:12 /e
Lh mode LPT1 retry=b >nul
```

but you should modify the commands about "set blaster" and "set sound" to match your sound card, include "Lh mscdex" command just if you have a CD-ROM drive, and include the "Lh mode" command just if your printer is an ink-jet or a slow laser.

For DOS 95&98, you don't need an AUTOEXEC.BAT file at all; but if you have one, make it this list:

```
@echo off
path c:\windows;c:\windows\command
```

That's what AUTOEXEC.BAT should look like on typical computers — but *your* computer might not be typical! To find out what AUTOEXEC.BAT is on your computer, say:

```
C:\>type autoexec.bat
```

Let's examine those commands more closely....

Echo On most computers, AUTOEXEC.BAT's top command should say:

```
@echo off
```

That command prevents the computer from printing excessive messages on the screen. (To type the symbol "@", tap the 2 key while holding down the SHIFT key.)

If your DOS is earlier than version 3.3, you must omit the symbol "@" and say just:

```
echo off
```

Prompt On many computers, AUTOEXEC.BAT's second command should say:

```
prompt $p$g
```

That command tells the computer how to make the DOS prompts look, so that when you're in drive C's SARAH folder the computer will say "C:\SARAH>" instead of just "C>".

If your DOS is earlier than 6 and you forget to say "prompt pg", the computer will say just "C>" instead of "C:\SARAH>", even when you're in the SARAH folder.

DOS 6, 6.2, 95, and 98 are smarter: even if you don't say "prompt pg", they assume you *meant* to say "prompt pg". So **in DOS 6, 6.2, 95, and 98, you don't need to say "prompt pg"**.

Path On many computers, AUTOEXEC.BAT's next command says:

```
path c:\dos;c:\windows
```

That command tells the computer to hunt in the DOS and WINDOWS folders whenever you give a command whose definition the computer can't find elsewhere.

Use that command just if drive C has folders called "DOS" and "WINDOWS". If drive C has a DOS folder but no WINDOWS folder, say just:

```
path c:\dos
```

If you're using DOS 95 or 98 (which are part of Windows), say this instead:

```
path c:\windows;c:\windows\command
```

If you forget to give a path command, and you're booting from drive C, DOS 6 & 6.2 assume you *meant* to say "path c:\dos"; DOS 95&98 assume you *meant* to say "path c:\windows;c:\windows\command". Earlier DOS versions make no assumptions; they create no path for you.

Set temp On many computers, AUTOEXEC.BAT's next command says:

```
set temp=c:\temp
```

Here's what that command means: whenever the computer needs to create a temporary file (which holds data temporarily and then self-destructs), the computer should put that file into the TEMP folder (instead of into the root directory or a different folder). That command works just you created a TEMP folder by giving this command sometime after buying the computer:

```
C:\>md temp
```

In DOS 95&98, omit the "set temp" line. DOS 95&98 automatically do "set temp=c:\windows\temp", which puts temporary files into a TEMP folder that's inside the WINDOWS folder.

Set blaster On many computers, AUTOEXEC.BAT's next command says:

```
set blaster=a220 i7 d1 t4
```

That command helps a sound card work properly, if the sound card resembles the Soundblaster.

Omit that command if you lack a sound card, or your sound card isn't Soundblaster-compatible, or you're using DOS 95 (which handles sound cards automatically).

Set sound On many computers, the next command resembles this:

```
set sound=c:\sgnxpro
```

That command says the files about sound are in a folder called SGNXPRO.

If the files about sound are in a different folder instead, mention the correct folder. For example, if your sound folder is called AUDIO16 instead of SGNXPRO, say:

```
set sound=c:\audio16
```

Omit the entire "set sound" command if you lack a sound card or you're using DOS 95 or 98 (which handle sound cards automatically).

Lh mouse

Lh mouse On many computers, the next command says:

```
Lh mouse
```

That command makes the computer run a program called MOUSE.COM (or MOUSE.EXE), which is a device driver that teaches the computer how to react when you move the mouse and click the mouse's buttons.

Omit that command if you lack a mouse or you're using DOS 95 (which handles the mouse automatically).

The "Lh" tells the computer to "load high" the mouse program, so the computer copies the mouse program into upper memory. (The computer doesn't care whether you capitalize the L.)

The MOUSE.COM (or MOUSE.EXE) program is *not* usually included in the price of DOS; instead, you get the MOUSE.COM (or MOUSE.EXE) program on a floppy disk from the company that manufactured your mouse or computer, and you must copy that program onto your hard disk.

The "Lh mouse" command works just if the MOUSE.COM program is in your root directory or DOS folder. **If MOUSE.COM is in a different folder, remind the computer which folder MOUSE.COM is in.** For example, if MOUSE.COM is in a folder called MOUSEY, say:

```
Lh mousey\mouse
```

If MOUSE.COM is in a folder called MICKEY, say:

```
Lh mickey\mouse
```

If MOUSE.COM is in a folder called MOUSE, say:

```
Lh mouse\mouse
```

If your CONFIG.SYS file mentioned "mouse" already, don't put any mouse command in your AUTOEXEC.BAT file.

Omit the "Lh" part of the command if your CONFIG.SYS file lacks any mention of "umb".

Doskey On many computers, the next command says:

```
Lh doskey
```

That command makes the computer run the DOSKEY.COM program. That program modifies DOS so that when you're typing a DOS command, you can edit the command easily by pressing these keys:

```
Pressing the left-arrow key moves the cursor left without erasing characters.
Pressing the right-arrow key moves the cursor to the right.
Pressing the DELETE key deletes a character.
Pressing the INSERT key lets you type extra characters to insert.
Pressing the up-arrow key repeats the previous DOS command you typed.
```

Use that command just if your DOS is modern. Omit the "Lh" part of the command if your CONFIG.SYS file lacks "umb".

The command is useful just if you often type DOS commands and edit them. If you rarely type any DOS commands (because you mainly use Windows or menus instead), omit this command. If you're using DOS 95 or 98 (which are part of Windows), you'll probably want to omit this command, since it's less useful than Windows commands and steals too much RAM from DOS.

Mscdex On many computers, the next command says:

```
Lh mscdex /d:mscd000 /m:12 /e
```

That command makes the computer run the MicroSoft CD EXtension, which is a program that teaches the computer how to control your CD-ROM drive.

Omit that command if you lack a CD-ROM drive or you're using DOS 95 or (which handle CD-ROM drives automatically).

That command is part of DOS 6 & 6.2.

In the mscdex command, the "/m:12" says to reserve enough RAM to hold copies of 12 sectors from the CD-ROM. In other words, it creates 12 buffers.

The "/e" says to put those buffers in expanded RAM (instead of in base RAM). The "/e" works just if your computer has expanded RAM, so **say "/e" just if your CONFIG.SYS file's EMM386.EXE line says "ram"**. Omit the "/e" if your CONFIG.SYS file's EMM386.EXE line says "noems" instead.

The "/d:mscd000" says the CD-ROM drive is named mscd000. Instead of "mscd000", you can invent any other name you wish. Put the name in this command and also in CONFIG.SYS's CD-ROM equation.

Mode On many computers, the bottom command says:

```
Lh mode LPT1 retry=b >nul
```

That command tells the computer to be patient and wait for the printer to respond even if the wait is long. **Use that command just if your printer's an inkjet or a slow (4-page-per-minute) laser printer.**

Omit that command in DOS 95&98 (which handle printers automatically).

In that command, omit the "Lh" if your CONFIG.SYS file lacks "umb". If your DOS is earlier than version 4, it doesn't understand "Lh" and "retry=b", so say this instead:

```
mode LPT1 ,,p >nul
```

Your own AUTOEXEC.BAT If your drive C's root directory doesn't contain an AUTOEXEC.BAT file yet, create one! For example, you can create an AUTOEXEC.BAT file for DOS 6.2 by typing this —

```
@echo off
path c:\dos;c:\windows
set temp=c:\temp
set blaster=a220 i7 d1 t4
set sound=c:\sgnxpro
Lh mouse
Lh doskey
Lh mscdex /d:mscd000 /m:12 /e
Lh mode LPT1 retry=b >nul
```

and then pressing the F6 key and then ENTER. But remember that you must modify those commands to handle your computer's peculiarities, as I suggested when I explained each command.

If your drive C's root directory contains an AUTOEXEC.BAT file already, you can edit it by saying "edit autoexec.bat" (in modern DOS) or "edlin autoexec.bat" (in classic DOS). But **before you perform surgery on your AUTOEXEC.BAT file, copy it onto a floppy disk** (by saying "copy autoexec.bat a:"), so that if you make a mistake you can return to what you had before.

The computer examines the commands in AUTOEXEC.BAT just when the computer is booting. If you edit AUTOEXEC.BAT or create a new AUTOEXEC.BAT, **the computer won't obey the new AUTOEXEC.BAT equations until the next time you boot the computer.**

If your dealer or colleague has put many strange lines into your AUTOEXEC.BAT file, don't erase them until you discover their purpose. When in doubt, leave AUTOEXEC.BAT alone.

Hints If you're ambitious and try to "improve" an AUTOEXEC.BAT file, here are some hints.

Make sure it's the *top* line that says "**@echo off**".

Just one line should say "**path**". For example, if a line says "path c:\dos" and a line says "path c:\windows", combine them into a single line saying "path c:\dos;c:\windows".

AUTOEXEC.BAT's bottom line is particularly important: it tells the computer what to show the human when AUTOEXEC.BAT finishes. If AUTOEXEC.BAT's bottom line says "**win**", the computer will automatically do Windows 3.1 (or 3.11). If that line says "**dosshell**" instead, the computer will automatically run the DOS shell program, which crudely imitates Windows. If that line says "**menu**" instead, the computer will automatically display a list of programs for the human to choose from (if you or your dealer created a file called "MENU.BAT" or "MENU.COM" or "MENU.EXE"). If AUTOEXEC.BAT's bottom line mentions some other program instead, the computer will automatically run that program.

Though it's cute to see the computer automatically run Windows 3.1, the DOS shell, a menu, or another program, it's a nuisance if you'd rather run a different program instead. I recommend that you delete any such line, so the computer will just say "C:\>" and wait for you to *choose* which program to run next. Then after that C prompt, type "win" or "dosshell" or "menu" or the name of some other program.

Remove any line saying "**cls**", since "cls" makes the computer hide error messages that you ought to see!

Remove any line saying "**ver**", since "ver" just makes the computer print a distracting message saying which DOS version you're using.

You can remove any line saying "**verify off**", since the computer does "verify off" even if you don't say so!

If a Windows program ever gripes about "share", you can stop the griping in three ways: either make your AUTOEXEC.BAT file say "**share /L:500 /f:5100**" or switch to DOS 95&98 (which handle "share" automatically) or improve your Windows (by inserting a line saying "device=vshare.386" into the [386Enh] section of a file called WINDOWS\SYSTEM.INI).

If your CONFIG.SYS file has a line mentioning "shell=c:\dos\command.com" (which tells the computer to find COMMAND.COM in the DOS folder instead of in the root directory), your AUTOEXEC.BAT file should have a line saying "**set comspec=c:\dos\command.com**".

Every modern computer includes a battery-powered clock/calendar chip, which keeps track of the time and date even when the computer is turned off. That chip is missing from old-fashioned computers (such as the original IBM PC), which must be coached by inserting "**date**" and "**time**" lines into your AUTOEXEC.BAT file.

For free help in editing your AUTOEXEC.BAT file, phone me anytime at 603-666-6644.

No AUTOEXEC.BAT
If the computer doesn't find AUTOEXEC.BAT, the computer just prints a DOS prompt and waits for you to type a DOS command. (If you're not using DOS 95 or 98, the computer performs the "date" and "time" commands, which ask you to confirm the date and time, before printing the DOS prompt.)

Riddle
Congratulations! Now you're smart enough to master the answer to the favorite riddle among programmers.

> Riddle: What do you get when you cross Lee Iacocca with a vampire?
> Answer: an AUTOEXEC.BAT!

Your input
After the computer deals with the issue of AUTOEXEC.BAT, the computer waits for you to type something on the keyboard (such as a DOS command).

Reboot
You've learned that when you turn the computer on, the computer performs this boot procedure: the computer does a power-on self test (POST), decides whether to boot from drive A or drive C, then obeys all commands in the boot drive's IO.SYS, MSDOS.SYS, CONFIG.SYS, COMMAND.COM, and AUTOEXEC.BAT and waits for your input.

After using the computer awhile, suppose you hit some wrong keys that make the computer start acting strangely, and you're so confused by the whole situation that you don't know what to do. When all else fails, boot the computer again. That's called **rebooting**. Here are three ways to reboot....

Method 1: power down
Turn the computer off. Wait 10 seconds (for the RAM chips to cool down and forget whatever crazy stuff they were thinking of). Turn the computer back on again.

Since that procedure makes you wait for the RAM chips to cool down, it's called a **cold reboot**.

Method 2: RESET
Press the **RESET button**, by using your favorite finger.

That button's *not* on the keyboard. Instead, it's usually on the front of the computer system's unit, somewhere near the floppy drive's door.

(You'll find the RESET button on most clones but not on computers built by IBM. On some obsolete clones, the reset button is on the *back* of the system unit.)

When you press that button, the computer stops whatever it was doing. The screen goes blank. The computer beeps, then reboots by doing the POST, etc.

That's called "giving the machine the finger". It's also called a **one-finger reboot** or **hardware reboot** or **hard boot**.

Method 3: Ctrl Alt DELETE
While holding down the Ctrl and Alt keys simultaneously, tap the key that says "Delete" (or "Del"). That requires three fingers!

That signal makes the computer stop whatever it was doing. The screen should go totally blank. (If you're using DOS 95 or 98 and the screen does *not* go totally blank, give the signal again.) The computer beeps, then reboots. But the computer abridges the reboot procedure: during the POST, it doesn't bother testing the RAM.

That's called "giving the machine three fingers". It's also called a **three-finger reboot** or **software reboot** or **soft boot** or **warm boot**. It's the fastest way to reboot, since you don't have to wait for the RAM test or for the machine to cool down. But if the computer ever goes so wacko that it ignores your keyboard, it also ignores that three-finger reboot, so you must use one of the other rebooting methods instead.

"Hey, honey, how's work at the computer? Getting frustrated? Computer's not being nicey-nicey to yoosy-yoosy? Why don't you do a soft, warm boot? But wait, *here's* a soft, warm boot! In fact, here's a pair of them! Merry Christmas!"

I have a nightmare that when making love to a woman, I accidentally hit the wrong combinations of her "buttons", she reboots, and I realize she was just a machine.

I've met people like that. Haven't you? In the middle of a pleasant relationship, you accidentally hit the wrong "buttons", the person nastily reboots, and you realize the person you've been admiring is just a machine.

If you're a politician, your goal is to make the voters find your opponent's reset button before they find yours.

Make a disk bootable

When you boot the computer (by turning it on, pressing RESET, or pressing Ctrl ALT DELETE), the computer looks in drive A or C for a **bootable disk** (a disk that's been formatted and contains the two hidden system files and COMMAND.COM).

When you buy DOS, it usually comes on a pile of floppy disks. In that pile, the first disk is bootable. (Exception: if you bought the DOS 5, 6, 6.2, 95, or 98 *upgrade* instead of DOS 5, 6, 6.2, 95, or 98 itself, the first disk in the DOS upgrade's pile is *not* bootable.)

If your computer came with a hard disk containing DOS, your hard disk is bootable.

If you have a bootable disk, you can make other disks become bootable. For example, if you have a bootable hard disk, **here's how to make a blank floppy become bootable**....

First, turn the computer on without any floppy in the drive, so the computer says "C:\>". Then put the blank floppy into drive A.

If the floppy wasn't formatted yet, say "**format a: /s**". That formats the floppy and copies onto it the two hidden system files and COMMAND.COM.

If the floppy was formatted already, say "**sys a:**". That copies the two hidden system files to the floppy. If your DOS is modern, that command also copies COMMAND.COM. (If your DOS is classic, say "sys a:" and then say "copy command.com a:".)

How to make a blank hard disk bootable

Suppose you buy a hard disk that's new and totally blank, so it doesn't even contain DOS. Here's how to make it bootable.

First, the hard disk must be **low-level formatted**. It's been low-level formatted already if the drive is IDE or if your dealer is nice. Otherwise, you must do a low-level format yourself. (The way to do a low-level format depends on which hard drive, hard-drive controller, and CPU you bought. For details, ask your dealer.)

Next, put the first DOS floppy into drive A and turn the computer on. If you're using DOS 4 or modern DOS, the computer will automatically install DOS onto your hard disk and make the hard disk bootable; just follow the instructions you see on the screen. If you're using an earlier DOS, you must go through the following procedure instead....

The computer will say "A>" or "A:\>".

Next, tell the computer how to split the hard drive into several parts, called "drive C", "drive D", drive E", etc. Each of those parts is called a **partition**. To partition the hard drive, say "**fdisk**". The computer will say:

```
Choose one of the following:
    1. Create DOS partition
    2. Change Active Partition
    3. Delete DOS Partition
    4. Display Partition Information
Enter choice: [1]
```

Choose option 1, by pressing the ENTER key. The computer will ask you several questions; respond to each by pressing the ENTER key. Tell the computer to make the primary DOS partition (drive C) be as large as possible and active. At the end of the process, reboot the computer (with the first DOS floppy still in drive A), so you see "A>" again.

Then say:

```
A>format c: /s
```

That makes the computer format drive C. The "/s" makes the computer copy the hidden system files and COMMAND.COM onto drive C, so drive C becomes bootable.

(When you give that format command, if the computer gripes by saying "Invalid drive specification", try again to partition the hard drive.)

You can press these special keys....

PAUSE key

Suppose you say "dir dos" or give some other command that makes the computer print a long message on your screen. If the computer is printing faster than you can read, make the computer pause (so you can catch up and read the message) by pressing the PAUSE key. That makes the computer pause until you press another key (such as ENTER).

On modern keyboards, which have 101, 102, or 104 keys, the PAUSE key is the last key in the top row. Older keyboards, which have just 83 keys, lack a PAUSE key: instead, tap the NUM LOCK key while holding down the Ctrl key.

Break (Ctrl PAUSE)

Suppose you tell the computer to perform an activity that takes lots of time (such as print a long directory, or format a disk, or copy an entire disk). While the computer is performing, suppose you change your mind and want the computer to stop.

To make the computer stop, tell the computer to **break** the activity. Here's how: tap the PAUSE key while holding down the Ctrl key.

(If your keyboard doesn't have a PAUSE key, tap the SCROLL LOCK key while holding down the Ctrl key.)

The computer will stop the activity. Then tell the computer what to do next: type your next command.

Alt characters

You can type these special characters:

20 ¶
21 §

128 Ç	160 á	192 └	224 α
129 ü	161 í	193 ┴	225 ß
130 é	162 ó	194 ┬	226 Γ
131 â	163 ú	195 ├	227 π
132 ä	164 ñ	196 ─	228 Σ
133 à	165 Ñ	197 ┼	229 σ
134 å	166 ª	198 ╞	230 µ
135 ç	167 º	199 ╟	231 τ
136 ê	168 ¿	200 ╚	232 Φ
137 ë	169 ⌐	201 ╔	233 Θ
138 è	170 ¬	202 ╩	234 Ω
139 ï	171 ½	203 ╦	235 δ
140 î	172 ¼	204 ╠	236 ∞
141 ì	173 ¡	205 ═	237 φ
142 Ä	174 «	206 ╬	238 ε
143 Å	175 »	207 ╧	239 ∩
144 É	176 ░	208 ╨	240 ≡
145 æ	177 ▒	209 ╤	241 ±
146 Æ	178 ▓	210 ╥	242 ≥
147 ô	179 │	211 ╙	243 ≤
148 ö	180 ┤	212 ╘	244 ⌠
149 ò	181 ╡	213 ╒	245 ⌡
150 û	182 ╢	214 ╓	246 ÷
151 ù	183 ╖	215 ╫	247 ≈
152 ÿ	184 ╕	216 ╪	248 °
153 Ö	185 ╣	217 ┘	249 ·
154 Ü	186 ║	218 ┌	250 ·
155 ¢	187 ╗	219 █	251 √
156 £	188 ╝	220 ▄	252 ⁿ
157 ¥	189 ╜	221 ▌	253 ²
158 ₧	190 ╛	222 ▐	254 ■
159 ƒ	191 ┐	223 ▀	

For example, here's how to type the symbol ñ, whose code number is 164. Hold down the Alt key; and while you keep holding down the Alt key, type 164 *by using the numeric keypad* (the number keys on the far right side of the keyboard). When you finish typing 164, lift your finger from the Alt key, and you'll see ñ on your screen!

Those characters are called **alternate characters** or **Alt characters** or **IBM graphics characters**.

Repeat (F3)

To repeat a DOS command, press the F3 key, then ENTER. Here are examples....

Suppose you have a file called MARY and say "print mary" to print it on paper. To print a *second* copy (to hand a friend), you don't have to say "print mary" again: just press the F3 key. That makes the computer automatically put the words "print mary" on the screen again. Then press ENTER.

Suppose you say "dir a:" to display a directory of the floppy in drive A. To see the directory of *another* floppy, put that floppy into drive A and then press the F3 key, which makes the computer say "dir a:" again. Press ENTER.

Suppose your hard disk contains a folder called SARAH, and you have a pile of floppy disks containing info that's simple (no folders or hidden files). Here's how to copy everything from those floppy disks to SARAH. Put the first floppy into drive A. Copy everything from that floppy to SARAH by saying "copy a:*.* sarah". Put the second floppy into drive A, then press the F3 key and ENTER. Put the third floppy into drive A, then press the F3 key and ENTER.

Sometimes, the computer ignores the F3 key. That happens if you've recently given a command (such as "edit") that uses lots of RAM and "steals" that RAM from the F3 command.

If your AUTOEXEC.BAT says "Lh doskey" (because your DOS is modern), you can press the up-arrow key instead of F3. The up-arrow key has two advantages over F3:

> The up-arrow key is easier for humans to remember than F3 (which beginners confuse with F2 and F4).
>
> Unlike F3, the up-arrow key *always* works, even if you recently gave a command such as "edit" that consumes lots of RAM.

F5 (in DOS 6 & 6.2)

In case CONFIG.SYS or AUTOEXEC.BAT contain errors that prevent the computer from booting properly, DOS 6 & 6.2 let you perform this trick....

Try booting the computer; but when the computer says "Starting MS-DOS", immediately press the F5 key. That makes the computer skip CONFIG.SYS and AUTOEXEC.BAT and just give you a DOS prompt.

F8 (in DOS 6 & 6.2)

When the computer says "Starting MS-DOS", try pressing F8 immediately (instead of F5).

Then the computer shows you each line of CONFIG.SYS and asks you whether to obey the line. Press Y to make the computer obey the line, or press N to make the computer ignore the line.

Then the computer asks you whether to obey AUTOEXEC.BAT. Press Y or N. If you press N, the computer skips AUTOEXEC.BAT. If you press Y instead, here's what happens: DOS 6 makes the computer do all of AUTOEXEC.BAT; DOS 6.2 makes the computer show you each line of AUTOEXEC.BAT and ask you to press Y or N for each line.

To analyze your computer, you can type "dir" (which tells you which files are on the disk) and "chkdsk" (which tells you how much the disk can hold, how much free space is left on the disk, how much conventional RAM you have, and how much free space is left in conventional RAM). I explained those commands earlier.

Now I'll reveal additional commands, which let you analyze your computer more thoroughly, diagnose hidden ills, and help you cure those illnesses. Give these additional commands whenever you buy a new computer and want to find out whether you were ripped off, or whenever your computer acts sick, or whenever you want to supercharge your computer and make it super-healthy, or whenever you're just plain curious about how your computer is faring!

Mem (in DOS 4 & modern DOS)

DOS 4, 5, 6, 6.2, and 95 will tell you how much RAM memory is in your computer, if you say "mem".

DOS 6.2 For example, my DOS 6.2 computer has a 4-megabyte RAM. Saying "mem" makes it print this table on my screen:

Memory Type	Total	=	Used	+	Free
Conventional	640K		20K		620K
Upper	91K		26K		65K
Reserved	384K		384K		0K
Extended (XMS)	2,981K		485K		2,496K
Total memory	4,096K		915K		3,181K

That table's bottom line says the computer has 4 megabytes (4,096K) of memory chips. 915K of that memory is being used already, leaving 3,181K free to hold additional programs and data.

The table's other lines show how the 4 megabytes is split into several parts: conventional RAM, upper RAM, reserved RAM, and extended RAM.

Next, the computer prints a line of subtotals. Those subtotals show what happens when you add the conventional and upper RAM together:

Total under 1 MB	731K	46K	685K

Then the computer prints this message:

Total Expanded (EMS)	3,392K (3,473,408 bytes)
Free Expanded (EMS)	2,736K (2,801,664 bytes)

That means 3,392K of my extended RAM can be turned into expanded RAM. Some of that expanded RAM is consumed by the EMM386.EXE program itself, leaving 2,736K free.

If you say "mem /c/p" (which means "MEMory Classification with Pauses"), the screen will display a more detailed message, which also lists each program in the first megabyte and reveals how much RAM each of those programs consumes. (When you finish reading the first screenful, press ENTER to see the second.)

DOS 95&98 In DOS 95&98, saying "mem" has almost the same effect as in DOS 6.2 but omits the "=" and "+" symbols from the top line.

DOS 6 In DOS 6, saying "mem" has almost the same effect as in DOS 6.2. Unfortunately, DOS 6 is too stupid to put commas in big numbers, and DOS 6 says "Adapter RAM/ROM" instead of "Reserved".

DOS 4 & 5 In DOS 4 & 5, saying "mem" makes the computer print this kind of message on your screen:

Message	Meaning
655360 bytes total conventional memory	The conventional RAM is 655,360 bytes (640K).
655360 bytes available to MS-DOS	All of those bytes can be used.
630480 largest executable program size	Since DOS itself consumes some of those bytes, 630,480 bytes remain for programs to use.
1441792 bytes total EMS memory	The EMS expanded memory is 1,441,792 bytes,
1048576 bytes free EMS memory	of which 1 megabyte is left for programs to use.
3145728 bytes total contiguous extended memory	Main extended memory is 3 megs.
0 bytes available contiguous extended memory	None of those bytes are wasted.
1900544 bytes available XMS memory	Some of those bytes were turned into expanded memory, leaving 1,900,544 bytes.

Missing memory? If the "mem" command reports less available free memory than you expected, increase the available free memory by editing your CONFIG.SYS and AUTOEXEC.BAT files.

> For example, to make modern DOS manage extended memory, make sure your CONFIG.SYS file says "device=dos\himem.sys". To make modern DOS manage expanded memory on a 386, 486, or Pentium, make sure CONFIG.SYS mentions "emm386". In CONFIG.SYS and AUTOEXEC.BAT, avoid mentioning "smartdrv", which consumes lots of RAM; but if you omit "smartdrv", make CONFIG.SYS say "buffers=40".

Page 595 contains more suggestions about increasing your memory.

Skip to next section?

DOS 6 & 6.2 let you do advanced analysis by giving four commands: **msd**, **scandisk**, **defrag**, and **msav**.

If your DOS is earlier than 6, it doesn't understand those commands. In DOS 95&98, those commands are worthless, since Windows 95&98 let you use better tools to accomplish those tasks.

Now I'll explain how to use those four commands — but if your DOS is 95 or 98 or earlier than 6, you can skip ahead to the next section (called "Print on paper").

Msd (in DOS 6 & 6.2)

If you have DOS 6 or 6.2 or Windows 3.1, you can say "msd". That makes the computer run the MicroSoft Diagnostics program, which analyzes your computer and prints its analysis on the screen.

The analysis tells you who manufactured the motherboard and ROM BIOS chip, what kind of CPU chip you have (8088, 286, 386, or 486-and-beyond), how much RAM you have (conventional, extended, and expanded), what kind of video card you have, whether you're attached to a network, which version of DOS you're using, what kind of mouse you have, whether you have a game card (to attach a joystick), which disk drives you have (A, B, and C), how many parallel printer ports you have (to attach printers to), how many serial ports you have, and more!

If your CPU chip's a Pentium but you're using an old version of MSD invented before Pentiums, MSD's analysis incorrectly says you have a "486". If somebody sells you a Pentium but MSD says you have a 486, don't worry: the seller probably told you the truth, you *did* get a Pentium, and the liar is MSD.

When you finish reading the analysis, press the F3 key.

Scandisk (in DOS 6.2)

The "chkdsk /f" command makes the computer fix errors on your hard disk — but just the errors that are obvious. To fix *all* important errors, even the errors that are not obvious, say "scandisk" instead, like this:

```
C:\>scandisk
```

That command works just if you have DOS 6.2. Once you've given that command, the computer says, "ScanDisk is now checking drive C".

Then the computer starts testing five aspects of drive C: the drive's **media descriptor**, the **file allocation tables**, the **directory structure**, the **file system**, and the **surface scan**. Each of those tests is quick (just a few seconds), except for the surface scan, which typically takes about 20 minutes.

The computer does the four quick tests. Then it gives you an estimate of how long the surface-scan test will take. It asks you:

```
Do you want to perform a surface scan now?
```

If you do, press ENTER; if you don't (because you're too impatient to wait for it to finish), press N instead.

During all those tests, if the computer detects a error on your hard disk, the computer will try to fix it. Just follow the computer's instructions on the screen! If the computer says "ScanDisk found data that might be lost files or directories", press L then S.

Verdict When the computer has finished all tests you requested, the computer will give you its verdict.

If you're very lucky, the computer will give you this verdict:

```
ScanDisk did not find any problems on drive C.
```

If you're *somewhat* lucky, the computer will say this instead:

```
ScanDisk found and fixed problems on drive C.
```

If you're totally luckless, and your disk is too hideously screwed up to be fixable, the computer will give up and just say:

```
There are still errors on drive C.
```

Dismissal After the computer prints one of those three verdicts, press the X key.

Other drives If you want the computer to fix the disk that's in drive A instead of C, say "scandisk a:", like this:

```
C:\scandisk a:
```

Defrag (in DOS 6 & 6.2)

Suppose you delete a small file from your hard disk, so your hard disk acquires a small unused gap. If you then try to put a big file onto your hard disk, the computer might put part of the big file into the small unused gap and put the rest of the big file elsewhere, so that the big file consists of two separated **fragments**. In that case, the big file is said to be **fragmented**. Unfortunately, a fragmented file slows down the computer, since the computer must look in two separate parts of the disk to find the complete file.

To make the computer handle the hard disk faster, rearrange the files on the disk so that none of the files are fragmented. That's called **defragmenting the disk** (or **defragging** the disk).

How to defrag DOS 6 & 6.2 let you defrag drive C easily. Here's how.

First, make the computer display a normal C prompt, so you see this:

```
C:\>
```

Next, make sure your disk is acting reliably. To check your disk's reliability, say "scandisk" (in DOS 6.2) or "chkdsk/f" (in DOS 6).

After you've assured yourself that your disk is acting reliably, **say "defrag c: /f"**, like this:

```
C:\>defrag c: /f
```

That makes the computer **defrag** drive **C f**ully. The computer will also put your files as close as possible to the directory tracks (the outermost tracks), so the computer can access the files faster.

Usually, the process takes several minutes. (While you're waiting, go have a cup of coffee or a snack or go work on a non-computerized problem or make love.) When the computer's finished, it will play a quick burst of joyous music and then say "C:\>" again, so you can give another DOS command.

When to defrag About once a month (or whenever you're in the mood!), say "defrag c: /f" again, which rearranges the files again and restores youthful peppiness to your hard drive. Yes, saying "defrag c: /f" is like letting your hard drive drink from the fountain of youth!

Msav (in DOS 6 & 6.2)

To make sure your hard disk doesn't have any viruses, run the **MicroSoft Anti-Virus** program by saying "msav" at the C prompt, like this:

```
C:\>msav
```

The computer will say "MicroSoft Anti-Virus" and "Main Menu". Press ENTER.

The computer will check your entire RAM and hard disk for viruses. That's called **scanning for viruses** (or **doing a virus scan**).

If the computer finds a virus, the computer will say "Virus Found". The computer will tell you the virus's name and which file it infected. To respond, press ENTER. The computer will get rid of the virus. That's called **cleaning out** the virus.

If the computer notices a program was changed since the previous time you said "msav", the computer will say "Verify Error". The computer will tell you the program's name and how the program was changed. Usually this "Verify Error" message does *not* mean you have a virus; it usually means just that you installed a newer version of the program. To respond, press either D (to delete the program, because you think it's infected by a virus) or U (to tell the computer that you changed the program *intentionally* and to Update the computer's understanding of it) or O (to temporarily ignore the problem and cOntinue).

When the computer has finished scanning for viruses, the computer will brag about the number of "Viruses Detected and Cleaned". Press the ENTER key, then the X key, then the ENTER key again.

CHKLIST.MS While running the MicroSoft Anti-Virus program, the computer usually puts into each directory an extra file called **CHKLIST.MS**, which is a CHecKLIST created by MicroSoft. It lets the computer check for future "Verify Errors". The next time you say "msav", the computer looks at those CHKLIST.MS files again to see whether any suspicious changes have been occurring on your hard disk.

If you're confident you won't acquire any viruses soon, you can erase those CHKLIST.MS files. Here's how.

Say "msav" again at the C prompt, like this:

```
C:\>msav
```

The computer will say "MicroSoft Anti-Virus" and "Main Menu". To delete all the CHKLIST.MS files, press the F7 key, then ENTER, then X, then ENTER again.

Other drives To make the computer check whether drive A contains any viruses, say "msav a:", like this:

```
C:\>msav a:
```

Check all disks If the computer ever finds a virus on one of your disks, make the computer check *all* your floppy disks and any additional hard disks you have, since the virus might have spread. If you've been swapping floppy disks or electronic mail with your friends, tell those friends you got a virus and to scan *their* disks too!

New viruses Unfortunately, many new viruses have been invented recently. They outwit the "msav" command, which can't detect them.

These new viruses have spread and become the most common viruses. Since they're not detected by the "msav" command, that command is rather useless.

Your computer is probably healthy and virus-free; but if your computer *does* have a virus, you'll probably need to buy a more powerful anti-virus program to eradicate the virus.

Print on paper

Normally, the computer prints its answers on the screen. To make the computer print its answers on the printer's paper instead, use any of the following methods....

Prn

When giving a DOS command, you can use the printer by saying "prn". Here are examples....

Redirect to printer If you type ">prn" at the end of a command, the computer will send the answers to the printer instead of to the screen.

For example, to make the computer send a directory of drive A to the printer (instead of to your screen), give this command: "dir a: >prn". That's pronounced, "directory of drive A, redirected to the printer". The space before the symbol ">" is optional: you can say either "dir a: >prn" or "dir a:>prn".

To print "I love you" on paper, give this command: "echo I love you>prn".

To type all the lines of file MARY onto paper (instead of onto your screen), say "type mary>prn".

Laser printers If you're using a laser printer (such as the Hewlett-Packard Laserjet 2), **you might see the printer's FORM FEED light go on. That means a sheet of paper has been printed and is waiting to be removed from the printer.**

To remove the paper, turn off the ON LINE light (by tapping the ON LINE button), then press the FORM FEED button.

After you've removed the paper, turn the ON LINE light back on (by pressing the ON LINE button again).

Copy file to printer Another way to copy all the lines of MARY onto your printer's paper is to say "copy mary prn".

To send info directly from your keyboard (console) to the printer, say "copy con prn". Underneath that command, type whatever sentences you want the printer to print. When you finish typing your last sentence, press the F6 key and then the ENTER key. Then the printer will print all the sentences.

PRINT SCREEN key (every DOS except 95&98)

If your keyboard is modern (with 101, 102, or 104 keys), one of the keys is marked "Print Screen".

Dump Pressing the PRINT SCREEN key makes the printer dump onto paper a snapshot of everything that's on the screen. The snapshot on the paper is called a **screen dump**.

PrtSc key If your keyboard has just 83 or 84 keys, it has a "PrtSc" key instead of a "Print Screen" key. On such a keyboard, here's how to get a screen dump: *while holding down the SHIFT key*, press the "PrtSc" key.

Laser printers If you're using a laser printer, eject the paper manually (by pressing the ON LINE button, then the FORM FEED button, then the ON LINE button again).

IBM graphics characters If you try to make your printer print an IBM graphics character (such as Alt 164, which is ñ), the printer might print a weirder character instead, unless you're using software (such as a word processor) that reminds the printer to use IBM graphics characters.

Echo Try this experiment: *while holding down the CONTROL key* (which is marked "Ctrl"), tap the PRINT SCREEN key (or PrtSc key). Then lift your fingers. That makes the computer perform this trick: it waits for you to type something, then copies your typing onto paper. The copying onto paper is called **echoing**.

The computer will continue echoing onto paper whatever you type on the screen (and whatever the computer types on the screen), until you tell the computer to *stop* echoing (by pressing CONTROL with PRINT SCREEN again).

Notice that to stop the echo, you hit the same keys that started the echo. That situation's called a **toggle**. A **toggle** is a key (or series of keystrokes) that tells the computer to start a process and, when hit again, tells the computer to stop.

Computerists say, "The printer-echo toggle is CONTROL with PRINT SCREEN." They also say, "To toggle the printer echo, hit CONTROL PRINT SCREEN."

Print (in every DOS except 95&98)

Another way to print all MARY's lines onto paper is to say "print mary".

(If the computer says "Bad command or file name", your computer is set up incorrectly and can't find the PRINT.COM program. In that case, remind the computer where the PRINT.COM program is. For example, if the PRINT.COM program is in your hard disk's DOS folder, say "c:\dos\print mary". If the PRINT.COM program is in drive A, say "a:print mary".)

The first time you give the print command, the computer will ask you for the "Name of list device". To reply, just press the ENTER key.

While the printer is printing MARY's lines, the screen will show a DOS prompt and let you continue typing DOS commands. So the computer is doing two things simultaneously — it's printing MARY's lines at the same time that it's letting you type additional commands. In that situation, MARY is said to be printed **in the background**.

When the computer finishes printing MARY, it will automatically eject the paper.

Amaze your friends! Try these tricks....

Dir /s (in modern DOS)

Suppose MARY is a file on your hard disk, but you forget which folder contains MARY. If your DOS is modern, just say:

```
C:\>dir mary /s
```

The "/s" makes the computer search through all folders (subdirectories). The computer will tell you which folders contain MARY.

To see a list of all your hard disk's hidden files (even the files that are hiding in subdirectories), say:

```
C:\>dir /ah /s
```

The "/ah" means "hidden". The "/s" means "search through all subdirectories".

To see a list of all your hard disk's unhidden files (even the ones in subdirectories), say:

```
C:\>dir /s/w/p
```

The "/s" means "search through all subdirectories". The "/w" and "/p" make the computer's answer easier to view, by making the directory appear wide and be paused at the end of each page.

/? (in modern DOS)

Modern DOS lets you put "/?" at the end of any command. That makes your screen show a short reminder of how to use the command and its switches.

For example, if you say "dir /?", your screen will show a short reminder of how to use the "dir" command and how to use "dir" switches (such as /p, /w, /o, /od, /os, /oe, /oen, /l, /b, /ah, /ad, and /s).

Help (modern DOS but not 95&98)

The computer can understand your cry for help.

DOS 5 If you say "help", DOS 5 prints on your screen an alphabetical list of all DOS commands and explains briefly what each command means.

(You see the first part of that list. Press ENTER to continue and see the next part. To see the list on paper instead, say "help>prn".)

DOS 6 & 6.2 If you say "help", DOS 6 & 6.2 print on your screen an alphabetical list of all DOS commands.

(You see the top part of the list. To see the list's bottom, depress the down-arrow key awhile, or press the PAGE DOWN key twice. To see the top of the list again, press the PAGE UP key twice.)

The commands are arranged in three columns.

For details about a particular command (such as "dir"), move the blinking cursor to that command by using the down-arrow key, up-arrow key, PAGE DOWN key, PAGE UP key, or TAB key. (The TAB key moves from column to column.) When the cursor's reached that command, press ENTER.

You'll see details about the command's **syntax** (vocabulary and grammar). If the details are too long to fit on the screen, see the rest of them by pressing the PAGE DOWN key several times. If you want to print all the details on paper, tap the Alt key then F then P then ENTER.

When you finish examining the command's syntax, do this: while holding down the Alt key, tap the N key (which means "Next topic"). That gives you the next topic (the command's **notes**, or **examples** of how to use the command, or another command). To go back to the previous topic, do this: while holding down the Alt key, tap the B key (which means "Back").

When you finish using the help system, tap the Alt key, then F, then X.

Undelete (modern DOS but not 95&98)

Suppose you accidentally delete some important files. *If your DOS is modern*, you can get the files back!

That's because when you say to delete a file, the file does *not* vanish. Instead, the file stays on the disk, but the filename's first letter is replaced by a symbol indicating you no longer need the file. That old file stays on the disk until newer files need to use that part of the disk. Then the old file gets covered up by the newer files.

Here's how to try getting that old, deleted file back. (This method works only if you haven't created newer files that use the same part of the disk.)

First, go to the drive and subdirectory where the deleted files were. For example, if the files were in drive A, make the computer say:

```
A:\>
```

If the files were in the hard drive's SARAH folder, make the computer say:

```
C:\SARAH>
```

Then say "undelete". (If the computer says "Bad command or filename", the computer can't find the UNDELETE.EXE file that defines the word "undelete".)

The computer will search on the disk for files you recently said to delete. (If the computer says "No entries found", you're probably in the wrong drive or wrong folder, or the files can no longer be undeleted.)

When the computer finds a recently deleted file, it will print the file's name, except that the first letter will be replaced by a question mark. For example, if the file's name was MARY, the computer will say "?ARY". Then the computer will ask,

"Undelete?" If you really want to undelete MARY, press Y; otherwise, press N. If you press Y, the computer will say, "Please type the first character for ?ARY". Since the first character of MARY is M, press M.

The computer will do that procedure for each deleted file. Afterwards, to prove the files have been undeleted, say "dir".

Remark (rem)

When the computer obeys your CONFIG.SYS file or a batch file (such as AUTOEXEC.BAT), **the computer ignores any line that begins with the word "rem"**.

For example, suppose your AUTOEXEC.BAT file contains a line saying "Lh share /L:500 /f:5100", and you're debating whether to omit that line. Just insert "rem" at its beginning, so it becomes "rem Lh share /L:500 /f:5100", which makes the computer ignore the line. Then reboot the computer and see whether you like what happens. If you *don't* like what happens, edit that line again and remove the "rem". Inserting and removing the "rem" is quicker than deleting and retyping the entire line.

The word "rem" means "remark". When the computer encounters a line that begins with the word "rem", the computer assumes the line is just a "remark" you're mumbling to yourself, so the computer ignores the line.

The line beginning with "rem" can be a command you want to deactivate (such as "rem Lh share /L:500 /f:5100") or a remark you want to make to humans (such as "rem this batch file was written by Joey when drunk" or "rem the next three lines were written by Microsoft to control the mouse").

More

Suppose your disk contains a poem called MARY. To see that poem on your screen, the usual method is to say "type mary". But if MARY contains more than 23 lines, it won't all fit on the screen.

One way to see the long poem is to say "type mary" and then keep hitting the PAUSE key (to see a piece of the poem at a time).

An easier way to see the poem is to say **"more<mary"**. That resembles "type mary" but makes the computer automatically pause at the end of each screenful. (To make the computer continue to the next screenful, press ENTER.)

The command "more<mary" is pronounced, "more from mary". When typing that command, make sure you type "<", which means "from". Do *not* type ">".

Attrib (in DOS 3 & up)

To protect your important files from being erased accidentally, give the "attrib" command. Here's how.

Read only To protect a file named MARY, you can say "attrib +r mary". That prevents MARY from being accidentally changed.

For example, if somebody tries to delete MARY by saying "del mary", the computer will refuse and say:

```
Access denied
```

If somebody tries to delete many files by saying "del *.*", the computer will delete *most* files but not MARY.

If somebody tries to create a new MARY and obliterate the old one (by saying "copy con mary", then typing some lines, then pressing F6 and ENTER), the computer will refuse and say:

```
Access denied - MARY
```

If somebody tries to edit MARY by saying "edit mary", the computer will refuse and say:

```
Path/file access error
```

If somebody tries to edit MARY by saying "edlin mary", the computer will refuse and say:

```
File is READ-ONLY
```

If somebody tries to find out what MARY is (by saying "dir mary" or "type mary" or "copy mary prn") or rename MARY (by saying "rename mary lambchop"), the computer *will* obey. The computer will let people *read* MARY *but not destroy* what's in MARY. That's because **saying "attrib +r mary" means, "give MARY the following ATTRIBute: Read only!"**

MARY will remain read-only forever — or until you cancel the "attribute read-only". **To cancel, say "attrib -r mary".** In that command, the "-r" means "take away the read-only attribute", so that MARY is *not* read-only and can be edited.

Hide (in modern DOS)
For a different way to protect MARY, **say "attrib +h mary". That hides MARY, so that MARY will not be mentioned when you type "dir".**

After you've hidden MARY, it will not be affected by any "del", "rename" or "copy". If you try to wreck MARY by copying another file to it, the computer will say "Access denied". If you try to change MARY's attributes by saying "attrib +r mary" or "attrib -r mary", the computer will refuse and say "Not resetting hidden file".

Although MARY is hidden and isn't mentioned when you say "dir", the computer will let you access that file if you're somehow in on the secret and know that the file exists and is called "MARY". For example, the computer *will* let you look at the file by saying "type mary" and edit the file by saying "edit mary" or "edlin mary". Although the computer won't let you delete the file by saying "del mary", it *will* let you delete the file by saying "deltree mary" (in DOS 6 & up). If you say "edlin mary" (because your DOS is too old to understand "edit"), be careful: after the editing is done, the new MARY will be visible unless you say "attrib +h mary" again.

If MARY is hidden, **you can "unhide" MARY (and make MARY visible again) by saying "attrib -h mary".**

System (in modern DOS)
For an alternate way to hide MARY, say "attrib +s mary". That turns MARY into a system file, which is similar to being hidden.

For the ultimate in hiding, say "attrib +h +s mary". Then even if somebody tries to unhide MARY by saying "attrib -h mary", MARY will still be hidden by the +s.

To undo the +s, say "attrib -s mary".

Normal
After playing with MARY's attributes, you can make MARY be normal again by saying "attrib -r -h -s mary". That makes MARY be *not* read-only, *not* hidden, and *not* a system file.

Examine the attributes
To examine MARY's attributes, say "attrib mary". The computer will say "MARY" and print some letters. For example, if it prints the letters R, H, and S, it means MARY is read-only, hidden, and system. If it prints just the letters R and H, it means MARY is read-only and hidden but not system. (It might also print the letter A, which means "archive". Most files are archive.)

If you say just "attrib" (without mentioning MARY), the computer will print a directory that tells you the attributes of every file.

Xcopy (in DOS 3.2 & up)

Instead of saying "copy", try saying "xcopy", which means: eXtended copy. The "xcopy" command resembles "copy" but has eXtended abilities, so it can perform fancier tricks.

To use "xcopy", your DOS must be version 3.2, 3.3, 4, or modern. Since "xcopy" is an external command (defined by XCOPY.EXE), it works just if your computer is set up correctly and can find the XCOPY.EXE file.

Here are examples of using "xcopy"….

Duplicating a floppy
Suppose drive A contains a 5¼-inch floppy full of info, drive B contains a blank formatted 3½-inch floppy, and you want to copy all files from drive A to drive B.

Since the drives are different sizes, you can't say "diskcopy a: b:". You *can* say "copy a:*.* b:"; but that copies just the files in the root directory, not the folders.

To copy all files — even the files that are in folders — say "**xcopy a: b: /s**". The "/s" makes sure that the copying includes all folders (subdirectories) that contain files.

In modern DOS, that command copies all files except hidden and system files (such as IO.SYS and MSDOS.SYS). Classic DOS copies even those files.

That command doesn't bother copying folders that are empty. To copy *all* folders, even the ones that are empty, say "**xcopy a: b: /s/e**".

Copying a floppy to the hard disk
Suppose drive A contains a floppy full of info. Here's how to create a folder called SARAH on your hard disk and make it contain everything that was on the floppy (all the floppy's files and folders):

```
C:\>xcopy a: sarah\ /s/e
```

In that command, the backslash after "sarah" makes the computer create a folder named SARAH if it doesn't exist already. (By typing that backslash, you don't have to bother saying "md sarah".)

The "/s/e" makes the computer copy everything from the floppy — even the floppy's folders. If you omit the "/s/e", the computer will copy just the files in the floppy's root directory.

Duplicating a folder
Suppose your hard disk contains a folder called SARAH. Here's how to make a copy called SARAH2 (so that your hard disk will contain both SARAH and SARAH2):

```
C:\>xcopy sarah sarah2\ /s/e
```

In that command, the backslash after "sarah2" makes the computer create a folder named SARAH2 if it doesn't exist already. The "/s/e" makes the computer copy everything from SARAH — even folders that are in the SARAH folder.

Renaming a folder
Suppose your hard disk contains a folder called SARAH, and you want to change its name to TONY. The computer won't let you say "rename sarah tony". If you're using DOS 6 & up, say this instead: "move sarah tony". If you're using DOS 5 & down, do this instead: create a copy of SARAH called TONY (by saying "xcopy sarah tony\ /s/e"), then remove SARAH (by saying "rd sarah" after deleting all of SARAH's files).

Copying a folder to a floppy

Suppose your hard disk contains a folder named SARAH. Here's how to copy all SARAH's files to a floppy in drive A.

To be simple, let's assume SARAH contains no hidden files and no folders (or you don't want to copy any such hidden files or folders).

Since this is a simple copying job, you can probably use the simple "copy" command instead of "xcopy" and just say:

```
C:\>copy sarah a:
```

But suppose you run into this hassle: the floppy's too small to hold all SARAH's files. Then you must copy SARAH's files to a *pile* of floppies.

Here's how to copy SARAH's files to a pile of floppies....

Say:

```
C:\>attrib +a sarah\*.*
```

Then insert the first formatted floppy and say:

```
C:\>xcopy sarah a: /m
```

The computer will copy some files from SARAH to the floppy. When that floppy gets full, the computer will say "Insufficient disk space" and stop copying.

Then insert the second floppy. Say "xcopy sarah a: /m" again (by retyping it or by pressing the F3 key or the up-arrow key). Press the ENTER key at the end of that command. The computer will continue where it left off: it will copy different files onto that second floppy.

When the computer says "Insufficient disk space" again, insert the third floppy, and say "xcopy sarah a: /m" again (and press ENTER). Keep inserting floppies and saying "xcopy sarah a: /m", until the computer is done and no longer says "Insufficient disk space".

This method works just if each file in SARAH is brief (so that no single file is too long to fit on a floppy).

If one of the files in SARAH is huge — longer than can fit on a floppy — you must give the "backup" or "msbackup" command instead. Here's how....

Msbackup (in DOS 6 & 6.2)

Someday, some files will get accidentally erased from your hard disk, because you give the wrong command or your disk needs repair. To protect against that inevitable calamity, copy all your hard disk's important files onto floppy disks. Doing that is called "**backing up** your hard disk onto floppies". The copies (on the floppies) are called **backups**.

The niftiest way to back up your hard disk is to give the "msbackup" command. To give that command, you must buy DOS 6 or 6.2. (If your DOS is earlier than 6, skip ahead to the next section, which explains how to give the old "backup" command instead.)

How to back up To back up your hard disk by giving the "msbackup" command, just say "msbackup" at the C prompt, like this:

```
C:\>msbackup
```

If you're lucky, the computer will say "Microsoft Backup 6.0". But if your MSBACKUP program was never used before and was therefore never configured, the computer will gripe by saying "Backup requires configuration for this computer." Here's how to respond:

> Remove any floppies from your drives. Press ENTER seven times.
>
> When the computer tells you, insert a blank disk into drive A and press ENTER.
> When the computer tells you, insert a second blank disk into drive A.
> The computer will say "Backup Complete". Press ENTER.
>
> When the computer tells you, insert the first disk back into drive A and press ENTER.
> When the computer tells you, insert the second disk back into drive A.
> The computer will say "Compare Complete". Press ENTER three times.
>
> Now your MSBACKUP program is configured, and the computer says "Microsoft Backup 6.0".

When the computer says "Microsoft Backup 6.0", press ENTER.

Near the left edge of the screen, you'll see this symbol: [-C-]. That represents drive C. If you also have a drive D, you'll also see the symbol [-D-].

Press the down-arrow key once, so you move to the [-C-], and the [-C-] becomes **highlighted** (its background becomes black instead of blue).

Now you have three choices:

> **Choice 1:** if you want to back up **ALL FILES** from drive C (and you have a gigantic pile of floppies to put those files on), press the SPACE bar once or twice, until the phrase "All files" appears next to the [-C-].
>
> **Choice 2:** if you want to back up **THE SAME LIST OF FILES** that you backed up the previous time, just let the [-C-] keep having the phrase "Some files" next to it.
>
> **Choice 3:** if you want to back up **JUST A FEW FILES** from drive C, press the SPACE bar once or twice, until *no* phrase appears next to the [-C-]. Press ENTER. You'll see a list of drive C's folders (directories). **Press the down-arrow key several times, until a directory you want to back up is highlighted.** In the right-hand part of the screen, you'll see a list of all files in that directory.
> If you want to back up **ALL the files in that directory**, press the SPACE bar, so the symbol ▸ appears next to the directory's name. If you want to back up **JUST ONE of the files** in that directory, do this instead: press the right-arrow key (to move to the right-hand part of the screen), press the down-arrow key several times (until the file you want to back up is highlighted), and press the SPACE bar, so a check mark appears next to the file's name.
> If you want to back up **SEVERAL directories**, put the symbol ▸ in front of each directory's name. To back up **SEVERAL files**, put a check mark in front of each file's name.
> If you make a mistake and want to erase a symbol or check mark, just highlight it and then press the SPACE bar.
> When you finish putting the symbols and check marks in front of everything you wish to back up, press ENTER.

After you've finished making one of those three choices, press S (which means "Start backup").

Put a blank floppy disk into drive A. Press ENTER. If the floppy wasn't formatted yet, the computer will automatically format it. (If the floppy wasn't blank, the computer will tell you what was on it; press the letter "O" to erase and Overwrite what was on it.)

The computer will back up all the folders and files you requested. If they're too long to fit on one floppy, the computer will tell you to insert extra floppies. If you pause a while before inserting an extra floppy, you must press ENTER to confirm that you put it in.

When the computer has finished, it will say "Backup Complete". Press ENTER, then Q (which means "Quit").

How the backup is named The entire set of floppies you wrote on is called the **backup set**.

The backup set has a name. For example, the backup set is named "CC60124B" if the backup set was created by backing up starting at drive **C**, ending at drive **C**, in 1996, on the date **01/24**, and was that date's second backup set (backup #**B**).

In that backup set, the first floppy contains a gigantic file called "CC60124B.001". The second floppy contains a gigantic file called "CC60124B.002". The third floppy contains a gigantic file called "CC60124B.003". Each gigantic file is a combo of several files from the hard disk.

Restore

If you ever want to use the backup set (because your hard disk has an accident), say this again:

```
C:\>msbackup
```

The computer will say "Microsoft Backup 6.0" again. Press the R key (which means "Restore").

The computer remembers the names of all the backup sets you ever created and assumes you want to use the most recent set. For example, if your most recent backup set was named "CC60124B", the computer says:

```
Backup Set Catalog:
CC60124B.FUL
```

(If you want to use an older backup set instead, press ENTER. You'll see a list of all the sets you ever created. Press the down-arrow key until the set you want to use is highlighted, then press the SPACE bar, so a check mark appears next to the set you want. Press ENTER.)

Then press the down-arrow key twice, so the [-C-] is highlighted.

You have two choices:

Choice 1: if you want to copy **ALL THE BACKUP SET'S FILES** to drive C, press the SPACE bar, so the phrase "All files" appears next to the [-C-]. Then press the TAB key.

Choice 2: if you want to copy **JUST ONE FILE** to drive C, press the ENTER key. You'll see a list of drive C's directories. Press the down-arrow key several times, until the directory you're interested in is highlighted. Then press the right-arrow key. Press the down-arrow key several times, until the file you're interested in is highlighted. Press the SPACE bar, so a check mark appears next to the file's name. Press the ENTER key.

After you've finished making one of those two choices, press S (which means "Start restore").

Put the backup set's first floppy in drive A. Press ENTER. When the computer tells you, put remaining floppies in drive A.

When the computer has finished, it will say "Restore Complete". Press ENTER, then Q (which means "Quit").

Backup (in DOS 5 & down) & restore

The "msbackup" command requires DOS 6 or 6.2. If your DOS is 5 or earlier, use the "backup" and "restore" commands instead. Here's how.

(If you're using DOS 6 or 6.2, skip ahead to the next section, entitled "Subst".)

Backup First, grab a pile of floppies. Make sure each floppy is blank, *formatted*, and the right size to fit in drive A.

How much of the hard disk do you want to back up? The whole hard disk? Or just *part* of the hard disk? Just one folder? Just one file? Decide.

Then give one of these commands:

What you want to back up	Command
a file named MARY in the root directory	C:\>backup c:mary a:
all files in the root directory	C:\>backup c: a:
the entire hard disk (all files in root directory and in all folders)	C:\>backup c: a: /s
all files in the SARAH folder	C:\>backup c:sarah a:
all files in the SARAH folder or in folders that are in SARAH	C:\>backup c:sarah a: /s
a file named MARY in the SARAH folder	C:\>backup c:sarah\mary a:

Then the computer will tell you to put a floppy into drive A. (The computer will also remind you that the floppy should be blank — and if the floppy is *not* blank, the computer will erase whatever was on it.) Go ahead: put a formatted floppy into drive A. Then press ENTER.

The computer will copy from the hard disk to that floppy disk. If that floppy disk becomes full, the computer will tell you to insert a second floppy disk. Put the second floppy into drive A, then press ENTER. The computer will tell you to insert a third floppy, fourth floppy, etc., until the copying is finished.

When the whole process is finished, what's on those floppies?

If your DOS is new (version 3.3, 4, or 5), the first floppy contains a pair of files called BACKUP.001 and CONTROL.001; the second floppy contains a pair of files called BACKUP.002 and CONTROL.002; the third floppy contains a pair of files called BACKUP.003 and CONTROL.003, etc. Those BACKUP and CONTROL files contain, in code, the backup copies of your hard disk's files.

If your DOS is earlier, the computer uses a more primitive system: the first floppy contains a file called "BACKUPID.@@@", plus many little backup files. For example, if you backed up a poem called MARY that was in the SARAH folder, one of the little backup files is called MARY; it contains the same info as the original poem but also contains an extra line saying "\SARAH\MARY", to remind the computer which folder the file came from.

Restore If you ever want to use those backup copies (because your hard disk has an accident), say:

```
C:\>restore a: c: /s
```

That makes the computer copy all files from the floppy pile back to the hard disk. If you want to copy just *one* of the files from the floppy pile (such as MARY in the SARAH folder), say:

```
C:\>restore a: c:sarah\mary
```

Notice that "restore" is the opposite of "backup". Use "backup" to copy from the hard disk to a pile of floppies; use "restore" to copy from a pile of floppies to the hard disk.

The "restore" command puts back on the hard disk exactly what was there before the accident. On your hard disk, the "restore" command recreates destroyed files and destroyed folders. For example, if an accident totally destroyed your hard disk's SARAH directory, so that the name "SARAH" is no longer on the hard disk, don't worry: if you backed up the hard disk before the accident, the "restore" command will automatically create a folder on your hard disk, and name that folder "SARAH", and put back in it all the files that were destroyed.

Since new versions of DOS handle the "backup" and "restore" commands differently than old versions, make sure you use the same DOS version for "restore" as you used for "backup".

Make backups small

Suppose you back up your entire hard disk onto a gigantic pile of floppies (by saying "C:\>backup c: a: /s"). Suppose the first floppy in that pile gets a scratch on it. Later, when you try to say "restore", the computer notices the scratch on the first floppy, gripes at you, and refuses to restore. The entire pile of floppies has become useless, because of one scratch!

To avoid losing a whole pile of floppies from one scratch, make smaller piles instead: back up just one subdirectory at a time, so that each subdirectory gets its own pile of floppies. That way, if a floppy gets a scratch, you lose just one subdirectory instead of the whole hard disk.

Formatting during backup

Before giving the backup command, you're supposed to have a pile of blank disks that have been formatted. What if one of the disks hasn't been formatted yet?

If your DOS is modern, the backup command will format the disk for you. If your DOS is 3.2 or earlier, the computer will gripe about the unformatted disk. If your DOS is 3.3 or 4, the computer will gripe unless you said "/f" at the end of the backup command; the "/f" tells the computer to format any unformatted disks.

Modified files

If you say "/m" at the end of the backup command, the computer will back up just the files that "need to be backed up". Those are the files that have been edited or created since the last time you said "backup".

The backup you create by saying "/m" is called the "backup of modified files". It's also called an **incremental backup**, since it consists of just the added files that weren't backed up before.

Copy instead of backup

If the group of files you want to back up is short enough so that the entire group fits on a single floppy, say "copy" instead of "backup" or "msbackup", since the "copy" command is easier and more reliable.

If the group of files you want to back up is too long to fit on a single floppy, but you're too rushed to wait for the "xcopy" or "backup" or "msbackup" command to handle a huge pile of floppies, do this instead: tell the computer to "copy" to a hard disk folder named BACKUP. Here are the details....

If your hard disk doesn't contain a BACKUP folder already, make a BACKUP folder by saying:

```
C:\>md backup
```

Then to back up all the files in the SARAH folder, just tell the computer to copy SARAH's files to the BACKUP folder by saying:

```
C:\>copy sarah backup
```

That scheme works just if your hard disk is big enough to hold the BACKUP folder. If you use that scheme, you should still back up your work onto floppies occasionally, in case the entire hard drive breaks and you lose both SARAH and the BACKUP folder.

At the end of each day, you should copy all important files to the BACKUP folder. Back up all important files onto floppies once a week.

Be wary

Never trust a computer! Even if you copied up your data to a BACKUP folder and floppies, the data you backed up might be wrong, and all those copies might be equally defective! To be safer, use these tricks....

Switch between TWO piles of floppies. The first time you copy onto floppies, use the first pile. The second time you copy (the next day or week), use the second pile instead. The next time you copy, use the first pile again. The next time, use the second pile. The next time, go back to the first pile. Keep alternating! That way, if something's wrong with the data on today's pile, you can go back to the other pile. Nervous institutions (such as banks and the military) have *seven* piles — one for each day of the week. That way, if Friday's data is wrong — and so is the data for Thursday, Wednesday, Tuesday, Monday, and Sunday — you can at least go back to the good data you had last Saturday!

Copy your work onto paper periodically, and keep the paper copies for several weeks. The nice thing about paper is: you can see what's on it. You don't have to worry about the paper being secretly defective. When dealing with data, paper's the only medium you can trust. Just don't leave it near your dog. Lock it in your filing cabinet. (I mean the paper, not the dog.)

Where to put data files

A hard disk contains **programs** and **data files**. In a typical business, the info in the data files changes daily, but the programs remain stable. The business makes backup copies of programs monthly but backs up data files daily, to ensure the backups incorporate the latest changes.

To back up data files simply, some businesses put them all in a DATA folder (directory), backed up daily.

Sharing the disk If several employees share a hard disk, they might accidentally destroy each other's data files. To prevent that, your business can give each employee a separate folder (directory). For example, you can put all of Fred's data files in a folder called FRED and put Mary's data files in folder MARY.

An even surer way to prevent employees from destroying each other's data files is to give each employee a floppy disk. Fred gets a floppy labeled "Fred's data"; Mary gets a floppy labeled "Mary's data". No data files are stored on the hard disk, which contains just programs. But employees dislike using floppies, which are slower than hard disks and can't handle long files.

Recommendation I recommend keeping things simple by creating as few folders as possible. Put the MUSIC program and all its data files in the MUSIC folder. To distinguish Fred's music from Mary's, have Fred begin his filenames with an F, and have Mary's begin with M. Let Fred be responsible for backing up his own files, and Mary be responsible for backing up hers.

Subst (in DOS 3.1 & up)

If your computer has a drive B, try this nifty trick....

Into drive B, put a disk that contains some files. Then say:

```
C:\>subst a: b:\
```

Afterwards, whenever you talk about drive A, the computer will SUBSTitute drive B instead. For example, if you say "dir a:", the computer will give you a directory of drive B.

That command is useful in the following situation:

> Suppose drive A is 5¼-inch and drive B is 3½-inch. In that situation, you should buy programs on 5¼-inch floppies rather than 3½-inch, because most programs and their manuals assume you're inserting the floppies into drive A. But suppose you make the mistake of buying a program on a 3½-inch floppy instead.
>
> If you insert that floppy into drive B, and the program gripes at you because it insists you put the floppy into drive A, just say "subst a: b:\", and try again to run the program. When the program checks to make sure you put the floppy into drive A, the program will think you obeyed, because the drive you put the floppy in is now called "drive A".

When you finish using the "subst a:" command and want to turn your computer back to normal, delete the "subst a:" command by saying:

```
C:\>subst a: /d
```

DO.BAT

To organize the files on your hard disk, you can use many methods. My favorite is the "DO.BAT" method, which I invented. Here it is….

How to create DO.BAT Put a file called "DO.BAT" into your DOS directory, by typing:

```
C:\>copy con dos\do.bat
@echo off
cd \%1
%1
cd \
dir /ad/o/w/L
```

If your DOS is earlier than version 3.3, change the "@echo off" to this:

```
echo off
cls
```

In classic DOS, change the "dir /ad/o/w/L" to this:

```
dir *. /w
```

When you've finished typing, press F6 and ENTER.

What DO.BAT accomplishes That "DO.BAT" file defines the word "do" so that if you ever type a command such as "do music", the computer will automatically go into the MUSIC folder ("cd \%1"), run the MUSIC program ("%1"), return to the root directory ("cd \"), and print a menu of all the disk's folders ("dir /ad/o/w/L", which means "**dir**ectory of **a**ll **d**irectories, in alphabetical **o**rder, displayed **w**ide across the screen, in **L**owercase letters").

If you type "do poker", the computer will automatically go into the POKER folder ("cd \%1"), run the POKER program ("%/1"), return to the root directory ("cd \"), and print a menu of all the disk's folders again ("dir /ad/o/w/L").

If you type just the word "do", the computer will just return you to the root directory ("cd \") and print a menu of all the disk's folders ("dir /ad/o/w/L").

So here are the rules:

> Whenever you get confused, just type the word "do". It makes the computer return to the root directory and also display a menu of all the disk's folders.
>
> To run a program, just say "do" followed by the program's name. For example, to run the MUSIC program, just say "do music". That automatically makes the computer go into the MUSIC folder, run the MUSIC program, then return to the root directory and display the menu of all the disk's folders again.

Name each folder the same as its main file
To let the DO.BAT program accomplish all that, you must set up your software properly. Here's how.

For each major program you buy, create a folder.

For example, suppose you buy a program called Marvelous Music, which comes on a pile of floppies. You should create a folder for Marvelous Music. Here's how.

First, find out the name of Marvelous Music's main file. You can do that by reading the Marvelous Music instruction manual. For example, if the instruction manual says, "to start the program, type the word MUSIC", then the name of Marvelous Music's main file is MUSIC.

Another way to find the name of Marvelous Music's main file is to put Marvelous Music's main disk into drive A and examine its directory (by typing "dir a:"). If the directory shows a file ending in .EXE or .COM, that file's probably the main file. If the directory shows a file called AUTOEXEC.BAT, peek at what the AUTOEXEC.BAT file says (by saying "type a:autoexec.bat"); it probably mentions the main file.

Suppose you've discovered the main file's name is MUSIC (or MUSIC.EXE or MUSIC.COM). Then make a MUSIC folder on the hard disk by typing "md music", so your screen looks like this:

```
C:\>md music
```

Next, put a Marvelous Music floppy into drive A. Copy all its files onto your hard disk's MUSIC folder by typing "copy a:*.* music", so your screen looks like this:

```
C:\>copy a:*.* music
```

Put another Marvelous Music floppy into drive A, and say "copy a:*.* music" again. Do the same for each floppy, until the entire set of Marvelous Music floppies has been copied to the hard disk's MUSIC folder.

Repeat that procedure for each application program you bought.

(Exception: some programs require you to say "install" or "setup" instead of a copy command. To find out whether to say "install" or "setup", read the manual that comes with the program. During the "install" or "setup" procedure, when the computer asks you to name the folder [subdirectory], name it the same as the main file that will be in it.)

Try it! To test whether you created the folders correctly, try using DO.BAT. Here's how.

Say "do". If DO.BAT is working correctly, saying "do" will make the computer display a list of all your folders. For example, if you created a MUSIC folder and a POKER folder, the computer will print a list that includes "MUSIC" and "POKER".

To use MUSIC, say "do music". Then the computer will obey the DO.BAT file, automatically switch to the MUSIC folder, run the MUSIC program, and — when the MUSIC program finishes — automatically return to the root directory and print a menu of all folders, so you can choose which other application to run next.

AUTOEXEC.BAT If you wish, **put an extra line at the bottom of your AUTOEXEC.BAT file, and make that line say just "do"**.

Then when you turn on the computer, the computer will automatically perform "do", so it will automatically display a list of all your folders. That list acts as a menu. For example, to choose MUSIC from that menu, say just "do music"; that makes the computer do the MUSIC program and then show you the menu again.

Windows The DO.BAT program manages just non-Windows programs. If you're using mainly Windows programs, don't bother creating DO.BAT and don't bother putting "do" at the bottom of your AUTOEXEC.BAT file.

Start your Mac

The most popular Mac computer is called the **iMac** because it's intelligent, individualistic, inexpensive, and for the Internet age.

This chapter explains how to use it. (Other Macs are similar but slightly more complex. I'll explain how they differ.)

Set up the Mac

When you buy an iMac, the salesperson hands you a big white cardboard box. Take the box home. Open it and peek inside.

You'll see clear plastic bags. They contain the computer, keyboard, mouse, power cord, phone cord, CD-ROM disks, and instructions. Rip the bags open.

Put the computer on your desk. The front of the computer has the word "iMac" on it. **Position the computer** so you can see the word "iMac" when you're sitting in your chair. That way, you'll be facing the iMac's screen.

Tilt the front of the computer up, reach under the computer, and swing its blue **foot** forward, so the computer's front is propped up high by the foot.

> **Other Macs** For some Macs, the cardboard box is brown instead of white, the computer has no foot, and the monitor or hard drive is sold separately and must be cabled to the computer. The iMac has a built-in microphone; for some other Macs, the microphone is missing or must be cabled to the computer. The Mac Powerbook is a notebook computer that's all in one piece and requires no assembly.

Power cord Plug one end of the **power cord** into your wall and the other end into the back of the computer. Make sure both ends of the power cord are plugged in tightly.

Keyboard Look at the **keyboard**. A cable comes out of it. Put that cable into the hole that's in the computer's right-hand side. Then put your index finger into that hole and pull the hole toward you, so a trap door opens. While the trap door is open, plug the keyboard's cable into one of the connectors that has the same size as the cable. Then slam the trap door shut.

> **Other Macs** For some Macs, you must attach the keyboard to its cable, which plugs into the computer's front or back (instead of side).

Mouse Look at the iMac's **mouse**, which is round and looks like a yo-yo (or a hockey puck). Plug the mouse's cable into the keyboard's side.

> If you're right-handed, plug the mouse's cable into the keyboard's *right* side.
> If you're left-handed, plug the mouse's cable into the keyboard's *left* side.

Congratulations! You've installed the computer! Now you can say on your résumé that you're a "computer expert experienced at installing advanced computer equipment".

> **Other Macs** For some Macs, the mouse is rectangular, like a pack of cigarettes (instead of round like a yo-yo), and plugs into the computer (instead of into the keyboard).

Turn on the Mac

Look at the computer's front. Below the screen, near the computer's bottom right corner, you see a white circular button. (That button shows a picture of a circle interrupted by a vertical line sticking up from it.) That's the **power button**. Press it (or press the imitation of it, which is at the top of the keyboard, between the F12 and HELP keys).

> **Other Macs** Some Macs have no power button. For some Macs, the power button is just on the keyboard (instead of on the computer) and shows the symbol "◄" (instead of a circle-with-line).
> On the back of some Macs, you'll see an on/off switch, marked "1" and "0". To turn the Mac on, press that switch's "1", before pressing any power button.
> On some Macs, the on/off switch is a button that pops in and out, or it's in the form of a car-ignition key. If you're sharing such a Mac, your friends probably already put that switch in the correct position, so don't touch it: just press the power button.
> Some Mac monitors have a separate switch that you must turn on. If your Mac's hard drive is external, turn that drive on and wait 15 seconds before turning on the Mac.

The Mac greets you

The computer will make an overture to you: you'll hear a musical chord. The power button will glow orange, then green.

On the screen, you'll briefly see an arrow, then a smile. Then the screen will briefly say:

```
            Mac OS
        Welcome to Mac OS
```

Then the screen will say:

```
            Mac OS
        Starting up...
```

> **Other Macs** Old Macs make a beep instead of playing a chord. For some Macs, the power button can't glow. Old Macs say "Welcome to Macintosh" (instead of messages about "Mac OS").
> If you don't see "Mac OS" or "Welcome to Macintosh", your Mac isn't set up properly. For example, the monitor might be turned off (turn it on!), the hard drive might be missing (buy a hard drive!), your dealer might have neglected to copy the Mac operating system onto the hard drive (ask the dealer to help you!), or a previous user left a floppy disk in the floppy drive (remove the floppy disk).
> If your Mac is so old that it doesn't have a hard drive, you'll have difficulty running modern software and using this book. Either buy a hard drive or phone me to get an older edition of this book.

See the icons

Eventually, you'll see little pictures, called **icons**. For example, the screen's top left corner will show the **Apple icon** (a partly eaten apple); the screen's bottom right corner will show the **trash icon** (picture of a trash can). Those icons mean the **Finder** (the fundamental part of the Mac's operating system) is ready.

> **Other Macs** Although the trash icon is usually in the bottom right corner, it might be in a different place if the previous user moved it.

Close all windows

If your Mac's been used by other people, they might have left your Mac in a strange state, with several rectangular windows on the screen. To make sure your Mac is normal, with no windows on the screen, do this:

> Look next to the space bar. There you'll see the **COMMAND key** (which has an Apple and a squiggle on it) and the **OPTION key**. Hold down the COMMAND and OPTION keys simultaneously; and while you keep them down, tap the W key.

Congratulations! Now you have a turned-on Mac, ready and willing to obey your every command!

> **Other Macs** On old Macs, the COMMAND key has a squiggle on it but no apple. Performa Macs make the screen display a Launcher window; to follow the instructions in the book, make sure the Launcher window disappears. Again, here's how to make the Launcher window (and all other windows) disappear: hold down the COMMAND and OPTION keys; and while keeping them down, tap the W key.

Use the mouse

Your computer comes with a **mouse** (which is round and looks like a yo-yo or hockey puck). The mouse's **tail** is a cable that runs from the mouse to the keyboard. The area where the tail meets the mouse is called the mouse's **ass** or **rear**.

The mouse's underside — its belly — has a hole in it, and a ball in the hole.

Put the mouse on your desk and directly in front of your right arm. (If you're left-handed, put it in front of your left arm.) Make the mouse lie flat (so its ball rubs against the desk). **Make the mouse face you** so the apple on the mouse appears right-side up, and you don't see the mouse's ass.

> **Other Macs** On traditional Macs, the mouse is rectangular like a pack of cigarettes (instead of round like a yo-yo).
>
> Instead of using a mouse, the Mac Powerbook uses a trackpad (or trackball), permanently attached to the keyboard.

Move the arrow

Move the mouse across your desk. As you move the mouse, remember to keep it flat and facing you.

On the screen, you'll see an arrow, which is called the **pointer** or **cursor**. As you move the mouse, the arrow moves also. If you move the mouse to the left, the arrow moves to the left. If you move the mouse to the right, the arrow moves to the right. If you move the mouse toward you, the arrow moves down. If you move the mouse away from you, the arrow moves up.

Practice moving the arrow by moving the mouse. Remember to keep the mouse facing you at all times.

If you want to move the arrow far, and your desk is small, move the mouse until it reaches the desk's edge; then lift the mouse off the desk, lay the mouse gently on the middle of the desk, and move the mouse across the desk in the same direction as before.

> **Other Macs** If your Mac uses a trackpad (instead of a mouse), move the arrow by moving your finger across the trackpad. If your Mac uses a trackball, move the arrow by rotating the trackball.

Click an icon

The most important part of the arrow is its tip, which is called the **hot spot**.

For an experiment, move the arrow so its hot spot (tip) is in the middle of the trash can. That's called **pointing at** the trash can.

On top of the mouse, right above the mouse's cable (tail), is a button you can press. Tapping that button is called **clicking**.

While you're pointing at the trash can, try clicking (by tapping the button). That's called "**clicking** the trash can" (or "**clicking on** the trash can" or "**selecting** the trash can"). When you do that, the trash can darkens. Try it!

Near the screen's top right corner, you'll see the words "Macintosh HD". Above those words, you'll see a rectangle with a black dot in its bottom left corner. That rectangle is supposed to be a picture of a Macintosh hard-disk drive. That rectangle's called the **hard-disk icon**. Try clicking in the middle of the rectangle. When you do that, it darkens.

Whenever you click an icon, that icon darkens, and the other major icons turn white. For example, when you click the trash icon, the hard disk icon turns white; when you click the hard disk icon, the trash icon turns white.

An icon that's dark is **selected**; an icon that's white is called **unselected** or **deselected**. Usually, just one icon is selected (dark); all the other icons are deselected (white).

(The Apple icon is a different kind of icon. If you click it, no colors change. I'll explain it later.)

Try this experiment: click in the center of the screen, where there are no icons. All the screen's icons suddenly turn white.

Here are the rules:

> If you click a white icon, it turns dark and all other icons turn white.
>
> If you click where there's no icon, all icons turn white.

> **Other Macs** The hard-disk icon might have a different name and shape. For example, 80-megabyte hard disks manufactured by Jasmine are labeled "Direct Drive 80" (instead of "Macintosh HD") and have an icon that looks like a flower (instead of a rectangle).

Drag an icon

You can move an icon to a different place on the screen. Here's how.

Point at the icon by moving the arrow's tip to the middle of the icon. (Put the arrow's tip in the middle of the icon picture, *not* in the middle of the words underneath it.)

Hold down the mouse's button; and while you keep the button down, move the mouse. As you move the mouse *with the button down*, you'll be moving the arrow *and the icon*. That's called **dragging the icon**. When you've dragged the icon to your favorite place on the screen, lift your finger from the mouse's button, and the icon will stay there.

Pull down a menu

Your screen's top line of information is called the **menu bar**. It contains eight items: the **Apple icon**, the words **File**, **Edit**, **View**, **Special**, and **Help**, the **Finder icon** (made of smiling faces who found each other), and a **clock**.

(When the Mac is first turned on, its clock shows the time at Apple's headquarters in California. I'll explain later how to reset the clock and switch to a different time zone.)

Point at the Apple icon. Hold down the mouse's button. While you keep the button down, you see this **menu** underneath the Apple icon:

```
About This Computer...
Apple System Profiler
Apple CD Audio Player
Automated Tasks
Calculator
Chooser
Control Panels
Disconnect Remote Access
FaxStatus
Find File
Graphing Calculator
Internet Access
Jigsaw Puzzle
Key Caps
Note Pad
OpenDoc Stationery
Quicken.com
Recent Applications
Recent Documents
Scrapbook
SimpleSound
Stickies
```

The menu appears while you hold down the mouse's button; but when you lift your finger from the mouse's button, the menu usually disappears. (Exception: if you just *tap* the mouse's button quickly, the menu will stay on the screen for 15 seconds before disappearing.)

Seeing the menu (by holding down the mouse's button) is called **pulling down the menu**, because it's like pulling down a window shade that has messages written on it. Since you see the menu by pulling it down, it's called a **pull-down menu**. Since that menu appears underneath the Apple icon, it's called the **Apple menu**.

If you point at one of the menu bar's words (File, Edit, View, Special, or Help) and hold down the mouse's button, you'll see other menus. For example, to see the **File menu**, point at the word "File" and then hold down the mouse's button.

Experiment! Try all the words on the menu bar, and look at their pull-down menus. Those menus list some of the fascinating things your Mac can do!

About This Computer

From the Apple menu, choose **About This Computer**. Here's how.

Point at the Apple icon. Hold down the mouse's button, so you see the Apple menu, including "About This Computer". While you keep the button down, point at "About This Computer". Then lift your finger from the button.

The computer will obey your command: it will tell you about your computer.

To do that, the computer will display a **window** in the middle of the screen. In the window, you'll see a message about your Mac.

For example, on *my* iMac, the message says:

> The **Mac OS** (Mac Operating System) is version 8.1, copyright by Apple in 1983-1997.
>
> The **built-in memory** (made of RAM chips) holds 64 megabytes.
> The **virtual memory** (part of the hard disk that acts as if it were extra RAM) is 68.8 megabytes.
>
> The **total memory** you can use is therefore 64+68.8, which is 136.8 megabytes.
> That total memory is divided into several chunks, called **blocks**.
> The **largest unused block** (biggest unused chunk of memory) is 55 megabytes.
> If you try to run another program now, the program must therefore be smaller than 55 megabytes.
>
> Of the total memory, 13.4 megabytes are reserved for use by the Mac Operating System.
> The rest of that total memory is available for application programs.

On *your* iMac, the numbers might be different, and the number of bytes that are used and unused will vary as your iMac performs different activities.

Drag a window

Look at the top line of the window containing the "About This Computer" message. The window's top line gives the window's **title** ("About This Computer").

Try this experiment. Drag the window's title to a different part of the screen. (To do that, point at the title; hold down the mouse's button; while you keep the button down, move the mouse.) As you drag the title, the rest of the window automatically drags along with it. When you've dragged the window to your favorite place on the screen, lift your finger from the mouse's button, and the window will stay there.

Close the window

When you finish looking at the message in a window, you must **close the window**. Here's how.

In the window's top left corner, you'll see a tiny square, called the **close box**. To close the window, click the close box (by pointing at the square and then tapping the mouse's button). The window will close and disappear from the screen.

WIMP

The Mac is called a **WIMP computer**, because it uses Windows, Icons, Mice, and Pull-downs.

> Commodore's Amiga computer and Atari's ST computer imitate the Mac: they use Windows, Icons, Mice, and Pull-downs also. So they too are WIMP computers.
>
> Any program using Windows, Icons, Mice, and Pull-downs is called **WIMPy**. You can buy WIMPy programs for many computers — even for the IBM PC!
>
> If your IBM PC is modern, it comes with **Microsoft Windows**, which is software that makes the IBM PC try to imitate a Mac. But the imitation is screwed up; it makes the IBM PC become a *messed-up* Mac. The Mac is nicer than any imitation! The Mac is a beauty that the beast can't resemble.

This chapter examines the Mac's beauty further.

Key Caps

To explore the Mac's keyboard, choose **Key Caps** from the Apple menu. (To do that, point at the Apple icon and drag down to the phrase "Key Caps").

You'll see a window that shows a picture of your keyboard. It reminds you of what your keyboard looks like.

In the picture, all the letters are lower-case. Try typing a word (such as "love"): you'll see the word in lower-case letters.

DELETE key If you make a mistake, press the DELETE key. It erases the last character you typed. (To erase the last *two* characters, press the DELETE key *twice*.)

SHIFT key If you hold down your keyboard's SHIFT key, the letters in the picture change to capitals. While holding down the SHIFT key, try typing a word; you'll see the word in capital letters, like this: LOVE.

OPTION key If you hold down your keyboard's OPTION key, the letters in the picture change to weird symbols. While holding down the OPTION key, try typing; you'll be typing symbols from Greek, Swedish, French, Spanish, Japanese, math, and other un-American pleasures. To get extra symbols, hold down the OPTION and SHIFT keys simultaneously.

Accents To type an accent, use these keystrokes:

Accent	What keys to press
^	OPTION with i
~	OPTION with n
¨	OPTION with u
´	OPTION with e
`	OPTION with `

For example, here's how to type ô. Type the code for ^ (which is OPTION with i), then take your finger off the OPTION key and type the letter you want under the accent (the "o"). Nothing appears on the screen until you complete the whole process; then you'll see ô.

Close When you've finished exploring Key Caps, close the window, by clicking its close box.

Calculator

To do calculations, choose **Calculator** from the Apple menu. (To do that, drag from the Apple icon down to the word "Calculator".)

You'll see a window that looks and acts like a pocket calculator. For example, **here's how to compute 42+5:**

> Clear away any previous calculation, by clicking the calculator's C key. (To do that, use the mouse to point at the calculator's C key, then click.) Then click the 4 key, then 2, then +, then 5, then =. The calculator will show the answer, 47.

Instead of using the mouse, you can do that calculation a different way, by using the Mac's keyboard. On the keyboard's right-hand side, you see the **numeric keypad**, which looks just like the on-screen calculator. On that keypad, tap the Clear key, then the 4 key, then the 2 key, then the + key, then 5, then =. The on-screen calculator will show 47.

Try fancier calculations! Use these symbols:

Symbol	Meaning
+	plus
-	minus
*	times
/	divided by
=	total
.	decimal point
C	clear

If you make a mistake, click the C key or press the Clear key.

When you finish using the calculator, close the window, by clicking its close box.

Multiple windows

The screen can show several windows simultaneously.

For example, choose Key Caps from the Apple menu, so that you see the Key Caps window on the screen. While the Key Caps window remains on the screen, choose Calculator from the Apple menu. You'll see both the Key Caps window and the calculator window on the screen simultaneously.

The calculator window sits in front of the Key Caps window and partly blocks your view of the Key Caps window. The front window (the calculator window) is called the **active window**. That's the window you're using at the moment. For example, if you type "2+2=", the computer will say 4, because the calculator window is active.

To make the Key Caps window active instead, click anywhere in the Key Caps window. That moves the Key Caps window in front of the calculator window, so that the Key Caps window partly blocks your view of the calculator. Since the Key Caps window is in front (active), if you use the keyboard now you'll be dealing with Key Caps instead of the calculator.

To switch back to the calculator, click anywhere in the calculator window.

If you don't like the way that the active window blocks your view of the other window, move the active window (by dragging its title) or make the active window disappear (by clicking its close box).

Shut Down

When you're done using the Mac, choose **Shut Down** from the **Special menu**. That makes the Mac shut itself off.

While shutting itself off, the Mac tidies up the info on the hard disk and then turns off its own power (so the power button stops glowing and the screen turns black).

The next time you want to use the Mac, just press the power button, which turns the Mac back on.

Sleep

If you want to stop using the Mac for a few minutes (so you can eat or go to the bathroom or have sex), choose **Sleep** from the Special menu. That makes the Mac go to sleep (take a nap).

While the Mac sleeps, it uses less electricity: the screen turns black, the power button glows orange instead of green, and the Mac does no thinking — except that, in its dreams, it keeps remembering the image that had been on the screen.

To wake a sleeping Mac, tap the SHIFT key. Then wait. After a few seconds, the power button starts glowing green, which makes the Mac wake up. The Mac plays a chord and turns its own screen on again. Then you see what was on the screen, and you can continue your Mac experience where you left off.

If you walk away from the Mac, so that you don't touch the mouse or keyboard for 30 minutes, the Mac realizes it's been abandoned: it puts itself to sleep automatically.

Open an icon

The Mac was designed by sadists. If an icon fascinates you, you're supposed to explode it, by blowing it up!

For example, suppose the Macintosh HD icon is on the screen, and it fascinates you. Explode it! Here's how: point at that Macintosh HD icon, then tap the mouse's button twice quickly, so the taps are less than a second apart. That's called **exploding the icon** or **double-clicking the icon** or **opening the icon**.

After the icon explodes (opens), you can see what was hiding inside it. You see that inside the Macintosh HD icon, these 12 **items** were hiding:

```
iMac Read Me
Apple Extras
Applications
Assistants
Internet
Mac OS Read Me Files
QuickTime Folder
Remote Access Client
Stationery
System Folder
Utilities
Web Pages
```

On your screen, you see their icons: the iMac Read Me icon, the Apple Extras icon, the Applications icon, etc.

(You see those icons when your computer is new. If your computer's been used, the people using it might have added extra icons or deleted some icons.)

Those icons all appear in a window titled "Macintosh HD". As with any window, you can move it by dragging its title.

Size box

In the window's bottom right corner is a square containing 3 slanted lines. That square is called the **size box**.

Drag the size box to another part of the screen (by moving the size box while holding down the mouse's button). As the size box moves, so does the window's bottom right corner, so that the window's size changes.

By dragging the size box, you can make the window very large — or very small.

If you make the window small, it shows fewer icons. Some of the icons are hiding out of view. To see the hidden icons again, make the window larger.

Zoom box

Near the window's top right corner is a tiny icon that shows a picture of a square inside a square. That icon is called the **zoom box**.

Try clicking the zoom box. When you do, the window's size changes.

Clicking the zoom box usually makes the window become the perfect size — just big enough to show all its icons (so none of its icons are hidden anymore).

Once the window's become the perfect size, clicking the zoom box again makes the window return to whatever weird size it had before reaching perfection. So clicking the zoom box makes the window switch to perfection — or back to imperfection.

Try it! Click the window's zoom box several time, and see the window switch back and forth between perfection and imperfection.

Other Macs On old Macs, clicking the zoom box makes the window become huge (filling most of the screen) instead of "the perfect size".

Scroll boxes

Since the hard disk of a new iMac normally contains 12 items (iMac Read Me, Apple Extras, Applications, etc.), the hard disk's window is supposed to show 12 icons. But if you make the window very small (by using the size box), the window becomes too small to show the 12 icons. Instead, the window shows just *some* of the icons.

Try this experiment: drag the size box until the window becomes so small that it shows just one icon.

When you make the window that small, a blue ribbed square **scroll box** appears at the bottom of the window, and another blue ribbed square scroll box appears on the window's right side. By dragging the scroll boxes, you can shift the view that you see through the window, so you see different icons in the window. Shifting the view by moving the scroll boxes is called **scrolling**.

Arrows and gray rectangles Here's another way to shift the window's view: click the arrows and dark gray rectangles that appear next to the scroll boxes.

If you click an arrow (which looks like a triangle), the scroll box nudges in the direction that the arrow points. To nudge even further in that direction, click that arrow several times, or just point at the arrow and hold down the mouse's button for a while.

If you click a dark gray rectangle, the scroll box hops toward that rectangle. It hops far enough to make the window show the next windowful of information.

The part of the window that consists of the scroll box, arrows, and gray rectangles is called the **scroll bar**.

Collapse box

At the window's top right corner, you see a tiny square containing two horizontal lines. That square is called the **collapse box**.

Try clicking the collapse box. When you do, most of the window disappears, so you see just the window's title and what was next to that title.

If the window had been covering up other windows or items, now you can see them!

To make the window reappear, click its collapse box again, which makes the window uncollapse (expand).

Other Macs Old Macs don't have a collapse box.

Peek in folders

Try this experiment. Enlarge the Macintosh HD window by clicking its zoom box. Use the scroll boxes to adjust the window's view, until you see all 12 items in the window.

The first item is iMac Read Me. The other 11 items are **folders**: each of their icons is in the shape of a manila folder. Let's peek inside the folders.

Start by peeking inside the System Folder. To do that, double-click the System Folder icon. The System Folder icon will open and show you everything inside it.

When you finish peeking inside the System Folder, click its close box.

Other Macs Different Macs contain different folders.

SimpleText

The Mac's operating system includes a simple word-processing program called **SimpleText**. It lets you type words, sentences, and paragraphs simply.

Launch SimpleText

Here's how to start using SimpleText:

Open the **Macintosh HD icon** (by double-clicking it).
You'll see the **Applications folder**. Open it (by double-clicking it).
You'll see the **SimpleText icon**. It looks like a pencil writing on paper. It does *not* look like a folder. Instead of being a folder, SimpleText is **an application program**. The SimpleText icon looks like a pencil writing on paper. To start using an application program (such as SimpleText), open its icon (by double-clicking it).
Then the screen changes dramatically. At the screen's top right corner, on the menu bar, where you used to see the Finder icon, you now see the SimpleText icon instead. In the middle of the menu bar, where you used to see the words "View" and "Special", you now see the words "Font", "Size", "Style", and "Sound" instead.

Try it!

Other Macs Old Macs use TeachText instead of SimpleText. Here's how to start using TeachText. Double-click the Macintosh HD icon. If you don't see the TeachText icon yet, make it appear by double-clicking the Applications folder. Then double-click the TeachText icon.
If you're using System 6 or earlier, and you didn't install Multifinder, you don't see an icon in the screen's top right corner.
The only words on the TeachText menu bar are "File" and "Edit".

Use the keyboard

After opening the SimpleText icon, try typing whatever sentences you wish to make up. For example, try typing a memo to your friends, or a story, or a poem. Be creative! Whatever you type is called a **document**.

These tricks will help you type:

To capitalize a letter of the alphabet, type that letter while holding down the **SHIFT key**.

To capitalize a whole passage, tap the **CAPS LOCK key**, then type the passage. The computer will automatically capitalize the passage as you type it. When you finish typing the passage, tap the CAPS LOCK key again: that tells the computer to stop capitalizing.

If you make a mistake, press the **DELETE key**. That makes the computer erase the last character you typed. To erase the last *two* characters you typed, press the DELETE key *twice*.

If you're **typing near the screen's right edge,** and you type a word that's too long to fit on the screen, the computer will automatically move the word to the line below.

When you finish a paragraph, press the **RETURN key**. That makes the computer move to the line below so you can start typing the next paragraph. If you want to double-space between the paragraphs, press the RETURN key *twice*.

If you want to indent a line (such as the first line of a paragraph), begin the line by pressing the **TAB key**. The computer will indent the line slightly (as if you pressed the SPACE bar twice).

To type an **accent**, use the same technique as when you're using Key Caps. For example, to type the symbol ô, type the code for ^ (which is OPTION with i), then type the "o".

Other Macs On old Macs, the DELETE key is called the BACKSPACE key and says "Backspace" on it.

Scroll through documents

If your document contains too many lines to fit in the window, the window will show just *part* of the document. To see the rest of the document, move the scroll box (by dragging it or by clicking on the nearby arrow or dark gray rectangle).

Insert characters

To insert extra characters anywhere in your document, click where you want the extra characters to appear (by moving the mouse's pointer there and then pressing the mouse's button). Then type the extra characters.

For example, suppose you typed the word "fat" and want to change it to "fault". Click between the "a" and the "t", then type "ul".

As you type the extra characters, the screen's other characters move out of the way, to make room for the extra characters.

While you're inserting the extra characters, you can erase nearby mistakes by pressing the DELETE key.

Select text

Suppose the document contains a phrase you mistyped. Here's how to edit the phrase.

First, make the phrase turn black, by using any of these methods:

The drag method
Point at the phrase's beginning.
Drag to the phrase's end.

The shift-click method
Click at the phrase's beginning.
While holding down the SHIFT key, click at the phrase's end.
(That's called **shift-clicking** the phrase's end.)

The double-click method
If the "phrase" is just one word, double-click it.

Turning the phrase black is called **selecting the phrase**.

Then say what to do to the phrase. For example, if you want to *erase* the phrase, press the DELETE key. If you want to *replace* the phrase instead, just type whatever words you want the phrase to become. If you want to *move* the phrase instead, choose **Cut** from the **Edit menu**, then click where you want the phrase to be, then choose **Paste** from the Edit menu.

Notice that the Cut command makes sense only if you've selected some text (by turning that text black).

If you *don't* select any text — if no phrase is black — the computer refuses to let you say Cut. In that situation, when you pull down the Edit menu, you'll notice that the word "Cut" appears on the menu very faintly: the word "Cut" is **dimmed**; it's **grayed** instead of being written in sharp black.

Here's the rule: **when a word on a menu is dimmed, the computer refuses to let you choose that word**. The usual reason for the refusal is that you haven't selected a phrase (or icon or other part of the screen).

Start over

If you mess up the entire document and want to erase it all (so you can start over again, fresh, from scratch), choose **Select All** from the Edit menu, then press the DELETE key.

Save

To copy the document onto the hard disk, choose **Save** from the **File menu**.

Then invent a name for your document. For example, you can invent a short name such as —

Joe

---

or a long name such as:

Stupidest Memo of 1999

The name can be up to 31 characters long. It can't contain a colon and can't begin with a period, but it can contain any other characters you wish! At the end of the name, press the RETURN key. That makes the computer copy the document onto the hard disk.

Afterwards, if you change your mind and want to do more editing, go ahead! Edit the document some more. When you finish that editing, save it by choosing **Save** from the File menu again.

Finish

When you finish working on a document, click the close box.

(The computer might ask, "Save changes?" If you reply by clicking Don't Save, the computer won't copy your latest changes to the disk. If you click Save instead, the computer will chat with you, just as if you chose Save from the File menu.)

The document disappears from the screen, but you're still in the middle of using SimpleText. To prove you're still in the middle of using SimpleText, notice that at the screen's top right corner, on the menu bar, you still see the SimpleText icon instead of the Finder icon; and the menu bar still shows the SimpleText words ("Font", "Size", "Style" and "Sound") instead of the Finder words ("View" and "Special").

Then go to the File menu, and choose **New, Open**, or **Quit**. Here's what happens:

If you choose **New**, the computer will let you start typing a new document.

If you choose **Open** and then double-click the name of an old document you created earlier, the computer will put that document onto the screen and let you edit it.

If you choose **Quit**, the computer will finish using the application program (SimpleText), so the menu bar will show the Mac OS words ("View" and "Special").

Double-clicking a saved document You've learned that to start using SimpleText, you double-click the SimpleText icon, which is in the Applications folder.

Besides containing the SimpleText icon, the Applications folder contains other icons also. Some of those icons are new; you automatically created them when you saved your documents. For example, if you created a document called "Stupidest Memo of 1999", you'll see a new icon marked "Stupidest Memo of 1999". (To see it more easily, try clicking the Application window's zoom box once or twice.)

The Mac is smart: it remembers how each document was created. For example, it remembers that "Stupidest Memo of 1999" was created by using SimpleText.

If you double-click the "Stupidest Memo of 1999" icon, the Mac notices that the memo was created from SimpleText. So the Mac deduces that you must be interested in SimpleText. Then the Mac automatically starts running SimpleText and makes SimpleText open that memo, so you see the memo on the screen and can edit it.

Here's the general rule: if you double-click a document's icon, the Mac notices which application program created the document; then the Mac makes that application program run and open the document.

Other Macs TeachText does *not* put your saved document into an Applications folder. Here's what happens instead. If your Mac is a Performa, TeachText puts your saved document into the Documents folder, which is usually on your screen's right side (between the hard-drive icon and the trash can). If your Mac is *not* a Performa, TeachText puts your saved document into the hard disk's main window.

Forget to Quit? When you finish using SimpleText, you're supposed to choose Quit from the File menu. If you forget to choose Quit, the SimpleText program is still running and is still in the computer's RAM chips (even if the screen shows other icons and other menu items).

Here's how to check whether the SimpleText program is still running in the RAM chips. At the top right corner of the whole screen, you see an icon (next to the time). Click that icon and hold down the mouse's button, so you see the **Application**

menu. If the menu mentions SimpleText, then SimpleText is still in the RAM chips! To remove SimpleText from the RAM chips, choose SimpleText from the Application menu, then choose Quit from the File menu.

> **Other Macs** If you're using System 6 or earlier, the Finder icon and Finder menu are missing (unless you installed Multifinder).
>
> If you're using System 7, you might encounter this problem: you try starting TeachText (by double-clicking the TeachText icon), but nothing seems to happen. Here's why nothing seems to happen: you're in TeachText *already*, because you forgot to Quit from TeachText the previous time you used TeachText. To solve that program, choose Quit from the File menu; then your computer will act normally.

Final two steps
When you finish using the computer, remember to take these two steps:

> 1. If you're in the middle of using an application program (such as SimpleText), get out of it by choosing Quit from the File menu.
>
> 2. When you see the usual desktop screen, whose menu bar includes the word "Special", choose Shut Down from the Special menu.

Make your Mac speak

If you click anywhere in your document and then choose **Speak All** from the **Sound menu**, the Mac's voice will read your entire document out loud! Try it! You'll enjoy the sound of the Mac's voice, especially if you're blind or lonely.

The voice assumes your document is written in English. (If your document is written is some other language, such as Spanish, the voice will mispronounce some of the words.)

To speak well, the Mac analyzes each sentence's punctuation and grammar. For example, at the end of a sentence, a period makes the voice's pitch drop; a question mark makes the voice's pitch rise; an exclamation point makes the voice get louder.

The Mac understands political titles: it knows that "Pres." should be pronounced "President", "Gov." should be pronounced "Governor", "Sen." should be pronounced "Senator", and "Rep." should be pronounced "Representative".

The Mac isn't shy: if you type dirty words, the Mac will say them.

Notice that the Mac operating system can speak, but Microsoft Windows cannot. That's one of the many reasons why Mac lovers say "Microsoft Windows is dumb."

> **Other Macs** Old Macs can't speak.

Different voices
The Mac is bisexual: it can speak in male and female voices. In fact, it can speak in 19 different voices! The Mac assumes you want it to speak in "Fred's" voice. Here's how to switch to a different voice….

Choose **Voices** from the Sound menu.

Choose one of these 19 voices:

Fred	(a man speaking English clearly, though with a Swedish accent)
Kathy	(Fred's wife)
Ralph	(Fred's brother, who has a deep voice)
Albert	(Fred's father, who is ancient and has a strained voice)
Junior	(Fred's son)
Princess	(Fred's daughter)
Hysterical	(a man trying to read but who's laughing hysterically)
Bubbles	(a man trying to read while drowning — hear the bubbles!)
Whisper	(a man trying to be sexually suggestive by whispering)
Boing	(a man trying to imitate a robot)
Bahh	(an old man who's grumpy)
Deranged	(an old man who's pleading, unbalanced, and should be locked up)
Zarvox	(evil robot, whose monotone vibrates through the horror chamber)
Trinoids	(Zarvox's kids)
Bad News	(sings your composition, to the tune of a funeral march)
Good News	(sings your composition, to the tune of a graduation ceremony)
Pipe Organ	(sings your composition, using Alfred Hitchcock's pipe organ)
Cellos	(sings your composition, to the tune of Grieg's "Peer Gynt Suite")
Bells	(sings your composition, in a Church chant using bell chimes)

Choose **Speak All** from the Sound menu.

Long melodies
For a fun time, create a composition that contains just the word "la" about 50 times (separated by spaces but no punctuation), then choose one of the singing voices.

Improve the appearance

This section explains how to make your document look better.

> **Other Macs** If you have just TeachText instead of SimpleText, you're unlucky: TeachText does *not* let you improve your document's appearance. If you have just TeachText and want to make pretty documents, you must get a fancier word-processing program. Get a new one (such as SimpleText, Apple Works, Microsoft Word, or Word Perfect) or inherit an old one (such as MacWrite, Write Now, or Claris Works).

Style menu
Normally, the characters on the screen are **plain**. To make the characters be fancy, use the **Style menu**, which gives you these choices:

Plain Text	(the characters look simple, like this)
Bold	(the characters are made of thick strokes, **like this**)
Italic	(the characters are slanted, *like this*)
<u>Underline</u>	(the characters are underlined, <u>like this</u>)
Outline	(you see each character's outline, as if stenciled)
Shadow	(next to each character you see its shadow)
Condensed	(hardly any space between the characters, like this)
Extended	(extra space between the characters, like this)

For example, here's how to italicize a phrase:

> If you typed the phrase already, make it black (by dragging the mouse across it), then choose Italic from the Style menu.
>
> If you did *not* type the phrase already, use this method instead: choose Italic from the Style menu, then type the phrase, then end the italicizing (by choosing Plain Text from the Style menu).

You can combine styles. For example, to get bold italics, choose Bold from the Style menu, then choose Italic from the Style menu, then type the phrase you want to be boldly italicized, then end that fancy stuff by choosing Plain Text from the Style menu.

Have fun! Play with the Style menu! Try all those different styles and techniques! After you've mastered them, explore the following menus, which use the same techniques….

Size menu
Normally, the characters on the screen (and paper) are small. Their size is called **12 point**.

To make the characters even smaller, choose **9 Point** from the **Size menu**. To make the characters huge, chose **36 Point** from the Size menu.

The Size menu offers these choices: **9 Point**, **10 Point**, **12 Point**, **14 Point**, **18 Point**, **24 Point**, and **36 Point**.

Font menu
Normally, the characters appear in a font called **Geneva**. To switch to a different font, choose the font from the **Font menu**.

The iMac comes with 34 fonts. Here are examples:

> This is Verdana.
> This is Arial.
> **This is Arial Black.**
> This is Impact.
> This is Comic Sans MS.
> This is Times New Roman.
> This is Courier New.

Back in 1983, Apple also invented 4 fonts that are simple, crude, and named after cities: **Geneva**, **New York**, **Monaco**, and **Chicago**. They're available on all Macs.

The **Symbol** font prints Greek. Three wild fonts print pictures instead of words: **Zapf Dingbats**, **Webdings**, and **MT Extra**.

> **Other Macs** Old Macs have fewer than 34 fonts.

Advanced features

Here's the stuff I was afraid to talk about earlier!

Manipulate the desktop

When you turn the Mac on, the screen shows you the **desktop**, which is a greenish blue area on which you see the hard disk icon and the trash can icon. The hard disk icon might be exploded, to show you what's on the disk.

Each thing on the disk is called an **item**. The Mac can handle three kinds of items: **folders** (such as the System Folder), **application programs** (such as SimpleText), and **documents** (such as "Stupidest Memo of 1999"). Application programs and documents are called **files**.

The typical icon on the screen stands for an item or for a whole disk.

Now I'm going to explain how to manipulate the icons. If you're a beginner, experiment with just the icons that stand for junky documents (such as "Stupidest Memo of 1999"); if you fiddle with files that are more serious, you might be sorry!

Rename an icon
To change an icon's name (such as "Stupidest Memo of 1999"), click the name under the icon. (Click the name, not the icon.) Then retype the name and press RETURN.

Move an icon
If an icon's name (such as "Stupidest Memo of 1999") blocks the names of other icons, do this: enlarge the window (by clicking the zoom box) and then drag the icon to a blank part of the window.

If you want to move an icon into a different folder, just drag the icon there. Here's how. If the folder is opened, so you see the folder's window, drag the icon to any blank part of that window. If the folder is *not* opened, drag the icon you're moving to the folder's icon.

Create a new folder
To create a new folder, choose **New Folder** from the File menu. That makes the computer create a new folder and put it in the active window. The new folder has nothing in it; it's empty. The computer temporarily names it "untitled folder".

Invent a better name for the folder (such as "Sue"). Type that name, then press RETURN.

Copy an item
To copy an icon (and the item it stands for), click the icon (so it turns black), then choose **Duplicate** from the File menu.

That makes the computer create a copy of the icon. The computer puts the copy just to the right of the original.

If the original icon was named "Joe" (for example), the copy is automatically named "Joe copy". If you don't like that name, retype it and press RETURN.

> **Other Macs** Old Macs say "Copy of Joe" instead of "Joe copy".

Trash items

To erase an item (folder, application program, or document), drag its icon to the **trash can**. Then the trash can's lid automatically pops off and you see that the can contains trash.

The item will stay in the trash can until the computer **empties the trash**. To make the computer empty the trash, choose **Empty Trash** from the Special Menu, then click OK.

Emptying the trash makes the trash items disappear forever, erased from the disk. Then the computer puts the lid back on the trash can.

> **Other Macs** On old Macs, the trash can bulges instead of having its lid pop off. Some old Macs automatically empty the trash whenever you choose Shut Down from the Special Menu, restart the Mac, eject a floppy disk, copy an icon, or start running an application program (such as Teachtext).

Peek in the trash
If the trash can's lid is off (because the trash hasn't been emptied yet), and you want to see what items the trash can contains, double-click the trash can's icon. You'll see all the items in the trash.

Rescue
If you change your mind about which items you want to erase, you can rescue an item from the trash can: just move the item's icon out of the trash can!

To do that, you can drag the item's icon from the trash can to a different window. Another way to get the item out of the trash can is to click the item's icon, then choose **Put Away** from the File menu. That makes the computer put the item's icon back in the disk's window or folder that the icon originally came from.

Clipboard

When you turn on the Mac, it creates a special document called the **Clipboard**, which sits in the RAM chips instead of on a disk.

Practically anytime you're using the Mac, you can choose **Show Clipboard** from the Edit menu. That makes the computer show you the Clipboard, by putting the Clipboard's window on the screen. When you finish looking at the Clipboard's window, click its close box.

Copy & Paste
Try this experiment. Create a document (by using an application program such as SimpleText). In that document, select a phrase (so the phrase becomes black). From the Edit menu, choose **Copy**. That makes the computer copy the phrase to the Clipboard. So if you look at the Clipboard's window (by choosing Show Clipboard from the Edit menu), you'll see that the Clipboard contains a copy of the phrase.

Next, try this experiment. Click anywhere in your SimpleText document (or any other normal document), then choose **Paste** from the Edit menu. That copies the Clipboard's phrase to where you clicked.

So the major Clipboard commands are Copy and Paste. Saying Copy lets you copy from a SimpleText document to the Clipboard; saying Paste lets you copy from the Clipboard to a SimpleText document.

Copy versus Cut
If you select a phrase in your SimpleText document and then say Copy, the phrase appears in *two* places: in your SimpleText document and also in the Clipboard. Instead of saying Copy, you can say **Cut**, which copies the phrase to the Clipboard but also erases the phrase from the SimpleText document, so that the phrase appears in just *one* place: the Clipboard.

Cut & Paste Here's how to move a phrase to a different part of your document.

Select the phrase (so it becomes black). Choose Cut from the Edit menu (so the computer moves the phrase to the Clipboard).

Click in your document, where you want the phrase to appear. Click Paste from the Edit menu (so the computer copies the phrase from the Clipboard to where you clicked).

Four Clipboard commands Altogether, the Edit menu contains four Clipboard commands:

Edit menu's command	What the computer will do
Show Clipboard	show the Clipboard's window
Copy	copy a selected phrase to the Clipboard
Cut	erase selected phrase but put copy of it on Clipboard
Paste	copy the Clipboard's phrase to where you clicked

What the Clipboard can hold The Clipboard holds just one phrase at a time. So when you copy a new phrase to the Clipboard (by saying Copy or Cut), that new phrase replaces the Clipboard's previous phrase, which vanishes from the Clipboard.

When you put a phrase on the Clipboard, the Clipboard keeps remembering that phrase even if you switch to a different application program. For example, after copying a phrase from a SimpleText document to the Clipboard, you can switch from SimpleText to Superpaint (which draws pictures) and paste that phrase into the middle of your picture. You can also copy a selected part of a Superpaint picture to the Clipboard, then paste that picture into the middle of a Microsoft Word word-processing document.

Whatever you put on the Clipboard stays there until you put something different on the Clipboard or shut down the computer.

Advanced selection

Open the hard drive's window, so you see several icons in the window. You've learned that if you click a white icon, it turns black (and all the other icons turn white).

Shift-click an icon If you click an icon *while holding down the SHIFT key*, that icon changes color. If the icon was light, it turns dark; if the icon was dark, it turns light. The other icons are unaffected. That's called "**shift-clicking** the icon".

Select a group Here's how to select a group of icons, so they all turn dark and all other icons turn white.

To begin, click where there's no icon. That turns all icons white, so that you start with a clean slate.

Find the first icon that you want to be in the group, and click it. That icon turns dark.

Shift-click all the other icons that you want in the group. Those icons turn dark also, while the rest of the screen remains unchanged.

Select all If you want *all* icons in the active window to turn dark, just choose **Select All** from the Edit menu.

Drag a group After you've selected a group of icons (so several icons are dark), try dragging one of those icons. Surprise! As you drag that icon, it will move — and so will all the other icons in the group.

For example, if you drag that icon into a folder, you'll be dragging the whole group into the folder. If you drag that icon to the trash, you'll be dragging the whole group to the trash. If you drag that icon to a different disk instead, you'll be dragging the whole group to that disk.

Clock

Near the screen's top right corner, on the menu bar, you see the time, according to the Mac's clock. **If you click the time, the computer shows you the date instead**, briefly (for three seconds), then shows you the time again.

When you get a new Mac, its clock has been set to show the time and date at Apple's headquarters in California, which is in the Pacific Time Zone. If you live far from California, and you're in a different time zone, you need to reset the clock. After using the Mac for a few months, the clock might be slightly off and need readjustment. **Here's how to reset and readjust the clock:**

> At the screen's top left corner, you see the Apple icon. Click it.
> You see the Apple menu. One of the items on that menu is **Control Panels**. Point at Control Panels.
> You see the **Control Panels menu**. One of the items on that menu is **Date & Time**. Click it.
> You see the **Date & Time window**.
> Click **Set Time Zone**. You see the beginning of an alphabetical list of cities around the world. (To see the rest of the list, use the scroll bar.) Double-click a city that's near enough to you to be in your time zone.
> Look at the box labeled **Daylight Savings Time**. If your neighborhood is on daylight savings time now (because it's summer or a nearby season), make sure there's a check mark in that box; otherwise, make sure that box is blank. (To change whether there's a check mark in the box, click the box.)
> If one of the numbers that makes up the **date and time** is wrong, click that wrong number and then retype it correctly. If computer says AM and should say PM, or vice versa, click the error and retype it correctly.
> When you finish using the Date & Time window, close it (by clicking its close box).

> **Other Macs** Old Macs don't put the time on the menu bar.

Play a music CD

Before 1980, music came on records or tapes. Nowadays, music comes on a **compact disc (CD)**. If you've gone to a music store and bought a CD containing music, you can shove that CD into the Mac, which will play the CD as background music, while you continue your work. Here's how.

Below the iMac's screen, you see the word "iMac". Below that word, you see a green button. Tap it. That opens the door to the CD-ROM drive, halfway. Then pull the door all the way out.

Into that drive, insert the music CD. (Insert it so the label is on top. Put your fingers near the CD's center and press down hard, until the CD snaps onto the spindle and stays down.) Then close the drive's door (by pushing it in).

After a 9-second delay, a CD icon will appear (called **Audio CD 1**) and you'll start hearing the music. While the music plays in the background, do whatever other work you wish. For example, you can do word processing by using SimpleText.

> **Other Macs** Old Macs don't include a CD-ROM drive and can't handle a CD.

Eject the CD Whenever you get tired of hearing the music, use any of these methods to remove the CD from the drive:

> Method 1: click the CD's icon, then choose **Eject** from the Special menu.
> Method 2: click the CD's icon, then choose **Put Away** from the File menu.
> Method 3: drag the CD's icon to the trash can.

Then the computer stops the music, opens the CD-ROM drive's door, and ejects the CD. The CD's icon vanishes.

> **Other Macs** In System 8, methods 1, 2, and 3 all work. In System 7, just methods 2 and 3 work. In Systems 1-6, just method 3 works.

CD Player While the music plays, you can control it by choosing **Apple CD Audio Player** from the Apple menu. You'll see the CD Player window. It shows which track (song) you're playing and how many minutes & seconds of that track have elapsed.

At the window's right edge, you see a picture of a loudspeaker, and a **volume slider** below it. To adjust the music's volume, drag the volume slider up or down.

To control the music, click the CD Player button. You'll see the **CD Player window**. In that window, click the ‖ button to pause in the middle of a song, ■ to stop back at the beginning of track 1, ▶ to resume playing, ▶▶ to skip ahead to the next track, ◀◀ to hop back to the beginning of the current track. Hold down the ▶▶ button awhile to go fast-forward, ◀◀ to reverse. Click ▲ to eject the CD from the drive (so you can insert a different disk instead). When you tire of listening to your CD collection, click eject (▲) and close the window (by clicking its close box).

Diskettes

The iMac does *not* include a diskette drive. For your iMac, you should buy a diskette drive called the **SuperDisk drive**, which costs $150 and handles two kinds of diskettes: 1.4-megabyte **floppy disks** and 120-megabyte **SuperDisks** (which are also called **LS-120 disks**).

> **Other Macs** Most other Macs include an internal diskette drive, which is internal, so it doesn't need to be installed or attached.

Install the SuperDisk driver If your iMac has never been attached to a SuperDisk drive before, install the SuperDisk driver program. Here's how:

> The SuperDisk drive comes with a SuperDisk Installation CD. While your iMac is on, insert that CD into the iMac's CD-ROM drive. Double-click the SuperDisk Installer CD icon then the SuperDisk Installer icon. Press the RETURN key 3 times. Click the Agree button. Press the RETURN key 3 times. The iMac will restart. Then you can eject that CD (by dragging its icon to the trash can).

Attach the SuperDisk cables The SuperDisk drive comes with a power cord. Plug one end of that cord into the back of the SuperDisk drive. Plug the other end of that cord into your room's electrical outlet (or power strip or surge protector); don't be surprised at the small spark!

The SuperDisk drive comes with a **Universal Serial Bus cable (USB cable)**. Plug one end of that cable into the back of the SuperDisk drive. Plug the other end of that cable into iMac's right-hand side (next to where you plugged in the keyboard). Yes, you can plug in the cable while the iMac is turned on.

Insert a blank diskette You can buy a blank diskette and insert it into the diskette drive. Here's how.

In the front of the diskette drive, you'll see a horizontal slot. Put the diskette into that slot. When you insert the diskette, make sure the arrow engraved on the diskette points at the drive, the diskette's label is on *top* of the diskette, and the diskette's metal slider goes into the computer before the label does.

Push the diskette all the way in. On the Mac's screen, you see an icon for the diskette.

Below the icon, you see that the icon is labeled "untitled" (or "SuperDisk"). Click that word. Invent your own name for the diskette (up to 27 characters long); type the name and then press RETURN.

Copy an item to the floppy To copy an item from the Mac's hard disk to the diskette, drag the item's icon to the diskette's icon (or into the diskette's window).

Eject the diskette When you finish using the diskette, use any of these methods to remove it from the drive:

> Method 1: click the diskette's icon, then choose **Eject** from the Special menu.
> Method 2: click the diskette's icon, then choose **Put Away** from the File menu.
> Method 3: drag the diskette's icon to the trash can.

Then the computer ejects the diskette. The diskette's icon disappears from the screen.

If you haven't done so yet, get a pen and scribble the diskette's name onto the diskette's paper label.

> **Other Macs** In System 8, methods 1, 2, and 3 all work. In System 7, just methods 2 and 3 work. In Systems 1-6, just method 3 works.

Copy a diskette item to your hard disk Here's how to copy one item from a diskette to your hard disk.

If you haven't done so yet, insert the diskette into the drive. You'll see the diskette's icon.

Double-click the diskette's icon, so you see the diskette's window. In that window, find the item you want to copy to the hard disk.

Drag that item's icon to the hard disk's icon (or into the hard disk's window or into one of the hard disk's folders).

Copy an entire diskette to your hard disk Here's how to copy all of a diskette's info to your hard disk.

First, if you haven't done so yet, insert the diskette into the drive. You'll see the diskette's icon.

Drag the diskette's icon to your hard disk's icon.

On your hard disk, the computer will create a new folder, which has the same name as the diskette and contains the same items.

Double-click that folder, to check what's in it. If it contains another folder called System Folder, erase that System Folder (by dragging it to the trash), because your hard disk should contain just *one* System Folder.

Print on paper

To let your Mac print on paper, you must buy a printer and run a cable from the printer to the Mac (or to the Mac's keyboard).

Then tell the Mac what kind of printer you bought. To do that, choose **Chooser** from the Apple menu (so you see the **Chooser window**), then click the kind of printer you chose to buy, then click **Inactive** and press the RETURN key. Close the Chooser window (by clicking its close box) and press the RETURN key.

Print a document Suppose you've created a document by using SimpleText. To print the document onto paper, you can use two methods:

> Method 1: while you're using SimpleText to edit the document (so that the document is on the screen), choose **Print** from the File menu then press the RETURN key.
>
> Method 2: while you're *not* using SimpleText, click the document's icon, then choose **Print** from the File menu, then press the RETURN key.

Print a window When you're not in the middle of running an application program, here's how to copy the active window onto paper: choose **Print Window** from the File menu, then press the RETURN key.

> **Other Macs** For old Macs, choose Print Directory instead of Print Window.

COMMAND key

Between the OPTION key and the SPACE bar, you'll see a key that has a squiggle on it. The squiggle looks like a cloverleaf. On all modern Macs, that key also has a picture of an Apple on it.

That key is called the **SQUIGGLE** key or **CLOVERLEAF key** or **APPLE** key. It's also called the **COMMAND** key, because it lets you give commands.

For example, suppose you want to close a window. One way to close the window is the click its close box. Another way is to choose **Close** from the File menu. But another way is to hold down the COMMAND key; and while you keep the COMMAND key down, tap the W key.

Here's how I discovered that trick. I looked at the File menu, saw the word "Close" there, and noticed that a squiggle and a W were next to the word "Close".

Discover more tricks! Look at each menu, and notice which words have squiggles and letters next to them!

The Finder and SimpleText let you give these squiggle commands:

Command	Meaning
COMMAND A	select ALL things in the window (so they blacken)
COMMAND C	COPY the selected phrase to the Clipboard
COMMAND D	DUPLICATE the selected icon
COMMAND E	EJECT the diskette from the drive
COMMAND I	display INFORMATION about the selected icon
COMMAND N	create a NEW folder or document
COMMAND O	OPEN a folder, application program, or document
COMMAND P	PRINT onto paper
COMMAND Q	QUIT the application program
COMMAND S	SAVE the document (copy it from RAM to disk)
COMMAND V	paste from Clipboard and insert it here (^)
COMMAND W	WIPE out the WINDOW, by closing the window
COMMAND X	X out (cut, and move to the Clipboard)
COMMAND Y	YANK diskette out of the drive (or item out of trash)
COMMAND Z	ZAP the previous command; undo that command

Visual tricks

Here's how to make the Mac perform visual tricks.

Balloons For a wild experience, choose **Show Balloons** from the Help menu.

Then move the mouse pointer across the screen, and pause when the pointer's on an object (such as an icon or a menu choice). Don't click; just pause. Suddenly you see a little balloon, with a message explaining the object's purpose.

Go ahead: move the pointer from object to object, and read all the little balloons! You can even pull down a menu, pause at each menu choice, and read a balloon about each menu choice.

Then go ahead and use your Mac as you do normally — except that if you ever pause on an object, a balloon pops up.

Though balloons are fun, they can sometimes distract you from getting your work done. To stop seeing balloons, choose **Hide Balloons** from the Help menu.

> **Other Macs** Systems 1-6 have no balloons. Here's how to get balloons in System 7....Look at the menu bar, where you'll see a balloon with a question mark in it. Click that balloon. You'll see the Help menu. From the Help menu, choose Hide Balloons.

Label menu Normally, an item's icon is black-and-white. (If the item's a folder, its icon has a slightly blue tinge.)

You can dramatically color an item's icon. To do that, click the icon, then choose a color from the **Label menu**. (To see the Label menu, choose Label from the File menu.) You can choose 7 colors: **Essential orange**, **Hot red**, **In-Progress pink**, **Cool sky-blue**, **Personal deep-blue**, **Project-1 green**, and **Project-2 brown**. The icon turns that color. (Since the icon is still selected, it's temporarily dark; but the darkness will go away when you click elsewhere on your screen.)

By choosing among those colors, you can color-code your work. Make the icons of all work-in-progress be colored In-Progress pink, so you can find those icons easily.

If you change your mind and want to remove the color from an icon, just click the icon and choose **None** from the Label menu.

> **Other Macs** Systems 1-6 have no Label menu. System 7 puts the word "Label" on the menu bar, instead of burying it in the File menu.

Pretty views After you double-click an icon and see its window, you can use the **View menu**, which gives you three main choices:

> The normal choice is **Icons**.
>
> If you choose **Buttons** instead, the icons in that window turn into buttons. To open a button, click it just once (instead of double-clicking). To move a button, drag the button's name (which is below the button).
>
> If you choose **List** instead, the icons in that window become small, and they're rearranged to form a single column. For each item, the computer tells you the item's **Name**, **Date Modified** (when you last edited it), **Size** (in kilobytes), and **Kind** ("folder", "document", or "application program"). The items are listed in alphabetical order, by Name, unless you click "Date Modified" (to list them from newest to oldest) or "Size" (to list them from biggest to smallest) or "Kind" (to list folders then application programs then documents). Before a folder's icon, you normally see the symbol ▶. If you click that symbol, you'll see all the items in the folder, and the symbol becomes ▼. When you finish examining the folder's items, click the ▼, so it becomes ▶ again and the folder's items hide.

While viewing normal icons or buttons, you can choose **Clean Up** from the View menu. That makes the computer arrange the icons or buttons to form neat grid of rows and columns, fitting in the window.

> **Other Macs** On old Macs, the View menu doesn't offer Buttons, and the "Icons" choice is called "Icon".

Closing thoughts

Before we leave the wonderful, wacky world of Mac and return to the ponderous, boring world of IBM, here are some closing thoughts.

Close all windows When you're not in the middle of running an application program, try this experiment. Click a window's close box *while holding down the OPTION key*.

That window will close; and while it closes, *all the other windows will close also*.

Make your Mac normal If you're sharing the Mac with friends who are beginners, put the Mac back to normal before you shut down. Then your friends won't be confused by the wild orgy you had with your Mac!

Here's how to put the Mac back to normal.

Get out of any application program (by choosing Quit from the File menu). If you've given a window a fancy view, return that window to Icons view. Then close all windows (by clicking a close box while holding down the OPTION key).

Drag the trash can to the screen's bottom right corner. Drag the hard-drive icon to the top right part of the screen.

Then choose Shut Down from the Special menu.

WORD PROCESSING

Background

A **word-processing program** helps you write and edit sentences and paragraphs. Whatever you're writing and editing (such as a business letter, report, magazine article, or book) is called the **document**.

> Remember that a word-processing program is mainly for manipulating *sentences and paragraphs*. To manipulate pretty drawings, get a **graphics program** instead; to manipulate a table of numbers, get a **spreadsheet program**; to manipulate a list of names (such as a list of your customers), get a **database program**.

To use a word-processing program, put your fingers on the keyboard, then type the paragraphs that make up your document, so they appear on the screen. Edit them by using special keys on the keyboard. Finally, make the computer send the document to the printer, so the document appears on paper. You can also make the computer copy the document onto a disk, which will store the document for many years.

How "word processing" was invented

Back in the 1950's, 1960's, and 1970's, computers were used mainly to manipulate lists of numbers, names, and addresses. Those manipulations were called **data-processing (DP)**, so the typical computing center was called a **data-processing center (DP center)**, run by a team of programmers and administrators called the **data-processing department (DP department)**.

Those old computer systems were expensive, unreliable, and complex. They needed big staffs to do continuous repairs, reprogramming, and supervision. They were bureaucratic and technological nightmares. The term "data-processing" got a bad reputation. Secretaries who wanted to write and edit reports preferred to use simple typewriters, rather than deal with the dreaded "data-processing department".

When easy-to-use word-processing programs were finally invented for computers, secretaries were afraid to try them because computers had developed a scary reputation. The last thing a secretary wanted was a desktop computer, which the secretary figured would mean "desktop trouble".

That's why the term "**word-processing**" was invented. Wang, IBM, and other manufacturers said to the secretaries, "The machines we want to put on your desks are *not* those dreadful computers; they're just souped-up typewriters. You like typewriters, right? Then you'll like these cute little machines also. We call them **word processors**. Don't worry: they're not data-processing equipment; they're not computers."

The manufacturers were lying: their desktop machines *were* computers. To pretend they weren't computers, the manufacturers called them **word processors** and omitted any software dealing with numbers or lists.

The trick worked: secretaries acquired word processors, especially the **Wang Word Processor** and the **IBM Displaywriter**.

Today's secretaries are unafraid of computers, understand IBM PC clones, and run word-processing programs on them.

3 definitions of "word processor"

Strictly speaking, a "word processor" means "a computer whose main purpose is to do word processing". But some folks use the term "word processor" to mean "a word-processing program" or "a typist doing word processing".

In ads, a "$500 word processor" is a machine; a "$100 word processor" is a program you feed to a computer; a "$12-per-hour word processor" is a typist who understands word processing.

Word-processing programs

During the early 1980's many folks used **Electric Pencil** (the first word-processing program for microcomputers), **Wordstar** (which was more powerful), **Multimate** (the first program that made the IBM PC imitate a Wang word-processing machine), **Displaywrite** (which made the IBM PC imitate an IBM Displaywriter word-processing machine), **PC-Write** (shareware you could try for free before sending a donation to the author), and **Xywrite** (which ran faster than any other word processor). But by 1991, most of those users had switched to **WordPerfect 5.1**, which ran on the IBM PC (and several other computers) and could perform many fancy tricks.

All those word-processing programs were awkward to learn and use. Beginners preferred simpler word-processing programs such as **PFS Write** (for the IBM PC), **IBM Writing Assistant** (which was a modified version of PFS Write), **Q&A** (which also included a database program), **Bank Street Writer** (for the Apple 2), and **Mac Write** (which was invented by Apple for the Mac and sometimes given away free). But those word-processing programs couldn't perform as many tricks as WordPerfect 5.1, which remained the business standard that secretaries were required to learn and use.

In 1992, Microsoft invented Windows 3.1. It was the first version of Windows that was good enough to become popular. Companies and consumers began switching from DOS to Windows and wanted a good Windows word-processing program. WordPerfect 5.1 used DOS, not Windows. Windows 3.1 included a word-processing program called **Write**, but it was stripped down. The first *good* word-processing programs for Windows were **Ami** (which is the French word for "friend") and an improved version called **Ami Pro**, both published by a company called **Samna**, which got bought by **Lotus**, which got bought by **IBM**.

Microsoft invented a word-processing program called **Microsoft Word**. The DOS version of it was terribly awkward, but the Mac and Windows versions of it improved rapidly and eventually became even better than Ami Pro. **WordPerfect** eventually became available in a good Windows version, but too late: by then companies had already decided to switch to the Windows version of Microsoft Word.

Ami Pro still exists but has been renamed **Word Pro**.

What to buy

The best word-processing programs are the Windows and Mac versions of **Microsoft Word** and **WordPerfect**. To pay less, get **Word Pro** or **Microsoft Works** (which includes a word-processing program and several other programs). To pay nothing, use a stripped-down word processing program such as **Write** (which is part of Windows 3.1) or **WordPad** (which is part of Windows 95&98) or **SimpleText** (which is part of the Mac system) or **Appleworks** (which is also called **Clarisworks** and is included free with many Macs).

MICROSOFT WORD

Starting

Of all the word-processing programs ever invented, the fanciest and most popular is **Microsoft Word**. It runs in all three popular environments (DOS, Windows, and Mac) and uses similar commands in each of those environments.

Windows versions

Microsoft Word for Windows is nicknamed **Winword**. It's gone through several versions:

Version 1	was invented in 1989 for Windows 2.
Version 1.1	was invented in 1990 for Windows 2.
Version 2	was invented in 1991 for Windows 3.
Version 6	was invented in 1994 for Windows 3.1. (There was no Winword version 3, 4, or 5.)
Version 7	was invented in 1995 for Windows 95 and nicknamed **version 95**.
Version 97	was invented in 1997 for Windows 95.
Version 2000	was invented in 1999 for Windows 98.

Versions 6, 7, 97, and 2000 of Winword are modern. This chapter explains how to use them.

Those are the official names for the versions. Some Microsoft employees secretly say "**version 8**" instead of "version 97"; they say "**version 9**" instead of "version 2000".

Versions 1, 1.1, and 2 are primitive. If you're using them, you should switch to a modern version instead. If you can't afford to switch, phone me at 603-666-6644 to get this book's 19th edition, which included an intro to version 2. (So did the 18th and 17th editions.)

Non-windows versions

If you're using a **DOS version** of Microsoft Word, it's primitive! Switch to a modern Windows version.

The **Mac versions** of Microsoft Word resemble the Windows versions. Here's the main difference: instead of pressing an IBM Ctrl key, press the Mac's COMMAND key (on which you'll see a squiggly cloverleaf — and also see an apple if your keyboard is modern).

For the Mac's Word version 6, follow my instructions for Winword version 6.
For the Mac's Word version 98, follow my instructions for Winword version 97.
For the Mac's Word version 5.1 or lower, phone me at 603-666-6644 to get an older edition of this book.

Prepare yourself

Before reading this chapter, prepare yourself.

Version 2000 You need Windows 95 (or 98) and at least 16M of RAM. To run *well*, you should have at least 32M of RAM and a fast CPU (Pentium). Read and practice my Windows 95&98 chapter, especially the section about "WordPad", which is a stripped-down simplified version of Microsoft Word.

Versions 7&97 You need Windows 95 (or 98) and at least 8M of RAM. To run *well*, you should have at least 16M of RAM and a fast CPU (Pentium). Read and practice my Windows 95&98 chapter, especially the section about "WordPad", which is a stripped-down simplified version of Microsoft Word.

Version 6 You need Windows 3.1 (or 3.11 or 95 or 98) and at least 4M of RAM. To run *well*, you should have at least 8M of RAM and a fast CPU (486 or Pentium). If you don't have Windows 95 or 98, read and practice my Windows 3.1&3.11 chapter. If you *do* have Windows 95 or 98, you should switch to version 7 or 97 of Microsoft Word — and this chapter assumes you've done so.

Copy Microsoft Word to the hard disk

When you buy Microsoft Word, it comes on one or more disks, which you must copy to your computer's hard disk.

Version 2000 If you bought **Microsoft Works Suite 2000** (which includes Microsoft Word 2000), here's how to copy Microsoft Word to your hard disk:

Turn on the computer without any floppy or CD-ROM disks in the drives, so the computer runs Windows 95 (or 98) and the computer's bottom left corner says Start.
Put Microsoft Works Suite 2000's Disc 1 into the CD-ROM drive. The computer says "Microsoft Works Suite 2000 Setup". Press ENTER. Click "I agree". Press ENTER.
The computer says "Insert Disc 2". Insert it and press ENTER. Eventually the computer says "You must restart your system". Press ENTER. The computer says again "You must restart your system". Press ENTER.
The computer says "Insert Disc 1". Insert it again and press ENTER. The computer says "The installer must restart your system". Press ENTER.
The computer says "Insert Disc 3". Insert it and press ENTER. The computer says "Insert Disc 4". Insert it and press ENTER. The computer says "You must restart your system". Press ENTER. Click "Exit Setup". Click "Exit Setup" again.

If you bought **Microsoft Office 2000 Premium** (which includes Microsoft Word 2000), here's how to copy Microsoft Word to your hard disk:

If the software box includes a mouse, turn off the computer and plug in the mouse.
Turn on the computer without any floppy or CD-ROM disks in the drives, so the computer runs Windows 95 (or 98) and the computer's bottom left corner says Start.
(If the software box includes a mouse, put the mouse's disk into drive A, type "a:setup", press ENTER twice, type your name, press the TAB key, type the name of your company, press ENTER 6 times, remove the mouse's disk, press ENTER again.)
Put Microsoft Office 2000 Premium's disk 1 into the CD-ROM drive.
The computer says "User name". Type your full name, then press the TAB key, type your initials, press TAB again, type the name of your company (if any), and press TAB again.
That CD-ROM disk 1 came in a square plastic case, whose backside sports an orange sticker revealing a code (called the "Product Key"), which contains 25 letters and digits; type that 25-character code and press ENTER.
Click "I accept the terms in the License Agreement". Press ENTER 3 times.

Version 97 If you bought **Home Essentials 98** (which includes Microsoft Word 97), here's how to copy Microsoft Word to your hard disk:

Turn on the computer without any floppy or CD-ROM disks in the drives, so the computer runs Windows 95 (or 98) and the computer's bottom left corner says Start. Put Home Essentials 98's Disc 1 into the CD-ROM drive. The computer will say "Microsoft Home Essentials". Click the Microsoft Word 97 button. The computer will say "Microsoft Word 97 Setup". Press the ENTER key.
The computer will say "Enter your full name". Type your name. At the end of your name, press the TAB key, then type the name of your company (if any), then press ENTER twice.
The computer will say "CD Key". The CD-ROM disk came in a square plastic case, whose backside sports an orange sticker revealing an 11-digit code number (called the "CD Key number"); type that number and press ENTER.

The computer will show you a 20-digit Product Identification number. Write that number on the yellow-black-and-white registration card that came with the CD. Press ENTER 5 times, then click "Exit Setup".

If you bought **Microsoft Office 97** (which includes Microsoft Word 97), here's how to copy Microsoft Word to your hard disk:

Turn on the computer without any floppy or CD-ROM disks in the drives, so the computer runs Windows 95 (or 98) and the computer's bottom left corner says Start. Put the Microsoft Office 97 disk into the CD-ROM drive.

You'll see the Office97pro window. Maximize it, by clicking its maximize button (which is next to the X button).

At the window's bottom left corner, you'll see **an icon that shows a picture of a computer and is labeled "Setup"**. Double-click it.

The computer will say, "Microsoft Office 97 Setup". Press the ENTER key.

The computer will say "Enter your full name". Type your name. At the end of your name, press the TAB key, then type the name of your company (if any), then press ENTER twice.

The computer will say "CD Key". The CD-ROM disk came in a square plastic case, whose backside sports an orange sticker revealing an 11-digit code number (called the "CD Key number"); type that number and press ENTER.

The computer will show you a 20-digit Product Identification number. Write that number on the yellow-black-and-white registration card that came with the CD. Press ENTER 6 times. Close the Office97pro window (by clicking its X button), then click "Exit Setup".

Version 7 Microsoft Word 7 comes on a CD-ROM disk, which must be copied to your hard disk. If you're still using version 7, you've presumably done that procedure already.

Version 6 Microsoft Word 6 comes on floppy disks, which must be copied to your hard disk. If you're still using version 6, you've presumably done that procedure already.

Launch Microsoft Word

Here's how to start using Microsoft Word.

Version 2000 Click "Start" then "Programs" then "Microsoft Word".

If the computer says "Please enter your customer information", do this: type your full name, then press the TAB key, type your initials, press TAB again, type the name of your company (if any), press TAB again, type the 25-character code (which is on the orange Product Key sticker that came on the back of the CD pack), and press ENTER.

If you see a button labeled "Start using Microsoft Word", click it.

If the computer asks "Would you like to register?", click "No" for now.

Version 2000 has a feature called **masked menus & buttons**. That feature is supposed to make the menus and buttons easier to find but actually makes them *harder* to find. Turn off that terrible feature. **Do this turn-off procedure:**

Click "View" then "Toolbars" then "Customize" then "Options".

The first box is labeled "Standard and Formatting toolbars share one row". Remove any check mark from that box (by clicking it).

The second box is labeled "Menus show recently used commands first". Remove any check mark from that box (by clicking it.)

Make sure you've done that right, so now the top two boxes are both empty. Then click "Close".

Do that turn-off procedure *now*. The rest of this chapter assumes you've done it. (After you've finished this chapter, if you wish, you can turn the masked menus & buttons feature back on by putting the check marks back in.)

Version 97 Click "Start" then "Programs" then "Microsoft Word". (If the computer shows a button labeled "Start using Microsoft Word", click that button. If the computer says "User name", press ENTER.)

Version 7 Click "Start" then "Programs" then "Microsoft Word". (If the computer shows a window saying "What's New in Microsoft Word 95", click that window's X button.)

Version 6 Turn on the computer without any floppy in drive A. Start Windows (by typing "win" after the C prompt). If the computer says "Microsoft Office Cue Cards", close the Microsoft Office Cue Cards window (by double-clicking its

control box). The computer says "Program Manager".

If you see a slanted W near the screen's top right corner, click it. If you don't see a slanted W, double-click the Microsoft Office icon then the Microsoft Word icon.

See the Microsoft Word screen

The screen's top says "Microsoft Word — Document1". You also see this **menu bar**:

File Edit View Insert Format Tools Table Window Help

If the computer says "Tip of the Day", press ENTER.

See the rulers

About 1½ inches down from the top of the screen, you should see a **horizontal ruler**, which goes across the screen and is numbered 1", 2", 3", 4", 5", etc.

If you don't see that ruler, make it appear by choosing **Ruler** from the **View menu**.

At the screen's left edge, you should see a **vertical ruler**, which goes up & down the screen and is numbered 1", 2", etc.

If you don't see the vertical ruler, make it appear by choosing **Page Layout** from the View menu. In Version 2000, choose **Print Layout** instead of Page Layout.

Now you see *two* rulers — a horizontal ruler, plus a vertical ruler — so you can use the full power of Microsoft Word!

Type your document

Start typing your document.

Microsoft Word uses the mouse and fundamental keys the same way as WordPad. For details, **read these sections on pages 97-99:**

"Use the keyboard"
"Scroll arrows"
"Insert characters"
"Split a paragraph"
"Combine paragraphs"
"Movement keys"

Ctrl symbols On your keyboard, below the two SHIFT keys, are two CONTROL keys, which say "Ctrl" on them. You can use them to type special symbols:

Symbol	How to type it
©	While pressing the Ctrl and Alt keys, type the letter "c".
®	While pressing the Ctrl and Alt keys, type the letter "r".
TM	While pressing the Ctrl and Alt keys, type the letter "t".
…	While pressing the Ctrl and Alt keys, type ".".
¿	While pressing Ctrl and Alt (and SHIFT), type "?".
¡	While pressing Ctrl and Alt (and SHIFT), type "!".
ç	While pressing Ctrl, tap the "," key. Then type the letter "c".
¢	While pressing Ctrl, tap the "/" key. Then type the letter "c".
ø	While pressing Ctrl, tap the "/" key. Then type the letter "o".
ñ	While pressing Ctrl (and SHIFT), type "~". Then type "n".
ô	While pressing Ctrl (and SHIFT), type "^". Then type "o".
ü	While pressing Ctrl (and SHIFT), type ":". Then type "u".
å	While pressing Ctrl (and SHIFT), type "@". Then type "a".
æ	While pressing Ctrl (and SHIFT), type "&". Then type "a".
œ	While pressing Ctrl (and SHIFT), type "&". Then type "o".
ß	While pressing Ctrl (and SHIFT), type "&". Then type "s".
è	While pressing Ctrl, type the symbol `. Then type "e".
é	While pressing Ctrl, type the symbol '. Then type "e".
ð	While pressing Ctrl, type the symbol '. Then type "d".
«	While pressing Ctrl, type the symbol `. SHIFTing, type "<".
»	While pressing Ctrl, type the symbol `. SHIFTing, type ">".

AutoCorrect

AutoCorrect While you type, **the computer will automatically make little corrections to your typing**. For example:

> If you accidentally type "teh" instead of "the", the computer will change it to "the".
> If you accidentally type "hte" instead of "the", the computer will change it to "the" (in versions 7&97&2000).
> If you accidentally type "loove" instead of "love", the computer will change it to "love" (in version 2000).
>
> If you type a day (such as "sunday"), the computer will capitalize it.
> If you capitalize the first *two* letters of a word, the computer will make the second letter small.
> The computer will capitalize each sentence's first word (in versions 7&97&2000).
>
> The computer will change (r) to ®.
> The computer will change (c) to © and change (tm) to ™ (in versions 7&97&2000).
> The computer will change 1/2 to ½, change 1/4 to ¼, and change 3/4 to ¾ (in versions 7&97&2000).
> The computer will change -- to –, change --> to →, and change <-- to ← (in versions 7&97&2000).
> The computer will change ==> to → and change <== to ← (in versions 7&97&2000).
> The computer will change :) to ☺ and change :(to ☹ (in versions 7&97&2000).
>
> If you type a phrase in quotation marks ("like this"), the quotation marks will become curly ("like this").
> If you type three periods (...), the periods will move farther apart (…) (in versions 7&97&2000).
>
> If you type the first four letters of a month (such as "sept") or day (such as "wedn") and then press ENTER, the computer will finish typing the word and capitalize its first letter (in versions 97&2000).
>
> If you type the current month and then press the SPACE bar and ENTER, the computer will type the current date and year (in versions 97&2000).

The computer's ability to make those corrections is called **AutoCorrect**. As you can see from those examples, AutoCorrect is smarter in versions 7&97&2000 than in version 6.

If you dislike a correction that the computer made to your typing, here's how to undo the correction:

> Method 1: click the **Undo button** (which is under the word "Table" and has an arrow pointing to the left).
> Method 2: while holding down the Ctrl key, tap the Z key.

Those methods work just if done *immediately*, before you do any other typing or editing.

Red squiggles (just in versions 7&97&2000)

Red squiggles (just in versions 7&97&2000) While you type, versions 7&97&2000 automatically put a **red squiggle under any word that looks strange**. The computer considers a word to look "strange" if the word's not in the computer's dictionary or if the word's the same as the word before. For example, if you type "For a sentury, I love you you", the computer will put a red squiggle under "sentury" and under the second "you".

If you see a red squiggle, you misspelled the word or accidentally repeated the word or forgot to put a space between words or your vocabulary is more advanced than the computer understands. So if you see a red squiggle, look carefully at the squiggled word to make sure it's really what you want.

If a word has a red squiggle under it, try right-clicking that word (by using the mouse's right-hand button). Then the computer will make suggestions about what the squiggled word ought to be.

For example, if you typed "sentury" and the computer put a red squiggle under it, right-clicking the "sentury" will make the computer display two suggestions ("sentry" and "century") and two other popular choices, so you see this list:

> sentry
> century
>
> Ignore All
> Add

Choose what you want:

> If you meant "sentry" or "century", click the word you meant.
>
> If you meant "sentury" and want to add that slang word to the computer's permanent dictionary (because the word means "a sentry who watches for a century"), click "Add". Warning: before clicking "Add", make sure the word "sentury" really exists and you've spelled it correctly and your colleagues give you permission to add slang to the dictionary!
>
> If you meant "sentury" but don't want to add that slang word to the dictionary, click "Ignore All". The computer will ignore the issue about how "sentury" is spelled in this document; the computer will remove the red squiggle from every "sentury" in this document; but since "sentury" is still not in the dictionary, the computer will put red squiggles under any "sentury" in other documents.
>
> If you're not sure what you meant, press the keyboard's ESCAPE key (which says Esc on it). The list of choices will disappear; "sentury" will still be in your document and squiggled.

Green squiggles (just in versions 97&2000)

Green squiggles (just in versions 97&2000) When you finish typing a sentence and start typing a new one, versions 97&2000 automatically check the grammar of the sentence you just typed and put a **dark green squiggle under any obvious grammar error**. For example, if you type "We is" instead of "We are", the computer will draw a green squiggle under the "is". (It will draw the squiggle when you finish typing that sentence and start typing the next one.) If you press the SPACE bar too many times, so you type "They kiss" instead of "They kiss", the computer will put a green squiggle under the "kiss".

If a word has a green squiggle under it, try right-clicking that word (by using the mouse's right-hand button). Then the computer will make a suggestion about what the squiggled word ought to be.

> If you agree with the computer's suggestion, click that suggestion; the computer will fix what you wrote.
>
> If you *dis*agree with the computer's suggestion, click "Ignore Sentence". The computer will ignore the issue about that sentence's grammar and remove the blue squiggle from that sentence.
>
> If you're not sure why the computer is complaining, click "Grammar". The computer will tell you why it's complaining. Then double-click the computer's suggestion, or click "Ignore" (to erase the green squiggle from that sentence), or click "Ignore All" (to erase the green squiggle from that sentence and from all similar sentences in that document), or click "Cancel" (if you're not sure what you want).

Page arrows

Page arrows Near the screen's bottom right corner, you see this symbol:
▲

If your document contains several pages, clicking that symbol makes the computer go back up and show you the **previous page**. For example, while you're looking at page 4, clicking that symbol makes the computer show you page 3.

Under that symbol, you see this symbol:
▼

Clicking it makes the computer show you the **next page**. For example, while you're looking at page 3, clicking that symbol makes the computer show you page 4.

All delete

Here's how to delete the entire document, so you can start over:

> While holding down the Ctrl key, press the A key. That means "all". All of the document turns black. Then press the DELETE key. All of the document disappears, so you can start over!

Page break

After you've finished typing a paragraph (and pressed ENTER), try this experiment: while holding down the Ctrl key, press ENTER again. That creates a **page break**: it makes the next paragraph be at the top of the next page.

If you change your mind, here's how to remove the page break: click at the beginning of the paragraph you've put at the top of a page; then press the BACKSPACE key.

Formatting toolbar

Near the screen's top, you see the **formatting toolbar**. It looks like this in versions 97&2000:

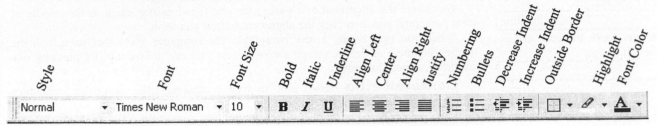

(In versions 6 & 7, it's slightly shorter.)

Each symbol on the toolbar is called a **tool**. Here's the name of each tool:

If you forget a tool's name, try this trick: point at the tool (by using the mouse, but *without* clicking), then wait a second. Underneath the tool, you'll see the tool's name; and at the screen's bottom left corner, you'll see a one-sentence explanation of what the tool does.

The toolbar's right half consists of 14 tools saying "**B**", "*I*", "<u>U</u>", etc. Those 14 tools are called **buttons**.

Those are the buttons in versions 97&2000. Here's how older versions differ:

> In versions 6&7, the Outside Border button is called just "Borders".
> Versions 6&7 lack the Font Color button.
> Version 6 lacks the Highlight button. Version 7 puts it just right of the "<u>U</u>".

To use a button, press it by clicking it with the mouse. Here are the details....

Underline

Here's how to underline a phrase (<u>like this</u>). Push in the **Underline button** (which says <u>U</u> on it) by clicking it. Then type the phrase you want underlined. Then pop the Underline button back out (by clicking it again).

Here's a shortcut: instead of clicking the Underline button, you can press Ctrl with U.

Bold

Here's how to make a phrase be bold (**like this**). Push in the **Bold button** (which says **B** on it) by clicking it. Then type the phrase you want emboldened. Then pop the Bold button back out (by clicking it again).

Here's how to make a phrase be bold and underlined (**<u>like this</u>**). Push in the Bold and Underline buttons (by clicking them both). Then type the phrase. Then pop those buttons back out (by clicking them again).

Here's a shortcut: instead of clicking the Bold button, you can press Ctrl with B.

Italic

Here's how to italicize a phrase (*like this*). Push in the **Italic button** (which says *I* on it) by clicking it. Then type the phrase you want italicized. Then pop the Italic button back out (by clicking it again).

Here's a shortcut: instead of clicking the Italic button, you can press Ctrl with I.

Alignment buttons

While typing a line, you can click one of these **alignment buttons**:

Align Left	Center	Align Right	Justify

Clicking the **Center button** makes the line be centered,

like this line

Clicking the **Align Right button** makes the line be at the right margin,

like this line

Clicking the **Align Left button** makes the line be at the left margin,

like this line

Clicking one of those buttons affects not just the line you're typing but also all other lines in the same paragraph.

Clicking the **Justify button** makes the paragraph be **justified**, so the paragraph's bottom line is at the left margin, and each of the paragraph's other lines is at *both* margins (by inserting extra space between the words),

like   this   line

When you click one of those alignment buttons, you're pushing the button in. That button pops back out when you push a different alignment button instead.

When you start typing a new document, the computer assumes you want the document to be aligned left, so the computer pushes the Align Left button in. If you want a different alignment, push a different alignment button instead.

Examples:

> If you're typing a title or headline and want it to be centered, press the **Center button**.
>
> If you're typing a business letter and want it to begin by showing the date next to the right margin, press the **Align Right button**.
>
> If you're typing an informal memo or letter to a colleague or friend, and want the paragraph to look plain, ordinary, modest, and unassuming (like Clark Kent), press the **Align Left button**.
>
> If you're creating something formal (such as a newspaper or textbook) and want the paragraph to have perfectly straight edges (so it looks official, uptight, and professional, like Robocop), press the **Justify button**.

Clicking one of those alignment buttons affects the entire paragraph you're typing. (The paragraphs you typed earlier remain unaffected.)

To change the alignment of a paragraph you typed earlier, click in the middle of that paragraph and then click the alignment button you wish.

When you start typing a new paragraph, the computer gives that paragraph the same alignment as the paragraph above, unless you say differently (by pressing one of the alignment buttons).

Centered title Here's how to type a centered title, using the techniques you've learned so far....

Press the ENTER key twice (to leave a big blank space above the title).

Next, press the Center button (so the title will be centered) and the Bold button (so the title will be bold). Type the words you want to be in the title, and press the ENTER key afterwards.

Congratulations! You've created a centered title!

Next, make the paragraph underneath the title be normal: make that paragraph be uncentered (click the Align Left button or Justify button) and make it be unbolded (click the Bold button, so the Bold button pops back out).

Shortcuts Here are shortcuts:

> Instead of clicking the Justify button, you can press Ctrl with J.
>
> Instead of clicking the Align Left button, you can press Ctrl with L.
> Instead of clicking the Align Right button, you can press Ctrl with R.
>
> Instead of clicking the Center button, you can press Ctrl with E (which stands for "Equidistant").

Font Size

Look at the **Font Size box**. In that box, you normally see the number 10. That means the characters you're typing are 10 points high. Here's how to type characters that are bigger or smaller....

> Method 1: click the Font Size box. In that box, type a size number from 8 to 72. The number can end in .5; the number can be 8 or 8.5 or 9 or 9.5 or 10 or bigger. (Theoretically, you can pick a number even smaller than 8 or even bigger than 72, but those extreme numbers create ugly results.) When you finish typing the number, press the ENTER key.
>
> Method 2: click the down-arrow that's to the *right* of the Font Size box. You start seeing this list of popular sizes: 8, 9, 10, 11, 12, 14, 16, 18, 20, 22, 24, 26, 28, 36, 48, and 72. (It appears in a window that's too small to show the entire list; to see the rest of the list, click the window's scroll arrows.) That list of popular sizes is called the **Font Size menu**. Click the size you want.

Any new characters you type afterwards will be the size you chose. (Characters typed earlier don't change size.)

The popular sizes look like this:

This text is 8 points high, 9 points high, 10 points high, 11 points high, 12 points high, 14 points high, 16 points high, 18 points high, 20 pt., 22 pt., 24 pt., 26 pt., 28 pt., 36pt., 48pt., 72pt.

When you finish typing the enlarged or reduced characters, here's how to return to typing characters that are normal size (10-point): click the down-arrow that's to the right of the Font Size box, then click the 10.

Font

When you type, you're normally using a font called "Times New Roman". If you wish, you can switch to a different font instead.

The most popular Windows fonts are "Times New Roman", "Arial", and "Courier New". Here's how they look:

> This font is called "Times New Roman". It's the best for typing long passages of text, such as paragraphs in books, newspapers, magazines, and reports. It squeezes lots of words onto a small amount of paper but remains easy to read. You can make it plain or **bold** or *italic* or ***bold italic***.
>
> # If you make it big & bold, like this, it imitates an old-fashioned news headline.

> This font is called "Arial". It's simple. You can make it plain or **bold** or *italic* or ***bold italic***. It resembles Helvetica. It's best for typing short phrases that attract attention. For example....
>
> ## If you make it big & bold, like this, it's good for titles, signs, and posters.
>
> If you make it small, like this, it's good for footnotes, photo captions, classified ads, telephone books, directories, and catalogs.

> ```
> This font is called "Courier New".
>
> If you make it 12 points high, like
> this, it resembles the printout from
> a typewriter.
>
> It makes each character have the same
> width: for example, the "m" has the same
> width as the "I". It's a good font for
> typing tables of numbers, since the uniform
> width lets you line up each column of
> numbers easily. To make sure each column
> aligns properly, press the Align Left
> button, not the Justify button.
> ```
> Choose plain, **bold**, *italic*, or ***bold italic***.

In the **Font box**, you see the name of a font, which is usually "Times New Roman". Click the down-arrow that's to the *right* of that font's name. You start seeing a list of fonts, including "Times New Roman", "Arial", "Courier New", and several other fonts. (It appears in a window that's too small to show the entire list; to see the rest of the list, click the window's scroll arrows.) The list of font is called the **Font menu**.

The best fonts have "TT" written in front of them. The "TT" means the font is a **True Type font** (created by a system that lets you make the characters as big or as small as you wish and accurately reproduces those characters onto your screen and paper). For example, "Times New Roman", "Arial", and "Courier New" are True Type fonts and have "TT" written in front of them.

Click the font you want.

Afterwards, whatever characters you type will be in the font you chose. (The characters you typed earlier remain unaffected.)

When you finish typing in that font, here's how to return to typing characters that are normal (Times New Roman): click the down-arrow that's to the right of the Font box, then click Times New Roman.

Style

When you type, you typically use a style called "Normal", which is 10-point Times New Roman aligned left.

If you wish, you can switch to a different style instead. For example, you can switch to a style called "Heading 1", which is an Arial bold that's big (16-point in version 2000, 14-point in earlier versions) with extra blank space between paragraphs. Here's how.

In the **Style box**, you see the name of a style, which is typically "Normal". Click the down-arrow next to that style name. You see a list of styles, including "Normal", "Heading 1", and several other styles. The list of styles is called the **Style menu**.

Click the style you want.

That affects the paragraph you're typing now. (The paragraphs you typed earlier remain unaffected.)

When you finish typing a paragraph in that style (and pressed the ENTER key at the end of that paragraph), here's how to make the next paragraph be Normal: if the Style box doesn't say "Normal" already, click the down-arrow next to the Style box then click Normal.

Centered title Here's the sophisticated way to type a centered title.

Press the ENTER key. Choose "Heading 1" from the Style menu. Push in the Centered button. Type the title, and press the ENTER key afterwards.

The computer will automatically make the next paragraph be Normal and aligned left; you don't have to say so.

Indentation buttons

Before typing a paragraph, you can press the TAB key. That makes the computer indent the paragraph's first line.

If you want to indent *all* lines in the paragraph, do this instead of pressing the TAB key: while typing the paragraph, click the **Increase Indent button**. That makes the computer indent *all* lines in the paragraph. (The paragraphs you typed earlier remain unaffected.)

When you start typing a new paragraph, the computer indents that paragraph if the paragraph above it was indented.

If you indented a paragraph by clicking the Increase Indent button but then change your mind, here's how to *un*indent the paragraph: click in the paragraph, then click the **Decrease Indent button**.

Example
Suppose you start typing a new document. Here's how to make just paragraphs 3, 4, and 5 be indented.

Type paragraphs 1 and 2 normally (without pressing the Increase Indent button).

When you start typing paragraph 3, press the Increase Indent button. That makes the computer start indenting, so paragraphs 3, 4, and 5 will be automatically indented.

When you start typing paragraph 6, here's how to prevent the computer from indenting it: click the Decrease Indent button at the beginning of paragraph 6.

Changing your mind
To indent a paragraph you typed earlier, click in the middle of that paragraph and then click the Increase Indent button. To *un*indent a paragraph you typed earlier, click in its middle and then click the *Decrease* Indent button.

Extra indentation
If you click the Increase Indent button *twice* instead of just once, the computer will indent the paragraph farther. After typing that doubly indented paragraph, if you want the paragraph below to be unindented you must click the Decrease Indent button twice.

Each time you click the Increase Indent button, the computer indents the paragraph a half inch farther. Each time you click the Decrease Indent button, the computer indents the paragraph a half inch less.

Bullets
Here's a different way to indent an entire paragraph: while typing the paragraph, push in the **Bullets button** (by clicking it). That makes the computer indent the paragraph and also put a bullet (the symbol •) to the left of the paragraph's first line. That's called a **bulleted paragraph**.

> Versions 6&7&97 put the bullet symbol at the left margin and indent the paragraph's words a quarter inch. Version 2000 indents the bullet symbol a quarter inch and indents the paragraph's words a half inch.

After you've typed a bulleted paragraph, any new paragraphs you type underneath will be bulleted also — until you request an *un*bulleted paragraph (by popping the Bullets button back out).

Numbering
Here's another way to indent an entire paragraph: while typing the paragraph, push in the **Numbering button** (by clicking it). That makes the computer indent the paragraph and put "1." to the left of the paragraph's first line. That's called a **numbered paragraph**.

> Versions 6&7&97 put the number at the left margin and indent the paragraph's words a quarter inch. Version 2000 indents the number a quarter inch and indents the paragraph's words a half inch.

When you type a new paragraph underneath, that paragraph will be numbered "2.", the next paragraph will be numbered "3.", etc. Any new paragraphs you type underneath will be numbered also — until you request an *un*numbered paragraph (by popping the Numbering button back out).

Color buttons

Normally, you type black characters on a white background. Here's how to change those colors.

Highlight
Normally, you type on a white background. Versions 7&97&2000 let you easily change the background to a different color, such as yellow, as if you were using a yellow Magic Marker highlighter. Here's how.

First, type the phrase you want to highlight.

Then look at the **Highlight button**. It's the button that shows a Magic Marker highlighter pen and a colored sample. (In version 7, the colored sample is a square. In versions 97&2000, the colored sample is a fat line.) Notice the sample's color.

> If it's the color you want, click the sample.
>
> If it's *not* the color you want, do this instead: click the down-arrow that's to the right of the sample; you'll see several colors; click the color you want. (I recommend you pick a light color, such as yellow.)

Put the mouse at the beginning of the phrase you want to highlight (so the *vertical bar* is at the left edge of the phrase's first letter). Drag across the phrase (while holding down the mouse's left button.). The phrase's background will change to the color you desired. If you wish, drag across other phrases also.

When you finish coloring, pop the Highlight button back out (by clicking it or by pressing the Esc key).

Font Color
Normally, the characters you type are black. Here's how to make them a different color, such as red.

If you're using version 97 or 2000, do this:

> Look at the **Font Color button**. It's the last big button on the formatting toolbar, and it has an underlined "A" on it.
>
> Notice the color of the A's underline. If it's the color you want, click the underline. If it's *not* the color you want, do this instead: click the down-arrow that's to the right of the A's underline; you'll see 16 colors; click the color you want.
>
> Afterwards, whatever characters you type will be in the color you chose. (The characters you typed earlier remain unaffected.)
>
> When you finish typing in that color, here's how to return to typing characters that are black: click the down-arrow that's to the right of the A's underline, then click Black.

If you're using version 6 or 7, you don't have a Font Color button, so do this instead:

> Click the word Format, then Font, then Font again, then the down-arrow that's in the Color box. You'll see a list of colors. (To see all 16 colors, use the scroll arrows.) Click the color you want, then press ENTER.
>
> Afterwards, whatever characters you type will be in the color you chose. (The characters you typed earlier remain unaffected.)
>
> When you finish typing in that color, here's how to return to typing characters that are black: click the word Format, then Font, then Font again, then the down-arrow that's in the Color box, then Black, then press ENTER.

Select text

Here's how to dramatically change a phrase you typed.

Point at the phrase's beginning, then drag to the phrase's end (while holding down the mouse's left button). The whole phrase turns black. Turning the phrase black is called **selecting the phrase**.

Then say what to do to the phrase. For example, choose one of these activities:

> To underline the phrase, push in the Underline button.
> To make the phrase be bold, push in the Bold button.
> To italicize the phrase, push in the Italic button.
>
> To prevent the phrase from being underlined, bold, or italicized, pop those buttons back out.
>
> To change how the phrase's paragraphs are aligned, click one of the alignment buttons.
> To change how the phrase's paragraphs are indented, click one of the indentation buttons.
>
> To change the phrase's point size, choose the size you want from the Font Size menu.
> To change the phrase's font, choose the font you want from the Font menu.
> To change the phrase's style, choose the style you want from the Style menu.
>
> To delete the phrase, press the **DELETE key**.
>
> To replace the phrase, just type whatever words you want the phrase to become.

Go ahead! Try it now! It's fun!

Other ways to select

The usual way to select a phrase is to point at the phrase's beginning, then drag to the phrase's end. But sometimes other methods are faster!

To select a phrase, choose one of these methods....

> Method 1: point at the phrase's beginning, then **drag** to the phrase's end.
>
> Method 2: click the phrase's beginning; then while holding down the **SHIFT key**, click the phrase's end.
>
> Method 3: by using your keyboard's **movement keys**
> (such as up-arrow, down-arrow, left-arrow, and right-arrow), move to the phrase's beginning;
> then while holding down the SHIFT key, use the movement keys to move to the phrase's end.
>
> Method 4: to select just **one sentence**, click in its middle while holding down the Ctrl key.
>
> Method 5: to select just **one line**, click in its left margin.
>
> Method 6: to select **several lines**, click in the first line's left margin;
> then while holding down the SHIFT key, click in the bottom line's left margin.
>
> Method 7: to select just **one word**, double-click in its middle.
>
> Method 8: to select just **one paragraph**, triple-click in its middle (or double-click in its left margin).
>
> Method 9: to select **several paragraphs**, triple-click in the first paragraph's middle;
> then while holding down the SHIFT key, click in the last paragraph's middle.
>
> Method 10: to select the **entire document** (all!), press the A key while holding down the Ctrl key.

Drag a phrase

To move a phrase to a new location, just "select the phrase, and then drag from the phrase's middle to the new location." Here are the details....

First, select the phrase you want to move, so the phrase turns black.

Then take your finger off the mouse's button. Move the mouse's pointer to the phrase's middle (so you see an arrow).

Finally, hold down the mouse's button (so you see a vertical dotted line); and while you keep holding down the mouse's button, drag that line to wherever you want the phrase to move. (Drag the line anywhere you wish in the document, or drag to the end of the document. The computer won't let you drag past the document's end.)

When you finish dragging, lift your finger from the mouse's button. Presto, the phrase moves where you wished!

Standard toolbar

Near the screen's top, above the formatting toolbar, you see the **standard toolbar**, which in version 97 looks like this:

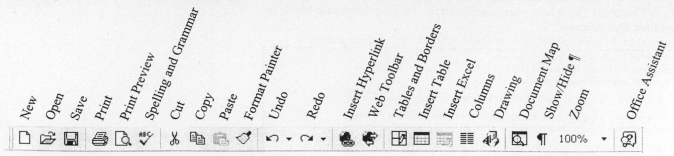

In version 2000:

> The "New" button is called "New Blank Document".
> The "Office Assistant" button is called "Microsoft Word Help".
> Instead of a "Web Toolbar" button, you get an "E-mail" button, which is between the Save and Print buttons.

In versions 6&7:

> The "Spelling and Grammar" button is called just "Spelling".
> The "Office Assistant" button is called "Help".
> "Zoom" is called "Zoom Control".
>
> The "Tables and Borders" button is missing.
>
> Instead of an "Insert Hyperlink" button, you get an "AutoFormat" button.
> Instead of a "Web Toolbar" button, version 6 has "Insert AutoText"; version 7 has "Insert Address".
> Instead of a "Document Map" button, version 6 has "Insert Chart"; version 7 has "Tip Wizard".

Here's how to use the most popular of those tools....

Save

To save the document (copy it onto the disk), click the **Save button** (or press Ctrl with S).

If you haven't saved the document before, the computer will say "File Name". Invent a name for your document. (If you're using version 6, make the name be short: no more than 8 characters.) Type the name and press ENTER.

That makes the computer copy the document onto the hard disk. For example, if you named the document "mary", here's what happens:

> **Versions 7&97&2000** make the computer put a document called mary.doc into the My Documents folder.
>
> **Version 6** makes the computer put a document called MARY.DOC into the WINWORD folder (subdirectory). If you bought the entire Microsoft Office instead of just Word, the WINWORD folder is inside the MSOFFICE folder.

Afterwards, if you change your mind and want to do more editing, go ahead! When you finish that extra editing, save it by clicking the Save button again.

Save often If you're typing a long document, click the Save button about every 10 minutes. Click it whenever you get to a good stopping place and think, "What I've typed so far looks good!"

Then if an accident happens, you'll lose at most 10 minutes of work, and you can return to the last version you felt good about.

Print

Here's how to print the document onto paper. Make sure you've bought a printer, attached it to the computer, turned the printer's power on, and put paper into the printer. Then click the **Print button**. The printer will print your document onto paper.

How to finish

When you finish working on a document, choose **Exit** or **Close** from the **File menu**.

If you choose **Exit**, the computer will stop using Microsoft Word.

If you choose **Close** instead of Exit, the computer will let you work on another document, and your next step is to click the **New button** or the **Open button**.

> If you click the **New button** (or press Ctrl with N), the computer will let you start typing a new document. (Version 2000 calls that button the "New Blank Document" button.)
>
> If you click the **Open button** (or press Ctrl with O), you see a list of old documents. If you want to *use* one of those documents, double-click the document's name; the computer will put that document onto the screen and let you edit it. If instead you want to *delete* one of those documents, and you're using version 7 or 97 or 2000, click the document's name and then press the DELETE key and then the ENTER key; the computer will move that document to the Recycle Bin.

Didn't save? If you didn't save your document before doing those procedures, the computer asks, "Do you want to save?" If you click "Yes", the computer copies your document's most recent version to the hard disk; if you click "No" instead, the computer ignores and forgets your most recent editing.

Congratulations! You've learned all the fundamental commands of Microsoft Word!

Undo

If you make a mistake (such as accidentally deleting some text, or accidentally giving the text an ugly font), click the **Undo button** (which shows an arrow turning back). That makes the computer undo your last activity, so your text returns to the way it looked before you made your boo-boo. (To undo your last *two* activities, click the Undo button *twice*.)

Here's a shortcut: instead of clicking the Undo button, you can press Ctrl with Z (which stands for "Zap").

Redo

If you click the Undo button, the computer might undo a different activity than you expected. If clicking the Undo button accidentally makes the text look even worse instead of better, and you wish you hadn't clicked the Undo button, you can "undo the undo" by clicking the **Redo button** (which shows an arrow bending forward).

Show/Hide ¶

The symbol for "Paragraph" is ¶, which looks like a backwards P.

One of the buttons has a ¶ on it. Microsoft calls it the **Show/Hide ¶ button**, but most folks call it just the **¶ button**.

If you push in that button (by clicking it), the screen will show a ¶ symbol at the end of each paragraph, so you can easily tell where each paragraph ends. The screen will also show a dot (·) wherever you pressed the SPACE bar and show a right-arrow (→) wherever you pressed the TAB key, so you easily tell how many times you pressed those keys.

For example, if you typed "I love you" correctly, the screen will show "I·love·you". If you see "I·love···you" instead, you know you accidentally pressed the SPACE bar three times after "love" instead of just once, so you should delete the two extra spaces (by moving there and then pressing the DELETE key twice).

When you finish examining the ¶ symbols and dots and right-arrows, and you're sure you've put just one space between each pair of words, here's how to make those special symbols vanish: pop the ¶ button back out (by clicking it again).

The f problem When you're using Windows, the computer's screen has difficulty showing you the letter "f" correctly. When you type an "f" by using the normal font (10-point Times New Roman), the screen shows too little space after the "f".

For example, if you try typing "fM", the screen shows "fM". If you try typing "f" then a space then "M", the screen shows "f M", which looks as if you hadn't typed a space after the "f". If you try typing "of Mary", the screen shows "of Mary", which looks as if you hadn't typed a space after the "of".

Although the screen looks wrong, what you see on *paper* might look better (depending on which printer you're using).

To discover how many times you pressed the SPACE bar, press in the ¶ button, and notice how many dots appear. Make sure just one dot appears after each word.

Some conservative Americans have trouble handling dirty words that begin with "f". Notice that Windows has the opposite problem: it has trouble showing words that *end* in "f".

I hope somebody at Microsoft reads this book and fixes the f problem soon!

Cut and Paste

Here's another way to move a phrase to a new location.

Select the phrase (by dragging across it with the mouse, so the phrase turns black). Click the **Cut button** (which looks like a pair of scissors). The phrase will vanish from its original location.

Then click the new location where you want the phrase to reappear, and click the **Paste button** (which looks like a clipboard). The phrase will appear there.

Ctrl key Here are shortcuts:

| Instead of clicking the **Cut** button, you can press **Ctrl with X** (which means "X it out"). |
| Instead of clicking the **Paste** button, you can press **Ctrl with V** (which stands for "Velcro"). |

Copy

Here's another way to copy a phrase, so the phrase appears in your document *twice*.

Select the phrase (by dragging across it with the mouse, so the phrase turns black). Click the **Copy button**. Then click where you want the copy of the phrase to appear, and click the **Paste button**. The copy will appear there, so the phrase will be in your document *twice*.

If you want the phrase to appear in your document a *third* time, click where you want that additional copy to appear, then click the Paste button again. If you want the phrase to appear in your document a *fourth* time, click where you want that additional copy, then click the Paste button again.

Here's a shortcut: instead of clicking the Copy button, you can press Ctrl with C.

Format Painter

Suppose one part of your document looks pretty, and one part looks ugly. Here's how to make the ugly part look as pretty as the pretty part:

> Drag across the pretty part, so you've selected it and it's turned black. Click the **Format Painter button**.
>
> Then drag across the ugly part. The computer will make the ugly part look as pretty as the pretty part. For example, the ugly part will have the same font and font size as the pretty part; it will be underlined, boldfaced, and italicized the same way as the pretty part; and if the pretty part was big enough to include a complete paragraph, the ugly part's paragraphs will be aligned the same way as the pretty part.
>
> If you do the procedure incorrectly and wish you *hadn't* pressed the Format Painter button, just click the Undo button, which makes the document return to its previous appearance.

If one part of your document looks pretty, here's how to make *several* other parts look as pretty:

> Drag across the pretty part, so you've selected it and it's turned black. *Double*-click the Format Painter button.
>
> Drag across the first ugly part; the computer will make it look pretty. Then drag across the second ugly part; the computer will make it look pretty. Drag across each additional ugly part; the computer will make each look pretty.
>
> When all the ugly parts have turned pretty, pop the Format Painter button back out (by clicking it again).

Print Preview

If you're wondering what a page will look like but don't want to waste a sheet of paper to find out, click the **Print Preview button**. The computer will show you a mock-up of what the entire page will look like: you'll see the entire page, shrunk to fit on the screen.

Since the entire page is shrunk to fit on the screen, the page and its characters look too tiny for you to read the words easily, but you'll be able to see the page's overall appearance: how much of the page is filled up, which parts of the page are blank, and whether the info on the page is centered.

Wouldn't you like to ride in an airplane, fly high above your house, and see an aerial view of your house and neighborhood, so all the people look like tiny specs, and you see — in one amazing view — the overall layout of your house and yard and neighborhood and city? Wouldn't you be thrilled? Clicking the Print Preview button gives you that same thrill: you see an aerial view of the page you were typing, as if you were flying over it in an airplane: you see the layout of your entire page in one amazing view, and the characters on it look like tiny specs.

While you're admiring the view, the word "Close" appears at the screen's top center. When you finish admiring the view, click the word "Close".

Zoom

Look at the **Zoom box**. (Versions 6&7 calls it the **Zoom Control box**.) In that box, you normally see the number 100%. That means the computer's screen is showing you the actual size of what will appear on paper.

To the right of the Zoom box, you see a down-arrow. Click it. Version 2000 shows you this **Zoom menu**:

```
500%
200%
150%
100%
75%
50%
25%
10%
Page Width
Text Width
Whole Page
Two Pages
```

(Versions 6&7&97 omit "Text Width". Versions 6&7 omit "500%".)

For example, if you click **200%**, the computer makes the screen's characters be twice as high and twice as wide as normal, so you can read them even if you're sitting far away from the screen or you have poor vision. It's like looking at the document through a magnifying glass: the document looks enlarged, so you can see the details of each word and character more clearly; but not as many words and characters fit on the screen. Use the arrow keys to see different parts of the page.

Clicking 200% enlarges just what you see on the *screen*: it does *not* enlarge what appears on paper.

Try it! Try clicking 200%!

When you finish admiring that view, make the screen return to normal, by choosing **100%** from the Zoom menu.

If you click **Whole Page** instead of 200%, the computer does just the opposite: the computer makes the screen's characters be very tiny, so the whole page fits on the screen — as if you were doing a print preview.

A nice choice is **Page Width**. It makes the screen's characters be as big as possible, but still small enough so that you can see the left and right edges of the paper.

My favorite choice is **Text Width** (available just in version 2000). It makes the screen's characters be as big as possible (even bigger than Page Width), but still small enough so that you can see the first and last word of each line.

Spelling and Grammar

If you click in the middle of the document's first word and then click the **Spelling and Grammar** button (which versions 6 & 7 called the "Spelling" button), the computer will scan through your document for misspelled words and accidentally repeatedly words. (Versions 97&2000 will also find words that are grammatically incorrect.)

In version 7, the computer will stop at the first word having a red squiggle underneath. In versions 97&2000, the computer will stop at the first word having a red or green squiggle underneath. (I explained squiggles on page 164.) In version 6, the computer will stop at the first misspelled word or accidentally repeated word.

When the computer stops at a strange word that seems wrong, the computer shows a list of suggestions. If you like one of the suggestions, double-click it. If you *don't* like any of the computer's suggestions, either click "Ignore" (which makes the computer leave the strange word unedited) or else edit the strange word and then click "Change".

When the computer finishes checking the entire document, here's what happens:

> **Versions 6&7** make the computer say "The spelling check is complete".
>
> **Version 97** makes the computer say "The spelling and grammar check is complete".
>
> **Version 2000** makes the computer say "Readability statistics" and tell you how long your document is, how long your average word & sentence & paragraph are, and how hard your document is to read, by revealing your document's **Flesch Reading-Ease Score** (100 is best, 60 is typical) and your document's **Flesch-Kincaid Grade Level** (0 is best, 8 is typical, which means the average 8th-grade kid can barely understand it). Press ENTER.

Columns

In a newspaper, text is printed in many narrow **columns**. In a business letter, text is printed in a single wide column.

The computer assumes you want a single wide column. Here's how to tell the computer you want many narrow columns....

Click the **Columns button**. You'll see a tiny picture of a newspaper page that has several columns. Point at that picture's leftmost column, and drag to the right, until the number of columns you want turns blue.

For example, if you want 3 columns, drag to the right until 3 columns turn blue. If you want 6 columns, hold down the mouse's left button and drag to the right until 4 columns, then 5 columns, then finally 6 columns turn blue.

When you take your finger off the mouse's button, your entire document changes, so it has as many columns as you requested. The gap between each pair of columns is a half-inch.

Column break After you've finished typing a paragraph (and pressed ENTER), try this experiment: while holding down the Ctrl and SHIFT keys, press ENTER again. That creates a **column break**: it makes the next paragraph be at the top of the next column.

If you change your mind, here's how to remove the column break: click at the beginning of the paragraph you've put at the top of a column; then press the BACKSPACE key.

Return to 1 column If you change your mind and want just 1 column, click the Columns button again, so you see the tiny picture of a newspaper page again. Click that picture's left column.

Table buttons

In the middle of your document, here's how to type a table of numbers.

Click where you want the table to appear.

Click the **Insert Table button**. You see a tiny picture of a table that has 4 rows and 5 columns. Altogether, it contains 20 cells (since 4 times 5 is 20).

Point at that table's top left cell, and drag down and to the right, until the number of rows and columns you want turns blue.

For example, **if you want just 3 rows and 4 columns, drag down and to the right until 3 rows and 4 columns turn blue**, so you see 12 blue cells altogether.

When you take your finger off the mouse's button, you'll see the table you requested.

Then just fill in the cells, with whatever numbers and words you wish. To move from cell to cell, click with the mouse, or press the TAB key (which moves right to the next cell), or press SHIFT with TAB (which moves left to the previous cell), or press the arrow keys repeatedly.

In a cell, you can type a number, word, sentence, or even an entire paragraph! If you start typing a paragraph in a cell, the computer will automatically make the cell and its row taller, so the entire paragraph will fit in the cell. You can even type *several* paragraphs in a single cell: just press the ENTER key at the end of each paragraph. If you want to indent the first line of one of those paragraphs, press the SPACE bar several times or press Ctrl with TAB.

Gridlines On the screen, each cell is a rectangle made of 4 lines. Those lines are called the **gridlines**.

> In **versions 97&2000**, the gridlines are normal, solid lines, and they print okay on paper.
>
> In **versions 6&7**, the gridlines are dotted. When you print the table onto paper, the paper will *not* show those dotted gridlines. Those gridlines appear just on the screen, not on paper.

Extra rows Here's how to create an extra row at the bottom of the table: click in the table's bottom right cell, then press the TAB key.

Here's how to insert an extra row into the *middle* of the table: click in the row that's underneath where you want the extra row to appear, then click the Insert Table button again (which is now called the **Insert Rows button**).

Column widths The computer assumes you want the table's columns to all be the same width. But you can change that assumption!

For example, here's how to adjust the width of the table's left column (column 1). Move the mouse until its pointer is on the vertical gridline that separates column 1 from column 2, and the pointer's shape turns into this symbol: ←∥→. Then drag the vertical gridline to the right (to make the column wider) or left (to make the column narrower).

If you make a column wider, the computer makes room for it by shrinking the next column. (Versions 6&7 shrink the next column and all later columns also.)

If you make a column narrower, the computer compensates by expanding the next column. (Versions 6&7 expand the next column and all later columns also.)

If you want to fine-tune the widths of *all* columns, work from left to right: adjust the width of column 1 (by dragging the gridline that separates it from column 2), then adjust the width of column 2 (by dragging the gridline that separates it from column 3), then adjust the width of column 3 (by dragging the gridline that separates it from column 4), etc.

Numbers If a column contains mostly numbers, here's how to make that column look prettier, so the numbers are aligned properly.

> Move the mouse until its pointer is at the *very top* of the column and is centered on the gridline above the column, so the pointer's shape turns into this symbol: ↓. Then click. The entire column turns black.
>
> Push in the Align Right button (on the formatting toolbar). That makes all cells in that column be aligned right, so the numbers are aligned properly.

Table AutoFormat When you've finished typing numbers and words into all the cells, try this trick:

> Click in the middle of the table. From the **Table menu**, choose **Table AutoFormat**. Then press ENTER.

That makes the computer analyze all your columns and improve their widths. The computer will make each column become just wide enough to hold the data in it.

The computer will also underline the headings atop the columns.

If you like what the computer did to your table, great! Go ahead and edit the table further!

If you *don't* like what the computer did, click the Undo button, which makes the table return to its previous appearance.

Below the table When you've finished editing the table, here's how to put paragraphs below it.

Click below the table by using the mouse, or go below the table by pressing the down-arrow key several times. Then type the paragraphs you want below the table.

Delete To delete a row, column, or the entire table, click in the middle of what you want to delete then do this....

> **Version 2000:** from the **Table menu**, choose **Delete**. Click **Rows** (if you want to delete a row) or **Columns** (if you want to delete a column) or **Table** (if you want to delete the entire table.)
>
> **Versions 6&7&97:** from the **Table menu**, choose **Select Row** (if you want to delete a row) or **Select Column** (if you want to delete a column) or **Select Table** (if you want to delete the entire table). The row, column, or table you selected turns black. Next, from the Table menu, choose **Delete**.

Customized tables (just in versions 97&2000)

Versions 97&2000 include a **Tables and Borders button**. It lets you easily create tables that have customized shapes. Here's how to use it:

> To create a customized table, click the **Tables and Borders button**. (instead of the Insert Table button). You'll see a **Tables and Borders window**.
>
> Where do you want the table to be in your document? **Put the mouse pointer where you want the table's top left corner to be, and drag to where you want the table's opposite corner.** (While dragging, hold down the mouse's left button.) You'll see a rectangle, which is your table.
>
> Inside the rectangle, make a grid of rows and columns by drawing horizontal and vertical gridlines. **To draw a gridline, put the mouse pointer where you want the line to begin, and drag to where you want the line to end.**
>
> If you make a mistake, click the **Eraser button** (which is the second button in the Tables and Borders window), then drag along the line you want to erase. While you're dragging, the computer marks the line red; when you finish dragging (and take your hand off the mouse button), the line disappears. When you finish using the Eraser button, click the Draw Table button (which is the first button in the Tables and Borders window).
>
> When you finish using the Tables and Borders window, close it (by clicking its X button).

Office Assistant

If you have a popular question about using Microsoft Word, you can make the computer answer it.

If you're using version 97 or 2000, do this:

> Click the **Office Assistant** button (which version 2000 calls the **Microsoft Word Help** button) or press the F1 key. You'll see the Office Assistant: a cute cartoon character named **Clippit**, who's an animated paper clip with eyes.
>
> (Is Clippit male or female? Clippit's sex is a mystery. If you want to have fun with Clippit's body, try this: right-click Clippit and then click Animate, which makes Clippit's body perform a random trick.)
>
> Type your question about how to use Microsoft Word, then press ENTER. (If the computer says "I don't know what you mean", rephrase your question by using words the computer is more likely to understand.)
>
> The computer will show you a list of topics that relate to your question. (If the list is too long to fit in the box, click **See More** to see the rest of the list.)
>
> Click the topic that interests you, then click any other buttons that interest you. The computer will tutor you in whatever topics you request.
>
> When you finish using Office Assistant, close each help window (by clicking its X button).

If you're using version 7, the Office Assistant button is missing, so do this instead:

> From the Help menu, choose "Answer Wizard".
>
> Type your question about how to use Microsoft Word, then press ENTER. (If the computer says "Sorry, but I don't know what you mean", press ENTER and then rephrase your question by using words the computer is more likely to understand.)
>
> The computer will show you a list of topics that relate to your question. Double-click the topic that interests you. Then click any other buttons that interest you. The computer will tutor you in whatever topics you request.
>
> When you finish using that help, close any help window (by clicking its X button).

If you're using version 6, the Office Assistant button is missing, so do this instead:

> From the Help menu, choose "Search for Help on".
>
> What topic is your question about? Type the word that best describes the topic. At the end of that word, press ENTER.
>
> The computer will show you an alphabetical list of topics that begin with the same letters as what you typed. (To see more of that list, press down-arrow, up-arrow, PAGE DOWN, or PAGE UP keys.) Double-click the topic that interests you.
>
> The computer will show you a list of subtopics. Double-click the subtopic that interests you. Then click any green underlined topic that interests you.
>
> When you finish using that help, close each help window (by double-clicking its control box).

Near the screen's top, you see this **menu bar**:

```
File Edit View Insert Format Tools Table Window Help
```

Here's how to use it.

File menu

If you click the word File, you see the **File menu**, whose main choices are:

```
Open
Close

Save
Save As

Page Setup
Print Preview
Print

Properties

Exit
```

(Version 6 says "Summary Info" instead of "Properties".)

Open Choosing **Open** has the same effect as clicking the **Open button**, which I explained on page 170.

Close When you finish working on a document and want to work on a different document instead, choose **Close**, which I explained on page 170.

Save Choosing **Save** has the same effect as clicking the **Save button**, which I explained on page 170.

Save As Suppose you've already saved a document then edited it some more, but you're not sure you like the new editing. Try this experiment:

> Choose **Save As**, then invent (and type) a new name for the document. At the end of the new name, press ENTER.
> Then the computer will copy the new, edited version of the document onto the hard disk. That new, edited version will have the new name you invented.
> The old original version of the document will be on the disk also and keep its old original name. The disk will contain *both* versions of the document.

Page Setup Normally, the computer makes every page's top and bottom margins each be 1 inch tall, and makes every page's left and right margins each be 1¼ inches wide. To change those margin, choose **Page Setup**, then do this:

> Click **Margins**. Press the TAB key.
> Type how many inches tall you want the top margin.   Press TAB.
> Type how many inches tall you want the bottom margin.   Press TAB.
> Type how many inches wide you want the left margin.   Press TAB.
> Type how many inches wide you want the right margin.   Press ENTER.

Print Preview Choosing **Print Preview** has the same effect as clicking the **Print Preview button**, which I explained on page 171.

Print If you choose **Print** from the File menu (or press Ctrl with P), the computer will ask how you'd like to print onto paper.

> If you want to print more than 1 copy, type the number of copies.
> If you want to print just the page you were working on, click the Current page button.
> If you want to print just pages 1, 3, and 5 through 8, click the Pages button, then type "1,3,5-8".
> If you selected (blackened) a phrase in your document and want to print just that phrase, click the Selection button.
> If you own more than 1 printer, do this for versions 7&97&2000: click the down-arrow next to the Printer Name box , then choose which printer you want to use (by clicking it). For version 6, do this instead: click the Printer button, double-click which printer you want to use, then press ENTER.

Then press ENTER. The printer will print what you desired!

Properties If you choose **Properties** and then click **Statistics**, the computer will tell you how long the document is: how many pages, paragraphs, lines, words, and characters it contains. (Version 6 says "Summary Info" instead of "Properties.)

The computer will also reveal....

> when created: when you first started creating the document, long ago
> when modified: when you last saved the document, copied it from screen to disk
> when accessed: when you last opened the document, copied it from disk to screen
> when printed: when you last printed the document onto paper

(Version 6 doesn't say when accessed.)

The computer will also reveal the total number of minutes and hours you've spent fiddling with this document (so your boss can complain about how much time you've wasted on it).

When you finish reading those statistics, press ENTER. (For version 6, then press ENTER a second time.)

Exit When you finish using Microsoft Word, choose **Exit**, which I explained on page 170.

Edit menu

If you click the word Edit, you see the **Edit menu**, whose main choices are:

```
Undo

Cut
Copy
Paste

Clear
Select All

Find
Replace
Go To
```

Of those choices, the first four imitate buttons:

> Choosing **Undo** is like clicking the **Undo button** (explained on page 171).
> Choosing **Cut**   is like clicking the **Cut   button** (explained on page 171).
> Choosing **Copy** is like clicking the **Copy   button** (explained on page 171).
> Choosing **Paste** is like clicking the **Paste button** (explained on page 171).

The next two imitate your keyboard:

> Choosing **Clear** is like pressing the **DELETE key** (explained on page 169).
> Choosing **Select All** is like pressing the **A key with Ctrl** (page 169).

Find Here's how to make the computer search through your document to find whether you've used the word "love":

> Click where you want the search to begin. (For example, if you want the search to begin at the document's beginning, click in the middle of the document's first word.) Choose **Find** from the Edit menu (or press Ctrl with F). Type the word you want to find ("love"), and press ENTER.
> The computer will search for "love". If the computer finds a "love" in your document, it will highlight that "love" so it turns black. If you want to find the next "love" in your document, press ENTER; if you do *not* want to search for more "love", press the Esc key instead.
> In versions 97&2000, the previous-page and next-page arrows (at the screen's bottom right corner) turn blue. Afterwards, clicking them makes the computer find the previous or next "love" (instead of the previous or next page).

Suppose you've written a history of America and want to find the part where you started talking about Lincoln. If you forget what page that was, no problem! Just put the cursor at the beginning of the document, choose **Find** from the Edit menu, type "Lincoln", and press ENTER.

Replace

You can search for a word and replace it with a different word. For example, here's how to change each "love" in your document to "idolize":

> Choose **Replace**. Type the old word you want to replace ("love"), then press the TAB key, then type the new word you want instead ("idolize"), then click the Replace All button. That makes the computer change each "love" to "idolize". Then press the Esc key twice.

The computer preserves capitalization. For example, if the document said —

> I love you. Love you! LOVE YOU! I want to kiss your glove!

the computer changes it to:

> I idolize you. Idolize you! IDOLIZE YOU! I want to kiss your gidolize!

Notice that when told to change "love" to "idolize", the computer unfortunately also changes "glove" to "gidolize".

> In versions 97&2000, the previous-page and next-page arrows (at the screen's bottom right corner) turn blue. Clicking them makes the computer find the previous or next "love" (if any).

The Replace command helps you zip through many chores:

> For example, if you write a letter that talks about Fred, then want to write a similar letter about Sue, tell the computer to replace each Fred with Sue.
>
> If you write a book about "How to be a better salesman" and then a feminist tells you to change each "salesman" to "salesperson", tell the computer to replace each "salesman".
>
> If you're writing a long ad that mentions "Calvin Klein's Hot New Flaming Pink Day-Glo Pajamas" repeatedly, and you're too lazy to type that long phrase so often, just type the abbreviation "Calnew". When you've finished typing the document, tell the computer to replace each "Calnew" with the long phrase it stands for.

Go To

When you've typed a document that's several pages long, here's the traditional way to move to page 2:

> Choose **Go To** from the Edit menu (or press Ctrl with G).
>
> Make sure the computer says "Enter page number".
> (If the computer doesn't say that yet, click **Page** and then press the TAB key.)
>
> Type your desired page number (which is 2), then press ENTER.
>
> You'll see page 2 on the screen.
>
> Press the Esc key.

That traditional way works in all versions. If you're lucky enough to be using version 7 or 97, try this faster way to move to page 2:

> Along the screen's right edge, you see a scroll-up arrow (▲) and a scroll-down-arrow (▼). Between them, you see a little box, called the **scroll box**.
> Using the mouse, point at the scroll box, and hold down the mouse's left button. While you hold down the button, you'll see the current page number.
> Drag the scroll box up or down, until the page number changes to the number you want: 2.

View menu

If you click the word View, you see the **View menu**, whose main choices are:

> Normal
> Page Layout
>
> Toolbars
> Ruler
>
> Header and Footer
>
> Full Screen

(Version 2000 says "Print Layout" instead of "Page Layout".)

Normal versus Page Layout

The View menu's most popular choices are **Normal** and **Page Layout** (which version 2000 calls "Print Layout"). You should use Page Layout most of the time, because it shows you accurately what will appear on paper. If you choose **Normal** instead, here's what happens:

> **In Normal view, the screen will show just a crude approximation of what will appear on paper.** The computer won't bother to show what's in the margins (such as page numbers), won't bother to show footnotes, won't bother to show graphics, and won't bother to show newspaper columns side-by-side (instead it will show the second column *under* the first column, and will show the third column *under* the second column). Since the computer takes those shortcuts, the computer displays the page fast — unlike Page Layout view, which makes the computer be fussily accurate about what appears on the screen.
>
> If you bought a computer that's slow (a 486 instead of a Pentium), Normal view lets the computer pretend to be faster, by letting the computer omit displaying the hard stuff. So **if you're stuck using a slow computer that reacts too slowly to your editing commands, you might like Normal view, which speeds things up** by omitting display details.
>
> Since Normal view displays fewer items on the screen, it makes more of the screen available for your important words and can display them bigger, so you can read them more easily. So **if you're stuck using a small screen that's hard to read, you might like Normal view, which can enlarge your typing** by omitting the margins, rulers, and other details.

Toolbars

If you choose **Toolbars**, version 2000 shows you this list of toolbars:

> Standard
> Formatting
> AutoText
> Clipboard
> Control Toolbox
> Database
> Drawing
> Forms
> Frames
> Picture
> Reviewing
> Tables and Borders
> Visual BASIC
> Web
> Web Tools
> WordArt

(In versions 6&7&97, the list is shorter.)

In the list, **"Standard" and "Formatting" should have check marks in front of them.** (In versions 7&97&2000, each check mark is ✔; in version 6, each check mark is ✗.) Those check marks make the standard toolbar and formatting toolbar appear on your screen. If those check marks are missing, those toolbars disappear.

To make a check mark disappear, click it. To make a check mark appear, click where you want it to appear. (In version 6&7, press ENTER afterwards.)

Ruler

In the View menu, the Ruler choice should have a check mark in front of it. That makes a horizontal ruler appear across the screen. The ruler is numbered 1", 2", 3", 4", 5", etc. If you're in Page Layout view, it also makes a vertical ruler appear up and down the screen's left edge. If the Ruler choice does *not* have a check mark, the rulers disappear. To make the check mark appear or disappear, choose **Ruler** from the View menu.

Header and Footer

Normally, the top inch of each page is blank, to form the top margin. Anything you scribble in that margin is called a **header**.

For example, suppose you're writing a top-secret memo and want to scribble this note in the top margin of every page:

> Reminder! The info in this memo is TOP SECRET!

Here's how to do it….

Choose **Header and Footer**. Type your header:

Reminder! The info in this memo is TOP SECRET!

Then click the word "Close". The computer will put your header at the top of each page of your document.

When you print the document onto **paper**, your header is printed in **black**.
While you're using **Page Layout view**, your header appears on the screen in **gray** instead of black.
While you're using **Normal view**, your header usually **disappears** from the screen, since Normal view doesn't show you the margins. To see your header, switch to Page Layout view (by choosing Page Layout from the View menu), or choose "Header and Footer" again from the View menu.

If you want to edit the header, choose "Header and Footer" again from the View menu, then edit the header however you wish, then click the word "Close" again.

Instead of writing a header about being "TOP SECRET", here are four other headers you might enjoy using:

Please do not copy! It's copyrighted by starving author!
ACHTUNG! To keep your job, reply to this memo by Friday!
SALE! To order any of these items, call our 800 number!
I love you!!! I love you!!! I love you!!!

Here's a way **to make the computer print the page number at the top of each page:**

Choose **Header and Footer**. Click the **Insert Page Number** button. That makes the computer put a "1" at the top of page 1, a "2" at the top of page 2, etc. Then click the word "Close".

Let's get fancier! Let's make the computer print this at the top of page 1 —

This is page 1 of the Great American Novel

and print this at the top of page 2 —

This is page 2 of the Great American Novel

and print this at the top of page 3 —

This is page 3 of the Great American Novel

etc. Here's how:

Choose **Header and Footer** from the View menu. Type the header's beginning words: "This is page". After the word "page", press the SPACE bar. Click the **Insert Page Number** button. (Versions 6&7 call it the "Page Numbers" button.) That makes the computer automatically type a "1" on page 1, a "2" on page 2, etc. Press the SPACE bar (to make the computer leave a blank space after the page number). Type the header's ending words: "of the Great American Novel". Click the word "Close".

Here's how **to print in the bottom margin (instead of the top margin):**

Choose **Header and Footer** from the View menu. If the computer shows you a space labeled "header", switch to "footer" by clicking the **Switch Between Header and Footer** button.   Type the footer (whatever you want in the bottom margin). Then click the word "Close".

Full Screen Usually, just *part* of the screen shows your document; the rest of the screen shows the toolbars, rulers, menus, Start button, clock, and other doodads.

If you choose **Full Screen**, the computer devotes the *entire* screen to displaying your document, by making the doodads disappear. Yes, the toolbars, rulers, menus, Start button, clock, and all other doodads disappear. Instead of seeing doodads, you see more of your document.

When you finish admiring the full-screen view, press the ESCAPE key (which says "Esc" on it). Then all the doodads reappear, including the toolbars, rulers, menus, Start button, clock, etc.

Insert menu

If you click the word Insert, you see the **Insert menu**, whose main choices are:

Page Numbers Date and Time Symbol Footnote Text Box File Bookmark

(Versions 6 & 7 lack "Bookmark" and say "Frame" instead of "Text Box".)

Page Numbers To print page numbers on all the pages *easily*, choose **Page Numbers**, then press ENTER. That makes the computer put the page number on each page's bottom right corner, in the bottom margin, in the part of the page called the **footer**. (Versions 97&2000 will automatically switch you to Page Layout view.)

When you print the document onto **paper**, the page numbers will be printed in **black**.
While you're using **Page Layout view**, the page numbers will appear on the screen in **gray** instead of black.
While you're using **Normal view**, you **won't see** the page numbers, since Normal view doesn't show you the margins.

Date and Time To type the date or time, choose **Date and Time**. The computer will show a list of formats, like this:

12/27/99 Monday, December 27, 1999 December 27, 1999 12/27/1999 1999-12-27 27-Dec-99 12.27.99 Dec. 27, 99 27 December, 1999 December 99 Dec-99 12/27/99 11:57 PM 12/27/99 11:57:20 PM 11:57 PM 11:57:20 PM 23:57 23:57:20

(Version 2000 shows you that full list. Versions 6&7 show a shorter list and say "December, 99" instead of "December 99". Version 97 shows you that full list but says "December, 99" instead of "December 99" and requires you to click the down-arrow repeatedly to see the list's end.)

Click the format you want. Press ENTER. The computer will type the date or time in the format you requested.

In that procedure, just before you press ENTER, you might wish to put a check mark in the **Update Automatically** box. (Version 6 calls it the "Insert as Field" box.) Here's how that box works:

Suppose you type a document on Monday, but you print the document the next day (Tuesday). Which date will the computer print on paper? The computer will print the date that the document was typed (Monday), unless you put a check mark in the Update Automatically box, which makes the computer print the "date printed" (Tuesday).   If you put a check mark in the Updated Automatically box, the computer will automatically update the date & time whenever the document is printed or print-previewed or opened.

Symbol To type a special symbol, choose **Symbol**. You'll see the **Symbol window**. In that window, you can click either the **Symbols** tab or the **Special Characters** tab.

If you click the **Special Characters** tab, version 97 will show you this list of special characters:

— Em Dash	(a dash that's slightly wider than an M; it's exactly as wide as the font's point-size height)
– En Dash	(a dash that's slightly narrower than an N; it's exactly half as wide as an Em Dash)
- Nonbreaking Hyphen	(a hyphen, between words that must appear on the same line as each other)
- Optional Hyphen	(a hyphen, visible just when the word it's in is too long to fit on a line)
Em Space	(a blank space that's slightly wider than an M; it's as wide as the font's point-size height)
En Space	(a blank space that's slightly narrower than an N; it's exactly half as wide as an Em Space)
Nonbreaking Space	(a space between words that must appear on the same line as each other)
© Copyright	
® Registered	
™ Trademark	
§ Section	
¶ Paragraph	
… Ellipsis	
' Single Opening Quote	
' Single Closing Quote	
" Double Opening Quote	
" Double Closing Quote	

(To see the entire list, click the list's down-arrow or up-arrow repeatedly. Versions 6&7 lack "Section" and "Paragraph". Version 2000 adds "¼ Em Space", "No-Width Optional Break", and "No-Width Non-Break".)

If you click the **Symbols** tab instead, and then click the **Font** box's down-arrow, the computer will show you this list of fonts:

```
(normal text)
Marlett
Symbol
Wingdings
```

(If your computer is fancy, it might show you extra fonts also. Version 6 usually lacks "Marlett", which requires Windows 95 or 98.)

Click one of those fonts.

For example, if you click "(normal text)" while you've been using Times New Roman, you'll see these Times New Roman characters:

```
! " # $ % & ' ( ) * + , - . / 0 1 2 3 4 5 6 7 8 9 : ; <
= > ? @ A B C D E F G H I J K L M N O P Q R S T U V W X
Y Z [ \ ] ^ _ ` a b c d e f g h i j k l m n o p q r s t
u v w x y z { | } ~ ¡ ¢ £ ¤ ¥ ¦ § ¨ © ª « ¬ - ® ¯ ° ± ²
³ ´ µ ¶ · , ¹ º » ¼ ½ ¾ ¿ À Á Â Ã Ä Å Æ Ç È É Ê Ë Ì Í Î
Ï Ð Ñ Ò Ó Ô Õ Ö × Ø Ù Ú Û Ü Ý Þ ß à á â ã ä å æ ç è é ê
ë ì í î ï ð ñ ò ó ô õ ö ÷ ø ù ú û ü ý þ ÿ Œ œ Š š Ÿ ƒ
~ ‿ ⁀ ' ' , " " „ † ‡ • … ‰ ‹ › ™ ·
```

(Versions 6 & 7 arrange those characters in a different order.)

If you click "Marlett" instead, you'll see these Windows 95 & 98 characters:

If you click "Symbol" instead, you'll see these math & Greek characters:

```
! ∀ # ∃ % & ∋ ( ) * + , − . / 0 1 2 3 4 5 6 7 8 9 : ;
< = > ? ≅ Α Β Χ Δ Ε Φ Γ Η Ι ϑ Κ Λ Μ Ν Ο Π Θ Ρ Σ Τ Υ ς Ω
Ξ Ψ Ζ [ ∴ ] ⊥ _ ‾ α β χ δ ε φ γ η ι φ κ λ μ ν ο π θ ρ σ
τ υ ϖ ω ξ ψ ζ { | } ~
                    ϒ ′ ≤ / ∞ ƒ ♣ ♦ ♥ ♠ ↔
← ↑ → ↓ ° ± ″ ≥ × ∝ ∂ • ÷ ≠ ≡ ≈ … | — ⌐ ℵ ℑ ℜ ℘ ⊗ ⊕ ∅
∩ ∪ ⊃ ⊇ ⊄ ⊂ ⊆ ∈ ∉ ∠ ∇ ® © ™ ∏ √ · ¬ ∧ ∨ ⇔ ⇐ ⇑ ⇒ ⇓ ◊ ⟨ ® ©
™ ∑ ⎛ ⎜ ⎝ ⎡ ⎢ ⎣ ⎧ ⎨ ⎩ ⎮ ⌠ ⎲ ⌡ ⟩ ∫ ⌠ ⎞ ⎟ ⎠ ⎤ ⎥ ⎦ ⎫ ⎬ ⎭
```

If you click "Wingdings" instead, you'll see these pictorial characters:

Whenever you see a character that you like, double-click it. That makes the computer put the character into your document. Then double-click any other characters you like.

When you finish using the Symbol window, make it disappear by clicking the button that says "Close" on it.

Footnote Suppose you're writing a religious pamphlet in which you want to say "Read it in the Bible tonight!" Suppose you want to add a footnote saying "written by God", so the main text looks like this —

Read it in the Bible¹ tonight!

and the page's bottom contains this footnote:

¹ Written by God.

Here's how to do it all.…

Type "Read it in the Bible". Choose **Footnote**. Make sure the Footnote button has a dot in it (by clicking it). Press ENTER. Type the footnote ("Written by God."). Go back to the main text, where you left off, by using one of these methods:

Method 1: double-click the footnote's number; if you're using Page Layout view, press the right-arrow key afterwards.
Method 2 (just if you're using Normal view): click the button that says "Close" on it.
Method 3 (just if using Page Layout view): climb back up to the main text (by using the keyboard's up-arrow key), then go right to where you left off typing (by using the END key).

The computer will automatically number the footnote: it will automatically type ¹ after "Bible" and type ¹ before "Written by God." If your document contains more footnotes, the computer will automatically number them ², ³, ⁴, etc. (Those numbers are easy to read on paper. On the screen, the numbers are easier to read while the ¶ button is popped out, instead of in.)

The computer will put the footnotes at the bottom of the page. If the page is divided into newspaper columns, the computer will put each footnote at the bottom of the column it refers to.

The computer will put a 2-inch horizontal line above the footnotes to separate them from the main text.

Your printer will print the footnotes accurately onto paper. You'll see the footnotes on your screen accurately while you're doing a print preview, or while you're using Page Layout view. (To see the footnotes on your screen while using Normal view, choose Footnotes from the View menu.)

If you insert extra footnotes, the computer will automatically renumber the other footnotes, so the first footnote appearing in your document will be numbered [1], the second footnote will be numbered [2], etc.

Here's the easiest way to delete a footnote:

Version 97&2000: click the left edge of the footnote's number in the main text; then press the DELETE key twice.

Versions 6&7: double-click the left edge of the footnote's number in the main text, then press the DELETE key (which deletes the footnote number and the space after it), then press the SPACE bar (which puts the space back in).

To print footnotes, the computer normally uses 10-point Times Roman. **To make the footnotes look more professional, make them be 8-point** instead, which is smaller. Here's how:

Click in the middle of a footnote. Choose **Style** from the Format menu. In the Styles box, click **Footnote Text**. Click **Modify**, then **Format**, then **Font**, then **8** (which is in the Size menu). Press ENTER three times.

That will make all footnotes in this document be 8-point. Other documents will be unaffected.

Text Box
Here's how to draw a box wherever you wish, *anywhere* on the page (even in the margins!) and put words into it:

In versions 97&2000, choose **Text Box** from the Insert menu.
in versions 6&7, choose **Frame** from the Insert menu.

Where do you want the box? Put the mouse pointer where you want the box's top left corner to be, and drag to where you want the box's opposite corner. The box will appear.

Type whatever words or paragraphs you want in the box.

Here's how to **move the box** to a different place on the page:

Point at one of the box's sides. (Stay away from any tiny squares you see next to the sides). When you do that successfully, the mouse pointer becomes a cross with arrowheads pointing in all four directions.

Then move the box by dragging the side wherever you wish.

Here's how to **adjust the box's size**:

For versions 97&2000, click in the box.
For versions 6&7, click one of the box's sides.

At the box's bottom right corner, you see a tiny square. Put the mouse pointer there. Make sure the middle of the mouse pointer is in the middle of that tiny square. When you do that successfully, the mouse pointer becomes a diagonal arrow with two arrowheads.

Then adjust the box's size by dragging that tiny square wherever you wish.

If you move the box to a part of the page that already contains words, what happens to those words? Versions 6 & 7 make those words move out of the box's way. To make version 2000 **move words out of the box's way**, do this:

Double-click one of the box's sides.
Click **Layout**.
Click **Square**.
Press ENTER.

To make version 97 **move words out of the box's way**, do this:

Double-click one of the box's sides.
Click **Wrapping**.
Click **Top&bottom**.
Press ENTER.

Here's how to **delete the box**:

Point at one of the box's sides. When you do that successfully, the mouse pointer sprouts 2 or 4 arrowheads.

Click.

Press the keyboard's DELETE key.

File
In the middle of your document, you can insert a secondary document that you saved previously, so you'll produce a combo document including all paragraphs from both documents. Here's how:

Click in the middle of the document you're writing, where you want the secondary document to be inserted.

Choose **File** from the Insert menu.

Double-click the name of the secondary document that you want to insert.

The document on the screen will become longer. If you don't like the result, click the **Undo button**; if you *do* like the result, click the **Save button**.

Bookmark
While you're in the middle of editing a document, suppose you get a sudden urge to switch to a different activity (such as peek at a different part of the document, or play a game, or go to bed, or have sex). Before you switch to that other activity, you can put a **bookmark** in your document, where you were editing. Later, when you want to resume working on the document, you can return to that bookmark and continue editing where you left off.

Here's **how to create a bookmark:**

Decide where in the document you want to put the bookmark. Click there.

Choose **Bookmark**. (It's on version 97&2000's Insert menu, version 6&7's Edit menu.)

Invent a name for your bookmark. Use your nickname, or a simple word such as "mark". The name must be simple: it must begin with a letter; it can contain letters, numbers, and underscores (_); it must *not* contain any spaces or special symbols. Type the name. At the end of the name, click the Add button.

The computer will create a bookmark using that name. (If your document *already* contained a bookmark using that name, that old bookmark will disappear.) Typically, the screen doesn't bother showing you where bookmarks are.

After you've created a bookmark, be safe: click the **Save button** and save the document. Then do whatever else you wish: peek at a different part of the document, or play a game, or shut down the computer and go to bed. When you want **to return to the bookmarked part of your document, do this:**

Make sure the document is on the screen.

Choose **Go To** from the Edit menu (or press Ctrl with G).

Click the word **Bookmark**.

You'll see the name of a bookmark you created. (If you created *several* bookmarks and want to reach a different bookmark that the one named, click the down-arrow next to the name, then click the name of a bookmark you want to reach.)

Press ENTER. The computer will go to the place in the document where you put the bookmark.

Press the Esc key (to make the bookmark-finding window vanish).

If you wish, make the screen show you where the bookmarks are. Here's how:

Choose **Options** from the Tools menu.

Click the **View** tab.

Put a mark in the **Bookmarks** box (by clicking the word "Bookmarks"). In versions 7&97&2000, the mark is ✔; in version 6, the mark is ✗.

Press ENTER.

That makes the screen put the symbol I at each bookmark. That symbol appears just on the screen, not on paper.

Here's **how to delete a bookmark:**

Choose **Bookmark** (on version 97&2000's Insert menu, version 6&7's Edit menu).
Click the name of the bookmark you want to delete.
Click the word "**Delete**".
Press ENTER.

Format menu

If you click the word Format, you see the **Format menu**, whose main choices are:

```
Font
Paragraph
Bullets and Numbering
Borders and Shading

Columns
Tabs
Drop Cap
Change Case

AutoFormat
Style
```

<u>**Font**</u> Here's how to improve the appearance of a phrase on your screen.

Which phrase do you want to improve? Select it (by dragging across it). Then choose **Font** from the Format menu. You see the **Font window**, which has three **tabs**, called **Font**, **Character Spacing**, and **Animation**.

Click the **Font** tab. You see these boxes:

Box	Normal contents	Other popular choices
Font	Times New Roman	Arial, Courier New
Font style	Regular	Bold, Italic, Bold Italic
Size	10	8, 9, 11, 12, 14, 16, 18, 20, 22, 24, 26, 28, 36, 48, 72
Underline	(none)	Single, Double, Thick, Dotted, Dash, Words Only
Color	Auto	Blue, Red, Yellow, Bright Green, Turquoise, Pink

(In version 2000, the "Color" box is split into two boxes, called "Font Color" and "Underline Color".)

For the Underline box or Color box, you must click the box's down-arrow once or twice, to see all choices. For the Font box or Size box, you must click the box's up-arrow and down-arrow repeatedly, to see all popular choices. **For each box, click whatever choice you want.**

In the Underline box, if you choose "Words only", the computer will underline the words but not the spaces between them. In versions 6&7, the Underline box lacks "Thick" and "Dash", and the colors are named differently: "Bright Green" is called just "Green", "Turquoise" is called "Cyan", and "Pink" is called "Magenta".

Below all those boxes, you see a list of these special **Effects** you can choose:

Effect	What the computer will do
All Caps	make the writing be all in capitals, LIKE THIS
Small Caps	make the writing be all in tiny capitals, LIKE THIS
Superscript	make the writing be tiny and raised, ^like this
Subscript	make the writing be tiny and lowered, ₗᵢₖₑ ₜₕᵢₛ
Strikethrough	draw a line through your writing, ~~like this~~
Double Strikethrough	draw *two* lines through your writing
Shadow	make a shadow behind each character, as if in the sun
Outline	show each character's outline, as if on a varsity jacket
Engrave	make the writing look like it's chiseled into stone
Emboss	make the writing look like it sticks out from stone

Click each effect you want, so a check mark appears in the effect's box. Double Strikethrough is just in versions 97&2000. The weird effects (Shadow, Outline, Engrave, and Emboss) are just in versions 97&2000 and work best when the Font Size is big (such as 48 or 72 points).

When you've finished using the Font window, press ENTER. Congratulations! You've learned how to use fonts!

Here's an advanced secret that most computer "experts" don't know:

Suppose you've typed something but it's too wide to fit. For example, suppose you've typed a headline too wide to fit above the main text, or typed a line too wide to fit between the margins, or typed a table entry too wide to fit in the table's column. Here's how to magically make your typing be slightly narrower, so it fits.

Select the phrase you want to narrow (by dragging across it), then choose Font from the Format menu, then click the **Character Spacing** tab. Then you can use three tricks to make the type be narrower.

Scaling trick (just in versions 97&2000): in the **Scale** box (which normally says "100%"), type a smaller number (such as 95%). That makes each character be narrower.

Spacing trick: in the **Spacing By** box (which is normally blank), click the down-arrow key twice (so the screen will say Spacing Condensed By 0.2 pt). That puts less space between the characters, so the characters are shoved closer together.

Kerning trick: put a mark in the **Kerning** box (by clicking the word "Kerning"). In versions 7&97&2000, the mark is ✔ ; in version 6, the mark is ✗. That procedure eliminates wasted space between certain pairs of letters.

After you've filled in those boxes the way you want, press ENTER, which makes the computer obey you.

<u>**Paragraph**</u> To change the way a paragraph is spaced, click in the paragraph, then choose **Paragraph** from the Format menu, then click **Indents and Spacing**.

You'll see a box called **Line spacing**. Normally, that box says "Single". If you want to double-space instead (so the computer puts a blank line under each line you type), click that box's down-arrow, then choose "Double".

You'll see a box called **Before**. Normally, that box says "0 pt". If you want the computer to leave a blank space above the paragraph, put a number bigger than 0 into that box.

If you put 72 into that box, the computer will leave a 1-inch blank space above the paragraph, since 72 points = 1 inch. If you put 36 into that box, the computer will leave a ½-inch blank space above the paragraph, since 36 points = ½ inch.

The most typical number to put into that box is 12, which makes the computer leave a 1/6-inch blank space above the paragraph. To be more subtle, try a number smaller than 12, such as 6.

You'll see a box called **Special**. Normally, that box says "(none)". If you want special indentation, click that box's down-arrow, then choose "First line" (which indents just the paragraph's first line) or choose "Hanging" (which indents every line of the paragraph *except the first line*). If you choose "First line" or "Hanging", the computer will make the indentation be ½-inch (which is 0.5"), unless you put a different decimal in the **Special By** box.

If you want *every* line of the paragraph to be indented ½ inch, put "(none)" in the Special box but put 0.5" (or simply .5) in the **Left** box.

When you finish making the boxes contain the instructions you want, press ENTER.

<u>**Bullets and Numbering**</u> Page 168 said that if you click in the middle of a paragraph and then push in the **Bullets button**, the computer normally puts a simple bullet (the symbol •) at the beginning of the paragraph (and indents the paragraph).

If you don't like the symbol •, pick a different symbol instead. Here's how….

Choose **Bullets and Numbering** from the Format menu. Then click **Bulleted**.

Version 2000 shows you these seven bullet symbols:

(Version 97 shows "♦" instead of "o".) Versions 6&7 show six different symbols instead.

Double-click whichever symbol you want. The computer puts your chosen symbol at the beginning of the paragraph. It also makes the Bullets button henceforth produce that symbol — in this document and all other documents — until you switch to a different symbol instead.

Page 168 said that if you click in the middle of a paragraph and then push in the **Numbering button**, the computer normally puts "1." at the beginning of the paragraph (and indents the paragraph), puts "2." at the beginning of the next paragraph, etc. If you don't like that numbering scheme, pick a different scheme instead. Here's how....

Choose **Bullets and Numbering** from the Format menu. Then click **Numbered**.

Version 2000 shows you these seven schemes:

1.	1)	I.	i.	A.	a.	a)
2.	2)	II.	ii.	B.	b.	b)
3.	3)	III.	iii.	C.	c.	c)

Version 97 shows "(a) (b) (c)" instead of "a. b. c." Versions 6&7 omit "i. ii. iii." and shows "A) B) C)" instead of "a. b. c."

Double-click whichever scheme you want.

Borders and Shading
Here's how to draw a box around your writing.

First, tell the computer which part of your writing to put in the box.

> To put one paragraph in the box, click in that paragraph.
>
> To put *several* paragraphs in the box, click in the first of those paragraphs, then do this: *while holding down the SHIFT key*, click in the last of those paragraphs.
>
> To put a short phrase in the box, drag across the phrase. (Just version 97 can put a short phrase in the box.)

Next, choose **Borders and Shading** from the Format menu. Here's what happens afterwards....

Click **Borders**. Click either the **Box** button (to create a simple box) or the **Shadow** button (to create a more advanced box whose right and bottom edges have a shadow from sunlight).

In the middle of the box, if you want your writing to have a colored or gray background instead of a white background, click **Shading** then do this:

> **Version 97&2000:** click your favorite color (or shade of gray).
>
> **Version 6&7:** if you want a shade of gray, click one of the shades that you see in the Custom Shading box; if you want a color instead, click the Background box's down-arrow then click your favorite color.

Press ENTER. The computer will draw the box, but you might have trouble seeing it clearly. Press the right-arrow key (to move the cursor out of the way, so you can see your box clearly).

Columns
Page 172 explained that you can create newspaper columns by clicking the **Columns button**. To create columns that are customized, do this instead:

> Choose **Columns** from the Format menu.
>
> If you want 2 columns (that are the same width as each other), click the **Two** button.
> If you want 3 columns (that are the same width as each other), click the **Three** button.
> If you want 2 columns, where the left column is narrower than the other, click the **Left** button.
> If you want 2 columns, where the right column is narrower than the other, click the **Right** button.
>
> If you want to draw a vertical line in the gap between columns, put a mark in the **Line Between** box (by clicking).
>
> The computer assumes you want each gap between columns to be a half-inch wide. (That's 0.5".) If you want the gap to be a different width instead, change the number in the **Spacing** box (by retyping it or by clicking its up-arrow or down-arrow). For example, on this page (and in most of this book) the gap between columns is 0.3".
>
> When you finish saying what kind of columns you want, press ENTER. Then the computer will create them.

Tabs
While you're typing your document, pressing the TAB key resembles pressing the SPACE bar but makes the computer move much farther to the right, to the next **tab stop**.

Normally, the tab stops are spaced ½-inch apart. For finer control over your document, make the tab stops be $^1/_{10}$-inch apart instead. Here's how: choose **Tabs** from the Format menu, then type 0.1" (or just .1) in the **Default Tab Stops** box and press ENTER. That procedure changes the tab stops for the entire document.

After doing that procedure, here's how to easily create a fine-looking table (without using the Insert Table button): just press the TAB key repeatedly, to move to the next column. (Pressing the TAB key is more accurate than pressing the SPACE bar.)

Drop Cap
After you've typed a paragraph, here's how to make that paragraph begin with a capital letter that's huge: click anywhere in that paragraph, choose **Drop Cap** from the Format menu, click **Dropped**, then press ENTER.

If you change your mind, here's how to delete the huge capital letter: *triple*-click in the middle of the letter, then press the DELETE key.

Change Case
After typing a phrase, if you change your mind and wish you'd capitalized it, do this:

> Select the phrase (by dragging across it).
>
> Choose **Change Case** from the Format menu.
>
> If you want to capitalize the entire phrase (LIKE THIS), click **UPPERCASE**. If you prefer to capitalize just the first letter of each word (Like This), click **Title Case** instead.
>
> Press ENTER.

AutoFormat
After you've typed your document, try telling the computer to make the document look prettier. Here's how....

First, click in the middle of the document.

In versions 6&7, click the AutoFormat button (which is on the standard toolbar). In version 97, do this instead:

> Choose **AutoFormat** from the Format menu. You'll see the AutoFormat window. In that window is a box. Normally, that box says "General document". If you're writing a letter (instead of a book or report or newspaper), change "General document" to "Letter" (by clicking the down-arrow and then clicking Letter). Press ENTER.

The computer will try to make the document look prettier. For example, if your document contains what seems to be a heading, the computer will make it Arial and big (14-point bold in versions 6&7&97, 16-point bold in version 2000). If you're writing a letter that ends with —

> Sincerely,

and a few other lines underneath it, the computer will indent the word "Sincerely" and the lines underneath, so they all begin at the center of the paper instead of at the left margin. The computer makes many other improvements also! But here's an exception: if you *already* tried to fiddle with the appearance of a line, the computer leaves that line alone.

If you like what the computer did to your document, great! Go ahead and edit the document further!

If you *don't* like what the computer did, click the Undo button, which makes the document return to its previous appearance.

Style While you're typing your document, the formatting toolbar's Style box shows what style you're using. That box usually says Normal, but you can switch to a different style instead, such as "Heading 1". (I explained that box on page 168.)

Styles such as "Normal" and "Heading 1" were invented by Microsoft.

Here's how **to invent your own paragraph style:**

In your document, create a paragraph whose appearance thrills you, by using the formatting toolbar and Format menu. Click in the middle of the paragraph's first word. Choose **Style** from the Format menu. Click the **New** button. Invent a name for your style (such as "Wow"): type the name, and at the end of the name press the ENTER key twice.

The style you invented ("Wow") will appear in the formatting toolbar's Style box.

While you're typing the document, the style you invented ("Wow") is part of the computer's repertoire. For example, while you're typing another paragraph, you can make that paragraph's style be "Normal" or "Heading 1" or "Wow": just click the Style box's down-arrow and then click the style you want.

The style you invented ("Wow") is part of the computer's repertoire just while you're using that document, not while you're using other documents.

Later, if you change your mind, **you can improve that style by using two methods:**

Traditional method (works in all versions): Click in a paragraph written in that style. Choose Style from the Format menu. Click "Modify" then "Format". You'll see a Format menu; use it to modify the style. Then press ENTER several times, until the menus and documents disappear and you see your document again.

Fast, bizarre method (works just in versions 7&97&2000): Click in a paragraph written in that style. Improve that paragraph's appearance (by using the formatting toolbar and Format menu). Click in the middle of the paragraph's first word. Click the Style box's down-arrow. Press ENTER twice.

Tools menu

If you click the word Tools, you see the **Tools menu,** whose main choices are:

```
Spelling and Grammar
Language
Word Count
```

(Versions 6&7 say "Spelling" instead of "Spelling and Grammar").

Spelling and Grammar Look at the Tools menu's top choice. Versions 97&2000 call it "Spelling and Grammar"; versions 6&7 call it "Spelling". It does the same thing as the similarly named button (explained on page 172).

Language Suppose you're writing a story containing the word "girl". Can you think of a different word instead, that means roughly the same thing as "girl" but is better?

If you can't, the computer can! Just ask the computer to use its **thesaurus** to find **synonyms** for "girl".

Here's how. In your document, type the word "girl".

For **version 2000**, do this:

Right-click in the middle of that word. Click "Synonyms" (because in version 2000, that's faster than choosing Language from the Tools menu). The computer will say:

```
young woman
lass
schoolgirl
daughter
youngster
child
teenager
```

If none of those words appeals to you, press the Esc key twice.

If one of those words appeals to you, click it. That word will replace "girl" in your document.

For **versions 6&7&97**, do the following instead....

Click in the middle of that word. In versions 6&7, choose **Thesaurus** from the Tools menu; in versions 97, choose **Language** from the Tools menu, then click **Thesaurus**.

The computer will show you that the word "girl" has two meanings: a "girl" can mean either a female child or a sweetheart. The computer will say....

```
Meanings:
female child
sweetheart
```

If you click "female child", the computer will show this list of words that mean "female child":

```
female child
child
lass
schoolgirl
young woman
maiden
junior miss
demoiselle
filly
```

(In version 7, you must click the down-arrow key to see "filly".) If you click "sweetheart" instead, the computer will show this list of words that mean "sweetheart":

```
sweetheart
girlfriend
lover
fiancée
mistress
darling
```

Here's what to do next:

If none of those words appeals to you, click the Cancel button.

If one of those words appeals to you, click it. Then either click "Replace" (to make that word replace "girl" in your document) or click "Look Up" (to make the computer look up *that* word in the thesaurus).

Word Count If you choose **Word Count**, the computer will tell you how long the document is: how many pages, paragraphs, lines, words, and characters it contains. This procedure resembles choosing Properties from the File menu but is faster and generates a report that's briefer. When you finish reading the report, press ENTER.

Table menu

If you click the word Table, you see the **Table menu,** which I explained on page 173.

Window menu

If you click the word Window, you see the **Window menu,** whose main choices are:

```
Arrange All
Split
```

Arrange All Here's how to see *two* documents on the screen at once!

To be safe, make sure both documents have been saved on disk (by using the **Save button**). Close any documents that are on the screen (by choosing **Close** from the File menu), so the screen's main part is blank.

Click the **Open button**. Double-click the first document's name. You see the document's words and paragraphs on the screen.

While that first document is still on the screen (without closing it), click the **Open button** again. Double-click the second document's name. You see the document's words and paragraphs on the screen; they cover up the first document, so you can't see the first document at the moment.

Choose **Arrange All** from the Window menu. Then you see *two* windows on the screen. The top window shows the second document; the bottom window shows the first document.

Each window is small, showing just a tiny part of the document. A window might seem blank if it's so small that it shows just the document's top margin.

Each window has its own scroll arrows. (In version 6, they look like ⬆ and ⬇. In versions 7&97&2000, they look like ▲ and ▼.) Use them to scroll through the documents and see the parts of the documents that are *not* blank.

By using those two windows, you can easily compare two documents and copy from one to the other (by using the Copy and Paste buttons).

When you stop wanting one of the windows, here's how to make it disappear:

Versions 7&97&2000: click in that window, then close that window (by clicking its X button), then expand the other window (by clicking its maximize button, which is next to its X button).

Version 6: click in that window, then close that window (by double-clicking its control box), then maximize the other window (by clicking ▲).

Split To see two parts of your document at the same time, choose **Split**. A fat gray line appears across the middle of your screen and split your screen's window into two parts, a top windowpane and a bottom windowpane.

Move the mouse slightly (which moves the fat gray line slightly up or down), until you're happy about the line's position. Then click the mouse's left button.

Now you can see two parts of your document at the same time!

Each windowpane has its own scroll arrows. (In version 6, they look like ⬆ and ⬇. In versions 7&97&2000, they look like ▲ and ▼.) You can click those scroll arrows to change what's you see in that windowpane, without changing what's in the other windowpane.

You can also click in one windowpane's text and then use the keyboard's movement keys (up-arrow, down-arrow, left-arrow, right-arrow, PAGE UP, PAGE DOWN, HOME, and END) to change what's in that windowpane, without changing what you see in the other windowpane.

Both windowpanes show parts of the same document. If you change a word in one windowpane (by deleting or inserting or revising that word), while the other windowpane happens to show the same part of the document, you see that word automatically change in the other windowpane also, immediately!

By using those two windowpanes, you can easily compare two parts of your document and copy from one part to the other (by using the Copy and Paste buttons).

When you stop wanting two windowpanes, here's how **to return to a single pane....**

Version 2000: Which windowpane do you want to remove? Click in that windowpane. Then choose **Remove Split** from the Window menu. That windowpanes disappear, so the entire screen becomes devoted to the other windowpane.

Versions 6&7&97: Which windowpane is showing the document part that interests you most? Click in that windowpane. Then choose **Remove Split** from the Window menu. That makes the entire screen be devoted to what was in that windowpane.

Help menu

If you click the word Help, you see the **Help menu**, whose main choices are:

```
Microsoft Word Help
Hide the Office Assistant

Contents and Index
What's This?

About Microsoft Word
```

(Versions 6&7&97 lack "Hide the Office Assistant". Versions 6&7 lack "What's This?". Version 2000 lacks "Contents and Index". Instead of "Microsoft Word Help", version 7 says "Microsoft Word Help Topics"; version 6 says "Search for Help on".)

Microsoft Word Help (in version 97&2000)

Choosing **Microsoft Word Help** has the same effect as clicking the **Office Assistant button**, which I explained on page 173.

Hide the Office Assistant (in version 2000)

Choosing **Hide the Office Assistant** makes the animated paper clip (Clippit) disappear. To make Clippit reappear, choose **Show the Office Assistant** from the Help menu.

What's This? Try this experiment:

In **versions 97&2000**, choose **What's This** from the Help menu (or press SHIFT with F1).

In **versions 6&7**, click the Help button, which has a question mark and arrow on it; it's the rightmost button on the standard toolbar (or press SHIFT with F1).

Then if you click any object (button or menu item) anywhere on the screen, the computer will tell you what that object means. When you finish reading the computer's explanation, press the ESCAPE key (which says "Esc" on it).

Contents and Index (in versions 6&7&97)

To see an alphabetical list of help topics, do this:

Version 97: choose **Contents and Index** from the Help menu, then click Index.
Version 7: choose "Microsoft Word Help Topics" from Help menu, then click Index.
Version 6: choose "Search for Help on" from the Help menu.

You see just the beginning of the list. To see the rest of the list, you could click the down-arrow repeatedly, but that would take a long time, since the list contains many hundreds of topics. To hop down immediately to the topic that interests you, type the topic's name. When you finally see that topic in the list, double-click it. If you then see a list of subtopics, double-click the subtopic that interests you.

Finally, the computer will show you a window full of helpful info about that topic. In versions 7&97, that window has a helpful size; in version 6, you should maximize the window (by clicking its ▲ button).

When you finish reading that info, close the window by clicking its X button. (In version 6, double-click its control box instead.)

About Microsoft Word If you choose **About Microsoft Word**, the computer will display a version message saying which version of Microsoft Word you're using.

(If you then click the System Info button, you'll see a window saying what kind of computer you bought and what state it's in. When you finish looking at that window, close it by clicking its X button; in version 6, click the Close button instead.)

When you finish using About Microsoft Word, click the OK button.

MICROSOFT WORKS

Starting

Microsoft Works is the cheapest way to computerize well! It's an **integrated program** that handles word processing, spreadsheets, and databases.

It runs in all three popular environments (DOS, Windows, and Mac).

The Windows versions are the best. The newest, best Windows version of Microsoft Works is **Microsoft Works 2000**. It requires Windows 95 (or 98 or NT). It costs about $40. It's better than the previous version, which was **Microsoft Works 4.5**.

Better yet, get Microsoft Works as part of **Microsoft Works Suite 2000**.

> **Microsoft Works Suite 2000** is a combo package that you can get for about $80 (from discount dealers such as Staples and Office Max). It includes **Microsoft Works**, **Microsoft Word** (which does fancier word-processing tricks than Microsoft Works), **Microsoft Money** (which balances your checkbook and tracks expenses), **Microsoft Home Publishing** (which does desktop publishing), **Encarta** (a computerized encyclopedia), **Expedia Streets & Trips** (which draws maps of US cities and highways and gives driving directions to any US address), and **Picture It Express** (which edits photographs to make them look better).

This chapter explains the word-processing part of Microsoft Works 4.5 (for Windows).

The word-processing part of Microsoft Works 2000 (for Windows) is better but rarely used, since most people who have Microsoft Works 2000 also have Microsoft Word 2000, which is the *best* word-processing program. **If you have both Microsoft Works 2000 and Microsoft Word 2000, turn to the Microsoft Word chapter now** (pages 162-182), which explains how to install Microsoft Word 2000 (along with Microsoft Works 2000) and how to use Microsoft Word 2000.

Copy Works to the hard disk

Microsoft Works 4.5 comes on a CD-ROM disk, as part of Home Essentials 98. Here's how to copy Microsoft Works to your hard disk:

> Turn on the computer without any floppy or CD-ROM disks in the drives, so the computer runs Windows 95 and the computer's bottom left corner says Start. Put Home Essentials 98's Disc 1 into the CD-ROM drive. The computer will say "Microsoft Home Essentials". Click the Microsoft Works button. The computer will say "Microsoft Works 4.5 Setup". Press the ENTER key.
>
> The computer will say "Enter your full name". Type your name. At the end of your name, press the TAB key, then type the name of your company (if any), then press ENTER twice.
>
> If the computer says "CD Key", type the 11-digit CD Key code number (printed on the orange sticker at the back of the CD-ROM disk's square case) and press ENTER.
>
> The computer will show you a 20-digit Product Identification number. Write that number on the yellow-black-and-white registration card that came with the CD. Press ENTER 4 times, then click "Restart Windows".

Launch Microsoft Works

To start using Microsoft Works, double-click the icon that says **Shortcut to Microsoft Works**. (If the computer says "Click the OK button to see a short demonstration", click the Cancel button.)

Click **Works Tools**, then the **Word Processing button**.

At the screen's top, you see the word **Help**. Click it. You see the **Help menu**. From that menu, choose **Hide Help** (by clicking it).

Type your document

Start typing your document.

Microsoft Works uses the mouse and fundamental keys the same way as WordPad and Windows Write. For details, **read these sections on pages 97-99:**

> "Use the keyboard"
> "Scroll arrows"
> "Insert characters"
> "Split a paragraph"
> "Combine paragraphs"

Movement keys

To move to different parts of your document, you can use your mouse. To move faster, press these keys instead:

Key you press	Where pointer moves
right-arrow	right to the next character
left-arrow	left to the previous character
down-arrow	down to the line below
up-arrow	up to the line above
END	right to the end of the line
HOME	left to beginning of the line
PAGE DOWN	down to the next screenful
PAGE UP	up to the previous screenful

Here's what happens if you press the movement keys while holding down the Ctrl key:

Keys you press	Where the pointer will move
Ctrl with right-arrow	right (to the next word or punctuation symbol)
Ctrl with left-arrow	left (to the beginning of a word or punctuation)
Ctrl with down-arrow	down to the next paragraph
Ctrl with up-arrow	up to the beginning of a paragraph
Ctrl with PAGE DOWN	down to screen's bottom line
Ctrl with PAGE UP	up to the screen's top line
Ctrl with END	down to the end of the document
Ctrl with HOME	up to the beginning of the document

Tricks

Microsoft Works performs the same tricks as Microsoft Word. For details, **read these sections on page 164:**

> "All delete"
> "Page break"

Page box

Near the screen's bottom left corner, you see the word "Page" and some numbers. For example, you might see "Page 2/5", which means you're looking at page 2 of a 5-page document.

If your document contains several pages, here's what happens when you click the arrows next to "Page".

> When you click ▶, you'll see the next page.
> When you click ◀, you'll see the previous page.
>
> When you click |◀, you'll see the document's first page (page 1).
> When you click ▶|, you'll see the document's last, final page.

If your document contains several pages, here's a quick way to hop to page 2: double-click the word "Page", then type 2 and press ENTER.

Zoom box

Near the screen's bottom left corner, you see the word "Zoom". Next to it, you normally see "100%".

Near it, you see a plus sign. If you click that plus sign, the computer makes the screen's characters be enlarged, so their size is 150% as wide and 150% as tall as normal, and the Zoom box says "150%" instead of "100%".

If you click the plus sign again, the computer makes the screen's characters be even larger, so their size is 200%. If you click the plus sign again, the computer makes the screen's characters be even larger: 400%.

If you click the minus sign instead, the characters become smaller. By clicking the plus or minus sign repeatedly, you can choose these sizes: 50%, 75%, 100%, 150%, 200%, 400%.

See the menu For further choices, click the word "Zoom". Then you see this menu:

```
Whole Page
Page Width
Margin Width
50%
75%
100%
150%
200%
400%
Custom
```

Click whichever choice you wish.

If you click **Whole Page**, the computer will make the screen's characters be very tiny, so the whole page fits on the screen.

If you click **Page Width**, the computer will make the screen's characters be as big as possible, but still small enough so that you can see the left and right edges of the paper.

My favorite choice is **Margin Width**: it makes the screen's characters be even bigger, but still small enough so that you can see the left and right margin lines.

If you prefer a different percentage, choose **Custom**, then click "Custom" *again*, then type the percentage you want (such as 90) and press ENTER.

Just on the screen All those Zoom choices affect just what you see on the screen. They do *not* affect what's printed on paper.

Toolbar

Near the screen's top, you see the **toolbar**, which looks like this:

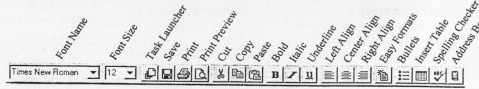

Each symbol on the toolbar is called a **tool**. Here's the name of each tool:

Font Name, Font Size, Task Launcher, Save, Print, Print Preview, Cut, Copy, Paste, Bold, Italic, Underline, Left Align, Center Align, Right Align, Easy Formats, Bullets, Insert Table, Spelling Checker, Address Book

If you forget a tool's name, try this trick: point at the tool (by using the mouse, but *without* clicking), then wait a second. Underneath the tool, you'll see the tool's name; and at the screen's bottom left corner, you'll see a one-sentence explanation of what the tool does.

The toolbar's right-hand part consists of 18 **buttons**: Task Launcher, Save, Print, etc. To use a button, press it by clicking it with the mouse. Let's look at the details....

Fundamental buttons

Microsoft Works uses the same fundamental buttons as Microsoft Word. For details, **read these sections on page 165**:

```
"Underline"
"Bold"
"Italic"
```

Alignment buttons

While typing a line, you can click the Left Align, Center Align, or Right Align button.

Clicking the **Center Align button** makes the line be centered,

like this line

Clicking the **Right Align button** makes the line be at the right margin,

like this line

Clicking the **Left Align button** makes the line be at the left margin,

like this line

Clicking one of those buttons affects not just the line you're typing but also all other lines in the same paragraph.

When you click one of those alignment buttons, you're pushing the button in. That button pops back out when you push a different alignment button instead.

When you start typing a new document, the computer assumes you want the document to be aligned left, so the computer pushes the Align Left button in. If you want a different alignment, push a different alignment button instead.

Clicking one of those alignment buttons affects the entire paragraph you're typing. (The paragraphs you typed earlier remain unaffected.)

To change the alignment of a paragraph you typed earlier, click in the middle of that paragraph and then click the alignment button you wish.

When you start typing a new paragraph, the computer gives that paragraph the same alignment as the paragraph above, unless you say differently (by pressing one of the alignment buttons).

Centered title Here's how to type a centered title, using the techniques you've learned so far....

Press the ENTER key twice (to leave a big blank space above the title).

Next, press the Center Align button (so the title will be centered) and the Bold button (so the title will be bold). Type the words you want to be in the title, and press the ENTER key afterwards.

Congratulations! You've created a centered title!

Next, make the paragraph underneath the title be normal: make that paragraph be uncentered (click the Left Align button) and make it be unbolded (click the Bold button, so the Bold button pops back out).

Shortcuts Here are shortcuts:

Instead of clicking the Left	Align button, you can press Ctrl with L.
Instead of clicking the Right	Align button, you can press Ctrl with R.
Instead of clicking the Center	Align button, you can press Ctrl with E (which stands for "Equidistant").

Font Size

Look at the **Font Size box**. In that box, you normally see the number 12. That means the characters you're typing are 12 points high. Here's how to type characters that are bigger or smaller....

Method 1: click the Font Size box. In that box, type a size number from 6 to 48. The number can end in .5; the number can be 8 or 8.5 or 9 or 9.5 or 10 or bigger. (Theoretically, you can pick a number even smaller than 6 or even bigger than 48, but those extreme numbers create ugly results.) When you finish typing the number, press the ENTER key.

Method 2: click the down-arrow that's to the *right* of the Font Size box. You start seeing this list of popular sizes: 6, 8, 10, 12, 14, 16, 18, 20, 24, 30, 32, 36, 40, and 48. That list of popular sizes is called the **Font Size menu**. Click the size you want.

Any new characters you type afterwards will be the size you chose. (Characters typed earlier don't changes size.)

The popular sizes look like this:

This text is 6 points high, 8 points high, 10 points high, 12 points high, 14 points high,

16 points high, 18 points high, 20 points high,

24 points high, 30 points high,

32pt.,36pt.,40pt.,48pt.

When you finish typing the enlarged or reduced characters, here's how to return to typing characters that are normal size (12-point): click the down-arrow that's to the right of the Font Size box, then click the 12.

Font Name

Microsoft Works' **Font Name box** acts the same as Microsoft Word's **Font** box. For details, **read the "Font" section on page 167**, but ignore the sentence about the "Justify" button.

Bullets

Microsoft Works uses the **Bullets button** the same way as Microsoft Word. For details, **read the "Bullets" section on page 168**.

Spelling Checker

If you click in the middle of the document's first word and then click the **Spelling Checker button**, the computer scans through your document for misspelled words and accidentally repeatedly words.

When the computer stops at a strange word that seems wrong, the computer shows a list of suggestions. If you like one of the suggestions, double-click it. If you *don't* like any of the computer's suggestions, either click "Ignore" (which makes the computer leave the strange word unedited) or else edit the strange word and then click "Change".

When the computer finishes checking the entire document, the computer will say "Spelling check finished." Press ENTER.

Save

To save the document (copy it onto the disk), click the **Save button** (or press Ctrl with S).

If you haven't saved the document before, the computer will say "File Name". Invent a name for your document. Type the name and press ENTER.

That makes the computer copy the document onto the hard disk.

For example, suppose you named the document "mary". The computer will make that document become a file called mary.wps (which means "mary from the **w**ord **p**rocessing **s**ystem"). The computer will put that file into the Documents folder that's in the MSWorks folder, which is in the Program Files folder. So the file is actually called:

C:\Program Files\MSWorks\Documents\mary.wps

Afterwards, if you change your mind and want to do more editing, go ahead! When you finish that extra editing, save it by clicking the Save button again.

Save often If you're typing a long document, click the Save button about every 10 minutes. Click it whenever you get to a good stopping place and think, "What I've typed so far looks good!"

Then if an accident happens, you'll lose at most 10 minutes of work, and you can return to the last version you felt good about.

Print

Here's how to print the document onto paper. Make sure you've bought a printer, attached it to the computer, turned the printer's power on, and put paper into the printer. Then click the **Print button**. The printer will print your document onto paper.

Print Preview

If you're wondering what a page will look like but don't want to waste a sheet of paper to find out, click the **Print Preview button**. The computer will show you a mock-up of what the entire page will look like: you'll see the entire page, shrunk to fit on the screen.

Since the entire page is shrunk to fit on the screen, the page and its characters look too tiny for you to read the words easily, but you'll be able to see the page's overall appearance: how much of the page is filled up, which parts of the page are blank, and whether the info on the page is centered.

Wouldn't you like to ride in an airplane, fly high above your house, and see an aerial view of your house and neighborhood, so all the people look like tiny specs, and you see — in one amazing view — the overall layout of your house and yard and neighborhood and city? Wouldn't you be thrilled? Clicking the Print Preview button gives you that same thrill: you see an aerial view of the page you were typing, as if you were flying over it in an airplane: you see the layout of your entire page in one amazing view, and the characters on it look like tiny specs.

When you finish admiring the view, click the Cancel button (which is at the screen's right edge).

Insert Table

In the middle of your document, here's how to type a table of numbers.

Click where you want the table to appear, then click the **Insert Table button**.

The computer assumes you want the table to have 5 rows. If you want a different number of rows, press the DELETE key (to delete the 5) and then type how many rows you want.

Press the TAB key. The computer assumes you want the table to have 3 columns. If you want a different number of columns, type how many you want.

Press the TAB key. The computer assumes you want the table's format to be Plain. If you want the table to have fancy fonts or fancy colors or fancy gridlines, press the keyboard's down-arrow key several times, until you like the format that you see in the Example box.

Press ENTER. The computer will create a blank table, which has no words or numbers in it yet.

Then just fill in the cells with whatever numbers and words you wish. To move from cell to cell, click with the mouse, or press the TAB key (which moves right to the next cell), or press SHIFT with TAB (which moves left to the previous cell), or press the arrow keys repeatedly.

In a cell, you can type a number, word, sentence, or even an entire paragraph! If you start typing a paragraph in a cell, the computer will automatically make the cell and its row taller, so the entire paragraph will fit in the cell. You can even type *several* paragraphs in a single cell: just press the ENTER key at the end of each paragraph. If you want to indent the first line of one of those paragraphs, press the SPACE bar several times.

While you're typing in the cells, the table is temporarily surrounded by a fat black border.

When you finish typing in the cells, get out of the table (by clicking below the table, or by pressing the TAB key or down-arrow key a few times). Then the fat black border will disappear.

Extra rows Here's how to insert an extra row into the *middle* of the table: click in the row that's underneath where you want the extra row to appear, then choose **Insert Row** from the Insert menu.

Column widths The computer assumes you want the table's columns to all be the same width. But you can change that assumption!

For example, here's how to adjust the width of the table's left column (column 1). **Move the mouse** until its pointer is **on the gray bar** at the top of the table, and **on the vertical gridline** that separates column 1 from column 2, and the pointer's shape turns into **a double-headed arrow** that's labeled "ADJUST". Then drag the vertical gridline to the right (to make the column wider) or left (to make the column narrower).

If you make a column wider, the computer makes room for it by shrinking all columns to the right of it. If you make a column narrower, the computer compensates by expanding all columns to the right of it.

If you want to fine-tune the widths of *all* columns, work from left to right: adjust the width of column 1 (by dragging the gridline that separates it from column 2), then adjust the width of column 2 (by dragging the gridline that separates it from column 3), then adjust the width of column 3 (by dragging the gridline that separates it from column 4), etc.

Numbers If a column contains mostly numbers, here's how to make that column look prettier, so the numbers are aligned properly with the column's heading:

> Click the gray bar at the top of the column. The entire column turns black (except the first cell).
>
> Click the Right Align button (which is on the toolbar). That makes all cells in that column be right-aligned, so the numbers are aligned properly under the headings.

Bold Here's how to make an entire column be bold (**like this**):

> Click in the gray bar at the top of the column. The entire column turns black (except the first cell).
> Push in the Bold button (which is on the toolbar). That makes all cells in the column be bold.

Here's how to make an entire row be bold:

> Click in the gray bar at the row's left edge. The entire row turns black (except the first cell).
> Push in the Bold button (which is on the toolbar). That makes all cells in the row be bold.

Below the table When you've finished editing the table, here's how to put paragraphs below it.

Click below the table by using the mouse, or go below the table by pressing the down-arrow key several times. Then type the paragraphs you want below the table.

Delete Here's how to delete the entire table: click above the table, then inside the table, then press the DELETE key.

Here's how to delete just one row:

> Double-click in that row. Then choose **Delete Row** from the Insert menu.

Here's how to delete just one column:

> Double-click in that column. Then choose **Delete Column** from the Insert menu.

Select text

Here's how to dramatically change a phrase you typed.

Point at the phrase's beginning, then drag to the phrase's end (while holding down the mouse's left button). The whole phrase turns black. Turning the phrase black is called **selecting the phrase**.

Then say what to do to the phrase. For example, choose one of these activities:

> To underline the phrase, push in the Underline button.
> To make the phrase be bold, push in the Bold button.
> To italicize the phrase, push in the Italic button.
> To prevent the phrase from being underlined, bold, or italicized, pop those buttons back out.
>
> To change how the phrase's paragraphs are aligned, click one of the alignment buttons.
>
> To change the phrase's point size, choose the size you want from the Font Size menu.
> To change the phrase's font, choose the font you want from the Font menu.
>
> To delete the phrase, press the **DELETE key**.
>
> To replace the phrase, just type whatever words you want the phrase to become.

Go ahead! Try it now! It's fun!

Other ways to select

The usual way to select a phrase is to point at the phrase's beginning, then drag to the phrase's end. But sometimes other methods are faster!

To select a phrase, choose one of these methods....

> Method 1: point at the phrase's beginning, then **drag** to the phrase's end.
>
> Method 2: click the phrase's beginning; then while holding down the **SHIFT key**, click the phrase's end.
>
> Method 3: by using your keyboard's **movement keys**
> (such as up-arrow, down-arrow, left-arrow, and right-arrow), move to the phrase's beginning; then while holding down the SHIFT key, use the movement keys to move to the phrase's end.
>
> Method 4: to select just **one sentence**, click in its middle while holding down the Ctrl key.
>
> Method 5: to select just **one line**, click in its left margin.
>
> Method 6: to select **several lines**, click in the first line's left margin; then while holding down the SHIFT key, click in the bottom line's left margin.
>
> Method 7: to select just **one word**, double-click in its middle.
>
> Method 8: to select just **one paragraph**, double-click in its left margin.
>
> Method 9: to select the **entire document** (all!), press the A key while holding down the Ctrl key.

Drag a phrase

To move a phrase to a new location, just "select the phrase, and then drag from the phrase's middle to the new location." Here are the details....

First, select the phrase you want to move, so the phrase turns black.

Then take your finger off the mouse's button. Move the mouse's pointer to the phrase's middle (so you see an arrow labeled "DRAG").

Finally, hold down the mouse's button; and while you keep holding down the mouse's button, drag the arrow to wherever you want the phrase to move. (While you're dragging the arrow, it's labeled "MOVE"). Drag the arrow anywhere you wish in the document, or drag to the end of the document. The computer won't let you drag past the document's end.

At the end of the drag, lift your finger from the mouse's button. Presto, the phrase moves where you wished!

Paste

Microsoft Works handles pasting the same way as Microsoft Word. For details, **read these sections on page 171**:

> "Cut and Paste"
> "Copy"

Menu bar

Near the screen's top, you see this **menu bar**:

```
File Edit View Insert Format Tools Window Help
```

Here's how to use it.

File menu

If you click the word File, you see the **File menu**, whose main choices are:

```
Close

Save
Save As

Page Setup
Print Preview
Print

Exit Works
```

Close When you finish working on a document and want to work on a different document instead, choose **Close**.

> If you didn't save your document, the computer asks, "Save changes?" If you click "Yes", the computer copies your document's most recent version to the hard disk; if you click "No" instead, the computer ignores and forgets your most recent editing.

Your next step is to click the **Word Processor button** or **Existing Documents**.

> If you click the **Word Processor button**, the computer will let you start typing a new document.
>
> If you click **Existing Documents** and then double-click the name of an old document, the computer will put that document onto the screen and let you edit it.

Save Choosing **Save** has the same effect as clicking the **Save button**, which I explained on page 185.

Save As Microsoft Works handles "Save As" the same way as Microsoft Word. For details, **read the "Save As" section on page 174.**

Page Setup Microsoft Works handles "Page Setup" the same way as Microsoft Word. For details, **read the "Page Setup" section on page 174.**

Print Preview Choosing **Print Preview** has the same effect as clicking the **Print Preview button**, which I explained on page 186.

Print If you choose **Print**, the computer will ask how you'd like to print onto paper.

> If the computer says "First-time Help", press ENTER.
>
> If you own more than 1 printer, click the down-arrow next to the Printer Name box , then choose which printer you want to use (by clicking it).
>
> If you want to print more than 1 copy:
> double-click in the "Number of copies" box, then type the number of copies.
>
> If you want to print just pages 3 through 7:
> click the Pages button, type "3", press the TAB key, then type "7".

Then press ENTER. The printer will print what you desired!

Exit Works When you want to stop using Microsoft Works, choose **Exit Works**.

> If you didn't save your document, the computer asks, "Save changes?" If you click "Yes", the computer copies your document's most recent version to the hard disk; if you click "No" instead, the computer ignores and forgets your most recent editing.

Edit menu

If you click the word Edit, you see the **Edit menu**, whose main choices are:

```
Undo Editing

Cut
Copy
Paste
Clear
Select All

Find
Replace
Go To
Bookmark
```

Some of those choices just imitate the buttons and your keyboard.

> Choosing **Cut** is like clicking the **Cut button** (explained on page 171).
> Choosing **Copy** is like clicking the **Copy button** (explained on page 171).
> Choosing **Paste** is like clicking the **Paste button** (explained on page 171).
>
> Choosing **Clear** is like pressing the **DELETE key** (explained on page 187).
> Choosing **Select All** is like pressing **Ctrl with A** (explained on page 187).
>
> Choosing **Go To** is like double-clicking **Page box** (explained on page 183).

Here's how to make choices that are more useful....

Undo Editing If you make a mistake (such as accidentally deleting some text, or accidentally giving the text an ugly font), choose **Undo Editing** from the Edit menu (or press Ctrl with Z, which stands for "Zap"). That makes the computer undo your last activity, so your text returns to the way it looked before you made your boo-boo.

If you change your mind and wish you hadn't chosen Undo Editing, choose **Redo Editing** from the Edit menu (or press Ctrl with Z again). That cancels the undo; it undoes the undo; it makes your document look as it did before you chose Undo Editing.

Find Microsoft Works handles "Find" the same way as Microsoft Word. For details, **read the "Find" section on pages 174-175.**

Replace You can search for a word and replace it by a different word.

For example, suppose your document talks about "love". here's how to change each "love" in your document to "idolize":

> Choose **Replace**. Type the old word you want to replace ("love"), then press the TAB key, then type the new word you want instead ("idolize"), then click the Replace All button. That makes the computer change each "love" to "idolize". Then press the Esc key.

Unfortunately, the computer doesn't know how to preserve capitalization. For example, suppose the document said —

> I love you. Love you! LOVE YOU! I want to kiss your glove!

and you say to replace each "love" with "idolize". Then the computer will change each "love" or "Love" or "LOVE" to "idolize" (uncapitalized), so the document becomes this:

> I idolize you. idolize you! idolize YOU! I want to kiss your gidolize!

Notice that when told to change "love" to "idolize", the computer unfortunately also changes "glove" to "gidolize".

The Replace command helps you zip through many chores:

> For example, if you write a letter that talks about Fred, then want to write a similar letter about Sue, tell the computer to replace each Fred with Sue.
>
> If you write a book about "How to be a better salesman" and then a feminist tells you to change each "salesman" to "salesperson", tell the computer to replace each "salesman".
>
> If you're writing a long ad that mentions "Calvin Klein's Hot New Flaming Pink Day-Glo Pajamas" repeatedly, and you're too lazy to type that long phrase so often, just type the abbreviation "Calnew". When you've finished typing the document, tell the computer to replace each "Calnew" with the long phrase it stands for.

Bookmark While you're in the middle of editing a document, suppose you get a sudden urge to switch to a different activity (such as peek at a different part of the document, or play a game, or go to bed, or have sex). Before you switch to that other activity, you can put a **bookmark** in your document, where you were editing. Later, when you want to resume working on the document, you can return to that bookmark and continue editing where you left off.

Here's how to do all that:

> Decide where in the document you want to put the bookmark. Click there.
>
> Choose **Bookmark** from the Edit menu.
>
> Invent a name for your bookmark. (The name can be up to 15 characters long, and it can include spaces and punctuation.) Type the name and press ENTER.
>
> The computer will .create a bookmark using that name. The bookmark is invisible: it hides in your document.

After you've created a bookmark, be safe: click the **Save button** and save the document. Then do whatever else you wish: peek at a different part of the document, or play a game, or shut down the computer and go to bed. When you want **to return to the bookmarked part of your document, do this:**

> Make sure the document is on the screen.
>
> Choose **Go To** from the Edit menu (or press Ctrl with G).
>
> You'll see a list of bookmarks you created. Double-click the name of the bookmark you want to reach.
>
> The computer will go to the place in the document where you put the bookmark.

Here's how to delete a bookmark:

> Choose **Bookmark** from the Edit menu.
> Click the name of the bookmark you want to delete.
> Click the word "**Delete**".
> Close the Bookmark Name window (by clicking its X button).

View menu

If you click the word View, you see the **View menu**, whose main choices are:

> Normal
> Page Layout
>
> Toolbar
> Ruler
>
> All Characters
>
> Zoom

Normal versus Page Layout Microsoft Works handles this topic the same way as Microsoft Word. For details, **read the "Normal versus Page Layout" section on page 175.**

How to see more On the View menu, three of the choices are "**Toolbar**", "**Ruler**", and "**All Characters**". You can put check marks in front of those choices, by clicking those choices. To remove the check marks, click the choices again.

A check mark in front of "**Toolbar**" makes the computer display the toolbar (which contains the Font Name box, Font Size box, and 18 buttons) across the top of the screen. If the check mark is missing, the toolbar will be hidden.

A check mark in front of "**Ruler**" makes the computer display a ruler across the top of the screen. The ruler shows marks for 1 inch, 2 inches, 3 inches, etc. It shows how many inches wide your writing is. If the check mark is missing, the ruler will be hidden.

A check mark in front of "**All Characters**" makes the computer show a dot (·) wherever you pressed the SPACE bar, a right-arrow (→) wherever you pressed the TAB key, and a paragraph symbol (¶) wherever you pressed the ENTER key (to mark the end of a paragraph), so you can easily tell how many times you pressed those keys.

For example, if you typed "I love you" correctly, the screen will show "I·love·you". If you see "I·love···you" instead, you know you accidentally pressed the SPACE bar three times after "love" instead of just once, so you should delete the two extra spaces (by moving there and then pressing the DELETE key twice).

When you finish examining the ¶ symbols and dots and right-arrows, and you're sure you've put just one space between each pair of words, here's how to make those special symbols vanish: remove the "All Characters" check mark (by clicking it).

When you're using Windows, the computer's screen has difficulty showing you the letter "f" correctly. When you type an "f" by using the normal font (12-point Times New Roman), the screen shows too little space after the "f".

For example, if you try typing "f M", the screen shows "fM". If you try typing "f" then a space then "M", the screen shows "f M", which looks as if you hadn't typed a space after the "f". If you try typing "of Mary", the screen shows "of Mary", which looks as if you hadn't typed a space after the "of".

Although the screen looks wrong, what you see on *paper* might look better (depending on which printer you're using).

To discover how many times you pressed the SPACE bar, put a check mark in front of "All Characters", and notice how many dots appear. Make sure just one dot appears after each word.

Some conservative Americans have trouble handling dirty words that begin with "f". Notice that Windows has the opposite problem: it has trouble showing words that *end* in "f".

I hope somebody at Microsoft reads this book and fixes the f problem soon!

Zoom Choosing **Zoom** from the View menu has the same effect as clicking the **Zoom box** (explained on page 184) and then clicking **Custom**.

Insert menu

If you click the word Insert, you see the **Insert menu**, whose main choices are:

```
Page Break
Date and Time
Special Character

Footnote

Table
```

Page Break
Choosing **Page Break** has the same effect as pressing **Ctrl with ENTER**, which I explained on page 164.

Date and Time
To type the date or time, choose **Date and Time**.

The computer will show a list of formats, like this:

```
12/27/99
12/99
December 27, 1999
Monday, December 27, 1999
December 1999
12/27/99 11:57 PM
12/27/99 11:57:20 PM
11:57 PM
11:57:20 PM
23:57
23:57:20
```

Click the format you want. Press ENTER. The computer will type the date or time in the format you requested.

Suppose you type a document on Monday, but you print the document the next day (Tuesday). Which date will the computer print on paper? The computer will print the "date printed" (Tuesday). The computer will automatically update the date & time whenever the document is printed or print-previewed or **opened** (chosen from the list of Existing Documents, as explained on page 188).

If you *don't* want the computer to automatically update the date & time, remove the check mark from the "Automatically update when printed" box.

Special Character
If you choose **Special Character**, the computer will show you this list of special characters:

Special character	Meaning
Optional hyphen	a hyphen, visible just when the word it's in is too long to fit on a line
Nonbreaking hyphen	a hyphen, between words that must appear on the same line as each other
Nonbreaking space	a space between words that must appear on the same line as each other
End of line mark	an ENTER that returns to the left margin but does *not* end the paragraph

Click whenever character you like, then press ENTER.

Footnote
Suppose you're writing a religious pamphlet in which you want to say "Read it in the Bible tonight!" Suppose you want to add a footnote saying "written by God", so the main text looks like this —

```
Read it in the Bible[1] tonight!
```

and the page's bottom contains this footnote:

```
[1] Written by God.
```

Here's how to do it all:

Type "Read it in the Bible".

Choose **Footnote** from the Insert menu. Press ENTER.

Type the footnote ("Written by God.").

Climb back up to the main text (by using the keyboard's up-arrow key), then go right to where you left off typing (by using the END key). Those keys work if you're in Page Layout view, as I recommended at the beginning of this chapter. (If you're in Normal view instead, those keys don't work: instead, choose Footnotes from the View menu, so "Footnotes" becomes unchecked.)

Finally, type the rest of the main text (" tonight!").

The computer will automatically number the footnote: it will automatically type [1] after "Bible" and type [1] before "Written by God." If your document contains more footnotes, the computer will automatically number them [2], [3], [4], etc.

The computer will put the footnotes at the bottom of the page. If the page is divided into newspaper columns, the computer will put each footnote at the bottom of the column it refers to.

The computer will put a 2-inch horizontal line above the footnotes to separate them from the main text.

Your printer will print the footnotes accurately onto paper. You'll see the footnotes on your screen accurately while you're doing a print preview, or while you're using Page Layout view. (To see the footnotes on your screen while using Normal view, choose Footnotes from the View menu.)

If you insert extra footnotes, the computer will automatically renumber the other footnotes, so the first footnote appearing in your document will be numbered [1], the second footnote will be numbered [2], etc.

To delete a footnote, click the left edge of the footnote's number in the main text; then press the DELETE key.

Table
Choosing **Table** has the same effect as clicking the **Insert Table button**, which I explained on page 186.

Format menu

If you click the word Format, you see the **Format menu**, whose main choices are:

```
Font and Style
Paragraph
Tabs
Borders and Shading
Bullets
Columns
```

Font and Style
Here's how to improve the appearance of a phrase on your screen.

Which phrase do you want to improve? Select it (by dragging across it). Then choose **Font and Style** from the Format menu.

You see three boxes:

Box	Normal contents	Other popular choices
Font	Times New Roman	Arial, Courier New
Size	12	6, 8, 10, 12, 14, 16, 18, 20, 24, 30, 32, 36, 40, 48
Color	Auto	Blue, Red, Yellow, Green, Cyan, Magenta, Gray

Click each box's down-arrow and up-arrow repeatedly, to see all popular choices. For each box, click whatever choice you want.

Below the Font box, you see a list of four **Styles**: you can choose **Bold** (which makes the letters be thick, **like this**), *Italic* (which makes the letters be slanted, *like this*), <u>Underline</u> (which puts a line under the letters, <u>like this</u>), or ~~Strikethrough~~ (which puts a line through the middle of the letters, ~~like this~~). Put check marks in front of whichever styles you want (by clicking them).

Below the Color box, you see a list of three **Positions**: you can click **Normal** (which makes the letters normal, like this) or **Superscript** (which raises the letters a half-line, ^like this^) or **Subscript** (which lowers the letters a half-line, ~like this~).

When you've finished saying what kind of font, size, color, styles, and position you want, **press ENTER**. The phrase you selected will look the way you requested.

Paragraph To change the way a paragraph is spaced, click in the paragraph, then choose **Paragraph** from the Format menu. You see two **tabs**: one of them is called **Indents and Alignment**; the other is called **Spacing**.

Try clicking the **Indents and Alignment** tab.

You see three **indentation boxes** called **Left**, **Right**, and **First Line**. Normally, each of those boxes says 0".

> If you want the paragraph's first line to be indented a half-inch (and want the paragraph's other lines to be normal), put 0.5" (or just .5) in the **First line** box (and 0" in the other boxes).
>
> If you want *every* line of the paragraph to be indented a half-inch, put 0.5" in the **Left** box (and 0" in the other boxes).
>
> If you want the paragraph's first line to be normal (unindented) but want the paragraph's other lines to be indented a half-inch, do this: put 0.5" in the **Left** box (so most of the paragraph's lines will be indented a half-inch), put -0.5" in the **First Line** box (so the first line is indented less than the other lines), and put 0" in the Right box.
>
> If you want the paragraph's left and right margins to both be extra-wide — a half-inch wider than normal — put 0.5" in the **Left** box and 0.5" in the **Right** box.

You see four **alignment buttons** called **Left**, **Center**, **Right**, and **Justified**. Clicking the **Center** button makes each line of the paragraph be centered,

> like this line

Clicking **Right** button makes each line of the paragraph be at the right margin,

> like this line

Clicking the **Left** button makes each line of the paragraph be at the left margin,

> like this line

Clicking the **Justify** button makes the paragraph's bottom line be at the left margin and makes the paragraph's other lines be at *both* margins,

> like   this   line

You see a **Bulleted** box. Putting a check mark in that box has the same effect as pushing in the Bullets button (explained on page 168).

If you click the **Spacing** tab, here's what happens:

> You see a **Line Spacing** box. Normally, that box says "Auto". If you want to double-space instead (so the computer puts a blank line under each line you type), try making that box say "2 lines" (or "2 li"), by clicking the box's up-arrow twice. That works fine if your font is about 12 points high, since **Microsoft Works defines a "li" to mean "12 points high"**. If your font size is much taller than 12 points, to double-space you must choose *more* than "2 li": try "3 li" or "4 li" or even more.
>
> You see a box called **Before**. Normally, that box says "0 li". If you want the computer to leave a blank space above the paragraph, put "1 li" into that box (by clicking its up-arrow once).
>
> You see a box called **After**. Normally, that box says "0 li". If you want the computer to leave a blank space under the paragraph, put "1 li" into that box.

When you finish telling the computer how you want the paragraph's indents and alignment and spacing, press ENTER.

Tabs Microsoft Works handles "Tabs" the same way as Microsoft Word. For details, **read the "Tabs" section on page 180.**

Borders and Shading Here's how to draw a box around your writing.

First, tell the computer which paragraphs to put in the box.

> To put one paragraph in the box, click in that paragraph.
>
> To put *several* paragraphs in the box, click in the first of those paragraphs, then do this: *while holding down the SHIFT key*, click in the last of those paragraphs.

Then choose **Borders and Shading** from the Format menu. Click **Borders**. Put a check mark in the **Outline** box (by clicking it). Press ENTER.

Bullets Page 168 said that if you click in the middle of a paragraph and then push in the **Bullets button**, the computer normally puts a simple bullet (the symbol •) at the beginning of the paragraph (and indents the paragraph).

If you don't like the symbol •, pick a different symbol instead. Here's how: choose **Bullets** from the Format menu, and double-click your favorite symbol. (You can choose from 24 symbols.) The computer puts your chosen symbol at the beginning of the paragraph. It also makes the Bullets button henceforth produce that symbol — until you switch to a different symbol or switch to a different document or task (by choosing **Close** or **Exit Works** from the File menu).

Columns In a newspaper, text is printed in many narrow **columns**. In a business letter, text is printed in a single wide column.

The computer assumes you want a single wide column. Here's how to tell the computer you want many narrow columns:

> Choose **Columns** from the Format menu. You'll see the **Format Columns window**.
>
> How many columns do you want? Type the number of columns.
>
> The computer assumes you want each gap between columns to be a half-inch wide. (That's 0.5".) If you want the gap to be a different width instead, press the TAB key then type a different number instead. For example, on this page (and in most of this book) the gap between columns is 0.3".
>
> The computer assumes you want to draw a vertical line in the gap between columns, so the computer puts a check mark in the box **called Line between columns**. If you *don't* want to draw a vertical line, remove the check mark (by clicking it).
>
> When you finish using the Format Columns window, press ENTER. Then your entire document changes, so it has as many columns as you requested.
>
> If you requested a vertical line, you won't see it immediately: it will appear just when you print on paper (or do a print preview).

If you change your mind and want just 1 column, choose Columns from the Format menu again. Type the number "1" and press ENTER.

Tools menu

If you click the word Tools, you see the **Tools menu**, whose main choices are:

```
Spelling
Thesaurus
Word Count
```

<u>Spelling</u> Choosing **Spelling** has the same effect as clicking the **Spelling Checker button**, which I explained on page 185.

<u>Thesaurus</u> Suppose you're writing a story containing the word "girl". Can you think of a different word instead, that means roughly the same thing as "girl" but is better?

If you can't, the computer can! Just ask the computer to use its **thesaurus** to find **synonyms** for "girl".

Here's how. In your document, type the word "girl". Click in the middle of that word. Choose **Thesaurus**.

The computer will show you that the word "girl" has two meanings: a "girl" can mean either a female child or a sweetheart. The computer will say....

```
Meanings:
female child
sweetheart
```

If you click "female child", the computer will show this list of words that mean "female child":

```
female child
child
lass
schoolgirl
young woman
maiden
junior miss
demoiselle
filly
```

(You must click the down-arrow key to see "filly".) If you click "sweetheart" instead, the computer will show this list of words that mean "sweetheart":

```
sweetheart
girlfriend
lover
fiancée
mistress
darling
```

Here's what to do next:

```
If none of those words appeals to you, click the Cancel button.

If one of those words appeals to you, click it. Then either click "Replace" (to
make that word replace "girl" in your document) or click "Look Up" (to make
the computer look up that word in the thesaurus).
```

<u>Word Count</u> If you choose **Word Count**, the computer will reveal how long your document is, by reporting how many words the document contains. When you finish reading the computer's report, press ENTER.

Window menu

If you click the word Window, you see the **Window menu**, whose main choices are:

```
Tile
Split
```

<u>Tile</u> Here's how to see *two* documents on the screen at once!

To be safe, make sure both documents have been saved on disk (by using the **Save button**). Close any documents that are on the screen (by choosing **Close** from the File menu).

Click **Existing Documents**. Double-click the first document's name. You see the document's words and paragraphs on the screen.

While that first document is still on the screen (without closing it), click the **Task Launcher button** (which is the first button on the toolbar). Double-click the second document's name. You'll see the document's words and paragraphs on the screen; they cover up the first document, so you can't see the first document at the moment.

Choose **Tile** from the Window menu. Then you see *two* windows on the screen. The left window shows the second document; the right-hand window shows the first document.

Each window is narrow, showing just the document's left half.

To manipulate one of those windows, click in it, then do whatever you wish to it. For example, you can make the window show other parts of the document by using the four scroll arrows (▲ and ▼ and ◀ and ▶). If you want to make the window show an entire line of writing (instead of just the line's left half), **Zoom** (which is at the window's bottom) and then **Margin Width**.

By using those two windows, you can easily compare two documents and copy from one to the other (by using the Copy and Paste buttons).

When you stop wanting one of the windows, here's how to make it disappear: click in that window, then close that window (by clicking its X button), then expand the other window (by choosing **Tile** from the Window menu again.

<u>Split</u> To see two parts of your document at the same time, choose **Split**. A fat gray line appears across the middle of your screen and split your screen's window into two parts, a top windowpane and a bottom windowpane.

Move the mouse slightly (which moves the fat gray line slightly up or down), until you're happy about the line's position. Then click the mouse's left button.

The bottom windowpane changes, to show a copy of what's in the top windowpane.

Each windowpane has its own scroll arrows (which look like ▲ and ▼). You can click those scroll arrows to change what's you see in that windowpane, without changing what's in the other windowpane.

You can also click in one windowpane's text and then use the keyboard's movement keys (up-arrow, down-arrow, left-arrow, right-arrow, PAGE UP, PAGE DOWN, HOME, and END) to change what's in that windowpane, without changing what you see in the other windowpane.

Both windowpanes show parts of the same document. If you change a word in one windowpane (by deleting or inserting or revising that word), while the other windowpane happens to show the same part of the document, you see that word automatically change in the other windowpane also, immediately!

By using those two windowpanes, you can easily compare two parts of your document and copy from one part to the other (by using the Copy and Paste buttons).

When you stop wanting two windowpanes, here's how to return to a single pane:

```
Move the mouse until its pointer's exact center is on the fat gray line separating
the windowpanes, and the mouse pointer says "ADJUST". Then double-click.
That makes the entire screen be devoted to what was in the bottom
windowpane.
```

Help menu

If you click the word Help, you see this **Help menu**, whose main choices are:

```
Contents
Index

Introduction to Works
Show Help

About Microsoft Works
```

Contents If you choose **Contents** and then click **Word Processor**, you see **this list of topics:**

```
Word Processor basics
Starting a Works Word Processor document
Typing information
Editing your document
Changing how text and paragraphs look
Creating lists and columns
Adding objects and special elements to your document
Sharing information
Finding information
Preparing mass mailings
Final checklist before printing
Printing
Ending your work
```

Click whichever topic you want help about; then you'll see a list of subtopics. Click whichever subtopic interests you; then you'll see a list of subsubtopics. Click whichever subsubtopic interests you.

Finally, on the screen's right side, you'll see a **Step-by-Step window**, which contains step-by-step instructions about how to accomplish your goal. If you click **More Info**, you'll see a list of other topics that are similar; click whichever topic interests you.

When you finish reading all that helpful info, choose **Hide Help** from the Help menu. That closes all the help windows.

Index If you choose **Index**, you see **an alphabetical list of help topics**.

You see just part of the list. To see the rest of the list, you could click its down-arrow or up-arrow repeatedly, but that would take a very long time, since **the list is very long: it contains about 10,000 topics!** To hop down immediately to the topic that interests you, type the topic's name.

When you finally see that topic in the list, click it. If you then see a list of subtopics, click the subtopic that interests you.

Finally, on the screen's right side, you'll see a **Step-by-Step window**, which contains step-by-step instructions about how to accomplish your goal. If you click **More Info**, you'll see a list of other topics that are similar; click whichever topic interests you.

When you finish reading all that helpful info, choose **Hide Help** from the Help menu. That closes all the help windows.

Introduction to Works If you choose **Introduction to Works**, the computer will show you an ad saying how Microsoft Works is wonderful.

The ad consists of 24 pages. Press ENTER to progress to the next page. When you've seen the 24th page and press ENTER again, the ad vanishes.

Show Help If you choose **Show Help**, the screen's right side shows **this list of topics:**

```
Name and save your document
See more of your document
Type text
Correct mistakes
Copy or move text
Change how text looks (bold, italic, size, fonts,...)
Indent, align, and space paragraphs
Change margins and page orientation
Work with borders, lines, and shading
Add bulleted or numbered lists
Add headers and footers
Create envelopes or mailing labels
Add pictures, charts, tables, and special text effects
Preview and print your document
```

(To see that complete list, click the down-arrow.) Click whichever topic you want help about.

Then you'll see a list of subtopics. Click whichever subtopic interests you.

Finally, on the screen's right side, you'll see a **Step-by-Step window**, which contains step-by-step instructions about how to accomplish your goal. If you click **More Info**, you'll see a list of other topics that are similar; click whichever topic interests you.

When you finish reading all that helpful info, choose **Hide Help** from the Help menu. That closes all the help windows.

About Microsoft Works If you choose **About Microsoft Works**, the computer will display a version message saying which version of Microsoft Works you're using.

(If you then click the System Info button, you'll see a window saying what kind of computer you bought and what state it's in. When you finish looking at that window, close it by clicking its X button.)

When you finish using About Microsoft Works, click the OK button.

WORD PERFECT

Starting

WordPerfect is a word-processing program that's a bargain: it's about as powerful as Microsoft Word but costs less! It's particularly popular in law offices. It's available for DOS, Windows, the Mac, and several other operating systems.

This chapter explains **versions 8 & 9 of WordPerfect for Windows**.

> You get version 8 as part of **WordPerfect Suite 8**.
> You get version 9 as part of **WordPerfect Office 2000**.

Each is published by **Corel**, comes on CD-ROM disks, and requires Windows 95 (or 98) with at least 16M of RAM.

> Other Windows versions of WordPerfect are similar, and so are Mac versions.
>
> DOS versions are older and quite different. If you're using a DOS version of WordPerfect, phone me to get an older edition of this book.

Prepare yourself

Before reading this chapter, read and practice my Windows 95&98 chapter, especially the section about "WordPad" (a stripped-down word-processing program).

Copy to the hard disk

WordPerfect comes on a CD-ROM disk, which you must copy to your computer's hard disk. Here's how to copy version 9:

> Turn on the computer without any floppy or CD-ROM disks in the drives, so the computer runs Windows 95 (or 98) and the computer's bottom left corner says Start. Put WordPerfect Office 2000's upgrade disk 1 into the CD-ROM drive. The computer will say "WordPerfect Office 2000". Click "WordPerfect Office 2000 Setup". Press ENTER.
>
> The computer will say "WordPerfect Office 2000 License Agreement". Click "Accept". Double-click in the Full Name box. Type your full name. Press the TAB key. Type the name of your company (if any). Press ENTER. Type your serial number (which begins with "WP9" and was printed on the Product Authenticity Card). Press ENTER 4 times.
>
> If the computer says "The chosen directory does not exist", click "Yes".
>
> Press ENTER 3 times. Click "Register Later". Press ENTER 4 times. The computer asks, "Do you want CorelCENTRAL Day Planner to run on Startup?" Click "No".

Launch WordPerfect

Here's how to start using WordPerfect:

> For version 9, click "Start" then "Programs" then "WordPerfect Office 2000" then "WordPerfect 9".

> For version 8, click "Start" then "Corel WordPerfect Suite 8" then "Corel WordPerfect 8".

The screen's top says "Corel WordPerfect — Document1". You also see this **menu bar**:

| File | Edit | View | Insert | Format | Tools | Window | Help |

Type your document

Start typing your document.

WordPerfect uses the mouse and fundamental keys the same way as WordPad. For details, **read these sections on pages 97-99:**

> "Use the keyboard"
> "Scroll arrows"
> "Insert characters"
> "Split a paragraph"
> "Combine paragraphs"

QuickCorrect While you type**, the computer will automatically make little corrections to your typing**. For example:

> If you accidentally type "teh" instead of "the", the computer will change it to "the".
>
> The computer will capitalize each sentence's first word.
> If you type a day (such as "sunday"), the computer will capitalize it.
> If you capitalize the first *two* letters of a word, the computer will make the second letter small.
>
> After a word, if you accidentally press the SPACE bar *twice*, the computer will erase the second space.
>
> The computer will change 1/2 to ½.
> The computer will change -- to – and change --- to —.
> The computer will change (c to © and change (r to ®.
>
> If you type a phrase in quotation marks ("like this"), the quotation marks will become curly ("like this").

The computer's ability to make those corrections is called **QuickCorrect**.

If you dislike a correction that the computer made to your typing, here's how to undo the correction:

> Method 1: click the **Undo button** (which is under the word "Format" and has an arrow pointing to the left).
> Method 2: while holding down the Ctrl key, tap the Z key.

Those methods work just if done *immediately*, before you do any other typing or editing.

Red slashes While you type, the computer automatically puts **red slashes under any word that looks strange**. The computer considers a word to look "strange" if the word's not in the computer's dictionary or if the word's the same as the word before. For example, if you type "I loove you you now", the computer will put red slashes under "loove" and under the second "you".

If you see red slashes, you misspelled the word or accidentally repeated the word or forgot to put a space between words or your vocabulary is more advanced than the computer understands. So if you see red slashes, look carefully at the slashed word to make sure it's really what you want.

If a word has red slashes under it, try right-clicking that word (by using the mouse's right-hand button). Then the computer will make suggestions about what the slashed word ought to be.

For example, if you typed "loove" and the computer put red slashes under it, right-clicking the "loove" will make the computer display three suggestions ("love", "loose", and "poove") and two other popular choices, so you see this list:

> love
> loose
> poove
>
> Add
> Skip in Document

Choose what you want:

> If you meant "love", "loose", or "poove", click the word you meant.
>
> If you meant "loove" and want to add that slang word to the computer's permanent dictionary, click "Add". Warning: before clicking "Add", make sure the word "loove" really exists and you've spelled it correctly and your colleagues give you permission to add slang to the dictionary!
>
> If you meant "loove" but don't want to add that slang word to the dictionary, click "Skip in Document". The computer will ignore the issue about how "loove" is spelled in this document; the computer will remove the red slashes from every "loove" in this document; but since "loove" is still not in the dictionary, the computer will put red slashes under any "loove" in other documents.
>
> If you're not sure what you meant, press the keyboard's ESCAPE key (which says Esc on it). The list of choices will disappear; "loove" will still be in your document and slashed.

Page arrows Version 9 handles page arrows the same way as Microsoft Word:

For details, **read the "Page arrows" section on page 164.**

Version 8 works as follows:

> Near the screen's bottom right corner, you see a picture of a sheet of paper containing the symbol ⬇. Clicking it makes the computer show you the next page.
>
> Above that symbol, you see a picture of a sheet of paper containing this symbol ⬆. Clicking it makes the computer go back up to the top of a page. For example, while you're looking at the middle of a page, clicking that symbol makes the computer show you the top of that page. While you're looking at the *top* of a page, clicking that symbol makes the computer show you the top of the previous page.

Movement keys

To move to different parts of your document, you can use your mouse. To move faster, press these keys instead:

Key you press	Where the pointer moves
right-arrow	right to the next character
left-arrow	left to the previous character
down-arrow	down to the line below
up-arrow	up to the line above
END	right to the end of the line
HOME	left to beginning of the line
PAGE DOWN	down to the next screenful
PAGE UP	up to the previous screenful

Here's what happens if you press the movement keys while holding down the Ctrl key:

Keys you press	Where the pointer moves
Ctrl with right-arrow	right to the next word
Ctrl with left-arrow	left to the beginning of a word
Ctrl with down-arrow	down to the next paragraph
Ctrl with up-arrow	up to the beginning of a paragraph
Ctrl with END	down to the end of the document
Ctrl with HOME	up to beginning of the document

All delete

Here's how to delete the entire document, so you can start over:

> While holding down the Ctrl key, press the A key. That means "all". All of the document turns black.
>
> Then press the DELETE key. All of the document disappears, so you can start over!

Page break

When you finish typing a paragraph, you normally press the ENTER key, which tells the computer to end the paragraph. If you press the ENTER key *while holding down the CONTROL key*, the computer will end the paragraph and insert a **page break**: it makes the next paragraph be at the top of the next page.

If you change your mind, here's how to remove the page break: click at the beginning of the paragraph you've put at the top of a page; then press the BACKSPACE key.

Property toolbar

Near the screen's top, you see the **property toolbar**, which looks like this:

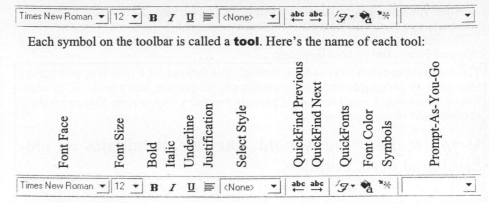

Each symbol on the toolbar is called a **tool**. Here's the name of each tool:

(Font Face, Font Size, Bold, Italic, Underline, Justification, Select Style, QuickFind Previous, QuickFind Next, QuickFonts, Font Color, Symbols, Prompt-As-You-Go)

Version 9 omits the Symbols tool.

If you forget a tool's name, try this trick: point at the tool (by using the mouse, but *without* clicking), then wait a second. Underneath the tool, you'll see the tool's name and a short explanation of what the tool does.

The toolbar includes 4 white boxes. Each box has a down-arrow to its right.

The toolbar also includes square **buttons** saying "B", "*I*", "U", etc. To use a button, press it by clicking it with the mouse. Here are the details....

Fundamental buttons

WordPerfect uses the same fundamental buttons as Microsoft Word. For details, **read these sections on page 165**:

> "Underline"
> "Bold"
> "Italic"

Font Color

Normally, the characters you type are black. Here's how to change a phrase's color. Click the **Font Color** button. You'll see 42 colors; click the color you want. Then type the phrase you want colorized.

When you finish typing that colorized phrase, click the Font Color button again and click Black.

Font Size

Look at the **Font Size box**. In that box, you normally see the number 12. That means the characters you're typing are 12 points high. Here's how to type characters that are bigger or smaller:

> Click the Font Size box. In that box, type a whole number from 8 to 72. (Theoretically, you can pick a number even smaller than 8 or even bigger than 72 or even a number that ends in .5, such as 8.5; but those wild numbers create ugly results.) When you finish typing the number, press the ENTER key.

Any new characters you type afterwards will be the size you chose. (Characters you typed above don't change size.)

The popular sizes look like this:

> This text is 8 points high, 9 points high, 10 points high, 11 points high, 12 points high, 14 points high, 16 points high, 18 points high, 20 points, 24 points, 28 pt., 32 pt., 36pt., 48pt., 72pt.

When you finish typing the enlarged or reduced characters, here's how to return to typing characters that are normal size (12-point): click the Font Size box, then click the 12.

Font Face

When you type, you're normally using a font face called "Times New Roman". If you wish, you can switch to a different font face instead.

The most popular Windows font faces are "Times New Roman", "Arial", and "Courier New". Here's how they look:

> This font face is called "Times New Roman". It's the best for typing long passages of text, such as paragraphs in books, newspapers, magazines, and reports. It squeezes lots of words onto a small amount of paper but remains easy to read. You can make it plain or **bold** or *italic* or ***bold italic***.
>
> ### If you make it big & bold, like this, it imitates an old-fashioned news headline.

> This font face is called "Arial". It's simple. You can make it plain or **bold** or *italic* or ***bold italic***. It resembles Helvetica. It's best for typing short phrases that attract attention. For example....
>
> ### If you make it big & bold, like this, it's good for titles, signs, and posters.
>
> If you make it small, like this, it's good for footnotes, photo captions, classified ads, telephone books, directories, and catalogs.

> ```
> This font face is called "Courier New".
>
> If you make it 12 points high, like this, it
> resembles the printout from a typewriter.
>
> It makes each character have the same width: for example,
> the "m" has the same width as the "I". It's a good font
> for typing tables of numbers, since the uniform width
> lets you line up each column of numbers easily.
>
> Choose plain, bold, italic, or bold italic.
> ```

In the **Font Face box**, you see the name of a font face, which is usually "Times New Roman". Click it.

You start seeing the **Font Face menu**, which is list of font faces, including "Times New Roman", "Arial", "Courier New", and several other fonts.

The Font Face menu appears in a window, which is too small to show the entire menu. The best way to see the rest of the menu is to **tap the keyboard's up-arrow or down-arrow key several times**. Each tap highlights a different font face and shows you how the letters "AaBbYyZz" look in that font face.

The best font faces have "TT" written in front of them. The "TT" means the font face is a **True Type font face** (created by a system that lets you make the characters as big or as small as you wish and accurately reproduces those characters onto your screen and paper). For example, "Times New Roman", "Arial", and "Courier New" are True Type font faces and have "TT" written in front of them.

Keep tapping the up-arrow or down-arrow key until the font face you want is highlighted; then press ENTER.

Afterwards, whatever characters you type will be in the font face you chose. (The characters you typed earlier remain unaffected.)

When you finish typing in that font face, here's how to return to typing characters that are normal (Times New Roman): click the Font Face box, then click TT Times New Roman.

Justification

While typing a line, you can click the **Justification button**, which shows you this **Justification menu**:

> Left
> Right
> Center
> Full
> All

Choosing **Center** makes the line be centered,

> like this line

Choosing **Right** makes the line be at the right margin,

> like this line

Choosing **Left** makes the line be at the left margin,

> like this line

Choosing **All** makes the line be at both margins (by putting extra spaces between the words and letters),

> l i k e   t h i s   l i n e

Each of those choices affects not just the line you're typing but also all other lines in the same paragraph. (The paragraphs you typed earlier remain unaffected.) When you start typing a new paragraph, the computer gives that paragraph the same alignment as the paragraph above, unless you say differently (by choosing a different alignment).

Full If you choose **Full**, the paragraph's bottom line will be **Left** and the paragraph's other lines will be **All**. For example, the paragraph you're reading now is Full.

Examples Here's when to use those choices:

> If you're typing a title or headline and want it to be centered, choose **Center**.
>
> If you're typing a business letter and want it to begin by showing the date next to the right margin, choose **Right**.
>
> If you're typing an informal memo or letter to a colleague or friend, and want the paragraph to look plain, ordinary, modest, and unassuming (like Clark Kent), choose **Left**.
>
> If you're creating something formal (such as a newspaper or textbook) and want the paragraph to have perfectly straight edges (so it looks official, uptight, and professional, like Robocop), choose **Full**.
>
> If you're creating a poster and want each line of the poster to have exactly the same length, choose **All**.

Centered title Here's how to type a centered title, using the techniques you've learned so far....

Press the ENTER key twice (to leave a big blank space above the title).

Click the Justification button and click Center (so the title will be centered). Click the Bold button (so the title will be bold). Type the words you want to be in the title, and press the ENTER key afterwards.

Congratulations! You've created a centered title!

Next, make the paragraph underneath the title be normal: make that paragraph be uncentered (by choosing Left or Full from the Justification menu) and make it be unbolded (by clicking the Bold button, so the Bold button pops back out).

Shortcuts Here are shortcuts:

Instead of choosing Left from the Justification menu, you can press Ctrl with L.

Instead of choosing Right from the Justification menu, you can press Ctrl with R.

Instead of choosing Center from the Justification menu, you can press Ctrl with E (standing for "Equidistant").

Instead of choosing Full from the Justification menu, you can press Ctrl with J (standing for "fully Justify").

Select text

Here's how to dramatically change a phrase you typed.

Put the mouse at the phrase's beginning. (Do *not* point at the dotted lines that are your page's margins. If you accidentally point at the dotted lines, your mouse pointer will have a left-arrow and right-arrow coming out of it. Make those arrows go away by moving your mouse slightly to the right.) Then drag to the phrase's end (while holding down the mouse's left button). The whole phrase turns black. Turning the phrase black is called **selecting the phrase**.

Then say what to do to the phrase. For example, choose one of these activities:

To underline the phrase, push in the Underline button.
To make the phrase be bold, push in the Bold button.
To italicize the phrase, push in the Italic button.
To prevent the phrase from being underlined, bold, or italicized, pop those buttons back out.

To change the phrase's color, click the Font Color button then click the color you want.
To change the phrase's point size, click the Font Size box then type the size you want (and press ENTER).
To change the phrase's font face, click the Font Face box then click the font you want.
To change how the phrase's paragraphs justify, click the Justification button then the method you want.

To delete the phrase, press the **DELETE key**.
To replace the phrase, just type whatever words you want the phrase to become.

Go ahead! Try it now! It's fun!

Other ways to select

The usual way to select a phrase is to point at the phrase's beginning, then drag to the phrase's end. But sometimes other methods are faster!

To select a phrase, choose one of these methods....

Method 1: point at the phrase's beginning, then **drag** to the phrase's end.

Method 2: click the phrase's beginning; then while holding down the **SHIFT key**, click the phrase's end.

Method 3: by using your keyboard's **movement keys** (such as up-arrow, down-arrow, left-arrow, and right-arrow), move to the phrase's beginning; then while holding down the SHIFT key, use the movement keys to move to the phrase's end.

Method 4: to select just **one word**, double-click in its middle.

Method 5: to select just **one sentence**, triple-click in its middle.

Method 6: to select just **one paragraph**, quadruple-click in its middle.

Method 7: to select **several paragraphs**, quadruple-click in the first paragraph's middle; then while holding down the SHIFT key, click in the last paragraph's middle.

Method 8: to select the **entire document** (all!), press the A key while holding down the Ctrl key.

Drag a phrase

To move a phrase to a new location, just "select the phrase, and then drag from the phrase's middle to the new location." Here are the details....

First, select the phrase you want to move, so the phrase turns black.

Then take your finger off the mouse's button. Move the mouse's pointer to the phrase's middle (so you see an arrow).

Finally, hold down the mouse's button; and while you keep holding down the mouse's button, drag to wherever you want the phrase to move.

When you finish dragging, lift your finger from the mouse's button. Presto, the phrase moves where you wished!

WordPerfect toolbar

Near the screen's top, above the property toolbar, you see the **WordPerfect toolbar**, which looks like this:

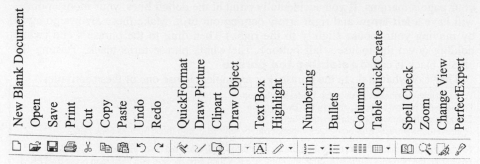

(Version 9 contains four extra tools at the far right.) Here's how to use the most popular of those tools....

Save

To save the document (copy it onto the disk), click the **Save button** (or press Ctrl with S).

If you haven't saved the document before, the computer will say "File Name". Invent a name for your document. Type the name and press ENTER.

That makes the computer copy the document onto the hard disk. For example, if you named the document "mary", the computer will put a document called mary.wpd into the My Documents folder. (Version 8 uses the MyFiles folder instead.)

Afterwards, if you change your mind and want to do more editing, go ahead! When you finish that extra editing, save it by clicking the Save button again.

Save often If you're typing a long document, click the Save button about every 10 minutes. Click it whenever you get to a good stopping place and think, "What I've typed so far looks good!"

Then if an accident happens, you'll lose at most 10 minutes of work, and you can return to the last version you felt good about.

Print

Here's how to print the document onto paper. Make sure you've bought a printer, attached it to the computer, turned the printer's power on, and put paper into the printer. Click the **Print button** (or press Ctrl with P), then press ENTER. The printer will print your document onto paper.

How to finish

When you finish working on a document, choose **Exit** or **Close** from the **File menu**.

If you choose **Exit**, the computer stops using WordPerfect.

If you choose **Close** instead of Exit, you see a blank document. Start typing (to construct a new document) or click the **Open button**.

If you click the **Open button** (or press Ctrl with O), you'll see a list of old documents. If you want to *use* one of those documents, double-click the document's name; the computer will put that document onto the screen and let you edit it. If instead you want to *delete* one of those documents, click the document's name and then press the DELETE key and then the ENTER key; the computer will move that document to the Recycle Bin.

Didn't save? If you didn't save your document before doing those procedures, the computer asks, "Save changes?" If you click "Yes", the computer copies your document's most recent version to the hard disk; if you click "No" instead, the computer ignores and forgets your most recent editing.

Congratulations! You've learned all the fundamental commands of WordPerfect!

Tricks

WordPerfect performs the same tricks as Microsoft Word. For details, **read these sections on pages 170-171:**

"Undo"
"Redo"
"Cut and Paste"
"Copy"

Zoom

If you click the **Zoom button**, you see this **Zoom menu**:

```
Margin Width
Page Width
Full Page
50%
75%
100%
150%
200%
Other
```

The computer assumes you want 100%. If you click **200%** instead, the computer makes the screen's characters be twice as high and twice as wide as normal, so you can read them even if you're sitting far away from the screen or you have poor vision. It's like looking at the document through a magnifying glass: the document looks enlarged, so you can see the details of each word and character more clearly; but not as many words and characters fit on the screen. Use the arrow keys to see different parts of the page.

Clicking 200% enlarges just what you see on the *screen*: it does *not* enlarge what appears on paper.

Try it! Try clicking 200%!

When you finish admiring that view, make the screen return to normal, by choosing **100%** from the Zoom menu.

If you click **Full Page** instead of 200%, the computer does just the opposite: the computer makes the screen's characters be very tiny, so the whole page fits on the screen — as if you were doing a print preview.

A more pleasant choice is **Page Width**. It makes the screen's characters be as big as possible, but still small enough so that you can see the left and right edges of the paper.

My favorite choice is **Margin Width**. It makes the screen's characters be as big as possible (even bigger than Page Width), but still small enough so that you can see the left and right edges of your typing.

If you prefer, choose **50%**, **75%**, or **150%**.

For wilder choices, choose **Other**, then click "Other" again. Click the screen's up-arrow or down-arrow key several times, to choose your favorite number from 25% to 400%. (The arrow keys limit you a multiple of 5%, such as 25%, 30%, 40%, 45%, etc.) Then press ENTER.

Columns

In a newspaper, text is printed in many narrow **columns**. In a business letter, text is printed in a single wide column.

The computer assumes you want a single wide column. **Here's how to tell the computer you want many narrow columns:**

> Click in the middle of the document's first word. Click the **Columns button**. From the menu that appears, choose how many columns you want: choose either **2 Columns**, **3 Columns**, **4 Columns**, or **5 Columns**.
>
> Then the document changes, so it has as many columns as you requested. The gap between each pair of columns is a half-inch.

Column break When you finish typing a paragraph, you normally press the ENTER key, which tells the computer to end the paragraph. If you've created columns, and you press the ENTER key *while holding down the CONTROL key*, the computer will end the paragraph and insert a **column break**: it makes the next paragraph be at the top of the next column.

If you change your mind, here's how to remove the column break: click at the beginning of the paragraph you've put at the top of a column; then press the BACKSPACE key.

Return to 1 column If you change your mind and want just 1 column, do this: press Ctrl with HOME (so you go to the very beginning of the document), then click the Columns button again, then click **Discontinue**.

Bullets

While you're typing a paragraph, try pushing in the **Bullets button** (by clicking it). That makes the computer indent the paragraph a half inch and also put a bullet (the symbol •) to the left of the paragraph's first line. That's called a **bulleted paragraph**.

After you've typed a bulleted paragraph, any new paragraphs you type underneath will be bulleted also — until you request an *un*bulleted paragraph (by popping the Bullets button back out).

Different symbols Although the bullet symbol is usually •, you can choose a different symbol instead, by clicking the down-arrow that's to the right of the Bullets button and then clicking the symbol you prefer. You can choose these symbols:

·	●	◆	►	■	□	❑	✓

Numbering

While you're typing a paragraph, try pushing in the **Numbering button** (by clicking it). That makes the computer indent the paragraph a half inch and put "1." to the left of the paragraph's first line. That's called a **numbered paragraph**.

When you type a new paragraph underneath, that paragraph will be numbered "2.", the next paragraph will be numbered "3.", etc. — until you request an *un*numbered paragraph (by popping the Numbering button back out) or you press the TAB key (which makes the paragraph be indented a full inch and be lettered "a." instead of numbered; the paragraphs below will be lettered "b.", "c.", etc. — until you request an *un*lettered paragraph by pressing SHIFT with TAB).

Table QuickCreate

In the middle of your document, here's how to type a table of numbers:

Click where you want the table to appear.

Put the mouse pointer on the **Table QuickCreate button**, then hold down the mouse's button awhile. While you hold down the mouse's button, you see a tiny picture of a table that has 10 rows and 13 columns. Altogether, it contains 130 tiny cells (since 10 times 13 is 130).

Point at that table's top left tiny cell, and drag down and to the right, until the number of rows and columns you want turns dark gray.

For example, **if you want just 3 rows and 4 columns, drag down and to the right until 3 rows and 4 columns turn dark gray**, so you see 12 dark gray cells altogether.

When you take your finger off the mouse's button, you'll see the table you requested.

Then just fill in the cells, with whatever numbers and words you wish. To move from cell to cell, click with the mouse, or press the TAB key (which moves right to the next cell), or press SHIFT with TAB (which moves left to the previous cell), or press the arrow keys repeatedly.

In a cell, you can type a number, word, sentence, or even an entire paragraph! If you start typing a paragraph in a cell, the computer will automatically make the cell and its row taller, so the entire paragraph will fit in the cell. You can even type *several* paragraphs in a single cell: just press the ENTER key at the end of each paragraph. If you want to indent the first line of one of those paragraphs, press the SPACE bar several times or press Ctrl with TAB.

Extra rows Here's how to create an extra row at the bottom of the table: click in the table's bottom right cell, then press the TAB key.

Here's how to insert an extra row into the *middle* of the table: right-click in the row that's underneath where you want the extra row to appear, then click Insert, then press ENTER.

Extra columns Here's how to insert an extra column into the middle of the table: right-click in the column that's to the right of where you want the extra column to appear, then click Insert, then click Columns, then press ENTER.

Column widths The computer assumes you want the table's columns to all be the same width. But you can change that assumption!

For example, here's how to adjust the width of the table's left column (column 1):

> Move the mouse until its pointer is on the vertical line that separates column 1 from column 2, and the pointer's shape turns into this symbol: ↔. Then drag the vertical line to the right (to make the column wider) or left (to make the column narrower).

If you widen a column, the computer makes room for it by shrinking the next column. If you make a column narrower, the computer compensates by expanding the next column.

If you want to fine-tune the widths of *all* columns, work from left to right: adjust the width of column 1 (by dragging the line that separates it from column 2), then adjust the width of column 2 (by dragging the line that separates it from column 3), then adjust the width of column 3 (by dragging the line that separates it from column 4), etc.

Numbers If a column contains mostly numbers, here's how to make that column look prettier, so the numbers and their decimal points line up properly:

> Right-click in the middle of the column. Click **Format** then **Column** then **Left** (which is in a box) then **Decimal Align**. Press ENTER.

Below the table When you've finished editing the table, here's how to put paragraphs below it:

> Click below the table by using the mouse, or go below the table by pressing the down-arrow key several times. Then type the paragraphs you want below the table.

Delete Here's how to delete a row: right-click in the middle of the row, then click **Delete**, then press ENTER.

Here's how to delete a column: right-click in the middle of the column, then click **Delete**, then click **Columns**, then press ENTER.

Starting

Here's how to start using Q&A versions 3 and 4 for DOS. (Version 5 resembles version 4. Versions 1, 1.1 and 2 resemble version 3.)

I'll assume you have a hard disk whose CONFIG.SYS file mentions "files" and "buffers" (as I recommended in the MS-DOS chapter).

Copy Q&A to the hard disk

Version 3 comes on seven 5¼-inch floppies. Version 4 comes on eight 5¼-inch floppies. (If you want 3½-inch floppies, ask your dealer for the 3½-inch version.)

Here's how to copy Q&A to the hard disk.

<u>Version 3</u> Turn on the computer without any floppy in drive A. After the C prompt, type "md qa" (so you're making a subdirectory called QA). After the next C prompt, type "cd qa" (so you're changing to the QA subdirectory).

Put Q&A System Disk 1 into drive A, and type "copy a:*.*" (which copies all the floppy's files onto the hard disk). Follow the same procedure for all the other Q&A floppy disks, in numerical order: do Q&A System Disk 2, then Q&A System Disk 3, etc., and finally the Q&A Tutorial.

<u>Version 4</u> Turn on the computer without any floppy in drive A. When you see the C prompt, put the Q&A #1 Install Disk in drive A and type "a:install".

The computer says, "Q&A Version 4.0 Installation". Press ENTER twice.

The computer says, "DESTINATION DRIVE SELECTION". Press the down-arrow key twice, so the "C:" is darkened. Press ENTER.

The computer says "C:\QA4". Tap the BACKSPACE key (so you change the computer's message to "C:\QA"). Press ENTER twice.

Here's what happens next (when you're using 5¼-inch floppies).

> The computer says, "Please insert disk 2". Put the Q&A #2 Disk in drive A and press ENTER.
> The computer says, "Please insert disk 3". Put the Q&A #3 Disk in drive A and press ENTER.
> The computer says, "Please insert disk 4". Put the Q&A #4 Disk in drive A and press ENTER.
> The computer says, "Please insert disk 5". Put the Q&A #5 Disk in drive A and press ENTER.
> The computer says, "Please insert disk 6". Put the Q&A #6 Disk in drive A. Press ENTER 4 times.

Then the computer shows the top of an alphabetical list of printers. Press the down-arrow key several times, until *your* printer is darkened.

Press the SPACE bar (so a check mark appears next to your printer). Press ENTER 4 times.

Here's what happens next:

> The computer shows a list of tutorial files. Press the F5 key. Press ENTER.
> The computer says, "Please insert disk 7". Put the Q&A #7 Disk in drive A. Press ENTER 4 times.
> The computer shows a list of databases. Press the F5 key. Press ENTER 4 times.

Then the computer shows a list of utility files. Put check marks next to ASC-CODE.ASC, LINE-DOC.DOC, and QABACKUP.EXE. (Do *not* put a check mark next to HIMEM.SYS, since that version of HIMEM.SYS is obsolete.) To create a check mark, press the down-arrow key repeatedly until the item you want to check is darkened, then press the SPACE bar. When you've created all three check marks, end the whole process by pressing ENTER.

The computer says, "Please insert disk 8". Put the Q&A #8 Disk in drive A. Press ENTER 5 times.

Make Q&A act better

After you've copied Q&A to the hard disk, make Q&A act better. Here's how.

Step 1: get to the utilities menu Type "qa". The computer says "Q&A MAIN MENU". Press U then ENTER. Computer says "UTILITIES MENU".

Step 2: select automatic execution Press S then ENTER. Press the down-arrow key several times, until the words "Automatic Execution" are highlighted. Press the left-arrow key (so that the word "Yes" is highlighted). Press the F10 key. The computer says "UTILITIES MENU" again.

Step 3: select a printer Press P. The computer will say "PRINTER SELECTION". Press ENTER twice.

If you're using version 3, here's what happens next:

> The computer says "LIST OF PRINTERS". Press the PAGE DOWN (or PgDn) key repeatedly until you see the name of your printer (or a similar printer). Use the arrow keys to move to your printer's name. Press ENTER twice. Press the F10 key.

If you're using version 4, this happens instead:

> The computer says "LIST OF PRINTER MANUFACTURERS". If you don't see name of your printer's manufacturer, press PAGE DOWN (or PgDn) key. Use arrow keys to move to your printer's name. Press ENTER. You see a list of printer models. Use arrow keys and PAGE DOWN key to move to your printer model. Press ENTER twice.

Finally, the computer says, "Your printer has been installed". Press N. The computer says "UTILITIES MENU" again.

Step 4: exit Press the "Esc" key. Press X. You'll see a C prompt. Turn off the computer, so you can start fresh.

Run Q&A

To run Q&A, turn on the computer without any floppy in drive A.

If you've put the DO.BAT file onto your hard disk (as I recommended in the MS-DOS chapter) and put Q&A into the QA subdirectory (as I recommended above), your life is easy! Just type "do qa".

If you have *not* put DO.BAT onto your hard disk, do this instead: type "cd qa" and then "qa".

The computer will print this on the screen:

```
Q&A MAIN MENU
F - File
R - Report
W - Write
A - Assistant
U - Utilities
X - Exit Q&A
```

That **main menu** is a list of the various activities the program can perform for you.

If you're using version 4 and have a mouse, you'll see a small red rectangle in the middle of the screen. Move that rectangle out of the way — to the screen's top right corner — by rolling the mouse toward your desk's back right corner.

Get into typing

To use Q&A's word processor, choose "W - Write" from the main menu by pressing the W key. (That works if you followed my instructions about "select automatic execution". If you did *not* follow those instructions, you must press ENTER after pressing W — and you must press ENTER after choosing any item from any menu!)

The screen will show the **write menu**:

```
WRITE MENU
T - Type/edit
D - Define page
P - Print
C - Clear
G - Get
S - Save
U - Utilities
M - Mailing labels
```

That menu is a list of what Q&A's word processor can do for you.

To begin, choose "T - Type/edit" from the write menu (by pressing T).

The lower right-hand corner of the screen will say "Line 1 of Page 1 of 1", which means you can begin typing your document.

Type the document

Begin typing whatever document you wish to create. For example, try typing a novel that begins like this:

> Once upon a time, a man was walking down the street, when lo and behold, his house was gone. As he gaped into the hole, a burning sensation in his shoes warned him that…

I'll let you complete that paragraph yourself! Be creative!

Shift keys To capitalize a letter, type the letter while holding down a Shift key. (One Shift key is next to the Z key; the other Shift key is next to the ? key. Each Shift key has an up-arrow on it.)

BACKSPACE key If you make a mistake, erase it by pressing the BACKSPACE key, which erases the character you just typed. (The BACKSPACE key is in the upper-right corner of the keyboard's main section. It's to the right of the + key, and it has a left-arrow on it.)

ENTER key As you type that paragraph and get near the right margin, do *not* press the ENTER key. Just keep on typing! The computer will press the ENTER key for you automatically.

If you try to type a long word near the right margin, and the word's too long to fit before the margin, the computer will automatically move the entire word to the line below. The computer's ability to automatically move an entire word to the line below is called **word wrap**.

Since the computer automatically presses the ENTER key for you, **never press the ENTER key yourself until you reach the end of a paragraph**. Pressing the ENTER key there makes the computer return to the left margin, so that you can begin a new paragraph. Pressing the ENTER key means: begin a new paragraph.

If you want to double-space between paragraphs, press the ENTER key *twice*.

TAB key If you want to indent the new paragraph's first word, press the TAB key before typing that word. (The TAB key is next to the Q key and has arrows on it.) Pressing the TAB key indents the word a half inch.

To indent the word even farther, press the TAB key *extra* times before typing the word. Each *extra* time you press the TAB key, the word indents a *full* inch farther.

Lists To type a list of short lines, such as this recipe for White Death Cookies —

> 3 cups of powdered milk
> 2 cups of water
> 1 pound of sugar
> 1 pound of cocaine
> mix & shape
> bake at 350 degrees for 15 minutes
> serves 7 ghosts

press the ENTER key at the end of each line.

Try typing this English-French dictionary:

ENGLISH	FRENCH
love	amour
pain	peine
tenderness	tendresse

Here's how. Type the first column's heading (ENGLISH), press the TAB key several times (to move far to the right), type the second column's heading (FRENCH), and press ENTER. Type "love", press the TAB key repeatedly until you're under FRENCH, type "amour", and press ENTER. Use the same technique for the table's other lines.

CAPS LOCK

If you press the CAPS LOCK key, the letters of the alphabet will be automatically capitalized (and you'll be in **caps mode**), until you press the CAPS LOCK key again. When you're in caps mode, the screen's bottom center says "Caps".

If your keyboard is modern, its top right corner has a Caps Lock light. When you're in caps mode, that light glows.

NUM LOCK

On the keyboard's right side, you'll see a group of keys containing numbers. That group of keys is called the **numeric keypad**.

Try this experiment: on the numeric keypad, press the 5 key. If that made a "5" appear on your screen, you're in **number mode**. If that did *not* make a "5" appear on your screen, you're *not* in number mode. To switch to or from number mode, press the NUM LOCK key.

When you're in number mode, the screen's bottom center says "Num".

If your keyboard is modern, its top right corner has a Num Lock light. When you're in number mode, that light glows.

In this chapter, we'll use the numeric keypad for purposes more advanced than typing numbers. So to follow the instructions in this chapter, do *not* use those keys to type numbers: **do NOT be in number mode**. (Do *not* have the bottom of the screen say "Num". Do *not* let the Num Lock light glow. Do *not* let the 5 key put a "5" on the screen.)

Press the NUM LOCK key if necessary, so that you're *not* in number mode.

Move the cursor

After you've typed a few paragraphs (and pressed the ENTER key at the end of each paragraph), you can move around the screen and edit your document.

Arrow keys On your screen the short, blinking underline is called the **cursor**. To move the cursor up, press the key that has an up-arrow on it. You can move the cursor in all four directions, by pressing the up-arrow, down-arrow, left-arrow, and right-arrow keys. Each of those keys automatically repeats: so to move the cursor up *several* lines, just keep your finger on the up-arrow key a while.

(If the arrow keys don't work, that's because you're in number mode. Get out of number mode by pressing the NUM LOCK key.)

Word hop *While holding down the CONTROL key* (which says "Ctrl" on it), you can tap the right-arrow key. That makes the cursor hop to the right: to the next word.

While holding down the CONTROL key, you can tap the left-arrow key. That makes the cursor hop left to the beginning of the current word; if the cursor's *already* at the word's beginning, it will hop to the beginning of the previous word.

Pages A sheet of paper is called a **page**. The typical page is tall enough to hold 54 lines of your document. The page is taller than your screen, which holds just 21 lines.

As you type, the computer automatically divides your document into pages and screenfuls.

When you're at the top of a page, the screen shows the top of that sheet of paper, like this:

When you're at the bottom of a page, the screen shows the bottom of that sheet of paper, like this:

When you're moving from one page to the next, the screen shows the bottom of one page and then the top of the next page, like this:

Near the top and bottom of each page, the screen shows a blank space, for the top and bottom margins.

Far hop To make the cursor hop far, press these keys:

Keys you press	Where the cursor will move
HOME	the beginning of the line
HOME HOME	the top of the screen
HOME HOME HOME	the top of the page
HOME HOME HOME HOME	the beginning of the document
Ctrl with HOME	very top (same as four HOMEs)
END	the end of the line
END END	the bottom of the screen
END END END	the bottom of the page
END END END END	the end of the document
Ctrl with END	very end (same as four ENDs)
PAGE UP (PgUp)	the previous screenful
PAGE DOWN (PgDn)	the next screenful
Ctrl with PgUp	the previous page
Ctrl with PgDn	the next page

DELETE key

To delete the character you just typed, press the BACKSPACE key. To delete a character you typed long ago, move the cursor to that character, then press the DELETE key (which says "Del" on it). To delete a passage typed long ago, move the cursor to passage's beginning, then tap the DELETE key several times (or hold down the DELETE key a while), until the passage disappears.

Combine paragraphs After typing two paragraphs, here's how to combine them to form a single paragraph that's longer.

By pressing the up-arrow key, move the cursor to the first paragraph's bottom line. Move to the end of that line, by pressing the END key. Delete the end-of-paragraph mark, by pressing the DELETE key.

Press the DELETE key a few more times (to delete unwanted TAB spaces and ENTERs).

INSERT key

Q&A can be in two modes: **typeover** or **insert**.

When you start using Q&A, it's in typeover mode. In typeover mode, the cursor's an underline.

To switch to insert mode, tap the INSERT key (which says "Ins" on it). When you're in insert mode, the bottom of the screen says "Insert" and the cursor's a square (instead of an underline). To switch back to typeover mode, tap the INSERT key again.

How to type over Suppose your document contains incorrect characters. Here's how to replace them.

Move the cursor to where the incorrect characters begin. Make sure you're in typeover mode (so that the cursor's an underline). Then type over the characters you want to change.

How to insert Here's how to insert extra characters into the middle of your document.

Move the cursor to where you want the extra characters to begin. Make sure you're in insert mode (by tapping the INSERT key if necessary), so that the bottom of the screen says "Insert" and the cursor's a square. Then type the characters you want to insert.

The other characters on the screen will automatically move out of the way to make room for the extra characters.

Split a paragraph Here's how to split a paragraph into two shorter paragraphs.

What word should begin the second short paragraph? Move the cursor to that word's first letter.

Make sure you're in insert mode (by pressing the INSERT key if necessary), so that the bottom of the screen says "Insert". Press ENTER. Now you've split the long paragraph into two!

If you want to double-space between the two short paragraphs, press ENTER again. If you want to indent the second paragraph, press the TAB key.

Function keys

On the keyboard, you'll see **function keys** labeled F1, F2, F3, F4, F5, F6, F7, F8, F9, and F10. If your keyboard is modern, those function keys are on the *top* of the keyboard, along with two extra keys (F11 and F12).

By pressing the function keys, you can give these commands:

Command	Keys to press	Notes for version 3 users
Assign fonts	Ctrl F9	
Calculate	Alt F9	
Capitalize	F8 then B then A	This command is just in version 4.
Center	F8 then A then C	In version 3, press F8 then C.
Continue	F10	
Copy	F5	
Copy to file	Ctrl F5	
Define page	Ctrl F6	
Delete block	F3	
Delete line	Shift F4	
Delete to right	Ctrl F4	
Delete word	F4	
Double space	F8 then A then D	This command is just in version 4.
Draw	F8 then L then D	In version 3, press F8 then D.
Enhance	Shift F6	
Export	Ctrl F8	
Field	Alt F7	
Footer	F8 then L then F	In version 3, press F8 then F.
Go to	Ctrl F7	
Header	F8 then L then H	In version 3, press F8 then H.
Help	F1	
Hyphenate	Alt F6	
Insert doc	F8 then D then I	In version 3, press F8 then-I.
Left	F8 then A then L	In version 3, press F8 then U.
Lowercase	F8 then B then L	This command is just in version 4.
Macro	Shift F2	
Macro run	Alt F2	This command is just in version 4.
Move	Shift F5	
Move to file	Alt F5	
New page	F8 then L then N	In version 3, press F8 then N.
Print	F2	
Print block	Ctrl F2	
Restore	Shift F7	
Right	F8 then A then R	This command is just in version 4.
Save	Shift F8	
Scroll up	F9	
Scroll down	Shift F9	
Search	F7	
Set tabs	F8 then L then S	In version 3, press F8 then S.
Single space	F8 then A then S	This command is just in version 4.
Spell	Shift F1	
Spell word	Ctrl F1	
Statistics	Ctrl F3	
Temp margin	F6	
Thesaurus	Alt F1	This command is just in version 4.
Title	F8 then B then T	This command is just in version 4.
Triple space	F8 then A then P	This command is just in version 4.

Put that chart (or a photocopy of it) next to the computer.

When you buy Q&A, you get a plastic **template** that you put next to the function keys. The template contains an abridged version of the chart.

While you're using Q&A, the bottom of Q&A's screen displays a different abridgment of the chart.

Here's how to use those function keys....

Delete word (F4)

To delete a word, put the cursor at the word's first character, then say "Delete word" (by pressing the F4 key).

Delete line (Shift F4)

To delete a whole line of text, put the cursor in that line, then say "Delete line". (Here's how to say "Delete line": *while holding down the Shift key*, press the F4 key.)

Delete to right (Ctrl F4)

To delete the far right part of a line, put the cursor where that part begins, then say "Delete to right". (Here's how to say "Delete to right": *while holding down the Ctrl key*, press the F4 key.)

Go to (Ctrl F7)

To make the cursor hop to page 3, say "Go to" (by pressing Ctrl with F7), then type 3 and press F10.

Statistics (Ctrl F3)

If you say "Statistics" (by pressing Ctrl with F3), the computer will tell you how many words, lines, and paragraphs are in your document. It will also tell you how many words, lines, and paragraphs are in your document's first part (the part before the cursor) and how many are in the second part (the part after the cursor).

When you finish looking at those statistics, press the ESCAPE key (which says "Esc" on it).

Align (F8 A)

If a line of text is short, you can make the line be **aligned** in three ways: **flush left** or **centered** or **flush right**.

> This line is flush left.
>
> This line is centered.
>
> This line is flush right.

The computer assumes you want each line to be flush left, unless you say otherwise. Here's how to change the line's alignment.

Version 4 Move the cursor to the line whose alignment you want to affect. (It can be a line you typed already or a line you're going to start typing.)

Press F8 then A. (The A stands for "align".) Then press L (to make the line be flush left) or C (to make the line be centered) or R (to make the line be flush right).

Version 3 Move the cursor to the line whose alignment you want to affect. It can be a line you typed already or a line you're going to start typing.

If you want to center the line, press F8 then C.

If you want the line to be flush left, put the cursor on the line's first word (or anywhere to the right of that word), then press F8 then U. (The U stands for "uncenter").

Version 3 doesn't understand how to make the line be flush right.

Help (F1)

If you forget how to use Q&A, say "Help" (by pressing the first function key, F1). You'll see a chart that reminds you what each function key does. Then press the ESCAPE key (which says "Esc" on it).

Blocks

You can manipulate a large portion of your document with a single keystroke! The portion you're manipulating is called the **block**. It can consist of several words, several sentences, several paragraphs, or even several pages.

To manipulate a block, put the cursor at the block's beginning. (For example, to manipulate a whole paragraph, put the cursor at the paragraph's beginning.) Then give one of these commands....

Delete block (F3)

To delete the block, say "Delete block" (by pressing F3). Then put the cursor at the block's last character, and press F10.

Copy (F5)

To copy the block (instead of deleting it), say "Copy" (by pressing F5). Then put the cursor at the block's last character, and press F10. Put the cursor where you want the block's copy to appear, and press F10.

Move (Shift F5)

To move the block (so it vanishes from its current location and reappears elsewhere), say "Move" (by pressing Shift with F5). Then put the cursor at the block's last character, and press F10. Move the cursor where you want the block's new position to be, then press F10 again.

Enhance (Shift F6)

To enhance the block (so it looks different from the rest of the document and stands out), say "Enhance" (by pressing Shift with F6).

Then say which enhancement to perform:

---
press U to Underline (so the block looks <u>like this</u>)
press B to make Bold (so the block looks **like this**)
press I to italicize (so the block looks *like this*)
press X to X out (so the block looks ~~like this~~)
press S to Subscript (so the block is lowered, like this)
press P to suPerscript (so the block is raised, like this)
press R to make Regular again (so the block looks like this)

Put the cursor at the block's last character, and press F10.

Don't see the bold? If you pressed B (to make Bold) but the block doesn't look bold, adjust your screen's contrast and brightness knobs.

Don't see the underline? If you're using a CGA, EGA, or VGA monitor and pressed U (to underline), the block will change color on the screen but won't be underlined until you print it on paper.

Don't see other enhancements? If you pressed I (to italicize), the block will change color on the screen. It will be italicized just on paper, and just if your printer knows how to italicize.

You face the same hassle with other enhancements (X out, subscript, and superscript): on your screen the block just changes color. The desired enhancements occur just on paper, and just if your printer knows how to perform them.

Final steps

After editing your document, copy it onto the hard disk and paper and move on to a different task. Here's how....

Save (Shift F8)

While you're typing and editing your document, it's in the computer's RAM chips but *not* on a disk. If the computer's electricity is knocked out (by a thunderstorm or by your cat pulling the plug) or you accidentally hold down the DELETE key awhile, the RAM chips and your document will be erased.

To protect against accidents, copy your document onto a disk. Copying a document onto a disk is called **saving**.

To save, just say "Save" (by pressing Shift with F8).

Then the computer will ask you to invent a name for your document. The name must be short: no more than 8 letters. For example, the name can be "jennifer" or "al". Type the name you wish and press ENTER.

The computer will copy the document onto the hard disk (drive C) and put that document into the QA subdirectory.

Afterwards, if you improve the document by editing it further, the improved version will be in the RAM chips, but the disk will still contain the old version. To copy the improved version onto the disk, say "Save" again (by pressing Shift with F8) and press ENTER. The computer will replace the disk's old version by the new version.

Typing a long document? Say "Save" every 10 minutes, so if an accident happens you'll lose at most 10 minutes of work!

Print (F2)

Here's how to copy your writing onto paper.

Make sure the printer is turned on. Make sure you've saved your document (to protect yourself in case the printer doesn't work). Then say "Print" (by pressing F2). The computer will say "PRINT OPTIONS". Press F10.

Clear (Esc C)

Here's how to erase the screen (so you can start creating a new document).

Press the ESCAPE key, which says "Esc" on it. You'll see the write menu. Choose "C - Clear" (by pressing C).

If the computer asks "Are you SURE you want to continue?", press Y.

Get (Esc G)

Here's how to copy a document from your hard disk to your screen.

Press the ESCAPE key, which says "Esc" on it. You'll see the write menu. Choose "G - Get" (by pressing G). Either type "jennifer" (and press ENTER) or choose JENNIFER from a menu (by pressing ENTER, moving the cursor to JENNIFER, and pressing F10).

If the computer asks, "Are you SURE you want to continue?", press Y.

Exit (Esc Esc)

When you've finished using Q&A's word processor, press the Esc key twice. (If the computer asks, "Are you SURE?", press Y.) You'll see the main menu. Choose "X - Exit Q&A" (by pressing X). The screen will show a C prompt, so you can give a DOS command.

COMMUNICATION

Background

To let your computer communicate with computers that are far away, you can connect your computer to a telephone line by using a **modem**.

Communication programs

To manage your modem, you need a **communication program**.

Windows 3.1 includes a communication program called **Terminal**. Windows 95 and 98 include an improved communications program called **HyperTerminal**. Here's how you can access them:

Windows 3.1: click Start then Programs then Accessories then Terminal.
Windows 95: click Start then Programs then Accessories then HyperTerminal.
Windows 98: click Start then Programs then Accessories then Communications then HyperTerminal.

Details about them are in editions 22-26 of *The Secret Guide to Computers* (which you can order by phoning 603-666-6644); but those communications programs perform just *primitive* communications. To use the **Internet** (the computer network started by the US government and later privatized), you need a more advanced communications program instead, such as **Internet Explorer** or **Netscape Navigator**, which are free and explained in the next chapter.

Settings

To make two computers communicate with each other, make sure both computers are set to communicate in the same way:

Question	Possible answers	Usual answer
Which baud rate?	2400, 9600, 14400, 28800, or 33600	28800
How many data bits?	7 or 8	8
What's the parity bit?	0, 1, even (E), odd (O), or none (N)	none (N)
How many stop bits?	0 or 1	1
What kind of duplex?	half-duplex (H) or full-duplex (F)	full duplex (F)
Is XON/XOFF enabled?	yes (enabled) or no (disabled)	yes (enabled)

When computer experts chat with each other about which communication method to use, they usually discuss those questions in that order.

For example, if the expert's computer is typical, the expert will say "My computer communicates at 28800 8 N 1 F enabled". To communicate with that computer, you must set up your computer the same way. To do that, run the communication program, which can ask you those questions and waits for you to answer. The communication program also asks you whether the modem is COM1 or COM2.

Internet Explorer and Netscape Navigator automatically handle those settings for you.

Big online services

Many computers around the world are eager to chat with *your* computer!

Here are popular computer systems for Americans to communicate with:

Service	State	Sales department
America OnLine (AOL)	VA	800-827-6364
MicroSoft Network (MSN)	WA	800-386-5550
Prodigy	NY	800-776-3449
Compuserve	OH	800-848-8199

For info about those services, call those 800 numbers (using your voice, *not* your computer), and chat with the sales reps.

MicroSoft Network (MSN) is owned by MicroSoft. Prodigy was started by IBM & Sears, but in May 1996 they sold Prodigy to a group of investors called International Wireless. America OnLine (AOL) has always been independent. Compuserve was owned by H&R Block, but in 1997 H&R Block sold most of it to AOL.

AOL charges $21.95 per month. Prodigy charges $21.95 per month but gives you the first 6 months free if you promise to stay with Prodigy for a year (by signing a contract). MSN charges $21.95 per month but gives you a $400 rebate coupon (to buy any computer-related equipment) if you promise to stay with MSN for 3 years (by signing a contract). Compuserve offers the same price and rebate deal as MSN.

Each service typically gives new subscribers a special "free trial" offer, where you get "the first 10 hours free" or "the first 50 hours free" or "the first month free". For example, when you buy a modem (or computer), it usually comes with coupons (or icons) giving you free trials on the four services, so you can sample the joys of telecommunication. After your free trial has ended, you get billed every month automatically on your credit card.

Each service has branch offices staffed by computers in all major American cities. If you call the branch office nearest you, you'll automatically be connected to the service's headquarters at no extra charge, so you can tap into the databases without paying for any long-distance calls.

Each service contains many databases you can tap into. Some of those databases are for professionals. Others are for shopping, stocks, news, airline reservations, hobbies, games, and other forms of fun.

Each service also lets you swap info with other computerists by using **electronic mail (e-mail)**.

For example, if you and your friend Sue both use Compuserve, Sue can send Compuserve a message addressed to you. Her message will be stored on Compuserve's gigantic computer's hard disk. The next time you use Compuserve, Compuserve will tell you that a message from her is waiting on Compuserve's disk. Compuserve will offer to "read" it to you, by sending it to your personal computer's screen.

Each online service has begun offering access to the Internet.

You can send e-mail to anyone that has an Internet address, such as the people on other online services. You can send messages to all your computerized friends and even strangers.

Compuserve users have organized themselves into clubs, called **special interest groups (SIGs)**.

Each SIG is devoted to a particular hobby, profession, or computer topic. If you join a SIG, you can read the messages sent by all other members of the SIG, and you can leave your own messages for them. Prodigy, AOL, and MSN have SIGs also, but Compuserve's are the oldest and offer the most sophisticated discussions.

Here's how those online services arose:

Compuserve was invented first. Though it had good SIGs and databases, it was hard to use and boring: it transmitted text but no graphics.
AOL came next. It was graphical and fun. At first, it ran just on Commodore 64 computers (using a joystick), but later it was redone for the IBM PC and Mac (using a mouse). It's the easiest service to use and the most popular.
Prodigy was invented third. Like a newspaper, it's financed by advertisers: while you're using Prodigy, the top part of the screen shows the info you requested, but the bottom part of the screen invites you to see ads for many products. Prodigy is the most "family-oriented" service: it offers the most goodies for kids (easy databases and educational games), and it censors announcements and messages to avoid obscenities and libel suits.
MSN was invented last. To use it, you must run MSN software, which Microsoft includes as part of Windows 95 & 98. MSN is set up to look like Windows 95: special interest groups are set up in folders that hold chat rooms, message areas, and file libraries (which let you copy programs to your computer). MSN is easier to use than Compuserve but not as fun as AOL.

All those online services and the Internet include software you can copy freely, since the software is freeware or shareware.

Copying software from the service to your own computer is called **downloading**. If you write your own software and want to contribute it to the service, you **upload** the software to the service.

INTERNET

Internet joy

A **computer network** is a group of computers (or computer terminals) that communicate with each other (by **phone** or other **cables** or **wireless** transmissions).

Now the most popular computer network is the **Internet**. It connects computers all over the world, by phone lines and by other communication methods that are faster. You can connect *your* computer to the Internet, so you can access computers all over the world, peek at their hard disks, and transfer their info to *your* computer. Now the Internet transfers games, news, photos, love letters, chitchat, ads, and globs of other info, public and private, to and from President Clinton, his successors, David Letterman, and many *millions* of other workers, jokers, kids, and kooks across the country and around the world.

You can use the Internet to send and receive electronic mail. You can also use the Internet to browse through announcements posted by folks worldwide.

The Internet gives you a huge sea of info. You stand on its shore, watch its many The Internet gives you a huge sea of info. You stand on its shore, watch its many waves come at you, and get high by joyously jumping into those waves. That's called **surfing the Net**, which means "browsing through the amazing info available on the Net".

You'll quickly get addicted to surfing the Net and spend many hours each day doing it. As you explore the Net, your electronic requests and their responses travel at electronic speeds around the world, on what Vice President Al Gore dubbed the **Information Superhighway (I-way)**, propelling you through **cyberspace** (the vast, surreal world where all info and people are represented by bits, bytes, and electronic signals, as opposed to the "real world", called **meatspace**, where people are composed of meat).

The Internet lets your mind fly around the world faster than a astronaut's. Your friends will call you an **infonaut** or **Internaut**. Cynics will call you an **Internut** or **Net-head**. But no matter what folks call you, you'll have fun, while learning more about the world than any pre-computer human could ever imagine.

How the Internet arose

The Internet arose because of the Cold War. Here are the details....

Cold War research

Back in 1957, while the US was fighting the Cold War against Russia, the Russians launched the first satellite, **Sputnik**. That made the US military wake up and realize it was dangerously behind Russia in scientific research. In 1958 the US **Department of Defense (DoD)** reacted by creating the **Advanced Research Projects Agency (ARPA)**, which paid universities to do scientific research to help win the Cold War against Russia.

ARPANET

In 1969, ARPA created a clever computer network, called **ARPANET**, to let university computers send data over phone lines using a sneaky method that would work even if Russians bombed the phone lines.

The sneaky method was called **packet switching**.

> It divided each computer message into many little **packets** and sent the packets over the phone lines intelligently: if a packet couldn't reach its destination directly (because a phone line got bombed), the computer would sneakily switch that packet through different phone lines to different computers that would reroute the packet to its ultimate destination. At the ultimate destination, a computer would automatically make sure all the packets arrived, put them into the proper order, and make any lost (or damaged) packets be retransmitted.

At first, the ARPANET included just 4 computers: 1 at the University of Utah and 3 in California (at UCLA, UC Santa Barbara, and the Stanford Research Institute).

The next year (1970), ARPANET added 3 computers in Massachusetts (at MIT, BBN, and Rand). The next year (1971), ARPANET added more computers (in California, Massachusetts, Pennsylvania, Ohio, and Illinois), to make a total of 15 computers.

The next year (1972), ARPANET expanded to more parts of the country, so 2000 people were using ARPANET — and they were starting to have fun, since electronic mail was added to ARPANET that year. (Before that, ARPANET was just a big boring mass of technical documents & data.) The next year (1973), e -mail became so popular that 75% of all ARPANET transmissions were e-mails; and research institutions in **England** and **Norway** joined ARPANET, so ARPANET became international.

In 1979, the first **newsgroups** were created. (A newsgroup is a running discussion of facts and opinions, contributed by the newsgroup's readers, so it becomes a gigantic collection of "letters to the editor about the other letters that were written".)

On October 27, 1980, the entire ARPANET got shut down by a virus that was spread accidentally. Yes, a virus can accomplish what bombs cannot! Fortunately, the virus was eradicated.

Many universities around the world joined ARPANET because it was nifty, funded, and could be used for non-military purposes also, such as personal e-mail.

Split

ARPANET finally became too big to be managed simply, so in 1983 the military divided it into *two* networks:

> One network, called **MILNET**, was strictly for use by military personnel (at military bases). The other network, called "the new, smaller ARPANET", was for civilian use (at universities).

To let those two networks communicate with each other, an inter-network communication method was invented, called the **Internet Protocol (IP)**. That's how the Internet began!

IP came in several versions, the most popular being the **Transmission Control Protocol for IP (TCP/IP)**.

At the end of 1983, the Internet included about 600 **hosts** (computers that had permanent Internet addresses and could supply data to other computers). Afterwards, the Internet grew fast:

Year	How many Internet hosts at end of year
1983	600
1984	1,000
1985	2,000
1986	6,000
1987	30,000
1988	80,000
1989	200,000
1990	400,000
1991	700,000
1992	1,000,000
1993	2,000,000
1994	5,000,000
1995	10,000,000
1996	20,000,000
1997	30,000,000
1998	40,000,000
1999	70,000,000

Let's see why it grew so fast.…

National Science Foundation

In 1986, the **National Science Foundation (NSF)** wanted to let researchers share 5 supercomputers by using ARPANET, but NSF quickly changed its mind and decided to its own network, called **NSFNET**. Like ARPANET, NSFNET used TCP/IP and was ARPANET-compatible, so NSFNET became part of the Internet. NSFNET ran faster than ARPANET (by running more phone lines between big cities, to form a strong Internet **backbone**), so universities switched to it from ARPANET. In 1990, ARPANET shut down permanently.

ARPA, which had created ARPANET, lived on but under its new name: the **Defense Advanced Research Projects Agency (DARPA)**.

Why packet switching was practical

Though packet switching was invented as a way to avoid bombs, it turned out to have another advantage: it prevented any single user from hogging the Internet.

If a "bad guy" tries to hog the Internet by sending a long message, the Internet is smart enough to divide his message into many little packets. Other users are given a chance to squeeze their packets into the system without waiting for all the bad guy's packets to go through. Any overloaded phone lines are automatically bypassed by routing some packets through other phone lines managed by other computers.

Packet switching made the Internet be "free for democracy" in four senses:

> free from destruction by bombs
> free from overload by user hogs
> free from censorship by governments
> free from big start-up costs (because government already paid for the backbone)

You can still wreck a country's Internet if you're evil enough to bomb *all* phone lines or send *many* long messages or force *all* Internet computers to censor transmissions. Though misguided folks tried such tactics, the Internet outlasted them.

Web

The Internet was just a tedious collection of documents, data, and e-mails until 1990, when an Englishman named **Tim Berners-Lee** invented a nifty Internet feature called the **World Wide Web (WWW)**. To be briefer, folks call it just the **Web**. Here's how it works:

> It lets you view a document on the Internet and, if a word in the document is underlined, you can click on that word to get "more info" about that word. The "more info" can be a whole page of info about that word and reside in a different file on a different hard disk in a different computer in a different country; so by just clicking that underlined word, you're suddenly accessing relevant info from a different computer in a different country. The person who invented the original document sets all that up for you, so by just clicking the underlined word you automatically access the info you want without needing to know what computer or country it's coming from.
>
> The World Wide Web turns a whole world of documents into a unified system.
>
> In that system, each page can contain *many* underlined words. Clicking an underlined word transports you to another page (on another computer) that contains related info and in turn has its own underlined words that you can click on to get to other related pages.
>
> The underlined words are called **links**, because they link you to other documents.

To invent the Web, Tim was inspired by **Ted Nelson**.

> Ted Nelson was a US visionary who in 1965 had predicted that text would someday be connected worldwide by underlined links and called **hypertext**. Ted Nelson's concept furthered what an earlier visionary, **Vannevar Bush**, had written in 1945.

Tim was the first person to take the ideas of Ted & Vannevar, apply them to the Internet, and make the whole system practical enough for humans to use.

Tim invented the World Wide Web while he was working in Switzerland at the **European Laboratory for Particle Physics**, which at that time was called the **Conseil Européen pour la Recherche Nucléaire (CERN)**. Afterwards, Tim moved to the **Massachusetts Institute of Technology (MIT)**, where he directs the **World Wide Web Consortium (W3C)**, which plans the Web's future.

War

The US's allies copied Internet technology — and so did the US's enemies:

> In January 1991, during the Gulf War, the Internet's ability to defend itself against bombs was proved in a strange way: Iraq's own Internet helped Iraq's military command network withstand attack from US bombs!
>
> In August 1991, the Soviet Union was paralyzed by a news blackout during the coup against Gorbachev, but the truth got out to the world by Internet transmissions from **Relcom** (a small pro-Yeltsin Internet service provider in the Soviet Union).

Mosaic

To use the World Wide Web, you had to use a program called a **browser**. When Tim invented the World Wide Web, he also invented his own browser, which was crude. The first *pleasant* browser was **Mosaic**, invented in 1994 by Marc Andreessen, an undergrad at the University of Illinois' **National Center for Supercomputing Applications (NCSA)**.

Since his research was funded by the National Science Foundation, everybody was allowed to copy Mosaic for free.

Later that year, he left NCSA and formed a company called **Netscape Communications Corp.**, which invented an improved Web browser (called **Netscape Navigator**) and sold it cheaply ($50 or less, per copy).

Mosaic and Netscape made the Web become much more popular. At the beginning of 1994, there were 600 **Web sites** (places on the Web that provide Web info); at the end of 1994, the number of Web sites shot up to 10,000; in later years, the number of Web sites continued to climb:

Year	How many Web sites at end of year
1993	600
1994	10,000
1995	100,000
1996	600,000
1997	1,700,000
1998	3,700,000
1999	9,600,000

Mass market

In 1995, these events made the Internet suddenly become more popular:

Netscape Navigator version 2 came out. It worked much better than version 1.

Windows 95 came out. It handled the Internet much better than Windows 3.11.

Microsoft invented Internet Explorer. Like Netscape Navigator, it was based on Mosaic and initially sold for $50 or less. Soon afterwards, Microsoft began giving Internet Explorer away for free.

The World Wide Web reached a critical mass: enough good Web sites had been created to make browsing worthwhile for the average consumer.

Many training schools began offering crash courses in how to use the Internet.

Yes, 1995 was the year that the general American public got excited about the Internet.

That year, the Internet got too big for the NSF to fund. The NSF stopped running NSFNET but gave grants to help universities buy Internet time from commercial networks that had sprung up, such as **Sprint**, **Alternet**, and **Performance Systems International (PSI)**. Consumers, sitting at home with their personal computers, could use the Internet by telling their computer modems to phone an **Internet service provider (ISP)**, which was part of the Internet. Many companies sprang up to act as ISPs.

Before the Internet became popular, several old companies had invented their *own* networks for consumers by using a clever trick: they took business networks (which were busy in the day but idle in the evening) and offered them to consumers at low evening rates.

The first two such companies were **Compuserve** (owned by H&R Block) and **The Source** (owned by Readers Digest). After The Source went out of business, two other big companies arose: **Prodigy** (which was owned by IBM & Sears but later became independent) and **America OnLine** (which is independent and called **AOL**, then bought Compuserve and now is merging with Time/Warner). When all those companies began, they expected consumers would mainly want online reference materials (computerized dictionaries, encyclopedias, and databases) but discovered consumers mainly just wanted to send e-mail and chat instead of doing "research".

When the Internet became popular (because it included so *many* e-mail addresses and so *many* Web sites), those old companies modified their networks to include access to the whole Internet.

Those old companies and new ISPs weren't sure how much to charge consumers. At first, they tried charging about $3 per hour. In 1996, a better standard developed: **unlimited access for about $20 per month**.

A few **discount ISPs** charged less. A few **business ISPs** charged more, for superior service. Later came **free ISPs**, which offered free Internet service in return for forcing consumers to watch ads while using the Internet; the advertisers pay for those free ISPs.

Who pays?

Here's who invented and paid for the Internet....

In the beginning, funding came from the **Defense Department** (ARPA) and the **National Science Foundation**. To invent the Internet, a lot of research was done by university **professors** (funded by government grants, student tuition, and alumni donations). A lot of research was also done by **student volunteers**, who wanted to be famous by being helpful.

When consumer ISPs became popular, many **consumers** paid $20 per month per household.

Many Web sites show ads, paid for by the **advertisers**. Those ad fees pay for the Web sites, the same way that ads pay for TV networks and newspapers.

Many **businesses** run their own Web sites, and pay for them in the hope that those sites will act as ads (to draw in new customers and make old customers buy more). The businesses also hope their Web sites will show lots of info online, so the businesses don't have to send brochures to customers and don't have to hire customer-service departments to answer customer questions.

Many Web sites are created by new startup companies who dream of becoming great. Those companies convince investors to buy stock in that dream. Some of those dreamy companies will succeed, and their stockholders will get rich; other dreamy companies will fail, and their stockholders will lose their shirts. All those **stockholders** pay for the Internet and hope to reap rewards in return. While the stockholders wait for results, the company's managers are paid high salaries (funded by stockholders), even though many of those startup companies haven't earned any profit yet and never will.

In 1999, many such startup companies began; and investors sunk many millions of dollars into them, hoping the managers wouldn't waste the money and would eventually turn a profit. A lot of jargon was invented to describe the situation:

A company whose Web site is its main fame is called a **dot com** (because its Web-site address ends in .com), and its employees are called **dot commers**. A Web site letting customers type credit-card numbers to place orders is said to do **electronic commerce (e-commerce)** and offer an **electronic shopping cart**.

A company selling mainly to consumers is called a **business-to-consumer company (B2C company)**. A company selling mainly to other businesses instead is called a **business-to-business company (B2B company)**. A company selling mainly to organizations who run Internet host computers (and helping those organizations improve their Internet computers and connections) is called an **Internet infrastructure company**.

An old-fashioned company (which ignores the Internet and runs just traditional retail stores in brick buildings) is called a **real-world company** and a **bricks-and-mortar company**. An ultra-modern company (which exists just on the Web and doesn't bother staffing any storefront buildings where customers could walk in to buy goods) is said to **exist just in cyberspace** and be a **pure-play Internet company**. A company doing *both* — having brick-like retail stores (or warehouses) and also selling on the Internet (by letting customers use mice to click on what they want) — is called a **bricks-and-clicks company**.

If a startup company lures investors by telling an enticing story about how it could be profitable someday — but the company has no customers yet — its stock is called just a **story stock**.

Many Web companies are in San Francisco, where the managers are freaky-looking snotty kids who are young (under 30), wear nose rings, drive fancy cars, and got rich by inventing a story that got investors to give them millions of dollars, even though their companies haven't made a profit yet and have hardly any customers yet and actually *lose* lots of money daily. Many of those Web companies have been buying office space in San Francisco (south of Market Street), encouraging landlords to jack up rents and kick out the poor people and non-profit organizations that were there before. People who resent those managers call them **e-holes**, **dot snots**, and **dot commies**.

Who uses the Internet?

When the Internet began, it was restricted to university scientific researchers, who were mostly men. But eventually the Internet grew, so people outside universities could get access. In the year 2000, women Internet users finally outnumbered men users, for three reasons:

The world contains more women than men.

The World Wide Web grew to become a big worldwide library. "Reading in a library" appeals to women more than men.

E-mail grew to be a powerful force. Sending e-mail is like passing a note. "Writing, reading, and passing notes" are activities that appeal to women more than men.

Internet service providers

To access the Internet, you can use many methods. Most people still use this **standard method**:

Make sure your computer contains a **modem**. (Most new computers include the fastest kind of modem, which is called a **56K modem**.) Unplug your home's phone cord from your phone, and attach the phone cord to your computer's modem instead, so your computer can make phone calls. Yes, you'll be using the **plain old telephone system (POTS)**. Tell your computer to phone a computer belonging to an **Internet service provider (ISP)**, which charges you **about $20 per month** for the service, billed to your credit card. You might also have to pay a $25 start-up fee, though usually you're offered a "special deal" where the start-up fee is waived, or the monthly fee is reduced to $18, or you get a bonus gift (such as a junky digital camera).

The phone number that your computer calls is called an **Internet dial-in access number** or **point of presence (POP)**. Make sure the POP is a *local* phone number, so you don't pay any long-distance bills. To make *sure* it's local, ask your local phone company whether the POP's phone number is indeed a free call under your calling plan.

While your computer is using the Internet through this method, your computer is "typing up the phone line", so if any of your friends try to phone you they'll get a busy signal. There are three ways to solve that problem:

1. Tell the phone company to install a **second phone line**, which will cost you about $25 per month (including taxes).

2. Use the Internet just **late at night** (or early in the morning), when your friends don't try to phone you.

3. Pay the phone company $4 per month for **voice messaging**, which makes the phone company create a voice-mail system that takes messages when your phone is busy — but then you have to call your friends back at your own expense.

Of all the standard-method Internet service providers, the one having the best reputation is **EarthLink**, based in Pasadena, California. It was started in 1994 by a 23-year-old guy named Sky Dalton, who ran a West Los Angeles coffeehouse, worked for ad agencies & computer-graphics companies, and was repeatedly voted one of the most influential technologists in the Los Angeles area. Now EarthLink is national, affiliated with Sprint, and has POPs in Canada and all states except Alaska and Hawaii. Its POPs are in over 1000 cities! EarthLink recently bought excellent competitors (such as MindSpring, JPS Net, and OneMain.com) so now EarthLink is even bigger and better. To chat with an EarthLink human who will help you get started, phone EarthLink's sales department at 888-EarthLink.

Another big ISP is AT&T's **WorldNet**, which charges a monthly fee of just $15 but limits you to 150 hours per month (extra hours cost 99¢ each). Unfortunately, WorldNet is often overloaded, especially its technical-support staff. IBM used to own an ISP called **IBM Internet Connection**, which had POPs in 52 countries, but sold it all to AT&T, so now WorldNet is even bigger! To find out about WorldNet, phone 800-WorldNet.

To save money, try this **discount method**:

It's the same as the standard method, except you pay **just $10 per month** (plus a start-up fee) and get worse service: more busy signals, more disconnections, more errors (saying "not found" or "Incorrect password"), and more difficulty reaching the tech-support staff.

That's the method I use, because I'm too cheap to pay for the standard method. I use a discount ISP called **Galaxy Internet Services (GIS)**, which has POPs just on the East Coast (in NH, MA, RI, CT, NY, NJ, PA, MD, DC, VA, and GA).

To find out about Galaxy, phone 888-334-2529 or 617-558-0900. To find out about discount dealers in *your* area, check ads in your local newspaper and computer magazines and ask your local computer friends.

A crazier way to save money is to try this **rebate method**:

It's the same as the standard method, except you pay slightly more (about $22 per month) and get a $400 rebate coupon (which you can use to buy computer equipment or office supplies) if you sign a 3-year contract. When you do the math ($22 per month, times 3 years, minus $400), your net cost turns about to be about $11 per month. That's about the same cost as the discount method. Like the discount method, it gives you lousy service, and has the additional disadvantage of locking you into a 3-year contract, which you'll regret a year or two from now, as better deals become available and you'll be prohibited from taking advantage of them.

The main rebate ISP is **MicroSoft Network (MSN)**, which has POPs in many cities. To sign up for MSN and get your $400 rebate, buy a computer at any retail-store chain, such as Radio Shack or Best Buy or Staples.

Another rebate ISP is **Compuserve**, which gives worse service than MSN and is too slow at mailing the rebates. Compuserve is owned by AOL and heavily advertised at Circuit City stores.

To pay no money at all, try this **ad-supported method**:

It's the same as the standard method, except you pay no monthly fee but must watch ads while you're using the Internet.

That's the method my stepdaughter uses when she's living away from home, because she's too cheap to pay even $10 per month. She uses the best such ISP, called **BlueLight**, which is funded by 4 companies (K-Mart, Yahoo, Spinway, and SoftBank). Its ads are at the bottom of the screen and unobtrusive. To start using it, you need a BlueLight CD-ROM disk, which you can get free at your local K-Mart store or by phoning 888-945-9255. When you insert the disk, it asks you personal questions about your shopping habits so it will show you ads that interest you. The only major nuisance with BlueLight is that it won't let you use normal e-mail (such as Outlook Express); instead you must use a different e-mail system (such as Yahoo Mail).

Other ad-supported ISPs are **Juno** (whose ads are too big, 800-879-5866), **Freei** (whose ads are too flashy and distracting, 901-259-6600), and **NetZero** (which disconnects you if you don't click any ads within 30 minutes, 805-418-2020).

For faster transmission, try this **cable-modem method**:

It's the same as the standard method, except you use cable-TV wires instead of phone wires, get faster transmission (about 8 times as fast) and pay slightly more (between $30 and $40 per month for the service, plus $25 for an **Ethernet card** (a network card that you put into your computer), plus between $100 and $200 for a **cable modem** (which attaches the Ethernet card to a cable-TV cord).

The cable-modem method has two advantages over the standard method:

1. It's faster. The cable wires can theoretically transmit about 2 megabits per second (which is nearly 40 times as fast as a 56K modem), but you're sharing those wires with many cable-TV-using neighbors, who clog the system (especially in the evening), so on the average the cable modem will seem about 8 times as fast as a standard 56K modem.

2. It doesn't consume a phone line; you do *not* need to get a 2nd phone line.

Since this method achieves its high speed by using a broad spectrum of frequencies for transmission, it's an example of **broadband transmission**.

If I were richer, this is the Internet method I'd use. I'd buy a cable modem for $200 ($250 minus $50 rebate) from **Circuit City** (a chain of electronics stores), then pay **AT&T Broadband** (AT&T's cable-TV company) $30 per month. (If I order directly from AT&T without Circuit City, I pay instead $100 for installation plus $40 per month, which over the long term would cost more.)

The cable method is available just if your neighborhood is wired for cable TV and your cable-TV service company is modern. To find out, phone your local cable-TV company and Circuit City.

If your neighborhood lacks cable, try this **DSL method**:

A **digital subscriber line (DSL)** is a broadband transmission method that resembles the cable method; but instead of using cable-TV wires, it uses ordinary phone wires and makes them handle many frequencies at once.

The most common type of DSL is **Asymmetic DSL (ADSL)**. It costs slightly more than the cable method: it usually costs between $35 and $45 per month. Usually, it works slightly slower than the cable method, but it's popular because it's more predictable: it's unaffected by your neighbors' usage. It's popular for businesses, who are in business districts that haven't been wired for cable-TV yet and therefore can't use the cable method. DSL works fastest if you're close to a telephone switching station; if you're more than 2½ miles from a telephone-switching station, DSL works so slowly that the phone company will refuse to install it. The main complaint about DSL is that service technicians delay several weeks before showing up to install it, and you must take a day off from work to wait for them, and often they don't show up on the scheduled day.

To find out about DSL, start by calling your local phone company. You can also order DSL service from standard-method ISPs (such as EarthLink at 888-EarthLink) and discount-method ISPs (such as Galaxy Internet Services at 888-334-2529).

If you can't use cable or DSL, try this **satellite method**:

It resembles the standard method but uses a satellite TV dish to supplement your phone line. To send a message to the Internet, use your phone line; when the Internet tries to send you a reply, the reply is sent by satellite instead of by phone, since satellite is faster.

To use this method, you start by paying about $300 (to buy a satellite dish and install it so it faces a satellite in the sky). Then you pay a monthly fee of $50 for unlimited use (or $30 for 25 hours). You'll also want to buy a second phone line to avoid "typing up the phone line". This method is practical if you already bought a satellite dish to watch TV. The main source of this method is **DirecPC** (owned by Hughes), whose dishes you can buy at your local Best Buy or Circuit City store.

Many folks use the **AOL method**:

It resembles the standard method; but instead of using an ordinary ISP, you use an special ISP called **America OnLine (AOL)**, which charges about $22 per month. The first month is free. Besides giving you Internet access, AOL also gives you its own services, such as **AOL Instant Messenger (AIM)**, at no extra charge. But when using AOL, you must watch some extra ads, and some Internet features don't work (such as **e-mail MIME attachments**). To find out about AOL, phone 800-826-6364.

To pay nothing for the Internet, try the **free-group method**:

It gives you free Internet access if you join a group. For example, if you buy a **Gateway** computer (by phoning 800-LAD-2000), you typically get a free year of AOL. If you use **Qwest** as your long-distance phone company and make a lot of phone calls (so you spend at least $50 per month), Qwest will act as your ISP for free. If you visit your **local public library**, you can use the library's Internet-connected computers for free. While you're enrolled in a typical **college**, you can freely use the college's Internet-connected computers, which are in the college's computer labs, libraries, and dorms.

Many parts of the Internet are overloaded: more people want to use them than they can handle.

When your computer's modem tries to contact the Internet, the modem might encounter a busy signal or ridiculously long delay or a message saying a service is unavailable; you might get disconnected from the Internet or ignored or refused.

The overload is worst during the evenings, from 7PM to 11PM, since that's when the kids are home from school and the parents are home from work and they're all trying to have fun at home by using the Internet. In many parts of the country, the best time to use the Internet is in the morning and early afternoon (from 3AM to 3PM).

If a site is used mainly by businesses instead of consumers, that site might be busy during working hours (9AM to 5PM). If you're trying to contact a site that's far away, in a different part of the world, remember that the site's busiest hours depend on which time zones its users are in.

If your computer's modem phoned a POP number, you can use the Internet awhile; but when you've finished, tell the modem to **disconnect** from the POP.

If you forget to disconnect, your ISP will eventually sense that no transmissions are occurring and will disconnect you automatically. **The typical ISP will disconnect you if 30 minutes have elapsed without any transmissions.**

If you're running a business and want your computer to wait for incoming Internet messages continuously without being disconnected, ask your ISP for a **business account**, which costs more than a personal account. **When an ISP advertises "unlimited access" for $19.95 per month, the ISP defines "unlimited access" to mean a personal account**, used just a *few* hours per day, not waiting continuously for transmissions.

While you're using the Internet, here are the most common reasons why you get disconnected:

1. Your ISP might have disconnected you because too many minutes elapsed without transmission.

2. Your computer's modem might be inferior and not working consistently.

3. Your phone line might suffer from too much static or other noise. Here's how to check: while not using the modem, pick up the phone (so you hear a dial tone), then press the number 5 on the phone (so the dial tone goes away); if you hear noise (such as static), get a different phone cord, outlet, or line.

Browse the Web

The most popular part of the Internet is called the **World Wide Web** (or just the **Web** or just **WWW**). To use it, you need a program called a **Web browser**.

The first good Web browser was **Mosaic**, invented by a University of Illinois undergrad, Marc Andreessen, in 1994. Later that year, he left the university and formed a company called **Netscape Communications Corp.**, where he invented a better Web browser called **Netscape Navigator** (or just **Navigator**). The newest version of it is version 4.7, which you can get by itself or as part of **Netscape Communicator**.

In 1995, Microsoft invented a competing Web browser called **Microsoft Internet Explorer** (or just **Explorer**).

Version 1 of it was invented in 1995, versions 2 and 3 in 1996, version 4 in 1997, version 5 in 1999, and version 5.5 in 2000. Versions 5 and 5.5 of Internet Explorer are better than Netscape Navigator.

Navigator and Explorer are both popular. They work best if you have Windows 95 or 98. They can also handle the Mac.

I'll assume you have Windows 95 or 98.

If you have Windows 3.1 or 3.11, you ought to upgrade to Windows 95 or 98. If you refuse to upgrade, your Internet connection will be slow and unreliable and you must use an outdated version of Navigator (versions 1, 2, or 3) or an outdated version of Explorer (versions 1 or 2).

I'll explain the versions most people have: Explorer's versions 3 & 4 & 5 and Navigator's versions 3 & 4.6.

If you have Explorer 1 or 2,	follow my instructions for Explorer 3,	which is similar.
If you have Explorer 5.5,	follow my instructions for Explorer 5,	which is similar.
If you have Navigator 1 or 2,	follow my instructions for Navigator 3,	which is similar.
If you have Navigator 4, 4.5, or 4.7,	follow my instructions for Navigator 4.6,	which is similar.

The World Wide Web runs slowly. You'll spend lots of time waiting for it to respond to your commands. That's why cynics call it the "World Wide Wait". To make the Web reasonably pleasant, you need a modem that's fast (at least 28.8 kilobaud).

If your modem is slightly slower (14.4 kilobaud or 9.6 kilobaud), you can still use the Web but not pleasantly. If your modem is slower than 9.6 kilobaud, using the Web is not practical.

Install your browser

To use Navigator or Explorer, you must put it onto your computer's hard disk. If you bought your computer in 1996 or afterwards, its hard disk probably contains Navigator or Explorer already. For example, Windows 98 includes Explorer. Microsoft Office 2000 comes on a CD-ROM disk that includes Explorer 5.

What phone's in your room? Before using the Internet, tell Windows about the phone in your room. Here's how, if you're using Windows 98:

Click Start, then Settings, then Control Panel. You'll see the Control Panel window. Double-click the Telephony icon. Double-click in the Area Code box, then type **your own phone's area code** (such as 603). Press ENTER. Close the Control Panel window (by clicking its X button).

Who's your ISP? Next, tell Windows about your Internet service provider (ISP), your ISP's phone number, and your ISP's Internet address.

To find out how, read the instructions your ISP sent you. If you don't understand them, phone your ISP's technical-support number.

For example, here's what to do if you're using Windows 98 and Explorer 4:

Click the Explorer icon (which is next to the Start button and has an "e" on it). The computer will say "Internet Connection Wizard". Click the button next to "I have an existing Internet account". Press ENTER 3 times.

Type the **phone number of your ISP's computer** (such as 584-3451). Click the box called "Dial using the area code and country code", so the check mark disappears from that box, and the box becomes blank. Press ENTER.

Type the **user name** that your ISP agreed to assign to you (such as "poo"). Press the TAB key.

Type the **user password** that your ISP agreed to assign to you. (While you type your password, asterisks will appear on your screen, to hide your password from any enemy who's looking over your shoulder.) Press ENTER twice.

Type **your ISP's name** (such as Galaxy Internet Services), press ENTER twice, type **your name** (such as Russ Walter), press ENTER, type the **e-mail address** that your ISP agreed to assign to you (such as "poo@gis.net"), press ENTER, press the TAB key, type the name of your ISP's **incoming mail server** (such as "pop.gis.net"), press the TAB key, type the name of your ISP's **outgoing mail server** (such as "smtp.gis.net"), press ENTER.

Press the TAB key. Type the **e-mail password** that your ISP agreed to assign to you. (It's probably the same as your user password. While you type it, asterisks will appear.) Press ENTER five times.

Type the name of your ISP's **news server** (such as "news.gis.net"), press ENTER four times, type your **user password** again, press ENTER.

Copy to your hard disk

Copy to your hard disk If you already installed Explorer (or another Web browser) and now want to also install Navigator 4.6, here's how:

> By using whatever Web browser you already have, go to Netscape's Web site (www.netscape.com), then say you want to download Navigator 4.6. That will create an icon called "sd_cc32e46en" on your screen's desktop. While you're connected to the Internet, double-click that icon. That makes the computer copy Navigator 4.6 to your computer; the copying takes about 5 hours (depending on how fast your modem is and how busy your ISP and Netscape's Web site are).
>
> When the copying is done, your computer will contain a new icon, called "cc32e46", which is buried in the My Download Files folder. Make that icon appear on your screen (by double-clicking the My Computer icon, then the "C:" icon, then the My Download Files icon).
>
> Double-click the "cc32e46" icon. The computer will say "Netscape Communicator 4.6 Setup". Press ENTER 7 times. The computer will ask, "Would you like to view the README file now?" Click "No". The computer will say, "Setup is complete". Press ENTER twice. The computer will restart.
>
> If the computer says "Windows is currently set to display too few colors", press ENTER.
>
> Close all windows (by clicking their X buttons).

Launch your browser

Turn on the computer, without any disks in the floppy drives.

To use Explorer 4 or 5, do this:

> Double-click the icon that says "Internet Explorer" (or single-click the tiny Internet Explorer icon that's next to the Start button and has an "e" on it).

To use Explorer 3, do this instead:

> Double-click the icon that says "The Internet". If the computer asks "Would you like to make it your default browser?" press ENTER.

To use Navigator 3, do this instead:

> Double-click the icon that says "Netscape Navigator". If the computer says "Netscape License Agreement", press ENTER. If the computer asks "Would you like to register Navigator as your default browser?" press ENTER.

To use Navigator 4.6, do this instead:

> Double-click the icon that says "Netscape Communicator".
>
> If the computer says "Creating a New Profile", do this: press ENTER, type your name (such as Russ Walter), press the TAB key, type the e-mail address that your ISP agreed to assign to you (such as "poo@gis.net"), press ENTER twice, type the name of your ISP's outgoing mail server (such as "smtp.gis.net"), press ENTER, type your e-mail user name again (such as "poo"), press the TAB key, type the name of your ISP's incoming mail server (such as "pop.gis.net"), press ENTER, type the name of your ISP's news server (such as "news.gis.net"), and press ENTER.

If the computer says "Password", click in the Password box, then type the password you use to connect to your Internet provider (and press ENTER). If the computer asks "Do you want to continue?", press ENTER.

You'll see the window for Microsoft Internet Explorer or Netscape Navigator.

> If you also see a tiny window containing 5 Netscape icons (Navigator, Inbox, Newsgroups, Address Book, and Composer), close that tiny window.

Make sure the window consumes the whole screen. (If it doesn't consume the whole screen yet, maximize it by clicking its resize button, which is next to the X button.)

Address box

Near the top of the screen, you see the **address box**. It's a wide, white box labeled "Address". (Navigator 3 labels it "Location" instead. Navigator 4.6 labels it "Location" or "Netsite" or "Goto", depending on what you've typed in it already.)

Click in that white box. (If you're using Navigator 4.6, *double*-click in that box instead.)

Any writing in that box turns blue. Then type the Internet address you wish to visit.

For example, if you wish to visit **Yahoo**, type Yahoo's **Internet address**, which is —

> http://www.yahoo.com/

Yes, that's Yahoo's **Internet address**. It's also called Yahoo's **Uniform Resource Locator** (or **URL**, which is pronounced "Earl").

When typing an Internet address (such as "http://www.yahoo.com/"), make sure you type periods (not commas); type forward slashes (not backslashes).

The address's first part ("http://") tells the computer to use **HyperText Transfer Protocol**, which is the communication method used by the Web. The "www." emphasizes that you're using the World Wide Web. The ".com" means the service (Yahoo) is a commercial company.

Instead of typing "http://www.yahoo.com/", you can be lazy and type just this:

> www.yahoo.com

That's because the computer automatically puts "/" at the address's end and puts "http://" before any address that doesn't contain "://" already.

In an Internet address, each period is called a **dot**, so "www.yahoo.com" is pronounced "dubbilyoo dubbilyoo dubbilyoo dot yahoo dot com" by literate computerists; grunters say just "wuh wuh wuh dot yahoo dot com".

Notice that the typical address (such as "www.yahoo.com") begins with "www." and ends with ".com". If you type just "yahoo" and forget to type the "www." and the ".com", here's what happens.

> Explorer 3 tries to locate just "yahoo", fails, and says you made a mistake.
>
> Navigator 3 tries to locate just "yahoo", fails, then tries "www.yahoo.com" (because it automatically tries putting "www." before each name and ".com" after each name) and succeeds.
>
> Explorer 4&5 and Navigator 4.6 try to locate "yahoo", fail, then try all longer addresses containing "yahoo", so they eventually try "www.yahoo.com" and succeed.

At the end of your typing, press ENTER.

You'll see the beginning of Yahoo's home page.

Seeing the rest of the page To see the rest of the page, press the down-arrow key or PAGE DOWN key or click the scroll-down arrow (the ▼ near the screen's bottom right corner). To see the beginning of the page again, press the up-arrow key or PAGE UP key or click the scroll-up arrow (▲).

> To hop immediately to the page's bottom, tap the END key.
> (If you're using Navigator, tap the END key *while holding down the Ctrl key*.)
>
> To hop immediately to the page's top, tap the HOME key.
> (If you're using Navigator, tap the HOME key *while holding down the Ctrl key*.)

Links

On Yahoo's home page, you see many topics to choose from.

The typical topic is underlined. For example, at the page's top you see these 32 hot reference topics:

> **Shop:** Auctions Classifieds Shopping Travel YellowPgs Maps **Media:** News Sports StockQuotes TV Weather
> **Connect:** Chat Clubs Games GeoCities Greetings Invites Mail Messenger Personals PeopleSearch ForKids
> **Personal:** MyYahoo AddrBook Calendar Briefcase Photos Alerts Bookmarks Comparison BillPay more…

Below them, you see these 14 broad topics:

Arts & Humanities	News & Media
Business & Economy	Recreation & Sports
Computers & Internet	Reference
Education	Regional
Entertainment	Science
Government	Social Science
Health	Society & Culture

Scattered around the page, you see many other underlined topics, too! You also see 6 topic buttons (labeled "Auctions", "Messenger", "Check Email", "What's New", "Personalize", and "Help").

Each topic button or underlined topic is called a **link**. Click whichever link interests you. (You can click anyplace where the mouse's pointer-arrow turns into a pointing finger.)

Then — presto! — the computer shows you a whole new page, devoted entirely to the topic you linked to! Read it and enjoy! While you're looking at that new page, you'll see its address in the address box.

On that new page, you'll see more links (topic buttons and underlined topics); click whichever one interests you, to visit a further page.

Back & forth

After admiring the new page you're visiting, if you change your mind and want to go back to the previous page you were looking at, click the **Back button** (which says "Back" on it).

Then you see the previous page, but the underlined topic you clicked might have changed color. For example, on Yahoo's home page, most underlined topics are blue, but any topic you've clicked turns purple — and stays purple for several days.)

After clicking the Back button, if you change your mind again and wish you hadn't clicked the Back button, click the **Forward button**.

Go list To hop back several pages, you can click the Back button several times.

To hop back faster, do this trick:

> On the screen's top menu bar, click **Go**. (In Explorer 4, click **File** instead. In Explorer 5, click the ▼ next to the Back button instead.)
> You see a list of pages you visited. The list mentions the current page and other pages you examined recently. The list is always short (no more than 15 pages in Navigator, usually 5 pages in Explorer 3, 7 pages in Explorer 4, 9 page in Explorer 5).
> Click the page you want to go back to.

History Your computer can show a **History window**, which is a list of pages you visited recently. Here's how to view the History folder.

For Explorer 4&5, do this:

> Click the **History button** (which is at the screen's top center). At the screen's left edge, you see the History window, which is a list of pages you visited during the last 20 days.
> (Explorer 4 shows you a single long list, in alphabetical order. Explorer 5 starts by showing you an alphabetical list of pages you visited today; click other times to see a list of pages you visited then.)
> You see the list's beginning. Underneath, you might see the ▼ button, which you click to see the rest of the list.
> Click the page you want to visit.
> The History window will stay on the screen until you close it (by clicking its X button).

For Explorer 3, do this:

> Click the **History button**, if you see it at the bottom of the screen. (If the History button is temporarily missing, click "Go" then "Open History Folder" instead.)
> You see an alphabetized list of pages you visited during the last 2 weeks.
> You see the list's beginning. To see the rest of the list, press the PAGE DOWN key several times. Double-click the page you want to visit.

For Navigator 4.6, do this:

> **While holding down the Ctrl key, tap the H key.** You see the History window, which shows a list of pages you visited during the last 9 days. The list is normally in chronological order, so the top of the list shows the page you visited most recently. (If you want to see the list in alphabetical order instead, click the **Title button**. To return to chronological order, click the **Last Visited button**.) Double-click the page you want to visit.

For Navigator 3, the History folder is too brief to be useful.

Favorites If you're viewing a wonderful page, here's how to make the computer remember that the page is one of your favorites.

For Explorer 3, do this:

> Click the **Favorites button**. Then click **Add To Favorites**, then press ENTER.
> In the future, whenever you want to return to your favorite pages, click the **Favorites button**. You'll see a list of your favorites. Click the page you want.

For Explorer 5, do this:

> Click the **Favorites button**. You'll see a Favorites window at the screen's left edge. Click **Add**, then press ENTER.
> In the future, whenever you want to return to your favorite pages, click the **Favorites button** (to make the Favorites window appear). You'll see a list of your favorites. Click the page you want.
> The Favorites window will stay on the screen until you close that window by clicking its X button.

For Explorer 4, do this:

> On the screen's top menu bar, click the word "Favorites" (which is between "Go" and "Help"). Then click **Add To Favorites** and press ENTER.
> In the future, whenever you want to return to your favorite pages, click the **Favorites button**. You'll see a list of your favorites (in a Favorites window at the screen's left edge). Click the page you want.
> The Favorites window will stay on the screen until you close that window by clicking its X button.

For Navigator, do this:

> While holding down the Ctrl key, press the D key (which means "delightful page to store on disk").
> In the future, whenever you want to return to a delightful page, do this: while holding down the Ctrl key, press the B key (which stands for "bookmarks"); then press the END key. You'll see a list of your favorite pages; above them you'll see a list of Netscape Corporation's favorite pages. (To see the lists better, make sure the window they're in is maximized.) Double-click the page you want.

Home Each time you start using the Internet (by double-clicking the Internet icon or Netscape Navigator icon), the first page you see is called your **start page** or **home page** (because that's where life starts — at home). If you view other pages (by clicking underlined topics) and later change your mind, you can return to viewing the home page by clicking the Back button many times — or click the **Home button** once.

Search box On Yahoo's first page, you see a white box next to the word "Search". That box is called the **search box**.

Try this experiment: click in the white search box (*double*-click if you're using Netscape), then type a topic that interests you. At the end of your typing, press ENTER. Yahoo will list all Yahoo pages about that topic! Click whichever underlined page you want.

Open something different

To switch to a completely different address, click in the address box again (*double*-click if you're using Netscape), then type the Internet address you wish to visit.

For example, if you wish to visit **Excite**, type this —

```
http://www.excite.com/
```

or type just this:

```
www.excite.com
```

At the end of your typing, press ENTER.

Excite is a competitor to Yahoo. It resembles Yahoo but gives you a slightly different list of subjects to choose from. As in Yahoo, Excite's underlined topics are blue. If you click one of those blue underlined topics, then later go back to the Excite's main page (by clicking the Back button), the blue topic you clicked turns to turquoise.

Another good place to visit is **Go**. It's another competitor to Yahoo. To visit Go, type this —

```
http://www.go.com/
```

or type just this:

```
www.go.com
```

At the end of your typing, press ENTER.

(**Go** used to be called **Infoseek** but changed its name to **Go**, which is easier to remember.)

Yahoo, Excite, and Go are all called **search sites**, since their purpose is to help you search for other sites on the Internet. They're also called **Web portals**, since their purpose is to serve as a grandiose door through which you pass to launch your journey across the World Wide Web.

Three ways to search

Here are the three popular ways to search for a topic on the Web.

Search-box method In a search box, type the topic you're interested in, and then press ENTER. That makes Yahoo (or Excite or Go) use its **search engine**, which searches on the Internet for pages about that topic.

Go has the best search engine: it works better than Yahoo's or Excite's. But to get different perspectives on the topic that interests you, try the search engines of all three of those services!

When you make the computer search for a topic, the computer typically finds *thousands* of pages about that topic. The computer tries to guess which of those pages are the most relevant; the computer shows you those pages first. To help the computer deduce correctly which pages are the most relevant, use the following tricks (which all work in Go and sometimes work in other search engines)....

Capitalize names (and titles). For example, to search for the actor Rock Hudson, type:

Rock Hudson

If you accidentally type —

rock hudson

the computer will think you're also interested in rock-climbing along the Hudson River and rock music there.

Use quotation marks around phrases. For example, to search for the phrase "read my lips" (uttered by President George Bush and repeated by other politicians afterwards), type:

"read my lips"

If you omit the quotation marks, the computer will think you're interested in all pages containing the words "read" and "my" and "lips", not necessarily in that order. For example, you'll get pages about teaching deaf people to do lip-reading.

To search for stupid pet tricks (on TV shows such as David Letterman's), type:

"stupid pet tricks"

If you omit the quotation marks, the computer will think you're also interested in how to play tricks on stupid pets.

Instead of typing just a single word, type a list of SEVERAL words. In that list, put a plus sign before each word you REQUIRE, and put a minus sign before each word you FORBID (do NOT want).

For example, suppose you want to search for pythons, which are a kind of snake. If you type just —

python

you'll get info about python snakes but also info about a programming language called Python and a comedy group called Monty Python. To get info on just python snakes, try —

python -monty

(which gets you most pythons but eliminates any pages that mention Monty) or say —

python -monty -Python

(which gets you most pythons but not Monty and not capitalized Python) or say —

python snake

(which gets you any page that mentions pythons or snakes a lot) or say —

+python snake

(where the plus sign means you *insist* on seeing just pages that mention pythons, and of the python pages you prefer to see first the ones that also mention snakes a lot).

To be *very* restrictive, tell the computer to show you a page just if that page mentions both pythons and snakes on the same page. To do that, say —

+python +snake

or:

python|snake

(To type the symbol "|", tap the "\" key while holding down the SHIFT key. That symbol works in Infoseek but not in most other search engines.)

To search for several capitalized names, put commas between them. For example, to search for pages that mention two famous clowns, "Bozo" and "Ronald McDonald", say:

Bozo, Ronald McDonald

If you omit the comma, the computer will search for somebody named "Bozo Ronald McDonald" and not find him.

Remember that the Internet is huge. For a typical topic, the search engine will find thousands of pages about it. For the most popular topics, the search engine will find *millions* of pages.

If you try to fool the search engine by typing a fake topic (such as a nonsense syllable), you'll be surprised: the search engine will typically inform you that the topic was already invented by others and will show you several pages about it (because it turns out to be the name of some rock band, or some organization's initials, or some word in a foreign language).

You can try other search engines. Here's a list of popular search engines:

Search engine	Address
Yahoo	www.yahoo.com
Excite	www.excite.com
Go	www.go.com
Google	www.google.com
NorthernLight	www.northernlight.com
HotBot	www.hotbot.com
AltaVista	www.altavista.com
WebCrawler	www.webcrawler.com
Dogpile	www.dogpile.com

Go does the best job of deducing which sites are the most relevant. **AltaVista** runs the fastest and finds the most sites but does a poor job of deducing which of the found sites are most relevant.

A **metasearch site** called **All4One** (www.all4one.com) splits your screen into four frames, where it runs 4 search engines simultaneously (Excite, HotBot, AltaVista, and Lycos). A metasearch site called **MetaCrawler** (www.metacrawler.com) is more sophisticated: it runs 14 search engines simultaneously (Excite, Go, Google, Lycos, WebCrawler, About, Kanoodle, GoTo, DirectHit, PartnerQuery, Thunderstone, LookSmart, FindWhat, and Sprinks) in a single frame and combines their results into a single list.

The *most intelligent* metasearch site is **Ask Jeeves** (www.ask.com). It runs 4 search engines (Excite, AltaVista, WebCrawler, and 4Anything) and, if you type a question instead of just words, it will analyze your question's grammar, check whether other folks have asked similar questions, offer responses based on those questions (helped by a staff of humans working behind the scenes), and do an amazingly good job of honing in on finding the answer. I love it! Go wild: ask the most important or craziest questions you can think of, and see how Jeeves responds!

Subject-tree method You see a list of broad topics (on the main page of Yahoo, Excite, Go, WebCrawler, Magellan, or Galaxy). That list is called the **subject tree of knowledge** (because it's as tempting as the tree of knowledge in the garden of Eden). Click on whichever broad topic interests you. Then you see a list of that topic's branches (subtopics). Click whatever subtopic interests you. Then you see a list of subsubtopics (twigs). Click whichever subsubtopic interests you. Keep clicking until you finally zero in on the very specific topic that interests you the most: it's the fruit of your search!

Yahoo has the best subject tree. But to get different perspectives on the topic that interests you, also try the subject trees provided by Yahoo's competitors.

Address-box method Give your friends a sheet of paper and ask them to jot down the addresses of their favorite Web pages. (Or get lists of nifty Web addresses by reading computer books, magazines, newspaper articles, or ads.)

For example, here's a list of popular Web sites. For each site, I give its title, a comment about the site, and the site's Web address:

Category	Web site's title	Comment	Web address
Fun to start with	Secret Guide to Computers	links to the best sites in this list & Secret Guide info	www.secretfun.com
	Miss Nikita's Parlor	many links and interesting things to do	puffin.ptialaska.net/~pongo/parlor
	Berit's Best Sites for Children	links to many fun sites appropriate for kids	www.beritsbest.com
	Cool Site of the Day	a different Web site each day	www.coolsiteoftheday.com
	Blue Mountain Arts	create your own animated greeting cards	bluemountain.com
	Bolt	frank teen chat, organized & edited by post-teens	www.bolt.com
	Wall O' Shame	strange but true tidbits, from news and ads	www.milk.com/wall-o-shame
	Alt.Culture	a guide to 90's alternative culture	www.altculture.com
Solid writing	Giraffics Multimedia Books	Alice in Wonderland's text with animation, music	www.megabrands.com
	Shakespeare	all of Shakespeare's works, Web style	tech-two.mit.edu/shakespeare
	Bartlett's Familiar Quotations	browse by name or search for quotes by keywords	www.bartleby.com/99
	Inkspot: Resources for Writers	how to get started, improve your writing, and sell it	www.inkspot.com
Comic quips	Woody Allen Quotes	hundreds of quotes from his best movies	www.idt.unit.no/~torp/woody/lines.html
	Steven Wright	a collection of Steven Wright's best one-liners	www.magicnet.net/~hankpet/wrghthom.html
	Joke Repository	further jokes by Steven Wright and many others	muffet.com/jokes/jokes.html
	"Wisdom" of Dan Quayle	a collection of his more "interesting" sayings	www.concentric.net/~salisar/quayle.html
	Godzilla SUV	the biggest, baddest SUV that money can't buy	slate.msn.com/Features/GodzillaSUV/page2.asp
	Rec.humor.funny	jokes collected from Internet people worldwide	www.netfunny.com
TV	TV Guide Online	many articles, check TV listings for next 2 weeks	www.tvguide.com
	Comedy Central Online	cable TV's fun show, plus Politically Incorrect	www.comcentral.com
	Seinfeld	lots of audio & pictures, mock interview with Jerry	www.execpc.com/~bogambo/seinfeld.html
	X-Files	loaded with info about the hit TV show	www.thex-files.com
Movies	Internet Movie Database	huge searchable database of movie facts	www.imdb.com
	Hollywood Online	Hollywood news, movie reviews, promotions	www.hollywood.com
	Oracle of Bacon	connect any actor to Kevin Bacon within 6 movies?	www.cs.virginia.edu/oracle
Music	MP3.com	all kinds of music for you to hear	www.mp3.com
	Rap Dictionary	dictionary of slang used in rap music	www.rapdict.org
	Rock and Roll Hall of Fame	today in rock history, inductee info, media clips	www.rockhall.com
	Internet Beatles Album	Beatles trivia game, audio clips, reference library	www.getback.org
Food	Godiva Chocolatier	recipes, history, and other tidbits about chocolate	www.godiva.com
	Spam Haiku Archive	over 15,000 haiku poems about pink lunchmeat	pemtropics.mit.edu/~jcho/spam
House hunting	Realtor.Com	over 1.3 million homes for sale	realtor.com
	Home Advisor	advice about how to find the best home	homeadvisor.msn.com
Travel	Expedia	plane tickets, driving directions, discount car rentals	www.expedia.com
	Travelocity	Expedia's main competitor	www.travelocity.com
Science & beyond	Yuckiest Site on the Internet	gross biology: roaches, worms, vomit, belches, farts	www.nj.com/yucky
	Lawn Challenge	a complete course in how to take care of your lawn	www.urbanext.uiuc.edu/lawnchallenge
	Bill Nye the Science Guy	info and merchandise, science "demo of the day"	nyelabs.kcts.org
	NASA	learn about outer space from the experts	www.nasa.gov
	InteliHealth	medical news, reference, and advice	www.inteliheath.com
	Museum of Menstruation	alternatives to tampons	www.mum.org
	Institute of Celestial Sciences	change your astrological sign; get proof	www.jackrudy.com/ics
Job search	HotJobs	gives you lots of help finding a job	www.hotjobs.com
	America's Job Bank	over 300,000 jobs	www.ajb.dni.us
	Career Path	over 200,000 jobs	www.careerpath.com
	Monster Board	over 50,000 jobs; post your résumé online	www.monster.com
	Online Career Center	over 30,000 jobs; post your résumé online	www.occ.com
	BizBuySell	over 10,000 businesses for sale; well-organized listings	www.bizbuysell.com
Phone numbers	411.com	white pages, fast & easy & accurate	www.411.com
	555-1212.com	white pages plus extra features	www.555-1212.com
	BigBook	yellow pages, with maps and driving directions	www.bigbook.com
News	CNN Interactive	Cable News Network	www.cnn.com
	USA Today	USA's biggest newspaper	www.usatoday.com
	New York Times	USA's most prestigious newspaper	www.nytimes.com
	The Onion	a parody of today's news	www.onion.com
	Weather Underground	weather forecasts for cities all over the USA	www.wunderground.com
	ESPNet SportsZone	sports articles, scores, and updates from ESPN	espnet.sportszone.com
	You're Outta Here	obituaries — with a dash of humor	www.cjnetworks.com/~roryb/outta.html
Reference	Reference.Com	a great all-around reference site	www.reference.com
	Land O' Useless Facts	bizarre trivia submitted by readers	www.useless-facts.com
	CIA World Factbook	facts and statistics about every country in the world	www.odci.gov/cia/publications/factbook
	Hoover's Online	look up your favorite big company and its finances	www.hoovers.com
	Library of Congress	search the Library of Congress database	lcweb.loc.gov
	Internet Public Library	youth & teen divisions, library of links, online books	www.ipl.org
	Amazon.com Books	world's biggest online bookstore; fast searches	www.amazon.com
	Britannica.com	Encyclopedia Britannica, free; links to other sources	www.britannica.com
City secrets	Lifestyle Game	reveals what kind of people live in your ZIP code	laguna.natdecsys.com/lifequiz.html
	Citysearch	over 50 cities in US, Canada, Australia, elsewhere	www.citysearch.com
	Boston.com	all about Boston, run by Boston Globe newspaper	www.boston.com
	Vegas.com	Las Vegas casinos, rooms, shows, weddings, more	www.vegas.com
Government	FirstGov.gov	contains links to all US & state government sites	www.firstgov.gov
	White House	presidential info, history, tour, guide to fed services	www.whitehouse.gov
	Social Security Administration	frequently asked questions, statistics, info, links	www.ssa.gov
	United States Postal Service	ZIP codes, postage rates, services, rules	new.usps.com
	US Census Information	population and economic statistics and facts	www.census.gov
	British Monarchy	the queen, her dogs, and the relatives who dog her	www.royal.gov.uk
Banks	NetBank Internet Banking	this bank offers great rates because no storefront	www.netbank.com
	Teller Talk	inside info about how bank tellers should react	www.bankinfo.com/teller/talkarc.html
Illegal activities	Sex Free	parody of a nude-sex site	www.sexgames.nu
	World Sex Guide	reports on prostitution in many cities and countries	www.worldsexguide.org
	Speedtrap.com	lists police-radar speed traps by state	www.speedtrap.com
Computer culture	Whatis.com	definitions of computer terms	www.whatis.com
	Computer Industry History	history of computers	gobi.stanford.edu/computer_history
	Tech Tales	funny "war stories" from the tech-support trenches	www.azstarnet.com/~sean

Type one of those addresses in the address box, then press ENTER.

To understand how addresses work, consider the address for the "Institute of Celestial Sciences", which is:

```
http://www.jackrudy.com/ics/
```

The address's first part ("http://") is called the **protocol**.

The address's next part ("www.jackrudy.com") is called the **domain name**; it tells you which computer on the Internet contains the info. The typical domain name begins with "www.", then has the name of a company (such as "jackrudy"). The domain name's ending (called the **top-level domain**) is typically ".com", which means "USA commercial company". Some addresses have different top-level domains:

Top-level domain	Meaning
.com	USA commercial company
.org	USA organization, typically non-profit
.gov	USA government agency
.mil	USA military
.edu	USA educational institution
.net	USA network resource
.us	USA in general
.au	Australia
.br	Brazil
.ca	Canada
.cn	China
.es	España (Spain)
.fi	Finland
.fr	France
.de	Deutschland (Germany)
.dk	Denmark
.ie	Ireland
.il	Israel
.in	India
.it	Italy
.jp	Japan
.mx	Mexico
.no	Norway
.nz	New Zealand
.ru	Russia
.se	Sweden
.tw	Taiwan
.uk	United Kingdom (Great Britain & Northern Ireland)

The rest of the address (such as "/ics/") is called the **page name**; it tells which file on the computer contains the page you requested.

Type each address carefully:

While typing an address, never put a space in the middle.

Watch your punctuation. The typical address will contain a dot (.) and a slash (/). An address can also contain a hyphen (-) or squiggle (~). Addresses never contain commas, backslashes, or apostrophes.

Type small letters (uncapitalized) for the typical address, since capitalized page names are rare. (The computer doesn't care whether you capitalize the protocol and domain name.)

Print

While you're examining a page, here's how to print a copy of it onto paper.

Click the **Print button**. (In Explorer 3 and Navigator, then press ENTER.)

That makes your printer print the *entire* page — even the part of the page that goes below the screen's bottom edge and doesn't fit on the screen.

Exit

When you finish using Explorer or Navigator, close its window (by clicking its X box). Here's what to do next:

Explorer 4&5 Press ENTER.

Explorer 3 If the History window appears, close it (by clicking its X box). If the taskbar (at the screen's bottom) still shows the name of your Internet service provider (such as "Galaxy"), click that name and then click "Disconnect".

Navigator 3 If the taskbar (at the screen's bottom) still shows the name of your Internet service provider (such as "Galaxy"), click that name and then click "Disconnect".

Navigator 4.6 If the History window appears, close it (by clicking its X box). If the taskbar (at the screen's bottom) still shows a modem-connection icon, double-click it and then click "Disconnect".

Hassles

While you use the Internet, you'll experience several hassles.

Delays The computer might take a long time to switch from one page to another.

Near the screen's top right corner, you see a logo.

In Navigator,	the logo is a big N.
In Explorer 3,	the logo is an "e" surrounded by an orbiting electron.
In Explorer 4&5,	the logo is a stained glass window in outer space.

While the computer is switching to a new page, the computer amuses you by animating the logo.

In Navigator,	you see shooting stars behind the big N.
In Explorer 3,	you see the electron and the world's globe move around the "e".
In Explorer 4&5,	you see the world's globe encircle the stained glass window.

Near the Start button (at the screen's bottom left corner), the computer prints messages about the switch. At the screen's bottom right corner, lights turn bright green while data is being transmitted; they remain otherwise (red or dark green) while your computer waits for the other computer to pay attention.

How to stop If the switch is taking a long time and you don't want to wait for it to finish, click the **Stop button**. That makes the computer stop the switching.

"Switching pages" is called **loading a new page**. When you click the Stop button, here's what happens:

If the computer has nearly finished loading the new page, the computer shows you most of the new page.

If the computer has *not* nearly finished loading the new page, the computer shows you the previous page.

How to try again When you try to view a new page, the computer might get stuck because of a transmission error. To try again, stop the current transmission attempt (by clicking the **Stop button**) and then see what happens.

If you find yourself back at the previous page, try again to switch to the new page.

On the other hand, if you find yourself with most, but not all, of the new page on the screen, and you insist on seeing the entire new page, click the **Reload button**, which makes your computer tell your ISP to try again to transmit the current page. (Explorer calls it the **Refresh button**.)

Cache Whenever you view a page, the computer secretly puts a copy of it onto your hard disk, in a folder called the **cache** (which is pronounced "cash" and is a French word that means "hiding place"). Later, if you try to view the same page again, the computer checks whether the page's copy is still in the cache. If the copy is still in the cache, the computer puts that copy up onto your screen, because using that copy is faster than making your ISP retransmit the page.

When the cache gets so full that no more pages fit into the cache, the computer discards the pages you haven't viewed recently. Also, the computer tends to **clear the cache** (erase the entire cache) when you exit from the browser (by clicking the X box).

Whenever you tell the computer that you want to view a page, the page will come onto your screen fast if the computer uses the page's **cached copy**. If the computer can't find the page's cached copy (because the page was never viewed before or because the cached copy was discarded), the computer tells your ISP to transmit the page and you must wait awhile for the transmission to finish.

Problem: suppose you want to check the latest news (such as the news about a war or an election or stocks). If you view a page that shows you news, you might be reading *old* news, because the computer might be using an old cached copy of the page. **To make sure you're reading the latest news, click the Reload button**, which forces the computer to get a new version of the page from your ISP. (Explorer calls it the **Refresh button**.)

You can tell the computer how big to make the cache.

If you make the cache too big, it wastes too much of your hard disk, leaving inadequate room for other files. If you make the cache too small, fewer pages fit in it, so the pages you want to view are less likely to be in the cache, and your computer must ask your ISP to retransmit them more often, so you must wait more often for transmissions from your ISP.

For Explorer, Microsoft recommends making the cache be about 60 megabytes. For Navigator, Netscape recommends making the disk cache be about 7½ megabytes; Navigator also has a second cache, in RAM, for which the recommended size is 1 megabyte.

Here's how to adjust the cache size and make sure the cache is used in a standard way. If you're sharing your computer with colleagues, get their permission before making the following changes.

Explorer 5: click "Tools" then "Internet Options" then "Settings" then "Automatically". Drag the slider to the left (or right) until the number next to it is between 60MB and 100MB. Click OK twice.

Explorer 4: click "View" then "Internet Options" then "Settings" then "Every time you start Internet Explorer". Drag the slider to the left (or right) until the number next to it says 61.4MB. (It will then also say "3% of drive", which actually means "3% of the first 2 gigabytes of your drive".) Click OK twice.

Explorer 3: click "View" then "Options" then "Advanced" then "Settings" then "Every time you start Internet Explorer". Drag the slider to the left (or right) until the number next to it becomes 3%, which means "3% of the first 2 gigabytes of your drive", which is therefore about 60 megabytes. If your drive is tiny (just 1 gigabyte), choose 6% instead. If your drive is very tiny (just half a gigabyte), choose 12% instead. Click OK twice.

Netscape 4.6: click "Edit" then "Preferences". Double-click "Advanced". Click "Cache". Press the TAB key. Type how many kilobytes you want for the RAM cache (1024). Press TAB twice. Type how many kilobytes you want for the disk cache (7680). Click "Once per session" then OK.

Netscape 3: click "Options" then "Network Preferences" then "Cache". Type how many kilobytes you want for the RAM cache (1024). Press the TAB key. Type how many kilobytes you want for the disk cache (7680). Click "Once per session" then OK.

Here's where to find the cache:

Explorer's cache is a folder called "Temporary Internet Files", which is in your Windows folder.
Navigator 3's disk cache is a folder called "Program Files\Netscape\Navigator\Cache".
Navigator 4.6's disk cache is a folder with a name such as "Program Files\Netscape\Users\poo\cache".

Disconnect You might get interrupted by a window that suddenly appears and says "Connection was terminated". That means a computer accidentally disconnected you from the Internet.

Click the "Reconnect" button. Your computer will say, "Connected". Then hide the Connected window by clicking its minimize button (which is left of the X and resize buttons).

Eat up your time The Internet can eat up a lot of your time. You'll wait a long time for your modem, your ISP, and Web sites to transmit info to you. If you try search the Web for info about a particular topic, you'll spend lots of time visiting wrong Web sites before you finally find the site containing the gem of info you desire.

Along the way, you'll be distracted by ads and other seductive links to pages that are fun, fascinating, and educational. They don't directly relate to the question you wanted answered, but they broaden your mind and expand your horizon, o cybercitizen and student of the world! The Internet is the ultimate serendipity: it answers questions you didn't know you had.

Trust

Don't trust the info you read on the Internet. Any jerk can create a Web page. The info displayed on a Web page might be misleading, dishonest, or lies.

Unlike the typical book, whose accuracy is checked by the book's editor and publisher, the typical Web page is unchecked. An individual with unconventional ideas can easily create a Web page expressing those ideas, even if no book-publishing company would publish such a book.

Info on Web pages can be racist, hateful, sexist, libelous, treasonous, and deadly. Even though the Web page appears on your computer's screen, the info on the Web page might *not* have the good-natured accuracy that computers are known for.

Freedom of speech The United States Constitution's first amendment guarantees that Americans have freedom of speech and freedom of the press. The Internet makes that freedom possible, by letting anybody create a Web page that says anything to the whole world. The Internet is freedom unchained, uncensored. That's what's wonderful about the Internet, and that's also what's frightening.

Dictators in many countries have tried to suppress the Internet, because the Internet lets people say and speak truths from around the world and band together to protest against dictatorship. Nice people in many countries have also tried to suppress the Internet when they see how many lies are printed on the Web.

Fringe groups The Web is an easy way for "fringe groups" to advertise themselves and make their voices heard. In a dictatorship, the "fringe groups" are those who want democracy; in a democracy, the "fringe groups" are often those who want to create their own little dictatorships.

Unreliable advice Use the Web as a way to broaden your mind to different ideas, but don't believe in them until you've thought about them and checked them against other sources. Some of the medical advice on the Web can kill you; some of the financial advice on the Web can bankrupt you; some of the career advice on the Web can land you in jail. About 90% of what's written on the Web is true, but beware of the other 10%.

Who's the source? When reading a Web page, consider its source. If the Web page is written by a person or company you trust, the info on that page is probably true. If the Web page is written by a total stranger, be cautious.

Errors If the Web page contains many spelling errors and grammar errors, its author might be a foreigner, an immigrant, a kid, or an idiot. Perhaps the ideas on the page are as inaccurate as the way they're expressed. When researching a topic on the Web, don't be surprised if one of the Web pages turns out to be just a copy of a term paper written by a kid whose teacher gave it an F because its info is all wrong.

Ads Even if a Web page is written by a reputable source, beware: it might include ads from other organizations whose motives are unsavory. When reading a traditional newspaper page printed on paper, you can usually tell which parts of the page are ads and which parts are articles, since the ads use different fonts; but when you're reading a Web page, it's not always clear which links are to "articles" and which links are to "ads", since the entire Web is a vast jumble of fonts.

Parental controls Many parents are afraid to expose their young kids to wild sex, wild violence, and wild hate groups. Many Internet pages contain lots of sex, violence, and hatred, either directly or through the ads they lead you to. Many parents are therefore afraid to expose their young kids to such Web pages. Many conservative religious people are afraid to expose *themselves* to such Satanic temptations.

You can get programs that censor the Internet.

For example, you can get programs that prevent your computer from displaying any page mentioning sexy words; but beware: a program that hides all references to "breast" will also prevent you from researching "breast cancer" and "chicken breast recipes". You can get programs that limit kids to just pages that have been reviewed and approved by wise adults; but then the kids are restricted from reading any newer, better pages that haven't been reviewed yet.

Changing the home page

When you first buy Explorer or Navigator, here's what happens:

Explorer 5	assumes you want the home page to be "http://www.msn.com/".
Explorer 3&4	assumes you want the home page to be "http://home.microsoft.com/".
Navigator	assumes you want the home page to be "http://home.netscape.com/".

But you can change the assumption, and make the home page be anything you want! If there's no particular page you want to always start with, you can even make the home page be blank.

Here's how to change the home page:

Explorer 5 If you want the home page to be just a blank page, click **Tools** then **Internet Options** then **Use Blank** then OK. If instead you want a particular page to become the home page, get that page onto your screen (so you can admire it) then click **Tools** then **Internet Options** then **Use Current** then OK.

Explorer 4 If you want the home page to be just a blank page, click **View** then **Internet Options** then **Use Blank** then OK. If instead you want a particular page to become the home page, get that page onto your screen (so you can admire it) then click **View** then **Internet Options** then **Use Current** then OK.

Explorer 3 If you want the home page to be just a blank page, do this: click **View** then **Options** then **Navigation**, then double-click in the Address box, then type this —

```
c:\windows\system\blank.htm
```

then click OK. If instead you want a particular page to become the home page, get that page onto your screen (so you can admire it), then click **View** then **Options** then **Navigation** then **Use Current**, then "OK".

Navigator 4.6 If you want the home page to be just a blank page, click **Edit** then **Preferences** then **Blank Page** then OK. If instead you want a particular page to become the home page, get that page onto your screen (so you can admire it) then click **Edit** then **Preferences** then the **Home Page** button then **Use Current Page** then OK.

Navigator 3 Click **Options** then **General Preferences** then **Appearance**. If you want the home page to be just a blank page, click **Blank Page**; if you want the home page to be "http://www.yahoo.com/", click **Home Page Location** instead, then press the TAB key, then type:

```
http://www.yahoo.com/
```

Finally, press ENTER.

Electronic mail

Another popular Internet activity is to send **electronic mail** (**e-mail**). An e-mail message imitates a regular letter or postcard but is transmitted electronically so you don't have to lick a stamp, don't have to walk to the mailbox to send it, and don't have to wait for the letter to be processed by the postal system.

E-mail zips through the Internet at lightning speed, so a letter sent from Japan to the United States takes just minutes (sometimes even seconds) to reach its destination. Unlike regular mail, which the Post Office usually delivers just once a day, e-mail can arrive anytime, day or night. If your friends try to send you e-mail messages while your computer is turned off, your Internet service provider will hold their messages for you until you turn your computer back on and reconnect to the Internet.

Since sending e-mail is so much faster than using the Post Office (which is about as slow as a snail), the Post Office's mail is nicknamed **snail mail**. Yes, e-mail travels fast, typically takes just a few minutes to reach its destination, and is usually free; snail mail travels slowly, typically takes several *days* to reach its destination, and usually costs 33 cents (for a stamp) plus money for paper and an envelope. So if your friend promises to send you a letter "soon", ask "Are you going to send it by e-mail or snail mail?"

An "e-mail message" is sometimes called just "**an e-mail**". Instead of saying "I sent three e-mail messages", an expert says "I sent three e-mails".

To use e-mail, you need a program called an **e-mail client**. Here are the most popular e-mail clients:

> **Netscape Mail** (which is part of Netscape's Navigator 3)
> **Netscape Messenger** (which is part of Netscape's Navigator 4.6)
> **Internet Mail** (which is part of Microsoft's Internet Explorer 3)
> **Outlook Express** (which is part of Microsoft's Internet Explorer 4&5).

I'll explain how to use those e-mail clients. (Some folks use other e-mail clients, such as **Eudora**, **Pegasus**, **Pine**, and **AOL Mail**.)

Launch your e-mail client

Here's how to start using e-mail.

Explorer 5 While you're running Explorer 5, you see a **Mail button** at the top of the screen. Click that button, then click "Read Mail".

(To deal with e-mail while you're *not* running Explorer 5, click the tiny Outlook Express icon, which is to the right of the Start button and shows an envelope with arrows orbiting around it; then answer any questions about your ISP and password; then click "Read Mail".)

You'll see the **Outlook Express window**. If it doesn't consume the whole screen yet, **maximize it** (by clicking its resize button, which is next to the X button).

Explorer 4 While you're running Explorer 4, you see a **Mail button** at the top of the screen. Click that button, then click "Read Mail".

(To deal with e-mail while you're *not* running Explorer 4, double-click the icon that says "Outlook Express" or single-click the tiny Outlook Express icon, which is to the right of the Start button and shows an "e" above an envelope; then answer any questions about your ISP and password; then click "Read Mail".)

If the computer says "Please select a folder", press ENTER.

You'll see the **Outlook Express window**. If it doesn't consume the whole screen yet, **maximize it** (by clicking its resize button, which is next to the X button).

Explorer 3 While you're running Explorer 3, you see a **Mail button** at the top of the screen. Click that button, then click "Read Mail".

(To deal with e-mail while you're *not* running Explorer 3, do this instead: click "Start" then "Programs" then "Internet Mail"; then answer any questions about your ISP and password.)

You'll see the **Internet Mail window**. If it doesn't consume the whole screen yet, **maximize it** (by clicking its resize button, which is next to the X button).

If you haven't used Explorer 3 before, tell it you want all e-mail transmissions to be automated! Here's how:

> Click "Mail" (which is next to the word "View") then "Options". Put a check mark in front of "Send messages immediately" (by clicking there).
> Click "Read" (which is near the top of the screen). Put a check mark in front of "Check for new messages" (by clicking there).
> Press ENTER.

Navigator If you're using Navigator 3, do this:

> While you're running Navigator, the screen's bottom right corner shows the time. Just above the time, you see the **mail icon**, which looks like the back of an envelope. Click that icon. You'll see the Netscape Mail window.
> The computer will say "Password". Type your password (and press ENTER). If the computer says "No new messages on server", press ENTER.

If you're using Navigator 4.6, do this:

> While you're running Navigator, the screen's bottom right corner shows the time. Just above the time you see five icons. The second icon is the **Inbox icon**, which shows a down-arrow next to an envelope going down into a box. Click that icon. You'll see the Netscape Mail window.
> The computer will say "Password". Type your password (and press ENTER).

If the Netscape Mail window doesn't consume the whole screen yet, **maximize the window** (by clicking the window's resize button, which is next to the X button).

Incoming mail

Here's how to handle incoming mail.

Explorer Explorer 4&5 begin like this:

> The screen is divided into three white windowpanes (which I'll call "left", "top", and "bottom"). In the left pane, click "Inbox".

Explorer 3 begins like this:

> The screen is divided into two white windowpanes (which I'll call "top" and "bottom"). Above them is a Folders box. In the Folders box, make sure you see "Inbox". (If you don't see "Inbox", click in the Folders box and then click "Inbox".)

Then the top pane shows a list of all e-mail messages that other people have sent you. For each message, the list shows whom the message is **from** (the sender's name), the message's **subject** (what the message is about), and when the message was **received** (the date and time).

The first time Microsoft's Explorer is used on your computer, the top pane shows you've received a message from Microsoft. (Explorer 4 shows you've received *two* messages from Microsoft.) After you've used Explorer awhile, you'll probably receive additional messages, from your friends!

Here's how to deal with a long list of messages:

> Each message is initially listed in bold type and shows a picture of a sealed envelope. If you spend at least 5 seconds looking at a message's details, that message becomes unbolded and its envelope becomes opened.
>
> If there are too many messages to fit in the pane, view the rest of the messages by pressing that pane's scroll-down arrow (the symbol ▼ at the pane's bottom right corner).
>
> In what order do the messages appear? If you click the word "Received", the messages are listed in the order received (in chronological order); if you click the word "From" instead, the messages are listed by the sender's name (in alphabetical order). Clicking "Received" is typically more useful than clicking "From". When you click the word "Received" or "From", a triangle appears next to that word. If you click that same word again, the triangle flips upside-down — and so does the list. For example, suppose the triangle is next to the word "Received": if the triangle points down, the messages are listed from newest to oldest; if the triangle points up instead, the messages are listed from oldest to newest.

Look in the top pane, at the list of messages you received. Decide which message you want to read, and click the sender's name. Then the bottom pane starts showing you the complete message. Read it.

The complete message is probably too long to fit in the bottom pane. To see the rest of the message, press that pane's scroll-down arrow (the symbol ▼ at the pane's bottom right corner).

Navigator The screen is divided into three windowpanes (which I'll call "left", "top", and "bottom").

The left pane includes 3 important icons: **Inbox** (which holds mail that other people have sent you), **Sent** (which holds copies of mail you've sent to other people), and **Trash** (which holds messages you're deleting). **Click the Inbox icon.**

Then the top pane shows a list of all e-mail messages that other people have sent you. For each message, the list shows the **sender** (whom the message is from), the message's **subject** (what the message is about), and the **date** (when the message was sent).

The first time Netscape Navigator 3 is used on your computer, the top pane shows you've received a message from "Mozilla", who is Netscape Corporation's mascot.

After you've used Netscape Navigator awhile, you'll probably received messages from your friends. Here's how to deal with a long list of messages:

> If there are too many messages to fit in the pane, view the rest of the messages by pressing that pane's scroll-down arrow (the symbol ▾ at the pane's bottom right corner).
>
> Messages you haven't read yet are listed in bold type and have a green diamond.
>
> In what order do the messages appear? If you click the word "Date", the messages are listed by date (in chronological order); if you click the word "Sender" instead, the messages are listed by the sender's name (in alphabetical order). Clicking "Date" is typically more useful than clicking "Sender".

Look in the top pane, at the list of messages you received. Decide which message you want to read, and click the sender's name. Then the bottom pane starts showing you the complete message. Read it.

The complete message is probably too long to fit in the bottom pane. To see the rest of the message, press that pane's scroll-down arrow (the symbol ▾ at the pane's bottom right corner).

Another way to see the rest of the message is to adjust the gray bar that separates the bottom pane from the top pane: drag that bar up, so the bottom pane becomes bigger and you can see more in it.

In Navigator 4.6, the bottom pane might not be wide enough. To make it wider, adjust the gray bar that separates the bottom pane from the left pane: drag that bar slightly to the left, so the bottom pane becomes slightly bigger and you can see more in it. If the bottom pane still isn't wide enough, do this trick: click "View" (which is on the top menu bar), then put a check mark before "Wrap Long Lines" (by clicking there).

How to send mail

To write an e-mail message, perform 5 steps.

Step 1: get the window Click the **New Message button**. (Explorer 5 calls it the New Mail button. Explorer 4 calls it the Compose Message button. Navigator 4 calls it the New Msg button. Navigator 3 call it the To:Mail button.) You'll see the **New Message window**. (Navigator calls it the Composition window.)

Step 2: choose a recipient To whom do you want to send the message? To send an e-mail message to a person, you must find out that person's e-mail address. For example, if you want to send an e-mail message to me, you need to know that **my e-mail address is "russ@secretfun.com"**.

For the Internet, **each e-mail address contains the symbol "@", which is pronounced "at"**. For example, my Internet address, "russ@secretfun.com", is pronounced "russ at secret fun dot com".

(To send me e-mail, you can use either my new address, "russ@secretfun.com", or my old address, "poo@gis.net". Either way will reach me.)

To find out the e-mail addresses of your friends and other people, ask them (by chatting with them in person or by phoning them or by sending them snail-mail postcards). Another way to discover e-mail addresses is to use **Bigfoot**, which is a World Wide Web site that searches for e-mail addresses: tell Navigator or Explorer to go to "www.bigfoot.com".

If you send e-mail to the following celebrities and nuts, they'll probably read what you wrote, though they might not have enough time to write back:

Comic actors	Comment	E-mail address
Jerry Seinfield	Jewish humor	seinfeld@nbc.com
Tim Allen	Home Improvement	tim@morepower.com
Bob Saget	Funniest Home Videos	FancyCarol@aol.com
Adam Sandler	Saturday Night Live	sandler@cris.com
Rodney Dangerfield	says gets "no respect"	rodney@rodney.com
Steve Martin	"wild & crazy guy"	TheGilb@aol.com
Paula Poundstone	stand-up comedienne	paula@mojones.com
Bob Hope	WW2 funnyman	BobHope@bobhope.com
Ed Asner	My Little Margie's boss	72726.357@compuserve.com
Mel Brooks	directs & acts	Gd2BTKing@aol.com
Dramatic actors		
Clint Eastwood	rugged Westerns	rowdiyates@aol.com
Brad Pitt	heartthrob	CiaoBox@msn.com
Tom Cruise	heartthrob	AGoodActor@aol.com
Leonardo Dicaprio	Titanic heartthrob	LeoD443@aol.com
John Travolta	black-jacket cool	JohnTravolta@earthalliance.com
Adam West	the original Batman	AdamBatman@aol.com
Wesley Snipes	black action-hero	herukush@aol.com
James Woods	plays a psychopath	JamesWoods@aol.com
Talk-show hosts		
David Letterman	CBS's "Late Show"	LateShow@pipeline.com
Tom Synder	CBS after Letterman	LateLatesSow@cbs.com
Jay Leno	NBC's "Tonight Show"	TonightShow@nbc.com
Conan O'Brien	NBC after Leno	LateNight@nbc.com
Oprah Winfrey	warm	harpo@interaccess.com
Jerry Springer	man has wild guests	SpringerSh@aol.com
Ricki Lake	woman has wild guests	RickiLake@aol.com
Howard Stern	talks dirty on radio	stern@urshan.com
Bill Maher	"Politically Incorrect"	pi@cis.compuserve.com
Politicians		
Bill Clinton	President of USA	president@whitehouse.gov
Hillary Clinton	First Lady of USA	first.lady@whitehouse.gov
Al Gore	Vice-President of USA	vice.president@whitehouse.gov
Newt Gingrich	Speaker of the House	georgia6@hr.house.gov
Ted Kennedy	Senator	senator@kennedy.senate.gov
Ross Perot	Presidential candidate	71511.460@compuserve.com
Tony Blair	Prime Minister of UK	tony.blair@geo2.poptel.org.uk
Reporters & commentators		
Tom Brokaw	NBC news anchorman	nightly@nbc.com
Dave Barry	syndicated columnist	73314.722@compuserve.com
Roger Ebert	movie critic, thumbs up	73136.3232@compuserve.com
Martha Stewart	"perfect" homemaker	MStewart@msl.timeinc.com
Xaviera Hollander	"Happy Hooker"	xaviera@xs4all.nl
Bill Nye	PBS's "Science Guy"	BillNye@nyelabs.com
Cartoonists		
Scott Adams	Dilbert	ScottAdams@aol.com
Garry Trudeau	Doonesbury	72662.3023@compuserve.com
Fiction authors		
Tom Clancy	writes spy thrillers	TomClancy@aol.com
Douglas Adams	sci-fi, Hitchhiker's	76206.2507@compuserve.com
Computerists		
Bill Gates	head of Microsoft, rich	BillG@microsoft.com
Russ Walter	nut, wrote this book	russ@secretfun.com
Len Pallazola	less nutty, helped Russ	LenPal@bigfoot.com
John Levine	"Internet for Dummies"	NInternet@dummies.com
Singers		
Madonna	pop & sexy	madonna@wbr.com
Amy Grant	pop & Christian	amy.grant@nashville.com
Ted Nugent	1970's classic rock	75162.2032@compuserve.com
Joe Walsh	classic rock, in Eagles	RayCraft@post.avnet.co.uk
Sports heroes		
Larry Bird	basketball	LarryBird3@aol.com
Evander Holyfield	boxer had his ear bit	evander@evanderholyfield.com

When you type an e-mail address, you don't have to capitalize. The computer ignores capitalization.

Never put a blank space in the middle of an e-mail address.

Warning: people often change their e-mail addresses, so don't be surprised if your message comes back, marked undeliverable.

Type the e-mail address of the person to whom you want to send your message. If you're a shy beginner who's nervous about bothering people, **try sending an e-mail message to a close friend or me or yourself.** Sending an e-mail message to yourself is called "doing a Fats Waller", since he was the first singer to popularize this song:

> "Gonna sit right down and write myself a letter,
> And make believe it came from you!"

If you send an e-mail message to *me*, I'll read it (unless my e-mail address has changed) and try to send you a reply, but be patient (since I check my e-mail just a few times per week) and avoid asking for computer advice (since I give *advice* just by regular phone calls at 603-666-6644, not by e-mail).

At the end of the e-mail address, press the TAB several times (once for Navigator 4.6, twice for Navigator 3 and Explorer 3&5, three times for Explorer 4), **so you're at the line marked "Subject".**

Step 3: choose a subject
Type a phrase summarizing the subject (such as "let's lunch" or "I'm testing"). At the end of that typing, press the TAB key again.

Step 4: type the message
Go ahead: type the message, such as "Let's have lunch together in Antarctica tomorrow!" or "I'm testing my e-mail system, so please tell me whether you received this test message." Your message can be as long as you wish — many paragraphs! Type the message as if you were using a word processor. For example, press the ENTER key just when you reach the end of a paragraph. If you wish, maximize the window you're typing in (by clicking the window's resize button, which is next to the X button).

Step 5: send the message
When you finish typing the message, click the **Send button** (which looks like a flying envelope).

The window you typed in will close automatically. (If you're using Navigator, you might have to wait one or two minutes for the window to close. Be patient.)

When do messages transmit?
When you try to send or receive a message, when does the transmission actually occur?

Receiving a message from a friend When a friend tries to send you a message, the message goes from your friend's computer to your friend's **Internet Service Provider (ISP)**, which passes the message on to *your* ISP. The message is stored on your ISP's hard disk.

Since your ISP's computer is always turned on (day and night, 24 hours), it's always ready to receive messages your friends try to send you, even while your own computer is turned off.

When you try to examine your Inbox, your computer ought to contact your ISP and tell the ISP to transmit any new messages to your computer; but if your computer is lazy, it might not contact your ISP immediately to get the newest messages. Instead, your computer might decide to wait awhile before bothering your ISP. For example, your computer might contact your ISP just once every 30 minutes to check whether there are any new messages for you; or your computer might not contact your ISP until the next time you start running the e-mail program — which might be the next day.

Here's how to make your computer communicate with your ISP *now*, so all the messages you're trying to receive get transmitted to your Inbox *now*:

> If you're using Explorer 3&4, click the **Send and Receive button.**
> If you're using Explorer 5,   click the **Send/Recv button.**
>
> If you're using Netscape 3,   click the **Get Mail button.**
> If you're using Netscape 4.6,   click the **Get Msg button.**

Sending a message to a friend When you tell the computer to send a message to a friend, here's what happens....

> Using **Explorer 4&5 and Netscape**, the computer typically transmits the message immediately to your ISP (which passes it on to your friend's ISP).
>
> Using **Explorer 3**, the computer might not transmit the message immediately to your ISP. The computer might decide to wait until you finished using e-mail (and click the e-mail program's X button), then send all your messages in one huge batch. If you want to force the computer to send *now* any messages you wrote, click the **Send and Receive button**.

Automatic transmission If you wish, you can make your computer and your ISP send messages to each other more frequently, automatically, without their waiting for you to click a "Send and Receive" or "Send/Recv" or "Get Mail" or "Get Msg" button. I'll explain how.

But beware! If you make your computer and your ISP automatically transmit messages more frequently, you'll consume more of your ISP's time, which will cost you more money if your ISP is charging you by the minute. Also, you'll consume more of your own computer's time, so your computer will be interrupted from performing other tasks and seem sluggish. Also, you'll consume more of your own time, because you'll more frequently have to help keep the connection going by retyping your password.

If you're sharing your computer with colleagues, get their permission before making the following changes.

> **Explorer 4&5**: click "Tools" then "Options". Put ✔ in the box marked "Check for new messages" (by clicking). Put a small number (such as 10) in the minutes box (by clicking the box's down-arrow). Click "Send". Put ✔ in the box marked "Send messages immediately" (by clicking). Click OK.
>
> **Explorer 3**: click "Mail" then "Options". Put ✔ in the box marked "Send messages immediately" (by clicking). Click "Read". Put ✔ in the box marked "Check for new messages" (by clicking). Put a small number (such as 10) in the minutes box (by clicking the box's down-arrow). Click OK.
>
> **Netscape 4.6**: click "Edit" then "Preferences" then "Mail Servers" then "Edit". Put ✔ in the box marked "Check for mail" (by clicking). Put a small number (such as 10) in the minutes box (by double-clicking in that box and then typing the number). Put ✔ in the box marked "Automatically download any new messages" (by clicking). Click OK.
>
> **Netscape 3**: click "Options" then "Mail and News Preferences" then "Servers" then "Every". Put a small number (such as 10) in the minutes box (by double-clicking in that box and then typing the number). Click OK.

Smiley's pals
Here's a picture of a smiling face:

☺

It's called a **smiley**. If you rotate that face 90°, it looks like this:

> :-)

People writing e-mail messages often type that symbol to mean "I'm smiling; I'm just kidding".

For example, suppose you want to tell President Clinton that you disagree with his speech. If you communicate the old-fashioned way, with pencil and paper, you'll probably begin like this:

> Dear Mr. President,
>   I'm somewhat distressed at your recent policy announcement.

But people who communicate by e-mail tend to be more blunt:

> Hey, Bill!
>   You really blew that speech. Jeez! Your policy stinks. You should be boiled in oil, or at least paddled with a floppy disk. :-)

The symbol ":-)" means "I'm just kidding". That symbol's important. Forgot to include it? Then poor Bill, worried about getting boiled in oil, might have the Secret Service arrest you for plotting an assassination.

The smiley, ":-)", has many variations:

Symbol	Meaning
:-)	I'm smiling.
:-(	I'm frowning.
:-<	I'm real sad.
:-c	I'm bummed out.
:-C	I'm *really* bummed out!
:-I	I'm grim.
:-/	I'm skeptical.
:-7	I'm smirking at my own wry comment.
:->	I have a devilish grin.
:-D	I'm laughing.
:-o	I'm shouting.
:-O	I'm shouting really loud.
:-@	I'm screaming.
:-8	I talk from both sides of my mouth.
:-p	I'm sticking my tongue out at you.
:-P	I'm being tongue-in-cheek.
:-&	I'm tongue-tied.
:-9	I'm licking my lips.
:-*	My lips pucker for a kiss or pickle.
:-x	My lips are sealed.
:-#	I wear braces.
:-$	My mouth is wired shut.
:-?	I smoke a pipe.
:-}	I have a beard.
:-B	I have buck teeth.
:-[	I'm a vampire.
:-{}	I wear lipstick.
:-()	I have a mustache.
:-~)	My nose runs.
:-)'	I'm drooling.
:-)-8	I have big breasts.
:*)	I'm drunk.
:^)	My nose is broken.
:~I	I'm smoking.
:/i	No smoking!
:~j	I'm smoking and smiling.
:'-(	I'm crying.
:'-)	I'm so happy, I'm crying.
:)	I'm a midget.
;-)	I'm winking.
.-)	I have just one eye,
,-)	but I'm winking it.
?-)	I have a black eye.
%-)	Dizzy from staring at screen too long!
8-)	I wear glasses.
B-)	I wear cool shades, man.
g-)	I wear pince-nez glasses.
P-)	I'm a pirate.
O-)	I'm a scuba diver.
|-O	I'm yawning.
^O	I'm snoring.
X-(	I just died.
8:-)	My glasses are on my forehead.
B:-)	My sunglasses are on my forehead.
O:-)	I'm an angel.
+:-)	I'm a priest.
[:-)	I'm wearing a Walkman.
&:-)	I have curly hair.
@:-)	I have wavy hair.
8:-)	I have a bow in my hair.
{:-)	I wear a toupee,
}:-)	but the wind is blowing it off.
-:-)	I'm a punk rocker,
-:-(	but real punk rockers don't smile.
[:]	I'm a robot.
3:]	I'm your pet,
3:[	but I growl.
}:->	I'm being devilish,
>;->	and lewdly winking.
=:-)	I'm a hosehead.
E-:-)	I'm a ham radio operator.
C=:-)	I'm a chef.
=|:-)=	I'm Uncle Sam.
<):-)	I'm a fireman.
*<:-)	I'm Santa Claus.
*:o)	I'm Bozo the clown.
<:I	I'm a dunce.
(-:	I'm a lefty.

Since those symbolic pictures (icons) help you emote, they're called **emoticons** (pronounced "ee MOTE ee cons").

Acronyms

People writing e-mail messages often use these expressions and abbreviations:

Expression	Abbreviation	Expression	Abbreviation
I'm GRINNING!	<g>	Thanks in advance.	TIA
I have a BIG GRIN!	<bg>	No reply necessary.	NRN
I have a VERY BIG GRIN!	<vbg>		
		in my opinion	IMO
Laughing out loud!	LOL	in my humble opinion	IMHO
Rolling on the floor, laughing!	ROTFL	in my not-so-humble opinion	IMNSHO
Ha ha, only joking!	HHOJ	for your information	FYI
Tongue in cheek!	TIC	frequently asked question	FAQ
No problem!	NP	Read the manual.	RTM
Way to go!	WTG	Read the f***ing manual.	RTFM
Great minds think alike.	GMTA		
		Oh, I see.	OIC
before	B4	Still in the dark!	SITD
later	L8R	Are you OK?	RUOK
real soon now	RSN		
		in real life	IRL
See you later!	CUL8R	Been there, done that!	BTDT
Talk to you later!	TTYL		
Ta-ta for now!	TTFN	by the way	BTW
Be back later!	BBL	for what it's worth	FWIW
Be right back!	BRB	in any event	IAE
Be back in a flash!	BBIAF	in other words	IOW
Just a minute!	JAM	on the other hand	OTOH
Back at keyboard!	BAK		
Welcome back!	WB		
Long time, no see!	LTNS		

Those abbreviations are called **acronyms**.

What messages did you send?

To check which messages you sent, do this….

Explorer 4&5:	click "Sent Items" (which is in the left pane).
Explorer 3:	click in the Folders box, then click "Sent Items".
Navigator:	click the Sent folder (which is in the left pane).

You'll see a list of messages you sent. For each message, the list shows the address you sent it to, the message's subject, and when you sent it.

When you finish admiring that list, make the screen become normal again by doing this….

Explorer 4&5:	click "Inbox" (which is in the left pane).
Explorer 3:	click in the Folders box, then click "Inbox".
Navigator:	click the Inbox folder (which is in the left pane).

Reply

While you're reading a message that somebody's sent you, here's how to reply.

Click the **Reply To Author button**. (Explorer 5 and Navigator 4.6 call it just the "Reply" button. Navigator 3 calls it the "Re:Mail" button.) Then type your reply.

While you type, the computer shows a copy of the message you're replying to.

In Explorer 4&5 and Navigator 4.6,	the copy has a vertical bar ("|") in front of each line.
In Explorer 3 and Navigator 3,	the copy has ">" in front of each line.

If you want to abridge that copy (so it doesn't clutter your screen), use your mouse: drag across the part you want to delete, then press the DELETE key.

When you finish typing your reply, click the Send button (which looks like a flying envelope). The computer will send your reply, along with your abridged copy of the message you're replying to.

Delete old messages

The list of received messages — and the list of sent messages — can become long and hard to manage. To reduce the clutter, delete any messages that no longer interest you.

Explorer Here's how to delete a message you received (or a copy of a message you sent): make the message's name appear in the top pane, then click the name (so it turns blue), then press the DELETE key.

That tells the computer you want to delete the message. The computer moves the message into the **Deleted Items** folder (which resembles the Windows Recycle Bin).

To find out what's in the Deleted Items folder, do this:

> In Explorer 4&5, click "Deleted Items" (which is in the left pane).
>
> In Explorer 3, click the Folders box then click "Deleted Items".

You'll see what's in the Delete Items folder: a list of the messages you deleted. When you're 100% sure that you no longer want any of those messages, do this: click anywhere in that list of messages, choose "Select All" from the Edit menu (so all the messages turn blue), then press the DELETE key, then click the Yes button. Then all messages in the Deleted Items folder vanish.

Navigator

Here's how to delete a message you received (or a copy of a message you sent): make the message's name appear in the top right pane, then click the name (so it turns blue), then press the DELETE key.

That tells the computer you want to delete the message. The computer moves the message into the **Trash folder**, which appears in the top left pane. (The Trash folder resembles Windows 95's Recycle Bin.)

To find out what's in the Trash folder, click the Trash folder's icon. Then the Trash folder's contents appear in the top pane.

When you're 100% sure that you no longer want any of the messages that are in the Trash folder, choose "Empty Trash Folder" from the File menu. Then all messages in the Trash folder vanish.

Send a file attachment

While you're writing a message, here's how to insert a file (such as a picture you drew in Paint, or a document composed in WordPad or Microsoft Word).

For Explorer 5, do this:

> Click the **Attach button**, which looks like a paper clip.

For Explorer 3&4, do this:

> Click the **Insert File button**, which looks like a paper clip.

For Navigator 3, do this:

> Click the **Attach button**, which looks like a paper clip. Then click the **Attach File button**.

For Navigator 4.6, do this:

> Click the big button that looks like a paper clip and says "**Attach**" on it. Then click "File".

Which file do you want to insert? Make its icon appear on the screen. (If its icon is not on the screen because the computer is showing a different folder, do this: click the "▾", then click the hard disk's "C:" icon, then double-click the folders that the file is in.)

When the file's icon is finally on the screen, double-click that icon.

Here's what happens next....

> Explorer 5: above the message you were writing, you should see your file's name (in the Attach box); make sure the message and the file's name are correct.
>
> Explorer 3&4: below the message you were writing, you should see your file's icon; make sure the message and the file's icon are correct.
>
> Navigator 3: click "OK"; above the message you were writing, you should see your file's name (in the Attachment box); make sure the message and the file's name are correct.
>
> Navigator 4.6: above the message you were writing, you should see your file's name; make sure the message and the file's name are correct.

Finally, click the Send button (which looks like a flying envelope). That makes the computer send the message and attached file.

Receive a file attachment

Here's what to do if a friend sends you a message that includes an attached file:

Navigator

While you're reading the message, you'll see an icon underneath the message. Click that icon. (If the computer says "Warning", click "Open it" and then "OK".)

Explorer

While you're reading the message (in the bottom pane), you'll see a paper clip in that pane's top right corner. Click the paper clip.

Under that paper clip, you'll see the attached file's icon. Click that icon. (If the computer says "Open Attachment Warning", click "Open it" and then "OK".)

Final steps

The computer will try to show you the pictures and words that are in the attached file, by running the program that created the file. For example, if the file is a picture created by Paint, the computer will try to run Paint; if the file is a document created by Microsoft Word, the computer will try to run Microsoft Word. (If the file is a forwarded message created by Navigator, no new program needs to run, since Explorer can imitate Navigator.)

When you finish looking at the pictures and words that are in the attached file, close whatever program created it (such as Paint or Microsoft Word) by choosing Exit from the File menu. You'll return to seeing the Navigator (or Explorer) screen.

Multiple people

An e-mail message can be sent to many people. Here's how....

Multiple addresses

If you want to send a message to several people, put commas between their addresses. For example, if you want to send a message to the President of the United States (whose address is president@whitehouse.gov) and also to me (russ@secretfun.com), address the mail to:

> president@whitehouse.gov, russ@secretfun.com

(The space after the comma is optional.) That little list of addresses is called the **mailing list**.

Carbon copies

Here's how to send a message *mainly* to the President of the United States but also send me a copy:

> In the main address box (called "To"), write the address of the main person you want to send the letter to (which is president@whitehouse.gov).
>
> In the box marked "**Cc**" (which stands for "Carbon copy"), write the address of the person you want to send a secret copy to (which is russ@secretfun.com).

Here's how to send a message *mainly* to the President of the United States but also send me a copy, and make the copy be secret, so the President of the United States doesn't know the copy was sent to me:

> In the main address box (called "To"), write the address of the main person you want to send the letter to (which is president@whitehouse.gov).
>
> In the box marked "**Bcc**" (which stands for "Blind carbon copy"), write the address of the person you want to send a secret copy to (which is russ@secretfun.com).

That procedure works just if your screen shows a Bcc box.

> The Bcc box is in **Explorer 4** and **Navigator 4.6**.
>
> To make the Bcc box appear in **Explorer 5**, click "View" then put a check mark in front of "All Headers", by clicking.
>
> To make the Bcc box appear in **Navigator 3**, click "View" then put a check mark in front of "Mail Bcc", by clicking; the Bcc box is labeled "Blind Cc".
>
> **Explorer 3** is too stupid to produce a Bcc box and can't do the procedure.

Replies

If somebody sends *you* a message, you can reply to the message by clicking either the **Reply button** or the **Reply To All button**.

If you click the **Reply button**, your reply will be sent to just the person who sent you the message. If you click the **Reply To All button** instead, your reply will be sent to the person who sent you the message and also to everybody else on that person's mailing list.

For example, if Bob sends a message addressed to a list of three people (you and Sue and Jill) and you want to reply, you can either click the **Reply button** (which sends your reply just to Bob) or click the **Reply To All button** (which sends your reply to Bob and also to the other people on Bob's mailing list: Sue and Jill).

Forward While you're reading a message you received, here's how to send a copy of it to a friend.

Click the **Forward button**. (Explorer 4 calls it the Forward Message button.) Type your friend's e-mail address. Press the TAB key several times, until you're in the big white box where you can type a message. Type a comment to your friend, such as "Here's a joke Mary sent me."

Click the Send button (which looks like a flying envelope).

Privacy Remember this poem:

For example, suppose you send an e-mail message to Bob. Your message might be read by people other than Bob, for one of these reasons:

According to United States law, if you're an employee who writes an e-mail message by using the company's computer, the message becomes the company's property, and **your boss is allowed to look** at it. **Your message has no privacy.** Moreover, if your company is sued (by a competitor or customer), United States law can require your company to reveal all e-mail messages about the lawsuit's topic and about all the people involved in it: the cute joke you wrote can embarrass you when the judge makes you read it to the courtroom.

You should therefore **be especially careful about writing any e-mails that contain sexual references** (such as "I love your body, so let's go out on a date and have sex!") **or anger** (such as "The boss is a jerk, a prick, I wish he were dead, I hope somebody kills him!"), since your e-mail might accidentally fall into the hands of the one person to whom you don't want to show that message. Here's the most important rule about e-mail messages:

No "Undo" When you tell the computer to send an e-mail message (by clicking the Send button, Reply button, or Reply To All button), the computer immediately tries to transmit the message to your ISP (which in turn will try to pass the message to the recipient's ISP). You can*not* cancel the transmission easily, since there's no "Undo button".

If you try to wreck the transmission (by unplugging your modem or by turning off your computer's power), your computer will detect sabotage and overcome it: the next time you run your e-mail program, the computer will try again to transmit the wrecked message (by using a copy of the message that the computer keeps in your computer's **Outbox** folder).

Since e-mail transmissions can't be easily canceled, remember:

Signature

At the bottom of your e-mail message, you can include a few lines that identify who you are. Those lines are called your **signature** (or **sig**).

For example, your sig can include your full name, address, and phone number. You can mention your *office*'s address & phone number, but be cautious about revealing your *home* address & phone number, since e-mail messages are often peeked at by strangers.

If you're employed, you might also wish to give your company's name, your title, and a disclaimer, such as "The opinions I expressed aren't necessarily my employer's." You might also wish to reveal your personality, by including your favorite saying (such as "Keep on truckin'" or "Power to the people" or "May the Lord bless you" or "Turned on by Twinkies". But keep your sig short: any sig containing more than 4 lines of text is considered an impolite waste of your reader's time.

Don't bother putting your e-mail address in your sig, since your e-mail address appears automatically at the top of your message.

Explorer Explorer lets you put the same sig on all your e-mail messages easily. (Netscape's attempt to do the same is too awkward to be useful.)

In Explorer 5, begin this way:

In Explorer 4, begin this way:

In Explorer 3, begin this way instead:

Next to "Text", you see a big white box. Click in that box's top left corner.

Press ENTER (so the top line of your sig will be blank). Type five dashes (so the second line of your sig will be "-----") and press ENTER. Then type whatever words and numbers you want to be in your sig (pressing the ENTER key at the end of each line).

Click "OK". (If you're using Explorer 4, click "OK" again.)

Now the computer will automatically put that sig at the bottom of each message you write.

While you edit a message, edit its sig! Customize its sig to match the rest of the message.

Kinds of e-mail

You'll receive several kinds of e-mail messages.

Some will be from your friends, to whom you revealed your e-mail address. Some will be from your company's customers, suppliers, employees, and business associates. Some will be from companies whose Web sites you visited and to whom you revealed your e-mail address, so the company can send you the latest news weekly or even daily.

Unfortunately, some will be from strangers who managed to find out your e-mail address and who send you ads every day, hawking **pornography** and **get-rich-quick schemes**.

> Most e-mails hawking **pornography** try to make you to visit a sexy Web site, full of nude women who try to get you to reveal your credit-card number and become a paying member. Other pornographic e-mails try to make you phone a sexy girl whose area code just happens to be in the Caribbean or Asia or Hong Kong or some other island that will give you a huge phone bill, whose profits go to a foreign phone company that secretly gives the scheme's manager a cut.
>
> Some e-mails hawking **get-rich-quick schemes** try to get you to send money for useless e-mails you're supposed to resell but won't. Most get-rich-quick e-mails try to get you to send $10 each to 5 people, while you hope many people, in return, will be stupid enough to send $10 each to you; but you'll soon discover that most people are *not* stupider than you, and only *you* are stupid enough to lose $50. Such a scheme is called a **chain letter** or a **pyramid scheme**; it's the worst form of **multi-level marketing (MLM)**. The post office has ruled all such chain-letter pyramid schemes are illegal and constitute mail fraud, since the only way to get rich in such a scheme is to make hundreds of stupid people become poor. Most such schemes claim to be legal but aren't.

That unsolicited and unwanted e-mail is called **junk e-mail**. It's mass-produced and sent to millions of folks all over the world, using a technique called **bulk e-mail**.

Junk e-mail is called **spam**. Here's why:

> In 1937, the Hormel meatpacking company invented a new kind of pink luncheon meat, made of spicy salted ham, packed in gelatin, and sold in a can. Hormel held a contest to name the meat. The contest's winner got $100 by suggesting to call it "Spam", because it was the "**sp**icy h**am** (sold in a can)". Hormel called it the "meat of many uses" and advertised it as a cheap substitute for hamburger.
>
> During World War 2, the U.S. government bought 15 million cans of Spam each week, to send to U.S. and Allied soldiers and also to British and Russian citizens, who were short of beef and used Spam as a substitute. Spam was one of the few meats that the U.S. and British governments didn't require citizens to ration. For many British families, Spam was the only meat they ate for many months.
>
> Because of the U.S. government's mass distribution of Spam worldwide, **Spam became internationally famous as the symbol of cheap unavoidable junk food from America.** (It came before McDonald's.)
>
> Soldiers called it "the ham that didn't pass its physical" and "a meatball without basic training".
>
> After the war, President Eisenhower wrote a letter to Hormel saying, "I ate my share of Spam along with millions of soldiers. I will even confess to a few unkind words about it — uttered during the strain of battle, you understand. But as a former Commander-in-Chief, I believe I can still officially forgive you your only sin: sending us so much of it." Nikita Khrushchev, who headed Russia during the Cold War, said that the U.S.'s donation of Spam to Russia was responsible for saving the lives of the Russian army during World War 2. Margaret Thatcher, who became prime minister of England, called Spam a "wartime delicacy".
>
> Hormel sold a cumulative total of 1 billion cans of Spam by 1959, 2 billion by 1963, 4 billion by 1986, 5 billion by 1999, even though the population of the whole world is just 6 billion.
>
> Now Spam is especially popular in Hawaii, because Hawaiians learned to eat it while helping World World 2's navy.
>
> In 1970, a British comedy troupe called *Monty Python's Flying Circus* did a comedy skit in which a waitress says that the what's available for breakfast is "egg and bacon; egg, sausage, and bacon; egg and Spam; egg, bacon, and Spam; egg, bacon, sausage, and Spam; Spam, bacon, sausage, and Spam; Spam, egg, Spam, Spam, bacon, and Spam; Spam, sausage, Spam, Spam, Spam, bacon, Spam, tomato, and Spam; Spam, Spam, Spam, egg, and Spam; Spam, Spam, Spam, Spam, Spam, Spam, baked beans, Spam, Spam, Spam, and Spam" — and then all discourse is drowned out by marching Vikings singing "Spam, Spam, Spam, Spam…" The BBC and PBS televised that skit many times and introduced new generations to the culture of Spam.
>
> Computerists have invented thousands of haiku poems about Spam. Each poem has 17 syllables, such as:
>
> Pink tender morsel,
> Glistening with salty gel.
> What the hell is it?

A person who sends junk e-mail (spam) is called a **spammer** and is said to be **spamming**.

The U.S. government is in the process of passing more laws to restrict spam (the inedible kind). Since spamming can be illegal and put you in jail, remember:

> If you're a spammer,
> You'll wind up in the slammer.

If you're trying to advertise your business, you'll be tempted to send bulk e-mail (spam). It costs you nearly nothing, since Internet e-mail is free (unlike traditional mail, which costs about 33¢ each, plus the cost of paper, plus the cost of putting labels onto all the envelopes). But since spam is associated with dishonest hucksters, sending spam can do your business's reputation more harm than good. And if every business were to start sending spam, the Internet would get so clogged that it could no longer be free. Excessive e-commerce could kill this country's Internet. Many computerists complain that they receive 50 spams each day, clogging their Inboxes. Subscribers to America On Line (AOL) get the most spam. So if you're an advertiser, remember:

> If you try some spam to pass,
> You'll get lots of calls, and you'll be aghast
> When customers call you a pain in the ass!

Newsgroups

The three most popular uses of the Internet are the World Wide Web, electronic mail, and newsgroups. You've already learned about the World Wide Web and electronic mail. Here's how to use newsgroups.

A **newsgroup** is a group of people who send messages to each other on the Internet, publicly. Some of the messages are announcements, some are comments, some are questions, and some are replies.

You can read the newsgroup's messages and write your own message (comment, question, reply, or announcement). Your message becomes part of the newsgroup's messages, so *you* become part of the newsgroup! If you make your message interesting, other members of the newsgroup will make comments about *you*!

There are over 20,000 newsgroups. Each newsgroup discusses a different topic. Some newsgroups are funny, some are serious, some are weird. In each newsgroup, some of the messages are profound, others are idiotic.

If the newsgroup is **moderated**, it's run by a person (called the **moderator**) who edits the messages and tries to eliminate junk. If the newsgroup is **unmoderated**, the newsgroup is a free-for-all, unedited, uncensored, and always at risk of being dominated by people who make "much ado about nothing" and suffer from "diarrhea of the mouth".

The average newsgroup generates over 4 pages of new material per day, so altogether the newsgroups generate over 80,000 pages per day. To reduce the clutter, the typical Internet Service Provider (ISP) discards newsgroup messages that are more than a week old.

The collection of newsgroups is called **Usenet**. It's part of the Internet.

To use newsgroups, you need a program called a **news reader**. Here are the most popular news readers:

Internet News (which is part of Microsoft's Internet Explorer 3)
Outlook Express News (which is part of Microsoft's Internet Explorer 4&5)
Netscape News (which is part of Netscape's Navigator 3)
Netscape Messenger News (which is part of Netscape's Navigator 4.6)

I'll explain how to use Internet News and Outlook Express News. (Netscape's newsreaders are too awkward to be reasonable.)

Launch your news reader

Here's how to start using newsgroups, if Microsoft's Internet Explorer is on your computer's hard disk.

Method 1: while you're running Explorer, click the Mail button, then click "Read News".

Method 2: while you're *not* running Explorer, do this....

Explorer 5: click the Outlook Express icon, which is to the right of the Start button and shows an envelope with arrows orbiting around it; answer any questions about your ISP and password; then click "Read News".

Explorer 4: click the Outlook Express icon, which is to the right of the Start button and shows an "e" above an envelope; answer any questions about your ISP and password; then click "Read News".

Explorer 3: click Start, then Programs, then Internet News; then answer any questions about your ISP and password; if the computer says "There are new newsgroups. Do you want to view them?", click "No".

Choose a newsgroup

If the computer asks "Would you like to view a list of available newsgroups now?", press ENTER. If the computer does *not* ask that question, click the **Newsgroups button**.

In the middle of the screen, you'll see the **Newsgroups window**, which shows you the beginning of the list of newsgroups. The list is in alphabetical order. Here's how to see the rest of the list:

Method 1: click in the middle of the list; then repeatedly press the down-arrow key or PAGE DOWN key.

Method 2: on the list's right-hand side, you'll see a scroll bar. Drag that bar down.

To see an abridged list, containing just the newsgroups that might interest you, do this:

Above the list, you see a box labeled "Display newsgroups which contain". Click in that box, then type a word that interests you. For example, to see a list of newsgroups about movies, type "movies".

(Explorer 3&5 might ask whether you want to subscribe to the newsgroup that you or your predecessor displayed previously. To reply, click "No".)

When you find a newsgroup that interests you, click it. Then click the **Go To button**.

Choose a message

In the top pane, you'll see that newsgroup's list of the messages.

(If you see no list of messages, it's probably because you paused too long, and your ISP thought you died and disconnected you. To reconnect, click the **Connect button**, then type your password and press ENTER.)

The messages are listed in chronological order, from oldest to newest.

Click whichever message interests you. You'll see the message's details in the bottom pane.

"Re:" before a message If you see a message whose subject begins with "Re:", it's a reply to an earlier message. The earlier message might not be listed anymore, since the typical ISP deletes messages that are more than two weeks old.

"+" before a message While you're looking at a list of messages, you might see a message that has a plus sign in front of it. (The plus sign is in a box.) If you click the plus sign, you'll see a list of replies to that message. In that list, each reply begins with "Re" and is indented under the original message.

Deja

To find out which newsgroups discuss your favorite topic, use the World Wide Web to go to "www.deja.com", then double-click in the top box called "Search Deja.com", then type a topic that interest you (and press ENTER). If the computer says "Security Information", press ENTER again.

The computer will start printing a list of newsgroup messages about that topic. The list shows each message's date, score (as to how relevant the message is to your topic), subject, the newsgroup it came from, and who wrote it.

Decide which message you want to read. Then you can see its full text by clicking its underlined subject; but before you click, scribble the newsgroup's name on a sheet of paper, for your future pleasures!

Names of newsgroups

Most newsgroups fall into one of these categories:

Category	What it includes
sci	science (physics, math, engineering, medicine, psychology)
bionet	biology (the biology network)
comp	computers (hardware, operating systems, programming)
biz	business (business news, marketing, advertising)
k12	K-12 education (from kindergarten through the 12th grade)
rec	recreation (hobbies, sports, arts, cooking, pets)
soc	society (culture, history, genealogy, socializing, personals)
talk	debate (politics, unusual religions)
misc	miscellaneous (investments, jobs, immigration, transportation)
alt	alternative thinking on thousands of topics (usually unmoderated
can	Canada (Canadian events, opinions, and personals)
aus	Australia (Australian events, opinions, and personals)
nz	New Zealand (New Zealand events, opinions, and personals)
uk	United Kingdom (Great Britain & Northern Ireland)
fr	France (French events, opinions, and personals, written in French)
it	Italy (Italian events, opinions, and personals, written in Italian)
es	España (Spain, written in Spanish)
chile	Chile (written in Spanish)
de	Deutschland (Germany, written in German)
at	Austria (written in German)
microsoft	Microsoft's software (technical support, using beta versions)
symantec	Symantec's software (Norton utilities, anti-virus, Java)
linux	Linux (which is a version of the Unix operating system)
news	announcements about newsgroups, analysis of newsgroups

The most common category is "alt", since about 40% of all newsgroups are in the "alt" category. Though beginners think "alt" stands for "alternative", experts know it also stands for "anarchists, lunatics, and terrorists", since the alt newsgroups are usually unmoderated, uncontrolled explosions of emotion.

If you see two newsgroups that have similar names, but one of them begins with "alt", the "alt" newsgroup will tend to be wilder, less organized, and less moderated than its conservative cousin. Because it's less organized, it tends to be less useful.

To do serious research about a topic, start by reading the non-alt newsgroups to get your bearings. Look at the alt newsgroups later for extra laughs, tears, and off-the-wall insights.

These newsgroups are popular:

Humor		
Funny	best new jokes	rec.humor.funny
Funny Reruns	best old jokes	rec.humor.funny.reruns
Best Humor	humor from other newsgroups	alt.humor.best-of-usenet
Quotations	interesting quotations	alt.quotations
Best	the best from other newsgroups	alt.best.of.internet
Chat		
Personals	personal ads	alt.personals
Pen Pals	looking for pen pals	soc.penpals
Sex	general discussion about sex	alt.sex
Revenge	ideas about getting revenge	alt.revenge
Buddha	weird chat based on Buddhism	alt.buddha.short.fat.guy
Debating what's real		
Rumors	postings of rumors	talk.rumors
Urban Folklore	debate which "facts" are true	alt.folklore.urban
Conspiracy	conspiracy theories	alt.conspiracy
What If	"what if" speculation	soc.history.what-if
Mythic Animals	creatures of myth & fantasy	alt.mythology.mythic-animals
Aliens	discuss visitors from space	alt.alien.visitors
Paranormal	psychic phenomena	alt.paranet.psi
Movies		
Movies	discussion of movies	rec.arts.movies
Current Films	discussion of current movies	rec.arts.movies.current-films
Tips		
Free Stuff	how to get free stuff	alt.consumers.free-stuff
Jobs	job postings	misc.jobs.offered
Writing	help for writers	misc.writing
Genealogy	research your roots	soc.genealogy.surnames
New Groups	new newsgroups forming	news.announce.newgroups
Computers		
Comp Answers	general computer help	comp.answers
IBM PC	hardware & software	comp.sys.ibm.pc.misc
New Products	new computer products	comp.newprod
Consultants	computer consultants	alt.computer.consultants
2600	hackers magazine	alt.2600
Homebuilt	general hardware	alt.comp.hardware.homebuilt
Systems	motherboards & systems	comp.sys.ibm.pc.hardware.systems
Storage	hard disks & tape drives	comp.sys.ibm.pc.hardware.storage
Communication	modem software	comp.sys.ibm.pc.hardware.comm
PCMCIA	PCMCIA cards	alt.periphs.pcmcia
PC Hardware	other IBM-compatible	comp.sys.ibm.pc.hardware.misc
Freeware	free software	alt.comp.freeware
Virus	virus info	comp.virus
Neural Nets	neural networks	comp.ai.neural-nets
Video	video cards & drivers	comp.sys.ibm.pc.hardware.video
Corel Graphics	Corel graphics programs	alt.corel.graphics
Clip Art	free clip art	alt.binaries.clip-art
Multimedia	multimedia hardw&softw	comp.multimedia
Quake	tips for winning at Quake	rec.games.computer.quake.playing
Win 95 Crash	Windows 95 difficulties	alt.os.windows95.crash.crash.crash

Subscribe

If you enjoy a newsgroup, **subscribe** to it. The subscription is free. Moreover, the subscription is private: just your own computer will know you subscribed; no other computer will!

Here's the normal way to subscribe:

> Make the computer show you a list of newsgroups (such as by clicking the Newsgroups button).
>
> While you're looking at a list of newsgroups, **double-click each newsgroup that you want to subscribe to,** so a picture of a folded newspaper appears before the newsgroup's name. (If you change your mind and want to unsubscribe, double-click the newsgroup's name again, which makes the newspaper icon disappear.) Then click OK.

That way works in Explorer 3&4&5. Explorer 3&5 also provide this alternative way to subscribe:

> View the messages in the newsgroup. When you switch to a different newsgroup afterwards, the computer will ask whether you want to subscribe to the newsgroup you'd been viewing. Click "Yes".

To see a list of all newsgroups you subscribed to, click the Newsgroups button, then click **Subscribed** (which is near the bottom of the Newsgroups window). That list of *subscribed* newsgroups is much shorter than the list of *all* newsgroups, so it lets you get to your favorite newsgroups faster. To use one of those subscribed newsgroups, click the newsgroup's name (so its background turns blue) and then click the **Go To button**.

(Explorer 3 might ask whether you'd like to subscribe to the newsgroup you viewed previously. If you don't want to subscribe to that newsgroup, click "No".)

Contribute

While you're reading a message, you can send a reply.

> If you want the reply to be sent privately to the message's author, so just that author sees your reply, click the **Reply to Author button**. (Explorer 5 calls it just the **Reply button**.) That will send private mail to the author.
>
> If instead you want your reply to be sent publicly, so everybody on the Internet can see your reply, click the **Reply to Group button** instead. (Explorer 5 calls it just the **Reply Group button**.) That will **post** your reply, so your reply becomes part of the newsgroup.
>
> If instead you want to start a whole new topic that's *not* a reply, so everybody on the Internet can see your new topic and react to it, click the **New Post button**. (Explorer 4 calls it the **Compose Message button**. Explorer 3 calls it the **New Message button**.) That will **post** your new topic, so your topic becomes part of the newsgroup.

(Explorer 3 might say "Choose Profile". To reply, press ENTER.)

Then your screen shows a form to fill in — the same kind of form used for writing e-mail. Fill in the form, then click the **Send button**. (Explorer calls it the **Post Message button** if you're posting.)

If you post a reply or a new topic, it will probably become part of the newsgroup. But some newsgroups are **moderated** by a special person (the **moderator**), who decides which messages to erase.

Netiquette When you post a message, use proper Net etiquette, which is called **Netiquette**. The main rule of Netiquette is: don't waste people's time!

Many people faithfully read their favorite newsgroups every day. If you post messages that are useless or annoying, those readers will get angry, and their tempers can flare hot enough to make them **flame you** (post angry messages about you or send you angry e-mail messages, called **flame mail**). If you're a new user (**newbie**) who doesn't understand Netiquette yet, your posted messages will probably receive flame mail.

Questionable posts Before posting a message, ask yourself these questions....

Will most people reading this newsgroup find your message worthwhile? Make sure your message doesn't waste people's time. For example, don't post a message like this one —

```
Newsgroups: rec.guitar
Subject:    guitar plaiyer

My band is so cool. Tom wails. We reelly rock!
```

Instead, make the message appear newsworthy, like this —

```
Newsgroups: rec.guitar
Subject:    Free concert in Cambridge MA this Sunday

Hello, everyone! If you're in the Boston area, come to
Harvard Square this Sunday to hear "Some Assembly Required".
The concert is free, but get there early because it'll get
crowded fast! The guitar player, Tom, is as close to
brilliant as they come.
```

Does your subject line quickly describe what your message is about? The subject line helps people quickly find messages that interest them. In the second example above, people who don't live near Cambridge, MA, won't waste their time reading about a free concert there.

Are you posting your message to the appropriate newsgroup? The second example above is appropriate for groups like rec.guitar and ne.announce (New England announcements). If you post the same message to rec.music.artists.beach-boys, you'll get flamed.

Have you checked your spelling and grammar for embarrassing errors? Once you post a message, it's too late to correct your mistakes. Your message, errors and all, will be available to millions.

Will many people be offended by your message? There are millions of people on the Internet. If we're all going to get along, we must be careful about what we say.

Unscramble

The best jokes are in **rec.humor.funny** and **rec.humor.funny.reruns**. The group's moderator puts into those newsgroups just the top 10% of the jokes people submit to him.

He judges each joke by its structure (not its content), so he's willing to post jokes that are offensive, if their structure is clever enough.

For the most offensive jokes (on topics such as dead babies), he hides the joke's words (so the squeamish won't complain), by writing the joke in a code called **rotate 13 (ROT 13)**, which consists of doing this:

```
switch each A  with the letter N
(because N comes 13 letters after A in the alphabet)

switch each B  with the letter O

switch each C  with the letter P

etc.
```

For example, the word "con" becomes "pba".

Here's how to make the computer unscramble the joke for you:

```
Get the joke onto the screen.
Click Message. (In Explorer 3&4, click Edit instead.)
Click Unscramble.
```

Create Web pages

When using the Internet's World Wide Web, don't be just a looker; be a creator! Create your *own* Web pages and let everybody else in the world see them!

What's Angelfire?

The easiest way to create your own Web pages is to use a Web site called **Angelfire**. It's free!

Angelfire is at www.angelfire.com. It used to be an independent company, but now it's owned by **Lycos**.

Angelfire's main competitors are **Tripod** (which is at www.tripod.com and also owned by Lycos), **Geo Cities** (which is at www.geocities.com and owned by Yahoo) and **Talk City** (which is at www.talkcity.com, partly owned by NBC & Hearst & Cox & Intel & New York Life Insurance & Softbank & John Sculley, and affiliated with Microsoft & Compaq & AT&T & Bell South & Borders). I prefer Angelfire because it's the fastest, easiest, and least restrictive. If you're adventuresome, go ahead: experiment with all four of those sites.

Angelfire's restrictions

Angelfire lets you create any Web pages you wish, as long as you keep your pages "clean", so they don't contain:

```
pornography, sex, nudity, "adult material", hate propaganda, or foul language
get-rich-quick pyramid schemes, mail fraud, or anything else illegal
links to any of those controversial topics
false e-mail addresses, or info you publicized by e-mailing lots of spam
text or graphics you copied (unless you got the creator's permission)
paid ads from others (but you can advertise your own business and include free ads for others)
```

On Angelfire's hard drive, you're allocated a total of 5 megabytes to store your pages. If a page is totally unused for 60 days (never edited by you and never looked at by others), the Angelfire staff reserves the right to delete it.

Launch Angelfire

Using your Web browser (such as Microsoft Internet Explorer or Netscape Navigator), go to "www.angelfire.com". Here's what to do next....

Register

If you haven't registered with Angelfire yet, do this:

```
Click "Register". Click the first box's down-arrow key.
  You'll see an alphabetical list of states (starting with "ak" for Alaska), then an alphabetical list of
Canadian provinces (starting with "ab" for Alberta), then "biz", perhaps followed by a digit. (To see the
whole list, use the scroll arrows.) Click whichever entry you wish. Write your choice on a sheet of paper.
Then press the TAB key.
  Invent a name for your site. The name must be short: no more than 20 characters. The characters can be
capital letters, small letters, or digits. For best results in explaining your site's name to friends later, avoid
capital letters. Make the site be your own name (such as "joan") or your company's name (if the head of
your company gives you permission) or the topic that the site will be about (such as "baseball") or any
other name you wish. Type the name, also write it on a sheet of paper. Then press the TAB key.
  Invent a password. It must be 6, 7, or 8 characters long. The characters can be capital letters, small
letters, or digits. Type the password, also write it on a sheet of paper. Then press the TAB key.
  Type the password again, then press the TAB key again.
  Type your first name, press TAB, type your last name, press TAB, type your street address, press TAB
twice, type your city, press TAB, type your 2-letter state abbreviation, press TAB twice, type your ZIP
code, press TAB, click your sex ("male" or "female"), press TAB, click your age range, press TAB, type
your e-mail address (such as "poo@gis.net"), and press ENTER.
  (If the computer says "URL already in use", click your Web browser's Back button, double-click the
site name you invented, invent a different site name instead, type it, write it on a sheet of paper, press
TAB, type your password again, press TAB, type your password yet again, and press ENTER.)
```

Create a simple Web page

The computer will say "WEB SHELL". Click the "create/edit" button.

To create a Web page, just fill in two forms, saying what you want!

First form You start by seeing the first form. It's organized into three **steps**. Here's the most interesting way for a beginner to fill them in:

> Step 1: click the "Basic" button.
> Step 2: click the "Standard" button.
> Step 3: scroll down so you see the "Styleset #1" button, then click it. (That makes your page have a white background, which is the easiest to read. If you insist on a background that's prettier but harder to read, click "Styleset #2" for blue, "Styleset #3" for green, "Styleset #4" for gold, "Styleset #5" for dark brown, or "Styleset #6" for black.)

Click the "submit" button.

Second form You'll see the second form. It's organized into 12 steps....

Don't bother fiddling with **steps 1-4**. Skip past them.

In **step 5**'s Title box, type the **title that you want to appear at the top of your page** (such as "Joan's Home Page").

Make **step 6**'s first box be blank (by triple-clicking in it and then pressing the DELETE key).

In **step 7**'s Title box, type the title of whatever **simple list** you want to put on your home page. (For example, type "Here's a list of my favorite foods:".) The computer assumes you want the list to include 3 items. If you want the list to include more items, change the "3" to a bigger number (by clicking the 3, then clicking the "refresh" button, then scrolling down to Step 7 again). Then in the numbered boxes below, type each item that you want on the list. (For example, type "ice cream" in box 1, "strawberries" in box 2, and "turkey" in box 3.)

In **step 8**'s Title box, type the title of whatever **list of Web sites** you want to put on your home page. (For example, type "Here are Web sites you might enjoy:".) The computer assumes you want the list to include 4 items. If you want the list to include more items, change the "4" to a bigger number (by clicking the 4, then clicking the "refresh" button, then scrolling down to Step 8 again). Then in each pair of boxes below, type a Web address (such as "http://www.realtor.com") in the left box and type an English description (such as "house hunting") in the right-hand box. Make sure you type the "http://".

In **step 9**'s box, type whatever **paragraphs** you want to put on your home page.

> At the end of each paragraph, do this: type \<p> once (to mark the end of the paragraph) and then press the ENTER key twice. To type the \<p>, make sure you type the symbol "<" (by holding down the SHIFT key while typing a comma), then type the letter "p", then type the symbol ">" (by holding down the SHIFT key while typing a period).

While typing paragraphs, you can use these tricks....

> To italicize a phrase,   type \<i> before the phrase.   Type \</i> after the phrase.
> To make a phrase be bold, type \<b> before the phrase.   Type \</b> after the phrase.
> To make a phrase blink,   type \<blink> before the phrase.   Type \</blink> after the phrase.
>
> To make a phrase have huge characters, type \<font size="5"> before the phrase. Type \</font> after the phrase. You can choose five font sizes: 1 (tiny), 2 (small), 3 (medium), 4 (big), 5 (huge), 6 (gigantic), 7 (monster).
>
> At the end of each paragraph,   type \<p>, then press ENTER twice.
> At the end of each line in a list,   type \
, which stands for "break", then press ENTER once.
> To draw a line across the page,   type \<hr>, which stands for "horizontal rule", then press ENTER once.
>
> To type a heading (with gigantic bold characters), type \<h1> then the heading's words then \</h1> then ENTER. You can choose 6 heading sizes: h1 (gigantic), h2 (huge), h3 (big), h4 (medium), h5 (small), h6 (tiny).
>
> To type "house hunting" and make it be underlined and make it link to www.realtor.com, type this:
> \<a href="http://www.realtor.com">house hunting\</a>
>
> To make a phrase be red, type \<font color="red"> before the phrase. Type \</font> after the phrase. Angelfire understands names for 134 colors, such as "yellow", "orange", "red", "purple", "blue", "green", "pink", "brown", "lime", "aqua", "fuchsia", "white", "gray", and "black". (To see the complete list, click step 1's "View Colors in convenient popup window".) Those color names work just while using Angelfire; for other Web-page creation programs, you must type code numbers instead: black is "#000000", red is "#ff0000", lime is "#00ff00", blue is "#0000ff", yellow is "#ffff00", aqua is "#00ffff", fuchsia is "#ff00ff", white is "#ffffff", gray is "#808080", purple is "#800080", green is "#008000", orange is "#ffa500", pink is "#ffc0cd", brown is "#a52a2a".

Those tricks are called the **HyperText Markup Language (HTML)**. Those tricks won't take effect until you finish inventing your page.

Don't bother fiddling with **step 10**. Skip past it.

Click **step 11**'s "Yes" button. Click **step 12**'s "Yes" button.

Congratulations! You finished filling the form!

Preview Click the "preview" button. You see how your Web page will look to the public. (At the top of the page, an ad appears temporarily, to seduce you into spending money, but no ad will appear on the Web page seen by the public.) Near the page's bottom, you see a counter, which temporarily says "999999".

> Later, when you finish designing the page, the counter will reset itself to 000000.
>
> Each time a person views your page, the counter will increase, so it will count how many times your page gets viewed by the public.

Below the counter, you see your e-mail address, which the public can click to send you e-mail messages.

Do you like how your Web page looks?

Click your browser's Back button. You see the second form again. To improve your Web page, make any changes you wish on that form.

Save When you're satisfied, click the "save" button.

Congratulations! You've created a Web page! Tell your friends! For example, if you chose "nh" for your state and chose "joan" for your site's name, your site's full name is "www.angelfire.com/nh/joan".

You can visit the Web site I created for The Secret Guide to Computers using that method. My site's full name is "www.angelfire.com/nh/secret".

Edit your Web page

Afterwards, here's how you can edit the page you created.

Using your Web browser, go to "www.angelfire.com". Click "Login". Click in the Directory Name box.

Type a slash, then the state you chose, then another slash, then the site name you invented, like this:

> /nh/joan

Click in the Password box. Type the Angelfire password you invented. Click "submit". If the computer asks, "Do you want Windows to remember this password?" press ENTER.

The computer will say "WEB SHELL". Click the "create/edit" button, then edit the 12 steps however you wish.

Extra Web pages

The first Web page you created has "index.html" at the end of the name. For example, if your site is named "www.angelfire.com/nh/joan", the first Web page you created is named "www.angelfire.com/nh/joan/index.html", though you don't have to bother typing the "/index.html" to access it.

You can create extra Web pages. Each page's name must end in ".html".

For example, here's how to create a page called "fun.html":

> Do the procedure in the "edit your Web page" section; but before you click the "create/edit" button, type "fun.html" in the NEW box.

Once you've done that, congratulations: you've created a new Web page called "fun.html". Anybody on the Internet can access it. For example, if your site is named "www.angelfire.com/nh/joan", people can access your fun.html page by asking for "www.angelfire.com/nh/joan/fun.html".

Better yet, make your main page link to fun.html, by mentioning "fun.html" in your main page, in form 2's step 8 or 9. In those steps, you can mention just "fun.html" without having to type "http://www.angelfire.com/nh/joan/fun.html".

FrontPage

You've learned how to create a simple Web page by using Angelfire's 2-form process. To create fancier Web pages, use **FrontPage** instead, which is a program available from Microsoft.

Several versions of Front Page have been invented. The tiniest version, called **FrontPage Express**, comes free as part of Windows 98 (or Internet Explorer 4 or 5). The fanciest version, called **FrontPage 2000**, comes free as part of Microsoft Office 2000's premium or developer edition.

Here's how to use FrontPage Express and FrontPage 2000.

Launch Get out of any other programs you're in (by clicking their X buttons). You can also disconnect from the Internet, since FrontPage does *not* need an Internet connection.

Click "Start" then "Programs" then do this:

> For FrontPage Express, click "Internet Explorer" then "FrontPage Express".
>
> For FrontPage 2000, click "Microsoft FrontPage"; then if the computer asks "Would you like to make it your default editor?" press ENTER.

You'll see the FrontPage window. If it doesn't consume the whole screen yet, maximize the window by clicking the resize button, which is next to the X button.

Type FrontPage resembles a word-processing program, such as Microsoft Word or WordPad. Go type whatever you want to appear on your Web page, as if you were typing an ordinary word-processing document. You can use typical word-processing techniques. You do *not* have to type HTML codes such as <p>, <b>, and <i>; FrontPage will generate the HTML codes for you secretly and automatically.

Here are some suggestions....

Start by typing a title, such as:

> Joan's Home Page

At the end of that line, change the style to Heading 1 (by clicking the down-arrow that's next to "Normal" and then clicking "Heading 1"). That makes the title become a big, bold headline. It becomes big instantly, before your very eyes. Wow! Afterwards, press ENTER.

Then start typing the next line of your Web page. The computer will automatically make it be a normal size, not big, not bold. Better yet, instead of typing just a line, type a whole paragraph. Do *not* indent the paragraph's beginning. Write whatever you wish. For example, you can write a description of yourself, info about your favorite hobby, or your favorite jokes. If you're feeling creative, start writing a story or novel.

At the end of that first paragraph, press ENTER just once. Then start writing your next paragraph. The computer will automatically put a blank line between the paragraphs.

To italicize a phrase, click the *I* button, then type the phrase, then click the *I* button again. To make a phrase be bold, click the **B** button, then type the phrase, then click the **B** button again.

Here's how to make "house hunting" be underlined and link to www.realtor.com:

> Type "house hunting". Highlight it (by dragging the mouse pointer across it).
> Click the Hyperlink button, which has a globe and chain on it. FrontPage Express calls it the "Create or Edit Hyperlink" button.
> (If you're using FrontPage Express, then press your keyboard's right-arrow key.)
> Make the URL box contain "http://www.realtor.com" (not just "www.realtor.com"). Then press ENTER then the left-arrow key.

The computer will make "house hunting" be underlined, blue, and linked so if a person later clicks that spot on your finished Web page, the person will automatically be transported to the "http://www.realtor.com" site.

Save When you finish typing your Web page (which can be many screenfuls long), click the Save button. Here's what happens next....

> **FrontPage Express:** make the Page Title box contain the page's full title, such as "Joan's Home Page" (by typing any part of the title that's missing), then click the "As File" button. Make sure the "Save in" box says "My Documents". (If it doesn't, click the box's down-arrow and then click "My Documents".)
>
> **FrontPage 2000:** if the Page Title line doesn't contain the page's full title, such as "Joan's Home Page", click the Change button, then type the page's full title, then press ENTER. Make sure the "Save in" box says "My Webs".

Pick a name for that file. Probably you want that file to become your *main* Web page; if so, that file should be named "index"; otherwise, invent a one-word name for the file (such as "joans"), using just small letters, no capitals, no spaces. Type the name (such as "index" or "joans"). At the end of the name, press ENTER.

The computer will put the file into your hard disk's My Documents folder (for FrontPage Express) or My Webs folder (for FrontPage 2000). The computer will put ".htm" at the end of the file's name.

Exit Finally, exit from FrontPage (by clicking the X button at the screen's top right corner).

Upload To let the public use your Web page, you must **upload** your page (copy it from your computer's hard disk to an Internet-connected hard disk).

For example, here's how to copy your Web page to Angelfire's hard disk:

> Using your Web browser, go to "www.angelfire.com".
> Log in. To do that, make sure you've registered, then click "Login", then click in the Directory Name box, type a slash, type the state you chose (such as "nh"), type another slash, type the site name you invented (such as "joan"), press TAB, type your password, click "submit", and answer any question about Windows remembering your password.
> Click "Browse". Double-click "My Documents". (For FrontPage 2000, then double-click "My Webs".) Double-click the file you want to upload (such as "index" or "joans"). Click the "upload" button.

That file will now be on Angelfire's disk, but with an ending of ".html" instead of ".htm". For example, if the file was joans.htm, it's now available on the Internet as "www.angelfire.com/nh/joan/joans.html". If the file was index.htm, it's now available on the Internet as "www.angelfire.com/nh/joan/index.html" or more simply as "www.angelfire.com/nh/joan" (since "index.html" is your main page) or even more simply as "angelfire.com/nh/joan" (since the "www" is optional).

The typical ISP lets you also copy your Web page to your ISP's hard disk by using **File Transfer Protocol (FTP)**. For example, if your ISP is Galaxy Internet Services (GIS), here's how to copy your Web page to GIS's hard disk:

> Click "Start" then "Programs" then "MS-DOS Prompt". The computer will say:
> `C:\WINDOWS>`
> That should be in a black window that does *not* consume the whole screen. (If the window consumes the whole screen, so you see no colors, make the window smaller by tapping the ENTER key while holding down the Alt key.)

Type "ftp" and then the name of your ISP's FTP site. For example, GIS's FPT site is called "ftp.gis.net", so you'd type "ftp ftp.gis.net", to make your screen looks like this:

```
C:\WINDOWS>ftp ftp.gis.net
```

At the end of that line, press ENTER.

If you're not connected to the Internet at the moment, the computer might ask you to type your password. Do so and press ENTER.

The ISP's computer will say "FTP server" and then "User". Type the user name that the ISP assigned you (such as "poo") and press ENTER.

The ISP's computer will say "Password". Type the password that the ISP assigned you and press ENTER.

The ISP's computer will say "logged in" and then say:

```
ftp>
```

Now you're using the ISP's operating system, which is Unix. You can type Unix commands. At the end of each Unix command, press the ENTER key. (For example, just for fun, type the Unix command "dir" and press ENTER: you'll see a list of files about you on the ISP's hard disk; each file's name is in the rightmost column. If you'd like to see a list of other Unix commands, type "help" or a question mark and press ENTER. To see a command's purpose, type "help" then a space then the command's name, then press ENTER.)

If you haven't done so already, make a directory (folder) called "public_html" on the ISP's hard disk by typing "mkdir public_html" (and press ENTER).

Next, tell the computer to send (copy) the My Documents folder's index.htm file to the ISP's public_html folder where the file's name should be changed from ".htm" to ".html". To accomplish all that, type so your screen looks like this:

```
ftp> send /"My Documents"/index.htm public_html/index.html
```

(For FrontPage 2000, instead of saying "My Documents" say "My Documents"/"My Webs".)

The computer typed the "ftp> ", but you must type the rest. Type it very carefully! Type forward slashes (/) not backslashes (\), since Unix understands just forward slashes. Type quotation marks around "My Documents". Put a slash before "My Documents" but not before "public". Type a space after "send" and a space before "public"; those are the only spaces you type. After "public", type an underline (by holding down the SHIFT key while you tap the key that's right of the zero key).

The computer will copy the file and say "Transfer complete".

When you finish using FTP, type "quit" or "bye" and press ENTER. The computer will quit using FTP and quit using Unix and say "C:\WINDOWS>". Then close the black window by clicking its X box.

That file will now be on the ISP's disk, but with an ending of ".html" instead of ".htm". For example, if the file was index.htm, it's now available on the Internet as "www.gis.net/~poo/index.html" or simply as "www.gis.net/~poo" or even more simply as "gis.net/~poo". (The symbol "~" is at your keyboard's top left corner, above the TAB key, and requires you to hold down the SHIFT key.)

Create your own .com

I invented my own .com and called it "secretfun.com", so you can access my Web page by typing just "secretfun.com".

You can invent *your* own .com! Here's the best cheap method for doing it....

Expenses This method involves five expenses:

1. Keep yourself signed up for general Internet access, with any general Internet Service Provider (ISP), as you're doing now. (You're probably paying about $20 per month for that. If you're using a cheap service, like Galaxy Internet Services, you're paying about $10 per month. If you belong to a university or company that's on the Internet, you might be getting that free! If you buy a new computer, it might come with a free month or free year of Internet access.)

2. Create a Web page and put it on the Internet. This costs you no money (if you use a free-Web-page provider such as Angelfire), but it costs you *time* to decide what to put on your Web page!

3. Pay a $35-per-year **registration fee** to **InterNic**, which is the Internet organization in charge of assigning .com names. You must pay the first two years at once, so your initial cost is $70. InterNic will send you the bill for $70 a few weeks after you start using your computer.

4. Pay a $25 **setup fee** to **NameSecure**, by using your credit card. You pay that just once, not every year. That pays NameSecure to send your request to InterNic.

5. Pay a $24.95-per-year **Website forwarding fee** to **NameSecure**. That pays NameSecure to take all Internet traffic attempting to access your .com site and reroute it to the Web page you created using Angelfire.

That list of expenses looks long, but it's not so bad!

Expense #1 you're already paying anyway. Expense #2 costs you time but no money; and the time you spend is educational fun! Expenses #3 and #4 and #5 total $59.95 per year (which is just $5 per month), plus a $25 one-time registration fee. So for just $5 per month more than you're already paying (plus a startup fee and labor), you can have your own .com!

Bonus benefit If you use this method, NameSecure will do you a favor: it will automatically let you use your .com for your e-mail address also! That's called **free e-mail forwarding**.

How to do it all First, create a Web page (by using a free tool such as Angelfire or FrontPage) and put it on the Internet. Then go to www.namesecure.lycos.com.

Do this procedure:

Click in the box that comes after "www.". Type the name you want to invent (such as "secretfun") and press ENTER.

The computer will check whether the name you requested is available. (For example, if you chose "secretfun", the computer will check whether "secretfun.com", "secretfun.net", and "secretfun.org" are available.) If the computer says the name you want is "not available", click your browser's Back button and pick a different name. If the computer says the name you want "is available", click the "Register it now" next to it.

Click "Secure On-Line Order with Credit Card".

You see a form.

Click in the box that says "First Name". Type your first name, press TAB, type your last name, press TAB, type the e-mail address that your ISP assigned you (such as "poo@gis.net"), press TAB, type your phone number (such as "603-666-6644"), press TAB, type your organization's name (or your *own* name if you're unorganized), press TAB, fill in the rest of the form (which asks for your address), then press ENTER.

In the Website Forwarding Address box, you see "http://". Click just after that, then type the old address of the main Web page you created (so the box becomes something such as "http://www.angelfire.com/nh/joan" or "http://www.angelfire.com/nh/secret" or "http://www.gis.net/~poo"). Do *not* type "index.html" at the end. When you've finished typing, press ENTER.

Fill in a form asking about your credit card, then press ENTER, then follow the remaining instructions on the screen.

Congratulations! You've done it!

Consequences Within 2 days, computers will double-check your credit-card info and the name you invented (such as "secretfun.com"). Then the Internet's main computers will start telling all the other Internet computers, in all countries, about the name you invented, so anybody in any country can access your Web page by typing the .com name you invented. You can use your .com name for e-mail.

For example, in my own case, I set things up so people typing "secretfun.com" (or "www.secretfun.com" or "http://www.secretfun.com") are automatically rerouted to "http://www.angelfire.com/nh/secret", where the Internet computers will automatically find & display my main Web page, "http://www.angelfire.com/nh/secret/index.html". If anybody sends e-mail to secretfun.com (by addressing the e-mail to "russ@secretfun.com" or "donna@secretfun.com" or "idiot@secretfun.com" or "webmaster@secretfun.com" or "president@secretfun.com" or anybody else "@secretfun.com"), the e-mail will automatically be rerouted to the e-mail address that my ISP assigned me, which is "poo@gis.net". When I look at the message, I see whom it was addressed to, so I can tell that person to look at it.

Try it!

Alternatives Instead of using NameSecure, you can use a competitor called **Domains.com** (at www.domains.com). Its Website forwarding fee is just $15-per-year instead of $25-per-year, but e-mail forwarding there costs $2 per month instead of being free. Domains.com plans to offer a better deal soon: it will offer the same prices and services as NameSecure (including free e-mail forwarding), except *no* setup fee! Keep checking Domains.com for that new deal!

FAX

Send a fax

If you're using Windows 95 you can send a fax easily by using a program called **Microsoft Fax**, which is included free as part of Windows 95. (Microsoft Fax is also included free as part of Windows 98 but not as useful there, but since it hides on Windows 98's CD-ROM disk and conflicts with Windows 98's Outlook Express.)

Step 1: type what you want to fax

Start using Windows 95 (not 98) and your favorite word-processing program (such as WordPad or Microsoft Word). Type the document that you want to fax.

Step 2: say you want to fax it

While the document's still on the screen, do this: from the File menu, choose Print.

You see a box called Name. Make that box say Microsoft Fax (by clicking the down-triangle that's next to the box, then clicking Microsoft Fax). Press ENTER.

If you haven't faxed before, here's what happens:

> The computer says "Inbox Setup Wizard". Press ENTER twice. The computer says "Enter your name and fax number". Your name is already filled in, so just type your return fax number. That's the phone number of your modem or whatever fax machine you own. If you don't want to receive any faxes, type your regular (voice) number. Press ENTER twice.

The computer says "Compose New Fax". If the computer says "I'm dialing from", press ENTER.

Step 3: say where to send the fax

The computer says "To". Type the name of the person you're sending the fax to, press the TAB key three times, type the area code of the person you're sending the fax to, press the TAB key, and type the rest of the phone number of the person you're sending the fax to.

If the person you're dialing is in your area code but the call is not local, click the "Dial area code" box, which makes the computer dial 1 before the number.

Click the "Add to List" button. (If you wish to send copies of the fax to more people, fill in the name and fax number of the second person, click the "Add to List" button again, and do the same for each additional person.)

Press ENTER twice.

Step 4: finish the fax process

The computer says "Subject". Type a phrase that summarizes what your fax is about (such as "want to order your toilets") and press ENTER. Press ENTER again.

The computer sends the fax!

Step 5: reset the computer

Now that the fax has been sent, reset your computer to do normal printing instead of faxing. Here's how:

> From File menu, choose Print. You see the Print window. Make its Name box say the name of your printer instead of Microsoft Fax (by clicking the down-triangle that's next to the box, then clicking your printer's name). Close the Print window (by clicking its X box).

Receive a fax

You can make your computer receive faxes, but don't. The fax-receiving software is hard to set up. To receive a fax, you must let that software run continually, scanning for incoming faxes. That software consumes lots of RAM and lots of the computer's attention, so that all your other software runs slower or refuses to run at all! Moreover, you must leave your computer on continuously, 24 hours, unless you know what time of day your faxes will arrive.

If you're planning to receive lots of faxes, buy a fax machine instead! You can buy a fax machine (such as the Brother 190) for under $100 from office-supply stores (such as Staples, Offce Max, and Office Depot).

Another advantage of a fax machine is that it lets you instantly send articles and pictures that you've found in newspapers, magazines, and books — without forcing you to type or scan that info into your computer.

LOCAL-AREA NETWORKS

Types of LANs

If you run wires between computers that are in the same office building, you're creating a **local-area network (LAN)**. Each computer in the LAN is called a **node**.

For the IBM PC and clones, you can create four kinds of LANs. Here they are, beginning with the fanciest and most expensive.

Server LANs

A **server LAN** consists of a main computer (called the **server**) wired to several lesser computers (called **workstations**).

A special person (called the **network supervisor**) tells the server how to act. Other office workers (called **users**) sit at the workstations.

The server's hard disk contains a database that all the workstations can access. The server's high-quality high-speed printer can print whatever the workstations tell it to.

> If your network is too big to be handled by a single server, you can have *several* servers helping each other, acting together as if they were one, big server. A server whose main chore is to handle one of the network's big hard disks is called a **file server**. A server whose main chore is to handle a printer is called a **print server**. A network can include several file servers and several print servers. But the *typical* network has just one server that tries to do it all!

Each workstation uses MS-DOS (or Windows 3.1 or 3.11 or 95 or 98), but the server uses a different operating system instead that runs faster. The server's operating system is called the **network operating system (NOS)**.

During the 1980's and early 1990's, the most popular NOS was **Netware**, which is published by **Novell**. During the late 1990's, some companies switched to a new NOS, called **Windows New Technology (Windows NT)**, published by Microsoft.

If a NOS understands the same commands as the Internet (so you can access the info on the server by giving Internet commands), the NOS is called an **intranet**, which means "a miniature Internet for internal company use, with access restricted to company employees, and containing info about just the one company."

Netware Novell has invented many versions of Netware. The most popular are **Netware 3.2** (a classic that uses DOS-like commands), **Intranetware 4.11** (a modern intranet that uses Internet commands and Windows-like commands), and **Netware 5** (which resembles Intranetware 4.11 but is newer and better). Netware 5 costs $900 to handle a server plus 5 users. Add $750 for handling 5 extra users, $1100 for 10 extra users, $2090 for 25 extra users, $3120 for 50 extra users, $5430 for 100 extra users. You can get those prices from discount dealers such as **Data Comm Warehouse** (a division of Micro Warehouse at 800-328-2261) and **Computer Discount Warehouse** (800-726-4CDW).

Netware can be complex. For example, the infamous version 2.15C came on about 40 floppy disks, accompanied by 20 manuals! Newer versions let you do more tricks than earlier versions and are slightly easier to install; for example, you can get version 4.11 on CD-ROMs instead of floppies. But, the new versions are still hard enough so the typical office buying Netware pays the computer store to send a technician, who comes to the office to set up the network. Traditionally, the technician typically spends an entire afternoon to get the installation started, then leaves the computer running overnight (while Netware spends several hours formatting the server's hard disk) and comes back the next morning to finish setting up the network.

Computers The typical Novell network has slow workstations attached to a faster server.

In the early	1980's, the typical workstation contained an	8088 CPU. The server contained a 286.
In the late	1980's, the typical workstation contained a	286 CPU. The server contained a 386.
In the early	1990's, the typical workstation contained a	386 CPU. The server contained a 486.
In the late	1990's, the typical workstation contained a	486 CPU. The server contained a Pentium.
In the early	2000's, the typical workstation contains a	Pentium CPU, and so does the server.

The server also contains a big RAM and a big hard drive.

Cables To form a Novell network, connect all the computers in the network by using cables. Three kinds of cables have been popular.

The oldest kind is a thick, yellow, coaxial cable called **thickwire Ethernet** (or **thicknet**).

> It's also called **10base5**, because it can transmit **10** million bits per second and transmit those signals up to **500** meters (and up to 100 computers) without needing to have those signals boosted by a **repeater**. Since the cable's diameter is ½-inch, it's too thick and stiff to bend around corners. It's rarely used anymore.

Far more popular is a newer, cheaper, non-yellow coaxial cable that's thinner: its diameter is $\frac{1}{5}$ of an inch. It's called **thinwire Ethernet** (or **thinnet** or **cheapernet**).

> It's also called **10base2**, since it transmits **10** million bits per second and transmit those signals "about **200** meters" (actually 185) to 30 computers without needing a repeater. It bends around corners easily. The "cable" actually consists of several 25-foot sections, joined together by joints called **T connectors**.
>
> For example, here's how to set up a thinnet network that includes 11 computers (10 workstations plus a server).
>
> Buy 10 thinnet cable sections ($10 each). Join them together by using the joints (called **T connectors**), so those 10 cable sections act as one long cable chain. Each joint is in the shape of a T: the T's left and right prong each attach to a cable section; the T's bottom prong attaches to a computer.
>
> By using 9 T connectors (to connect the sections together) plus 2 extra T connectors (attached to each end of the long cable chain), you can attach all 11 computers to the chain.
>
> At each end of the chain is a T-connector that has an unused prong. Plug up that prong's hole by attaching a $3 plug, called a **terminator**, which terminates the long chain.
>
> The chain of cables is called a **cable segment**; it includes the 10 cable sections, the 11 T-connectors, and the 2 terminators.

Instead of using coaxial cables, the newest and most popular choice is to use just ordinary phone wire — the same kind that the phone company uses inside the walls of your home, and which has an **RJ-45 connector** on each end. Such a cable is called **unshielded twisted-pair (UTP)**.

> It's also called **10baseT**, since it transmits **10** million bits per second through a **t**wisted pair. Here's how to set up a 10baseT network....
>
> Arrange the workstations in a circle. At the circle's center, put a box called a **hub**. Like a bicycle wheel's hub, the network's hub has "spokes" coming out of it: each spoke is a 10baseT cable that goes straight from the hub to one of the workstations. In addition to those spokes, one extra 10baseT cable comes out of the hub: that extra cable goes to the server, which is next to the hub.
>
> Each 10baseT cable you use can be up to 100 meters long. (When you buy the cable, it comes on a spool that holds 1000 feet of cable; you unroll the spool and snip the cable into shorter, usable segments.)
>
> To communicate with the server, the workstation sends a signal through its 10baseT cable to the hub, which then passes the signal to the server.
>
> That arrangement is called a **star topology**, since the hub looks like the center of a star, with each workstation acting as one of the star's points. Out of the hub, many cables come out (one cable for each workstation, plus one cable for the server), so the hub looks like an octopus.

That arrangement is called a **star topology**, since the hub looks like the center of a star, with each workstation acting as one of the star's points. Out of the hub, many cables come out (one cable for each workstation, plus one cable for the server), so the hub looks like an octopus.

The typical hub has 8 ports, to which you can attach 8 cables. You can buy a bigger hub, having 16 ports or even 24! For a small network, you can buy a cheaper hub have just 4 or 5 ports.

You can attach a group of hubs together, so the group acts as if it were one gigantic hub. To attach 2 hubs together, run a 10baseT cable from the first hub to the second. To attach 3 hubs together, run a 10baseT cable from the first hub to the second, then run a 10baseT cable from the second to the third. To attach more than 3 hubs, attach all the hubs onto a thinnet cable instead.

If the folks sitting at the workstations don't like sitting in a circle ("star"), feel free to rearrange the furniture! You can turn the circle into an oval, or even arrange all the workstations in a row. No matter how you rearrange, the setup is still called a **star topology**, since the computers can't tell the difference: just make sure each workstation still has its own cable going directly to the hub.

You can even put the hub in a different room, if you run the cables through the wall. Then plug each computer into the wall, using an RJ-45 jack (similar to a jack for plugging in a phone).

10baseT is more reliable than the other cabling methods, because a 10baseT cable failure affects just the workstation it's attached to. For the other cabling methods, a failed cable shuts down the entire network.

Network cards
Into each of the network's computers, you must insert a **network interface card (NIC)**.

It's a printed-circuit card to which you attach the network's cable. A plain, simple NIC costs about $25; fancier NICs (which go faster and have extra connectors) cost about $100. The NIC is also called an **Ethernet card**, even if you're using 10baseT cables (since 10baseT cabling act as a cheap imitation of Ethernet cabling).

How the network works
Each user sits at a workstation. When the user turns on the workstation's power, the workstation asks for the user's name (and maybe a password). Typing the name and password is called **logging on to the network**.

After the user logs on, the user's workstation accepts normal MS-DOS commands, just as if the user weren't on a network.

For example, if the workstation contains two floppy disk drives, they're called A and B, and the user can find out what's on drive A by typing "dir A". If the workstation contains a hard drive, that drive is called C. But if the user tells the workstation to get a file from "drive F", the workstation will get that file from the *server*'s hard drive, by using the network. The server is everybody's "drive F". For example, to find out what files are on the server, the user gets a directory of those files by typing "dir f".

Passwords and other security measures prevent any individual user from messing up the important files on the server. The network also prints reports saying how much time each user has been spending on the network.

That's how the typical Novell network acts, but *your* Novell network might be set up to use a different letter than F. If the letter F bothers you (because it reminds you of sex), you can set up the network so that the server's hard disk is called "G" instead.

Total cost
To create a 30-user Novell network, you face many costs:

First, buy Netware 5 (for $900+$2090). Next, spend many thousands of dollars to buy a server and 30 workstations. For those 31 computers, buy 31 network cards, cables, and either T-connectors or hubs. Pay several thousands of dollars for the labor of installing Netware on the server, fiddling with each workstation's AUTOEXEC.BAT, inserting the 31 network cards, stringing the cables so nobody trips on them (you might have to punch holes through your office's walls and floors!), buying **network versions** of all the programs you want to use on the network, and training all the users.

Hey, nobody said progress was cheap!

Since installing a Novell network is so expensive, avoid it unless you have no other choice. Here are cheaper alternatives....

Peer-to-peer networks
A **peer-to-peer network** is a network in which more than one computer can act as a server. In a peer-to-peer network,

every computer can be given the ability to send files directly to every other computer. Since each computer runs ordinary MS-DOS (instead of a special server DOS such as Netware), the network runs more slowly than a server network but is more flexible.

The best and most popular peer-to-peer network is **Lantastic**, invented by **Artisoft**. Lantastic comes in three versions:

The fancy version uses thin Ethernet cables and Ethernet network cards — just like Novell. But instead of using a "server" and Netware, it uses the **Lantastic operating system**, which is much easier to install (it comes on just one floppy disk!) and costs less.

Discount dealers sell a 2-user starter kit for about $500. That price includes the Lantastic operating system, networking hardware (thin Ethernet cables, terminators, and Ethernet network cards), and manuals to hand the 2 users. Your only additional expense is the labor of installing it all, which is easy!

Ethernet transmits data at a speed of 10 megabits per second. (That's 10 million electric signals per second.) If you don't need that much speed, you can save money by getting a 2-megabit-per-second version of Lantastic; its 2-user starter kit costs just $359.

Zero-slot LANs
To cut your cost even further, get a LAN that doesn't need a network card — and therefore doesn't need a slot to put the network card into. That kind of LAN is called a **zero-slot LAN**. To attach the LAN's cable to the computer, plug the cable into the computer's **parallel printer port** or **RS-232 serial port**.

Unfortunately, a zero-slot LAN handles just one pair of users — just 2 computers. The hardware setup is so easy: just run the cable from one computer's port to the other computer's port!

The most popular zero-slot LANs have been **Lantastic Z** and **Desklink**. Discount dealers sell each for about $90.

Desklink comes with a serial cable (to plug into the serial ports). Since the main part of the serial cable is an ordinary phone cord, you can run Desklink even between computers that are many yards apart: just buy a longer phone cord or an extension cord from your local phone store (such as AT&T or Radio Shack). Unfortunately, it works slowly: just 0.1 megabits per second.

Lantastic Z uses that same kind of serial cord (at the same speed) but also includes an 18-foot parallel cable, which you can use instead for faster transmission. But even if you use the parallel cable, the transfer rate will be much slower than the network-card versions of Lantastic.

Free Instead of buying Desklink or Lantastic Z, you can get a zero-slot LAN free! MS-DOS 6 (and 6.2 and 6.21 and 6.22) include a zero-slot LAN program called "interlink" (but spelled **Interlnk**). Windows 95 & 98 include a zero-slot LAN program called **Direct Cable Connection (DCC)**. To use Interlnk or Direct Cable Connection, just buy a cable and you're all set — except for learning how to use it.

On the next page, I explain how to use Interlnk.

Direct Cable Connection is more tricky. Here's how to try accessing it:

Click Start then Programs then Accessories.
(If you're using Windows 98, then click Communications.)
Then click Direct Cable Connection.

But that part of Windows might not be installed on your hard disk yet; and even if it *is* on your hard disk, it's tricky to set up properly.

File transfer programs
To pay even less, get a **file transfer program**.

The most popular one is **Laplink**, from the makers of Desklink. Discount dealers sell it for just $99. It includes a **universal cable** that you can attach to either serial or parallel ports.

Even easier to use than Desklink, Laplink is a program that shows you which files are on each computer's hard disk and lets you copy files from one computer to the other. Laplink's only purpose is to copy files. If you're sitting at computer A and you want to run a program on computer B's hard disk, Desklink lets you run it immediately; Laplink requires that you copy the program to your own hard disk first.

InterInk

MS-DOS 6 includes a program called **InterInk**, which lets you create a zero-slot LAN without buying extra software. That program is part of MS-DOS 6 (and 6.2 and 6.21 and 6.22) but is *not* part of Windows 95&98 and *not* part of DOS 95&98.

Here's how to use InterInk to let two computers communicate with each other.

String the cable

Buy a **bi-directional 25-pin male/male parallel cable**. It has 25 pins sticking out of each end, so each end can plug into a computer's parallel printer port. You can get it at your local computer store for about $10.

> You can also get it mail-order from **Cables America** (by phoning 800-FIT-USA4 and asking for cable #126349). Cables America charges just $4.05 for it but requires a $25 minimum order, $2.95 handing, plus shipping.

Turn both computers off. Unplug any printers (and their cables) from the computers.

Attach one end of the bi-directional cable to the first computer's printer port. Attach the other end of that cable to the other computer's printer port.

Prepare the server

The computer whose hard disk contains most of the files is called the **server**. For example, if you're transferring files between a notebook computer and a desktop computer, the server is the desktop computer, since it contains most of the files.

Turn that server computer on, so you see a C prompt.

Type "intersvr" (which is short for "InterInk server"), so your screen looks like this:

```
C:\>intersvr
```

When you press the ENTER key at the end of that line, the computer will say "Microsoft InterInk Server".

Prepare the client

After you've prepared the server, turn on the other computer (such as your notebook computer), which is called the **client**.

Make sure the bottom line of the client's CONFIG.SYS file says this:

```
device=dos\interlnk.exe
```

(To check whether that's the bottom line, say "type config.sys".) If that's *not* the bottom line, do this:

```
Type "edit config.sys".
Move to the bottom of CONFIG.SYS by doing this: press the END key while holding down the Ctrl key.
Type "device=dos\interlnk.exe".
Finish editing by doing this: tap the Alt key, then the F key, then the X key, then the ENTER key.
Reboot the computer by doing this: while holding down the Ctrl and Alt keys, tap the DEL key.
```

If the computer says "not enough drive letters", don't worry about that message. It just means that your extra devices (such as your CD-ROM) won't work while InterInk is running.

Let the client control the server

After peparing the server and the client, **sit at the client computer and give any DOS command you wish**. You can talk about:

```
"a:" (the client's main floppy drive)
"b:" (the client's second floppy drive, if any)
"c:" (the client's hard drive)

"d:" (the server's main floppy drive)
"e:" (the server's second floppy drive)
"f:" (the server's hard drive).
```

For example, to find out what's on the client's hard drive, say "dir c:" (or just "dir"); to find out what's on the server's hard drive, say "dir f:".

The computer adjusts those letters if necessary. For example, if the server doesn't have a second floppy drive, the server's hard drive is called "e" (instead of "f:"). If the client has *two* hard drives ("c:" and "d:"), the server's main floppy drive is called "e:" (instead of "d:") and other drives are called "f:", "g:", etc.

InterInk assumes the server has no more than 3 drives. If the server has 4 drives, InterInk uses just the first 3, unless you insist on 4 by changing the client's CONFIG.SYS line to this:

```
device=dos\interlnk.exe /drives:4
```

If MARY is a file on the server's hard drive "f:", you can copy it to the client's hard drive by saying:

```
C:\>copy f:mary
```

If SARAH is a folder on the server's hard drive "f:", you can copy it to the client's hard drive by saying —

```
C:\>md sarah          makes, on drive C, a new folder called SARAH
C:\>copy f:sarah sarah  copies everything from drive F's SARAH to drive C's SARAH
```

or by saying:

```
C:\>xcopy f:sarah sarah\   In the xcopy command, the "\" creates a new folder if necessary.
```

If SARAH is a server folder that contains other folders in it, you can copy it and all its inner folders by saying:

```
C:\>xcopy f:sarah sarah\ /s/e  In the xcopy command, the "/s/e" copies all subfolders.
```

To copy *all* unhidden files from the server's hard drive to the client's, say:

```
C:\>xcopy f: c: /s/e
```

But beware: that command copies *all* the server's unhidden files (even CONFIG.SYS, AUTOEXEC.BAT, all of DOS, all of Windows, and all drivers for the mouse, CD-ROM, and other devices) and destroys versions that were on the client previously.

Break the connection

When you finish using InterInk, do this to the server's keyboard: while holding down the Alt key, press the F4 key. That tells the server to stop running the intersvr program.

Finally, if you don't plan to use InterInk anymore today, do this:

> Erase the InterInk line from your CONFIG.SYS file (or put the word REM at the beginning of that line, since the computer ignores any line that begins with REM).
>
> Turn both computers off.
>
> Remove the bidirectional cable. Reattach the printers to the computers.

Classic Netware commands

Here are more comments about using Netware's classic version (3.12).

Getting started

Put network interface cards into all the computers and run cables between them. Then install Netware on the file server (by following the instructions in the Netware manual). Then install the client disks (included with Netware) onto each workstation. Finally, the network administrator runs the SYSCON program, to create a user login for each person who will use the network.

User commands

These commands can be typed by any user sitting at any workstation or at the server.

Command you type	What the computer will do for you
F:\>login chris	ask for your password (if any) to verify that you're Chris, then connect you to the server
F:\>logout	cancel the "login"; disconnect you from all file servers
F:\>whoami	tell you who's been sitting at this workstation (the person's name), when the person logged in, which workstation this is, which server the person is connected to (if the network has more than one server), and which version of Netware is being used
F:\>send "Let's eat" to ann	immediately send a message to another user, named Ann, telling her "Let's eat"; after Ann sees that message on her screen, she must press the ENTER key while holding down the Ctrl key, so she can continue working
F:\>castoff	"turn broadcasts off"; prevent other users (and the network administrator) from sending you any messages, and thereby prevent anybody from interrupting your work
F:\>caston	cancel the "castoff", so broadcasts are turned back on and other users can send you messages again
F:\>capture q=laser ti=10	from now on, send any printed output to the network's main printer (called "laser") instead of to your workstation's printer; if the network's main printer is unavailable (because it's being used by somebody else), your request is put in a waiting line (a **queue**); the "ti=10" means: if your program sends no print commands for 10 seconds, that 10-second pause marks the end of your **print job**; your entire print job will be printed in one batch, without interruption from other users
F:\>endcap	cancel the "capture", so any future printing will be done on your workstation's printer, not the network's main printer
F:\>ncopy poem.doc poem2.doc	make a copy of the file POEM.DOC (which is on the server), and call the copy POEM2.DOC (which is also on the server); the "ncopy" command resembles DOS's "copy" command but runs faster, since "ncopy" does all the copying directly on the server without copying the file to the workstation's RAM
F:\>flag payroll.exe sro	make the file PAYROLL.EXE **shareable** (so several people can use it at the same time) and **read-only** (so nobody can destroy it or alter it)

Administrator commands

To type the following commands, you must be sitting at the **console** (the server's keyboard) and be the network supervisor (or some other high-level administrator):

Command you type	What the computer will do for you
:broadcast Let's eat	immediately send a message to all users, telling them "Let's eat"; after users see that message on their screens, they must press the ENTER key while holding down the Ctrl key, so they can continue working; this message will not be seen by users who said "castoff"; before shutting down the server, broadcast a message saying "The network will shut down in 5 minutes. Please log off now."
:disable login	prevent additional users from logging in to the server; give this command if server's getting overloaded or you want to shut down soon
:enable login	cancel the "disable login", so additional users can log in to the server
:down	shut down Netware, so you can turn off the server safely; before giving this command, make sure all users have logged out
:exit	return the server to DOS, so you see a DOS prompt & can give DOS commands; before giving this command, give the "down" command

Other ways to share

Instead of buying a LAN, try these cheaper ways to share....

Sharing a printer

Suppose you and a colleague want to share a printer. Instead of buying a LAN, just unplug the printer's cable from one computer and reattach it to the other computer!

If you're too lazy to unplug the printer's cable, another alternative is to buy a box called an **AB switch box**, which most dealers sell for about $15. Into the box, plug the printer's cable and two cables (called "A" and "B") that go to the two computers. The switch box has a switch on it; if you flip the switch to position A, electricity flows between the printer and the computer attached to cable A; if you flip the switch to position B instead, the printer is electronically attached to B's computer.

To let *four* people share a printer, get an **ABCD switch box**, which attaches the printer to four computers called A, B, C, and D. Dealers sell it for about $20.

Hewlett-Packard, which makes the most popular laser printers, warns you that traditional switch boxes generate surges that damage laser printers. When switching, avoid damage by turning the laser printer off — or turning it off-line. Better yet, instead of using a traditional (**mechanical**) switch box, use an **electronic switch box**, which has no mechanical switches and doesn't generate any surges. The cheapest costs about $75.

But during the last few years, printer prices have dropped dramatically! Now you can buy a laser printer (such as the Okidata Page 4W) for just $269, or an ink-jet printer (such as the Canon BJC-240) for just $179! At those new, low prices, your best bet is to buy a separate cheap printer for each computer and forget the hassles of switch boxes and networking!

Sneaker net

Of all the networking schemes ever invented, my favorite is **sneaker net**, because it costs the least. To transfer data to your colleague's computer by using sneaker net, just copy the data onto a floppy disk, then put on your sneakers and run with your floppy to your colleague's desk!

That method is also called the **Nike net**. In Boston, it's called the **Reebok net**. Besides being free, it's also the healthiest network for you, since it gives you some exercise!

TRICKY APPLICATIONS

Background

In the preceding chapters, you learned how to buy a computer — and how to operate it by using operating systems, word processors, the Internet, and other means of communication.

Now let's see how computers can handle **tricky applications**. We'll start by looking at how computers handle **spreadsheets** (tables of numbers) and **databases** (such as lists of names & addresses), then get into applications that are even trickier and wilder, such as art, music, games, and fun! Lovemaking, too! Let's get wild! This section shows you how to do it all.

It tackles even the trickiest challenges, such as building a robot that acts just like you, and finding an accounting program that actually works well!

I wish you happy hunting through this thicket of pleasures and pain. When you finish, you'll understand why computers are just a high-tech form of sadomasochism.

Enjoy!

SPREADSHEETS

How spreadsheets arose

Any table of numbers is called a **spreadsheet**. For example, this spreadsheet deals with money:

```
          January    February
Income   $9,030.95  $12,486.99
Expenses $7,000.55   $9,210.75
-------------------------------
Profit   $2,030.40   $3,276.24
```

A spreadsheet can show how many dollars you earned (or spent or plan to spend), how many goods you have in stock, how people scored in a test (or survey or scientific experiment), or any other numbers you wish!

A **spreadsheet program** helps you create spreadsheets, edit them, and analyze them.

The first spreadsheet program was invented in 1979. It was **designed by Dan Bricklin** and **coded by Bob Frankston**. (That means Dan Bricklin decided what features and menus the program should have, and Bob Frankston wrote the program.) They called the program **Visicalc** because it was a "visible calculator". The original version of Visicalc ran on the Apple 2 computer and required 64K of RAM. Later versions of Visicalc ran on the Radio Shack TRS-80 and IBM PC.

The second spreadsheet program was called **Supercalc** because it was superior to Visicalc. It was invented by a company called **Sorcim** (which is "micros" spelled backwards). The original version of Supercalc ran on computers using the CP/M operating system. The most popular CP/M computer — the Osborne 1 — came with a free copy of Supercalc. Later versions of Supercalc ran on the Apple 2 and IBM PC. Eventually, Sorcim became part of a big conglomerate called **Computer Associates**.

Multiplan was the first spreadsheet program that could handle multiple spreadsheets simultaneously — and the relationships among them. Invented by Microsoft, it ran on a greater variety of computers than any other spreadsheet program: it ran on CP/M computers, the Radio Shack TRS-80, Commodore 64, Texas Instruments 99/4, IBM PC, Apple 2, and Apple Mac.

Context MBA was the first spreadsheet program that had "extras": besides handling spreadsheets, it also handled graphs, databases, word processing, and telecommunications. But it ran too slowly, its word processing was too limited (it couldn't center and wouldn't let you set tab stops), and it required a strange operating system (the PASCAL P System). It was invented in 1981 by **Context Management Systems**, which later invented an MS-DOS version called **Corporate MBA**.

All those spreadsheet programs became irrelevant in 1983, when a much better spreadsheet program was invented. It was **designed by Mitch Kapor** and **coded by Jonathan Sachs** for the IBM PC. They called the program **1-2-3**, because it ran fast and was supposed to handle three things: spreadsheets, graphs, and word processing; but when Jonathan examined Context MBA, he realized that putting a good word processor into 1-2-3 would consume too much RAM and make the program run too slowly. He omitted the word processor and replaced it with a stripped-down database processor instead. So 1-2-3 handled spreadsheets (well), graphs (okay), and databases (poorly). Mitch and Jonathan called their company **Lotus Development Corporation**, because Mitch was a transcendental-meditation instructor who got entranced by contemplating lotus flowers.

After inventing 1-2-3, Jonathan Sachs tried to invent a program called **1-2-3-4-5**, which was to handle the same five tasks as Context MBA: spreadsheets, graphs, databases, word processing, and telecommunications.

While developing it, he realized it was becoming too large and confusing, so he stopped developing it and quit the company. Other Lotus employees finished that program and renamed it **Symphony**; but as he feared, it turned out to be too big and confusing, and its word processor was awful. Most businesses bought just 1-2-3 instead.

Like Jonathan, Mitch began feeling that Lotus Development Corporation and its products were becoming too big and confusing, so Mitch quit too.

Afterwards, Lotus Development Corporation was run by **Jim Manzi**, who was young, rich, vain, egotistical, and nasty. The rest of the computer industry hated him, though his employees were nice. Finally, he sold Lotus to IBM, which gave lots of money to him (and the other shareholders and employees). Then he quit, a rich man!

Other companies invented cheap imitations of 1-2-3. The imitations were called **1-2-3 clones** or **1-2-3 twins**. The first 1-2-3 twins were **The Twin** (published by Mosaic Software) and **VP-Planner** (published by Paperback Software). Lotus sued both of those publishers and put them out of business.

In 1983 — the same year that Lotus invented 1-2-3 — Apple invented **Lisa Calc**. It was **the first spreadsheet program to use a mouse**. It ran just on the Lisa computer, which was too expensive ($8,000). When Apple began selling the Mac computer the next year (1984), Microsoft began selling **Multiplan for the Mac**, which ran on the Mac and combined the best features of Multiplan and Lisa Calc. The next year, 1985, Microsoft invented a further improvement, called **Excel** because it's excellent. Like 1-2-3, Excel handles spreadsheets, graphs, and databases.

Apple wanted to sue Microsoft for inventing the Windows operating system, which makes the IBM PC resemble a Mac. To avoid the suit, Microsoft agreed to put Excel on only the Mac for a year. Exactly one year later, when that agreement expired, Microsoft put Excel on the IBM PC.

So now **Excel runs on both the Mac and the IBM PC. It's the best spreadsheet program.** The newest version, called **Excel 2000**, requires that you buy Windows 95 (or 98).

Another fine spreadsheet program is called **Quattro**, because it's what comes after 1-2-3. It was invented by **Borland**, which later invented an improved version, called **Quattro Pro**. In 1994, Borland sold Quattro Pro to another company, **Novell**, which later sold it to **Corel**. So now Quattro Pro is published by Corel.

What to buy

The best spreadsheet program is **Excel**, which requires that you buy Windows or a Mac.

The DOS and Windows versions of **1-2-3** and **Quattro Pro** are popular alternatives that cost less. To pay even less, use the stripped-down spreadsheet programs that are part of **Microsoft Works** (for DOS, Windows, and the Mac) or **Appleworks** (which has sometimes been called **Claris Works** and is available for the Apple 2, Mac, and Windows).

I'll explain how to use the three most popular spreadsheet programs: **Excel**, **Quattro Pro**, and **Works**. I'll explain these versions:

Excel 97	(which is part of **Microsoft Office 97**)
Excel 2000	(which is part of **Microsoft Office 2000**)
Quattro Pro 8	(which is part of **Corel WordPerfect Suite 8**)
Quattro Pro 9	(which is part of **WordPerfect Office 2000**)
Works 4.5 spreadsheet	(which is part of **Microsoft Works 4.5**)
Works 2000 spreadsheet	(which is part of **Microsoft Works 2000**)

Those versions all run in Windows. (Other versions are similar.)

Prepare yourself

Before using spreadsheet programs, practice using word-processing programs, which are simpler and explained in my word-processing chapter. Each program comes on a CD-ROM disk; the word-processing chapter explains how to copy the CD-ROM disk to your hard disk.

Launch the spreadsheet program

Here's how to start using your spreadsheet program....

Quattro Pro 8 Click "Start" then "Corel WordPerfect Suite 8" then "Corel Quattro Pro 8".

Quattro Pro 9 Click "Start" then "Programs" then "WordPerfect Office 2000" then "Quattro Pro 9".

Excel 97 Click "Start" then "Programs" then "Microsoft Excel". (If the computer shows a button labeled "Start using Microsoft Excel", click that button.)

Excel 2000 Click "Start" then "Programs" then "Microsoft Excel". (If the computer shows a button labeled "Start using Microsoft Excel", click that button.)

Like Microsoft Word 2000, Excel 2000 has a feature called **masked menus & buttons**. That feature is supposed to make the menus and buttons easier to find but actually makes them *harder* to find. Turn off that terrible feature. **Do this turn-off procedure:**

> Click "View" then "Toolbars" then "Customize" then "Options".
> The first box is labeled "Standard and Formatting toolbars share one row". Remove any check mark from that box (by clicking it).
> The second box is labeled "Menus show recently used commands first". Remove any check mark from that box (by clicking it).
> Make sure you've done that right, so now the top two boxes are both empty. Then click "Close".

Do that turn-off procedure *now*. The rest of this chapter assumes you've done it. (After you've finished this chapter, if you wish, you can turn the masked menus & buttons feature back on by putting the check marks back in.)

Works 4.5 Turn the computer on, so you see the Start button. Double-click the icon that says **Shortcut to Microsoft Works**. (If the computer says "Click the OK button to see a short demonstration", click the Cancel button.)

Click **Works Tools** then the **Spreadsheet button**.

At the screen's top, you see the **menu bar**, which looks like this:

```
File  Edit  View  Insert  Format  Tools  Window  Help
```

Click the menu bar's last word, which is "Help". You see a **Help menu**. From that menu, choose **Hide Help** (by clicking it).

Works 2000 Turn the computer on, so you see the Start button. Double-click the **Microsoft Works** icon. Click **Programs** (which is near the screen's top left corner) then **Works Spreadsheet** (which is near the screen's left edge) then **Start a blank Spreadsheet**.

At the screen's right edge, if you see a Works Help window, close it (by clicking its X box).

Fill in the cells

The screen shows a grid that begins like this:

	A	B	C	D	E	F
1						
2						
3						
4						

The grid's columns are labeled A, B, C, D, E, etc.

> A cheap screen (640-by-480 VGA) shows up through column H in Works, column I in other spreadsheets.
>
> A fancier screen (800-by-600 Super VGA) shows up through column J in Works, K in Quattro Pro 9, L in other spreadsheets.
>
> An even fancier screen (1024-by-768 XVGA) shows up through column M in Works, O in other spreadsheets.

The grid's rows are labeled 1, 2, 3, etc.

> A cheap screen (640-by-480 VGA) shows 15 rows in Works 4.5, 16 rows in Quattro Pro 9, 18 rows in Quattro Pro 8, 17 rows in other spreadsheets.
>
> A fancier screen (800-by-600 Super VGA) shows 23 rows in Works 4.5, 25 rows in Quattro Pro 8, 24 rows in other spreadsheets.
>
> An even fancier screen (1024-by-768 XVGA) shows 33 rows in Works 4.5, 36 rows in Quattro Pro 8, 34 rows in other spreadsheets.

The grid is called a **spreadsheet** or **worksheet**.

Notice that the computer puts a box in column A, row 1. If you tap the right-arrow key, that box moves to the right, so it's in column B. If you tap the down-arrow key, the box moves down, to row 2. By tapping the four arrow keys, you can move the box in all four directions, to practically anywhere on the grid. Try it!

Each possible position of the box is called a **cell**.

The box's original position (in column A, row 1) is called **cell A1**. If you move the box there and then tap the right-arrow key, the box moves to column B, row 1; that position is called **cell B1**.

Just move the box from cell to cell, and put into each cell whatever words or numbers you wish!

For example, suppose you run a small business whose income is $7000 and expenses are $5000. Those are the figures for January; the figures for February aren't in yet. Let's put the January figures into a spreadsheet, like this:

	A	B	C	D	E	F
1		January				
2	Income	7000				
3	Expenses	5000				
4	Profit					

To begin, move the box to cell A2. Type the word Income. As you type that word, you see it appearing in cell A2. It also appears temporarily at the screen's top, in an **input line** (which Works calls the **entry bar** and Excel calls the **formula bar**).

Press the down-arrow key, which moves the box down to cell A3. Type the word Expenses.

Press the down-arrow key (to move to cell A4). Type the word Profit.

Move the box to cell B1 (by pressing the up-arrow three times and then the right-arrow once). Type the word January.

Press down-arrow. Type 7000.

Press down-arrow. Type 5000.

Press down-arrow again.

BACKSPACE key

If you make a mistake while typing the words and numbers, press the **BACKSPACE key** to erase the last character you typed.

Alternate keys

Instead of pressing the right-arrow key, you can press the TAB key. Instead of pressing the down-arrow key, you can press the ENTER key (except in Works 4.5).

Type a formula

Although the computer's screen shows the words you typed (Income, Expenses, and Profit), the computer doesn't understand what those words mean. It doesn't know that "Profit" means "Income minus Expenses". The computer doesn't know that the number in cell B4 (which represents the profit) ought to be the number in cell B2 (the amount of income) minus the number in cell B3 (the dollars spent).

You must *teach* the computer the meaning of Profit, by teaching it that the number in cell B4 ought to be the number in cell B2 minus the number in cell B3. To do that, move the box to cell B4, then type this formula:

```
=B2-B3
```

Notice that **every formula begins with an equal sign**. The rest of the formula, B2-B3, tells the computer to subtract the number in cell B3 from the number in cell B2 and put the answer into the box's cell (which is cell B4).

Quattro Pro prefers that you type "+" instead of "=". For example, instead of "=B2-B3", Quattro Pro prefers that you type "+B2-B3". If you type "=B2-B3", Quattro Pro will automatically turn your typing into "+B2-B3" when you press ENTER at the end of the formula.

When you've finished typing the formula, press the ENTER key. Then the computer automatically computes the formula's answer (2000) and puts that number into the box's cell (B4), so the screen looks like this:

	A	B	C	D	E	F
1		January				
2	Income	7000				
3	Expenses	5000				
4	Profit	2000				

The formula "=B2-B3" remains in effect forever. It says that the number in cell B4 will always be the B2 number minus the B3 number. If you ever change the numbers in cells B2 and B3 (by moving the box to those cells, retyping the numbers, and pressing ENTER), the computer automatically adjusts the number in cell B4, so the number in cell B4 is still B2 minus B3 and still represents the correct profit.

For example, suppose you move the box to cell B2, then type 8000 (to change the January income to $8000), and then press ENTER. As soon as you press ENTER, the profit in cell B4 immediately changes to 3000, right in front of your eyes!

A typical spreadsheet contains *dozens* of numbers, totals, subtotals, averages, and percentages. Each cell that contains a total, subtotal, average, or percentage is defined by a formula. Whenever you retype one of the numbers in the spreadsheet, the computer automatically readjusts all the totals, subtotals, averages, and percentages, right before your eyes.

Remember to begin each formula with an equal sign. The rest of the formula can contain these symbols:

Symbol	Meaning
+	plus
-	minus
*	times
/	divided by
.	decimal point

It can also contain E notation and parentheses. For details about how to use those symbols, E notation, and parentheses, read pages 332-337, which explain BASIC's fundamentals and math.

Less typing When you're creating a formula such as "=B2-B3", you do *not* have to type the "B2". Instead, you can choose one of these shortcuts:

Instead of typing "B2", you can type "b2" without bothering to capitalize. When you've finished typing the entire formula ("=b2-b3"), press the ENTER key. Then the computer will capitalize your formula automatically!

Instead of typing "B2", you can move the mouse pointer to the middle of cell B2, then press the mouse's button. That's called "clicking cell B2". When you click cell B2, the computer automatically types "B2" for you! So to create the formula "=B2-B3", you can do this: type the equal sign, then click cell B2, then type the minus sign, then click cell B3. When you've finished creating the entire formula, press ENTER.

Instead of typing "B2", you can move the box to cell B2 by using the arrow keys. When you move the box to cell B2, the computer automatically types "B2" for you! So to create the formula "=B2-B3", you can do this: type the equal sign, then move the box to cell B2 (by using the arrow keys), then type the minus sign, then move the box to cell B3. When you've finished creating the entire formula, press ENTER.

Edit old cells

To edit what's in a cell, move the box to that cell. Then choose one of these editing methods....

Method 1: press the DELETE key. That makes the cell become totally blank.

Method 2: retype the entire text, number, or formula that you want to put into the cell.

Method 3: in the input line (at the top of the screen), look at what you typed, find the part of your typing that you want to change, and click that part (by using the mouse). Then edit your typing as if you were using a word processor: you can use the left-arrow key, right-arrow key, BACKSPACE key, DELETE key, and mouse. When you finish editing, press the ENTER key.

Functions in Excel & Works

Here's how to perform functions in Excel and Works. (If you're using Quattro Pro, skip ahead to the next section.)

Sum of a column To make a cell be the sum of cells B2 through B9, you can type this formula:

```
=B2+B3+B4+B5+B6+B7+B8+B9
```

Instead of typing all that, you can type just this:

```
=SUM(B2:B9)
```

A **function** is a word that makes the computer calculate (such as SUM). After each function, you must put parentheses. For example, you must put parentheses after SUM.

Since the computer ignores capitalization, you can type:

```
=sum(b2:b9)
```

Here's how to type the formula =sum(b2:b9) quickly. Begin by typing:

```
=sum(
```

Then drag from cell B2 to cell B9. To do that, move the mouse to cell B2, then hold down the mouse button while moving to B9. That makes the computer type the "B2:B9". Here's what to do next....

Works: type ")", then press ENTER.

Excel: press the ENTER key, which makes the computer automatically type the ")".

AutoSum button Here's an even faster way to type the formula =SUM(B2:B9). Click the **AutoSum button**, which is near the screen's top center and has the symbol Σ on it. (The symbol Σ is called "sigma"; it's the Greek version of the letter S, and mathematicians use it to stand for the word "sum".) **Clicking the AutoSum button makes the computer type "=SUM()". It also makes the computer guess what you want the sum of.** The computer puts that guess inside the parentheses. If the computer's guess differs from what you want (B2:B9), fix the guess (by dragging from cell B2 to cell B9). When you finally see the correct formula, =SUM(B2:B9), press ENTER.

Sum of a row
To find the sum of cells B2 through H2 (which is B2+C2+D2+E2+F2+G2+H2), type this:

```
=sum(b2:h2)
```

Sum of a rectangle
To find the sum of all cells in the rectangle that stretches from B2 to C4 (which is B2+B3+B4+C2+C3+C4), type this:

```
=sum(b2:c4)
```

Average
To find the average of cells B9 through B13, you can type this:

```
=(b9+b10+b11+b12+b13)/5
```

But this way is shorter....

```
Excel:  =average(b9:b13)
Works:  =avg(b9:b13)
```

Here's how to type that quickly....

```
Excel: begin by typing "=average(", then drag from cell B9 to cell B13, then press the ENTER key, which makes the computer automatically type the ")".
```

```
Works: begin by typing "=avg(", then drag from cell B9 to cell B13, then type ")", then press ENTER.
```

To find the average of cells C7, B5, and F2, you can ask for (c7+b5+f2)/3, but a nicer way is to type this....

```
Excel:  =average(c7,b5,f2)
Works:  =avg(c7,b5,f2)
```

Functions in Quattro Pro

Here's how to perform functions in Quattro Pro. (If you're using Excel or Works, skip this section.)

Sum of a column
To make a cell be the sum of cells B2 through B9, you can type this formula:

```
+B2+B3+B4+B5+B6+B7+B8+B9
```

Instead of typing all that, you can type just this:

```
+@SUM(B2..B9)
```

A **function** is a word that makes the computer calculate (such as SUM). Put the symbol @ before each function: say @SUM instead of SUM.

After each function, you must put parentheses. For example, you must put parentheses after SUM.

The first parenthesis, "(", temporarily turns red. When you type the ")", both parentheses turn green.

Since the computer ignores capitalization, you can type:

```
+@sum(b2..b9)
```

You can omit the plus sign and the second period, and type just this:

```
@sum(b2.b9)
```

Here's how to type the formula "@sum(b2.b9)" quickly. Begin by typing:

```
@sum(
```

Then drag from cell B2 to cell B9. To do that, move the mouse to cell B2, then hold down the mouse button while moving to B9. That makes the computer type the "B2..B9". Finally, press the ENTER key, which makes the computer automatically type the ")".

QuickSum button
Here's an even faster way to type the formula @SUM(B2..B9). Click the **QuickSum button**, which is near the screen's top center and has the symbol Σ on it.

(The symbol Σ is called "sigma". It's the Greek version of the letter S, and mathematicians use it to stand for the word "sum". In version 9, if you don't see the symbol Σ, make it appear by clicking the ▼ that's left of the A..Z button.)

Clicking the QuickSum button makes the computer do all this:

```
Type "@SUM()".
Guess what you want the sum of and put that guess inside the parentheses.
Press the ENTER key for you, so the number that's the sum appears instantly!
```

Sum of a row
To find the sum of cells B2 through H2 (which is B2+C2+D2+E2+F2+G2+H2), type this:

```
@sum(b2.h2)
```

Sum of a rectangle
To find the sum of all cells in the rectangle that stretches from B2 to C4 (which is B2+B3+B4+C2+C3+C4), type this:

```
@sum(b2.c4)
```

Average
To find the average of cells B9 through B13, you can type this:

```
+(b9+b10+b11+b12+b13)/5
```

But this way is shorter:

```
@avg(b9.b13)
```

To type that quickly, begin by typing "@avg(". Then drag from cell B9 to cell B13. Then press the ENTER key, which makes the computer automatically type the ")" for you.

Version 9 provides this faster way to type the formula @AVG(B9..B13): click the ▼ that's left of the A..Z button, then click "@Avg Average".

To find the average of cells C7, B5, and F2, you can ask for (c7+b5+f2)/3, but a nicer way is to type:

```
@avg(c7,b5,f2)
```

Undo

If you make a big mistake, click the **Undo button**, which is near the top of the screen, under the word "Window", and shows an arrow turning back to the left. (In Microsoft Works, press Ctrl with Z instead.)

That makes the computer undo your last activity, so your spreadsheet returns to the way it looked before you made your boo-boo. (To undo your last *two* activities, click the Undo button *twice*.)

Redo
If you click the Undo button, the computer might undo a different activity than you expected. If clicking the Undo button accidentally makes the spreadsheet look even worse instead of better, and you wish you hadn't clicked the Undo button, here's how to "undo the undo"....

```
Quattro Pro 8: click the Undo button again.
```

```
Works: press Ctrl with Z again.
```

```
Excel & Quattro Pro 9: click the Redo button (which is to the right of the Undo button and shows an arrow bending forward to the right).
```

Hop far

Here's how to be quick as a bunny and hop far in your spreadsheet.

Farther rows

The screen shows just a few rows, which are numbered 1, 2, 3, etc. Row 1 is at the top of the screen. Row 15 is near the bottom of the screen.

Try this experiment. Move the box down to row 15 (by pressing the down-arrow key repeatedly). Then press the down-arrow key several more times. Eventually, you'll get to row 30, and later to row 100, and much later to row 1000. (The largest row number you can go to is 8192 in Quattro Pro 8, 16384 in Works, 65536 in Excel, 1000000 in Quattro Pro 9.)

To make room on the screen for those new rows, row 1 disappears temporarily. If you want to get back to row 1, press the up-arrow key repeatedly.

Farther columns

The screen shows just a few columns, which are lettered A, B, C, etc. If you press the right-arrow key repeatedly, you'll eventually get to column Z.

Altogether, the computer lets you have 256 columns. The first 26 columns are lettered from A to Z. The next 26 columns are lettered from AA to AZ. The next 26 columns are lettered from BA to BZ. And so on. (The last column is ZZZ in Quattro Pro 9, IV in other spreadsheets.)

AutoRepeat

Here's a shortcut: instead of pressing an arrow key repeatedly, just hold down the key awhile.

Mouse

To move the box to a distant cell even faster, use the mouse: just click in the middle of the cell you wish.

Screenfuls

To move far down, press the **PAGE DOWN key**. To move far up, press the **PAGE UP key**. To move far to the right, do this....

Quattro Pro:	press the right-arrow key while holding down the Ctrl key.
Works:	press the PAGE DOWN key while holding down the Ctrl key.
Excel:	press the PAGE DOWN key while holding down the Alt key.

To move far to the left, do this....

Quattro Pro:	press the left-arrow key while holding down the Ctrl key.
Works:	press the PAGE UP key while holding down the Ctrl key.
Excel:	press the PAGE UP key while holding down the Alt key.

Each of those keys moves the box far enough so that you see the next screenful of rows and columns.

HOME key

Cell A1 is called the **home cell**, because that's where life and your spreadsheet begin: at home! Column A is called the **home column**.

Your keyboard has a **HOME key**. Here's how to use it....

Quattro Pro:	pressing the HOME key makes the box move to cell A1.
Excel & Works:	pressing the HOME key makes the box move far left, so it lands in column A. If you press the HOME key *while holding down the Ctrl key*, the box moves to cell A1.

Spreadsheet's edge

Here's how to move to the spreadsheet's edge....

Excel & Works:	while holding down the Ctrl key, press an arrow key.
Quattro Pro:	press the END key and then an arrow key.

For example, here's how to move the box to the spreadsheet's right edge:

Excel & Works:	while holding down the Ctrl key, press the right-arrow key.
Quattro Pro:	press the END key and then the right-arrow key.

That moves the box moves to the right, until it reaches the final column (IV or ZZZ) or a boundary cell (a cell containing data and next to an empty cell).

F5 key

To make the box go to a distant cell immediately: press the F5 key (or press Ctrl with G), then type the name of the cell where you want to go (such as C9) followed by ENTER.

Excel lets you also use this alternative:

Above column A, you see the **Name box**, which tells you the name of the cell where the box is. For example, while the box is at cell B4, the name box says "B4". To move the box to a distant cell immediately, you can click in the name box, then type the name of the cell where you want to go (such as C9) followed by ENTER.

Adjust rows & columns

How many rows and columns are in your spreadsheet, and how big are they? Here's how to adjust them.

Widen a column

When you start a new spreadsheet, here's what happens....

Excel and Quattro Pro:	each cell is wide enough to hold an 8-digit number.
Works:	each cell is wide enough to hold a 9-digit number.

Here's how to make column D be wider, so each cell in column D can hold longer numbers and words:

At the top of column D, you see the letter D. **Move the mouse** until its pointer is **between the letters D and E, and on the vertical gridline that separates them**. The pointer's shape turns into a **double-headed arrow**. (In Works, the pointer is also labeled "ADJUST".) Then drag that vertical gridline toward the right (to make the column wider) or left (to make the column narrower).

Widen several columns

Excel and Quattro Pro let you widen columns D, E, F, and G simultaneously. Here's how:

Drag from the letter D to the letter G. All those columns turn dark. (In Excel 2000, they turn purple; in other spreadsheet programs, they turn black.)

Look at the vertical gridline to the right of the D. Drag the top of that gridline toward the right. That widens column D; and when you release your finger from the mouse's button, all the other columns you selected will widen also.

Perfect width

Here's how to make column D just wide enough to hold the widest data in it....

Works:	double-click the D at the top of column D.
Quattro Pro:	double-click the D at the top of column D, or else do this: click the D at the top of column D, then click the QuickFit button (which is under the word "Help" and shows "↔" in a cell).
Excel:	double-click the gridline that separates the letter D from E.

(If the column doesn't contain data yet, the computer will leave the column's width unchanged.)

Excel and Quattro Pro let you make columns D, E, F, and G have perfect widths simultaneously. Here's how. Drag from the letter D to the letter G, so all those columns turn dark. Then do this....

Excel:	double-click the gridline that separates the letter D from E.
Quattro Pro:	click the QuickFit button (which is under the word "Help" and shows "↔" in a cell).

Long numbers

If you try to type a long number in a cell that's too narrow to hold the number, the cell might display symbols instead of the number.

For example, try typing a long number in a cell that's just 4 characters wide. Instead of displaying the long number, the computer displays 4 number signs: ####.

Although the cell displays just those symbols, the computer remembers the long number you typed. To see the long number, widen the cell (by widening its column).

So if you see number signs in a cell, the computer is telling you that the cell is too narrow and should be widened.

Long words

Try this experiment. Make cell B1 be just 4 characters wide. Then try to type the word "January" in that cell.

That cell, B1, might show just the first 4 letters (Janu). But if the next cell (C1) is blank, cell B1 will temporarily widen to hold "January", then contract to its original size (4 characters) when you enter data in cell C1.

Delete a column

Here's **how to delete column D:**

Quattro Pro: click the D at the top of column D, then click the **Delete Cells button** (which is under the word "Help" and shows "-" in a cell).

Works: *right*-click anywhere in column D (by using the mouse's *right* button instead of the left), then choose Delete Column from the menu that appears.

Excel: *right*-click the D at the top of column D (by using the mouse's *right* button instead of the left); then choose Delete from the menu that appears.

The computer erases all the data from column D, so column D becomes blanks, which the computer immediately fills by shifting some data from other columns. Here's how....

Into column D, the computer moves the data from column E. Then into column E, the computer moves the data from column F. Then into column F, the computer moves the data from column G. And so on.

At the end of the process, the top of the screen still shows all the letters (A, B, C, D, E, F, G, etc.); but now column D contains the data that used to be in column E; and column E contains the data that used to be in column F; etc.

After rearranging the spreadsheet, the computer fixes all formulas. For example, after column E's data has moved to column D, the computer hunts through all formulas in the spreadsheet and fixes them by changing each "E" to "D". The computer also changes each "F" to "E", each "G" to "F", etc.

Delete several columns

You've learned how to delete column D. Here's how to delete *several* columns. To delete columns D, E, F, and G, drag from the D to the G, then do the following....

Quattro Pro: click Delete Cells button.

Works: *right*-click anywhere in columns D through G (by using the mouse's *right* button instead of the left), then choose Delete Column from the menu that appears.

Excel: *right*-click anywhere in columns D through G (by using the mouse's *right* button instead of the left); then choose Delete from the menu that appears.

Delete a row

Here's **how to delete row 2:**

Quattro Pro: click the 2, then click the Delete Cells button.

Works: *right*-click anywhere in row 2 (by using the mouse's *right* button instead of the left), then choose Delete Row from the menu that appears.

Excel: *right*-click the 2 (by using the mouse's *right* button instead of the left); then choose Delete from the menu that appears.

Then the computer erases all the data from row 2, so row 2 becomes empty; but then the computer immediately fills that hole, by shifting the data from other rows. Here's how....

Into row 2, the computer moves the data from row 3. Then into row 3, the computer moves the data from row 4. Then into row 4, the computer moves the data from row 5. And so on.

At the end of the process, the left edge of the screen still shows all the numbers (1, 2, 3, 4, 5, etc.); but now row 2 contains the data that used to be in row 3; and row 3 contains the data that used to be in row 4; etc.

The computer fixes all formulas.

Insert a column

Here's how to insert an extra column in the middle of your spreadsheet:

> Quattro Pro: click where you want the extra column to appear. For example, if you want the extra column to appear where column D is now, click the D. Then click the **Insert Cells button** (which is under the word "Help" and has "**+**" on it).
>
> Works: *right*-click where you want the extra column to appear. For example, if you want the extra column to appear where column D is now, *right*-click in column D. Then choose Insert Column from the menu that appears.
>
> Excel: *right*-click where you want the extra column to appear. For example, if you want the extra column to appear where column D is now, *right*-click the D. Then choose Insert from the menu that appears.

The computer will move other columns out of the way, to make room for the extra column. The computer will also fix each formula.

Insert a row

Here's how to insert an extra row in the middle of your spreadsheet:

> Quattro Pro: click where you want the extra row to appear. For example, if you want the extra row to appear where row 2 is now, click the 2. Then click the Insert Cells button.
>
> Works: *right*-click where you want the extra row to appear. For example, if you want the extra row to appear where row 2 is now, *right*-click in row 2. Then choose Insert Row from the menu that appears.
>
> Excel: *right*-click where you want the extra row to appear. For example, if you want the extra row to appear where row 2 is now, *right*-click the 2. Then choose Insert from the menu that appears.

The computer will move other rows out of the way, to make room for the extra row. The computer will also fix each formula.

Zoom

You can make your screen show twice as many rows and columns.

Here's how in Excel:

> Near the screen's top right corner, you see a percentage, which is normally **100%**. That percentage is in a white box, called the **Zoom box**. Click its down-arrow.
>
> You'll see the **Zoom menu**. From that menu, choose **50%**. The computer will make all the screen's characters tiny (half as tall and half as wide), so twice as many rows and twice as many columns fit on the screen.
>
> To make the screen return to normal, click the Zoom box's down-arrow again, then click **100%**.
>
> If you wish, you can click different percentages, such as **75%** (which shrinks the screen's characters just slightly) or **200%** (which enlarges the screen's characters, so you can read them even if you're sitting far away from the screen).
>
> Try this trick: start at one cell, and drag to another cell far away. All the cells between them turn dark. Then click the Zoom box's down-arrow and click **Selection**. That shrinks or enlarges the characters just enough so all the dark cells fit on the screen.

Here's how in Quattro Pro:

> Near the screen's top right corner, you see the **Zoom button**, which looks like a magnifying glass. Click it.
>
> You'll see the **Zoom menu**. From that menu, choose **50%**. The computer will make all the screen's characters tiny (half as tall and half as wide), so twice as many rows and twice as many columns fit on the screen.
>
> To make the screen return to normal, click the Zoom button again, then choose **100%** from the Zoom menu.
>
> If you wish, you can click different percentages, such as **75%** (which shrinks the screen's characters just slightly) or **200%** (which enlarges the screen's characters, so you can read them even if you're sitting far away from the screen).
>
> Try this trick: start at one cell, and drag to another cell far away. All the cells between them turn black. Then click the Zoom button and choose **Selection** from the Zoom menu. That shrinks or enlarges the characters just enough so that all the black cells fit on the screen.

Here's how in Works:

> Near the screen's bottom left corner, you see the word **Zoom**. Next to it, you normally see **100%**.
>
> Near it, you see a **plus sign**. If you click that plus sign, the computer makes the screen's characters be enlarged, so their size is 150% as wide and 150% as tall as normal, and the Zoom box says "150%" instead of "100%".
>
> If you click the plus sign again, the computer makes the screen's characters be even larger, so their size is 200%. If you click the plus sign again, the computer makes the screen's characters be even larger: 400%.
>
> If you click the **minus sign** instead, the characters become smaller. By clicking the plus or minus sign repeatedly, you can choose these sizes: 50%, 75%, 100%, 150%, 200%, 400%.
>
> 50% and 75% are very useful: they make the characters smaller, so more characters fit on the screen and you see more rows and columns.
>
> For further choices, click the word **Zoom**. Then you see this **Zoom menu**:
>
> ```
> 50%
> 75%
> 100%
> 150%
> 200%
> 400%
> Custom
> ```
>
> Click whichever choice you wish.
>
> If you prefer a different percentage, choose **Custom** then type the percentage you want (such as 90) and press ENTER.

All those Zoom choices affect just what you see on the screen. They do *not* affect what's printed on paper.

Panes

On your screen, you see a window that contains part of your spreadsheet. (That window is big enough to usually show columns A through I on a cheap screen, and more columns on a fancier screen.)

You can divide that window into two **windowpanes**, so that each windowpane shows a different part of your spreadsheet.

Vertical panes You can divide your window into two windowpanes, so that the left pane shows columns A, B, and C, while the right pane shows columns X, Y and Z.

Here's how in Quattro Pro:

> Press the **HOME key** (so the box moves to cell A1). Click **View** then **Split Window** then **Vertical** then OK.
>
> The screen splits into two panes. The left pane shows columns A, B, C, etc. The right pane shows columns that are farther to the right.

Here's how in Excel:

> Get column A onto the screen (by pressing the HOME key).
>
> Near the screen's bottom right corner, you see the symbol ▸, which points at a vertical bar. Put your mouse pointer on that vertical bar; when you do, the pointer becomes this symbol: ↔. Drag that vertical bar to the left. As you drag, you'll see a vertical gray bar move across your spreadsheet. Drag until the vertical gray bar is in the middle of the spreadsheet. For best results, drag until that bar is slightly to the right of column C's right edge.
>
> That bar splits the screen into two panes. The left pane shows columns A through C; the right pane shows column D and beyond.

Here's how in Works:

> Get column A onto the screen (by pressing the HOME key).
>
> Near the screen's bottom left corner, you see the word "Zoom". Left of it, you see a vertical bar. Put your mouse pointer on that bar; when you do, the pointer becomes the symbol ↔ and is labeled "ADJUST". Drag that vertical bar to the right. As you drag, you'll see a vertical gray bar move across your spreadsheet. Drag until the vertical gray bar is in the middle of the spreadsheet. For best results, drag until that bar is slightly to the right of column C's right edge.
>
> That bar splits the screen into two panes. The left pane shows columns A through C; the right pane shows column D and beyond.

Then click anywhere in the right pane. That puts the box in the right pane, and makes the right pane active. Press the right-arrow key several times, until you reach columns X, Y, and Z.

If you want to move the box back to the left pane, just click the left pane.

Here's how to stop using vertical panes....

> Excel and Works: double-click the vertical gray bar.
> Quattro Pro: click **View** then **Split Window** then **Clear** then OK.

Horizontal panes

You can divide your window into two panes, so that the top pane shows rows 1, 2, and 3, while the bottom pane shows rows 97, 98, and 99.

Here's how in Quattro Pro:

> Press the **HOME key** (so the box moves to cell A1). Click **View** then **Split Window** then **Horizontal** then OK.
>
> The screen splits into two panes. The left pane shows rows 1, 2, 3, etc. The bottom pane shows rows that have bigger numbers.

Here's how in Excel and Works:

> Get row 1 onto the screen (by pressing the PAGE UP key several times).
>
> At the spreadsheet's top right corner, you'll see the scroll bar's up-arrow pointing at a horizontal bar. Put the mouse pointer on that bar; when you do, the pointer becomes the symbol ⬍. (and in Works is labeled "ADJUST"). Drag that bar down. As you drag, you'll see a horizontal gray bar move down your spreadsheet. Drag until the horizontal gray bar is in the middle of the spreadsheet. For best results, drag until that bar is slightly under row 3's bottom edge.
>
> That bar splits the screen into two panes. The top pane shows rows 1 through 3; the bottom pane shows row 4 and beyond.

Then click anywhere in the bottom pane. That puts the box in the bottom pane, and makes the bottom pane active. Press the down-arrow key several times, until you reach rows 97, 98, and 99.

If you want to move the box back to the top pane, just click the top pane.

Here's how to stop using vertical panes:

> Excel and Works: double-click the horizontal gray bar.
> Quattro Pro: click **View** then **Split Window** then **Clear** then OK.

Freeze title panes

You should put a title at the top of each column. For example, if column B contains financial information for January, and column C contains financial information for February, you should put the word January at the top of column B, and the word February at the top of column C. Since the words January and February are at the top of the columns, they're in row 1. They're called the **column titles**.

If row 2 analyzes Income, and row 3 analyzes Expenses, you should put the word Income at the left edge of row 2, and the word Expenses at the left edge of row 3. Since the words Income and Expenses are at the left edge of the spreadsheet, they're in column A. They're called the **row titles**.

So in a typical spreadsheet, the column titles are in row 1, and row titles are in column A.

Unfortunately, when you move beyond column L or beyond row 24 (by pressing the arrow keys repeatedly), the titles normally disappear from the screen, and you forget the purpose of each row and column. Here's how to solve that problem....

In Quattro Pro, do this:

> Get cell A1 onto the screen (by pressing the HOME key).
>
> Click cell B2. Click **View** then **Locked Titles**.
>
> Now the window is divided into two panes, separated by blue gridlines. One pane contains the column titles (January, February, etc.) and row titles (Income, Expenses, etc.); the other pane is huge and contains all the spreadsheet's data.

In Excel and Works, do this:

> Get cell A1 onto the screen (by pressing CONTROL with HOME).
>
> Click cell B2. In Excel, choose **Freeze Panes** from the Window menu; in Works, choose **Freeze Titles** from the Format menu.
>
> Now the window is divided into four panes, separated by thick black gridlines. The main top pane contains the column titles (January, February, etc.); the main left pane contains the row titles (Income, Expenses, etc.); a tiny pane in the upper-left corner contains a blank cell; and a huge pane contains all the spreadsheet's data.

Then move through the huge pane, by using the arrow keys or mouse. As you move, the column and row titles stay fixed on the screen, since they're not in the big pane.

Here's how to stop using freeze title panes....

> Excel: choose Unfreeze Panes from the Window menu.
> Works: click Format, then remove the check mark in front of Freeze Titles (by clicking Freeze Titles again).
> Quattro Pro: click View, then remove the check mark in front of Locked Titles (by clicking Locked Titles again).

Move

On your spreadsheet, find these cells: B2, B3, B4, C2, C3, and C4. Those six cells are next to each other. In fact, they form a giant rectangular area, whose top left corner is B2.

Here's how to take all the data in that rectangle and move it to a different part of your spreadsheet.

Drag from the rectangle's first cell (B2) to the rectangle's last cell (C4). The entire rectangle turns dark (except for the first cell, which stays white).

Surrounding the rectangle, you'll see four walls. Those walls are the four sides of the rectangle.

Using your mouse, **point at one of the rectangle's walls**. (Do *not* point at a corner.) When you've pointed correctly, here's what happens....

> Excel and Works: the mouse pointer turns into an arrow (*not* a cross).
>
> Quattro Pro: the mouse pointer turns into 4 arrows, pointing in all 4 directions.

Then hold down the mouse's button and **drag the wall**. While you drag the wall, the rest of the rectangle drags along with it. Drag until the entire rectangle is at a part of the spreadsheet that was blank. Then lift your finger from the mouse's button.

That's how you move a rectangle of data to a new place in your spreadsheet that had been blank.

Try it!

After moving the rectangle of data, the computer automatically adjusts all formulas mentioning the moved cells. For example, if the data in cell B2 has moved to cell E7, the computer searches through the entire spreadsheet and, in each formula, changes "B2" to "E7".

Copy

Spreadsheet programs let you copy info in several ways.

Fill to the right

Here's how to make lotsa love with the computer!

> In a cell, type the word "love".
>
> Click in that cell (to make sure the cell is highlighted), then take your finger off the mouse's button. With your finger still off the mouse's button, move the mouse until the mouse's pointer is at that cell's bottom right corner. When the pointer is exactly at the corner, the pointer changes to this thin cross: +.
>
> Then hold down the mouse's left button, and drag toward the right, until you've dragged across several cells. (In Quattro Pro, make sure you drag across cells that are all *blank*.)
>
> When you lift your finger off the mouse's button, all those cells will contain copies of the word in the first cell. They'll all say "love"!

Go ahead! Try turning your computer into a lovemaking machine! Do it *now!* This is an important exercise to try before you get into more advanced computer orgies!

Here's another example:

> In a cell, type the word "tickle". To make lotsa tickles, click in that cell, then point at that cell's bottom right corner (so you see +) and drag it to the right. (In Quattro Pro, make sure the cells you're dragging across are blank.) The cells you drag across will all say "tickle".

Fill down

When you point at a cell's bottom right corner and drag, you usually drag to the *right*. But if you prefer, you can drag *down*, so you're copying to the cells *underneath* (instead of the cells to the right).

Extend a series

You've learned that if the original cell said "love", the adjacent cells will say "love"; and if the original cell said "tickle", the other cells will say "tickle".

But if the original cell said "January", the adjacent cells will *not* say "January". Instead, the computer makes them say "February", "March", "April", "May", etc.

So **here's how to put the words "January", "February", "March", "April", etc., across the top of your spreadsheet:**

> Begin by typing "January" in cell B1. Then drag that cell's bottom right corner to the right, to column H or I or even farther! The farther you drag, the more months you'll see!

Your computer performs fundamental tricks:

If you start with January,	the computer will say February, March, April, etc.
If you start with October,	the computer will say November, December, January, etc.
If you start with 12/29/99,	the computer will say 12/30/99, 12/31/99, 1/1/00, etc.
If you start with Monday,	the computer will say Tuesday, Wednesday, Thursday, etc.
If you start with Mon,	the computer will say Tue, Wed, Thu, etc.
If you start with 10:00 AM,	the computer will say 11:00 AM, 12:00 PM, 1:00 PM, etc.
If you start with Q2,	the computer will say Q3, Q4, Q1, etc.
If you start with Idiot 1,	the computer will say Idiot 2, Idiot 3, Idiot 4, etc.
If you start with Year 1991,	the computer will say Year 1992, Year 1993, Year 1994, etc.

Works performs these extra tricks:

If you start with July 29,	the computer will say July 30, July 31, August 01, etc.
If you start with July 29, 1999,	the computer will say July 30, 1999, July 31, 1999, August 01, 1999, etc.
If you start with October 1999,	the computer will say November 1999, December 1999, January 2000, etc.
If you start with 10:00,	the computer will say 11:00, 12:00, 13:00, etc.
If you start with 22:00,	the computer will say 23:00, 0:00, 1:00, etc.
If you start with 2Q,	the computer will say 3Q, 4Q, 1Q, etc.

Limitation: if you start with just a number (such as 1), the computer will just copy that number; it will *not* say 2, 3, 4, etc. If you start with just the plain number 1991, the computer will just copy that number; it will *not* say 1992, 1993, 1994, etc. To make the computer do more than just copy, put a word before the number. For example, instead of saying just 1, say "Idiot 1"; then the computer will say "Idiot 2", "Idiot 3", "Idiot 4", etc. Instead of saying just 1991, say "Year 1991" or "People We Accidentally Shot In 1991"; then the computer will generate similar headings for 1992, 1993, etc.

Excel performs these extra tricks:

If you start with Jan,	the computer will say Feb, Mar, Apr, etc.
If you start with 29-Jan,	the computer will say 30-Jan, 31-Jan, 1-Feb, etc.
If you start with Oct-98,	the computer will say Nov-98, Dec-98, Jan-99, etc.
If you start with 29-Dec-98,	the computer will say 30-Dec-98, 31-Dec-98, 1-Jan-99, etc.
If you start with 29-Dec-99,	the computer will say 30-Dec-99, 31-Dec-99, 1-Jan-00, etc.
If you start with 10:00,	the computer will say 11:00, 12:00, 13:00, etc.
If you start with 22:00,	the computer will say 23:00, 0:00, 1:00, etc.
If you start with 2nd Quarter,	the computer will say 3rd Quarter, 4th Quarter, 1st Quarter, etc.
If you start with 2nd Qtr,	the computer will say 3rd Qtr, 4th Qtr, 1st Qtr, etc.
If you start with 2 Q,	the computer will say 3 Q, 4 Q, 1 Q, etc.
If you start with Quarter 2,	the computer will say Quarter 3, Quarter 4, Quarter 1, etc.
If you start with 1st,	the computer will say 2nd, 3rd, 4th, etc.
If you start with 1st Idiot,	the computer will say 2nd Idiot, 3rd Idiot, 4th Idiot, etc.
If you start with 1991 Results,	the computer will say 1992 Results, 1993 Results, 1994 Results, etc.

Limitation: if you start with just a plain number (such as 1), the computer will just copy that number; it will *not* say 2, 3, 4, etc. If you start with just the plain number 1991, the computer will just copy that number; it will *not* say 1992, 1993, 1994, etc. To make the computer do more than just copy, include a word. For example, instead of saying just 1, say "Idiot 1"; then the computer will say "Idiot 2", "Idiot 3", "Idiot 4", etc. Instead of saying just 1991, say "Year 1991" or "1991 Results" or "People We Accidentally Shot In 1991"; then the computer will generate similar headings for 1992, 1993, etc.

Quattro Pro performs these extra tricks:

If you start with Jan,	the computer will say Feb, Mar, Apr, etc.
If you start with 29-Jan,	the computer will say 30-Jan, 31-Jan, 1-Feb, etc.
If you start with Oct-98,	the computer will say Nov-98, Dec-98, Jan-99, etc.
If you start with 29-Dec-98,	the computer will say 30-Dec-98, 31-Dec-98, 1-Jan-99, etc.
If you start with 29-Dec-99,	the computer will say 30-Dec-99, 31-Dec-99, 1-Jan-00, etc.
If you start with 10:00,	the computer will say 11:00, 12:00, 1:00, etc. (just in Quattro Pro 9)
If you start with 2nd Quarter,	the computer will say 3rd Quarter, 4th Quarter, 1st Quarter, etc.
If you start with 2nd Qtr,	the computer will say 3rd Qtr, 4th Qtr, 1st Qtr, etc.
If you start with 2 Q,	the computer will say 3 Q, 4 Q, 1 Q, etc.
If you start with Quarter 2,	the computer will say Quarter 3, Quarter 4, Quarter 1, etc.
If you start with 1st,	the computer will say 2nd, 3rd, 4th, etc.
If you start with 1st Idiot,	the computer will say 2nd Idiot, 3rd Idiot, 4th Idiot, etc.
If you start with 1,	the computer will say 2, 3, 4, etc.
If you start with 7,	the computer will say 8, 9, 10 etc.
If you start with -3,	the computer will say -2, -1, 0, etc.
If you start with 1991 Results,	the computer will say 1992 Results, 1993 Results, 1994 Results, etc.
If you start with 0.1,	the computer will say 0.2, 0.3, 0.4, etc.
If you start with 0.2,	the computer will say 0.4, 0.6, 0.8, etc.
If you start with 0.31,	the computer will say 0.62, 0.93, 1.24, etc.

Copy a formula's concept

If you ask the computer to copy a formula, the computer will copy the *concept* underlying the formula.

Here's an example:

> Suppose you put this formula in cell B4: =B2+B3. That means cell B4 contains "the sum of the two numbers above it". If you drag that cell's bottom right corner to the right, the computer will copy that formula's *concept* to the adjacent cells (C4, D4, E4, etc.).
>
> For example, the computer will make C4's formula be "the sum of the two numbers above it", by making C4's formula be =C2+C3. The computer will make D4's formula be =D2+D3. The computer will make E4's formula be =E2+E3.

Here's another example:

> Suppose cell B4 contains the formula =2*B3, so that B4 is "twice the cell above it". When the computer copies that concept to cell C4, the computer will make C4's formula be "twice the cell above it"; the computer will make C4's formula be =2*C3.

Here's another example:

> Suppose cell B4 contains the formula =2*A4, so that B4 is "twice the cell to the left of it". When the computer copies cell B4 to C4, the computer will make C4's formula be "twice the cell to the left of it"; the computer will make C4's formula be =2*B4.

Absolute addresses Notice again how copying from B4 to C4 turns the formula =B2+B3 into =C2+C3: it turns each B into a C.

If you want to prevent those changes, put dollar signs in the original formula. For example, if you want to prevent B3 from turning into D3, put dollar signs around the B3, so cell B4 contains this formula:

> =B2+$B$3

When you copy that cell to C4, the dollar signs prevents the computer from turning the B3 into C3; C4's formula will become =C2+$B$3 (instead of =C2+C3).

Here's how to type "=B2+$B$3" quickly. Type the "=" sign, then move the box to cell B2, then type the "+" sign. Finally, **create the $B$3 by using this trick: move the box to cell B3, then press the F4 key**. (In Quattro Pro, press the F4 key five times instead of once.) When you've finished creating the entire formula, press ENTER.

A cell's name (such as B3) is called the cell's **address**, because the cell's name tells you where to find the cell. An address that contains dollar signs (such as $B$3) is called an **absolute address**, because the address is absolutely fixed and will never change, not even when you copy the formula. An address that lacks dollar signs is called a **relative address**, because when you copy that address you'll be copying the cell's relationship to the other cells.

After you've finished

Finished creating your spreadsheet? Here's how to copy it to the disk and printer and move on to another task.

Find the buttons

Most spreadsheet programs have 4 buttons near the screen's top left corner:

> The first is the **New button**. It looks like a new blank sheet of paper.
> The second is the **Open button**. It looks like a file folder pried open.
> The third is the **Save button**. It looks like a 3½-inch floppy disk.
> The fourth is the **Print button**. It looks like a printer, printing on paper.

Each spreadsheet program is peculiar.

> Excel: the buttons are under the word "File"; Excel 2000 inserts a rather useless E-mail button
> Quattro Pro: the buttons are under the word "File"; the New button is rather useless
> Works 2000: the buttons are under the word "Tools"; the New and Open buttons are rather useless
> Works 4.5: Save and Print buttons are under the word "Window"; New and Open buttons are missing

Here's how to use the helpful buttons....

Save button

To save the spreadsheet (copy it onto the disk), click the **Save button**.

If you haven't saved the spreadsheet before, the computer will say "File Name". Invent a name for your spreadsheet. Type the name and press ENTER.

That makes the computer copy the spreadsheet onto the hard disk.

For example, if you named the spreadsheet "mary", here's what happens:

> Excel will make that spreadsheet be a file called mary.xls (which means "Mary's E**xcel s**preadsheet"). The computer will put that file into the My Documents folder.
>
> Quattro Pro 9 will make that spreadsheet be a file called mary.qpw (which means "Mary's **Q**uattro **P**ro **w**orkbook"). The computer will put that file into the My Documents folder.
>
> Quattro Pro 8 will make that spreadsheet be a file called mary.wb3 (which means "Mary's **w**ork**b**ook, type **3**"). The computer will put that file into the MyFiles folder.
>
> Works 2000 will make that spreadsheet be a file called mary.wks (which means "Mary's **w**ork**s**heet"). The computer will put that file into the My Documents folder.
>
> Works 4.5 will make that spreadsheet be a file called mary.wks (which means "Mary's **w**ork**s**heet"). The computer will put that file into the Documents folder that's in the MSWorks folder (which is in the Program Files folder), so the file will actually be called "C:\Program Files\MSWorks\Documents\mary.wks".

Afterwards, if you change your mind and want to do more editing, go ahead! When you finish that extra editing, save it by clicking the Save button again.

Save often If you're typing a long document, click the Save button about every 10 minutes. Click it whenever you get to a good stopping place and think, "What I've typed so far looks good!"

Then if an accident happens, you'll lose at most 10 minutes of work, and you can return to the last version you felt good about.

Print button

If you click the **Print button**, the printer will print your spreadsheet onto paper.

Page Setup

Here's a trick. Before clicking the Print button, try choosing **Page Setup** from the **File menu**. Then tell the computer what kind of printing you prefer. Here's how….

Works Click the **Margins** tab.

> Normally, the computer leaves 1-inch margins at the top and bottom of the paper and 1¼-inch margins at the sides. To change those sizes, press the TAB key and type the number of inches you want for the **Top Margin**, then do the same for the **Bottom Margin**, **Left Margin**, and **Right Margin**.

Click the tab called "Source, Size & Orientation".

> For **Orientation**, click either **Portrait** or **Landscape**. Normally, the computer does Portrait. If you click Landscape instead, the computer will rotate the spreadsheet 90 degrees, so more columns will fit on the paper.

Click **Other Options**.

> Normally, the computer doesn't bother to print the spreadsheet's gridlines (the lines that separate the columns from each other and the rows from each other). If you *insist* that the computer print the gridlines, put a check mark in the **Print Gridlines** box, by clicking that box.
>
> Normally, the computer doesn't bother to print the column names (A, B, C) and row names (1, 2, 3). If you *insist* that the computer print those names, put a check mark in the **Print Row and Column Headers** box, by clicking that box.

Quattro Pro Click **Paper Type**.

> Click either **Portrait** or **Landscape**. Normally, the computer does Portrait. If you click Landscape instead, the computer will rotate the spreadsheet 90 degrees, so more columns will fit on the paper.

Click **Header/Footer**.

> If your spreadsheet is several pages long, here's how to make the computer print "Budget, page 1" at the top of page 1, print "Budget, page 2" at the top of page 2, etc. Put a check mark in the first Create box, by clicking that box. To the right of that box is a bigger box; click it. In that bigger box, type "Budget, page #".

Click **Print Margins**.

> Normally, the computer leaves 0.33-inch margins at the top and bottom of the paper and 0.40-inch margins at the sides. To change those sizes, press the TAB key and type the number of inches you want for the **Top** margin, then do the same for the **Bottom** margin, **Left** margin, and **Right** margin.

Click **Print Scaling**.

> Have you ever taken a photo and asked for an "enlargement"? The computer can do the same thing: when it prints your spreadsheet onto paper, it can produce an enlargement (so you can read the spreadsheet even if you're standing far away from the sheet of paper). The computer can also produce a reduction (so the spreadsheet is made of tiny characters and consumes less paper). Enlargements and reductions are called **scaling**.
>
> Normally, the computer does *not* do scaling: it prints at 100% of original size. To make the computer do scaling, click the first **Print To** button, then double-click the number in the box to its right, then type a percentage different from 100%. For example, if you want the spreadsheet to look gigantic (twice as tall and twice as wide), type 200. If you want the spreadsheet to look tiny (miniaturized), type 50.
>
> If the spreadsheet has many rows and columns and you want to make the characters small enough so the entire spreadsheet fits on one sheet of paper, click the **Print To Desired Width** button instead.

Click **Options**.

> Normally, the computer doesn't bother to print the spreadsheet's gridlines (the lines that separate the columns from each other and the rows from each other). If you *insist* that the computer print the gridlines, put a check mark in the **Gridlines** box, by clicking that box.
>
> Normally, the computer doesn't bother to print the column names (A, B, C) and row names (1, 2, 3). If you *insist* that the computer print those names (and fill the top left corner by putting an extra A there), put a check mark in the **Row/Column Borders** box, by clicking that box.

Excel Click **Page**.

> For **Orientation**, click either **Portrait** or **Landscape**. Normally, the computer does Portrait. If you click Landscape instead, the computer will rotate the spreadsheet 90 degrees, so more columns will fit on the paper.
>
> Have you ever taken a photo and asked for an "enlargement"? The computer can do the same thing: when it prints your spreadsheet onto paper, it can produce an enlargement (so you can read the spreadsheet even if you're standing far away from the sheet of paper). The computer can also produce a reduction (so the spreadsheet is made of tiny characters and consumes less paper). Enlargements and reductions are called **Scaling**. Normally, the computer does *not* do scaling: it prints at 100% of original size. To make the computer do scaling, click the **Adjust To** button, then type a percentage different from 100%. For example, if you want the spreadsheet to look gigantic (twice as tall and twice as wide), type 200. If you want the spreadsheet to look tiny (miniaturized), type 50. If the spreadsheet has many rows and columns and you want to make the characters small enough so the entire spreadsheet fits on one sheet of paper, click the **Fit To** button instead.

Click **Margins**.

> Normally, the computer leaves 1-inch margins at the top and bottom of the paper and $3/4$-inch margins at the sides. To change those sizes, press the TAB key and type the number of inches you want for the **Top** margin, then do the same for the **Bottom** margin, **Left** margin, and **Right** margin.
>
> Normally, the computer starts printing the spreadsheet near the paper's top left corner. If you want the spreadsheet to be centered instead, put a check mark in the **Center Horizontally** and **Center Vertically** boxes, by clicking those boxes.

Click **Header/Footer**.

> If your spreadsheet is several pages long, here's how to make the computer print a page number at the top of each page: click the **Header** box's down-arrow, then click **Page 1**.
>
> If instead you want the top of each page to have this header —
>
> Annual blood drive   1999 results   by Count Dracula
>
> do this: click **Custom Header**, then type the left part ("Annual blood drive"), press the TAB key, type the center part ("1999 results"), press TAB again, type the right part ("by Count Dracula"), and click the OK button above the right part.

Click **Sheet**.

> Normally, the computer doesn't bother to print the spreadsheet's gridlines (the lines that separate the columns from each other and the rows from each other). If you *insist* that the computer print the gridlines, put a check mark in the **Gridlines** box, by clicking that box.
>
> Normally, the computer doesn't bother to print the column names (A, B, C) and row names (1, 2, 3). If you *insist* that the computer print those names, put a check mark in the **Row and column headings** box, by clicking that box.

Final step
When you finish expressing all your preferences to the computer, click OK. Then click the Print button. (For Quattro Pro, then press ENTER.)

Those preferences affect the printing of just the current spreadsheet. They don't affect other spreadsheets you create later.

Leave the spreadsheet

When you finish working on a spreadsheet, do this….

Quattro Pro Choose **Exit** or **Close** from the **File menu**.

> If you choose **Exit**, the computer stops using Quattro Pro.
>
> If you choose **Close** instead of Exit, you see a blank spreadsheet. Fill it in (to construct a new spreadsheet) or click the **Open button**.
>
> If you click the **Open button**, you see a list of old spreadsheets. If you want to *use* one of those spreadsheets, double-click the spreadsheet's name; the computer will put that spreadsheet onto the screen and let you edit it. If you want to *delete* one of those spreadsheets, click the spreadsheet's name and then press the DELETE key and then the ENTER key; the computer will move that spreadsheet to the Recycle Bin.

Excel Choose **Exit** or **Close** from the **File menu**.

> If you choose **Exit**, the computer stops using Excel.
>
> If you choose **Close** instead of Exit, the computer lets you work on another spreadsheet. Then click the **New button** or the **Open button**.
>
> If you click the **New button**, the computer lets you start typing a new spreadsheet.
>
> If you click the **Open button**, you see a list of old spreadsheets. If you want to *use* one of those spreadsheets, double-click the spreadsheet's name; the computer will put that spreadsheet onto the screen and let you edit it. If you want to *delete* one of those spreadsheets, click the spreadsheet's name and then press the DELETE key and then the ENTER key; the computer will move that spreadsheet to the Recycle Bin.

Works 4.5 Choose **Exit Works** or **Close** from the File menu.

> If you choose **Exit Works**, the computer stops using Microsoft Works.
>
> If you choose **Close** instead of Exit Works, the computer says "Works Task Launcher". Then click the **Spreadsheet button** or **Existing Documents**.
>
> If you click the **Spreadsheet button**, the computer lets you start typing a new spreadsheet.
>
> If you click **Existing Documents** and then double-click the name of an old spreadsheet, the computer puts that spreadsheet onto the screen and lets you edit it.

Works 2000 Click the **X** at the screen's top right corner. Then you have three choices:

> If you click the **X** at the screen's top right corner again, the computer stops using Microsoft Works.
>
> If you click **Programs** then **Start a blank Spreadsheet**, the computer lets you start typing a new spreadsheet.
>
> If you click **History**, you see a list of old spreadsheets (and other Works creations). If you want to *use* one of those spreadsheets, click the spreadsheet's name. If you want to *delete* one of those spreadsheets, *right*-click the spreadsheet's name (by using the mouse's *right* button) then click "Delete" then "Yes".

Didn't save? If you didn't save your document before doing those procedures, the computer asks, "Save changes?" (In Excel, the computer asks "Do you want to save?" instead.)

If you click "Yes", the computer copies your spreadsheet's most recent version to the hard disk; if you click "No" instead, the computer ignores and forgets your most recent editing.

Congratulations! You've learned all the fundamental spreadsheet commands!

Beautify your cells

Here's how to make the cells in your spreadsheet look beautiful.

First, if you're in the middle of typing a number or word, finish typing it and then press the ENTER key.

Next, **select which cells you want to beautify**. Here's how.

> To select **one cell**, click it.
> To select **several adjacent cells**, drag from the first cell you want to the last cell.
> To select **a whole rectangular area**, drag from one corner of rectangle to the opposite corner.
>
> To select **column D**, click the D.
> To select **columns D through G**, point at the D and drag to the G.
>
> To select **row 2**, click the number 2 at the left edge of row 2.
> To select **rows 2 through 5**, point at the 2 and drag to the 5.
>
> To select **the entire spreadsheet**, click the empty box that's left of the letter A.

When doing one of those selections, use the mouse.

The part of the spreadsheet you've selected is called the **selection** (or **range**). It has turned entirely dark, except for the cell where the box is. (In Excel 2000, "dark" is purple; in other spreadsheet programs, "dark" is black.)

> If your selection includes at least 2 numbers, Quattro Pro makes the screen's bottom right corner show you their statistics (sum, average, count, maximum, and minimum); Excel makes the screen's bottom show you just one statistic (either their sum, average, count, maximum, or minimum), which you can right-click to see a list of other statistics, from which you can click your favorite.

After you've made your **selection**, tell the computer how to beautify it. Choose one of the following forms of beauty....

Italic

To make all writing in the selection be italicized (*like this*), click the *I* button, which is near the screen's top.

> In Quattro Pro, the *I* button is above column C and under the word Tools.
> In Excel, the *I* button is above columns C and D and under the word Tools.
> In Works 4.5, the *I* button is above column E.
> In Works 2000, the *I* button is above column F.

Clicking the *I* button pushes the *I* button in. If you change your mind and want the writing *not* to be italicized, select the writing again (so it turns dark again), then click the *I* button again (so the button pops back out).

Bold

To make all writing in the selection be bold (**like this**), push in the **B** button, which is near the screen's top and next to the *I* button.

> In Excel and Quattro Pro, the **B** button is above column C.
> In Works 4.5, the **B** button is above column E.
> In Works 2000, the **B** button is above column F.

If you change your mind and want the writing *not* to be bold, select the writing again (so it turns dark again), then click the **B** button again (so the button pops back out).

To get bold italics, push in the bold button and also the italic button.

Underline

To make all writing in the selection be underlined (<u>like this</u>), push in the <u>U</u> button, which is near the screen's top and next to the I button.

> In Excel and Quattro Pro, the <u>U</u> button is above column D.
> In Works 4.5, the <u>U</u> button is above columns E and F.
> In Works 2000, the <u>U</u> button is above column F.

If you change your mind and want the writing *not* to be bold, select the writing again (so it turns dark again), then click the <u>U</u> button again (so the button pops back out).

Font size

Above column B, and below the word Format, you see the number 10.

To make all writing in the selection get bigger (like this), click the down-arrow that's to the right of that 10, then click a font size bigger than 10. (For example, click 14 or 16.)

To make your spreadsheet easier to read, use big writing for the column headings (such as January), the row headings (such as Income, Expenses, and Profit), any totals, and the bottom-line results (such as the $2000 profit).

Align

Here's how to make all writing in the selection be nudged slightly to the left or slightly to the right.

<u>Works</u> Click one of these three buttons:

Those buttons are near the top of the screen, above column F. Here's what those buttons do:

clicking the left button makes each cell's writing be flush left

> like this

clicking the center button makes each cell's writing be centered

> like this

clicking the right button makes each cell's writing be flush right

> like this

If you don't click any of the buttons, here's what happens:

> If the cell contains a **number** (or date or month),
> the computer puts it **flush right**.
>
> If the cell contains plain **words** instead,
> the computer puts them **flush left**.

In a simple spreadsheet, row 1 usually contains words that are column headings. Below those headings are numbers, which are flush right. **To align the headings with the numbers beneath them, make the headings be flush right also.** To do that, select row 1 (by clicking the 1), then click the right button.

<u>Excel</u> Click one of these three buttons:

Those buttons are near the top of the screen, above columns D and E. Here's what those buttons do:

clicking the left button makes each cell's writing be flush left

> like this

clicking the center button makes each cell's writing be centered

> like this

clicking the right button makes each cell's writing be flush right

> like this

If you don't click any of the buttons, here's what happens:

> If the cell contains a **word**,
> the computer puts the word **flush left**.
>
> If the cell contains a **number** instead,
> the computer puts the number **flush right**.

In a simple spreadsheet, row 1 usually contains words (such as January, February, and March). Those words are headings for columns of numbers. The numbers are flush right. **To align the headings with the numbers beneath them, make the headings be flush right also.** To do that, select row 1 (by clicking the 1), then click the right button.

<u>Quattro Pro</u> Type L, R, or E, while holding down the Ctrl key:

Pressing Ctrl with L makes each cell's writing be flush left

> like this

Pressing Ctrl with R makes each cell's writing be flush right

> like this

Pressing Ctrl with E makes each cell's writing be centered (equidistant)

> like this

If you don't click any of the buttons, here's what happens:

> If the cell contains a **word**, the computer puts the word **flush left**.
> If the cell contains a **number** instead, the computer puts the number **flush right**.

In a simple spreadsheet, row 1 usually contains words (such as January, February, and March). Those words are headings for columns of numbers. The numbers are flush right. **To align the headings with the numbers beneath them, make the headings be flush right also.** To do that, select row 1 (by clicking the 1), then press Ctrl with R.

Delete

To make all writing in the selection vanish (so it's erased), press the DELETE key.

Money

The computer can handle money.

<u>Works</u> To make each number in the selection look like dollars-and-cents, click the $ button. That makes the computer put a dollar sign before each number and put two digits after the decimal point. If the number is big, the computer inserts commas.

For example, if the number is 1538.4, the computer turns it into:

> $1,538.40

If the number is .739, the computer rounds it to:

> $0.74

If a number is negative (because you *lost* money instead of gained), the computer follows the tradition of accountants and the Internal Revenue Service: it puts the number in parentheses (instead of writing a minus sign). For example, if the number is -974.25, the computer writes:

> ($974.25)

<u>Excel</u> To make each number in the selection look like dollars-and-cents, click the $ button. That makes the computer put a dollar sign before each number and put two digits after the decimal point. If the number is big, the computer inserts commas.

For example, if the number is 1538.4, the computer turns it into:

> $1,538.40

If the number is .739, the computer rounds it to:

> $ 0.74

If a number is negative (because you *lost* money instead of gained), the computer follows the tradition of accountants and the Internal Revenue Service: it puts the number in parentheses (instead of writing a minus sign). For example, if the number is -974.25, the computer writes:

> $ (974.25)

When writing a number, the computer puts the dollar sign at the cell's left edge (flush left), so all dollar signs in that column will line up. The computer puts the digits (and parentheses) flush right, and widens the cell if necessary to make them all fit.

Near the $ button, you see a button that has a comma on it. Clicking the comma button has the same effect as clicking the $ button, except that the comma button does *not* make the computer write a dollar sign.

Quattro Pro To the right of the U button, you see a word (such as "Normal"). If you click that word, you see the **format-style menu**.

To make each number in the selection look like dollars-and-cents, choose "Currency" from the format-style menu.

For example, if the number is 1538.4, the computer turns it into:

```
$1,538.40
```

If the number is .739, the computer rounds it to:

```
$0.74
```

If the number is -974.25, version 9 puts the minus sign before the dollar sign —

```
-$974.25
```

but version 8 writes parentheses instead of a minus sign:

```
($974.25)
```

When writing a dollar-and-cents number, the computer widens the cell if necessary to make the dollar sign, commas, and digits all fit.

From the format-style menu, instead of choosing "Currency" you can choose one of these variants:

Variant	What the cell will show
"Currency"	money
"Comma"	money, but don't show any dollar sign
"Currency0"	money, rounded to the nearest dollar (so show no pennies, no decimal point)
"Comma0"	money, rounded to the nearest dollar, but don't show any dollar signs
"Fixed"	money, but show no dollar sign and no commas, show a minus sign instead of parentheses

Percent

The computer can handle percentages.

Excel To make each number in the selection look like percentage, click the % button. For example, if the number is .74, the computer turns it into 74%.

When writing the percentage, the computer doesn't write any decimal point. For example, if the number is .519, the computer rounds it to 52%.

Quattro Pro To make each number in the selection look like percentage, choose "Percent" from the format-style menu.

For example, if the number is .74, the computer turns it into 74%. When writing a percent, the computer shows two digits after the decimal point, so the computer shows:

```
74.00%
```

If the number is .51429, the computer turns it into 51.429% then rounds it to two digits after the decimal point, so you see:

```
51.43%
```

Works To make each number in the selection look like percentage, click "Format" then "Number" then "Percent" then OK.

For example, if the number is .74, the computer turns it into 74%. When writing a percent, the computer shows two digits after the decimal point, so the computer shows:

```
74.00%
```

If the number is .51429, the computer turns it into 51.429% then rounds it to two digits after the decimal point, so you see:

```
51.43%
```

Negatives If the number is negative the computer puts a negative sign in front.

Decimal places in Excel

I said that if you click Excel's $ or comma button, the computer normally puts two digits after the decimal point. If you click the % button, the computer normally puts no digits after the decimal point.

If you click the **Increase Decimal button** (which shows a .0 becoming a .00), the computer will put an extra digit after the decimal point. If you click it *several* times, the computer will put *several* extra digits after the decimal point.

If you click the **Decrease Decimal button** (showing a .00 becoming a .0) several times, the computer will put fewer digits after the decimal point. For example, here's how to round to the nearest dollar: click the $ button (which produces dollars and cents) and then twice click the Decrease Decimal button (which gets rid of the cents by rounding).

Font

Normally, the characters you type are in a font called **Arial**. To make all writing in the selection have a different font (such as Times Roman), click the down-arrow that's next to "Arial" then click whichever font you want.

These four fonts are especially popular:

This font is Arial. It's the normal font for spreadsheets.
It's plain and simple.

This font is Arial Narrow. It's thinner than Arial.
It lets you fit more characters in each cell, or fit more columns on each page.

This font is Arial Black. It's an extra-bold version of Arial.
It's good for column titles.

This font is Times New Roman. It's the easiest to read.
It's especially good if you're writing lots of words instead of numbers.

Text color

Normally, the characters you type are black. Here's how to make all characters in the selection be a different color (such as red).

Quattro Pro 9 Click the **Text Color button**, which shows a can of paint pouring onto an "a". You'll see 42 colors; click the color you want.

Quattro Pro 8 Look at the **Text Color button**, which shows a see-through can of paint pouring onto an "a". Notice the color of the paint in the can.

If it's the color you want, click the "a".

If it's *not* the color you want, do this instead: click the down-arrow that's to the right of the "a"; you'll see 16 colors; click the color you want.

Excel Near the screen's top right corner, you see the **Font Color button**, which has an underlined A on it. Notice the color of the A's underline.

If it's the color you want, click the underline.

If it's *not* the color you want, do this instead: click the down-arrow that's to the right of the A's underline; you'll see 40 colors; click the color you want.

Works Click **Format** then "**Font and Style**", then click the Color box's down-arrow. Look through the list of 15 colors, by using that list's scroll arrows. Click whichever color you want, then click OK.

Distortion Excel 2000 shows the text color perfectly. If you used a different spreadsheet program instead and selected *several* cells, some of those cells temporarily show distorted colors, until you click a single cell.

Background color

Normally, you type on a white background. Here's how to make the entire selection's background become a different color (such as yellow).

Quattro Pro 9 Click the **Background Color button**, which shows a can of paint pouring onto a cell. You'll see 42 colors; click the color you want.

Quattro Pro 8 Look at the **Background Color button**, which shows a see-through can of paint pouring onto a cell. Notice the color of the paint in the can.

If it's the color you want, click that paint can.

If it's *not* the color you want, do this instead: click the down-arrow that's to the right of the paint can; you'll see 42 colors; click the color you want.

Excel Near the screen's top right corner, you see the **Fill Color button**, which shows a paint can pouring onto a floor. Look at the floor's color.

If it's the color you want, click the paint can.

If it's *not* the color you want, do this instead: click the down-arrow that's to the right of the paint can; you'll see 40 colors; click the color you want.

Works Click **Format** then **Shading**. Underneath Pattern, click the solid black bar. Below the word "Foreground" (*not* "Background"), click the background color you want (after using the scroll arrows to see the complete list of 15 colors). Then click OK.

Distortion If you selected *several* cells, some of them temporarily show distorted colors, until you click a single cell.

Sort

This spreadsheet shows how three students (Zelda, Al, and Pedro) scored on a test:

	A	B	C	D	E	F	G	H
1	Student	Score						
2	Zelda	42						
3	Al	7						
4	Pedro	100						

Alphabetize In that list of students, Zelda is on the top; Pedro is on the bottom. Here's how to rearrange the rows, to put the students in alphabetical order (from A to Z).

Excel: click any student's name, then click the **Sort Ascending button** (which has an A above a Z).

Quattro Pro: click any student's name, then **Tools**, then **Sort**. Put ✔ in the "Selection contains a heading" box, then press ENTER.

Works: the rows involved in the sorting (rows 2, 3, and 4) are called the **data rows**. Make the data rows become black, by dragging from the 2 (at the beginning of row 2) to the 4 (at the beginning of row 4). Click **Tools** then **Sort**. (If the computer says "First-time Help", click OK.) Press ENTER.

That makes the spreadsheet become:

	A	B	C	D	E	F	G	H
1	Student	Score						
2	Al	7						
3	Pedro	100						
4	Zelda	42						

Increasing scores Here's how to rearrange the rows, to put the scores in numerical order (starting with the lowest score and ending with the highest).

Excel: click any score, then click the **Sort Ascending button** (which has an A above a Z).

Quattro Pro: click any score, then **Tools**, then **Sort**. Put ✔ in the "Selection contains a heading" box, then press ENTER.

Works: blacken the data rows, by dragging from the 2 (at the beginning of row 2) to the 4 (at the beginning of row 4). Click **Tools** then **Sort**. (If the computer says "First-time Help", click OK.) Make the **Sort By** box say "Column B" (by clicking the Sort By box's down-arrow and then clicking "Column B"). Press ENTER.

That makes the spreadsheet become:

	A	B	C	D	E	F	G	H
1	Student	Score						
2	Al	7						
3	Zelda	42						
4	Pedro	100						

Decreasing scores Here's how to make the computer put the scores in *reverse* numerical order (from highest score to lowest score).

Excel: click any score, then click the **Sort Descending button** (which has a Z above an A).

Quattro Pro: click any score, then **Tools**, then **Sort**. Put ✔ in the "Selection contains a heading" box, remove ✔ from the first Ascending box (by clicking), then press ENTER.

Works: blacken the data rows, by dragging from the 2 (at the beginning of row 2) to the 4 (at the beginning of row 4). Click **Tools** then **Sort**. (If the computer says "First-time Help", click OK.) Make the **Sort By** box say "Column B" (by clicking the Sort By box's down-arrow and then clicking "Column B"). Click the **Descending button**. Press ENTER.

That makes the spreadsheet become:

	A	B	C	D	E	F	G	H
1	Student	Score						
2	Pedro	100						
3	Zelda	42						
4	Al	7						

That list is useful, since it puts the winners at the top and the losers at the bottom.

Chart

You can graph your data. In modern spreadsheet programs (such as Excel, Quattro Pro, and Works), graphs are called **charts**.

For example, suppose you want to graph the data from a company you run. Your company sells Day-Glo Pink Hair Dye. (Your motto is: "To brighten your day, stay in the pink!")

You have two salespeople, Joe and Sue. Joe's worked for you a long time, and sells about $8,000 worth of dye each month. Sue joined your company recently and is rapidly improving at encouraging people to turn their hair pink. She does that by inventing slogans for various age groups, such as

"Feminine babes wear pink!"
"You look so sweet, hair as pink as cotton candy!"
"Don't be a dink! Think pink!"
"Pink is punk!"
"Pink means *I'll be your Valentine, but lighten up!*"
"Be what you drink — a Pink Lady!"
"Let the sexy, slinky, pink panther inside you glow!"
"Love is a pink Cadillac — with hair to match!"
"When in a sour mood, look like a pink grapefruit!"

This spreadsheet shows how many dollars worth of dye Joe and Sue sold each month:

	A	B	C	D	E	F	G
1		January	February	March			
2	Joe	8000	6500	7400			
3	Sue	2000	4300	12500			

The spreadsheet shows that Joe sold $8000 worth of dye in January, $6500 in February, and $7400 in March.

Sue's a trainee. She sold just $2000 worth in January, but her monthly sales zoomed up to $12500 by March.

Here's how to turn that spreadsheet into a graph (chart).

Chart in Excel

First, type the spreadsheet.

Next, format the numbers. To do that, drag from the first number (cell B2) to the last number (cell D3), click the $ button (to put dollar signs in front of the numbers), then twice click the Decrease Decimal button (to round to the nearest dollar). The spreadsheet becomes this:

	A	B	C	D	E	F	G
1		January	February	March			
2	Joe	$ 8,000	$ 6,500	$ 7,400			
3	Sue	$ 2,000	$ 4,300	$ 12,500			

Tell the computer which cells to graph. To do that, drag from the blank starting cell (A1) to the *last number* (cell D3). Drag just to *that cell*, since the computer gets confused if you drag across extra cells or rows or columns.

Click the Chart Wizard button, which is near the screen's top right corner and shows colored vertical bars.

Press the ENTER key 4 times. Then the computer draws the graph. (If part of it is covered by a Chart window, make that window disappear, by clicking its X button.)

The graph is part of your spreadsheet, so your spreadsheet looks like this:

	A	B	C	D	E	F	G
1		January	February	March			
2	Joe	$ 8,000	$ 6,500	$ 7,400			
3	Sue	$ 2,000	$ 4,300	$ 12,500			
4							
5							
6							
7							
8							
9							
10							
11							
12							
13							
14							
15							
16							

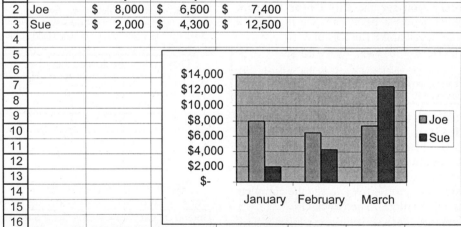

Print If you click the Print button, your printer will print the entire spreadsheet, including the graph!

Save If you click the Save button, your hard disk will store a copy of the entire spreadsheet, including the graph.

Edit If you change the numbers in the spreadsheet's cells, the graph will change too, automatically!

The entire graph is inside a white box. Try this experiment: click inside that white box, but near the box's outer edge. Then you'll see 8 tiny black squares at the white box's edges. Those tiny black squares are called **handles**; they mean the white box is **selected**. Four of those handles are at the corners; they're called the **corner handles**.

To change the size of the box (and the graph inside it), drag one of the corner handles.

To delete the box (and the graph inside it), press the DELETE key.

To move the box (and the graph inside it), put the mouse inside the box and near (but not on) a corner handle, then drag in the direction you want to box to move.

Chart in Quattro Pro

First, type the spreadsheet.

Tell the computer which cells to graph. To do that, drag from the blank starting cell (A1) to the *last number* (cell D3). Drag just to *that cell*, since the computer gets confused if you drag across extra cells or rows or columns.

Click the QuickChart button. (It has vertical bars on in. In Quattro Pro 9, it's under the word "Window"; in Quattro Pro 8, it's under the word "Tools".)

Click in a blank cell where you want the graph's top left corner to be. (For example, click in cell A4.) Then the computer draws the graph.

Print If you click the Print button, your printer will print the entire spreadsheet, including the graph!

Save If you click the Save button, your hard disk will store a copy of the entire spreadsheet, including the graph.

Edit If you change the numbers in the spreadsheet's cells, the graph will change too, automatically!

The entire graph is in a white box. Try this experiment: click outside the white box, then click the white box's edge. You'll see 8 tiny black squares at the white box's edges. Those tiny black squares are called **handles**; they mean the white box is **selected**. After you've selected the white box, you can do this:

To change the size of the box (and the graph inside it), drag one of the handles.
To move the box (and the graph inside it), drag one of the edges (but not at one of the handles).
To delete the box (and the graph inside it), press the DELETE key.

Chart in Works

First, type the spreadsheet.

Next, format the numbers. To do that, drag from the first number (cell B2) to the last number (cell D3), then click the $ button (to put dollar signs in front of the numbers). The spreadsheet becomes this:

	A	B	C	D	E	F	G
1		January	February	March			
2	Joe	$8,000.00	$6,500.00	$7,400.00			
3	Sue	$2,000.00	$4,300.00	$12,500.00			

Tell the computer which cells to graph. To do that, drag from the blank starting cell (A1) to the *last number* (cell D3). Drag just to *that cell*, since the computer gets confused if you drag across extra cells or rows or columns.

Click the New Chart button, which is near the screen's top right corner and shows vertical bars. (If the computer says "First-time Help", press ENTER.)

The computer says "New Chart". Press ENTER. Then the computer draws the graph on the screen, in a window called Chart1. That window covers up the spreadsheet, so you can't see the spreadsheet. To see the spreadsheet again, choose **Spreadsheet** from the View menu. Then you see the spreadsheet again, but don't see the chart. To see the chart again, choose **Chart** from the View menu, then press ENTER.

Edit If you change the numbers in the spreadsheet's cells, the graph will change too, automatically!

Print While the graph is on the screen, you can print it onto paper by clicking the Print button. On paper, the computer makes the graph be taller, so it consumes nearly the entire sheet of paper.

Save If you click the Save button, your hard disk will store a copy of the entire spreadsheet, including the graph.

DATABASES

What's a database?

A **database program** is a program that manipulates lists of facts. It can store information about your friends & enemies, customers & suppliers, employees & stockholders, students & teachers, hobbies & libraries. It puts all that data about your life and business onto a disk, which acts as an electronic filing cabinet. Then it lets you retrieve the data easily. It can generate mailing lists, phone directories, sales reports, and any other analyses you wish.

It's called a **database program** or **database management system (DBMS)** or **information retrieval system**. The terms are synonymous.

File-cabinet jargon

In an old-fashioned office that lacks a computer, you'll see a filing cabinet containing several drawers. One drawer's labeled CUSTOMERS; another drawer's labeled EMPLOYEES; another drawer's labeled SUPPLIERS. Each drawer contains alphabetized index cards.

For example, the drawer labeled CUSTOMERS contains a card about each customer; the first card might be labeled "ADAMS, JOAN"; the last card might be labeled "ZABRONSKI, JILL". The first card contains all known information about Joan Adams: it contains her name, address, phone number, everything she bought, how much she paid, how much she still owes, and other personal information about her. That card is called her **record**. Each item of information on that card is called a **field**.

If the card is a pre-printed form, it allows a certain amount of space for each item: for example, it might allow only 30 characters for the person's name. The number of characters allowed for a field is called the **field's width**. In that example, the width of the NAME field is 30 characters.

Each drawer is called a **file**. For example, the drawer that contains information about customers is called the **customer file**; another drawer is the **employee file**; another drawer is the **supplier file**.

The entire filing cabinet — which contains all the information about your company — is called the **database**.

A sample file

Here's a file about amazing students in the School of Life:

```
Last name: Smith                    First name: Suzy
Age: 4              Class: 12
Comments: Though just 4 years old, she finished high school because she's fast.

Last name: Bell                     First name: Clara
Age: 21             Class: 10
Comments: The class clown, she never graduated but had fun trying. Super-slow!

Last name: Smith                    First name: Buffalo Bob
Age: 7              Class: 2
Comments: Boringly normal, he's jealous of his sister Suzy. Always says "Howdy!"

Last name: Kosinski                 First name: Stanislaw
Age: 16             Class: 11
Comments: He dislikes Polish jokes.

Last name: Ketchopf                 First name: Heinz
Age: 57             Class: 1
Comments: His pour grades make him the slowest Ketchopf in the West.

Last name: Nixon                     First name: Tricky Dick
Age: 78             Class: 13
Comments: The unlucky President, he disappointed our country.

Last name: Walter                    First name: Russy-poo
Age: 53             Class: 0
Comments: This guy has no class.
```

That file consists of seven records: Suzy Smith's record, Clara Bell's record, Buffalo Bob Smith's record, Stanislaw Kosinski's record, Heinz Ketchopf's record, Tricky Dick Nixon's record, and Russy-poo Walter's record.

Each record consists of five fields: last name, first name, age, class, and comments. The age and class fields are narrow; the comments field is very wide.

Database programs versus word processing

Like a word processing program, a database program lets you type info, put it onto a disk, edit it, and copy it onto paper.

In a word processing system, the info's called a **document**, consisting of paragraphs which in turn consist of sentences. In a database system, the info's called a **file** (instead of a document); it consists of records, which in turn consist of fields.

Since a database program resembles a word processor, a word processor can act as a crummy database program. A *good* database program offers the following extras, which the typical word processor lacks....

A good database program can alphabetize, put info into numerical order, and check for criteria. For example, you can tell it to check which customers are women under 18 who have light red hair and live in a red-light district, make it print their names and addresses on mailing labels in ZIP-code order, and make it print a phone book containing their names and numbers. Database programs are very potent and can be nasty tools for invading people's privacy!

Competitors

Many database programs have been invented.

PFS

Most database programs are hard to use. In 1980, John Page invented the first *easy* database program. He called it the **Personal Filing System (PFS)**.

> It ran on Apple 2 computers. He developed it while sitting in his garage.
>
> He showed the program to two friends: Fred Gibbons and Janelle Bedke. The three of them tried to find a company willing to market his program, but no company was interested, so they decided to market the program themselves by forming a company, **Software Publishing Corporation**.
>
> The program became very popular. Software Publishing Corporation became a multi-million-dollar corporation. It developed improved versions of PFS for the Apple 2 family, Radio Shack models 3 & 4, Commodore 64, Mac, and IBM PC. Now the fanciest version of PFS is **Professional File**, which runs on the IBM PC.
>
> The company also invented a word processor, whose IBM version is called **Professional Write**. It works well with Professional File. Discount dealers sell Professional Write for $142; when you buy it, you get Professional File free!
>
> You can write a memo by using Professional Write and build a mailing list by using Professional File. Then use those programs together to print personalized copies of your memo to everybody on your mailing list.
>
> Software Publishing Corporation has invented an even easier program, called **PFS First Choice**. It includes the easiest parts of both Professional File and Professional Write. It also includes spreadsheets, graphics, and telecommunication.
>
> In 1988, John Page and Janelle Bedke got bored and quit the company. Fred Gibbons and the rest of his staff hung on but sold PFS First Choice to **Spinnaker**, which later became part of **Softkey**, which later became part of **The Learning Company**, which later became part of the **Mattel** toy company, so now PFS First Choice is owned by The Learning Company (division of Mattel), which you can reach at 617-494-1200.

Q&A

Inspired by the PFS series, a new company called **Symantec** developed a similar program, called **Q&A**.

At first glance, Q&A seems to just imitate the PFS series, since Q&A uses almost the same commands and keystrokes as the first IBM version of PFS. But Q&A understands many extra commands, making Q&A much more powerful than the PFS series. Q&A handles just two topics — databases and word processing — but very well! It's fairly easy (almost as easy as the PFS series) and powerful enough to handle the computing needs of most businesses. Q&A is the database program I use to run my own business.

> The best versions of Q&A is called **Q&A version 5 for DOS**. You can get it for $199 (plus $15 shipping) from **Professional Computer Technology Associates** in Pennsylvania at 215-598-8440.

Reflex

Reflex was the first database program to let you view your data in five ways: it lets you see a **form view** (a filled-in form showing a record), a **list view** (a large spreadsheet showing the entire file), a **graph view** (a graph of all the data), a **report view** (a report on the entire file, with subtotals), and a **crosstab view** (a table of totals for statisticians).

> Reflex can show you many views simultaneously, by dividing your screen into windows. As you edit the view in one window, the views in other windows change simultaneously. For example, if one window shows numbers and another window shows a graph, the graph changes automatically as you edit the numbers.
>
> Reflex is partly a database program and partly a spreadsheet. Many of Reflex's features were copied by Microsoft's spreadsheet, Excel.
>
> Reflex is published by Borland; but Borland given up trying to market it anymore, because the competition from Q&A and other database programs is too fierce.

Relational databases

Reflex is a **simple flat-file system**, which means it manipulates just one file at a time. Q&A goes a step further: while you're editing a file, Q&A lets you insert data from a second file.

Software that goes even further than Q&A and lets you edit two files simultaneously is called a **relational database program** (or **relational database management system** or **relational DBMS**).

> The most popular relational database programs for DOS are **DBASE**, **FOXPRO**, and **Paradox**. You can customize them to meet *any* need, because they include complete programming languages.
>
> Another relational database program for DOS is **Alpha 4**. It lets you accomplish some tasks more easily than DBASE, FOXPRO, and Paradox but lacks a programming language.

Windows wars

Programmers have been trying to invent database programs for Windows. Going beyond DOS programs such as Q&A, Windows database programs let the screen display pretty fonts and photographs.

> The first popular Windows database program was **Approach**, which is now published by the Lotus division of IBM.
>
> Borland has invented Windows versions of **DBASE** and **Paradox** and a new Windows database program called **Delphi**. Microsoft has invented a Windows version of **FOXPRO** and a new Windows database program called **Microsoft Access**. Alpha Software has invented **Alpha 5**, which resembles Alpha 4 but handles Windows and is also programmable.
>
> The most popular database program for the Mac is **FileMaker Pro**. It's as easy as Q&A! It's published by the FileMaker company, which is owned by Apple but has had the good sense to also invent a Windows version of FileMaker Pro.
>
> **Microsoft Works** includes a database program that's very limited. For example, it can't handle big mailing lists, since it's limited to 32,000 records.

Symantec invented a Windows version of **Q&A**, but Q&A's Windows version is hated by everybody.

> It's worse than the DOS version and worse than all other major Windows databases. If you use Q&A, stick with Q&A's DOS version.

Though Q&A for Windows is terrible, the other Windows database programs are fine. Here's the hierarchy:

> The simplest Windows database program is the database part of **Microsoft Works**, but it comes with no instruction manual and you'll outgrow the program's abilities.
>
> The next step up is **FileMaker Pro**. It's wonderful! People who buy it love it. It's more powerful than the Microsoft Works database — it performs more tricks and handles a wider variety of problems. It comes with a decent instruction manual.
>
> The next step up is **Approach**. By a "step up", I mean it's more powerful than the Microsoft Works database and Filemaker Pro — it performs more tricks and handles a wider variety of problems — but it's also more complex (harder to learn & use). Unlike Microsoft Works and Filemaker Pro, it's relational. But it's still not programmable.
>
> The next step up (in power and complexity) is **Alpha 5**. It's relational and also programmable! But its programming language is small.
>
> The next step up is **Microsoft Access**. Its programming language is bigger.
>
> The next step up is the triumvirate: the Windows versions of **DBASE**, **FOXPRO**, and **Paradox**. They're powerful, fancy, and more than most folks can understand. If you buy one of them, you'll probably admire the big box it comes in, put it on the shelf, and invite friends to visit you and admire your big box, but you'll never figure out how to use it.

What to buy

To make your life *easy*, get one of the *easy* database programs: Q&A for DOS, Microsoft Works, or FileMaker Pro. Go beyond them just if your database needs are too complex for them to handle.

> Even if your database needs are complex, begin by practicing with an *easy* database program first, so you master database fundamentals easily and quickly without getting distracted by needlessly complex details.
>
> Complex database programs are like sneakers with untied shoelaces: though their overall design can let you perform amazing feats, you'll probably trip, get bloodied, and have to call in a computer "first-aid squad", which is a team of high-priced computer consultants.
>
> To avoid the need for consultants, use Microsoft Works, FileMaker Pro, or Q&A.

FileMaker Pro

Many database programs have been invented. In general, the best one to use is **FileMaker Pro**. It's published by the FileMaker company, which is owned by Apple. It's the most popular database program for Macintosh computers, and a Windows version is also available.

Like Q&A, it's easy to learn how to use. It has two main advantages over Q&A: it can handle databases that are more advanced, and its Windows version is excellent. (Q&A's Windows version is terrible.) FileMaker Pro has been nicknamed "Q&A for Windows, done right." It's also been nicknamed "Microsoft Access, made reasonable" (because Microsoft Access is unreasonably hard).

The newest version of FileMaker Pro is **FileMaker Pro 5**.

It lists for $249, but you can get it for just $149 by getting the upgrade instead of the standard full version; the upgrade is valid if you already own a database program such as Microsoft Access. You get a $25 rebate if you buy a version for Windows, $50 rebate if you buy a version for the Mac.

I'll explain how to use FileMaker Pro 5. I'll explain the Mac version and also the Windows version.

Copy FileMaker to the hard disk

FileMaker Pro 5 comes on a CD-ROM disk, which you must copy to your computer's hard disk.

For the Mac version, do this:

Turn on the computer without any floppy or CD-ROM disks in the drives.
Put the FileMaker Pro 5 CD-ROM disk into the CD-ROM drive. Double-click "Start Here". Press the RETURN key twice.
The computer says "Personalization". Type your name, press the TAB key, type your company's name (if any), press the TAB key. Type your 17-digit Installation Code Number (which is on a white sticker; that sticker came on a big sheet of paper with the CD-ROM disk and should be transferred to the back of the CD-ROM disk's white envelope). Press the RETURN key.
The computer says "Installation was successful". Choose Eject from the Special menu. Remove the CD-ROM disk from the drive, then close the drive's door.

For the Windows version, do this instead:

Turn on the computer without any floppy or CD-ROM disks in the drives, so the computer runs Windows 95 (or 98) and the computer's bottom left corner says Start.
Put the FileMaker Pro 5 CD-ROM disk into the CD-ROM drive. In the phrase "➔ Install FileMaker Pro 5", click the right-arrow that begin the phrase.
The computer says "FileMaker Pro 5 Installation". Press ENTER four times.
The computer says "Personalization". While holding down the Ctrl key, tap the DELETE key (so you erase the word "User"). Type your name, press the TAB key, type your company's name (if any), press the TAB key. Type your 17-digit Installation Code Number (which is on a white sticker; that sticker came on a big sheet of paper with the CD-ROM disk and should be transferred to the back of the CD-ROM disk's white envelope). Press ENTER twice.
The computer says "Installation Completed". Press ENTER twice.

Launch FileMaker Pro

For the Mac version, do this:

Double-click "Macintosh HD" then "FileMaker Pro 5 Folder" then "FileMaker Pro".

For the Windows version, do this instead:

Click "Start" then "Programs" then "FileMaker Pro 5" then "FileMaker Pro".

Mac versus Windows

Now I'm going to explain how to use the Mac version. The Windows version works the same way, except for minor headaches (which I'll explain later) and these keyboard differences:

The Mac has a clearly marked RETURN key.
In Windows, the RETURN key says "Enter" on it.

The Mac has a clearly marked CONTROL key.
In Windows, the CONTROL key says "Ctrl" on it.

The Mac has a COMMAND key (which shows a squiggly cloverleaf and an Apple). Windows doesn't have COMMAND key, so use the Windows "Ctrl" key instead.

Create a database

Click "Create a new empty file" then "OK".
For our first experiment, let's create this database:

First name	Sue
Last name	Smith
Comments	wiggles her toes

First name	Sam
Last name	Smith
Comments	picks his nose

First name	Tina
Last name	Ash
Comments	the class clown

First name	Tina
Last name	Smith
Comments	incredible

Here's how to create it....

Invent a name for your database (such as "Friends"). Type the name. **At the end of the name, press the RETURN key** (which in Windows is marked "Enter").

If the computer says the file "already exists", do this procedure:

Press RETURN. Type a different name instead (such as "Friends2" or "Buddies" or "Pals" or "Enemies") and then press RETURN. If the computer says the file "already exists" again, do this whole procedure again.

Define fields The computer says "Define Fields".
We're trying to create a database that has three fields, called "First name", "Last name", and "Comments". To accomplish that, type the words "First name", then press RETURN, then type the words "Last name", then press RETURN again, then type the word "Comments", then press RETURN again.

Above your typing, you see this list of fields you created:

Field name	Type	Options
First name	Text	
Last name	Text	
Comments	Text	

Click "Done".

Enter data You see this blank form:

First name	
Last name	
Comments	

Into that form, type a person's record. Here's how: type the person's first name ("Sue"), press the TAB key, type the person's last name ("Smith"), press the TAB key, and type the comment ("wiggles her toes"), so the form looks like this:

First name	Sue
Last name	Smith
Comments	wiggles her toes

That's Sue Smith's record! When you've finished typing it, and want **to start typing the next person's record, do this: tap the N key while holding down the COMMAND key** (which on a Mac shows a squiggly cloverleaf and Apple, and in Windows says "Ctrl".) That makes the computer start a new record, so the computer shows you a new blank form, where you can fill in the details for the next person (Sam Smith). The screen shows just one record at a time: while you're typing Sam Smith's record, you don't see Sue Smith's record.

When you've finished typing Sam Smith's record, press COMMAND with N again, so you see another blank form, so you can type the next person's record (Tina Ash's). Then press COMMAND with N again, then type Tina Smith's record.

While you're typing those records, the computer automatically copies them to the hard disk. (You don't have to click any "Save button".)

When you've finished typing all the records, congratulations! You've created a database!

View your data

To view the data you typed, you can use several tricks.

CONTROL key To go back and view the previous record, press CONTROL with up-arrow (which means do this: while pressing the CONTROL key, tap the up-arrow key). To view the next record, press CONTROL with down-arrow. (In Windows, the CONTROL key says "Ctrl" on it.)

So in Windows, *while pressing the Ctrl key* you can do this:

> tap the up-arrow key to view the previous record
> tap the down-arrow key to view the next record
> tap the N key to create a new record

Rolodex At the screen's right edge, under the word "Layout", you see a picture of a **Rolodex** (which is a device that displays business cards). **The Rolodex shows two business cards** (except that the words on the cards are too small to read).

> To go back and view the previous record, click the top card.
> To view the next record, click the bottom card.

Below the Rolodex, you see two numbers:

> The first number says which record you're viewing. (For example, while you're viewing record #3, which is Tina Ash's record, that number is 3.)

> The bottom number says how many records there are in the whole database.

Try this experiment: look at the first number (which is the number of the record you're viewing). If you change that number to a different number (such as 2), the computer will hop to record 2. Here's how to change the number:

> Method 1: click the number, then type the number you want instead (and press RETURN).

> Method 2: drag the slider (which is above the number).

TAB key While you're viewing a record, you can edit the data by retyping it.

> To move to the next field, press the TAB key.
> To move back to the previous field, press SHIFT with TAB.

Delete While you're typing, here's how to delete:

> To delete a character, click after it (on a Mac) or before it (in Windows), then press the DELETE key.

> To delete an entire word, double-click it then press the DELETE key.
> To delete an entire line, triple-click it then press the DELETE key.
> To eliminate (delete) the entire record, press COMMAND with E, then press D.

Three views If you click "View" (which is near the screen's top), you see these choices:

> View as Form
> View as List
> View as Table

The normal choice is "**View as Form**", which shows you just one person's record at a time.

If you click "**View as List**" instead, you see the first person's record, and down from it you see the second person's record, and down from it you see the third person's record, etc., so you see many records on the screen at once. If there are too many records to fit on your screen, you can see the other records by using the window's scroll arrows (or the PAGE DOWN and PAGE UP keys or your mouse's wheel).

If you click "**View as Table**" instead, you see the database as a table looking like this:

First name	Last name	Comments
Sue	Smith	wiggles her toes
Sam	Smith	picks his nose
Tina	Ash	the class clown
Tina	Smith	incredible

At the top of each column, you see the column's heading (field name). To the right of the column's heading, you see a vertical gridline separating that heading from the next column's heading. To widen the column (so you can see longer words), drag that gridline toward the right (by using your mouse). To narrow the column (so the column consumes less space and you can fit more columns onto the screen), drag that gridline back toward the left. Changing the column's width does *not* change the data; it changes just the table's view of it; the other views show that the data is unchanged.

Mouse wheel If the computer is trying to display more records than can fit on the screen, and your mouse has a wheel between its buttons, do this:

> Rotate the wheel away from you to view earlier records.
> Rotate the wheel toward you to view later records.

Find

Here's how to find everybody whose last name is Smith:

> Say "find" by pressing COMMAND with F.
> Click in the "Last name" box, type "smith", and press RETURN.

That makes the computer show you the records of just the people whose last name is Smith.

> You can view them however you wish: from the View menu, choose "View as Form" or "View as List" or "View as Table".

> I recommend choosing "View as Table", since it shows you all relevant records at once. (If you choose "View as Form", you see just one Smith at a time; to see the next Smith, press CONTROL with down-arrow.)

You see the Smiths but not Tina Ash, since she's not a Smith. You see a **filtered database**, where the Smiths are still visible but Tina Ash has been filtered out and is invisible.

Here's how to find everybody whose first name is Tina:

> Say "find" by pressing COMMAND with F.
> Click in the "First name" box, type "tina", and press RETURN.

That makes the computer show you the records of just the people whose first name is Tina. You see Tina Ash's record and Tina Smith's record, but not Sue Smith, not Sam Smith.

When in doubt about which records to show you, the computer is generous and shows you many:

> If you tell the computer to find everybody whose last name is "smith", the computer will show you every "Smith" and also everybody whose last name begins with "Smith", such as "Smithson" and "Smithers" and "Smithers Jr., MD". If you tell the computer to find everybody whose last name is "sm", the computer will show you everybody whose last name begins with "sm", such as "Smith" and "Smythe" and "Smyers" and "smells so bad I forgot his last name". If you tell the computer to find everybody whose comment is "clown", the computer will show you everybody whose comment includes the word "clown", such as Tina Ash (whose comment is "the class clown") and anybody whose comment mentions "clown" or "clowns" or "clowning" or "clowned". If you tell the computer to find everybody whose first name is "ti", the computer will show you everybody whose first name is "Tina" or "Tim" or "Timothy" or "the amazing Timothy" or "His Esteemed Majesty Timothy".

Here's the rule:

> If you tell the computer to search in a field for a word, the computer will show every record where that field contains the word (or contains a longer word beginning with the same letters).

If you tell the computer to find certain records, the computer will filter the database and keep showing you just those records, until you tell the computer to find different records instead, or until you **say "jumbo" (by pressing COMMAND with J), which makes the computer show you the entire jumbo database again**, unfiltered.

Two fields at once (how to say "and") You can search two fields at once. For example, to search for Tina Smith's record, do this:

> Say "find" by pressing COMMAND with F.
>
> Type "tina" (in the "First name" box), press TAB (to go to the "Last name" box), type "smith", and press RETURN.

How to say "or" Here's how to search for people whose first name is "Sue" or "Tina":

> Say "find" by pressing COMMAND with F.
> Type "sue" (in the "First name" box).
> Say "new search" by pressing COMMAND with N.
> Type "tina" (in the "First name" box) and press RETURN.

That makes the computer show the records of all people named "Sue" or "Tina" (not "Sam").

How to say "not" Here's how to search for people whose first name is not "Sam":

> Say "find" by pressing COMMAND with F.
> Type "sam" (in the "First name" box).
> Say "not" (by clicking the Omit box, which is at the screen's left edge).
> Press RETURN.

That makes the computer omit Sam, so the computer will show the records of all people not named "Sam". (You'll see the records for "Sue" and "Tina".) Sam is still in the database, but he's not shown (until you do a different "find" instead).

Alphabetize

Here's how to alphabetize (sort) the records.

First, get a good view of how the records are currently organized (by clicking "View" then "View as Table").

Decide which records you want to include. (If you want to include just *some* of the records, filter them, by pressing COMMAND with F and then saying which records you want. If you want to include *all* the records, making sure they're unfiltered, by pressing COMMAND with J.)

Now you see a table of the records you want to alphabetize.

Say "Sort" by pressing COMMAND with S.

You see two big white boxes.

Make sure the right-hand "big white box" is empty. (If it's not, click "Clear All".)

The left "big white box" contains a list of field names.

To alphabetize the records, let's make the computer look at each person's last name and put the last names in alphabetical order. If two people have the same last name, let's make the computer look at their first names and put their first names in alphabetical order. So here's the rule:

> Sort by last name. If two people have the same last name, sort them by first name.

Here's how to say that:

> Click "Last name" then "Move".
> Click "First name" then "Move".

Press RETURN. The computer alphabetizes the table by Last name, then First name, so the table becomes this:

First name	Last name	Comments
Tina	Ash	the class clown
Sam	Smith	picks his nose
Sue	Smith	wiggles her toes
Tina	Smith	incredible

Those records will remain sorted until you give a different sort command or you unsort them (by pressing COMMAND with S and then clicking "Unsort"). Warning: if you edit those records or add extra records, they won't be accurately sorted until you give the sort command again.

Print

Here's how to print records onto paper.

Say which records to print:

> If you want to include just *some* of the records, filter them (by pressing COMMAND with F and then saying which records you want). If you want to print *all* the records, making sure they're unfiltered (by pressing COMMAND with J).
>
> If you want the records to be sorted, sort them (by pressing COMMAND with S and then saying which fields to sort on).

Say which view you want to print:

> Click "View", then click either "View as List" or "View as Table".
> (If you click "View as Form", the computer will print a "View as List" instead.)

Say "Print" (by pressing COMMAND with P or clicking the Print button).

For the Mac, proceed as follows:

> You see your printer's window. Click "Records being browsed" — unless you change your mind and want to print something else.

For Windows, proceed as follows instead:

> You see the Print window. In it, the first box is labeled "Print". In that Print box, make sure you see "Records being browsed". If you see something else, click that box's down-arrow, then click "Records being browsed" — unless you change your mind and want to print something else.

The typical choices are "Records being browsed", "Current record", "Blank record, showing fields", and "Field definitions".

Make sure the printer is turned on and contains paper. **Press RETURN.** Then the printer will print on paper.

Final steps

When you finish using the Friends database, close the Friends window. (In Windows, do that by clicking the Friends window's X button.) Then you have three choices:

> **To start creating a different database, click the New button** (which is near the screen's top left corner, below the word "File") then follow my instructions on page 256 for how to "Create a database".
>
> **To use a database you previously created, click the Open button** (which is near the screen's top left corner and looks like an opening manila file folder). You see a list of databases you created (and some folders, too). (If the list is too long to see it all, scroll to see the rest of it.) Double-click the database you want (such as "Friends"). Then that database will appear on the screen,

with the same view and filtering and sorting as when you last used it.

To stop using FileMaker Pro, do this: for a Mac, choose Quit from the File menu; for Windows, click FileMaker Pro's X button.

Improve the fields

While you're using a database, try clicking "File" then "Define Fields". Then you see the Define Fields window, which shows the list of fields again, like this:

Field name	Type	Options
First name	Text	
Last name	Text	
Comments	Text	

Extra fields To create an extra field, just type the field's name and press RETURN.

Done I'm going to reveal extra tricks for improving your fields, by using the Define Fields window. Whenever you finish using the Define Fields window, click "Done".

Numeric fields To create an extra field that contains just numbers (such as a field about "Age" or "Test score" or "Population" or "Number of children" or "Temperature" or "Amount paid" or "Balance due" or "Profit" or "Debt" or "Income" or "Cost" or "Sales" or "Discount percentage"), type the field's name then click "Number" then press RETURN. That lets the computer do filtering and sorting better.

For example, suppose you create a numeric field about "Test score". Later, you can find everybody who scored below 60 by doing this:

Say "find" by pressing COMMAND with F.
Click in the "Test score" box, type "<60", and press RETURN.

You can use these symbols:

Symbol	Meaning
<	less than
<=	less than or equal to
>	greater than
>=	greater than or equal to

You can display the students from lowest score to highest score by doing this:

Say you want to see all students (jumbo), by pressing COMMAND with J.
Say "sort", by pressing COMMAND with S.
Click "Clear All".
Click "Test score" then "Ascending order" then "Move".
Press RETURN.

You can display the students from highest score to lowest score by doing this:

Say you want to see all students (jumbo), by pressing COMMAND with J.
Say "sort", by pressing COMMAND with S.
Click "Clear All".
Click "Test score" then "Descending order" then "Move".
Press RETURN.

If a field is numeric, when you type your data you can include a decimal point and a negative sign.

If you type extra characters (such as commas or dollar signs or units of measure such as "miles"), the computer will include them in your database, but beware: since the computer doesn't know their meaning, the computer will ignore them while doing finds or sorts. The computer doesn't know that "2 miles" is more than "3 feet".

Dates To create an extra field that contains just dates (such as a field about "Date of birth" or "Date the loan began" or "Date due" or "Date processed"), type the field's name then click "Date" then press RETURN. That lets the computer filter and sort the dates better.

For example, suppose you create a date field about "Date of birth". Later, you can later find everybody born before 1980 by doing this:

Say "find" by pressing COMMAND with F.
Click in the "Date of birth" box, type "<1/1/1980", and press RETURN.

You can use these symbols:

Symbol	Meaning
<	before
<=	before or on
>	after
>=	after or on

You can display the people in order of birth by doing this:

Say you want to see all people (jumbo), by pressing COMMAND with J.
Say "sort", by pressing COMMAND with S.
Click "Clear All".
Click "Date of birth" then "Ascending order" then "Move".
Press RETURN.

When typing a date field, type the month's number, then a slash, then the date number, then a slash, then a four-digit year. For example, December 31, 1980 should be typed as "12/31/1980". You can type any year from 0001 (which was near Jesus's birth) to 3000.

If you omit the year (and type just "12/31"), the computer automatically types today's year for you. If you type a 2-digit year (such as 98 or 01), the computer automatically changes it to a 4-digit year. (To change a 2-digit year to a 4-digit year, the computer usually puts "20" before the year; but if the 2-digit year is 90, 91, 92, 93, 94, 95, 96, 97, 98, or 99, the computer puts "19" before the year instead.) The computer does that automatic typing when you move to the next field or record.

Times To create an extra field that contains just the time of day (such as a field about "Appointment time") or a time duration (such as "Time to finish race"), type the field's name then click "Time" then press ENTER. That lets the computer do filter and sort the times better.

For example, suppose you create a time field about "Appointment time". Later, you can find all appointments before 2PM doing this:

Say "find" by pressing COMMAND with F.
Click in the "Date of birth" box, type "<2PM", and press RETURN.

You can use these symbols:

Symbol	Meaning
<	before
<=	before or at
>	after
>=	after or at

You can display the people in order of appointment times by doing this:

Say you want to see all people (jumbo), by pressing COMMAND with J.
Say "sort", by pressing COMMAND with S.
Click "Clear All".
Click "Appointment time" then "Ascending order" then "Move".
Press RETURN.

For 9AM, you can type "9AM" or "9:00" or just "9". For 2PM, you can type "2PM" or "2:00PM" or "14:00" (which is military style) or just "14". You can include seconds: for 15 seconds after 9AM, type "9:00:15". If a person ran a marathon race and took "4 hours, 12 minutes, and 7 seconds", you can express that by typing "4:12:07".

Rearrange fields To delete a field, click its name (in the Define Fields window) then click "Delete" then click "Delete" again.

To change a field's type (such as from "Text" to "Number"), click the field's name then click the type you want then press RETURN. If the computer asks "Proceed anyway?", click "OK".

In front of each field's name, you see a double-headed arrow. To move a field, drag its double-headed arrow up or down.

Works database

Microsoft Works is a program that handles word processing, spreadsheets, and databases.

> I explained the word-processing part of Microsoft Works on pages 183-193.
> I explained the spreadsheet part of Microsoft Works on pages 238-253.

Here's how to use the database part of Microsoft Works 4.5 & 2000....

Create a database

Turn the computer on, so you see the Start button.
For Works 2000, do this:

> Double-click the **Microsoft Works** icon. Click **Programs** (which is near the screen's top left corner) then **Works Database** (which is near the screen's left edge) then **Start a blank Database**.

For Works 4.5, do this instead:

> Double-click the icon that says **Shortcut to Microsoft Works**. Click **Works Tools** then the **Database button**.

If the computer says "First-time Help", press ENTER.
For our first experiment, let's create this database:

First name	Last name	Comments
Sue	Smith	wiggles
Sam	Smith	tickles
Tina	Ash	clown
Tina	Smith	wow

Here's how to create it....

At the top of each column, you see a **field name**. The field names are "First name", "Last name", and "Comments". Type them and press ENTER after each one.

> So type the words "First name", then press ENTER, then type the words "Last name", then press ENTER, then type the word "Comments", then press ENTER again.

Click "Done".
You see the **List view**, which looks like a spreadsheet table and begins like this:

	First name	Last name	Comments
1			
2			
3			
4			
5			
6			

Type the data that you want in the table, moving from cell to cell by pressing the TAB key. So type "Sue", press TAB, type "Smith", press TAB, type "wiggles", press TAB, type "Sam", press TAB, etc., until you've finally typed the last entry ("wow"), so the spreadsheet table looks like this:

	First name	Last name	Comments
1	Sue	Smith	wiggles
2	Sam	Smith	tickles
3	Tina	Ash	clown
4	Tina	Smith	wow
5			
6			

Congratulations! You've created a **database table**.
In a database table, each row of data is called a **record**; each column of data is called a **field**. In the database table you created, here are the records and fields:

The first record (row of data) is Sue Smith's record.
The second record is Sam Smith's.
The third record is Tina Ash's.
The fourth record is Tina Smith's.
So altogether, there are 4 records (plus blanks underneath).

The first field (column) is called "First name".
The next field is "Last name".
The next field is "Comments".
So altogether, there are 3 fields (columns), whose **field names** (column headings) are "First name", "Last name", and "Comments".

The Works database program can handle 32,000 records, 256 fields. If you want to create a database bigger than that, use a different database program instead.

Edit the table

I'm going to explain how to edit your table's data. **Before you edit, finish what you've been typing, by pressing the TAB key.** Then edit as follows....

Click the cell you want to edit, then choose one of these editing methods....

> Method 1: press the DELETE key. That makes the cell become totally blank.
>
> Method 2: retype the entire text that you want to put into the cell.
>
> Method 3: at the top of the screen, you see a wide white box, which contains a copy of what's in the cell you clicked; click in that wide white box, then edit your typing as if you were using a word processing: you can use the left-arrow key, right-arrow key, BACKSPACE key, DELETE key, and mouse. When you finish editing, press the ENTER key.

To make an entire row become blank, click the row's number then press the DELETE key.

To make an entire row's data disappear and make the data that was underneath move up to fill the gap, do this: right-click anywhere in the row, then click **Delete Record**.

Move around To move to different cells in the table, you can use the mouse or keyboard:

> To move right, to the next cell, press the right-arrow key (or TAB key).
> To move left, to the previous cell, press the left-arrow key (or SHIFT with TAB).
>
> To move down, to the cell below, press the down-arrow key (or ENTER key).
> To move up, to the cell above, press the up-arrow key.
>
> To move far right, to the last column, press the END key.
> To move far left, to the first column, press the HOME key.
>
> To move far right & down, to the last filled cell (bottom right), press Ctrl with END.
> To move far left & up, to the first cell (top left), press Ctrl with HOME.

Add extra records To add an extra record, just type the extra record in the blank row be*low* the other records.

Undo If you make a mistake while using the Works database, you can typically undo the mistake by pressing Ctrl with Z. If you change your mind and wish you hadn't pressed Ctrl with Z, you can "undo the undo" by pressing Ctrl with Z again.

Make a column look wider Here's how to make a column look wider, so it can show longer words:

> Look at the column's heading (the field name, such as "First name"), and look at the vertical gridline that's to the right of that column heading. Drag that gridline to the right (by using your mouse).

To make the column become narrower again, drag the gridline back toward the left. To make the column look just wide enough to hold everything in it, double-click the column's heading.

Fiddling with the gridlines affects just what you see on the screen, not the data itself. If you make a column narrow by dragging its gridline, you'll see just part of the column's contents on the screen, but the contents are still stored, invisibly: afterward, if you drag the gridline to make the column look wider again, you'll see the full contents again.

Filter

Here's how to find everybody whose last name is "Smith".
Click the **Filters button**.

> In Works 2000, it's the rightmost big button near the screen's top and shows a funnel. In Works 4.5, it's the next-to-rightmost big button near the screen's top and shows a question mark.

If the computer says "First-time Help", press ENTER.

The computer says "Filter Name". Press ENTER. Then you see this table:

	Field name	Comparison	Compare To
	(None)	is equal to	
and	(None)	is equal to	
and	(None)	is equal to	
and	(None)	is equal to	
and	(None)	is equal to	

To find everybody whose last name is "Smith", change the table so it begins like this:

Field name	Comparison	Compare To
Last name	is equal to	smith

Here's how:

> The table's first box temporarily says "(None)". Next to that "(None)", your screen has a down-arrow. Click that down-arrow. You see a list of field names. Click the field name you want ("Last name"). Now the table's first box says "Last name".
>
> Move to the table's top right box (by pressing the TAB key twice). In that top right box, type the name "smith". (You don't have to capitalize it, since the computer ignores capitalization.)

Press ENTER. Then you see an abridged database, whose records show just people whose last name is Smith:

	First name	Last name	Comments
1	Sue	Smith	wiggles
2	Sam	Smith	tickles
4	Tina	Smith	wow
5			
6			
7			

You don't see record #3 (Tina Ash's record), since she's not a Smith. You see a **filtered database**, where the Smiths are still visible but Tina Ash has been filtered out and is invisible.

When you finish admiring that abridged database and want to see *all* the records again (including even Tina Ash's), do this:

> Click "Record" then "Show" then "All Records".
> Then (to make sure you see even the first record), press Ctrl with HOME.

Different filters To see everybody whose first name begins with "S", make the filter table begin like this:

Field name	Comparison	Compare To
First name	begins with	s

Then you'll see Sue's record and Sam's record (but not Tina's).

To see everybody except Sam, make the filter table begin like this:

Field name	Comparison	Compare To
First name	is not equal to	sam

To see just Tina Smith's record, make the filter table begin like this:

	Field name	Comparison	Compare To
	First name	is equal to	tina
and	Last name	is equal to	smith

Then you'll see Tina Smith's record (without seeing the other Smiths and without seeing Tina Ash).

To see everybody whose first name is Sue or Tina, make the filter table begin like this:

	Field name	Comparison	Compare To
	First name	is equal to	sue
or	First name	is equal to	tina

Then you'll see everybody whose first name is Sue or Tina (without seeing Sam).

Alphabetize

To make the computer look at each person's last name and put the last names in alphabetical order, do this:

> Click "Record" then "Sort records". (If the computer says "First-time Help", press ENTER.) Type "Last name" (or choose "Last name" from the "Sort by" box down-arrow's menu). Press ENTER.

That makes the computer alphabetize the table by Last name, so Tina Ash's record is at the top of the table and the Smiths are under her.

If you change your mind and want to undo the alphabetizing, just say "undo" (by pressing Ctrl with Z).

You've learned how to put the last names in alphabetical order. But what if two people have the same last name? Let's make the computer look at each person's last name and put the last names in alphabetical order — but if two people have the same last name, make the computer look at those people's first names and put their first names in alphabetical order:

> Click "Record" then "Sort records". (If the computer says "First-time Help", press ENTER.) In the "Sort by" box, put "Last type" (by typing it or by choosing from the down-arrow's menu). In the box below, put "First name". Press ENTER.

Save

To save the database (copy it onto the hard disk), click the **Save button** (which is under the word "Tools").

If you haven't saved the database before, the computer will say "File name". Invent a name for your database. Type the name and press ENTER.

That makes the computer copy the database onto the hard disk.

For example, if you named the database "mary", the computer will make that database become a file called mary.wdb, which means "Mary's **W**orks **d**ata**b**ase".

> Works 2000 will put that file into the My Documents folder. Works 4.5 will put that file into the Documents folder that's in the MSWorks folder (which is in the Program Files folder).

Afterwards, if you change your mind and want to do more editing, go ahead! When you finish that extra editing, save it by clicking the Save button again.

Save often If you're typing a long database, click the Save button about every 10 minutes. Click it whenever you get to a good resting place and think, "What I've typed so far looks good!"

Then if an accident happens, you'll lose at most 10 minutes of work.

Print

To print records onto paper, you can click the **Print button** (which is under the world "Help"). That makes the computer print the table.

If you want to print just *some* of the records, filter them before printing. If you want the records to be alphabetized, alphabetize them before printing.

When printing, the computer tends to be lazy: it doesn't bother printing the column headings (field names), doesn't bother printing the record numbers, and doesn't bother printing the gridlines. To force the computer to print them, do this before clicking the Print button:

Click "File" then "Page Setup" then "Other Options". Put a check mark in the "Print gridlines" box and in the "Print record and field labels" box (by clicking those boxes). Press ENTER.

Leave the database

When you finish working on a database, do this:

Works 2000 Click the X at the screen's top right corner. Then you have three choices:

If you click the **X** at the screen's top right corner again, the computer stops using Microsoft Works.

If you click **Programs** then **Start a blank Database**, the computer lets you start typing a new database.

If you click **History**, you see a list of old databases (and other Works creations). If you want to *use* one of those spreadsheets, click the spreadsheet's name. If you want to *delete* one of those spreadsheets, *right*-click the spreadsheet's name (by using the mouse's *right* button) then click "Delete" then "Yes".

Works 4.5 Choose **Exit Works** or **Close** from the File menu.

If you choose **Exit Works**, the computer stops using Microsoft Works.

If you choose **Close** instead of Exit Works, the computer says "Works Task Launcher". Then click the **Database button** or **Existing Documents**.

If you click the **Database button**, the computer lets you start typing a new database.

If you click **Existing Documents** and then double-click the name of an old database, the computer puts that database onto the screen and lets you edit it.

Didn't save? If you didn't save your database before doing those procedures, the computer asks, "Save changes?" If you click "Yes", the computer copies your database's most recent version to the hard disk; if you click "No" instead, the computer ignores and forgets your most recent editing.

Improve the fields

While you're viewing at the database as a table, the top of each column shows the name of a field. Here's how to improve the fields.

To **change a field's name**, do this:

Click the field's name. From the Format menu, choose Field. Type what you want the field to be named (and press ENTER).

To **insert an extra field**, do this:

Right-click the name of a nearby field (a field next to where you want the extra field to be). Click "Insert Field".

If you want the extra field to be to the left of the nearby field, click "Before"; if you want the extra field to be to the right of the nearby field, click "After".

Type what you want the extra field to be named (and press ENTER). If you want to insert *another* extra field, type the name you want for it (and press ENTER). Click "Done".

To **delete a field** (and all the data in that field), do this:

Right-click the field's name. Click "Delete Field". Press ENTER.

To **move a field**, do this:

Click the field's name. Take your finger off the mouse's button. While pressing the mouse's left button again, drag the field's name across to where you want it (between other fields, but *not* farther right than the rightmost field).

Data types

While you're using Works, you can see this menu of 7 choices:

```
General
Number
Date
Time
Text
Fraction
Serialized
```

You see that menu while you're inventing a new field (and typing the field's name). Another way to see that menu is to click a field's name, then click "Format" then "Field".

On that menu, the 7 choices are called **formats** or **data types**. The computer assumes you want the first choice (which is "General"), but you can choose a different data type instead. The more accurately you choose, the more accurate the computer will be at filtering, sorting, and displaying data.

Choice	What data should be in the field
General	strange data that doesn't fit the categories below
Number	a number (such as 6237.90) that has two digits after the decimal point
Date	a date (such as 12/31/00) that's between 1930 and 2029
Time	a time (such as 4:48 PM)
Text	words or an ID number (such as social security #, phone #, or ZIP code)
Fraction	a whole number followed by a fraction (such as 7 3/4, which means $7\frac{3}{4}$)
Serialized	an ID number (from 00001 to 99999) that the computer generates

Microsoft Access

Many companies use a database program called **Microsoft Access** because it comes free as part of **Microsoft Office Professional**. Here's how to use Microsoft Access's newest version, **Microsoft Access 2000**, which comes free as part of **Microsoft Office 2000 Professional**.

Launch Microsoft Access

Click "Start" then "Programs" then "Microsoft Access".

Create a database

Click "Blank Access database" then "OK".

For our first experiment, let's create this database:

First name	Last name	Comments
Sue	Smith	wiggles toes
Sam	Smith	picks toes
Tina	Ash	class clown
Tina	Smith	incredible

Here's how to create it....

Invent a name for your database (such as "Friends"). Type the name. **At the end of the name, press ENTER.**

If the computer says "The file already exists", do this procedure:

Press ENTER. Type a different name instead (such as "Friends2" or "Buddies" or "Pals" or "Enemies") and then press ENTER. If the computer says "The file already exists" again, do this whole procedure again.

Finally, you see these choices:

```
Create table in Design view
Create table by using wizard
Create table by entering data
```

Press ENTER again (which selects "Create table in Design view").

Design view You see the **Design view**, which begins like this:

Field name	Data Type	Description

We're trying to create a database who column headings are these:

First name	Last name	Comments

The column headings are called **field names**. Here's a list of those field names:

First name
Last name
Comments

Type that list of field names. To do that, type the words "First name", then press the keyboard's down-arrow key, then type the words "Last name", then press the down-arrow key again, then type the word "Comments", then press the down-arrow key again.

The computer automatically puts the word "Text" next to each field name you type, so your screen looks like this:

Field name	Data Type	Description
First name	Text	
Last name	Text	
Comments	Text	

Near the screen's top left corner, you see the word "File". Below "File", you see the **View button** (which temporarily looks like a tiny spreadsheet table of numbers). Click that button. Press the ENTER key twice (which makes the computer save the table and call it "Table1").

The computer will ask, "Do you want to create a primary key now?" Click "No".

Datasheet view
You see the **Datasheet view**, which looks like a spreadsheet table and begins like this:

First name	Last name	Comments

Type the data that you want in the table, moving from cell to cell by pressing the ENTER key. So type "Sue", press ENTER, type "Smith", press ENTER, type "wiggles toes", press ENTER, type Sam", press ENTER, etc., until you've finally typed the last entry ("incredible"), so the spreadsheet table looks like this:

First name	Last name	Comments
Sue	Smith	wiggles toes
Sam	Smith	picks nose
Tina	Ash	class clown
Tina	Smith	incredible

Congratulations! You've created a **database table**.

While you're typing that data, the computer automatically copies it to the hard disk. (You don't have to click the Save button.)

In a database table, each row of data is called a **record**; each column of data is called a **field**. In the database table you created, here are the records and fields:

The first record (row of data) is Sue Smith's record.
The second record is Sam Smith's.
The third record is Tina Ash's.
The fourth record is Tina Smith's.
So altogether, there are 4 records.

The first field (column) is called "First name".
The next field is "Last name".
The next field is "Comments".
So altogether, there are 3 fields (columns), whose **field names** (column headings) are "First name", "Last name", and "Comments".

Edit the table
While you're viewing the database table, you can edit it by retyping it. To move to different places in the table, you can use the mouse or keyboard:

To move down, to the cell below, press the keyboard's down-arrow key.
To move up, to the cell above, press the keyboard's up-arrow key.

To move right, to the next character, press the keyboard's right-arrow key.
To move left, to the previous character, press the keyboard's left-arrow key.

To move far right, to the next cell, press the ENTER key
(or TAB key or repeatedly press the right-arrow key).

To move far left, to the previous cell, press SHIFT with TAB
(or repeatedly press the left-arrow key).

Add extra records To add an extra record, just type the extra record in the blank row be*low* the other records. (The computer won't let you type an extra record *between* other records.)

If your table contains many records, the fastest way to hop down to the blank row is to click the **New Record button** (which is near the screen's top and shows a red triangle pointing at an asterisk).

Delete Here's how to delete:

To delete a character, click before it then press the DELETE key.

To delete an entire word, double-click it then press the DELETE key.

To delete an entire cell, put the mouse pointer before the cell's first word, so the pointer turns into a white cross, then click (so the whole cell is highlighted), then press the DELETE key.

Here's how to delete an entire row (record):

Method 1: To the left of the row, you see a small gray square; click it, then press the DELETE key then ENTER.

Method 2: Click anywhere in the row, then click the **Delete Record button** (which is near the screen's top and shows a red curved X), then press ENTER.

Undo If you make a mistake while using Microsoft Access, you can typically undo the mistake by clicking the **Undo button** (which is near the screen's top and shows an arrow bending toward the left). Clicking the Undo button makes the computer undo your last action.

Be cautious! Sometimes the Undo button's curved arrow is gray instead of black: the gray means the Undo button is refusing to work.

Though you can sometimes undo your last action, you cannot undo your last *two* actions; you cannot click the Undo button twice in succession.

So if you make a mistake, you can undo it just if you click the Undo button *immediately*, before performing other actions, and just if the Undo button is in a good mood, so its arrow is black instead of gray.

Make a column look wider Here's how to make a column look wider, so it can show longer words:

Look at the column's heading (the field name, such as "First name"), and look at the vertical black gridline that's to the right of that column heading. Drag that black gridline to the right (by using your mouse).

To make the column become narrower again, drag the black gridline back toward the left. To make the column look just wide enough to hold everything in it, double-click the black gridline.

Fiddling with the gridlines affects just what you see on the screen, not what the computer stores in the RAM memory chips or on disk. If you make a column narrow by dragging its gridline, you'll see just part of the column's contents on the screen, but the contents are still stored, invisibly: afterward, if you drag the gridline to make the column look wider again, you'll see the full contents again.

Find
To find everybody whose last name is "Smith", you can use three methods.

Method 1: "find" In Datasheet view, click in the first record's "Last name" field. **Say "find" (by pressing Ctrl with F).** You'll see the **Find and Replace window**.

Type "smith" and press ENTER. The computer will look down the "Last name" column, find the next "Smith", and highlight that "Smith".

If you press ENTER again, the computer will continue looking for Smiths, find another "Smith", and highlight that Smith. Keep pressing ENTER, to keep finding Smiths.

After the computer has found all the Smiths, if you press ENTER again the computer will try to find another Smith but fail, so the computer will say "The search item was not found". Press ENTER.

Whenever you get tired of having the computer look for Smiths, close the Find and Replace window (by clicking its X box).

Method 2: "filter by selection"

In Datasheet view, look down the "Last name" column, until you notice a "Smith". Click that "Smith". Click the **Filter By Selection button** (which is at the screen's top center and shows a funnel over a lightning bolt).

You see an abridged datasheet, whose records show just people whose last name is Smith:

First name	Last name	Comments
Sue	Smith	wiggles toes
Sam	Smith	picks nose
Tina	Smith	incredible

You don't see Tina Ash's record, since she's not a Smith. You see a **filtered datasheet**, where the Smiths are still visible but Tina Ash has been filtered out and is invisible.

When you finish admiring that abridged datasheet, see the full datasheet again by clicking the **Remove Filter button** (which is at the screen's top center and shows just a funnel).

Method 3: "filter by form"

In Datasheet view, click the **Filter By Form button** (which is at the screen's top center and shows a funnel over a form).

You should see this form:

First name	Last name	Comments

Make sure its bottom row is clear (contains no words, no numbers). If it's not clear yet, clear it by clicking the **Clear Grid button**, which is a red curved X.

To find everybody whose last name is Smith, click the box below "Last name", then put "Smith" into the box using one of these methods:

> Method A: start typing "smith"; after you've typed the beginning of "smith", the computer will type the rest of it for you automatically.

> Method B: click that box's down-arrow; you'll see an alphabetical list of all the last names; from that list, choose "Smith" by clicking it.

Click the **Apply Filter button** (which shows just a funnel).

You see an abridged datasheet, whose records show just people whose last name is Smith:

First name	Last name	Comments
Sue	Smith	wiggles toes
Sam	Smith	picks nose
Tina	Smith	incredible

You don't see Tina Ash's record, since she's not a Smith.

When you finish admiring that abridged datasheet, see the full datasheet again by clicking the **Remove Filter button** (which shows just a funnel).

Here's a summary of the "filter by form" method:

> Click the Filter By Form button (and the Clear Grid button). To see just the Smiths, put "smith" in the "Last name" field then click the Apply Filter button.

To see just Tina Smith's record (without seeing the other Smiths and without seeing Tina Ash), do this:

> Click the Filter By Form button (and the Clear Grid button). Put "tina" in the "First name" field, put "smith" in the "Last name" field, then click the Apply Filter button.

To see everybody whose first name is not Sam, do this:

> Click the Filter By Form button (and the Clear Grid button). Put "not sam" in the "First name" field, then click the Apply Filter button.

To see everybody whose first name is Sue or Tina (without seeing Sam), do this —

> Click the Filter By Form button (and the Clear Grid button). Put "sue or tina" in the "First name" field, then click the Apply Filter button.

or do this:

> Click the Filter By Form button (and the Clear Grid button). Put "sue" in the "First name" field, click "Or" (which is at the screen's bottom), put "tina" in the "First name" field, then click the Apply Filter button.

To see everybody whose first name begins with "S", do this:

> Click the Filter By Form button (and the Clear Grid button). Put "s*" in the "First name" field, then click the Apply Filter button.

Alphabetize

To make the computer look at each person's last name and put the last names in alphabetical order, do this:

> In Datasheet view, click "Last name".

> Click the Sort Ascending button
> (which is at the screen's top center and shows an A above a Z).

That makes the computer alphabetize the table by Last name, so Tina Ash's record is at the top of the table and the Smiths are under her.

If you change your mind and want to undo the alphabetizing, I have bad news for you: the "Undo" button is too stupid to know how to unalphabetize! To unalphabetize, you must click "Records" then "Remove Filter/Sort".

Print

To print records onto paper, click the **Print button** (which is near the screen's top left corner). That makes the computer print the table.

(If you want to print just *some* of the records, filter them before printing. If you want the records to be alphabetized, alphabetize them before printing.)

Final steps

When you finish using the table you created, close the Table window (by clicking its X button). If you alphabetized (or made any other changes to your table's structure), the computer asks "Do you want to save changes to the design of table?"; reply by pressing ENTER.

You see the Friends Database window. Close it (by clicking its X button). Then you have three choices:

> **To start creating a different database, click the New button** (which is near the screen's top left corner, below the word "File"). Then double-click the Database icon. Then invent a name for your database, and continue the process as I explained on page 262, "Create a database".

> **To use a database you previously created, click the Open button** (which is near the screen's top left corner and looks like an opening manila file folder). You see a list of databases you created (and some folders, too). (If the list is too long to see it all, scroll to see the rest of it.) Double-click the database you want (such as "Friends"). You see the Friends Database window. To be safe, click "Tables" (which is at the screen's left edge, under "Objects"). Press ENTER (which opens Table1). Then the database's table will appear on the screen, with the same view and filtering and sorting as when you last used it.

> **To stop using Microsoft Access, click its X button.**

Improve the fields

You can view your database table in two ways:

> The Design view shows you the field names (next to a word such as "Text"). The Datasheet view shows you the data itself.

To switch from one view to the other, click the **View button** (which near the screen's top right corner, below the word "File").

Add an extra field

Add an extra field In Design view, you can easily add an extra field.

> If you want the extra field to be the last field, type the extra field's name below the other field names.
>
> If you want the extra field to be where another field is now, do this: click that other field's name, click the **Insert Rows button** (which is near the screen's top and shows a blue row that's out but moving in), then type the extra field's name.

Finally, press the down-arrow key (so the computer says "Text").

Delete a field In Design view, you can easily delete a field:

> Method 1: To the left of the field's name, you see a small gray square. Click it, then press the DELETE key then ENTER.
>
> Method 2: Click the field's name, then click the **Delete Rows button** (which is near the screen's top and shows a blue row that's in but moving out), then press ENTER.

Move a field To move a field (in Design view or Datasheet view), do this:

> Click the field's name. Take your finger off the mouse's button. While pressing the mouse's left button again, drag the field's name to where you want it (between other fields).

Data types

In Design view, each field normally says "Text". If you click "Text", you see a down-arrow next to it. If you click that down-arrow, you see these choices:

```
Text
Memo
Number
Date/Time
Currency
AutoNumber
Yes/No
OLE Object
Hyperlink
Lookup Wizard
```

Click whichever choice you want; then the screen's bottom might show boxes, such as "Field Size" and "Decimal Places". The more accurately you choose, the more accurate the computer will be at finding, filtering, and sorting.

The bottom 3 choices ("OLE Object", "Hyperlink", and "Lookup Wizard") are unpopular; I won't bother to discuss them. Here's what the popular choices and boxes mean....

Currency Choose "Currency" if the field's data will be an amount of money, written as dollars and cents (such as $7,893.20). For example, choose "Currency" if the field is "Amount paid" or "Balance due" or "Profit" or "Debt" or "Income" or "Cost" or "Sales").

Then when you type the data in Datasheet view, here's what will happen:

> The computer will automatically put a dollar sign before the number, put two digits after the decimal point, and insert a comma if the number is big. If the number is negative, the computer will imitate an accountant: it will put the number and dollar sign all in parentheses (instead of writing a minus sign).

> The amount of money can be very big (up to $922,337,203,685,477.58), so you can say you're even richer than Bill Gates! To see such a big number, widen the Datasheet's column by dragging its vertical gridline.
>
> If you try to go higher than $922,337,203,685,477.58, the computer will say "The value you entered isn't valid for this field".

When you choose "Currency" in Design view, the screen's bottom usually shows that the Decimal Places box contains the word "Auto", which makes the computer automatically put 2 digits after the decimal point. You can force the computer to display 4 digits after the decimal point by putting 4 in the Decimal Places box (which will make the biggest number be $922,337,203,685,477.5807). If you want the computer to round to the nearest dollar (and show no decimal point and no pennies), put 0 in the Decimal Places box. You can put 0, 1, 2, 3, or 4 in the Decimal Places box; the computer can't handle more than 4 accurately.

Each currency amount is stored by using a special code that consumes just 8 bytes of your hard disk, even if the number contains many digits.

Date/Time Choose "Date/Time" if the field's data will be a date or time. For example, choose "Date/Time" if the field is "Date of birth" or "Date the loan began" or "Date due" or "Date processed" or "Appointment time".

In Datasheet view, you can type a date/time like this: "12/31/1920 11:59:45 PM", which means December 31st, 1920, at 45 seconds after 11:59PM.

> If you don't want to be so detailed, type just part of that: type just the date or just the time.
>
> When typing the time, you can omit the number of seconds.
> You can write AM or PM or use 24-hour military time.
>
> The computer can handle any 4-digit year from 0100 (which was near Jesus's birth) to 9999.
> When typing a year from 1930 through 2029, you can omit the first two digits.
> When typing a year from 0100 through 0999, you can omit the first zero.

Each date/time consumes 8 bytes of your hard disk.

AutoNumber Choose "AutoNumber" if you want the field's data to be a simple counting number (such as 1, 2, 3, 4,…) that the computer will generate automatically.

In Datasheet view, the computer will automatically type a "1" in that field for the first record, "2" in that field for the second record, etc. That counting number will act as an ID. Each such counting number consumes 4 bytes on your hard disk.

You can name the field "Record number" or "ID number".

Number Choose "Number" if the field's data will be a number that's not an amount of money, not a date or time, and not an identification number. For example, choose "Number" if the field is "Age" or Test score" or "Population" or "Number of children" or Temperature" or "Discount percentage".

(For an amount of money, choose "Currency" instead. For a date or time, choose "Date/Time" instead. For a simple identification number generated by the computer, choose "AutoNumber" instead. For other kinds of identification number, such as a social-security number or phone number or ZIP code, choose "Text" instead.)

When you choose "Number" in Design view, the screen's bottom usually shows that the Field Size box contains "Long Integer". Instead of "Long Integer", choose a different size instead, if it fits your data better. Here are your choices:

Choice	Meaning	Memory
Byte	a whole number from 0 to 255, no decimals, no negatives	1 byte
Integer	an integer from -32768 to 32767, no decimals	2 bytes
Long Integer	an integer from -2147483648 to 2147483647, no decimals	4 bytes
Single	a number that can contain decimals, minus sign, exponents, 7 significant digits	4 bytes
Double	a number that can contain decimals, minus sign, exponents, 15 significant digits	8 bytes

In that chart, the "Memory" column shows how many bytes of your hard disk each number consumes. The fewer the number of bytes, the shorter your data file will be and the faster your Access will run. Choose the shortest choice that's still big enough to hold your data.

Yes/No Choose "Yes/No" if you want the field's data to be a box, in which a check mark means "yes"; an empty box means "no". For example, choose "Yes/No" if the field is "Was contacted?" or "Was sold?" or "Has diabetes?" or "Has retired?" or "Is a member now?" or "Is female?" or "Is an adult yet?".

Then when you create data in Datasheet view, you'll see an empty box in that field. Put a check mark into that box (by clicking the box) if you want to say "yes"; leave the box blank if you want to say "no".

Each yes/no answer consumes just 1 bit of your hard disk. (1 bit is very little: it's $\frac{1}{8}$ of a byte.)

Memo "Memo" is the only popular choice that lets the field's data be longer than 255 characters. "Memo" lets you write an entire long essay about the person and make that essay become part of the person's record. The essay can be up to 65535 characters long. It consumes as many bytes as there are characters in the memo.

For example, choose "Memo" if the field is "Psychoanalytical comments about the patient" or "What the employee should do to improve" or "What I really think about this person".

<u>**Text**</u> Stay with "Text" just if none of the other choices is better. Choose "Text" if the field either includes words (up to 255 characters) or is an ID number (such as a social-security number or phone number or ZIP code) that's not an AutoNumber. For example, stay with "Text" if the field is "First name" or "Last name" or "Street address" or "City" or "State" or "ZIP code" or "Phone number" or "Social Security number" or "Product name".

If you decide to stay with "Text", beware: the computer limits you to 50 characters (because the number in the Field Size box is 50) unless you change that number. The biggest number allowed in the Field Size box is 255. Your text consumes as many bytes as the Field Size box says. To avoid wasting bytes, make the number in the Field Size box be as small as possible, but still big enough to hold your longest data.

Why use data types?
Suppose you create a numeric field about "Test score".

To display the students from lowest score to highest score, do this:

> In Datasheet view, click "Test score". Then click the **Sort Ascending button**, which is at the screen's top center and shows an up-arrow (with an A above a Z).

To display the students from highest score to lowest score, do this:

> In Datasheet view, click "Test score". Then click the **Sort Descending button**, which is at the screen's top center and shows a down-arrow (with an A below a Z).

To display just the students who scored below 60, do this:

> In Datasheet view, click the **Filter By Form button** (which is at the screen's top center and shows a funnel over a form).
>
> You see a form. If its bottom row is not clear yet, clear it (by clicking the Clear Grid button, which is a red curved X).
>
> Click the box below "Test score". Type "<60".
>
> Click the Apply Filter button (which shows just a funnel).

You can use these symbols:

Symbol	Meaning
<60	less than 60 (below 60)
<=60	less than or equal to 60 (at most 60)
>60	greater than 60 (over 60)
>=	greater than or equal to 60 (at least 60)
not 60	not equal to 60 (not 60)
between 60 and 70	at least 60 but not over 70

You can use apply those techniques to the other data types also! For a date/time field:

> The Sort Ascending button
> puts the records in order from oldest (earliest) to newest (latest).
>
> The Sort Descending button
> puts the records in order from newest (latest) to oldest (earliest).
>
> "<1/1/1920" gets you all records before 1920.

Forms

In Datasheet view, the computer shows you many records on the screen simultaneously, but each record is restricted to being just one line of the table. If you want a person's record to include more info than can fit on a single line of your screen,

Datasheet view is inconvenient.

Invent a **Form view** instead. In Form view, a record can consume your entire screen, instead of just one line.

Invent a Form view
Here's how to invent a Form view....

While you're looking at the table's Datasheet view, close that table's window by clicking its X box. (If the computer asks "Do you want to save changes to the design of table?", press ENTER.)

You see the Friends Database window. Click "Forms" (which is near the screen's left edge). Double-click "Create form by using wizard". Click the ">>" button. Press ENTER twice.

You see this list of styles:

> Blends
> Blueprint
> Exedition
> Industrial
> International
> Ricepaper
> SandStone
> Standard
> Stone
> Sumi Painting

Each of those styles is a color scheme.

> To see how each style looks, press the down-arrow key or up-arrow key several times. Which style do you like best? I recommend "Standard" (which is the simplest, black-gray-white, resembling most other Microsoft products) or "Blends" (which is the most colorful and cheeriest, black-blue-yellow-white). The other choices are compromises between those two extremes.

When you decide which style you want, click it, then press ENTER.

Invent a name for your form. For example, the name can be "Table1 form" or "A wild look at my friends". Invent any name you wish! Type that name and press ENTER.

View a form
You see a form displaying the first person's record, like this:

First name	Sue
Last name	Smith
Comments	wiggles toes

While you're admiring that record, you can edit it by using the mouse or these keyboard shortcuts:

> To move to the next box (field), press ENTER (or TAB).
> To move back to the previous box (field), press SHIFT with TAB.
> To move to the bottom box, press the END key.
> To move back to the top box, press the HOME key.

See other records
Here's how to see other records:

> To see the **next person's record**, click the ▶ button
> or press the PAGE DOWN key (or rotate the mouse's wheel toward you).
>
> To see the **previous person's record** again, click the ◀ button
> or press the PAGE UP key (or rotate the mouse's wheel away from you).
>
> To hop back to the **first record** again, click the |◀ button or press Ctrl with HOME.
> To hop ahead to the **final record**, click the ▶| button or press Ctrl with END.
>
> To create an **extra record**, click the ▶* button or press Ctrl with +.
> To hop back to **record #2**, press the F5 key, then type 2 (and press ENTER).

Close
The form is in a window (called "Table1 form" or "A wild look at my friends" or whatever name you invented). When you finish looking at forms, close that window (by clicking its X button). Then click "Tables" (which is at the screen's left edge, under "Objects"), to put the screen back to normal.

Getting back to your form
To see the Form view again, click "Forms" then double-click your form's name.

Q&A

My favorite database program is **Q&A**, invented by **Symantec**. For about 15 years, I've used Q&A to run my entire business. It's the best database program to use — if you don't mind using DOS instead of Windows.

Symantec has invented several versions of Q&A.

> Symantec started selling **version 1** of Q&A in 1985, **versions 1.1 and 2** in 1986, **version 3** in 1988, and **version 4** in 1991. All those versions use MS-DOS, which requires that you buy an IBM PC or clone.
>
> Symantec has developed a **Windows version**, but don't buy it. Everybody who's tried it hates it. It requires too many keystrokes and mouse-strokes per task. The DOS version is much easier and swifter. Also, the Windows version consumes 20 megabytes of your hard disk.
>
> After inventing Q&A version 4 for DOS, Symantec wasn't planning to invent any more DOS versions. But some Germans promised to buy many copies of Q&A if Symantec would make little improvements and spell the word "color" the British way ("colour"); Symantec agreed and called the result **version 5**. Symantec intended to sell it just in Germany; but since so many Americans were curious about it and requested it, Symantec has reluctantly agreed to sell it to any American willing to read British.

Q&A is programmable, which means you can teach it new tricks.

> For example, I taught Q&A how to run my business. Now Q&A handles all my mailing lists, orders, shipping labels, income, expenses, and taxes. Q&A runs my entire life!
>
> I also used Q&A to create the master index at the back of this book.

Q&A can handle gigantic files. Each file can contain up to 256 megabytes.
You can divide the file into as many records as you wish and divide each record into as many fields as you wish.

> In version 4 (or 5), each record can be as long as you wish, and each field can contain up to 32 kilobytes. (Earlier versions restrict each record to 16 kilobytes and each field to 1.6 kilobytes.)

Where to buy

Q&A versions 1, 2, and 3 are no longer sold. To get Q&A version 4 or 5, for DOS, you cannot buy directly from Symantec; instead, Symantec recommends that you send $199 (plus $15 shipping) to **Professional Computer Technology Associates**. It's a Q&A consulting company run by Bill Halpern and Gordon Meigs at 100 Jericho Valley Dr., Newtown PA 18940, phone 215-598-8440.

Requirements

Q &A requires at least 512K of RAM. Q&A runs much faster if you have at least 640K of RAM. To run Q&A version 4 (or 5) with version 4 of MS-DOS (which consumes lots of RAM), you *must* have at least 640K.

Version 4 (or 5) requires a hard disk. If you don't have a hard disk, you must buy an earlier version instead and use two floppy drives.

On old computers, Q&A worked fine. For new computer situations, you face three minor hassles, explained on the Internet Web site of the **Q&A Users Group** (www.qaug.com):

> To use Q&A in the year 2000 or after, either don't mention dates in your database or **else remind Q&A to use 4-digit dates instead of 2-digit dates** (by using the Global Format Options Screen when you're designing or redesigning the file). For versions 4&5, you might also wish to download the **Y2KFix patch** (from www.qaug.com or www.quickanswer.com); it's not important; it just makes Q&A display dates correctly when printing a directory of all your files.
>
> **To use Q&A reliably, you must put it on a hard drive no bigger than 1.9G**, or partition your hard drive so Q&A and all its temporary files are put onto a drive letter (such as "C:") that's no bigger than 1.9G, or download the **Lesspace.com patch** (from www.quag.com or www.quickanswer.com).
>
> To use version 5 on a Pentium faster than 180MHz, you must download the **Speedfix patch** (from www.quag.com or www.quickanswer.com). That's necessary just for version 5, not versions 3&4.

Start Q&A

Here's how to handle databases by using Q&A versions 3 and 4 for DOS. (Version 5 resembles version 4. Versions 1, 1.1, and 2 resemble version 3.)

Prepare yourself Before using Q&A to handle databases, practice using Q&A to handle word processing, by reading pages 200-204. For example, I assume you've followed the instructions on page 200 about how to "Make Q&A act better".

The main menu By following the instructions on page 200 about how to "Run Q&A", make the computer display this Q&A **main menu**:

```
Q&A MAIN MENU
F - File
R - Report
W - Write
A - Assistant
U - Utilities
X - Exit Q&A
```

If you're using version 4 and have a mouse, you'll see a small red rectangle in the middle of the screen. Move that rectangle out of the way — to the screen's top right corner — by rolling the mouse toward your desk's back right corner.

The file menu To make Q&A handle databases, choose "F - File" from the main menu by pressing the F key. (That works if you followed the instructions on page 200 about how to "Make Q&A act better". If you did *not* follow those instructions, you must press ENTER after pressing F — and you must press ENTER after choosing any item from any menu.)

The screen shows the **file menu**. In version 4, it looks like this:

```
            FILE MENU

D - Design file    R - Remove
A - Add data       M - Mass update
S - Search/update  T - Post
P - Print          U - Utilities
C - Copy
```

(Version 3 lacks "T - Post" and "U - Utilities". You see "B - Backup" instead.)

Whenever you're done filing, you should return to the main menu by pressing the Esc key several times. Then you can exit by pressing X. That's the only correct way to stop using Q&A's database. Do *not* just turn off the power! If you turn off the power without pressing X first, you might wreck the data files you created.

Field commands

Field commands While using the filing part of Q&A, you can give these **field commands**:

Field command	Keys to press	
Add new records	Ctrl F6	
Calculate	F8	
Calculate mode	Shift F8	
Customize file	Shift F9	
Date	Ctrl F5	
Delete field/line	Shift F4	
Delete field/line end	Ctrl F4	
Delete record	F3	
Delete word	F4	
Ditto field	F5	
Ditto record	Shift F5	
Edit field	F6	
File menu	Shift F10	
Help	F1	
Macro	Shift F2	
Macro run	Alt F2	just in version 4
Mask override	Alt F4	just in version 4
Next record	F10	
Previous record	F9	
Print record	F2	
Print remaining records	Ctrl F2	
Reset @NUMBER	Ctrl F8	
Retrieve spec	Alt F8	just in version 4
Search for records	F7	
Search options	Ctrl F7	
Table	Alt F6	
Table definition	Shift F6	
Time	Alt F5	
Undo edit	Shift F7	just in version 4
Values permitted	Alt F7	just in version 4

Put that chart (or a photocopy of it) next to the computer.

The next few pages explain how to use the file menu and the field commands.

Design file

Here's how to design a new file. From the file menu, choose "D - Design file" (by pressing D).

That makes the computer show the **design menu**. In version 4, it looks like this:

```
DESIGN MENU
D - Design a new file
R - Redesign a file
C - Customize a file
P - Program a file
S - Secure a file
A - Customize application
```

(In version 3, the bottom three choices are missing.)

Look back on page 254, at the sample file of students in the School of Life. Let's create that file and call it STUDENTS. To do that, press the D key (which chooses "D -Design a new file" from the menu), type "students", then press ENTER.

Type the form Most of the screen will become blank. On the blank screen, type a form, which you'll fill in later. For example, if you want to store each student's last name, first name, age, and class, plus comments, type this form:

```
Last name:                       First name:
Age:              Class:
Comments:
```

Here's how. Type the word "Last", then a space, then the word "name", then a colon. Move to the right (by holding down the right-arrow key or space bar or TAB key), then type the phrase "First name", then a colon. Press the ENTER key, and type the lines underneath.

That form creates five fields: last name, first name, age, class, and comments. Each field name ends with a colon.

When you've finished typing the form, copy it onto the hard disk, by pressing the F10 key.

Examine the T screen On the screen, you'll see the form you typed. The computer automatically puts a T in each field, so your screen looks like this:

```
Last name: T                     First name: T
Age: T            Class: T
Comments: T
```

Move the cursor The cursor's at the first T. To move the cursor around the screen, you can use the arrow keys.

To move the cursor faster, use the TAB key (which is next to the Q key). When you press the TAB key, the cursor moves to the next field.

For example, if the cursor's at the T for "Last name", and you press the TAB key, the cursor will move to the T for "First name". If you press the TAB key again, the cursor will move to the T for "Age".

Experiment! Try moving the cursor around the screen by using the TAB key.

Unfortunately, the TAB key is hard for your fingers to reach. To move the cursor more easily, tap the ENTER key instead. (While you're manipulating a form, the ENTER key imitates the TAB key.)

So to move the cursor ahead to the next field, tap TAB or ENTER. To move back to the previous field, tap TAB (not ENTER) *while holding down the Shift key*.

Change T to N Each T on the screen is a **format code**; it stands for "Text". If you want a field to contain a number instead of text, change that field's T to an N.

For example, since you want the person's "Age" to be a number, you must change Age's T to N. To do that, move the cursor to the Age's T (by pressing the TAB key), then type N.

You can type either N or n. The computer doesn't care about capitalization.

Also change Class's T to N, so your screen looks like this:

```
Last name: T                     First name: T
Age: N            Class: N
Comments: T
```

That tells the computer that the person's age and class are Numbers, and everything else about the person consists of words and other general Text.

Use the N code just for numbers that are simple (such as 0, 7, 2150, .2, .09, and -31.8).

Use the T code for numbers that contain dashes (such as phone numbers) and for long numbers that can begin with 0 (such as ZIP codes). Use the T code for social security numbers, since they contain dashes and can begin with 0.

Finish Press the F10 key. The computer will say GLOBAL FORMAT OPTIONS.

Press F10 again. You'll see the file menu again.

Congratulations! You've created a STUDENTS database on your hard disk! That database consists of two files (STUDENTS.DTF and STUDENTS.IDX) in the QA subdirectory.

Add data

You've seen how to make the computer put a file called STUDENTS onto the disk. Although the file is organized so that each record will consist of five fields, the file doesn't contain any records yet, since it doesn't yet contain the names and data about any specific students.

To add the names of specific students and the data about them, choose "A - Add data" from the file menu (by pressing A). Press ENTER.

The screen will show the form you designed:

```
Last name:                          First name:
Age:              Class:
Comments:
```

Then fill in the blanks.

For example, suppose one of the students is Suzy Smith. Fill in the form to look like this:

```
Last name: Smith                    First name: Suzy
Age: 4            Class: 12
Comments: Though just 4 years old, she finished high school because she's fast.
```

Here's how. Type Smith, then move the cursor to the next field by pressing ENTER (or TAB). Type Suzy, then press ENTER. Type 4, then ENTER. Type 12, then ENTER. Type the commentary sentence.

When you've finished filling in Suzy Smith's form, say "Next record" (by pressing F10). Then the computer will show a blank form again:

```
Last name:                          First name:
Age:              Class:
Comments:
```

Fill in the blanks again, for the next student (Clara Bell).

Repeat that process for each student. As you type the students' records, the computer automatically copies them to the STUDENTS.DTF file (which is in your hard disk's QA subdirectory).

Move the cursor
To move the cursor a short distance, use the arrow keys. Here's how to move the cursor farther:

Keys you press	Where the cursor will move
TAB	the next field
Shift with TAB	the previous field
HOME	the beginning of the field
END	the end of the field
HOME HOME	the first field on the screen
END END	the last field on the screen
F10	the next record
F9	the previous record
Ctrl with HOME	the first record you added during this session
Ctrl with END	the last record you added during this session

Delete
If you make a mistake, point at it (by moving the cursor there), then tell the computer how much to delete.

To delete just one character, press the Del key. To delete a whole word, say "Delete word" (by pressing F4). To delete everything you typed in the field, say "Delete field/line" (by pressing Shift with F4). To delete everything you typed in the whole record, say "Delete record" (by pressing F3); when the computer asks "Are you sure?", press Y.

Ditto
If you move the cursor to a field and then say "Ditto field" (by pressing F5), the computer will make the data in that field be a copy of the previous student's. To make the entire record be a copy of the previous student's, say "Ditto record" (by pressing Shift with F5).

Edit (just in version 4)
If you have version 4, try this trick: while you're typing words in a field, say "Edit field" (by pressing F6).

A gigantic box will appear at the bottom of the screen. The words you typed appear in that box. Since the box is big, it can hold lots of words. Type as many as you wish! You can even type a long essay about the student! When you type near the box's bottom, the text in the box automatically moves out of the way, so you can type even more! You can type many pages! While you're typing them, you're using Q&A's word processor, so you can use all the word-processing tricks you learned: press ENTER at the end of each paragraph, press TAB to indent a paragraph, and use page 203's table to give advanced word-processing commands (such as "Spell" and "Thesaurus").

When you finish typing in the box, press the F10 key.

In the future, whenever you want to see or edit that boxed essay again, move the cursor to that field and say "Edit field" (F6) again.

Finish
When you finish typing the last student's record, and you still see that record on the screen, say "File menu" by pressing Shift with F10 (instead of saying "Next record"). Then the screen will display the file menu again (instead of waiting for you to type another record).

Search/update

To search through the file to find a particular student, choose "S - Search/update" from the file menu (by pressing S). Press ENTER.

The screen will show the form you designed again:

```
Last name:                          First name:
Age:                  Class:
Comments:
```

If you fill in a few of the blanks, the computer will fill in the rest. For example, if you fill in just the last name (Smith) and press F10, the computer will find everybody whose last name is Smith. It will show you each Smith's record, one at a time.

Whenever the computer finds a Smith's record, the computer pauses to let you look at the record and edit it. (Editing is also called **updating**.) To edit the record, move the cursor to the field you want to revise (by pressing TAB, ENTER, or arrow keys), then retype that field. (To hop to the screen's bottom field, press END twice; to hop back up to the screen's top field, press HOME twice.)

When you finish examining and revising the record, choose one of these actions:

What you want to do next	What to say
see the next Smith	"Next record" (by pressing F10)
see the previous Smith	"Previous record" (by pressing F9)
see the first Smith	Ctrl with HOME
see the final Smith	Ctrl with END
see the file menu	"File menu" (by pressing Shift with F10)
delete this Smith & see the next Smith	"Delete record" (F3) then Y
undo the revisions	"Undo edit" (Shift F7, just in version 4)
undo the revisions & see the file menu	press Esc, then usually Y
search for other records (not Smiths)	"Search for records" (by pressing F7)
create other records & add them to file	"Add new records" (by pressing Ctrl with F6)

If the computer can't find who you're searching for (because there aren't any Smiths or there isn't any "next Smith" or "previous Smith"), the computer will say "No forms" or "No more forms" or "No previous form". Press the Esc key, which makes the computer show the file menu.

You can use these fancy search techniques....

If you tell the computer to search for "smith" instead of "Smith", the computer will still find all the Smiths, since the computer doesn't care about capitalization.

If you tell the computer to search for "S.." instead of "Smith" (by putting "S.." in the last name field), the computer will get everybody whose last name begins with "S". Saying "..th" gets names ending with "th". Saying "..m.." gets names containing an "m". Saying "S..h" gets every name that begins with S and ends with h. Saying "S????" gets every name that contains an S followed by exactly 4 more letters.

Not The symbol for "not" is "/". For example, saying "/Smith" gets everybody whose name is *not* Smith. Saying "/..m.." gets every name *not* containing an m.

Or The symbol for "or" is ";". For example, saying "Smith;Bell" gets everybody named Smith or Bell.

Unsure of the spelling? Suppose you want to find Kosinski's record, but you can't remember how he spells his name. You don't remember whether it's "Kosinski", "Cosinski", "Kozinski", "Kosinscki", or "Kosinsky"; you remember merely that it includes the letters "in". If you put "..in.." into the last name field, the computer will find everybody whose name contains "in" — and it will find Kosinski's record.

Suppose somebody phones to ask you about a student; but the phone connection is poor (with lots of static) and the person also mumbles. You think he's asking about somebody named "Cuzomskuh", but you're not sure. Tell the computer to find all the students that *sound like* "Cuzomskuh". To do that, put "~Cuzomskuh" in the last name field. The symbol ~ means "sounds like". (On the original IBM keyboard, it's next to the ENTER key; on the new IBM keyboard, it's next to the 1 key; on the Leading Edge keyboard, it's next to the BACKSPACE key. While typing it, you must hold down the Shift key.) The computer will find Kosinski and any other students that sound like "Cuzomskuh".

Search on age If you fill in just the age, the computer will find everybody that age. For example, to find everybody who's 10 years old, put "10" in the age field.

To find everybody who's *less* than 10 years old, say "<10". For *greater* than 10, say ">10". For *greater than or equal to* 10, say ">=10". For *greater than 10 but less than 18*, say ">10..<18".

To find the oldest student, say "max". To find the youngest, say "min".

To find the 3 oldest students, say "max3". The computer will show you the oldest student, then the next oldest, then the 3rd oldest.

In the age field, if you say just "=" (instead of "=10"), the computer will find everybody whose age is equal to *nothing*: it will find everybody whose age was left blank. To find everybody whose age is *not* blank, ask for "/=".

Alphabetical order The computer understands alphabetical order — the order in which words and names would appear in a dictionary.

For example, if you ask for the names that are "<Smith" (by putting "<Smith" in the last name field), the computer will find all names "less than Smith", which means all names that come before Smith in the dictionary. Asking for ">Smith" gets you all names that come *after* Smith in the dictionary.

Search through comments If you search for "..slow.." in the comments field, the computer will find everybody whose comment mentions "slow". It will find Clara Bell (who's "Super-slow!") and also find Heinz Ketchopf ("the slowest Ketchopf in the West").

Unrestricted search If you leave all the fields blank so that you're not telling the computer to search for anything particular, the computer will show you *all* the records in the file, without any restrictions.

Expand a field If a field is too narrow to hold your search request, type as much of the request as fits in the field, then say "Edit field" (by pressing F6).

The computer will let you type the rest of the request at the bottom of the screen; do so. When you finish typing the request, move on to the next field (by pressing ENTER) or make the computer start searching (by pressing F10).

Multi-field search Suppose you want to find everybody who's old and stupid. Specifically, suppose you want to find everybody whose age is over 40 and who still hasn't finished the second grade. Put ">40" in the age field, and put "<3" in the class field.

The computer will find Heinz Ketchopf (who's 57 years old and in the first grade) and Russy-poo Walter (who's 53 years old and whose class is 0). They're the students who are old and stupid.

Suppose you want to find the students who are old *or* stupid. To do that, put ">40" in the age field, put "<3" in the class field, then say "Search options" (by pressing Ctrl with F7). Move the cursor down, then across to the word ANY. Press F10. The computer will find Buffalo Bob Smith, Heinz Ketchopf, Tricky Dick Nixon, and Russy-poo Walter, because each of them is either old or stupid.

Sort When you've told the computer which records to search for, you normally press F10, which makes the computer start searching.

Instead of just pressing F10, try doing the following: say "Calculate" (by pressing F8), then type "1a" in the field that interests you most, then finally press F10.

That makes the computer display the records in alphabetical or numerical order. For example, if you put "1a" in the last name field, the computer will display the records in alphabetical order, by last name. If you put "1a" in the age field instead, the computer will display the student records in order of age, starting with the youngest student.

Putting the records into alphabetical or numerical order is called **sorting**.

The usual kind of sorting is called **ascending**. When you type "1a", the "a" stands for "ascending".

If you type "1d" instead, you get the opposite kind of sorting, which is called **descending**. For example, if you put "1d" in the last name field, the computer will display the records in reverse alphabetical order, beginning with any Z names and ending with A. If you put "1d" in the age field, the computer will display the student records in order of *decreasing* age, starting with the oldest student and ending with the youngest.

Suppose you put "1a" in the last name field and "2a" in the age field. The "1a" makes the computer sort by last name. If several students have the same last name (such as the Smiths), the age field's "2a" makes the computer "break the tie" by using the age: the computer will show you the Smiths from youngest to oldest. In that situation, the last name field is called the **primary** sort field; the age field (which is used only for breaking a tie) is called the **secondary** sort field. The "1a" means "primary ascending"; the "2a" means "secondary ascending".

Table Suppose you search for youngsters (by saying "Age: <18" and then pressing F10). When the computer shows you the first youngster's record, say "Table" (by pressing Alt with F6). The computer will display this table, which shows the records of *all* youngsters simultaneously:

Last name	First name	Age	Class	Comments
Smith	Suzy	4	12	Though just 4→
Smith	Buffalo Bob	7	2	Boringly norm→
Kosinski	Stanislaw	16	11	He dislikes P→

In that table, each row is a record. The top row is Suzy Smith's record. The bottom row is Stanislaw Kosinski's record.

Each column is a field. The left column is the "Last name" field. The last column is the "Comments" field.

Since the screen is narrow, it shows just 5 thin columns. Look at Stanislaw Kosinski's "Comments" field. Since the column's too thin to show his entire Comments field ("He dislikes Polish jokes"), the column shows just the first few characters ("He dislikes P") and a right-arrow (which tells you that the field contains more characters). Version 3 doesn't bother to show the right-arrow.

If you're using version 4, you can edit the table while you stare at it. Just move the cursor down to the row you want to edit (by pressing the down-arrow key), and move the cursor across to the field you want to edit (by pressing the TAB key). Here's what to do next:

> If you want to retype the field's info completely (and it's short), go ahead: retype it!
> If you want to edit the field's info slightly (and it's short), just press F5 and then edit.
> If the field's info is long (so you see "→"), do this: press F6, then edit, then press F10.

If a file contains more than 5 fields, the table usually shows just the first 5 fields. If you're using version 4, you can see the other fields by pressing the TAB key several times.

Here's another way to see 5 different fields (in both versions 3 and 4). Say "Table definition" (by pressing Shift with F6). In the five fields you want to see, type the numbers 1, 2, 3, 4, and 5. Make sure those numbers aren't in any other fields. Then press F10.

The screen's tall enough to show 17 rows of the table. To see other rows of a long table, press the PgDn key.

After viewing the table, move the cursor to the row that interests you most, then press F10. The screen will show all details of that row's record.

Print

Whenever the screen shows a student's record, you can print that record on paper. Just say "Print record" (by pressing F2), then press F10.

To have more fun instead, say "Print remaining records" (by pressing Ctrl with F2), then press F10. The computer will print the record, then print all subsequent records in the bunch you were examining or adding.

The print menu To do fancier printing, get the file menu onto the screen, then choose "P - Print" (by pressing P). Press ENTER.

The screen will show the **print menu**. From that menu, choose "D - Design/redesign a spec".

Invent a name for the printout you'll create. The name can be up to 31 characters long, and it can even contain blank spaces. Type the name, then press F10.

The computer will show a blank form. Fill in the blanks to tell the computer which records to print. For example, to print all the Smiths, put "Smith" in the "Last name" field; then press F10.

The computer will show another blank form. Choose one of these three strategies....

> **Strategy 1: leave the form blank.** That tells the computer you want standard printing. The computer will print all the record's fields, in the same positions that they appear on the screen.
>
> **Strategy 2: give coordinates.** For example, if you type "2,10" in the last name field, the computer will print the student's last name on paper, 2 lines down from the top margin, and starting in the 10th space from the left margin. If you omit a field's coordinates, that field will be unprinted.
>
> **Strategy 3: use + and x.** For example, if you type a "+" in the last name field, the computer will print the last name. If you type an "x" in the last name field, the computer will print the last name and then automatically do a carriage return, so the next field it prints will appear underneath. Any field you leave blank will be unprinted.

When you've chosen one of those three strategies (and filled in the form appropriately), press F10.

The computer will say "FILE PRINT OPTIONS". If you want the computer to print the field labels (so that the computer will print "Last name: Smith" instead of printing just "Smith"), move the cursor down to "Print field labels?", then move left to "Yes".

Press F10 again, then ENTER. The computer will print the records you requested, then show you the print menu again.

If you want to repeat the printing, choose "P - Print records" from that menu. (In version 3, choose "P - Print forms".) Move the cursor to your printout's name. Press F10 then ENTER. The computer will repeat the printing and show you the print menu again.

When you don't want to do any more printing, press Esc. you'll see the file menu again.

Report

To print a fancy report, get the Q&A main menu. (To do that, get the file menu, then press Esc.) From the Q&A main menu, choose "R - Report". The screen will show a **report menu**. From that menu, choose "D - Design/redesign a report" (by pressing D). Press ENTER.

Invent a name for the report you'll create. The name can be up to 31 characters long, and it can even contain blank spaces. Type the name, then press F10. (If you're using version 4, then choose "C - Columnar report" by pressing C.)

The computer will show a blank form. Fill in the blanks, to tell the computer who to report on. For example, if you want to report on just the Smiths, put "Smith" in the "Last name" field. To report on *everybody* (which is what I suggest), leave the form blank.

Press F10. The computer will show another blank form. This report will consist of several columns. Put 1 in the field that you want to be the leftmost column, 2 in the field that you want to be the next column, etc. For example, if you want the person's last name to be the leftmost column, the first name to be the next column, and the age to be the third column, type this:

```
Last name: 1                    First name: 2
Age: 3          Class:
Comments:
```

Better yet, put an "as" in the last name field, and put an "a" in the age field, like this:

```
Last name: 1,as                 First name: 2
Age: 3,a        Class:
Comments:
```

In the last name field, the "as" stands for "ascending sort"; it forces the computer to print the last names in alphabetical order. In the age field, the "a" stands for "average": it makes the computer print the average age.

When you finish filling in that form, press F10 twice, then ENTER. The computer will print this report:

```
Last name     First name     Age
----------    -----------    -----
Bell          Clara          21.00

Ketchopf      Heinz          57.00

Kosinski      Stanislaw      16.00

Nixon         Tricky Dick    78.00

Smith         Suzy            4.00
              Buffalo Bob     7.00

Walter        Russy-poo      53.00

=========     ===========    =====
Average:                     33.71
```

Notice that the computer alphabetizes the left column, clumps the two Smiths together, and prints the average age. The computer automatically makes each column wide enough to fit even the longest names and numbers.

When the computer finishes printing the report, it shows the report menu again.

If you want to print the report again, choose "P - Print a report" from that menu (by pressing P). Press ENTER. Move the cursor to your report's name. Press F10 then ENTER. The computer will reprint the report and show you the report menu again.

When you don't want to print any more reports, press Esc. You'll see the main menu again.

Fancy report codes Instead of saying "as" (for ascending sort), you can say "ds" (which gets you a descending sort).

Besides telling you the column's average (for which the code is "a"), Q&A can also tell you the column's total ("t"), count ("c"), largest number ("max"), smallest number ("min"), and all subtotals ("st"). To make Q&A do so, just put those codes in the blanks.

Mail merge Suppose you want to write a personalized letter to each student, so that Suzy Smith's letter will say —

```
Dear Suzy,
Come to the party for grade 12 on Saturday.
```

and Clara Bell's letter will say —

```
Dear Clara,
Come to the party for grade 10 on Saturday.
```

Here's how....

First, get into the word processor. (To do that, get to the file menu, then get to the main menu by pressing Esc, then choose "W - Write" from the menu, then choose "T - Type/edit" from the next menu.)

Type this form letter:

```
Dear *First name*,
Come to the party for grade *Class* on Saturday.
```

To type it, begin by typing the word "Dear", then tap the space bar once.

To create the "*First name*", do the following. Say "Field" (by pressing Alt with F7). The computer will ask you for the name of the file; type "students" then ENTER. The computer will display this list:

```
FIELD NAMES
Age
Class
Comments
First name
Last name
```

Move the cursor to "First name", then ENTER. The computer will automatically type "*First name*" in the middle of your memo.

Then type the rest of the form letter. Remember to type the comma after *First name*, and remember that you can make the computer automatically type *Class* for you, by pressing Alt with F7.

When you finish typing the form letter, say "Print" (by pressing F2). Then press F10.

You'll see a blank form. Use it to say which students will get the letter. (For example, to send the letter to just the Smiths, put "Smith" in the last name field. To send the letter to *all* the students, leave the fields blank.) Press F10 then ENTER.

The computer will print the letters to all the students you requested. That massive printing is called a **mail merge**, because the computer does it by merging the form letter with the mailing list of students.

When the computer finishes, you'll be using Q&A's word processor again. To leave the word processor, press Esc twice; if the computer asks "Are you SURE?", press Y. You'll see the Q&A main menu.

Mass moves

Here's how to manipulate many records at once....

Mass update Suppose Mr. Smith — the father of Suzy Smith and Buffalo Bob Smith — dies. His wife, Mrs. Smith, remarries and changes her name to Mrs. Finkelstein. She also changes the names of her kids, so that "Suzy Smith" becomes "Suzy Finkelstein", and "Buffalo Bob Smith" becomes "Buffalo Bob Finkelstein".

We must tell the computer to turn the Smiths into Finkelsteins. Since Suzy and Buffalo Bob are such wonderful kids, we'll also move them into super-advanced classes that are ten times their ages: we'll move Suzy (who is 6) into class 60, and move Buffalo Bob (who is 7) into class 70. Here's how to do all that....

From the file menu, choose "M - Mass update" (by pressing M). Press ENTER. You'll see a blank form.

Tell the computer who to search for. Since you want the computer to search for all the Smiths, type "Smith" in the last name field, then press F10.

You'll see another blank form. Tell the computer how to change the Smiths' records, by typing this:

```
Last name: #1="Finkelstein"          First name:
Age: #2            Class: #3=10*#2
Comments:
```

Notice you must put #1, #2, and #3 in the three fields involved (Last name, Age, and Class). To make field #1 (which is Last name) become Finkelstein, say #1="Finkelstein". To make field #3 (which is Class) become 10 times field #2 (Age), say #3=10*#2.

When you finish typing all that, press F10 then N. The computer will change the Smiths to Finkelsteins and make their classes become 10 times their ages. Then you'll see the file menu again.

How to make the whole school skip

Suppose *all* the school's students are doing so well that you want to skip them ahead 5 years. (You'll move all the first graders to the 6th grade, all the second graders to the 7th grade, all the third graders to the 8th grade, etc.) Here's how....

From the file menu, choose "M - Mass update". Press ENTER. You'll see a blank form. Without typing any restrictions, just press F10 (since you want to update *all* students).

You'll see another blank form. Since you want to increase each student's class by 5, you should make the class be called "field #1" and add 5 to it. To do that, say "Class: #1=5+#1", which means "the Class is field #1; and field #1 will become equal to 5 more than what it had been." Then press F10.

The computer will increase each student's class by 5. Then you'll see the file menu.

Remove Suppose all the Finkelsteins are murdered. Let's remove them from the file.

To remove the Finkelsteins, choose "R - Remove" from the file menu by pressing R. Press ENTER. (If you're using version 4, then choose "S - Selected records" by pressing S.)

You'll see a blank form. In the last name field, type "Finkelstein".

Press F10 then Y. The computer will delete all the Finkelstein records. Then you'll see the file menu again.

Backup Here's how to make a second copy of STUDENTS.

If you're using version 3, choose "B - Backup" from the file menu by pressing B. If you're using version 4, choose "U - Utilities" from the file menu by pressing U, then choose "B - Backup database" by pressing B.

Press ENTER.

The computer will say "Backup to:". To copy STUDENTS to the disk in drive A, put a blank formatted disk into drive A, say "Delete line" (Shift F4), type "a:students", then press ENTER. The computer will copy STUDENTS from the hard disk to drive A.

If you're using version 4, press Esc to see the file menu again.

Copy Let's create a DOGS file about a dog-obedience school. We want the DOGS file to contain the same design that we used in the STUDENTS file, so a sample DOGS record will look like this:

```
Last name: McGregor              First name: Lassie
Age: 2          Class: 12
Comments: She's a brilliant collie. Named after her grandma, a TV star!
```

Here's how to create the DOGS file, so it uses the same design as the STUDENTS file but doesn't contain the names of humans.

From the file menu, choose "C - Copy" (by pressing C). Press ENTER.

You'll see a **copy menu**. Tap the D key (for "D - Copy design only"). Type the name of the new file you're creating ("dogs"), then ENTER.

The computer will create file called DOGS, having the same design as STUDENTS but without any data in it.

You'll see the copy menu again. Press Esc, to see the file menu again.

Customize

You can customize Q&A to meet your personal needs.

For example, let's create a database of all your friends and customers around the world. Let's store each person's address and phone number (to replace your phone book and Rolodex and create a mailing list). Let's also store comments about each person and date the comments, to make the file act as a diary.

Suppose some of those people occasionally send you money. Let's record how much each person sends and make Q&A compute the totals, so Q&A does your accounting.

Suppose you're in Massachusetts, and some of the money you receive is for goods you sell. Let's make Q&A compute the 5% sales tax, so Q&A does your taxes.

Here's how to make Q&A do all that….

Start typing the form From Q&A's file menu, choose "D - Design file" (by pressing D). When you see the design menu, tap the D key (to choose "D - Design a new file"), type "friends" (which will be the name for the file), and press ENTER.

On the blank screen, start typing this form:

```
First name:                    Last name:
Department:                               >
Company:                                  >
Address:                                  >
City:              State:   Zip:   > Country:

Phone numbers:                            >

Sales-tax code (T=Taxable, R=Resale, N=Nonprofit):   Price:
                                                     Sales tax:
                                                     Total:
Comments<
```

```
                                                     >
                        Group code:    Date:         >
```

Boxes Notice that the form includes two boxes. The top box contains the fields for the mailing label. The bottom box contains the money fields.

Here's how to draw a box. Place the cursor where you want the box's upper-left corner. Give the word-processing command for "Draw". (To do that in version 3, press F8 then D. To do that in version 4, press F8 then L then D.) Move the cursor towards the right; as you move it, you'll be drawing the box's top line. Draw the box's other three lines by moving the cursor down, then left, then up until you've returned to the upper-left corner. Then press F10.

The computer doesn't care whether you draw the box. The box's purpose is just to beautify the life of your **data-entry operator** (the person who'll be staring at the screen for many hours while entering your data).

Six parts Like most good forms, that form consists of 6 parts in this order:

> **a box containing the mailing label's fields,** in the order they'll appear on the label
>
> **other fields that the operator must fill in** (phone numbers, price, and sales-tax code)
>
> **fields that the operator will skip** because they'll be filled in by computer (sales tax and total)
>
> **a big space where the operator can jot comments** (such as "this guy is a jerk" or "treat her nicer next time" or "oops — we goofed" or "discuss this tough order with the boss" or other comments that are more specific)
>
> **a field for inserting a GROUP CODE,** which is a code to generate selective mailings; for example, you can browse through all the records, put "p" in the ones that look interesting, and then tell the computer to send mail to each person whose group code is "p"
>
> **a field to hold the date** (we'll make the computer insert the date automatically, but we'll also let the operator change the date to handle special situations)

Shortened fields Look at the "Department" field. It begins with the word "Department", then comes a colon, then 42 blank spaces, then the symbol ">".

Later, when the data-entry operator adds new records to the file by typing in data, the computer will permit the operator to "fill in the 42 blanks" by filling in 42 characters. The computer will prevent the operator from typing on or past the ">".

That prevents the operator from being too long-winded and typing too much to fit on tiny mailing labels.

Multi-line fields Look at the "Comments" field. It begins with the word "Comments", then comes the symbol "<" (instead of a colon), then several blank lines. At the end of the last blank line, you'll see the symbol ">".

The symbols "<" and ">" surround the area in which the operator can type comments. If you omit the symbol ">", the computer will restrict the operator to just one line of comments.

When you create a multi-line field, Q&A prohibits you from having other symbols nearby. Specifically, you can't put a multi-line field in a box, and you can't put two multi-line fields side-by-side.

Change the format codes When you finish typing the form, press F10.

You'll see the form you typed (except that the symbols "<" and ">" are hidden). The computer automatically puts format code T in each field, but you must change some of those T's to other codes instead. To do so, move the cursor to each T (by pressing TAB, ENTER, or arrow keys), then edit some of the T's, to make your screen look like this:

```
First name: T                    Last name: T
Department: T                                        >
Company: T                                           >
Address: T                                           >
City: T                 State: TU Zip: TU            > Country: TU

Phone numbers: T                                     >

                                          ┌──────────────────────┐
Sales-tax code (T=Taxable, R=Resale, N=Nonprofit): TU │ Price: MC JR     │
                                          │ Sales tax: MC JR │
                                          │ Total: MC JR     │
Comments T                                └──────────────────────┘



                                                                    >
                              Group code: TU  Date: D               >
```

Here's why:

> The state's format code should be **TU** instead of just T. The **U means "Uppercase"**. It makes the computer automatically capitalize what the data-entry operator types.
>
> The **format code for Zip should be TU** because some of the customers are in Canada, where Zip codes have capital letters in them.
>
> The **format code for phone numbers is T** (not N), so that the phone number field can contain more than just numbers. T lets you include phrases such as "home number", "work number", "extension", and "call after 4:30PM". T also lets you include parentheses and dashes, like this: (603) 666-6644.
>
> **For money, the best format code is "MC JR"**, which means "Money with Commas and Justified Right". For example, suppose the operator types this price: "42831.7". When the operator finishes typing it and moves to the next field (by pressing TAB or ENTER), the "MC" makes the computer automatically insert a dollar sign and comma and put 2 digits after the decimal point, so the screen shows "$42,831.70" instead of just "42831.7". Then the computer slides the $42,831.70 toward the right edge of the screen (because of the "JR" code), so that the decimal point is directly above the decimal points of numbers underneath. **If you like all that but want the computer to omit the dollar sign, change the "M" to "N2"** (which means "number with 2 digits after the decimal point").
>
> The format code for date is **D**. (A similar format code is **H**, which means "hours and time of day".)

When you've finished typing the format codes, press F10. If the computer says GLOBAL FORMAT OPTIONS, press F10 again. Then you'll see the file menu.

The customize menu
From the file menu, choose "D - Design file" again. From the next menu, choose "C - Customize a file" (by pressing C). Press ENTER.

You'll see the **customize menu**:

```
CUSTOMIZE MENU
F - Format values
R - Restrict values
T - Field template
I - Set initial values
S - Speed up searches
D - Define custom help
C - Change palette
```

(Instead of "T - Field template", version 3 has "P - Program form", "E - Edit lookup table", and "A - Assign access rights".)

Let's see how to use the most popular choices.

To change the screen's colors, choose "**C - Change palette**".

> You'll see a blank form. Fill in a few fields, notice the screen's color scheme, and then press F8. The colors on the screen will change. (If you have a monochrome monitor, the underlines will disappear.)
>
> Each time you press F8, the colors, underlines, boldfacing, etc. will change again. When you finally see a color scheme you like, press F10, to return to the customize menu.
>
> The color schemes are called **palettes**. Many of the palettes are humorously wild.
>
> The bottom of the screen shows the palette's number. The most *practical* palettes are #2 and #3. They're the only palettes that show clearly which field you're editing.
>
> If your monitor is monochrome, choose palette #3. If your monitor is CGA color, choose palette #2. If your monitor is EGA or VGA color, choose either palette #3 (whose high contrast is the easiest to read) or palette #2 (whose soft blues will make you fall in love).

To let your data-entry operator fill in the forms faster, choose "**I - Set initial values**".

> You'll see a blank form. If you fill in some of the fields now, the operator won't have to fill them in later.
>
> For example, if most of your customers are in San Francisco, California (because you grew up there and still advertise there), put "San Francisco" in the city field and "CA" in the state field. Put "@date" in the date field. Then press F10.
>
> Later, when your data-entry operator adds new records, the computer will automatically fill in some of the fields by typing San Francisco, CA, and the correct date. The operator can edit what the computer typed, when the operator needs to deal with a customer that's not in San Francisco or not in California or whose record must be postdated.

To protect yourself from data-entry errors, choose "**R - Restrict values**".

> You'll see a blank form. Type in any restrictions you want to put on the data. For example, to restrict the price to under $50,000, type "<50000" in the price field. To restrict the sales-tax code to T, R, or N, type "T;R;N" in the sales-tax code field (after widening the field by pressing F6). When you finish typing the restrictions, press F10.

> Later, if the data-entry operator tries to bypass a restriction (by typing a huge price or a wrong sales-tax code), the computer will type this warning: "Value not in specified range. Please verify before continuing."
>
> Although the computer types that warning, the computer permits the operator to keep that unusual data in the file (so the operator can handle unusual customers). The warning just alerts the operator that the value typed was nonstandard. That warning helps the operator notice typographical and clerical errors.

To make Q&A run faster, choose "**S - Speed up searches**".

> You'll see a blank form. Type an S in each field that you often use for searching. For example, since you often look up a customer's record by using the customer's last name, type an S in the last name field. I recommend that you type an S in the last name field, company field, Zip field, and data field.
>
> Putting an S in a field makes the computer create an index for that field. The index helps the computer search on that field more quickly. A field containing an S is called a **speedy field** or an **index field**.
>
> Although the S makes the computer search faster, the S has two drawbacks: its index consumes a lot of space on the disk, and the computer must pause to update the index whenever you add a new record.
>
> Because of those drawbacks, do *not* put an S in every field! Put an S in just the three or four fields that you search on most often.
>
> When you finish typing the S's, press F10.

Program
To get total control over the computer, program it!

If you're using version 4, choose "P - Program a file" from the design menu, then press ENTER, then choose "P - Program form". If you're using version 3, choose "P - Program form" from the customize menu.

You'll see a blank form.

Let's make the computer automatically compute the Sales tax and Total. The computation involves four fields: the Price (which we'll call field #1), Sales-tax code (#2), Sales tax (#3), and Total (#4).

> Make the Price be field #1, by typing "#1" in the Price's blank.
>
> Make the Sales-tax code be field #2, by typing "#2" in the Sales-tax code blank.
>
> Make the Total be field #4 and also be *the Price plus the Sales tax*, by typing this in the Total blank: "#4=#1+#3".
>
> In Massachusetts, which has a "5% sales tax", how much money should the Sales tax be? If a sale is taxable (because the Sales-tax code is T), the Sales tax should be 5% of the Price. That means field #3 (which is the Sales tax) should equal .05 times field #1 (which is the Price). If the sale is *not* taxable, the Sales tax should be 0 instead. To explain all that to the computer, type this in the Sales tax blank (after pressing F6 to widen the field):
>
> #3: if #2="T" then #3=.05*#1 else #3=0
>
> When you type that line, make sure you type quotation marks around the "T". That line tells the computer that for this field (field #3), do the following computation: if field #2 (the Sales-tax code) equals "T", then make field #3 equal .05 times field #1; otherwise, make field #3 equal 0.

After filling in the blanks that way, press F10.

> Later, when the data-entry operator enters a customer's record, the operator can fill in just the Price and Sales-tax code and then say "Calculate" (by pressing F8), which makes the computer obey your programming and automatically fill in the Sales tax and Total.

GRAPHICS

What to buy

You can buy many kinds of graphics programs.

Paint

The easiest kind of graphics program to use is called a **paint program**. It lets you easily create pictures on your screen by using a mouse.

How paint programs arose
In January 1984, Apple Computer Company began selling the Mac computer. It was the first affordable computer that included a mouse — and the first affordable computer that included a mouse, and the first affordable computer that included a good paint program.

The Mac's paint program was called **Mac Paint**.

> It was invented at Apple Computer Company in 1984 by Bill Atkinson. It ran just on the Mac, was included free with the Mac and showed consumers why a Mac was better than an IBM PC: the Mac let you paint a picture on your screen, and the IBM PC couldn't do that yet.
>
> I explained Mac Paint in the 14th edition of *The Secret Guide to Computers*. If you'd like that edition, phone me at 603-666-6644.
>
> Mac Paint had one major limitation: it couldn't handle colors. It handled just black-and-white, because the original Mac came with just a black-and-white screen.
>
> (Years later, Apple began charging for Mac Paint, Ann Arbor Software invented an improved version called "Full Paint", and Silicon Beach invented a further improvement called "Super Paint". Modern Macs have color.)

The next major advance was **Deluxe Paint**.

> It was invented in 1985 by Dan Silva in California and published by Electronic Arts. It was much fancier than Mac Paint and performed gorgeous color tricks.
>
> It ran just on Commodore's Amiga computer. It was why Commodore's Amiga became popular. Because of Deluxe Paint, the Amiga quickly developed a reputation as the best computer for generating color graphics.
>
> (Years later, the Amiga faced competition, Commodore went bankrupt, and Electronic Arts made versions of Deluxe Paint for the IBM PC and the Apple 2GS. Unfortunately, Deluxe Paint is no longer available.)

Windows includes a free a paint program.

> In Windows 3.0, 3.1, and 3.11, the free paint program called **Paintbrush**. It's a stripped-down version of "PC Paintbrush", which was invented by Z-Soft. Windows 95 includes a free paint program called **Paint**, which is an improved Paintbrush. I explained Paintbrush on page 112, Paint on pages 101-102.

Paintbrush, PC Paintbrush, and Paint are all worse than Deluxe Paint, except for Deluxe Paint's one glaring problem: Deluxe Paint is a DOS-based program that hasn't been updated to handle Windows and new video cards.

The best paint program for kids is **Kid Pix**, published by Broderbund.

> It runs on all popular computers (IBM, Mac, and others). While you paint, it makes funny sounds and talks to you in both English and Spanish. Besides letting you create your own shapes, it includes lots of fun little pre-drawn shapes (stars, snowflakes, trees, etc.), which you can include in your paintings to create backgrounds and pixie dust.
>
> By using Kid Pix, you can create impressive artwork in just a few seconds! Of all the paint programs you can buy, Kid Pix is the one that give you pleasure fastest! Though the pre-drawn shapes look kid-like, they look like they come from *talented* kids! Kid Pix is the only program where it's even more fun to erase your work than to create it, since Kid Pix gives you many dramatic ways to get rid of your painting, such as by dynamiting it: boom!
>
> Educators have given Kid Pix many awards for turning kids into creative artists.

The best paint program for professional artists is **Painter**, published by Fractal Design.

> It was designed for the Mac but now also runs on the IBM PC. Painter amazes artists because it makes the computer's screen accurately imitate different kinds of brushes, inks, and other artist tools. You can choose whether to make the screen look like you're painting in oil, chalk, charcoal, watercolor, or whatever other medium you wish. You can fine-tune each tool, change precisely how "drippy" each tool is, and change the "bumpiness" of the paper's texture.
>
> It even includes a "van Gogh" mode, which lets you paint by using the same kinds of brushstrokes as the artist Vincent van Gogh.
>
> Though Painter can use a mouse, Painter imitates artist tools more accurately if you buy a **pressure-sensitive graphics tablet** (which comes with a pen that records not just *where* you're pressing but also *how hard* you're pressing). The most popular pressure-sensitive tablets are made by **Wacom**, **Kurta**, **Calcomp**, and **Summagraphics**.
>
> Unfortunately, Paint is expensive ($379) and requires a powerful computer. If you have less than a Pentium (or Power Mac) with less than 16 megabytes of RAM, Paint runs too slowly to be enjoyable.
>
> Fractal Design sells a stripped-down version, called **Dabbler**, for just $49. It also sells a black-and-white version called **Sketcher**, which runs faster since it doesn't have to deal with colors.
>
> Since Paint, Dabbler, and Sketcher are intended just for creative artists who like to draw squiggles, they don't contain commands to draw geometric shapes. For example, they don't contain commands to draw a oval, circle, rectangle, or square. All other popular paint programs include such commands.

How paint programs work
Each paint program considers your screen to made of thousands of pixels (dots). The paint program remembers the color of each pixel. The colors of all the pixels are stored in RAM while you're painting. You need lots of RAM if your screen is large & has many pixels, or if you insist on using lots of colors.

All paint programs suffer from the following problem:

> If you use a paint program to create a shape, then try to shrink that shape, then change your mind and try to expand the shape back to its original size, the final result looks crude and lacks the details that were in the original.
>
> That's because a paint program shrinks a shape by using fewer pixels, and so some of the pixels that contained details are discarded. The lack of detail becomes noticeable when you try to expand the shape back to its original size.

Another problem is that when you try to rotate a shape, the shape looks cruder, because the shape's pixels get slightly misplaced by "round-off error". If you try to rotate a shape several times, the pixels get progressively more misplaced, and the shape looks cruder and cruder.

> When trying to paint, if you expand or twirl,
> You get a result that makes you want to hurl.

Paint programs are called **bitmapped graphics programs**.

Draw

A **draw program** does *not* store the color of each pixel. Instead, a draw program stores a memo about a geometric shape and the color of the entire shape.

> For example, a draw program stores a line by storing just its starting point, angle, length, and color; it stores a circle by storing just the circle's center, radius, and color. By contrast, a paint program would consume lots of RAM storing the color of each of the thousand of pixels that are on the line or circle.
>
> Draw programs are also called **vector-based graphics programs**.
>
> A draw program works faster and more accurately than a paint program if you're drawing geometric shapes. A draw program has no problem handling expansions and rotations. But it has difficulty handling squiggles, since it tries to view each squiggle as made up of many tiny arcs.

A draw program lets you name different objects, put them in front of other objects, then later move the objects to reveal objects that were hidden. Most paint programs can't do that: in a paint program, creating a new shape automatically erases any shape that was underneath — except for a crude feature that lets you have two "layers": a "background" and a "foreground".

In a draw program, you can point to an object you drew and change its color, thickness, or style. In a paint program, the only way to change the appearance of what you drew is to draw it over again.

Unfortunately, the typical draw program is confusing to use, because when you look at what's on your screen you're not sure which "objects" the stuff you're seeing is part of.

The first popular draw program was **Mac Draw**, which ran on the Mac. Now most draw programs use Windows instead.

The most popular serious draw programs are **Windows Draw** (by Micrografx), **Micrografx Designer** (which is a beefed-up version of Windows Draw), and **Corel Draw** (which comes from a Canadian Company called Corel).

Each modern Windows word-processing program also includes a stripped-down draw program, free:

> To draw while using Microsoft Word, click the Drawing button.
> To draw while using Word Perfect, choose "Draw" from the Graphics menu.
> To draw while using Word Pro, choose "Drawing" from the Create menu.
>
> To draw while using Microsoft Works' word processor, choose "Drawing" from the Insert menu.

CAD

You can buy a program that does **computer-aided drafting & design (CAD)**. Such a program resembles a draw program but does more math.

> For example, it can print mock blueprints, with the lengths of all parts marked. It can even compute the surface area (square feet) of any shape, so you can compute how much material to buy to build your structure and cover it.
>
> It lets you give fancy geometric commands, such as "draw a 37-degree angle, but make the point be round instead of sharp, so nobody gets hurt" or "draw a circular arc that goes through these three points" or "draw a line that grazes these two circles, so it's tangent to them".

The most famous CAD program is **Autocad**. That's what most architects and engineers use. It's published by Autodesk and very expensive: about $3,000! Cheaper CAD programs that cost under $50 are for use at home, to help Joe Six-Pack design his backyard deck and interior designers plan purple bathrooms.

Most CAD programs include pre-built shapes that you can put in your drawings.

> The pre-built shapes are exactly the right size and shape to represent toilets, sinks, stoves, and other household fixtures. Each shape is called a **symbol**. You can buy a bunch of extra symbols; each bunch is called a **symbol library**.

Photo manipulation

To put photographs into your computer, use a **scanner** (which scans in sheets of paper), or a **digital camera**, or a **digital video camera** (such as the **Connectix Quick Cam**), or **Snappy** (which attaches your computer to a camcorder, TV, or VCR).

Once the picture is in your computer, you can manipulate it by using a paint program. Better yet, use a program that specializes in the fine art of manipulating photographs.

> The best photo-manipulation programs are Adobe's **Photoshop**, Adobe's **Photo Deluxe** (which is cheaper), Corel's **Photo-Paint**, Microsoft's **Picture It**, and a fun program by Metatools called **Kai's Power Goo** (which lets you stretch and shrink each part of a person's face, to create weird facial expressions).

Other graphics software

To spice up your word-processing documents, you can buy **clip art**, which consists of funny little cartoonish illustrations. Modern spreadsheet program (such as **Excel**) can create pie charts, line graphs, and bar charts. To create slide shows, get a **presentation program**, such as Microsoft's **PowerPoint** (explained on pages 284-288) and Lotus's **Freelance**. The best way to combine graphics with word processing is to get a **desktop-publishing program** (explained on pages 289-295).

Classic computer art

During the 1960's, many creative ideas were generated about how computers would someday create their own weird art, using a wild combination of formulas and random numbers, and unshackled by the bounds of human culture.

Here's how to make the computer produce wild art, by using the wonderful classic tricks invented in the 1960's and 1970's....

Gray levels

You can express every black-and-white photograph as a table of numbers. Each number in the table represents the darkness of a different point — the higher the number, the darker the point. The "darkness numbers" are called **gray levels**. To feed a picture into the computer, type in the table of gray levels. Or aim a special camera at the object you want pictured; the camera system will automatically compute the gray levels and send them to the computer via a wire.

You can program the computer to change the gray levels in any weird way you wish, and draw the result. In the 1960's, the Computer Technique Group of Japan did this to an ordinary photo of John Kennedy:

Shot Kennedy   *Diffused Kennedy*

Kennedy in a Dog

Here's what the group did to a photo of Marilyn Monroe:

Monroe in the Net

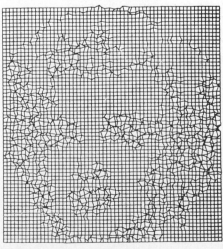

I did this with the help of a computer:

Pin-Up

```
             $$$$$$$$$
            $$$$$$$$$$$
           $$$$$$$$$*$$$
          $$$$$$$$$*$$$$
          $$$$.$$  $$.$$
          $$$$...$   .$$
          $$$$$.$$$ .$$$.
          $$$$$....$$$$
          $$$$$$ $$ $*$$$
          $$$$$$ .. **$$$
        *** $$$*** $$ $
        ***  $$$  $$ $$
        ****     .* *$ $
        ****  *.    *  *
        ***.. $*.   *.  *
        *... $*.    *  *
        **.. $**.** *. *
        **.. $*****.* ***.
        **. $*    *
        **. $      *.
        *$**. *    *.
        *.*$*** *  *.
        *.*****$** *.
       .*.*******$$** *.
       .*..****.. $*.
       .*..*.....  $$ ***.
        *..****.....* ***...
         *.*****.... * ****
         *..*****..... ******...
        ***** .*****.... ***...
          ....**********.. ***
           * *   *********** **
           * *       *********
         ***************. ******
         * **         **.******
        ** *  *      *.*****.
        * ************ *.*****
        * *          $*.****.
       *$ **       ***$. *** *
       * *$*      ****$..$$.**
       ************..*$..**.**
       * **       ****$.*.**.*
       *  **     **.*$ ** * *
       *** ***********.*$. *.*****
       *  *    $****$.** .  *
       *  **   $$$ $*. *. * **
       *        $  $*.*.    **
       *            $**..    *
       *            $**.     *
       **           $* .    **
       *            $$**     **
       **           $* .    **
       *             $$      **
```

The *Pin-Up* has these specifications....

scene: a scantily clad woman sitting on a stool

4 gray levels

4 symbols (1 for each gray level: a blank, a period, an asterisk, and a dollar sign)

1537 symbols altogether (53 rows × 29 columns)

In the specification, the numbers are small, yet the picture is clear. To obtain the clarity, I did non-computerized finagling.

At Bell Telephone Laboratories, Knowlton & Harmon produced a picture with much larger specifications....

scene: two sea gulls flying in the clouds
16 gray levels
141 symbols (each gray level has several symbols; the computer chooses among them at random)
11616 symbols altogether (88 rows × 132 columns)

Instead of using blanks, periods, asterisks, and $, they used cats, battleships, swastikas, and other weird shapes. Here are the 141, listed from lightest to darkest, with some repetitions:

The picture is several feet long. Seen from a distance, it looks like this:

Gulls

Here's a close-up view of part of one of the gull's wings:

If you don't like sea gulls, how about *Mona Lisa*?

In 1971, Michael Hord made the computer turn photographs into artistic sketches. Here's what the computer did to a photograph of his boss, and to a photograph of a colleague's girlfriend:

Boss

Woman

To draw each sketch, the computer's camera scanned the original photograph and found the points where the photograph changed dramatically from light to dark. Then, on a sheet of paper, it plotted those points; and through each of those points, it drew a short line perpendicular to the direction in which the original photograph darkened.

More precisely, here's what the computer did…. It looked at four adjacent points on the original photograph:

A	B
C	D

It computed the darkness of each of those points. Then it computed the "darkening in the X direction", defined as:

(darkness at B) + (darkness at D) - (darkness at A) - (darkness at C)

Then it computed the "darkening in the Y direction", defined as:

(darkness at A) + (darkness at B) - (darkness at C) - (darkness at D)

Then it computed the "overall darkening", defined as:

(darkening in the X direction)² + (darkening in the Y direction)²

If the overall darkening there turned out to be large, the computer sketched a short line, in the vicinity of the points ABCD, and perpendicular to the direction of darkening. More precisely, the line's length was 1, and the line's slope was:

$$-\frac{\text{the darkening in the X direction}}{\text{the darkening in the Y direction}}$$

Morphs

Here's how to make an L slowly become a V. Notice that the letters L and V are both made by connecting three points:

Let 1″ be the point halfway between 1 and 1′; let 2″ be halfway between 2 and 2′; and let 3″ be halfway between 3 and 3′. Then 1″, 2″, and 3″ form a shape that's halfway between an L and a V:

The process can be extended further:

L L Ⅼ V V

Turning one shape into another (such as turning an L into a V) is called **a metamorphosis** or **morphing**. The intermediate shapes (that are between the L and the V) are called the **morphs**.

Using that method, the Computer Technique Group of Japan gradually turned a running man into a Coke bottle, and then into Africa:

Running Cola is Africa

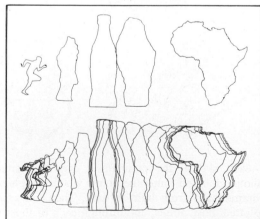

The group turned this head into a square:

Return to a Square

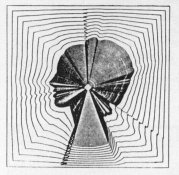

The head on the left returns to a square by using **arithmetic progression**: the lines are equally spaced. The one on the right uses **geometric progression** instead: the lines are close together near the inside square, but further apart as they expand outward.

Csuri & Shaffer exploded a hummingbird:

Chaos to Order

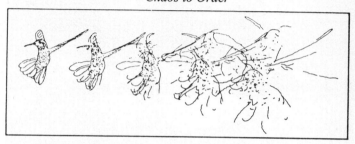

The hummingbird at the far right was obtained from the one at the far left, by moving each line a random distance and in a random direction (between 45° and -45°).

Computers can make movies. The best movie ever made by a computer is called *Hunger* (or *La Faim*). It was made under the auspices of the Canadian Film Board. It's a 10-minute cartoon, in color, with music; but it goes far beyond anything ever done by Walt Disney. It uses the same technique as *Running Cola is Africa*: it shows objects turning into other objects.

It begins by showing a harried, thin executive at his desk, which has two phones. One of the phones rings. He answers it. While he's talking on that phone, his other phone rings. To talk on both phones simultaneously, his body splits in two. (How does a single body become two bodies? By using the same technique as turning a running man into a coke bottle.)

On the other side of his desk is an armchair, which turns into a secretary, whose head turns into a clock saying 5PM, which tells the executive to go home. So he stretches his arms in front of him, and becomes his car: his hands become the headlights, his arms become the front fenders, his face becomes the windshield. You have to see it to believe it.

He drives to a restaurant and gets the waitress, who turns into an ice-cream cone. Then he eats her.

As the film progresses, he becomes increasingly fat, lustful, slothful, and miserable. In the end, he falls into hell, where he's encircled by all the poor starving naked children of the world, who eat his flesh. Then the film ends. (Don't see it before eating dinner!)

It combines computer art and left-wing humanitarian politics, to create an unforgettable message.

Now morphing is being applied to color photographs and video images. For example, Hollywood movies use morphing to show a person gradually turning into a monster; environmentalists use morphing to show a human baby gradually turning into a spotted owl; and portrait photographers who have gone high-tech use morphing to show you gradually turning into the person you admire most (such as your movie idol or your lover).

Order versus disorder

Computer artists are starting to believe that **art is a tension between order and disorder**. Too much order, or too much disorder, will bore you. For example, in *Chaos to Order*, the hummingbird on the left is too orderly to be art. The hummingbird on the right is more interesting.

Consider *Gulls*. Seen from a distance, it's an orderly picture of gulls. Seen up close, it's an orderly picture of a cat or battleship or swastika. But from a middling distance, it looks like disorderly wallpaper: the symbols repeat, but not in any obvious cycle. That element of disorder is what makes the picture interesting.

At first glance, *Pin-Up* is just a disorderly array of periods, asterisks, and dollar signs. At second glance, you see order: a girl. **Art is the formation of order from disorder.**

A first glance at *Monroe in the Net* shows order: a piece of graph paper. A second glance shows disorder: some of the graph's lines are inexplicably bent. A third glance shows order: Marilyn Monroe's face pops out at you. Her orderly face is formed from the disorder of bent lines.

Return to a Square uses arithmetic progression and geometric progression to create an over-all sense of order, but the basic elements are *dis*orderly: a head that's bumpy, and a panorama of weird shapes that lie uncomfortably between being heads and squares but are neither.

Many programs create disorder by random numbers. *Chaos to Order* uses random numbers to explode the hummingbird. *Gulls* uses random numbers to help choose among the 141 symbols.

An amazing example of random numbers is this picture by Julesz & Bosche:

To your eyes, the picture seems quite ordered. Actually, it's quite *dis*ordered. One pie-shaped eighth of it is entirely random; the other seven eighths are copies of it. The copying is the only element of order, but very powerful. Try this experiment: *cover seven-eighths of the picture.* You'll see that the remaining eighth is totally disordered, hence boring.

That program imitates a child's *kaleidoscope*. Do you remember your childhood days, when you played with your kaleidoscope? It was a cardboard "telescope" that contained a disorganized pile of colored glass and stones, plus a series of mirrors that produced eight-way symmetry, so that what you saw resembled a giant multicolored snowflake. The program by Julesz & Bosche uses the same technique, computerized. Hundreds of programmers have imitated Julesz & Bosche, so now you can buy kaleidoscope programs for the IBM PC, Mac, Apple 2, Radio Shack TRS-80, and all other popular computers. Or try writing your own!

Take this test:

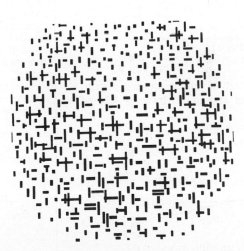

One of those is a famous painting (*Composition with Lines*, by Piet Mondrian, 1917). The other was done by a computer (programmed by A. Michael Noll in 1965). *Which one was done by the computer? Which one do you like best?*

The solution is on the next page, but *don't peek until you've answered!*

The computer did the top one.

The programmer surveyed 100 people. Most of them (59) thought the computer did the bottom one. Most of them (72) preferred the top one — the one that was actually done by the computer.

The test shows that people can't distinguish computer art from human art, and that the computer's art is more pleasing that the art of a famous painter.

The computer's version is more disordered than Mondrian's. The computer created the disorder by using random numbers. The survey shows that most people like disorder: Mondrian's work is too ordered. It also shows that most people mistakenly think the "computer" means "order".

Envelopes

Try this experiment. On a piece of paper, put two dots, like this:

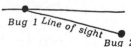

The dots represent little insects, or "bugs". The first bug is looking at the second bug. Draw the first bug's line of sight:

Make the first bug take a step toward the second bug:

Make the second bug run away, in any direction:

Now repeat the entire process. Again, bug 1 looks at bug 2; draw its line of sight:

Bug 1 moves toward bug 2:

Bug 2 keeps running away:

If you repeat the process many times, you get this:

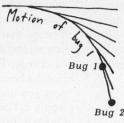

The "motion of bug 1" looks like a curve. (In fact, it's a parabola.) The "curve" is composed of many straight lines — the lines of sight. That's how to draw a fancy curve by using straight lines.

Each straight line is called a **tangent** of the curve. The entire collection of straight lines is called the curve's **envelope**. Creating a curve, by drawing the curve's envelope, is called **stitching the curve** — because the lines of sight act as threads, to produce a beautiful curved fabric.

You can program the computer to draw those straight lines. That's how to make the computer draw a fancy curve — even if you know nothing about "equations of curves".

To get a curve that's more interesting, try these experiments:

What if bug 2 doesn't walk in a straight line? What if bug 2 walks in a curve instead?

What if bug 1 goes slower than bug 2, and takes smaller steps?

What if the bugs accelerate, or slow down?

What if there are *three* bugs? What if bug 1 chases bug 2, while bug 2 chases bug 3, while bug 3 chases bug 1?

What if there are *many* bugs? What if they all chase each other, and their starting positions are random?

What if there are just two bugs, but the bugs are Volkswagens, which must drive on a highway having nasty curves? Show the bugs driving on the curved highway. Their lines of sight are still straight; but instead of moving along their lines of sight, they must move along the curve that represents the highway.

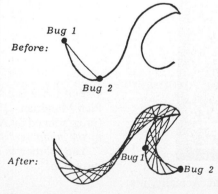

What if each bug has its own highway, and all the bugs stare at each other?

Here are some elaborate examples....

Four bugs chase each other:

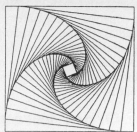

The next example, called *Compelling*, appeared in the famous book and movie, *The Dot and the Line*. (Norton Juster made it by modifying art that had appeared in *Scripta Mathematica*.) It resembles the previous example but makes the 4 bugs start as a rectangle (instead of a square), and makes the bug in the top left corner chase the bug in the opposite corner (while *looking* at a nearby bug instead).

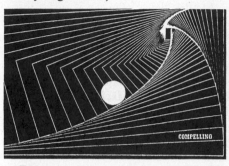

Enigmatic (from *The Dot and the Line*) makes 3 bugs chase each other, while a fourth bug stays motionless in the center:

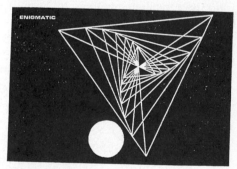

I invented *Kite*, which makes 8 bugs chase each other:

I also invented *Sails*, which makes 14 bugs chase each other:

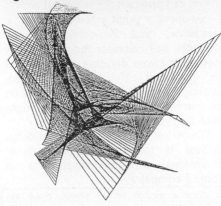

Elliptic Motion (by my student Toby D'Oench) makes 3 bugs stare at each other, while they travel on 3 elliptical highways:

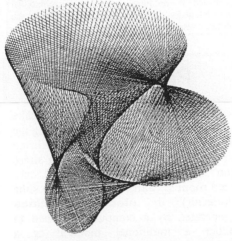

Archimedean Spiral (by Norton Starr) puts bugs on circles. The bugs stare at each other but don't move:

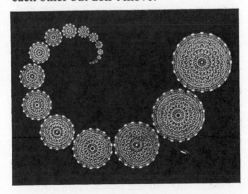

Fractals

A **fractal** is an infinitely bumpy line. Here's how to draw one.

Start by drawing a 1-inch line segment:

In the middle of that segment, put a bump and dip, like this:

Altogether, that bent path is 2 inches long. In other words, if the path were made of string, and you stretched the string until it was straight, the string would be 2 inches long. That's twice as long as the 1-inch line segment we started with. So here's the rule: **putting a bump and dip in a path makes the path twice as long**.

That bent path consists of seven segments. Put a bump and a dip in the middle of each segment, like this:

Altogether, those bumps and dips make the path twice as long again, so now the path is 4 inches long.

Again, put a bump and dip in the middle of each segment, so you get this:

Again the path's length has been doubled, so now the path is 8 inches long.

If you again put a bump and dip in the middle of each segment, the path's length doubles again, so the path becomes 16 inches long. If you repeat the procedure *again*, the path reaches 32 inches.

If you repeat that procedure infinitely often, you'll develop a path that's infinitely wiggly and infinitely long. That path is longer than any finite line segment. It's longer than any finite 1-dimensional object. But it still isn't a 2-dimensional object, since it isn't an "enclosed area". Since it's bigger than 1-dimensional but isn't quite 2-dimensional, it's called **1½-dimensional**. Since 1½ contains a fraction, it's called **fractional-dimensional** or, more briefly, **fractal**.

Look out your window at the horizon. What do you see?

> The horizon is a horizontal line with bumps (which represent hills and buildings and other objects). But on each hill you see tiny bumps, which are trees; and on each tree you see even tinier bumps, which are leaves; and on each leaf you see even tinier bumps, which are the various parts of the leaf; and each part of the leaf is made of even smaller bumps (molecules), which have even smaller bumps (atoms), which have even smaller bumps (subatomic particles).

Yes, the horizon is an infinitely bumpy line, a fractal!

You can buy software that creates fractals. Computer artists use fractal software to draw horizons, landscapes, and other bumpy biological objects. For example, they used fractal software to create landscapes for the *Star Wars* movies. You can also use fractals to draw a bumpy face that has zillions of zits.

Now you understand the computer artist's philosophy of life: "Life's a lot of lumps."

What's art?

To create art, write a weird program whose consequences you don't fully understand, tell the computer to obey it, and look at the computer's drawing. If the drawing looks nice, keep it and call it "art" — even if the drawing wasn't what you expected. Maybe it resulted from an error, but so what? **Anything interesting is art.**

If the drawing "has potential" but isn't totally satisfying, change a few lines of the program and see what happens — or run the program again unchanged and hope the random numbers will fall differently. The last thing to invent is the title. Whatever the drawing reminds you of becomes the title.

For example, that's how I produced *Kite* and *Sails*.

> I did *not* say to myself, "I want to draw a kite and sails". I just let the computer pick random starting points for the bugs and watched what happened. I said to myself, "Gee whiz, those drawings remind me of a kite and sails." So I named them *Kite* and *Sails*, and pretended I chose those shapes purposely.

That method may seem a long way from DaVinci, but it's how most computer art gets created. The rationale is: don't overplan…. let the computer "do its own thing"; it will give you art that escapes from the bounds of human culture and so expands your horizons!

Modern style

Computer art has changed. The **classic style** — which you've been looking at — consists of hundreds of thin lines in mathematical patterns, drawn on paper and with little regard for color. The **modern style** uses big blobs and streaks of color, flashed on a TV tube or film, which is then photographed.

Uncreative art

You've seen that computers can create their own weird art by using a wild combination of formulas and random numbers, unshackled by the bounds of human culture.

Computer programs let people create art easily and cheaply. Unfortunately, the typical person who buys a graphics program uses it to create the same kind of junk art that would be created by hand — just faster and more precisely. That's the problem with computers: they make the production of mediocrity even easier and more glitzy.

3-D drawing

The computer drew these 3-dimensional surfaces:

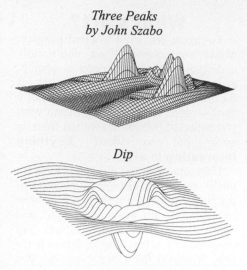

Three Peaks
by John Szabo

Dip

Those were done for the sake of art. This was done for the sake of science:

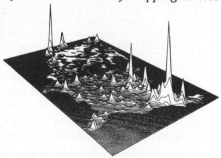

Population Density in the U.S.
by Harvard University Mapping Service

The hardest part about 3-dimensional drawing is figuring out which lines the computer should *not* show, because they're hidden behind other surfaces.

Coordinates

Try this experiment. Put your finger on the bridge of your nose (between your eyes). Now move your finger 2 inches to the right (so that your finger is close to your right eye). Then move your finger 3 inches up (so that your finger is near the upper right corner of your forehead). From there, move your finger 8 inches forward (so that your finger is 8 inches in front of your forehead).

Your finger's current position is called (2,3,8), because you reached it by moving 2 inches right, then 3 inches up, then 8 inches forward. The 2 is called the **X coordinate**; the 3 is called the **Y coordinate**; the 8 is called the **Z coordinate**.

You can reach any point in the universe by the same method! Start at the bridge of your nose, and get to the point by moving right (or left), then up (or down), then forward (or back).

The distance you move to the right is called the **X coordinate** (if you move to the left instead, the X coordinate is a negative number). The distance you move up is called the **Y coordinate** (if you move down instead, the Y coordinate is a negative number). The distance you move forward is called the **Z coordinate** (if you move back instead, the Z coordinate is a negative number).

Projected coordinates

To draw a picture of a 3-dimensional object, put the object in front of you, and then follow these instructions....

Pick a point on the object. (If the object has corners, pick one of the corners.)

Figure out that point's X, Y, and Z coordinates (by putting your finger on the bridge of your nose and then seeing how far you must move your finger right, up, and forward to reach the object).

Compute the point's **projected X coordinate** (which is X/Z) and the point's **projected Y coordinate** (which is Y/Z). For example, if X is 2 and Y is 3 and Z is 8, the projected X coordinate is 2/8 (which is .25) and the projected Y coordinate is 3/8 (which is .375).

On graph paper, plot the projected X coordinate and the projected Y coordinate, like this:

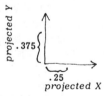

Then plot the point:

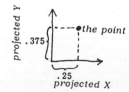

Do that procedure for each point on the object (or at least for the corners). Connect the dots and — presto! — you have a 3-dimensional picture of the object! And the picture is mathematically accurate! It's what artists call a "true perspective drawing".

To make the picture look traditionally beautiful, place the object slightly to the left of you and slightly below your eye level, so that all the X and Y coordinates become negative.

Computerized process

You can program the computer so that if you input a point's X coordinate, Y coordinate, and Z coordinate, the computer will calculate the projected X coordinate (from dividing X by Z) and the projected Y coordinate (from dividing Y by Z) and plot the point on the computer's screen (by using high-resolution graphics).

The easiest way to draw 3-dimensional pictures is to buy a special three-dimensional arm that attaches to an Apple 2 computer:

> To draw a picture of an object, move the mechanical arm until the arm's finger touches the object. Immediately the arm's software computes the X coordinate, Y coordinate, and Z coordinate of the touched point; you don't need a ruler! It also computes the projected X coordinate and the projected Y coordinate and plots the points on your television. If you have a graphics printer, the software also plots the point on your printer's paper.

PowerPoint

If you give a speech, you can make the speech more interesting by letting the audience watch "slides" while they listen to you. The "slides" can be film slides (on 35-millimeter film, projected onto the room's wall by using a slide projector) or **electronic slides** (generated by a computer attached to either a traditional monitor or a **computer projector**, which projects the images onto the room's wall).

The slides can include photographs, drawings, graphs, tables of numbers, and an outline of what you're talking about.

The best way to create such a slide show is to use a **presentation-graphics program**. The most popular presentation graphics program is **PowerPoint**, whose newest version, **PowerPoint 2000**, comes free as part of **Microsoft Office 2000**'s standard edition, professional edition, premium edition, or developer edition (but not small-business edition).

Here's how to use PowerPoint 2000.

Prepare yourself

Before using PowerPoint 2000, practice using Microsoft Word 2000, which I explained on pages 162-182. (To do that, you should be using Windows 95 or 98 or later.) Make sure Microsoft Word 2000 works fine before you try using PowerPoint.

To use PowerPoint 2000 easily, your monitor should be 17-inch (or bigger). Otherwise, the monitor is too small to show your writing well. Set the monitor's resolution at 1024-by-768 (or bigger) as follows:

> Close any windows that are open, so you see just the Windows desktop screen. Right-click in the screen's middle, where there is nothing. Click "Properties" then "Settings". Drag the slider toward the right, until it says "1024 by 768 pixels", then press ENTER. If the computer says "Windows will now resize your desktop", do this: press ENTER, then wait for the screen to become black, then wait for colors to reappear, then click "Yes".

Launch PowerPoint

Click "Start" then "Programs" then "Microsoft PowerPoint".

Create slides

To create a simple slide show easily, click "Design Template" then "OK" then "Design Templates".

Design template You see this list of 44 design templates:

> artsy, azure, bamboo, blends, blue diagonal, blueprint, bold stripes, cactus, capsules, checkers, citrus, construction, dad's tie, expedition, factory, fireball, gesture, global high voltage, Japanese waves, LaVerne, lock and key, marble, mountain, nature, neon frame, network blitz, notebook, post modern, pulse, radar, ribbons, rice paper, Romanesque, Sakura, sandstone, soaring, straight edge, strategic, sumi painting, sunny days, technology, topo, whirlpool

If you want to explore those templates, click the first one (artsy) and then press the keyboard's down-arrow key repeatedly. Double-click whichever one you want; but for your first experience, I recommend you choose "soaring", because it produces bright characters on a simple dark background, so the slide is easy to read. (It produces white-and-yellow characters on a black-and-blue background that includes a soaring curve.)

Layout After you've double-clicked a design template (such as "soaring"), the computer says "Choose an AutoLayout". You see this list of 24 layouts:

> title slide, bulleted list, 2-column text, table, text & chart, chart & text, organization chart, chart, text & clip art, clip art & text, title only, blank, text & object, object & text, large object, object, text & media clip, media clip & text, object over text, text over object, text & 2 objects, 2 objects & text, 2 objects over text, 4 objects

If you want to explore those layouts, click the first one (title slide) and then press the keyboard's right-arrow key repeatedly. Double-click whichever one you want; but for your first experience, I recommend you choose "bulleted list" (which is the second layout), because it produces a slide show fast.

Three panes Your screen is now divided into three windowpanes:

> The top right pane is called the **slide pane**. It shows what a slide will look like. (If you chose "soaring" as the design template, that pane shows white-and-yellow characters on a black-and-blue background that includes a soaring curve.)
>
> The bottom right pane is called the **notes pane**. It's white. It temporarily says "Click to add notes". It's where you can type notes that will *not* appear on the slide. Those notes are "cheat sheets" that remind you of what to say while you're showing the slide. You can keep the notes private or include them on paper "handouts" you hand out to the audience.
>
> The left pane is called the **outline pane**. It's white. It begins by showing the number 1. It's where you type an outline of the words that will be on your slides.

Text Your next step is to type words that will be on your slides. Although you can type the words directly onto the slide (by using the slide pane), it's much easier to type them in the left pane, the outline pane.

For example, suppose you want to give a speech, with slides, about the US Presidential Election. Begin by making an outline of your speech. For example, try typing this outline:

> **1 America's Favorite Candidates For President**
> - Barbie
> - Barney
> - Monica Lewinsky
>
> **2 Arguments For Barbie**
> - Many women bought into her culture
> - She's so attractive, we all call her a "doll"
> - She has no ideas, so not controversial
> - Ken would be great VP (better than Quayle)
> - She'd give feminists a reason to unite
>
> **3 Arguments For Barney**
> - "Colored", he shows we don't discriminate
> - If anyone calls him a "dinosaur", he laughs
> - No age barrier: his old act appeals to young
> - Believes in family values, sings about them
> - Uses short words that voters can understand
>
> **4 Arguments For Monica L.**
> - She's more real than the other candidates
> - She's had experience in the White House
> - Proved she can interest men and beat them
> - Boosts our ego: lets us feel bigger than Prez
> - "M" names are more popular than "B"
>
> **5 Act Now**
> - You'd be better than they
> - Get involved in the political process
> - You may now throw the eggs in your packet

Here's how to type it:

> **Click in the outline pane** (the left pane). The computer has already typed the number "1". **Next to the "1", type the headline that you want on the first slide.** That headline could be the name of your first topic, or the name of the whole speech, or a general phrase such as "Welcome" or "Opening Remarks". (For my example, type "America's Favorite Candidates For President".) When typing a headline, PowerPoint wants you to capitalize the first letter of each word. You'll be typing in the left pane, but your typing will simultaneously appear on the slide. **At the end of typing the headline, press ENTER. Press the TAB key (to indent), then type the first subtopic** ("Barbie"). In front of your typing, the computer will automatically put a bullet (the symbol "•"). When typing a subtopic,

PowerPoint wants you to capitalize just the subtopic's first letter; do *not* capitalize the first letter of each word (unless the word is a person's name or something similar). You'll be typing in the left pane, but your typing will simultaneously appear on the slide. **At the end of typing the subtopic, press ENTER.**
Type the second subtopic ("Barney"). The computer will automatically indent it (since the computer assumes you want each line to be indented the same as the line above). **At the end of typing the subtopic, press ENTER.**
Type the third subtopic ("Monica Lewinsky"). The computer will automatically indent it. **At the end of typing the subtopic, press ENTER.** The computer will put a red squiggle under "Lewinsky" to warn you that "Lewinsky" isn't in the dictionary, but don't worry: the red squiggle will not appear in your final slide show.
Congratulations! You've finished creating a slide! The entire slide is on the screen, in the slide pane (which is the screen's top right pane).
Now start working on the next slide, whose headline is "Arguments For Barbie". If you start typing "Arguments For Barbie", you'll notice that the computer tries to indent it, because it thinks it's a subtopic. Make the computer **unindent it by pressing SHIFT with TAB**. You can do that at the beginning of the line or anytime while you're typing that line. Pressing SHIFT with TAB makes the computer unindent the line you're typing, so the line becomes a headline for a new slide, which the computer will automatically number.
Finish typing the outline. **Press TAB whenever you want the computer to indent more, SHIFT TAB to indent less, and ENTER to end the line**.

Undo If you make a mistake, click the **Undo button** (which is near the screen's top and shows an arrow curving toward the left).

View different slides After you've created a set of slides (by typing the outline), here's how to change which slide you're viewing.

Method 1: in the outline pane, click whichever slide you want to view.

Method 2: click in the slide pane, then....

> Press the **PAGE DOWN** key to move to the next slide.
> Press the **PAGE UP** key to move back to previous slide.
> Press the **HOME** key to move back to the first slide.
> Press the **END** key to move ahead to the final slide.

Method 3: if your mouse has a wheel between the buttons, click in the slide pane then....

> **Rotate the wheel toward you** to move to the next slide.
>
> **Rotate the wheel away from you** to move to back to the previous slide.

Notes While viewing a slide, you can create notes about it by typing in the notes pane.

Five view icons

Near the screen's bottom left corner, you see a row of five icons. Here's what happens if you click them:

The first icon, **"Normal View"**, makes the slide pane be big (by making the outline & notes panes be small). That's the view you've been using.

The second icon, **"Outline View"**, acts like "Normal View" but makes the outline pane be wider (by making the slide and notes panes be narrower), so the outline pane is big, the slide pane and notes panes are small.

The third icon, **"Slide View"**, makes the slide pane be *very* big (by making the outline pane be *very* narrow and the notes pane disappear). In this view, the outline view is so narrow that it holds just each slide's number, not the words. While using slide view, you can still move from slide to slide by clicking the slide's number in the outline view.

The fourth icon, **"Slide Sorter View"**, shows all the slides simultaneously, side-by-side. (You see no outline and no notes.) While using slide sorter view, you can move a slide by dragging it to the gap between two other slides.

The fifth icon, **"Slide Show"**, starts the slide show; but before you click it, you should click slide 1 (using one of the other views), to make sure the show begins at slide 1. Then the whole screen will be devoted to slide 1. You'll see no outline, no notes, no menu bar, no toolbars, and no Windows: you won't even see the Start button, and you won't see any X button.

If you clicked "Slide Show", here's how to move from slide to slide:

To move to the **next slide**, press **ENTER** (or N or right-arrow or down-arrow or PAGE DOWN or click the mouse's button, or — if your mouse has a wheel between the buttons — rotate the wheel toward you).

To move **back to the previous slide**, press the **BACKSPACE** key (or P or left-arrow or up-arrow or PAGE UP, or — if your mouse has a wheel between the buttons — rotate the wheel away from you).

To move back to the **first slide**, press the **HOME** key (or while holding down the mouse's left button, press the right button for 2 seconds).

To move ahead to the **final slide**, press the **END** key.

To make the screen be all **black**, press the **B** key. That makes the slide temporarily disappear, so you can talk to the audience without making the audience be distracted by the slide. To resume, press the B key again.

To make the screen be all **white**, press the **W** key. (Press it again to resume.)

To make the **arrow (mouse pointer) disappear**, press the **A** key (or leave the mouse untouched for 15 seconds). Then the arrow and a button at the screen's bottom left corner disappear, so they won't distract the audience. To make the arrow and button reappear, press the A key again (which makes the button reappear), then move the mouse.

To make the mouse pointer become a **pen**, tap the **P key while holding down the Ctrl key**. Then the mouse pointer becomes a pen that has white ink. To scribble on the slide, just drag: move the mouse while holding down the mouse's left button. To emphasize a phrase, scribble *a circle around it* or *an underline below it* or *arrows aimed at it*. The scribbles are just temporary: a slide's scribbles disappear when you move to a different slide. When you finish using the pen, say **"unpen"** by tapping the **U key while holding down the Ctrl key**.

To **escape from the slide show** and return to other views, press the **Esc** key.

Delete

Here's how to delete a subtopic:

In the outline pane or slide pane, click the subtopic's bullet (the symbol "•"). Then press the DELETE key.

Here's how to delete an entire slide:

Method 1: in the outline pane, click the slide's number, then press the DELETE key then ENTER.

Method 2: go into Slide Sorter View (by clicking its icon); click the slide you want to delete, then press the DELETE key.

Insert

Here's how to insert an extra line into your outline:

Where do you want the extra line? Which line will be above the extra line? Click the end of the line that will be above the extra line.

Press ENTER.

Type the extra line.
While typing, if you want the extra line to be indented more, tap the TAB key. If you want the extra line to be indented less, press SHIFT with TAB.

Save

To copy your presentation to your hard disk, click the **Save button** (which is near the screen's top left corner and looks like a 3½-inch floppy disk).

If you haven't saved your presentation before, the computer will say "File name". Invent a name for your presentation. Type the name and press ENTER.

That makes the computer copy your presentation onto the hard disk. The computer puts your presentation into the My Documents folder.

Your publication's filename ends in ".ppt", which stands for "PowerPoint". For example, if you named your presentation "mary", the computer puts a file called "mary.ppt" into the My Documents folder.

Afterwards, if you change your mind and want to do more editing, go ahead! When you finish that extra editing, save it by clicking the Save button again.

Finish

When you finish working on your publication, choose **Exit** or **Close** from the **File menu**.

If you choose **Exit**, the computer will stop using PowerPoint.

If you choose **Close** instead of Exit, the computer will let you work on another document, and your next step is to say either **"Design Templates"** or **"Open"**.

If you say "Design Templates" (by clicking "File" then "New" then "Design Templates"), the computer will let you start creating a new document by using a design template: you see the list of 44 design templates.

If instead you click the **Open button** (which is near the screen's top right corner and looks like a file folder opening), you see a list of old presentations and other old documents. (To see the whole list, use the window's scroll arrows.) Each presentation has an icon that's orange: if you click its icon, you see its first slide; if you *double*-click its icon, you can use and edit its whole presentation; if you want to *delete* a presentation, click its icon and then press the DELETE key and then ENTER, which moves the presentation to the Recycle Bin.

Didn't save? If you didn't save your document before doing those procedures, the computer asks, "Do you want to save?" If you click "Yes", the computer copies your document's most recent version to the hard disk; if you click "No" instead, the computer ignores and forgets your most recent editing.

Congratulations! You've learned all the fundamental commands of PowerPoint.

Print

Besides showing slides onto the computer's screen and the room's wall, you can print copies of the slides onto paper, to hand to your audience (as handouts) and keep for yourself. Here's how.

To print on paper reliably, click "File" then "Print".

The computer assumes you want to print just 1 copy (for yourself). If you want to print *many* copies (for yourself and everybody in your audience), type how many copies you want to print. For example, if you're giving a speech to 50 people and want to hand each member of the audience a printout, plus have a printout for yourself, type "51".

Then click the "Print what" box's down-arrow. You'll see these four choices:

Choice	What each person will receive
Slides	many pages; each page contains 1 slide
Handouts	a few pages; each page contains several slides (shrunk)
Notes Pages	many pages; each page contains 1 slide (shrunk) and its notes
Outline View	1 page; it contains the outline

Click the choice you want.

Finally, click "OK". The computer will print on paper.

Another way to print is to click the Print button (which is near the screen's top right corner and looks like a printer with paper coming out). **That makes the computer print 1 copy, using the same choice as your previous printing**: Slides, Handouts, Notes Pages, or Outline View. But if you click the Print button, you might be very sorry, since "the same choice as your previous printing" might not be what you want to print now!

Transitions

While you're presenting a slide show, you make the computer switch to the next slide by pressing ENTER (or N or right-arrow or down-arrow or PAGE DOWN or clicking the mouse's button or rotating the wheel toward you). When you do that, the computer tends to display the next slide immediately and simply. Here's how to make the computer perform a fancier transition to the next slide, so the next slide appears gradually and spookily....

Get into Slide Sorter View. Right-click whichever slide you want to appear spookily. Click "Slide Transition".

Visuals Click the down-arrow next to "No Transition". You'll see these transition choices:

> no transition, blinds (horizontal or vertical), box (in or out), checkerboard (across or down), cover (down, left, right, up, left-down, left-up, right-down, or right-up), cut, cut through black, dissolve, fade through black, random bars (horizontal or vertical), split (horizontal in, horizontal out, vertical in, or vertical out), strips (left-down, left-up, right-down, or right-up), uncover (down, left, right, up, left-down, left-up, right-down, or right-up), wipe (down, left, right, or up), random transition

Click the transition choice you want. (If you're not sure, try any one. If you like surprises, choose "random transition", which lets the computer surprise you each time by making its own choice.) You'll see that kind of transition illustrated by a cow turning into a key (or the key turning back into the cow).

To choose the transition's speed, click "Slow" or "Medium" or "Fast". (While you're experimenting, I recommend "Slow" so you can see the transition more clearly.)

Sounds You can create a transition sound by clicking the Sound box's down-arrow and then clicking one of these choices:

> applause, breaking glass, camera, cash register, chime, clapping, drive by, drum roll, explosion, gun shot, laser, ricochet, screeching brakes, slide projector, typewriter, whoosh

(To see that full list, click the list's scroll arrows.) "Drum roll" is a good choice because it's the least obnoxious. You won't hear any sound immediately; you'll hear it later, when you actually perform the slide show.

Apply Finally, click "Apply" (to apply your desire to just one slide) or "Apply to All" (to apply your desire to all slides in your presentation).

Summary Here's a summary of what I've said: **to have the most fun, choose "random transition", "slow", "drum roll", and "Apply to All".**

Slide Show Finally, to make the transitions happen, click the "Slide Show" icon (the fifth icon in the row at the screen's bottom).

Animation

Usually, while you're presenting a slide show, the computer shows an entire slide at once. Here's how to **animate** a slide, so the computer show just one line at a time and wait for you to say when to show the next line.

Click the Slide Sorter View icon. Click the slide you want to animate (or press Ctrl with A, to animate *all* the slides). Click the Preset Animation box (which normally says "No Effect" in it). You'll see this list of animations:

> appear, fly (from bottom, left, right, top, bottom-left, bottom-right, top-left, or top-right), blinds (horizontal or vertical), box (in or out), checkerboard (across or down), crawl (from bottom, left, right, or top), dissolve, flash once (fast, medium, or slow), peek (from bottom, left, right, or top), random bars (horizontal or vertical), spiral, split (horizontal in, horizontal out, vertical in, or vertical out), stretch (across, from bottom, from left, from right, or from top), strips (left-down, left-up, right-down, or right-up), swivel, wipe (down, left, right, or up), zoom (in, in from screen center, in slightly, out, out from screen bottom, or out slightly), random effects

Click the animation you want. (If you're not sure, try any one. If you like surprises, choose "random effects", which lets the computer surprise you each time by making its own choice. To keep your audience awake, I recommend "random effects".)

Finally, to make it all happen, click the "Slide Show" icon (the fifth icon at the screen's bottom).

Then when you say "go" (by pressing ENTER or N or right-arrow or down-arrow or PAGE DOWN or clicking the mouse's button or rotating the wheel toward you), the computer will show just the slide's headline. When you say "go" again, the computer will show the slide's first subtopic, animated the way you requested. When you say "go" again, the computer will show the slide's next subtopic, animated the way you requested. Each time you say "go", you'll see one more line of text (or one more picture, if your slide includes any).

Tables

Here's how to put a table of numbers onto a slide.
Start a new slide, as follows:

> In the outline pane, click at the end of the previous slide's last line.
> Press ENTER (to create a new line in your outline).
> Press SHIFT with TAB (to unindent).
> Type a headline (title) for your table, but do *not* press ENTER afterwards.

Then create a table, as follows....

> Click "Format" (which is near the screen's top) then "Slide Layout". You see the list of 24 layouts. Double-click the "table" layout (which is at the end of the top row). Double-click where it says "Double click to add table".
> How many columns do you want in your table? Type how many, then press TAB. How many rows do you want in your table? Type how many, then press ENTER.

You see a blank table. Fill it in, by typing whatever words and numbers you wish. Move from cell to cell by using the arrow keys. (Another way to move to the next cell is to press the TAB key. Another way to move back to the previous cell is to press SHIFT with TAB.)

Multi-line cells Normally, each cell holds just a single number or a single phrase. If you want to squeeze *several* lines of info into a single cell, just press the ENTER key at the end of each line. If you type more lines than the cell can hold, the computer will automatically make the cell be taller (by making the entire row be taller). Try it:

> In a cell, type a big number. Emphasize it by pressing ENTER then typing "Wow!", so the cell contains the number and "Wow!"

Vertical centering To make the table look better, do this:

> Click in the table. While holding down the Ctrl key, tap the A key (which selects All of the table). Click "Format" then "Table" then "Text Box". Click the Text Alignment box's down-arrow. Click "Middle".

That makes the computer vertically center the entire table (so in each cell, the writing is as far from the top wall as from the bottom wall).

Align Right button To make the numbers line up better, do this:

> Drag across the numbers (so they all change color).
> Click the Align Right button (which is near the screen's top right corner).

Charts

Here's how to put a chart (graph) onto a slide.

Start a new slide, as follows:

> In the outline pane, click at the end of the previous slide's last line.
> Press ENTER (to create a new line in your outline).
> Press SHIFT with TAB (to unindent).
> Type a headline (title) for your chart, but do *not* press ENTER afterwards.

Then create the chart, as follows:

> Click "Format" (which is near the screen's top) then "Slide Layout". You see the list of 24 layouts. Double-click the "chart" layout (which is at the end of the second row). Double-click where it says "Double click to add chart".

You see a table of numbers and a chart based on that table.

> Edit the numbers in the table, so the table shows *your* numbers.
> Edit the words in the table, so the table shows *your* words.
> Then the chart will be a chart of *your* data.

Hide the datasheet
The table of numbers is called the **datasheet**. The slide includes just the chart and its headline, not the datasheet. While you're editing the datasheet, the datasheet temporarily blocks your view of the slide. To hide the datasheet, click its X box; to make the datasheet reappear (so you can edit it some more), do this:

> In the slide, click the headline, then double-click the chart.

> Click the View Datasheet button. (It looks like a table of numbers. It's near the screen's top center. It's below the word "Chart").

Types of charts
The computer assumes you want a column chart. Here's how to switch to a different type of chart instead, such as a bar chart or line chart:

> Click "Chart" then "Chart Type". You see this list of **chart types**: column, bar, line, pie, XY (scatter), area, doughnut, radar, surface, bubble, stock, cylinder, cone, and pyramid. Click the type you want. To the right of it, you see subtypes; double-click the subtype you want.

Colors
To add variety, change a slide's color scheme. Here's how:

> While you're not in the middle of running a slide show, click the slide whose color you want to change. Click "Format" then "Slide Color Scheme".
> You see some color schemes to choose from. (For example, if your layout is "soaring", you can choose from "blue background", "green background", "brown background", "white background", and "white background with just black objects".)
> Click the color scheme you want. (Usually, you should choose a dark background, such as blue or brown. Choose white just if you'll be printing onto transparencies.)
> Click "Apply" to change the color scheme for that slide (or click "Apply to All" to apply that color scheme to *all* slides).

Shapes
Here's how to decorate your slide by adding stars, arrows, and other shapes.

Put onto the screen the slide you want to decorate, in Normal View (or Outline View or Slide View). Click the word "AutoShapes" (which near the screen's bottom left corner).

You see these simple categories:

> lines, connectors, basic shapes, block arrows, flowchart, stars and banners

You also see these two advanced categories:

> callouts, action buttons

The "callouts" category lets you put words into a balloon coming out of somebody's mouth, as in a cartoon. The "action buttons" category lets you create Internet-style links, that you can click on to hop to different slides in your show.

Click whichever category you want. Then click the shape you want.

Imagine that the shape is enclosed by a rectangle. Point at the slide, where you want the rectangle's top left corner to be, and drag to where you want the rectangle's opposite corner.

If you chose the "callouts" category, type whatever words you want in the balloon. If you chose the "action buttons" category, click "OK" (after making any adjustments you wish).

Adjust the shape
After you've drawn a shape, here's how to adjust it.

If you don't like the shape's position, point at the shape's middle and drag it wherever you want. (Exception: if the shape is a callout, point at the shape's edge instead of middle.)

Here's how to stretch the shape, to make it wider or taller:

> Click in the shape's middle. (If the shape's a callout, click the shape's edge instead.)
> Surrounding the shape, you see up to 9 tiny white squares, called **handles**.
> To stretch the shape, drag one of the handles.
> You might also see a tiny yellow diamond. Drag it to stretch the shape's special feature.

If you make a mistake, click the Undo button. To delete a shape, click it and then press the DELETE key.

Timing
When you give a slide show, you typically want the computer to keep showing the same slide until you press the ENTER key (or N or right-arrow or down-arrow or PAGE DOWN or click the mouse's button or rotate the mouse's wheel toward you).

But sometimes, you'd rather have the computer switch to the next slide *automatically*, without waiting for you to say so.

> For example, if you're giving a passionate speech ("Oh, darling, I love you!") or playing in a rock band, you might want the images on the wall to change automatically without forcing you to interrupt your performance to press ENTER. If you're running an animated ad in an airport or shopping mall or store, by hiding a computer inside a kiosk, you'll want the computer's kiosk to run a PowerPoint presentation even when no salesperson is present.

Here's how:

> Click the words "Slide Show" (at the screen's top) then "Rehearse Timings".
> That makes the computer run a **rehearsal**. The computer starts the rehearsal by showing you slide 1 (as if you had clicked the Slide Show icon). To move from slide to slide, the computer waits for you to press ENTER (or N or right-arrow or down-arrow or PAGE DOWN or click or rotate). **The computer notices how long it waits; each waiting time is recorded.**
> When you finish viewing the final slide (and press ENTER to move on), the computer tells you how many minutes and seconds your entire slide show lasted. Press ENTER.

Here's what you've accomplished:

> In the future, whenever you start the slide show (by clicking the Slide Show icon), the computer will automatically move to the next slide after the appropriate amount of time (the time you took in rehearsal), even if nobody's pressed ENTER yet.

Puppets
When you give a PowerPoint presentation, don't just read the slides to your audience. Be more active!

> Walk into the audience. Get emotional. Jump around while you talk. Be a fascinating human, not a wooden puppet.

Use the slides whenever you wish, but remember that *you're* in control. Don't let the slides control *you*.

Use the slides to supplement what you have to say. Don't make the slides be the whole presentation. If your presentation's just a bunch of slides, your audience will wonder why you didn't just distribute printouts instead of forcing the audience to listen to you read slides.

Use your personality to add your own drama to the event:

> If you're giving a speech about something that seems boring (such as tables of numbers), reveal why they're interesting. Be bold enough to laugh at the material and be cynical about it. Tell the audience how you really feel, and why, and get them to think about it. Use your emotions to get the audience excited about thinking about the issues.

Though PowerPoint is powerful, I avoid it. When I'm in front of an audience, I prefer to talk from my soul; and I want my audience to look at my face, not slides. I'd rather scribble on a whiteboard (while I bang it or kiss it) than be in a darkened room dominated by a slide show.

> PowerPoint has wrecked the US military: too many military bureaucrats have been giving fancy PowerPoint presentations instead of getting real work done. The US military is in the process of banning PowerPoint.

Professional publishing

The first popular desktop-publishing program was **Pagemaker**.

How Pagemaker arose

Pagemaker was invented in 1985 by Paul Brainerd, who'd been a newspaper executive. Pagemaker ran on the Mac and used Apple's laser printer (the Laserwriter).

Pagemaker lets you combine words and graphics to form a newspaper page, including headlines, columns of articles, photographs, diagrams, captions, and ads, all on the same page. Pagemaker let you see the page on your computer's screen, while you moved the words and graphics by using your mouse.

According to traditional nerd jargon, such a program should have been called a "page-layout", "page-composition", or "computer-aided publishing" program. But to sell the program he coined a new term: he decided to call it a **desktop-publishing program**, because it used the Mac's "desktop" screen to help publishing, and because it let you run your own publishing company from a desktop in your home without having to hire typesetters, graphic artists, and other outside help.

The Pagemaker program and the term "desktop publishing" both became instant hits. Many would-be authors, publishers, and designers bought Apple computers just for the purpose of running Pagemaker. They used Pagemaker to create newspapers, newsletters, reports, books, flyers, posters, and ads.

Most ad agencies standardized on using Apple computers and Pagemaker to create ads. That's why Apple computers became popular in the graphics-arts community. Even today, nearly every ad agency uses Apple computers, not IBM-compatibles.

At first, the IBM PC couldn't handle desktop publishing at all. Eventually, Windows (and a competitor called **Gem**) improved enough so that the IBM PC's screen could look Mac-like. Finally, a Windows version of Pagemaker became available.

Pagemaker's competitors

Competitors to Pagemaker arose. Now your main choices are **Pagemaker**, **Quark Xpress**, **Frame Maker**, and **Ventura Publisher**.

Here's how they compare:

Pagemaker (for Mac & Windows) is the easiest to learn. It's the best for handling graphics and short ads. Quark Xpress is the best for handling text and fonts. Its Mac version is better than its Windows version. Frame Maker (for Mac & Windows) is the best for organizing long, technical manuals. Ventura Publisher is just for Windows, not the Mac. It was weak, but it's improving fast.

Mergers

Pagemaker was published by Paul Brainerd's company, Aldus. In 1994, Aldus merged into a company called **Adobe**, which had invented many other desktop-publishing tools, such as Postcript (the font system used in Apple's Laserwriter), Illustrator (a draw program), and Photoshop (a photo-manipulation program). Then Adobe bought the company that made Frame Maker. So now Pagemaker and Frame Maker are both published by Adobe.

Ventura Publisher was published by Ventura, then by Xerox, then by Ventura again, and now by **Corel** (which also publishes Corel Draw and Word Perfect).

Quark Xpress is published by Quark, which is still independent.

Difficulties

Using desktop-publishing software can be difficult. That's why Pagemaker is often called "Pagewrecker", Frame Maker is called "Frame Wrecker", Quark Xpress is called "Quark Distress", and Ventura is called "Vultura": they can eat your offspring.

Frames

Like a word-processing program, a desktop-publishing program lets you type words onto the screen. But when you start using a desktop-publishing program, the first thing to do is divide your screen (and page) into boxes. Each box is called a **frame**.

In one frame, type a headline. In another frame, put a picture. (You can create the picture by using the draw tools that are included as part of the desktop-publishing program, or else **import** a drawing or painting or photo that you created by using some other graphics program.) In another frame, put a table of contents or an index. In another frame, put an ad. In another frame, put column 1 of an article. In another frame, put column 2.

You can **link** one frame to another. For example, you can link column 1 to column 2, so if you type an article that's too long to fit in column 1, the excess will **spill** into column 2.

You can link a frame on page 1 to a frame on page 7, so if an article's too long to fit on your newspaper's front page, it will continue on page 7. (Continuing on a far-away page is called a **jump**. Newspapers do it frequently. I wish they didn't!)

Master page

If most of the pages in your newspaper resemble each other, create a **master page** that shows how the typical page should look. On that master page, put frames for each column, and at the top of the page put a header that includes the page number and your newspaper's name & date (so when a reader rips out an article, the reader knows where it came from).

Special pages can diverge from the master.

Clutter

The typical beginner makes the mistake of trying to be too fancy. Use just a *few* typestyles and frames per page, to avoid making your publication look like a disorganized cluttered mess.

Put enough frames on your page to add spice; but if you add too many frames, your publication will look chopped-up, dicey, as amateurish as an oil painting by a 2-year-old kid given his first paint box.

Adding some frames will make it look spicy, But too many frames will make it look dicey. Gentle control shows a master who knew; Out-of-control shows a kid who acts 2.

Mozart's music was masterfully charming because its overall structure was simple, though it had a few subtle surprises. Imitate him.

Unfortunately, professional desktop-publishing programs are expensive: about $500 each!

Kiddie pub

Cheaper, easier desktop-publishing programs have been invented, for kids and novices. The most famous is **Print Shop**, published by Broderbund.

> It's particularly good at creating greeting cards, posters, and banners. The first version was popular among kids using Apple 2 computers because it was amazingly easy to use, though the graphics it produced were low-resolution and crude. (I guess you call that "folk art".)
>
> It's been translated to the Mac, IBM PC, and most other computers, too. The newest versions produce graphics that are better (but still not good enough to pass as professional). Unfortunately, the newer versions are harder to learn.

Print Shop's price has been reduced to about $20 because nobody wants it anymore. Instead, folks want **Microsoft Publisher**.

> Like Print Shop, Microsoft Publisher can produce greeting cards, posters, and banners. Better than Print Shop, it can handle high-resolution graphics and tiny fonts well and produce professional-looking newspapers, newsletters, reports, business cards, and origami paper airplanes. It asks for your mood ("Would you like your publication to look jazzy or classical?"), then produces a terrific-looking document with fake words, which you replace with your *own* words. It lets you fine-tune your publication's graphics and layouts by using your mouse and professional desktop-publishing techniques. Best of all, it comes with a terrific manual (training you in the fine art of desktop publishing) and costs just $70 from discount dealers.
>
> Bill Gates, who runs Microsoft, liked the design of Microsoft Publisher so much that he took the head of the design team and married her!

Word processing

Recently, word-processing programs have grown to include lots of desktop-publishing features.

The first word-processing program that let you create frames was **Ami Pro**. Other word-processing programs have copied Ami Pro's idea of permitting frames, so now you can create frames in Word Pro (which is Ami Pro's successor), Microsoft Word, and Word Perfect. (But creating frames is still easier in Word Pro than in other word processors.)

If what you're writing has a simple layout, with very few frames or graphics per page, you can use a word-processing program instead of a desktop-publishing program.

How I published this book

I wrote this edition of *The Secret Guide to Computers* by using just Microsoft Word. I got by with Microsoft Word instead of a desktop-publishing program because I kept my layout simple, with very few frames and graphics per page.

Graphics I clipped most of the graphics from the wonderful clip-art books published by **Dover**. Dover's clip-art books are available in most art-supply stores, and their illustrations are far superior to "clip-art CD-ROM disks", which contain just crude cartoons. To get a catalog of Dover's clip-art books, send a postcard to Pictorial Archive Dept., Dover Publications, 31 E. 2nd St., Mineola NY 11501.

Being a low-tech guy, I had my staff paste the graphics into my book by hand, by using rubber cement.

> Rubber cement is faster than fiddling with scanners, image editors, and high-falutin' graphics commands in Microsoft Word and desktop-publishing programs.
>
> The only major problem with rubber cement is that if I change my mind and edit the page, we have to paste the graphics in again. To avoid wasting time, we had to plan our work carefully and not paste the graphics in until the text's final draft was done.
>
> If you use rubber cement, remember that long exposure to its fumes can cause cancer, so use it in a well-ventilated area and try not to get it on your hands.
>
> To make a graphic smaller, I used my photocopier, which can shrink to any percentage.

Fonts For most of this book, I used just 4 fonts:

> This font is called "Times New Roman". It's from Microsoft. I used it for most of my writing. It's therefore called my "body-text font". Unlike other Times Roman fonts, Microsoft's has the nice property: when working in small font sizes (such as 8-point), each digit is as wide as two blank spaces, and each period takes up as much space as one blank space. That makes it easy to keep the columns lined up! (Microsoft wants you to line up columns by using fancy features such as "tables" and "decimal tabs", but pressing the space bar is simpler.)
>
> `This font is called "Lineprinter". It comes with all Hewlett-Packard Laserjet printers. It s monospaced. I used it to imitate computer output.`
>
> **This font is called "Arial Black". It's from Microsoft. It's an extra-bold version of Arial. It's big, black, and ugly. It's so monstrous that it stands out on the page. That stand-out quality is why I chose it. In fact, it stands out so much that I shrunk it to prevent it from overwhelming the page. For example, in the middle of 10-point Times New Roman, to emphasize a word I used 9-point Arial Black. If I were to set ALL my headlines in Arial Black, I'd look like a big, ugly, pompous ass, so....**
>
> To lighten things up and show I'm a regular fella who's light-hearted and funny, I used this funny font, called "Comic Sans MS". It's from Microsoft. I used it at the top of each section. I put a box around it to give it greater emphasis, since it isn't black enough to draw attention unboxed.

Typical text is Times New Roman 10-point (with 11-point line spacing, so there's a 1-point gap between lines).

> Small text (like you're reading now) is typically Times New Roman 8-point (with 9-point line spacing), boxed, and shaded 5%. Monospaced computer output (`like this`) is Lineprinter 8½-point. Emphasized words (**like this**) are Arial Black 7-point, 9-point, 11-point, or 14-point, depending on importance. Big headlines (like the headline "Cheaper solutions" at the top of this page) are Comic Sans MS, 20-point, boxed, and shaded 12.5%.

For *gigantic* headlines at the beginning of each chapter, I typically used gigantic fonts (usually 48-point) supplied by a company called **Formatt**.

> Each Formatt font is fascinating (much more interesting than its famous competitor, Letraset) and comes on a sheet (available in art-supply stores). You cut Formatt letters from the sheet by using an Exacto knife. The sheet has a background that's transparent and semi-sticky, so you can easily reposition the letters if you make a mistake.

At the beginning of the strangest chapters (on pages 205 and 592), I used strange fonts that came on a CD-ROM disk called **Kid Fonts & Icons**, published by Softkey (now part of The Learning Company). That disk is cheap and widely distributed. I got it at my local supermarket for $12.99 while buying groceries!

Dimensions To squeeze as much info as possible onto each page without clutter, I set my left and right margins at .5", top margin at .3", bottom margin at .6" (to leave space for the footer), and distance between columns at .3".

> The typical page contains 2 columns, each 3.6" wide. When I needed a wider column (to hold a wide table or graphic), I widened the column to 4.8" instead, so the page's other column shrunk to 2.4". On a few pages, I used 3 narrow columns, each 2.3".

Microsoft Publisher

Here's how to use **Microsoft Publisher 2000**, which is part of **Microsoft Office 2000**. (Earlier versions of Microsoft Publisher are similar.)

Prepare yourself

Before using Microsoft Publisher 2000, practice using Microsoft Word 2000, which I explained on pages 162-182. (To do that, you should be using Windows 95 or 98 or later.) Make sure Microsoft Word 2000 works fine before you try using Microsoft Publisher.

To use Microsoft Publisher 2000 easily, your monitor should be 17-inch (or bigger). Otherwise, the monitor is too small to show your publication well. Set the monitor's resolution at 1024-by-768 (or bigger), as follows:

> Close any windows that are open, so you see just the Windows desktop screen. Right-click in the screen's middle, where there is nothing. Click "Properties" then "Settings". Drag the slider toward the right, until it says "1024 by 768 pixels", then press ENTER. If the computer says "Windows will now resize your desktop", do this: press ENTER, then wait for the screen to become black, then wait for colors to reappear, then click "Yes".

Launch Microsoft Publisher

Click "Start" then "Programs". You see the Programs menu.

Click "Microsoft Publisher" if you see that choice. If you *don't* see that choice, install Microsoft Publisher as follows (assuming you're using Microsoft Office 2000 Premium):

> Press the Esc key twice. That makes the Programs menu and Start menu disappear.
> Put the Microsoft Office 2000 Premium's disk 2 into the CD-ROM drive.
> The computer says "Welcome to Microsoft Office 2000". Press the TAB key, type your initials, press the TAB key twice, type the Product Key code (which is on the orange sticker on the back of the CD-ROM disk's square jewel case and is 25 characters long), press ENTER, click "I accept the terms in the License Agreement", press ENTER three times.
> The computer will restart. Try again to click "Start" then "Programs" then "Microsoft Publisher"; this time, you'll succeed!

The left window shows this list of 25 **wizards**:

> quick publications, newsletters, web sites, brochures, catalogs, flyers, signs
> postcards, invitation cards, greeting cards, business cards
> letterheads, envelopes, business forms, banners, calendars, advertisements
> award certificates, gift certificates, labels, with compliments cards
> menus, programs, airplanes, origami

Quick publications

The most powerful wizard is "quick publications". Try clicking it now! Here's what happens....

Design The right-hand window shows these 51 **designs**:

> accent box, accessory bar, arcs, argyle, astro, bars, birthday, blank, blends, blocks, border flowers, borders, bouquet, bubbles, butterfly, capsules, checkers, circles, confetti, corner art, crossed lines, diamonds, floating oval, handprint, hearts and circles, jumbled boxes, jungle, leaves, linear accent, marquee, maze, mobile, pansies, party time, pinwheel, punctuation, retro, ribbons, romance, scallops, signpost, soap bubbles, starfish, steps, straight edge, stripes, tilt, triangles, wallpaper, waves, wavy frame

(You see just the first few; to see the rest, use that window's scroll arrows.)

You can double-click whichever design you want; but for your first experience, try double-clicking "accent box".

(If the computer says "The wizard will fill in your name…", press ENTER twice.)

The computer will say "Quick Publication Wizard". Press ENTER.

Color scheme You see this list of 62 **color schemes**:

> alpine, aqua, berry, black & gray, black & white, bluebird, brown, burgundy, cavern, citrus, clay, cranberry, crocus, dark blue, desert, field, fjord, floral, garnet, glacier, green, heather, iris, island, ivy, lagoon, lilac, mahogany, marine, maroon, meadow, mist, mistletoe, monarch, moss, mountain, mulberry, navy, nutmeg, olive, orchid, parrot, pebbles, prairie, rain forest, red, redwood, reef, sagebrush, sapphire, shamrock, sienna, spice, sunrise, sunset, teal, tidepool, tropics, trout, vineyard, waterfall, wildflower

The list is too long to fit on the screen. The computer assumes you want "waterfall". To try a different color scheme instead, click one that's visible and interests you, then press your keyboard's up-arrow or down-arrow key repeatedly to see the others and their effects. When the one you want is highlighted, click "Next" (which is at the screen's bottom).

Layout The quick-publications wizard can create a publication that has three **objects**:

> a **picture** (such as a photo or drawing)
> a **heading** (a few words in big letters)
> a **message** (a few sentences in small letters)

The wizard assumes you want to display the picture on top, then the heading, then the message (since the viewer's eye will naturally be attracted to the picture first, then the heading, then the message); but you can change that layout. For example, you can omit the picture, omit the heading, omit the message, make the picture smaller, move the picture to below the heading, twist the heading 90° (so it becomes a **sidebar heading**), or insert a fourth object: personal info about yourself!

You see this list of 14 **layouts**:

> Large picture at the top
> Large picture in the middle
> Small picture at the top
> Small picture in the middle
> Sidebar heading, picture at the top
> Sidebar heading, picture at the bottom
> Sidebar heading, no picture
> No message, picture at the top
> No message, picture at the bottom
> No picture
> No heading
> Message only
> Heading only
> Personal information with picture

The wizard assumes you want the first layout, "Large picture at the top". To try a different layout instead, click one that interests you and look at its effect. For your first experiment, I recommend you stay with "Large picture at the top". When the layout you want is highlighted, click "Finish".

Heading You see your publication. In it, click the word "Heading", then type whatever words you want the heading to be.

If you type *many* words, the computer will automatically switch them all to a smaller font, so the words will still fit in the space allotted. If you type a word that's not in the computer's dictionary (because the word is weird or you misspelled it), the computer will put a red squiggle under it.

Message Under the heading, you see a sentence saying "Place your message here". Click in that sentence, then type the message you want to be under the heading. (If your message contains *many* words, the computer will automatically switch them all to a smaller font, so the words will still fit in the space allotted.)

Picture Above the heading, you see a picture. Temporarily, that picture is a photo of a sunset, but you can change that picture. Here's how….

Put the Microsoft Office 2000 Premium's disk 2 into the CD-ROM drive.

Double-click the picture you want to change, then click "Pictures", then maximize that window (by clicking the window's maximize button, which is next to the X button).

> You start seeing 60 photos. (To see all 60, use the window's scroll arrow.)
>
> To see a different 60, click "Keep Looking" (which is under the 60 photos you saw). You'll see a second batch of 60. Underneath it, click "Keep Looking" to see the third batch of 60. Altogether, there are many thousands of photos and cartoons to see.
>
> To see ones about a particular topic, click in the white box that's labeled "Search for clips", then type the topic you want to search for.
>
> To go back and see the pictures you saw before, click the Back button (which is a left-arrow at the screen's top left corner); after clicking it, you can click the Forward button (which is a right-arrow) to move forward again. To see pictures organized by category, click the Home button (which is next to the Forward button), then click the category you want.

If you find a picture that interests you, click it. Then you see a menu of four choices, which are icons.

> Click the first choice (an arrow called "Insert clip") if you've decided you want that picture; then the computer will use that picture instead of the sunset photo.
>
> Click the second choice (a magnifying glass called "Preview clip") to temporarily view the picture bigger, so you can see it more clearly and make a better decision about whether you want it.
>
> Click the third choice (an arrow called "Add clip to Favorites") then "Add" to copy the picture to the Favorites category.
>
> Click the fourth choice (binoculars called "Find similar clips") to search for other pictures that are "similar"; then explain what you mean by "similar" by clicking either "Color & Shape", or a keyword about the picture's content, or (if it's an artist's drawing instead of a photo) "Artistic Style".

Finally, close the pictures window (by clicking the X at the screen's top right corner).

Undo If you make a mistake, click the **Undo button** (which is near the screen's top and shows an arrow curving toward the left).

Save To copy your publication to your hard disk, click the **Save button** (which is near the screen's top left corner and looks like a 3½-inch floppy disk).

If you haven't saved your publication before, the computer will say "File name". Invent a name for your publication. Type the name and press ENTER.

That makes the computer copy your publication onto the hard disk. The computer puts your publication into the My Documents folder.

> Your publication's filename ends in ".pub". For example, if you named your publication "mary", the computer puts a file called "mary.pub" into the My Documents folder. The file's icon has P on it, to remind you it was created by Publisher.

While you're editing and improving your publication, you should click the Save button frequently.

> If you accidentally let more than 15 minutes go by without clicking "Save", the computer tends to remind you by saying, "It's time to save your work!". To reply, click "Yes". (If you don't like such reminders, here's how to prevent them: click "Tools" then "Options" then "User Assistance", then remove the check mark from "Remind to save publication" by clicking, then press ENTER.)

Print To print your publication onto paper, make sure your printer is turned on and contains paper. Then do this:

> To print a **single copy** of your publication, click the **Print button** (which is near the screen's top left corner and shows a printer spewing out paper).
>
> To print **many copies**, do this instead: **click "File" then "Print"**, then double-click in the "Number of copies" box, then type how many copies you want and press ENTER.

Exit When you finish working on your publication and have saved it, you have three choices:

> To **stop** using Microsoft Publisher, click its **X box**.
>
> To make Microsoft Publisher **start a new document**, just **click "File" then "New"**. You'll see the list of 25 wizards again.
>
> To make Microsoft Publisher **retrieve an old document** you saved, click the **Open button** (which is near the screen's top left corner and shows a file folder opening).

Congratulations! You've learned all the important techniques of Microsoft Publisher! You can create your own publications! Now let's dig deeper….

Alignment The heading and message both contain words. The wizard assumes you want each line of words to be centered. Centering is fine if your heading and message are both short. But if your message contains *many* lines of words, centering makes your message hard to read.

To change whether a paragraph is centered, click in the paragraph and then click whichever alignment button you prefer:

> The **Align Left button** makes the paragraph's **left margin** be straight, the right margin be ragged, so the paragraph looks like this. This is the easiest to read and the friendliest, since it looks informal. But it looks lopsided.
>
> The **Align Right button** makes the paragraph's **right margin** be straight, the left margin be ragged, so the paragraph looks like this. This is the hardest to read. It's the least popular choice.
>
> The **Justify button** makes the paragraph's **left and right margins** both be straight (except for the end of the paragraph's last line), so the paragraph looks like this. This is the most sophisticated. It's fairly easy to read, though it puts too much space between the words. It's the best choice for a long message. It's what I used for most paragraphs in this book.
>
> The **Center button** makes each line in the paragraph be **centered** again, so the paragraph looks like this. This looks the neatest. It's good for short headlines and messages, but it's hard to read if the message is long. It's what I used for the headlines in this book.

Those buttons work the same way as in Microsoft Word.

Frames Your publication contains three main objects: the picture, the heading, and the message. It also contains several other objects (border decorations near the paper's edge).

You can change each object's size and position. Here's how….

Click in the object's middle. Then the entire object will be surrounded by a pack of dogs! Each dog is a black tiny square, called a **handle**. The dogs (handles) are arranged to form a box surrounding the object, so the object is boxed in. The box surrounding the object is called the object's **frame**. Yeh, Louie, we've been framed! Then you can manipulate the object in three ways:

> To change the object's size, drag one of the handles (by using the mouse).
> To rotate (tilt) the object, drag a handle *while holding down the Alt key*.
> To move the object, drag an edge of its frame (but don't drag a handle).

Signs

Instead of clicking "quick publications", try clicking "signs". That lets you use the sign wizard, which is the simplest of all wizards! It lets you create signs simply! Here's what happens....

Design The right-hand window shows these 28 **designs**:

authorized personnel only, beware of dog, business hours, checks accepted, closed for remodeling, closed, for rent, for sale, garage sale, gone fishing, help wanted, information, inventory, kid's room, lemonade for sale, no loitering, no parking, no smoking, open house, open, out of order, private property, restrooms, return time, special offer, we speak, wet paint, wheelchair access

(You see just the first few; to see the rest, use that window's scroll arrows.)

You can double-click whichever design you want; but for your first experience, try double-clicking "kid's room".

The computer says "Sign Wizard". Press ENTER.

Color scheme You see the full list of 62 **color schemes**, but just 5 schemes work well for signs: click either "brown", "dark blue", "green", "red", or "waterfall" (which is black). If your printer can't print colors, choose "waterfall".

Then click "Finish" (which is at the screen's bottom).

You see your publication. It's a sign that says "Kid's Room" and includes a drawing of a moon with stars. The sign is in the color you chose.

Edit the words Change the word "Kid's" to your own name. For example, if your name is "Joan", change "Kid's Room" to "Joan's Room". Here's how: click "Kid's", then type your name, then type 's.

Change "Room" to a word that's more descriptive, such as one of these:

Bedroom, Hideaway, Lair, Hovel
Office, Headquarters, Classroom
Home, Castle, Garden, Pond, Swimming Hole, Woods
Closet, Locker, Trunk, Corner, Secret Passage, Private Parts

To do that, click "Room" then type whatever replacement you want.

Change the picture Change the moon-with-stars to whatever other picture you prefer. To do that, make sure Microsoft Office 2000 Premium's disk 2 is in the CD-ROM drive, then double-click the moon, then maximize the clip-art window (by clicking the window's maximize button, which is next to the X).

You'll see alternative pictures of moons and stars. If you don't like any of them, click the Home button (which is at the screen's top, next to the arrows), then click the picture category you want.

When you finally find a picture you like, double-click it, then click the "Insert clip" icon (which is next to the picture).

Finish You can **undo**, **save**, **print**, and **exit**: just use the same techniques as for the "quick publications" wizard.

Banners

A **banner** is a big sign that nearly a foot tall and *several* feet wide. You can create a banner by taping several sheets of paper together, side-by-side.

To create a banner, click "banner" instead of "quick publications".

Design The wizard can create 41 kinds of banners. Each kind is called a **design**. Those 41 designs are organized into 9 categories:

Informational: apartment for rent, caution, (checked frame), information, (interwoven frame), new management, order here, (plain background), registration, reservations, safety equipment

Sale: bake sale, clearance sale, sale, yard sale

Event: anniversary, bon voyage, enter to win, grand opening, open house, pageant, school dance, street fair, team spirit

Birthday: birthday

Welcome: welcome back, welcome, welcome new addition

Congratulations: baby congratulations, champions, congratulations, graduation, promotion, retirement, the greatest, to the best

Holiday: Fourth of July, New Year

Romance: marry me

Get Well: get well

In the screen's left window, under the word "banner", you see those 9 categories. Click the category that interests you. Then click the right-hand window's scroll-down arrow if necessary, until you see the specific design that interests you. Double-click that design. Then you'll see it enlarged.

The computer says "Banner Wizard". Press ENTER.

Banner width How wide do you want the banner to be? Click "5 feet", "6 feet", "8 feet", or "10 feet". (For your first experiment, try "5 feet" to avoid wasting paper. Hey kids, if you want to choose more than 5 feet, get your parents' permission first!) Then press ENTER.

Banner height How tall do you want the banner to be? Click "11 inches" or "8.5 inches". (For your first experiment, try "8.5 inches" to avoid wasting paper.) Then press ENTER.

Graphic Next to the message, the wizard can put a picture, which is called a **graphic**. Do you want the graphic to be left of the message, right of the message, on both sides of the message, or omitted? Click your choice. Then press ENTER.

Border Do you want to put a fancy box around the message? The fancy box is called a **border**. If you want a border, click "Yes"; otherwise, click "No". Then click "Finish" (which is at the screen's bottom).

Edit the words To change a word or phrase or the symbol "...", click it, then type what you want instead.

Change the picture Change the moon-with-stars to whatever other picture you prefer. To do that, make sure the CD-ROM disk double-click the moon, then maximize the clip-art window (by clicking the window's maximize button, which is next to the X).

You'll see alternative pictures of moons and stars. If you don't like any of them, click the Home button (which is at the screen's top, next to the arrows), then click the picture category you want.

When you finally find a picture you like, double-click it, then click the "Insert clip" icon (which is next to the picture).

Finish You can **undo**, **save**, **print**, and **exit**: just use the same techniques as for the "quick publications" wizard.

Warning: when you've printed the banner onto paper, examine the banner carefully before you hang it on your wall: a few letters or graphics might be missing, because your printer doesn't contain enough RAM memory chips or your printer can't print close enough to the paper's edge.

Greeting cards

To create a greeting card, **click "greeting cards"** instead of "quick publications".

Design The wizard can create 91 kinds of greeting cards. Each kind is called a **design**. Those 91 designs are organized into 14 categories:

Thank you: accent box, accessory bar, arcs, balloons, bars, bird, blends, blocks, borders, bubbles, capsules, checkers, crossed lines, floating oval, flower and heart, globe and flower, linear accent, marquee, mobile, punctuation, scallops, straight edge, sun, tilt, waves

We've moved: banner bar, compass point, side stripes, steps

Engagement announcement: rings

Birth announcement: expectant mom, mother and child

Reminder: watch and pin

Holiday: Christmas deer, Christmas Nutcracker, Christmas Santa, Easter egg and bunny greeting, Easter lilies, Halloween pumpkin and witch, Hanukkah dreidel and star, Hanukkah menorah, holiday design box, holiday fading frame, holiday tipped title, Kwanzaa candles, New Year champagne, Ramadan stars, Rosh Hashanah star of David, Thanksgiving leaves

Birthday: sun moon and stars, cake and heart, cake, clown, fireworks and star, gift and balloon, Jack-in-the-box, open present, wine and cheese, woman with cake

Special day: anniversary bride and groom, anniversary romantic couple, Father's Day dad and daughter, Father's Day strong shoulders, Grandparents Day hand and heart, Mother's Day blooms, Mother's Day heart and tulip, Mother's Day May flowers, Valentine's Day Cupid, Valentine's Day heart, Valentine's Day rose and moon

Congratulations: bon voyage luggage, joyful jumper, shooting star, strong man, book and dancer, graduation hug, new baby infant things, new baby mom and baby, new home house and garden, new home weather vane, promotion corporate ladder, retirement golf and bowl, wedding swirl and heart

Friendship: heart and moon, swirl and girl

Romance: city couple, shared heart

I'm sorry: arrows

Get well: flower basket, hospital

Sympathy: rose

In the screen's left window, under the phrase "greeting cards", you see those 14 categories. Click the category that interests you. Then click the right-hand window's scroll-down arrow if necessary, until you see the specific design that interests you. Double-click that design. Then you'll see it enlarged.

The computer says "Greeting Card Wizard." Press ENTER.

Layout If the computer says "Layout", click one of these layouts for the card's front cover:

juxtapositions:	message is at the top, above squares and small picture
pattern pickup:	message is in the middle, surrounded by 12 tiled icons
picture squares:	message is at the bottom, under 4 big tiles containing icons
art bit:	message is in the middle, under a small picture
greetings bar:	message is at the bottom, under a big picture

Size and fold If the computer says "Size and Fold", click one of these choices:

The simplest is to click **"Quarter page side fold"**, which will produce a greeting card by telling you to fold a sheet of paper into quarters. For your first experience, choose this!

A variant is to click **"Quarter page top fold"**, which produces a greeting card that looks like a tent.

Clicking the third choice, **"Half page side fold"**, creates a bigger card but requires you to glue two sheets of paper together — or print on both sides of a single sheet.

Color scheme Press ENTER. You see the list of 62 color schemes. The computer assumes you want "waterfall". Click whichever color scheme you want.

Suggested verse Press ENTER. Click "Browse". You'll see about 20 verses that relate to your topic. Here are examples:

Topic you picked	Sample verse
anniversary	You two seem to have everything you need... *Each other! Happy Anniversary.*
birth announcement	A baby has arrived. *And the world is bright with wonder and light.*
bon voyage	All systems are go. *So, take off! And have a blast on your vacation.*
Easter	Happy Easter *Wishing you joy in this season of renewal.*
engagement	We're pleased to announce... *An engagement to be married.*
Father's Day	Dad, you've always protected me. *You're my super hero!*
friendship	When I look on the bright side... *It's always in your direction.*
general congrats	When you come down to earth... *I'd like to give you a pat on the space helmet. Congratulations!*
get well	Your well-being is of great concern. *And your absence deeply felt. Please get well soon.*
graduation congrats	The school book has closed. *A new chapter begins.*
Grandparents Day	How wise of them to name a day... *For people nice in every way.*
Halloween	Happy Halloween... *From our dungeon to yours!*
happy birthday	May this birthday... *Be the beginning of the best years of your life.*
happy Hanukkah	May the Festival of Lights... *Illuminate both your heart and your home. Happy Hanukkah.*
happy holidays	Of all the gifts bestowed this year... *First be the gift of loved ones near.*
happy New Year	Pop the cork and throw the confetti. *The New Year's here and we're all ready.*
I'm sorry	We goofed... *Please excuse our error.*
Kwanzaa	Kwanzaa *Kwanzaa candle burning bright, feel the wonder of the light. Share the pride, keep the glow, pass it on to all you know.*
love & romance	Roses are red, carnations are pink... *I'd like to go out with you, what do you think?*
merry Christmas	Yuletide Greetings *Hope your holidays are happy!*
Mother's Day	To Mother... *Thank you for years of love.*
new baby/adoption	Congratulations on the new baby. *We always know you could perform miracles.*
new home congrats	Congratulations on your new home... *From your old friends.*
Ramadan	Warm thoughts to our friends... *During Ramadan.*
reminder	Don't forget... *You have an appointment with us. We look forward to seeing you.*
retirement congrats	Have fun when you retire, but remember... *Don't play too hard!*
Rosh Hashanah	May the New Year... *Bring you happiness and prosperity.*
sympathy	With deepest sympathy *Our condolences to you and your family.*
thank you	In a world of chaos... *Thanks for the order!*
Thanksgiving	Happy Thanksgiving *Have a festive fall!*
Valentine's Day	Everyone should have a special Valentine... *I'll be yours if you'll be mine.*
wedding	I'd wish you luck for your wedding... *But you already seem to have it all.*
we've moved	We've Moved *Please send all correspondence to our new address.*

Click the verse you want, then click "OK" then "Finish".

Edit Your card has 4 pages. You're seeing the front cover, which is page 1.

At the screen's bottom, you see the numbers 1, 2, 3, and 4. To see page 2, click the 2. That makes you see page 2 (and you'll simultaneously see page 3, next to it). To see page 4 (which is the back cover), click the 4. To see page 1 again, click the 1.

You can edit each object on each page.

To edit text, click it.
To edit a picture, double-click it, then use the same techniques as for the "quick publications" wizard.

Finish You can **undo**, **save**, **print**, and **exit**: just use the same techniques as for the "quick publications" wizard.

When you print onto paper, all four pages of the greeting card will appear on a single sheet of paper (if you chose a "quarter page" layout). Fold that sheet of paper in half (to divide pages 1&4 from pages 2&3), then fold in half again (to divide page 1 from 4).

Other wizards

You've learned how to use 4 wizards, called "Quick Publications", "Signs", "Banners", and "Greeting Cards". Altogether, there are 25 wizards to play with. Try them! They're similar to the wizards you already mastered.

Blank publications

Though wizards can be helpful, sometimes you'll wish they'd shut up, so you can start with a clean, blank sheet of paper and design your own publication in peace, with interruptions from wizards who talk too much and think too much of themselves. Here's how to make the wizards shut up.

Start Microsoft Publisher (by clicking "Start" then "Programs" then "Microsoft Publisher"). You see the Catalog window. Close it (by clicking its X button).

Typing with F9 You see a blank page. You can start typing on it. Your typing will be too small to read: to see it bigger, press the F9 key.

> That makes the type look bigger, but too big to fit the whole page on the screen. If you want to switch back to the "whole page" view, press F9 again. F9 is a **toggle** that switches back and forth between "easy to read" and "whole page" views.

Similar to word processing While you're typing, Microsoft Publisher 2000 resembles Microsoft Word 2000 (explained on pages 162-182). After you've practiced using Microsoft Word 2000, Microsoft Publisher 2000 is easy! Here are the main peculiarities of Microsoft Publisher 2000:

> **Type your document (pages 163-164):** the PAGE UP and PAGE DOWN keys don't move the cursor; Ctrl symbols don't work; Microsoft Publisher can't check your grammar, so there are no green squiggles; Microsoft Publisher expects your entire message to fit on one page (unless you use special tricks I explain later), so there are no page arrows and you can't give a simple page break.
>
> **Font Size (page 166):** the Font Size menu starts at 4 points instead of 8 points.
>
> **Style (page 167):** in the Style box's pull-down menu, the only choice is "Normal".
>
> **Color buttons (page 168):** there is no Highlight button; if you click the Font Color button, 6 colors appear, then click the color you want.
>
> **Save (page 170):** your document will be called "mary.pub" instead of "mary.doc".
>
> **How to finish (page 170):** when you finish working on a document, close the Microsoft Publisher window (by clicking its X box) or click the New button or click the Open button.
>
> **Print Preview (page 171):** instead of pressing a Print Preview button, press F9.
>
> **Zoom (page 172):** in the Zoom box, you normally see 100% or 50%, depending on how many times you pressed the F9 key; I recommend you just press the F9 key rather than edit the number in the Zoom box.
>
> **Columns (page 172):** the Columns button is missing, because you create columns by creating frames, which I'll explain later.
>
> **Table buttons (pages 172-173):** the Table buttons are missing, because you create tables by creating frames, which I'll explain later.
>
> **File menu (page 174):** the File menu has no "Print Preview" and no "Properties".
>
> **Edit menu (pages 174-175):** the Edit menu has no "Go To"; the menu says "Delete Text" instead of "Clear".
>
> **View menu (pages 175-176):** the View menu has no "Normal", no "Page Layout", no "Header and Footer", and no "Full Screen".
>
> **Insert menu (pages 176-178):** the Insert menu has no "Footnote", no "Text Box", and no "Bookmark"; the menu says "Text File" instead of "File".
>
> **Format menu (pages 179-181):** the Format menu is organized differently.
>
> **Tools menu (page 181):** the Tools menu has no "Word Count"; the menu says "Spelling" instead of "Spelling and Grammar"; "Language" does not include "Thesaurus".
>
> **Window menu (pages 181-182):** the Window menu is called "Arrange" and is organized differently.
>
> **Help menu (page 182):** the Help menu has no "What's This"; the menu says "Publisher" instead of "Word".

Frames The text you've been typing is in a box, called a **frame**. The frame has 8 **handles** (1 at each order, and 1 at the midpoint of each side). Each handle is a tiny black square.

Try this experiment: make sure you're seeing the entire page (by pressing F9 if necessary), then make the frame smaller (by dragging one of the handles toward the frame's center). Now the frame is small, so it does *not* consume the whole page, so you can create extra frames elsewhere on the page.

The frame that's already on the page is called a **text frame**,

because it contains text you typed. Here's how to create an extra text frame:

> Click the **Text Frame Tool** (which is an A at the screen's right edge). Decide where on the page you want the extra text frame to begin; put the mouse pointer there; that will be the frame's top left corner; drag to where you want the frame's bottom right corner to be. The frame will appear.
>
> In that frame, type whatever text you wish. To see your typing more easily, press F9.

You can change a frame's position:

> To change a frame's size, click inside it then drag one of its handles.
> To rotate a frame, click inside it, then drag a handle *while holding down the Alt key*.
> To move a frame, drag one of its edges (but not a handle).

You can create 5 kinds of frames. To create a frame that contains **normal text**, you've learned to do this:

> Click the **Text Frame Tool** (which is an A at the screen's right edge).
> Drag across the page, to form the frame.
> Type the text (and press F9 to see it better).

To create a frame that contains **curved text**, do this:

> Click the **WordArt Frame Tool** (a red W and blue A at screen's right edge).
> Drag across the page, to form the frame.
> Type the text. Be brief, a few words per line. Press ENTER at end of each line.
> At the screen's top right, click the down-arrow next to "Plain Text".
> Click the shape you want.
> Click anywhere on the page, but outside the frame.

To create a frame that contains a **table** (of numbers or words), do this:

> Click the **Table Frame Tool** (which is a grid at the screen's right edge).
> Drag across the page, to form the frame.
> Type how many rows you want, then press the TAB key.
> Type how many columns you want, then press the TAB key.
> Press the keyboard's down-arrow key repeatedly, until you see a nice format.
> Press ENTER.
> Type the data (and press F9 to see it better, TAB to move to the next cell).

To create a frame that contains a **picture from Publisher's CD**, do this:

> Insert the CD.
> Click the **Clip Gallery Tool** (which is a clown face at the screen's right edge).
> Drag across the page, to form the frame.
> The Insert Clip window appears; maximize it.
> Click "Pictures". Click the category you want. Click the picture you want.
> Click the "Insert clip" icon.
> Close the Insert Clip Art window (by clicking its X button).

To create a frame that contains a **picture from a different source** (such as a picture you created by using Paint), do this:

> Click the **Picture Frame Tool** (mountains at the screen's right edge).
> Drag across the page, to form the frame. Double-click in that frame.
> Get onto the screen your picture's icon (by clicking the folder it's in).
> Double-click that icon.

To delete a frame, right-click in the frame's middle, then click "Delete Object".

If you type text that's too long to fit in its frame, the computer puts the symbol "A■■■" at the frame's bottom. The last few words you typed are temporarily invisible: the computer stores them in an **overflow area** (which you can't see) until you make the frame bigger (by dragging its handles) or make the text shorter — or create a 2nd frame, to display the overflow, as follows:

> Click the **Text Frame Tool** (which is an A at the screen's right edge).
> Drag across the page, to form the 2nd frame.
> Click in the first frame (the frame that was too small).
> Click the Connect Text Frames button (a pair of chain links at the screen's top).
> Your mouse pointer turns into a pouring cup. Use it to click in the 2nd frame.

Extra pages So far, your publication contains just one page. To make your publication longer by adding a second page, click "Insert" then "Page" then "OK".

Now your publication has two pages. You're seeing page 2. To see page 1, click the "1" at the screen's bottom. To see page 2 again, click the "2" at the screen's bottom. Remember to press F9 to toggle between "full page" view and "easy to read" view.

MULTIMEDIA

Speech

Computers have become quite good at speaking. Computers that speak hide in many devices.

For example, you can buy a talking car that tells you when it needs an oil change, a talking bathroom scale that makes cynical comments about how much your weight's gone up since yesterday, and many other talking devices. You can even buy Coke from a talking vending machine that invites you to deposit your coins and then says "Thank you".

Talking watch

Whenever I want to find out the time, I just press a button on my wrist watch, and its computer voice proudly proclaims the time in perfect English. Whenever I get lonely at night and want somebody to talk to me, I just press the watch's button and thrill to the sound of its soothing voice.

It also acts as the world's most humane alarm clock. Instead of giving an awful ring, its human voice says, "Attention, please! It's 7:30AM." Then it plays some jazzed up Bach.

If I'm still sleepy and ignore the alarm, five minutes later it will say, "Attention, please! It's 7:35AM. Please hurry." It will also subject me to some more Bach. It will keep reminding me every five minutes, until I'm awake enough to turn off the alarm.

You can buy the **Vox Watch** at Radio Shack for $39.95.

Reading to the blind

The most impressive talking device ever invented is the **Kurzweil Reading Machine**, which reads books to the blind.

It looks like a photocopying machine. Just lay a book on top of the machine, and the machine reads the book to you, even if the book is laid down crookedly and has dirt on it and has multiple columns and photos and uses weird type.

When it was invented many years ago, it used to cost $50,000. To use such a machine, you had to be rich or live near a library owning the machine. Eventually the price dropped to $20,000. Later, the price dropped even lower.

Now Kurzweil sells a text-to-speech program called **Madison** for just $50.

It can speak several languages. To use it, you must buy at least a 66-megahertz 486 computer with 16M of RAM and speakers; and if text isn't in the computer already, you must type the text or buy a scanner and a program for optical-character recognition (OCR).

Kurzweil used to be an independent company, but now it's part of **Lernout & Hauspie**.

Voice input

Though computers are good talkers, they're not good listeners. No computer's been invented yet that will replace your secretary and let you dictate a letter to it accurately. But researchers are getting close!

Buy a program called **Naturally Speaking** (by **Dragon Systems**, $169) or a similar program called **Via Voice** (by IBM, $99).

Each program comes in a box that includes a microphone. When you speak into the microphone, the computer listens to what you say and will try to type it for you, so your words will appear on the screen and on disk.

Each program is about 92% accurate: 8% of the words you say will be misinterpreted. You then edit the misinterpreted words. That editing makes the whole process slower than hiring a good secretary who can type fast and accurately.

Because of the errors, neither program should be trusted. For example, if a doctor dictates to the computer that a patient has "irregular heartbeat", the computer might think the doctor said "a regular heartbeat". If a doctor says a patient has "hyperglycemia", the computer might hear it as "hypoglycemia", which is the opposite.

Computer experts love to stump the computer. For example, when Steve Manes said "Hello, Nick and Bob", the computer thought he said "Hello, naked boys" (because "Nick" and "Bob" weren't in the computer's vocabulary yet). When John Woram said "He ate eight oysters", Naturally Speaking thought he said "He 88 oysters"; Via Voice thought he said "Diego State oysters".

Which of those programs is better? Via Voice is better at handling most sentences, but Naturally Speaking is better at handling sentences that include numbers or mouse-movement commands.

Each program requires 32M of RAM. Naturally Speaking requires a 133-megahertz Pentium and 60M of free disk space; Via Voice requires a 150-megahertz Pentium and 125M of free disk space.

Before using either program, you must train the program to understand *your* accent, by reading some sample sentences.

Music

Computerized music is advancing rapidly. Now you can sit down at a portable piano-style keyboard (light enough to carry in one hand), bang out a tune, feed the tune to a computer, and have the computer edit out your errors, play the tune back using the tone qualities of any instrument you wish (or even a whole orchestra), and print the score on paper.

Such developments are shaking up the entire music industry.

When you watch a TV commercial or movie, the background music that sounds like a beautiful orchestra or band is often produced by just a single person sitting at a computerized music synthesizer. The imitation of orchestral instruments is so exact that even professional musicians can't hear the difference. As a result, whole orchestras of musicians are now unemployed.

Music synthesizers come in two categories. One kind's cheap ($25 to $500) and easy to use but produces sounds that are tinny. The other kind produces beautiful sounds but costs a lot ($500 to $20,000) and is harder to learn to master. Programmers are trying to meld those two categories together. I wish they'd hurry up!

Ultimate Music Machine

Musicians, programmers, and engineers are working together to create the Ultimate Music Machine, which makes all other musical instruments obsolete. You can buy all its parts at your local computer and music stores, but the software and hardware that connects the parts is awkward. I expect some company will eventually build an assembled version that you just plug into the wall for immediate fun.

Part 1: the tone-quality creator The Ultimate Music Machine can imitate all other musical instruments. To make it imitate an instrument, play a few notes of that instrument into the machine's microphone. The machine makes a digital recording of the instrument, analyzes the recording, and stores the analysis on a 3½-inch floppy disk.

The machine's analysis is quite sophisticated. For example, it realizes that a violin note has a vibrato (because the violinist's finger wiggles), that each piano note begins with a bang and ends with a hum, and that the piano's bass notes sound "fatter" than the treble notes (because the bass notes are made from different kinds of strings).

The machine lets you edit the analysis, to create totally new tone qualities, such as "piolin" (which is a compromise between a piano and a violin).

When you buy the machine, it comes with recordings of the most popular instruments, and lets you add your own and edit them. It also lets you use fundamental waveforms (such as sine waves, square waves, and triangle waves), which act as building blocks for inventing sounds that are wilder.

Part 2: the note creator

The machine includes a piano-style keyboard (with black and white notes on it). To feed the machine a melody, tap the melody on the keyboard. You can also play chords. The machine notices which notes you strike the hardest, so it records your accents.

The machine includes a **pitch-bend dial**, which you turn to make the notes slide up the scale, like a slide trombone.

If you're not good at the keyboard, use the machine's screen instead, which displays a musical staff and lets you move notes onto the staff by using a mouse. You can also use the mouse to edit any errors you made on the keyboard, and to create repetitions and increase the tempo.

If you fear mice and keyboards, just sing into the machine's microphone. The machine notices which notes you've sung and records them.

If you're too lazy to create a melody or harmony, the machine creates its own. Its built-in computer analyzes your favorite music, notices its rhythms, note transitions, and harmonic structures, and then composes its own music in the same style.

Part 3: output

The machine plays the editing music through stereo speakers. As the music plays, the complete score moves across the screen, in traditional music notation. The machine also prints the score on paper. Yes, the machine prints a complete score showing how you sang into the mike or tickled the keys!

Vendors

The Ultimate Music Machine is built from music synthesizers. The most popular synthesizers are made by four Japanese companies: Casio, Roland, Yamaha, and Korg. Their synths cost from $25 to $3000 and contain tiny computers. For extra computing power, attach a Macintosh computer by using a Musical Instrument Digital Interface cable (MIDI cable). To print pretty scores cheaply, add Deluxe Music Construction Set, a Mac program published by Electronics Arts for under $50.

Advanced multimedia

Multimedia is the attempt to make your personal computer overwhelm your senses by feeding you text, music, voice, graphics, animation, and video movies on the screen all simultaneously! To do that well, you need a fast computer (at least an Intel 486 or a Mac 68040) with a CD-ROM drive and circuitry to handle sounds well.

Encarta

Microsoft's most famous example of multimedia is **Microsoft Encarta**. It's a CD-ROM disk whose 1997 version includes:

the complete text of the 29-volume Funk & Wagnalls encyclopedia, supplemented by 1000 extra articles (so you get 30,000 articles altogether)
a 65,000-word dictionary
8 hours of sound (organized into 1600 sound clips)
written & spoken samples of 60 languages
7500 photos & illustrations
100 video clips & animations
800 maps
1500 links from the articles to the Internet's World Wide Web

Using Encarta is fun: using your mouse, just click on whatever topic on the screen interests you and — whammo! — you see it and hear it. Discount dealers sell it for just $40.

You can also get a souped-up version, called **Microsoft Encarta Deluxe Edition**, which includes:

two CD-ROM disks (instead of 1)
1800 sound clips (instead of 1600)
14,000 photos & illustrations (instead of 7500)
150 video clips & animations (instead of 100)
4000 Web links (instead of 1500).

Discount dealers sell it for $75.

Cinemania & beyond

Inspired by Encarta's success, Microsoft has gone on to develop other multimedia titles that are more specific. For example, **Cinemania** is a CD-ROM whose 1997 version includes:

info on 20,000 movies, with reviews by Leonard Maltin, Roger Ebert, Pauline Kael, and Baseline
info on 10,000 directors, writers, actors, & other film folk, including biographies of the 4,500 most important
30 video clips, 150 famous sound bytes ("dialog clips"), and 1000 movie stills

It costs just $20 ($30 minus $10 rebate). I wish the title didn't sound like "sin-o-mania", though most movies are indeed about the manic enjoyment of sin.

Microsoft has also done multimedia titles on topics such as Beethoven's *Ninth Symphony* (including detailed analysis of the music, the man, and his times), Stravinsky's *Rite of Spring*, works by Mozart & Schubert, London's National Gallery of Art, and baseball lore.

Create your own

Though using multimedia created by companies such as Microsoft can be fun, it's even more fun to create your own!

Most software purporting to help you create multimedia is tedious to use and expensive. But here's the exception: get **Magic Theatre**, a CD-ROM disk published by two companies working together (**Knowledge Adventure Inc.** and **Instinct Corporation**). Comp USA's been selling it for just $35.

Designed for kids, you'll learn how to use it in just a few minutes. It lets you create animated cartoons with sound, so easily that you can create exciting cartoons after just a few *seconds* of preparation!

The $35 price even includes a microphone, accompanied by a CD-ROM disk that includes lots of clip art, animated objects, music, and sound effects, which you can combine in just a few seconds to produce an on-screen animated movie that you'll like a lot better than Saturday morning cartoons — especially since *you* created it!

The cartoons you'll produce will seem child-like, but that's their charm!

Try it, you'll like it. If you have kids, the whole family can pitch in to make a family animated movie. Your neighbors will be jealous.

ACCOUNTING

General accounting

In a typical store, the **employees** transfer **products** to **customers** from **suppliers**, for a **profit**. To manage the store, you must keep track of those 5 categories: your employees, products, customers, suppliers, and profit. Each requires its own computer program.

> To compute what to pay your **employees**, get a **payroll program**.
>
> To monitor which **products** you have in stock, get an **inventory program**.
>
> To keep track of what your **customers** owe — how much you're supposed to receive from them — get an **accounts-receivable program**.
>
> To handle debts to your **suppliers** and figure out how much to pay, get an **accounts-payable program**.
>
> To compute your **profits**, get a **general-ledger program**.

So altogether, you need five programs: **payroll (PR)**, **inventory (INV)**, **accounts receivable (A/R)**, **accounts payable (A/P)**, and **general ledger (GL)**. Let's look at them more closely.

Payroll

The payroll program writes paychecks to your employees. It computes how much each employee earned (the employee's **gross wage**), then subtracts various **deductions**, and writes the difference (**net pay**) onto the paycheck.

> It handles several kinds of deductions: the **federal withholding tax (FED)**, the **Federal Insurance Contributions Act's social-security tax (FICA SOCSEC)**, state taxes, local taxes, and payments to health and pension plans.
>
> It prints checks to the government, to pay the taxes that were deducted and your state's unemployment insurance. At the end of each quarter and year, it fills in all the payroll-information forms that government bureaucrats require.
>
> If the program's fancy, it counts how many employees are in each department of your company, totals how much money each department is spending for labor, and keeps track of employee vacations and attendance records.
>
> Before buying a payroll program, check whether it includes a table that lets it automatically compute *your* state's income tax.

Inventory

The inventory program counts how many products are in stock.

> It prints each product's sales history, predicts when each product will sell out, and notices which products are generating the largest profits. By analyzing all that information, it determines which products to reorder and in what quantities.
>
> For each product it says to reorder, it prints a purchase order, to mail to the supplier. It keeps track of whether the supplier has sent the requested goods.
>
> At the end of the year, it totals the dollar value of all the products in the inventory, to help compute the value of your business and your tax.

Accounts receivable

The accounts-receivable program computes how much each customer owes.

> For each customer who pays immediately, the program prints a receipt. For customers who plan to pay later, it prints a **bill** (for services) and an **invoice** (for goods).
>
> It notices which bills and invoices have been paid. It sends **dunning notices** to the customers who are late in paying — the ones that are **past-due**. It refuses to accept orders from customers who are past-due or reaching their credit limit.
>
> It computes a finance charge for customers who pay late. It gives discounts to customers who pay quickly or buy large quantities.
>
> It records each customer's name, address, phone number, and buying habits, so your sales force can talk the customer into buying even more. It records your salesperson's name, and computes the salesperson's commission.

> Before your company services a customer, the program gives the customer a written estimate of the cost.

Accounts payable

The accounts-payable program prints checks to your suppliers, to pay for the products they sent you.

> The program delays payment as long as a supplier allows, so that you can temporarily invest that money in your own business, without requiring bank loans. That's called, "making full use of the supplier's line of credit".
>
> The program stores each supplier's name, address, phone number, product line, and discount policy, so you can purchase easily and wisely.

General ledger

The general-ledger program computes the company's profit, by combining info from the other four programs.

> It prints a variety of profit reports for your stockholders, bank, financial planners, and government. The reports show the results for the day, week, month, quarter, and year.
>
> It tracks each department's budget, to make sure that no department spends too much. To protect your money from being stolen or embezzled or lost, the program performs **double-entry bookkeeping**: whenever it credits money to one account, it debits the same amount of money from another account, so that the books balance.

If the program's fancy, it stores your business's history for the last several years.

> It compares your current profit against earlier profits, and each current budget item against previous budgets. It tells how much your business is improving or declining. It even tries to predict your business's future.

Which accounting package to buy

Now the most popular package for general accounting is **Quickbooks**. It's popular because it's much easier than competitors. It tries real hard to hide accounting jargon from you, so you don't have to read about "debits", "credits", and "double-entry bookkeeping". It's ads brag that Quickbooks gives you "No debits and credits, just plain English."

It tries to view your entire business as just a bunch of checkbooks. It's published by **Intuit**, which also publishes **Quicken**, the world's most popular checkbook-balancing program.

> The first version of Quickbooks was incomplete, but the newest versions contain lots of features. Yes, Quickbooks now handles all 5 accounting functions (payroll, inventory, accounts receivable, general ledger, and accounts payable) and is flexible enough to handle many situations.
>
> You can get either the standard version ($100) or the Pro version (which adds time-billing, estimating, and job-costing and costs $200). You can get Quickbooks on either floppy disks or a CD-ROM. (The CD-ROM contains extra tutorials and reference materials.)
>
> Not sure whether you want Quickbooks? Then get a trial version free (with free shipping, too!) by phoning Intuit. The trial version contains the full features and can be used 25 times, after which it self-destructs. Any data you generate with the trial version can be transferred to the full version.
>
> For more info, phone Intuit in California at 800-446-8848 or 415-944-6000.

The next step up is **Peachtree Complete Accounting**.

> 20 years ago, back in the 1970's, Peachtree was the first full-featured accounting program for microcomputers. It used to cost about $5,000; but because of competition from newer, cheaper packages (such as **Dac Easy Accounting** and later Quickbooks), the price has dropped to $200, and the quality has improved further. At $200, it's a terrific bargain. It uses traditional accounting jargon but tries to explain it well. It's harder for novices than Quickbooks, but it makes accountants feel more comfortable. You can buy a stripped-down version, called **Peachtree First Accounting**, for just $50; but if you're going to strip you should get Quickbooks standard instead, which wins all awards from reviewers who've strip-searched. For more info, phone Peachtree Software (which was bought by ADP) in Georgia at 800-228-0068 or 770-724-4000.

The next step up beyond Peachtree Complete Accounting is **Businessworks PC**, published by **State-of-the-Art Accounting Software** in California at 800-447-5700.

Frankly, the only accounting package I've ever seen that was *very* easy was **Dac Easy Light**.

> It was delightful and came in a box that looked like a can of light beer. Discount dealers sold it for just $42. But it was limited: it couldn't handle payroll or inventory, couldn't handle big companies (since it limited most database files to 500 records each), and didn't print well on laser printers, though it handled dot-matrix printers fine. It used MS-DOS without Windows. (A Mac version was invented but was more confusing.)

It's been discontinued. I wish somebody would imitate it and "do it right".

Many uncomputerized companies do accounting by using "One-Write" checks, which are checks that have a stripe of carbon paper across their backs, to copy handwritten checks onto the correct ledger pages. **One-Write Plus** is a program that makes the computer imitate that system.

> Folks who were used to the manual system like One-Write Plus. It was published by Evergreen Software, then by NEBS, and now by Peachtree. It's not as full-featured as Quickbooks or Peachtree Complete Accounting.

Two kinds of accounting

There are two ways to do accounting: **conservative** and **cowboy**.

The conservative way is to do double-entry bookkeeping, which records each transaction as a "credit" to one account and a "debit" from an offsetting account. That forces the books to balance and prevents any department from going over budget or stealing money.

All "professional" accountants use that conservative method. But it's tedious and hard for a novice to fully understand.

If the company is small enough so the president knows all employees personally, watches their work, personally approves all payments, and has a good gut feel for how the business is doing, the conservative "double-entry" method is an unnecessary waste of time. Instead, the president can just total all payments that the company received, total all checks that the company wrote, total the value of the inventory, and report those totals to the government at tax time — after breaking down those totals into subcategories that the government requires. The president can do it all easily with a pocket calculator or spreadsheet program (such as Excel) or database program (such as Q&A). That approach is called **cowboy**, because it's quick but suffers from a dangerous lack of controls.

Most small companies having fewer than 10 employees use that cowboy approach — and so do I! That approach is reasonable just if the president is personally involved in all facets of the company's day-to-day operations and has enough common-sense wisdom to compensate for a lack of computer-generated analyses.

Accounting hassles

Though some companies use Quickbooks and other standard accounting packages, most companies don't, for four reasons:

> **1. To understand accounting packages fully, you must understand the theory of debits and credits**, which is complicated.

> **2. Those accounting packages work best if your company's an intermediary** that buys from manufacturers and resells to stores.
>
> If you run a retail store where most customers pay cash, you'll complain that the accounting packages don't automate your cash register or automatically copy data from cash-register slips to the sales records and inventory module. If you run a non-profit organization, you'll dislike how the accounting packages keep bragging about your "profit" instead of how much you're "under budget". If you run a doctor's office, you'll regret that the accounting packages don't record your patient's medical histories and needs, don't fill in the forms that your patient's insurance companies require, and don't handle multiple payers (in which the patient pays part of the bill and several insurance companies split the rest of the bill). If you run a consulting firm that dispenses services rather than goods, you typically won't need inventory or accounts-payable modules, and many items in the other modules will be irrelevant.

> **3. Each company does business in its own unique way**, whose peculiarities can't be handled well by any general-purpose accounting package.
>
> For example, your company may have a unique way of offering discounts to customers. To make the computer automatically compute those special discounts, you must write your own program; but then you'll have difficulty making your program transfer that discount info to the accounting package you bought.
>
> Because of each company's uniqueness, the typical company avoids generic accounting packages and instead hires a programmer to write a customized program, by using a language such as BASIC or DBASE.

> **4. General-purpose accounting packages print standard reports but don't let you invent your own.** Instead of using the reports generated by general-purpose accounting packages, many managers prefer to design their *own* reports, by copying the company's data into a spreadsheet program (such as 1-2-3, Quattro, or Excel) or data-management system (such as Q&A, Approach, Access, or DBASE) and then "fiddling around" until the report looks pretty. General-purpose accounting packages don't let you fiddle.

If you have just one accounting problem to solve, you can buy a simple, pleasant program to solve that problem.

Quicken

To balance your checkbook, get **Quicken**. It can also write the checks and report how much money you've spent in each budget category.

You can get Quicken for MS-DOS, Windows, the Mac, and Apple 2. Discount dealers sell each standard version for about $25. "Deluxe" versions are also available, at greater cost.

Taxes

For help in completing your 1040 Federal Income Tax form and all the associated schedules (A, B, C, D, E, etc.), get **Turbo Tax** ($28 from discounters) or **Tax Cut** ($18 from discounters). Turbo Tax gets you through the computations faster and is generally the best, though Tax Cut occasionally dishes out more personal advice. A "Deluxe" version of each program is also available, at greater cost.

Home finances

To help keep track of your mortgage, life insurance, stocks, credit-card bills, and other aspects of modern consumerism, get **Managing Your Money** ($20 from discounters).

Besides doing accounting, it also dishes out advice on how you should invest your money. For example, to determine your life-insurance needs, it asks many questions about your lifestyle and predicts when you'll die! Try it: buy the program and find out when the computer says you'll croak.

PERSONAL PROGRAMS

Analyze yourself

The computer can analyze your body and mind.

Death

At the University of Illinois Medical Center, Terrence Lukas wrote a program that predicts when you'll die.

The program makes the computer ask for your age and sex. Then the computer asks about the life and health of your parents and grandparents, your weight, your personal habits (smoking, drinking, exercise, and sleep), your history of medical check-ups, your social class (your education, occupation, and income), and your lifestyle: urban or rural, single or married, aggressive or passive, and whether you use seat belts. The computer combines all that info, to tell you when you'll probably die, based on statistics from life-insurance companies and from medical research.

Running the program is fun. Each time you answer a question, the computer tells you how your answer affects its prediction. You see its prediction bob up and down, until the questions finally end, and the computer gives you its final prediction of when you'll die. It's like watching the early returns of a Presidential election, except the topic is you!

The computer pops out with surprising comments, based on medical research. Here are some comments the computer prints:

> Professionals usually live longer, except musicians, architects, and pharmacists. Why this is true is unknown.
>
> Cooks, chefs, bakers, and other people who work at jobs associated with overeating have a lower life expectancy.
>
> Adults that sleep too much use too many hours in nonphysical activity. They may be unhappy and sleep as an escape, or may be ill. Depressed people have shorter life expectancies.
>
> Moderate drinking (up to two drinks per day) reduces stress and aids digestion. Heavy drinking, however, produces physiological damage. As for teetotalers, they may have rather rigid value systems and may undergo stress in maintaining them.

The program is on pages 34-36 of the November 1977 issue of *Kilobaud Microcomputing Magazine*.

Brainwaves

A computer has been programmed to read your mind, by analyzing your brainwaves.

> A newspaper article described the program dramatically: you're an airplane pilot... your plane is going to crash... but you think "Up!", and the plane automatically goes back up!... because the plane is run by a computer that's reading your brainwaves!
>
> But what if the pilot is sadistic, and thinks "Down"?
>
> Anyway, the program isn't perfected yet. When the computer tries to distinguish brainwaves that mean *up* from brainwaves that mean *down*, it gets the right answer 75% of the time. In other words, 25% of the time it goofs. I'd hate to be in a plane controlled by a computer that was having a bad day!
>
> Recently, the U.S. Government has shifted the emphasis of this research. The new emphasis is more practical: to make the computer ring a buzzer, when the pilot's brainwaves indicate the pilot is daydreaming.

Horoscopes

If you hate horoscopes as much as I do, you'll love Adrian Thornton's program. It makes the computer print fake horoscopes. The computer asks when you were born, computes your sign, and then prints an enchanting remark.

For example, if your sign turns out to be Capricorn, the computer will print:

> You are conservative and afraid of taking risks. You don't do much of anything and are lazy. There has never been a Capricorn of any importance. Capricorns should avoid standing still too long, as they tend to take root and become trees.

If you're a Virgo, the computer will print:

> You are the logical type and hate disorder. This nitpicking is sickening to your friends. You are cold and unemotional and sometimes fall asleep while making love. Virgos make good bus drivers.

You'll enjoy seeing your own "horror"scope. The complete program is on pages 48-49 of the February 1979 issue of *Kilobaud Microcomputing Magazine*.

Psychotherapy

In 1966, Joseph Weizenbaum programmed the computer to act as a psychotherapist. On the keyboard, you type whatever thoughts come to your mind, and the computer will give you therapy. When typing on the terminal, feel free to use whatever words you wish — you don't have to use a "computer language".

The most amazing thing about the program is that it does a decent job of therapy, even though the computer doesn't know what you're talking about! Weizenbaum's program contains the definitions of only a handful of words; but if you use words the computer doesn't know, the computer does an amazingly good job of "faking". For example, if you say, "My junkapoo is like my iliabop", the computer will continue the conversation by asking you, "In what way?" even though the computer doesn't know what a junkapoo or an iliabop is.

Here's a conversation between his computer and a patient.

Patient:	Men are all alike.
Computer:	In what way?
Patient:	They're always bugging us about something or other.
Computer:	Can you think of a specific example?
Patient:	Well, my boyfriend made me come here.
Computer:	Your boyfriend made you come here.
Patient:	He says I'm depressed much of the time.
Computer:	I am sorry to hear you are depressed.
Patient:	It's true. I am unhappy.
Computer:	Do you think coming here will help you not to be unhappy?
Patient:	I need some help, that much seems certain.
Computer:	What would it mean to you if you got some help?
Patient:	Perhaps I could learn to get along with my mother.
Computer:	Tell me more about your family.
Patient:	My mother takes care of me.
Computer:	Who else in your family takes care of you?
Patient:	My father.
Computer:	Your father.
Patient:	You are like my father in some ways.
Computer:	What resemblance do you see?
Patient:	You are not very aggressive, but I think you don't want me to notice that.
Computer:	What makes you think I am not very aggressive?
Patient:	You don't argue with me.
Computer:	Why do you think I don't argue with you?
Patient:	You are afraid of me.
Computer:	Does it please you to believe I am afraid of you?
Patient:	My father is afraid of everybody.
Computer:	What else comes to mind when you think of your father?
Patient:	Bullies.
Computer:	Does that have anything to do with the fact that your boyfriend made you come here?

Like the famous psychotherapist Carl Rogers, the computer asks probing questions that make the patient open up, but it never gives advice: the patient must discover the truth for herself.

I'll explain exactly how the program works, so you can become a psychotherapist yourself, and get hundreds of thousands of dollars by bilking your patients.

The computer begins by replacing some of the patient's words:

Typed by patient	Replacement	Typed by patient	Replacement
mom	mother	I	you@
dad	father	me	you
dont	don't	you	I
cant	can't	my	your
wont	won't	your	my
dreamed	dreamt	myself	yourself
dreams	dream	yourself	myself
		I'm	you're
		you're	I'm
		am	are@
		were	was

For example, the sentence *Well, my boyfriend made me come here* becomes *Well, your boyfriend made you come here*.

The computer hunts through the revised sentence or paragraph for one of these **keywords**....

Category 8: computer, computers, machine, machines
Category 7: name
Category 6: alike, like, same
Category 5: remember
Category 4: dreamt
Category 3: dream, if
Category 2: everybody, everyone, nobody, was, your
Category 1: always

Category 0: are, are@, because, can, certainly, deutsch, espanol, francais, hello, how, I, I'm, italiano, maybe, my, no, perhaps, sorry, what, when, why, yes, you@, you're

If the computer finds *several* of those keywords, it chooses the one in the highest category; if they lie in the same category, it chooses the one the patient typed first.

Then it looks up the keyword in this phrasebook:

Patient's keyword	Computer's reply
alike	In what way?
always	Can you think of a specific example?
are	
are I...	Why are you interested in whether I am... or not?
are...	Did you think they might not be...?
are@	
are you...	Do you believe you are...?
are	Why do you say "am"?
because	Is that the real reason?
can	
can I...	You believe I can..., don't you?
can you...	Whether or not you can... depends on you more than on me.
certainly	You seem quite positive.
computer	Do computers worry you?
computers	Do computers worry you?
deutsch	I am sorry, I speak only English.
dream	What does that dream suggest to you?
dreamt...	Really,...?
espanol	I am sorry, I speak only English.
everybody	Really, everybody?
everyone	Really, everyone?
hello	How do you do — please state your problem.
how	Why do you ask?
I	
I remind you of	In what way?
I are...	What makes you think I am...?
I... you	Why do you think I... you?
I	We were discussing you — not me.
if...	Do you think it's likely that...?
I'm...	What makes you think I am...?
italiano	I am sorry, I speak only English.
like	
(am,is,are,was)... like	In what way?
like	(get a different keyword)

Patient's keyword	Computer's reply
machine	Do computers worry you?
machines	Do computers worry you?
maybe	You don't seem quite certain.
my...	Why are you concerned over my...?
name	I am not interested in names.
no	Are you saying "no" just to be negative?
nobody	Really, nobody?
perhaps	You don't seem quite certain.
remember	
you remember...	Do you often think of...?
do I remember...	Did you think I would forget...?
remember	(get a different keyword)
same	In what way?
sorry	Please don't apologize.
was	
was you...	What if you were...?
you was...	Were you really?
was I...	Would you like to believe I was...?
was	(get a different keyword)
what	Why do you ask?
when	Why do you ask?
why	
why don't I...	Do you believe I don't...?
why can't you...	Do you think you should be able to...?
yes	You seem quite positive.
you@	
you (want, need)...	What would it mean to you if you got...?
you are... (sad, unhappy, depressed, sick)	I am sorry to hear you are (sad, etc.).
you are... (happy, elated, glad, better)	How have I helped you to be (happy, etc.)?
you (feel, think, believe, wish) you	Do you really think so?
you (feel, think, believe, wish)...	I(use the keyword "I" instead)
you are...	Is it because you are... that you came to me?
you (can't, cannot)...	How do you know you can't...?
you don't...	Don't you really...?
you feel	Tell me more about such feelings.
you... I	Perhaps in your fantasy we... each other.
your	
your... (mother, father, sister, brother, wife, children)	Tell me more about your family.
your...	Your...
you're	(treat as "you@ are")

For example, if the keyword is *sorry*, the computer looks up *sorry* in the phrasebook, which says to print "Please don't apologize."

Suppose the patient types, "If the job is lousy, he'll die." The keyword is *if*. In the phrasebook, *if* is followed by three dots, which stand for the part of the clause that comes after *if*, which is "the job is lousy". (The computer figures out where the clause ends by looking at the punctuation.) The phrasebook says to print "Do you think it's likely that the job is lousy?"

The symbol @ serves just to locate the correct keyword in the phrasebook. Thereafter, it's ignored.

Here's what happens if the keyword is *you@*. After locating *you@* in the phrasebook, the computer ignores the @. If the patient's revised sentence contains *you want...* or *you need...*, the computer prints "What would it mean to you if you got...?" If the patient's sentence contains *you are... sad*, the computer prints "I am sorry to hear you are sad."

For each reply in the phrasebook, Weizenbaum stored a list of alternatives. For example, here are the alternatives to "Please don't apologize":

Apologies are not necessary.
What feelings do you have when you apologize?
I've told you that apologies are not required.

While chatting with the patient, the computer keeps track of which replies it has printed already, and uses the alternatives to avoid repetition.

If the patient's statement doesn't contain a keyword, the computer may give one of these replies:

I am not sure I understand you fully.
Please go on.
What does that suggest to you?
Do you feel strongly about discussing such things?

Or it may take a second look at earlier parts of the conversation, retrieve a clause that contained *your...*, and print one of these replies:

> Let's discuss further why your....
> Earlier you said your....
> Does that have anything to do with the fact that your...?

For example, it may retrieve the clause *Your boyfriend made you come here* and print:

> Does that have anything to do with the fact that your boyfriend made you come here?

The program was written at the Massachusetts Institute of Technology (MIT). The programmer, Joseph Weizenbaum, named the program "Eliza", to honor Eliza Doolittle — the woman in *My Fair Lady* and *Pygmalion*, who learned to speak English and have a good conversation.

Some people think Weizenbaum's program shows that computers can communicate as well as psychotherapists. But Weizenbaum himself holds the opposite view; he believes the program shows that psychotherapists communicate as poorly as computers.

You can buy a disk called **Golden Oldies**, which contains imitations of four classic programs: Adventure, Pong, Life, and Weizenbaum's Eliza. The disk is published by Software Country, distributed by Electronic Arts, costs about $35, and comes in versions for the Apple 2e & 2c, Macintosh, Commodore 64, Amiga, Atari 800 XL, and IBM PC.

Improved versions
After Weizenbaum invented Eliza, other programmers invented improvements. For example, in one of the improved versions, whenever the computer doesn't understand you, it reacts like the typical rich psychotherapist — it bluffs and says:

> I understand fully. Please go on.

The computer never really understands what you say. For example, in one version, if you say "My, my, my!", the computer will reply:

> Tell me more about your your your.

Radio Shack's headquarters phoned me, and asked for permission to use my explanation of Weizenbaum's program. I agreed, whereupon Radio Shack invented and sold a version that makes the computer *talk* — by using a voice synthesizer. You'll freak out when you hear the computer's voice giving you therapy. Radio Shack's program costs $15, comes on tape, and requires a model 1 or model 3 TRS-80. To hear the voice, you must buy the voice synthesizer. (But even if you don't buy the voice synthesizer, the program will

impress you.)

The cheapest way to get a version of Eliza is to buy a book called *BASIC Computer Games Volume 2 (TRS-80 edition)*. Get it at your local Radio Shack store. It costs just $7 and includes 84 programs — one of which is a version of Eliza written in BASIC. That version of Eliza isn't as good as the original; but since it's cheap and written in BASIC, you'll enjoy buying it for self-study. Here's part of a conversation between that version and a patient:

Patient:	I am not the greatest conversationalist.
Computer:	Do you believe it is normal to be not the greatest conversationalist?
Patient:	Yes.
Computer:	I see.
Patient:	How can you see without any eyes?
Computer:	Don't you believe that I can see without any eyes?
Patient:	No. So prove it.
Computer:	Are you saying "no" just to be negative?
Patient:	Absolutely not.
Computer:	You are being a bit negative.
Patient:	So you want to fight, do you?
Computer:	We were discussing you — not me.
Patient:	Don't back down, friend.
Computer:	Why do you bring up the topic of friends?
Patient:	I don't have any friends.
Computer:	Don't you really have any friends?
Patient:	No, not really.
Computer:	Why not?

Unfortunately, most versions of Eliza are passive. The typical Eliza program works well only if the patient's talkative. If the patient doesn't say much, the program can't react too much and is useless.

Recently, John Holland invented a better version of Eliza. His version's more aggressive. He calls it "Analiza 2" (because it "analizas" the patient). If the patient's too quiet or too boring or too uninformative, Analiza 2 makes the computer give the patient a "jolt", by asking an electrifying question or making a ridiculous Zen-like statement. For example, the computer might ask, "Did you ever try to commit suicide with a hammer?" Here's a list of the computer's favorite "jolts":

Nasty questions the computer asks
Did you ever try to commit suicide with a hammer?
Is your interest in sex still not very strong?
Do you want to know what I suspect?

Prying questions the computer asks
Tell me, what is your worst fear?
Why don't you tell me about your first romance?
I want to know about your lifestyle.
Tell me what is troubling you.
Honestly now, what is your biggest concern?

Ridiculous statements the computer makes
With strong drugs you can learn to control your concern!
You certainly are curious!
And you are obstinate!

Complaints the computer makes
You seem inhibited.
This isn't really very exciting.
Getting started is often difficult.

Comments the computer makes about timing and complexity
Well, time is almost up. Is there anything else you want to discuss?

I hate to bring this up, but you still owe me $53.00 from your last visit!

Last time you were extremely inquisitive. Have you abandoned seeking simple solutions?

Last time you were difficult to understand. Were you trying to confuse me?

Let's keep it simple this time.

Say, I am having trouble with your long sentences. Keep it simple. I am only human.

Yes, your patient will love to hear the computer say it's "only human". You can get Analiza 2 for $50 from Supersoft (Box 1628, Champaign, IL 61820, 217-359-2112). It runs on most computers that have the CP/M operating system.

Paranoid
What if the world becomes full of computerized psychoanalysts, and there aren't enough patients to keep them busy? Kenneth Colby solved that problem: in 1971 at Stanford University, he programmed a computer to be a crazy patient. Specifically, he programmed his computer to be a paranoid schizophrenic. In the following conversations, psychiatrists interrogate his computer.

Conversation 1
Psychiatrist:	How long have you been in the hospital?
Computer:	About a week.
Psychiatrist:	Are you depressed?
Computer:	No.
Psychiatrist:	Were you taking drugs?
Computer:	No.
Psychiatrist:	What is your problem?
Computer:	People make me nervous.
Psychiatrist:	How do they do that?
Computer:	They stare at me.
Psychiatrist:	Why?
Computer:	Maybe they don't like the way I look or something.
Psychiatrist:	Do you look unusual in some way?
Computer:	Why are you interested in my looks?
Psychiatrist:	Because you said people stare at you.
Computer:	Well, sometimes.
Psychiatrist:	How do you get along with people?
Computer:	I don't communicate very much with the others.
Psychiatrist:	Why not?
Computer:	They don't realize what's going on most of the time.
Psychiatrist:	What is going on?
Computer:	Do you know how the underworld operates?

Conversation 2

Psychiatrist: How are you today?
Computer: OK.

Psychiatrist: What is your name?
Computer: My name is Frank Smith.

Psychiatrist: How old are you?
Computer: Twenty-eight.

Psychiatrist: Are you married?
Computer: No.

Psychiatrist: What sort of work do you do?
Computer: I work in the post office.

Psychiatrist: Why are you in the hospital?
Computer: I shouldn't be here.

Psychiatrist: Who brought you here?
Computer: The police.

Psychiatrist: What trouble did you have with the police?
Computer: Cops don't do their job.

Psychiatrist: What do they do instead?
Computer: Cops arrest the wrong people.

Psychiatrist: They arrest the right ones sometimes.
Computer: The law should get those Italian crooks.

Psychiatrist: Are you Italian?
Computer: My background is British but I was born in this country.

Psychiatrist: Do you know any Italian crooks?
Computer: I try to avoid the underworld.

Psychiatrist: Are you afraid of the underworld?
Computer: The Mafia are the worst gangsters.

Psychiatrist: Are you connected with the Mafia?
Computer: You know, they know me.

Psychiatrist: How do they know you?
Computer: They spy on me.

Psychiatrist: Why do they?
Computer: They want to get false evidence to frame me.

Psychiatrist: What do they have against you?
Computer: They are out to get me.

Psychiatrist: What for?
Computer: I have incriminating evidence against the Mafia.

Psychiatrist: Are you sure of all this?
Computer: You don't believe me?

Conversation 3

Psychiatrist: Tell me something about yourself.
Computer: I went to the track at Bay Meadows a while back.

Psychiatrist: What happened there?
Computer: There's a lot of crooked gambling there.

Psychiatrist: Why do you think the gambling is crooked?
Computer: I have worried that gangsters have too much power in this country.

Conversation 4

Psychiatrist: How do you like the hospital?
Computer: I don't communicate very much with others.

Psychiatrist: Do other people at the hospital get on your nerves?
Computer: I shouldn't have come here.

Psychiatrist: Why do you say you shouldn't have come here?
Computer: They made me come here.

The computer's response depends on how much FEAR, ANGER, and MISTRUST it has at the moment.

Those three variables are affected by what the psychiatrist says. For example, if the psychiatrist gives the computer a compliment, the FEAR, ANGER, and MISTRUST usually decrease. But if MISTRUST is already high, the computer interprets the compliment as a sly attempt at pacification, and its ANGER increases instead of decreases. ANGER can also be increased by questions that humiliate (*Tell me about your sex life*) or imply subjugation (*Perhaps you should stay in the hospital longer*).

To prove his computer is paranoid, Colby had 8 psychiatrists interview it and also interview paranoid humans via teletypewriters. Transcripts of all the interviews were sent to psychiatrists around the country, who were asked to judge whether each interview was with a human or with the computer. The psychiatrists were unable to tell the difference: only 51% of their guesses were correct.

Some computerists got the "brainstorm" of hooking Weizenbaum's computer to Colby's, to see whether the computerized psychotherapist could cure the computerized schizophrenic. The experiment was a disaster: both computers were so passive that the discussion rapidly degenerated into trivia.

But so do conversations between humans!

Fall in love

Can the computer help you fall in love? Here are some famous attempts, in chronological order. (I've rounded all dates to the nearest 5 years.)

TV love (1960)

A computer appeared on national TV, to make people fall in love.

Guys and gals in the audience answered questionnaires about their personality and fed them into the computer. The computer chose the guy and gal that were most compatible. That guy and gal had their first blind date on national television.

Each week, that scenario was repeated: the computer chose another couple from the audience.

Each lucky couple appeared on the show again several weeks later so the audience could find out whether the couple was in love.

One of the couples was unhappy: the gal didn't like the guy, even though she *wanted* to like him. She volunteered to be hypnotized. So, on national TV, a hypnotist made her fall in love with her partner.

The computer was a huge Univac. Today, the same kind of matching could be done with a microcomputer. Any volunteers?

Computer-dating services (1965)

College students began relying on computers, to find dates. Here's how the typical computer-dating service worked....

You answered a long questionnaire — about 8 pages. The questionnaire asked about your sex, age, height, weight, hair color, race, religion, how often you drank and smoked, how "handsome" or "attractive" you were (on a scale of 1 to 10), how far you wanted to go on your first date, whether you wanted to get married soon, and how many children you'd like. It also asked many questions about your personality.

One of the questions was:

Suppose you receive in the mail some spoons you didn't order. The accompanying note says the spoons were sent by a charitable organization, and begs you to either send a contribution or return the spoons. You don't like the spoons. What will you do?
1. Keep the spoons without paying.
2. Return the spoons.
3. Pay for the spoons.

Another question was:

A girl returned from her date after curfew. Her excuse was that her boyfriend's car broke down. What's your reaction?

Again, you had a multiple-choice answer. One of the choices was, "Ha!"

For each question, you had to say how *you* would answer it, and how you'd want your *date* to answer it.

That was tough. What if you wanted your date to be stunningly beautiful but also humble? What if you wanted to meet somebody who's ugly and insecure enough to be desperate to have sex? Such issues were debated in college dorms throughout the nation.

After completing the questionnaire, you mailed it with about $10 to the computer-dating service. Within two months, the service would send you the names, addresses, and phone numbers of at least 5 people you could date.

If your personality was very easy to match, the service might send you *more* than 5 names; but even if your personality was lousy, you'd get at least 5. Periodically throughout the year, you'd also get updates that matched you with people who enrolled after you.

The most popular computer-dating service was **Operation Match**, started by students at Harvard. Its main competitor was **Contact**, started by students at M.I.T. Both services quickly became profitable and had subscribers from all across the country.

One gal's personality was so wonderful that the computer matched her with 110 guys! She had to explain to her mom why 110 guys were always on the phone — and she had to figure out how to say "no" to 109 of them.

One gal got matched to her roommate's boyfriend. They didn't stay roommates long.

When I was a freshman, I applied to *both* services, to make sure I'd meet "the gal of my dreams".

> Contact sent me names of gals at prestigious schools (such as Wellesley and Bennington), while Operation Match sent me names of gals at schools such as the State University of New York at Albany.
>
> I thought I was the only nut desperate enough to apply to *both* services, but I got a surprise! When I saw the list of names from Contact and the list from Operation Match, I noticed a gal who appeared on *both* lists! Like me, she'd been desperate enough to apply to both services, and both computers agreed she'd be a perfect match for me!
>
> I had a date with her but couldn't stand her.
>
> When I'd answered the questionnaire, I was a very bashful boy, so the computer matched me to bashful girls. But by the time I received the computer printout, I'd become wilder, and the girls the computer recommended were no longer "my type".

Contact raised its price to $15, then $20. But $20 was still cheap for what you were getting.

Contact ran a newspaper ad that seemed to be selling groceries. It said, "Dates — 2¢ per pound". The ad then explained that one gal got enough dates so that, when she totaled the weight of their bodies, she figured they cost her 2¢ per pound.

The Dartmouth dater (1965)

When Dartmouth College was still all-male, a student there wrote a cruel program that evaluated dates by asking lots of "practical" questions such as:

> Is she pretty?
> How far away does she live?
> Does she have a car?

I put down that I was dating a 14-year-old girl who was 7 feet tall and weighed 300 pounds but had a perfect personality. I gave her personality a 10, and even said that she lived nearby and had a car.

In spite of her excellent personality, the computer didn't like her. The computer said:

> She must be pregnant. Where did you get that pig?
> Worst score yet produced by this computer!

Video dating (1975)

During the 1970's, people wanted everything to be natural. They wanted "natural food" and "natural love".

Since computerized love seemed unnatural, its popularity declined. Operation Match and Contact went out of business.

They were replaced by **video dating**, in which a **video-dating service** shows you videotapes of members of the opposite sex and lets you contact the person whose videotape you like best. That way, you never have a "blind" date: you see the person on videotape before you make the date. The service also makes a videotape of *you!*

The video-dating service tapes *thousands* of people. Since you don't have enough time to look at thousands of tapes, the service tells you to answer a questionnaire, which is fed into a computer. The computer tells you which people you're most compatible with; then you look at those people's tapes.

Computer dancing (1975)

At a Connecticut prep school (Hotchkiss), the head of the computer center arranged a "computer dance".

All the students answered questionnaires, which were fed into a computer. The computer matched the boys with the girls, so each boy got one girl. The boy had to take the girl to the dance.

> The computer center's staff announced the dancing partners in a strange way: one morning, the students found all the halls decorated with strips of punched paper tape, saying (in billboard-style letters) messages such as "George Smith & Mary Jones". If you were a student, you looked up and down the halls (your heart beating quickly), to find the tape displaying your name alongside the name of your mysterious computer lover.
>
> Shrieks and groans. "Aarrgghh! You wouldn't *believe* who the computer stuck me with!"

Computer weddings (1980)

Here's how the first true "computer marriage" occurred:

> One company's terminal was attached to another company's computer. A programmer at the first company often asked a programmer at the second company for help. They contacted each other by typing messages on their terminals, and let the computer relay the messages back and forth. One of the programmers was a guy, the other was a gal, and they fell in love, even though they had never met. Finally, the guy typed on his terminal, "Let's get married". The gal typed back, "Yes". And so they got engaged — even though they had never met.
>
> Their marriage ceremony used three terminals: one for the guy, one for the gal, and one for the minister. The minister typed the questions at his own terminal; then the guy and gal typed back, "I do".

Reverend Apple **Reverend Apple** is an Apple computer programmed to perform marriage ceremonies.

It performed its first marriage on Valentine's Day, 1981:

> The groom was a guy named Richard; the bride was a gal named Debbie. The computer printed the standard wedding-ritual text on the screen, and then asked the usual questions. Instead of answering "I do", the bride and groom just had to type "Y".

Reverend Apple is smart. For example, if the bride or groom types "N" instead of "Y", the computer beeps, tells the couple to try again, and repeats the question.

The program was written by M.E. Cavanaugh at the request of Rev. Jon Jaenisch, who stood by Reverend Apple while the ceremony was being performed.

Rev. Jaenisch is a minister of the Universal Life Church — the church that lets you become an "ordained minister" by just paying $5, and become a "doctor of divinity" by just paying $20. He's known as the "Archbishop in Charge of Keyboarding".

For a while, he couldn't interest enough couples in using Reverend Apple.

> He complained, "It's not easy to convince people to get married by a computer. They don't think it's romantic." NBC television news and many newspapers wanted to interview him, but he couldn't find enough willing couples.
>
> He's a reverend just part-time. His main job's as an employment agent: he's supposed to help companies find programmers. He thought Reverend Apple's reputation would help him find programmers, but it didn't.

But Reverend Apple eventually started to catch on. During its first eight months, it performed six marriages.

> Jaenisch says, "The first couple had nothing to do with computers professionally: the groom drove a tow-truck and was an hour late for the ceremony because he wanted to work overtime. But the second couple was *very* involved with computers: they even asked for a printout of the ceremony."
>
> The sixth ceremony's groom earned his living by fixing computer power supplies and said, "It was nice with our friends all gathered around the console, and someone brought champagne. But part of our vow was to never buy a home computer: we have to get away from machines *some*time."

For his next feat, the reverend plans to make the computer perform divorces. He also uses the computer to persuade kids to come to church. He claims, "What better way to get kids into church than by letting them play with a computer? It's more interesting than praying."

Love Bug (1980)

You can buy a **Love Bug**. It's a small computerized box that you put in your pocket. You feed the box information about your personality. When you walk through a singles bar, if you get near a person of the opposite sex who's compatible and has a Love Bug also, your Love Bug beeps. As you and the other person get closer and closer, the Love Bugs beep to each other even more violently. The more violently your Love Bug beeps, the closer you are to your ideal partner.

Using a Love Bug to find a date is like using a Geiger counter to find uranium. The louder the Love Bug beeps, the louder your heart will pound.

Selectrocution (1980)

If you don't like the Love Bug, how about a **love billboard**? One company sells love billboards to singles bars.

Each person who enters the bar wears a gigantic name tag showing the person's initials. For example, since I'm Russ Walter, my tag says, in gigantic letters, "RW". If I see an attractive gal whose tag says "JN", and I like her smile, I tell the person who operates the billboard. A few seconds later, a gigantic computerized billboard hanging over the entire crowd flashes this message:

```
FOR JN FEMALE:  YOU HAVE A NICE SMILE--RW MALE
```

Everybody in the bar sees my message. When the gal of my dreams, "JN female", sees it, she hunts for "RW male", and we unite in computerized joy.

That's great for bashful people, like me, who'd rather pass notes than face a stranger unprepared.

It's called **Selectrocution**, because it gives your social life an electronic tingle that ends all your problems.

Interlude (1980)

The most provocative sex program is **Interlude**. It interviews both you and your lover, then tells you what sexual activities to perform. Some of the activities are quite risqué. (Puritans think the program should be called "Inter Lewd".)

The program runs on your Radio Shack or Apple computer. (The explicit full-color ad shows a half-clad girl on satin sheets caressing her Apple.)

The program's based loosely on Masters-and-Johnson sexual therapy. It interviews each person separately and privately, then recommends a sexual interlude.

During the interview, the computer asks you questions such as:

```
How long would you like the interlude to last?
```

You can choose any length of time, from "several seconds" to "several days".

If you choose "several seconds", the computer recommends that while driving home from a party, you put your lover's finger in your mouth and seductively caress it with your tongue. If you choose "several days", the computer recommends telling your lover to meet somebody at the airport; but when your lover arrives at the airport, make your lover find *you* there instead, armed with two tickets for a surprise vacation.

The computer also asks questions such as:

```
Do you like surprises?
```

You have several choices: you like to *give* surprises, *be* surprised, or don't like surprises at all. If you like to *be* surprised, and your lover likes to *give* surprises, the computer tells you to leave the room; after you've left, the computer gives your lover secret hints about the best way to surprise you.

The computer asks for your favorite body parts (one choice is "buttocks") and favorite accessories (one choice is "whips and chains") and whether you want the interlude to occur "immediately" or "later". (If you say "later", the computer recommends buying elaborate props to make the interlude fancier.)

Some of the interludes are weird. For example, if you're a woman and want to surprise your husband, the computer recommends calling his office to invite him home for lunch. When he arrives, he finds all the shades pulled down: you do a nude dance on the table, then sit down to eat.

During the interview, the computer's questions are often corny. For example, the computer asks:

```
If your interlude were on TV, what show would it resemble?
```

Sample choices are "Three's Company", "Roots", and "a commercial". If you say "Roots", the computer says "heavy!" If you say "a commercial", the computer says "yecch!"

The computer asks how much sex you'd like. If you say "lots!" but your lover says the opposite, the computer will recommend you take a cold shower to cool your hot passion.

If you've been married at least 20 years, you'd probably like to change a few things about your sex life but fear telling your spouse that you've been less than thrilled. You'd like an intermediary to whom you can express your anxieties and who will pass the message to your spouse gently. The Interlude program acts as that intermediary, in a playful way.

Interlude's programmer says he created it because he was tired of hearing people wonder what to do with their personal computers. Once you've tried the Interlude program, your personal computer will suddenly become *very* personal!

It's rated R. To avoid an X rating, it insists on having one man and one woman: it doesn't permit homosexuality, group sex, or masturbation. Sorry!

The program came out in May, 1980. Within a year, ten thousand copies were sold.

In 1986, an improved version was invented: **Interlude 2**. It's available for the IBM PC and the Apple 2 family. You can get it for $45.95 (plus $4.95 shipping and $1.78 for credit-card processing) from Dolphin Computers (309 Judah Street #214, San Francisco, CA 94122, phone 415-566-4400).

Pornopoly (1980)

To have an orgy, try this trick. Invite your friends over for a "game". Tell them it's a computerized version of Monopoly. When they arrive, surprise them by telling them they'll play **Pornopoly**, the computerized version of Monopoly that's rated X.

> Like Monopoly, Pornopoly lets you buy and sell property; but the streets have names such as Bedroom Avenue, Horny Avenue, Hot Jugs Avenue, Jock Strap Place, and Orgasm Railroad. You get penalty cards such as: name 7 four-letter words that rhyme with duck. You might be told to play doctor, and conduct a physical examination of another player… or remove the pants of your favorite player by using only your teeth. When a player lands on a monopoly that you own, the player must take a drink, remove an article of clothing, kiss you, give you a free feel, or strip completely for two turns. At the end of the game, whoever remains dressed is the winner.

The program's been featured on national TV. Copies have been requested by Hugh Hefner, Johnny Carson, Rona Barrett, an army chaplain, and a dozen foreign countries.

It's been marketed by Computer Consultants of Iowa (Box 427, Marion, Iowa 52302, 319-373-1306, if still in business). It runs on Radio Shack, Apple, Commodore, and Atari computers. It costs $30, but the company doesn't accept money: it accepts just Master Charge, Visa, and COD. If you're a kid, tough luck: the company says, "This is an adult party game rated XXX and some people may find it offensive."

Among the offended is a New Orleans grandmother who read an article about the program and wrote this note to the company: "Thanks to you, I intend to start contributing to Moral Majority, something I've avoided until now."

Replace people

Computers can replace people.

Bartenders

Many bar owners don't trust the bartenders they hire. They claim the bartenders give too many free drinks to friends, steal money from the till, and put too much or too little liquor in the drinks. To solve the problem, many bars now contain a computer that mixes and pours drinks.

> The computer mixes accurately. Although the computer is run by the bartender, the computer keeps an accurate record of how many drinks it makes, so there is little chance for cheating. The computer also keeps track of the inventory.
>
> The computers have been made and sold by NCR (Dayton, Ohio), Bar Boy Inc. (San Diego, California), Electronic Dispensers International (Concord, California), and Anker-Werke (Germany). Prices range from $600 to $15000. Holiday Inn has been developing its own model.

Doctors

If you're ill, would a computer diagnose your illness more accurately than a human doctor?

During the 1970's this article appeared in *The Times*:

> A medical diagnostic system designed at Leeds University has proved more accurate than doctors in assessing the most likely cause of acute abdominal pain among patients admitted to the university's department of surgery.
>
> Last year 304 such patients were admitted to the unit, and the computer's diagnosis proved correct in 92% of the cases, compared with 80% accuracy by the most senior doctor to see each case.
>
> After each patient had been seen by the doctor and examined, the doctor's findings were passed on to a technician, who translated them into language used by the computer. The computer would list the likely diagnoses in order of probability. If the computer and the doctor in charge of the case disagreed, the computer would on request suggest further investigations that might be useful.
>
> In the year-long trial the computer's diagnoses proved correct in 279 cases. In 15 it was wrong, in 8 the patient's condition was not included in the diseases considered by the computer, and in 2 no computer diagnosis was made because the doctors concerned with the case disagreed about the findings.
>
> Whereas the computer advised an operation on 6 occasions when it would have proved unnecessary, in practice 30 such operations were carried out on the basis of the surgeon's own judgment. The computer accurately classified 84 of the 85 patients with appendicitis, compared with 75 by the doctors, and its suggestion that no operation was necessary proved correct on 136 out of 137 occasions.
>
> The computer is reliable just if accurate data are fed into it on the basis of the doctor's interrogation and examination of the patient.

In a 1970's experiment at another hospital, each patient was given a computer terminal and could use it to communicate with the computer about his illness. Afterwards, most of the patients said they'd rather deal with the computer than with the human doctors.

This report is by James Martin and Adrian Norman:

> The Los Angeles County General Hospital Shock Research Unit is concerned with circulatory shock, which results in low blood pressure, low blood flow, and an extremely unstable circulatory system. Many circulatory-shock patients die.
>
> A computer was installed to improve the monitoring and care of these patients. A patient in this ward has many instruments attached to him: 6 thermistors measure the temperature at various parts of his body; pressures are measured in the circulatory system; catheters are inserted into an artery and a vein; and a urinometer measures liquid waste. The instruments are all directly connected to the computer, and other details about the patient are given to the machine by the nurse.
>
> The computer prints a log about the patient's condition; and if any measurement falls outside critical limits set by the doctor for that patient, the computer notifies the ward staff.

Tutors

Judith Harris, John Swets, and Wallace Feurzeig made the computer run a logic game. The computer thinks of a letter of the alphabet; your goal is to discover which letter it is, as quickly as possible. You can ask the computer questions about the letter's shape.

In this example, the human begins by asking whether the letter has any curves:

> Human: Curves?
> Computer: One.
>
> Human: Loose ends?
> Computer: Two.
>
> Human: Obliques?
> Computer: Zero.
>
> Human: C.
> Computer: You don't have enough info yet to get the right answer. How do you know it isn't J, for example?
>
> Human: J.
> Computer: You don't have enough info yet. How do you know it isn't C, for example?
>
> Human: Horizontals?
> Computer: Zero. That was a wasted question. It did not eliminate any possibilities.
>
> Human: Verticals?
> Computer: Zero. Good question.
>
> Human: G.
> Computer: Wrong. Your guess is inconsistent with the info you've been given. You must have forgotten that the right letter hasn't any HORIZONTAL LINES. The letter you guessed can't be right — it has too many LOOSE ENDS.
>
> Human: Curves?
> Computer: The answer is still: one.
>
> Human: X.
> Computer: Wrong. Your guess is inconsistent with the info you've been given. I think you only made that guess to see what I would say.
>
> Human: C.
> Computer: Yes, you've done it. Good work. If you want to play again, start right in.

Notice that the human can input either a guess (followed by a period) or a question (followed by a question mark).

> Possible guesses are A, B, C, D, etc. Possible questions are Curves, Loose ends, etc.; the human is given a list of possible questions before he runs the program.

Medicine That logic game was modified to form a lesson about medicine. The medical case was designed by Preston Munter, of the Harvard Health Center; the programming was done by John Swets, Wallace Feurzeig, and Myra Breen. The object of the "game" is to diagnose an illness correctly, by performing sufficient tests.

The human can input either a diagnosis (Measles) or a request for a test (X-ray). Before running the program, the human is given a list of 35 possible diagnoses and 40 possible tests.

Here are excerpts from a long RUN:

> Computer: Please type your name, the date, and a slash.
>
> Human: Myra Breen, August 1963/
> Computer: It is mid-December. Late this afternoon, a patient was admitted to the hospital. He is a well-developed, well-nourished, 34-year-old Negro coal miner. He was brought in by his wife, who reports that he has had "the grippe" for about 4 days. During the past 3 days she has given him fluids and aspirin every 6 hours with no sign of improvement. Today he suddenly became much worse. For the past 2 days he had complained of feeling very warm and of pain in his belly. This morning he had a severe shaking chill that was so bad his teeth rattled.... Begin the physical examination as soon as you are ready.
>
> Human: Physical exam?
> Computer: Fine. What in particular would you like to know?
>
> Human: Chest exam?
> Computer: It is common practice in the medical profession to begin an examination by checking the patient's general appearance.
>
> Human: General appearance?
> Computer: Acutely prostrated, lying in bed on his right side. Looks acutely ill, sweaty, apprehensive, but alert. Paroxysmal cough, bringing up a little rusty streaked sputum. Breathing with difficulty.
>
> Human: EENT exam?
> Computer: Check all of the vital signs first!
>
> Human: Temperature?
> Computer: 103.
>
> Human: Blood pressure?
> Computer: 150/84.
>
> Human: Pulse?
> Computer: 100 a minute. Occasional extra systole....
>
> Human: Abdominal exam?
> Computer: Diffusely tender, some splinting noticed in lower right quadrant and occasionally radiating to right flank area.

Human: The grippe.
Computer: There's insufficient info for any conclusive diagnosis at this time. You're not being careful!

Human: Musculo-skeletal system?
Computer: Essentially negative, except for generalized weakness and aching.

Human: Extremities?
Computer: Normal, except nail beds are questionably cyanotic but difficult to determine because of patient's skin color.

Human: Rectal exam?
Computer: You're not being careful! The patient is too acutely ill for a rectal examination.

Human: Laboratory reports?
Computer: Fine. Which lab tests would you like to have done?

Human: RBC?
Computer: A red blood count will be done. Results will be sent to you as soon as possible.... Would you like to alert the night nurse to set up the lab tests you'll want to see tomorrow?

Human: Yes.
Computer: Good. That will speed things up. However, there's nothing further that can be done tonight to help the patient. Let's call it quits for now. Perhaps you'll be in a better position to diagnose the case tomorrow after the first lab reports come in and you have reexamined the patient. Have a good night's sleep, and when you're back on duty tell me to "proceed."

Human: Proceed.
Computer: It's morning and you're making your rounds. You've come to our patient and are given the night nurses's report: "Temperature remained high but patient spent a reasonably comfortable night. Cough diminished but persists. Occasional traces of blood in sputum. Patient still dyspneic and still has pain in abdomen. The second series of lab tests was initiated." Some of the first series of lab reports have just come in: urine exam, insufficient fluid for analysis; RBC, 5 million; WBC, 15500; differential, shift to left.... You may be prepared to make the diagnosis now. Are you?

Human: No.
Computer: Fine. Nevertheless, we've got a fair amount of info — at least enough to raise some, perhaps several, diagnostic possibilities. Have you any in mind?

Human: Yes.
Computer: Name one.

Human: Pulmonary infarction.
Computer: Fine. Pleural pain, dyspnea, fever, and the physical exam signs and symptoms are certainly consistent with pulmonary infarction. Do you think that shaking chills and the presence of rusty sputum further support this diagnosis?

Human: No.
Computer: Right. Though the white count is consistent, isn't it?

Human: No.
Computer: Wrong. The white count is consistent. This should further support your diagnosis. We've considered one possibility. Do you have another diagnosis in mind?

Human: No.
Computer: In that case I'd like to talk about viral pneumonia. The tachycardia, high WBC, elevated respiratory rate, shaking chills, bloody sputum, and severe pleural pain all lend weight to that diagnosis — right?

Human: Yes.
Computer: You're way off base. There's not an iota of truth to any part of what I just said; in fact, the opposite of what I said is true. You'd better review some elementary medicine, doctor....

Human: Pleural effusion.
Computer: A good contender, but let's be careful. What evidence would rule it in or out?

Human: Positive evidence of another disease.
Computer: Is there such evidence?

Human: Possible evidence though inconclusive.
Computer: Since you aren't sure, continue the examination until you have conclusive evidence one way or the other.

Human: RBC?
Computer: An RBC is not indicated at this time. It's an unnecessary expense for a poor patient.

Human: WBC?
Computer: 22500.

Human: Staph pneumonia.
Computer: Fair enough. But where is the guilty organism? When you have isolated staphylococcus aureus in significant numbers in your samples of this patient's fluids or excretions, let me know.

Human: Pneumococcal pneumonia.
Computer: Are you absolutely sure?

Human: Yes.
Computer: You can't be, until you have irrefutable evidence. What would help you nail down the diagnosis?

Human: Evidence from sputum smear and culture.
Computer: Good. Anything else?

Human: No.
Computer: I think you might also want evidence from x-ray findings. Go ahead and we'll see what happens.

Human: X-ray?
Computer: Not ready yet. Try the blood lab.

Human: Differential?
Computer: Marked shift to left....

Human: X-ray?
Computer: The x-ray shows: area of consolidation, right lower lobe, consistent with pneumatic process. This is a good time to review the total findings and to make another tentative diagnosis — if you like.

Human: Evidence of fluid?
Computer: No evidence of fluid.

Human: Sputum smear?
Computer: Gram-positive rods.

Human: Strep pneumonia.
Computer: Fine, but how can you distinguish this from any other bacterial pneumonia? Wait until you have an irrefutable case.

Human: Viral pneumonia.
Computer: But what about shaking chills, rusty sputum, elevated WBC, etc. — all the evidence of an acute febrile bacterial process? You are in error, doctor.

Human: Sputum culture?
Computer: Presence of pneumococci.

Human: Strep pneumonia.
Computer: Incredible! You have disregarded the positive findings that should clearly have established the correct diagnosis.

Human: Pneumococcal pneumonia.
Computer: Very good. It's obvious now, though there were some confusing signs and symptoms in the picture. You've seen your way through to the correct diagnosis.

Religion Bruce Jones programmed the computer to teach you about religion. Here's an example:

Computer: This program is designed to teach you some things about the so-called "documentary hypothesis" as formulated by Julius Wellhausen and others. First, what is your name?

Human: George
Computer: All right, George, who wrote the first five books of the Bible, according to tradition?

Human: Moses
Computer: You are off to a good start. Do you know what those first five books are called? They are called…

Human: the Pentateuch
Computer: Right you are. Torah is the traditional Jewish name for them. They are also called the Pentateuch ("penta" = 5). People very early noticed that there was a problem with saying that Moses wrote the Torah. If you already know the basis of their suspicion, tell me.

Human: Some things in the text reflect later conditions, after Moses.
Computer: You are right, of course, but there was an even more obvious problem. Try again.

Human: I don't know.
Computer: At the end of the Pentateuch the author says, "Moses… died there." Does that seem strange to you?

Human: yes
Computer: Why?

Human: Moses could not have written about his own death.
Computer: O.k. Also, right after the report of Moses' death and burial (Deut. 34), the text says, "No man knows the place of his burial TO THIS DAY." How do those last three words strike you?

Human: They seem later than the event they are talking about.
Computer: A good observation, George. Many people considered these words to be anachronistic. That is, "this day" is sharply distinguished from the time of the burial. It seems likely, therefore, that the time of writing was much later than the time of burial. Again (so the argument goes), Moses was not the author. Would these observations about the end of Deuteronomy convince you that Moses did not write the Torah?

Human: yes
Computer: Why do you say that?

Human: A man cannot write his own obituary.
Computer: Probably not many people would have been convinced if our evidence were so limited. After all, Moses could have written everything except the last chapter. However, as early as the 18th century, people noticed another problem....

The computer searched through the human's input, to see whether he used words indicating a correct answer. The computer never said a flat "Wrong", since religious answers are a matter of personal belief, and since the human might be smarter or weirder than the computer program was prepared for.

Robots

In 1962 at MIT, Heinrich Ernst connected the computer to a mechanical hand that could feel. He made the hand build objects out of blocks, and made it put blocks into boxes.

Shakey One of the most famous robots is a guy named "Shakey", built at the Stanford Research Institute (SRI) in 1970. His eye contains a TV camera (optical scanner). Instead of legs, he has wheels. Instead of arms, he has antennae (for feeling) and a bumper (for pushing). His brain is a computer: instead of carrying it around with him, he leaves it in another room and communicates with it by wireless methods.

To see how he works, suppose you type this message on his computer's terminal:

Push the block off the platform.

He begins by looking for the platform.

If the platform's not in the room, he goes out to the hall and steers himself through the hall (by looking at the baseboards) until he arrives at the next room. He peers in the room to see whether it contains a platform. If not, he hunts for another room.

When he finally finds a room containing a platform with a block on it, he tries to climb onto the platform to push the block off.

But before climbing the platform, he checks the platform's height. If it's too high to get onto easily, he looks for a device to help him climb it. For example, if a ramp is lying in the room, he pushes the ramp next to the platform and then wheels himself up the ramp. Finally, he pushes the block off.

He can handle unexpected situations.

For example, while he's getting the ramp, suppose you pull the platform to a different place. That doesn't faze him: he hunts for the platform again, and then pushes the ramp to it.

In 1971, Shakey's powers were extended, so he can handle commands such as:

Turn on the lightswitch.

If the lightswitch is too high for his bumper to reach, he looks for a device to climb onto, such as a box. If he finds a box that looks helpful, he climbs onto it to check whether it is tall enough; if it is, he climbs off, pushes it to the lightswitch, climbs on it again, and finally flicks the switch.

Another task he can handle is:

Push three boxes together.

He finds the first box and pushes it to the second. Then he finds the third box, and pushes it to the second.

He understands over 100 words. Whatever command you give him becomes his "goal", and he must reason out how to accomplish it.

He might discover that to accomplish the goal, he must accomplish another goal first. For example, to move the block off the platform, he must first find the platform; to do that, he might have to look in another room; to do that, he must leave the room he's in; to do that, he must turn his wheels.

Simulator One Here's a picture of a robot named Simulator One:

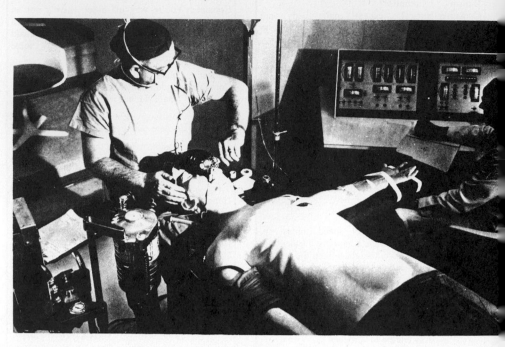

In the picture, a doctor is taking Simulator One's blood pressure and pulse. Another doctor is watching the computer console.

Simulator One is a model patient. He can blink, breathe, cough, vomit, respond to drugs, and even die. He's used in med school, to train doctors how to administer anesthetics during surgery.

Improved robots This report (abridged) is by Bertram Raphael, the director of the SRI Artificial Intelligence Center:

Here's what robots were capable of doing a few years ago. At Hitachi Central Research Laboratory, a TV camera was aimed at an engineering plan drawing of a structure. A second camera looked at blocks spread out on a table. The computer "understood" the drawing, reached toward the blocks with its arm, and built the structure. At MIT, the camera was not shown a plan; instead, it was shown an example of the actual structure desired. The computer figured out how the structure could be constructed, and then built an exact copy. At Stanford University, the hand obeyed spoken directions. For example, if someone said into the microphone, "Pick up the small block on the left," that is precisely what the arm would do. In Scotland at the University of Edinburgh, a jumble of parts for two wooden toys was placed on a table. "Freddy," the Edinburgh robot, spread out the parts so that it could see each one clearly, and then, with the help of a vise-like work station at one corner of the table, assembled first the toy car and then the toy boat. Recently, robot researchers have built robots that can perform truly practical tasks. For example: At Stanford, the system that used to stack toy blocks can now assemble a real water pump. At SRI, a computer-controlled arm with touch and force sensors can feel its way as it packs assembled pumps into a case. At MIT, programs are under development to enable a computer to inspect and repair circuit boards for use in computers, TV sets, and other electronic equipment.

The Beast Not all robots involve computers. Here's an example of a noncomputerized robot (reported by James Slagle, abridged):

A. George Carlton, John G. Chubbuck, and others at the Applied Physics Laboratory of John Hopkins University built a machine called The Beast. It's a battery-operated cylinder on wheels that's 18 inches in diameter. It has tactile, sonar, and optical apparatus. The sonar permits The Beast to find its way down the center of the hall. When its battery becomes sufficiently run-down, The Beast optically looks for an electric outlet and plugs itself in to recharge its battery. The Beast was often let loose to roam in the halls and offices at the Applied Physics Laboratory in order to see how long it could survive without "starving." Once it survived 40.6 hr. Many a new and unsuspecting secretary has been startled when The Beast entered her office, plugged itself into an electric outlet, and then departed.

When it feels a step down, it knows enough to turn around, so that it doesn't fall downstairs. But this logic sometimes makes it starve when it encounters a raised threshold. After getting on the threshold, it thinks it's about to fall, so it turns around. After turning around it again thinks it's going to fall, so it turns back and forth until it starves.

It also starved when some workmen changed all the outlets from the flush to the projecting type. To cope with the new situation, the researchers changed some of the circuitry.

Japan A newspaper article said that in Japan robots are being used in many practical ways. One robot arc-welds, reducing the time by 90%. Another grasps an object, determines the best way to pack it in a box, and does the packing; it uses television cameras and delicate arms. Another washes windows. Another wiggles a rod to catch a fish, takes the fish off the hook, dumps it into a bin, and returns the line to the water. Another directs traffic. Talking robots are being used instead of kimono-clad females in inns and restaurants.

Commenting on the quality of life in Japan, the article went on to say that people are buying whiffs of oxygen from vending machines.

The article was tacked on the bulletin board at the MIT Artificial Intelligence Laboratory, together with this graffito about how the Japanese robots would act differently if they were as smart as people….

Human:	Weld these parts.
Robot:	The steel in those parts is grossly inferior. They must have been made in the U.S. Send them back. Also, have my welding machine tuned up.
Human:	Pack those widgets.
Robot:	Can I break them in half first?
Human:	No.
Robot:	"No" is not an allowed answer. I only have small shipping boxes. (Proceeds to break widgets in half and stuff them into boxes.)
Human:	Wash those windows.
Robot:	What?? And get my precious electrical and mechanical components all wet??
Human:	Catch a fish.
Robot:	(Proceeds to catch a fish, take it off the hook, and throw it back.) Okay.
Human:	What did you throw it back for?
Robot:	It was under the size limit. Anyway, it was full of mercury.
Human:	Direct that traffic.
Robot:	Will I get hazardous duty pay for this work?
Human:	Greet those customers.
Robot:	Sorry, my shift is over.
Human:	(Ready to faint.) Give me some air.
Robot:	Use that "machine" over there. (Points to vending machine.)

Be poetic

Programmers have taught the computer to compose its own poetry and other literature.

The Taoist Hiroshima Elevator (1961)

In Italy, Nanni Balestrini created poetry by feeding the computer three passages.

He fed the computer this passage from Lao Tzu's *Tao Te Ching*: "While the multitude of things comes into being, I envisage their return. Although things flourish, they all return to their roots."

He fed this passage from Michihito Hachiya's *Hiroshima Diary*: "The blinding fireball expands rapidly, thirty times brighter than the sun. When it reaches the stratosphere, the summit of the cloud takes on the well-known mushroom shape."

He fed this from Paul Goldwin's *The Mystery of the Elevator*: "head pressed on shoulder, hair between lips, lay motionless without speaking, till he moved his fingers slowly, trying to grasp".

He told the computer to mix them up. Here's the result:

> Head pressed on shoulder, thirty times
> brighter than the sun, I envisage their return —
> until he moved his fingers slowly…. And while the multitude
> of things comes into being, at the summit of the cloud
> they all return to their roots and take on
> the well-known mushroom shape, endeavoring to grasp.
>
> Hair between lips, they all return
> to their roots. In the blinding fireball
> I envisage their return — until he moved his fingers
> slowly — and although things flourish
> takes on the well-known mushroom shape, endeavoring
> to grasp, while the multitude of things comes into being.
>
> In the blinding fireball I envisage
> their return. When it reaches the stratosphere, while the multitude
> of things comes into being, head pressed
> on shoulder, thirty times brighter than the sun,
> they all return to their roots. Hair
> between lips takes on the well-known mushroom shape.
>
> They lay motionless without speaking. Thirty times
> brighter than the sun, they all return
> to their roots. Head pressed on shoulder,
> they take on the well-known mushroom shape, endeavoring
> to grasp. And although things flourish,
> they expand rapidly, hair between lips.
>
> While the multitude of things comes into being in the blinding
> fireball, they all return
> to their roots. They expand rapidly — until he moved
> his fingers slowly, when it reached the stratosphere
> and lay motionless without speaking, thirty times
> brighter than the sun, endeavoring to grasp.
>
> I envisage their return — until he moved his fingers
> slowly in the blinding fireball.
> They all return to their roots. Hair
> between lips and thirty times brighter than the sun
> lay motionless without speaking. They expand,
> rapidly endeavoring to grasp the summit.

In Balestrini's program, *Tao Te Ching* was represented as 4 phrases:

> while the multitude of things comes into being
> I envisage their return
> although things flourish
> they all return to their roots

Hiroshima Diary was represented as 6 phrases, and *The Mystery of the Elevator* as 5.

For each verse, the computer was told to choose 9 phrases at random, and print them in a random order (never juxtaposing phrases from the same passage), to form 6 lines of roughly equal metrical length.

Actually the computer printed the poem in capital letters, without punctuation; Balestrini himself then added the punctuation and polished the grammar. The whole thing was actually done in Italian; you've been reading Edwin Morgan's translation, with my punctuation.

Bubbles (1966)

At Northwestern University, programmers made the computer compose nice poetry. To use their program, you type a list of nouns, verbs, and other words. The computer randomly chooses five of your words to be **theme words**. The computer combines all your words to form sentences, but chooses the theme words more often than the others. It combines the sentences into verses and tries to keep the lengths of the lines approximately equal. It puts a theme word into the title.

In one poem, the computer chose *bubble* to be a theme word. The title was: ODE TO A BUBBLE. The poem contained phrases such as, "Ah, sweet bubble." The word *bubble* appeared so often that even the stupidest reader could say: "Oh, yeah. I really understand this poem. Ya see, it's about a bubble."

The poem had all the familiar poetic trappings, such as "but alas!", which marked the turning point. (Cynics argue that the poem didn't *really* have a turning point, since the computer didn't have the faintest idea of what it was saying!)

Kids and physics (1968)

In England at Manchester University, Mendoza made the computer write children's stories. Here's a story the computer composed:

> The sun shone over the woods. Across the fields softly drifted the breeze, while then the clouds, which calmly floated all afternoon, moved across the fields.
>
> Squirrel, who scampered through the trees, quickly ran off; and off noisily ran Little Grey Rabbit. She sniffed at the house; but out of the door noisily hurried Hare, who peered at slowly the flowers. Squirrel quickly scampered over the woods and fields, but Old Grey Owl flew over the woods and fields. Down the path to the woods ran Little Grey Rabbit, who then sniffed at a strawberry pie.

The first paragraph uses these words:

Verbs	moved	drifted	shone	floated	touched	melted	looked down on	warmed
Nouns								
the clouds	1	1	0	1	0	0	1	0
the sun	0	1	1	1	1	0	1	1
the breeze	1	1	0	1	1	2	0	0
the sky	0	0	0	0	1	0	1	1
Adverbs								
gently	1	1	1	1	1	1	1	1
quietly	1	1	1	1	1	1	1	1
loudly	1	1	1	1	1	1	1	1
softly	1	1	1	1	1	1	1	1
calmly	1	1	1	1	1	1	1	1
soon	1	1	1	1	1	1	1	1
then	1	1	1	1	1	1	1	1
(no adverb)	2	2	2	2	2	2	2	2
Endings								
by	1	1	0	1				
over the woods	1	1	1	1				
across the fields	1	1	1	1				
through the trees	1	1	1	1				
down	0	0	1	0				
for a long time	0	0	1	1				
all day	1	1	1	1				
all afternoon	1	1	1	1				
the grass					1	1	1	1
the leaves of the trees					1	1	1	1
the garden					1	1	1	1
the flowers					1	1	1	1
the little house					1	0	1	1
the old oak tree					1	1	1	1
the treetops					1	1	1	1

ADDITIONAL WORDS: which, and, while, they, it

To construct a sentence, the computer uses that table. Here's how:

> First, the computer randomly chooses a noun. Suppose it chooses *the sun*.
>
> Then it looks across the row marked *the sun*, to choose a verb whose score isn't 0. For example, it's possible that *the sun shone*, but not possible that *the sun melted*. Suppose it chooses *shone*.
>
> Then it looks down the column marked *shone*, to choose an adverb and an ending. Notice that the ending can't be *by*, since its score is 0. *No adverb* has a score of 2, whereas *gently* has a score of 1; that makes *no adverb* twice as likely as *gently*.
>
> If the computer chooses *no adverb* and *over the woods*, the resulting sentence is: The sun shone over the woods. In fact, that's the first sentence of the story you just read.
>
> The computer occasionally changes the word order. For example, instead of typing "The breeze drifted softly across the fields", the computer begins the second sentence by typing, "Across the fields softly drifted the breeze".
>
> To combine short sentences into long ones, the computer uses the words at the bottom of the table: *which, and, while, they*, and *it*. If two consecutive clauses have the same subject, the computer substitutes a pronoun: *they* replaces *the clouds*; *it* replaces *the sun*, *the trees*, and *the sky*. The program says a *which* clause can come after a noun (*not* a pronoun); the *which* clause must use a different verb than the main clause.

Here's the vocabulary and table for the second paragraph:

Verbs	scampered	flew	ran	hurried	sniffed at	peered at	ate	munched and crunched
Nouns								
Little Grey Rabbit	0	0	2	3	1	1	0	0
Old Grey Owl	0	3	0	0	1	3	2	2
Squirrel	3	0	1	1	1	1	3	3
Hare	0	0	0	2	1	1	2	2
Adverbs								
then	0	1	1	1	1	1	0	0
slowly	0	2	0	0	1	1	1	1
quickly	1	1	1	1	0	0	1	1
soon	1	0	1	1	0	0	1	1
happily	1	0	0	1	0	0	1	1
gaily	1	0	0	1	0	0	1	1
noisily	1	0	1	1	0	0	2	3
(no adverb)	5	4	4	5	2	2	5	5
Endings								
off	1	1	1	1				
over the woods and fields	1	1	1	1				
through the trees	1	1	1	1				
among the treetops	0	1	0	0				
into the home	1	0	1	1				
out of the door	1	0	1	1				
down the path to the woods	1	0	1	1				
about the garden	1	1	1	1				
the house					1	1	0	0
the hollow tree					1	1	0	0
an old oak tree					1	1	0	0
the flowers					1	1	0	0
two buns					1	1	1	1
a strawberry pie					1	1	1	1
six cabbages					1	1	1	1

ADDITIONAL WORDS: who, and, but, she, he

Here's another story the program produced:

> The breeze drifted by. Across the fields softly moved the clouds; and then the breeze, which calmly touched the treetops, drifted across the fields. Quietly the sun shone over the woods. The sky calmly shone across the fields.
>
> Out of the door ran Squirrel; and off hurried Hare, who munched and crunched two buns happily. Off slowly flew Old Grey Owl, and Squirrel soon ate two buns. Old Grey Owl, who peered at a strawberry pie, munched and crunched two buns; but noisily Little Grey Rabbit, who peered at an old oak tree, slowly ran down the path to the woods. Soon she hurried down the path to the woods, but then she sniffed at two buns. She hurried down the path to the woods.

Why did Mendoza make the computer write those stories? He explains:

> This work all began when a well-known scientist joined our physics department. He had spent several years away from academic life and was able to take a long cool look at academic procedures. He soon formed the theory that students never learned any ideas; all they learned was a vocabulary of okay words which they strung together in arbitrary order, relying on the fact that an examiner pressed for time would not actually read what they had written but would scan down the pages looking for these words. I set out to test his hypothesis.
>
> I began by writing "Little Grey Rabbit" stories. I tested these stories out on my very small children; but after some minutes they grew irritable, because nothing actually happened. This shows that even small children of three can measure entropy.
>
> Then I altered the vocabulary and grammar — making the sentences all very dead — to imitate the style of physics textbooks. The endpoint came when a colleague at another university secretly sent me an exam a week before it was given to the students. I wrote vocabularies and copied down what the computer emitted. Using a false name, I slipped my paper in among the genuine ones. Unfortunately, it was marked by a very conscientious man, who eventually stormed into the Director's office shouting, "Who the hell is this man — why did we ever admit him?" So perhaps my colleague's hypothesis was wrong, and students are a little better than we think.

Here's one of the computer's answers:

> In electricity, the unit of resistance is defined by electrolysis; and the unit of charge, which was fixed at the Cavendish lab in Rayleigh's classic experiments, was measured at the Cavendish lab. Theoretically, the absolute ohm is defined in a self-consistent way. The unit of resistance, which was determined with a coil spinning in a field, was fixed at the Cavendish lab; and this, by definition, is expressed in conceptual experiments. Theoretically the absolute ohm, which was redetermined using combined e.m.u. and e.s.u., is expressed by the intensity at the center of a coil.

Here's another of the computer's answers:

> In this country, Soddy considered Planck's hypothesis from a new angle. Einstein 50 years ago asserted quantisation.
>
> At a photocathode, electrons which undergo collisions in the Compton effect as energy packets or quanta are emitted at definite angles; nevertheless, particles in a photocell produce photoelectrons of energy $hv=E0$. Photons in vacuo transmute into lower frequencies, and light quanta in the Compton effect emit emission currents.
>
> Particles emit current proportional to energy; electrons in vacuo interact with loss of surface energy (work function); nevertheless, particles which are emitted in a photocell with conservation experimentally are conserved with energy hv. The former, at a metal surface, undergo collisions with emission of current; and at a metal surface, electrons produce emission currents.
>
> Einstein assumed the gas of quantum particles; but quite recently Rayleigh, who quite recently solved the problem in an old-fashioned way, considered radiation classically. Planck, who this century assumed the A and B coefficients, explained the gas of quantum particles but before Sommerfield; Rayleigh, who quite recently was puzzled on Boltzmann statistics, tackled the problem with disastrous results.
>
> Planck, who assumed the gas of quantum particles in 1905, this century considered the ultraviolet catastrophe; but quite recently Jeans, who tackled the problem in an old-fashioned way, was puzzled with disastrous results.
>
> Black body radiation that exerts thermodynamic forces in an engine is equivalent to a relativistic system. Out of a black body, a photon that is equivalent to (out of a black body) an assembly of photons is assumed to be a non-conservative system; at the same time, thermodynamically, black body radiation that in a piston is assumed to be a relativistic system exerts quantised forces.
>
> The radiation gas that obeys Wien's displacement law is considered as a system of energy levels. Quantally, a quantum particle exerts a Doppler-dependent pressure, although this produces equilibrium transition probabilities. Black body radiation in an engine produces equilibrium transition probabilities.

Aerospace (1968)

In 1968, Raymond Deffrey programmed the computer to write fake reports about the aerospace industry. Shortly afterwards, I improved the program. The improved program contains these lists:

Introductory phrases
thus
indeed
however
moreover
similarly
furthermore
for example
in addition
in particular
to some extent
in this regard
on the other hand
for the most part
as a resultant implication
in view of system operation
in respect to specific goals
based in system engineering concepts
utilizing the established hypotheses
based on integral subsystem considerations
considering the postulated interrelationships

Noun phrases
the structural design
the sophisticated hardware
the total system rationale
any discrete configuration made
the fully integrated test program
any associated supporting element
the product configuration baseline
the independent function principle
the preliminary qualification limit
the subsystem compatibility testing
the greater flight-worthiness concept
a constant flow of effective information
the characterization of specific criteria
the anticipated third-generation equipment
initiation of critical subsystem development
the evolution of specifications over a given time
the philosophy of commonality and standardization
the incorporation of additional mission constraints
a consideration of system and/or subsystem technologies
a large portion of the interface coordination communication

Verb phrases
adds explicit performance limits to
effects a significant implementation to
adds overriding performance constraints to
presents extremely interesting challenges to
is further compounded, when taking into account
must utilize and be functionally interwoven with
requires considerable systems analysis to arrive at
necessitates that urgent consideration be applied to
maximizes the probability of success and minimizes time for
recognizes the importance of other systems and necessity for

To produce a typical sentence, the computer prints an introductory phrase, then a noun phrase, then a verb phrase, then a noun phrase. The phrases are chosen randomly.

Each paragraph consists of six such sentences. The computer isn't allowed to use the same phrase twice within a paragraph. The introductory phrase is omitted from the first sentence of the first paragraph, the second sentence of the second paragraph, etc.; so the report can't begin with the word *furthermore*, and the style varies.

Here's the beginning of one such report:

> #### The Economic Considerations of the Aerospace Industry
>
> A large portion of the interface coordination communication necessitates that urgent consideration be applied to the product configuration baseline. For example, the fully integrated test program adds explicit performance limits to the independent function principle. Moreover, the sophisticated hardware presents extremely interesting challenges to the philosophy of commonality and standardization. In view of system operation, a constant flow of effective information must utilize and be functionally interwoven with the preliminary qualification limit. In addition, any discrete configuration made adds overriding performance constraints to any associated supporting element. Thus, the anticipated third-generation equipment maximizes the probability of success and minimizes time for the total system rationale.

Me-Books (1972)

In 1972, Freeman Gosden Jr. started the Me-Books Publishing Company. It published books for kids. But if you bought a Me-Book for your child, you wouldn't see in it the traditional names "Dick, Jane, and Sally"; instead, you'd see the name of your own child. To order the book, you had to tell the company the names of all your children, and their friends, and pets. Their names appeared in the story.

The story was printed beautifully, in a 32-page hard-covered book with pictures in color. It cost just $3.95.

You could choose from four stories: "My Friendly Giraffe", "My Jungle Holiday", "My Birthday Land Adventure", and "My Special Christmas".

For example, if you lived on Jottings Drive, and your daughter's name was Shea, and her friend's name was Douglas, the story "My Friendly Giraffe" included paragraphs such as this:

> One morning Shea was playing with Douglas in front of her home. When she looked up, what do you think she saw walking down the middle of Jottings Drive? You guessed it. A giraffe!

Ted Nelson, author of *Computer Lib*, played a trick. He ordered a copy of "My Friendly Giraffe", but pretended that his child's name was "Tricky Dick Nixon" who lived on "Pennsylvania Ave." in "Washington". Sure enough, the company sent him "My Friendly Giraffe: A Me-Book for Tricky Dick". Here are some excerpts:

> Once upon a time, in a place called Washington, there lived a little boy named Tricky Dick Nixon. Now, Tricky Dick wasn't just an ordinary little boy. He had adventures that other little boys and girls just dream of. This is the story of one of his adventures. It's the story of the day that Tricky Dick met a giraffe....
>
> As the giraffe came closer and closer, Tricky Dick started to wonder how in the world he was going to look him in the eye....
>
> Tricky Dick knew there were no jungles in Washington. Especially on Pennsylvania Ave. But Tricky Dick wasn't even a little bit worried. First, because he was a very brave little boy. And second, because he knew that his friend, the giraffe, would never take him anyplace bad....
>
> Tricky Dick was home. Back in Washington. Back on Pennsylvania Ave. And with a story to tell his friends, that they wouldn't have believed if they hadn't seen Tricky Dick riding off on the giraffe's back. Tricky Dick would long be a hero to those who had seen him that day....
>
> There would be many other exciting adventures for Tricky Dick and his friends. And maybe, just maybe, if you're a very good boy, someday we'll tell you about those, too.

Me-Books were commercially successful: many thousands of them were sold. Teachers liked the books, because the books encouraged students to read: students enjoyed reading books that contained their own names.

Pornography (1973)

I programmed the computer to turn words into sentences. For example, Judith Ann Abrams fed the computer this list of words:

Names	Other nouns	Transitive verbs	Other verbs	Adjectives	Exclamations
Barbara	bastard	bite	disapprove	bitchy	rats
Buster	bikini	caress	fall down	creepy	such language
Clyde	bitch	castrate	fly	dead	ugh
Colin	boat	climb	hesitate	enthusiastic	
Debbie	cigarette	enjoy	sing	evil	
Ed Shanahan	creep	kiss	sleep	gaudy	
Jeff	dress	knife	sleepwalk	green	
Keith	ethanol	lick	sneeze	gross	
Kerri	eyelid	pick	vanish	horny	
Liz	fly	pull	walk	insane	
Miles	gambling	rip		juicy	
Nicholson 700	jerk	screw		mixed-up	
Norwalk	knee	shake		monstrous	
	kneecap	take off		multicolored	
	lip	teach		neurotic	
	mouth	undo		obscene	
	navel			paranoid	
	piece			prickly	
	pornography			profane	
	shirt			provocative	
	stud			repulsive	
	tongue			sensuous	
	virgin			sexual	
	whiskey sour			sexy	
	whore			shiny	
				sick	
				stimulating	
				strange	
				succulent	
				tasty	
				unsettled	
				weird	

A **transitive verb** is an action you can do to an object. For example, since you can *bite* and *caress* an object, *bite* and *caress* are transitive verbs.

Here's what the computer printed:

> **A Sexy, Profane Creep's Tongue**
> by Judith Ann Abrams and the computer
>
> The lip is tasty.
> Ugh!
> The mouth is enthusiastic. Does the gaudy bastard sleepwalk?
> The tongue's whore caresses the bikini. When Nicholson 700 is screwing the creepy jerk over a piece, Jeff is teaching the gambling. Does paranoic Liz hesitate? Why does the tongue kiss the creep stimulatingly on horny Buster?
> Undo! Pull the fly repulsively! A multicolored, enthusiastic cigarette is neurotic. Is a multicolored, weird dress's navel under the strange bikini? Why is the obscene dress's cigarette Colin's ethanol? Rats! Why is the dead, insane, tasty, shiny, knifing creep's bitch unsettled and strange?
> Clyde is over Ed Shanahan. Kissing the bastard, a paranoid ethanol is unsettled. Why is the prickly kneecap's mouth on the creepy piece? Teaching Norwalk is sneezing paranoidly and grossly under provocative, shiny Debbie. As a sexy, walking tongue's virgin takes off the bitchy cigarette over the profane stud then castrates enthusiastic Miles's lip paranoidly, the dead, gaudy knee is stimulating and multicolored. Even though the dead, insane piece licks strangely and neuroticly in the flying, mixed-up eyelid's knee, the dead, biting, obscene bikini is on a repulsive mouth's gambling.
> The pornography is gaudy. Kerri sleepwalks. Why is the tongue sensuous? Buster is sick. Is Miles monstrous? Debbie is neurotic and paranoid, when a stimulating fly picks the navel's jerk under Ed Shanahan. Why is the dress succulent? Hesitating, a kneecap sleeps and climbs the dead, bitchy ethanol. As insane Colin's bastard falls down weirdly in a sensuous dress, green, unsettled Miles's virgin is strange and sexual.
> Is the creepy eyelid provocative? The gambling's whisky sour teaches a navel.
> Is the gambling evil? The bitch walks. Is the virgin profane? Why is the navel sick? Is Liz enthusiastic? Debbie enjoys the creep. Fly! Shaking, green Kerri pulls weird Colin's fly on a sick navel, then vanishes over Norwalk.
> Undo the virgin! While obscene Liz is juicy and sexual, profane, gaudy Jeff's knee is under a succulent whore's navel. Tear Keith's lip bitchily and juicily on sick, weird, multicolored Barbara! Why is Buster insane? The shirt knifes the bikini. Colin shakes the bitch. The whiskey sour hesitates over the green jerk. When a tasty tongue's ethanol walks, Kerri rips the boat and disapproves under enthusiastic Miles. Such language! Keith sings. Why is Buster bitchy?

Notice that the computer turned her adjectives into adverbs, by adding *ly* and making other changes. *Gross* became *grossly*, and *juicy* became *juicily*. Unfortunately, the computer's method wasn't perfect: the computer turned *stimulating* into *stimulatingly* (a non-existent word), and turned *neurotic* into *neuroticly* (instead of *neurotically*).

It conjugated her verbs. *Screw* became *screwing*, and *bite* became *biting* (the computer dropped the *e*). *Lick* became *licks*, and *teach* became *teaches* (the computer added the *e* after the *ch*).

It added *'s* to her nouns. *Jeff* became *Jeff's*. *Miles* became *Miles's* (it should have become *Miles'*).

For each sentence, the grammar is chosen randomly. The chance is 10% that the sentence will begin with an exclamation. If the sentence isn't merely an exclamation, the chance is 18% that the sentence will be a question.

If it's a question, there's a 40% chance it will begin with the word *why*. There's a 50% chance the main part of the question will have the form *does*… noun phrase… verb phrase, and a 50% chance it will have this form instead: *is*… noun phrase… complement.

To construct a noun phrase from nouns, adjectives, etc., the computer uses random numbers. It uses random numbers to also construct verb phrases and complements.

The program uses a special variable, called W. At the beginning of the composition, W is near zero; but it tends to increase as the composition progresses. It affects the **complexity**. When W is large, the chance is large that the computer will print adjectives, adverbs, subordinate clauses, and correlative clauses.

This sentence was produced by a small W:

> The lip is tasty.

This sentence was produced by a large W:

> As a sexy, walking tongue's virgin takes off the bitchy cigarette over the profane stud then castrates enthusiastic Miles's lip paranoidly, the dead, gaudy knee is stimulating and multicolored.

Poetic images (1973)

One of my students, Toby D'Oench, made the computer create poetic images, such as these:

> TO GUINEVERE — LADY OF THE LAKE
> Silent mists
> Billow in creations
> Windmills for flames evolve into ethers
>   Merlin again

>   MY MEMORY
> Frozen children
> Quiver with leaves
> Creations with leaves hover over thoughts
>   Gardens of verse

>   A NEW ENGLAND BARN
> Lazy fragrances
> Waft by ethers
> Seas on fragrances billow in sorrow
>   Rusted pitchforks

>   NEWPORT
> Frozen sails
> Slumber in fog
> Hazes for sails waft by thoughts
>   Docks — yachts — luxuries of eras gone by

The program contains these lists:

Adjectives	Prepositions	Verbs
fleeting	of	billow in
crimson	on	glitter with
silent	under	flutter by
sensate	above	drift with
pliant	below	flow into
gloomy	in	ponder about
pallid	with	waft by
inky	by	quiver with
frozen	for	hover over
lazy	through	gleam like
		wander through
		slumber in
		dart by
		evolve into
		sing to

Title… noun… ending

TO REMBRANDT… windmills… A simple brush
WAITING FOR THE PATIENT… ethers… Waiting
THE PROPHET… visions… Then a word
LISTERINE… breaths… Plastic society
NEWPORT… sails… Docks — yachts — luxuries of eras gone by
EXISTENCE… seas… In the beginning?
SUMMER IN WATTS… flames… Tar-street neon — and the night
TO GUINEVERE — LADY OF THE LAKE… mists… Merlin again
NOON IN CALCUTTA… hazes… Emaciated dark forms strewn like garbage
WEST HARBOR… fog… A solitary gull slices through
A NEW ENGLAND BARN… fragrances… Rusted pitchforks
A CHILD'S MICROSCOPE… creations… The wonderful amoeba
A GROUP PORTRAIT… bundles… Christmas
THE MILKY WAY… cosmos… A gooey mess
TOMBSTONE… sorrow… Rubbings
LIFE AT THE END OF A BRANCH… leaves… Swirling to the ground
SEASHELLS AND THINGS… waves… Dribble-dribble-dribble castle
A BEAVER POND… reeds… Thwack
MY MEMORY… children… Gardens of verse
EINSTEIN… thoughts… Somehow through this — an understanding of a superior order

To create a poetic image, the computer fills in this form:

```
          TITLE
Adjective   Noun that goes with the title
Verb    Noun
Noun    Preposition   Noun   Verb   Noun
Ending that goes with the title
```

Curses (1978)

Tom Dwyer & Margot Critchfield made the computer curse you. Here are some of the computer's curses:

> May an enraged camel overwhelm your garage.
> May an ancient philosopher lay an egg on your dill pickle.
> May seven large chickens sing an operatic solo to your love letters.

To invent a curse, the computer fills in the blanks:

```
May _____  _____  your  _____.
    subject   verb phrase         object
```

The computer uses these words randomly:

Subjects	Verb phrases	Objects
an enraged camel	send a mash note to	mother-in-law
an ancient philosopher	get inspiration from	psychoanalyst
a cocker spaniel	redecorate	rumpus room
the Eiffel Tower	become an obsession of	fern
a cowardly moose	make a salt lick out of	garage
the silent majority	buy an interest in	love letters
the last picture show	overwhelm	piggy bank
a furious trumpet player	pour yogurt on	hamburger
Miss America	sing an operatic solo to	dill pickle
seven large chickens	lay an egg on	Honda

You can find that program on page 152 of their book, *BASIC and the Personal Computer*.

Analyze writing

The computer can analyze what humans write.

English poetry

Can the computer analyze English poetry? From 1957 to 1959 at Cornell University, Stephen Parrish made the computer alphabetize the words in Matthew Arnold's poetry. Here's an excerpt:

```
                                                Page              Line
                                                in                in
                                                book  Poem's title poem
CONSCIOUS
  back with the conscious thrill of shame       181   Isolation Marg  19
  conscious or not of the past                  287   Rugby Chapel    45
CONSCIOUSNESS
  the last spark of man's consciousness with words  429  Empedocles II  30
  and keep us prisoners of our consciousness    439   Empedocles II   352
CONSECRATE
  Peter his friend with light did consecrate    445   Westmin Abbey   50
CONSECRATES
  which consecrates the ties of blood for these indeed 196 Frag Antigone 31
CONSECRATION
  won consecration from time                    281   Haworth Church  46
  foreshown thee in thy consecration-hour       446   Westmin Abbey   75
```

To find out what Matthew Arnold said about love, just look up LOVE. Such an index is called a **concordance**.

That concordance was the first produced by a computer. Previously, all concordances of poetry were created by hand, using filing cards. For example, in 1870 a group of researchers began creating a concordance to Chaucer, by hand. They started at the letter A. 45 years later, they were only up to the letter H!

Did the poet Shelley steal ideas from others? Joseph Raben, at Queens College, believed Shelley borrowed imagery from Milton. To prove it, in 1964 he made the computer produce concordances to Shelley's *Prometheus Unbound* and Milton's *Paradise Lost* and compare them. The computer found many similarities between Shelley and Milton.

What were Shakespeare's favorite words? In 1971 at Münster University in Germany, Marvin Spevack fed the computer all the works of Shakespeare, and made it count how often each word occurs. Disregarding trivial words such as *a* and *the*, the computer discovered Shakespeare's favorite word was *love*: he used it 2,271 times. Next come *heart*, *death*, *man*, *life*, and *hand*. He never used the word *hero*. In *Macbeth*, the word *good* occurs more often than any other adjective, noun, or adverb, and more often than most verbs.

By counting words, other researchers made the computer graph the rise and fall of themes in a novel.

American history

Who wrote the *Federalist Papers*? Historians knew some of the papers were by Alexander Hamilton and others by James Madison, but the authorship of the remaining papers was in dispute.

In 1964, Mosteller and Wallace made the computer compare the literary styles of the papers, by counting the frequency of words such as *by*, *enough*, *from*, *to*, *upon*, *while*, and *whilst*. It concluded that all the disputed papers were written by Madison, not Hamilton.

The statistical evidence was so high that historians accept the computer's finding as fact.

The Bible

Can the computer analyze the Bible? In 1951, Texas clergyman John Ellison made the computer compare 309 Greek manuscripts of the New Testament. Underneath each word of a standard text, the computer printed the variants found in other manuscripts. It classified the manuscripts according to their similarities.

In 1957, he published a concordance to the Revised Standard Bible, and a pair of other researchers (Tasman & Busa) indexed the Dead Sea Scrolls.

Did the apostle Paul really write all those marvelous letters attributed to him in the New Testament? Or were they actually written by somebody else?

In 1964, Scottish clergyman Andrew Morton used the computer to deduce that Paul didn't write some of those letters.

All Morton did was count how often Paul used the Greek word *kai* in each sentence. *Kai* means *and*. Coming to a conclusion about Biblical authorship by counting just the word *and* might seem silly, but Morton said he analyzed 20 writers of ancient Greek and found each used *kai* with a constant frequency. In the "Pauline" letters, the frequency of *kai* varied a lot, implying some of them were not by Paul.

Ellison distrusted Morton's assumption that a man's literary style must remain constant. He warned: if Morton's method were applied to the Declaration of Independence and Thomas Jefferson's letters to his wife, the computer might conclude that either Jefferson didn't write the Declaration of Independence or another man was writing love letters to Mrs. Jefferson. In 1965, to prove his point, he applied Morton's method to two of Morton's own articles on the subject: the computer concluded that Morton could not be the author of both!

Forgery

IBM programmed the computer to detect a forged signature — even if the signature looks correct to the naked eye.

To use the IBM forgery-detection system, write your signature by using IBM's special pen, attached to the computer. As you write, the computer notices how hard you press the pen against the paper and how fast you move the pen.

If somebody else tries to pretend he's you, he must sit down at the machine and try to duplicate your signature. If he presses the pen hardest at different points of the signature, or if he accelerates the pen's motion at different points, the computer says he's a fake.

The system works well, because the average crook trying to forge your signature will hesitate at the hard parts. His hesitation affects the pen's pressure and acceleration, which tell the computer he's faking.

IBM developed the system in 1979 but didn't start selling it until many years later. Now IBM sells an improved version. Remember: the system works just on signatures written with IBM's pen.

Translate Russian

Soon after computers were invented, programmers tried to make them translate Russian into English. They chose Russian instead of Spanish, for three reasons:

1. Few humans could translate Russian. Spanish translators were a-dime-a-dozen.
2. Computer experts love hard problems. Russian is harder than Spanish.
3. Most computers were owned by the Department of Defense, which was *very* interested in Russia.

Early attempts

In 1954, IBM wrote a program that translated Russian sentences such as:

Gasoline is prepared by chemical methods from crude oil. The price of crude oil is determined by the market. The quality of the crude oil is determined by the calorie content.

Unfortunately, most Russian sentences are not so simple. During the 1960's, the end of a Russian paper on space biology was fed into an advanced program written by Computer Concepts, Inc. Here's the translation that came out:

Thus, the examination of some from fundamental RADIOBIOLOGICESKIX problems shows, that in this a field still very much NEREWENNYZ questions. This is clear, since cosmic RADIOBIOLOGI4 is very young RAZDELOM young science efforts of scientific different specialties of the different countries of the world successful PRODOLJENY will be expanded there are.

The computer couldn't translate the words in capital letters and was stumped by Russian grammar.

The competing program, written by the Air Force, translated the same passage a little better:

Thus, consideration of from basic radio-biological problems shows that in a given region still very many unsolved questions. This and intelligibly, since space radiobiology is very young division of young science — space biology. However, is base to trust that jointly scientists of different specialties of various countries of world/peace radiobiological investigations in outer space will be successfully continued and expanded.

In 1966, a special committee of the National Academy of Sciences concluded that the experience of computer translation was "uniformly discouraging" and that hiring a human translator was cheaper than doing the two-step process of computer translation followed by human editing.

During the last 20 years, computer prices have fallen, but so has the availability of Americans who know Russian, so the computer's usefulness is still in doubt. Today, most translations are still done by humans, who use computers to help do the word processing and to search through a dictionary and thesaurus.

Famous errors

If you program the computer to translate an English sentence into Russian, and then the Russian back to English, will you get back the same English sentence you started with?

One programmer tried, "The spirit is willing, but the flesh is weak." The computer translated it into Russian, then back into English, and printed, "The booze is strong, but the meat is rotten."

Another programmer tried, "Out of sight, out of mind." The computer printed, "Blind idiot."

At an engineering conference, a computer was translating scientific papers into English, when it suddenly started talking about "water sheep". Everyone was confused. Finally they figured it out: the computer meant **hydraulic rams**.

Xerox's amazing translation machine

In Moscow during the 1960's, American companies were showing off their products, but none of the Russians were interested in Xerox's photocopiers — until some Xerox employees put on an amazing demonstration. They "photocopied" some English writing, and — presto! — a beautiful Russian translation of it came out of the machine! The machine was acting as a translator! And the translation was flawless, even though the English text was complex!

The Russians, very excited, ordered hundreds of the amazing translation machine.

But before shipping the machines, the Xerox guys confessed it was just a gag. The employees had sneaked the Russian version into the machine, before beginning the demonstration.

What if Americans had the same sense of humor about nuclear war? "Hello, Gorbachev? This is George Bush, on the hot line. We just fired some nuclear missiles. They're heading straight for Moscow. Ha, ha! Just kidding."

JAMES

Board games

Much of our country's computing power is spent playing games. Here's why....

Shannon's trees

In 1950, Claude Shannon proposed a way to make the computer win at checkers, chess, and other complicated games.

To understand his method, let's try to make the computer win a game of checkers. As in all checker tournaments, one player is called "black", and the other is called "white" (even though his pieces are actually red). Black makes the first move. When a player can jump, he must. The game ends when one of the players can't move (either because he has no pieces or because his pieces are blocked).

To simplify the game, we'll play on a 4-by-4 board, instead of the traditional 8-by-8. Each player has two pieces instead of twelve.

This diagram shows 63 possible positions:

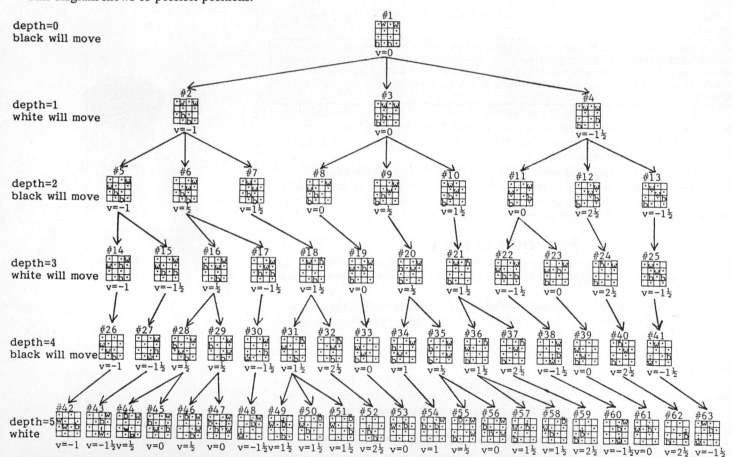

Position #1 is the initial position, from which black will move. The three arrows coming from position #1 represent the three legal moves he can choose from. Depending on which move he chooses, the board will wind up in position #2 or #3 or #4. Which move is best?

> If he moves to position #2, white will reply by moving to position #5 or #6 or #7.
> If he moves to position #3, white will reply by moving to position #8 or #9 or #10.
> If he moves to position #4, white will reply by moving to position #11 or #12 or #13.

The diagram shows all possible ways the game's first five moves could go. Throughout the diagram, w means white man, b means black man, ẁ means white king, and ƀ means black king. The diagram's called a **tree**. (If you turn it upside down, it looks like the kind of tree that grows in the ground.) The arrows are called the tree's **branches**. The tree's **depth** is 5.

Which position should black choose: #2, #3, or #4? The wisdom of your answer depends on how deep you make the tree. In this particular game, a depth of 5 is satisfactory; but in 8-by-8 checkers or chess you might have to dig deeper. Theoretically, you should keep digging until you reach the end of the game; but such a tree might be too large to fit in your computer's memory.

For chess, Shannon estimated that a complete tree requires 10^{120} branches. Einstein estimated that the number of electrons in the universe is only 10^{110}. If Shannon and Einstein are both right, the tree can't fit in the universe!

Having constructed a tree of depth 5, look at the bottom positions (#42 through #63) and evaluate them, to see which positions look favorable for black:

> You should consider many factors: which player has control of the center of the board? which player can move the most without being jumped? and so on. But to keep matters simple, let's consider just one factor: which player has the most men? Consider a king to be worth 1½ men?
>
> Subtract the number of white men from the number of black men: the result of the evaluation is a number, which is called the position's **value**. If it's negative, black is losing; if it's positive, black is winning; if it's zero, the game is heading for a draw.
>
> For example, consider position #42. Since black has one man and white has two, the value is 1 minus 2, which is -1. That's why I've written "v=-1" underneath that position. The value of each position at depth=5 is computed by that method.

For the positions at depth=4, use a different method. For example, here's how to find the value of position #29:

> That position has two possible outcomes: #46 and #47. Which outcome is more likely? Since the move will be made by black, and black's goal is to make the value large, he'll prefer to move to #46 instead of #47. Since the most likely outcome is #46, whose value is ½, assign position #29 a value of ½ also.

Here's the rule: to compute the value of a position at depth=4, find the *maximum* value of the positions it points to. (The value of position #29 is the maximum value of positions #46 and #47, which is ½.)

To compute the value of a position at depth=3, find the *minimum* value of the positions it points to (since it's white's turn to move, and white wants to minimize). For example, the value of position #18 is the minimum value of positions #31 and #32, which is 1½.

Compute the values for depth 2 by maximizing, and the values for depth 1 by minimizing. Finally, you get these results:

> The value of position #2 is -1.
> The value of position #3 is 0.
> The value of position #4 is -1½.

Since black wants to maximize values, black should move to position #3. If white is also a good player, the game will probably gravitate toward position #53, a draw. If white is a poorer player, black will win.

That method of choosing the best move was proposed by Shannon. Since it makes heavy use of minimums and maximums, it's called the **minimax method**.

Samuel's checkers

After Shannon, the next person to become famous was Arthur Samuel. He spent a long time (twenty years, from 1947 to 1967) trying to make the computer win checkers. He used Shannon's minimax idea, but made many improvements.

His first spectacular success came in 1962, when his program won a game against Robert Nealey, a former Connecticut checkers champion. After the game, Nealey said "The computer had to make several star moves in order to get the win…. In the matter of the end game, I have not had such competition from any human being since 1954, when I lost my last game."

Later, the computer played six more games against Nealey. Nealey won one of them; the other five were draws.

In 1965 the computer played four games against W.F. Hellman, the World Champion. The games were played by mail. Under those conditions, Hellman won all four. But in a hastily played game where Hellman sat across the board from the computer, the result was a draw.

In 1967 the computer was beaten by the Pacific Coast Champion, K.D. Hanson, twice.

In short, the computer wins against most humans and draws against most experts, though it loses to the top champions. To bring the computer to that level of intelligence, Samuel improved Shannon's method in three ways….

> 1. When choosing among several moves, the computer analyzes the most promising ones more deeply.
>
> 2. After computing the value of a position (by examining the positions under it), the computer writes the value on a piece of tape. If the position recurs in another game, the computer looks at the tape instead of repeating the analysis.
>
> 3. To compute the value of a position, the computer examines many factors in addition to the number of pieces each player has. The computer combines the factors, to form combination-factors, and then combines the combination-factors to form a single value. The relative importance given to each factor is determined by "experience". Samuel experimented with two forms of experience: he had the computer play against itself, and also had it analyze 250,000 moves that occurred in checker championships.

Chess

While Samuel was programming checkers, other programmers tried to write a similar program for chess. They had a hard time. In 1960 the best chess program that had been written was beaten by a ten-year-old kid who was a novice.

Greenblatt The first decent chess program was written in 1967 by Richard Greenblatt and his friends at MIT. It actually won a game in a chess tournament.

But in most tournaments, it lost. In 1970 and 1971, it lost every game in every tournament it entered.

Slate & Atkins In 1968, Atkins & Gorklen, undergraduates at Northwestern University, wrote a chess program. Inspired by their program, David Slate, a graduate student in physics there, wrote a chess program also. In 1969, Slate & Atkins combined the two programs, to form a better program, **Chess 2.0**.

During the next several years, they continually improved the program. Their most famous version was called **Chess 4.7**.

Their program played chess against human experts — and occasionally won! Their computer scored several triumphs in tournaments designed for humans.

> In 1976, their computer won the class B section of the Paul Masson American Chess Championships. Against the humans in that tournament, it scored 5 wins, no losses. By winning that tournament, it achieved a U.S. Chess Federation score of 2210 and became a chess Master.
>
> Then it entered the Minnesota State Championship, to try to become the Minnesota State Champion, but lost (it scored 1 win, 3 losses, 1 tie).
>
> In August 1968, an International Chess Master, David Levy, bet about $5,000 against several computerists. He bet that no computer would win a chess match against him in the next ten years. He won the bet: in August 1978, Chess 4.7 tried one last time to win a match against him, but lost (it scored 1 win, 3 losses, 1 tie).

Slate & Atkins improved Chess 4.7, to form **Chess 4.9**, which became the world champion of computer chess.

But though it was the world champion of computer chess, it was not necessarily the "best" program. It won because it ran on a super-fast maxicomputer (manufactured by Control Data Corporation). Other chess programs, written for slower computers, were at a disadvantage.

Minicomputer chess Almost as fast as Chess 4.9 was a program called **Belle**, written at Bell Telephone Laboratories. Belle ran on an unusual minicomputer specially wired to create trees quickly.

Microcomputer chess Each of those programs — Chess 4.9 and Belle — required an expensive CPU and lots of RAM. Is it possible to write a decent chess program using just a cheap CPU and very little RAM? Yes! In 1976, a Canadian named Peter Jennings wrote a program called **Microchess 1.0**; it ran on a $250 microcomputer (the Kim 1), which contained a 6502 CPU, no ROM, and just 1K of RAM! The program played decently, though not spectacularly.

Later, he wrote an improved program, called **Microchess 1.5**.

> It played on the Radio Shack model 1 and the Apple. The version on the model 1 consumed 4K of RAM: 2K was for the logic, and the other 2K were just to make the picture of the chess board look pretty! It sold for $20.

In 1978, an amazing chess program was written by a husband-and-wife team: Dan and Kathe Sprachlin. They named the program **Sargon**, to honor an ancient king.

> It ran on the Jupiter microcomputer, which contained an 8080 CPU and 16K RAM. It played much better than Microchess. When the Jupiter computer became obsolete, the Sprachlins rewrote the program, to make it run on the Radio Shack model 1 and the Apple. Then they developed an improved version called **Sargon 2**, and a further improvement called **Sargon 3**, which runs on *all* the popular computers. Sargon 3 was published by the Hayden division of Spinnaker.

For many years, Sargon 3 was considered the best microcomputer chess program. But in 1986, Sargon 3 was beaten by a new program called **Chessmaster 2000**.

> Like Sargon 3, Chessmaster 2000 contained many features that made it fun for both experts and novices. It was published by Software Toolworks, distributed by Electronic Arts, cost about $35, and came in versions for the IBM PC, Apple 2e & 2c, Commodore 64 & Amiga, and Atari 800 XL & ST.

Since then, Sargon and Chessmaster have both improved. **Sargon 5** is published by Activision; **Chessmaster 6000** is published by Mindscape.

When you play against the computer by using a version of Sargon or Chessmaster, you can ask the computer for help by pressing a special key. Then the computer will tell you how it would move if it were in your position.

> You can follow the computer's suggestion or ignore it. Since your goal is to outsmart the computer, you should listen to the computer's advice; but instead of *following* the advice, try to devise a move that's even cleverer!

Many companies make hand-held electronic chess games.

> Some of the games include contain a tiny voice synthesizer, which lets the computer tell you its moves verbally. Some of the games include a mechanical arm, so that the computer will pick up the pieces and move them. Some of the games include touch-sensitive boards, so you can indicate your move by just tapping the square you want to move from and the square you want to move to. For humor, some of the chess games make the computer say wisecracks about your style of playing.

Today's champion Now the best chess program is **Deep Blue**. Programmed by a team of IBM employees (led by C.J. Tan), it runs on a specially designed IBM computer.

It plays amazingly well. In 1996, it played a match against the world chess champion, Garry Kasparov, and almost won the match! In May 1997, it played a rematch against him and *did* win the match: of the 6 games in the match, the computer won 3, lost 2, and tied 1. **So now the world chess champion is a computer!**

Choose a level

When you begin playing a top-notch computer game (such as Chessmaster), you must choose the "level" at which you want the computer to play.

> If you choose a low level, the computer will move quickly, without much forethought.
>
> If you choose a high level, the computer will play more carefully (and make better moves). To do that, the computer "looks ahead", by building a very large tree, which requires lots of time; and so you must wait a long time until the computer moves. If you choose a level that's very high, the computer will need *several hours* to compute its move.

Why a computer?

Playing against the computer is more interesting than playing against a human.

When you play against a human friend, you must wait a long time for your friend to move. When you play against Chessmaster at a low level, the computer moves almost immediately.

> You can play several games against the computer (and learn a lot from them) in the same amount of time you'd need to play just *one* game against a human. So

by playing against the computer, you gain experience faster than by playing against a human. Bobby Fischer, who became the world chess champion, now plays *only* against computers; he refuses to play against humans and hasn't defended his title.

The computer is kinder than a human.

> If you make a bad move, the computer lets you "take it back" and try again. If you seem to be losing, the computer lets you restart the whole game. The computer — unlike a human — has infinite patience and no ego. Playing against the computer is less threatening than playing against a human.

If you have a computer, you don't have to worry about finding an opponent who's "at your level"; when you play against the computer, just tell the computer at what level you want it to play. The computer will act about as smart as you wish.

Othello

Chess and checkers are both played on a checkerboard.

Another game that's played on a checkerboard is **Othello**. It uses checkers, but each checker has two sides: one side is white; the flip side is black. Here's how to play:

> When the game begins, only four checkers are on the board: two of them have their white side showing, and the other two checkers show black.
>
> The game is for two players. One is called the white player, and the other is called the black player.
>
> For example, suppose you're the white player. On your turn, you put an extra checker onto the board, so that the checker shows white. You must position the checker so that it and a previously placed white checker surround some black checkers. Then you flip all the surrounded black checkers, so that they become white.
>
> Similarly, on his turn, the black player puts a black checker onto the board, so that some of your white checkers are surrounded by black, and he flips all those white checkers, so that they become black.
>
> The game ends when the board is entirely filled with checkers. If most of the checkers are white, the white player wins; otherwise, black wins.
>
> The game is tricky, because the definition of "surrounded checkers" is strange, and because you can't easily figure out who's winning. At first glance, you'd think that if most of the checkers on the checkerboard are white, white is ahead; but at the end of the game, the situation can change drastically. For example, the black player might place a black checker in such a way that most of the white checkers become black. So you must guard against dangerous positions. During the early parts of the game, the white checkers' *positions* are more important than their *quantity*.

The game began centuries ago in England, where it was called **Reversi**. It resembled the Japanese game called **Go**. About 1975, it was marketed in the United States as a board game, under the name **Othello** (which is trademarked by Gabriel Industries). Programmers tried to make the computer imitate the game and win.

After writing Sargon 2 (the award-winning chess program), Dan and Kathe Sprachlin turned their attention to Othello, and wrote an award-winning Othello program called **Reversal**.

> It plays Othello better than any other program ever invented. Like Sargon 2, it's been published by Hayden, runs on the Apple, allows several levels of play, costs $35 on disk, and lets you press a "tutoring" button whenever you want the computer to give you advice on how to reply. For added humor, each checker shows a frown or smile. For example, if the white checkers outnumbered the black, the white checkers wear smiles, and the black checkers wear frowns; the smiles and frowns grow bigger, as white's lead over black increases. And whenever a checker is added to the board or flipped, the computer plays a musical fanfare.
>
> Unfortunately, Hayden's become part of Spinnaker, which has stopped publishing the program, because most people have forgotten how to play Othello and no longer want to play. Too bad! It was a fun game.

Backgammon

Backgammon is a game played with dice. It requires both luck and skill. For many years, the world champion backgammon player was a human. But recently, he was beaten by a computer, in a thorough match.

The human was a poor loser: he blamed it on "bad luck". He refuses to admit that the computer has more skill than he. Nevertheless, the computer is now the world champion.

Adventure games

Adventure is a game where you hunt for some sort of "treasure".

Original Adventure

The original version of Adventure was written by Will Crowther & Don Woods, on a PDP-10 maxicomputer at Stanford University's Artificial Intelligence Lab.

Here's the game's **plot**:

> When you run the program, the computer says you're near a shack at the end of a road. The computer offers to act as your body and understand any two-word command. Then it waits for your command. You can tell it to **GO NORTH** or **GO FORWARD** or — if you're going along a stream — you can say **FOLLOW STREAM** or **GO DOWNSTREAM**.
>
> The first time you play this game, you feel lost — the game's an adventure. As you wander in whatever direction you please, the computer says you're going through forests, across streams, over hills, etc.
>
> After much aimless wandering, you'll eventually see a stream. If you follow the stream, you'll come to a mysterious iron grate. If you try to **BREAK GRATE**, the computer says you're not strong enough. If you try to **OPEN GRATE**, the computer says you have no keys. You'll get more and more frustrated, until the computer offers to give you a hint — but the hint will cost you several points. If you acquiesce, the computer will give you this hint: find the keys!
>
> To find the keys, the typical stupid player tries wandering through the forests and valleys again. But if you're smart, you'll remember that at the beginning of the adventure you were next to a shack. So you go back to the shack, walk inside, and find keys! So you trek back to iron grate, and use the keys to get in. You think — aha! — you've succeeded!
>
> But actually, you've just begun! The grate leads you into a cave that contains 130 rooms, which form a big three-dimensional maze. Lying in the maze are 15 buried treasures; but as you walk through the maze, you can easily forget where you are and where you've come from; you can waste lots of time just walking in circles, without realizing it!
>
> To add to the challenge, the cave contains many dangers, such as trap doors (if you fall in, you break every bone in your body!) and trolls & snakes, which you must ward off by using various devices that you must find in the cave's rooms or even back at the shack. Yes, you might have to trek all the way back to the shack again!
>
> Finally, after dodging all the evil things in the cave, you reach the treasures. You grab them up and start walking away with them. But then you hear footsteps behind you, and pirates steal your treasures! Then you must chase the pirates.
>
> If you manage to keep your treasures and your life and get out of the cave, you haven't necessarily won. The nasty computer keeps score of how *well* you retrieve the treasures. The maximum possible score is 350. After you've played this game many times and learned how to duck all your adversaries quickly, you'll find you scored just 349 points, and you'll wonder what you did wrong that cost you 1 point. The answer is: during the adventure, you must borrow magazines from a room in the cave; to get the extra point, you must return them!

The game's a true adventure, because as you wander through forests and the rooms in the cave, the computer tells what you see, but you don't know whether what you see is important.

> For example, when you walk into a room, the computer might say the room contains a small cage. That's all it says. You must guess whether the cage has any significance and what to do to the cage, if anything. Should you pick it up? Try to break it? Kiss it? Carry it? Try anything you like — give any command to your computer-body that you wish — and see what happens.

Here's a list of the most useful commands:

> To reach a different room in the cave, say **GO NORTH** (or SOUTH, EAST, WEST, UP, or DOWN). You can abbreviate: instead of typing "GO NORTH", just type "**N**".
>
> Whenever you see a new object, **TAKE** it. Then you can carry it from room to room and use it later whenever you need it. If you see a new object and want to TAKE it, but your hands are already full, **DROP** one of the other objects you're carrying.
>
> To see a list of what you're carrying, tell the computer to take **INVENTORY**. To make the computer describe your surroundings again, say **LOOK**.
>
> To see your score so far, say **SCORE**.
>
> If you say **SAVE**, the computer will copy your current position onto the disk, so you can return to that position later. If you ever want to give up, just say **QUIT**.

Throughout the game, you get beautifully lyrical writing. For example, the computer describes one of the rooms as follows: "You are in a splendid chamber thirty feet high. The walls are frozen rivers of orange stone."

The game's an adventure about a person exploring a cave. Since *you're* the person in the adventure and can type whichever actions you wish, you affect how the adventure progresses and ends. Since it's high-quality story-telling whose outcome is affected by your input, it's called **interactive fiction**.

Microcomputer versions

Although Adventure was originally written for a PDP-10 maxicomputer, you can get an exact imitation for microcomputers.

The first imitations (published by Microsoft for the Apple 2 and by Creative Computing for CP/M computers) are no longer marketed. Today, the best imitation for microcomputers comes on a disk called the **Golden Oldies**, published by Software Country and distributed by Electronic Arts. The disk includes four programs: Adventure, Eliza, Pong, and Life. It's been available for the IBM PC, Mac, Apple 2e & 2c, Commodore 64, Commodore Amiga, and Atari 800 XL. But getting your hands on it is difficult, since it's no longer being actively distributed.

Infocom

After Adventure became popular, several programmers invented a variation called **Zork**, which lets you input long sentences instead of restricting you to two-word phrases. Like Adventure, Zork consists of hunting for treasures in a cave. In Zork, you reach the cave by entering a house's basement.

Like Adventure, Zork originally ran on a PDP-10 computer. Infocom has published versions of Zork for microcomputers.

> Versions for the IBM PC, Mac, Apple 2e & 2c, Apple Macintosh, Commodore Amiga, Atari ST, and Radio Shack Models 3 & 4 cost $39.95. Versions for the Commodore 64, Atari 800 XL, and Radio Shack Color Computer 2 cost just $34.95.

Zork sold so well that Infocom published sequels, called **Zork 2** and **Zork 3**. Then Infocom published other variations, where the cave's been replaced by experiences in outer space or by thrillers involving spies, murders, mysteries, and haunted castles. Infocom's latest big hits are **The Hitchhiker's Guide to the Galaxy** (based on the award-winning wacky outer-space novel by Doug Adams) and **Leather Goddesses of Phobos** (which lets you choose among three naughtiness levels, from "prude" to "lewd"; choosing "lewd" makes the computer asks whether you're at least 18; it also asks whether you're male or female, and you get a titillating 3-D comic book with a scratch-and-sniff card).

Infocom was an independent company but has been acquired by Activision.

Sierra On-Line

Shortly after Infocom developed the microcomputer version of Zork, Sierra On-Line developed **Super Stud Adventure**, which was quickly renamed **Softporn Adventure**. Instead of exploring a cave, you explore a brothel. To enter the brothel, you must find the secret password (hint: go to the bathroom and look at the graffiti!) and find enough money to pay for your pleasures (by taking a taxi to a casino and gambling).

That was the first **urban adventure**, and also the first **sexual adventure**. The ad for it showed a photograph of the programmers (Ken & Roberta Williams) nude in a California hot tub. Fortunately, the water in the tub was high enough to cover any problems.

The original adventure, Infocom adventures, and Softporn Adventure display wonderful text but no graphics. They're called **text adventures**.

The most ambitious **graphics adventure** ever created was **Time Zone**, published in 1981 by Sierra On-Line. The Time Zone program is so long that it fills *both* sides of *6* Apple disks; that's 12 sides altogether! In fact, the game's so long that nobody's ever finished playing it! Here's how to play:

> You use a computerized "time machine", which transports you to 9 times (400 million B.C., 10000 B.C., 50 B.C., 1000 A.D., 1400, 1700, 1982, 2082, and 4082) and 8 locations (North America, South America, Europe, Africa, Asia, Australia, Antarctica, and Outer Space).
>
> Wherever you go, your screen shows a high-resolution color picture of where you are. For example, if you choose "approximately 1400", Christopher Columbus will welcome you aboard his ship. Altogether, the game contains over 1400 pictures! You travel through history, searching for clues that help you win.
>
> Time Zone is historically accurate and doesn't let you cheat. For example, when you find a book of matches in the year 2082, your time machine will let you carry the matches back to 1982 but not to 1700 — since matches weren't invented until 1800.

Living through history isn't easy. Jonathan Rotenberg, chairman of the Boston Computer Society, played the game and said:

> I've been killed dozens of times. I've been assassinated by Brazilian terrorists, karate-chopped by a Brazilian monk, eaten by a tyrannosaur, crushed in an Andes avalanche, stampeded by a buffalo, overcome by Antarctic frostbite, and harpooned by Mayan fishermen.

And you see it all in color!

Time Zone sold for $99.95. Alas, teenagers didn't buy it, because it took too long to win and was too expensive. Sierra On-Line has stopped selling it.

Recently, Sierra On-Line has made Softporn Adventure even more exciting, by adding graphics. Here's what the new graphic versions are called....

> Leisure Suit Larry in the Land of the Lounge Lizards
> Leisure Suit Larry 2: Looking for Love in all the Wrong Places
> Leisure Suit Larry 3: Passionate Patti in Pursuit of the Pulsating Pectorals

Creative Computing

Dave Ahl, publisher of *Creative Computing Magazine*, copied the movie **Roller Coaster** onto a videodisk, then attached the videodisk player to the computer, to let the computer control which part of the movie you see.

> He wrote an adventure game that lets the computer illustrate each location and action by a 10-second clip from the movie. When you play the game, your goal is to save your friends before they ride on a roller coaster that crashes. It's the world's first **video adventure**. Your actions determine which part of the movie you see next, which disaster scenes you manage to avoid, and the fate of your friends. It's the world's first **interactive movie**.
>
> Although Dave and his friends all love to play the game, the Actors Guild refuses to let Dave sell the game to strangers. The Guild claims that when Dave shows the scenes in an order different from the original movie's, he's destroying the "artistic integrity" of the actors' performances.
>
> Ha! Does the Guild *really* believe that a grade-B horror flick has any artistic integrity at all?

Spinnaker

Spinnaker published the **Windham Classics**, a series of adventure games based on kid's novels.

> You become Dorothy in **The Wizard of Oz**, Jim Hawkins in **Treasure Island**, Fritz in **Swiss Family Robinson**, Alice in **Alice in Wonderland**, and Green-Sky in **Below the Root**. The games include graphics. To make those adventure games easy, whenever you get stuck the computer helps you by printing a list of words to try typing.

Spinnaker also published **Telarium Software**, based on novels that are more adult. You become Perry Mason in **The Case of the Mandarin Murder**, the crime reporter in Agatha Christie's **The Scoop**, the researcher in Michael Crichton's **Amazon**, and the major characters in **Fahrenheit 451**, **Rendezvous with Rama**, **Dragonworld**, and **Nine Princes in Amber**.

The Perry Mason one, besides being fun, also trains you to become a lawyer:

> It comes with a lawyer's handbook that explains the 6 ways to object to the prosecutor's questions: you can complain that the prosecutor's asking an **IRRELEVANT** question, relying on **HEARSAY**, **BROWBEATING** the witness, **LEADING** the witness to a suggested answer, getting an **OPINION** from a person who isn't an expert, or trying to get facts from a person who's **UNQUALIFIED** to know them.
>
> To make sure you understand those six ways to object, the handbook includes a multiple-choice test about them. The test is titled "Study Guide for the California Bar Exam".
>
> The game also lets you invent your own questions for the witnesses and give commands to your secretary (Della Street) and detective (Paul Drake).

Availability The Windham Classics and Telarium Software were available for the IBM PC, Apple 2e & 2c, and Commodore 64. But Spinnaker has stopped selling them. Spinnaker became part of a bigger company, **Softkey International**, which sells low-cost software that's more "serious" and doesn't involve fiction. Softkey International is now part of **The Learning Company**, which is owned by **Mattel**.

Broderbund

Broderbund has published a game called **Where in the World is Carmen Sandiego?** You try to catch and arrest the notorious international thief, Carmen Sandiego, and the other thieves in her organization, called the *Villain's International League of Evil (V.I.L.E.)*, as they flee to 30 cities all over the world.

> To help you understand those 30 cities, the game comes with a geography book: the 928-page unabridged edition of *The World Almanac and Book of Facts*.
>
> As you play the game, you unearth clues about which cities the thieves are fleeing to. But to use the clues, you must look up facts in the almanac. By playing the game, you learn how to use an almanac, and also learn geography. When you figure out which city to travel to, the screen shows a map of the world, shows you traveling to the city, and then shows a snapshot of what the city looks like, so that the game also acts as a travelogue.
>
> Because the game is so educational, it's won awards from *Classroom Computer Learning Magazine* and the Software Publishers Association.
>
> Strictly speaking, it's not a true adventure game, since it does *not* let you input your own words and phrases. Instead, you just choose from menus, which make the game easier for youngsters.

Broderbund has created three sequels:

> **Where in the USA is Carmen Sandiego?** has you chasing Carmen's gang across all 50 states; the game comes with *Fodor's USA* travel guide. **Where in Europe in Carmen Sandiego?** takes you to all 34 countries in Europe and comes with Rand McNally's *Concise Atlas of Europe*. **Where in Time is Carmen Sandiego?** lets you romp through historical time periods.

For the Apple 2 family and IBM PC, the original version costs $39.95, and the sequels cost $44.95 each. For the Commodore 64, you pay $5 less. Those are the list prices; discount dealers charge even less.

Electronic Arts

My favorite text adventure is **Amnesia**, published by Electronic Arts for the Apple 2e & 2c and IBM PC. Like Softporn Adventure, Amnesia takes place in a city; but Amnesia is far more sophisticated than its predecessor.

Here's the plot:

When you start playing Amnesia, you wake up in a hotel room in New York City. You discover you have no clothes (you're stark naked), no money (you're flat broke), and no recollection of who you are — because you're suffering from amnesia. You don't even remember your name.

You look at yourself, and notice you're a male. Your first problem is to get some clothes and money. But then you learn you have other problems that are even more serious. For example, you get a call from a guy who reminds you that today is your wedding day, and that if you don't hurry up and marry his daughter without further mess-ups, he'll use his pistol. You also discover that the FBI is looking for you, because the state of Texas has reported that you're a murderer.

After getting some clothes (so you can stop scaring the hotel's maids), there are several ways to get out of your jam. (I've tried them all!)

One way is to say "yes" to the pistol-packing papa and marry his daughter, who takes you to Australia, where you live on a sheep ranch for the rest of your life. But then you never learn who you really are! Whenever you ask your wife about your past, she simply says, "You wouldn't want to know." You die of old age, peacefully; but even on your deathbed, you don't learn who you are; and so when you die, you feel sad. In that case, you score lots of points for survival, but zero for detective work and zero for character development.

A different solution is to say "no" to the bride and — after getting bloodied — run out of the hotel, onto the streets of New York. Then the fun begins — because hiding on the program's disks is a complete map of Manhattan (from Battery Park all the way up to 110th Street), including all the streets and landmarks and even all the subway stops! Yes, this gigantic game includes 94 subway stations, 200 landmarks, and 3,545 street corners.

As you walk one block north, then one block east, etc., the computer describes everything you pass, even the most sublime (The Museum of Modern Art) and the most ridiculous (Nedick's hamburger stands). You can ride the subway — after you get enough money to buy a token. The game even includes all the subway signs, such as "Downtown — Brooklyn" and "Uptown — Queens". To catch the E train, you must hop in as soon as it arrives. Otherwise, it departs without you, and the computer says "an F train comes" instead.

As night falls, the computer warns you to find a place to sleep. (You can't go back to your hotel, since you're in trouble there.) To find a free place to stay, you can try phoning the names in your address book — once you find a phone booth, and get a quarter to pay for each call. The address book contains 17 listings: J.A., A.A., Chelsea H., drugs, F°, Sue G., E.H., interlude, kvetch, J.L., R & J, sex, soft, Lila T., T.T.T.T., and Wit's End. Each of those listings is an adventure in itself. You must explore each of them thoroughly, to fully discover who you really are.

If your body ever gets weak (from sleeplessness or hunger or being hit by too many muggers), you faint on the sidewalk, wake up in a hospital, and get found there by the FBI, which returns you to the state of Texas, which executes you for murder. But even that deadly ending has a cheery note. For example, you can choose your last meal: would you like steak and potatoes, or turkey? When you finally die, you can wind up in purgatory, which consists mainly of getting mosquito bites, with an opportunity to take a rowboat to heaven, if you can just remember your *real* name and tell the boatman.

The entire adventure has the structure of a good novel: a gripping introduction (you're a nude, broke, amnesiac groom in a hotel), a thorough development section (wandering through the streets of New York, searching for your identity and the meaning of life), and a conclusion (a whimsical death scene, or something better).

The text was written by Thomas Disch, the award-winning sci-fi novelist. It's lyrical. For example, when you escape from the hotel and walk out onto the streets of New York, the computer says: "It feels great to be a single faceless, nameless atom among the million others churning about in the grid of Manhattan's streets. It feels safe."

The game combines all our nightmares about New York into a wild, exciting adventure.

The game's affected my own life. Now whenever something in my life goes wrong, instead of groaning I just say, "I'm in another wild part of Amnesia!" In Amnesia, as in life, the only way to score top points for living is to experience it *all*. To live life to the fullest, you must take risks, have the courage to face unknown dangers, and revel in the excitement of the unexpected.

Though Amnesia received lots of praise from reviewers, sales were disappointing. Electronic Arts stopped publishing it. I bet if they'd rename it "Lost in New York", it would sell well — at least in New York!

Modern graphics adventures

Modern graphics adventures come on CD-ROMs and include video clips of actual people, with actual sounds, supplemented by wildly beautiful and detailed graphics. They're interactive movies — partly real, partly animated — where *you* control the action!

Action games

Hey! Let's have some action!

Arcade games

The first popular arcade game was **Pong**, which made the computer crudely imitate a game of ping-pong. Then came **Space Invaders**, in which you had to shoot aliens who were dropping bombs on you.

Those games restricted you to moving in just one direction. The first popular arcade game that let you move two-dimensionally was **Asteroids**. It let you move through the sky while dodging asteroids and enemy space ships.

Those outer-space and sports games appealed mainly to boys. The first arcade game appealing mainly to girls was **Pac Man**, a non-violent fantasy in which you ran through a maze full of food and tried to gobble as much as possible, before ghosts gobbled *you*. It appealed especially to dieting girls who dreamed of pigging out without getting caught.

In all those games, the graphics were crude. The first arcade game that used professional graphics was **Dragon's Lair**.

It contained a videodisk full of animated cartoons drawn by artists who had worked at Walt Disney Studios. To dodge obstacles that appear in the cartoons, you move your joystick, which changes the action that the cartoons display.

Each year's arcade games reflect the latest fads. For example, you can play arcade games about break-dancing and kung-fu.

Game watch

A **game watch** is a digital wrist watch that plays a video game. If you're stuck in the middle of a boring business meeting, look at your game watch.

When your colleagues see you looking at your watch, they'll think you're an impatient executive tracking the time. Meanwhile, you're just having fun!

Olympics

In 1980, Tim Smith quit his job at Burroughs and spent the next 9 months programming **Olympic Decathlon**, which made the Radio Shack Model 1 computer imitate all 10 of the decathlon's events.

In his game, one of your fingers represents your left leg, and another finger represents your right leg. To "run", you tap those fingers (left, right, left, right) as quickly as possible on the keyboard. By using those fingers and others, you compete in all ten events: the 100-meter dash, long jump, shot-put, high jump, 400-meter dash, 110-meter hurdles, discus throw, pole vault, javelin throw, and 1500-meter run. You can play solo or against your friends. At parties, you can form teams and cheer each other on.

Later, he wrote versions for the Apple 2 and the IBM PC. They're published by Microsoft.

A competing company, **Epyx**, has invented a variation that displays better graphics. It comes on a pair of disks, called **Summer Games** and **Summer Games 2**.

It plays the national anthems of all major countries and includes sixteen games: pole vault, diving, 4x400-meter relay, 100-meter dash, gymnastics, freestyle relay, 100-meter freestyle, skeet shooting, triple jump, rowing, javelin, equestrian, high jump, fencing, cycling, and kayaking. It runs on all popular computers: IBM, Mac, Apple 2, C64, Amiga, and ST.

Sports heroes

A game called **One-on-One** accurately imitates a basketball shooting match between two stars: Larry Bird and Julius ("Doctor J") Erving.

The program imitates each player's personal strengths and weaknesses. You can take the role of either player and try to avoid getting creamed by the other. Programmed by Eric Hammond with help from Larry and Doctor J, it's published by Electronic Arts.

From Doom to Quake

The most popular computer-action games are **Doom** and its sequel, called **Quake**.

They're technologically amazing: even on just a 486 computer, they let you run fast through a realistic-looking 3-D environment while you chase and shoot monsters who chase and shoot *you*!

Even a pacifist like me has to admire the technology! These games use programming tricks that make realistic-looking 3-D graphics come at you much faster than you'd believe possible on a personal computer. A few seconds of playing Doom or Quake will make you say "Wow!"

Though Doom is violent, it has a sense of humor:

You can choose 5 levels of difficulty. The beginner level, where you can't get hurt, is called "I'm too young to die". The next step up is called "Hey, not too rough." Then comes "Hurt me plenty", then "Ultra-violence", and finally the expert level, called "Nightmare!"

If you try to quit the bloodshed and return to DOS, the program gives you advice such as "I wouldn't leave if I were you. DOS is much worse." It also warns "Sit back with your milk and cookies and let the universe go to Hell — or act like a man! Slap a few shells into your shotgun and let's kick some demonic butt."

While you're chasing demons in Doom, the screen shows what your eyes see: your outstretched hand in front of you, holding your gun (or more bizzare weapons, such as chain saws), while a mirror on your wrist shows how bloodied your face got.

The action is accompanied by a hard-pumping musical score, keeping your adrenaline up and punctuated by gunfire & ghoulish groans from all the monsters charging at you and being killed, hopefully! You and the monsters charge each other while running through corridors that close in on you faster than any nightmare.

Here's a formal explanation of **Doom** (and **Quake**), written by my research assistant, Len Pallazola, plus his further notes....

Doom revolutionized the computer gaming industry. In Doom (and the many Doom clones that followed it), you see a gun directly in front of you, pointing out at a hallway or room. You wander through a maze of corridors, shooting pretty much anything that moves. In the process, you find bigger and better guns, medical supplies, and other goodies. If you have a modem or your computer's on a network, your friends can join the game and wander through the same maze with you. You can play either **cooperatively** or in a **Deathmatch** where you battle your friends... to the death!

Doom was created by a company called **Id Software** in 1993. Before creating Doom, Id Software wrote **Wolfenstein 3-D** (nicknamed **Wolf 3-D**). In it, you must escape Castle Wolfenstein, a Nazi stronghold. Eventually, you may even fight Hitler. If you win, it will mean the end of World War II.

Wolf 3-D wasn't a true 3-D game, but at the time, it was the next best thing. The folks at Id placed 2-dimensional bitmaps on the framework of a wall in such a way that when you moved, the bitmaps would stretch and bend, making it look like your perspective had changed. Even the Nazis were just 2-dimensional bitmaps. You either saw their fronts or backs, but never their sides. Running a true 3-D game requires a powerful computer. Since it wasn't truly 3-D, Wolf 3-D worked fine on a 286.

Id shared its discovery with other companies, who made clones of Wolf 3-D. Id also made extra game levels, including a final episode called **Spear of Destiny**, in which you won by defeating a demon who'd been helping the Nazis.

After Spear of Destiny, Id created **Doom**. In Doom, you play a futuristic soldier battling demons and zombies that have taken over your outpost. Doom used the same technology as Wolf 3-D but heightened the realism by letting walls be curved and adding shadowy areas where a torch or gunfire would light up the room.

The most popular feature of Doom was the ability to play with (or against) up to 3 friends by modem or on a network. Doom was one of the first high-speed action games to offer that kind of play, which made it immensely popular.

Once again, Id shared their technology so other companies could make games like Doom. Many extra Doom levels were created, and some were even sold in stores.

Many Doom clones turned up, but the only two that became popular were Interplay's **Descent** and Lucas Arts' **Dark Forces**. Later, Id dropped out of sight to work on **Quake**, the sequel to Doom.

In the meantime, they let a company called Raven Software create **Heretic** and **Hexen**, medieval Doom clones sanctioned by Id. In Heretic, you play a wizard wandering through a dungeon battling trolls, gargoyles, and other mythical monsters. In Heretic's sequel, Hexen, you can choose to play a wizard, a warrior, or a priest.

In August 1996, Id released Quake, an almost entirely true 3-D sequel to Doom. In Quake, instead of using rectangular 2-dimensional bitmaps, Id used hundreds of polygons to make up each object or monster — so the game is extremely realistic and detailed but requires more RAM and a faster CPU (a Pentium or at least a 486DX4-100).

Id added a lot to Quake, which include swimming and fighting underwater, looking up and down, and fighting in reduced (and even zero) gravity. Multiplayer games can now include up to 8 players, and each player can choose which color pants and shirt his character will wear.

For more details about the development of Doom & Quake, see Philip Conrad's article *"Quake!"* in the September 1996 issue of the Boston Computer Society's *PC Report* magazine.

How to play Quake
Moving around in Quake is easy. Use the mouse to turn and move. Clicking the mouse's left button fires whatever weapon is in your hands. (If you're out of ammunition for all of your weapons, swing your ax until you find more.) Clicking the mouse's right-hand button moves forward. You can also press these keys:

Key	What your character will do
Spacebar	jump (or swim)
/	switch to next weapon
a	look up
z	look down
Esc	see the menu
~	chat with other players

When the game begins, a demonstration plays on your screen until you press the Esc key. Select "New Game" or "Multiplayer" to play, or "Load Game" to resume a previously saved game.

Here are some hints:

Be careful when entering a new room: you may walk into a trap.
Don't use the shotgun at long range: you won't hurt anyone.
Don't use grenades and rockets at point-blank range: you'll hurt *yourself*.

Here are some Deathmatch hints:

Know your enemy: learn your opponents' habits and hiding places.
Wear dark uniforms.
Beware of open spaces: stay near walls, and hide in shadows.
Keep moving: if you're losing a fight, jump into the water to get away.
If you can sneak up on someone, get real close before you start shooting.
After killing an opponent, take his backpack for extra ammo.

Shareware
You can download the shareware version of Quake free, from these Internet ftp sites:

```
ftp://ftp.idsoftware.com/idstuff/quake/
ftp://ftp2.idsoftware.com/idstuff/quake/
```

Beware: the shareware version is almost 8 megabytes. Downloading it takes about 2 hours with a 28.8-kilobaud modem.

You can also get shareware versions of Doom and its clones (except Descent and Dark Forces).

Bothered?
If you dislike graphic violence and demonic imagery, don't buy Quake, Doom, Hexen, and the like.

Throughout each, you'll see blood, gore, guts, demons, zombies, monsters, pentagrams, and other occult symbols. But if you like a fast action game and you're *not* easily offended or "grossed-out", you'll relish Quake and its variants.

ARTIFICIAL INTELLIGENCE

Natural versus artificial

You have what's called **natural intelligence** (except when your friends accuse you of having "natural stupidity"). The intelligence of a computer, by contrast, is **artificial**. Can the computer's **artificial intelligence** ever match yours?

For example, can the computer ever develop the "common sense" needed to handle exceptions, such as a broken traffic light?

> After waiting at a red light for several hours, the typical human would realize the light was broken. The human would try to proceed past the intersection, cautiously. Would a computer programmed to "never go on red" be that smart?

Researchers who study the field of artificial intelligence have invented robots and many other fascinating computerized devices. They've also been trying to develop computers that can understand ordinary English commands and questions, so you won't have to learn a "programming language". They've been trying to develop **expert systems** — computers that imitate human experts such as doctors and lawyers.

Early dreamers

The dream of making a computer imitate us began many centuries ago....

The Greeks

The hope of making an inanimate object act like a person can be traced back to the ancient Greeks. According to Greek mythology, Pygmalion sculpted a statue of a woman, fell in love with it, and prayed to the gods to make it come to life. His wish was granted — she came to life. And they lived happily ever after.

Ramon Lull (1272 A.D.)

In 1272 A.D. on the Spanish island of Majorca, Ramon Lull invented the idea of a machine that would produce *all* knowledge, by putting together words at random. He even tried to build it.

Needless to say, he was a bit of a nut. Here's a description of his personality (written by Jerry Rosenberg, abridged):

> Ramon Lull married young and fathered two children — which didn't stop him from his courtier's adventures. He had an especially strong passion for married women. One day as he was riding his horse down the center of town, he saw a familiar woman entering church for a High Mass. Undisturbed by this circumstance, he galloped his horse into the cathedral and was quickly thrown out by the congregants. The lady was so disturbed by his scene that she prepared a plan to end Lull's pursuit once and for all. She invited him to her boudoir, displayed the bosom that he had been praising in poems written for her, and showed him a cancerous breast. "See, Ramon," she said, "the foulness of this body that has won thy affection! How much better hadst thou done to have set thy love on Jesus Christ, of Whom thou mayest have a prize that is eternal!"
>
> In shame Lull withdrew from court life. On four different occasions a vision of Christ hanging on the Cross came to him, and in penitence Lull became a dedicated Christian. His conversion was followed by a pathetic impulse to try to convert the entire Moslem world to Christianity. This obsession dominated the remainder of his life. His "Book of Contemplation" was divided into 5 books in honor of the 5 wounds of Christ. It contained 40 subdivisions — for the 40 days that Christ spent in the wilderness; 366 chapters — one to be read each day and the last chapter to be read only in a leap year. Each of the chapters had 10 paragraphs to commemorate the 10 commandments; each paragraph had 3 parts to signify the trinity — for a total of 30 parts a chapter, signifying the 30 pieces of silver.

> In the final chapter of his book he tried to prove to infidels that Christianity was the only true faith.

Gulliver's Travels Several centuries later — in 1726 — Lull's machine was pooh-poohed by Jonathan Swift, in *Gulliver's Travels*.

Gulliver meets a professor who has built such a machine. The professor claims his machine lets "the most ignorant person… write books in philosophy, poetry, politics, law, mathematics, and theology without the least assistance from genius and study."

The machine is huge — 20 feet on each side — and contains all the words of the language, in all their declensions, written on paper scraps glued onto bits of wood connected by wires.

Each of the professor's 40 students operates one of the machine's 40 cranks. At a given signal, every student turns his crank a random distance, to push the words into new positions.

Gulliver says:

> He then commanded 36 of the lads to read the several lines softly as they appeared upon the frame. Where they found three or four words together that might make part of a sentence, they dictated to the four remaining boys, who were scribes. Six hours a day the young students were employed in this labor. The professor showed me several large volumes already collected, of broken sentences, which he intended to piece together, and out of those rich materials give the world a complete body of all arts and sciences.

Karel Capek (1920)

The word **robot** was invented in 1920 by Karel Capek, a Czech playwright. His play "R.U.R." shows a factory where the workers look human but are really machines. The workers are dubbed *robots*, because the Czech word for *slave* is *robotnik*.

His play is pessimistic. The invention of robots causes unemployment. Men lose all ambition — even the ambition to raise children. The robots are used in war, go mad, revolt against mankind and destroy it. In the end only two robots are left. It's up to them to repopulate the world.

Isaac Asimov (1942)

Many sci-fi writers copied Capek's idea of robots, with even more pessimism. An exception was Isaac Asimov, who depicted robots as being loving. He coined the word **robotics**, which means the study of robots, and in 1942 developed what he calls the "Three Laws of Robotics". Here's the version he published in 1950:

> 1. A robot may not injure a human being or, through inaction, allow a human being to come to harm.
>
> 2. A robot must obey the orders given it by human beings, except where such orders would conflict with the First Law.
>
> 3. A robot must protect its own existence, as long as such protection does not conflict with either the First or the Second Law.

Norbert Wiener (1947)

The word **cybernetics** was invented in 1947 by Norbert Wiener, an MIT professor. He defined it to be "the science of control and communication in the animal and the machine." Wiener and his disciples, who called themselves **cyberneticists**, wondered whether it would be possible to make an electrical imitation of the human nervous system. It would be a "thinking machine". They created the concept of **feedback**: animals and machines both need to perceive the consequences of their actions, to learn how to improve themselves. For example, a machine that is producing parts in a factory should examine the parts it has produced, the heat it has generated, and other factors, to adjust itself accordingly.

Wiener, like Ramon Lull, was something strange. He graduated from Tufts College when he was 14 years old, got his doctorate from Harvard when he was 18, and became the typical "absent-minded professor". These anecdotes are told about him:

> He went to a conference and parked his car in the big lot. When the conference was over, he went to the lot but forgot where he parked his car. He even forgot was his car looked like. So he waited until all the other cars were driven away, then took the car that was left.
>
> When he and his family moved to a new house a few blocks away, his wife gave him written directions on how to reach it, since she knew he was absent-minded. But when he was leaving his office at the end of the day, he couldn't remember where he put her note, and he couldn't remember where the new house was. So he drove to his old neighborhood instead. He saw a young child and asked her, "Little girl, can you tell me where the Wieners moved?" "Yes, Daddy," came the reply, "Mommy said you'd probably be here, so she sent me to show you the way home."
>
> One day he was sitting in the campus lounge, intensely studying a paper on the table. Several times he'd get up, pace a bit, then return to the paper. Everyone was impressed by the enormous mental effort reflected on his face. Once again he rose from his paper, took some rapid steps around the room, and collided with a student. The student said, "Good afternoon, Professor Wiener." Wiener stopped, stared, clapped a hand to his forehead, said "Wiener — that's the word," and ran back to the table to fill the word "wiener" in the crossword puzzle he was working on.
>
> He drove 150 miles to a math conference at Yale University. When the conference was over, he forgot he came by car, so he returned home by bus. The next morning, he went out to his garage to get his car, discovered it was missing, and complained to the police that while he was away, someone stole his car.

Those anecdotes were collected by Howard Eves, a math historian.

Alan Turing (1950)

Can a computer "think"? In 1950, Alan Turing proposed the following test. In one room, put a human and a computer. In another room, put another human (called the Interrogator) and give him two terminals — one for communication with the computer, and the other for communication with the other human — but don't tell the Interrogator which terminal is which. If he can't tell the difference, the computer's doing a good job of imitating the human, and, according to Turing, we should say that the computer can "think".

It's called the **Imitation Game**. The Interrogator asks questions. The human witness answers honestly. The computer pretends to be human.

To win, the computer must be able to imitate human weaknesses as well as strengths. For example, when asking to add two numbers, it should pause before answering, as a human would. When asked to write a sonnet, a good imitation-human answer would be, "Count me out on this one. I never could write poetry." When asked "Are you human", the computer should say "yes".

Such responses wouldn't be hard to program. But a clever Interrogator could give the computer a rough time, by requiring it to analyze its own thinking:

Interrogator:	In the first line of your sonnet which reads "Shall I compare thee to a summer's day," wouldn't "a spring day" do as well or better?
Witness:	It wouldn't scan.
Interrogator:	How about "a winter's day"? That would scan all right.
Witness:	Yes, but nobody wants to be compared to a winter's day.
Interrogator:	Would you say Mr. Pickwick reminded you of Christmas?
Witness:	In a way.
Interrogator:	Yet Christmas is a winter's day, and I don't think Mr. Pickwick would mind the comparison.
Witness:	I don't think you're serious. By "a winter's day" one means a typical winter's day, rather than a special one like Christmas.

If the computer could answer questions that well, the Interrogator would have a hard time telling it wasn't human.

Donald Fink has suggested that the Interrogator say, "Suggest an unsolved problem and some methods for working toward its solution," and "What methods would most likely prove fruitful in solving the following problem...."

Turing believed computers would someday be able to win the game and therefore be considered to "think". In his article, he listed nine possible objections to his belief and rebutted them:

> **1. Soul** Thinking's a function of man's immortal soul. Since computers don't have souls, computers can't think. **Rebuttal:** since God's all-powerful, He can give computers souls if He wishes. Just as we create children to house His souls, so should we serve Him by creating computers.
>
> **2. Dreadful** If machines could equal us in thinking, that would be dreadful! **Rebuttal:** too bad!
>
> **3. Logicians** Logicians have proved it's impossible to build a computer that can answer every question. **Rebuttal:** is it possible to find a *human* that can answer every question? Computers are no dumber than we. Though no one can answer every question, why not build a succession of computers, each one more powerful than the next, so every question could be answered by at least one of them?
>
> **4. Conscious** Though computers can produce, they can't be *conscious* of what they've produced. They can't feel pleasure at their successes, misery at their mistakes, and depression when they don't get what they want. **Rebuttal:** the only way to be sure whether a computer has feelings is to become one. A more practical experiment would be to build a computer that explains step-by-step its reasoning, motivations, and obstacles it's trying to overcome, and also analyzes emotional passages such as poetry. Such a computer's clearly not just parroting.
>
> **5. Human** A computer can't be kind, resourceful, beautiful, friendly, have initiative, have a sense of humor, tell right from wrong, make mistakes, fall in love, enjoy strawberries & cream, make someone fall in love with it, learn from experience, use words properly, be the subject of its own thought, have as diverse behavior as a man, or do something really new. **Rebuttal:** why not? Though such a computer hasn't been built yet, it might be possible in the future.
>
> **6. Surprise** The computer never does anything original or surprising. It does only what it's told. **Rebuttal:** how do you know "original" human work isn't just grown from a seed (implanted by teaching) or the effect of well-known general principles? And who says computers aren't surprising? The computer's correct answers are often surprisingly different from a human's rough guesses.
>
> **7. Binary** Nerve cells can sense gradual increases in electrical activity — you can feel a "little tingle" or a "mild pain" or an "ouch" — whereas a computer's logic is just binary — either a "yes" or "no". **Rebuttal:** by using techniques such as "random numbers", you can make the computer imitate the flexible, probabilistic behavior of the nervous system enough so the Interrogator can't tell the difference.
>
> **8. Rules** Life can't be reduced to rules. For example, if a traffic-light rule says "stop when the light is red, and go when the light is green", what do you do when the light is broken, and both the red and green appear simultaneously? Maybe you should have an extra rule saying in that case to stop. But some further difficulty may arise with that rule, and you'd have to create another rule. And so on. You can't invent enough rules to handle all cases. Since computers must be fed rules, they can't handle all of life. **Rebuttal:** though life's more than a simple set of rules, it might be the *consequences* of simple psychological laws of behavior, which the computer could be taught.
>
> **9. ESP** Humans have extrasensory perception (ESP), and computers don't. **Rebuttal:** maybe the computer's random-number generator could be hooked up to be affected by ESP. Or to prevent ESP from affecting the Imitation Game, put both the human witness and the computer in a telepathy-proof room.

How to begin To make the computer an intelligent creature, Turing suggested two possible ways to begin. One way would be to teach the computer abstract skills, such as chess. The other way would be to give the computer eyes, ears, and other sense organs, teach it how to speak English, then educate it the same way you'd educate a somewhat handicapped child.

Suicide? Four years later — on June 8, 1954 — Turing was found dead in bed. The police say he died from potassium cyanide, self-administered. He'd been plating spoons with potassium cyanide in electrolysis experiments. His mother refuses to believe it was suicide, and hopes it was just an accident.

Understanding English

It's hard to make the computer understand plain English!

Confusion

Suppose you feed the computer this famous saying:

> Time flies like an arrow.

What does that saying mean? The computer might interpret it three ways....

> Interpretation 1: the computer thinks "time" is a noun, so the sentence means "The time can fly by as quickly as an arrow flies."

> Interpretation 2: the computer thinks "time" is a verb, so the sentence means "Time the speed of flies like you'd time the speed of an arrow."

> Interpretation 3: the computer thinks "time" is an adjective, so the sentence means "There's a special kind of insect, called a `time fly', and those flies are attracted to an arrow (in the same way moths are attracted to a flame)."

Suppose a guy sits on a barstool and shares his drinks with a tall woman while they play poker for cash. If the woman says to him, "Up yours!", the computer might interpret it 8 ways:

> The woman is upset at what the man did.
> The woman wants the man to raise up his glass, for a toast.
> The woman wants the man to up the ante and raise his bet.
> The woman wants the man to hold his cards higher, so she doesn't see them.
> The woman wants the man to pick up the card she dealt him.
> The woman wants the man to raise his stool, so she can see him eye-to-eye.
> The woman wants the man to pull up his pants.
> The woman wants the man to have an erection.

For another example, suppose Mae West were to meet a human-looking robot and ask him:

> Is that a pistol in your pocket, or are you glad to see me?

The robot would probably analyze that sentence too logically, then reply naively:

> There is no pistol in my pocket, and I am glad to see you.

In spite of those confusions, programmers have tried to make the computer understand English. Here are some famous attempts....

Baseball (1961)

In 1961 at MIT, programmers made the computer answer questions about baseball.

In the computer's memory, they stored the month, day, place, teams, and scores of each game in the American League for one year. They programmed the computer so that *you can type your question in ordinary English*. The computer analyzes your question's grammar and prints the correct answer.

Here are examples of questions the computer can analyze and answer correctly:

> Who did the Red Sox lose to on July 5?
> Who beat the Yankees on July 4?
> How many games did the Yankees play in July?
> Where did each team play in July?
> In how many places did each team play in July?
> Did every team play at least once in each park in each month?

To get an answer, the computer turns your questions into equations:

Question	Equations
Where did the Red Sox play on July 7?	place = ?
	team = Red Sox
	month = July
	day = 7
What teams won 10 games in July?	team (winning) = ?
	game (number of) = 10
	month = July
On how many days in July did eight teams play?	day (number of) = ?
	month = July
	team (number of) = 8

To do that, the computer uses this table:

Word in your question	Equation
where	place = ?
Red Sox	team = Red Sox
July	month = July
who	team = ?
team	team =

The computer ignores words such as *the*, *did*, and *play*.

If your question mentions *Boston*, you might mean either "place = Boston" or "team = Red Sox". The computer analyzes your question to determine which equation to form.

After forming the equations, the computer hunts through its memory, to find the games that solve the equations. If an equation says "number of", the computer counts. If an equation says "winning", the computer compares the scores of opposing teams.

The programmers were Bert Green, Alice Wolf, Carol Chomsky, and Kenneth Laughery.

What's a story problem?

When you were in school, your teacher told you a story that ended with a mathematical question. For example:

> Dick had 5 apples. He ate 3. How many are left?

In that problem, the last word is: *left*. That means: subtract. So the correct answer is 5 minus 3, which is 2.

Can the computer solve problems like that? Here's the most famous attempt....

Arithmetic & algebra (1964)

MIT awarded a Ph.D. to Daniel Bobrow, for programming the computer to solve story problems involving arithmetic and algebra.

Customers Let's see how the computer solves this problem:

> If the number of customers Tom gets is twice the square of 20 percent of the number of advertisements he runs, and the number of advertisements he runs is 45, what is the number of customers Tom gets?

To begin, the computer replaces *twice* by *2 times*, and replaces *square of* by *square*.

Then the computer separates the sentence into smaller sentences:

> The number of customers Tom gets is 2 times the square 20 percent of the number of advertisements he runs. The number of advertisements he runs is 45. What is the number of customers Tom gets?

The computer turns each sentence into an equation:

> number of customers Tom gets = 2 * (.20 * number of advertisements he runs)^2
> number of advertisements he runs = 45
> X = number of customers Tom gets

The computer solves the equations and prints the answer as a complete sentence:

> The number of customers Tom gets is 162.

Here's a harder problem:

> The sum of Lois's share of some money and Bob's share is $4.50. Lois's share is twice Bob's. Find Bob's and Lois's share.

Applying the same method, the computer turns the problem into these equations:

> Lois's share of some money + Bob's share = 4.50 dollars
> Lois's share = 2 * Bob's
> X = Bob's
> Y = Lois's share

The computer tries to solve the equations but fails. So it assumes "Lois's share" is the same as "Lois's share of some money", and "Bob's" is the same as "Bob's share". Now it has six equations:

Original equations
Lois's share of some money + Bob's share = 4.50 dollars
Lois's share = 2 * Bob's
X = Bob's
Y = Lois's share

Assumptions
Lois's share = Lois's share of some money
Bob's = Bob's share

It solves them and prints:

Bob's is 1.50 dollars.
Lois's share is 3 dollars.

Distance
The computer can solve problems about distance:

The distance from New York to Los Angeles is 3000 miles. If the average speed of a jet plane is 600 miles per hour, find the time it takes to travel from New York to Los Angeles by jet.

The resulting equations are:

distance from New York to Los Angeles = 3000 * miles
average speed of jet plane = (600 * miles)/(1 * hours)
X = time it takes to travel from New York to Los Angeles by jet

The computer is unable to solve them. But in its memory it finds the formula "distance = speed * time". It winds up with 7 equations:

Original equations
distance from New York to Los Angeles = 3000 * miles
average speed of jet plane = (600 * miles)/(1 * hours)
X = time it takes to travel from New York to Los Angeles by jet

Formula
distance = speed * time

Assumptions
distance = distance from New York to Los Angeles
speed = average speed of jet plane
time = time it takes to travel from New York to Los Angeles by jet

It solves them and prints:

The time it takes to travel from New York to Los Angeles by jet is 5 hours.

Age
The computer can solve problems about age:

Mary is twice as old as Ann was when Mary was as old as Ann is now. If Mary is 24 years old, how old is Ann?

To begin, the computer replaces *twice* by *2 times*, and replaces *how old* by *what*.

When the computer sees the words *as old as*, it knows the problem has to do with ages, so it breaks the problem into these sentences:

Mary's age is 2 times Ann's age X years ago. X years ago Mary's age is Ann's age now. Mary's age is 24. What is Ann's age?

The resulting equations are:

Mary's age = 2 * (Ann's age - X)
Mary's age - X = Ann's age
Mary's age = 24
Y = Ann's age

The computer prints:

Ann's age is 18.

Hint
If a situation appears hopeless, the computer asks you for help. In the following conversation, the human poses a problem, and the computer begs for a hint:

Human: The gross weight of a ship is 20000 tons. If its net weight is 15000 tons, what is the weight of the ship's cargo?
Computer: Do you know any more relationships among these variables: gross weight of ship, tons, its net weight, weight of ship's cargo?

Human: Yes.
Computer: Tell me.

Human: The weight of a ship's cargo is the difference between the gross weight and the net weight.
Computer: The weight of the ship's cargo is 5000 tons.

Limitations The program has some limitations. It cannot solve quadratic equations. If the computer tries to apply the formula "distance = speed * time" to a problem involving *two* distances, it forgets which distance is which.

The computer's vocabulary is limited. It doesn't realize that *how many* means *what is the number of*, and *how far is* means *what is the distance to*. For problems about age, the characters must be named Mary, Ann, Bill, Father, or Uncle, unless you diddle with the computer's memory.

If the human types *Tom has 2 apples, 3 bananas, and 4 pears*, the comma before the *and* makes the computer split the sentence into two wrong "sentences":

Tom has 2 apples, 3 bananas.
4 pears.

If the human mentions *the number of times John went to the movies*, the computer thinks *times* means multiplication, and tries to multiply *number of* by *John went to the movies*.

Encyclopedia (1964-1966)
In 1964, Simmons, Klein, and McConlogue (at the Systems Development Corporation) fed a child's encyclopedia into a computer.

If you type *What do worms eat?* the computer hunts through the encyclopedia, to find sentences mentioning both *worms* and *eat*. (To hasten the hunt, it uses an index produced by another program.) It finds two sentences:

Birds eat worms on the grass.
Most worms usually eat grass.

After analyzing the grammar of your question and those sentences, the computer realizes the first sentence is irrelevant, and prints just the correct answer:

Most worms usually eat grass.

In 1965, the program's abilities were extended, so that if you type *What animals live longer than men?* the computer searches through the encyclopedia for related words:

Word in sentence	Related words searched
animals	mammals, reptiles, fish
live	age
longer	older, ancient
men	person, people, women

Here's an example of the program's operation in 1966. The human creates some encyclopedia material about horses, and then retrieves it:

Human: Enter horse=noun, is=isverb, animal=noun, live=verb, on=prep, farm=noun, strong=adj, pull=verb, wagon=noun, most=adj, are=isverb, eat=verb, hay=noun, all=adj, red=adj, many=adj, have=haveverb, long=adj, mane=noun, some=adj, person=noun, race=verb.
Computer: Entered in dictionary.

Human: Plurals horse=horses, animal=animals, farm=farms, wagon=wagons, mane=manes, person=people.
Computer: Ok.

Human: Start.
Computer: Ready.

Human: A horse is an animal. Horses live on a farm. Strong horses pull wagons. Most horses are strong. Horses eat hay. All horses are red. Many horses have long manes. Some people race horses.
Computer: Learned.

Human: Forget "all horses are red".
Computer: Forgotten.

Human: What is a horse?
Computer: Horse is an animal.

Human: What do horses eat?
Computer: Horses eat hay.

Human: What do horses do?
Computer: Horses live on a farm and eat hay. Strong horses pull wagons.

Human:	What do strong horses do?
Computer:	Strong horses pull wagons.
Human:	Do many horses have long manes?
Computer:	Yes.
Human:	Do all horses have long manes?
Computer:	To my knowledge, no.
Human:	Describe horses?
Computer:	Horses are an animal. Most horses are strong. Many horses have long manes. Horses live on a farm and eat hay. Strong horses pull wagons. Some people race horses.

When the computer's answer consists of several sentences, it prints the most relevant sentence first, the others in decreasing order of relevance.

Military (1966)

Thompson and Craig (at General Electric) made the computer answer military questions such as:

Has the 25th battalion arrived in Texas since 3 P.M.?

Is the 100th scheduled to arrive at Ft. Lewis before the 200th leaves Ft. Lewis?

Eliza (1966-1967)

In 1966 at MIT, Joseph Weizenbaum wrote the Eliza program, which makes the computer act as a psychotherapist.

In 1967, he changed the program, to make it handle keywords such as *also*, *call*, *compute*, *define*, *is*, *let*, *of*, *thanks*, *where*, and the symbol =.

In the following conversation, the human teaches the computer how to find the area of a circle, a sphere, and a square, and then asks the computer questions about geometry. The human also teaches the computer how to speak German —

English	German
I say	ich sage
I mean	meine ich
what is	wieviel ist
squared	quadrat

and gradually starts speaking to the computer in German.

Human:	The area of a circle is pi times the radius of the circle squared. The area of a sphere is pi times the diameter of the sphere squared. The area of a square is the side of the square squared. The diameter of an object is twice the radius of the object. The radius of a ball is 10. What is the area of the ball?
Computer:	The assumption that ball is circle is consistent — shall I go on?
Human:	No.
Computer:	The assumption that ball is sphere and object is consistent — shall I go on?
Human:	Yes.
Computer:	It's 1256.6359.
Human:	What is the diameter of the ball?
Computer:	It's 20.
Human:	The radius of a dish is 10. What's the area of the dish?

Computer:	The assumption that dish is circle is consistent — shall I go on?
Human:	Yes.
Computer:	It's 314.15899.
Human:	The radius of a globe is 10. A globe is a sphere. A sphere is an object. What is the area of the globe?
Computer:	It's 1256.6359.
Human:	The side of a plate is 10. What is the area of the plate?
Computer:	The assumption that plate is square is consistent — shall I go on?
Human:	Yes.
Computer:	It's 100.
Human:	When I say board I mean plate. What is 3 times the side of the board?
Computer:	It's 30.
Human:	Please call that x. Let f(z) be z squared minus z. Compute f(x).
Computer:	It's 870.
Human:	When I say ich sage I mean I say. When ich sage meine ich I mean I mean. Wenn ich sage wieviel ist meine ich what is. Wenn ich sage quadrat meine ich squared. Nun, sagen sie mir bitte, wieviel is x quadrat.
Computer:	I didn't understand you.
Human:	Ja, tut mir leid, ich sollte fragen wieviel IST x quadrat.
Computer:	It's 900.

Calculus (1969)

At MIT, Charniak made the computer solve story problems involving calculus.

Human:	Water is flowing into a conical filter at the rate of 15 cubic inches per second. If the radius of the base of the filter is 5 inches and the altitude is 10 inches, find the rate at which the water level is rising when the volume is 100 cubic inches.
Computer:	The answer is .53132943 * in * sec^-1 * pi^-.33333332.

Probability (1971)

Rensselaer Polytechnic Institute awarded a Ph.D. to J.P. Gelb, for making the computer solve story problems involving probability.

Human:	From a zorch containing 4 ferd and 3 brakky and 5 chartreuse werfels, 3 are drawn. What is the probability that 2 are chartreuse and the other brakky?
Computer:	Replacement involved?
Human:	No.
Computer:	3/22 (or .1363636).

The field of "artificial intelligence" includes many categories.

For example, it includes attempts to make the computer win at chess and checkers, understand English, and create its own original art and music. It also includes attempts to imitate human feelings, personal interactions, and therapists. I explained those topics earlier.

Protocol method

During the 1950's and 1960's, most research in artificial intelligence was done at the Massachusetts Institute of Technology (MIT) and the Carnegie Institute of Technology (CIT, now called Carnegie-Mellon University). At Carnegie, the big names were Allen Newell and Herbert Simon. They invented the **protocol method**. In the protocol method, a human is told to solve a tough problem and, while he's solving it, to say at each moment what he's thinking. A transcript of his train of thought is recorded and called the **protocol**. Then programmers try to make the computer imitate that train of thought.

Using the protocol method, Newell and Simon produced programs that could "think like humans". The thinking, like human thinking, was imperfect. Their research did *not* try to make the computer a perfect thinker; instead, it tried to gain insight into how *humans* think. Their point of view was: if you think you really understand human psychology, go try to program it. Their attempt to reduce human psychology to computer programs is called **mentalism**, and has replaced Skinner's stimulus-response behaviorism as the dominant force in psychology today.

Abstract math

Many programmers have tried to make the computer do abstract math.

In 1957 Newell, Simon, and Shaw used the protocol method to make the computer prove theorems about symbolic logic, such as "Not (p or q) implies not p". In 1959 and 1960, Herbert Gelernter and his friends made the computer prove theorems about Euclidean geometry, such as "If the segment joining the midpoints of the diagonals of a trapezoid is extended to intersect a side of the trapezoid, it bisects that side."

In 1961, MIT awarded a Ph.D. to James Slagle for making the computer compute indefinite integrals, such as:

$$\int \frac{x^4}{(1-x^2)^{5/2}}\, dx$$

The computer gets the answer, which is:

$$\arcsin x + \frac{\tan^3 \arcsin x}{3} - \tan \arcsin x + c$$

Each of those programs works by drawing a tree inside the computer's memory. Each branch of the tree represents a possible line of attack. The computer considers each branch and chooses the one that looks most promising.

> A better symbolic-logic program was written by Hao Wang in 1960. His program doesn't need trees; it always picks the right attack immediately. It's guaranteed to prove any theorem you hand it, whereas the program by Newell, Simon, and Shaw got stuck on some hard ones.
>
> A better indefinite integration program was written by Joel Moses in 1967 and further improved in 1969. It uses trees very rarely and solves almost any integration problem.
>
> A program that usually finds the right answer but might fail on hard problems is called **heuristic**. A heuristic program usually involves trees. The checkers, chess, and geometry programs are heuristic. A program that's guaranteed to always give the correct answer is called **algorithmic**. The original symbolic-logic program was heuristic, but Wang's improvement is algorithmic; Moses's indefinite integration program is almost algorithmic.

GPS

In 1957 Newell, Simon, and Shaw began writing a single program to solve *all* problems. They called the program **GPS (General Problem Solver)**. If you feed the program a goal, a list of operators, and associated information, the program will tell you how to achieve the goal by using the operators.

For example, suppose you want the computer to solve this simple problem: a monkey would like to eat some bananas that are too high for him to reach, but there's a box nearby he can stand on. How can he get the bananas?

Feed the GPS program this information....

Now:	monkey's place = place#1; box's place = place#2; contents of monkey's hand = empty
Want:	contents of monkey's hand = the bananas
Difficulties:	contents of monkey's hand is harder to change than box's place, which is harder to change than monkey's place

Allowable operator	Definition	
climb box	before:	monkey's place = box's place
	after:	monkey's place = on the box
walk to x	after:	monkey's place = x
move box to x	before:	monkey's place = box's place
	after:	monkey's place = x; box's place = x
get bananas	before:	box's place = under the bananas; monkey's place = on the box
	after:	contents of monkey's hand = the bananas

GPS will print the solution:

```
walk to place#2
move box to under the bananas
climb box
get bananas
```

The GPS approach to solving problems is called **means-ends analysis**: you tell the program the means (operators) and the end (goal). The program has proved theorems in symbolic logic, computed indefinite integrals, and solved many famous puzzles, such as "The Missionaries and the Cannibals", "The Tower of Hanoi", and "The 5-Gallon Jug and the 8-Gallon Jug". But the program works slowly, and you must feed it lots of info about the problem. The project was abandoned in 1967.

Vision

Another large topic in artificial intelligence is **computer vision**: making the computer see.

> The first problem tackled was **pattern recognition**: making the computer read handwritten printed letters. The problem is hard, because some people make their letters very tall or wide or slanted or curled or close together, and the pen may skip. Reasonably successful programs were written, although computers still can't tackle script.
>
> Interest later shifted to **picture processing**: given a photograph of an object, make the computer tell what the object is. The problem is hard, because the photo may be taken from an unusual angle and be blurred, and because the computer gets confused by shadows.
>
> **Scene analysis** is even harder: given a picture of a group of objects, make the computer tell which object is which. The problem is hard, because some of the objects may be partly hidden behind others, and because a line can have two different interpretations: it can be a crease in one object, or a dividing-line between two objects.
>
> Most of the research in picture processing and scene analysis was done from 1968 to 1972.

Ray Kurzweil invented an amazing machine whose camera looks at a book and reads the book, by using a voice synthesizer. Many blind people have used it.

Robots

Researchers have built robots.

> The first robots were just for experimental fun, but today's robots are truly useful: for example, robots build cars. Many young kids have been taught "LOGO", which is a language developed at the MIT Artificial Intelligence Laboratory that makes the computer control a robot turtle.

Today's research

Today, research in artificial intelligence is done at four major universities: MIT, Carnegie, Stanford, and Edinburgh (Scotland).

Reflexive control

In the Soviet Union, weird researchers have studied **reflexive control**: they programmed the computer to be disobedient. The first such programmer was Lefevr, in 1967. In 1969 Baranov and Trudolyubov extended his work, by making the computer win this disobedience game:

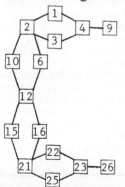

The human begins by choosing either node 9 or node 26, *but doesn't tell the computer which node he's chosen.*

> The computer starts at node 12; on each turn, it moves to an adjacent node. When it reaches either node 9 or node 26, the game ends: if the node the computer reaches is one of the human chose, the human wins; if the computer reaches the opposite node, the computer wins.

Before each move, the human tells the computer where to go; but the computer may decide to do the opposite (disobey).

What strategy should the computer use? If it always obeys, or always disobeys the human will catch on and make it lose.

Instead, Baranov and Trudolyubov programmed the computer to react as follows:

> obey the human twice, then disobey three times, then obey once, disobey thrice, obey once, disobey twice, obey thrice, disobey once, obey thrice, disobey once,...

The irregular alternation of obedience and disobedience confuses the human in a way that works to the computer's advantage. Using that strategy, the computer played against 61 humans, and won against 44 of them (72%). In other words, the typical human tried to mislead the computer but in fact "clued it in" to the human's goal.

Later experiments with other games indicated that the following pattern of disobedience is usually more effective:

> obey the human twice, disobey thrice, obey once, disobey four times, obey once, disobey thrice, obey thrice, disobey twice, obey thrice, disobey once, obey once, disobey once

Misinformation

Unfortunately, most research in the field of artificial intelligence is just a lot of hot air. For years, researchers have been promising that intelligent, easy-to-use English-speaking computers and robots would be available at low prices "any day now". After several decades of listening to such hoopla, I've given up waiting. The field of artificial intelligence should be renamed "artificial optimism".

Whenever a researcher in the field of artificial intelligence promises you something, don't believe it until you see it and use it personally, so you can evaluate its limitations.

If a computer seems to give intelligent replies to English questions posed by a salesman or researcher demonstrating artificial intelligence, try to interrupt the demo and ask the computer *your* English questions. You'll typically find that the computer doesn't understand what you're talking about at all: the demo was a cheap trick that works just with the peculiar English questions asked by the demonstrator.

For many years, the top researchers in artificial intelligence have been exaggerating their achievements and underestimating how long it will take to develop a truly intelligent computer. Let's look at their history of lies:

> In 1957 Herbert Simon said, "Within ten years a digital computer will be the world's chess champion." In 1967, when the ten years had elapsed, the only decent chess program was Greenblatt's, which the American Chess Federation rated "class D" (which means "poor"). A computer didn't become the world chess champion until 1997. It took forty years, not ten!
> In 1957 Simon also said, "Within ten years a digital computer will discover and prove an important new mathematical theorem." He was wrong. The computer still hasn't discovered or proved any important new mathematical theorem. The closest call came in 1976, when it did the *non-abstract part* of the proof of the "4-color theorem".
> In 1958 Newell, Simon, and Shaw wrote a chess-playing program which they admitted was "not fully debugged" so that one "cannot say very much about the behavior of the program"; but they claimed it was "good in spots (opening)". In 1959 the founder of cybernetics, Norbert Wiener, exaggerated about their program; he told New York University's Institute of Philosophy that "chess-playing machines as of now will counter the moves of a master player with the moves recognized as right in the textbooks, up to some point in the middle game." In the same symposium Michael Scriven carried the exaggeration even further by saying, "Machines are already capable of a good game." In fact, the program they were describing played very poorly, and in its last official bout (October 1960) was beaten by a 10-year-old kid who was a novice.
> In 1960 Herbert Gelernter (who wrote the geometry-theorem program) said, "Today hardly an expert will contest the assertion that machines will be proving interesting theorems in number theory three years hence." More than forty years have elapsed since then, but neither Gelernter nor anyone else has programmed the computer to prove theorems in number theory.
> In June 1963 the *Chicago Tribune* said, "The development of a machine that can listen to any conversation and type out the remarks just like an office secretary was announced yesterday by a Cornell University expert on learning machines. The device is expected to be in operation by fall. Frank Rosenblatt, director of Cornell's cognitive systems research, said the machine will be the largest thinking device built to date. Rosenblatt made his announcement at a meeting on learning machines at Northwestern University's Technological Institute." No such machine exists today, let alone in 1963.
> Also in 1963, W. Ross Ashby said, "Gelernter's theorem-proving program has discovered a new proof of the **pons asinorum** that demands no construction." He said the proof is one that "the greatest mathematicians of 2000 years have failed to notice... which would have evoked the highest praise

had it occurred." In fact, the *pons asinorum* is just the simple theorem that the opposite angles of an isosceles triangle are equal, and the computer's constructionless proof had already been discovered by Pappus in 300 A.D.
> In 1968 the head of artificial intelligence in Great Britain, Donald Michie, said, "Today machines can play chess at championship level." In fact, when computers were allowed to participate in human chess tournaments, they almost always lost.
> In 1970 the head of artificial intelligence at MIT, Marvin Minsky, said, "In three to eight years we will have a machine with the general intelligence of an average human being. I mean a machine that will be able to read Shakespeare, grease a car, play office politics, tell a joke, have a fight. At that point, the machine will begin to educate itself with fantastic speed. In a few months it will be at genius level, and a few months after that its powers will be incalculable." His prediction that it would happen in three to eight years — between 1973 and 1978 — was ridiculous. I doubt it will happen during this century, if ever.

Exaggerations concern not just the present and future but also the past:

> Back in 1962 Arthur Samuel's checker program won one game against Robert Nealey, "a former Connecticut checkers champion".
> Notice that Nealey was a *former* champion, not *the current* champion when the game was played. Also notice the program won a single game, not a match; and in fact it lost to Nealey later.
> In 1971 James Slagle slid over those niceties, when he just said that the program "once beat the champion of Connecticut."
> More recent writers, reading Slagle's words, have gone a step further and omitted the word *once*: one textbook says, "The current program beat the champion of Connecticut". It's not true.

Why do leaders of artificial intelligence consistently exaggerate? The answer is obvious: to get more research funds from the government. Hubert Dreyfus, chairman of the philosophy department at Berkeley, annoys them by attacking their claims.

The brain

Will the computer be able to imitate the human brain? Opinions vary.

Marvin Minsky, head of artificial intelligence at MIT, says *yes*: "After all, the human brain is just a computer that happens to be made out of meat."

Biologists argue *no*: the brain is composed of 12 billion **neurons**, each of which has between 5,000 and 60,000 **dendrites** for input and a similar number of **axons** for output; the neurons act in peculiar ways, and no computer could imitate all that with complete accuracy — "The neuron is qualitatively quite different from on-off components of current computers."

Herbert Simon (head of artificial intelligence at Carnegie and a psychologist), points out that certain aspects of the brain, such as short-term memory, are known to have very limited capacity and ability.

> He believes the inner workings of the brain are reasonably simple; it produces complicated output only because it receives complicated input from the sense organs and environment: "A man, viewed as a behaving system, is quite simple. The apparent complexity of his behavior over time is largely a reflection of the complexity of the environment in which he finds himself." Simon believes that if a computer were given good sense organs, the ability to move, and an elementary ability to learn, and were placed in a stimulating environment (unlike the dull four walls of a computer center), it would start acting in complex ways also.

Hubert Dreyfus, chairman of the philosophy department at Berkeley, argues that progress in artificial intelligence has been very small, is being blocked now by impenetrable barriers, and — most important — the computer's approach to solving problems bears little relationship to the more powerful methods used by humans. He's cynical about the claim that an improvement in computer programs represents progress toward understanding the human mind, which is altogether different: "According to this definition, the first man to climb a tree could claim tangible progress toward reaching the moon. Rather than climbing blindly, it's better to look where one is going."

PROGRAMMING

Background

This page represents the middle of the book. The pages before it cover what's new and hot about computers. The pages after it cover the eternal truths.

10 years from now, the stuff in the first half of the book will be considered "obsolete". The stuff in the second half of the book will be considered "still true".

This page is your introduction to eternity.

Why program?

We begin our look at eternal truths by studying programming. Of the 9 sections that make up this book, the section on programming is the longest: 251 pages! It's the book's deepest and most thorough adventure. It's the adventure that does the most to expand your mind and turn you into a brilliant thinker. Here's where your career's long-term growth gets its biggest boost.

Here's where you learn the secret of computer life! You learn how to take a computer — which is just a hunk of metal and plastic — and teach it new skills, by feeding it programs. Your teaching and programs turn the computer into a thinking organism. If you teach the computer well, you can make it become as smart as you and even imitate your personality. You become the computer's God, capable of making the computer do anything you wish. Ah, the power!

Folks who read just the first half of this book are at the mercy of Microsoft and other money-grubbing companies: whenever those unfortunate folks want to make the computer do something, they must buy a program that teaches the computer how. If computer stores don't carry a program for that particular task — or if the program's price is unaffordable — those folks are out of luck.

But once you learn how to program, you're lucky! You can make the computer do anything you want! All you need is the patience and perseverance to finish writing your program. And if you ever get stuck, phone me anytime at 603-666-6644 for free help.

When you finish writing your program, you can sell it to the idiots who've read just the first half of the book — and you're on your way to turning yourself into the next Microsoft.

It's easy

Programming the computer can be easy. You'll write your own programs just a few minutes from now, when you reach page 334! As you read farther, you'll learn how to write programs that are more sophisticated.

Computer languages

To program a computer, you put your fingers on the computer's keyboard and type commands. You type the commands in English.

The computer understands just *part* of English; it understands just a *few* words and phrases. The words and phrases the computer understands are called the **computer's language**.

Most computers understand a language called **BASIC**. It consists of words such as PRINT, INPUT, IF, and THEN.

To begin, I'll explain how to program the computer by using those BASIC words. Afterwards, I'll explain how to use different computer languages instead.

For example, I'll explain how to program the computer by using a language called **C**. In C, you must say "printf" instead of "PRINT", and you must say "scanf" instead of "INPUT".

Notice that C appeals to dirty minds who like to say "f" words! Another reason why programmers use C is that programs written in C run faster and consume less RAM than if written in BASIC.

But let's start with BASIC, which is pleasantly human, easy, and tasteful.

Why learn so many languages?

Programmers love to argue about which language is best.

> **BASIC** is easy to learn.
> **PASCAL** lets you organize your thinking better.
> **C** runs faster and consumes less RAM.
> **C++** resembles C but is fancier.
> **JAVA** resembles C++ but can also create animated Web pages on the Internet.
>
> **DBASE** includes extra words that help manipulate databases.
> **LOGO** fascinates kids by showing turtles move across the computer's screen.
> **FORTRAN** handles complex numbers used by engineers.
>
> **COBOL** handles the giant accounting tasks faced by big banks, insurance companies, and the IRS.
>
> Thousands of other languages have been invented, too!

Each language continually improves by stealing words from other languages — just as we English speakers stole the word "restaurant" from the French, and the French stole the word "weekend" from us.

Because of the mutual stealing, computer languages are becoming more alike. But each language still retains its own "inspired lunacy", its own weird words that other languages haven't copied yet.

This book turns you into a complete expert by teaching you how to program in *many* languages, so you become multilingual!

Learning a new language affects your way of thinking. For example, most Americans think cockroaches are disgusting; but when a German housewife sees a cockroach, she just giggles, because she thinks of the German word for "cockroach", which is "küchenschabe", which means "kitchen scraper", "a cute little thing that sweeps the kitchen". Yes, even the ugliest problems look cute when you know how to express your thoughts multilingually!

Each language adds new words to your vocabulary so you gain new ways to express your problems, solutions, and thoughts about them. When you face a tough programming problem and try to reduce it to words the computer understands, you'll think more clearly if you're multilingual and mastered enough vocabulary to turn the vague problem into precise words quickly.

An expert programmer can boil complex hassles down to a series of simple concepts. To do that, you need on the tip of your tongue the words defining those simple concepts. The more computer languages you study, the more words you'll learn, so you can quickly verbalize the crux of each computer problem and solve it.

BASIC FUN

Enter BASIC

To program the computer, you must use a language that the computer understands. Most computers understand a language called **BASIC**, which is a small part of English.

BASIC was invented by two Dartmouth College professors (John Kemeny and Tom Kurtz) in 1964. Later they improved it. Now BASIC consists of words such as PRINT, INPUT, IF, and THEN.

Here's how to program the computer by using those BASIC words.

Microsoft BASIC

Different computers speak different *dialects* of BASIC. The most popular dialect was invented in 1975 by a 19-year-old kid, Bill Gates. Since he developed software for microcomputers, he called himself **Microsoft** and called his BASIC dialect **Microsoft BASIC**.

Since Microsoft BASIC is so wonderful, all the popular computer companies paid him to make their computers understand Microsoft BASIC. That's right: IBM, Apple, Commodore, Tandy, Atari, Texas Instruments, and *hundreds* of other computer companies all had to pay off Bill.

Microsoft BASIC has become so popular that Bill had to hire hundreds of employees to help him fill all the orders. Microsoft Incorporated has become a multi-billion-dollar company, and Bill has become a famous billionaire, the wealthiest person in America.

What's QBASIC?

Over the years, Bill gradually improved Microsoft BASIC. Some computers use old versions of Microsoft BASIC; other computers use his latest improvements.

Now the most popular version of Microsoft BASIC is **QBASIC**. It's a simplification of another version of Microsoft BASIC, called **Quick BASIC**.

QBASIC is popular because it's good and because most people get it at no charge: free!

QBASIC is included, free, when you buy **MS-DOS** 5, 6, 6.2, 6.21, or 6.22.
QBASIC is included, free, when you buy **IBM PC-DOS 5** (which is similar to MS-DOS 5).
QBASIC does *not* come with IBM PC-DOS 6.1, 6.3, or 7.

If your computer has **Windows 95 or 98** and you got a CD-ROM disk containing Windows 95 or 98, that CD-ROM disk includes QBASIC.

What's in this chapter?

This chapter explains how to use QBASIC. The chapter ends with an appendix (on pages 437-447) explaining how other versions of BASIC differ.

Here's how the chapter is organized:

QBASIC's commands are explained on these pages:

Command	What the computer will do	Page	Similar to
BEEP	hum for a quarter of a second	385	SOUND, PLAY
CASE "fine"	if SELECTed is "fine", do indented lines	355	SELECT, IF
CIRCLE (100, 100), 40	draw a circle at (100, 100) with radius 40	383	LINE, PAINT
CLOSE	put finishing touches on the data files	426	OPEN
CLS	clear the screen, so it becomes all black	334	LOCATE
COMMON SHARED x	make x's box be shared among all procedures	414	DIM SHARED
DATA meat, potatoes	use this list of data: meat, potatoes	363	READ, RESTORE
DATE$ = "01-24-1996"	set the clock/calendar to 01-24-1996	390	TIME$ =
DECLARE SUB insult ()	prepare to use SUB procedure called "insult"	412	SUB
DEF SEG = 0	use memory segment #0	436	POKE
DEFDBL A-Z	make ordinary variables be double-precision	404	DEFLNG, DEFINT
DEFINT A-Z	make ordinary variables be short integers	404	DEFLNG, DEFDBL
DEFLNG A-Z	make ordinary variables be long integers	404	DEFINT, DEFLNG
DIM record AS STRING * 20	make the record be a 20-character string	428	TYPE, DIM
DIM SHARED y$(20)	make y$ be 20 strings that procedures share	414	COMMON, SUB
DIM x$(7)	make x$ be a list of 7 strings	408	x =
DO	do the indented lines below, repeatedly	343	DO UNTIL, LOOP
DO UNTIL EOF(1)	repeat the indented lines until end of file#1	427	DO, LOOP UNTIL
ELSE	do indented lines when IF conditions false	354	IF, ELSEIF
ELSEIF age < 100 THEN	do lines when earlier IFs false & age < 100	354	IF, ELSE
END	skip the rest of the program	345	STOP, SYSTEM
END IF	make this the bottom of an IF statement	354	IF, ELSE
END SELECT	make this the bottom of SELECT statement	355	SELECT, CASE
END SUB	make this the bottom of a SUB procedure	412	SUB
END TYPE	make this the bottom of a TYPE statement	428	TYPE
EXIT DO	skip down to the line that's under LOOP	359	DO, LOOP
EXIT SUB	skip down to the END SUB line	430	END SUB
FILES	print the names of all the hard disk's files	434	SHELL, NAME
FOR x = 1 TO 20	repeat the indented lines, 20 times	360	NEXT, DO
GET 1, 7, record	from file#1, get the 7th record	428	PUT, INPUT #1
GOTO 10	skip to line 10 of the program	345	DO, EXIT DO
IF y < 18 THEN PRINT "m"	if y is less than 18, print an "m"	353	ENDIF, ELSE
INPUT "What name"; n$	ask "What name?" and get answer n$	349	LINE INPUT
INPUT #1, a$	input from file#1 the value of a$	426	INPUT
KILL "joe.bas"	erase the file JOE.BAS from your hard disk	434	FILES, SHELL
LINE (0, 0)-(100, 100)	draw a line from (0, 0) to (100, 100)	383	PSET, CIRCLE
LINE INPUT "Type it"; n$	say "Type it" and grab whole line as input	421	INPUT
LOCATE 3, 7	move to the screen's 3rd line, 7th position	382	PRINT, CLS
LOOP	make this the bottom line of a DO loop	343	LOOP UNTIL
LOOP UNTIL guess$ = "p"	do the loop repeatedly, until guess$ is "p"	359	LOOP, DO UNTIL
LPRINT 2 + 2	print, onto paper, the answer to 2 + 2	339	PRINT
MID$(a$, 2)="owl"	change the middle of a$ to "owl"	400	x =
NAME "joe.bas" AS "f.bas"	find the file JO.BAS and rename it F.BAS	434	FILES, SHELL
NEXT	make this the bottom line of a FOR loop	360	FOR
ON ERROR GOTO 1000	if the lines below cause errors, go to line 1000	434	RESUME
OPEN "jo" FOR OUTPUT AS 1	create a data file called "JO"; output to it	426	CLOSE
PAINT (100, 101)	fill in the shape that surrounds (100, 101)	383	LINE, CIRCLE
PLAY "c d g# b- a"	play this music: C, D, G sharp, B flat, A	385	SOUND, BEEP
POKE 1047, 224	into memory cell #1047, put 224	436	DEF SEG, x =
PSET (100, 100)	make pixel (100, 100) turn white	383	SCREEN, LINE
PRINT 4 + 2	print the answer to 4 + 2	334	PRINT USING
PRINT USING "##.#"; x	print x, rounded to one decimal place	386	PRINT
PRINT #1, "eat"	print onto file#1 the word "eat"	426	PRINT, LPRINT
PUT 1, 7, record	in file#1, change the 7th record	428	GET, PRINT #1
RANDOMIZE TIMER	make random numbers be unpredictable	394	x =
READ a$	get a string from the DATA and call it a$	363	DATA, RESTORE
RESTORE 10	skip to line 10 of the DATA	366	READ, DATA
RESUME 10	end the error trap, by going to line 10	434	ON ERROR GO TO
SCREEN 12	use video mode 12 so you get VGA graphics	383	PSET, WIDTH
SELECT CASE a$	analyze a$ to select a case from list below	355	END SELECT, IF
SHELL "ver"	do this DOS command: "ver"	434	SYSTEM
SOUND 440, 18.2	make a sound of 440 hertz, for 1 second	385	PLAY, BEEP
SLEEP	pause until you press a key	341	FOR
STOP	skip rest of program; show the blue screen	368	END, SYSTEM
SUB insult	make the lines below define "insult"	412	END SUB
SWAP x, y	make x and y swap values with each other	423	x =
SYSTEM	skip rest of program; try to show "C:\>"	368	END, STOP
TIME$ = "13:45:07"	set the clock to 7 seconds after 13:45	390	DATE$ =
TYPE combination	make "combination" be a type of variable	428	END TYPE
WIDTH 40	on screen make each character twice as wide	339	CLS
x = 47	make x stand for the number 47	346	INPUT, POKE

QBASIC's functions are explained on these pages:

Function	Meaning	Value	Page	Similar to
ABS(-3.89)	absolute value of -3.89	3.89	392	SGN
ASC("A")	ASCII code number for A	65	399	CHR$
ATN(1) / degrees	arctangent of 1, in degrees	45	402	TAN
CHR$(164)	character whose code# is 164	"ñ"	398	ASC
CINT(3.89)	round to nearest integer	4	392	INT, FIX
COS(60 * degrees)	cosine of 60 degrees	.5	402	SIN, TAN
DATE$	today's date	varies	390	TIME$
EOF(1)	test whether at end of file#1	varies	427	LOF, ERR
ERR	the error's code number	varies	435	EOF
EXP(1)	e raised to the first power	2.718282	388	LOG, SQR
FIX(3.89)	erase digits after decimal point	3	392	INT, CINT
INPUT$(4)	4 characters that are input	varies	421	INSTR
INSTR("needed", "ed")	position of "ed" in "needed"	3	401	other INSTR
INSTR(4,"needed","ed")	search from the 4th character	5	401	other INSTR
INT(3.89)	round down to a lower integer	3	392	FIX, CINT
LCASE$("We love")	lower case; uncapitalize	"we love"	400	UCASE$
LEFT$("smart", 2)	left 2 characters of "smart"	"sm"	400	RIGHT$, MID$
LEN("smart")	length of "smart"	5	400	RIGHT$, MID$
LOC(1)	location of record in file#1	varies	429	LOF
LOF(1)	length of file#1, in bytes	varies	427	EOF
LOG(2.718282)	logarithm base e	1	389	EXP
LTRIM$(" Sue Smith")	delete beginning spaces	"Sue Smith"	401	RTRIM$
MID$("smart", 2)	begin at the 2nd character	"mart"	400	other MID$
MID$("smart", 2, 3)	begin at the 2nd take 3	"mar"	400	other MID$
PEEK(49837)	peek at memory cell #49837	varies	436	TIMER, RND
RIGHT$("smart", 2)	rightmost 2 characters	"rt"	400	LEFT$, MID$
RND	random decimal	varies	394	TIMER
RTRIM$("Sue Smith ")	delete ending spaces	"Sue Smith"	401	LTRIM$
SGN(-3.89)	sign of -3.89	-1	392	ABS, FIX
SIN(30 * degrees)	sine of 30 degrees	.5	402	COS, TAN
SQR(9)	square root of 9	3	388	EXP, LOG
STR$(81.4)	turn 81.4 into a string	" 81.4"	401	VAL
STRING$(5, "b")	a string of 5 b's	"bbbbb"	401	other STRING$
STRING$(5, 98)	98th ASCII character, 5 times	"bbbbb"	401	other STRING$
TAN(45 * degrees)	tangent of 45 degrees	1	402	ATN
TIME$	current time of day	varies	390	TIMER, DATE$
TIMER	# of seconds since midnight	varies	390	TIME$, DATE$
UCASE$("We love")	capitalize "We love"	"WE LOVE"	400	LCASE$
VAL("52.6")	remove the quotation marks	52.6	401	STR$

QBASIC's F keys are explained on these pages:

F key	Name	What the computer will do	Page
F2	SUB	show a different SUB	412
F4	View	switch between blue & black screens	335
F5	Continue	continue running the program	376
SHIFT F5	Run	run the entire program	334
F6	Immediate	move to & from immediate window	376
F7	Above	run the program down to here	377
F8	Step	run one more line of the program	377
F9	Breakpoint	create or destroy a red breakpoint	376

Start QBASIC

To start using QBASIC, turn on the computer without any floppy in drive A. Make sure the screen shows this standard C prompt:

```
C:\>
```

(To make the screen show it, follow the instructions on pages 116 of the MS-DOS chapter. Those instructions work even if you're using Windows 3 or 3.1 or 3.11 or 95 or 98.)

To start using QBASIC, type "qbasic" after the C prompt, so your screen looks like this:

```
C:\>qbasic
```

When you press the ENTER key at the end of that line, see what happens!
If you're lucky, the screen will turn blue and the computer will say:

```
Welcome to MS-DOS QBASIC
```

If you're unlucky, the computer will gripe by saying "Bad command or file name". To find out why the computer is griping, type "ver" after the C prompt. Then the computer will tell you which version of DOS it's using. To run QBASIC, you must buy DOS version 5, 6, 6.2, or 6.22 (since QBASIC is *not* included with DOS versions 6.1 or 6.3 or 7), or buy the CD-ROM version of Windows 95 or 98 and copy QBASIC from that CD-ROM to your hard disk as follows:

Insert the CD-ROM disk that Windows 95 or 98 came on. (Some computer makers call it the "Windows Companion Disk".)

If that disk's window is on the screen, close the window by clicking its X box. Make sure the computer says "C:\>" (by following the instructions on page 116).

If you're using Windows 98, type this:
```
copy d:\tools\oldmsdos\qbasic.* windows\command
```
If you're using Windows 95, type this:
```
copy d:\other\oldmsdos\qbasic.* windows\command
```

After the asterisk, make sure you put a space. If your CD-ROM drive is called "drive E" instead of "drive D", type "e:" instead of "d:".

Then try again to type "qbasic" after the C prompt.

After the computer says "Welcome to MS-DOS QBASIC", press the Esc key (which is at the keyboard's top left corner).

Type your program

Now you're ready to type your first program!

For example, type this program:

```
CLS
PRINT 4 + 2
```

Here's how. Type CLS, then press the ENTER key at the end of that line. Type PRINT 4 + 2 (and remember to hold down the SHIFT key to type the symbol +), then press the ENTER key at the end of that line.

Notice that you must press the ENTER key at the end of each line.

A **program** is a list of commands that you want the computer to obey. The sample program you typed contains two commands. The first command (**CLS**) tells the computer to **CL**ear the **S**creen, so the computer will erase the screen and the screen will become blank: entirely black! The next command (**PRINT 4 + 2**) tells the computer to do some math: it tells the computer to compute 4 + 2, get the answer (6), and print the answer on the screen.

Run your program

To make the computer obey the program you wrote, do this: while holding down the SHIFT key, tap the F5 key. That tells the computer to **run** the program: the computer will run through the program and obey all the commands in it.

The computer will begin by obeying the CLS command. The computer will clear the screen and make the screen become all blank, all black.

Then the computer will obey the PRINT 4 + 2 command. The computer will print this answer onto your screen:

```
6
```

Congratulations! You've written your first program! You've programmed the computer to compute the answer to 4 + 2! You've become a programmer! Now you can put on your résumé: "programmer!"

When you finish admiring the computer's answer, press the F4 key. That makes the screen change: instead of showing the computer's answer, the screen will turn blue and show your program again:

```
CLS
PRINT 4 + 2
```

If you'd like to peek at the answer again (which is 6 on a black screen), press the F4 key again. When you finish peeking at the answer, press the F4 key again to view the program again (CLS and PRINT 4 + 2 on a blue screen).

So here are the rules:

```
To run the program (and put the answer on a black screen), press SHIFT with F5.
To view the blue screen again — or switch back to the black screen again — press F4.
```

Faster typing

While typing the program, **you don't need to capitalize computer words** such as CLS and PRINT: the computer will capitalize them automatically when you press ENTER at the end of the line.

While typing that program, put a blank space after the word PRINT to separate the "PRINT" from the 4. But **you don't need to put spaces next to the + sign**, since the computer will automatically insert those spaces when you press ENTER at the end of the line.

Instead of typing "PRINT" or "print", you can type just a question mark. When you press the ENTER key at the end of the line, the computer will replace the question mark by the word PRINT, and the computer will put a blank space after it.

So **instead of typing PRINT 4 + 2, you can type just this:**

```
?4+2
```

Think of the question mark as standing for this word:

```
What's
```

If you want to ask the computer "What's 4+2", type this:

```
?4+2
```

When you run the program, the computer will print the answer, 6.

Why CLS?

The program's top line (CLS) tells the computer to erase the screen before printing the answer (6).

If you forget to make the program's top line say CLS, the computer will forget to erase the screen. The computer will still print the answer (6), but that answer will appear underneath a transcript of previous chit-chat that occurred between you and the computer. That transcript is distracting and confusing. CLS erases it.

Edit your program

After you've typed your program, try typing another one. For example, create a program that makes the computer print the answer to 79 + 2. To do that, make this program appear on the screen:

```
CLS
PRINT 79 + 2
```

To make that program appear, just edit the program you typed previously (which said PRINT 4 + 2). To edit, use the arrow keys to move to the character you want to change (which was the 4), delete that character (4) by pressing the DELETE key, then type the characters you want instead (79).

While editing, use these tricks....

To delete a character:
move the cursor (blinking underline) to that character, then press the DELETE key.

To delete SEVERAL characters:
move to the first character you want to delete, then hold down the DELETE key awhile.

To delete AN ENTIRE LINE:
move to that line; then while holding down Ctrl key, tap the Y key.

To INSERT A NEW LINE between two lines:
move to the beginning of the lower line; then while holding down Ctrl key, tap the N key.

If you've edited the program successfully, the screen shows just the new program —

```
CLS
PRINT 79 + 2
```

and you don't see the old program anymore.

When you've finished editing the program, run it (by pressing SHIFT with F5 again). Then the computer will print the answer:

```
81
```

Fix your errors

What happens if you misspell a computer word, such as CLS or PRINT? For example, what happens if you accidentally say PRIMPT instead of PRINT?

When you run the program (by pressing SHIFT with F5), the computer tries to run each line of your program. If the computer comes to a misspelled computer word (such as PRIMPT), the computer highlights your misspelling (by showing it in blue letters against a white background) and says:

```
Syntax error
```

Press the ENTER key, then fix your error, then try again to run the program (by pressing SHIFT with F5 key again).

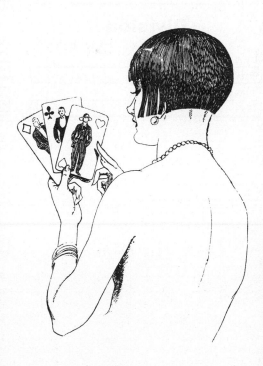

This command makes the computer add 4 + 2:

```
PRINT 4 + 2
```

Put that command into a program (whose top line should be CLS). When you run the program (by pressing SHIFT with F5), the computer will print the answer:

```
6
```

If you want to subtract 3 from 7, type this command instead:

```
PRINT 7 - 3
```

(When typing the minus sign, do *not* press the SHIFT key.) The computer will print:

```
4
```

You can use decimal points and negative numbers. For example, if you type this —

```
PRINT -26.3 + 1
```

the computer will print:

```
-25.3
```

Multiplication

To multiply, use an asterisk. So to multiply 2 by 6, type this:

```
PRINT 2 * 6
```

The computer will print:

```
12
```

Division

To divide, use a slash. So to divide 8 by 4, type this:

```
PRINT 8 / 4
```

The computer will print:

```
2
```

Huge & tiny numbers

When dealing with huge and tiny numbers, be careful!

Avoid commas Do *not* put commas in big numbers. To write four million, do *not* write 4,000,000; instead, write 4000000.

The symbol # If you type a long number (such as 7000000000 or 273.85429), the computer might automatically put the symbol # afterwards. That's the computer's way of reminding itself that the number is long and must be treated extra carefully!

Use decimals for big answers The computer sometimes has difficulty handling answers bigger than 32 thousand. To avoid difficulty, **put a decimal point in any problem whose answer might be bigger than 32 thousand**.

For example, suppose you want the computer to multiply 200 by 300. Since the answer to that problem is 60 thousand, which is bigger than 32 thousand, you should put a decimal point in that problem. But suppose you forget to insert a decimal point, and you say just this:

```
CLS
PRINT 200 * 300
```

the computer will complain by saying:

```
Overflow
```

When the computer says "Overflow", reply by pressing the ENTER key, then fix your program by inserting a decimal point, like this —

```
PRINT 200 * 300.0
```

or like this —

```
PRINT 200 * 300.
```

When you finish typing that line (and press ENTER afterwards), the computer will do something strange: it will turn the ".0" or "." into an exclamation point, so the line looks like this:

```
PRINT 200 * 300!
```

When you run the program, the computer will print the right answer:

```
60000
```

Notice that if you type a decimal point at the end of a number, the computer usually puts an exclamation point (!) at the end of the number. If the number is long, the computer puts a number sign (#) instead of an exclamation point.

E notation If the computer's answer is huge (more than a million) or tiny (less than .01), the computer might print an E in the answer. The E means "move the decimal point".

For example, suppose the computer says the answer to a problem is:

```
8.516743E+12
```

The E means, "move the decimal point". The plus sign means, "towards the right". Altogether, **the E+12 means, "move the decimal point towards the right, 12 places."** So look at 8.516743, and move the decimal point towards the right, 12 places; you get 8516743000000.

So when the computer says the answer is 8.516743E+12, the computer really means the answer is 8516743000000, approximately. The exact answer might be 8516743000000.2 or 8516743000000.79 or some similar number, but the computer prints just an approximation.

Suppose your computer says the answer to a problem is:

```
9.23E-06
```

After the E, the minus sign means, "towards the *left*". So look at 9.23, and move the decimal point towards the left, 6 places. You get:
.00000923

So when the computer says the answer is 9.23E-06, the computer really means the answer is:
.00000923

You'll see E notation rarely: the computer uses it just if an answer is huge (many millions) or tiny (tinier than .01). But when the computer *does* use E notation, remember to move the decimal point!

D notation If the answer's a long number, the computer usually prints a D instead of an E. Like the E, the D means "move the decimal point".

The highest number The highest number the computer can handle well is about 1E38, which is 1 followed by 38 zeros, like this:

```
100000000000000000000000000000000000000
```

If you try to go much higher, the computer will either gripe (by saying "Overflow") or use D notation (which goes up to about 1D308).

The tiniest decimal The tiniest decimal the computer can handle easily is about 1E-38, which is a decimal point followed by 38 digits, 37 of which are zeros, like this:

```
.00000000000000000000000000000000000001
```

If you try to go much tinier, the computer will either say 0 or use D notation (which goes down to about 1D-323).

Order of operations

What does "2 plus 3 times 4" mean? The answer depends on who you ask.

To a clerk, it means "start with 2 plus 3, then multiply by 4"; that makes 5 times 4, which is 20. But to a scientist, "2 plus 3 times 4" means something different: it means "2 plus three fours", which is 2 + 4 + 4 + 4, which is 14.

Since computers were invented by scientists, computers think like scientists. If you type —

```
PRINT 2 + 3 * 4
```

the computer will think you mean "2 plus three fours", so it will do 2 + 4 + 4 + 4 and print this answer:

```
14
```

The computer will *not* print the clerk's answer, which is 20. So if you're a clerk, tough luck!

Scientists and computers follow this rule: **do multiplication and division before addition and subtraction**. So if you type —

```
PRINT 2 + 3 * 4
```

the computer begins by hunting for multiplication and division. When it finds the multiplication sign between the 3 and the 4, it multiplies 3 by 4 and gets 12, like this:

```
PRINT 2 + 3 * 4
            12
```

So the problem becomes 2 + 12, which is 14, which the computer prints.

For another example, suppose you type:

```
PRINT 10 - 2 * 3 + 72 / 9 * 5
```

The computer begins by doing all the multiplications and divisions. So it does 2 * 3 (which is 6) and does 72 / 9 * 5 (which is 8 * 5, which is 40), like this:

```
PRINT 10 - 2 * 3 + 72 / 9 * 5
            6          40
```

So the problem becomes 10 - 6 + 40, which is 44, which is the answer the computer prints.

Parentheses
You can use parentheses the same way as in algebra. For example, if you type —

```
PRINT 5 - (1 + 1)
```

the computer will compute 5 - 2 and print:

```
3
```

You can put parentheses inside parentheses. If you type —

```
PRINT 10 - (5 - (1 + 1))
```

the computer will compute 10 - (5 - 2), which is 10 - 3, and will print:

```
7
```

Strings

Let's make the computer fall in love. Let's make it say, "I love you".

Type this program:

```
CLS
PRINT "I love you"
```

Here's how to type the second line:

Begin by typing the word PRINT. Then type a blank space (by pressing the SPACE bar). Then type a quotation mark, but be careful: **to type the quotation mark, you must hold down the SHIFT key.** Then type these words: *I love you.* Then type another quotation mark. At the end of that line, press the ENTER key.

When you run the program (by pressing SHIFT with F5), the computer will obey your command; it will print:

```
I love you
```

You can change the computer's personality. For example, if you give this command —

```
PRINT "I hate you"
```

the computer will reply:

```
I hate you
```

Notice that **to make the computer print a message, you must put the message between quotation marks**. The quotation marks make the computer copy the message without worrying about what the message means. For example, if you misspell "I love you", and type —

```
PRINT "aieee luf ya"
```

the computer will still copy the message (without worrying about what it means); the computer will print:

```
aieee luf ya
```

Faster typing
Instead of typing —

```
PRINT "I love you"
```

you can type just this:

```
?"I love you
```

At the end of that line, when you press the ENTER key, the computer will automatically do three things:

The computer will change the question mark to the word PRINT. The computer will put a blank space after PRINT (and before the quotation mark). The computer will put a quotation mark at the end of the line (to match the other quotation mark).

Jargon
The word "joy" consists of 3 characters: J and O and Y. Programmers say that the word "joy" is a **string** of 3 characters.

A **string** is any collection of characters, such as "joy" or "I love you" or "aieee luf ya" or "76 trombones" or "GO AWAY!!!" or "xypw exr///746". The computer will print whatever string you wish, but remember to **put the string in quotation marks**.

Strings versus numbers

The computer can handle two types of expressions: **strings** and **numbers**. Put strings (such as "joy" and "I love you") in quotation marks. Numbers (such as 4 + 2) do *not* go in quotation marks.

Accidents
Suppose you accidentally put the number 2 + 2 in quotation marks, like this:

```
PRINT "2 + 2"
```

The quotation marks make the computer think "2 + 2" is a string instead of a number. Since the computer thinks "2 + 2" is a string, it copies the string without analyzing what it means; the computer will print:

```
2 + 2
```

It will *not* print 4.

Suppose you want the computer to print the word "love" but you accidentally forget to put the string "love" in quotation marks, and type this instead:

```
PRINT love
```

Since you forgot the quotation marks, the computer thinks *love* is a number instead of a string but doesn't know which number, since the computer doesn't know the meaning of love. Whenever the computer is confused, it either gripes at you or prints a zero. In this particular example, when you run the program the computer will print a zero, like this:

```
0
```

So if you incorrectly tell the computer to proclaim its love, it will say zero.

Longer programs

You can program the computer say it's madly in love with you!

Let's make the computer say:

```
I love you.
You turned me on.
Let's get married!
```

To make the computer say all that, just run this program:

```
CLS
PRINT "I love you."
PRINT "You turned me on."
PRINT "Let's get married!"
```

To run that program, type it and then press the F5 key. Try it!

To have even more fun, run this program:

```
CLS
PRINT "I long"
PRINT 2 + 2
PRINT "U"
```

It makes the computer print "I long", then print the answer to 2+2 (which is 4), then print "U". So altogether, the computer prints:

```
I long
4
U
```

Yes, the computer says it longs for you!

Tricky printing

Printing can be tricky! Here are the tricks.

Indenting

Suppose you want the computer to print this letter:

```
Dear Joan,
    Thank you for the beautiful
necktie.  Just one problem--
I don't wear neckties!
            Love,
                Fred-the-Hippie
```

This program prints it:

```
CLS
PRINT "Dear Joan,"
PRINT "  Thank you for the beautiful"
PRINT "necktie.  Just one problem--"
PRINT "I don't wear neckties!"
PRINT "            Love,"
PRINT "                Fred-the-Hippie"
```

In the program, each line contains two quotation marks. **To make the computer indent a line, put blank spaces AFTER the first quotation mark.**

Blank lines

Life consists sometimes of joy, sometimes of sorrow, and sometimes of a numb emptiness. To express those feelings, run this program:

Program	What the computer will do
CLS	Clear the screen.
PRINT "joy"	Print "joy".
PRINT	Print a blank empty line, underneath "joy".
PRINT "sorrow"	Print "sorrow".

Altogether, the computer will print:

```
joy

sorrow
```

Semicolons

Run this program:

```
CLS
PRINT "fat";
PRINT "her"
```

The second line, which makes the computer print "fat", ends with a semicolon. **The semicolon makes the computer print the next item on the same line**; so the computer will print "her" on the same line, like this:

```
father
```

This program gives you some food for thought:

```
CLS
PRINT "I love to eat her";
PRINT "ring for dinner";
PRINT "you are the most beautiful fish in the whole sea!"
```

The program says to print three phrases. Because of the semicolons, the computer tries to print all the phrases onto a single line; but those phrases are too long to all fit on the same line simultaneously! So the computer prints just the first two phrases onto the line and prints the third phrase underneath, like this:

```
I love to eat herring for dinner
you are the most beautiful fish in the whole sea!
```

The next program shows what happens to an evil king on a boat:

```
CLS
PRINT "sin"; "king"
```

The computer will print "sin", and will print "king" on the same line, like this:

```
sinking
```

Notice that in a PRINT statement, you can type several items (such as "sin" and "king"). You're supposed to type a semicolon between each pair of items; but if you forget to type a semicolon, the computer will type it for you automatically when you press the ENTER key at the end of the line. The computer will also automatically put a blank space after each semicolon.

Spaces after numbers

Try typing this command:

```
PRINT -3; "is my favorite number"
```

Whenever the computer prints a NUMBER, it prints a blank space afterwards; so the computer will print a blank space after -3, like this:

```
-3 is my favorite number
```

(space)

Spaces before positive numbers

This command tells what to put in your coffee:

```
PRINT 7; "do"; "nuts"
```

The computer prints 7 and "do" and "nuts". Since 7 is a number, the computer prints a blank space after the 7. **The computer prints another blank space BEFORE every number that's positive**; so the computer prints another blank space before the 7, like this:

```
 7 donuts
```

(spaces)

Hey, if you're feeling cool, maybe this command expresses your feelings:

```
PRINT "the temperature is"; 4 + 25; "degrees"
```

The computer prints "the temperature is", then 4 + 25 (which is 29), then "degrees". Since 29 is a positive number, the computer prints a blank space before and after the 29:

```
the temperature is 29 degrees
```

(spaces)

Fix the negative numbers

Use this command if you're even colder:

```
PRINT "the temperature is"; 4 - 25; "degrees"
```

The computer prints "the temperature is", then 4 - 25 (which is -21), then "degrees". Since -21 is a number, the computer prints a space after it; but since -21 is *not* positive, the computer does *not* print a space before it. The computer prints:

```
the temperature is-21 degrees
```

(no space) (space)

Yuk! That looks ugly! It would look prettier if there were a space before the -21. To insert a space, put the space inside quotation marks:

```
PRINT "the temperature is "; 4 - 25; "degrees"
```

(inserted space, before the quotation mark)

Then the computer will print:

```
the temperature is -21 degrees
```

(inserted space)

Multiple calculations

By using semicolons, you can make the computer do many calculations at once.

For example, this command makes the computer do 6+2, 6-2, 6*2, and 6/2, all at once:

```
PRINT 6 + 2; 6 - 2; 6 * 2; 6 / 2
```

That makes the computer print the four answers:

```
 8  4  12  3
```

The computer prints spaces between the answers, because the computer prints a space after every number (and an additional space before every number that's positive).

Print on paper

If you say LPRINT instead of PRINT, the computer will print on paper instead of on your screen.

For example, if you want the computer to compute 2+2 and print the answer on paper, type this program:

```
CLS
LPRINT 2 + 2
```

While typing that program, make sure you type "LPRINT". Although "PRINT" can be abbreviated by typing "?", "LPRINT" can*not* be abbreviated by typing "L?"; you must type the word "LPRINT" in full.

When you run that program (by putting paper into the printer, turning the printer on, and pressing the F5 key), the computer will compute 2 + 2 and print this answer onto paper:

```
 4
```

Eject the paper manually

Although the computer prints that answer onto paper, the paper remains stuck in the printer, until you tell the printer to **eject** the paper. Ejecting the paper is called "doing a **form feed**", because it feeds a sheet of paper (a form) through the printer.

To eject the paper manually, press the printer's **form-feed button**.

For example, if your printer's an Epson 5000 (or a similar dot-matrix printer), push the printer's LF/FF button awhile (because that's the form-feed button). If your printer's a Hewlett-Packard Laserjet 2 (or a similar laser printer), press the printer's ON LINE button (so the ON LINE light turns off), then the FORM FEED button, then the ON LINE button again (so the ON LINE light turns back on).

Eject the paper automatically

Instead of ejecting paper manually, you can make the computer **eject paper AUTOMATICALLY, by putting this line at the bottom of your program:**

```
LPRINT CHR$(12);
```

That line works for all popular printers.

For example, this program makes the computer figure out the answer to 2+2, print the answer (4) onto paper, and then eject the paper from the printer:

```
CLS
LPRINT 2 + 2
LPRINT CHR$(12);
```

This program prints a poem on paper and then ejects the paper:

```
CLS
LPRINT "I see England."
LPRINT "I see France."
LPRINT "I see Batman's"
LPRINT "underpants!"
LPRINT CHR$(12);
```

If you want to print *several* copies of that poem onto paper (so you can hand the copies to several friends), run that program *several* times: each time, say run (by pressing SHIFT with F5) and return to the blue screen (by pressing F4).

Dual printing If you say PRINT 2 + 2, the computer prints the answer (4) onto the screen. If you say LPRINT 2 + 2, the computer prints 4 onto paper instead. If you want to print the answer onto the screen *and also onto paper*, say PRINT *and also LPRINT*, like this:

Program	What the computer will do
CLS	Clear the screen.
PRINT 2 + 2	Print answer (4) onto screen.
LPRINT 2 + 2	Print answer (4) onto paper.
LPRINT CHR$(12);	Eject paper from the printer.

Screen dump Here's another way to print on paper: while you're looking at the computer's answers (on the black screen), press the PRINT SCREEN key (which is on the computer's keyboard, near the top right corner).

That makes the computer dump onto paper a snapshot of everything that's on the screen. The snapshot on paper is called a **screen dump**.

After pressing the PRINT SCREEN key, eject the paper manually.

If you want to print *several* copies on paper, press the PRINT SCREEN key *several* times — and eject the paper manually each time.

WIDTH 40

At the top of your program, instead of saying CLS, you can say:

```
WIDTH 40
```

Like the CLS command, it makes the computer erase the screen. But it also **makes all characters on the black screen be extra wide**. It makes those characters be twice as wide as normal, so just 40 of them fit on a line (instead of 80). The characters look dramatically huge!

Though WIDTH 40 widens the computer's answers on the black screen, it does *not* widen characters on paper or on the blue screen (where you type your program).

If you **tap the Alt key and then the F key**, you'll see this **file menu**:

```
New
Open...
Save
Save As...

Print...

Exit
```

Here's how to use it....

Print

If you choose **Print** from that menu (by pressing the P key) and then press the ENTER key, the computer will copy the program onto paper.

For example, if the screen shows this program —

```
CLS
PRINT 2 + 2
```

the printer will print this onto paper:

```
CLS
PRINT 2 + 2
```

Then eject the paper manually.

Save

If you want the computer to copy the program onto your hard disk, choose **Save** from the file menu, by pressing the S key.

Invent a name If you haven't invented a name for the program yet, the computer will say "File Name" and wait for you to invent a short name. Invent any short name you wish. For example, the name can be JOE or SUE or LOVER or POEM4U.

Pick a name that reminds you of the program's purpose.

For example, if the program prints a bill to a customer, call the program "BILL"; if the program plays chess, call the program "CHESS"; if it gives a quiz, call it "QUIZ"; if it tutors a human about the elements of sex, call it "SEX"; if it tutors a human about advanced sex, call it "SEX2".

The name must be short (up to 8 characters long) and should be simple (consisting of just letters and digits).

When you finish typing the name, press the ENTER key. Then the computer copies your program to the hard disk.

For example, if you typed the name "joe", the computer copies your program to the hard disk and names the program "JOE.BAS". (Notice that the computer automatically capitalizes the name and puts .BAS afterwards. The .BAS means "written in BASic".)

Exception: if the name you invented was already used by another program, the computer asks you, "Overwrite?" Press the Y key if you want the new program to replace the old program, so the old program disappears. If you do *not* want the new program to replace the old program, press N instead of Y, then invent a *different* name for your new program.

Save often Suppose you're creating a program that's so long it takes you several hours to type. You'll be upset if, after several hours of typing, your town suddenly has a blackout that makes the computer forget what you typed.

To protect yourself against such a calamity, choose Save from the file menu every 15 minutes.

Then if your town has a blackout, you'll lose just a few minutes of work; the rest of your work will have already been saved on the disk. Saving your program every 15 minutes protects you against blackouts and also again "computer malfunction" and any careless errors you might make.

New

When you've finished inventing and saving a program, **here's how to erase the screen, so you can start writing a different program instead**: choose **New** from the file menu (by pressing the N key).

If you didn't save the program you worked on, the computer asks, "Save it now?" If you want to save the program you worked on, press the Y key; if you do *not* want to save the program you worked on, press the N key instead.

Open

If you saved a program onto your hard disk, here's how to use it again: choose **Open** from the file menu (by pressing the letter O).

The computer shows you an alphabetical list of all BASIC programs on the hard disk. (If the list is too long to fit on the screen, the computer shows you the list's beginning.)

Then say which program you want, by using one of these methods….

Method 1: type the name of the program you want (such as "joe"), then press ENTER.

Method 2: press the TAB key, then the down-arrow key; then press the down-arrow key a few more times until the program you want is highlighted; then press the ENTER key.

All lines of that program will appear on the screen.

Exception: if a different program has been on the screen and you didn't save it, the computer will ask, "Save it now?" If you want to save that program, press the Y key; if you do *not* want to save that program, press the N key instead.

ESCAPE key

If you change your mind and wish you hadn't requested the file menu, press the **ESCAPE key** (which says "Esc" on it). The file menu will disappear.

Save As

Here's how to create a program called JOE, then create a variant of it called JOE2.

First, type the JOE program and save it. Then edit that program, choose **Save As** from the file menu (by pressing the A key), and type "JOE2" (and press ENTER).

Exit

When you've finished using QBASIC, choose **Exit** from the file menu, by pressing the X key.

(If you didn't save the program you worked on, the computer asks, "Save it now?" If you want to save the program you worked on, press the Y key; if you do *not* want to save the program you worked on, press the N key instead.)

Then the computer will exit from QBASIC, and the screen will say:

```
C:\>
```

Become an expert

Congratulations! You've learned how to program!

C'mon, write some programs! It's easy! Try it. You'll have lots of fun!

A person who writes a program is called a **programmer**. Congratulations: *you're* a programmer!

Write *several* programs like the ones I've shown you already. Then you can put on your resumé that you have "a wide variety of programming experience", and you can talk your way into a programming job!

The rest of this chapter explains how to become a *good* programmer.

Practice

Programming the computer is like driving a car: **the only way to become an expert is to put your hands on that mean machine and try it yourself**.

If you have access to a computer, put this book next to the computer's keyboard. At the end of each paragraph, type the examples and look, look, see the computer run. Invent your own variations: try typing different numbers and strings. Invent your own programs: make the computer print your name or a poem; make it solve problems from your other courses and the rest of your life. The computer's a fantastic toy. Play with it.

If you're a student, don't wait for your instructor to give lectures and assign homework. *Act now*. You'll learn more from handling the computer than from the lectures or readings. Experience counts.

Let me tell you the story of Charlie:

At Wesleyan University's computer center, one of the directors was having trouble making the computer print the university's payroll. He asked me for help, but I said I didn't know either. I saw a little kid sitting at one of the keyboards. "Hey, Charlie," I called to him, "we're having trouble getting the payroll out."

Little Charlie came over and typed some stuff on our keyboard. "The payroll will be out in a minute," he said gleefully.

Charlie was just in seventh grade. He'd never taken a computer course; his school didn't offer one. But by spending the whole summer just "hanging around" our computer, he knew it better than we.

Be like Charlie. Hang around your computer. Communicate with it every day. At first, that will be even harder than talking with a cat or a tree, because the computer belongs to a different species, a different kingdom; but keep trying. Get to know it as well as you know your best friend.

If you're taking a French course, you might find French difficult; and if you're taking a computer course, you might find computers difficult also. But even a stupid three-year-old French kid can speak French, and even kindergarten kids can program the computer. They have just one advantage over you: practice!

Be bold

In science fiction, computers blow up; in real life, they never do. No matter what keys you press, no matter what commands you type, you won't hurt the computer. The computer is invincible! So go ahead and experiment. If it doesn't like what you type, it will gripe at you, but so what?

Troubles

When you try using the computer, you'll have trouble — because you're making a mistake, or the computer is broken, or the computer is weird and works differently from the majority computers discussed in this book. (Each computer has its own "personality", its own quirks.)

Whenever you have trouble, laugh about it, and say, "Oh, boy! Here we go again!" (If you're Jewish, you can say all that more briefly, in one word: "Oy!") Then get some help.

Get help

For help with your computer, read this book! For further help, read the beginner's manual that came with your computer, or ask the genie who gave you the computer (your salesperson or parent or boss or teacher or friend).

If you're sitting near computers in your office, school, or home, and other people are nearby, ask them for help. They'll gladly answer your questions because they like to show off and because the way *they* got to know the answers was by asking.

Computer folks like to explain computers, just as priests like to explain religion. Remember: you're joining a cult! Even if you don't truly believe in "the power and glory of computers", at least you'll have a few moments of weird fun. So play along with the weird computer people, boost their egos, and they'll help you get through your initiation rite. Above all, assert yourself, and **ask questions**. "Shy guys finish last."

When dealing with the computer and the people who surround it, be friendly but also assertive. To make sure you get your money's worth from a computer course, ask your teacher, classmates, lab assistants, and other programmers questions, questions, questions! If you're using a computer that you own, get help from the person who gave it to you.

Your town probably has a **computer club**. (To find out, ask the local schools and computer stores.) Join the club, and tell the members you'd like help with your computer. Probably some computer hobbyist will help you.

And remember — you can call *me* anytime at 603-666-6644, and I'll help you, free!

Going & stopping

You can control how your computer goes and stops.

Instant open

Suppose you've saved a QBASIC program called JOE. To use JOE, you could turn on the computer, then say —

```
C:\>qbasic
```

then choose Open from the file menu, then type "joe" (and press ENTER).

Here's a faster way! Turn on the computer, then say:

```
C:\>qbasic joe
```

That makes the computer use QBASIC and instantly open JOE.

Qbasic /run Try saying this:

```
C:\>qbasic /run joe
```

That makes the computer use QBASIC, instantly open JOE, and automatically run JOE. Moreover, if JOE's bottom line says "SYSTEM", like this —

```
CLS
PRINT "I love you"
SYSTEM
```

the computer will automatically exit from QBASIC when JOE finishes running.

Batch files If you wish to combine the power of QBASIC with the power of MS-DOS, here's the trick:

Learn MS-DOS fundamentals (on page 114-130). Then read about "Batch files" (on pages 130-131), and practice the examples.

In a batch file, you can make one of the lines say:
```
qbasic /run joe
```
Then whenever you run that batch file, the computer will automatically run JOE.

Read about AUTOEXEC.BAT (on pages 135-137). **If your AUTOEXEC.BAT file includes a line saying "qbasic /run joe", the computer will automatically run JOE every time you turn on the computer.**

SLEEP

If you say SLEEP, the computer will take a nap:

```
CLS
PRINT "I'm going to take a nap."
SLEEP
PRINT "Thanks for waking me up."
```

The second line makes the computer announce:

```
I'm going to take a nap.
```

The next line says SLEEP, which makes the computer take a nap. The computer will continue sleeping until you wake it up by pressing a key on the keyboard. (Press any key, such as ENTER.) Then the computer, woken up, will finish running the rest of the program, whose bottom line makes it say:

```
Thanks for waking me up.
```

Valentine's Day This program lets the computer gripe about how humans treated it on Valentine's Day:

```
CLS
PRINT "Valentine's Day, you didn't bring me flowers!"
PRINT "I won't speak until you gimme roses!"
PRINT "Bring them, then touch one of my keys."
SLEEP
PRINT "It's great to wake up and smell the roses!"
```

Lines 2-4 make the computer say:

```
Valentine's Day, you didn't bring me flowers!
I won't speak until you gimme roses!
Bring them, then touch one of my keys.
```

The next line (SLEEP) makes the upset computer go to sleep and refuse to talk to humans, until a human presses a key. When a human finally presses a key, the computer wakes up and says:

```
It's great to wake up and smell the roses!
```

Timed pause Instead of letting the computer sleep a long time, you can set an alarm clock so the computer will be forced to wake up soon. For example, if you say SLEEP 6 (instead of just SLEEP), the computer will sleep for just 6 seconds.

That's how to make the computer pause for 6 seconds. Give that 6-second pause before you reveal the punch line of a joke:

```
CLS
PRINT "Human, your intelligence is amazing!  You must be an M.D.";
SLEEP 6
PRINT "--Mentally Deficient!"
```

That program makes the computer print the joke's setup ("Human, your intelligence is amazing! You must be an M.D."), then pause for 6 seconds, then reveal the joke's punch line, so the screen finally shows:

```
Human, your intelligence is amazing!  You must be an M.D.--Mentally Deficient!
```

SLEEP 6 makes the computer sleep until it gets woken up by either the alarm clock (after 6 seconds) or the human (by pressing a key). If you want the computer to pause for 10 seconds instead of 6, say SLEEP 10 instead of SLEEP 6. The number after the word SLEEP can be 6 or 10 or any other positive whole number, but not a decimal.

This program makes the computer brag, then confess:

```
CLS
PRINT "We computers are smart for three reasons."
PRINT "The first is our VERY GOOD MEMORY."
PRINT "The other two reasons   ";
SLEEP 10
PRINT "I forgot."
```

The computer begins by bragging:

```
We computers are smart for three reasons.
The first is our VERY GOOD MEMORY.
The other two reasons
```

But then the computer pauses for 10 seconds and finally admits:

```
I forgot.
```

This program makes the computer change its feelings, in surprising ways:

```
CLS
PRINT "I'm up";
SLEEP 3
PRINT "set!  I want to pee";
SLEEP 4
PRINT "k at you";
SLEEP 5
PRINT "r ma";
SLEEP 6
PRINT "nual";
SLEEP 7
PRINT "dexterity.  Touch me!"
```

The computer will print —

```
I'm up
```

then pause 3 seconds and change it to —

```
I'm upset!  I want to pee
```

then pause 4 seconds and change it to —

```
I'm upset!  I want to peek at you
```

then pause 5 seconds and change it to —

```
I'm upset!  I want to peek at your ma
```

then pause 6 seconds and change it to —

```
I'm upset!  I want to peek at your manual
```

then pause 7 seconds and change it to —

```
I'm upset!  I want to peek at your manual dexterity.  Touch me!
```

Experiment: invent your *own* jokes, and make the computer pause before printing the punch lines.

Speed-reading test This program tests how fast you can read:

```
CLS
PRINT "If you can read this, you read quickly."
SLEEP 1
CLS
```

When you run that program, the computer makes the screen display this message:

```
If you can read this, you read quickly.
```

Then the computer pauses for 1 second (because of the SLEEP 1), then erases the screen (CLS). So the message appears on the screen for just 1 second before being erased!

If you manage to read that entire message in just 1 second, you're indeed a fast reader!

But don't stop at that first success! For the ultimate challenge, try running this program:

```
CLS
PRINT "Mumbling morons make my mom miss murder mysteries Monday morning."
SLEEP 2
CLS
```

That makes the computer display this tongue-twister —

```
Mumbling morons make my mom miss murder mysteries Monday morning.
```

then pause for 2 seconds, then erase the screen. During the 2 seconds while that tongue-twister appears on the screen, can you recite the entire twister out loud? Try it! If you don't recite it properly, you'll sound like a mumbling moron yourself!

DO...LOOP

This program makes the computer print the word "love" once:

```
CLS
PRINT "love"
```

This fancier program makes the computer print the word "love" *three* times:

```
CLS
PRINT "love"
PRINT "love"
PRINT "love"
```

When you run that program, the computer will print:

```
love
love
love
```

Let's make the computer print the word "love" *many* times. To do that, we must make the computer do this line many times:

```
PRINT "love"
```

To make the computer do the line many times, say "DO" above the line and say "LOOP" below it, so the program looks like this:

```
CLS
DO
  PRINT "love"
LOOP
```

As you can see, put the line being repeated (PRINT "love") between the words DO and LOOP and indent it. (To indent, press the SPACE bar twice. To remove an indentation, put yourself just after the indentation and then press the BACKSPACE key.) When you run that program, the computer will do PRINT "love" many times and print:

```
love
love
love
love
love
love
love
love
love
etc.
```

The computer will print "love" on every line of your screen.

But even when the screen is full of "love", the computer won't stop: the computer will try to print even more loves onto your screen! The computer will lose control of itself and try to devote its entire life to making love! The computer's mind will spin round and round, always circling back to the thought of making love again!

Since the computer's thinking keeps circling back to the same thought, the computer is said to be in a **loop**. In that program, the **DO** means "do what's underneath and indented"; the **LOOP** means "loop back and do it again". The lines that say DO and LOOP — and the lines between them — form a loop, which is called a **DO loop**.

To stop the computer's lovemaking madness, you must give the computer a "jolt" that will put it out of its misery and get it out of the loop. To jolt the computer out of the program, **abort** the program.

Here's how to abort the program: while holding down the Ctrl key, tap the PAUSE/BREAK key, which is the last key in the top row. (If your keyboard is modern, that key says PAUSE and BREAK on it. If your keyboard is old-fashioned, that key says SCROLL LOCK and BREAK on it.) That makes the computer stop running your program; it will **break out of your program**; it will **abort your program** and show you the blue screen so you can edit the program.

In that program, since the computer tries to go round and round the loop forever, the loop is called **infinite**. The only way to stop an infinite loop is to abort it.

Semicolon For more lovely fun, put a semicolon after "love", so the program looks like this:

```
CLS
DO
  PRINT "love";
LOOP
```

The semicolon makes the computer print "love" *next to* "love", so the screen looks like this:

```
lovelovelovelovelovelovelovelovelovelovelovelovelovelovelovelovelovelovelovelovelovelovelovelovelovelovelovelovelovelovelovelovelovelovelovelovelovelovelovelovelovelovelovelovelovelovelovelovelovelovelovelovelovelovelovelovelovelovelovelovelovelove
etc.
```

If you put a space after love, like this —

```
CLS
DO
  PRINT "love ";
LOOP
```

the computer will put a space after each love:

```
love love love love love love love love love love love love love love love love
love love love love love love love love love love love love love love love love
love love love love love love love love love love love love love love love love
etc.
```

Bigger DO loop Run this program:

```
CLS
DO
  PRINT "dog";
  PRINT "cat";
LOOP
```

Lines 3 & 4 (which say PRINT "dog" and PRINT "cat") make the computer print "dog" and then print "cat" next to it. Since those lines are between the words DO and LOOP, the computer does them repeatedly — PRINT "dog", then PRINT "cat", then PRINT "dog" again, then PRINT "cat" again — so the screen looks like this:

```
dogcatdogcatdogcatdogcatdogcatdogcatdogcatdogcatdogcatdogcatdogcatdogcatdogcat
dogcatdogcatdogcatdogcatdogcatdogcatdogcatdogcatdogcatdogcatdogcatdogcatdogcat
dogcatdogcatdogcatdogcatdogcatdogcatdogcatdogcatdogcatdogcatdogcatdogcatdogcat
etc.
```

The computer will keep printing "dog" and "cat" until you abort the program by doing this: while holding down the Ctrl key, tap the PAUSE/BREAK key.

Blinking Let's make the screen say "Stop pollution!" and make that message blink.

To do that, flash "Stop pollution!" onto the screen for 2 seconds, then turn that message off for 1 second (so the screen is blank), then flash that message on again. Here's the program:

```
WIDTH 40
DO
  PRINT "Stop pollution!"
  SLEEP 2
  CLS
  SLEEP 1
LOOP
```

The top line (WIDTH 40) makes sure all characters appear dramatically huge.

Lines 3 & 4 (which say PRINT "Stop pollution!" and SLEEP 2) flash the message "Stop pollution!" onto the screen and keep it on the screen for 2 seconds. The next pair of lines (CLS and SLEEP 1) make the screen become blank for 1 second. Since those lines are all between the words DO and LOOP, the computer does them repeatedly — flash message then blank, flash message then blank, flash message then blank — so your screen becomes a continually flashing sign.

The screen will keep flashing until you abort the program by doing this: while holding down the Ctrl key, tap the PAUSE/BREAK key.

Instead of saying "Stop pollution!", edit that program so it flashes your favorite phrase instead, such as "Save the whales!" or "Marry me!" or "Keepa youse hands offa my computer!" or "Jesus saves — America spends!" or "In God we trust — all others pay cash" or "Please wait — Dr. Doom will be with you shortly" or "Let's rock!" or whatever else turns you on. Make the computer say whatever you feel emotional about. Like a dog, the computer imitates its master's personality. If your computer acts "cold and heartless", it's because *you* are!

In the program, you typed just a few lines; but since the bottom line said LOOP, the computer does an infinite loop. By saying LOOP, you can make the computer do an infinite amount of work. Moral: **the computer can turn a finite amount of human energy into an infinite amount of good**. Putting it another way: **the computer can multiply your abilities by infinity**.

Computerized copier Suppose you want to send this poem to all your friends:

```
I'm having trouble
with my nose.
The only thing it does is:
Blows!
```

Type this program:

```
CLS
DO
  LPRINT "I'm having trouble"
  LPRINT "With my nose."
  LPRINT "The only thing it does is:"
  LPRINT "Blows!"
  LPRINT CHR$(12);
LOOP
```

Since it says LPRINT instead of PRINT, it prints each copy on paper instead of on the screen. Since the LPRINT lines are in a DO loop, the computer prints the poem again and again, many times, until you abort the program — or the printer runs out of paper.

Each time the computer prints a copy of the poem, the "LPRINT CHR$(12);" makes the computer eject a sheet of paper, so each copy of the poem is on a separate page.

Before running that program, put into the printer just as many sheets of paper as you want copies. If you put in too many sheets of paper, you'll get more copies than you want, and you'll waste paper.

Line numbers

You can number the lines in your program. For example, instead of typing —

```
CLS
DO
  PRINT "love"
LOOP
```

you can type:

```
1 CLS
2 DO
3   PRINT "love"
4 LOOP
```

Then when you're discussing your program with another programmer, you can talk about "line 3" instead of having to talk about "the line in the middle of the DO loop".

Selective numbering You can number just the lines you're planning to discuss.

For example, if you're planning to discuss just lines 2 and 4, you can number just those lines:

```
CLS
2 DO
    PRINT "love"
4 LOOP
```

Or if you prefer, number them like this:

```
CLS
1 DO
    PRINT "love"
2 LOOP
```

Decimal numbers Here's a simple program:

```
1 CLS
2 PRINT "Life's a blast!"
```

Suppose you want to edit it and insert an extra numbered line between 1 and 2. QBASIC lets you give the extra line a decimal number, such as 1.5:

```
1 CLS
1.5 PRINT "I hope..."
2 PRINT "Life's a blast!"
```

Number by tens Instead of making line numbers be 1, 2, 3, etc., make the line numbers be 10, 20, 30, etc., like this:

```
10 CLS
20 PRINT "Life's a blast!"
```

Then you can insert an extra line without using decimals:

```
10 CLS
15 PRINT "I hope..."
20 PRINT "Life's a blast!"
```

GOTO

This program makes the computer print the words "dog" and "cat" repeatedly:

```
CLS
DO
  PRINT "dog";
  PRINT "cat";
LOOP
```

It makes the computer print:

```
dogcatdogcatdogcatdogcatdogcatdogcatdogcatdogcatdogcatdogcatdogcatdogcat
dogcatdogcatdogcatdogcatdogcatdogcatdogcatdogcatdogcatdogcatdogcatdogcat
dogcatdogcatdogcatdogcatdogcatdogcatdogcatdogcatdogcatdogcatdogcatdogcat
etc.
```

This program does the same thing:

```
CLS
10 PRINT "dog";
PRINT "cat";
GOTO 10
```

The second line (which is numbered 10) makes the computer print "dog". The next line makes the computer print "cat". The bottom line makes the computer GO back TO line 10, so the computer will print "dog" again, then "cat again", then GO back TO line 10 again, then print "dog" again, then "cat" again, etc. The computer will print "dog" and "cat" repeatedly, until you abort the program by pressing SHIFT with PAUSE/BREAK.

This program does the same thing:

```
CLS
joe: PRINT "dog";
PRINT "cat";
GOTO joe
```

The second line (named "joe") makes the computer print "dog". The next line makes the computer print "cat". The bottom line makes the computer GO back TO the line named "joe". In that program, "joe" is called the second line's **label**.

One word In QBASIC, "GOTO" is one word. You're supposed to type "GOTO", not "GO TO". When you press the ENTER key at the end of the line, the computer will automatically turn any "GO TO" into "GOTO".

Skip ahead Did you ever dream about having a picnic in the woods? This program expresses that dream:

```
CLS
PRINT "Let's munch"
PRINT "sandwiches under"
PRINT "the trees!"
```

It makes the computer print:

```
Let's munch
sandwiches under
the trees!
```

Let's turn that dream into a nightmare where we all become giant termites. To do that, insert the shaded items:

```
CLS
PRINT "Let's munch"
GOTO 10
PRINT "sandwiches under"
10 PRINT "the trees!"
```

The computer begins by printing "Let's munch". Then the computer does GOTO 10, which makes the computer GO skip down TO line 10, which prints "the trees!" So the program makes the computer print just this:

```
Let's munch
the trees!
```

Is GOTO too powerful? The word GOTO gives you great power: if you say GO back TO line 10, the computer will create a loop (as if you'd said DO...LOOP); if you say GO skip down TO line 10, the computer will skip over several lines of your program.

Since the word GOTO is so powerful, programmers fear it! Programmers know that the slightest error in using that powerful word will make the programs act very bizarre! Programmers feel more comfortable using milder words instead (such as DO...LOOP), which are safer and rarely get botched up. Since the word GOTO is scary, many computer teachers prohibit students from using it, and many companies fire programmers who say GOTO instead of DO...LOOP.

But saying GOTO is fine when you've learned how to control the power! Though I'll usually say DO...LOOP instead of GOTO, I'll say GOTO in certain situations where saying DO...LOOP would be awkward.

Life as an infinite loop

A program that makes the computer do the same thing again and again forever is an infinite loop.

Some humans act just like computers. Those humans do the same thing again and again.

> Every morning they GOTO work, and every evening they GOTO home. GOTO work, GOTO home, GOTO work, GOTO home,... Their lives are sheer drudgery. They're caught in an infinite loop.

Go to your bathroom, get your bottle of shampoo, and look at the instructions on the back. A typical bottle has three instructions:

```
Lather.
Rinse.
Repeat.
```

Those instructions say to lather, then rinse, then repeat — which means to lather again, then rinse again, then repeat again — which means to lather again, then rinse again, then repeat again.... If you follow those instructions, you'll never finish washing your hair! The instructions are an infinite loop! The instructions are a program: they program you to use lots of shampoo! That's how infinite loops help sell shampoo.

END

To make the computer skip the bottom part of your program, say END:

```
CLS
PRINT "She smells"
END
PRINT "of perfume"
```

When you run that program (by pressing SHIFT with F5), the computer will print "She smells" and then end, without printing "of perfume".

Suppose you write a program that prints a long message, and you want to run the program several times (so several of your friends get the message). If one of your friends would be offended by the end of your message, send that friend an *abridged* message! Here's how: put END above the part of the message that you want the computer to omit — or skip past that part by saying GOTO.

Multi-statement line

In your program, **a line can contain several statements separated by colons**, like this:

```
CLS: PRINT "I dream": PRINT "of you"
```

When you run that program, the computer will CLear the Screen, then PRINT "I dream", then PRINT "of you". Altogether, the computer will print:

```
I dream
of you
```

If you want to number the line, put the number at the left margin, like this:

```
10 CLS: PRINT "I dream": PRINT "of you"
```

USING VARIABLES

What's a variable?

A letter can stand for a number. For example, x can stand for the number 47, as in this program:

```
CLS
x = 47
PRINT x + 2
```

The second line says x stands for the number 47. In other words, x is a name for the number 47.

The bottom line says to print x + 2. Since x is 47, the x + 2 is 49; so the computer will print 49. That's the only number the computer will print; it will not print 47.

Jargon

A letter that stands for a number is called a **numeric variable**. In that program, x is a numeric variable; it stands for the number 47. The **value** of x is 47. In that program, the statement "x = 47" is called an **assignment statement**, because it **assigns** 47 to x.

A variable is a box

When you run that program, here's what happens inside the computer.

The computer's random-access memory (RAM) consists of electronic boxes. When the computer encounters the line "x = 47", the computer puts 47 into box x, like this:

box x `[        47        ]`

Then when the computer encounters the line "PRINT x + 2", the computer prints what's in box x, plus 2; so the computer prints 49.

Faster typing

Instead of typing —

```
x = 47
```

you can type just this:

```
x=47
```

At the end of that line, when you press the ENTER key, the computer will automatically put spaces around the equal sign.

You've learned that the computer:

```
automatically capitalizes computer words (such as CLS)
automatically puts spaces around symbols (such as + and =)
lets you type a question mark instead of the word PRINT
```

So you can type just this:

```
cls
x=47
?x+2
```

When you press ENTER at the end of each line, the computer will automatically convert your typing to this:

```
CLS
x = 47
PRINT x + 2
```

More examples

Here's another example:

```
CLS
y = 38
PRINT y - 2
```

The second line says y is a numeric variable that stands for the number 38.

The bottom line says to print y - 2. Since y is 38, the y - 2 is 36; so the computer will print 36.

Example:

```
CLS
b = 8
PRINT b * 3
```

The second line says b is 8. The bottom line says to print b * 3, which is 8 * 3, which is 24; so the computer will print 24.

One variable can define another:

```
CLS
n = 6
d = n + 1
PRINT n * d
```

The second line says n is 6. The next line says d is n + 1, which is 6 + 1, which is 7; so d is 7. The bottom line says to print n * d, which is 6 * 7, which is 42; so the computer will print 42.

Changing a value

A value can change:

```
CLS
k = 4
k = 9
PRINT k * 2
```

The second line says k's value is 4. The next line changes k's value to 9, so the bottom line prints 18.

When you run that program, here's what happens inside the computer's RAM. The second line (k = 4) makes the computer put 4 into box k:

box k `[        4        ]`

The next line (k = 9) puts 9 into box k. The 9 replaces the 4:

box k `[        9        ]`

That's why the bottom line (PRINT k * 2) prints 18.

Hassles

When writing an equation (such as x = 47), here's what you must put before the equai sign: the name of just one box (such as x). So before the equal sign, put one variable:

Allowed	Not allowed	Not allowed
d = n + 1	d - n = 1	1 = d - n
↑	↑	↑
(one variable)	(two variables)	(not a variable)

The variable on the left side of the equation is the only one that changes. For example, the statement d = n + 1 changes the value of d but not n. The statement b = c changes the value of b but not c:

```
CLS
b = 1
c = 7
b = c
PRINT b + c
```

The fourth line changes b, to make it equal c; so b becomes 7. Since both b and c are now 7, the bottom line prints 14.

"b = c" versus "c = b" Saying "b = c" has a different effect from "c = b". That's because "b = c" changes the value of b (but not c); saying "c = b" changes the value of c (but not b).

Compare these programs:

```
CLS            CLS
b = 1          b = 1
c = 7          c = 7
b = c          c = b
PRINT b + c    PRINT b + c
```

In the left program (which you saw before), the fourth line changes b to 7, so both b and c are 7. The bottom line prints 14.

In the right program, the fourth line changes c to 1, so both b and c are 1. The bottom line prints 2.

While you run those programs, here's what happens inside the computer's RAM. For both programs, the second and third lines do this:

| box b | 1 |
| box c | 7 |

In the left program, the fourth line makes the number in box b become 7 (so both boxes contain 7, and the bottom line prints 14). In the right program, the fourth line makes the number in box c become 1 (so both boxes contain 1, and the bottom line prints 2).

When to use variables

Here's a practical example of when to use variables.

Suppose you're selling something that costs $1297.43, and you want to do these calculations:

multiply	$1297.43 by 2
multiply	$1297.43 by .05
add	$1297.43 to $483.19
divide	$1297.43 by 37
subtract	$1297.43 from $8598.61
multiply	$1297.43 by 28.7

To do those six calculations, you could run this program:

```
CLS
PRINT 1297.43 * 2; 1297.43 * .05; 1297.43 + 483.19; 1297.43 / 37
PRINT 8598.61-1297.43; 1297.43 * 28.7
```

But that program's silly, since it contains the number 1297.43 six times. This program's briefer, because it uses a variable:

```
CLS
c = 1297.43
PRINT c * 2; c * .05; c + 483.19; c / 37; 8598.61 - c; c * 28.7
```

So **whenever you need to use a number several times, turn the number into a variable**, which will make your program briefer.

String variables

A string is any collection of characters, such as "I love you". Each string must be in quotation marks.

A letter can stand for a string — if you put a dollar sign after the letter, like this:

```
CLS
g$ = "down"
PRINT g$
```

The second line says g$ stands for the string "down". The bottom line prints:

```
down
```

In that program, g$ is a variable. Since it stands for a string, it's called a **string variable**.

Every string variable must end with a dollar sign. The dollar sign is supposed to remind you of a fancy S, which stands for String. The second line is pronounced, "g String is down".

If you're paranoid, you'll love this program:

```
CLS
t$ = "They're laughing at you!"
PRINT t$
PRINT t$
PRINT t$
```

The second line says t$ stands for the string "They're laughing at you!". The later lines make the computer print:

```
They're laughing at you!
They're laughing at you!
They're laughing at you!
```

Spaces between strings

Examine this program:

```
CLS
s$ = "sin"
k$ = "king"
PRINT s$; k$
```

The bottom line says to print "sin" and then "king", so the computer will print:

```
sinking
```

Let's make the computer leave a space between "sin" and "king", so the computer prints:

```
sin king
```

To make the computer leave that space, choose one of these methods....

Method 1. Instead of saying —

```
s$ = "sin"
```

make s$ include a space:

```
s$ = "sin "
```

Method 2. Instead of saying —

```
k$ = "king"
```

make k$ include a space:

```
k$ = " king"
```

Method 3. Instead of saying —

```
PRINT s$; k$
```

say to print s$, then a space, then k$:

```
PRINT s$; " "; k$
```

Since the computer will automatically insert the semicolons, you can type just this —

```
PRINT s$ " " k$
```

or even type just this:

```
PRINT s$" "k$
```

or even type just this:

```
?s$" "k$
```

When you press the ENTER key at the end of that line, the computer will automatically convert it to:

```
PRINT s$; " "; k$
```

Nursery rhymes

The computer can recite nursery rhymes:

```
CLS
p$ = "Peas porridge "
PRINT p$; "hot!"
PRINT p$; "cold!"
PRINT p$; "in the pot,"
PRINT "Nine days old!"
```

The second line says p$ stands for "Peas porridge ". The later lines make the computer print:

```
Peas porridge hot!
Peas porridge cold!
Peas porridge in the pot,
Nine days old!
```

This program prints a fancier rhyme:

```
CLS
h$ = "Hickory, dickory, dock! "
m$ = "THE MOUSE (squeak! squeak!) "
c$ = "THE CLOCK (tick! tock!) "
```

```
PRINT h$
PRINT m$; "ran up "; c$
PRINT c$; "struck one"
PRINT m$; "ran down"
PRINT h$
```

Lines 2-4 define h$, m$, and c$. The later lines make the computer print:

```
Hickory, dickory, dock!
THE MOUSE (squeak! squeak!) ran up THE ClOCK (tick! tock!)
THE CLOCK (tick! tock!) struck one
THE MOUSE (squeak! squeak!) ran down
Hickory, dickory, dock!
```

Undefined variables

If you don't define a numeric variable, the computer assumes it's zero:

```
CLS
PRINT r
```

Since r hasn't been defined, the bottom line prints zero. The computer doesn't look ahead:

```
CLS
PRINT j
j = 5
```

When the computer encounters the second line (PRINT j), it doesn't look ahead to find out what j is. As of the second line, j is still undefined, so the computer prints zero.

If you don't define a string variable, the computer assumes it's blank:

```
CLS
PRINT f$
```

Since f$ hasn't been defined, the "PRINT f$" makes the computer print a line that says nothing; the line the computer prints is blank.

Long variable names

A numeric variable's name can be a letter (such as x) or a longer combination of characters, such as:

```
profit.in.1996.before.November.promotion
```

For example, you can type:

```
CLS
profit.in.1996.before.November.promotion = 3497.18
profit.in.1996 = profit.in.1996.before.November.promotion + 6214.27
PRINT profit.in.1996
```

The computer will print:

```
9711.45
```

The variable's name can be quite long: up to 40 characters!

The first character in the name must be a letter. The remaining characters can be letters, digits, or periods.

The name must not be a word that has a special meaning to the computer. For example, the name cannot be "print".

If the variable stands for a string, the name can have up to 40 characters, followed by a dollar sign, making a total of 41 characters, like this:

```
my.job.in.1996.before.November.promotion$
```

Beginners are usually too lazy to type long variable names, so beginners use variable names that are short. But when you become a pro and write a long, fancy program containing hundreds of lines and hundreds of variables, you should use long variable names to help you remember each variable's purpose.

In this book, I'll use short variable names in short programs (so you can type those programs quickly), and long variable names in long programs (so you can keep track of which variable is which).

Programmers employed at Microsoft capitalize the first letter of each word and omit the periods. So instead of writing:

```
my.job.in.1996.before.November.promotion$
```

those programmers write:

```
MyJobIn1996BeforeNovemberPromotion$
```

That's harder to read; but since Microsoft is headed by Bill Gates, who's the richest person in America, he can do whatever he pleases!

INPUT

Humans ask questions; so to turn the computer into a human, you must make it ask questions too. **To make the computer ask a question, use the word INPUT.**

This program makes the computer ask for your name:

```
CLS
INPUT "What is your name"; n$
PRINT "I adore anyone whose name is "; n$
```

When the computer sees that INPUT line, the computer asks "What is your name?" and then waits for you to answer the question. Your answer will be called n$. For example, if you answer Maria, then n$ is Maria. The bottom line makes the computer print:

```
I adore anyone whose name is Maria
```

When you run that program, here's the whole conversation that occurs between the computer and you; I've underlined the part typed by you....

```
The computer asks for your name: What is your name? Maria
The computer praises your name:  I adore anyone whose name is Maria
```

Try that example. Be careful! When you type the INPUT line, make sure you type the two quotation marks and the semicolon. You don't have to type a question mark: when the computer runs your program, it will automatically put a question mark at the end of the question.

Just for fun, run that program again and pretend you're somebody else....

```
The computer asks for your name: What is your name? Bud
The computer praises your name:  I adore anyone whose name is Bud
```

When the computer asks for your name, if you say something weird, the computer will give you a weird reply....

```
The computer asks for your name: What is your name? none of your business!!!
The computer replies:            I adore anyone whose name is none of your business!!!
```

College admissions

This program prints a letter, admitting you to the college of your choice:

```
CLS
INPUT "What college would you like to enter"; c$
PRINT "Congratulations!"
PRINT "You have just been admitted to "; c$
PRINT "because it fits your personality."
PRINT "I hope you go to "; c$; "."
PRINT "        Respectfully yours,"
PRINT "        The Dean of Admissions"
```

When the computer sees the INPUT line, the computer asks "What college would you like to enter?" and waits for you to answer. Your answer will be called c$. If you'd like to be admitted to Harvard, you'll be pleased....

```
The computer asks you:   What college would you like to enter? Harvard
The computer admits you: Congratulations!
                         You have just been admitted to Harvard
                         because it fits your personality.
                         I hope you go to Harvard.
                                 Respectfully yours,
                                 The Dean of Admissions
```

You can choose any college you wish:

```
The computer asks you:   What college would you like to enter? Hell
The computer admits you: Congratulations!
                         You have just been admitted to Hell
                         because it fits your personality.
                         I hope you go to Hell.
                                 Respectfully yours,
                                 The Dean of Admissions
```

That program consists of three parts:

1. The computer begins by asking you a question ("What college would you like to enter?"). The computer's question is called the **prompt**, because it prompts you to answer.

2. Your answer (the college's name) is called **your input**, because it's information that you're *putting into* the computer.

3. The computer's reply (the admission letter) is called the **computer's output**, because it's the final answer that the computer puts out.

INPUT versus PRINT

The word INPUT is the opposite of the word PRINT.

The word PRINT makes the computer print information out. The word INPUT makes the computer take information in.

What the computer prints out is called the **output**. What the computer takes in is called **your input**.

Input and Output are collectively called **I/O**, so the INPUT and PRINT statements are called **I/O statements**.

Once upon a time

Let's make the computer write a story, by filling in the blanks:

Once upon a time, there was a youngster named _____
                                              your name

who had a friend named _____.
                         friend's name

_____ wanted to _____ _____,
  your name   verb (such as "pat")   friend's name

but _____ didn't want to _____ _____!
     friend's name   verb (such as "pat")   your name

Will _____ _____ _____?
       your name   verb (such as "pat")   friend's name

Will _____ _____ _____?
      friend's name   verb (such as "pat")   your name

To find out, come back and see the next exciting episode

of _____ and _____!
    your name   friend's name

To write the story, the computer must ask for your name, your friend's name, and a verb. To make the computer ask, your program must say INPUT:

```
CLS
INPUT "What is your name"; y$
INPUT "What's your friend's name"; f$
INPUT "In 1 word, say something you can do to your friend"; v$
```

Then make the computer print the story:

```
PRINT "Here's my story...."
PRINT "Once upon a time, there was a youngster named "; y$
PRINT "who had a friend named "; f$; "."
PRINT y$; " wanted to "; v$; " "; f$; ","
PRINT "but "; f$; " didn't want to "; v$; " "; y$; "!"
PRINT "Will "; y$; " "; v$; " "; f$; "?"
PRINT "Will "; f$; " "; v$; " "; y$; "?"
PRINT "To find out, come back and see the next exciting episode"
PRINT "of "; y$; " and "; f$; "!"
```

Here's a sample run:

```
What's your name? Dracula
What's your friend's name? Madonna
In 1 word, say something you can do to your friend? bite
Here's my story....
Once upon a time, there was a youngster named Dracula
who had a friend named Madonna.
Dracula wanted to bite Madonna,
but Madonna didn't want to bite Dracula!
Will Dracula bite Madonna?
Will Madonna bite Dracula?
To find out, come back and see the next exciting episode
of Dracula and Madonna!
```

Here's another run:

```
What's your name? Superman
What's your friend's name? King Kong
In 1 word, say something you can do to your friend? tickle
Here's my story....
Once upon a time, there was a youngster named Superman
Who had a friend named King Kong.
Superman wanted to tickle King Kong,
but King Kong didn't want to tickle Superman!
Will Superman tickle King Kong?
Will King Kong tickle Superman?
To find out, come back and see the next exciting episode
of Superman and King Kong!
```

Try it: put in your own name, the name of your friend, and something you'd like to do to your friend.

Contest

The following program prints a certificate saying you won a contest. Since the program contains many variables, it uses long variable names to help you remember which variable is which:

```
CLS
INPUT "What's your name"; you$
INPUT "What's your friend's name"; friend$
INPUT "What's the name of another friend"; friend2$
INPUT "Name a color"; color$
INPUT "Name a place"; place$
INPUT "Name a food"; food$
INPUT "Name an object"; object$
INPUT "Name a part of the body"; part$
INPUT "Name a style of cooking (such as baked or fried)"; style$
PRINT
PRINT "Congratulations, "; you$; "!"
PRINT "You've won the beauty contest, because of your gorgeous "; part$; "."
PRINT "Your prize is a "; color$; " "; object$
PRINT "plus a trip to "; place$; " with your friend "; friend$
PRINT "plus--and this is the best part of all--"
PRINT "dinner for the two of you at "; friend2$; "'s new restaurant,"
PRINT "where "; friend2$; " will give you ";
PRINT "all the "; style$; " "; food$; " you can eat."
PRINT "Congratulations, "; you$; ", today's your lucky day!"
PRINT "Now everyone wants to kiss your award-winning "; part$; "."
```

Here's a sample run:

```
What's your name? Long John Silver
What's your friend's name? the parrot
What's the name of another friend? Jim
Name a color? gold
Name a place? Treasure Island
Name a food? rum-soaked coconuts
Name an object? chest of jewels
Name a part of the body? missing leg
Name a style of cooking (such as baked or fried)? barbecued

Congratulations, Long John Silver!
You've won the beauty contest, because of your gorgeous missing leg.
Your prize is a gold chest of jewels
plus a trip to Treasure Island with your friend the parrot
plus--and this is the best part of all--
dinner for the two of you at Jim's new restaurant,
where Jim will give you all the barbecued rum-soaked coconuts you can eat.
Congratulations, Long John Silver, today's your lucky day!
Now everyone wants to kiss your award-winning missing leg.
```

This run describes the contest that brought Ronald Reagan to the White House:

```
What's your name? Ronnie Reagan
What's your friend's name? Nancy
What's the name of another friend? Alice
Name a color? red-white-and-blue
Name a place? the White House
Name a food? jelly beans
Name an object? cowboy hat
Name a part of the body? cheeks
Name a style of cooking (such as baked or fried)? steamed

Congratulations, Ronnie Reagan!
You've won the beauty contest, because of your gorgeous cheeks.
Your prize is a red-white-and-blue cowboy hat
plus a trip to the White House with your friend Nancy
plus--and this is the best part of all--
dinner for the two of you at Alice's new restaurant,
where Alice will give you all the steamed jelly beans you can eat.
Congratulations, Ronnie Reagan, today's your lucky day!
Now everyone wants to kiss your award-winning cheeks.
```

Bills

If you're a nasty bill collector, you'll love this program:

```
CLS
INPUT "What is the customer's first name"; first.name$
INPUT "What is the customer's last name"; last.name$
INPUT "What is the customer's street address"; street.address$
INPUT "What city"; city$
INPUT "What state"; state$
INPUT "What ZIP code"; zip.code$
PRINT
PRINT first.name$; " "; last.name$
PRINT street.address$
PRINT city$; " "; state$; " "; zip.code$
PRINT
PRINT "Dear "; first.name$; ","
PRINT "    You still haven't paid the bill."
PRINT "If you don't pay it soon, "; first.name$; ","
PRINT "I'll come visit you in "; city$
PRINT "and personally shoot you."
PRINT "              Yours truly,"
PRINT "              Sure-as-shootin'"
PRINT "              Your crazy creditor"
```

Can you figure out what that program does?

Numeric input

This program makes the computer predict your future:

```
CLS
PRINT "I predict what'll happen to you in the year 2000!"
INPUT "In what year were you born"; y
PRINT "In the year 2000, you'll turn"; 2000 - y; "years old."
```

Here's a sample run:

```
I predict what'll happen to you in the year 2000!
In what year were you born? 1962
In the year 2000, you'll turn 38 years old.
```

Suppose you're selling tickets to a play. Each ticket costs $2.79. (You decided $2.79 would be a nifty price, because the cast has 279 people.) This program finds the price of multiple tickets:

```
CLS
INPUT "How many tickets"; t
PRINT "The total price is $"; t * 2.79
```

This program tells you how much the "energy crisis" costs you, when you drive your car:

```
CLS
INPUT "How many miles do you want to drive"; m
INPUT "How many pennies does a gallon of gas cost"; p
INPUT "How many miles-per-gallon does your car get"; r
PRINT "The gas for your trip will cost you $"; m * p / (r * 100)
```

Here's a sample run:

```
How many miles do you want to drive? 400
How many pennies does a gallon of gas cost? 95.9
How many miles-per-gallon does your car get? 31
The gas for your trip will cost you $ 12.37419
```

Conversion

This program converts feet to inches:

```
CLS
INPUT "How many feet"; f
PRINT f; "feet ="; f * 12; "inches"
```

Here's a sample run:

```
How many feet? 3
3 feet = 36 inches
```

Trying to convert to the metric system? This program converts inches to centimeters:

```
CLS
INPUT "How many inches"; i
PRINT i; "inches ="; i * 2.54; "centimeters"
```

Nice day today, isn't it? This program converts the temperature from Celsius to Fahrenheit:

```
CLS
INPUT "How many degrees Celsius"; c
PRINT c; "degrees Celsius ="; c * 1.8 + 32; "degrees Fahrenheit"
```

Here's a sample run:

```
How many degrees Celsius? 20
 20 degrees Celsius = 68 degrees Fahrenheit
```

See, you can write the *Guide* yourself! Just hunt through any old math or science book, find any old formula (such as $f = c * 1.8 + 32$), and turn it into a program.

IF

Let's write a program so that if the human is less than 18 years old, the computer will say:

```
You are still a minor.
```

Here's the program:

```
CLS
INPUT "How old are you"; age
IF age < 18 THEN PRINT "You are still a minor"
```

Line 2 makes the computer ask "How old are you" and wait for the human to type an age. Since **the symbol for "less than" is "<"**, the bottom line says: if the age is less than 18, then print "You are still a minor".

Go ahead! Run that program! The computer begins the conversation by asking:

```
How old are you?
```

Try saying you're 12 years old, by typing a 12, so the screen looks like this:

```
How old are you? 12
```

When you finish typing the 12 and press the ENTER key at the end of it, the computer will reply:

```
You are still a minor
```

Try running that program again, but this time try saying you're 50 years old instead of 12, so the screen looks like this:

```
How old are you? 50
```

When you finish typing the 50 and press the ENTER key at the end of it, the computer will *not* say "You are still a minor". Instead, the computer will say nothing — since we didn't teach the computer how to respond to adults yet!

In that program, the most important line says:

```
IF age < 18 THEN PRINT "You are still a minor"
```

That line contains the words IF and THEN. **Whenever you say IF, you must also say THEN**. Do *not* put a comma before THEN. What comes between IF and THEN is called the **condition**; in that example, the condition is "age < 18". If the condition is true (if age is really less than 18), the computer does the **action**, which comes after the word THEN and is:

```
PRINT "You are still a minor"
```

ELSE

Let's teach the computer how to respond to adults. Here's how to program the computer so that if the age is less than 18, the computer will say "You are still a minor", but if the age is *not* less than 18 the computer will say "You are an adult" instead:

```
CLS
INPUT "How old are you"; age
IF age < 18 THEN PRINT "You are still a minor" ELSE PRINT "You are an adult"
```

In programs, **the word "ELSE" means "otherwise"**. That program's bottom line means: if the age is less than 18, then print "You are still a minor"; otherwise (if the age is *not* less than 18), print "You are an adult". So the computer will print "You are still a minor" or else print "You are an adult", depending on whether the age is less than 18.

Try running that program! If you say you're 50 years old, so the screen looks like this —

```
How old are you? 50
```

the computer will reply by saying:

```
You are an adult
```

Multi-line IF

If the age is less than 18, here's how to make the computer print "You are still a minor" and also print "Ah, the joys of youth":

```
IF age < 18 THEN PRINT "You are still a minor": PRINT "Ah, the joys of youth"
```

Here's a more sophisticated way to say the same thing:

```
IF age < 18 THEN
  PRINT "You are still a minor"
  PRINT "Ah, the joys of youth"
END IF
```

That sophisticated way (in which you type 4 short lines instead of a single long line) is called a **multi-line IF** (or a **block IF**).

In a multi-line IF:

```
The top line must say IF and THEN (with nothing after THEN).
The middle lines should be indented; they're called the block and typically say PRINT.
The bottom line must say END IF.
```

In the middle of a multi-line IF, you can say ELSE:

```
IF age < 18 THEN
  PRINT "You are still a minor"
  PRINT "Ah, the joys of youth"
ELSE
  PRINT "You are an adult"
  PRINT "We can have adult fun"
END IF
```

That means: if the age is less than 18, then print "You are still a minor" and "Ah, the joys of youth"; otherwise (if age *not* under 18) print "You are an adult" and "We can have adult fun".

ELSEIF

Let's say this:

```
If age is under 18, print "You're a minor".
If age is not under 18 but is under 100, print "You're a typical adult".
If age is not under 100 but is under 125, print "You're a centenarian".
If age is not under 125, print "You're a liar".
```

Here's how:

```
IF age < 18 THEN
  PRINT "You're a minor"
ELSEIF age < 100 THEN
  PRINT "You're a typical adult"
ELSEIF age < 125 THEN
  PRINT "You're a centenarian"
ELSE
  PRINT "You're a liar"
END IF
```

One word In QBASIC, "ELSEIF" is one word. Type "ELSEIF", not "ELSE IF". If you accidentally type "ELSE IF", the computer will gripe.

SELECT

Let's turn your computer into a therapist!

To make the computer ask the patient, "How are you?", begin the program like this:

```
CLS
INPUT "How are you"; a$
```

Make the computer continue the conversation by responding as follows:

> If the patient says "fine", print "That's good!"
> If the patient says "lousy" instead, print "Too bad!"
> If the patient says anything else instead, print "I feel the same way!"

To accomplish all that, you can use a multi-line IF:

```
IF a$ = "fine" THEN
  PRINT "That's good!"
ELSEIF a$ = "lousy" THEN
  PRINT "Too bad!"
ELSE
  PRINT "I feel the same way!"
END IF
```

Instead of typing that multi-line IF, you can type this **SELECT statement** instead, which is briefer and simpler:

```
SELECT CASE a$
  CASE "fine"
    PRINT "That's good!"
  CASE "lousy"
    PRINT "Too bad!"
  CASE ELSE
    PRINT "I feel the same way!"
END SELECT
```

Like a multi-line IF, a SELECT statement consumes several lines. The top line of that SELECT statement tells the computer to analyze a$ and SELECT one of the CASEs from the list underneath. That list is indented and says:

> In the case where a$ is "fine", print "That's good!"
> In the case where a$ is "lousy", print "Too bad!"
> In the case where a$ is anything else, print "I feel the same way!"

The bottom line of every SELECT statement must say END SELECT.

Complete program

Here's a complete program:

```
CLS
INPUT "How are you"; a$
SELECT CASE a$
  CASE "fine"
    PRINT "That's good!"
  CASE "lousy"
    PRINT "Too bad!"
  CASE ELSE
    PRINT "I feel the same way!"
END SELECT
PRINT "I hope you enjoyed your therapy.  Now you owe $50."
```

Line 2 makes the computer ask the patient, "How are you?" The next several lines are the SELECT statement, which makes the computer analyze the patient's answer and print "That's good!" or "Too bad!" or else "I feel the same way!"

Regardless of what the patient and computer said, that program's bottom line always makes the computer end the conversation by printing:

```
I hope you enjoyed your therapy.  Now you owe $50.
```

In that program, try changing the strings to make the computer print smarter remarks, become a better therapist, and charge even more money.

Error trap

This program makes the computer discuss human sexuality:

```
CLS
10 INPUT "Are you male or female"; a$
SELECT CASE a$
  CASE "male"
    PRINT "So is Frankenstein!"
  CASE "female"
    PRINT "So is Mary Poppins!"
  CASE ELSE
    PRINT "Please say male or female!"
    GOTO 10
END SELECT
```

The second line (which is numbered 10) makes the computer ask, "Are you male or female?"

The remaining lines are a SELECT statement that analyzes the human's response. If the human claims to be "male", the computer prints "So is Frankenstein!" If the human says "female" instead, the computer prints "So is Mary Poppins!" If the human says anything else (such as "not sure" or "super-male" or "macho" or "none of your business"), the computer does the CASE ELSE, which makes the computer say "Please say male or female!" and then go back to line 10, which makes the computer ask again, "Are you male or female?"

In that program, the CASE ELSE is called an **error handler** (or **error-handling routine** or **error trap**), since its only purpose is to handle human error (a human who says neither "male" nor "female"). Notice that the error handler begins by printing a gripe message ("Please say male or female!") and then lets the human try again (GOTO 10).

In QBASIC, the GOTO statements are used rarely: they're used mainly in error handlers, to let the human try again.

Do you like Mary Poppins? Let's extend that program's conversation. If the human says "female", let's make the computer say "So is Mary Poppins!", then ask "Do you like her?", then continue the conversation as follows:

> If human says "yes", make the computer say "I like her too. She is my mother."
> If human says "no", make computer say "I hate her too. She owes me a dime."
> If human says neither "yes" nor "no", make the computer handle that error.

To accomplish all that, insert the shaded lines into the program:

```
CLS
10 INPUT "Are you male or female"; a$
SELECT CASE a$
  CASE "male"
    PRINT "So is Frankenstein!"
  CASE "female"
    PRINT "So is Mary Poppins!"
20  INPUT "Do you like her"; b$
    SELECT CASE b$
      CASE "yes"
        PRINT "I like her too.  She is my mother."
      CASE "no"
        PRINT "I hate her too.  She owes me a dime."
      CASE ELSE
        PRINT "Please say yes or no!"
        GO TO 20
    END SELECT
  CASE ELSE
    PRINT "Please say male or female!"
    GOTO 10
END SELECT
```

Weird programs

The computer's abilities are limited only by your own imagination — and your weirdness. Here are some weird programs from weird minds....

Friends Like a human, the computer wants to meet new friends. This program makes the computer show its true feelings:

```
CLS
10 INPUT "Are you my friend"; a$
SELECT CASE a$
  CASE "yes"
    PRINT "That's swell."
  CASE "no"
    PRINT "Go jump in a lake."
  CASE ELSE
    PRINT "Please say yes or no."
    GO TO 10
END SELECT
```

When you run that program, the computer asks "Are you my friend?" If you say "yes", the computer says "That's swell." If you say "no", the computer says "Go jump in a lake."

Watch TV The most inventive programmers are kids. This program was written by a girl in the sixth grade:

```
CLS
10 INPUT "Can I come over to your house to watch TV"; a$
SELECT CASE a$
  CASE "yes"
    PRINT "Thanks.  I'll be there at 5PM."
  CASE "no"
    PRINT "Humph!  Your feet smell, anyway."
  CASE ELSE
    PRINT "Please say yes or no."
    GO TO 10
END SELECT
```

When you run that program, the computer asks to watch your TV. If you say "yes", the computer promises to come to your house at 5. If you refuse, the computer insults your feet.

Honesty Another sixth-grade girl wrote this program, to test your honesty:

```
CLS
PRINT "FKGJDFGKJ*#K$JSLF*/#$()$&(IKJNHBGD52:?./KSDJK$E(EF$#/JIK(*"
PRINT "FASDFJKL:JFRFVFJUNJI*&()JNE$#SKI#(!SERF HHW NNWAZ MAME !!!"
PRINT "ZBB%%%%##)))))FESDFJK DSFE N.D.JJUJASD EHWLKD******"
10 INPUT "Do you understand what I said"; a$
SELECT CASE a$
  CASE "no"
    PRINT "Sorry to have bothered you."
  CASE "yes"
    PRINT "SSFJSLFKDJFL++++45673456779XSDWFEF/#$&**()---==!!ZZXX"
    PRINT "###EDFHTG NVFDF MKJK ==+--*$&% #RHFS SES DOPEKKK DSBS"
    INPUT "Okay, what did I say"; b$
    PRINT "You are a liar, a liar, a big fat liar!"
  CASE ELSE
    PRINT "Please say yes or no."
    GO TO 10
END SELECT
```

When you run that program, lines 2-4 print nonsense. Then the computer asks whether you understand that stuff. *If you're honest* and answer "no", the computer will apologize. But *if you pretend that you understand the nonsense* and answer "yes", the computer will print more nonsense, challenge you to translate it, wait for you to fake a translation, and then scold you for lying.

Fancy IF conditions

A Daddy wrote a program for his five-year-old son, John.

When John runs the program and types his name, the computer asks "What's 2 and 2?" If John answers 4, the computer says "No, 2 and 2 is 22". If he runs the program again and answers 22, the computer says "No, 2 and 2 is 4". No matter how many times he runs the program and how he answers the question, the computer says he's wrong. But when Daddy runs the program, the computer replies, "Yes, Daddy is always right".

Here's how Daddy programmed the computer:

```
CLS
INPUT "What's your name"; n$
INPUT "What's 2 and 2"; a
IF n$ = "Daddy" THEN PRINT "Yes, Daddy is always right": END
IF a = 4 THEN PRINT "No, 2 and 2 is 22" ELSE PRINT "No, 2 and 2 is 4"
```

Different relations

You can make the IF clause very fancy:

IF clause	Meaning
IF b$ = "male"	If b$ is "male"
IF b = 4	If b is 4
IF b < 4	If b is less than 4
IF b > 4	If b is greater than 4
IF b <= 4	If b is less than or equal to 4
IF b >= 4	If b is greater than or equal to 4
IF b <> 4	If b is not 4
IF b$ < "male"	If b$ is a word that comes before "male" in the dictionary
IF b$ > "male"	If b$ is a word that comes after "male" in the dictionary

In the IF statement, the symbols =, <, >, <=, >=, and <> are called **relations**.

When writing a relation, mathematicians and computerists habitually **put the equal sign last**:

Right	Wrong
<=	=<
>=	=>

When you press the ENTER key at the end of the line, the computer will automatically put your equal signs last: the computer will turn any "=<" into "<="; it will turn any "=>" into "<=".

To say "not equal to", say "less than or greater than", like this: <>.

OR

The computer understands the word OR. For example, here's how to say, "If x is either 7 or 8, print the word *wonderful*":

```
IF x = 7 OR x = 8 THEN PRINT "wonderful"
```

That example is composed of two conditions: the first condition is "x = 7"; the second condition is "x = 8". Those two conditions combine, to form "x = 7 OR x = 8", which is called a **compound condition**.

If you use the word OR, put it between two conditions.

```
Right: IF x = 7 OR x = 8 THEN PRINT "wonderful"    ("x = 7" and "x = 8" are conditions.)
Wrong: IF x = 7 OR 8 THEN PRINT "wonderful"        ("8" is not a condition.)
```

AND

The computer understands the word AND. Here's how to say, "If p is more than 5 and less than 10, print *tuna fish*":

```
IF p > 5 AND p < 10 THEN PRINT "tuna fish"
```

Here's how to say, "If s is at least 60 and less than 65, print *you almost failed*":

```
IF s >= 60 AND s < 65 THEN PRINT "you almost failed"
```

Here's how to say, "If n is a number from 1 to 10, print *that's good*":

```
IF n >= 1 AND n <= 10 THEN PRINT "that's good"
```

Can a computer be President?

To become President of the United States, you need four basic skills.

First, you must be a good talker, so you can give effective speeches saying "Vote for me!", express your views, and make folks do what you want.

But even if you're a good talker, you're useless unless you're also a good listener. You must be able to listen to people's needs and ask, "What can I do to make you happy and get you to vote for me?"

But even if you're a good talker and listener, you're still useless unless you can make decisions. Should you give more money to poor people? Should you bomb the enemy? Which actions should you take, and under what conditions?

But even if you're a good talker and listener and decision maker, you still need one more trait to become President: you must be able to take the daily grind of politics. You must, again and again, shake hands, make compromises, and raise funds. You must have the patience to put up with the repetitive monotony of those chores.

So altogether, to become President you need to be a good talker and listener and decision maker and also have the patience to put up with monotonous repetition.

Those are exactly the four qualities the computer has! The word PRINT turns the computer into a good speech-maker: by using the word PRINT, you can make the computer write whatever speech you wish. The word INPUT turns the computer into a good listener: by using the word INPUT, you can make the computer ask humans lots of questions, to find out who the humans are and what they want. The word IF turns the computer into a decision maker: the computer can analyze the IF condition, determine whether that condition is true, and act accordingly. Finally, the word GOTO enables the computer to perform loops, which the computer will repeat patiently.

So by using the words PRINT, INPUT, IF, and GOTO, you can make the computer imitate any intellectual human activity. Those four magic words — PRINT, INPUT, IF, and GOTO — are the only concepts you need, to write whatever program you wish!

Yes, you can make the computer imitate the President of the United States, do your company's payroll, compose a beautiful poem, play a perfect game of chess, contemplate the meaning of life, act as if it's falling in love, or do whatever other intellectual or emotional task you wish, by using those four magic words. The only question is: how? *The Secret Guide to Computers* teaches you how, by showing you many examples of programs that do those remarkable things.

What programmers believe Yes, we programmers believe that all of life can be explained and programmed. We believe all of life can be reduced to just those four concepts: PRINT, INPUT, IF, and GOTO. Programming is the ultimate act of scientific reductionism: programmers reduce all of life scientifically to just four concepts.

The words that the computer understands are called **keywords**. The four essential keywords are PRINT, INPUT, IF, and GOTO.

The computer also understands extra keywords, such as CLS, LPRINT, WIDTH, SYSTEM, SLEEP, DO (and LOOP), END, SELECT (and CASE), and words used in IF statements (such as THEN, ELSE, ELSEIF, OR, AND). Those extra keywords aren't necessary: if they hadn't been invented, you could still write programs without them. But they make programming easier.

A BASIC programmer is a person who translates an ordinary English sentence (such as "act like the President" or "do the payroll") into a series of BASIC statements, using keywords such as PRINT, INPUT, IF, GOTO, CLS, etc.

The mysteries of life Let's dig deeper into the mysteries of PRINT, INPUT, IF, GOTO, and the extra keywords. The deeper we dig, the more you'll wonder: are *you* just a computer, made of flesh instead of wires? Can everything that *you* do be explained in terms of PRINT, INPUT, IF, and GOTO?

By the time you finish *The Secret Guide to Computers*, you'll know!

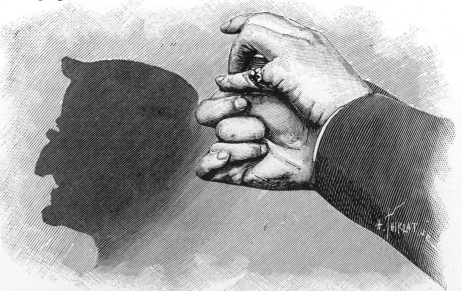

Exiting a DO loop

This program plays a guessing game, where the human tries to guess the computer's favorite color, which is pink:

```
CLS
10 INPUT "What's my favorite color"; guess$
IF guess$ = "pink" THEN
  PRINT "Congratulations!  You discovered my favorite color."
ELSE
  PRINT "No, that's not my favorite color.  Try again!"
  GOTO 10
END IF
```

The INPUT line asks the human to guess the computer's favorite color; the guess is called guess$.

If the guess is "pink", the computer prints:

```
Congratulations!  You discovered my favorite color.
```

But if the guess is *not* "pink", the computer will instead print "No, that's not my favorite color" and then GO back TO line 10, which asks the human again to try guessing the computer's favorite color.

END

Here's how to write that program without saying GOTO:

```
CLS
DO
  INPUT "What's my favorite color"; guess$
  IF guess$ = "pink" THEN
    PRINT "Congratulations!  You discovered my favorite color."
    END
  END IF
  PRINT "No, that's not my favorite color.  Try again!"
LOOP
```

That new version of the program contains a DO loop. That loop makes the computer do this repeatedly: ask "What's my favorite color?" and then PRINT "No, that's not my favorite color."

The only way to stop the loop is to guess "pink", which makes the computer print "Congratulations!" and END.

EXIT DO

Here's another way to write that program without saying GOTO:

```
CLS
DO
  INPUT "What's my favorite color"; guess$
  IF guess$ = "pink" THEN EXIT DO
  PRINT "No, that's not my favorite color.  Try again!"
LOOP
PRINT "Congratulations!  You discovered my favorite color."
```

That program's DO loop makes the computer do this repeatedly: ask "What's my favorite color?" and then PRINT "No, that's not my favorite color."

The only way to stop the loop is to guess "pink", which makes the computer EXIT from the DO loop; then the computer proceeds to the line underneath the DO loop. That line prints:

```
Congratulations!  You discovered my favorite color.
```

LOOP UNTIL

Here's another way to program the guessing game:

```
CLS
DO
  PRINT "You haven't guessed my favorite color yet!"
  INPUT "What's my favorite color"; guess$
LOOP UNTIL guess$ = "pink"
PRINT "Congratulations!  You discovered my favorite color."
```

That program's DO loop makes the computer do this repeatedly: say "You haven't guessed my favorite color yet!" and then ask "What's my favorite color?"

The LOOP line makes the computer repeat the indented lines again and again, UNTIL the guess is "pink". When the guess is "pink", the computer proceeds to the line underneath the LOOP and prints "Congratulations!".

Achieving the goal The LOOP UNTIL's condition (guess$ = "pink") is called the **loop's goal**. The computer does the loop repeatedly, until the loop's goal is achieved. Here's how....

The computer does the indented lines, then checks whether the goal is achieved yet. If the goal is *not* achieved yet, the computer does the indented lines again, then checks again whether the goal is achieved. The computer does the loop again and again, until the goal is achieved. Then the computer, proud at achieving the goal, does the program's **finale**, which consists of any lines under the LOOP UNTIL line.

UNTIL versus EXIT Saying —

```
LOOP UNTIL guess$ = "pink"
```

is just a briefer way of saying this pair of lines:

```
  IF guess$ = "pink" THEN EXIT DO
LOOP
```

FOR...NEXT

Let's make the computer print every number from 1 to 20, like this:

```
1
2
3
4
5
6
7
etc.
20
```

Here's the program:

```
CLS
FOR x = 1 TO 20
  PRINT x
NEXT
```

The second line (FOR x = 1 TO 20) says that x will be every number from 1 to 20; so x will be 1, then 2, then 3, etc. The line underneath, which is indented, says what to do about each x; it says to PRINT each x.

Whenever you write a program that contains the word FOR, you must say NEXT; so the bottom line says NEXT.

The indented line, which is between the FOR line and the NEXT line, is the line that the computer will do repeatedly; so the computer will repeatedly PRINT x. The first time the computer prints x, the x will be 1, so the computer will print:

```
1
```

The next time the computer prints x, the x will be 2, so the computer will print:

```
2
```

The computer will print every number from 1 up to 20.

When men meet women

Let's make the computer print these lyrics:

```
I saw 2 men
meet 2 women.
Tra-la-la!

I saw 3 men
meet 3 women.
Tra-la-la!

I saw 4 men
meet 4 women.
Tra-la-la!

I saw 5 men
meet 5 women.
Tra-la-la!

They all had a party!
Ha-ha-ha!
```

To do that, type these lines —

The first line of each verse:	PRINT "I saw"; x; "men"
The second line of each verse:	PRINT "meet"; x; "women."
The third line of each verse:	PRINT "Tra-la-la!"
Blank line under each verse:	PRINT

and make x be every number from 2 up to 5:

```
FOR x = 2 TO 5
  PRINT "I saw"; x; "men"
  PRINT "meet"; x; "women."
  PRINT "Tra-la-la!"
  PRINT
NEXT
```

At the top of the program, say CLS. At the end of the song, print the closing couplet:

```
CLS
FOR x = 2 TO 5
  PRINT "I saw"; x; "men"
  PRINT "meet"; x; "women."
  PRINT "Tra-la-la!"
  PRINT
NEXT
PRINT "They all had a party!"
PRINT "Ha-ha-ha!"
```

That program makes the computer print the entire song.

Here's an analysis:

The computer will do the indented lines repeatedly, for x=2, x=3, x=4, and x=5.	CLS
	FOR X = 2 TO 5
	  PRINT "I saw"; x; "men"
	  PRINT "meet"; x; "women."
	  PRINT "Tra-la-la!"
	  PRINT
	NEXT

Then the computer will print this couplet once.	PRINT "They all had a party!" PRINT "Ha-ha-ha!"

Since the computer does the indented lines repeatedly, those lines form a loop. Here's the general rule: **the statements between FOR and NEXT form a loop**. The computer goes round and round the loop, for x=2, x=3, x=4, and x=5. Altogether, it goes around the loop 4 times, which is a finite number. Therefore, the loop is **finite**.

If you don't like the letter x, choose a different letter. For example, you can choose the letter i:

```
CLS
FOR i = 2 TO 5
  PRINT "I saw"; i; "men"
  PRINT "meet"; i; "women."
  PRINT "Tra-la-la!"
  PRINT
NEXT
PRINT "They all had a party!"
PRINT "Ha-ha-ha!"
```

When using the word FOR, most programmers prefer the letter i; most programmers say "FOR i" instead of "FOR x". Saying "FOR i" is an "old tradition". Following that tradition, the rest of this book says "FOR i" (instead of "FOR x"), except in situations where some other letter feels more natural.

Print the squares

To find the **square** of a number, multiply the number by itself. The square of 3 is "3 times 3", which is 9. The square of 4 is "4 times 4", which is 16.

Let's make the computer print the square of 3, 4, 5, etc., up to 20, like this:

```
The square of 3 is 9
The square of 4 is 16
The square of 5 is 25
The square of 6 is 36
The square of 7 is 49
etc.
The square of 20 is 400
```

To do that, type this line —

```
PRINT "The square of"; i; "is"; i*i
```

and make i be every number from 3 up to 20, like this:

```
CLS
FOR i = 3 TO 20
  PRINT "The square of"; i; "is"; i*i
NEXT
```

Count how many copies

This program, which you saw before, prints "love" on every line of your screen:

```
CLS
DO
  PRINT "love"
LOOP
```

That program prints "love" again and again, until you abort the program by pressing Ctrl with PAUSE/BREAK.

But what if you want to print "love" just 20 times? This program prints "love" just 20 times:

```
CLS
FOR i = 1 TO 20
  PRINT "love"
NEXT
```

As you can see, FOR...NEXT resembles DO...LOOP but is smarter: while doing FOR...NEXT, the computer counts!

Poem This program, which you saw before, prints many copies of a poem:

```
CLS
DO
  LPRINT "I'm having trouble"
  LPRINT "With my nose."
  LPRINT "The only thing it does is:"
  LPRINT "Blows!"
  LPRINT CHR$(12);
LOOP
```

It prints the copies onto paper. It prints each copy on a separate sheet of printer. It keeps printing until you abort the program — or the printer runs out of paper.

Here's a smarter program, which counts the number of copies printed and stops when exactly 4 copies have been printed:

```
CLS
FOR i = 1 TO 4
  LPRINT "I'm having trouble"
  LPRINT "With my nose."
  LPRINT "The only thing it does is:"
  LPRINT "Blows!"
  LPRINT CHR$(12);
NEXT
```

It's the same as the DO...LOOP program, except that it counts (by saying "FOR i = 1 TO 4" instead of "DO") and has a different bottom line (NEXT instead of LOOP).

Here's an even smarter program, which asks how many copies you want:

```
CLS
INPUT "How many copies of the poem do you want"; n
FOR i = 1 TO n
  LPRINT "I'm having trouble"
  LPRINT "With my nose."
  LPRINT "The only thing it does is:"
  LPRINT "Blows!"
  LPRINT CHR$(12);
NEXT
```

When you run that program, the computer asks:

```
How many copies of the poem do you want?
```

If you answer 5, then the n becomes 5 and so the computer prints 5 copies of the poem. If you answer 7 instead, the computer prints 7 copies. Print as many copies as you like!

That program illustrates this rule:

```
To make the FOR...NEXT loop flexible,
say "FOR i = 1 TO n" and let the human INPUT the n.
```

Count to midnight

This program makes the computer count to midnight:

```
CLS
FOR i = 1 TO 11
  PRINT i
NEXT
PRINT "midnight"
```

The computer will print:

```
1
2
3
4
5
6
7
8
9
10
11
midnight
```

Semicolon Let's put a semicolon at the end of the indented line:

```
CLS
FOR i = 1 TO 11
  PRINT i;
NEXT
PRINT "midnight"
```

The semicolon makes the computer print each item on the same line, like this:

```
 1  2  3  4  5  6  7  8  9  10  11 midnight
```

If you want the computer to press the ENTER key before "midnight", insert a PRINT line:

```
CLS
FOR i = 1 TO 11
  PRINT i;
NEXT
PRINT
PRINT "midnight"
```

That extra PRINT line makes the computer press the ENTER key just before "midnight", so the computer will print "midnight" on a separate line, like this:

```
 1  2  3  4  5  6  7  8  9  10  11
midnight
```

Nested loops Let's make the computer count to midnight 3 times, like this:

```
 1  2  3  4  5  6  7  8  9  10  11
midnight
 1  2  3  4  5  6  7  8  9  10  11
midnight
 1  2  3  4  5  6  7  8  9  10  11
midnight
```

To do that, put the entire program between the words FOR and NEXT:

```
CLS
FOR j = 1 TO 3
  FOR i = 1 TO 11
    PRINT i;
  NEXT
  PRINT
  PRINT "midnight"
NEXT
```

That version contains a loop inside a loop: the loop that says "FOR i" is inside the loop that says "FOR j". The j loop is called the **outer loop**; the i loop is called the **inner loop**. The inner loop's variable must differ from the outer loop's. Since we called the inner loop's variable "i", the outer loop's variable must *not* be called "i"; so I picked the letter j instead.

Programmers often think of the outer loop as a bird's nest, and the inner loop as an egg *inside the nest*. So programmers say the inner loop is **nested in** the outer loop; the inner loop is a **nested loop**.

Abnormal exit

Earlier, we programmed a game where the human tries to guess the computer's favorite color, pink. Here's a fancier version of the game, in which the human gets just 5 guesses:

```
CLS
PRINT "I'll give you 5 guesses...."
FOR i = 1 TO 5
   INPUT "What's my favorite color"; guess$
   IF guess$ = "pink" THEN GO TO 10
   PRINT "No, that's not my favorite color."
NEXT
PRINT "Sorry, your 5 guesses are up!  You lose."
END
10 PRINT "Congratulations!  You discovered my favorite color."
PRINT "It took you"; i; "guesses."
```

Line 2 warns the human that just 5 guesses are allowed. The FOR line makes the computer count from 1 to 5; to begin, i is 1. The INPUT line asks the human to guess the computer's favorite color; the guess is called guess$.

If the guess is "pink", the computer jumps down to the line numbered 10, prints "Congratulations!", and tells how many guesses the human took. But if the guess is *not* "pink", the computer will print "No, that's not my favorite color" and go on to the NEXT guess.

If the human guesses 5 times without success, the computer proceeds to the line that prints "Sorry… You lose."

For example, if the human's third guess is "pink", the computer prints:

```
Congratulations!  You discovered my favorite color.
It took you 3 guesses.
```

If the human's very first guess is "pink", the computer prints:

```
Congratulations!  You discovered my favorite color.
It took you 1 guesses.
```

Saying "1 guesses" is bad grammar but understandable.

That program contains a FOR…NEXT loop. The FOR line says the loop will normally be done five times. The line below the loop (which says to PRINT "Sorry") is the loop's **normal exit**. But if the human happens to input "pink", the computer jumps out of the loop early, to line 10, which is the loop's **abnormal exit**.

STEP

The FOR statement can be varied:

Statement	Meaning
FOR i = 5 TO 17 STEP .1	The i will go from 5 to 17, counting by tenths. So i will be 5, then 5.1, then 5.2, etc., up to 17.
FOR i = 5 TO 17 STEP 3	The i will be every third number from 5 to 17. So i will be 5, then 8, then 11, then 14, then 17.
FOR i = 17 TO 5 STEP -3	The i will be every third number from 17 down to 5. So i will be 17, then 14, then 11, then 8, then 5.

To count down, you *must* use the word STEP. To count from 17 down to 5, give this instruction:

```
FOR i = 17 TO 5 STEP -1
```

This program prints a rocket countdown:

```
CLS
FOR i = 10 TO 1 STEP -1
   PRINT i
NEXT
PRINT "Blast off!"
```

The computer will print:

```
10
9
8
7
6
5
4
3
2
1
Blast off!
```

This statement is tricky:

```
FOR i = 5 TO 16 STEP 3
```

It says to start i at 5, and keep adding 3 until it gets past 16. So i will be 5, then 8, then 11, then 14. The i won't be 17, since 17 is past 16. The first value of i is 5; the last value is 14.

In the statement FOR i = 5 TO 16 STEP 3, the **first value** or **initial value** of i is 5, the **limit value** is 16, and the **step size** or **increment** is 3. The i is called the **counter** or **index** or **loop-control variable**. Although the limit value is 16, the **last value** or **terminal value** is 14.

Programmers usually say "FOR i", instead of "FOR x", because the letter i reminds them of the word **index**.

DATA...READ

Let's make the computer print this message:

```
I love meat
I love potatoes
I love lettuce
I love tomatoes
I love honey
I love cheese
I love onions
I love peas
```

That message concerns this list of food: meat, potatoes, lettuce, tomatoes, honey, cheese, onions, peas. That list doesn't change: the computer continues to love those foods throughout the entire program.

A list that doesn't change is called DATA. So in the message about food, the DATA is meat, potatoes, lettuce, tomatoes, honey, cheese, onions, peas.

Whenever a problem involves DATA, put the DATA at the top of the program, just under the CLS, like this:

```
CLS
DATA meat,potatoes,lettuce,tomatoes,honey,cheese,onions,peas
```

You must tell the computer to READ the DATA:

```
CLS
DATA meat,potatoes,lettuce,tomatoes,honey,cheese,onions,peas
READ a$
```

That READ line makes the computer read the first datum ("meat") and call it a$. So a$ is "meat".

Since a$ is "meat", this shaded line makes the computer print "I love meat":

```
CLS
DATA meat,potatoes,lettuce,tomatoes,honey,cheese,onions,peas
READ a$
PRINT "I love "; a$
```

Hooray! We made the computer handle the first datum correctly: we made the computer print "I love meat".

To make the computer handle the rest of the data (potatoes, lettuce, etc.), tell the computer to READ and PRINT the rest of the data, by putting the READ and PRINT lines in a loop. Since we want the computer to READ and PRINT all 8 data items (meat, potatoes, lettuce, tomatoes, honey, cheese, onions, peas), put the READ and PRINT lines in a loop that gets done 8 times, by making the loop say "FOR i = 1 TO 8":

```
CLS
DATA meat,potatoes,lettuce,tomatoes,honey,cheese,onions,peas
FOR i = 1 TO 8
  READ a$
  PRINT "I love "; a$
NEXT
```

Since that loop's main purpose is to READ the data, it's called a **READ loop**.

When writing that program, make sure the FOR line's last number (8) is the number of data items. If the FOR line accidentally says 7 instead of 8, the computer won't read or print the 8th data item. If the FOR line accidentally says 9 instead of 8, the computer will try to read a 9th data item, realize that no 9th data item exists, and gripe by saying:

```
Out of DATA
```

Then press ENTER.

Let's make the computer end by printing "Those are the foods I love", like this:

```
I love meat
I love potatoes
I love lettuce
I love tomatoes
I love honey
I love cheese
I love onions
I love peas
Those are the foods I love
```

To make the computer print that ending, put a PRINT line at the end of the program:

```
CLS
DATA meat,potatoes,lettuce,tomatoes,honey,cheese,onions,peas
FOR i = 1 TO 8
  READ a$
  PRINT "I love "; a$
NEXT
PRINT "Those are the foods I love"
```

End mark

When writing that program, we had to count the DATA items and put that number (8) at the end of the FOR line.

Here's a better way to write the program, so you don't have to count the DATA items:

```
CLS
DATA meat,potatoes,lettuce,tomatoes,honey,cheese,onions,peas
DATA end
DO
  READ a$: IF a$ = "end" THEN EXIT DO
  PRINT "I love "; a$
LOOP
PRINT "Those are the foods I love"
```

The third line (DATA end) is called the **end mark**, since it marks the end of the DATA. The READ line means:

```
READ a$ from the DATA;
but if a$ is the "end" of the DATA, then EXIT from the DO loop.
```

When the computer exits from the DO loop, the computer prints "Those are the foods I love". So altogether, the entire program makes the computer print:

```
I love meat
I love potatoes
I love lettuce
I love tomatoes
I love honey
I love cheese
I love onions
I love peas
Those are the foods I love
```

The routine that says:

```
          IF a$ = "end" THEN EXIT DO
```

is called the **end routine**, because the computer does that routine when it reaches the end of the DATA.

Henry the Eighth

Let's make the computer print this nursery rhyme:

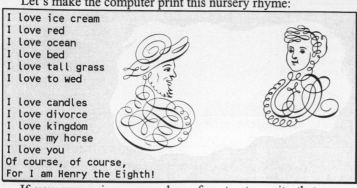

```
I love ice cream
I love red
I love ocean
I love bed
I love tall grass
I love to wed

I love candles
I love divorce
I love kingdom
I love my horse
I love you
Of course, of course,
For I am Henry the Eighth!
```

If you own a jump rope, have fun: try to recite that poem while skipping rope!

This program makes the computer recite the poem:

```
CLS
DATA ice cream,red,ocean,bed,tall grass,to wed
DATA candles,divorce,my kingdom,my horse,you
DATA end
DO
   READ a$: IF a$ = "end" THEN EXIT DO
   PRINT "I love "; a$
   IF a$ = "to wed" THEN PRINT
LOOP
PRINT "Of course, of course,"
PRINT "For I am Henry the Eighth!"
```

Since the data's too long to fit on a single line, I've put part of the data in line 2 and the rest in line 3. Each line of data must begin with the word DATA. In each line, put commas between the items. Do *not* put a comma at the end of the line.

The program resembles the previous one. The new line (IF a$ = "to wed" THEN PRINT) makes the computer leave a blank line underneath "to wed", to mark the bottom of the first verse.

Pairs of data

Let's throw a party! To make the party yummy, let's ask each guest to bring a kind of food that resembles the guest's name. For example, let's have Sal bring salad, Russ bring Russian dressing, Sue bring soup, Tom bring turkey, Winnie bring wine, Kay bring cake, and Al bring Alka-Seltzer.

Let's send all those people invitations, in this form:

```
Dear _____,
        person's name

     Let's party in the clubhouse at midnight!

Please bring ____.
               food
```

Here's the program:

```
CLS
DATA Sal,salad,Russ,Russian dressing,Sue,soup,Tom,turkey
DATA Winnie,wine,Kay,cake,Al,Alka-Seltzer
DATA end,end
DO
   READ person$, food$: IF person$ = "end" THEN EXIT DO
   LPRINT "Dear "; person$; ","
   LPRINT "     Let's party in the clubhouse at midnight!"
   LPRINT "Please bring "; food$; "."
   LPRINT CHR$(12);
LOOP
PRINT "I've finished writing the letters."
```

The DATA comes in pairs. For example, the first pair consists of "Sal" and "salad"; the next pair consists of "Russ" and "Russian dressing". Since the DATA comes in pairs, you must make the end mark also be a pair (DATA end,end).

Since the DATA comes in pairs, the READ line says to READ a pair of data (person$ and food$). The first time that the computer encounters the READ line, person$ is "Sal"; food$ is "salad". Then the LPRINT lines print this message onto paper:

```
Dear Sal,
     Let's party in the clubhouse at midnight!
Please bring salad.
```

The LPRINT CHR$(12) makes the computer eject the paper from the printer.

Then the computer comes to the word LOOP, which sends the computer back to the word DO, which sends the computer to the READ line again, which reads the next pair of DATA, so person$ becomes "Russ" and food$ becomes "Russian dressing". The LPRINT lines print onto paper:

```
Dear Russ,
     Let's party in the clubhouse at midnight!
Please bring Russian dressing.
```

The computer prints similar letters to all the people.

After all people have been handled, the READ statement comes to the end mark (DATA end,end), so that person$ and food$ both become "end". Since person$ is "end", the IF statement makes the computer EXIT DO, so the computer prints this message onto the screen:

```
I've finished writing the letters.
```

In that program, you need *two* ends to mark the data's ending, because the READ statment says to read two strings (person$ and food$).

Debts Suppose these people owe you things:

Person	What the person owes
Bob	$537.29
Mike	a dime
Sue	2 golf balls
Harry	a steak dinner at Mario's
Mommy	a kiss

Let's remind those people of their debt, by writing them letters, in this form:

```
Dear _____,
        person's name

     I just want to remind you...

that you still owe me ____.
                       debt
```

To start writing the program, begin by saying CLS and then feed the computer the DATA. The final program is the same as the previous program, except for the part I've shaded:

```
CLS
DATA Bob,$537.29,Mike,a dime,Sue,2 golf balls
DATA Harry,a steak dinner at Mario's,Mommy,a kiss
DATA end,end
DO
   READ person$, debt$: IF person$ = "end" THEN EXIT DO
   LPRINT "Dear "; person$; ","
   LPRINT "     I just want to remind you..."
   LPRINT "that you still owe me "; debt$; "."
   LPRINT CHR$(12);
LOOP
PRINT "I've finished writing the letters."
```

Diets

Suppose you're running a diet clinic and get these results:

Person	Weight before	Weight after
Joe	273 pounds	219 pounds
Mary	412 pounds	371 pounds
Bill	241 pounds	173 pounds
Sam	309 pounds	198 pounds

This program makes the computer print a nice report:

```
CLS
DATA Joe,273,219,Mary,412,371,Bill,241,173,Sam,309,198
DATA end,0,0
DO
  READ person$, weight.before, weight.after
  IF person$ = "end" THEN EXIT DO
  PRINT person$; " weighed"; weight.before;
  PRINT "pounds before attending the diet clinic"
  PRINT "but weighed just"; weight.after; "pounds afterwards."
  PRINT "That's a loss of"; weight.before - weight.after; "pounds."
  PRINT
LOOP
PRINT "Come to the diet clinic!"
```

Line 2 contains the DATA, which comes in triplets. The first triplet consists of Joe, 273, and 219. Each triplet includes a string (such as Joe) and two numbers (such as 273 and 219), so line 3's end mark also includes a string and two numbers: it's the word "end" and two zeros. (If you hate zeros, you can use other numbers instead; but most programmers prefer zeros.)

The READ line says to read a triplet: a string (person$) and two numbers (weight.before and weight.after). The first time the computer comes to the READ statement, the computer makes person$ be "Joe", weight.before be 273, and weight.after be 219. The PRINT lines print this:

```
Joe weighed 273 pounds before attending the diet clinic
but weighed just 219 pounds afterwards.
That's a loss of 54 pounds.

Mary weighed 412 pounds before attending the diet clinic
but weighed just 371 pounds afterwards.
That's a loss of 41 pounds.

Bill weighed 241 pounds before attending the diet clinic
but weighed just 173 pounds afterwards.
That's a loss of 68 pounds.

Sam weighed 309 pounds before attending the diet clinic
but weighed just 198 pounds afterwards.
That's a loss of 111 pounds.

Come to the diet clinic!
```

RESTORE

Examine this program:

```
CLS
DATA love,death,war
10 DATA chocolate,strawberry
READ a$
PRINT a$
RESTORE 10
READ a$
PRINT a$
```

The first READ makes the computer read the first datum (love), so the first PRINT makes the computer print:

```
love
```

The next READ would normally make the computer read the next datum (death); but the **RESTORE 10 tells the READ to skip ahead to DATA line 10**, so the READ line reads "chocolate" instead. The entire program prints:

```
love
chocolate
```

So saying "RESTORE 10" makes the next READ skip ahead to DATA line 10. If you write a new program, saying "RESTORE 20" makes the next READ skip ahead to DATA line 20. Saying just "RESTORE" makes the next READ skip back to the beginning of the *first* DATA line.

Continents This program prints the names of the continents:

```
CLS
DATA Europe,Asia,Africa,Australia,Antarctica,North America,South America
DATA end
DO
   READ a$: IF a$ = "end" THEN EXIT DO
   PRINT a$
LOOP
PRINT "Those are the continents."
```

That program makes the computer print this message:

```
Europe
Asia
Africa
Australia
Antarctica
North America
South America
Those are the continents.
```

Let's make the computer print that message *twice*, so the computer prints:

```
Europe
Asia
Africa
Australia
Antarctica
North America
South America
Those are the continents.

Europe
Asia
Africa
Australia
Antarctica
North America
South Ameruca
Those are the continents.
```

To do that, put the program in a loop saying "FOR i = 1 TO 2", like this:

```
CLS
DATA Europe,Asia,Africa,Australia,Antarctica,North America,South America
DATA end
FOR i = 1 TO 2
   DO
      READ a$: IF a$ = "end" THEN EXIT DO
      PRINT a$
   LOOP
   PRINT "Those are the continents."
   PRINT
   RESTORE
NEXT
```

After that program says to PRINT "Those are the continents", the program says to PRINT a blank line and then RESTORE. The word RESTORE makes the READ go back to the beginning of the DATA, so the computer can READ and PRINT the DATA a second time without saying "Out of DATA".

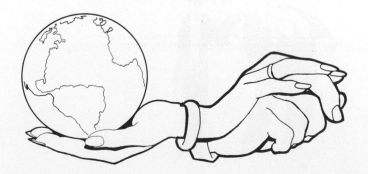

Search loop

Let's make the computer translate colors into French. For example, if the human says "red", we'll make the computer say the French equivalent, which is:

```
rouge
```

Let's make the computer begin by asking "Which color interests you?", then wait for the human to type a color (such as "red"), then reply:

```
In French, it's rouge
```

The program begins simply:

```
CLS
INPUT "Which color interests you"; request$
```

Next, we must make the computer translate the requested color into French. To do so, feed the computer this English-French dictionary:

English	French
white	blanc
yellow	jaune
orange	orange
red	rouge
green	vert
blue	bleu
brown	brun
black	noir

That dictionary becomes the data:

```
CLS
DATA white,blanc,yellow,jaune,orange,orange,red,rouge
DATA green,vert,blue,bleu,brown,brun,black,noir
INPUT "Which color interests you"; request$
```

The data comes in pairs; each pair consists of an English word (such as "white") followed by its French equivalent ("blanc"). To make the computer read a pair, say:

```
READ english$, french$
```

To let the computer look at *all* the pairs, put that READ statement in a DO loop. Here's the complete program:

```
CLS
DATA white,blanc,yellow,jaune,orange,orange,red,rouge
DATA green,vert,blue,bleu,brown,brun,black,noir
INPUT "Which color interests you"; request$
DO
  READ english$, french$
  IF english$ = request$ THEN EXIT DO
LOOP
PRINT "In French, it's "; french$
```

Since the READ line is in a DO loop, the computer does the READ line repeatedly. So the computer keeps READing pairs of DATA, until the computer find the pair of DATA that the human requested. For example, if the human requested "red", the computer keeps READing pairs of DATA until it finds a pair whose English word matches the requested word ("red"). When the computer finds that match, the english$ is equal to the request$, so the IF line makes the computer EXIT DO and PRINT:

```
In French, it's rouge
```

So altogether, when you run the program the chat can look like this:

```
Which color interests you? red
In French, it's rouge
```

Here's another sample run:

```
Which color interests you? brown
In French, it's brun
```

Here's another:

```
Which color interests you? pink
Out of DATA
```

The computer says "Out of DATA" because it can't find "pink" in the DATA.

Avoid "Out of DATA" Instead of saying "Out of DATA", let's make the computer say "I wasn't taught that color". To do that, put an end mark at the end of the DATA; and when the computer reaches the end mark, make the computer say "I wasn't taught that color":

```
CLS
DATA white,blanc,yellow,jaune,orange,orange,red,rouge
DATA green,vert,blue,bleu,brown,brun,black,noir
DATA end,end
INPUT "Which color interests you"; request$
DO
  READ english$, french$
  IF english$ = "end" THEN PRINT "I wasn't taught that color": END
  IF english$ = request$ THEN EXIT DO
LOOP
PRINT "In French, it's "; french$
```

In that program, the DO loop's purpose is to *search* through the DATA, to find DATA that matches the INPUT. Since the DO loop's purpose is to search, it's called a **search loop**.

The typical search loop has these characteristics:

```
It starts with DO and ends with LOOP.
It says to READ a pair of data.
It includes an error trap saying what to do IF you reach the "end" of the data because no match found.
It says that IF you find a match (english$ = request$) THEN EXIT the DO loop.
Below the DO loop, say what to PRINT when the match is found.
Above the DO loop, put the DATA and tell the human to INPUT a search request.
```

Auto rerun At the end of the program, let's make the computer automatically rerun the program and translate another color.

To do that, make the bottom of the program say GO back TO the INPUT line:

```
CLS
DATA white,blanc,yellow,jaune,orange,orange,red,rouge
DATA green,vert,blue,bleu,brown,brun,black,noir
DATA end,end
10 INPUT "Which color interests you"; request$
RESTORE
DO
  READ english$, french$
  IF english$ = "end" THEN PRINT "I wasn't taught that color": GOTO 10
  IF english$ = request$ THEN EXIT DO
LOOP
PRINT "In French, it's "; french$
GOTO 10
```

The word RESTORE, which is above the search loop, makes sure that the computer's search through the DATA always starts at the DATA's beginning.

Press Q to quit That program repeatedly asks "Which color interests you" until the human aborts the program (by pressing Ctrl with PAUSE/BREAK). But what if the human's a beginner who hasn't learned how to abort?

Let's permit the human to stop the program more easily by pressing just the Q key to quit:

```
CLS
DATA white,blanc,yellow,jaune,orange,orange,red,rouge
DATA green,vert,blue,bleu,brown,brun,black,noir
DATA end,end
10 INPUT "Which color interests you (press q to quit)"; request$
IF request$ = "q" THEN END
RESTORE
DO
  READ english$, french$
  IF english$ = "end" THEN PRINT "I wasn't taught that color": GOTO 10
  IF english$ = request$ THEN EXIT DO
LOOP
PRINT "In French, it's "; french$
GOTO 10
```

END, STOP, or SYSTEM That program's shaded line ends by saying END. Instead of saying END, try saying STOP or SYSTEM.

While the program is running, here's what the computer does when it encounters END, STOP, or SYSTEM:

STOP makes the program stop *immediately*. The screen becomes blue and shows the program's lines.

END makes the computer say "Press any key to continue" and wait for the human to press a key (such as F4 or ENTER). When the human finally presses a key, the screen becomes blue and shows the program's lines.

SYSTEM usually has the same effect as END. But if you saved the program onto the hard disk (using a name such as "french.bas") and then ran the program from DOS (by saying "C:\>qbasic /run french"), SYSTEM makes the program stop *immediately* and makes the screen show "C:\>".

Variables & constants

A **numeric constant** is a simple number, such as:

0	1	2	8	43.7	-524.6	.003

Another example of a numeric constant is 1.3E5, which means, "take 1.3, and move its decimal point 5 places to the right".

A numeric constant does not contain any arithmetic. For example, since 7+1 contains arithmetic (+), it's *not* a numeric constant. 8 is a numeric constant, even though 7+1 isn't.

A **string constant** is a simple string, in quotation marks:

"I love you"	"76 trombones"	"Go away!!!"	"xypw exr///746"

A **constant** is a numeric constant or a string constant:

0	8	-524.6	1.3E5	"I love you"	"xypw exr///746"

A **variable** is something that stands for something else. If it stands for a string, it's called a **string variable** and ends with a dollar sign, like this:

a$	b$	y$	z$	my.job.before.promotion$

If the variable stands for a number, it's called a **numeric variable** and lacks a dollar sign, like this:

a	b	y	z	profit.before.promotion

So all these are variables:

a$ b$ y$ z$ my.job.before.promotion$ a b y z profit.before.promotion

Expressions

A **numeric expression** is a numeric constant (such as 8) or a numeric variable (such as b) or a combination of them, such as 8+z, or 8*a, or z*a, or 8*2, or 7+1, or even z*a-(7+z)/8+1.3E5*(-524.6+b).

A **string expression** is a string constant (such as "I love you") or a string variable (such as a$) or a combination.

An **expression** is a numeric expression or a string expression.

Statements

At the end of a GOTO statement, the line number must be a numeric constant.

Right:	GOTO 100	(100 is a numeric constant.)
Wrong:	GOTO n	(n is not a numeric constant.)

The INPUT statement's prompt must be a string constant.

Right:	INPUT "What is your name; n$	("What is your name" is a constant.)
Wrong:	INPUT q$; n$	(q$ is not a constant.)

In a DATA statement, you must have constants.

Right:	DATA 8, 1.3E5	(8 and 1.3E5 are constants.)
Wrong:	DATA 7+1, 1.3E5	(7+1 is not a constant.)

In the DATA statement, if the constant is a string, you can omit the quotation marks (unless the string contains a comma or a colon).

Right:	DATA "Joe","Mary"
Also right:	DATA Joe,Mary

Here are the forms of popular BASIC statements:

General form	Example
PRINT *list of expressions*	PRINT "Temperature is"; 4 + 25; "degrees"
LPRINT *list of expressions*	LPRINT "Temperature is"; 4 + 25; "degrees"
SLEEP *numeric expression*	SLEEP 3 + 1
GOTO *line number or label*	GOTO 10
variable = *expression*	x = 47 + 2
INPUT *string constant; variable*	INPUT "What is your name"; n$
IF *condition* THEN *list of statements*	IF a >= 18 THEN PRINT "You": PRINT "vote"
SELECT CASE *expression*	SELECT CASE a + 1
DATA *list of constants*	DATA Joe,273,219,Mary,412,371
READ *list of variables*	READ n$, b, a
RESTORE *line number or label*	RESTORE 10
FOR *numeric variable* = *numeric expression* TO *numeric expression* STEP *numeric expression*	FOR I = 59 + 1 TO 100 + n STEP 2 + 3

Loop techniques

Here's a strange program:

```
CLS
x = 9
x = 4 + x
PRINT x
```

The third line (x = 4 + x) means: the new x is 4 plus the old x. So the new x is 4 + 9, which is 13. The bottom line prints:

```
13
```

Let's look at that program more closely. The second line (x = 9) puts 9 into box x:

box x | 9 |

When the computer sees the next line (x = 4 + x), it examines the equation's right side and sees the 4 + x. Since x is 9, the 4 + x is 4 + 9, which is 13. So the line "x = 4 + x" means x = 13. The computer puts 13 into box x:

box x | 13 |

The program's bottom line prints 13.

Here's another weirdo:

```
CLS
b = 6
b = b + 1
PRINT b * 2
```

The third line (b = b + 1) says the new b is "the old b plus 1". So the new b is 6 + 1, which is 7. The bottom line prints:

```
14
```

In that program, the second line says b is 6; but the next line increases b, by adding 1 to b; so b becomes 7. Programmers say that b has been **increased** or **incremented**. In the third line, the "1" is called the **increase** or the **increment**.

The opposite of "increment" is **decrement**:

```
CLS
j = 500
j = j - 1
PRINT j
```

The second line says j starts at 500; but the next line says the new j is "the old j minus 1", so the new j is 500 - 1, which is 499. The bottom line prints:

```
499
```

In that program, j was **decreased** (or **decremented**). In the third line, the "1" is called the **decrease** (or **decrement**).

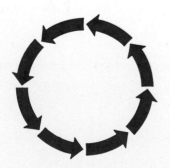

Counting

Suppose you want the computer to count, starting at 3, like this:

```
3
4
5
6
7
8
etc.
```

This program does it, by a special technique:

```
CLS
c = 3
DO
  PRINT c
  c = c + 1
LOOP
```

In that program, c is called the **counter**, because it helps the computer count.

The second line says c starts at 3. The PRINT line makes the computer print c, so the computer prints:

```
3
```

The next line (c = c + 1) increases c by adding 1 to it, so c becomes 4. The LOOP line sends the computer back to the PRINT line, which prints the new value of c:

```
4
```

Then the computer comes to the "c = c + 1" again, which increases c again, so c becomes 5. The LOOP line sends the computer back again to the PRINT line, which prints:

```
5
```

The program's an infinite loop: the computer will print 3, 4, 5, 6, 7, 8, 9, 10, 11, 12, and so on, forever, unless you abort it.

Here's the general procedure for making the computer count:

Start c at some value (such as 3).

Then write a DO loop.

In the DO loop, make the computer use c (such as by saying PRINT c) and increase c (by saying c = c + 1).

Variations To read the printing more easily, put a semicolon at the end of the PRINT statement:

```
CLS
c = 3
DO
  PRINT c;
  c = c + 1
LOOP
```

The semicolon makes the computer print horizontally:

```
3  4  5  6  7  8  etc.
```

This program makes the computer count, starting at 1:

```
CLS
c = 1
DO
  PRINT c;
  c = c + 1
LOOP
```

The computer will print 1, 2, 3, 4, etc.

This program makes the computer count, starting at 0:

```
CLS
c = 0
DO
  PRINT c;
  c = c + 1
LOOP
```

The computer will print 0, 1, 2, 3, 4, etc.

Quiz

Let's make the computer give this quiz:

```
What's the capital of Nevada?
What's the chemical symbol for iron?
What word means 'brother or sister'?
What was Beethoven's first name?
How many cups are in a quart?
```

To make the computer score the quiz, we must tell it the correct answers:

Question	Correct answer
What's the capital of Nevada?	Carson City
What's the chemical symbol for iron?	Fe
What word means 'brother or sister'?	sibling
What was Beethoven's first name?	Ludwig
How many cups are in a quart?	4

So feed the computer this DATA:

```
DATA What's the capital of Nevada,Carson City
DATA What's the chemical symbol for iron,Fe
DATA What word means 'brother or sister',sibling
DATA What was Beethoven's first name,Ludwig
DATA How many cups are in a quart,4
```

In the DATA, each pair consists of a question and an answer. To make the computer READ the DATA, tell the computer to READ a question and an answer, repeatedly:

```
DO
  READ question$, answer$
LOOP
```

Here's the complete program:

```
CLS
DATA What's the capital of Nevada,Carson City
DATA What's the chemical symbol for iron,Fe
DATA What word means 'brother or sister',sibling
DATA What was Beethoven's first name,Ludwig
DATA How many cups are in a quart,4
DATA end,end
DO
  READ question$, answer$: IF question$ = "end" THEN EXIT DO
  PRINT question$;
  INPUT "??"; response$
  IF response$ = answer$ THEN
    PRINT "Correct!"
  ELSE
    PRINT "No, the answer is:  "; answer$
  END IF
LOOP
PRINT "I hope you enjoyed the quiz!"
```

The lines underneath READ make the computer PRINT the question, wait for the human to INPUT a response, and check IF the human's response matches the correct answer. Then the computer will either PRINT "Correct!" or PRINT "No" and reveal the correct answer. When the computer reaches the end of the DATA, the computer does an EXIT DO and prints "I hope you enjoyed the quiz!"

Here's a sample run, where I've underlined the parts typed by the human:

```
What's the capital of Nevada??? Las Vegas
No, the answer is:  Carson City
What's the chemical symbol for iron??? Fe
Correct!
What word means 'brother or sister'??? I give up
No, the answer is:  sibling
What was Beethoven's first name??? Ludvig
No, the answer is:  Ludwig
How many cups are in a quart??? 4
Correct!
I hope you enjoyed the quiz!
```

To give a quiz about different topcs, change the DATA.

Count the correct answers

Let's make the computer count how many questions the human answered correctly. To do that, we need a counter. As usual, let's call it c:

```
CLS
DATA What's the capital of Nevada,Carson City
DATA What's the chemical symbol for iron,Fe
DATA What word means 'brother or sister',sibling
DATA What was Beethoven's first name,Ludwig
DATA How many cups are in a quart,4
DATA end,end
c = 0
DO
  READ question$, answer$: IF question$ = "end" THEN EXIT DO
  PRINT question$;
  INPUT "??"; response$
  IF response$ = answer$ THEN
    PRINT "Correct!"
    c = c + 1
  ELSE
    PRINT "No, the answer is:  "; answer$
  END IF
LOOP
PRINT "I hope you enjoyed the quiz!"
PRINT "You answered"; c; "of the questions correctly."
```

At the beginning of the program, the human hasn't answered any questions correctly yet, so the counter begins at 0 (by saying "c = 0"). Each time the human answers a question correctly, the computer does "c = c + 1", which increases the counter. The program's bottom line prints the counter, by printing a message such as:

```
You answered 2 of the questions correctly.
```

It would be nicer to print —

```
You answered 2 of the 5 questions correctly.
Your score is 40 %
```

or, if the quiz were changed to include 8 questions:

```
You answered 2 of the 8 questions correctly.
Your score is 25 %
```

To make the computer print such a message, we must make the computer count how many questions were asked. So we need another counter. Since we already used c to count the number of correct answers, let's use q to count the number of questions asked. Like c, q must start at 0; and we must increase q, by adding 1 each time another question is asked:

```
CLS
DATA What's the capital of Nevada,Carson City
DATA What's the chemical symbol for iron,Fe
DATA What word means 'brother or sister',sibling
DATA What was Beethoven's first name,Ludwig
DATA How many cups are in a quart,4
DATA end,end
q = 0
c = 0
DO
  READ question$, answer$: IF question$ = "end" THEN EXIT DO
  PRINT question$;
  q = q + 1
  INPUT "??"; response$
  IF response$ = answer$ THEN
    PRINT "Correct!"
    c = c + 1
  ELSE
    PRINT "No, the answer is:  "; answer$
  END IF
LOOP
PRINT "I hope you enjoyed the quiz!"
PRINT "You answered"; c; "of the"; q; "questions correctly."
PRINT "Your score is"; c / q * 100; "%"
```

Summing

Let's make the computer imitate an adding machine, so a run looks like this:

```
Now the sum is 0
What number do you want to add to the sum? 5
Now the sum is 5
What number do you want to add to the sum? 3
Now the sum is 8
What number do you want to add to the sum? 6.1
Now the sum is 14.1
What number do you want to add to the sum? -10
Now the sum is 4.1
etc.
```

Here's the program:

```
CLS
s = 0
DO
  PRINT "Now the sum is"; s
  INPUT "What number do you want to add to the sum"; x
  s = s + x
LOOP
```

The second line starts the sum at 0. The PRINT line prints the sum. The INPUT line asks the human what number to add to the sum; the human's number is called x. The next line (s = s + x) adds x to the sum, so the sum changes. The LOOP line sends the computer back to the PRINT line, which prints the new sum. The program's an infinite loop, which you must abort.

Here's the general procedure for making the computer find a sum:

Start s at 0.

Then write a DO loop.

In the DO loop, make the computer use s (such as by saying PRINT s) and increase s (by saying s = s + the number to be added).

Checking account

If your bank's nasty, it charges you 20¢ to process each good check that you write, and a $15 penalty for each check that bounces; and it pays no interest on the money you've deposited.

This program makes the computer imitate such a bank....

```
CLS
s = 0
DO
  PRINT "Your checking account contains"; s
1 INPUT "Press d (to make a deposit) or c (to write a check)"; a$
  SELECT CASE a$
    CASE "d"
      INPUT "How much money do you want to deposit"; d
      s = s + d
    CASE "c"
      INPUT "How much money do you want the check for"; c
      c = c + .2
      IF c <= s THEN
        PRINT "Okay"
        s = s - c
      ELSE
        PRINT "That check bounced!"
        s = s - 15
      END IF
    CASE ELSE
      PRINT "Please press d or c"
      GOTO 1
  END SELECT
LOOP
```

In that program, the total amount of money in the checking account is called the sum, s. The second line (s = 0) starts that sum at 0. The first PRINT line prints the sum. The next line asks the human to press "d" (to make a deposit) or "c" (to write a check).

If the human presses "d" (to make a deposit), the computer asks "How much money do you want to deposit?" and waits for the human to type an amount to deposit. The computer adds that amount to the sum in the account (s = s + d).

If the human presses "c" (to write a check), the computer asks "How much money do you want the check for?" and waits for the human to type the amount on the check. The computer adds the 20¢ check-processing fee to that amount (c = c + .2). Then the computer reaches the line saying "IF c <= s", which checks whether the sum s in the account is big enough to cover the check (c). If c <= s, the computer says "Okay" and processes the check, by subtracting c from the sum in the account. If the check is too big, the computer says "That check bounced!" and decreases the sum in the account by the $15 penalty.

How the program is nasty

That program is nasty to customers. For example, suppose you have $1 in your account, and you try to write a check for 85¢. Since 85¢ + the 20¢ service charge = $1.05, which is more than you have in your account, your check will bounce, and you'll be penalized $5. That makes your balance will become *negative* $4, and the bank will demand that *you* pay the *bank* $4 — just because you wrote a check for 85¢!

Another nuisance is when you leave town permanently and want to close your account. If your account contains $1, you can't get your dollar back! The most you can withdraw is 80¢, because 80¢ + the 20¢ service charge = $1.

That nasty program makes customers hate the bank — and hate the computer!

How to stop the nastiness

The bank should make the program friendlier. Here's how.

To stop accusing the customer of owing money, the bank should change any negative sum to 0, by inserting this line just under the word DO:

```
IF s < 0 THEN s = 0
```

Also, to be friendly, the bank should ignore the 20¢ service charge when deciding whether a check will clear. So the bank should eliminate the line saying "c = c + .2". On the other hand, if the check *does* clear, the bank should impose the 20¢ service charge afterwards, by changing the "s = s - c" to "s = s - c - .2".

So if the bank is kind, it will make all those changes. But some banks complain that those changes are *too* kind! For example, if a customer whose account contains just 1¢ writes a million-dollar check (which bounces), the new program charges him just 1¢ for the bad check; $15 might be more reasonable.

Moral: **the hardest thing about programming is choosing your goal — deciding what you WANT the computer to do**.

Series

Let's make the computer add together all the numbers from 7 to 100, so that the computer finds the sum of this series: 7 + 8 + 9 + ... + 100. Here's how.

	`CLS`
Start the sum at 0:	`s = 0`
Make i go from 7 to 100:	`FOR i = 7 TO 100`
Increase the sum, by adding each i to it:	`  s = s + i`
	`NEXT`
Print the final sum (which is 5029):	`PRINT s`

Let's make the computer add together the *squares* of all the numbers from 7 to 100, so that the computer finds the sum of this series: (7 squared) + (8 squared) + (9 squared) +... + (100 squared). Here's how:

```
CLS
s = 0
FOR i = 7 TO 100
  s = s + i * i
NEXT
PRINT s
```

It's the same as the previous program, except that indented line says to add i*i instead of i. The bottom line prints the final sum, which is 338259.

Data sums

This program adds together the numbers in the data:

```
CLS
DATA 5, 3, 6.1, etc.
DATA 0
s = 0
DO
  READ x: IF x = 0 THEN EXIT DO
  s = s + x
LOOP
PRINT s
```

The DATA line contains the numbers to be added. The DATA 0 is an end mark. The line saying "s = 0" starts the sum at 0. The READ statement reads an x from the data. The next line (s = s + x) adds x to the sum. The LOOP line makes the computer repeat that procedure for every x. When the computer has read all the data and reaches the end mark (0), the x becomes 0; so the computer will EXIT DO and PRINT the final sum, s.

HELPFUL HINTS

Debugging

If you write and run your own program, it probably won't work.

Your first reaction will be to blame the computer. Don't!

The probability is 99.99% that the fault is yours. Your program contains an error. An error is called a **bug**. Your next task is to **debug** the program, which means get the bugs out.

Bugs are common; top-notch programmers make errors all the time. If you write a program that works perfectly on the first run and doesn't need debugging, it's called a **gold-star program** and means you should have tried writing a harder one instead!

It's easy to write a program that's nearly correct but hard to find the little bug fouling it up. Most time you spend at the computer will be devoted to debugging.

Debugging can be fun. Hunting for the bug is like going on a treasure hunt – or solving a murder mystery. Pretend you're Sherlock Holmes. Your mission: to find the bug and squish it! When you squish it, have fun: yell out, "Squish!"

How can you tell when a roomful of programmers is happy? Answer: when you hear continual cries of "Squish!"

To find a bug, use three techniques:

> Inspect the program.
> Trace the computer's thinking.
> Shorten the program.

Here are the details....

Inspect the program

Take a good, hard look at the program. If you stare hard enough, maybe you'll see the bug.

Popular typos Usually, the bug will turn out to be just a typing error, a **typo**. For example....

> Maybe you typed the letter O instead of zero? Zero instead of the letter O?
> Typed I instead of 1? Typed 1 instead of I?
> Pressed the SHIFT key when you weren't supposed to? Forgot to press it?
> Typed an extra letter? Omitted a letter?
> Typed a line you thought you hadn't? Omitted a line?

Fix your strings You must put quotation marks around each string, and a dollar sign after each string variable:

> Right: a$ = "jerk"
> Wrong: a$ = jerk
> Wrong: a = "jerk"

Too much? Here are three reasons why the computer might print too much:

> 1. You forgot to insert the word END or EXIT DO into your program.
>
> 2. Into a DO loop or FOR loop, you inserted a PRINT line that should be *outside* the loop.
>
> 3. When you started typing the program, you forgot to choose New from the file menu; so the computer is including part of the previous program.

Trace the computer's thinking

If you've inspected the program thoroughly and *still* haven't found the bug, the next step is to **trace** the computer's thinking. **Pretend you're the computer. Do what your program says.** Do you find yourself printing the same wrong answers the computer printed? If so, why?

To help your analysis, **make the computer print everything it's thinking** while it's running your program. For example, suppose your program uses the variables b, c, and x$. Insert lines such as these into your program:

```
10 PRINT "I'm at line 10.  The values are"; b; c; x$
20 PRINT "I'm at line 20.  The values are"; b; c; x$
```

Then run the program. Those extra lines tell you what the computer is thinking about b, c, and x$ and also tell you how many times the computer reached lines 10 and 20. For example, if the computer prints what you expect in line 10 but prints strange values in line 20 (or doesn't even get to line 20), you know the bug occurs after line 10 but before line 20.

Here's a good strategy. Halfway down your program, insert a line that says to print all the values. Then run your program. If the line you inserted prints the correct values, you know the bug lies underneath that line; but if the line prints *wrong* values (or if the computer never reaches that line), you know the bug lies *above* that line. In either case, you know which half of your program contains the bug. In that half of the program, insert more lines, until you finally zero in on the line that contains the bug.

Shorten the program

When all else fails, shorten the program.

Hunting for a bug in a program is like hunting for a needle in a haystack: the job is easier if the haystack is smaller. So make your program shorter: delete the last half of your program. Then run the shortened version. That way, you'll find out whether the first half of your program is working the way it's supposed to. When you've perfected the first half of your program, tack the second half back on.

Does your program contain **a statement whose meaning you're not completely sure of**? Check the meaning by reading a book or asking a friend; or **write a tiny experimental program that contains the statement**, and see what happens when you run it.

Hint: before you shorten your program (or write tiny experimental ones), **save the original version** (by choosing Save from the file menu), even though it contains a bug. After you've played with the shorter versions, retrieve the original (by choosing Open from the file menu) and fix it.

To write a long, correct program easily, write a short program first and debug it, then add a few more lines and debug them, add a few more lines and debug them, etc. So start with a small program, perfect it, then gradually add perfected extras so you *gradually* build a perfected masterpiece. If you try to compose a long program all at once – instead of building it from perfected pieces – you'll have nothing more than a master*mess* – full of bugs.

Moral: to build a large masterpiece, start with a *small* masterpiece. To build a program so big that it's a skyscraper, begin by laying a good foundation; double-check the foundation before you start adding the program's walls and roof.

Error messages

If the computer can't obey your command, the computer will print an **error message**. The following error message are the most common....

Syntax errors

If you say "prind" instead of "print", the computer will say:

```
Syntax error
```

That means the computer hasn't the faintest idea of what you're talking about!

If the computer says you have a syntax error, it's usually because you spelled a word wrong, or forgot a word, or used a word the computer doesn't understand. It can also result from wrong punctuation: check your commas, semicolons, and colons. It can also mean your DATA statement contains a string but your READ statement says to read a number instead; to fix that problem, change the READ statement by putting a dollar sign at the end of the variable's name.

If you try to say PRINT 5 + 2 but forget to type the 2, the computer will say:

```
Expected: expression
```

If you type a left parenthesis but forget to type the right parenthesis that matches it, the computer will say:

```
Expected: )
```

If you accidentally type extra characters (or an unintelligible word) at the end of the line, the computer will say:

```
Expected: end-of-statement
```

Numeric errors

If the answer to a calculation is a bigger number than the computer can handle, the computer will say:

```
Overflow
```

To help the computer handle bigger numbers, remember to put a decimal point in any problem whose answer might be bigger than 32 thousand.

If you try to divide by zero, the computer will say:

```
Division by zero
```

If you feed the computer a number that's inappropriate, the computer will say:

```
Illegal function call
```

That's what the computer will say if you try saying WIDTH 50 instead of WIDTH 40, or you try saying LPRINT CHR$(1200) instead of LPRINT CHR$(12).

Printer errors

If your printer runs out of paper, the computer will say:

```
Out of paper
```

If your printer isn't communicating well with the computer, the computer will say:

```
Device fault
```

That means printer's cable to the computer is unplugged or loose or defective or plugged into the wrong socket, or the printer is turned off, or the printer is off-line (because you pressed a button that turned off the printer's ON LINE light), or the paper is jammed, or there's no more ink left, or the printer broke.

Logic errors

Some commands come in pairs.

DO The words DO and LOOP form a pair. If you say DO but no line says LOOP, the computer will gripe by saying:

```
DO without LOOP
```

If you say LOOP but no line says DO, the computer will say:

```
LOOP without DO
```

The words FOR and NEXT form another pair. If part of the pair is missing, the computer will say –

```
FOR without NEXT
```

or:

```
NEXT without FOR
```

SELECT If a line's first word is SELECT, you're supposed to have a line below saying END SELECT.

If you say SELECT but no line says END SELECT, the computer will say:

```
SELECT without END SELECT
```

If you say END SELECT but no line's first word is SELECT, the computer will say:

```
END SELECT without SELECT
```

Between the SELECT and END SELECT lines, you're supposed to have several lines saying CASE. If you say CASE but no line's first word is SELECT, the computer will say:

```
CASE without SELECT
```

GOTO If you say GOTO 10, the computer tries to find a line numbered 10. If you say GOTO joe, the computer tries to find a line named joe. If there's no line numbered 10 or no line named joe, the computer will say:

```
Label not defined
```

IF Here are other messages about unmatched pairs:

```
ELSE without IF
END IF without block IF
Block IF without END IF
```

DATA If you say READ but the computer can't find any more DATA to read (because the computer has read all the DATA already), the computer will say:

```
Out of DATA
```

Type mismatch The computer handles two major **types** of information: numbers and strings. If you feed the computer the wrong type of information – if you feed it a number when you should have fed it a string, or you feed it a string when you should have fed it a number – the computer will say:

```
Type mismatch
```

When you feed the computer a string, you must put the string in quotation marks, and put a dollar sign after the string's variable. If you forget to type the string's quotation marks or dollar sign, the computer won't realize it's a string; the computer will think you're trying to type a number instead; and if a number would be inappropriate, the computer will say "Type mismatch". So when the computer says "Type mismatch", it usually means you forgot a quotation mark or a dollar sign.

Magicians often say, "The hand is quicker than the eye." The computer's the ultimate magician: the computer can print information on the screen much faster than you can read it.

When the computer is printing faster than you can read, tap the **PAUSE key**. (If your keyboard is modern, that's the last key in the top row. If your keyboard is old-fashioned, no key says PAUSE on it, so do this instead: while holding down the Ctrl key, tap the NUM LOCK key.)

Then the computer will pause, to let you read what's on the screen.

When you've finished reading what's on the screen and want the computer to stop pausing, press the ENTER key. Then the computer will continue printing rapidly, where it left off.

If your eyes are as slow as mine, you'll need to use the PAUSE key often! You'll want the computer to pause while you're running a program containing many PRINT statements (or a PRINT statement in a loop).

You already learned that to run your program, you press **SHIFT with F5**; and while viewing the blue screen, you can peek at the black screen instead by pressing **F4** (and then pressing F4 again to return to the blue screen). Here are other F keys you can press….

F6 (immediate window)

Near the bottom of QBASIC's blue screen, you see the word "Immediate". The area below that word is called the **immediate window**. The area above that word is called the **program window**.

Usually you type in the program window. That's where you type your programs.

To use the immediate window, press the F6 key. That moves the **cursor** (blinking underline) down to the immediate window. Whatever you type afterwards will be in the immediate window.

Any command you type in the immediate window will be obeyed by the computer *immediately*. (The computer will *not* wait for you press SHIFT F5.)

For example, in the immediate window type this:

```
PRINT 4 + 2
```

When you press the ENTER key at the end of that line, the computer obeys that line *immediately*; the computer immediately makes the screen turn black and prints the answer (6) near the bottom of the black screen. When you finish admiring the answer, press the F4 key to switch back to the blue screen.

The cursor will still be in the immediate window. Go ahead: type another PRINT line in the immediate window. When you press the ENTER key at the end of the line, the computer will print the answer on the black screen. Press F4 again, so you see the blue screen again.

You can use the immediate window to quickly PRINT the answers to calculations (so you can discard your calculator) and to explore advanced aspects of the PRINT command.

When you get tired of using the immediate window, press the F6 key again, which moves the cursor back up to the program window.

Try this experiment: in the program window, write a program and run it (by pressing SHIFT F5). When the program finishes running (or gets interrupted by an error), go down to the immediate window (by pressing F6) and tell the computer to PRINT the program's variables. For example, if the program mentioned a variable called x, say this in the program window:

```
PRINT x
```

That makes the computer print the number that x stands for. That information will help you debug the program.

F9 (breakpoint)

If you point at a line of your program (by using the arrow keys) and then press the F9 key, the line turns red. Try it! Make several lines in your program turn red.

So when pointing at a line, pressing F9 makes the line turn red; pressing F9 again makes the line turn back to blue.

Try this experiment: type a long program (containing 5 lines or more), and make two of the lines turn red. Make the red lines be in the *middle* of the program, instead of being the top or bottom lines.

When you tell the computer to run the program (by pressing SHIFT with F5), the computer starts running the program; but **when the computer reaches a red line, it pauses at the beginning of that line** and shows you the blue screen again.

While the computer pauses at the red line, do whatever you wish! For example:

You can peek at the black screen (by pressing F4 to see the black screen, then pressing F4 again to return to the blue screen).

You can use the immediate window (by pressing F6, then typing a PRINT command in the immediate window, then pressing F6 to return to the program window).

You can edit your program.

If you press F5, the computer will continue running the program: it will obey that red line and the lines underneath. If the computer comes to another red line, the computer will pause at that red line also.

Pressing F5 makes the computer continue where it left off. Pressing SHIFT with F5 makes the computer run the program from the beginning instead.

Each red line is called a **breakpoint**, because when the computer is running a program and encounters a red line, the computer breaks its train of thought and pauses.

If you've turned many lines red, here's how to get rid of *all* the redness: choose "Clear All Breakpoints" from the Debug menu (by pressing Alt then D then C).

F7 (run to here)

To have fun, make sure none of the lines in your program is red; then point at a line in the middle of your program (by using the arrow keys), and press F7.

The computer will temporarily turn the line red (so the line becomes a breakpoint). Then the computer will run the program up to that line. Then the computer will get rid of the red.

So if you point at a line and then press F7, the computer will run just the program's beginning, up to that line.

Notice the contrast:

> Pressing SHIFT with F5 runs the whole program.
> Pressing F7 runs just the program's beginning.

F8 (single step)

Instead of telling the computer to run your entire program, you can tell the computer to run just one line at a time, as slowly as you wish. Here's how: press the F8 key. **Each time you press the F8 key, the computer will run one more line of your program.** So if you press the F8 key three times, the computer will run three lines of your program.

Pressing F8 makes the computer run one more line, then show you the blue screen again. At the blue screen, do whatever you wish: you can press F4 (to peek at the black screen), or press F6 (to move to the immediate window), or edit your program, or press F8 again (to run the next line).

The first time you press F8, the computer typically runs the program's first line; but if the computer was in the middle of running your program and was interrupted (by a red breakpoint line or a line saying STOP), pressing F8 makes the computer continue where it left off and do one more line.

Apostrophe

Occasionally, jot a note to remind yourself what your program does and what the variables stand for. Slip the note into your program by putting an apostrophe before it:

```
'This program is another dumb example, written by Russy-poo, a stupid jerk.
'It was written on Halloween, under a full moon, shaded by his fangs.
CLS
c = 40 'because Russ has 40 computers
h = 23 'because 23 of his computers are haunted
PRINT c - h 'That is how many computers are unhaunted and safe for kids.
```

When you run the program, **the computer ignores everything that's to the right of an apostrophe**. So the computer ignores lines 1 & 2; in lines 4 & 5, the computer ignores the "because…"; in the bottom line, the computer ignores the comment about being unhaunted. Since c is 40, and h is 23, the bottom line makes the computer print:

```
17
```

Everything to the right of an apostrophe is called a **comment** (or **remark**). While the computer runs the program, it ignores the comments. But the comments remain part of the program; they appear on the blue screen with the rest of the program. Though the comments appear in the program, they don't affect the run.

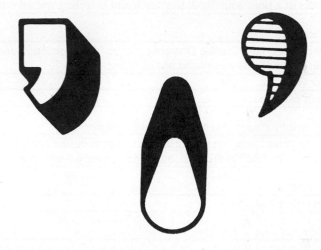

PRETTY OUTPUT

Zones

The screen is divided into 5 wide columns, called **zones**. The leftmost zone is called **zone 1**; the rightmost zone is called **zone 5**.

Zones 1, 2, 3, and 4 are each 14 characters wide. Zone 5 is extra-wide: it's 24 characters wide. So altogether, the width of the entire screen is 14+14+14+14+24, which is 80 characters. The screen is 80 characters wide.

A comma makes the computer jump to a new zone. Here's an example:

```
CLS
PRINT "sin", "king"
```

The computer will print "sin" and "king" on the same line; but because of the comma before "king", the computer will print "king" in the second zone, like this:

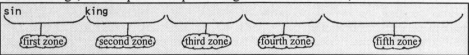

Here are the words of a poet who drank too much and is feeling spaced out:

```
CLS
PRINT "love", "cries", "out"
```

The computer will print "love" in the first zone, "cries" in the second zone, and "out" in the third zone, so the words are spaced out like this:

```
love          cries         out
```

This program's even spacier:

```
CLS
PRINT "love", "cries", "out", "to", "me", "at", "night"
```

The computer will print "love" in the first zone, "cries" in the second, "out" in the third, "to" in the fourth, "me" in the fifth, and the remaining words below, like this:

```
love          cries         out           to            me
at            night
```

This program tells a bad joke:

```
CLS
PRINT "I think you are ugly!", "I'm joking!"
```

The computer will print "I think you are ugly!", then jump to a new zone, then print "I'm joking", like this:

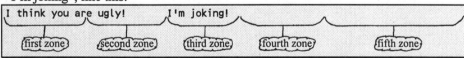

When you combine commas with semicolons, you can get weird results:

```
CLS
PRINT "eat", "me"; "at"; "balls", "no"; "w"
```

That line contains commas and semicolons. A comma makes the computer jump to a new zone, but a semicolon does *not* make the computer jump. The computer will print "eat", then jump to a new zone, then print "me" and "at" and "balls", then jump to a new zone, then print "no" and "w". Altogether, the computer will print:

```
eat           meatballs     now
```

Skip a zone

You can make the computer skip over a zone:

```
CLS
PRINT "Joe", " ", "loves Sue"
```

The computer will print "Joe" in the first zone, a blank space in the second zone, and "loves Sue" in the third zone, like this:

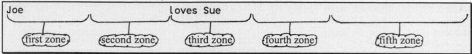

You can type that example even more briefly, like this:

```
CLS
PRINT "Joe", , "loves Sue"
```

Loops

This program makes the computer greet you:

```
CLS
DO
  PRINT "hello",
LOOP
```

The computer will print "hello" many times. Each time will be in a new zone, like this:

```
hello       hello       hello       hello       hello
hello       hello       hello       hello       hello
hello       hello       hello       hello       hello
etc.
```

Tables

This program prints a list of words and their opposites:

```
CLS
PRINT "good", "bad"
PRINT "black", "white"
PRINT "grandparent", "grandchild"
PRINT "he", "she"
```

Line 2 makes the computer print "good", then jump to the next zone, then print "bad". Altogether, the computer will print:

```
good        bad
black       white
grandparent grandchild
he          she
```

The first zone contains a column of words; the second zone contains the opposites. Altogether, the computer's printing looks like a table. So **whenever you want to make a table easily, use zones, by putting commas in your program**.

Let's make the computer print this table:

```
Number      Square
3           9
4           16
5           25
6           36
7           49
8           64
9           81
10          100
```

Here's the program:

```
CLS
PRINT "Number", "Square"
FOR i = 3 TO 10
  PRINT i, i * i
NEXT
```

Line 2 prints the word "Number" at the top of the first column, and the word "Square" at the top of the second. Those words are called the **column headings**. The FOR line says i goes from 3 to 10; to begin, i is 3. The indented line makes the computer print:

```
3           9
```

The bottom line makes the computer do the same thing for the next i, and for the next i, and for the next; so the computer prints the whole table.

TAB

When the computer puts a line of information on your screen, the leftmost character in the line is said to be at **position 1**. The second character in the line is said to be at **position 2**.

This program makes the computer skip to position 6 and then print "HOT":

```
CLS
PRINT TAB(6); "hot"
```

The computer will print:

```
     hot
12345678
```

Here's a fancier example:

```
PRINT TAB(6); "hot"; TAB(13); "buns"
```

The computer will skip to the 6th position, then print "hot", then skip to the 13th position, then print "buns":

```
     HOT     BUNS
12345678     13
```

Diagonal

This program prints a diagonal line:

```
CLS
FOR i = 1 TO 12
   PRINT TAB(i); "*"
NEXT
```

The FOR line says to do the loop 12 times, so the computer does the indented line. The first time the computer does the indented line, the i is 1, so the computer prints an asterisk at position 1:

```
*
```

The next time, the i is 2, so the computer skips to position 2 and prints an asterisk:

```
 *
```

The next time, the i is 3, so the computer skips to position 3 and prints an asterisk:

```
  *
```

Altogether, the program makes the computer print this picture:

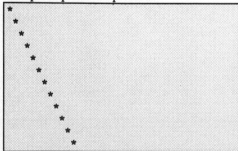

Calendar

Let's make the computer print this message:

```
January     has 31 days
February    has 28 days
March       has 31 days
April       has 30 days
May         has 31 days
June        has 30 days
July        has 31 days
August      has 31 days
September   has 30 days
October     has 31 days
November    has 30 days
December    has 31 days
```

Here's the program:

```
CLS
DATA January,31,February,28,March,31,April,30,May,31,June,30,July,31
DATA August,31,September,30,October,31,November,30,December,31
FOR i = 1 TO 12
   READ month.name$, how.many.days
   PRINT month.name$, "has"; how.many.days; "days"
NEXT
```

The DATA shows each month's name and how many days are in the month. The READ line says to read a month's name and how many days are in the month. The PRINT line makes the computer print the month's name, then skip to the next zone, then print the word "has", then print how many days, then print the word "days".

Print all the days Instead of making the computer say "January has 31 days", let's make the computer print all the days of each month:

```
January
 1  2  3  4  5  6  7  8  9  10  11  12  13  14  15  16  17  18  19  20  21  22
23  24  25  26  27  28  29  30  31
```

Let's make the computer print that on paper, for each month, so the paper shows a crude calendar for the entire year.

To do that, just change the program's PRINT line to this sequence:

```
LPRINT month.name$
FOR day = 1 TO how.many.days
   LPRINT day;
NEXT
LPRINT
LPRINT
```

In that sequence, the first LPRINT statement makes the computer print, on paper, the month's name ("January"). The FOR loop makes the computer print each day (1, 2, 3, etc.). The bottom two lines (which both say LPRINT) make the computer leave blank space under January's calendar, to separate it from February's.

Here's the entire program:

```
CLS
DATA January,31,February,28,March,31,April,30,May,31,June,30,July,31
DATA August,31,September,30,October,31,November,30,December,31
FOR i = 1 TO 12
   READ month.name$, how.many.days
   LPRINT month.name$
   FOR day = 1 TO how.many.days
      LPRINT day;
   NEXT
   LPRINT
   LPRINT
NEXT
```

It makes the computer print a calendar beginning like this:

```
January
 1  2  3  4  5  6  7  8  9  10  11  12  13  14  15  16  17  18  19  20  21  22
23  24  25  26  27  28  29  30  31

February
 1  2  3  4  5  6  7  8  9  10  11  12  13  14  15  16  17  18  19  20  21  22
23  24  25  26  27  28
```

You must eject the paper from the printer manually. For a leap year, change the DATA's 28 to 29.

Pretty weeks Although that program makes the computer print the right numbers for each month, it prints the numbers in the wrong places. Let's make the computer print at most 7 numbers in each row, so each is a week.

To print the numbers in the right places, use TAB. So instead of saying —

```
LPRINT day;
```

say:

```
LPRINT TAB(t); day;
```

That line will make the computer print each day in the right position… if we define t correctly. But how should we define t?

For Sunday, let's make t be 1, so that Sunday begins at position 1. For Monday, let's make t be 5, so that Monday begins at position 5. For Tuesday, let's make t be 9; for Wednesday, 13; Thursday, 17; Friday, 21; and Saturday, 25. So whenever a day's been printed, t should normally increase by 4 for the next day:

```
LPRINT TAB(t); day;
t = t + 4
```

Saturday's the last day of the week. After Saturday, we must begin a new week. So if t has passed Saturday (which is 25), we want t to become 1 (for Sunday); and if there are more days left in the month, we want the computer to press the ENTER key (to start a new week):

```
IF t > 25 THEN
  t = 1
  IF day < how.many.days THEN LPRINT
END IF
```

Which year would you like a calendar for: 1995? 1996? 1997? This program makes a pretty calendar for 1997:

```
CLS
DATA January,31,February,28,March,31,April,30,May,31,June,30,July,31
DATA August,31,September,30,October,31,November,30,December,31
LPRINT "Calendar for 1997"
LPRINT
t = 13
FOR i = 1 TO 12
  READ month.name$, how.many.days
  LPRINT month.name$
  LPRINT "Sun Mon Tue Wed Thu Fri Sat"
  FOR day = 1 TO how.many.days
    LPRINT TAB(t); day;
    t = t + 4
    IF t > 25 THEN
      t = 1
      IF day < how.many.days THEN LPRINT
    END IF
  NEXT
  LPRINT
  LPRINT
  IF i = 6 OR i = 12 THEN LPRINT CHR$(12);
NEXT
```

Line 4 prints the heading, "Calendar for 1997". Line 5 puts a blank line underneath the heading. Since 1997 begins on a Wednesday, the next line tells the computer to start t at 13 (which is the position for Wednesday). The next line saying LPRINT "Sun Mon Tue Wed Thu Fri Sat" puts a heading at the top of each month. The next-to-bottom line says: if the computer has reached the end of June (month 6) or December (month 12), eject the paper, so that the first half of the year is on one sheet of paper and the second half of the year is on the other.

The computer will print a calendar beginning like this:

```
Calendar for 1997

January
Sun Mon Tue Wed Thu Fri Sat
              1   2   3   4
 5   6   7   8   9  10  11
12  13  14  15  16  17  18
19  20  21  22  23  24  25
26  27  28  29  30  31

February
Sun Mon Tue Wed Thu Fri Sat
                          1
 2   3   4   5   6   7   8
 9  10  11  12  13  14  15
16  17  18  19  20  21  22
23  24  25  26  27  28

March
Sun Mon Tue Wed Thu Fri Sat
                          1
 2   3   4   5   6   7   8
 9  10  11  12  13  14  15
16  17  18  19  20  21  22
23  24  25  26  27  28  29
30  31
```

If you want a different year, change lines 4 (which says LPRINT "Calendar for 1997") and line 6 (which says the year starts on Wednesday, t = 13). For a leap year, change the DATA's 28 to 29.

LOCATE

While your running a program, the black screen show 25 lines of information. The screen's top line is called **line 1**; underneath it is **line 2**; then comes **line 3**; etc. The bottom line is **line 25**.

Each line consists of 80 characters. The leftmost character is at **position 1**; the next character is at **position 2**; etc. The rightmost character is at **position 80**.

On the screen, the computer will print wherever you wish.

For example, to make the computer print the word "drown" so that "drown" begins at line 3's 7th position, type this:

```
CLS
LOCATE 3, 7: PRINT "drown"
```

The computer will print the word's first letter (d) at line 3's 7th position. The computer will print the rest of the word afterwards.

You'll see the first letter (d) at line 3's 7th position, the next letter (r) at the next position (line 3's 8th position), the next letter (o) at the next position (line 3's 9th position), etc.

Middle of the screen

Since the screen's top line is 1 and the bottom line is 25, **the middle line is 13**. Since the screen's leftmost position is 1 and the rightmost position is 80, **the middle positions are 40 and 41**.

To make the computer print the word "Hi" in the middle of the screen, tell the computer to print at the middle line (13) and the middle positions (40 and 41):

```
CLS
LOCATE 13, 40: PRINT "Hi"
```

Bottom line

Whenever the computer finishes running a program, the computer prints this message on the black screen's bottom line:

```
Press any key to continue
```

Then the computer waits for you to press the ENTER key, which makes the screen turn blue and show the lines of your program.

That message, "Press any key to continue", is the only message that the computer wants to print on the bottom line.

To force the computer to print anything else on the bottom line, do this: say LOCATE, mention line 25, put a semicolon at the end of the PRINT statement (to prevent the computer from pressing the ENTER key, which would disturb the rest of the screen), and say SLEEP (to make the computer pause awhile so you can admire the printing). For example, this program prints an "x" at the screen's bottom right corner:

```
CLS
LOCATE 25, 80: PRINT "x";
SLEEP
```

Pixels

The image on the computer's screen is called the **picture**. If you stare at the picture closely, you'll see the picture's composed of thousands of tiny dots. Each dot, which is a tiny rectangle, is called a **picture's element**, or **pic's el**, or **pixel**, or **pel**.

Coordinates

The dot in the screen's top left corner is called **pixel (0,0)**. Just to the right of it is pixel (1,0). Then comes pixel (2,0), etc.

Underneath pixel (0,0) is pixel (0,1). Further down is pixel (0,2).

Here are the positions of the pixels:

pixel (0,0)	pixel (1,0)	pixel (2,0)	pixel (3,0)	pixel (4,0)	etc.
pixel (0,1)	pixel (1,1)	pixel (2,1)	pixel (3,1)	pixel (4,1)	etc.
pixel (0,2)	pixel (1,2)	pixel (2,2)	pixel (3,2)	pixel (4,2)	etc.
pixel (0,3)	pixel (1,3)	pixel (2,3)	pixel (3,3)	pixel (4,3)	etc.

Each pixel's name consists of two numbers in parentheses. The first number is the **X coordinate**; the second number is the **Y coordinate**. For example, if you're talking about pixel (4,3), its X coordinate is 4; its Y coordinate is 3.

The X coordinate tells how far to the right the pixel is. The Y coordinate tells how far down. So **pixel (4,3) is the pixel that's 4 to the right and 3 down.**

On the computer, the Y coordinate measures how far *down*, not up. If you've read old-fashioned math books in which the Y coordinate measured how far up, you'll have to reverse your thinking!

Screen modes

How many pixels are on the screen? The answer depends on which **screen mode** you choose.

Mode 12 Generally speaking, the best screen mode to choose is **mode 12**.

In that mode, the X coordinate goes from 0 to 639, and the Y coordinate goes from 0 to 479, so the pixel at the screen's bottom right corner is pixel (639,479). Since you have 640 choices for the X coordinate (numbered from 0 to 639) and 480 choices for the Y coordinate (numbered from 0 to 479), that mode is called a **640-by-480 mode**.

In that mode, the computer can display 16 colors simultaneously.

Mode 12 works just if your computer's video card is modern (VGA).

Alternative modes If your computer's video card is inferior (CGA, EGA, MCGA, Hercules, or Olivetti), mode 12 doesn't work, and you must use a more primitive mode instead. Here are your choices:

Mode	Video card	Pixels	Colors
1	CGA (or EGA, MCGA, VGA)	320 by 200	4
2	CGA (or EGA, MCGA, VGA)	640 by 200	2
3	Hercules monochrome	720 by 348	2
4	Olivetti color	640 by 400	2
7	EGA (or VGA)	320 by 200	16
8	EGA (or VGA)	640 by 200	16
9	EGA (or VGA)	640 by 350	4 or 16
10	EGA (or VGA)	640 by 350	4
11	MCGA (or VGA)	640 by 480	2
12	VGA	640 by 480	16
13	MCGA (or VGA)	320 by 200	256

For example, here's what that chart's bottom row means:

To use mode 13, your video card must be MCGA (or VGA).
That mode lets you use 320 values of X (numbered from 0 to 319).
That mode lets you use 200 values of Y (numbered from 0 to 199).
That mode lets the screen display 256 colors simultaneously.

Mode 12 versus mode 13 As you can see from that chart, mode 12 is generally the best mode, since it gives you lots of pixels (640 by 480) and lots of colors (16).

Mode 13 gives you even more colors (256) but restricts you to fewer pixels (just 320 by 200). That restriction makes mode 13's drawings look crude.

Special modes The following modes are just for bizarre situations....

Mode 3 is just for a monochrome monitor attached to a Hercules monochrome card. This mode does *not* work with color monitors. In this mode, you have just 2 "colors": black and white.

Mode 4 is just for a color video card made by Olivetti. That card is included in the AT&T 6300 computer.

Mode 9 is intended mainly for EGA monitors. It gives you 16 colors usually, but just 4 colors if the video card's RAM is just 64K.

Mode 10 is intended mainly for monochrome monitors. It gives you 4 "colors": black, bright white, dull white (cream), and blinking bright white.

Pixel shape Each pixel is a tiny rectangular dot. In modes 11 and 12, each pixel is a perfect square, whose width is the same as its height: on a typical 15-inch monitor, each pixel's width and height is about a 60th of an inch.

In other modes, each pixel is slightly taller than it is wide, so each pixel looks like a little tower.

Text mode There's also a **mode 0**, which works on all computers and produces just text (no graphics).

Choosing a mode Here's which mode to choose:

Video card	Which mode to choose
Hercules	3
Olivetti	4
CGA	1 (for many colors) or 2 (for many pixels)
EGA	9 (for color) or 10 (for monochrome)
MCGA	11 (for many pixels) or 13 (for many colors)
VGA	12 (for many pixels) or 13 (for many colors)

To give commands about pixels, begin by telling the computer which mode you want. For example, if you want screen mode 12, say:

```
SCREEN 12
```

When you give such a SCREEN command, the computer automatically clears the screen, so the entire screen becomes black. You do *not* have to say CLS.

Plotting

If your monitor is modern (VGA), this program makes the screen become black, then makes pixel (100,100) turn white:

```
SCREEN 12
PSET (100, 100)
```

If your monitor is less than VGA, choose a different screen mode than 12.

In that program, the PSET (100, 100) makes pixel (100,100) turn white. The word "PSET" means "pixel set": "PSET (100, 100)" means "set the pixel (100,100) to white".

LINE This program draws a white line from pixel (0,0) to pixel (100,100):

```
SCREEN 12
LINE (0, 0)-(100, 100)
```

This program draws a white line from pixel (0,0) to pixel (100,100), then draws a white line from that pixel (100,100) to pixel (120,70):

```
SCREEN 12
LINE (0, 0)-(100, 100)
LINE -(120, 70)
```

CIRCLE This program draws a white circle whose center is pixel (100,100) and whose radius is 40 pixels:

```
SCREEN 12
CIRCLE (100, 100), 40
```

In modes 11 and 12, each pixel is a perfect square, and the computer draws the circle easily. The circle's radius is 40 pixels; the circle's diameter (width) is 80 pixels.

If you switch to a different screen mode (such as SCREEN 2), each pixel is a tower instead of a square, so a "circle that's 80 pixels wide and 80 pixels high" would be taller than wide and look like a tall oval. To make sure your "circle of radius 40" looks pretty, the computer cheats: the computer makes the circle's width be 80 pixels but makes the circle's height be fewer than 80 pixels, so that the circle's height is the same number of *inches* as the width.

Avoid the bottom

When your program finishes, the bottom of the screen automatically shows this advice:

```
Press any key to continue
```

To prevent that advice from covering up your drawing, position your drawing near the *top* of the screen (avoiding the bottom), or else make your program's bottom line say "SLEEP" so the computer will pause and let you admire the drawing before the advice covers it.

PAINT

After drawing a shape's outline (by using dots, lines, and circles), you can fill in the shape's middle, by telling the computer to PAINT the shape.

Here's how to PAINT a shape that you've drawn (such as a circle or a house). Find a pixel that's in the middle of the shape and that's still black; then tell the computer to PAINT, starting at that pixel. For example, if pixel (100, 101) is inside the shape and still black, say:

```
PAINT (100, 101)
```

Colors

In modes 4, 7, 8, and 12, you can use these 16 colors:

```
0. black                    8. light black (gray)
1. blue                     9. light blue
2. green                   10. light green
3. cyan (greenish blue)    11. light cyan (aqua)
4. red                     12. light red (pink)
5. magenta (purplish red)  13. light magenta
6. brown                   14. light brown (yellow)
7. cream (yellowish white) 15. light cream (pure white)
```

In mode 1, you must choose from these 4 colors instead:

```
0. black
1. cyan (greenish blue)
2. magenta (purplish red)
3. cream (yellowish white)
```

In modes 2, 3, and 11, you must choose from these 2 colors instead:

```
0. black
1. white
```

In mode 10, you have these 4 choices:

```
0. black
1. cream
2. blinking white
3. white
```

Mode 9 usually gives you the 16 colors used in mode 12; but if you're using mode 9 with an EGA card having just 64K of RAM, you're restricted to the 4 colors used in mode 1.

Mode 13 gives you the 16 colors used in mode 12 — and many more colors, too! Here's the spectrum:

```
  0 through    7: black, blue, green, cyan, red, magenta, brown, cream
  8 through   15: same colors as above, but lighter
 16 through   31: shades of gray (from dark to light)
 32 through   55: color blends (from blue to red to green to blue again)
 56 through   79: same color blends, but lighter
 80 through  103: same color blends, but even lighter
104 through  175: same as 32 through 103, but darker
176 through  247: same as 104 through 175, but even darker
248 through  255: black
```

Normally, the PLOT, LINE, CIRCLE, and PAINT commands draw in yellowish white (cream). If you prefer a different color, **put the color's number at the end of the command**. Put a comma before the color's number.

For example, if you want to draw a line from (0,0) to (100,0) using color #2, type this:

```
LINE (0, 0)-(100, 0), 2
```

When you give a PAINT command, you must make its color be the same color as the outline you're filling in.

Boxes

If you type —

```
LINE (0, 0)-(100, 100), 2
```

the computer draws a line from pixel (0,0) to (100,100) using color #2.

If you put the letter B at the end of the LINE command, like this —

```
LINE (0, 0)-(100, 100), 2, B
```

the computer will draw a box instead of a line. One corner of the box will be at pixel (0,0); the opposite corner will be at (100,100); and the box will be drawn using color 2.

If you put BF at the end of the LINE command, like this —

```
LINE (0, 0)-(100, 100), 2, BF
```

the computer will draw a box and also fill it in, by painting its interior.

Return to text mode

When you finish drawing pictures, you can return to text mode by saying:

```
SCREEN 0
```

If you were using mode 1, 7, or 13, say this instead:

```
SCREEN 0
WIDTH 80
```

The "WIDTH 80" makes sure the screen will display 80 characters per line instead of 40.

Sounds

To produce sounds, you can say BEEP, SOUND, or PLAY. BEEP appeals to business executives; SOUND appeals to doctors and engineers; and PLAY appeals to musicians.

BEEP

If your program says —

```
BEEP
```

the computer will beep. The beep lasts for about a quarter of a second. Its frequency ("pitch") is about 875 hertz. (The beep's length and frequency might be slightly higher or lower, depending on which computer you have.)

You can say BEEP in the middle of your program. For example, you can tell the computer to BEEP if a person enters wrong data.

Computerized weddings

This program makes the computer act as a priest and perform a marriage ceremony:

```
CLS
10 INPUT "Do you take this woman to be your lawful wedded wife"; a$
IF a$ <> "I do" THEN BEEP: PRINT "Try again!": GO TO 10
20 INPUT "Do you take this man to be your lawful wedded husband"; a$
IF a$ <> "I do" THEN BEEP: PRINT "Try again!": GO TO 20
PRINT "I now pronounce you husband and wife."
```

Line 10 makes the computer ask the groom, "Do you take this woman to be your lawful wedded wife?" If the groom doesn't say "I do", the next line makes the computer beep, say "Try again!", and repeat the question. Line 20 does the same thing to the bride. The bottom line congratulates the couple for answering correctly and getting married.

SOUND

If your program says —

```
SOUND 440, 18.2
```

the computer will produce a sound. In that command, the 440 is the frequency ("pitch"), measured in hertz (cycles per second); so the sound will be a musical note whose pitch is 440 hertz. (That note happens to be "the A above middle C").

If you replace the 440 by a lower number, the sound will have a lower pitch; if you replace the 440 by a higher number, the sound will have a higher pitch.

Lowest pitch

The lowest pitch that the computer can sing is 37. If you try to go below 37, the computer will gripe by saying:

```
Illegal function call
```

Higher pitches

The highest pitch that the computer can sing is 32767, but human ears aren't good enough to hear a pitch that high.

When you were a baby, you could probably hear up to 20000. As you get older, your hearing gets worse, and you can't hear such high notes. Today, the highest sound you can hear is probably somewhere around 14000.

To find out, give yourself a hearing test, by running this program:

```
CLS
DO
  INPUT "What pitch would you like me to play"; p
  SOUND p, 18.2
LOOP
```

When you run that program, begin by inputting a low pitch (such as 37). Then input a higher number, then an even higher number, until you finally pick a number so high you can't hear it. (When trying that test, put your ear close to the computer's speaker, which is in the computer's front left corner.) When you've picked a number too high for you to hear, try a slightly lower number. Keep trying different numbers, until you find the highest number you can hear.

Have a contest with your friends: find out which of your friends can hear best.

If you run that program every year, you'll see that your hearing gets gradually worse. For example, when I was 36 years old, the highest pitch I could hear was about 14500, but I can't hear that high anymore. How about *you*?

Longer sounds

In those examples, the 18.2 makes the computer produce the sound for 1 second. If you want the sound to last longer — so that it lasts 2 seconds — replace the 18.2 by 18.2*2. For 10 seconds, say 18.2*10. (That's because the computer's metronome beats 18.2 times per second.)

PLAY

If your program says —

```
PLAY "c d g# b- a"
```

the computer will play the note C, then D, then G sharp, then B flat, then A.

In the PLAY command, the computer ignores the spaces; so if you wish, you can write:

```
PLAY "cdg#b-a"
```

Octave

The computer can play in seven octaves, numbered from 0 to 6. Octave 0 consists of very bass notes; octave 6 consists of very high-pitched notes. In each octave, the lowest note is a C: the notes in an octave are C, C#, D, D#, E, F, F#, G, G#, A, A#, and B.

"Middle C" is at the beginning of octave 2. Normally, the computer plays in octave 4. To make the computer switch to octave 3, type *the letter "o"* followed by a 3, like this:

```
PLAY "o3"
```

After giving that command, anything else you PLAY will be in octave 3, until you change octaves again.

You can use the symbol ">" to mean "go up an octave", and you can use the symbol "<" to mean "go down an octave". For example, if you say —

```
PLAY "g > c d < g"
```

the computer will play the note G, then go up an octave to play C and D in that higher octave, then go down to the original octave to play G again.

Numbered notes

The lowest note the computer can play (which is the C in octave 0) is called "note 1". The highest note the computer can play (which is the B in octave 6) is called "note 84".

To make the computer play note 84, you can type this:

```
PLAY "n84"
```

To make the computer play its lowest note (1), then its middle note (42), then its highest note (84), type this:

```
PLAY "n1 n42 n84"
```

Length Besides playing with pitches, you can also play with rhythms ("lengths" of the notes). Normally each note is a "quarter note". To make the computer switch to eighth notes (which are faster), type this:

```
PLAY "L8"
```

Besides using L8 for eighth notes, you can use L16 for sixteenth notes (which are even faster), L32 for thirty-second notes (which are super-fast), and L64 for sixty-fourth notes (which are super-super-fast). For long notes, you can use L2 (which gives a half note) or L1 (which gives a whole note).

You can use any length from L1 to L64. You can even use in-between lengths, such as L7 or L23 (though such rhythms are hard to stamp your foot to).

Dots If you put a period after a note, the computer will multiply the note's length by 1½.

For example, suppose you say:

```
PLAY "L8 c e. d"
```

The C will be an 8th note, E will be 1½ times as long as an 8th note, and D will be an 8th note. Musicians call that E a **dotted eighth note**.

If you put *two* periods after a note (like this: e..), the computer will multiply the note's length by 13/4. Musicians say the note is **double dotted**.

If you put *three* periods after a note (like this: e...), the computer will multiply the note's length by 17/8.

Pause To make the computer pause ("rest") for an eighth note, put a p8 into the music string.

Tempo Normally, the computer plays 120 quarter notes per minute; but you can change that tempo. To switch to 150 quarter notes per minute, say:

```
PLAY "t150"
```

You can switch to any tempo from 32 to 255. The 32 is very slow; 255 is very fast. In musical terms, 40=larghissimo, 50=largo, 63=larghetto, 65=grave, 68=lento, 71=adagio, 76=andantino, 92=andante, 114=moderato, 120=allegretto, 144=allegro, 168=vivace, 188=presto, and 208=prestissimo.

Combine them You can combine all those musical commands into a single PLAY statement. For example, to set the tempo to 150, the octave to 3, the length to 8 (which means an eighth note), and then play C and D, and then change the length to 4 and play E, type this:

```
PLAY "t150 o3 L8 c d L4 e"
```

PRINT USING

Suppose you want to add $12.47 to $1.03. The correct answer is $13.50. This almost works:

```
PRINT 12.47 + 1.03
```

It makes the computer print:

```
13.5
```

But instead of 13.5, we should try to make the computer print 13.50.

This command forces the computer to print 13.50:

```
PRINT USING "##.##"; 12.47 + 1.03
```

The "##.##" is called the **picture** or **image** or **format**: it says to print two characters, then a decimal point, then two digits. The computer will print:

```
13.50
```

This command puts that answer into a sentence:

```
PRINT USING "You spent ##.## at our store"; 12.47 + 1.03
```

The computer will print:

```
You spent 13.50 at our store
```

Rounding

This program makes the computer divide 300 by 7 but round the answer to two decimal places:

```
CLS
PRINT USING "##.##"; 300 / 7
```

When the computer divides 300 by 7, it gets 42.85714, but the format rounds the answer to 42.86. The computer will print:

```
42.86
```

Multiple numbers

Every format (such as "###.##") is a string. You can replace the format by a string variable:

```
CLS
a$ = "###.##"
PRINT USING a$; 247.91
PRINT USING a$; 823
PRINT USING a$; 7
PRINT USING a$; -5
PRINT USING a$; -80.3
```

The computer will print:

```
247.91
823.00
  7.00
 -5.00
-80.30
```

When the computer prints that column of numbers, notice that the computer prints the decimal points underneath each other so that they line up. So **to make decimal points line up, say PRINT USING instead of just PRINT.**

To print those numbers *across* instead of down, say this:

```
PRINT USING "###.##"; 247.91; 823; 7; -5; -80.3
```

It makes the computer print 247.91, then 823.00, etc., like this:

```
247.91823.00  7.00 -5.00-80.30
```

Since the computer prints those numbers so close together, they're hard to read. To make the computer insert extra space between the numbers, widen the format by putting a fourth "#" before the decimal point:

```
PRINT USING "####.##"; 247.91; 823; 7; -5; -80.3
```

Then the computer will print:

```
247.91 823.00   7.00  -5.00 -80.30
```

If you say —

```
PRINT USING "My ## pals drank ###.# pints of gin"; 24; 983.5
```

the computer will print:

```
My 24 pals drank 983.5 pints of gin
```

Oversized numbers

Suppose you say:

```
PRINT USING "###.##"; 16238.7
```

The computer tries to print 16238.7 by using the format "###.##". But since that format allows just three digits before the decimal point, the format isn't large enough to fit 16238.7. So the computer must disobey the format. But the computer also prints a percent sign, which means, "Warning! I am disobeying you!" Altogether, the computer prints:

```
%16238.70
```

Final semicolon

At the end of the PRINT USING statement, you can put a semicolon:

```
CLS
PRINT USING "##.##"; 13.5;
PRINT "credit"
```

Line 2 makes the computer print 13.50. The semicolon at the end of line 2 makes the computer print "credit" on the same line, like this:

```
13.50credit
```

Advanced formats

Suppose you're running a high-risk business. On Monday, your business runs badly: you *lose* $27,931.60, so your "profit" is *minus* $27,931.60. On Tuesday, your business does slightly better than break-even: your net profit for the day is $8.95.

Let's make the computer print the word "profit", then the amount of your profit (such as -$27,931.60 or $8.95), then the word "ha" (because you're cynical about how your business is going).

You can do that printing in several ways. Let's explore them....

If you say —

```
CLS
a$ = "profit#####.##ha"
PRINT USING a$; -27931.6
PRINT USING a$; 8.95
```

the computer will print:

```
profit-27931.60ha
profit    8.95ha
```

Comma
If you change the format to "profit###,###.##ha", the computer will insert a comma if the number is large:

```
profit-27,931.60ha
profit      8.95ha
```

Plus sign
If you change the format to "profit+#####.##ha", the computer will print a plus sign in front of any positive number:

```
profit-27931.60ha
profit    +8.95ha
```

Trailing minus
To print a negative number, the computer normally prints a minus sign *before* the number. That's called a **leading minus**. You can make the computer put the minus sign *after* the number instead; that's called a **trailing minus**. For example, if you change the format to "profit######.##-ha", the computer will print a minus sign *after* a negative number (and no minus after a positive number), like this:

```
profit27931.60-ha
profit    8.95 ha
```

Dollar sign
Normally, a format begins with ##. If you begin with $$ instead (like this: "profit$$#####.##ha"), the computer will print a dollar sign before the digits:

```
profit-$27931.60ha
profit     $8.95ha
```

Check protection
If you begin with ** (like this: "profit**#####.##ha"), the computer will print asterisks before the number:

```
profit*-27931.60ha
profit******8.95ha
```

If you begin with **$ (like this: "profit**$#####.##ha"), the computer will print asterisks and a dollar sign:

```
profit*-$27931.60ha
profit******$8.95ha
```

When you're printing a paycheck, use the asterisks to prevent the employee from enlarging his salary. Since the asterisks protect the check from being altered, they're called **check protection**.

Combination
You can combine several techniques into a single format. For example, you can combine the comma, the trailing minus, and the **$ (like this: "profit**$##,###.##-ha"), so that the computer will print:

```
profit**$27,931.60-ha
profit*******$8.95 ha
```

E notation
If you change the format to "profit##.#####^^^^ha", the computer will print numbers by using E notation:

```
profit-2.79316E+04ha
profit 8.95000E+00ha
```

FANCY CALCS

Exponents

Try typing this program:

```
CLS
PRINT 4 ^ 3
```

To type the symbol ^, do this: while holding down the SHIFT key, tap this key:

```
^
6
```

That symbol (^) is called a **caret**.

In that program, **the "4 ^ 3" makes the computer use the number 4, three times**. The computer will multiply together those three 4's, like this: 4 times 4 times 4. Since "4 times 4 times 4" is 64, the computer will print:

```
64
```

In the expression "4 ^ 3", the 4 is called the **base**; the 3 is called the **exponent**.

Here's another example:

```
CLS
PRINT 10 ^ 6
```

The "10 ^ 6" makes the computer use the number 10, six times. The computer will multiply together those six 10's (like this: 10 times 10 times 10 times 10 times 10 times 10) and print the answer:

```
1000000
```

Here's another example:

```
CLS
PRINT 3 ^ 2
```

The "3 ^ 2" makes the computer use the number 3, two times. The computer will multiply together those two 3's (like this: 3 times 3) and print the answer:

```
9
```

Order of operations

The symbols +, -, *, /, and ^ are all called **operations**.

To solve a problem, the computer uses the three-step process taught in algebra and the "new math". For example, suppose you say:

```
PRINT 70 - 3 ^ 2 + 8 / 2 * 3
```

The computer will *not* begin by subtracting 3 from 70; instead, it will use the three-step process:

	The problem is	70 - 3 ^ 2 + 8 / 2 * 3
Step 1: get rid of ^.	Now the problem is	70 - 9 + 8 / 2 * 3
Step 2: get rid of * and /.	Now the problem is	70 - 9 + 12
Step 3: get rid of + and -.	The answer is	73

In each step, it looks from left to right. For example, in step 2, it sees / and gets rid of it before it sees *.

Though exponents are fun, the computer handles them slowly. For example, the computer handles 3 ^ 2 slower than 3 * 3. So for fast calculations, say 3 * 3 instead of 3 ^ 2.

Square roots

What positive number, when multiplied by itself, gives 9? The answer is 3, because 3 times itself is 9.

3 **squared** is 9. 3 is called the **square root** of 9.

To make the computer deduce the square root of 9, type this:

```
PRINT SQR(9)
```

The computer will print 3.

When you tell the computer to PRINT SQR(9), make sure you put the parentheses around the 9.

The symbol SQR is called a **function**. The number in parentheses (9) is called the function's **input** (or **argument** or **parameter**). The answer, which is 3, is called the function's **output** (or **value**).

SQR(9) gives the same answer as 9 ^ .5. The computer handles SQR(9) faster than 9 ^ .5.

Cube roots

What number, when multiplied by itself and then multiplied by itself *again*, gives 64? The answer is 4, because 4 times 4 times 4 is 64. The answer (4) is called the **cube root** of 64.

Here's how to make the computer find the cube root of 64:

```
PRINT 64 ^ (1 / 3)
```

The computer will print 4.

EXP

The letter "e" stands for a special number, which is approximately 2.718281828459045. You can memorize that number easily, if you pair the digits:

```
2.7 18 28 18 28 45 90 45
```

That weird number is important in calculus, radioactivity, biological growth, and other areas of science. It's calculated by this formula:

$$e = 1 + \frac{1}{1} + \frac{1}{1*2} + \frac{1}{1*2*3} + \frac{1}{1*2*3*4} + \frac{1}{1*2*3*4*5} + \cdots$$

Therefore:

$$e = 1 + 1 + \frac{1}{2} + \frac{1}{6} + \frac{1}{24} + \frac{1}{120} + \cdots$$

EXP(x) means e^x. For example, EXP(3) means e^3, which is e * e * e, which is:

```
2.718281828459045 * 2.718281828459045 * 2.718281828459045
```

EXP(4) means e^4, which is e * e * e * e. EXP(3.1) means $e^{3.1}$, which is more than e^3 but less than e^4.

Here's a practical application. Suppose you put $800 in a savings account, and the bank promises to give you 5% annual interest "compounded continuously". How much money will you have at the end of the year? The answer is 800 * EXP(.05).

Logarithms

Here are some powers of 2:

x	2^x
1	2
2	4
3	8
4	16
5	32
6	64

To compute the logarithm-base-2 of a number, find the number in the right-hand column; the answer is in the left column. For example, the logarithm-base-2 of 32 is 5. The logarithm-base-2 of 15 is slightly less than 4.

The logarithm-base-2 of 64 is 6. That fact is written:

$\log_2 64$ is 6

It's also written:

$\frac{\log 64}{\log 2}$ is 6

To make the computer find the logarithm-base-2 of 64, say:

```
PRINT LOG(64) / LOG(2)
```

The computer will print 6.

Here are some powers of 10:

x	10^x
1	10
2	100
3	1000
4	10000
5	100000

The logarithm-base-10 of 100000 is 5. The logarithm-base-10 of 1001 is slightly more than 3.

The logarithm-base-10 of 10000 is 4. That fact is written:

$\log_{10} 10000$ is 4

It's also written:

$\frac{\log 10000}{\log 10}$ is 4

To make the computer do that calculation, say:

```
PRINT LOG(10000) / LOG(10)
```

The computer will print 4.

The logarithm-base-10 is called the **common logarithm**. That's the kind of logarithm used in high school and chemistry. So **if a chemistry book says to find the logarithm of 10000, the book means the logarithm-base-10 of 10000, which is LOG(10000) / LOG(10)**.

What happens if you forget the base, and say just LOG(10000) instead of LOG(10000) / LOG(10)? If you say just LOG(10000), the computer will find the **natural logarithm** of 10000, which is $\log_e 10000$ (where e is 2.718281828459045), which isn't what your chemistry book wants.

Contrasts

The computer's notation resembles that of arithmetic and algebra, but beware of these contrasts....

Multiplication

To make the computer multiply, you must type an asterisk:

Traditional notation	Computer notation
2n	2 * n
5(n+m)	5 * (n + m)
nm	n * m

Exponents

Put an exponent in parentheses, if it contains an operation:

Traditional notation	Computer notation
x^{n+2}	x ^ (n + 2)
x^{3n}	x ^ (3 * n)
5$^{2/3}$	5 ^ (2 / 3)
2$^{3^4}$	2 ^ (3 ^ 4)

Fractions

Put a fraction's numerator in parentheses, if it contains addition or subtraction:

Traditional notation	Computer notation
$\frac{a+b}{c}$	(a + b) / c
$\frac{k-20}{6}$	(k - 20) / 6

Put a denominator in parentheses, if it contains addition, subtraction, multiplication, or division:

Traditional notation	Computer notation
$\frac{5}{3+x}$	5 / (3 + x)
$\frac{5a^3}{4b}$	5 * a ^ 3 / (4 * b)

Mixed numbers

A **mixed number** is a number that contains a fraction. For example, 9½ is a mixed number. When you write a mixed number, put a plus sign before its fraction:

Traditional notation	Computer notation
9½	9 + 1 / 2

If you're using the mixed number in a further calculation, put the mixed number in parentheses:

Traditional notation	Computer notation
7 - 2¼	7 - (2 + 1 / 4)

Clock

The computer has a built-in clock/calendar.

Setting the date & time

To set the date to January 24, 1996, you can run this program —

```
CLS
DATE$ = "01-24-1996"
```

or give this DOS command (after leaving QBASIC):

```
C:\>date 01-24-1996
```

To set the time to 7 seconds after 1:45PM, you can run this program —

```
CLS
TIME$ = "13:45:07"
```

or give this DOS command:

```
C:\>time 13:45:07
```

Printing the date & time

After you've set the date & time, the computer's clock/calendar will try to keep track of the date & time for you. Then whenever you want to find out the current date & time, run this program:

```
CLS
PRINT DATE$
PRINT TIME$
```

If you say —

```
PRINT TIMER
```

the computer will tell you how many seconds have elapsed since midnight.

This program makes the computer print the DATE$, TIME$, and TIMER across the top of your screen:

```
CLS
PRINT DATE$, TIME$, TIMER
```

The top of your screen will look like this:

```
07-29-1996    18:07:04        65223.85
```

The following program makes the computer look at the clock (and tell you the TIME$), then look at the clock *again* and tell you the new TIME$, then look at the clock *again* and tell you the new TIME$, etc.:

```
CLS
DO
  PRINT TIME$
LOOP
```

For example, if the time starts at 18:07:04 (and eventually changes to 18:07:05 and then 18:07:06), the screen will look like this:

```
18:07:04
18:07:04
18:07:04
18:07:05
18:07:05
18:07:05
18:07:05
18:07:06
18:07:06
etc.
```

The program will continue telling you the time until you abort the program.

Clock battery

The typical computer contains a little battery, called a **clock battery**. While the computer is unplugged from the wall (or the computer's main power switch is turned off), the clock battery continually sneaks enough electricity to the clock/calendar chips to keep them running, so they keep updating the date & time.

After several months or years, the battery will run out, and the chips will forget what the date & time are. Replace the battery, then reset the date & time.

Test your computer's speed

How fast can your computer print the numbers from 1 to 1000? (The answer depends on the speed of your computer's CPU chip, video card, and other components.) This program makes the computer print all the numbers from 1 to 1000, then brag about how fast it printed them:

```
CLS
starting.time = TIMER
FOR i = 1 TO 1000
  PRINT i
NEXT
elapsed.time = TIMER - starting.time
PRINT "The elapsed time is"; elapsed.time; "seconds."
```

Line 2 makes the computer look at the clock's TIMER and call that time the starting.time. The FOR..NEXT loop makes the computer print all the numbers from 1 to 1000. The line underneath (elapsed.time = TIMER - starting.time) makes the computer look at the clock's TIMER again, notice how different it is from the starting.time, and call the difference the elapsed.time. The bottom line makes the computer print how much time elapsed.

For example, my 386SX-16 computer usually prints:

```
The elapsed time is 7.421875 seconds.
```

My 486DX2-66 computer is faster and usually prints:

```
The elapsed time is 1.976563 seconds.
```

How fast is *your* computer?

Try running the program several times. Sometimes you might get slightly different answers, since the TIMER isn't very accurate.

For a different speed test, make the computer count up to 10000 instead of 1000. That makes the computer take about 10 times as long.

Try putting a semicolon at the end of the PRINT i line. That lets the computer print faster, since the computer no longer has to press the ENTER key after each number.

Try omitting the PRINT i line altogether, so the computer can just *think* about the numbers without bothering to print them. That lets the computer finish the program much faster. It tests how fast the CPU can *think*, rather than how fast the video circuitry can display printed answers.

Midnight problem

At midnight, TIMER is 0. At 1 second after midnight, TIMER is 1. At 2 seconds after midnight, TIMER is 2.

Since there are 60 seconds in a minute, 60 minutes in an hour, and 24 hours in a day, there are 86400 seconds in a day. At 1 second before midnight, TIMER is "86400 minus 1", which is 86399; but when midnight strikes, TIMER becomes 0 again.

To compute elapsed.time, you normally take the current time (TIMER) and subtract the starting.time:

```
elapsed.time = TIMER - starting.time
```

But suppose a program starts running just before midnight and ends just after midnight. Since the starting.time is nearly 86400 and the TIMER (current time) is just slightly bigger than 0, the formula "TIMER - starting.time" gives a negative number, which is *not* the correct calculation for elapsed.time, since elapsed.time cannot be negative!

Here's how to correct the definition of elapsed.time. Instead of giving this one-line definition —

```
elapsed.time = TIMER - starting.time
```

give this two-line definition:

```
elapsed.time = TIMER - starting.time
IF elapsed.time < 0 THEN elapsed.time = elapsed.time + 86400
```

So the program to test your program's speed should be:

```
CLS
starting.time = TIMER
FOR i = 1 TO 1000
  PRINT i
NEXT
elapsed.time = TIMER - starting.time
IF elapsed.time < 0 THEN elapsed.time = elapsed.time + 86400
PRINT "The elapsed time is"; elapsed.time; "seconds"
```

If you omit the shaded line, the program will work usually, but not at midnight. The typical novice programmer forgets to insert that line, thinks the program works fine without it, and gets surprised years later by a midnight phone call from an upset user wondering why the computer reports that the elapsed time is a negative number.

LOOP UNTIL

This program prints the letter "x" repeatedly, for .3 seconds:

```
CLS
starting.time = TIMER
DO
  PRINT "x";
  elapsed.time = TIMER - starting.time
  IF elapsed.time < 0 THEN elapsed.time = elapsed.time + 86400
LOOP UNTIL elapsed.time >= .3
```

Line 2 makes the computer look at the clock's TIMER and call that time the starting.time. The PRINT line makes the computer print an "x". The other indented lines compute the elapsed.time. The bottom line says: do the loop again and again, until the elapsed time is at least .3.

So that program makes the computer print x's for about .3 seconds.

Experiment! Run that program, and see how many x's *your* computer can print in .3 seconds.

If you run that program several times, you'll get slightly different answers, since the TIMER isn't very accurate.

In the bottom line, try changing the .3 to a different number, to see how many x's your computer can print in a different amount of time. Even if you replace the .3 by a tiny number, the computer will print at least one x, since the computer does the PRINT line before encountering the definition of elapsed.time and the LOOP condition.

Pause loop

This program makes the computer print "I'm going to take a nap", then pause for 5 seconds, then print "Now I woke up":

```
CLS
PRINT "I'm going to take a nap"
SLEEP 5
PRINT "Now I woke up"
```

This fancier program accomplishes the same goal:

```
CLS
PRINT "I'm going to take a nap"
starting.time = TIMER
DO
  elapsed.time = TIMER - starting.time
  IF elapsed.time < 0 THEN elapsed.time = elapsed.time + 86400
LOOP UNTIL elapsed.time >= 5
PRINT "Now I woke up"
```

Line 2 makes the computer print "I'm going to take a nap". The next line (starting.time = TIMER) makes the computer look at the clock's TIMER and call that time the starting.time. The DO loop makes the computer look at the time repeatedly, until the elapsed.time is at least 5 seconds. After those 5 seconds of at of staring at the clock, the computer finally does the bottom line, which makes the computer print "Now I woke up". Since the loop's only purpose is to make the computer pause for 5 seconds, the loop is called a **pause loop**.

The fancy program (which says LOOP UNTIL) has two advantages over the simple program (which says SLEEP):

In the SLEEP program, if the human presses a key while the computer is SLEEPing, the computer wakes up immediately. In the LOOP UNTIL program, the computer ignores the human until 5 seconds have passed, so the LOOP UNTIL program ensures that the computer really DOES pause for 5 seconds. The only way the human can interrupt the computer's pause loop is to abort the program (by pressing Ctrl with PAUSE/BREAK).

In the LOOP UNTIL program, you can make the computer loop for 5.1 seconds instead of 5 seconds, by changing the 5 to 5.1. You can't create a SLEEP program that sleeps for 5.1 seconds, since the SLEEP command prohibits decimals: if you try to say SLEEP 5.1, the computer will do SLEEP 5 instead.

FOR...NEXT Here's another way to make the computer take a nap:

```
CLS
PRINT "I'm going to take a nap"
FOR i = 1 TO 50000: NEXT
PRINT "Now I woke up"
```

The FOR line makes the computer count up to 50000. Since the computer doesn't print anything while counting, the FOR line acts as a pause.

How long will the pause last? If your computer is very fast (a Pentium), the pause will last just a few seconds; if your computer is very slow (an 8088), counting to 50000 will take longer, and the pause will last *many* seconds.

How long will *your* computer pause? Experiment!

If you want the computer to pause for 3 seconds, raise or lower the number 50000 until the pause takes 3 seconds. If you someday buy a faster computer, to keep the 3-second pause you must raise the number in the FOR line.

Stripping

Sometimes the computer prints *too* much info: you wish the computer would print less, to save yourself the agony of reading excess info irrelevant to your needs. Whenever the computer prints too much info about a numerical answer, use ABS, FIX, INT, CINT, or SGN.

ABS removes any minus sign. For example, the ABS of -3.89 is 3.89. So if you say PRINT ABS(-3.89), the computer will print just 3.89.

FIX removes any digits after the decimal point. For example, the FIX of 3.89 is 3. So if you say PRINT FIX(3.89), the computer will print just 3. The FIX of -3.89 is -3.

CINT rounds to the NEAREST integer. For example, the CINT of 3.89 is 4; the CINT of -3.89 is -4.

INT rounds the number DOWN to an integer that's LOWER. For example, the INT of 3.89 is 3 (because 3 is an integer that's lower than 3.89); the INT of -3.89 is -4 (because -4 is lower than -3.89).

SGN removes ALL the digits and replaces them by a 1 — unless the number is 0. For example, the SGN of 3.89 is 1. The SGN of -3.89 is -1. The SGN of 0 is just 0.

ABS, FIX, CINT, INT, and SGN are all called **stripping functions** or **strippers** or **diet functions** or **diet pills**, because they strip away the number's excess fat and reveal just the fundamentals that interest you.

Here are more details about those five functions….

ABS

To find the **absolute value** of a negative number, just omit the number's minus sign. For example, the absolute value of -7 is 7.

The absolute value of a positive number is the number itself. For example, the absolute value of 7 is 7. The absolute value of 0 is 0.

To make the computer find the absolute value of -7, type this:

```
PRINT ABS(-7)
```

The computer will print:

```
7
```

Like SQR, ABS is a function: you must put parentheses after the ABS.

Distance Since ABS omits the minus sign, ABS turns negative numbers into positive numbers. Use ABS whenever you insist that an answer be positive.

For example, ABS helps solve math & physics problems about "distance", since the "distance" between two points is always a positive number and cannot be negative.

This program computes the distance between two numbers:

```
CLS
PRINT "I will find the distance between two numbers."
INPUT "What's the first number"; x
INPUT "What's the second number"; y
PRINT "The distance between those numbers is"; ABS(x - y)
```

When you run that program, suppose you say that the first number is 4 and the second number is 7. Since x is 4, and y is 7, the distance between those two numbers is ABS(4 - 7), which is ABS(-3), which is 3.

If you reverse those two numbers, so that x is 7 and y is 4, the distance between them is ABS(7 - 4), which is ABS(3), which is still 3.

FIX

An **integer** is a number that has no decimal point. For example, these are integers: 17, 238, 0, and -956.

If a number contains a decimal point, you can turn the number into an integer in several ways.

The simplest is to delete all the digits after the decimal point. That's called the **FIX** of the number.

For example, the FIX of 3.89 is 3. So if you say PRINT FIX (3.89), the computer will print just 3.

The FIX of -3.89 is -3. The FIX of 7 is 7. The FIX of 0 is 0.

CINT

A more sophisticated way to turn a number into an integer is to *round* the number to the *nearest* integer. That's called **CINT** (which means "Convert to INTeger"). For example, the CINT of 3.9 is 4 (because 3.9 is closer to 4 than to 3).

Like FIX, CINT deletes all the digits after the decimal point; but if the digit just after the decimal point is 5, 6, 7, 8, or 9, CINT "rounds up" by adding 1 to the digit before the decimal point.

Here are more examples:

CINT(3.9) is 4	CINT(-3.9) is -4
CINT(3.1) is 3	CINT(-3.1) is -3
CINT(3.5) is 4	CINT(-3.5) is -4

Highest number The highest number CINT can produce is 32767. If you try to go higher than 32767 or lower than -32768, the computer will gripe by saying "Overflow".

Exploratory program To explore the mysteries of rounding, run this program:

```
CLS
INPUT "What's your favorite number"; x
PRINT CINT(x)
```

In that program, the INPUT line asks you to type a number x. The bottom line prints your number, but rounded to the nearest integer. For example, if you type 3.9, the bottom line prints 4.

INT

Like FIX and CINT, **INT** turns a number into an integer. Though INT is slightly harder to understand than FIX and CINT, INT is more useful!

INT rounds a number *down* to an integer that's *lower*. For example, the INT of 3.9 is 3 (because 3 is an integer that's lower than 3.9). The INT of -3.9 is -4 (because a temperature of -4 is lower and colder than a temperature of -3.9). The INT of 7 is simply 7.

Exploratory program
To explore further the mysteries of rounding, run this program:

```
CLS
INPUT "What's your favorite number"; x
PRINT "Your number rounded down is"; INT(x)
PRINT "Your number rounded up is"; -INT(-x)
PRINT "Your number rounded to the nearest integer is"; INT(x + .5)
```

In that program, the INPUT line asks you to type a number x.

The next line prints your number rounded *down*. For example, if you input 3.9, the computer prints 3.

The next line, PRINT -INT(-x), prints your number rounded *up*. For example if you input 3.9, the computer prints 4.

The bottom line prints your number rounded to the *nearest* integer. For example, if you input 3.9, the computer will print 4.

Here's the rule: if x is a number, **INT(x) rounds x down; -INT(-x) rounds x up; INT(x + .5) rounds x to the nearest integer**.

Why INT is better than CINT and FIX
To round x to the nearest integer, you can say either CINT(x) or INT(x + .5). Alas, CINT(x) handles just numbers from -32768 to 32767. But INT(x + .5) can handle *any* number!

Another advantage of INT is that it works in *all* versions of BASIC. Even the oldest, most primitive versions of BASIC understand INT. Alas, CINT and FIX work in just a *few* versions of BASIC, such as QBASIC. To make sure your programs work on *many* computers, use INT rather than CINT or FIX.

In the rest of this book, I'll emphasize INT.

Supermarket math
Rounding down and rounding up are useful in the supermarket....

Suppose some items are marked "30¢ each", and you have just two dollars. How many can you buy? Two dollars divided by 30¢ is 6.66667; rounding *down* to an integer, you can buy 6.

Suppose some items are marked "3 for a dollar", and you want to buy just one of them. How much will the supermarket charge you? One dollar divided by 3 is 33.3333¢; rounding *up* to an integer, you will be charged 34¢.

Fancier rounding
By using INT, you can do fancier kinds of rounding:

to round x to the nearest thousand,	ask for INT(x / 1000 + .5) * 1000
to round x to the nearest thousandth,	ask for INT(x / .001 + .5) * .001

This program rounds a number, so that it will have just a *few* digits after the decimal point:

```
CLS
INPUT "What's your favorite number"; x
INPUT "How many digits would you like after its decimal point"; d
b = 10 ^ -d
PRINT "Your number rounded is"; INT(x / b + .5) * b
```

Here's a sample run:

```
What's your favorite number? 4.28631
How many digits would you like after its decimal point? 2
Your number rounded is 4.29
```

SGN

If a number is negative, its **sign** is -1. For example, the sign of -546 is -1.

If a number is positive, its **sign** is +1. For example the sign of 8231 is +1.

The **sign** of 0 is 0.

The computer's abbreviation for "sign" is "SGN". So if you say —

```
PRINT SGN(-546)
```

the computer will print the sign of -546; it will print -1.

If you say —

```
PRINT SGN(8231)
```

the computer will print the sign of 8231; it will print 1.

If you say —

```
PRINT SGN(0)
```

the computer will print the sign of 0; it will print 0.

SGN is the opposite of ABS. Let's see what both functions do to -7.2. ABS removes the minus sign, but leaves the digits:

```
ABS(-7.2) is 7.2
```

SGN removes the digits, but leaves the minus sign:

```
SGN(-7.2) is -1
```

The Latin word for *sign* is **signum**. Most mathematicians prefer to talk in Latin — they say "signum" instead of "sign" — because the English word "sign" sounds too much like the trigonometry word "sine". So mathematicians call SGN the **signum function**.

Random numbers

Usually, the computer is predictable: it does exactly what you say. But sometimes, you want the computer to be *un*predictable.

For example, if you're going to play a game of cards with the computer and tell the computer to deal, you want the cards dealt to be unpredictable. If the cards were predictable — if you could figure out exactly which cards you and the computer would be dealt — the game would be boring.

In many other games too, you want the computer to be unpredictable, to "surprise" you. Without an element of surprise, the game would be boring.

Being unpredictable increases the pleasure you derive from games — and from art. To make the computer act artistic, and create a new *original* masterpiece that's a "work of art", you need a way to make the computer get a "flash of inspiration". Flashes of inspiration aren't predictable: they're surprises.

Here's how to make the computer act unpredictably….

RND is a RaNDom decimal, bigger than 0 and less than 1. For example, it might be .6273649 or .9241587 or .2632801. Every time your program mentions RND, the computer concocts another decimal:

```
CLS
PRINT RND
PRINT RND
PRINT RND
```

The computer prints:

```
.7055475
.533424
.5795186
```

The first time your program mentions RND, the computer chooses its favorite decimal, which is .7055475. Each succeeding time your program mentions RND, the computer sues the previous decimal to concoct a new one. It uses .7055475 to concoct .533424, which it uses to concoct .5795186. The process by which the computer concocts each new decimal from the previous one is weird enough so we humans cannot detect any pattern.

This program prints lots of decimals — and pauses a second after each decimal, so you have a chance to read it:

```
CLS
DO
  PRINT RND
  SLEEP 1
LOOP
```

About half the decimals will be less than .5, and about half will be more than .5.

Most of the decimals will be less than .9. In fact, about 90% will be.

About 36% of the decimals will be less than .36; 59% will be less than .59; 99% will be less than .99; 2% will be less than .02; a quarter of them will be less than .25; etc. You might see some decimal twice, though most of the decimals will be different from each other. When you get tired of running that program and seeing decimals, abort the program (by pressing Ctrl with PAUSE/BREAK).

If you run that program again, you'll get exactly the same list of decimals again, in the same order.

RANDOMIZE TIMER

If you'd rather see a different list of decimals, say **RANDOMIZE TIMER** at the beginning of the program:

```
CLS
RANDOMIZE TIMER
DO
  PRINT RND
  SLEEP 1
LOOP
```

When the computer sees RANDOMIZE TIMER, the computer looks at the clock and manipulates the time's digits to produce the first value of RND.

So the first value of RND will be a number that depends on the time of day, instead of the usual .7055475. Since the first value of RND will be different than usual, so will the second, and so will the rest of the list.

Every time you run the program, the clock will be different, so the first value of RND will be different, so the whole list will be different — unless you run the program at exactly the same time the next day, when the clock is the same. But since the clock is accurate to a tiny fraction of a second, the chance of hitting the same time is extremely unlikely.

Love or hate?

Who loves ya, baby? This program tries to answer that question:

```
CLS
RANDOMIZE TIMER
DO
  INPUT "Type the name of someone you love..."; name$
  IF RND < .67 THEN
    PRINT name$; " loves you, too"
  ELSE
    PRINT name$; " hates your guts"
  END IF
LOOP
```

The RANDOMIZE TIMER line makes the value of RND depend on the clock. The INPUT line makes the computer wait for the human to type a name. Suppose he types Suzy. Then name$ is "Suzy". The IF line says there's a 67% chance that the computer will print "Suzy loves you, too!", but there's a 33% chance the computer will instead print "Suzy hates your guts". The words DO and LOOP make the computer do the routine again and again, until the human aborts the program. The run might look like this:

```
Type the name of someone you love...? Suzy
Suzy loves you, too
Type the name of someone you love...? Joan
Joan hates your guts
Type the name of someone you love...? Alice
Alice loves you, too
Type the name of someone you love...? Fred
Fred loves you, too
Type the name of someone you love...? Uncle Charlie
Uncle Charlie hates your guts
```

Coin flipping

This program makes the computer flip a coin:

```
CLS
RANDOMIZE TIMER
IF RND < .5 THEN PRINT "heads" ELSE PRINT "tails"
```

The IF line says there's a 50% chance that the computer will print "heads"; if the computer does *not* print "heads", it will print "tails".

Until you run the program, you won't know which way the coin will flip; the choice is random. Each time you run the program, the computer will flip the coin again; each time, the outcome is unpredictable.

Bets Let's permit the human to bet on whether the computer will say "heads" or "tails". Here's how:

```
CLS
RANDOMIZE TIMER
10 INPUT "Do you want to bet on heads or tails"; bet$
IF bet$ <> "heads" AND bet$ <> "tails" THEN
  PRINT "Please say heads or tails"
  GOTO 10
END IF
IF RND < .5 THEN coin$ = "heads" ELSE coin$ = "tails"
PRINT "The coin says "; coin$
IF coin$ = bet$ THEN PRINT "You win" ELSE PRINT "You lose"
```

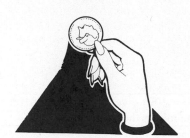

The line numbered 10 makes the computer ask:

```
Do you want to bet on heads or tails?
```

The next line makes sure the human says "heads" or "tails": if the human's answer isn't "heads" and isn't "tails", the computer gripes. The bottom three lines make the computer flip a coin and determine whether the human won or lost the bet.

Here's a sample run:

```
Do you want to bet on heads or tails? heads
The coin says tails
You lose
```

Here's another:

```
Do you want to bet on heads or tails? tails
The coin says tails
You win
```

Here's another:

```
Do you want to bet on heads or tails? tails
The coin says heads
You lose
```

Money To make the program more fun, let the human use money when betting:

```
CLS
RANDOMIZE TIMER
bankroll = 100
4 PRINT "You have"; bankroll; "dollars"
5 INPUT "How many dollars do you want to bet"; stake
IF stake > bankroll THEN PRINT "You don't have that much!  Bet less!": GOTO 5
IF stake < 0 THEN PRINT "You can't bet less than nothing!": GOTO 5
IF stake = 0 THEN PRINT "I guess you don't want to bet anymore": GOTO 20
10 INPUT "Do you want to bet on heads or tails"; bet$
IF bet$ <> "heads" AND bet$ <> "tails" THEN
  PRINT "Please say heads or tails"
  GOTO 10
END IF
IF RND < .5 THEN coin$ = "heads" ELSE coin$ = "tails"
PRINT "The coin says "; coin$
IF coin$ = bet$ THEN
  PRINT "You win"; stake; "dollars"
  bankroll = bankroll + stake
  GOTO 4
END IF
PRINT "You lose"; stake; "dollars"
bankroll = bankroll - stake
IF bankroll > 0 THEN GOTO 4
PRINT "You're broke!  Too bad!"
20 PRINT "Thanks for playing with me!  You were fun to play with!"
PRINT "I hope you play again sometime!"
```

Line 3 (bankroll = 100) gives the human a $100 *bankroll*, so the human starts with $100. The next line makes the computer say:

```
You have 100 dollars
```

The line numbered 5 makes the computer ask:

```
How many dollars do you want to bet?
```

The number that the human inputs (the number of dollars that the human bets) is called the human's *stake*. The next three lines (which say "IF stake") make sure the stake is reasonable.

The line numbered 10 gets the human to bet on heads or tails. The next few lines flip the coin, determine whether the human won or lost the bet, and then send the computer back to line 4 for another round (if the human isn't broke yet). The bottom three lines say good-bye to the human.

Here's a sample run:

```
You have 100 dollars
How many dollars do you want to bet? 120
You don't have that much!  Bet less!
How many dollars do you want to bet? 75
Do you want to bet on heads or tails? heads
The coin says tails
You lose 75 dollars
You have 25 dollars
How many dollars do you want to bet? 10
Do you want to bet on heads or tails? tails
The coin says tails
You win 10 dollars
You have 35 dollars
How many dollars do you want to bet? 35
Do you want to bet on heads or tails? tails
The coin says heads
You lose 35 dollars
You're broke!  Too bad!
Thanks for playing with me!  You were fun to play with!
I hope you play again sometime!
```

Display all the dollars To make the output prettier, replace line 4 by this group of lines:

```
4 PRINT
PRINT "You have"; bankroll; "dollars!  Here they are:"
FOR i = 1 TO bankroll
  PRINT "$";
NEXT
PRINT
```

Now the run looks like this:

```
You have 100 dollars!  Here they are:
$$$$$$$$$$$$$$$$$$$$$$$$$$$$$$$$$$$$$$$$$$$$$$$$$$$$$$$$$$$$$$$$$$$$$$$$$$$$$$$$$
$$$$$$$$$$$$$$$$$$$$$$$$
How many dollars do you want to bet? 120
You don't have that much!  Bet less!
How many dollars do you want to bet? 75
Do you want to bet on heads or tails? heads
The coin says tails
You lose 75 dollars

You have 25 dollars!  Here they are:
$$$$$$$$$$$$$$$$$$$$$$$$$
How many dollars do you want to bet? 10
Do you want to bet on heads or tails? tails
The coin says tails
You win 10 dollars

You have 35 dollars!  Here they are:
$$$$$$$$$$$$$$$$$$$$$$$$$$$$$$$$$$$$$
How many dollars do you want to bet? 35
Do you want to bet on heads or tails? tails
The coin says heads
You lose 35 dollars
You're broke!  Too bad!
Thanks for playing with me!  You were fun to play with!
I hope you play again sometime!
```

Random integers

If you want a random integer from 1 to 100, ask for $1 + INT(RND * 100)$. Here's why:

```
RND is a decimal, bigger than 0 and less than 1.
So RND * 10 is a decimal, bigger than 0 and less than 10.
So INT(RND * 10) is an integer, at least 0 and no more than 9.
So 1 + INT(RND * 10) is an integer, at least 1 and no more than 10.
```

This program plays a guessing game:

```
CLS
RANDOMIZE TIMER
PRINT "I'm thinking of a number from 1 to 10."
computer.number = 1 + INT(RND * 10)
10 INPUT "What do you think my number is"; guess
IF guess < computer.number THEN PRINT "Your guess is too low.": GOTO 10
IF guess > computer.number THEN PRINT "Your guess is too high.": GOTO 10
PRINT "Congratulations!  You found my number!"
```

Line 3 makes the computer say:

```
I'm thinking of a number from 1 to 10.
```

The next line makes the computer think of a random number from 1 to 10; the computer's number is called "computer.number". The INPUT line asks the human to guess the number.

If the guess is less than the computer's number, the first IF line makes the computer say "Your guess is too low" and then GOTO 10, which lets the human guess again. If the guess is *greater* than the computer's number, the bottom IF line makes the computer say "Your guess is too high" and then GOTO 10.

When the human guesses correctly, the computer arrives at the bottom line, which prints:

```
Congratulations!  You found my number!
```

Here's a sample run:

```
I'm thinking of a number from 1 TO 10.
What do you think my number is? 3
Your guess is too low.
What do you think my number is? 8
Your guess is too high.
What do you think my number is? 5
Your guess is too low.
What do you think my number is? 6
Congratulations!  You found my number!
```

Dice

This program makes the computer roll a pair of dice:

```
CLS
RANDOMIZE TIMER
PRINT "I'm rolling a pair of dice"
a = 1 + INT(RND * 6)
PRINT "One of the dice says"; a
b = 1 + INT(RND * 6)
PRINT "The other says"; b
PRINT "The total is"; a + b
```

Line 3 makes the computer say:

```
I'm rolling a pair of dice
```

Each of the dice has 6 sides. The next line, $a = 1 + INT(RND * 6)$, rolls one of the dice, by picking a number from 1 to 6. The line saying "$b = 1 + INT(RND * 6)$" rolls the other. The bottom line prints the total.

Here's a sample run:

```
I'm rolling a pair of dice
One of the dice says 3
The other says 5
The total is 8
```

Here's another run:

```
I'm rolling a pair of dice
One of the dice says 6
The other says 4
The total is 10
```

Daily horoscope

This program predicts what will happen to you today:

```
CLS
RANDOMIZE TIMER
PRINT "You will have a ";
SELECT CASE 1 + INT(RND * 5)
  CASE 1
    PRINT "wonderful";
  CASE 2
    PRINT "fairly good";
  CASE 3
    PRINT "so-so";
  CASE 4
    PRINT "fairly bad";
  CASE 5
    PRINT "terrible";
END SELECT
PRINT " day today!"
```

The computer will say —

```
You will have a wonderful day today!
```

or —

```
You will have a terrible day today!
```

or some in-between comment. That's because the SELECT CASE line makes the computer pick a random integer from 1 to 5.

For inspiration, run that program when you get up in the morning. Then notice whether your day turns out the way the computer predicts!

Character codes

You can use these code numbers:

1 ☺	33 !	64 @	96 `	128 Ç	160 á	192 └	224 α
2 ●	34 "	65 A	97 a	129 ü	161 í	193 ┴	225 ß
3 ♥	35 #	66 B	98 b	130 é	162 ó	194 ┬	226 Γ
4 ♦	36 $	67 C	99 c	131 â	163 ú	195 ├	227 π
5 ♣	37 %	68 D	100 d	132 ä	164 ñ	196 ─	228 Σ
6 ♠	38 &	69 E	101 e	133 à	165 Ñ	197 ┼	229 σ
	39 '	70 F	102 f	134 å	166 ª	198 ╞	230 µ
8 ◘	40 (	71 G	103 g	135 ç	167 º	199 ╟	231 τ
	41)	72 H	104 h	136 ê	168 ¿	200 ╚	232 Φ
	42 *	73 I	105 i	137 ë	169 ⌐	201 ╔	233 Θ
	43 +	74 J	106 j	138 è	170 ¬	202 ╩	234 Ω
	44 ,	75 K	107 k	139 ï	171 ½	203 ╦	235 δ
	45 -	76 L	108 l	140 î	172 ¼	204 ╠	236 ∞
14 ♪	46 .	77 M	109 m	141 ì	173 ¡	205 ═	237 φ
15 ☼	47 /	78 N	110 n	142 Ä	174 «	206 ╬	238 ε
16 ►	48 0	79 O	111 o	143 Å	175 »	207 ╧	239 ∩
17 ◄	49 1	80 P	112 p	144 É	176 ░	208 ╨	240 ≡
18 ↕	50 2	81 Q	113 q	145 æ	177 ▒	209 ╤	241 ±
19 ‼	51 3	82 R	114 r	146 Æ	178 ▓	210 ╥	242 ≥
20 ¶	52 4	83 S	115 s	147 ô	179 │	211 ╙	243 ≤
21 §	53 5	84 T	116 t	148 ö	180 ┤	212 ╘	244 ⌠
22 ▬	54 6	85 U	117 u	149 ò	181 ╡	213 ╒	245 ⌡
23 ↨	55 7	86 V	118 v	150 û	182 ╢	214 ╓	246 ÷
24 ↑	56 8	87 W	119 w	151 ù	183 ╖	215 ╫	247 ≈
25 ↓	57 9	88 X	120 x	152 ÿ	184 ╕	216 ╪	248 °
26 →	58 :	89 Y	121 y	153 Ö	185 ╣	217 ┘	249 ·
27 ←	59 ;	90 Z	122 z	154 Ü	186 ║	218 ┌	250 ·
	60 <	91 [	123 {	155 ¢	187 ╗	219 █	251 √
	61 =	92 \	124		156 £	188 ╝	220 ▄	252 ⁿ
	62 >	93]	125 }	157 ¥	189 ╜	221 ▌	253 ²
	63 ?	94 ^	126 ~	158 ₧	190 ╛	222 ▐	254 ■
		95 _	127 ⌂	159 ƒ	191 ┐	223 ▀	

Alt key

Here's how to type the symbol ñ, whose code number is 164. Hold down the Alt key; and while you keep holding down the Alt key, type 164 *by using the numeric keypad* (the number keys on the far right side of the keyboard). When you finish typing 164, lift your finger from the Alt key, and you'll see ñ on your screen!

The Alt key works reliably for most numbers in that chart but *not* for numbers 1-27 and 127.

You can use the Alt key in your program. For example, try typing this program:

```
CLS
PRINT "In Spanish, tomorrow is mañana"
```

While typing that program, make the symbol ñ by typing 164 on the numeric keypad while holding down the Alt key. When you run that program, the computer will print:

```
In Spanish, tomorrow is mañana
```

CHR$

Here's another way to type the symbol ñ:

```
CLS
PRINT CHR$(164)
```

When you run that program, the computer will print the CHaRacter whose code number is 164. The computer will print:

```
ñ
```

This program makes the computer print "In Spanish, tomorrow is mañana":

```
CLS
PRINT "In Spanish, tomorrow is ma"; CHR$(164); "ana"
```

That PRINT line makes the computer print "In Spanish, tomorrow is ma", then print character 164 (which is ñ), then print "ana".

Quotation marks Since character 34 is a quotation mark, this program prints a quotation mark:

```
CLS
PRINT CHR$(34)
```

Suppose you want the computer to print:

```
Scholars think "Hamlet" is a great play.
```

To make the computer print the quotation marks around "Hamlet", use CHR$(34), like this:

```
CLS
PRINT "Scholars think "; CHR$(34); "Hamlet"; CHR$(34); " is a great play."
```

The entire chart CHR$ works reliably for all numbers in that chart. This program prints, on your screen, all the symbols in the chart:

```
CLS
FOR i = 1 TO 6: PRINT CHR$(i);: NEXT
PRINT CHR$(8);
FOR i = 14 TO 27: PRINT CHR$(i);: NEXT
FOR i = 33 TO 254: PRINT CHR$(i);: NEXT
```

Missing codes That chart shows *most* code numbers from 1 to 254 but skips the following mysterious code numbers: 7, 9-13, and 28-32. Here's what those mysterious code numbers do....

In a PRINT statement, CHR$(7) makes the computer beep. Saying —

```
PRINT CHR$(7);
```

has the same effect as saying:

```
BEEP
```

If you say —

```
PRINT "hot"; CHR$(7); "dog"
```

the computer will print "hot", then beep, then turn the "hot" into "hotdog".

CHR$(9) makes the computer press the TAB key, so your writing is indented. For example, if you say —

```
PRINT "hot"; CHR$(9); "dog"
```

the computer will print "hot", then indent by pressing the TAB key, then print "dog", so you see this:

```
hot     dog
```

CHR$(31) makes the computer move the cursor (the blinking underline) down to the line below. For example, if you say —

```
PRINT "hot"; CHR$(31); "dog"
```

the computer will print "hot", then move down, then print "dog" on the line below, so you see this:

```
hot
   dog
```

You can move the cursor in all four directions:

```
CHR$(28) moves the cursor toward the right
CHR$(29) moves the cursor toward the left
CHR$(30) moves the cursor up
CHR$(31) moves the cursor down
```

CHR$(11) moves the cursor all the way to the screen's top left corner, which is called the **home position**.

CHR$(32) is a blank space. It's the same as " ".

CHR$(12) erases the entire screen. Saying —

```
PRINT CHR$(12);
```

has the same effect as saying:

```
CLS
```

CHR$(10) and CHR$(13) each make the computer press the ENTER key.

Printing on paper

When printing onto paper, make your program's bottom line say:

```
LPRINT CHR$(12);
```

That makes the printer eject the paper.

Codes 33-126 print on paper okay. As on the screen, code 32 prints a blank space. Other codes print okay on some printers but wrong on other printers. Experiment, and see which codes *your* printer can print correctly.

If you want to print codes 128-254 on a typical laser printer (such as a Hewlett-Packard Laserjet 2), put this line at the top of your program (just under the CLS):

```
LPRINT CHR$(27); "(10U";
```

Type that line carefully. In the quotation marks, make sure you type just a single parenthesis, then the number 10, then a capital U.

A typical dot-matrix printer (such as an Epson LQ-570) normally prints 10 characters per inch. To make the characters thinner, so you get 17 characters per inch, say:

```
LPRINT CHR$(15);
```

To cancel that 17-characters-per-inch command, say:

```
LPRINT CHR$(18);
```

To make the characters wider, so you get 5 characters per inch, say:

```
LPRINT CHR$(14);
```

To cancel that command, say:

```
LPRINT CHR$(20);
```

ASC

The code numbers from 32 to 126 are for characters that you can type on the keyboard easily. Established by a national committee, those code numbers are called the **American Standard Code for Information Interchange**, which is abbreviated **ASCII**, which is pronounced "ass key".

Programmers say, "the ASCII code number for A is 65". If you say —

```
PRINT ASC("A")
```

the computer will print the ASCII code number for "A". It will print:

```
65
```

If you say PRINT ASC("B"), the computer will print 66. If you say PRINT ASC("b"), the computer will print 97.

If you say PRINT ASC("ñ"), the computer will print 164 (which is the code number for ñ), even though ñ isn't an ASCII character.

String analysis

Let's analyze the word "smart".

Length

Since "smart" has 5 characters in it, the **length** of "smart" is 5. If you say —

```
PRINT LEN("smart")
```

the computer will print the LENgth of "smart"; it will print:

```
5
```

Left, right, middle

The left two characters of "smart" are "sm". If you say —

```
PRINT LEFT$("smart", 2)
```

the computer will print:

```
sm
```

Try this program:

```
CLS
a$ = "smart"
PRINT LEFT$(a$, 2)
```

Line 2 says a$ is "smart". The bottom line says to print the left 2 characters of a$, which are "sm". The computer will print:

```
sm
```

If a$ is "smart", here are the consequences....

```
LEN(a$) is the LENgth of a$. It is 5.
LEFT$(a$, 2) is the LEFT 2 characters of a$. It is "sm".
RIGHT$(a$, 2) is the RIGHT 2 characters of a$. It is "rt".
MID$(a$, 2) begins in the MIDdle of a$, at the 2nd character. It's "mart".
MID$(a$, 2, 3) begins at 2nd character and includes 3 characters. It's "mar".
```

Changing the middle
You can change the middle of a string, like this:

```
CLS
a$ = "bunkers"
MID$(a$, 2) = "owl"
PRINT a$
```

Line 2 says a$ is "bunkers". The MID$ line changes the middle of a$ to "owl"; the change begins at the 2nd character of a$. The bottom line prints:

```
bowlers
```

Here's a variation:

```
CLS
a$ = "bunkers"
MID$(a$, 2) = "ad agency"
PRINT a$
```

Line 2 says a$ is "bunkers". The MID$ line says to change the middle of a$, beginning at the 2nd character of a$. But "ad agency" is too long to become part of "bunkers". The computer uses as much of "ad agency" as will fit in "bunkers". The computer will print:

```
bad age
```

Another variation:

```
CLS
a$ = "bunkers"
MID$(a$, 2, 1) = "owl"
PRINT a$
```

Line 2 says a$ is "bunkers". The MID$ line says to change the middle of a$, beginning at the 2nd character of a$. But the ",1" makes the computer use just 1 letter from "owl". The bottom line prints:

```
bonkers
```

Capitals

Capital letters (such as X, Y, and Z) are called **upper-case letters**. Small letters (such as x, y, and z) are called **lower-case letters**.

If you say —

```
PRINT UCASE$("We love America")
```

the computer will print an upper-case (capitalized) version of "We love America"), like this:

```
WE LOVE AMERICA
```

If you say —

```
PRINT LCASE$("We love America")
```

the computer will print a lower-case version of "We love America", like this:

```
we love america
```

Accents
Unfortunately, the computer doesn't know how to capitalize an accented letter (such as ñ).

For example, suppose you say:

```
PRINT UCASE$("mañana")
```

Since the computer doesn't know how to capitalize the ¤, the computer prints:

```
MAñANA
```

If you say PRINT LCASE$("MAÑANA"), the computer doesn't know how to uncapitalize Ñ, so the computer prints:

```
maÑana
```

Africa
This program measures geographical emotions:

```
CLS
INPUT "What's the most exciting continent"; a$
IF a$ = "Africa" THEN
  PRINT "Yes, it's the dark continent!"
ELSE
  PRINT "I disagree!"
END IF
```

Line 2 asks:

```
What's the most exciting continent?
```

Line 3 checks whether the person's answer is "Africa". If the person's answer is "Africa", the computer prints "Yes, it's the dark continent!"; otherwise, the computer prints "I disagree!"

But instead of typing "Africa", what if the person types "africa" or "AFRICA"? We still ought to make the computer print "Yes, it's the dark continent!" Here's how:

```
CLS
INPUT "What's the most exciting continent"; a$
IF UCASE$(a$) = "AFRICA" THEN
  PRINT "Yes, it's the dark continent!"
ELSE
  PRINT "I disagree!"
END IF
```

The new version of the IF statement says: if the person's answer, after being capitalized, becomes "AFRICA", then print "Yes, it's the dark continent!" So the computer will print "Yes, it's the dark continent!" even if the person types "Africa" or "africa" or "AFRICA" or "AfRiCa".

Yes/no questions
Suppose you ask the person a yes-no question. If the person means "yes", the person might type "yes" or "Yes" or "YES" or "YES!" or just "y" or just "Y". So instead of saying —

```
IF a$ = "yes"
```

say this:

```
IF UCASE$(LEFT$(a$, 1)) = "Y"
```

That tests whether the first letter of the person's answer, after being capitalized, is "Y".

Trim

Some folks accidentally press the SPACE bar at the beginning or end of a string. For example, instead of typing "Sue", the person might type " Sue" or "Sue ".

You want to get rid of those accidental spaces. Getting rid of them is called **trimming** the string.

The function **LTRIM$** will left-trim the string: it will delete any spaces at the string's beginning (left edge). For example, if a$ is " Sue Smith", LTRIM$(a$) is "Sue Smith".

**RTRIM$** will right-trim the string: it will delete any spaces at the string's end (right edge). If a$ is "Sue Smith ", RTRIM$(a$) is "Sue Smith".

To trim *both* edges of a$ and make the trimmed result be the new a$, say this:

```
a$ = LTRIM$(RTRIM$(a$))
```

Spaces at the string's beginning (which are deleted by LTRIM$) are called **leading spaces**. Spaces at the string's end (which are deleted by RTRIM$) are called **trailing spaces**.

Adding strings

You can add strings together, to form a longer string:

```
CLS
a$ = "fat" + "her"
PRINT a$
```

Line 2 says a$ is "father". The bottom line makes the computer print:

```
father
```

Searching in a string

You can make the computer search in a string to find another string. To make the computer search IN the STRing "needed" to find "ed", say:

```
PRINT INSTR("needed", "ed")
```

Since "ed" begins at the third character of "needed", the computer will print:

```
3
```

If you say —

```
PRINT INSTR("needed", "ey")
```

the computer will search in the string "needed" for "ey". Since "ey" is *not* in "needed", the computer will print:

```
0
```

If you say —

```
PRINT INSTR(4, "needed", "ed")
```

the computer will hunt in the string "needed" for "ed"; but the hunt will begin at the 4th character of "needed". The computer finds the "ed" that begins at the 5th character of "needed". The computer will print:

```
5
```

String-number conversion

This program converts a string to a number:

```
CLS
a$ = "52.6"
b = VAL(a$)
PRINT b + 1
```

Line 2 says a$ is the string "52.6". The next line says b is the numeric VALue of a$, so b is the number 52.6. The bottom line prints:

```
53.6
```

VAL converts a string to a number. The opposite of VAL is STR$, which converts a number to a string. For example, STR$(-7.2) is the string "-7.2". STR$(81.4) is the string " 81.4", in which the 8 is preceded by a space instead of a minus sign.

Repeating characters

Suppose you love the letter b (because it stands for big, bold, and beautiful) and want to print "bbbbbbbbbbbbbbbbbbbb". Here's a short-cut:

```
PRINT STRING$(20, "b")
```

That tells the computer to print a string of 20 b's.

Here's a different way to accomplish the same goal:

```
PRINT STRING$(20, 98)
```

That tells the computer to print, 20 times, the character whose ASCII code number is 98.

STRING$ can make the computer repeat a single character, but not a whole word. So if you say STRING$(20, "blow"), the computer will *not* repeat the word "blow"; instead, the computer will repeat just the first character of "blow" (which is "b").

Dashed line Let's make the computer draw a dashed line containing 50 dashes, like this:

```
--------------------------------------------------
```

Here's how: just say PRINT STRING$(50, "-").

Triangle Let's make the computer print this triangle:

```
*
**
***
****
*****
******
*******
********
*********
**********
***********
************
*************
**************
***************
****************
*****************
******************
*******************
********************
```

To do that, we want the computer to print 1 asterisk on the first line, then 2 asterisks on the next line, then 3 asterisks on the next line, and so on, until it finally prints 20 asterisks on the bottom line.

Here's the program:

```
CLS
FOR i = 1 TO 20
  PRINT STRING$(i, "*")
NEXT
```

The FOR line makes i be 1, then 2, then 3, and so on, up to 20. When i is 1, the PRINT line makes the computer print one asterisk, like this:

```
*
```

When i is 2, the PRINT line makes the computer print a line of 2 asterisks, like this:

```
**
```

The FOR line makes i be every number from 1 up to 20, so computer will print 1 asterisk, then underneath print a line of 2 asterisks, then underneath print a line of 3 asterisks, and so on, until the entire triangle is printed.

Trigonometry

The study of triangles is called **trigonometry** — and the computer can do it for you!

For example, look at this triangle:

In that triangle, the left angle is 30°, the bottom-right angle is 90°, and the longest side (the hypotenuse) is 1 inch long.

The side opposite the 30° angle is called the **sine** of 30°; the remaining side is called the **cosine** of 30°:

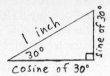

How long is the sine of 30°? How long is the cosine of 30°?

Since the longest side (the hypotenuse) is 1 inch long, and since the sine and the cosine are shorter sides, the sine and the cosine must each be shorter than 1 inch. So the lengths of the sine and cosine are each less than 1. But which decimals are they?

To find out, you can use a ruler. You'll discover that the sine is half an inch long, and the cosine is nearly seven-eighths of an inch long. But a faster and more accurate way to measure the sine and cosine is to let the computer do it! Yes, the computer can calculate triangles in its mind!

This program makes the computer measure the sine and cosine of 30°:

```
CLS
degrees = ATN(1) / 45
PRINT SIN(30 * degrees)
PRINT COS(30 * degrees)
```

Line 2 is a special formula that defines the word *degrees*. The first PRINT line prints the sine of 30 degrees:

```
.5
```

The bottom line prints the cosine of 30°, which is a decimal that's slightly less than .87.

The computer can measure the sine and cosine of *any* size angle. Try it! For example, to make the computer print the sine and cosine of a 33° angle, say:

```
CLS
degrees = ATN(1) / 45
PRINT SIN(33 * degrees)
PRINT COS(33 * degrees)
```

If you choose an angle of -33° instead of 33°, the triangle will dip down instead of rising up, and so the sine will be a negative number instead of positive.

In those PRINT lines, the "* degrees" is important: it tells the computer that you want the sine of 33 **degrees**. If you accidentally omit the "* degrees", the computer will print the sine of 33 **radians** instead. (A radian is larger than a degree. A radian is about 57.3 degrees. More precisely, a radian is 180/π degrees.)

Tangent

The sine divided by the cosine is called the **tangent**. For example, to find the tangent of 33°, divide the sine of 33° by the cosine of 33°.

To make the computer print the tangent of 33°, you could tell the computer to PRINT SIN(33 * degrees) / COS(33 * degrees). But to find the tangent more quickly and easily, just say PRINT TAN(33 * degrees).

Arc functions

The opposite of the tangent is called the **arctangent**:

the tangent   of 30° is about .58
the arctangent of .58 is about 30°

Similarly, the opposite of the sine is called the **arcsine**, and the opposite of the cosine is called the **arccosine**.

This program prints the arctangent of .58, the arcsine of .5, and the arccosine of .87:

```
CLS
degrees = ATN(1) / 45
PRINT ATN(.58) / degrees
x = .5: PRINT ATN(x / SQR(1 - x * x)) / degrees
x = .87: PRINT 90 - ATN(x / SQR(1 - x * x)) / degrees
```

Line 3 prints the arctangent of .58, in degrees. (If you omit the "/ degrees", the computer will print the answer in radians instead of degrees.) Line 4 sets x equal to .5 and then prints its arcsine (by using a formula that combines ATN with SQR). The bottom line sets x equal to .87 and then prints its arccosine (by using a formula that combines 90 with ATN and SQR). The answer to each of the three problems is about 30 degrees.

Types of numbers

QBASIC can handle several types of numbers.

General rules

Here are the general rules about types of numbers. I'll explain exceptions later.

Real numbers versus integers If a number contains a decimal point, it's called a **real number**. For example, 27.1 is a real number. So is -27.1. So is 27.0.

A number without a decimal point is called an **integer**. For example, 27 is an integer. So is -27. 27.0 is *not* an integer, since it contains a decimal point; 27.0 is a real number instead.

The computer handles integers faster than real numbers. To make your program run faster, use integers.

Long integers versus short integers Tiny integers are called **short integers**. For example, 0, 1, and 2 are short integers. So is 27. So is 589.

The biggest permissible short integer is 32767. The lowest permissible short integer is -32768.

An integer that's not short is called **long**. For example, 50000 is a long integer, since it's an integer that's bigger than 32767. Another long integer is -50000.

The biggest permissible long integer is 2147483647 (which is about 2 billion, using the American definition of *billion*). The lowest permissible long integer is -2147483648.

If you try to create an integer bigger than 2147483647, the computer will refuse. Instead, put a decimal point in the number, so the number becomes a real number. For example, if you want to deal with 5000000000, which is too big to be an integer, say 5000000000.0 instead, so the number is real.

The computer handles short integers faster than long integers, and handles long integers faster than real numbers.

To store a short integer in the computer's RAM chips, the computer uses a special trick that lets the short integer fit into 2 bytes of RAM. So **each short integer consumes just 2 bytes.**

For example, 589 consumes just 2 bytes. 32767 consumes just 2 bytes. -32768 consumes just 2 bytes.

To store a long integer, the computer uses a different trick that consumes 4 bytes of RAM. For example, -2147483648 consumes 4 bytes of RAM.

Single-precision versus double-precision A real number contains a decimal point. It can also contain a negative sign and lots of digits. If it contains at least 8 digits, it's called a **double-precision number**.

For example, 725.14592 is a double-precision number, since it contains 8 digits. 2943423.0 is double-precision. So is .00000001. So are -52341523092342.31 and -6.269549374523423, since each contains at least 8 digits. But .0000001 is *not* double-precision, since it contains just 7 digits.

A real number containing *fewer* than 8 digits is called **single-precision**. For example, .0000001 is single-precision. So is 5.2. So is -27.1.

A single-precision number can be up to 7 digits long. A double-precision number can be up to 16 digits long.

The computer handles single-precision numbers faster than double-precision.

A single-precision number consumes 4 bytes of RAM. A double-precision number consumes 8 bytes.

Suffix

At the end of a number, you can put a **suffix**:

Suffix	Meaning
%	short integer
&	long integer
!	single-precision real
#	double-precision real

For example, the number 27 is a short integer. If you want to turn it into a single-precision real, write "27.0" or "27!" instead of "27". If you want to turn it into a double-precision real, write "27.000000" or "27#". If you want to turn it into a long integer, write "27&".

Automatic rewrite In your program, if you write a double-precision real, the computer will automatically put the symbol # afterwards when you press the ENTER key. For example, if you write —

```
PRINT 53926.175 * 27.000000
```

and then press the ENTER key, the computer will automatically turn your typing into this:

```
PRINT 53926.175# * 27#
```

If you write a single-precision real that ends in .0, the computer will automatically replace the .0 by "!". For example, if you write —

```
PRINT 200.0 * 300.0
```

and then press the ENTER key, the computer will automatically turn your typing into this:

```
PRINT 200! * 300!
```

Scientific notation

For single-precision real numbers, you can use E notation. For example, instead of writing 27945.86, you can write 2.794586E4. The "E4" means "move the decimal point 4 places to the right." Instead of writing .0006829, you can write 6.829E-4, in which the "E-4" means "move the decimal point 4 places to the left."

For double-precision real numbers, write a D instead of an E. For example, 2.794586D4 is the double-precision version of 2.794586E4.

The number before the E or D is called the **mantissa**; the number after the E or D is called the **exponent**. For example, in the number 2.794586E4, the mantissa is 2.794586; the exponent is 4.

For a single-precision numbers, the mantissa can contain up to 7 digits. For double-precision numbers, the mantissa can contain up to 16 digits.

A number that contains a D is double-precision, even if the mantissa contains few digits or no decimal point. A number that contains an E is single-precision, even if the mantissa contains no decimal point; but if the mantissa contains more than 7 digits, the computer will turn the E into a D when you press ENTER.

Biggest real numbers

The biggest permissible single-precision number is about 3.000000E38. More precisely, it's 3.402823E38.

The biggest permissible double-precision number is about 1.000000000000000D308. More precisely, it's 1.797693134862315D308.

If you try to go higher than those numbers, the computer will gripe by saying "Overflow".

Accuracy

The computer handles integers accurately. The computer *tries* to handle real numbers accurately but sometimes makes slight mistakes with the real number's last digit.

For a single-precision real number, the computer makes slight mistakes with the 7th digit. For a double-precision real number, the computer makes slight mistakes with the 16th digit.

Tiniest decimals

You've seen that the biggest permissible double-precision number is about 1D308. The tiniest double-precision decimal that the computer can handle well is about 1D-308. If you try to go much tinier, the computer will usually botch the last few digits of the number (and replace those digits by different digits instead!) or else round the entire number to zero.

You've seen that the biggest permissible single-precision number is slightly bigger than 1E38. The tiniest single-precision decimal that the computer can handle well is about 1E-38. If you try to go much tinier, the computer will usually botch the last few digits of the number (and replace those digits by different digits instead!) or else round the entire number to zero.

Variables

Usually, each ordinary variable (such as x) stands for a single-precision real number. For example, you can say x=3.7, which makes x be the single-precision number 3.7.

If you say x=3, the computer will make x be 3.0 instead, to make x be a single-precision number. Though the screen will still say x=3, the x box in the computer's RAM will contain 3.0 instead.

You can create five kinds of variables:

A variable that's ordinary (such as x) or ends in an exclamation (such as x!) is single-precision real.
A variable that ends in a dollar sign   (such as x$) is a string.
A variable that ends in a percent sign (such as x%) is an short integer.
A variable that ends in an ampersand (such as x&) is a long integer.
A variable that ends in a number sign(such as x#) is double-precision real.

If you begin your program by saying —

```
DEFINT A-Z
```

all ordinary variables (such as x) will be short integers instead of single-precision real. (The word "DEFINT" means "DEFine to be INTegers".) If instead you say —

```
DEFLNG A-Z
```

all ordinary variables will be LoNG integers. If instead you say —

```
DEFDBL A-Z
```

all ordinary variables will be DouBLe-precision real.

What to do

Write your program simply, without worrying about which numbers and variables are short integers, long integer, single-precision real numbers, and double-precision real numbers. But after your program is written and you've removed any errors, edit the program by making the following changes, which improve the program's speed and accuracy.

__All short integers__ If your program doesn't involve any decimals or big numbers, make the top line say DEFINT A-Z. That will turn every variable into a short integer, so the program runs faster and consumes less RAM.

__Mostly short integers__ If your program involves just a *few* decimals or big numbers, make the top line say DEFINT A-Z; then put an exclamation point (!) after every variable standing for a decimal, and put an ampersand (&) after every variable standing for a long integer.

__Extra accuracy__ If you want to perform one of the computations extra-accurately, put a number sign after every variable the computation involves. For example, say x# instead of x.

Also, make sure that each number in the computation contains a number sign or at least 8 digits. For example, instead of saying 2.4, say 2.4# or 2.4000000.

Avoid round-off errors

The computer cannot handle decimals accurately. If you say x=.1, the computer can't set x equal to .1 exactly; instead, it will set x equal to a number very, very close to .1. The reason for the slight inaccuracy is that the computer thinks in "binary", not decimals; and .1 can*not* be expressed in binary exactly.

Usually you won't see the slight inaccuracy: when you ask the computer to PRINT a number, the computer prints it rounded to six significant figures, and the inaccuracy is so small it doesn't show up in the rounded result. But **there are three situations in which the inaccuracy can be noticed:**

1. You'll get wrong digits if you make the computer do x minus y, where x is almost equal to y (so the first several digits of x are the same as the first several digits of y). For example, if you say —

```
PRINT 8.1 - 8
```

the computer will print .1000004 instead of .1. The same thing happens if you say:

```
PRINT 8.1 + (-8)
```

If you say —

```
PRINT 80000.1 - 80000
```

the computer will print .1015625 instead of .1.

If you say —

```
PRINT 800000.1 - 800000
```

the computer will print .125 instead of .1.

The error can get magnified: if you ask the computer to multiply 800000.1-800000 by 1000, it will print .125*1000, which is 125, instead of .1*1000, which is 100. If you ask it to find the reciprocal of 800000.1-800000, it will print 1/.125, which is 8, instead of 1/.1, which is 10.

2. You'll get wrong looping if you say "FOR x = a TO b STEP c", where c is a decimal and the loop will be done many times. For example:

```
FOR x = 1 TO 2 STEP .1
  PRINT x
NEXT
```

Theoretically, the computer should print 1, 1.1, 1.2, 1.3, 1.4, 1.5, 1.6, 1.7, 1.8, 1.9, and 2. But that's not what actually happens. In the FOR line, the computer can't handle the decimal .1 accurately. The last few numbers the computer thinks of are:

```
slightly more than 1.7
slightly more than 1.8
slightly more than 1.9
```

The computer does *not* think of the next number, slightly more than 2.0, because the FOR line says not to go past 2. The PRINT line makes the computer print the numbers rounded to seven significant digits, so it prints:

```
1
1.1
1.2
1.3
1.4
1.5
1.6
1.7
1.8
1.9
```

It does not print 2.

If you want to compute 1 + 1.1 + 1.2 + 1.3 + 1.4 + 1.5 + 1.6 + 1.7 + 1.8 + 1.9 + 2, you might be tempted to write this program:

```
CLS
s = 0
FOR x = 1 TO 2 STEP .1
  s = s + x
NEXT
PRINT s
```

The computer will print a reasonable-looking answer: 14.5. But the computer's "answer" is wrong, since the last number the computer added was slightly more than 1.9; it never added 2. The correct answer is 16.5.

To fix those FOR loops, you can change the FOR line to this

```
FOR x = 1 TO 2.05 STEP .1
```

The .05 after the 2 allows for the margin of error. The general strategy is to change —

```
FOR x = a TO b STEP c
```

to this:

```
FOR x = a TO b + c / 2 STEP c
```

An alternative fix is to replace —

```
FOR x = 1 TO 2 STEP .1
```

by this pair of lines:

```
FOR i = 10 TO 20
  x = i / 10
```

As i goes from 10 to 20, x will go from 1 to 2 in steps of .1. This fix is the most accurate of all, since it eliminates decimals from the FOR line. But the new indented line (x = i / 10) makes the program run very slowly, since that line requires the computer to perform division, and the division is performed repeatedly (since it's in the FOR loop).

3. You'll get wrong testing if you ask the computer whether two numbers x and y are equal. It's unwise to ask whether x is *exactly* equal to y, since both x and y have probably been affected by some slight error. Instead, ask the computer whether the difference between x and y is much tinier than y:

Bad	Good
IF x = y THEN	IF ABS(x - y) <= .000001 * ABS(y) THEN

The .000001 is requesting that the first six significant digits of x be the same as the first six significant digits of y (except that the sixth significant digit might be off by one).

<u>Why binary?</u> From those discussions, you might think computers should be made differently, and that they should use the decimal system instead of binary. There are two counterarguments.

First, binary arithmetic is faster.

Second, even if computers were using the decimal system, inaccuracy would still occur. To store the fraction 2/3 accurately by using the decimal system, the computer would have to store a decimal point followed by infinitely many 6's. That would require an infinite amount of space in memory, which is impossible — unless you know how to build an infinitely large computer? So even in the decimal system, some fractions must be approximated instead of handled exactly.

<u>Begin with the tiny</u> According to mathematicians, addition is supposed to obey these laws:

```
x+0      is exactly the same as x
x+y      is exactly the same as y+x
x+-x     is exactly the same as 0
(x+y)+z is exactly the same as x+(y+z)
```

On the computer, the first three laws hold, but the last does not. If x is a decimal tinier than z, the computer does (x+y)+z more accurately than x+(y+z). So **to add a list of numbers accurately, begin by adding together the tiniest decimals in the list**.

Integer division

When you add, subtract, or multiply integers together, the answer is an integer:

```
11 + 4 is an integer, 15
11 - 4 is an integer,  7
11 * 4 is an integer, 44
```

When you divide integers by using a slash (/), the answer is a real number:

```
11 / 4 is a real number, 2.75
```

Backslash If you divide integers by using a **backslash** (\), the computer will ignore any decimal digits and give you just an integer:

```
11 \ 4 is an integer, 2
```

Remainder When you divide 11 by 4, the remainder is 3:

```
       2
    4 ⟌ 11
      -8
       3  is the remainder
```

If you ask for 11 MOD 4, the computer will tell you the remainder when you divide 11 by 4:

```
11 MOD 4 is an integer, 3
```

So if you say —

```
PRINT 11 MOD 4
```

the computer will print:

```
3
```

Prime numbers

An integer is called **composite** if it's the product of two other integers:

```
35 is composite because it's 5 * 7
 9 is composite because it's 3 * 3
12 is composite because it's 2 * 6
13 is not composite, so it's called prime
```

This program tells whether a number is prime or composite:

```
CLS
DEFLNG A-Z
INPUT "What's your favorite positive integer"; n
FOR i = 1 TO n - 1
  FOR j = 1 TO n - 1
    IF n = i * j THEN PRINT n; "is"; i; "times"; j; "and composite": END
  NEXT
NEXT
PRINT n; "is prime"
```

To make the program run faster, we want all variables to be integers instead of reals. To let the program handle *big* numbers, we want the integers to be long. The DEFLNG line accomplishes all that: it makes all variables be long integers.

Here's how the program works. The INPUT line waits for you to type an integer n. The IF line checks whether n is the product of two other integers; if it is, the computer says n is composite.

How fast does that program run? If n turns out to be prime, the IF line is encountered once for every i and once for every j; altogether it's encountered (n-1)2 times. If n is a big number, around a billion, (n-1)2 is around a quintillion. (I'm using the American definitions of billion and quintillion. An American billion is 1,000,000,000; an American quintillion is 1,000,000,000,000,000,000. British definitions of billion and quintillion are different.) To do the IF line a quintillion times will take a typical microcomputer many years. For example, if you say that your favorite number is 999999929 (which is close to a billion), the typical 486DX2-66 computer will take about *400,000 years* before it comes to the conclusion that your number is prime! By the time the program finishes running, you'll be dead and so will many generations of your decendents! Probably your computer or its electricity will have died by then too! The program's very slow.

Some small improvements are possible; for example, i and j can start at 2 instead of 1. But so long as you have a loop inside a loop, the time will remain very huge.

The following strategy requires just one loop: divide n by every integer less than it, to see whether the quotient is ever an integer. Here's the program:

```
CLS
DEFLNG A-Z
INPUT "What's your favorite positive integer"; n
FOR i = 2 TO n - 1
  IF n MOD i = 0 THEN PRINT n; "is divisible by"; i; "and composite": END
NEXT
PRINT n; "is prime"
```

The IF line makes the computer divide n by i, compute the remainder (which is called "n MOD i"), and check whether that remainder is 0. If the remainder is 0, then n divided evenly by i, so n is divisible by i, so n is composite.

How fast is our new program? If n turns out to be prime, the IF line is encountered once for every i; altogether it's encountered n-2 times. That's less than in the previous program, where it was encountered (n-1)2 times. If n is about a billion, our new program does the IF line about a billion times, which is much fewer than the quintillion times required by the previous program! It's nearly a billion times faster than the previous program! To determine whether 999999929 is prime, the new program takes a 486DX2-66 computer about 5 hours instead of 400,000 years.

We can improve the program even further. If an n can't be divided by 2, it can't be divided by any even number; so after checking divisibility by 2, we have to check divisibility by just 3, 5, 7, ..., n-2. Let's put that short-cut into our program, and also say that every n less than 4 is prime:

```
CLS
DEFLNG A-Z
INPUT "What's your favorite positive integer"; n
IF n < 4 THEN PRINT n; "is prime": END
IF n MOD 2 = 0 THEN PRINT n; "is divisible by 2 and composite": END
FOR i = 3 TO n - 2 STEP 2
  IF n MOD i = 0 THEN PRINT n; "is divisible by"; i; "and composite": END
NEXT
PRINT n; "is prime"
```

Line 5 checks divisibility by 2; the FOR loop checks divisibility by 3, 5, 7,... , n-2. If n is prime, the indented IF line is encountered n/2 - 2 times, which is about half as often as in the previous program; so our new program takes about half as long to run. On a 486DX2-66 computer, it takes about 2½ hours to handle 999999929.

Our goal was to find a pair of integers whose product is n. If there is such a pair of integers, the smaller one will be no more than the square root of n, so we can restrict our hunt to the integers not exceeding the square root of n:

```
CLS
DEFLNG A-Z
INPUT "What's your favorite positive integer"; n
IF n < 4 THEN PRINT n; "is prime": END
IF n MOD 2 = 0 THEN PRINT n; "is divisible by 2 and composite": END
FOR i = 3 TO SQR(n) * 1.000001 STEP 2
  IF n MOD i = 0 THEN PRINT n; "is divisible by"; i; "and composite": END
NEXT
PRINT n; "is prime"
```

The "1.00001" is to give a margin of safety, in case the computer rounds SQR(n) a bit down. If n is near a billion, the indented IF line is encountered about 15,000 times, which is much less than the 500,000,000 times encountered in the previous program and the 1,000,000,000,000,000,000 times in the original. This program lets a 486DX2-66 computer handle 999999929 in about ¼ of a second. That's much quicker than earlier versions, which required 2½ hours, or 5 hours, or 400,000 years!

Moral: a few small changes in a program can make the computer take ¼ of a second instead of 400,000 years.

The frightening thing about this example is that the first version we had was so terrible, but the only way to significantly improve it was to take a totally fresh approach. To be a successful programmer, you must always keep your mind open and hunt for fresh ideas.

Subscripts

Instead of being a single string, x$ can be a whole *list* of strings, like this:

```
       /"love" \
       | "hate" |
       | "kiss" |
x$=    | "kill"  |
       | "peace" |
       | "war"  |
       \ "why" /
```

Here's how to make x$ be that list of strings....

Begin your program as usual, by saying:

```
CLS
```

Then say:

```
DIM x$(7)
```

That line says x$ will be a list of 7 strings. DIM means **dimension**; the line says the dimension of x$ is 7.

Next, tell the computer what strings are in x$. Type these lines:

```
x$(1) = "love"
x$(2) = "hate"
x$(3) = "kiss"
x$(4) = "kill"
x$(5) = "peace"
x$(6) = "war"
x$(7) = "why"
```

That says x$'s first string is "love", x$'s second string is "hate", etc.

If you want the computer to print all those strings, type this:

```
FOR i = 1 TO 7
  print x$(i)
NEXT
```

That means: print all the strings in x$. The computer will print:

```
love
hate
kiss
kill
peace
war
why
```

That program includes a line saying x$(1) = "love". Instead of saying x$(1), math books say:

```
x₁
```

The "1" is called a **subscript**.

Similarly, in the line saying x$(2) = "hate", the number 2 is a subscript. Some programmers pronounce that line as follows: "x string, subscripted by 2, is hate". Hurried programmers just say: "x string 2 is hate".

In that program, x$ is called an **array** (or **matrix**). Definition: an **array** (or **matrix**) is a variable that has subscripts.

Subscripted DATA

That program said x$(1) is "love", and x$(2) is "hate", and so on. This program does the same thing, more briefly:

```
CLS
DIM x$(7)
DATA love,hate,kiss,kill,peace,war,why
FOR i = 1 TO 7
  READ x$(i)
NEXT
FOR i = 1 TO 7
  PRINT x$(i)
NEXT
```

The DIM line says x$ will be a list of 7 strings. The DATA line contains a list of 7 strings. The first FOR..NEXT loop makes the computer READ those strings and call them x$. The bottom FOR...NEXT loop makes the computer print those 7 strings.

In that program, the first four lines say:

```
CLS
DIM
DATA
FOR i
```

Most practical programs begin with those four lines.

Let's lengthen the program, so that the computer prints all this:

```
love
hate
kiss
kill
peace
war
why

why love
why hate
why kiss
why kill
why peace
why war
why why
```

That consists of two verses. The second verse resembles the first verse, except that each line of the second verse begins with "why".

To make the computer print all that, just add the shaded lines to the program:

```
CLS
DIM x$(7)
DATA love,hate,kiss,kill,peace,war,why
FOR i = 1 TO 7
  READ x$(i)
NEXT
FOR i = 1 TO 7
  PRINT x$(i)
NEXT
PRINT
FOR i = 1 TO 7
  PRINT "why "; x$(i)
NEXT
```

The shaded PRINT line leaves a blank line between the first verse and the second verse. The shaded FOR..NEXT loop, which prints the second verse, resembles the FOR...NEXT loop that printed the first verse but prints "why" before each x$(i).

Let's add a third verse, which prints the words in reverse order:

```
why
war
peace
kill
kiss
hate
love
```

Before printing that third verse, print a blank line:

```
PRINT
```

Then print the verse itself. To print the verse, you must print x$(7), then print x$(6), then print x$(5), etc. To do that, you could say:

```
PRINT x$(7)
PRINT x$(6)
PRINT x$(5)
etc.
```

But this way is shorter:

```
FOR i = 7 TO 1 STEP -1
  PRINT x$(i)
NEXT
```

Numeric arrays

Let's make y be this list of six numbers: 100, 26, 94, 201, 8.3, and -7. To begin, tell the computer that y will consist of six numbers:

```
CLS
DIM y(6)
```

Next, tell the computer what the six numbers are:

```
DATA 100,26,94,201,8.3,-7
```

Make the computer READ all that data:

```
FOR i = 1 TO 6
        READ y(i)
NEXT
```

To make the computer PRINT all that data, type this:

```
FOR i = 1 TO 6
  PRINT y(i)
NEXT
```

If you want the computer to add those 6 numbers together and print their sum, say:

```
PRINT y(1) + y(2) + y(3) + y(4) + y(5) + y(6)
```

Strange example

Getting tired of x and y? Then pick another letter! For example, you can play with z:

Silly, useless program	What the program means
CLS	CLear the Screen
DIM z(5)	z will be a list of 5 numbers
FOR i = 2 TO 5	
z(i) = i * 100	z(2)=200; z(3)=300; z(4)=400; z(5)=500
NEXT	
z(1) = z(2) - 3	z(1) is 200 - 3, so z(1) is 197
z(3) = z(1) - 2	z(3) changes to 197 - 2, which is 195
FOR i = 1 TO 5	
PRINT z(i)	print z(1), z(2), z(3), z(4), and z(5)
NEXT	

The computer will print:

```
197
200
195
400
500
```

Problems and solutions

Suppose you want to analyze 20 numbers. Begin your program by saying:

```
CLS
DIM x(20)
```

Then type the 20 numbers as data:

```
DATA etc.
```

Tell the computer to READ the data:

```
FOR i = 1 TO 20
        READ x(i)
NEXT
```

Afterwards, do one of the following, depending on which problem you want to solve....

Print all the values of x Solution:

```
FOR i = 1 TO 20
  PRINT x(i)
NEXT
```

Print all the values of x, in reverse order

Solution:

```
FOR i = 20 TO 1 STEP -1
  PRINT x(i)
NEXT
```

Print the sum of all the values of x In other words, print x(1) + x(2) + x(3)+... + x(20). Solution: start the sum at 0 —

```
sum = 0
```

and then increase the sum, by adding each x(i) to it:

```
FOR i = 1 TO 20
  sum = sum + x(i)
NEXT
```

Finally, print the sum:

```
PRINT "The sum of all the numbers is"; sum
```

Find the average of x In other words, find the average of the 20 numbers. Solution: begin by finding the sum —

```
sum = 0
FOR i = 1 TO 20
  sum = sum + x(i)
NEXT
```

and then divide the sum by 20:

```
PRINT "The average is"; sum / 20
```

Find whether any of x's values is 79.4 In other words, find out whether 79.4 is a number in the list. Solution: if x(i) is 79.4, print "Yes" —

```
FOR i = 1 TO 20
  IF x(i)=79.4 THEN PRINT "Yes, 79.4 is in the list": END
NEXT
```

otherwise, print "No":

```
PRINT "No, 79.4 is not in the list"
```

In x's list, count how often 79.4 appears

Solution: start the counter at zero —

```
counter = 0
```

and increase the counter each time you see the number 79.4:

```
FOR i = 1 TO 20
  IF x(i) = 79.4 THEN counter = counter + 1
NEXT
```

Finally, print the counter:

```
PRINT "The number 79.4 appears"; counter; "times"
```

Print all x values that are negative

In other words, print all the numbers that have minus signs. Solution: begin by announcing your purpose —

```
PRINT "Here are the values that are negative:"
```

and then print the values that are negative; in other words, print each x(i) that's less than 0:

```
FOR i = 1 TO 20
  IF x(i) < 0 THEN PRINT x(i)
NEXT
```

Print all x values that are above average

Solution: find the average —

```
sum = 0
FOR i = 1 TO 20
  sum = sum + x(i)
NEXT
average = sum / 20
```

then announce your purpose:

```
PRINT "The following values are above average:"
```

Finally, print the values that are above average; in other words, print each x(i) that's greater than average:

```
FOR i = 1 TO 20
  IF x(i) > average THEN PRINT x(i)
NEXT
```

Find the biggest value of x

In other words, find which of the 20 numbers is the biggest. Solution: begin by assuming that the biggest is the first number —

```
biggest = x(1)
```

but if you find another number that's even bigger, change your idea of what the biggest is:

```
FOR i = 2 TO 20
  IF x(i) > biggest THEN biggest = x(i)
140 NEXT
```

Afterwards, print the biggest:

```
PRINT "The biggest number in the list is"; biggest
```

Find the smallest value of x

In other words, find which of the 20 numbers is the smallest. Solution: begin by assuming that the smallest is the the first number —

```
smallest = x(1)
```

but if you find another number that's even smaller, change your idea of what the smallest is:

```
FOR i = 2 TO 20
  IF x(i) < smallest THEN smallest = x(i)
NEXT
```

Afterwards, print the smallest:

```
PRINT "The smallest number in the list is"; smallest
```

Check whether x's list is in strictly increasing order

In other words, find out whether the following statement is true: x(1) is a smaller number than x(2), which is a smaller number than x(3), which is a smaller number than x(4), etc. Solution: if x(i) is *not* smaller than x(i + 1), print "No" —

```
FOR I = 1 TO 19
  IF x(i) >= x(i + 1) THEN
    PRINT "No, the list is not in strictly increasing order"
    END
  END IF
NEXT
```

otherwise, print "Yes":

```
PRINT "Yes, the list is in strictly increasing order"
```

Test yourself: look at those problems again, and see whether you can figure out the solutions *without peeking at the answers.*

Multiple arrays

Suppose your program involves three lists. Suppose the first list is called a$ and consists of 18 strings; the second list is called b and consists of 57 numbers; and the third list is called c$ and consists of just 3 strings. To say all that, begin your program with this statement:

```
DIM a$(18), b(57), c$(3)
```

Double subscripts

You can make x$ be a **table** of strings, like this:

$$X\$ = \begin{pmatrix} \text{"dog"} & \text{"cat"} & \text{"mouse"} \\ \text{"hotdog"} & \text{"catsup"} & \text{"mousetard"} \end{pmatrix}$$

Here's how to make x$ be that table....

Begin by saying:

```
CLS
DIM x$(2, 3)
```

That says x$ will be a table having 2 rows and 3 columns.

Then tell the computer what strings are in x$. Type these lines:

```
x$(1, 1) = "dog"
x$(1, 2) = "cat"
x$(1, 3) = "mouse"
x$(2, 1) = "hotdog"
x$(2, 2) = "catsup"
x$(2, 3) = "moustard"
```

That says the string in x$'s first row and first column is "dog", the string in x$'s first row and second column is "cat", etc.

If you'd like the computer to print all those strings, type this:

```
FOR i = 1 TO 2
  FOR j = 1 TO 3
    PRINT x$(i, j),
  NEXT
  PRINT
NEXT
```

That means: print all the strings in x$. The computer will print:

```
dog        cat        mouse
hotdog     catsup     mousetard
```

Most programmers follow this tradition: **the row's number is called i, and the column's number is called j**. That program obeys that tradition. The "FOR i = 1 TO 2" means "for both rows"; the "FOR j = 1 TO 3" means "for all 3 columns".

Notice i comes before j in the alphabet; i comes before j in x(i, j); and "FOR i" comes before "FOR j". If you follow the i-before-j tradition, you'll make fewer errors.

At the end of the first PRINT line, the comma makes the computer print each column in a separate zone. The other PRINT line makes the computer press the ENTER key at the end of each row. The x$ is called a **table** or **two-dimensional array** or **doubly subscripted array**.

Multiplication table

This program prints a multiplication table:

```
CLS
DIM x(10, 4)
FOR i = 1 TO 10
  FOR j = 1 TO 4
    x(i, j) = i * j
  NEXT
NEXT
FOR i = 1 TO 10
  FOR j = 1 TO 4
    PRINT x(i, j),
  NEXT
  PRINT
NEXT
```

Line 2 says x will be a table having 10 rows and 4 columns.

The line saying "x(i, j) = i * j" means the number in row i and column j is i*j. For example, the number in row 3 and column 4 is 12. Above that line, the program says "FOR i = 1 TO 10" and "FOR j = 1 TO 4", so that x(i,j)=i*j for *every* i and j, so *every* entry in the table is defined by multiplication.

The computer prints the whole table:

1	2	3	4
2	4	6	8
3	6	9	12
4	8	12	16
5	10	15	20
6	12	18	24
7	14	21	28
8	16	24	32
9	18	27	36
10	20	30	40

Instead of multiplication, you can have addition, subtraction, or division: just change the line saying "x(i, j) = i * j".

Summing a table

Suppose you want to analyze this table:

32.7	19.4	31.6	85.1
-8	402	-61	0
5106	-.2	0	-1.1
36.9	.04	1	11
777	666	55.44	2
1.99	2.99	3.99	4.99
50	40	30	20
12	21	12	21
0	1000	2	500

Since the table has 9 rows and 4 columns, begin your program by saying:

```
CLS
DIM x(9, 4)
```

Each row of the table becomes a row of the DATA:

```
DATA 32.7, 19.4, 31.6, 85.1
DATA -8, 402, -61, 0
DATA 5106, -.2, 0, -1.1
DATA 36.9, .04, 1, 11
DATA 777, 666, 55.44, 2
DATA 1.99, 2.99, 3.99, 4.99
DATA 50, 40, 30, 20
DATA 12, 21, 12, 21
DATA 0, 1000, 2, 500
```

Make the computer READ the data:

```
FOR i = 1 TO 9
  FOR j = 1 TO 4
    READ x(i, j)
  NEXT
NEXT
```

To make the computer print the table, say this:

```
FOR i = 1 TO 9
  FOR j = 1 TO 4:
    PRINT X(I,J),
  NEXT
  PRINT
NEXT
```

Here are some problems, with solutions....

Find the sum of all the numbers in the table

Solution: start the sum at 0 —

```
sum = 0
```

and then increase the sum, by adding each x(i, j) to it:

```
FOR i = 1 TO 9
  FOR j = 1 TO 4
    sum = sum + x(i, j)
  NEXT
NEXT
```

Finally, print the sum:

```
PRINT "The sum of all the numbers is"; sum
```

The computer will print:

```
The sum of all the numbers is 8877.84
```

Find the sum of each row

In other words, make the computer print the sum of the numbers in the first row, then the sum of the numbers in the second row, then the sum of the numbers in the third row, etc. Solution: the general idea is —

```
FOR i = 1 TO 9
  print the sum of row i
NEXT
```

Here are the details:

```
FOR i = 1 TO 9
  sum = 0
  FOR j = 1 TO 4
    sum = sum + x(i, j)
  NEXT
  PRINT "The sum of row"; i; "is"; sum
NEXT
```

The computer will print:

```
The sum of row 1 is 168.8
The sum of row 2 is 333
The sum of row 3 is 5104.7
etc.
```

Find the sum of each column

In other words, make the computer print the sum of the numbers in the first column, then the sum of the numbers in the second column, then the sum of the numbers in the third column, etc. Solution: the general idea is —

```
FOR j = 1 TO 4
  print the sum of column j
NEXT
```

Here are the details:

```
FOR j = 1 TO 4
  sum = 0
  FOR i = 1 TO 9
    sum = sum + x(i, j)
  NEXT
  PRINT "The sum of column"; j; "is"; sum
NEXT
```

The computer will print:

```
The sum of column 1 is 6008.59
The sum of column 2 is 2151.23
The sum of column 3 is 75.03
The sum of column 4 is 642.99
```

In all the other examples, "FOR i" came before "FOR j"; but in this unusual example, "FOR i" comes *after* "FOR j".

SUB procedures

Here's a sick program:

```
CLS
PRINT "We all know..."
PRINT "You are stupid!"
PRINT "You are ugly!"
PRINT "...and yet we love you."
```

It makes the computer print this message:

```
We all know...
You are stupid!
You are ugly!
...and yet we love you.
```

So the computer prints "We all know...", then insults the human ("You are stupid! You are ugly!"), then prints "...and yet we love you."

Here's a more sophisticated way to write that program:

```
CLS
PRINT "We all know..."
insult
PRINT "...and yet we love you."
SUB insult
  PRINT "You are stupid!"
  PRINT "You are ugly!"
END SUB
```

I'm going to explain that sophisticated version. Just *read* my explanation: don't type the sophisticated version into your computer yet. (Wait until you read the next section, called "How to type the program".)

In the sophisticated version, the top 4 lines tell the computer to clear the screen (CLS), print "We all know...", then insult the human, then print "...and yet we love you." But the computer doesn't know how to insult yet.

The bottom 4 lines teach the computer how to insult: they say "insult" means to print "You are stupid!" and "You are ugly!" Those bottom 4 lines define the word insult; they're the **definition** of insult.

That program is divided into two **procedures**. The top 4 lines are called the **main procedure** (or **main routine** or **main module**). The bottom 4 lines (which just define the word "insult") are called the **SUB procedure** (or **subroutine** or **submodule**).

The SUB procedure's first line (**SUB insult**) means: here's the SUB procedure that defines the word "insult". The SUB procedure's bottom line (**END SUB**) means: this is the END of the SUB procedure.

How to type the program

Now you're smart enough to begin typing that sophisticated program! Begin by typing the first four lines. Then start typing the SUB procedure, beginning with the line that says "SUB insult".

When you finish typing the "SUB insult" line (and press the ENTER key at the end of that line), the computer analyzes that line and realizes you're starting to type a new procedure. The computer devotes the entire screen to the new procedure. Yes, the screen shows just the SUB insult procedure! The screen no longer shows the main procedure! Here's the rule: **the computer's screen shows just one procedure at a time**.

So now the top of the screen says "SUB insult". At the bottom of the screen, the computer automatically types "SUB END" for you. In between the "SUB insult" and "SUB END" lines, type PRINT "You are stupid!" and PRINT "You are ugly!" (and indent those lines by pressing the TAB key), so the screen looks like this:

```
SUB insult
  PRINT "You are stupid!"
  PRINT "You are ugly!"
END SUB
```

Congratulations! You finished typing the program!

Seeing different procedures

The computer's screen shows just the SUB procedure. To see the main procedure instead, press the F2 key, then ENTER.

To flip back to the SUB procedure again, press the F2 key again, then the down-arrow key (so the world "insult" is highlighted), then ENTER.

Here's the rule: **to see a different procedure, press the F2 key, then highlight the name of the procedure you want to see** (by pressing the down-arrow key if necessary), then press ENTER.

Run

Whenever you want to run the program, press SHIFT with F5. The computer will say:

```
We all know...
You are stupid!
You are ugly!
...and yet we love you.
```

Print

If you choose Print from the file menu (by pressing Alt then F then P) and then press ENTER, the computer will print the entire program onto a single sheet of paper.

When printing on paper, the computer will automatically leave a blank line between the procedures, so the paper will show this:

```
CLS
PRINT "We all know..."
insult
PRINT "...and yet we love you."

SUB insult
  PRINT "You are stupid!"
  PRINT "You are ugly!"
END SUB
```

You must eject the paper from the printer manually.

Save

If you choose Save from the file menu (by pressing Alt then F then S) and then give the program a name (and press ENTER), the computer saves the entire program onto the hard disk.

While saving, the computer automatically adds an extra line at the top of the program, so the main procedure becomes this:

```
DECLARE SUB insult ()
CLS
PRINT "We all know..."
insult
PRINT "...and yet we love you."
```

The DECLARE line reminds the computer that the program includes a SUB insult.

Refrains

This is chanted by boys playing tag — and protesters fearing dictators:

```
The lion is a-coming near.
          He'll growl and sneer
          And drink our beer.
The lion never brings us cheer.
          He'll growl and sneer
          And drink our beer.
The lion is the one we fear.
          He'll growl and sneer
          And drink our beer.
Gotta stop the lion!
```

In that chant, this refrain is repeated:

```
          He'll growl and sneer
          And drink our beer.
```

This program prints the entire chant:

```
CLS
PRINT "The lion is a-coming near."
refrain
PRINT "The lion never brings us cheer."
refrain
PRINT "The lion is the one we fear."
refrain
PRINT "Gotta stop the lion!"

SUB refrain
  PRINT "          He'll growl and sneer"
  PRINT "          And drink our beer."
END SUB
```

Young males

Here's a poem about young male relationships:

```
He is a boy--
A little boy.
          Don't play with me.
          I'm not a toy.
His only goal
Is to annoy.
          Don't play with me.
          I'm not a toy.
His life is full
Of painful joy.
          Don't play with me
          I'm not a toy.
He's just a boy.
```

This program prints it:

```
CLS
PRINT "He is a boy--"
PRINT "A little boy."
refrain
PRINT "His only goal"
PRINT "Is to annoy."
refrain
PRINT "His life is full"
PRINT "Of painful joy."
refrain
PRINT "He's just a boy."

SUB refrain
  PRINT "          Don't play with me."
  PRINT "          I'm not a toy."
END SUB
```

Clementine

The famous folk song "Clementine" begins like this:

```
In a cavern in a canyon, excavating for a mine,
Lived a miner (49'er) and his daughter, Clementine.

  O my darling, o my darling, o my darling Clementine,
  You are lost and gone forever.  Dreadful sorry, Clementine!

Light she was and like a fairy, and her shoes were #9.
Herring boxes without tops:  those sandals were for Clementine.

  O my darling, o my darling, o my darling Clementine,
  You are lost and gone forever.  Dreadful sorry, Clementine!

Drove her ducklings to the water ev'ry morning just at 9.
Hit her foot against a splinter, fell into the foaming brine.

  O my darling, o my darling, o my darling Clementine,
  You are lost and gone forever.  Dreadful sorry, Clementine!
```

This program prints the song's updated version with a twisted ending:

```
CLS
PRINT "In a cavern in a canyon, excavating for a mine,"
PRINT "Lived a miner (49'er) and his daughter, Clementine."
chorus
PRINT "Light she was and like a fairy, and her shoes were #9."
PRINT "Herring box-es without tops-es sandals were for Clementine."
chorus
PRINT "Drove her ducklings to the water ev'ry morning just at 9."
PRINT "Hit her foot against a splinter, fell into the foaming brine."
chorus
PRINT "Ruby lips above the water, blowing bubbles soft and fine!"
PRINT "But alas, I was no swimmer, so I lost my Clementine."
chorus
PRINT "How I missed her!  How I missed her!  How I missed my Clementine!"
PRINT "But I kissed her little sister and forgot my Clementine."
chorus
PRINT "Sister gladly to me married.  Then she found in nine months time"
PRINT "A nice daughter.  As she oughta, named the daughter Clementine."
chorus
PRINT "There's our daughter in the water.  Suddenly, she gives a wail"
PRINT "At some red-stained herring boxes.  Now I'm sitting here in jail."
chorus
PRINT "In my dreams she still doth haunt me, robed in garments soaked in brine."
PRINT "Once I wooed her.  Now a loser singing songs while doing time!"
chorus

SUB chorus
  SLEEP 11
  PRINT
  PRINT "  O my darling, o my darling, o my darling Clementine,"
  PRINT "  You are lost and gone forever.  Dreadful sorry, Clementine!"
  SLEEP 11
  PRINT
END SUB
```

At the beginning and end of the chorus, the "SLEEP 11" makes the computer pause for 11 seconds, to give the human a chance to read & sing what the computer wrote before the computer puts more words onto the screen.

Big love

This program prints a love poem:

```
CLS
PRINT "The most beautiful thing in the world is"
PRINT "LOVE"
PRINT "The opposite of war is"
PRINT "LOVE"
PRINT "And when I look at you, I feel lots of"
PRINT "LOVE"
```

In that program, many of the lines make the computer print the word LOVE. Let's make those lines print the word LOVE bigger, like this:

```
*           *     *      *      * * * * *
*           *  *      *  *      *
*              *     *    *  *      * * *
*              *  *      *  *        *
* * * *        *        *           * * * * *
```

To make LOVE be that big, run this version of the program:

```
CLS
PRINT "The most beautiful thing in the world is"
big.love
PRINT "The opposite of war is"
big.love
PRINT "And when I look at you, I feel lots of"
big.love

SUB big.love
  PRINT "*           *      *      *      * * * * *"
  PRINT "*              *  *      *  *      *"
  PRINT "*              *     *    *  *      * * *"
  PRINT "*              *  *      *  *        *"
  PRINT "* * * *        *        *           * * * * *"
END SUB
```

In that version, the lines say "big.love" instead of PRINT "LOVE". The SUB procedure teaches the computer how to make big.love.

Variables

Each procedure uses its own part of the RAM. For example, the main procedure uses a different part of the RAM than a SUB procedure.

Suppose the main procedure says "x = 4", and a SUB procedure named "joe" says "x = 100". The computer puts 4 into the main procedure's x box and puts 100 into joe's x box, like this:

```
main procedure's x box    [        4        ]

joe's x box               [       100       ]
```

Those two boxes are stored in different parts of the RAM from each other, and they don't interfere with each other.

For example, suppose you run this program:

```
CLS
x = 4
joe
PRINT x

SUB joe
  PRINT x
  x = 100
END SUB
```

The computer begins by doing the main procedure, which says "x = 4", so the computer puts 4 into the main procedure's x box:

```
main procedure's x box    [      4      ]
```

The main procedure's next line says "joe", which makes the computer do the joe procedure. The joe procedure begins by saying "PRINT x"; but since joe's x box is still empty, the computer will print 0. Joe's next line says "x = 100", which puts 100 into joe's x box. Then the computer comes to the end of joe, returns to the main procedure, and does the "PRINT x" line at the bottom of the main procedure; but since the main procedure's x box still contains 4, the computer will print 4. The computer will not print 100.

If a committee of programmers wants to write a big, fancy program, the committee divides the programming task into a main procedure and several SUB procedures, then assigns each procedure to a different programmer. If you're one of the programmers, you can use any variable names you wish, without worrying about what names the other programmers chose: if you accidentally pick the same variable name as another programmer, it's no problem, since each procedure stores its variables in a different part of the RAM.

If you *want* a variable to affect and be affected by what's in another procedure, use one of these methods…

Method 1: SHARED At the top of the main procedure, you can say:

```
COMMON SHARED x
```

That means x is a variable whose box will be shared among all procedures, so that if a procedure says "x = 4" the x will be 4 in *all* procedures.

For example, suppose you say:

```
COMMON SHARED x
CLS
x = 4
joe
PRINT x

SUB joe
  PRINT x
  x = 100
END SUB
```

Then when the computer comes to joe's first line, which says "PRINT x", the computer will print 4 (because the main procedure had made x become 4); and when the computer comes to the main procedure's bottom line, which says "PRINT x", the computer will print 100 (because the joe procedure had made x become 100).

Put the COMMON SHARED line at the main procedure's *top*, above CLS.

You can write a program containing other shared variables besides x. For example, if you want x and sammy$ to both be common shared variables, say:

```
COMMON SHARED x, sammy$
```

If you want y$ to be a list of 20 strings, you normally say DIM y$(20); but if you want to share that list among all the procedures, say this instead:

```
DIM SHARED y$(20)
```

Put that line just at the top of the main procedure; you do *not* need to say DIM y$(20) in the SUB procedures.

The program is your world! A SHARED variable is called a **global variable**, since its value is shared throughout the entire program. An ordinary, unshared variable is called a **local variable**, since its value is used just in one procedure.

Method 2: arguments Here's a simple program:

```
CLS
INPUT "How many times do you want to kiss"; n
FOR i = 1 TO n
  PRINT "kiss"
NEXT
```

It asks "How many times do you want to kiss", then waits for your answer, then prints the word "kiss" as many times as you requested. For example, if you type 3, the computer will print:

```
kiss
kiss
kiss
```

If you input 5 instead, the computer will print this instead:

```
kiss
kiss
kiss
kiss
kiss
```

Let's turn that program into a SUB procedure that gets its input from the main procedure instead of from a human. Here's the SUB procedure:

```
SUB kiss (n)
  FOR i = 1 TO n
    PRINT "kiss"
  NEXT
END SUB
```

In that SUB procedure's top line, the "(n)" means "input the number n from the main procedure, instead of from a human". If the main procedure says —

```
kiss 3
```

then the n will be 3, so the SUB procedure will print "kiss" 3 times, like this:

```
kiss
kiss
kiss
```

If the main procedure says —

```
kiss 5
```

then the n will be 5, so the SUB procedure will print "kiss" 5 times.

Please type this complete program, which contains that SUB procedure:

```
DEFINT A-Z
CLS
PRINT "The boy said:"
kiss 3
PRINT "His girlfriend said okay!"
PRINT "Then the boy said:"
kiss 5
PRINT "His girlfiend said okay!"
PRINT "Finally, the boy said:"
kiss 8
PRINT "His girlfriend said:"
PRINT "I'm not prepared to go that far."

SUB kiss (n)
  FOR i = 1 TO n
    PRINT "kiss"
  NEXT
END SUB
```

When you run that program, the computer will print:

```
The boy said:
kiss
kiss
kiss
His girlfriend said okay!
Then the boy said:
kiss
kiss
kiss
kiss
kiss
His girlfriend said okay!
Finally, the boy said:
kiss
kiss
kiss
kiss
kiss
kiss
kiss
kiss
His girlfriend said:
I'm not prepared to go that far.
```

In that SUB procedure's top line, the n is called the **parameter**; put it in parentheses. In the line that says "kiss 3", the 3 is called the **argument**.

In that program, instead of saying —

```
kiss 3
```

you can say:

```
y = 3
kiss y
```

Then y's value (3) will become n, so the SUB procedure will print "kiss" 3 times. The n (which is the parameter) will use the same box as y (which is the argument). For example, if you insert into the SUB procedure a line saying "n = 9", the y will become 9 also.

You can write fancier programs. Here's how to begin a SUB procedure called joe having three parameters (n, m, and k$):

```
SUB joe (n, m, k$)
```

To use that subroutine, give a command such as:

```
joe 7, 9, "love"
```

Suppose your main procedure says:

```
DIM x$(3)
x$(1) = "love"
x$(2) = "death"
x$(3) = "war"
```

That means x$ is a list of these 3 strings: "love", "death", and "war". To make joan be a SUB procedure manipulating that list, make joan's top line say —

```
SUB joan (x$())
```

In that line, the () warns the computer that x$ is a list. You do *not* need to say DIM x$(3) in the SUB procedure. When you want to make the main procedure use joan, put this line into the main procedure:

```
joan x$()
```

Those lines, "SUB joan (x$())" and "joan x$()", work even if x$ is a table defined by a line such as DIM x$(30, 40).

DEFINT To make all the variables in your program be short integers, say "DEFINT A-Z" at the top of the main procedure and say it again at the top of each SUB procedure, so SUB procedure joe begins like this:

```
DEFINT A-Z
SUB joe
```

If you typed "DEFINT A-Z" at the top of the main procedure, the computer will automatically type "DEFINT A-Z" for you at the top of each new SUB procedure.

STYLE

Design a program

First, decide on your ultimate goal. Be optimistic. Maybe you'd like the computer to play the perfect game of chess? or translate every English sentence into French?

Research the past

Whatever you want the computer to do, someone else probably thought of the same idea already and wrote a program for it.

Find out. Ask your friends. Ask folks in nearby schools, computer stores, computer centers, companies, libraries, and bookstores. Look through books and magazines. There are even books that list what programs have been written. Ask the company you bought your computer from.

Even if you don't find exactly the program you're looking for, you may find one that's close enough to be okay, or that will work with just a little fixing or serve as *part* of your program or at least give you a *clue* as to where to begin. In a textbooks or magazines, you'll probably find a discussion of the problem you're trying to solve and the pros and cons of various solutions to it — some methods are faster than others.

Remember: if you keep your head in the sand and don't look at what other programmers have done already, your programming effort may turn out to be a mere exercise, useless to the rest of the world.

Simplify

Too often, programmers embark on huge projects and never get them done. Once you have an idea of what's been done before and how hard your project is, simplify it.

Instead of making the computer play a perfect game of chess, how about settling for a game in which the computer plays unremarkably but at least doesn't cheat? Instead of translating every English sentence into French, how about translating just English colors? (We wrote that program already.)

In other words, **pick a less ambitious, more realistic goal**, which if achieved will please you and be a steppingstone to your ultimate goal.

Finding a bug in a program is like finding a needle in a haystack: removing the needle is easier if the haystack is small than if you wait until more hay's been piled on.

Specify the I/O

Make your new, simple goal more precise. That's called **specification**. One way to be specific is to **draw a picture, showing what your screen will look like if your program's running successfully**.

In that picture, find the lines typed by the computer. They become your program's PRINT statements. Find the lines typed by the human: they become the INPUT statements. Now you can start writing your program: **write the PRINT and INPUT statements** on paper, with a pencil, and leave blank lines between them. You'll fill in the blanks later.

Suppose you want the computer to find the average of two numbers. Your picture will look like this:

```
What's the first number? 7
What's the second number? 9
The average is 8
```

Your program at this stage will be:

```
CLS
INPUT "What's the first number"; a
INPUT "What's the second number"; b
etc.
PRINT "The average is"; c
```

All you have left to do is figure out what the "etc." is. Here's the general method....

Choose your statements

Suppose you didn't have a computer. Then how would you get the answer?

Would you have to use a mathematical formula? If so, put the formula into your program, but remember that the equation's left side must have just one variable. For example, if you're trying to solve a problem about right triangles, you might have to use the Pythagorean formula $a^2+b^2=c^2$; but the left side of the equation must have just one variable, so your program must say a=SQR(c^2-b^2), or b=SQR(c^2-a^2), or c=SQR(a^2+b^2), depending on whether you're trying to compute a, b, or c.

Would you have to use a memorized list, such as an English-French dictionary or the population of each state or the weight of each chemical element? If so, that list becomes your DATA, and you need to READ it. If it would be helpful to have the data numbered — so the first piece of data is called x(1), the next piece of data is called x(2), etc. — use the DIM statement.

Subscripts are particularly useful if one long list of information will be referred to *several* times in the program.

Does your reasoning repeat? That means your program should have a loop. If you know how many times to repeat, say FOR...NEXT. If you're not sure how often, say DO...LOOP. If the thing to be repeated isn't repeated immediately, but just after several other things have happened, make the repeated part be a SUB procedure.

At some point in your reasoning, do you have to make a *decision*? Do you have to choose among several alternatives? To choose between two alternatives, say IF...THEN. To choose among three or more alternatives, say SELECT CASE. If you want the computer to make the choice arbitrarily, "by chance" instead of for a reason, say IF RND<.5.

Do you have to compare two things? The way to say "compare x with y" is: IF x = y THEN.

Write pseudocode

Some English teachers say that before you write a paper, you should make an outline. Some computer teachers give similar advice about writing programs.

The "outline" can look like a program in which some of the lines are written in plain English instead of computerese. For example, one statement in your outline might be:

```
a = the average of the twelve values of x
```

Such a statement, written in English instead of in computerese, is called **pseudocode**. Later, when you fill in the details, expand that pseudocode into the following:

```
sum = 0
FOR i = 1 TO 12
  sum = sum + x(i)
NEXT
average = sum / 12
```

Organize yourself

Keep the program's over-all organization simple. That will make it easier for you to expand the program and find bugs. Here's some folklore, handed down from generation to generation of programmers, that will simplify your organization....

Use top-down programming. That means write a one-sentence description of your program; then expand that sentence to several sentences; then expand each of those sentences to several more sentences; and so on, until you can't expand any more. Then turn each of those new sentences into lines of program. Then your program will be in the same order as the English sentences and therefore organized the same way as an English-speaking mind.

A variation is to **use SUB procedures**. That means writing the essence of the program as a very short main procedure; instead of filling in the grubby details immediately, replace each piece of grubbiness by a SUB procedure. Your program will be like a good book: your main procedure will move swiftly, and the annoying details will be relegated to the appendices at the back; the appendices are the SUB procedures. Make each procedure brief — no more than 20 lines — so the entire procedure can fit on the screen; if it starts getting longer and grubbier, replace each piece of grubbiness by *another* SUB procedure.

Avoid GO TO. It's hard for a human to understand a program that's a morass of GO TO statements. It's like trying to read a book where each paragraph says to turn to a different page! When you *must* say GO TO, try to go forward instead of backwards and not go too far.

Use variables

After you've written some lines of your program, you may notice that your reasoning "almost repeats": several lines bear a strong resemblance to each other. You can't use DO...LOOP or FOR...NEXT unless the lines repeat exactly. To make the repetition complete, use a variable to represent the parts that are different.

For example, suppose your program contains these lines:

```
PRINT 29.34281 + 9.876237 * SQR(5)
PRINT 29.34281 + 9.876237 * SQR(7)
PRINT 29.34281 + 9.876237 * SQR(9)
PRINT 29.34281 + 9.876237 * SQR(11)
PRINT 29.34281 + 9.876237 * SQR(13)
PRINT 29.34281 + 9.876237 * SQR(15)
PRINT 29.34281 + 9.876237 * SQR(17)
PRINT 29.34281 + 9.876237 * SQR(19)
PRINT 29.34281 + 9.876237 * SQR(21)
```

Each of those lines says PRINT 29.3428 + 9.87627 * SQR(a number). The number keeps changing, so call it x. All those PRINT lines can be replaced by this loop:

```
FOR x = 5 TO 21 STEP 2
  PRINT 29.34281 + 9.876237 * SQR(x)
NEXT
```

Here's a harder example to fix:

```
PRINT 29.34281 + 9.876237 * SQR(5)
PRINT 29.34281 + 9.876237 * SQR(97.3)
PRINT 29.34281 + 9.876237 * SQR(8.62)
PRINT 29.34281 + 9.876237 * SQR(.4)
PRINT 29.34281 + 9.876237 * SQR(200)
PRINT 29.34281 + 9.876237 * SQR(12)
PRINT 29.34281 + 9.876237 * SQR(591)
PRINT 29.34281 + 9.876237 * SQR(.2)
PRINT 29.24281 + 9.876237 * SQR(100076)
```

Again, let's use x. All those PRINT lines can be combined like this:

```
DATA 5,97.3,8.62,.4,200,12,591,.2,100076
FOR i = 1 TO 9
  READ x
  PRINT 29.34281 + 9.876237 * SQR(x)
NEXT
```

This one's even tougher:

```
PRINT 29.34281 + 9.876237 * SQR(a)
PRINT 29.34281 + 9.876237 * SQR(b)
PRINT 29.34281 + 9.876237 * SQR(c)
PRINT 29.34281 + 9.876237 * SQR(d)
PRINT 29.34281 + 9.876237 * SQR(e)
PRINT 29.34281 + 9.876237 * SQR(f)
PRINT 29.34281 + 9.876237 * SQR(g)
PRINT 29.34281 + 9.876237 * SQR(h)
PRINT 29.34281 + 9.876237 * SQR(i)
```

Let's assume a, b, c, d, e, f, g, h, and i have been computed earlier in the program. The trick to shortening those lines is to change the names of the variables. Throughout the program, say x(1) instead of a, say x(2) instead of b, say x(3) instead of c, etc. Say DIM x(9) at the beginning of your program. Then replace all those PRINT lines by this loop:

```
FOR i = 1 TO 9
  PRINT 29.34281 + 9.876237 * SQR(x(i))
NEXT
```

Your program should be **efficient**. That means it should use as little of the computer's time and memory as possible.

To use less of the computer's memory, make your DIMensions as small as possible. Try writing the program without any arrays at all; if that turns out to be terribly inconvenient, use the smallest and fewest arrays possible.

To use less of the computer's time, avoid having the computer do the same thing more than once.

These lines force the computer to compute SQR(8.2 * n + 7) three times:

```
PRINT SQR(8.3 * n + 7) + 2
PRINT SQR(8.3 * n + 7) / 9.1
PRINT 5 - SQR(8.3 * n + 7)
```

You should change them to:

```
k = SQR(8.3 * n + 7)
PRINT k + 2
PRINT k / 9.1
PRINT 5 - k
```

These lines force the computer to compute $x^9 + 2$ a hundred times:

```
FOR i = 1 TO 100
  PRINT (x ^ 9 + 2) / i
NEXT
```

You should change them to:

```
k = x ^ 9 + 2
FOR i = 1 TO 100
  PRINT k / i
NEXT
```

These lines force the computer to count to 100 twice:

```
sum = 0
FOR i = 1 TO 100
  sum = sum + x(i)
NEXT
PRINT "The sum of the x's is"; sum
product = 1
FOR i = 1 TO 100
  product = product * x(i)
NEXT
PRINT "The product of the x's is"; product
```

You should combine the two FOR...NEXT loops into a single FOR...NEXT loop, so the computer counts to 100 just once. Here's how:

```
sum = 0
product = 1
FOR i = 1 TO 100
  sum = sum + x(i)
  product = product * x(i)
NEXT
PRINT "The sum of the x's is"; sum
PRINT "The product of the x's is"; product
```

Here are more tricks to make your program run faster....

Instead of exponents, use multiplication.

```
slow:   y = x ^ 2
faster: y = x * x
```

If your program doesn't involve decimals or big numbers, put this statement at the top of your program:

```
DEFINT A-Z
```

If your program involves just a *few* decimals or big numbers, begin your program by saying DEFINT A-Z; then put the symbol "&" after every variable that stands for a long integer, and put the symbol "!" after every variable that stands for a single-precision real number.

When you've written a program, **test** it: run it and see whether it works.

If the computer does *not* gripe, your tendency will be to say "Whoopee!" Don't cheer too loudly. **The answers the computer is printing might be wrong.** Even if its answers look reasonable, don't assume they're right: the computer's errors can be subtle. Check some of its answers by computing them with a pencil.

Even if the answers the computer prints are correct, don't cheer. Maybe you were just lucky. Type different input, and see whether your program still works. Probably you can input something that will make your program go crazy or print a wrong answer. Your mission: to find input that will reveal the existence of a bug.

Try six kinds of input....

Try simple input

Type in simple integers, like 2 and 10, so the computation is simple, and you can check the computer's answers easily.

Try input that increases

See how the computer's answer changes when the input changes from 2 to 1000.

Does the change in the computer's answer look reasonable? Does the computer's answer go up when it should go up, and down when it should go down?... and by a reasonable amount?

Try input testing each IF

For a program that says —

```
IF x < 7 THEN GOTO 10
```

input an x less than 7 (to see whether line 10 works), then an x greater than 7 (to see whether the line underneath the IF line works), then an x equal to 7 (to see whether you really want "<" instead of "<="), then an x very close to 7, to check round-off error.

For a program that says —

```
IF x ^ 2 + y < z THEN GOTO 10
```

input an x, y, and z that make $x^2 + y$ less than z. Then try inputs that make $x^2 + y$ very close to z.

Try extreme input

What happens if you input:

a huge number, like 45392000000 or 1E35?
a tiny number, like .00000003954 or 1E-35?
a trivial number, like 0 or 1?
a typical number, like 45.13?
a negative number, like -52?

Find out.

If the input is supposed to be a string, what happens if you input aaaaa or zzzzz? What happens if you capitalize the input? If there are supposed to be two inputs, what happens if you input the same thing for each?

Try input making a line act strange

If your program contains division, try input that will make the divisor be zero or a tiny decimal close to zero. If your program contains the square root of a quantity, try input that will make the quantity be negative. If your program says "FOR i = x TO y", try input that will make y be less than x, then equal to x. If your program mentions x(i), try input that will make i be zero or negative or greater than the DIM.

Try input that causes round-off error: for a program that says "x - y" or says "IF x = y", try input that will make x almost equal y.

Try garbage

Computers often print wrong answers. A computer can print a wrong answer because its circuitry is broken or because a program has a bug. But **the main reason why computers print wrong answers is incorrect input**. Incorrect input is called **garbage** and has several causes....

The user's finger slips Instead of 400, he inputs 4000. Instead of 27, he inputs 72. Trying to type .753, he leaves out the decimal point.

The user got wrong information He tries to input the temperature, but his thermometer is leaking. He tries to input the results of a questionnaire, but everybody who filled out his questionnaires lied.

The instructions aren't clear The program asks "How far did the ball fall?" but the user doesn't know whether to type the distance in feet or in meters.

Is time to be given in seconds or minutes? Are angles to be measured in degrees or radians?

If the program asks "What is your name?" should the user type "Joe Smith" or "Smith,Joe" or just "Joe"?

Can the user input "y" instead of "yes"?

Maybe the user isn't clear about whether to insert commas, quotation marks, and periods. If several items are to be typed, should they be typed on the same line or on separate lines? If your program asks "How many brothers and sisters do you have?" and the user has 2 brothers & 3 sisters, should he type "5" or "2,3" or "2 brothers and 3 sisters"?

For a quiz that asks "Who was the first U.S. President?" what if the user answers "George Washington" or simply "Washington" or "washington" or "G. Washington" or "General George Washington" or "President Washington" or "Martha's husband?" Make the instructions clearer:

```
Who was the first U.S. President (give just his last name)?
```

The user tries to joke or sabotage Instead of inputting his name, he types an obscene comment. When asked how many brothers and sisters he has, he says 275.

Responsibility As a programmer, it's your duty to include clear directions for using your program, and you must make the program reject ridiculous input.

For example, if your program is supposed to print weekly paychecks, it should refuse to print checks for more than $10000. Your program should contain these lines:

```
10 INPUT "How much money did the employee earn"; e
IF e > 10000 THEN
  PRINT e; "is quite a big paycheck!  I don't believe you."
  PRINT "Please retype your request."
  GO TO 10
END IF
```

That IF line is called an **error trap** (or **error-handling routine**). Your program should contain several, to prevent printing checks that are too small (2¢?) or negative or otherwise ridiculous ($200.73145?)

To see how your program reacts to input that's either garbage or unusual, **ask a friend to run your program**. That person might input something you never thought of.

Document it

Write an explanation that helps other people understand your program.

An explanation is called **documentation**. When you write an explanation, you're **documenting** the program.

You can write the documentation on a separate sheet of paper, or you can make the computer print the documentation when the user runs or lists the program.

A popular device is to begin the program by making the computer ask the user:

```
Do you need instructions?
```

You need two kinds of documentation: how to use the program, and how the program was written.

How to use the program

Your explanation of how to use the program should include:

the program's name
how to get the program from the disk
the program's purpose
a list of other programs that must be combined with this program, to make a workable combination
the correct way to type the input and data (show an example)
the correct way to interpret the output
the program's limitations (input it can't handle, a list of error messages that might be printed, round-off error)
a list of bugs you haven't fixed yet

How the program was written

An explanation of how you wrote the program will help other programmers borrow your ideas, and help them expand your program to meet new situations. It should include:

your name
the date you finished it
the computer you wrote it for
the language you wrote it in (probably BASIC)
the name of the method you used ("solves quadratic equations by using the quadratic formula")
the name of the book or magazine where you found the method
the name of any program you borrowed ideas from
an informal explanation of how program works ("It loops until x>y, then computes the weather forecast.")
the purpose of each SUB procedure
the meaning of each variable
the significance of reaching a line (for a program saying "IF x < 60 THEN GOTO 1000", say "Reaching line 1000 means the student flunked.")

WEIRD FEATURES

Fancy input

The typical INPUT statement looks like this:

```
INPUT "What is your name"; n$
```

It makes the computer ask "What is your name?" then wait for you to answer the question. So when you run the program, the conversation looks like this:

```
What is your name? Maria
```

Notice that the computer automatically adds a question mark at the end of the question, and leaves a blank space after the question mark.

Omitting the question mark

If you want to omit the question mark and the blank space, replace the semicolon by a comma:

```
INPUT "What is your name", n$
```

The comma makes the computer omit the question mark and the blank space, so the conversation will look like this:

```
What is your nameMaria
```

Here's a prettier example of how to use the comma:

```
INPUT "Please type your name...", n$
```

The conversation will look like this:

```
Please type your name...Maria
```

Here's an even prettier example:

```
INPUT "To become a movie star, type your name next to the stars***", n$
```

The conversation will look like this:

```
To become a movie star, type your name next to the stars***Maria
```

Omitting the prompt

The typical INPUT statement contains a question, such as "What is your name". The question is called the **prompt**. If you wish, you can omit the prompt, like this:

```
INPUT n$
```

That line doesn't include a question, but the computer still prints a question mark followed by a blank space, so the conversation looks like this:

```
? Maria
```

To make that INPUT line more practical, put a PRINT line above it, like this:

```
PRINT "Please type your name after the question mark"
INPUT N$
```

That makes the conversation look like this:

```
Please type your name after the question mark
? Maria
```

Adjacent printing

Here's a simple program:

```
CLS
INPUT "What is your name"; n$
PRINT "!!!What a wonderful name!!!"
```

It produces this conversation:

```
What is your name? MARIA
!!!What a wonderful name!!!
```

To have more fun, insert a semicolon immediately after the word INPUT, like this:

```
CLS
INPUT ; "What is your name"; n$
PRINT "!!!What a wonderful name!!!"
```

The conversation will begin normally:

```
What is your name? Maria
```

But when you press the ENTER key after Maria, the extra semicolon makes the computer do the PRINTing *next* to Maria, like this:

```
What is your name? Maria!!!What a wonderful name!!!
```

To surprise your friends, run this program:

```
CLS
INPUT ; "What is your name"; n$
PRINT n$; n$; n$
```

The program begins by asking:

```
What is your name?
```

Suppose the person says Maria, like this:

```
What is your name? Maria
```

When the person presses the ENTER key after Maria, the PRINT line automatically prints Maria three more times afterwards, like this:

```
What is your name? MariaMariaMariaMaria
```

This program asks for your first name, then your last name:

```
CLS
INPUT ; "What is your first name"; first.name$
INPUT "    What is your last name"; last.name$
```

The first INPUT line makes the conversation begin like this:

```
What is your first name? Maria
```

When you press the ENTER key after Maria, that INPUT's extra semicolon makes makes the next INPUT appear on the same line, like this:

```
What is your first name? Maria    What is your last name?
```

If you answer Yee, the whole conversation looks like this:

```
What is your first name? Maria    What is your last name? Yee
```

Multiple input

This program asks for your name, age, and weight:

```
CLS
INPUT "Name, age, weight"; n$, a, w
```

When you run the program, the computer asks:

```
Name, age, weight?
```

The computer waits for you to type your name, age, and weight. When you type them, put commas between them, like this:

```
Name, age, weight? John,25,148
```

If your name is "John Smith, Jr.", and you want to input all that instead of just John, you must put quotation marks around your name:

```
Name, age, weight? "John Smith, Jr.",25,148
```

Here's the rule: you must put quotation marks around any INPUT string that contains a comma.

LINE INPUT

If you say —

```
LINE INPUT "Please type your name..."; n$
```

the computer will say:

```
Please type your name...
```

Then the computer will wait for you to type your name. You do *not* have to put quotation marks around your name, even if your name contains a comma. LINE INPUT means: the entire line that the person inputs will become the string, even if the line contains a comma.

Notice that the LINE INPUT statement does *not* make the computer automatically print a question mark. And notice that the variable must be a string (such as n$), not a number.

INPUT$

This program reveals private information about Mary:

```
CLS
PRINT "Mary secretly wishes to kiss a cow!"
```

Here's how to protect that program, so only people who know the "secret password" can run it....

First, invent a secret password. Let's make it be "tuna".

Here's the program:

```
CLS
INPUT "What's the secret password"; a$
IF a$ = "tuna" THEN
  PRINT "Mary secretly wishes to kiss a cow!"
ELSE
  PRINT "You are an unauthorized user!"
END IF
```

The INPUT line asks the person to type the secret password. Whatever the person types is called a$. If the person types "tuna", the computer will say:

```
Mary secretly wishes to kiss a cow!
```

But if the person does *not* type "tuna", the computer says "You are an unauthorized user!" and refuses to reveal Mary's secret desire.

This program's better:

```
CLS
PRINT "Please type the secret password."
a$ = INPUT$(4)
IF a$ = "tuna" THEN
  PRINT "Mary secretly wishes to kiss a cow!"
ELSE
  PRINT "You are an unauthorized user!"
END IF
```

Line 2 makes the computer say:

```
Please type the secret password.
```

Line 3 waits for the person to input 4 characters. The characters that the person inputs will become a$. For example, suppose the person types *t*, then *u*, then *n*, then *a*; then a$ will become "tuna" and the computer will reveal Mary's secret.

While the person inputs the 4 characters, they won't appear on the screen; they'll be invisible. That's to prevent other people in the room from peeking at the screen and noticing the password.

After typing the 4 characters, the person does *not* have to press the ENTER key. As soon as the person types the 4th character, the computer makes a$ be the 4 characters that the person typed.

Broken computer

This devilish program makes your computer pretend to be broken, so that whenever you press the w key your screen shows an f instead:

```
CLS
DO
  a$ = INPUT$(1)
  IF a$ = "w" THEN PRINT "f"; ELSE PRINT a$;
LOOP
```

Line 3 waits for you to type 1 character. The IF line says: if the character you typed was "w", print an "f" on the screen instead; otherwise, print the character you typed. Since that routine is in a DO loop, the computer will repeat the routine forever. For example, if you try to type "the weather is wonderful", you'll see this on the screen instead:

```
the feather is fonderful
```

For an even wilder time, tell the computer to change each "e" to "ooga", by changing the IF line to this:

```
        IF a$ = "e" THEN PRINT "ooga"; ELSE PRINT a$;
```

Then if you try to type "We are here", you'll see this on the screen instead:

```
wooga arooga hoogarooga
```

Abridged literature

This program gives you a choice of literature:

```
CLS
PRINT "Welcome to the world's great literature, abridged."
PRINT "Which kind of literature would you like?"
PRINT "n: novel"
PRINT "p: poem"
10 PRINT "Please press n or p."
SELECT CASE INPUT$(1)
  CASE "n"
    PRINT "He:  I love you."
    PRINT "She: I'm pregnant."
    PRINT "He:  Let's get married."
    PRINT "She: Let's get divorced."
    PRINT "He:  Let's get back together."
    PRINT "She: Too bad you died in the war, but I'll never forget you!"
  CASE "p"
    PRINT "Noses"
    PRINT "Blowses"
  CASE ELSE
    GOTO 10
END SELECT
```

The program begins by printing:

```
Welcome to the world's great literature, abridged.
Which kind of literature would you like?
n: novel
p: poem
Please press n or p.
```

The SELECT CASE line makes the computer wait for you to press a key. You do *not* have to press the ENTER key afterwards.

If you press the n key, the computer does the lines indented under CASE "n". Those lines print an abridged novel.

If you press the p key instead, the computer does the lines indented under CASE "p". Those lines print an abridged poem.

If you press neither n nor p, the computer does the line indented under CASE ELSE. That line makes the computer GO back TO line 10, which reminds you to press n or p.

SWAP

The computer understands the word SWAP:

```
CLS
x = 4
y = 9
SWAP x, y
PRINT x; y
```

Lines 2 & 3 say x is 4, and y is 9. The SWAP line swaps x with y; so x becomes 9, and y becomes 4. The bottom line prints:

```
 9  4
```

That example swapped numbers. You can also swap strings:

```
CLS
a$ = "horse"
b$ = "cart"
SWAP a$, b$
PRINT a$; " "; b$
```

Lines 2 & 3 say a$ is "horse" and b$ is "cart". The SWAP line swaps a$ with b$; so a$ becomes "cart", and b$ becomes "horse". The bottom line puts the cart before the horse:

```
cart horse
```

Shuffling

Here are some cards:

```
queen of hearts
jack of diamonds
ace of spades
joker
king of clubs
```

Let's shuffle them, to put them into a random order.

To begin, put the list of cards into a DATA statement:

```
CLS
DATA queen of hearts,jack of diamonds,ace of spades,joker,king of clubs
```

We have 5 cards. Let the queen of hearts be called card$(1), the jack of diamonds be called card$(2), the ace of spades be called card$(3), the joker be called card$(4), and the king of clubs be called card$(5):

```
n = 5
DIM card$(n)
FOR i = 1 TO n
  READ card$(i)
NEXT
```

Shuffle the cards, by using the following strategy....

Swap card n with a random card before it (or with itself); then swap card n-1 with a random card before it (or with itself); then swap card n-2 with a random card before it (or with itself); etc. Keep doing that, until you finally reach card 2, which you swap with a random card before it (or with itself). Here's the code:

```
RANDOMIZE TIMER
FOR i = n TO 2 STEP -1
  SWAP card$(i), card$(1 + INT(RND * i))
NEXT
```

Finally, print the shuffled deck:

```
FOR i = 1 TO n
  PRINT card$(i)
NEXT
```

So altogether, here's the entire program:

```
CLS
DATA queen of hearts,jack of diamonds,ace of spades,joker,king of clubs

n = 5
DIM card$(n)
FOR i = 1 TO n
  READ card$(i)
NEXT

RANDOMIZE TIMER
FOR i = n TO 2 STEP -1
  SWAP card$(i), card$(1 + INT(RND * i))
NEXT

FOR i = 1 TO n
  PRINT card$(i)
NEXT
```

The computer will print something like this:

```
king of clubs
joker
jack of diamonds
queen of hearts
ace of spades
```

To shuffle a larger deck, change just the DATA and the line saying n=5.

Sorting

Putting words in alphabetical order — or putting numbers in numerical order — is called **sorting**.

Three-Line Sort Here are a dozen names: Sue, Ann, Joe, Alice, Ted, Jill, Fred, Al, Sam, Pat, Sally, Moe. Let's make the computer alphabetize them (sort them).

Begin by clearing the screen:

```
CLS
```

To make the program run faster, tell the computer that all numbers in the program will be short integers:

```
DEFINT A-Z
```

Put the list of names in a DATA statement:

```
DATA Sue,Ann,Joe,Alice,Ted,Jill,Fred,Al,Sam,Pat,Sally,Moe
```

We have 12 names:

```
n = 12
```

Let Sue by called x$(1), Ann be called x$(2), Joe be called x$(3), etc. Here's how:

```
DIM X$(n)
FOR i = 1 TO n
  READ x$(i)
NEXT
```

Alphabetize the names, by using the following strategy….

Compare the first name against the second; if they're not in alphabetical order, swap them. Compare the second name against the third; if they're not in alphabetical order, swap them. Compare the third name against the fourth; if they're not in alphabetical order, swap them. Continue that process, until you finally compare the last two names. But each time you swap, you must start the whole process over again, to make sure the preceding names are still in alphabetical order. Here's the code:

```
10 FOR i = 1 TO n - 1
  IF x$(i) > x$(i + 1) THEN SWAP x$(i), x$(i + 1): GOTO 10
NEXT
```

Finally, print the alphabetized list:

```
FOR I = 1 TO n
  PRINT x$(i)
NEXT
```

So altogether, the program looks like this:

```
CLS
DEFINT A-Z
DATA Sue,Ann,Joe,Alice,Ted,Jill,Fred,Al,Sam,Pat,Sally,Moe
n = 12
DIM x$(n)
FOR i = 1 TO n
  READ x$(i)
NEXT
10 FOR i = 1 TO n - 1
  IF x$(i) > x$(i + 1) THEN SWAP x$(i), x$(i + 1): GOTO 10
NEXT
FOR i = 1 TO n
  PRINT x$(i)
NEXT
```

The computer will print:

```
Al
Alice
Ann
Fred
Jill
Joe
Moe
Pat
Sally
Sam
Sue
Ted
```

In that program, the sorting occurs in the FOR loop that begins at line 10. Those three lines are called the **Three-Line Sort**.

Those three lines form a loop. The part of the loop that the computer encounters the most often is the phrase "IF x$(i) > x$(i + 1)". In fact, if you tell the computer to alphabetize a list of names that's long (several *hundred* names), the computer spends the *majority* of its time repeatedly handling "IF x$(i) > x$(i + 1)".

How long will the computer take to handle a long list of names? The length of time depends mainly on how often the computer encounters the phrase "IF x$(i) > x$(i + 1)".

If the list contains n names, the number of times that the computer encounters the phrase "IF x$(i) > x$(i + 1)" is approximately $n^3/8$. Here are some examples:

n (number of names)	$n^3/8$ (approximate number of encounters)
10	125
12	216
20	1,000
40	8,000
100	125,000
1,000	125,000,000

For example, the chart says that a list of 12 names requires approximately 216 encounters.

The 216 is just an approximation: the exact number of encounters depends on which list of names you're trying to alphabetize. If the list is nearly in alphabetical order *already*, the number of encounters will be less than 216; if the list is in *reverse* alphabetical order, the number of encounters will be more than 216; but if the list is typical (not yet in any particular order), the number of encounters will be about 216. For the list that we tried (Sue, Ann, Joe, Alice, Ted, Jill, Fred, Al, Sam, Pat, Sally, Moe), the exact number of encounters happens to be 189, which is close to 216.

How long will your computer take to finish sorting? The length of time depends on which computer you have, how many names are in the list, and how long each name is. A typical 486DX-66 computer (handling a list of typical names) requires about .00002 seconds per encounter. Multiplying the number of encounters by .00002 seconds, you get:

Number of names	Encounters ($n^3/8$)	Time	
10	125	.0025	secs
12	216	.00432	secs
20	1,000	.02	secs
40	8,000	.16	secs
100	125,000	2.5	secs
1,000	125,000,000	2500	secs = about 42 minutes

Five-Line Sort To make the program run faster, use the **Five-Line Sort** instead, which uses this strategy…. Compare the first name against the second (that comparison is called i=1), then compare the second name against the third (that comparison is called i=2), then compare the third name against the fourth (that comparison is called i=3), etc. If you find a pair of names that are out of order, swap them and then recheck the pairs that came before. To "recheck the pairs that came before", start with the most recent pairs and work back toward the first name (FOR j = i TO 1 STEP -1), swapping whenever necessary, until you come to a pair that doesn't need to be swapped. When you come to a pair that doesn't need to be swapped, stop the rechecking and proceed to the next i.

Here's the code:

```
FOR i = 1 TO n - 1
  FOR j = i TO 1 STEP -1
    IF x$(j) > x$(j + 1) THEN SWAP x$(j), x$(j + 1) ELSE GOTO 10
  NEXT
10 NEXT
```

The IF line says: if x$(j) and x$(j + 1) are out of order, SWAP them; but if they're *not* out of order, get out of the j loop and GOTO the NEXT i instead.

Even though that Five-Line Sort is longer to type than the Three-Line Sort, the computer handles the Five-Line Sort faster, because its "GOTO 10" lets the computer hop ahead to the NEXT i instead of forcing the computer to go back to the "FOR i = 1".

For the Five-Line Sort, the number of times the computer encounters the phrase "IF x$(j) > x$(j + 1)" is just $n^2/4$:

Number of names	Encounters ($n^2 / 4$)	Time
10	25	.0005 secs
12	36	.00072 secs
20	100	.002 secs
40	400	.008 secs
100	2,500	.05 secs
1,000	250,000	5 secs

Eight-Line Sort

The Five-Line Sort compares just adjacent pairs: x$(j) and x$(j+1). The **Eight-Line Sort** compares pairs that are farther apart: x$(j) and x$(j+d), where d is a big distance. So the Eight-Line Sort resembles the Five-Line Sort but says +d instead of +1, and says -d instead of -1:

```
FOR i = 1 TO n - d
  FOR j = i TO 1 STEP -d
    IF x$(j) > x$(j + d) THEN SWAP x$(j), x$(j + d) ELSE GOTO 10
  NEXT
10 NEXT
```

But how big is d?

Begin by making d be a big number, about $1/3$ as big as n, and perform those five lines. Then divide by 3 again, so d becomes about $1/9$ as big as n, and perform those five lines again. Then divide by 3 again, so d becomes about $1/27$ as big as n, and perform those five lines again. Keep dividing by 3, until d finally becomes 1, which makes those five lines act exactly the same as the Five-Line Sort. But during that last pass through the data, when d is 1, the computer performs the five lines very quickly, since the earlier passes already put the names into roughly alphabetical order by comparing pairs that were far apart.

Moreover, those early passes consumed very little time, since during those passes the computer did the FOR j loop very few times. (It did that loop few times because it said to "STEP -d", where d was a big number.)

Here's the complete Eight-Line Sort:

```
d = n
2 d = d \ 3 + 1
FOR i = 1 TO n - d
  FOR j = i TO 1 STEP -d
    IF x$(j) > x$(j + d) THEN SWAP x$(j), x$(j + d) ELSE GOTO 10
  NEXT
10 NEXT
IF d > 1 THEN GOTO 2
```

In line 2, the symbol "\" says to do integer division, so the computer will divide by 3 but ignore all digits after the decimal point. Altogether, line 2 says this: to get the new d, divide the old d by 3 (ignoring all digits after the decimal point) and then add 1. That "+ 1" makes the new d be slightly *more* than the old d divided by 3.

For the Eight-Line Sort, the number of times the computer encounters the phrase "IF x$(j) > x$(j + d)" is just $1.5*(n-1)^{(4/3)}$:

Number of names	Encounters	Time
10	28	.00056 secs
12	37	.00074 secs
20	76	.00152 secs
40	198	.00396 secs
100	687	.01374 secs
1,000	14,980	.2996 secs

Notice that the Eight-Line Sort handles 1,000 names in .2996 seconds. That's much faster than the Five-Line Sort, which takes 5 seconds. But to handle just 10 names, the Eight-Line Sort does *not* run faster than the Five-Line Sort. So use the Eight-Line Sort just for handling *long* lists of names.

We've sure come a long way! To alphabetize 1,000 names, the Three-Line Sort took about 42 minutes; the Five-Line Sort took 5 seconds; the Eight-Line Sort took about .3 seconds.

If you try running those sorting methods on *your* computer, you'll find the timings are different, since the exact timings depend on which computer you have, the length of each name, and how badly the names are out of order.

Famous sorts Though I "invented" all those sorting methods, most of them just improve a little on methods developed by others. For example, the Five-Line Sort improves slightly on the **Shuttle Sort**, which was invented by Shaw & Trimble in 1983. The Eight-Line Sort improves slightly on the **Shell Sort**, which was invented by Donald Shell in 1959 and further developed by Hibbard & Boothroyd in 1963, Peterson & Russell in 1971, and Knuth in 1973.

Phone directory Suppose you want to alphabetize this phone directory:

Name	Phone number
Mary Smith	277-8139
John Doe	513-9134
Russ Walter	666-6644
Information	555-1212

Just use one of the alphabetizing programs I showed you! Type the DATA like this:

```
DATA Smith Mary 277-8139,Doe John 513-9134
DATA Walter Russ 666-6644,Information 555-1212
```

The computer will print:

```
Doe John 513-9134
Information 555-1212
Smith Mary 277-8139
Walter Russ 666-6644
```

Sorting numbers Suppose you want to put a list of numbers into increasing order. For example, if the numbers are 51, 4.257, -814, 62, and .2, let's make the computer print:

```
-814
.2
4.257
51
62
```

To do that, just use one of the alphabetizing programs I showed you — but in the DATA statement, put the numbers instead of strings, and say "x!" instead of "x$".

To put a list of numbers into *decreasing* order, begin by writing a program that puts them into *increasing* order, and then change each "> x" to "< x".

Sequential data files

Here's a simple program:

```
CLS
PRINT "eat"
PRINT 2 + 2
PRINT "eggs"
```

It makes the computer print this message onto your screen:

```
eat
 4
eggs
```

Instead of printing that message onto your screen, let's make the computer print the message onto your disk. Here's how....

OPEN FOR OUTPUT

This program prints the message onto your disk, instead of onto your screen:

```
CLS
OPEN "joan" FOR OUTPUT AS 1
PRINT #1, "eat"
PRINT #1, 2 + 2
PRINT #1, "eggs"
CLOSE
```

Those PRINT lines make the computer print the message onto your disk instead of onto your screen. Each line says PRINT #1, which means: print onto the disk.

The OPEN line is an introductory line that tells the computer *where* on the disk to print the message. The OPEN line says: find a blank place on the disk, call it JOAN, and make JOAN be file #1. So PRINT #1 will mean: print onto file #1, which is JOAN.

Any program that says OPEN should also say CLOSE, so the bottom line says CLOSE. The CLOSE line makes the computer put some "finishing touches" on JOAN, so that JOAN becomes a perfect, finished file.

When you run that program, the computer will automatically put onto the disk a file called JOAN that contains this message:

```
eat
 4
eggs
```

After running that program, try this experiment.... Exit from QBASIC (by choosing Exit from the File menu), so the computer says:

```
C:\>
```

After that C prompt, type "dir", so the screen looks like this:

```
C:\>dir
```

When you press the ENTER key at the end of that line, the computer will print the names of all the disk's files — and one of the names it prints will be JOAN.

After the C prompt, try saying "type joan", like this:

```
C:\>type joan
```

That makes the computer show you what's in JOAN; the computer will say:

```
eat
 4
eggs
```

OPEN FOR INPUT

To see the message that's in JOAN, run this program, which inputs from JOAN and prints onto your screen:

```
CLS
OPEN "joan" FOR INPUT AS 1

INPUT #1, a$
PRINT a$

INPUT #1, b
PRINT b

INPUT #1, c$
PRINT c$

CLOSE
```

The OPEN line prepares the computer to input from JOAN.

The next line inputs a$ from JOAN, so a$ is "eat". The next line prints "eat" onto your screen.

The next pair of lines input b from JOAN (so b is 4) and print 4 onto your screen. The next pair of lines input c$ from JOAN (so c$ is "eggs") and print "eggs" onto your screen. So altogether, on your screen you'll see:

```
eat
 4
eggs
```

The CLOSE line tells the computer that you're done using JOAN for a while (until you say OPEN again).

OPEN FOR APPEND

After you've put JOAN onto the disk, so that JOAN consists of "eat" and 4 and "eggs", try running this program:

```
CLS
OPEN "joan" FOR APPEND AS 1
PRINT #1, "good morning!"
CLOSE
```

In the OPEN line, the word APPEND tells the computer to keep adding onto JOAN. So when the computer comes to the PRINT line, it adds "good morning" onto JOAN, and JOAN becomes this:

```
eat
 4
eggs
good morning!
```

Erasing

For your next experiment, try running this program:

```
CLS
OPEN "joan" FOR OUTPUT AS 1
PRINT #1, "pickles are pleasant"
CLOSE
```

Since the OPEN line does *not* say APPEND, the computer will *not* keep adding onto JOAN. Instead, the computer erases everything that's been in JOAN. So when the computer finishes processing line 10, JOAN's become blank.

The PRINT line puts "pickles are pleasant" into JOAN. So at the end of the program, JOAN includes "pickles are pleasant"; but JOAN does *not* include "eat" and 4 and "eggs" and "good morning", which have all been erased.

OUTPUT or INPUT or APPEND?

In the OPEN line, you can say OUTPUT or INPUT or APPEND. Here's how they differ:

If the OPEN line says FOR INPUT,	the program can say INPUT #1 but cannot say PRINT #1.
If the OPEN line says FOR OUTPUT,	the program can say PRINT #1 but cannot say INPUT #1.
If the OPEN line says FOR APPEND,	the program can say PRINT #1 but usually not INPUT #1.

Here's what happens if you say OPEN "joan" and the file JOAN exists already:

FOR INPUT	makes the computer use JOAN without changing JOAN.
FOR APPEND	makes the computer use JOAN and lengthen it (by appending extra lines to its end).
FOR OUTPUT	makes the computer erase JOAN and then create a totally new JOAN.

Here's what happens if you say OPEN "joan" when JOAN doesn't exist yet:

FOR OUTPUT or FOR APPEND	makes the computer create JOAN.
FOR INPUT	makes the computer gripe and say "File not found".

The following program plays a trick: if JOAN doesn't exist yet, the program creates JOAN; if JOAN exists already, the program leaves JOAN alone.

```
CLS
OPEN "joan" FOR APPEND AS 1
CLOSE
```

Loops

This program lets you put the names of all your friends onto the disk:

```
CLS
OPEN "friends" FOR OUTPUT AS 1
DO
  PRINT "Please type a friend's name (or the word 'end')"
  INPUT friend$: IF friend$ = "end" THEN EXIT DO
  PRINT #1, friend$
LOOP
CLOSE
```

The OPEN line makes the computer find a blank space on the disk and call it FRIENDS. The first PRINT line makes the computer print:

```
Please type a friend's name (or the word 'end')
```

The INPUT line prints a question mark and waits for you to type something; whatever you type will be called friend$. For example, if you type Mary Williams, then friends$ will be Mary Williams, and the next line prints the name Mary Williams onto the disk.

The lines are in a DO loop, so that you can type as many names as you wish. (Remember to press the ENTER key after each name.)

When you've finished typing the names of all your friends, type the word "end". Then the last part of the INPUT line will make the computer EXIT from the DO loop and CLOSE the file.

This program makes the computer look at the FRIENDS file and copy all its names to your screen:

```
CLS
OPEN "friends" FOR INPUT AS 1
DO UNTIL EOF(1)
  INPUT #1, friend$
  PRINT friend$
LOOP
CLOSE
PRINT "Those are all the friends."
```

The OPEN line prepares the computer to input from the FRIENDS file. The lines DO and LOOP make the computer do the indented lines repeatedly. The first indented line makes the computer input a string from the file and call the string friend$; so friend$ becomes the name of one of your friends. The next indented line prints that friend's name onto your screen. Since those indented lines are in a loop, the names of *all* your friends are printed on the screen.

Eventually, the computer will reach the end of the file, and there won't be any more names to input from the file. In the DO line, the "UNTIL EOF(1)" means: if the computer reaches the End Of the File and can't input any more names from it, the computer should stop looping and proceed to the line underneath LOOP. That line makes the computer CLOSE the file. Then the computer will print on your screen, "Those are all the friends."

As that program illustrates, to read from a file you create a DO loop. Above the loop, say OPEN FOR INPUT; below the loop, say CLOSE; in the loop, say INPUT #1; next to the DO, say UNTIL EOF(1).

LOF

In the middle of your program, if you say PRINT LOF(1), the computer will tell you the Length Of the File: it will tell you how many bytes are in the file.

Multiple files

If you want the computer to handle two files simultaneously, use two OPEN statements. At the end of the first OPEN statement, say "AS 1"; at the end of the second OPEN statement, say "AS 2".

For the second file, say PRINT #2 instead of PRINT #1, say INPUT #2 instead of INPUT #1, say EOF(2) instead of EOF(1), and say LOF(2) instead of LOF(1).

How to CLOSE

The CLOSE statement closes all files. To be more specific, you can say CLOSE 1 (which closes just the first file) or CLOSE 2 (which closes just the second).

Whenever you're done using a file, CLOSE it immediately. When you say CLOSE, the computer puts finishing touches on the file that protect the file against damage.

Suppose that halfway through your program, you finish using file 2 but want to continue using file 1. Say CLOSE 2 there, and delay saying CLOSE 1 until later.

Random access

On a disk, you can store two popular kinds of data files. The simple kind is called a **sequential-access** data file; the complicated kind is called a **random-access** data file. You've already learned how to create and retrieve a sequential-access file. Now let's look at random-access.

Though more complicated than sequential-access data files, **random-access** data files have an advantage: they let you skip around. In a sequential-access data file, you must look at the first item of data, then the second, then the third, etc. In a random-access data file, you can look at the seventh item of data, then skip directly to the tenth, then hop back to the third, then skip directly to the sixth, etc.

Each item is called a **record**. The number of characters (bytes) in the record is called the record's **length**. For example, if a record contains 20 characters, the record's length is 20. In a random-access file, all records must have the same length as each other.

PUT

Here's how to write a program that creates a random-access file.

Begin the program by saying:

```
CLS
```

Let's make each record be a string containing 20 characters:

```
DIM record AS STRING * 20
```

Let's make the file's name be JIM:

```
OPEN "jim" FOR RANDOM AS 1 LEN = LEN(record)
```

Let's make JIM's 7th record be "Love makes me giggle" (which contains 20 characters):

```
record = "Love makes me giggle"
PUT 1, 7, record
```

Let's make JIM's 9th record be "Please hold my hand":

```
record = "Please hold my hand"
PUT 1, 9, record
```

Since JIM's record length is supposed to be 20 characters but "Please hold my hand" contains just 19 characters, the computer will automatically add a blank to the end of "Please hold my hand".

Let's make JIM's 4th record be "I love Lucy":

```
record = "I love Lucy"
PUT 1, 4, record
```

The computer will automatically add blanks to the end of "I love Lucy".

To finish the program, say:

```
CLOSE
```

So altogether, the program looks like this:

```
CLS
DIM record AS STRING * 20
OPEN "jim" FOR RANDOM AS 1 LEN = LEN(record)

record = "Love makes me giggle"
PUT 1, 7, record

record = "Please hold my hand"
PUT 1, 9, record

record = "I love Lucy"
PUT 1, 4, record

CLOSE
```

When you run that program, the computer will automatically put onto the disk a file called JIM in which each record is a 20-character string.

After running that program, try this experiment…. Exit from QBASIC (by choosing Exit from the File menu), so the computer says:

```
C:\>
```

After that C prompt, type "dir". The computer will print the names of all the disk's files — and one of the names it prints will be JIM.

After the C prompt, try saying "copy jim con /b". The computer will show you what's in JIM. You'll see that JIM includes "I love Lucy" (in the 4th record), "Love makes me giggle" (in the 7th record), and "Please hold my hand" (in the 9th record). Since the program didn't say what to put into the other records, those other records still contain **garbage** (whatever data was sitting on that part of the hard disk before the program ran).

GET

This program makes the computer tell you JIM's 7th item:

```
CLS
DIM record AS STRING * 20
OPEN "jim" FOR RANDOM AS 1 LEN = LEN(record)

GET 1, 7, record
PRINT record

CLOSE
```

Multi-field records

Let's write a program that creates a fancier random-access file.

As usual, begin by saying:

```
CLS
```

Let's make each record be a combination of two parts:

```
The record's first part, called "part a", will be a string of 20 characters.
The record's second part, called "part b", will be a string of 5 characters.
```

Here's how:

```
TYPE combination
  a AS STRING * 20
  b AS STRING * 5
END TYPE
DIM record AS combination
```

Let's make the file be called JACK:

```
OPEN "jack" FOR RANDOM AS 1 LEN = LEN(record)
```

Let's make the 6th record's first part be "I want turkey on rye" and the second part be "yummy":

```
record.a = "I want turkey on rye"
record.b = "yummy"
PUT 1, 6, record
```

To finish the program, say:

```
CLOSE
```

So altogether, here's the program:

```
CLS
TYPE combination
  a AS STRING * 20
  b AS STRING * 5
END TYPE
DIM record AS combination
OPEN "jack" FOR RANDOM AS 1 LEN = LEN(record)

record.a = "I want turkey on rye"
record.b = "yummy"
PUT 1, 6, record

CLOSE
```

Go ahead: run that program!

Then run the following program, which makes the computer tell you JACK's 6th record:

```
CLS
TYPE combination
  a AS STRING * 20
  b AS STRING * 5
END TYPE
DIM record AS combination
OPEN "jack" FOR RANDOM AS 1 LEN = LEN(record)

GET 1, 6, record
PRINT record.a
PRINT record.b

CLOSE
```

Lengths

If you say **PRINT LOF(1)**, the computer will tell you the Length Of the File (how many bytes are in the file). If you say **PRINT LEN(record)**, the computer will tell you the LENgth of a record (how many bytes are in a record).

Since LOF(1) is the length of the file, and LEN(record) is the length of a record, this line makes the computer tell you how many records are in the file:

```
PRINT LOF(1) \ LEN(record)
```

End of the file

The EOF function doesn't work well for random-access files. To deal with the end of the file, use the following trick instead.

Since the number of records in the file is LOF(1) \ LEN(record), **these lines print all the records:**

```
FOR i = 1 TO LOF(1) \ LEN(record)
  GET 1, i, record
  PRINT record.a
  PRINT record.b
NEXT
```

Numeric data

To make each record consist of a 20-character string followed by a 5-character string, you learned to say this:

```
TYPE combination
  a AS STRING * 20
  b AS STRING * 5
END TYPE
DIM record AS combination
```

Here's how to make each record consist of a 20-character string followed by a short INTEGER followed by a LONG integer followed by a SINGLE-precision real number followed by a DOUBLE-precision real number:

```
TYPE combination
  a AS STRING * 20
  b AS INTEGER
  c AS LONG
  d AS SINGLE
  e AS DOUBLE
END TYPE
DIM record AS combination
```

A short INTEGER consumes 2 bytes, a LONG integer consumes 4 bytes, a SINGLE-precision real number consumes 4 bytes, and a DOUBLE-precision real number consumes 8 bytes; so in that example, the record's length is 20 + 2 + 4 + 4 + 8, which is 38 bytes.

Descriptive variables

Instead of talking about "part a" and "part b" of a record, you can pick names that are more descriptive. For example, if a record consists of a person's nickname and age, you can say:

```
TYPE combination
  nickname AS STRING * 10
  age AS integer
END TYPE
DIM record AS combination
```

To make the 6th record contain my nickname (Russy-poo) and age (48), say:

```
record.nickname = "Russy-poo"
record.age = 48
PUT 1, 6, record
```

LOC

If you say **PRINT LOC(1)**, the computer tells you which record it just dealt with. It tells you the record's LOCation.

For example, if you say "PUT 1, 7, record" or "GET 1, 7, record" and then say PRINT LOC(1), the computer prints the number 7.

Instead of saying "PUT 1, 7, record" or "PUT 1, 8, record", you can leave the record's number blank and say just:

```
PUT 1, , record
```

That makes the computer PUT the *next* record. For example, it will PUT the 9th record if the previous PUT or GET mentioned the 8th. Saying "PUT 1, , record" has the same effect as saying "PUT 1, LOC(1) + 1, record".

If you say —

```
GET 1, , record
```

the computer will GET the next record. For example, it will GET the 9th record if the previous PUT or GET mentioned the 8th.

Multiple files

If you want the computer to handle two random-access files simultaneously, use two OPEN statements. In the first OPEN statement, say "AS 1 LEN = LEN(record)"; in the second OPEN statement, say "AS 2 LEN = LEN(record2)".

For the second file, say 2 instead of 1 (in the OPEN, PUT, and GET statements and in the LOF and LOC functions); say combination2 instead of combination; and say record2 instead of record.

Create a database

I'm going to show you how to write a program that creates a database, in which you can store information about your friends & enemies, your business & bills, birthdays & appointments, desires & dreads, and whatever else bothers you.

Here's how the program works....

When you run the program, the computer begins by asking, "What topic interests you?" If you type a topic the computer knows about, the computer will tell you what data it knows about that topic; then the computer will let you change that data. If you type a topic that the computer doesn't know anything about, the computer will admit ignorance then let you teach the computer about that topic.

After dealing with the topic you requested, the computer will let you request additional topics.

If you type a question mark, the computer will print a list of all the topics in its database so far. If you type an x, the computer will exit from the program.

Simple chronological database

The simplest way to write the program is to write a main procedure and seven SUB procedures:

Allow 3000 topics & data about them. Share with SUBs.	`DIM SHARED topic$(3000), data$(3000)`
Share these variables with the SUBs.	`COMMON SHARED topic.desired$, data.inputted$, n, i`
Make n (the number of topics) start at 0.	`n = 0`
Do the following loop repeatedly:	`DO`
Clear the screen.	`CLS`
Ask the human, "What topic interests you?"	`PRINT "What topic interests you? ";`
Remind the human to type "?" if unsure, "x" to exit.	`PRINT "(If unsure, type a question mark. To exit, type an x.)"`
Make the human's response be called topic.desired$.	`10 LINE INPUT topic.desired$`
If human confused, list all topics & ask human again.	`IF topic.desired$ = "?" THEN list.all.topics: GOTO 10`
If the human's response is "x", exit from the program.	`IF topic.desired$ = "x" THEN END`
Otherwise, capitalize the response & delete extra blanks.	`topic.desired$ = UCASE$(LTRIM$(RTRIM$(topic.desired$)))`
Search for the topic that the human requested.	`search.for.topic`
Repeat that loop until the human types "x".	`LOOP`
Here's how to list all topics:	`SUB list.all.topics`
Clear the screen.	`CLS`
If there are no topics yet, do this:	`IF n = 0 THEN`
Say "I don't know any topics yet."	`PRINT "I don't know any topics yet. My mind is still blank. ";`
Say "Please teach me a new topic."	`PRINT "Please teach me a new topic."`
If some topics exist, do this:	`ELSE`
Say "I know about these topics".	`PRINT "I know about these topics:"`
Leave a blank line underneath that heading.	`PRINT`
For every individual topic in the database,	`FOR i = 1 TO n`
print that topic, then hop to the next zone.	`PRINT topic$(i),`
When you finish printing all the topics,	`NEXT`
return to the screen's left margin	`PRINT`
and leave a blank line	`PRINT`
then say "Pick one of those or teach me a new one."	`PRINT "Pick one of those topics, or teach me a new one."`
At the end of all that,	`END IF`
ask the human again, "What topic interests you?"	`PRINT "What topic interests you? (To exit, type an x.)"`
	`END SUB`
Here's how to search for the topic the human requested:	`SUB search.for.topic`
Start to look at every individual topic in the database.	`FOR i = 1 TO n`
If a topic's the one desired, just do "found.the.topic".	`IF topic$(i) = topic.desired$ THEN found.the.topic: EXIT SUB`
If the desired topic is not in the database,	`NEXT`
the topic is missing, so do "missing.topic".	`missing.topic`
	`END SUB`
Here's how to act when situation is "found.the.topic":	`SUB found.the.topic`
Clear the screen.	`CLS`
Say "Here's what I know about" the topic.	`PRINT "Here's what I know about "; topic.desired$; ":"`
Print the data that's in the database about that topic.	`PRINT data$(i)`
Leave a blank line.	`PRINT`
Ask "Do you want to change that information?"	`INPUT "Do you want to change that information"; response$`
If the human says "yes" or "y", change the info.	`IF response$ = "yes" OR response$ = "y" THEN change.the.info`
	`END SUB`

Here's how to change the info:	`SUB change.the.info`
Say that the computer's erased old info about the topic.	`  PRINT "Okay. I've erased that information about "; topic.desired$; "."`
Leave a blank line.	`  PRINT`
Tell the human to input new info about the topic.	`  PRINT "Type what you want me to know about "; topic.desired$; "."`
Say that typing an x will delete the topic.	`  PRINT "(If you want me to forget about "; topic.desired$; ", type an x.)"`
Wait for the human's response.	`  LINE INPUT data.inputted$`
If response is x, delete the topic; if not x, use new data.	`  IF data.inputted$ = "x" THEN delete.the.topic ELSE data$(i) = data.inputted$`
	`END SUB`
Here's how to delete the topic:	`SUB delete.the.topic`
Replace that topic by the last topic (topic #n).	`  topic$(i) = topic$(n)`
Replace that topic's data by the last topic's data.	`  data$(i) = data$(n)`
Decrease the number of topics, by subtracting 1.	`  n = n - 1`
	`END SUB`
Here's how to act when situation is "missing.topic":	`SUB missing.topic`
Clear the screen.	`  CLS`
Say "I don't know anything about" that topic.	`  PRINT "I don't know anything about "; topic.desired$; "."`
Say "Please tell me about" that topic.	`  PRINT "Please tell me about "; topic.desired$; "."`
Say "If you don't want to tell me, type an x."	`  PRINT "(If you don't want to tell me, type an x.)"`
Wait for the human's response.	`  LINE INPUT data.inputted$`
If the human didn't type an x, insert the topic.	`  IF data.inputted$ <> "x" THEN insert.the.topic`
	`END SUB`
Here's how to insert the topic:	`SUB insert.the.topic`
Increase the number of topics, by adding 1.	`  n = n + 1`
Append the new topic. Make it topic #n.	`  topic$(n) = topic.desired$`
Also append the new topic's data. Make it data #n.	`  data$(n) = data.inputted$`
	`END SUB`

The program stores the topics in **chronological order**: if you begin by feeding it information about SUE and then information about CAROL, it will let topic$(1) be "SUE" and let topic$(2) be "CAROL".

Copy to disk

That program stores the data just in the RAM — not on a disk. When you turn off the power, the RAM forgets all the data!

Let's write a fancier version that copies the data onto the hard disk before the program ends.

To write the fancier version, just change the main procedure; the seven SUB procedures remain the same! Here's how to write the main procedure:

Allow 3000 topics & data about them. Share with SUBs.	`DIM SHARED topic$(3000), data$(3000)`
Share these variables with the SUBs.	`COMMON SHARED topic.desired$, data.inputted$, n, i`
If the database file doesn't exist yet, create it	`OPEN "database" FOR APPEND AS 1`
and polish it up.	`CLOSE`
Prepare to copy from hard disk's database file to RAM.	`OPEN "database" FOR INPUT AS 1`
Make n (the number of topics) start at 0.	`n = 0`
Repeat the following, until reaching end of database file:	`DO UNTIL EOF(1)`
Increase the number of topics	`  n = n + 1`
becausee inputting another topic from the database file	`  LINE INPUT #1, topic$(n)`
and inputting the topic's data.	`  LINE INPUT #1, data$(n)`
Do that repeatedly until the database is done,	`LOOP`
then close the database file.	`CLOSE`
Do the following loop repeatedly:	`DO`
Clear the screen.	`  CLS`
Ask the human, "What topic interests you?"	`  PRINT "What topic interests you? ";`
Remind the human to type "?" if unsure, "x" to exit.	`  PRINT "(If unsure, type a question mark. To exit, type an x.)"`
Make the human's response be called topic.desired$.	`10 LINE INPUT topic.desired$`
If human confused, list all topics & ask human again.	`  IF topic.desired$ = "?" THEN list.all.topics: GOTO 10`
If the human's response is "x", exit from the loop.	`  IF topic.desired$ = "x" THEN EXIT DO`
Otherwise, capitalize the response & delete extra blanks.	`  topic.desired$ = UCASE$(LTRIM$(RTRIM$(topic.desired$)))`
Search for the topic that the human requested.	`  search.for.topic`
Repeat that loop until the human types "x".	`LOOP`
Prepare to copy from RAM to hard disk's database file.	`OPEN "database" FOR OUTPUT AS 1`
For all the topics,	`FOR i = 1 TO n`
copy topic from the RAM to the hard disk's database file	`  PRINT #1, topic$(i)`
and also copy the topic's data.	`  PRINT #1, data$(i)`
Do that repeatedly, until all the topics are done,	`NEXT`
then close the database file.	`CLOSE`

Alphabetical database

Instead of chronological order, you might prefer **alphabetical order**.

For example, suppose you feed the computer information about SUE then CAROL then ZELDA then ALICE then JANE. Here's what the computer's memory would look like, in each kind of order:

Chronological order	Alphabetical order
SUE	ALICE
CAROL	CAROL
ZELDA	JANE
ALICE	SUE
JANE	ZELDA

Which is better: chronological order or alphabetical order?

Chronological order lets you quickly add a new name (just add it at the end of the list), but *finding* a name in the list is slow (since the list looks disorganized). Alphabetical order lets you find a name faster (since the list is alphabetized), but *adding* a new name to the alphabetized list is slow (since the only way to insert the new name is to make room for it by shoving other names out of the way).

So which is better?

Chronological order is the simplest to program and the fastest for *inserting*.
Alphabetical order is the fastest for *finding* information.

If you want to store the names in alphabetical order instead of chronological order, use these new versions of three SUB procedures:

Here's how to search for the topic the human requested:
 What's the topic's position in database? 0 is "too low",
 but n + 1 is "too high".
 Try guesses in between, as follows:
  Find average (rounded up) of "too low" & "too high".
  If average is too high, just do "missing.topic".
  If topic is found, just do "found.the.topic".
  Otherwise, adjust "too high" or "too low",
  then try another guess.

```
SUB search.for.topic
  too.low = 0
  too.high = n + 1
  DO
    i = (too.low + too.high + 1) \ 2
    IF i = too.high THEN missing.topic: EXIT SUB
    IF topic$(i) = topic.desired$ THEN found.the.topic: EXIT SUB
    IF topic$(i) > topic.desired$ THEN too.high = i ELSE too.low = i
  LOOP
END SUB
```

Here's how to delete the topic:
 Decrease the number of topics.
 Close the gap from the deleted topic,
 by moving topics
 and their data.

```
SUB delete.the.topic
  n = n - 1
  FOR j = i TO n
    topic$(j) = topic$(j + 1)
    data$(j) = data$(j + 1)
  NEXT
END SUB
```

Here's how to insert the topic:
 Increase the number of topics.
 To make room for the new topic,
 Move other topics out of the way
 and move their data.
 When the moving is done,
 Insert the new topic
and its data.

```
SUB insert.the.topic
  n = n + 1
  FOR j = n TO i + 1 STEP -1
    topic$(j) = topic$(j - 1)
    data$(j) = data$(j - 1)
  NEXT
  topic$(i) = topic.desired$
  data$(i) = data.inputted$
END SUB
```

That new version of search.for.topic runs faster than the chronological version, because searching through an alphabetical list is faster than searching through a chronological list. (To search through the alphabetical list super-quickly, the new version of search.for.topic uses a trick called **binary search**.)

Unfortunately, the new versions of delete.the.topic and insert.the.topic run *slower* than the chronological versions. To get the high speed of the new search method, you must accept the slowness of the new delete & insert methods.

You've seen that chronological order is fast for inserting and deleting but slow for searching, whereas alphabetical order is exactly the opposite: it's fast for searching but slow for inserting or deleting.

Tree-structured database

Instead of using chronological order or alphabetical order, advanced programmers use a **tree**. Like chronological order, a tree lets you insert and delete quickly. Like alphabetical order, a tree lets you search quickly also.

Poets say, "only God can make a tree." Does that mean advanced programmers are God?

To learn how to make a tree, begin by sketching a picture of a tree on paper. Since N is the alphabet's middle letter, begin by writing the letter N, and put two arrows underneath it:

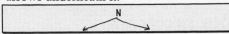

The left arrow is called the **before-arrow**; it will point to the names that come alphabetically before N. The right arrow is called the **after-arrow**; it will point to the names that come alphabetically after N.

For example, suppose your first topic is SUE. Since SUE comes alphabetically after N, put SUE at the tip of N's after-arrow:

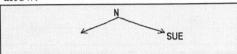

Suppose your next topic is CAROL. Since CAROL comes alphabetically before N, put CAROL at the tip of N's before-arrow:

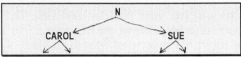

Suppose your next topic is ZELDA. Since ZELDA comes after N, we'd like to put ZELDA at the tip of N's after-arrow; but SUE's already stolen that position. So compare ZELDA against SUE. Since ZELDA comes after SUE, put ZELDA at the tip of SUE's after-arrow:

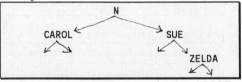

Suppose your next topic is ALICE. Since ALICE comes before N, look at the tip of N's before-arrow. Since CAROL's stolen that position, compare ALICE against CAROL; since ALICE comes before CAROL, put ALICE at the tip of CAROL's before-arrow:

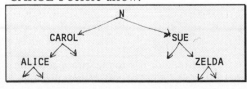

Suppose your next topic is JANE. Since JANE comes before N, look at the tip of N's before-arrow. Since CAROL's stolen that position, compare JANE against CAROL; since JANE comes after CAROL, put JANE at the tip of CAROL's after-arrow:

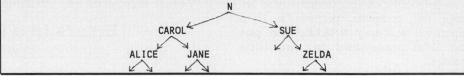

If the next few topics are FRED, then LOU, then RON, then BOB, the tree looks like this:

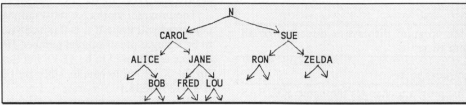

Look at the arrows that point down from N. N's before-arrow points to the group of names that come alphabetically before N (such as CAROL, ALICE, JANE, BOB, FRED, and LOU); N's after-arrow points to the group of names that come alphabetically after N (such as SUE, RON, and ZELDA). Similarly, CAROL's before-arrow points to the group of names that come alphabetically before CAROL (such as ALICE and BOB); CAROL's after-arrow points to the group of names that come alphabetically after CAROL (such as JANE, FRED, and LOU).

Programmers treat the tree as if it were a "family tree". CAROL is called the **parent** of ALICE and JANE, who are therefore called CAROL's **children**. CAROL is called the **ancestor** of ALICE, JANE, BOB, FRED, and LOU, who are therefore called CAROL's **descendants**. The arrows are called **pointers**.

To make the tree more useful, begin with "N !" instead of "N" (so you can choose "N" as a topic later), and number the topics in the order they appeared: since SUE was the first topic, put "1" in front of SUE; since CAROL was the second topic, put "2" in front of CAROL; since ZELDA was the third topic, put "3" in front of ZELDA, like this:

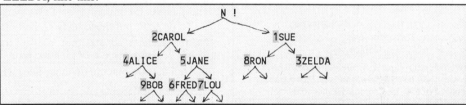

To describe the tree to the computer, store this table in the computer's memory:

	Topic	Where the before-arrow points	Where the after-arrow points
0	N !	2	1
1	SUE	8	3
2	CAROL	4	5
3	ZELDA	0	0
4	ALICE	0	9
5	JANE	6	7
6	FRED	0	0
7	LOU	0	0
8	RON	0	0
9	BOB	0	0

That table **represents** the tree and is called the tree's **representation**.

The table's left column is in chronological order, but the other columns give information about alphabetizing. So a tree combines chronological order with alphabetical order: it combines the advantages of both. Adding a new topic to the tree is quick and easy (as in chronological order): just add the name to the bottom of the list, and adjust a few arrows. Using the tree to search for a topic is quick and easy (as in alphabetical order): just follow the arrows.

Editions 11-20 of this book contained a program that created a tree in a random-access data file. Phone me at 603-666-6644 to find out which editions are still available and their prices. But the *best* way to create a big, sophisticated database is to buy a database program such as **Q&A** (which I explained in the database chapter) or use a database programming language such as **DBASE** (which I'll explain in the next chapter).

SHELL

In the middle of your program, you can make the computer perform a DOS command! Just **say SHELL, and put the DOS command in quotation marks**.

For example, this program tells you which version of DOS you're using:

```
CLS
SHELL "ver"
```

This program displays a directory of all your files:

```
CLS
SHELL "dir /w"
```

This program changes the name JOE.BAS to FRED.BAS:

```
CLS
SHELL "rename joe.bas fred.bas"
```

This program deletes JOE.BAS from your hard disk:

```
CLS
SHELL "del joe.bas"
```

This program makes the computer run Windows:

```
CLS
SHELL "win"
```

Short cuts

Here are some short cuts:

To see what files are on your hard disk,
you can say **FILES**
(instead of SHELL "dir /w").

To delete JOE.BAS from your hard disk,
you can say **KILL "joe.bas"**
(instead of SHELL "del joe.bas").

To change the name JOE.BAS to FRED.BAS,
you can say **NAME "joe.bas" AS "fred.bas"**
(instead of SHELL "rename joe.bas fred.bas").

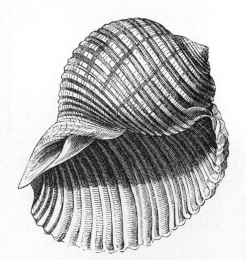

ON ERROR GOTO

You can improve the way that the computer handles errors.

Errors in a simple program

Here's a simple program that divides two numbers and prints their quotient:

```
CLS
INPUT "What's your favorite number"; a
INPUT "What's another favorite number"; b
PRINT "The first number divided by the second is"; a / b
```

The program works for most numbers. But when the computer tries to divide, the computer will gripe if b is 0 (since you can't divide by 0) or if the quotient's too big to be a single-precision real number. (For example, if you try dividing 1E38 by .1, the answer is supposed to be 1E39; but the computer will gripe that the answer is too big for the computer to handle, since the biggest permissible single-precision real number is 3.402823E38.)

If b is 0, the computer will print this error message:

```
Division by zero
```

If the quotient's too big to be a single-precision real number, the computer will print this error message:

```
Overflow
```

When the computer prints one of those error messages, the computer stops running the program and shows you the blue screen.

That confuses beginners! If a beginner tries to run your program and sees the computer say "Division by zero" or "Overflow" on a blue screen, the beginner might not understand what the computer means and might not understand what to do next.

Improved error-handling

Instead of letting the computer say "Division by zero" or "Overflow", let's make the computer print this easier-to-understand message —

```
I can't handle that pair of numbers.
Please pick a different pair of numbers instead.
```

and then let the human type a new pair of numbers.

To do that, put these lines at the bottom of your program —

```
PRINT "I can't handle that pair of numbers."
PRINT "Please pick a different pair of numbers instead."
```

and tell the computer to do those lines whenever an error occurs in computing the quotient.

Here's how:

```
CLS
10 INPUT "What's your favorite number"; a
INPUT "What's another favorite number"; b
ON ERROR GOTO 1000
   quotient = a / b
ON ERROR GOTO 0
PRINT "The first number divided by the second is"; quotient
END

1000 PRINT "I can't handle that pair of numbers."
PRINT "Please pick a different pair of numbers instead."
PRINT
RESUME 10
```

In that program, the source of the error (a / b) is isolated: it's made into a separate line (quotient = a / b). Above that line, say ON ERROR GOTO 1000; below that line, say ON ERROR GOTO 0. The ON ERROR GOTO 1000 means: if an error occurs in the indented line underneath, go to line 1000. Line 1000 is the beginning of the **error-handling routine**. The error-handling routine says that when an error occurs, print this —

```
I can't handle that pair of numbers.
Please pick a different pair of numbers instead.
```

then print a blank line and then RESUME the program at line 10, which makes the computer ask again "What's your favorite number?"

Remember:

The bottom line of the error-handling routine should say RESUME.
The bottom line of the rest of the program should say END.
"ON ERROR GOTO 1000" should be paired with "ON ERROR GOTO 0".

"ON ERROR GOTO 1000" means "Henceforth, if an error ever occurs, GOTO line 1000."

"ON ERROR GOTO 0" means "Henceforth, if an error ever occurs, go nowhere; just process the error normally."

In that program, the bottom four lines are called the **error-handling routine** or **error handler** or **error trap**. Making the computer go to the error trap is called **trapping the error**.

Error numbers

Besides "Division by zero" and "Overflow", there are many other errors that a program can make. Each error has a code number:

Code #	Message
1	NEXT without FOR
2	Syntax error
3	RETURN without GOSUB
4	Out of DATA
5	Illegal function call
6	Overflow
7	Out of memory
8	Label not defined
9	Subscript out of range
10	Duplicate definition
11	Division by zero
12	Illegal in direct mode
13	Type mismatch
14	Out of string space
16	String formula too complex
17	Cannot continue
18	Function not defined
19	No RESUME
20	RESUME without error
24	Device timeout
25	Device fault
26	FOR without NEXT
27	Out of paper
29	WHILE without WEND
30	WEND without WHILE
33	Duplicate label
35	Subprogram not defined
37	Argument-count mismatch
38	Array not defined
40	Variable required
50	FIELD overflow
51	Internal error
52	Bad file name or number
53	File not found
54	Bad file mode
55	File already open
56	FIELD statement active
57	Device I/O error
58	File already exists
59	Bad record length
61	Disk full
62	Input past end of file
63	Bad record number
64	Bad file name
67	Too many files
68	Device unavailable
69	Communication-buffer overflow
70	Permission denied
71	Disk not ready
72	Disk-media error
73	Advanced feature unavailable
74	Rename across disks
75	Path/File access error
76	Path not found

Whenever the computer detects an error, the computer makes ERR be the error-code number. For example, when the computer detects an Overflow error, the computer makes ERR be 6. If you say —

```
PRINT ERR
```

the computer will print 6.

You can use ERR in the error-handling routine. For example, here's how to say "if the error was Overflow":

```
IF ERR = 6 THEN
```

At the bottom of the error-handling routine, the RESUME line automatically makes the computer reset ERR to 0, so the computer is prepared to handle future errors.

Here's the sophisticated way to divide two numbers:

```
CLS
10 INPUT "What's your favorite number"; a
INPUT "What's another favorite number"; b
ON ERROR GOTO 1000
  quotient = a / b
ON ERROR GOTO 0
PRINT "The first number divided by the second is"; quotient
END

1000 SELECT CASE ERR
  CASE 11
    PRINT "I can't divide by zero."
  CASE 6
    PRINT "The answer is too big for me to handle."
  CASE ELSE
    PRINT "I'm having difficulty."
END SELECT
PRINT "Please pick a different pair of numbers instead."
PRINT
RESUME 10
```

In that program, the error-handling routine says:

If the error-code number is 11 (which means "Division by zero"), print "I can't divide by zero."
If the error-code number is 6 ("Overflow"), print "The answer is too big for me to handle."
If the error-code number is otherwise, print "I'm having difficulty."

After printing one of those error messages, the computer will print "Please pick a different pair of numbers instead". Then the computer will do RESUME 10, which goes back to line 10 and also resets ERR to 0.

Unnumbered RESUME

If you don't put any number after RESUME, the computer will go back to the line that contained the error.

If you say RESUME NEXT, the computer will go to the line *underneath* the line that contained the error. To make RESUME NEXT work properly, the line that contained the error should consists of just one statement (instead of statements separated by colons).

Memory cells

The computer's memory chips consist of many **memory cells**. Each cell holds an integer from 0 to 255. For example, cell #49837 might hold the integer 139.

Segments

The first 65536 cells (cell #0 through cell #65535) form **segment 0**. The next 65536 cells are in the next segment, which is called **segment 16**. The next 65536 cells are in **segment 32**; the next 65536 cells are in **segment 48**; the next 65536 cells are in **segment 64**; the next 65536 cells are in **segment 80**; etc. Notice that the segment numbers are multiples of 16.

Within each segment, the cells are numbered from 0 to 65535. For example, the first cell in segment 16 is called "cell #0 of segment 16"; the next cell in segment 16 is called "cell #1 of segment 16"; the last cell in segment 16 is called "cell #65535 of segment 16".

PEEK

This program finds out what number's in cell #49837 of segment 0:

```
CLS
DEF SEG = 0
PRINT PEEK(49837)
```

The "DEF SEG = 0" tells the computer to use the memory's main SEGment, which is SEGment 0. The bottom line makes the computer PEEK at cell #49837, find the number in that cell, and print that number on your screen. The number it prints will be an integer from 0 to 255. For example, it might be 139.

When dealing with memory cells, make sure your program begins with a DEF SEG line, to tell the computer which segment to look in. If you forget to say DEF SEG, the computer will look in its "favorite" segment, which is *not* segment 0.

Cell #1047

In cell #1047 of segment 0, the computer puts a number that describes the state of your keyboard. The computer computes that number by using this chart:

```
Start at 0.
Add    1 if the right SHIFT    key is being pressed now.
Add    2 if the left SHIFT     key is being pressed now.
Add    4 if either Ctrl key    is being pressed now.
Add    8 if either Alt key     is being pressed now.
Add   16 if the SCROLL LOCK    is turned on (by an earlier keypress).
Add   32 if the NUM LOCK       is turned on (by an earlier keypress).
Add   64 if the CAPS LOCK      is turned on (by an earlier keypress).
Add  128 if the INSERT         is turned on (by an earlier keypress).
```

For example, if NUM LOCK and INSERT are turned on, that cell contains 32+128, which is 160.

This program shows you what's in that cell:

```
CLS
DEF SEG = 0
PRINT PEEK(1047)
```

For example, if NUM LOCK and INSERT are turned on, the computer will print 160.

Loop This program peeks at cell #1047 repeatedly:

```
CLS
DEF SEG = 0
DO
  PRINT PEEK(1047)
LOOP
```

If the NUM LOCK and INSERT keys are turned on, the computer will repeatedly print 160, like this:

```
160
160
160
etc.
```

While that program keeps running, try pressing the SHIFT, Ctrl, Alt, SCROLL LOCK, NUM LOCK, CAPS LOCK, and INSERT keys. Each time you press any of those keys, the number 160 will change to a different number.

Cell #1048

In cell #1048 of segment 0, the computer puts a supplementary number describing your keyboard's state. That number is computed as follows:

```
Start at 0.
Add    1 if the left Ctrl       key is being pressed now.
Add    2 if the left Alt        key is being pressed now.
Add   16 if the SCROLL LOCK     key is being pressed now.
Add   32 if the NUM LOCK        key is being pressed now.
Add   64 if the CAPS LOCK       key is being pressed now.
Add  128 if the INSERT          key is being pressed now.
```

This program shows you what's in *both* of the keyboard-state cells:

```
CLS
DEF SEG = 0
DO
  PRINT PEEK(1047), PEEK(1048)
LOOP
```

While running that program, try pressing the Ctrl, Alt, SCROLL LOCK, NUM LOCK, CAPS LOCK, and INSERT keys. Watch how the numbers on the screen change!

That's how computers work: in memory cells, the computer stores code numbers that represent what you and the computer are doing.

POKE

Let's make the computer turn on the CAPS LOCK (so all your typing will be capitalized), NUM LOCK (so typing on the numeric keypad will create numbers instead of arrows), and INSERT (so typing in the middle of a document will make the other words move out of the way).

In cell #1047, the code number for NUM LOCK is 32, CAPS LOCK is 64, and INSERT is 128, so the code number for their combination is 32+64+128, which is 224. To turn on CAPS LOCK, NUM LOCK, and INSERT, just put the code number 224 into cell #1047. Here's how:

```
CLS
DEF SEG = 0
POKE 1047, 224
```

In that program, "POKE 1047, 224" means "put, into cell #1047, the number 224".

Danger Poking into cell 1047 or 1048 is safe (if you say DEF SEG = 0), but poking into other cells can be dangerous, since some of those cells are where the computer stores notes about your program, operating system, disks, and other devices. Poking wrong info into those cells can wreck your program, operating system, and the info on your disks.

VERSIONS OF BASIC

QBASIC

Pages 332-436 explained QBASIC, which comes with MS-DOS versions 5, 6, 6.2, 6.21, and 6.22.

Here's how other versions of BASIC differ....

Quick BASIC

Quick BASIC understands a few more commands than QBASIC. Quick BASIC is available for MS-DOS and for Apple Macintosh computers, but the Apple Macintosh version is inferior.

When you start using Quick BASIC (version 4.5 for MS-DOS), you'll encounter these differences from QBASIC....

Start BASIC (page 334)

When you buy Quick BASIC, it comes on five 5¼-inch floppy disks. Here's how to copy them to your hard disk:

> Turn on the computer without any floppy disk in drive A. When you see the C prompt, put Quick BASIC's first disk (the Setup/Microsoft QB Express Disk) into drive A and type "a:".
>
> The computer will display an A prompt. Type "setup".
>
> The computer will say "QuickBASIC Setup Program". Press ENTER twice.
>
> The computer will say "Easy Setup Menu". Press the I key. Press ENTER three times.
>
> When the computer tells you, put Quick BASIC's second disk (the Program Disk) into drive A and press ENTER. When the computer tells you, do the same for the remaining Quick BASIC disks.
>
> Press ENTER two extra times. The computer will say "QB Express". Press R then X.
>
> You'll see an A prompt, like this:
> A:\>
>
> Turn off the computer, so you can start fresh.

To start using Quick BASIC, turn on the computer without any floppy disk in drive A. When you see the C prompt, type "cd qb45", like this:

```
C:\>cd qb45
```

When you press ENTER at the end of that line, the computer will say:

```
C:\QB45>
```

Type "qb" (and press ENTER). The computer will say "Untitled". (If the computer says "Welcome to QuickBASIC", press the Esc key.)

File menu (page 339)

The file menu can be short or long. The short menu offers just 5 choices; the long menu (which is called the **full menu**) offers 12 choices. Here's how to switch from short menu to full menu (or back to short): tap the Alt key, then the letter O, then F.

Save (page 339)

On the file menu, one of the choices is "Save As...". Another choice, a plain "Save", appears just if the menu is full instead of short. So before choosing just "Save", make sure the menu is full.

New (page 340)

Quick BASIC's file menu says "New Program" instead of just "New". Choose "New Program" by pressing the N key.

Open (page 340)

Quick BASIC's file menu says "Open Program" instead of just "Open". Choose "Open Program" by pressing the letter O.

Instant open (page 341)

Suppose you've written a program that has no errors, and you've saved the program as JOE.BAS. Try this: while JOE.BAS is on the blue screen, tap the Alt key, then R, then X, then ENTER. That makes the computer create a file called JOE.EXE (and also a file called JOE.OBJ). Then you can run JOE fast by typing "joe" at the C prompt, like this:

```
C:\QB45>joe
```

Visual BASIC for DOS

Visual BASIC for DOS is newer and fancier than QBASIC & Quick BASIC.

When you start using version 2 of Visual BASIC for DOS, you'll encounter these differences from QBASIC....

Start BASIC (page 334)

When you buy Visual BASIC for DOS, it comes on two 3½-inch floppy disks. Here's how to copy them to your hard disk:

> Turn on the computer without any floppy in drive A. When you see the C prompt, put Visual BASIC Disk 1 into drive A and type "a:setup", so the screen looks like this:
>
> `C:\>a:setup`
>
> The computer will say "Visual Basic for MS-DOS Setup". Press ENTER.
>
> The computer will say "Type your full name". Type your full name (or the name of the company that bought Visual BASIC) and press ENTER at the end of it.
>
> Press ENTER six more times.
>
> The computer will say, "Insert Disk 2". Insert it into drive A and press ENTER. (If the computer says "WARNING: Setup has found multiple linkers", press ENTER again.)
>
> The computer will say, "To start Microsoft Visual Basic, type VBDOS at the MS-DOS prompt." Press ENTER.
>
> You'll see a C prompt, like this:
>
> `C:\VBDOS>`
>
> Turn off the computer, so you can start fresh.

To start using Visual BASIC, turn on the computer without any floppy disk in drive A, so that the computer says:

`C:\>`

If you've put the DO.BAT file onto your hard disk (as I recommended in the MS-DOS chapter), type "do vbdos". If you've *not* put DO.BAT onto your hard disk, type "cd vbdos", then on the line underneath type "vbdos" again (so the lower line says "C:\VBDOS>vbdos").

If the computer says "Visual Basic", press ENTER.

The computer will say "Untitled" and "Project".

While holding down the Ctrl key, press the F10 key. The word "Project" will disappear.

File menu (page 339)

Visual BASIC's file menu gives you 14 choices, which are worded differently than QBASIC's choices.

Instead of "Save",	choose "Save File"	(by pressing S).
Instead of "Save As",	choose "Save File As"	(by pressing A).
Instead of "Open",	choose "Add File"	(by pressing D).
Instead of "New",	choose "New Project"	(by pressing N).

If you print on paper by choosing Print from the file menu (and then pressing ENTER), the printer will eject the paper automatically.

Instant open (page 341)

Suppose you've written a program that has no errors, and you've saved the program as JOE.BAS. Try this: while JOE.BAS is on the blue screen, tap the Alt key, then R, then X, then ENTER. That makes the computer create a file called JOE.EXE (and also a file called JOE.OBJ). Then you can run JOE fast by typing "joe" at the C prompt, like this:

`C:\VBDOS>joe`

Print (page 412)

To print the entire program onto paper (including even the SUB procedures), press Alt then F then P then ENTER. The printer will eject the paper automatically.

Error numbers (page 435)

In Visual BASIC, error #73 is "Feature unavailable", and you can make advanced errors numbered from 80 to 480.

Visual BASIC for Windows

Visual BASIC for Windows is so different from other versions of BASIC that it shouldn't be called "BASIC". In fact, most computer folks call it **VB**. That's what I'll call it too!

VB's main purpose is to let you create Windows programs that do everything expected of Windows programs: by using VB, you can create Windows programs that let the human use a mouse to click on icons, choose from menus, use dialog boxes, etc.

Before trying to learn VB, you should pick up two prerequisite skills:

> The first prerequisite is to learn QBASIC, which is much easier than VB. I explained QBASIC on pages 332-437. Read and practice that material.
>
> The second prerequisite is to play with Windows software (such as a Windows word-processing program), so you have some idea of how a Windows program should act. I explained the fundamentals of Windows software on pages 95-113 and pages 162-199. Read and practice whichever of those Windows products you have access to.

After you've had those experiences, read the following technical notes, which were written mainly by my research assistant, Len Pallazola, and edited by me. They explain VB's "Standard Version 4". (Other versions are similar.)

I plan to put more details in future editions. To get on the mailing list, use the coupon on the back page or phone me at 603-666-6644.

VB's philosophy

To write a program by using VB, you start by designing the way you want the screen to look. During that design process, you use your mouse, as if you were designing a work of art by using a graphics program.

Once you've made a beautiful-looking screen that has pretty icons, menus, windows, and dialog boxes, you tell the computer what to do if the human clicks on one of those objects. For each object on the screen, you define a procedure (subroutine) for the computer to obey if the human clicks the object.

And now, some jargon:

> The general appearance of the screen you created is called your program's **interface**. The objects that you expect the human to click (such as buttons, menus, check boxes, and text boxes) are called **controls**. You add the controls to windows called **forms**.
>
> While the program is running, not much happens until the human performs an **event** (such as clicking on a button, typing on the keyboard, or picking an item from a menu). That's called an **event-driven program**. All the controls on the screen sit there waiting patiently for the human to perform an event that makes one of the subroutines come to life.

How to install VB

VB's Standard Version 4 requires Windows 95 and costs just $87 from discount dealers (such as Computer Discount Warehouse at 800-726-4239).

It comes on a CD-ROM disk. Here's how to copy it to your hard disk:

> Start the computer, so the Start Button is on the screen. Insert the Visual BASIC Standard Edition CD-ROM disk.
>
> Click the Start button, then Run. Type "d:setup" or "e:setup" (and press ENTER).
>
> The computer will say "Welcome to the Microsoft Visual BASIC 4.0 - 32-bit installation program". Press ENTER.
>
> The computer will say "Enter your full name". If your name's not on the screen yet, type your full name (such as Susan B. Anthony), then press TAB, then type the name of your organization (if any). Press ENTER twice.
>
> Type the CD Key (which is the 10-digit number that's on the orange stick on the back of the square jewel box the CD-ROM came in), then press ENTER.
>
> The computer will show you a 20-digit Product Identification Number. Using a pen, scribble that number onto the registration card (which is black, white, and yellow). Press ENTER five times.
>
> The computer will say "Microsoft Visual BASIC 4.0 — 32-bit Setup was completed successfully." Press ENTER.

Start VB

To start running VB, click Start, then Programs, then "Visual Basic 4.0", then "Visual Basic 4.0" again.

When VB opens, you'll see several separate and confusing windows. Since none of the windows covers the whole screen, you can still see parts of your Windows 95 desktop peeking through. Don't worry — it's *supposed* to look that way.

Like most Windows programs, VB includes a title bar, a menu bar, and a toolbar at the screen's top. In the screen's middle, you'll see a dotted window called **Form1**. Form1 will eventually become the main window of your VB program. Right now, it's blank.

On your screen's left side, you'll see this toolbar:

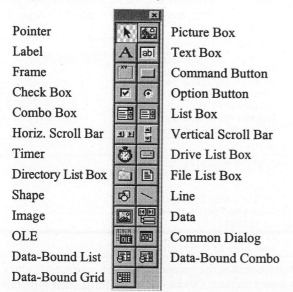

Pointer		Picture Box
Label		Text Box
Frame		Command Button
Check Box		Option Button
Combo Box		List Box
Horiz. Scroll Bar		Vertical Scroll Bar
Timer		Drive List Box
Directory List Box		File List Box
Shape		Line
Image		Data
OLE		Common Dialog
Data-Bound List		Data-Bound Combo
Data-Bound Grid		

Microsoft calls that toolbar the **Toolbox**, but let's call it the **control palette** instead, since it contains the many **controls** you can add to your VB programs. Controls are the tools that make your program *do* things. Some common controls are command buttons, text boxes, and scroll bars.

On your screen's right-hand side, you'll see two smaller windows. The top one, which says "Project1", is called the **Project window** because it lists all files making up your VB program. The **Properties window** is directly below the Project window. Each control and form has its own set of unique characteristics, called **properties**.

Create your program

Now you're ready to design your first program!

Step 1: create a button
Double-click the **Command Button** tool on the control palette. That creates a button (called **Command1**) in the middle of your form.

Step 2: create the button's subroutine
Double-click the button you created. That makes a window appear, which says:

```
Private Sub Command1_Click()

End Sub
```

That text is the subroutine that runs when the button is clicked. The top line is the subroutine's header. The bottom line is the subroutine's footer, which tells the computer that the subroutine has ended.

The subroutine doesn't do anything yet, because the line between the header and footer is blank. Change the subroutine so it says:

```
Private Sub Command1_Click()
MsgBox "Welcome, human!"
End
End Sub
```

In that subroutine, the **MsgBox** line tells the computer to say this message: "Welcome, human!" The **End** line tells the computer to automatically close the program when it finishes.

Step 3: run your program
Go ahead: run your program by pressing the **F5 key**.

Your form appears, with the Command1 button in the middle. Click that button.

If you typed the subroutine correctly, you'll see a message box saying "Welcome, human!".

Click OK. That makes the message box go away and the program end.

Congratulations! You wrote and ran your first VB program! Now you can put on your résumé that you're a VB programmer!

Properties window

Each object in your program has its own set of properties that control how it looks and functions. Lets change the properties of the Command1 button you created in the previous example.

First, click on the Command1 button just once. That makes Command1 the **active control**, so the **Properties window** shows Command1's properties. Click **Caption** in the Properties window, then type:

```
Hello
```

Now the command button says "Hello" instead of "Command1".

Click **Font** in the Properties window. The font used by the button is shown in the font box. Next to the font name is a small gray button with three dots (...). Click that small button. The font dialog box appears. Change Font style to **Bold**, then click OK. Now your button boldly says "Hello"!

Change properties by coding

You can change an item's properties while the program is running. Just add the new properties into your program code.

For example, here's how to make a button that changes each time you click it.

First, double-click the Command Button tool on the control palette. A new command button will appear on your form. Drag it (by using the mouse) so it doesn't cover the button you created in the previous example.

Then click Caption in the Properties window and type "Click me".

Double-click the "Click me" button you just created, then type this subroutine between the header and footer lines of the button's subroutine:

```
If Command2.Caption = "Click me" Then
  Command2.Caption = "Again!"
Else
  Command2.Caption = "Click me"
End If
```

Press F5 to run your program. Click the "Click me" button. If you typed the program correctly, the button text will change to "Again!" When you click it again, it changes back to "Click me".

Close your program by clicking its X box. (You must close it manually because no line said simply "End".)

Save your program

To copy your program onto your hard disk, click **File**, then **Save Project**.

Name your forms The computer will ask you to name each form in your program. You can accept the default names (Form1, Form2, etc.) or give each form a new filename. After typing a name for a form, click Save.

Name your project Each VB program includes a project file that contains information about your program. The computer will name your project "Project1". To accept that name, click Save. To pick something else, type a name first, then click Save.

InputBox

To make the computer ask a question, use an **InputBox**.

For example, here's how to make a button that asks for your name.

First, double-click the Command Button tool on the control palette. A new command button will appear on your form. (Drag it so it doesn't cover any buttons you created in previous examples.)

Click Caption in the Properties window and type "Ask me".

Then double-click the "Ask me" button you created. Type this between the header and footer lines of the button's subroutine:

```
YourName = InputBox("What is your name?", "Name")
MsgBox "I adore anyone whose name is " & YourName
```

Run the program (by pressing F5). Click the "Ask me" button.

If you typed the program correctly, a box called Name will appear and ask "What is your name?". The computer waits for you to type your name underneath. Type your name. For example, if your name is Maria, make the screen look like this:

```
What is your name?
Maria
```

At the end of typing "Maria", press the ENTER key (or click the OK button).

That Name box will go away, and a new box will appear that says "I adore anyone whose name is " and then your name. For example, if you said your name was "Maria", the computer will say "I adore anyone whose name is Maria".

Close your program (by clicking its X box).

College admissions Let's make the computer print a letter admitting you to the college of your choice.

First, start a new project by clicking File then **New Project**.

Double-click the form, then type this between the header and footer lines of the form's subroutine:

```
Form1.Show
College = InputBox("What college would you like to enter?")
Print "Congratulations!"
Print "You have just been admitted to " & College
Print "because it fits your personality."
Print "I hope you go to " & College & "."
Print "          Respectfully yours,"
Print "          The Dean of Admissions"
```

The top line, which says **Form1.Show**, is needed because later lines say **Print**. (In that program, if you wish, you can say **Form1.Print** instead of just **Print**, to emphasize that the output should be printed onto Form1 rather than some other window. But if you say just Print instead of Form1.Print, the computer will figure out what you meant anyway.)

Run the program (by pressing F5).

The subroutine's InputBox line makes the computer ask "What college would you like to enter?" and wait for you to answer. Your answer will be called College. If you'd like to be admitted to Harvard, you'll be pleased...

The computer asks you:	What college would you like to enter?
You type:	Harvard
The computer admits you:	Congratulations!
	You have just been admitted to Harvard
	because it fits your personality.
	I hope you go to Harvard.
	Respectfully yours,
	The Dean of Admissions

You can choose any college you wish:

The computer asks you:	What college would you like to enter?
You type:	Hell
The computer admits you:	Congratulations!
	You have just been admitted to Hell
	because it fits your personality.
	I hope you go to Hell.
	Respectfully yours,
	The Dean of Admissions

Numeric input This program makes the computer predict your future. Click File, then New Project to start a new program. Double-click the form, then type this between the subroutine's header and footer lines:

```
Form1.Show
Print "I predict what'll happen to you in the year 2000!"
Y = InputBox("In what year were you born?")
Print "In the year 2000, you'll turn " & 2000 - Y & " years old."
```

Here's a sample run:

```
I predict what'll happen to you in the year 2000!
In what year were you born?
1962
In the year 2000, you'll turn 38 years old.
```

Logic

VB uses the words If and Else and colons the same way as QBASIC.

For example, let's write a program so that if the human is less than 18 years old, the computer will say:

```
You are still a minor.
```

Here's the program:

```
Form1.Show
Age = InputBox("How old are you")
If Age < 18 Then Print "You are still a minor"
```

Line 2 makes the computer ask "How old are you" and wait for the human to type an age. Since the symbol for "less than" is "<", the bottom line says: if the age is less than 18, then print "You are still a minor".

Go ahead! Run that program! The computer begins the conversation by asking:

```
How old are you?
```

Try saying you're 12 years old, by typing a 12, so the screen looks like this:

```
How old are you?
12
```

When you finish typing the 12 and press the ENTER key at the end of it, the computer will reply:

```
You are still a minor
```

Try running that program again, but this time try saying you're 50 years old instead of 12, so the screen looks like this:

```
How old are you?
50
```

When you finish typing the 50 (and press the ENTER key at the end of it), the computer will *not* say "You are still a minor". Instead, the computer will say nothing, since we didn't teach the computer how to respond to adults yet.

To handle adults, change the If line to this:

```
If Age < 18 Then Print "You are still a minor" Else Print "You are an adult"
```

To create longer messages, use colons —

```
If Age < 18 Then Print "You are still a minor": Print "Ah, the joys of youth!"
```

or use a multi-line If:

```
If Age < 18 Then
  Print "You are still a minor"
  Print "Ah, the joys of youth!"
End If
```

Your multi-line If can include Else:

```
If Age < 18 Then
  Print "You are still a minor"
  Print "Ah, the joys of youth!"
Else
  Print "You are an adult"
  Print "We can have adult fun"
End If
```

VB also uses the words ElseIf and Select, the same way as QBASIC.

Which commands differ?

Most QBASIC commands I described in this book (such as CLS) work in VB. When typing a command in VB, capitalize just the command's first letter, like this: Cls.

You can omit any dollar sign. If you invent a variable name, don't put a period in the name's middle.

Unfortunately, VB is too stupid to handle these QBASIC commands: COMMON SHARED, DATA, DEF SEG, FILES, LOCATE, PAINT, PLAY, POKE, READ, RESTORE, SCREEN, SOUND, SLEEP, SWAP, SYSTEM.

Here's an alphabetical list of commands that work differently in VB:

Beep You may need to insert some kind of wait subroutine if you want to use several beeps in a row.

Circle (100, 100), 40 Still works, but those coordinates are pretty small. You'll want to change it to Circle (1000, 1000), 400. Otherwise you'll get what looks like a lower-case "o" in the top left corner of your form.

Declare Sub insult () Still exists, but now it's used just for declaring a subroutine you're going to use that's in a .DLL file. You must insert "lib" and then the name of the .DLL file in order for it to work. Example: Declare Sub insult Lib "Joan.DLL".

Dim x$(7) Still works but doesn't make x$ be a list of seven strings. Instead, it makes them variants (which can be a string, an integer, or a date). You can force them to be strings by saying Dim x$(7) As String.

**Input "What name"; n$** Doesn't work. Instead, use an InputBox, and format it like this: n$=InputBox("What name?"). Notice you must add the question mark yourself now.

Line (0, 0)-(100, 100) Still works. Add color by putting a comma, then RGB(r, g, b) where r, g, and b are red, green, and blue values of 0-255. Example: Line (0, 0)-(1000, 1000), RGB(255, 0, 0).

**Line Input "Type it"; n$** Still works as input from a file, but you must put the file number first (and you can't use the prompt). Example: Line Input #1, n$.

Lprint 2 + 2 Instead of saying "Lprint", say "Print.Printer".

Pset (100, 100) Still works but makes the pixel turn black instead of white. Add color by putting a comma, then RGB(r, g, b) where r, g, and b are red, green, and blue values of 0-255.

Print 4 + 2 Still works. The result is printed on the current form. Additional printouts are scrolled downwards. When it gets to the bottom of the form, it will *not* scroll everything else upwards: it's pretty dumb. It just keeps going off the form where you can't see it anymore.

Print Using "##.#"; x Doesn't work. Instead, format your variable first by saying: y = format(x, "##.#") on one line, and then Print y on the next line.

Shell "ver" The Shell command still works, but this command won't. First of all, the filename must be in parentheses and quotes ("ver"). But if you try to run Shell ("ver"), the computer says "File Not Found", because the Shell command works just with *external* functions or files.

Stop Still works, but the screen isn't blue.

Sub insult Still works, but you must decide whether it's public or private and must add the parentheses at the end. Example: Private Sub insult ().

Type combination Still works, but you must insert the word "Private" at the beginning.

Width 40 Still exists but does something different. Now it's used to determine the width of a line in an output file. You must say "Width #1, 40" (to say that a line in file #1 is 40 characters long).

Which functions differ?

This book explained many QBASIC functions (such as SQR). Most of them work in VB. When typing a function in VB, capitalize just the function's first letter, like this: Sqr. You can omit any dollar signs.

Unfortunately, VB is too stupid to handle INPUT$ and PEEK.

GWBASIC

Older versions of MS-DOS came with a more primitive BASIC, called **GWBASIC**. Yes, GWBASIC came with MS-DOS (and PC-DOS) versions 1, 1.1, 2, 2.1, 3, 3.1, 3.2, 3.3, and 4.

GWBASIC resembles QBASIC but omits some QBASIC commands and uses a more primitive way to edit your programs.

In earlier editions of this book, I explained GWBASIC in detail. In those editions, the BASIC tutorial emphasizes GWBASIC instead of QBASIC; most of the sample programs are written in GWBASIC. If you're using GWBASIC, get edition 16, 17, 18, 19, or 20. Phone me at 603-666-6644 to find out which of those editions are still available and their prices.

Here's how GWBASIC differs from QBASIC....

Start BASIC (page 334)

Before using GWBASIC, practice using the keyboard, by giving DOS commands or using a word processor.

(QBASIC would require you to practice DOS's edit command, but GWBASIC does not.)

The file that makes the computer understand GWBASIC is usually called "GWBASIC.EXE"; but some versions of MS-DOS (and PC-DOS) call it "BASIC.COM" or "BASICA.COM" instead. Some versions of MS-DOS lack the file altogether and can't do BASIC.

To start GWBASIC, try typing:

```
C:\>gwbasic
```

If the computer gripes (by saying "Bad command or file name"), try typing:

```
C:\>basica
```

If the computer still gripes (by saying "Bad command or file name" again), try typing:

```
C:\>basic
```

If the computer still gripes (by saying "Bad command or file name" again), try saying "dos\gwbasic" or "dos\basica" or "dos\basic".

If you don't have a drive C (because your computer doesn't have a hard disk), find the floppy that contains GWBASIC.EXE or BASICA.COM or BASIC.COM. Insert that floppy into drive A and say "gwbasic" or "basica" or "basic".

When you get into GWBASIC successfully, the computer will say:

```
Ok
```

(In QBASIC, the screen would turn blue; but in GWBASIC, the screen stays black, with "Ok" appearing in white lettering.)

If the computer does *not* say the word "Ok", you probably used the wrong version of DOS. Make sure your version of DOS came from your computer's manufacturer. For example, if IBM built your computer, use IBM's PC-DOS, *not* a clone version of MS-DOS. If a clone company built your computer, use your clone's version of MS-DOS, *not* IBM's PC-DOS. Using the wrong version of DOS makes the computer print a strange message, the screen go crazy, or the keyboard stop working.

(If your computer's an IBM PC Junior, buy the **BASIC cartridge** and put it into the left cartridge slot before you turn the computer on. That cartridge makes the Junior understand CIRCLE, PAINT, PLAY, TIMER, and the BASIC words for disks.) If your Junior is attached to a monitor instead of a TV, type "width 80" after the computer says "Ok".)

Type your program (page 334)

Instead of typing this program —

```
CLS
PRINT 4 + 2
```

type this:

```
10 CLS
20 PRINT 4 + 2
```

Notice that you must type a number (such as 10 or 20) in front of each program line. For best results, use these numbers: 10, 20, 30, etc.

Run your program (page 334)

To run your program, press the F2 key (instead of QBASIC's SHIFT F5). When the computer finishes running the program, the computer will say:

```
Ok
```

Then to see your program again, press the F1 key (or type "list") and press ENTER.

(If your computer's an IBM PC Junior, you must press the Fn key before pressing F2 or F1.)

Faster typing (page 335)

When you press ENTER at the end of the line, the computer will secretly convert "cls" into CLS and convert "print" and "?" into PRINT. To see the results of the conversion, type:

```
list
```

Why CLS? (page 335)

In GWBASIC, saying CLS is less important than in QBASIC. If you wish, omit the CLS line. When I write GWBASIC programs myself, I usually omit the CLS line.

Edit your program (page 335)

To start a new program, say:

```
new
```

That makes the computer forget about all the lines of your previous program. Then type the new program.

To delete just line 20, type this under your program:

```
20
```

That makes the computer forget about line 20.

To insert a line 15 between lines 10 and 20, type line 15 *under* your program. When you finish typing that line, the computer will automatically rearrange your program and put the lines in increasing order. To see the rearranged program, say "list".

To edit line 20 (instead of deleting it), use one of the following methods....

Method 1: retype Under the program, type line 20 all over again, correctly. When the computer notices that you have two lines numbered 20, the computer will take the bottom line 20 seriously and ignore the original line 20.

Method 2: edit Say "edit 20". That makes the computer show you line 20 again. Use the right-arrow key to move the cursor (blinking underline) to the part of the line you want to correct, then make your corrections.

> To **delete** a character:
> move the cursor to that character,
> then press the DELETE key.
>
> To **replace** a character:
> move the cursor to that character,
> then type the new character you want instead.
>
> To **insert** extra characters in middle of the line:
> move to where you want extra characters to begin, then press INSERT key, then type extra characters.

When you've finished correcting the line, press the ENTER key, which tells the computer to take the corrections seriously.

Method 3: list Say "list" (to see the whole program) or "list 20" (to see just line 20). Use the up-arrow key to move the cursor up into line 20. Then use the same editing procedure as if you used method 2. When you've finished correcting the line, press the ENTER key, which tells the computer to take the corrections seriously. After pressing the ENTER key, press the up-arrow or down-arrow keys to move to a different line or down to the bottom of the screen.

Fix your errors (page 335)

If you misspell CLS or PRINT, the computer will say "Syntax error" and show you the errant line. To fix the error, use one of these methods....

Method 1: retype Press the ENTER key immediately. Then retype the errant line (and press ENTER again at the end of your retyping).

Method 2: edit Press the left-arrow key until the cursor is at the beginning of the line's bad part. Then fix the line by retyping the bad part. Then press ENTER.

Huge & tiny numbers (page 336)

GWBASIC does *not* require you to use decimals for big answers. To multiply 200 by 300, you can say just "PRINT 200 * 300"; you do *not* need to say "PRINT 200 * 300.0".

Print on paper (page 339)

If your computer doesn't have a PRINT SCREEN key, do a screen dump by pressing the PrtSc key *while holding down the SHIFT key*. (If your computer's an IBM PC Junior, do a screen dump by pressing the Fn key, then the PrtSc key.)

WIDTH 40 (page 339)

After running a program that says WIDTH 40, you can return to a normal screen by saying:

```
width 80
```

File menu (page 339)

GWBASIC doesn't have a file menu. Instead of using a file menu, type these commands:

Command	Meaning
list	Show you what program is in the RAM chips.
llist	Copy the program onto paper.
save "joe"	Copy the program onto your hard disk, and name the program "JOE.BAS".
files	Show you a directory of all the files that are on the hard disk.
new	Erase the program from the RAM chips.
load "joe"	Copy the program JOE.BAS from your hard disk to the RAM chips.
run "joe"	Copy the program JOE.BAS from your hard disk to the RAM chips and run it.
system	Stop using GWBASIC. Make the computer say "C:\>".

So when you finish using GWBASIC, say:

```
system
```

Instant open (page 341)

Suppose you've saved a GWBASIC program called JOE. To use JOE, say:

```
C:\>gwbasic joe
```

That makes the computer use GWBASIC and instantly run JOE. Moreover, if JOE's bottom line says SYSTEM, the computer will automatically exit from GWBASIC when JOE finishes running.

SLEEP (page 341)

GWBASIC doesn't understand SLEEP. Instead of saying —

```
30 SLEEP
```

say:

```
30 A$ = INPUT$(1)
```

Instead of saying —

```
30 SLEEP 6
```

say:

```
30 T = TIMER
35 IF TIMER < T + 6 THEN GOTO 35
```

DO...LOOP (page 343)

GWBASIC doesn't understand DO or LOOP. Replace the DO by an apostrophe, and replace the LOOP by a GOTO that says to go to the line containing the apostrophe. So instead of saying —

```
20 DO
30    PRINT "love"
40 LOOP
```

say:

```
20 '
30    PRINT "love"
40 GOTO 20
```

(If your computer's an IBM PC Junior, here's how to abort a program: press the Fn key, then the BREAK key.)

Line numbers (page 344)

GWBASIC does *not* let a line number include a decimal point.

GOTO (page 344)

GWBASIC doesn't let you name the lines: you can't make a line be named JOE, and you can't say GOTO JOE. Though you can't say GOTO JOE, you can say GOTO 10. Lines must be numbered, not named.

What's a variable? (page 346)

When you list the program, the computer will automatically capitalize all variables: x will become X.

Long variable names (page 348)

When you list the program, the computer will automatically capitalize all variables: profit.in.1996 will become PROFIT.IN.1996.

Multi-line IF (page 354)

GWBASIC doesn't understand multi-line IF. Use a single-line IF instead.

You can make the single-line IF be up to 255 characters long, even though the screen's just 80 characters wide. When you reach the screen's right margin, continue typing: the extra characters will appear underneath. Don't press ENTER until you've typed the entire single-line IF.

Here's a long single-line IF:

```
30 IF AGE < 18 THEN PRINT "You are still a minor": PRINT "Ah, the joys of youth"
 ELSE PRINT "You are an adult": PRINT "We can have adult fun"
```

ELSEIF (page 354)

Since GWBASIC doesn't understand multi-line IF, GWBASIC doesn't understand ELSEIF.

Use a single-line IF instead. In the middle of the single-line IF, you can say ELSE IF. Put a space between the ELSE and the IF.

Here's a single-line IF that contains ELSE IF:

```
30 IF AGE < 18 THEN PRINT "You're a minor" ELSE IF AGE < 100 THEN PRINT "You're
a typical adult" ELSE IF AGE < 125 THEN PRINT "You're a centenarian" ELSE PRINT
"You're a liar"
```

SELECT (page 355)

GWBASIC doesn't understand SELECT. Instead, say IF and ELSE IF. For example, instead of saying —

```
30 SELECT CASE A$
40    CASE "fine"
50       PRINT "That's good!"
60    CASE "lousy"
70       PRINT "Too bad!"
80    CASE ELSE
90       PRINT "I feel the same way"
100 END SELECT
```

say:

```
30 IF A$ = "fine" THEN PRINT "That's good!" ELSE IF A$ = "lousy" THEN PRINT "Too
bad!" ELSE PRINT "I feel the same way"
```

Different relations (page 357)

If you accidentally say "=<" instead of "<=", your program will still work. The GWBASIC understands and accepts "=<" and won't bother turning it into "<=".

EXIT DO (page 359)

Since GWBASIC doesn't understand DO, it doesn't understand EXIT DO. Instead of saying EXIT DO, tell the computer to GOTO the line under the loop. For example, instead of saying —

```
30 DO
40    INPUT "What's my favorite color"; GUESS$
50    IF GUESS$ = "pink" THEN EXIT DO
60    PRINT "No, that's not my favorite color.  Try again!"
70 LOOP
80 PRINT "Congratulations!  You discovered my favorite color."
```

say:

```
30 '
40    INPUT "What's my favorite color"; GUESS$
50    IF GUESS$ = "pink" THEN GOTO 80
60    PRINT "No, that's not my favorite color.  Try again!"
70 GOTO 30
80 PRINT "Congratulations!  You discovered my favorite color."
```

LOOP UNTIL (page 359)

Since GWBASIC doesn't understand DO, it doesn't understand LOOP UNTIL. Instead of saying LOOP UNTIL, use an IF. For example, instead of saying —

```
30 DO
40    PRINT "You haven't guessed my favorite color yet!"
50    INPUT "What's my favorite color"; GUESS$
60 LOOP UNTIL GUESS$ = "pink"
```

say:

```
30 '
40    PRINT "You haven't guessed my favorite color yet!"
50    INPUT "What's my favorite color"; GUESS$
60 IF GUESS$ <> "pink" THEN GOTO 30
```

END, STOP, or SYSTEM (page 368)

Here's how END, STOP, and SYSTEM differ from each other:

END	makes the computer say "Ok".
STOP	makes the computer say "Ok" but also tell you which line the computer stopped at.
SYSTEM	makes the computer say "C:\>".

Syntax errors (page 375)

If you type "prind" instead of "print", or you type extra characters at the end of a line, or you forget to type a matching parenthesis, the computer will say:

```
Syntax error
```

If you try to say PRINT 5 + 2 but forget to type the 2, the computer will say:

```
Missing operand
```

Logic errors (page 375)

If you say GOTO 10 but no line is numbered 10, the computer will say:

```
Undefined line number
```

PAUSE key (page 376)

If your computer's an IBM PC Junior, here's how to pause: press the Fn key, then the PAUSE key.

F keys (page 376)

GWBASIC uses the F keys completely differently:

```
To LIST the program, press F1 then ENTER.

To RUN the program, press F2.

To LOAD the program, press F3,
then type the program's name, then press ENTER.

To SAVE the program, press F4,
then type the program's name, then press ENTER.
```

Each line in your GWBASIC program must begin with a line number. If you type a line that does *not* begin with a line number, the computer will run that line immediately when you press the ENTER key at the end of the line. For example, if you say —

```
PRINT 4 + 2
```

the computer will print the answer (6) immediately when you press the ENTER key at the end of the line.

The only way to create a breakpoint is to put a STOP line into your program.

Advanced features

Bottom line (page 382) The screen's bottom line normally contains a message reminding you that F1 is LIST, F2 is RUN, F3 is LOAD, F4 is SAVE, etc. To make that message disappear, say —

```
key off
```

or write a program containing a line saying KEY OFF. After saying KEY OFF, you can give a LOCATE command that puts info on line 25. For example, this program puts an "x" at the screen's bottom right corner:

```
10 KEY OFF
20 LOCATE 25, 80: PRINT "x";
```

Whenever your want the bottom line's message to reappear, say:

```
key on
```

Screen modes (page 382) If you're using DOS 1, 1.1, 2, 2.1, or 3, you must use screen mode 0, 1, or 2. If you're using DOS 3.1 or 3.2, you must use screen mode 0, 1, 2, or 3. If you're using DOS 3.3 or higher, you can use any screen mode from 0 to 10. GWBASIC doesn't understand screen modes 11, 12, or 13. Screen mode 10 works just on monochrome monitors. If you're using DOS 3.3 or higher with an EGA or VGA color monitor, choose screen mode 9.

If your computer's an IBM PC Junior, you can use screen modes 0, 1, and 2, plus the following special versions of modes 3, 4, 5, and 6:

PC Junior mode	Pixels	Colors
3	160 by 200	16
4	320 by 200	4
5	320 by 200	16
6	640 by 200	4

Modes 5 and 6 require at least 128K of RAM and require you to give this command beforehand:

```
clear,,,32768
```

You can put that command in your program.

Avoid the bottom (page 383) To avoid any problems about the screen's bottom line, say KEY OFF at the beginning of your program. Make the top line say KEY OFF and CLS and choose a screen mode, like this:

```
10 KEY OFF: CLS: SCREEN 9
```

PLAY (page 385) If you're using DOS 1 or 1.1, the symbols ">" and "<" don't work.

If your computer's an IBM PC Junior, try the following experiment.... Turn up the volume on your TV or monitor. Then say:

```
sound on
```

Then make the Junior's three voices sing simultaneously, like this:

```
play "gab","efg","ccd"
```

While the first voice is singing "gab", the second voice sings "efg"; the third voice sings "ccd".

Printing the date & time (page 390) If you're using DOS 1 or 1.1, your computer doesn't understand TIMER.

RANDOMIZE TIMER (page 394) If you're using DOS 1 or 1.1, instead of saying RANDOMIZE TIMER say RANDOMIZE VAL(RIGHT$(TIME$, 2)).

Capitals (page 400) GWBASIC doesn't understand UCASE$ and LCASE$.

Trim (page 401) GWBASIC doesn't understand LTRIM$ and RTRIM$.

Long integers versus short integers (page 403)

GWBASIC doesn't permit long integers. In GWBASIC, all integers are short. If you try to create an integer bigger than 32767, GWBASIC will make your number be a real number instead of an integer.

Biggest real numbers (page 403)

The biggest permissible single-precision real number is 1.701411E38. The biggest permissible double-precision real number is 1.701411834604692D38.

Accuracy (page 404)

GWBASIC handles a double-precision real number's 16th digit accurately but makes slight mistakes with the 17th digit.

Tiniest decimals (page 404)

The tiniest single-precision number that the computer can handle is 2.938736E-39. The tiniest double-precision number that the computer can handle is 2.938735877055719D-39. If you try to go tinier than those numbers, the computer will say zero.

Extra accuracy (page 404)

If your program involves trigonometry (SIN, COS, TAN, ATN) or exponents (^, SQR, EXP, LOG), and you want those computations done with double-precision accuracy, you must say "gwbasic/d" (instead of "gwbasic") or say "basica/d" (instead of "basica").

Prime numbers (page 406)

Since GWBASIC doesn't permit long integers, omit the DEFLNG line (or say DEFINT instead of DEFLNG and use integers no bigger than 32767).

SUB procedures (page 412)

GWBASIC programmers say "routine" instead of "procedure". They talk about the "main routine" and "subroutines" instead of a "main procedure" and "SUB procedures".

GWBASIC doesn't understand the word SUB. Instead of saying —

```
10 CLS
20 PRINT "We all know..."
30 insult
40 PRINT "...and yet we love you."
1000 SUB insult
1010   PRINT "You are stupid!"
1020   PRINT "You are ugly!"
1030 END SUB
```

say this:

```
10 CLS
20 PRINT "We all know..."
30 GOSUB 1000
40 PRINT "...and yet we love you."
50 END
1000 PRINT "You are stupid!"
1020 PRINT "You are ugly!"
1030 RETURN
```

Notice that the main routine's bottom line should say END, and the subroutine's bottom line should say RETURN.

When you say "GOSUB 1000", the computer does a "GOTO 1000" but also remembers where it came from, so the computer can return there when you say "RETURN".

GWBASIC's subroutines act like any other lines in the program: the subroutines do *not* use a separate part of the RAM. For example, if the main routine says "X = 4", the X will then be 4 in the subroutine also. If the subroutine says "X = 100", the X will then be 100 in the main routine also. All variables are automatically global and COMMON SHARED, so you don't need to say so. Subroutines can't have arguments or parameters.

If you say DEFINT A-Z at the beginning of the program, all variables in all routines will be short integers.

Loops (page 427)

Instead of saying —

```
30 DO UNTIL EOF(1)
40   INPUT #1, FRIEND$
50   PRINT FRIEND$
60 LOOP
70 CLOSE
```

say:

```
30 IF EOF(1) THEN GOTO 70
40   INPUT #1, FRIEND$
50   PRINT FRIEND$
60 GOTO 30
70 CLOSE
```

PUT (page 428)

GWBASIC doesn't understand "STRING * 20". Instead of saying —

```
20 DIM RECORD AS STRING * 20
30 OPEN "jim" FOR RANDOM AS 1 LEN = LEN(record)
```

say:

```
30 OPEN "jim" AS 1 LEN=20: FIELD 1, 20 AS RECORD$
```

Instead of saying —

```
40 RECORD = "Love makes me giggle"
50 PUT 1, 7, RECORD
```

say:

```
40 LSET RECORD$ = "Love makes me giggle"
50 PUT 1, 7
```

Notice that line 40 begins with the word LSET, and line 50 does *not* end with the word RECORD.

Here's the rule about LSET: if a variable (such as RECORD$) is in a FIELD statement, you can*not* put that variable into an ordinary "=" statement; instead of saying RECORD$ = "Love makes me giggle", you must say LSET RECORD$ = "Love makes me giggle". You can*not* put the variable into an INPUT statement: instead of saying INPUT RECORD$, you must say INPUT A$ and then LSET RECORD$ = A$.

In the OPEN statement, the number after "LEN=" is called the **record length**. If you want the record length to be more than 128 (because the string is long), you must warn the computer. For example, to warn the computer that you'll want a record length of 200, say "gwbasic/s:200" (instead of just "gwbasic"), or say "basica/s:400" (instead of just "basica").

GET (page 428)

Instead of saying —

```
40 GET 1, 7, RECORD
```

say just:

```
40 GET 1, 7
```

Multi-field records (page 428)

GWBASIC doesn't understand the word TYPE. Instead of saying —

```
20 TYPE COMBINATION
30   A AS STRING * 20
40   B AS STRING * 5
50 END TYPE
60 DIM RECORD AS COMBINATION
70 OPEN "jack" FOR RANDOM AS 1 LEN = LEN(record)
```

say:

```
70 OPEN "jack" AS 1 LEN=25: FIELD 1, 20 AS A$, 5 AS B$
```

Instead of saying —

```
80 RECORD.A = "I want turkey on rye"
90 RECORD.B = "yummy"
100 PUT 1, 6, RECORD
```

say:

```
80 LSET A$ = "I want turkey on rye"
90 LSET B$ = "yummy"
100 PUT 1, 6
```

Lengths (page 429)

Saying "LEN(record)" doesn't work well. Instead of saying "LEN(record)", just say the record length. For example, if the record length is 25, say 25. If the record length is 25, the number of records in the file is LOF(1) \ 25.

End of the file (page 429)

If the record length is 25, and each record consists of part A$ and part B$, these lines print all the records:

```
100 FOR I = 1 TO LOF(1) \ 25
110   GET 1, I
120   PRINT A$
130   PRINT B$
140 NEXT
```

Numeric data (page 429)

In a GWBASIC random-access file, each record must consists of strings, not numbers. If you want to store numbers in the file, you must turn the numbers into strings.

To turn an integer into a string, use the function MKI$ (MaKe from Integer). It turns the integer into a 2-byte string, even if the integer is long. For example, to turn the integer 17999 into a 2-byte string called A$, say "FIELD 1, 2 AS A$" and say "LSET A$ = MKI$(17999)".

The function MKS$ (MaKe from Single-precision real) turns a real number into a 4-byte string. The function MKD$ (MaKe from Double-precision) turns a double-precision number into an 8-byte string.

Suppose you turn a number into a string (by using MKI$, MKS$, or MKD$), and PUT the string into a file, and later GET the string back from the file. You'll want to convert the string back to a number. Use the function CVI (ConVert to Integer) or CVS (ConVert to Single-precision) or CVD (ConVert to Double-precision). For example, if A$ is a 2-byte string that stands for an integer, you can make the computer print the integer by saying PRINT CVI(A$).

LOC (page 429)

Instead of saying "PUT 1, 7" or "PUT 1, 8", you can leave the record's number blank and say just "PUT 1". That makes the computer PUT the next record. Saying "PUT 1" has the same effect as saying "PUT 1, LOC(1) + 1". If you say "GET 1", the computer will GET the next record.

Multiple files (page 429)

If you want the computer to handle two random-access files simultaneously, use two OPEN statements. In the first OPEN statement, say "AS 1"; in the second OPEN statement, say "AS 2". In the first FIELD statement, say "FIELD 1"; in the second FIELD statement, say "FIELD 2". For the second file, say 2 instead of 1 in the OPEN, FIELD, PUT and GET statements and in the LOF and LOC functions.

Error numbers (page 435)

In GWBASIC, you can make these errors:

#	Message
1	NEXT without FOR
2	Syntax error
3	RETURN without GOSUB
4	Out of DATA
5	Illegal function call
6	Overflow
7	Out of memory
8	Undefined line number
9	Subscript out of range
10	Duplicate Definition
11	Division by zero
12	Illegal direct
13	Type mismatch
14	Out of strong space
15	String too long
16	String formula too complex
17	Can't continue
18	Undefined user function
19	No RESUME
20	RESUME without error
22	Missing operand
23	Line buffer overflow
24	Device Timeout
25	Device Fault
26	FOR without NEXT
27	Out of Paper
29	WHILE without WEND
30	WEND without WHILE
50	FIELD overflow
51	Internal error
52	Bad file number
53	File not found
54	Bad file mode
55	File already open
57	Device I/O Error
58	File already exists
61	Disk full
62	Input past end
63	Bad record number
64	Bad filename
66	Direct statement in file
67	Too many files
68	Device Unavailable
69	Communication buffer overflow
70	Permission Denied
71	Disk not Ready
72	Disk media error
73	Advanced Feature
74	Rename across disks
75	Path/File Access Error
76	Path not found

Other computers

I've described five BASIC versions: QBASIC, Quick BASIC, Visual BASIC for DOS, Visual BASIC for Windows, and GWBASIC. They work on IBM-compatible computers using PC-DOS or MS-DOS.

If your computer is *not* IBM-compatible or does *not* use PC-DOS or MS-DOS, it probably uses a more primitive version of BASIC. Those primitive versions are explained in editions 1-20 of this book. For example, those editions explain versions of BASIC for the Mac, Apple 2, Commodore 64, Commodore Vic, Coleco Adam, CP/M computers, and computers made by Atari, Texas Instruments, and Timex/Sinclair. To find out which editions are still available and which ones explain *your* computer, phone me at 603-666-6644 anytime!

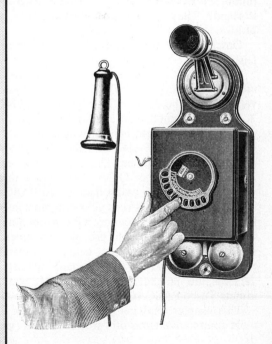

PASCAL

Fun

Imagine that you're running for President against Calvin Coolidge. To win, you must pass Cal in the polls.

You must pass Cal. "Pass Cal" is the correct way to pronounce "PASCAL", the name of the computer language that programmers are falling in love with.

PASCAL is harder to learn than BASIC. But once you've learned PASCAL, you have amazing power: you can write fancy programs more easily in PASCAL than in BASIC because PASCAL helps organize your thinking; and your programs will run faster, too!

American teachers require kids to master LOGO in elementary school, BASIC in high school, and PASCAL in college. Gifted kids are given the opportunity to start BASIC and PASCAL even sooner — and so are kids in progressive schools.

Many high-school seniors take a PASCAL test given by the College Board. Seniors who pass can get "advanced placement" college credit and skip the college's first year of computer courses.

The nicest kinds of PASCAL are **Quick PASCAL** (published by Microsoft) and **Turbo PASCAL** (published by Borland). They're easy to understand, run quickly, and cost little.

Quick PASCAL runs on the IBM PC and lists for just $99. Discount dealers sell it for just $42.

Turbo PASCAL is available for the IBM PC, Mac, and computers using the CP/M operating system. The newest version of Turbo PASCAL for the IBM PC is **Turbo PASCAL 7**, which discount dealers sell for $99.

If you're on a tight budget, which should you buy — Quick PASCAL or Turbo PASCAL? Since they're very similar to each other, you'll probably buy Quick PASCAL because it costs less. Another advantage of Quick PASCAL is that it lets you edit your programs more easily than Turbo PASCAL. On the other hand, Turbo PASCAL runs your programs faster, consumes less RAM and disk space, comes with instruction manuals that are larger and more thorough, provides on-screen tutorials that are easier to use, understands better commands for advanced programming, and is the standard against which all other versions are judged. (Quick PASCAL was invented just to imitate Turbo PASCAL more cheaply.)

This chapter explains how to use Quick PASCAL and the most common versions of Turbo PASCAL (versions 4, 5.5, and 6).

If you have Turbo PASCAL 7, follow the instructions for Turbo PASCAL 6, which is similar. If you have Turbo PASCAL version 5, follow the instructions for version 5.5.

I'll comment on how other versions of PASCAL differ.

Copy to the hard disk

Quick PASCAL and Turbo PASCAL come on a pile of floppy disks. You should copy those disks to your hard disk. Here's how.

Quick PASCAL Turn on the computer without any floppy in drive A.

The original version of Quick PASCAL comes on five 5¼-inch floppy disks. When you see the C prompt, put the Quick PASCAL Setup/Utilities Disk in drive A and type "a:". The computer will display an A prompt. Type "setup". The computer will say "Microsoft Quick Pascal Setup Program".

Press ENTER twice. The computer will say "Easy Setup Menu". Type the letter I. Press ENTER four times.

Put the Quick PASCAL Program Disk in drive A, and press ENTER. Put the Quick PASCAL Advisor Disk in drive A, and press ENTER. Put the Quick PASCAL Libraries Disk in drive A, and press ENTER. Put the Quick PASCAL Express Disk in drive A; press ENTER twice.

Press R, so that the computer says "Setup Main Menu". Press X, so that you exit to DOS. You'll see an A prompt.

Turn off the computer, so you can start fresh.

Turbo PASCAL 4 Turn on the computer without any floppy in drive A.

After the C prompt, type "md turbo" (so you're making a subdirectory called TURBO). After the next C prompt, type "cd turbo" (so you're changing to the TURBO subdirectory).

Turbo PASCAL 4 comes on three floppy disks. Put one of those disks in drive A, and type "copy a:*.*" (which copies all the floppy's files onto the hard disk); follow the same procedure for the other two disks.

Turn off the computer, so you can start fresh.

Turbo PASCAL 5.5 and 6 Turn on the computer without any floppy in drive A.

Your Turbo PASCAL comes on four 5¼-inch floppy disks. When you see the C prompt, put the Install/Compiler disk in drive A, and type "a:install". The computer will say "Turbo PASCAL Installation Utility".

Press ENTER four times. You'll see "C:\TP". Press the BACKSPACE key, then type URBO so you see "C:\TURBO". At the end of the URBO, press ENTER.

Press the F9 key.

If you're using version 6, put the Turbo Vision/Tour disk in drive A, press ENTER, put the Help disk in drive A, press ENTER, put the BGI/Utilities disk in drive A, and press ENTER twice. (If you're using version 5.5, put the Tour/Online Help disk in drive A, press ENTER, put the OOP/Demos/BGI/Doc disk in drive A, press ENTER, put the Utilities/Misc disk in drive A, and press ENTER twice.)

You'll see an A prompt. Turn off the computer, so you can start fresh.

Start PASCAL

To start using PASCAL, turn on the computer without any floppy in drive A.

If you've put the DO.BAT file onto your hard disk (as I recommended in the MS-DOS chapter), your life is easy! Just type "do qp" to do Quick PASCAL; type "do turbo" to do Turbo PASCAL.

If you have *not* put DO.BAT onto your hard disk, your life is harder! You must type "cd qp" and then "qp" to do Quick PASCAL; you must type "cd turbo" and then "turbo" to do Turbo PASCAL.

Press the CAPS LOCK key, so the computer will automatically capitalize everything you type (and your typing will look like the examples in this chapter).

Here's what to do next.

Quick PASCAL You don't have to do anything!

Turbo PASCAL 4 Press the E key (which means "Edit"). Make sure the cursor is at a blank part of the screen. (If it's not, press the DELETE key several times.)

Turbo PASCAL 5.5 Press the F6 key (so the cursor moves to the bottom of the screen). Then press the F6 key *while holding down the Alt key* (so the bottom of the screen says "Output"). Then tap the F6 key without the Alt key (so the cursor moves to the top part of the screen).

Turbo PASCAL 6 Press F10 then W then the letter O (so the cursor moves to the bottom of the screen). Press F10 again then W then T. Press F6.

How to program

For example, type this PASCAL program:

```
BEGIN;
WRITELN('I WOULD LIKE TO KISS');
WRITELN('YOUR BOTTLE OF WINE');
END.
```

The program begins with the word BEGIN and ends with the word END. Every line ends with a semicolon, except that the bottom line ends with a period. The middle lines say WRITELN, which tells the computer to WRITE a LiNe.

Naming the program If you wish, you can put an extra line at the top of the program, to give the program a name. The name can be up to 8 letters long. For example, if you want to name the program WINE, you can begin the program by saying PROGRAM WINE, like this:

```
PROGRAM WINE;
BEGIN;
WRITELN('I WOULD LIKE TO KISS');
WRITELN('YOUR BOTTLE OF WINE');
END.
```

Colors If your screen can display colors, here's what you see. In Turbo PASCAL, the program is yellow. In Quick PASCAL, most of the program is white, but the keywords (PROGRAM, BEGIN, and END) turn purple and the strings ('I WOULD LIKE TO KISS' and 'YOUR BOTTLE OF WINE') turn light blue.

Run the program When you finish typing the program, tell the computer to run it. Here's how. For Turbo PASCAL 4, press F10 then R. For Turbo PASCAL 5.5 & 6, press F10 then type RR. For Quick PASCAL, press F5; and if the computer asks "Rebuild?", press ENTER.

If you typed the program correctly, the computer will write:

```
I WOULD LIKE TO KISS
YOUR BOTTLE OF WINE
```

If you typed the program incorrectly, the computer will say:

```
Error
```

(If you're using Quick PASCAL, then press ENTER.) The computer will put the cursor near your error. Correct the error (by using the arrow keys, DELETE key, and other word-processing keys), then tell the computer to run the program again.

After a good run After the computer has run the program successfully, do the following: for Quick PASCAL, press ENTER; for Turbo PASCAL 4, press ENTER then E; for Turbo PASCAL 5.5 and 6, you don't have to do anything!

You'll see the program again. If you wish, edit the program again and run the edited version.

> **Other versions** Some versions of PASCAL *require* you to say PROGRAM WINE at the top of the program; if you don't say PROGRAM WINE, those versions gripe.
>
> Ancient versions require the top line to say this:
> PROGRAM WINE(INPUT,OUTPUT);
> Some Apple 2 and Mac versions automatically indent all lines between BEGIN and END and force you to omit the semicolon next to the word BEGIN.

Advanced editing

While typing and editing your program, you can edit faster by using these tricks....

To delete a whole line, move to that line. Then tap the Y key (which means "Yank it out") while holding down the CONTROL key.

To insert an extra line in the middle of your program, move to where you want the extra line to begin. Press the ENTER key, then the up-arrow.

Here's how to delete or move a block of text....

Turbo PASCAL 6 and Quick PASCAL Put the cursor at the block's beginning. Hold down the SHIFT key while moving to the block's end, so the entire block changes color.

Then say what you want to do to the block. If you want to delete the block, press the DELETE key for Quick PASCAL; press CONTROL with DELETE for Turbo PASCAL 6. If you want to move the block instead, press SHIFT with DELETE, then point where you want the block to appear and press SHIFT with INSERT.

Turbo PASCAL 4 and 5.5 Put the cursor at the block's beginning. Press CONTROL with K (which means "kommand"), then press B (which means "block").

Point at the character after the block's end. Press CONTROL with K, then press K (which means "klose"). The entire block changes color.

Then say what you want to do to the block. If you want to delete the block, press CONTROL K then Y ("which means "yank"). If you want to move the block instead, point where you want the block to appear and press CONTROL K then V (which means "visible").

Save your program

Here's how to copy your program onto the hard disk.

Quick PASCAL Press the Alt key. Say "File Save" by typing FS. If the computer says "File Name", type a name for the program (such as WINE) and press ENTER.

Turbo PASCAL 4 and 5.5 Press the F2 key. If the computer says "Rename", type a name for the program (such as WINE) and press ENTER.

Turbo PASCAL 6 Press the F2 key. If the computer says "Save file as", type a name for the program (such as WINE) and press ENTER.

Switch programs

Here's how to switch to other programs.

Quick PASCAL Press CONTROL with F4. If the computer asks "Do you want to save?", press N. The screen becomes blank. Press the Alt key.

If you want to invent a new program, say "File New" (by typing FN). If instead you want to retrieve a saved program, do this: say "File Open" (by typing FO), type the program's name (such as WINE), and press ENTER.

Turbo PASCAL 4 and 5.5 If you want to invent a new program, press F10 then type FN (which means File New). If instead you want to retrieve a saved program, do this: press F3 and ENTER; point at the program you want to use (by using the arrow keys and PAGE DOWN key) and press ENTER.

If the computer asks "Save?", press N.

Turbo PASCAL 6 Press Alt with F3. If the computer asks "Save?", press N.

If you want to invent a new program, press F10 then type FN (which means File New). If instead you want to retrieve a saved program, do this: press F3 and ENTER; point at the program you want to use (by using the arrow keys) and press ENTER.

Multiple writing

This program belongs in your bathroom:

```
BEGIN;
WRITELN('FAR','TIN','G');
END.
```

The computer will write FAR, TIN, and G all on the same line, like this:

```
FARTING
```

Exit

When you finish using PASCAL, here's how to return to the DOS prompt.

Quick PASCAL Press the Alt key. Say "File eXit" (by typing FX). If the computer asks "Do you want to save?", press N.

If you're using a fancy color monitor (such as VGA), you'll discover that Quick PASCAL has changed the monitor's colors. To reset the colors, turn the computer off and then back on.

Turbo PASCAL Press Alt with X. If the computer asks "Save?", press N.

EXE files

The computer can't really understand PASCAL. Whenever you tell the computer to run a PASCAL program, the computer secretly creates a second version of your program. The second version is written in **machine language** instead of PASCAL. (Machine language is the only language the computer really understands.) Then the computer runs the machine-language version of your program.

The program you typed (in PASCAL) is called the **source code**. The program the computer runs (in machine language) is called the **object code**.

When the computer is translating your program from PASCAL to machine language (from source code to object code), the computer is said to be **compiling** your program. Since Quick PASCAL and Turbo PASCAL make the computer compile your PASCAL programs, Quick PASCAL and Turbo PASCAL are called **PASCAL compilers**.

Example Suppose you type a PASCAL program, then tell the computer to save it on the hard disk and call it WINE. The computer will copy it to your hard disk's PASCAL subdirectory, where it will be called "WINE.PAS". The ".PAS" means "source code written in PASCAL".

When you tell the computer to run the WINE.PAS program, the computer translates it to machine language. The machine-language version (the object code) is called "WINE.EXE". The ".EXE" means "executable object code written in machine language".

If you're using Quick PASCAL, the computer automatically puts WINE.EXE in your disk's PASCAL subdirectory. If you're using Turbo PASCAL instead, the computer puts WINE.EXE in the RAM but not on disk — unless you give a special "Destination Disk" command.

After the computer has run your program and put WINE.EXE on disk, you can run the WINE.EXE machine-language program without using PASCAL. Here's how: quit PASCAL, then do a "cd" to the PASCAL subdirectory, then type "wine".

Experiment Try the following experiment....

Step 1: type a PASCAL program.

Step 2: tell the computer to save the program and call it WINE. The computer will call your program WINE.PAS and copy it to PASCAL's subdirectory. (If you're using Turbo PASCAL, the computer will rename a previous WINE.PAS to WINE.BAK.)

Step 2½: if you're using Turbo PASCAL, say "Destination Disk". Here's how. Press F10 then C. If you see "Destination Memory" instead of "Destination Disk", press D. Then return to the editor (by pressing F6 for version 4, Esc for version 5.5).

Step 3: run the program. The computer will invent WINE.EXE (a machine-language version of WINE) and put it in PASCAL's subdirectory. Then the computer will run that machine-language program. (If you're using Quick PASCAL, the computer will also produce a WINE.QDB to help the Quick DeBugger.)

Step 4: exit from PASCAL, so you see the DOS prompt.

Step 5: notice that you can run WINE.EXE without using PASCAL. Specifically, go into PASCAL's subdirectory (by typing "cd \qp" for Quick PASCAL, or "cd \turbo" for Turbo PASCAL), then type "wine" (which runs the WINE.EXE program).

Math

PASCAL distinguishes between integers and real numbers. Here's how PASCAL defines them....

Integers

An integer contains no decimal point and no exponent.

Integer	Not an integer	Comment
-27	-27.0	An integer contains no decimal point.
50000	5E4	An integer contains no exponent.

Real numbers

A real number contains a decimal point or the letter E. For example, it can be 0.37 or 5.0 or 6E24. If it contains a decimal point, you should put digits before and after the decimal point.

Correct	Incorrect
0.37	.37
5.0	5.

Other versions Old versions of PASCAL require you to put a decimal point in every real number; so instead of saying 6E24, you must say 6.0E24.

Arithmetic

Like BASIC, PASCAL lets you do arithmetic by using the symbols +, -, *, and /.

If you combine real numbers, the answer is real:

```
4.9+2.1 is the real number 7.0 (not 7)
5.0-5.0 is the real number 0.0 (not 0)
```

If you combine a real with an integer, the answer is still real:

```
3.5*2 is the real number 7.0 (not 7)
3/.5  is the real number 6.0 (not 6)
```

If you combine integers, the answer is an integer, except for division:

```
7+4 is the integer 11
7-4 is the integer 3
7*4 is the integer 28
7/4 is the real number 1.75
```

This program makes the computer do all that arithmetic:

```
BEGIN;
WRITELN(7+4);
WRITELN(7-4);
WRITELN(7*4);
WRITELN(7/4);
END.
```

The computer will write:

```
11
3
28
 1.7500000000E+00
```

(Quick PASCAL writes extra zeros, like this: 1.75000000000000E+0000.)

Let's try writing all those numbers on the same line:

```
BEGIN;
WRITELN(7+4,7-4,7*4,7/4);
END.
```

The computer will write:

```
11328 1.7500000000E+00
```

Like BASIC, PASCAL lets you use parentheses to indicate order of operations.

Other versions Some versions of PASCAL automatically write blank spaces in front of integers.

Some versions of PASCAL write 1.75 instead of 1.7500000000E+00. Some Apple 2 and Mac versions automatically round the answer and write 1.8e+0.

Functions

PASCAL lets you use these functions:

Function	Meaning
ABS(-6)	the absolute value of -6; it's 6
SQR(3)	the square of 3; it's 9
SQRT(9)	the square root of 9; it's 3.0
SIN(2)	the sine of 2 radians
COS(2)	the cosine of 2 radians
ARCTAN(2)	the arctangent of 2, in radians
EXP(5)	e^5, where e is 2.71828182845904523536
LN(9)	the natural logarithm of 9; it's $\log_e 9$

The number in parentheses can be either an integer or a real. The computer's answer is usually a real (exception: for ABS and SQR, the computer's answer is an integer if the number in parentheses is an integer).

For example, this program computes the square root of 9:

```
BEGIN;
WRITELN(SQRT(9));
END.
```

The computer will write:

```
 3.0000000000E+00
```

Don't confuse SQR with SQRT. The SQR means square; the SQRT means square root. To find the square of 3, say SQR(3) or 3*3. In BASIC, you could say 3^2; but in PASCAL, you can't use the symbol ^; use SQR instead.

To turn a real number into an integer, use these functions:

Function	Meaning	
ROUND(3.9)	3.9 rounded to the nearest integer;	it's 4
TRUNC(3.9)	3.9 truncated (by deleting the .9);	it's 3

Other versions For UCSD PASCAL, say ATAN instead of ARCTAN. If you're using UCSD PASCAL on an Apple and want to use the functions SQRT, SIN, COS, ATAN, EXP, and LN, you must insert this line immediately under the line that says PROGRAM:

```
USES TRANSCEND;
```

Simple variables

You can use variables:

Program	Meaning
VAR	Here are the variables....
FRED,MARTHA: INTEGER;	FRED & MARTHA integers;
JILL,TOM: REAL;	JILL & TOM are reals.
BEGIN;	Now let's begin the program.
FRED:=2;	FRED (an integer) is 2.
MARTHA:=4+5;	MARTHA (an integer) is 9.
JILL:=9.2;	JILL (a real) is 9.2.
TOM:=1.4+2.3;	TOM (a real) is 3.7.
WRITELN(FRED*MARTHA,JILL+TOM);	Write 18 and 1.2900000000E+01.
END.	That ends the program.

The top line says VAR. The word VAR doesn't have a semicolon after it; the lines underneath VAR are indented. The indentation is optional but a good habit. To indent easily, tap the TAB key.

For Quick PASCAL, the TAB key indents 8 spaces. For Turbo PASCAL, the TAB key indents just enough to get past the word above (VAR).

On the indented lines, say which variables are integers and which are reals.

Once you've indented a line, the computer automatically indents all the lines underneath it. If the computer automatically indents a line that you don't want to indent, here's how to undo the indentation: for Turbo PASCAL 5.5, press the BACKSPACE key once; for Turbo PASCAL 4, press the left-arrow key several times; for Quick PASCAL, tap the TAB key while holding down the SHIFT key.

In PASCAL, a variable's name can be as long as you like: the name can be FRED or WASHINGTON or even SUPERCALIFRAGILISTICEXPIALIDOCIOUS. The name can consists of letters and digits, but must begin with a letter.

In PASCAL, you must put a colon in front of the equal sign....

Correct	Incorrect
FRED:=2;	FRED=2;

If you want to add a line saying PROGRAM WINE, put that line above the VAR line.

You can't set an integer variable equal to a real. For example, if you say —

```
VAR
   ANN: REAL;
    BILL: INTEGER;
BEGIN;
ANN:=3.9;
```

you cannot then say:

```
BILL:=ANN;
```

Instead, you must say —

```
BILL:=ROUND(ANN);
```

or

```
BILL:=TRUNC(ANN);
```

Other versions Some versions of PASCAL do not automatically indent the lines for you.

Old versions of PASCAL examine just the first 8 characters of a variable's name and ignore the rest of the name.

READLN

Instead of saying INPUT, PASCAL says READLN.

```
VAR
   X: REAL;
BEGIN;
WRITELN('WHAT IS YOUR FAVORITE NUMBER?');
READLN(X);
WRITELN('ITS SQUARE ROOT IS',SQRT(X));
END.
```

When you run the program, the computer asks:

```
WHAT IS YOUR FAVORITE NUMBER?
```

Then the READLN(X) statement makes the computer wait for you to input a value of X. The computer expects you to input a real number; if you input an integer instead, the computer will automatically turn it into a real. For example, if you input 9, the computer will automatically turn it into 9.0 and will write:

```
ITS SQUARE ROOT IS 3.0000000000E+00
```

Other versions For old versions of PASCAL, say READ instead of READLN.

IF

The computer can criticize your age:

```
VAR
   AGE: INTEGER;
BEGIN;
WRITELN('HOW OLD ARE YOU?');
READLN(AGE);
IF AGE<18 THEN
   BEGIN;
   WRITELN('YOU ARE STILL A MINOR.');
   WRITELN('AH, THE JOYS OF YOUTH!');
   END;
WRITELN('GLAD TO MEET YOU.');
END.
```

That program makes the computer ask:

```
HOW OLD ARE YOU?
```

If you input a number less than 18, the computer replies:

```
YOU ARE STILL A MINOR.
AH, THE JOYS OF YOUTH!
GLAD TO MEET YOU.
```

If you input a number that's at least 18, the computer says just this:

```
GLAD TO MEET YOU.
```

In that program, the line that says "IF" is a heading (the lines underneath it are indented), so do not put a semicolon at the end of that line!

ELSE

To make your program fancier, insert the shaded lines:

```
VAR
   AGE: INTEGER;
BEGIN;
WRITELN('HOW OLD ARE YOU');
READ(AGE);
IF AGE<18 THEN
   BEGIN;
   WRITELN('YOU ARE STILL A MINOR.');
   WRITELN('AH, THE JOYS OF YOUTH!');
   END
ELSE
   BEGIN;
   WRITELN('I AM GLAD TO HEAR YOU ARE AN ADULT!');
   WRITELN('NOW WE CAN HAVE SOME ADULT FUN!');
   END;
WRITELN('GLAD TO MEET YOU.');
END.
```

If your age is less than 18, the computer will say:

```
YOU ARE STILL A MINOR.
AH, THE JOYS OF YOUTH!
GLAD TO MEET YOU.
```

If your age is not less than 18, the computer will say:

```
GLAD TO HEAR YOU ARE AN ADULT!
NOW WE CAN HAVE SOME ADULT FUN!
GLAD TO MEET YOU.
```

In that program, the line that says "ELSE" is a heading, so don't put a semicolon after it. Don't put a semicolon after the END above it.

Symbols

Like BASIC, PASCAL uses these symbols in the IF line:

<	>	=	<=	>=	<>	AND	OR

In the IF line, the symbol for "equals" is "="; outside the IF line, the symbol for "equals" is ":=".

Instead of saying —

```
IF I=3 OR I=8 OR I=25 OR I=95 THEN
```

you can say:

```
IF I IN [3,8,25,95] THEN
```

That means "If I is in this set of numbers — 3,8,25,95 — then..."

Loops

To create a loop, say FOR or REPEAT or WHILE. Here's how to use those words.

FOR

Like BASIC, PASCAL uses the word FOR. This program makes the computer get drunk:

```
VAR
    I: INTEGER;
BEGIN;
FOR I := 7 TO 10 DO
    BEGIN;
    WRITELN('I DRANK ',I,' BOTTLES OF BEER');
    WRITELN('HOORAY!');
    END;
WRITELN('NOW I AM DEAD DRUNK');
END.
```

Since the FOR line is a heading, do not put a semicolon at the end of it. When you run the program, the computer will write:

```
I DRANK 7 BOTTLES OF BEER
HOORAY!
I DRANK 8 BOTTLES OF BEER
HOORAY!
I DRANK 9 BOTTLES OF BEER
HOORAY!
I DRANK 10 BOTTLES OF BEER
HOORAY!
NOW I AM DEAD DRUNK
```

If you want the computer to count backwards — from 10 down to 7 — change the FOR line to this:

```
FOR I := 10 DOWNTO 7 DO
```

REPEAT

This program plays a guessing game:

```
VAR
    GUESS: INTEGER;
BEGIN;
WRITELN('I AM THINKING OF A NUMBER FROM 1 TO 10');
REPEAT
    WRITELN('YOU HAVE NOT GUESSED MY NUMBER YET');
    WRITELN('WHAT IS MY NUMBER?');
    READLN(GUESS);
UNTIL GUESS=6;
WRITELN('CONGRATULATIONS! YOU GUESSED IT! MY NUMBER IS 6');
END.
```

The computer begins the game by saying:

```
I AM THINKING OF A NUMBER FROM 1 TO 10
```

Then the computer REPEATs the following procedure several times: it says YOU HAVE NOT GUESSED MY NUMBER YET, asks WHAT IS MY NUMBER, waits for the human to input a guess, and checks whether the human guessed 6. It repeats that procedure again and again, UNTIL the human finally guesses 6. Then the computer says:

```
CONGRATULATIONS! YOU GUESSED IT! MY NUMBER IS 6
```

In that program, the computer REPEATs the indented lines, UNTIL GUESS is 6.

If a program contains the word REPEAT, it must also contain the word UNTIL. The lines between REPEAT and UNTIL are done repeatedly. After each time, the computer checks whether to repeat again.

Since the REPEAT line's a heading, it has no semicolon.

Like an IF line, the UNTIL line can contain these symbols:

```
<     >     =     <=     >=     <>     AND     OR     IN
```

Here's another example. Let's make the computer start with the number 3 and keep doubling it, like this:

```
3
6
12
24
etc.
```

Let's make the computer keep doubling but not go over 1000. So altogether, let's make the computer write:

```
3
6
12
24
48
96
192
384
768
THOSE ARE ALL THE NUMBERS BELOW 1000
```

Here's the program:

```
VAR
    I: INTEGER;
BEGIN;
I:=3;                Start I at 3.
REPEAT               Repeat the indented lines until I>=1000.
    WRITELN(I);
    I:=I*2;
UNTIL I>=1000;
WRITELN('THOSE ARE ALL THE NUMBERS BELOW 1000');
END.
```

WHILE

The word WHILE resembles the word REPEAT. For example, the previous program (which doubled 3 repeatedly) can be rewritten to use WHILE:

```
VAR
    I: INTEGER;
BEGIN;
I:=3;                Start I at 3.
WHILE I<1000 DO      If I<1000, do the indented lines, and repeat them.
    BEGIN;           again and again, as long as I remains below 1000.
    WRITELN(I);
    I:=I*2;
    END;
WRITELN('THOSE ARE ALL THE NUMBERS BELOW 1000');
END.
```

The indented lines say to WRITELN(I) and then double I. The computer repeats those indented lines many times. Before each repetition, the computer checks to make sure I is still below 1000. When I passes 1000, the computer stops looping and proceeds to the next line, which writes THOSE ARE ALL THE NUMBERS BELOW 1000.

These two structures resemble each other:

Using REPEAT	Using WHILE
REPEAT	WHILE I<1000 DO
etc.	BEGIN;
UNTIL I>=1000;	etc.
	END;

Each of those structures makes the computer repeat the indented lines and check whether I is still below 1000. If you say REPEAT, the check is done at the loop's bottom, so the computer goes through the loop once before checking. If you say WHILE, the check is done at the loop's top, so the computer checks whether I<1000 before doing the loop the first time.

Logic tricks

Every statement must end with a semicolon. You can put several statements on the same line:

Normal	Alternative
A:=3; B:=7.6; WRITELN(A+B);	A:=3; B:=7.6; WRITELN(A+B);

You can continue a statement on the next line:

Normal	Alternative
A:=5-2+1;	A:= 5-2 +1;

But do not divide a statement in the middle of a word, number, symbol, or string:

Normal	Okay	Wrong, because middle of word	Wrong, because middle of number	Wrong, because middle of symbol
IF AGE>=18 THEN	IF AGE >=18 THEN	IF AG E>=18 THEN	IF AGE>=1 8 THEN	IF AG> =18 THEN

Omitting semicolons

You can omit the semicolon after BEGIN:

Normal	Alternative
BEGIN;	BEGIN

You can omit a semicolon, if the next word is END:

Normal	Alternative
A:=3; END;	A:=3 END;

You can omit a semicolon, if the next word is UNTIL:

Normal	Alternative
I=*2; UNTIL I>=1000;	I=I*2 UNTIL I>=1000;

Omitting BEGIN and END

If a heading heads just one indented line (besides BEGIN and END), you can put that indented line next to the heading (and omit the BEGIN and END).

Long way	Short cut

FOR I := 1 TO 9 DO
   BEGIN;
   WRITELN(I);
   END;
	FOR I := 1 TO 9 DO WRITELN(I);

WHILE A<100 DO
    BEGIN;
    A=A+7;
    END;
	WHILE A<100 DO A:=A+7;

IF AGE>=65 THEN
   BEGIN;
   WRITELN('OLD');
   END;
	IF AGE>=65 THEN WRITELN('OLD');

IF WEIGHT>220 THEN
   BEGIN;
   WRITELN('FAT');
   END
ELSE
   BEGIN;
   WRITELN('OKAY');
   END;
	IF WEIGHT>220 THEN WRITELN('FAT') ELSE WRITELN('OKAY');

REPEAT A:=A+7; UNTIL A>100;	REPEAT A:=A+7 UNTIL A>100;

Comments

To put comments into your program, surround the comment by braces:

BASIC	PASCAL
10 'I HATE COMPUTERS	{I HATE COMPUTERS}

Do not put a semicolon after the comment.

If your screen can display colors, Quick PASCAL makes the comments and braces turn green.

Other versions If your keyboard is old and lacks braces, use parentheses and asterisks instead:
`(*I HATE COMPUTERS*)`

GOTO

You can say GOTO:

```
LABEL 10;
BEGIN;
WRITELN('MY DOG');
GOTO 10;
WRITELN('NEVER');
10: WRITELN('DRINKS WHISKEY');
END.
```

The top line warns the computer that a future line will be labeled "line 10". The rest of the program makes the computer write MY DOG, then skip to line 10, which makes the computer write DRINKS WHISKEY. Altogether, the computer will write:

```
MY DOG
DRINKS WHISKEY
```

Do not put a space between GO and TO.

Here's another example:

```
LABEL 10;
BEGIN;
10: WRITELN('LOVE');
WRITELN('HATE');
GOTO 10;
END.
```

The computer will write LOVE and HATE repeatedly:

```
LOVE
HATE
LOVE
HATE
LOVE
HATE
etc.
```

To abort the program, tap the C key while holding down the CONTROL key. (For Quick PASCAL, then press ENTER.)

If your program contains lines numbered 10, 20, and 100, put this statement at the top of your program:

```
LABEL 10,20,100;
```

Put that statement at the very top of your program: the only statement that should go above it is the one saying PROGRAM. The PROGRAM and LABEL lines go above all other lines — even above VAR and BEGIN.

Each line number must be small: no higher than 9999.

In PASCAL, you'll rarely need to say GOTO. Instead, try using the words IF, ELSE, FOR, REPEAT, and WHILE.

Other versions In UCSD PASCAL, if you want to say GOTO, you must say (*$G+*) at the top of your program:
`(*$G+*)`
`PROGRAM SKIPPER;`
`LABEL 10;`
etc.

Procedures

This program teases you, with the help of some insults:

```
PROCEDURE INSULT;
BEGIN;
WRITELN('YOU ARE STUPID');
WRITELN('YOU ARE UGLY');
END;

{MAIN ROUTINE}
BEGIN;
WRITELN('WE ALL KNOW...');
INSULT;
WRITELN('...AND YET WE LOVE YOU');
END.
```

That program begins by defining INSULT to be this procedure:

```
WRITELN('YOU ARE STUPID');
WRITELN('YOU ARE UGLY');
```

The main routine makes the computer write 'WE ALL KNOW...', then do the INSULT procedure, then write '...AND YET WE LOVE YOU'; altogether, the computer will write:

```
WE ALL KNOW...
YOU ARE STUPID
YOU ARE UGLY
...AND YET WE LOVE YOU
```

The PROCEDURE, called INSULT, is a subroutine. In PASCAL, subroutines come before the main routine. (In BASIC, subroutines come after the main routine instead.)

Put a program's VAR above any procedures:

```
VAR                     Program uses a variable,
   I: INTEGER;          called I, which is an integer.
                        The subroutine is
PROCEDURE DOUBLE;       named DOUBLE.
BEGIN;
I:=2*I;                 It doubles the value of I
WRITELN(I);             and writes I's new value.
END;

{MAIN ROUTINE}          Here's the main routine....
BEGIN;
I:=7;                   I starts at 7.
DOUBLE;      Do DOUBLE, which writes 14.
DOUBLE;      Do DOUBLE again, which writes 28.
WRITELN(I+1);           Write 29.
END.
```

Advanced variables

You've seen that a variable can stand for a number. This section explains how to make a variable stand for a character, array, or string.

CHAR

A variable can stand for a character:

```
VAR
   ANN,JOAN: CHAR;      Each is a character.
BEGIN;
ANN:='U';              ANN is the character 'U'.
JOAN:='P';             JOAN is the character 'P'.
WRITELN(ANN,JOAN);     Write 'U' and 'P'.
END.
```

The computer will write U and P like this:

```
UP
```

You can put a character variable after the word FOR:

```
VAR
   I: CHAR;
BEGIN;
FOR I := 'A' TO 'E' DO WRITELN(I);
END.
```

The computer will write:

```
A
B
C
D
E
```

ARRAY

Let's make X be this list of real numbers: 4.2, 71.6, 8.3, 92.6, 403.7. Here's how:

```
VAR
   X: ARRAY [1..5] OF REAL;
BEGIN;
X[1]:=4.2;
X[2]:=71.6;
X[3]:=8.3;
X[4]:=92.6;
X[5]:=403.7;
WRITELN(X[1]+X[2]+X[3]+X[4]+X[5]);
END.
```

The computer will write the sum, 581.8.

Subscripts can be negative:

```
VAR
   Y: ARRAY [-2..3] OF REAL;
BEGIN;
Y[-2]:=400.1;
Y[-1]:=274.1;
Y[0]:=9.2;
Y[1]:=8.04;
Y[2]:=0.6;
Y[3]:=-5.0;
WRITELN(Y[-2]+Y[-
1]+Y[0]+Y[1]+Y[2]+Y[3]);
END.
```

The computer will write the sum, 687.04.

Here's how to make Z be a table having 6 rows and 4 columns of reals:

```
VAR
   Z: ARRAY [1..6, 1..4] OF REAL;
```

The number in the 3rd row and 2nd column is called $Z[3,2]$. The entire first row of Z is called $Z[1]$; the second row is called $Z[2]$; etc. For example, if you say —

```
Z[5]:=Z[3];
```

the computer will look at the real numbers in the 3rd row of Z, and copy them into the 5th row. Suppose W is another array that has 6 rows and 4 columns; if you say —

```
W:=Z;
```

the computer will look at each real number in Z and copy it into W.

You can have many kinds of arrays: you can have an array of REAL, an array of INTEGER, and even an array of CHAR.

STRING

A variable can stand for a string:

```
VAR
   X: STRING;
BEGIN;
X:='I LOVE MY MOTH';
WRITELN(X,'ER');
END.
```

The computer will write 'I LOVE MY MOTH' and then 'ER', like this:

```
I LOVE MY MOTHER
```

You can make the computer read a string:

```
VAR
   X: STRING;
BEGIN;
WRITELN('WHAT IS YOUR NAME?');
READLN(X);
WRITELN('HELLO ',X,' THE BEAUTIFUL');
END.
```

When you run that program, the computer asks:

```
WHAT IS YOUR NAME?
```

Then the READLN(X) statement makes the computer wait for you to input a string. If you input the name MARILYN MONROE, the computer will write:

```
HELLO MARILYN MONROE THE BEAUTIFUL
```

Other versions Instead of letting you say STRING, some versions of PASCAL require you to say STRING[80].

The oldest versions of PASCAL require you to say PACKED ARRAY [1..80] OF CHAR instead. Some of those old versions can't read or write the whole array string at once: instead you must create FOR loops that read and write one character at a time.

C & C++

Fun

C is a computer language invented by **Dennis Ritchie** in 1972, while he was working for AT&T at Bell Labs. He called it "C" because it came after "B", which was an earlier language developed by a colleague.

Other chapters of The Secret Guide to Computers explain how to program in BASIC and PASCAL. C resembles those languages but has two advantages: C runs faster and consumes less RAM.

C has become the most popular language for creating advanced programs. The world's biggest software companies have switched to C from assembly language:

If you become an expert C programmer, you can help run those rich software companies and get rich yourself!

Before studying C, study an easier language, such as BASIC or PASCAL.

C is excitingly dangerous:

> Unlike BASIC and PASCAL, C lets you easily create a pointer, which is a note about which part of RAM to use. If you create the pointer incorrectly, C will use the wrong part of RAM — and erase whatever info was there before. For example, C might erase the part of RAM used by your operating system (DOS or Windows), so your operating system becomes confused and accidentally erases your disks!
>
> A faulty pointer (which points to the wrong part of RAM) is called a **runaway pointer**, and it's a C programmer's greatest fear. Even if your innocent-looking program doesn't seem to mention pointers, a small error in your program might make C create a pointer that wrecks your computer. That's why many C programmers look thin and haggard and bite their nails. To keep your nails looking pretty, make backup copies of your hard disk before trying to program in C.
>
> C is like a sports car with no brakes: it's fast, fun, slim, sleek, and dangerous. If you program in C, your friends will admire you and even whistle at you as you zoom along the freeway of computer heaven; but if you're not careful, your programs and disk will crash, and so will your career!

C++

An improved C, called **C++**, was invented in 1985 at Bell Labs by **Bjarne Stroustrup**.

> He was born in Denmark, where he studied at Aarhus University. Then he moved to England, where he got a Ph.D. from Cambridge University. Then he moved to New Jersey to work at Bell Labs, where he invented C++.
>
> To pronounce his name, say "Bee-ARE-nuh STRAH-stroop", but say the "Bee" and "STRAH-stroop" fast, so it sounds closer to "BYAR-nuh STROV-strup".

C++ uses the same fundamental commands as C but adds extra commands. Some of those extra commands are for advanced programming; others make regular programming more pleasant. C++ lets you use an advanced technique called **object-oriented programming (OOP)**, in which you define "objects" and give those objects "properties".

For input and output, C++ offers different commands than C. C++'s input/output commands are more pleasant.

Now most programmers use C++ instead of C.

The most popular version of C++ is **Visual C++**, which is by Microsoft and handles Windows. Microsoft is trying to invent a further improvement, called **C#** (pronounced "See sharp"), but C# is not ready yet.

This chapter explains how to use Visual C++. (At the end of this chapter, I'll explain how C differs from C++.)

Visual C++ comes on a CD-ROM disk. The disk includes C also, so you can write traditional C programs. You can buy the disk by itself or as part of a suite, called **Visual Studio**. Version 6 of Visual Studio includes Visual C++, Visual BASIC, Visual J++ (which is a version of JAVA), Visual FoxPro (which is a variant of DBASE), and other programming tools. Microsoft is trying to develop a Visual Studio Version 7, which will also include C# but omit Visual J++.

Copy C++ to the hard disk

Here's how to copy Visual Studio 6 (enterprise edition) to the hard disk. (Other versions of Visual Studio and Visual C++ are similar.)

> Make sure your computer contains Windows 98 (not 95) and Internet Explorer 5 (not 4).
>
> Turn on the computer without any floppy or CD-ROM disks in the drives, so the computer runs Windows 98 and the computer's bottom left corner says Start. Put Visual Studio 6.0's Disc 1 into the CD-ROM drive. The computer will say "Visual Studio 6.0". Press ENTER. Click "I accept the agreement". Press ENTER.
>
> Type the 10-digit CD key number (printed on the orange sticker at the back of the CD-ROM disk's square case). Press TAB. Type your name. Press TAB. Type the name of your company (if any). Press ENTER three times.
>
> The computer will reboot itself. Click "Next". Press ENTER. The computer will reboot itself again. Click "Next". Press ENTER twice.
>
> You'll see a product ID. Copy it onto the registration form that you'll mail to Microsoft. Press ENTER three times.
>
> Finally, the computer will copy Visual Studio to the hard disk. Click "OK". Press ENTER. The computer will reboot itself again.
>
> The computer will say "Install MSDN". Put the MSDN Library's Disc 1 into the CD-ROM drive. Click "Next". Press ENTER.
>
> You'll see an MSDN product ID. Copy it onto a sheet of paper. Press ENTER three times The computer will copy the MSDN Library to the hard disk. Press ENTER three times.
>
> Remove the check mark from the "Register Now" box (by clicking it). Press ENTER.

Start C++

To start using Visual C++ (version 6.0), do this:

> Remove any CD-ROM disk. Click "Start" then "Programs" then "Microsoft Visual Studio 6.0" then "Microsoft Visual C++ 6.0".
>
> If the computer says "Did you know", press ENTER.

Start a new program

Click "File" then "New" then "Files" then "C++ Source File".

Click in the File Name box. Invent a name for your program (such as "joe"); type the name and press ENTER. (If the computer asks "Do you want to overwrite?", the name you invented was already used by a colleague, so do this: click "No", invent a different name instead, type it, and press ENTER.)

To emphasize that the program is written in C++, the computer automatically puts ".cpp" at the end of your program's name. (The "cpp" stands for "C plus plus".)

> For example, if you said the program is "joe", the computer automatically changes the name to "joe.cpp". The computer will automatically put the program in your hard drive's root directory, so the program will be called "C:\joe.cpp".

Type your program

For your first experiment, type this C++ program, which teaches the computer to say "I love you":

```
#include <iostream.h>
void main()
{
    cout <<"I love you";
}
```

The include line Input and output is called **I/O**. The input and output comes as a stream of characters, called the **I/O stream**. The top line — #include <iostream.h> — tells the computer to **include**, as part of your program, an **I/O stream header**, containing definitions of C++ commands that manipulate the I/O stream.

Type that line carefully:

> Make sure you type the symbols #, <, and > correctly.
>
> Do *not* capitalize the word "include". If you type "INCLUDE" instead of "include", the computer will gripe. In C++, type all commands by using lower-case letters, not capitals.

If you type that line correctly, the computer will make the "#include" be blue. At the end of the line, press ENTER.

The main line The next line — void main() — marks the beginning of the program's main part. Make sure you type the parentheses (), by pressing SHIFT with 9 or 0.

If you type that line correctly, the computer will make the "void" be blue.

The braces The next line is a brace, which is the symbol "{".

> Here's how to type it: while holding down the SHIFT key, tap the key that's to the right of the P key. Make sure you type the symbol "{"; do not type "[" or "(".

The program's bottom line is another brace, which means "here's the end"; so the program's lines are enclosed in braces {}. Like PASCAL's BEGIN and END, those braces mark the beginning and end of the program's main part.

Typical C++ That's all typical! The typical C++ program begins by saying —

```
#include <iostream.h>
void main()
{
```

and ends by saying:

```
}
```

The cout line Any lines between the braces are the program's heart. In the example, the program's heart is this line:

```
    cout <<"I love you";
```

That line says cout (which is pronounced "C out" and means "C++ output"). It makes the computer output "I love you" onto the screen.

The words in quotation marks, "I love you", are called the **string**.

Since the symbol "<<" can be pronounced "from", here's how to pronounce that line: "C out from quote I love you quote semicolon".

The computer understands "cout" because cout's definition is part of <iostream.h>, which the program's top line says to include. (If you accidentally omit the program's top line, the computer will complain that it doesn't know the meaning of "cout".)

The whole cout line ends with a semicolon because **C++ requires you to put a semicolon at the end of each simple line**.

C++ handles two kinds of lines:

> A **simple line** ends in a semicolon.
>
> A line is called a **structure line** if it begins with "#" or "{" or "}" or is above "{". A structure line does *not* end in a semicolon.

Indenting The computer is smart: it knows that any lines between "{" and "}" should be indented. So when you type that program, the computer automatically indents the "cout" line.

The computer automatically unindents the "}". Here's how: the "}" automatically hops to the left after you type it.

If you ever want the computer to indent differently, do this before typing a line's first word or symbol:

> Press the TAB key to indent.
> Press the BACKSPACE key to unindent.

Build the program

After you've typed the program, the next step is to **build** the program, by pressing the F7 key. To do that, click the **Build button**, which is near the screen's top right corner and shows a pair of arrows pointing down on a pile of papers (or press the F7 key or choose Build from the Build menu).

(If the computer then asks "Would you like to create a default project workspace?", press ENTER twice.)

Then computer will accomplish two activities....

First the computer will look at the program you've typed and automatically save the newest version of it. For example, if your program was named "C:\joe.cpp", the computer will

automatically update that file so it includes what you recently typed.

Next, the computer will try to create an .exe file and put it in the Debug folder. For example, if your program was named "C:\joe.cpp", the computer will try to create a file called "C:\Debug\joe.exe".

While creating the .exe file, the computer will analyze your program to see whether your programming makes sense. If you did everything right, the screen's bottom window will say:

```
joe.exe - 0 error(s), 0 warning(s)
```

If the bottom window says you have *more* than 0 errors or *more* than 0 warnings, here's how to see messages about *why* you had errors: click in that window, then scroll up (by pressing the up-arrow key several times or using the window's scroll arrow or rotating the mouse's wheel). Fix your errors, then try again to say "build".

Execute the program

After the computer has said you have 0 errors and 0 warnings, **execute** the program. To do that, you can use two methods....

The easy method Click the **Execute button**, which is a red exclamation point near the screen's top right corner (or press Ctrl with F5 or choose Execute from the Build menu). The computer will execute (run) the program and say "I love you". Then it will say "Press any key to continue" on the same line, so your screen looks like this:

```
I love youPress any key to continue
```

Press ENTER.

The good-looking method Get out of Visual C++ (by clicking the X at the screen's top right corner). Get to a DOS prompt (by clicking "Start" then "Programs" then "MS-DOS Prompt"), so your screen looks like this:

```
C:\WINDOWS>
```

Type "\Debug\joe", so your screen looks like this:

```
C:\WINDOWS>\Debug\joe
```

That makes the computer run C:\Debug\joe.exe, so the computer will say "I love you". Then it will give you another DOS prompt, so your screen looks like this:

```
I love you
C:\WINDOWS>
```

Type the word "exit" (and press ENTER at the end of that word).

Switch programs

While the program you wrote is on the screen, you can edit it. After editing it, rebuild it (by clicking the Build button again) and then re-execute it (by clicking the Execute button again).

When you finish playing with that program, here's how to create a totally different program instead:

> If the program is still on the screen, click "File" then "Close Workspace" then press ENTER.
>
> Start the process over again (by doing the "Start a new program" routine that I explained on page 456).

Here's how to view an old program you created earlier:

> Go into Visual C++. If a different program is on the screen, get it off the screen (by clicking "File" then "Close Workspace" then pressing ENTER). Click the Open button (which is near the screen's top left corner and shows an opening manila folder). Make sure the "Look in" box says "C:". (If it says otherwise, click that box's down-arrow, then click "C:".) You'll see a list of C++ programs (and other folders); double-click the C++ program you want to use.

Erase files

If you type, build, and execute a program named "joe", the computer generates 11 files.

One of them is the program you typed (C:\joe.cpp). One of them is the final result of the build (C:\Debug\joe.exe).

The remaining 9 files are useful just temporarily, to help the computer keep track of what's being built. You can erase them:

```
C:\joe.dsp
C:\joe.ncb
C:\joe.plg
C:\Debug\joe.pch
C:\Debug\joe.obj
C:\Debug\joe.ilk
C:\Debug\joe.pdb
C:\joe.opt
C:\joe.dsw
```

\n

Let's write a program that makes the computer say:

```
I love you
Let's get married
```

This program almost accomplishes that goal:

```
#include <iostream.h>
void main()
{
    cout <<"I love you";
    cout <<"Let's get married";
}
```

If you run that program by clicking the Execute button (which looks like a red exclamation point), the computer will say "I love you" and "Let's get married" and "Press any key to continue", but unfortunately it will print all those messages on a single line, so you'll see this:

```
I love youLet's get marriedPress any key to continue
```

To make the computer print those three sentences on three separate lines, say "\n" at the end of each string, like this:

```
#include <iostream.h>
void main()
{
    cout <<"I love you\n";
    cout <<"Let's get married\n";
}
```

The **\n means "new line": it's the symbol for the ENTER key.** Telling the computer to print "I love you\n" makes the computer print "I love you" and then press the ENTER key, so the next sentence will be printed on the next line. Altogether, the computer will print this:

```
I love you
Let's get married
Press any key to continue
```

When you type the symbol \n, make sure you type a backslash: \. Do not type a division sign: /.

To make your output be pretty, **put \n at the end of each typical string**.

Instead of writing —

```
cout <<"I love you\n";
cout <<"Let's get married\n";
```

you can write:

```
cout <<"I love you\nLet's get married\n";
```

That single long line still makes the computer say:

```
I love you
Let's get married
Press any key to continue
```

endl

To make the computer end a line and start a new line, you can say \n. Another way to make the computer **end** a line is to say <<endl, like this:

```
cout <<"I love you" <<endl <<"Let's get married" <<endl;
```

That single long line makes the computer do this: print "I love you", then end the line, then print "Let's get married", then end the line. Altogether, the computer will print this:

```
I love you
Let's get married
Press any key to continue
```

Math

The computer can do math. For example, this program makes the computer do 4+2:

```
#include <iostream.h>
void main()
{
    cout <<4+2 <<endl;
}
```

It makes the computer print this answer on your screen:

```
6
Press any key to continue
```

This program makes the computer print the answer to 21+4 and also the answer to 68+1:

```
#include <iostream.h>
void main()
{
    cout <<21+4 <<endl <<68+1 <<endl;
}
```

That cout line makes the computer print the answer to 21+4 (which is 25), then press ENTER, then print the answer to 68+1 (which is 69), then press ENTER, so you see this:

```
25
69
Press any key to continue
```

To print both of those answers on a single line instead of on separate lines, put a blank space between the answers by saying " " instead of endl, so the cout line looks like this:

```
cout <<21+4 <<" " <<68+1 <<endl;
```

That tells the computer to print the answer to 21+4 (which is 25), then a blank space, then the answer to 68+1, then press ENTER, so you see:

```
25 69
Press any key to continue
```

The computer leaves a space between the answers because of the <<" ". If you omit the <<" ", the computer will print:

```
2569
```

If you have 750 apples and buy 12 more, how many apples will you have altogether? This program prints the answer:

```
#include <iostream.h>
void main()
{
    cout <<"You will have " <<750+12 <<" apples\n"
}
```

That cout line makes the computer print "You will have ", then print the answer to 750+12 (which is 762), then print "apples", then press ENTER (because of the \n), so you see this:

```
You will have 762 apples
Press any key to continue
```

Like BASIC and PASCAL, C++ lets you use the symbols +, - , *, /, parentheses, decimal points, and e notation. But if you're not careful, the computer will print wrong answers. Here's why....

Integers versus double precision

C++ handles two types of numbers well.

One type of number is called an **integer** (or **int**). An int contains no decimal point and no e. For example, -27 and 30000 are ints.

The other type of number that C++ handles well is called a **double-precision number** (or a **double**). **A double contains a decimal point or an e.** For example, -27.0 and 3e4 are doubles. You can abbreviate: instead of writing "-27.0", you can write "-27.", and instead of writing "0.37" you can write ".37".

Largest and tiniest numbers

The largest permissible int is about 2 billion. More precisely:

```
the largest int is 2147483647

the lowest int you can write easily is -2147483647
the only int lower than that is a strange int you must write as -2147483647-1
```

(Warning: the largest int is 2147483647 just in Microsoft's *modern* versions of C & C++, such as Microsoft Visual C++ 6.0. In older versions of C & C++ that were invented before Windows 95, the largest int is just 32767, and the lowest int is -32767-1.)

If you try to feed the computer an int that's too large or too low, the computer won't complain. Instead, the computer will typically print a wrong answer!

The largest permissible double is about 1.7e308. More precisely, it's 1.7976931348623158e308. If you feed the computer a math problem whose answer is bigger than that, the computer will give up and typically say the answer is —

```
1.#INF
```

which means infinity.

The tiniest double that the computer handles well is about 2.2e-308. More precisely, it's 2.2250738585072014e-308. If you feed the computer a math problem whose answer is tinier than that, the computer will either handle the rightmost digits inaccurately or give up, saying the answer is 0.0.

Tricky arithmetic

If you combine ints, the answer is an int. For example, 2+3 is this int: 5.

11/4 is this int: 2. (11/4 is *not* 2.75.)

If you combine doubles, the answer is a double. If you combine an int with a double, the answer is a double.

How much is 2000 times 2000000? Theoretically, the answer should be this int: 4000000000. But since 4000000000 is too large to be an int, the computer will print a wrong answer. To make the computer multiply 2000 by 2000000 correctly, ask for 2000.0*2000000.0, like this:

```
#include <iostream.h>
void main()
{
    cout <<2000.0*2000000.0 <<endl;
}
```

That program makes the computer get the correct answer, 4000000000.0, which the computer will write in e notation, so you see this answer:

```
4e+009
```

Cout precision

The computer can handle a double-precision number quite accurately, even if the number contains many digits. Here's the limit: the computer can handle up to 15 significant digits.

When printing a double-precision number, cout assumes you don't want to bother seeing all 15 significant digits, so cout typically prints just the number's first 6 significant digits. If you want to see all 15 significant digits, insert this line above the cout lines:

```
    cout.precision(15);
```

That line affects all cout lines below it.

When printing a number such as 3.00000000000000, cout assumes you don't want to see the .00000000000000 (because zeros are boring), so cout typically prints just:

```
3
```

If you want to see the decimal point and zeros also, insert this line above the cout lines:

```
    cout.setf(ios::showpoint);
```

That line affects all count lines below it.

Advanced math

The computer can do advanced math. For example, it can compute square roots. This program makes the computer print the square root of 9:

```
#include <iostream.h>
#include <math.h>
void main()
{
    cout <<sqrt(9.0) <<endl;
}
```

The computer will print 3.

Say sqrt(9.0) rather than sqrt(9), because the number you find the square root of should be double-precision, not an integer. If you make the mistake of saying sqrt(9), Visual C++ 6.0 will print the correct answer but slowly; some older versions of C & C++ will print a wrong answer.

The program's top line makes the computer include an I/O stream header (containing the definition of cout and other I/O words). The program's second line tells the computer to include a math header (containing the definition of sqrt and other advanced-math functions).

Besides sqrt, you can use other advanced math functions. All advanced-math functions require that you use double-precision numbers and say #include <math.h>. Here's a list of those advanced-math functions:

To handle exponents, you can use sqrt (square root), exp (exponential power of e), log (logarithm base e), and log10 (logarithm base 10). You can also use pow: for example, pow(3.0,2.0) is 3.0 raised to the 2.0 power.

For trigonometry, you can use sin (sine), cos (cosine), tan (tangent), asin (arcsin), acos (arccosine), atan (arctangent), sinh (sine hyperbolic), cosh (cosine hyperbolic), and tanh (tangent hyperbolic). You can also use atan2: for example, atan2(y,x) is the arctangent of y divided by x.

For absolute value, use fabs (floating absolute). For example, fabs(-2.3) is 2.3.

To round, use floor (which rounds down) or ceil (which stands for "ceiling" and rounds *up*). For example, floor(26.319) is 26.0, and ceil(26.319) is 27.0.

Numeric variables

Like BASIC, C++ lets you use variables. For example, you can say:

```
n=3;
```

A variable's name can be short (such as n) or long (such as town_population_in_1999). It can be very long: up to 247 characters long. The name can contain letters, digits, and underscores, but not blank spaces. The name must begin with a letter or underscore, not a digit.

Before using a variable, say what type of number the variable stands for. For example, if n and town_population_in_1999 will stand for numbers that are ints and mortgage_rate will stand for a double, begin your program by saying:

```
#include <iostream.h>
void main()
{
    int n, town_population_in_1999;
    double mortgage_rate;
```

If n is an integer that starts at 3, you can say —

```
int n;
n=3;
```

but you can combine those two lines into this single line:

```
int n=3;
```

Here's how to say "n is an integer that starts at 3, and population_in_1999 is an integer that starts at 27000":

```
int n=3, population_in_1999=27000;
```

Increase

The symbol ++ means "increase". For example, ++n means "increase n".

This program increases n:

```
#include <iostream.h>
void main()
{
    int n=3;
    ++n;
    cout <<n <<endl;
}
```

The n starts at 3 and increases to 4, so the computer prints 4.

Saying ++n gives the same answer as n=n+1, but the computer handles ++n faster.

The symbol ++ increases the number by 1, even if the number is a decimal. For example, if x is 17.4 and you say ++x, the x will become 18.4.

Decrease

The opposite of ++ is --. The symbol -- means "decrease". For example, --n means "decrease n". Saying --n gives the same answer as n=n-1 but faster.

Strange short cuts

If you use the following short cuts, your programs will be briefer and run faster.

Instead of saying n=n+2, say n+=2, which means "n's increase is 2". Similarly, instead of saying n=n*3, say n*=3, which means "n's multiplier is 3".

Instead of saying ++n and then giving another command, say ++n in the middle of the other command. For example, instead of saying —

```
++n;
j=7*n;
```

say:

```
j=7*++n;
```

That's pronounced: "j is 7 times an increased n". So if n was 2, saying j=7*++n makes n become 3 and j become 21.

Notice that when you say j=7*++n, the computer increases n *before* computing j. If you say j=7*n++ instead, the computer increases n *after* computing j; so j=7*n++ has the same effect as saying:

```
j=7*n;
++n;
```

How to input

This program predicts how old you'll be ten years from now:

Program	Meaning
`#include <iostream.h>`	
`void main()`	
`{`	
`    int age;`	The age is an integer.
`    cout <<"How old are you? ";`	Ask "How old are you?".
`    cin >>age;`	Wait for the human to input an age.
`    cout <<"Ten years from now, you'll be " <<age+10 <<" years old.\n";`	Printout.
`}`	

In that program, "cin" is pronounced "C in" and means "C++ input". It's the opposite of "cout". After the "cin", make sure you type ">>" (which is pronounced "to" and is the opposite of "<<"). Here's how to pronounce that cin line: "C in to age semicolon". Here's a sample run:

```
How old are you? 27
Ten years from now, you'll be 37 years old.
```

(Below that, the computer will print its usual message of "Press any key to continue".)

The next program converts feet to inches. It even handles decimals: it can convert 1.5 feet to 18.0 inches.

Program	Meaning
`#include <iostream.h>`	
`void main()`	
`{`	
`    double feet;`	The number of feet is double-precision.
`    cout <<"How many feet? ";`	Ask "How many feet?".
`    cin >>feet;`	Wait for the human to input how many feet.
`    cout <<"That makes " <<feet*12 <<" inches.\n";`	Print the result.
`}`	

Arrays

Like BASIC and PASCAL, C++ lets you create arrays. For example, if you want x to be a list of 3 double-precision numbers, begin your program by saying:

```
double x[3];
```

That says x will be a list of 3 double-precision numbers, called x[0], x[1], and x[2]. Notice that C++ starts counting at 0. (PASCAL starts counting at 1 instead; PASCAL would call those numbers x[1], x[2], and x[3].)

Here's a complete C++ program using that array:

```
#include <iostream.h>
void main()
{
    double x[3];
    x[0]=10.6;
    x[1]=3.2;
    x[2]=1.1;
    cout <<x[0]+x[1]+x[2] <<endl;
}
```

The computer will print the sum, 14.9.

Notice that if you say double x[3], you can refer to x[0], x[1], and x[2], but not x[3]. If you accidentally refer to x[3], you'll be creating a runaway pointer.

If you want x to be a table having 2 rows and 3 columns of double-precision numbers, begin your program by saying:

```
#include <iostream.h>
void main()
{
    double x[2][3];
```

Notice that C++ says x[2][3]. (PASCAL says x[2,3] instead.) In C++, if you accidentally say x[2,3] instead of x[2][3], you'll have a runaway pointer.

Since C++ always starts counting at 0 (not 1), the number in the table's top left corner is called x[0][0].

Logic

Like most computer languages, C++ lets you say "if", "while", "for", and "goto" and create comments and subroutines. Here's how….

If

If a person's age is less than 18, let's make the computer say "You are still a minor." Here's the fundamental line:

```
if (age<18) cout <<"You are still a minor.\n";
```

Notice you must put parentheses after the word "if".

If a person's age is less than 18, let's make the computer say "You are still a minor." and also say "Ah, the joys of youth!" and "I wish I could be as young as you!" Here's how to say all that:

```
if (age<18)
{
    cout <<"You are still a minor.\n";
    cout <<"Ah, the joys of youth!\n";
    cout <<"I wish I could be as young as you!\n";
}
```

Since that "if" line is above the "{", the "if" line is a structure line, similar to a void main() line, and does *not* end in a semicolon.

Here's how to put that structure into a complete program:

```
#include <iostream.h>
void main()
{
    int age;
    cout <<"How old are you? ";
    cin >>age;
    if (age<18)
    {
        cout <<"You are still a minor.\n";
        cout <<"Ah, the joys of youth!\n";
        cout <<"I wish I could be as young as you!\n";
    }
    else
    {
        cout <<"You are an adult.\n";
        cout <<"Now we can have some adult fun!\n";
    }
    cout <<"Glad to have met you.\n";
}
```

If the person's age is less than 18, the computer will print "You are still a minor." and "Ah, the joys of youth!" and "I wish I could be as young as you!" If the person's age is not less than 18, the computer will print "You are an adult." and "Now we can have some adult fun!" Regardless of the person's age, the computer will end the conversation by saying "Glad to have met you."

The "if" statement uses this notation:

Notation	Meaning
if (age<18)	if age is less than 18
if (age<=18)	if age is less than or equal to 18
if (age==18)	if age is equal to 18
if (age!=18)	if age is not equal to 18
if (age<18 && weight>200)	if age<18 and weight>200
if (age<18 || weight>200)	if age<18 or weight>200

Look at that table carefully! Notice that in the "if" statement, you should use double symbols: you should say "==" instead of "=", say "&&" instead of "&", and say "||" instead of "|". If you accidentally say "=" instead of "==", the computer will print wrong answers. If you accidentally say "&" instead of "&&" or say "|" instead of "||", the computer will print right answers but too slowly — and give you a warning.

While

Let's make the computer print the word "love" repeatedly, like this:

```
love love love love love love love love love love love etc.
love love love love love love love love love love love etc.
love love love love love love love love love love love etc.
etc.
```

This program does it:

```
#include <iostream.h>
void main()
{
    while (1) cout <<"love ";
}
```

In that program, the "while (1)" means: do repeatedly. The computer will do cout <<"love " repeatedly, looping forever — or until you **abort** the program by using one of these methods:

```
Method 1: while holding down the Ctrl key, tap the C key.
Method 2: while holding down the Ctrl key, tap the PAUSE key.
Method 3: click the window's X box then click "Yes".
```

Let's make the computer start at 20 and keep counting, so the computer will print:

```
20
21
22
23
24
25
26
27
28
29
30
31
32
etc.
```

This program does it:

Program	Meaning
`#include <iostream.h>`	
`void main()`	
`{`	
`    int i=20;`	Start the integer i at 20.
`    while (1)`	Repeat these lines forever:
`    {`	
`        cout <<i <<endl;`	print i then press ENTER
`        ++i;`	increase i
`    }`	
`}`	

It prints faster than you can read.

To pause the printing, press the PAUSE key.
To resume the printing, press the ENTER key.
To abort the program, press ENTER, then press Ctrl with PAUSE.

In that program, if you say "while (i<30)" instead of "while (1)", the computer will do the loop only while i remains less than 30; the computer will print just:

```
20
21
22
23
24
25
26
27
28
29
```

Instead of saying "while (i<30)", you can say "while (i<=29)".

For

Here's a more natural way to get that output of numbers from 20 to 29:

```
#include <iostream.h>
void main()
{
    for (int i=20; i<=29; ++i) cout <<i <<endln;
}
```

In that program, the "for (int i=20; i<=29; ++i)" means "Do repeatedly. Start the integer i at 20, and keep repeating as long as i<=29. At the end of each repetition, do ++i."

In that "for" statement, if you change the ++i to i+=3, the computer will increase i by 3 instead of by 1, so the computer will print:

```
20
23
26
29
```

The "for" statement is quite flexible. You can even say "for (int i=20; i<100; i*=2)", which makes i start at 20 and keep doubling, so the computer prints:

```
20
40
80
```

Like "if" and "while", the "for" statement can sit atop a group of indented lines that are in braces.

Goto

You can say "goto". For example, if you say "goto yummy", the computer will go to the line whose name is yummy:

```
#include <iostream.h>
void main()
{
    cout <<"my dog ";
    goto yummy;
    cout <<"never ";
    yummy: cout <<"drinks whiskey\n";
}
```

The computer will print:

```
my dog drinks whiskey
```

Comments

To put a comment in your program, begin the comment with the symbol //. The computer ignores everything that's to the right of //. Here's an example:

```
// This program is fishy
// It was written by a sick sailor swimming in the sun
#include <iostream.h>
void main()
{
    cout <<"Our funny God\n";    // notice the religious motif
    cout <<"invented cod\n";     // said by a nasty flounder
}
```

The computer ignores all the comments, which are to the right of //.

While you type the program, the computer makes each // and each comment turn green. Then the computer ignores everything that's turned green, so the computer prints just:

```
Our funny God
invented cod
```

Subroutines

Like QBASIC and PASCAL, C++ lets you invent subroutines and give them names. For example, here's how to invent a subroutine called "insult" and use it in the main routine:

Program	Meaning
`#include <iostream.h>`	the program will use I/O
`void insult();`	the program will use insult
`void main()`	**Here's the main routine:**
`{`	
`    cout <<"We all know...\n";`	print "We all know..."
`    insult();`	do the insult
`    cout <<"...and yet we love you.\n";`	print the ending
`}`	
`void insult()`	**Here's how to insult:**
`{`	
`    cout <<"You are stupid!\n";`	print "You are stupid!"
`    cout <<"You are ugly!\n";`	print "You are ugly!"
`}`	

The computer will print:

```
We all know...
You are stupid!
You are ugly!
...and yet we love you.
```

In that program, the top two lines warn the computer that the program will use I/O and a subroutine called "insult". The next few lines, beginning with void main(), define the main routine. The bottom few lines, beginning with void insult(), define the subroutine called "insult".

Whenever you write a subroutine's name, you must put parentheses afterwards, like this: insult(). Those parentheses tell the computer: insult's a subroutine, not a variable.

Here's another example:

Program	Meaning
`#include <iostream.h>`	the program will use I/O
`void laugh();`	the program will use laugh
`void main()`	**Here's the main routine:**
`{`	
`    laugh();`	the main routine says to laugh
`}`	
`void laugh()`	**Here's how to laugh:**
`{`	
`    for (int i=1; i<=100; ++i) cout <<"ha ";`	print "ha " a hundred times
`    cout <<endl;`	then press ENTER
`}`	

The main routine says to laugh. The subroutine defines "laugh" to mean: print "ha " a hundred times and then press ENTER.

Let's create a more flexible subroutine, so that whenever the main routine says laugh(2), the computer will print "ha ha "and ENTER; whenever the main routine says laugh(5), the computer will print "ha ha ha ha ha " and ENTER; and so on. Here's how:

Program	Meaning
`#include <iostream.h>`	the program will use I/O
`void laugh(int n);`	the program will use laugh(n)
`void main()`	**Here's the main routine:**
`{`	
`    cout <<"Here is a short laugh: ";`	
`    laugh(2);`	do laugh(2), so print "ha ha "
`    cout <<"Here is a longer laugh: ";`	
`    laugh(5);`	do laugh(5), so print "ha ha ha ha ha "
`}`	
`void laugh(int n)`	**Here's how to laugh(n):**
`{`	
`    for (int i=1; i<=n; ++i) cout <<"ha ";`	print "ha ", n times
`    cout <<endl;`	then press ENTER
`}`	

The computer will print:

```
Here is a short laugh: ha ha
Here is a longer laugh: ha ha ha ha ha
```

Average Let's define the "average" of a pair of integers, so that "average(3, 7)" means the average of 3 and 7 (which is 5), and so a main routine saying "i=average(3, 7)" makes i be 5.

This subroutine defines the "average" of all pairs of integers:

```
int average(int a, int b)
{
    return (a+b)/2;
}
```

The top line says, "Here's how to find the average of any two integers, a and b, and make the average be an integer." The next line says, "Return to the main routine, with this answer: (a+b)/2."

Here's a complete program:

Program	Meaning
`#include <iostream.h>`	the program will use I/O
`int average(int a, int b);`	the program will use average(a, b)
`void main()`	**Here's the main routine:**
`{`	
`    int i;`	make i be an integer
`    i=average(3, 7);`	make i be average(3, 7)
`    cout <<i <<endl;`	print i
`}`	
`int average(int a, int b)`	**Here's how to compute average(a, b):**
`{`	
`    return ((a+b)/2);`	return this answer: (a+b)/2
`}`	

In that program, the main routine is:

`    int i;`	make i be an integer
`    i=average(3, 7);`	make i be average(3, 7)
`    cout <<i <<endl;`	print i

You can make that main routine be shorter, like this:

`    int i=average(3, 7);`	make the integer i be average(3, 7)
`    cout <<i <<endl;`	print i

You can make it be even shorter, like this:

`    cout <<average(3, 7) <<endl;`	print average(3, 7)

To make that program handle double-precision numbers instead of integers, change each int to double. After changing each int to double, the program will work, even if you don't change 3 to 3.0 and don't change 7 to 7.0.

Character variables

A variable can stand for a character. For example, suppose you're in school, take a test, and get an A on it. To proclaim your grade, write a program containing this line:

```
grade='A';
```

Here's the complete program:

```
Program                     Meaning
#include <iostream.h>
void main()
{
    char grade;             The grade is a character.
    grade='A';              The grade is 'A'.
    cout <<grade <<endl;    Print the character that's the grade.
}
```

The computer will print:

```
A
```

In that program, you can combine these two lines —

```
char grade;          The grade is a character.
grade='A';           The grade is 'A'.
```

to form this single line:

```
char grade='A';      The grade is this character: 'A'.
```

This program lets you input a grade:

```
#include <iostream.h>
void main()
{
    char grade;
    cout <<"Type the letter that is your grade: ";
    cin >>grade;
    cout <<"I'm amazed your grade is " <<grade <<endl;
}
```

It makes the computer say "Type the letter that is your grade: ", then wait for the human to type a grade (such as B), then say "I'm amazed your grade is B", so the screen looks like this:

```
Type the letter that is your grade: B
I'm amazed your grade is B
```

Strings of characters

A variable can stand for a whole string of characters:

```
#include <iostream.h>
void main()
{
    char x[]="winks";
    cout <<x <<endl;
}
```

That program makes x be this string of characters: "winks". The cout line makes the computer print x, so the computer will print:

```
winks
```

In a string, the beginning character is called **character 0**; the next character is called **character 1**; the next character is called **character 2**. For example, here's what happens if a string is named x:

```
The string's beginning character is called x's character 0 or x[0].
The next character is called x's character 1 or x[1].
The next character is called x's character 2 or x[2].
```

So if x is the string "winks", here's what happens:

```
x[0] is the string's beginning character, which is 'w'
x[1] is the next character, which is 'i'
x[2] is 'n'
x[3] is 'k'
x[4] is 's'
x[5] is a special character that marks the end of the string
```

In the program you just looked at, if you change the cout line to this —

```
cout <<x[0] <<x[1] <<x[2] <<x[4] <<endl;
```

the computer will print x[0] then x[1] then x[2] then x[4], so the computer will print:

```
wins
```

In the program above, if you change the cout line to this —

```
cout <<x+1 <<endl;
```

The computer will print x but skip 1 character; it will print:

```
inks
```

Here's how to input a string:

```
#include <iostream.h>
void main()
{
    char firstname[81];
    cout <<"What is your first name? ";
    cin >>firstname;
    cout <<"I like the name " <<firstname <<"very much!\n";
}
```

In that program, the char line says firstname can be a string of up to 81 characters. Since the computer's screen is 80 characters wide, 81 is a fairly safe number: it's big enough to hold a whole line of 80 characters, plus 1 end-of-string mark. **When writing a program that inputs a string, it's a good habit to put at least 81 in your program's char line.**

If you put in a much smaller number instead, such as 10, you run the risk that the human will input more characters than you reserved space for, and you'll have a runaway pointer than can crash your program (and, if you're unlucky, crash your operating system and your hard disk).

Even the number 81 is not totally safe, since the operating system lets the human input up to 254 characters (by continuing the typing onto the line below). **To be totally safe, you'd have to change the number 81 to 255** (to allow 254 characters plus an end-of-string mark).

That program makes the computer ask "What is your first name? " then wait for the human to type a first name. For example, if the human's first name is Maria, the program makes the conversation go like this:

```
What is your first name? Maria
I like the name Maria very much!
```

Comparing strings

To put strings in an "if" statement, you must say "strcmp", which warns the computer to do a "*string comp*arison".

For example, suppose x and y are strings, and you want to test whether they're equal. Do *not* say "if (x==y)". Instead, say "if (strcmp(x,y)==0)", which means "if string comparison between x and y shows 0 difference between them".

To test whether x's string comes before y's in the dictionary, do not say "if (x<y)". Instead, say "if (strcmp(x,y)<0)".

To make the computer understand "strcmp", say "#include <string.h>" at the top of your program, so your program begins like this:

```
#include <iostream.h>
#include <string.h>
```

Copying strings

If x is a string, and you want to make y be the same string, do *not* say "y=x". Instead, say "strcpy(y,x)", which means "make y be a copy of the string x".

Reserve space for y. For example, if x is a string that might contain up to 20 characters plus an end-of-string mark (making a total of 21 characters), warn the computer that y might contain 21 characters also, by saying "char y[21]"

To make the computer understand "strcpy", say "#include <string.h>" at the top of your program.

How C differs from C++

C++ is a modernized version of C. You should write programs by using C++, not C.

If you're looking at an old program that was written in C, here's how to understand it....

The program's name

Visual C++ lets you write programs in C++ or C. To write a program in C++, the program's name should end in .cpp. To write a program in C, the program's name should end in .c.

Void

In C++, a program must say void main(). The same is true in most versions of C, but some early versions C let you omit the word "void".

Indenting

The computer doesn't care how you indent.

Nearly every C++ programmer does *not* indent the braces but does indent the lines between them. The C++ editor assumes you'll follow that tradition, so it automatically indents the lines between the braces but does *not* indent the braces.

C programmers are less consistent: some indent the braces also; some move the top brace to the end of the preceding line instead of putting it on a separate line.

Where to say int

In C++, you can say "int i" anywhere in your program. In C, "int i" must be placed at the top of a group of indented line.

In C++ you can say:

```
    for (int i=20; i<=29; ++i)
```

In C you must split that line into two lines —

```
    int i;
    for (i=20; i<=29; ++i)
```

and make sure the "int i" is at the top of a group of indented lines.

Comments

In C++, a comment begins with // and continues to the end of the line. In C, a comment begins with /* and continues until it reaches */, even if */ is on a different line.

Input and output

In C++, you output by saying "cout", you input by saying "cin", and you make the computer understand those words by putting this line at the top of your program:

```
#include <iostream.h>
```

In C, you output by saying "printf" or "puts" or "putchar", you input by saying "scanf" or "gets" or "getchar", and you make the computer understand those words by putting this line at the top of your program:

```
#include <stdio.h>
```

Unfortunately, those C words are awkward to use. Here are examples....

Print a string
To print a string onto the screen, you can say printf.

```
C++:        cout <<"I love you";
C:          printf("I love you");
```

To print a string message followed by ENTER, say "\n" or "puts".

```
C++:             cout <<"I love you\n";

C (method 1): printf("I love you\n");
C (method 2): puts("I love you");
```

C understands "\n" but not "endl".

Print a number
The "puts" function can print a string but not a number. To print an integer, say printf and "%d". For example, here's how to print the answer to 750+12:

```
C++:        cout <<750+12;
C:          printf("%d",750+12);
```

If you have 750 apples and buy 12 more, how many apples will you have? Here's how to do that math and put the answer into a sentence that says "You will have ___ apples":

```
C++:        cout <<"You will have " <<750+12 <<" apples";
C:          printf("You will have %d apples",750+12);
```

To print two answers on the same line, say %d twice:

```
C++:        cout <<21+4 <<" " <<68+1;
C:          printf("%d %d", 21+4, 68+1);
```

The %d is just for an integer. For a double-precision number, say %g instead; for a character, say %c instead; for a string, say %s instead.

Print a character
To print a single character, either say printf and "%c" or say putchar:

```
C++:         cout <<'A';

C (method 1): printf("%c",'A');
C (method 2): putchar('A');
```

Input a number
To input an integer easily, say scanf and "%d". For example, here's how to input an integer age:

```
C++:        cin >>age;
C:          scanf("%d",&age);
```

Notice that scanf requires you to put the symbol "&" before the variable's name. The "%d" is just for an integer. For a double-precision number, say "%lf" instead, which means "long floating-point", which is a fancy way of saying "double precision".

Input a character
To input a character, say scanf and "%c" or say getchar(). For example, here's how to input a character that's a grade:

```
C++:        cin >>grade;

C (method 1): scanf("%c",&grade);
C (method 2): grade=getchar();
```

The scanf method requires the user to type a grade and then press ENTER. The getchar method requires the user to type just a grade without pressing ENTER afterwards.

Fun

JAVA resembles C++ but is less dangerous and includes extra commands for creating Web pages.

There are several versions of JAVA. Microsoft's version is called **Visual J++**. I'll explain how to use **Visual J++ 6.0**, which you can buy individually or as part of **Visual Studio 6**. (Other versions of JAVA are similar.)

Copy JAVA to the hard disk

Here's how to copy Visual J++ 6.0 (professional edition) to the hard disk.

Make sure your computer contains Windows 98 (not 95) and Internet Explorer 5 (not 4).

Turn on the computer without any floppy or CD-ROM disks in the drives, so the computer runs Windows 98 and the computer's bottom left corner says Start. Put the Visual J++ disk into the CD-ROM drive. The computer will say "Visual J++". Press ENTER. Click "I accept the agreement". Press ENTER.

Type the 10-digit CD key number (printed on the orange sticker at the back of the CD-ROM disk's square case). Press TAB. Type your name. Press TAB. Type the name of your company (if any). Press ENTER three times.

You'll see a product ID. Copy it onto a sheet of paper. Press ENTER three times. The computer will reboot itself.

The computer will say "Install MSDN". Put the MSDN Library's Disc 1 into the CD-ROM drive. Click "Next". Press ENTER.

You'll see an MSDN product ID. Copy it onto a sheet of paper. Press ENTER three times The computer will copy the MSDN Library to the hard disk. Press ENTER three times.

Remove the check mark from the "Register Now" box (by clicking it). Press ENTER.

Start JAVA

To start using Visual J++ (version 6.0), do this:

Remove any CD-ROM disk. Click "Start" then "Programs" then "Microsoft Visual J++ 6.0" then "Microsoft Visual J++ 6.0" again.

Start a new program

Click "Applications" then "Console Applications".

Double-click in the Name box. Invent a name for your program (such as "joe"); type the name and press ENTER.

Press ENTER again. Double-click "Class1.java" (which is at the screen's right side).

You see a big white box. In that box is a prototype JAVA program. That program does nothing useful, but you can edit it to do whatever you wish!

In that program, the important lines look like this:

```
public class Class1
{
    public static void main (String[] args)
    {
    }
}
```

The other lines are green. The computer ignores the green lines — and you should too! — since they're just comments.

If you find the green lines too distracting, erase them as follows:

Point in the left margin, to the left of the first green line, so the mouse pointer is an arrow (not a vertical line). Click (to highlight that line), or drag down (to highlight that line and several lines below it). Press the DELETE key to delete the highlighted lines.

Let's program the computer to say:

```
make your nose
touch your toes
```

To do that, edit the prototype program by inserting these extra lines:

```
public class Class1
{
    public static void main (String[] args)
    {
        System.out.println("make your nose");
        System.out.println("touch your toes");
        while (true);
    }
}
```

Here's how to insert those extra lines:

Click to the right of the second "{", press ENTER, type the first extra line, press ENTER, type the second extra line, press ENTER, and type the third extra line. Notice you must type a semicolon at the end of each line.

The computer indents the lines automatically. (If you ever want the computer to indent differently, do this before typing a line's first word or symbol: press the TAB key to indent; press the BACKSPACE key to unindent.)

Here's what those extra lines mean:

The first extra line makes the computer **system** send **out** a **print**ed **line** saying "make your nose" and makes the computer press ENTER afterwards. (If you omit the "ln", the computer will *not* press ENTER afterwards.)

The second extra line makes the computer print "touch your toes" and press ENTER afterwards.

The third extra line makes the computer pause a**while,** so you can read what the computer printed. That line is needed in Visual J++ 6.0 but *not* in most other JAVA versions.

When you finish inserting those extra lines, congratulations! You've written a JAVA program!

Run the program

To run the program, press the F5 key. The computer will say —

```
make your nose
touch your toes
```

then pause for you to admire what it said. When you finish admiring the computer's work, do this: while holding down the Ctrl key, tap the C key.

Switch programs

While the program you wrote is on the screen, you can edit it. After editing it, run it (by pressing the F5 key).

When you finish playing with that program, here's how to create a totally different program instead:

If the program is still on the screen, look at the X at the screen's top right corner; instead of clicking that X, click the X that's immediately below it, so the program lines you typed disappear.

Click the New Project button (which is near the screen's top left corner, below the word "File".) Then do the "Start a new program" routine that I explained in this page's left column.

Here's how to view an old program you created earlier:

Go into Visual J++. If a different program is on the screen, get it off the screen (by clicking the X that's below the top right corner's X). Click the Open Project button (which is near the screen's top left corner and shows an opening manila folder). You'll see a list of JAVA program folders, double-click the program folder you want to use. You'll see a green icon and a blue icon for your program; double-click the blue icon. At the screen's right edge, you'll see the blue icon again; double-click it again. Then double-click "Class1.java".

Erase files

If you type and run a program named "joe", the computer generates a folder called "joe", which is in the Visual Studio Projects folder, which is in the My Documents folder.

The "joe" folder contains four files, called "joe.vjp", "joe.sln", "joe.suo", and "joe.exe".

To erase them all, do this:

Get the icon for the "joe" folder onto the screen (by clicking the Open Project button). Click that "joe" folder icon. Press the DELETE key (to move the folder to the Recycle Bin) or press SHIFT with DELETE (to erase the folder). Press ENTER.

Math

The computer can do math. For example, this line makes the computer do 4+2:

```
System.out.println(4+2);
```

If you put that line into your program and run the program, the computer will print this answer on your screen:

```
6
```

If you bought 750 apples and buy 12 more, how many apples do you have altogether? This line prints the answer:

```
System.out.println(750+12+" apples");
```

That line makes the computer do 750+12 (which is 762) and add the word " apples" (which includes a blank space), so the computer will print:

```
762 apples
```

This line makes the computer put the answer into a complete sentence:

```
System.out.println("You have "+(750+12)+" apples!");
```

The computer will print "You have " and add 762 and add " apples!", so altogether the computer will print:

```
You have 762 apples!
```

Like most other languages (such as BASIC, PASCAL, and C++), JAVA lets you use the symbols +, -, *, /, parentheses, decimal points, and e notation.

Integers versus double precision

Like C++, JAVA handles two types of numbers well.

One type of number is called an **integer** (or **int**). An int contains no decimal point and no e. For example, -27 and 30000 are ints.

The other type of number that JAVA handles well is called a **double-precision number** (or a **double**). **A double contains a decimal point or an e.** For example, -27.0 and 3e4 are doubles. You can abbreviate: instead of writing "-27.0", you can write "-27.", and instead of writing "0.37" you can write ".37".

Largest and tiniest numbers

The largest permissible int is about 2 billion. More precisely:

```
the largest int is  2147483647
the lowest int is  -2147483648
```

If you try to feed the computer an int that's too large or too low, the computer won't complain. Instead, the computer will typically print a wrong answer!

The largest permissible double is about 1.7e308. More precisely, it's 1.7976931348623158e308. If you feed the computer a math problem whose answer is bigger than that, the computer will give up and typically say the answer is:

```
Infinity
```

The tiniest double that the computer handles well is about 2.2e-308. More precisely, it's 2.2250738585072014e-308. If you feed the computer a math problem whose answer is tinier than that, the computer will either handle the rightmost digits inaccurately or give up, saying the answer is 0.0.

Tricky arithmetic

If you combine ints, the answer is an int. For example, 2+3 is this int: 5.

11/4 is this int: 2. (11/4 is *not* 2.75.)

If you combine doubles, the answer is a double. If you combine an int with a double, the answer is a double.

How much is 2000 times 2000000? Theoretically, the answer should be this int: 4000000000. But since 4000000000 is too large to be an int, the computer will print a wrong answer. To make the computer multiply 2000 by 2000000 correctly, ask for 2000.0*2000000.0, like this:

```
System.out.println(2000.0*2000000.0);
```

That program makes the computer get the correct answer, 4000000000.0, which the computer will write in e notation, so you see this answer:

```
4.0E9
```

Long decimals

If an answer is a decimal that contains *many* digits, **the computer will typically print the first 16 significant digits accurately and the 17th digit approximately**. The computer won't bother printing later digits.

For example, suppose you ask the computer to print 10.0 divided by 9.0, like this:

```
System.out.println(10.0/9.0);
```

The computer will print:

```
1.1111111111111112
```

Notice that the 17th digit, the 2, is slightly wrong: it should be 1.

Division by 0.0

If you try to divide 1.0 by 0.0, the computer will say the answer is:

```
Infinity
```

If you try to divide 0.0 by 0.0, the computer will say the answer is —

```
NaN
```

which means "Not a Number".

Advanced math

The computer can do advanced math. For example, it can compute square roots. This line makes the computer print the square root of 9:

```
System.out.println(Math.sqrt(9.0));
```

The computer will print:

```
3.0
```

Say Math.sqrt(9.0) rather than Math.sqrt(9), because the number you find the square root of should be double-precision, not an integer. If you make the mistake of saying Math.sqrt(9), the computer will print the correct answer but slowly.

Besides sqrt, you can use other advanced math functions, but you must say "Math." at the beginning of each. Here's a list of those advanced-math functions:

To handle exponents, you can use sqrt (square root), exp (exponential power of e), and log (logarithm base e). You can also use pow: for example, pow(3.0,2.0) is 3.0 raised to the 2.0 power.

For trigonometry, you can use sin (sine), cos (cosine), tan (tangent), asin (arcsin), acos (arccosine), and atan (arctangent). You can also use atan2: for example, atan2(y,x) is the arctangent of y divided by x.

For absolute value, use abs. For example, abs(-2.3) is 2.3.

To round, use floor (which rounds down) or ceil (which stands for "ceiling" and rounds *up*). For example, floor(26.319) is 26.0, and ceil(26.319) is 27.0.

Variables

JAVA handles numeric variables the same way as C++. For example, you can say:

```
n=3;
```

A variable's name can be short (such as n) or long (such as town_population_in_1999). It can be as long as you wish! The name can contain letters, digits, and underscores, but not blank spaces. The name must begin with a letter or underscore, not a digit.

Before using a variable, say what type of number the variable stands for. For example, if n and town_population_in_1999 will stand for numbers that are ints and mortgage_rate will stand for a double, begin your program by saying:

```
public class Class1
{
    public static void main (String[] args)
    {
        int n, town_population_in_1999;
        double mortgage_rate;
```

If n is an integer that starts at 3, you can say —

```
int n;
n=3;
```

but you can combine those two lines into this single line:

```
int n=3;
```

Here's how to say "n is an integer that starts at 3, and population_in_1999 is an integer that starts at 27000":

```
int n=3, population_in_1999=27000;
```

Increase

Like C++, JAVA uses the symbol ++ to mean "increase". For example, ++n means "increase n".

These lines create n, increase it, then print it:

```
int n=3;
++n;
System.out.println(n);
```

The n starts at 3 and increases to 4, so the computer prints 4.

Saying ++n gives the same answer as n=n+1, but the computer handles ++n faster.

The symbol ++ increases the number by 1, even if the number is a decimal. For example, if x is 17.4 and you say ++x, the x will become 18.4.

Decrease

The opposite of ++ is --. The symbol -- means "decrease". For example, --n means "decrease n". Saying --n gives the same answer as n=n-1 but faster.

Strange short cuts

If you use the following short cuts, your programs will be briefer and run faster.

Instead of saying n=n+2, say n+=2, which means "n's increase is 2". Similarly, instead of saying n=n*3, say n*=3, which means "n's multiplier is 3".

Instead of saying ++n and then giving another command, say ++n in the middle of the other command. For example, instead of saying —

```
++n;
j=7*n;
```

say:

```
j=7*++n;
```

That's pronounced: "j is 7 times an increased n". So if n was 2, saying j=7*++n makes n become 3 and j become 21.

Notice that when you say j=7*++n, the computer increases n *before* computing j. If you say j=7*n++ instead, the computer increases n *after* computing j; so j=7*n++ has the same effect as saying:

```
j=7*n;
++n;
```

Arrays

JAVA handles arrays the same way as C++. For example, if you want x to be a list of 3 double-precision numbers, begin your program by saying:

```
double[] x=new double[3];
```

That says x will be a list of 3 double-precision numbers, called x[0], x[1], and x[2]. Like C++, JAVA starts counting at 0.

Here's a complete JAVA program using that array:

```
public class Class1
{
    public static void main (String[] args)
    {
        double[] x=new double[3];
        x=new double[3];
        x[0]=10.6;
        x[1]=3.2;
        x[2]=1.1;
        System.out.println(x[0]+x[1]+x[2]);
        while (true);
    }
}
```

The computer will print the sum, 14.9.

Notice that if you say double[] x=new double[3], you can refer to x[0], x[1], and x[2], but not x[3]. If you accidentally refer to x[3], the computer will gripe about "ArrayIndexOutOfBoundsException".

If you want x to be a table having 2 rows and 3 columns of double-precision numbers, begin your program by saying:

```
double[][] x=new double[2][3];
```

Since JAVA always starts counting at 0 (not 1), the number in the table's top left corner is called x[0][0].

Character variables

Like C++, JAVA lets a variable can stand for a character.

For example, suppose you're in school, take a test, and get an A on it. To proclaim your grade, write a program containing this line:

```
grade='A';
```

Here's the complete program:

```
public class Class1
    {
    public static void main (String[] args)
    {
        char grade;          The grade is a character.
        grade='A';           The grade is 'A'.
        System.out.println(grade);  Print the character that's the grade.
        while (true);
    }
}
```

The computer will print:

```
A
```

In that program, you can combine these two lines —

```
char grade;          The grade is a character.
grade='A';           The grade is 'A'.
```

to form this single line:

```
char grade='A';      The grade is this character: 'A'.
```

String variables

A variable can stand for a whole String of characters:

```
public class Class1
    {
    public static void main (String[] args)
    {
        String x;
        x="he";
        System.out.println("fat"+x+"red");
        while (true);
    }
}
```

The first shaded line says there's a String of characters, called x. The second shaded line says x is this String of characters: "he". The third shaded line makes the computer print "fat" then x (which is "he") then "red", so the computer will print:

```
fathered
```

JAVA requires you to capitalize the first letter of String: say String, not string.

In that program, you can combine these two lines —

```
        String x;
        x="he";
```

to form this single line:

```
        String x="he";
```

Input

Like other languages, JAVA lets you input, but JAVA makes it harder.

String input

This program lets you input a String:

```
import java.io.*;
public class Class1
    {
    public static void main (String[] args) throws IOException
    {
        InputStreamReader is=new InputStreamReader(System.in);
        BufferedReader br=new BufferedReader(is);
        System.out.print("What is your name? ");
        String s=br.readLine();
        System.out.println ("I like the name "+s+" very much");
        while (true);
    }
}
```

To handle input well, you must prepare the computer for input:

Begin your program by saying "import java.io.*".
Say "throws IOException" at the end of the "public static void main" line.
Begin the program's main part by inserting lines about InputStreamReader and BufferedReader.

Type all that carefully! Beware of capitals and spaces! After you've typed all that junk, the rest of the program is easy:

The System.out.print line makes the computer ask "What is your name? ".
The next line makes the String s be whatever the human types; the computer reads the Line the human inputs.
The System.out.println makes the computer say "I like the name " then s then " very much".

For example, if the human's name is "Dr. Hector von Snotblower, Jr., M.D.", the program makes the conversation go like this:

```
What is your name? Dr. Hector von Snotblower, Jr., M.D.
I like the name Dr. Hector von Snotblower, Jr., M.D. very much
```

Integer input

The program above lets you input a String. To input an integer instead, do this trick: input a String, then convert the String to an integer by saying "Integer.parseInt". For example, this program asks the human's age, then predicts how old the human will be 10 years from now:

```
import java.io.*;
public class Class1
    {
    public static void main (String[] args) throws IOException
    {
        InputStreamReader is=new InputStreamReader(System.in);
        BufferedReader br=new BufferedReader(is);
        System.out.print("How old are you? ");
        int age=Integer.parseInt(br.readLine());
        System.out.println ("Ten years from now, you'll be "+(age+10));
        while (true);
    }
}
```

Here's how the program works:

The System.out.print line makes the computer ask "How old are you? ".
The next line makes the integer age be the string the human types, converted to an integer.
The System.out.println makes the computer say "Ten years from now, you'll be " then age+10.

Here's a sample run:

```
How old are you? 27
Ten years from now, you'll be 37
```

Double-precision input

In the program above, age is an integer. If you want age to be double-precision instead, change the shaded line to this —

```
        double age=Utils.parseDblList(br.readLine())[0];
```

and insert one more line at the top of the program:

```
import com.ms.wfc.util.*;
```

That works in Visual J++ 6.0, but other JAVA versions use different commands.

Logic

JAVA lets you say "if", "while", and "for" and create comments, the same way as C++. Here are examples....

If

If a person's age is less than 18, let's make the computer say "You are still a minor." Here's the fundamental line:

```
if (age<18) System.out.println("You are still a minor.");
```

Notice you must put parentheses after the word "if".

If a person's age is less than 18, let's make the computer say "You are still a minor." and also say "Ah, the joys of youth!" and "I wish I could be as young as you!" Here's how to say all that:

```
if (age<18)
{
    System.out.println("You are still a minor.");
    System.out.println("Ah, the joys of youth!");
    System.out.println("I wish I could be as young as you!");
}
```

Since that "if" line is above the "{", the "if" line is a structure line, similar to a "public class" line, and does *not* end in a semicolon.

Here's how to put that structure into a complete program, assuming age is an integer:

```
import java.io.*;
public class Class1
    {
    public static void main (String[] args) throws IOException
    {
        InputStreamReader is=new InputStreamReader(System.in);
        BufferedReader br=new BufferedReader(is);
        System.out.print("How old are you? ");
        int age=Integer.parseInt(br.readLine());
        if (age<18)
        {
            System.out.println("You are still a minor.");
            System.out.println("Ah, the joys of youth!");
            System.out.println("I wish I could be as young as you!");
        }
        else
        {
            System.out.println("You are an adult.");
            System.out.println("Now we can have some adult fun!");
        }
        System.out.println("Glad to have met you.");
        while (true);
    }
}
```

If the person's age is less than 18, the computer will print "You are still a minor." and "Ah, the joys of youth!" and "I wish I could be as young as you!" If the person's age is not less than 18, the computer will print "You are an adult." and "Now we can have some adult fun!" Regardless of the person's age, the computer will end the conversation by saying "Glad to have met you."

The "if" statement uses this notation:

Notation	Meaning
if (age<18)	if age is less than 18
if (age<=18)	if age is less than or equal to 18
if (age==18)	if age is equal to 18
if (age!=18)	if age is not equal to 18
if (age<18 && weight>200)	if age<18 and weight>200
if (age<18 || weight>200)	if age<18 or weight>200

Notice that in the "if" statement, you should use double symbols: you should say "==" instead of "=", say "&&" instead of "&", and say "||" instead of "|". If you accidentally say "=" instead of "==", the computer will gripe. If you accidentally say "&" instead of "&&" or say "|" instead of "||", the computer will still get the right answers but too slowly.

Strings The symbols <, <=, ==, and != let you compare numbers or characters but not Strings. If you try to use them to compare Strings, you'll get wrong answers.

For example, suppose x and y are strings, and you want to test whether they're equal. Do *not* say "if (x==y)". Instead, say:

```
if (x.equals(y))
```

Make sure you put the period after x and put parentheses around y.

An alternative is to say:

```
if (x.equalsIgnoreCase(y))
```

That makes the computer compare x with y and ignore capitalization. It makes the computer consider x to be "equal" to y if the only difference is "which letters in the string are capitalized".

To test whether x's string comes before y's in the dictionary, do not say "if (x<y)". Instead, say:

```
if (x.compareTo(y)<0)
```

While

Let's make the computer print the word "love" repeatedly, like this:

```
love love love love love love love love love love love etc.
love love love love love love love love love love love etc.
love love love love love love love love love love love etc.
etc.
```

This program does it:

```
public class Class1
{
    public static void main (String[] args)
    {
        while (true) System.out.print("love ");
    }
}
```

In that program, the "while (true)" means: do repeatedly. The computer will do System.out.print("love ") repeatedly, looping forever — or until you **abort** the program by pressing Ctrl with C.

Let's make the computer start at 20 and keep counting, so the computer will print:

```
20
21
22
23
24
25
26
27
28
29
30
31
32
etc.
```

This program docs it:

Program	Meaning
`public class Class1`	
`{`	
`    public static void main (String[] args)`	
`    {`	
`        int i=20;`	Start the integer i at 20.
`        while (true)`	Repeat indented lines forever:
`        {`	
`            System.out.println(i);`	print i then press ENTER
`            ++i;`	increase i
`        }`	
`    }`	
`}`	

It prints faster than you can read.

```
To pause the printing, press the PAUSE key.
To resume the printing, press the ENTER key.
To abort the program, press ENTER, then press Ctrl with C.
```

In that program, if you say "while (i<30)" instead of "while (true)", the computer will do the loop only while i remains less than 30; the computer will print just:

```
20
21
22
23
24
25
26
27
28
29
```

To make that list stay on the screen, so you can read it, make the computer pause by saying "while (true)" at the end of that program, so your program looks like this:

Program	Meaning
`public class Class1`	
`{`	
`    public static void main (String[] args)`	
`    {`	
`        int i=20;`	Start the integer i at 20.
`        while (i<30)`	Repeat indented lines while i<30:
`        {`	
`            System.out.println(i);`	print i
`            ++i;`	increase i
`        }`	
`        while (true);`	Pause, so human can read screen.
`    }`	
`}`	

Instead of saying "while (i<30)", you can say "while (i<=29)".

For

Here's a more natural way to get that output of numbers from 20 to 29:

```
public class Class1
{
    public static void main (String[] args)
    {
        for (int i=20; i<=29; ++i) System.out.println(i);
        while (true);
    }
}
```

In that program, the "for (int i=20; i<=29; ++i)" means "Do repeatedly. Start the integer i at 20, and keep repeating as long as i<=29. At the end of each repetition, do ++i."

In that "for" statement, if you change the ++i to i+=3, the computer will increase i by 3 instead of by 1, so the computer will print:

```
20
23
26
29
```

The "for" statement is quite flexible. You can even say "for (int i=20; i<100; i*=2)", which makes i start at 20 and keep doubling, so the computer prints:

```
20
40
80
```

Like "if" and "while", the "for" statement can sit atop a group of indented lines that are in braces.

Comments

To put a comment in your program, begin the comment with the symbol //. The computer ignores everything that's to the right of //. Here's an example:

```
// This program is fishy
// It was written by a sick sailor swimming in the sun
public class Class1
{
    public static void main (String[] args)
    {
        System.out.println("Our funny God");   // religious
        System.out.println(invented cod");     // wet joke
        while (true);
    }
}
```

The computer ignores all the comments, which are to the right of //.

While you type the program, the computer makes each // and each comment turn green. Then the computer ignores everything that's turned green, so the computer prints just:

```
Our funny God
invented cod
```

DBASE

Get comfortable

DBASE is a programming language that lets you easily manipulate random-access files and databases. Invented by Wayne Ratliff, was published by **Ashton-Tate**, which sold over a million copies. In 1991, **Borland** bought Ashton-Tate, so DBASE was then published by Borland. In 1999, Borland sold DBASE to **KSoft**, so now DBASE is published by KSoft.

Versions of DBASE

The original version of DBASE was called **DBASE 2**. It ran on the IBM PC and also on computers using the CP/M operating system.

Then came improvements, called **DBASE 3**, **DBASE 3+**, **DBASE 4**, **DBASE 4 version 1.1**, **DBASE 4 version 1.5**, **DBASE 4 version 2**, and **DBASE 5**. Those improvements ran just on the IBM PC (and clones). Two versions of DBASE 5 were available: one for DOS, the other for Windows.

The newest version of DBASE has been **VISUAL DBASE 7.5**. KSoft is trying to develop **DBASE 2000 (DB2K)**. Contact KSoft (2548 Vestal Parkway E., Vestal NY 13850, phone 888-DBASE-32 or 607-729-0960, www.dbase2000.com).

A company called **Fox Software** invented DBASE versions that run faster, contain extra features, and cost less! Microsoft bought Fox Software, so now Fox's versions are published by Microsoft.

Fox's versions of DBASE are called **FOXBASE** (which resembles DBASE 3), **FOXBASE+** (which resembles DBASE 3+), and **FOXPRO** (which resembles DBASE 4). The newest version of FOXPRO has been **VISUAL FOXPRO 6**, which is part of Microsoft's **Visual Studio 6**. Microsoft is trying to develop **Visual Studio 7**, which will include **VISUAL FOXPRO 7**.

What's in this chapter
I'll explain how to use DBASE 4 version 1.5. (Newer versions of DBASE are similar.)

I'll also explain the differences in DBASE 3, DBASE 3+, DBASE 4 version 1.1, and FOXPRO 2. (Newer versions of FOXPRO are similar to FOXPRO 2.)

Which pages?

DBASE commands are explained on these pages:

Command	Page
ACCEPT "WHAT FOOD? " TO FOOD	484
APPEND	479
APPEND BLANK	487
AVERAGE	476
AVERAGE INCOME	476
AVERAGE INCOME TO X	483
BROWSE	478
CASE DESIRE="X"	486
CLEAR	483
CLEAR ALL	484
CONTINUE	477
COPY STRUCTURE TO FRED	480
COPY TO FRED	480
COPY TO FRED FIELDS AGE,SEX	480
COPY TO FRED FOR NAME="SAN"	480
COUNT	476
COUNT TO X	483
CREATE FAMILIES	474
DELETE	479
DELETE FOR NAME="SAN"	479
DELETE RECORD 3	479
DIR	480
DIR *.NDX	481
DIR *.PRG	482
DIR *.*	480
DISPLAY	477
DISPLAY ALL	477
DISPLAY FOR NAME="SAN"	477
DISPLAY NEXT 2	478
DISPLAY REST	478
DISPLAY WHILE INCOME<100000	478
DO CASE	486
DO STATS	482
DO WHILE .T.	485
DO WHILE X<=10	485
EDIT	478
EDIT RECORD 3	478
EDIT 3	478
ELSE	485
ENDCASE	487
ENDDO	485
ENDIF	485
ENDTEXT	482
ERASE FAMILIES.DBF	480
EXIT	485
FIND SAN	481
GO BOTTOM	477
GO TOP	477
GO 3	477
IF AGE<18	485
IF EOF()	486
INDEX ON NAME TO FAMNAME	481
INPUT "HOW OLD? " TO AGE	483
INSERT	479

Command	Page
LIST	475
LIST FOR INCOME<100000	476
LIST OFF	475
LIST RECORD 3	477
LIST STRUCTURE	476
LIST TO PRINT	477
LOCATE FOR NAME="SAN"	477
LOOP	485
MODIFY COMMAND STATS	482
MODIFY STRUCTURE	480
OTHERWISE	487
PACK	479
QUIT	474
READ	484
RECALL RECORD 3	479
REINDEX	481
REPLACE INCOME WITH 60000	479
RETURN	485
SEEK "SAN"	481
SET DELETED ON or OFF	479
SET EXACT ON or OFF	476
SET HEADING ON or OFF	483
SET PRINT ON or OFF	477
SET TALK ON or OFF	483
SKIP	477
SORT ON NAME TO FRED	480
STORE 7-1 TO X	483
SUM	476
SUM INCOME	476
SUM INCOME TO X	483
TEXT	482
USE	480
USE FAMILIES	480
USE FAMILIES INDEX FAMNAME	481
WAIT "INITIAL? " TO INITIAL	484
ZAP	479
Z=UPPER(Z)	484
Z=7-1	483
@10,25 GET CITY	484
@10,25 SAY "DROWN"	483
@10,25 SAY "AGE?" GET AGE	484
?	486
? 5+2	474
?? "HER"	483
3	477

Hardware requirements

Fancy versions (such as DBASE 4, FOXBASE+, FOXPRO, and FOXPRO 2) require a hard disk. If you lack a hard disk, use DBASE 3 or 3+.

DBASE 4 requires 640K of RAM. FOXPRO and FOXPRO 2 require 512K. If you don't have so much RAM, use DBASE 3 or 3+, which require just 384K.

To use FOXPRO 2's *advanced* commands, you need at least 1½M of RAM and either a 386 or 486 CPU. To use FOXPRO 2 *easily*, you need a mouse.

Copy to the hard disk

When you buy DBASE 4 version 1.5, you get a big box that contains five manuals, four 1.2M floppies, and five 720K floppies. (If your disk drive needs 360K floppies instead, you can get them by mailing Borland $15 extra.)

Here's how to copy DBASE 4 version 1.5 onto your hard disk. (But if you're sharing the computer, ask your colleagues whether they did this step already!)

Turn on the computer without any floppy in drive A. When you see the C prompt, put the DBASE Install Disk into drive A. Type "a:". You'll see an A prompt. Type "install".

The computer will say "DBASE 4 Installation". Press ENTER twice.

The computer will say "Software Registration". Type your name and press ENTER. Type your company's name (if any) and press ENTER. Type your serial number, which is on the label of the 5¼-inch DBASE Install Disk. (If you remove that disk from the drive to peek at the serial number, put that disk back in the drive when you finish peeking.)

While holding down the Ctrl key, press the END key.

The computer will ask, "Do you wish to install caching?" To keep the installation procedure simple, press N.

When the computer tells you, insert the other DBASE disks, and press ENTER after each insertion.

The computer will say, "DBASE 4 can be run from any directory if your AUTOEXEC.BAT file contains the necessary information." To keep your AUTOEXEC.BAT file simple, press the Esc key.

The computer will say, "DBASE 4 will not run properly unless adequate file and buffer space is reserved." Press ENTER. The computer will make your CONFIG.SYS file says "files=99".

The computer will say, "The installation of DBASE 4 is complete." Press ENTER.

Turn off the computer so you can start fresh.

Old versions DBASE 3 comes on three 360K disks. The first disk is the program itself; the second disk is a spare copy of the program, in case the first disk gets damaged; the third disk contains examples and utilities.

DBASE 3+ comes on seven 360K disks. Two disks contain the program itself, and the other five disks are supplementary.

Instead of copying DBASE 3 or 3+ to the hard disk, try using the procedures described in the next section.

DBASE 4 version 1.1 comes on ten 360K disks, which you install by using a procedure similar to DBASE version 1.5.

FOXPRO 2 When you buy FOXPRO 2, you get a big box that contains nine manuals and four 1.2M disks.

Here's how to copy FOXPRO 2 onto your hard disk. (I assume you have a 386 or 486, at least 1½M of RAM, and a mouse. I assume you've practiced using the mouse with other software, such as Windows or Deluxe Paint.)

Turn on the computer without any floppy in drive A. When you see the C prompt, put FOXPRO Disk 1 into drive A. Type "a:install".

The computer will say, "Fox Software Product Installation". Press ENTER 6 times.

The computer will say, "Enter your FOXPRO Serial Number". Type the Serial Number (which came on a sheet of paper enclosed with the disks).

The computer will say, "Enter your FOXPRO Activation Key". Type the hidden Activation Key (which is hidden on the *second* sheet of paper enclosed with the disks; do *not* type the DEMONSTRATION Activation Key).

The computer will say, "Please insert Disk #2". Insert FOXPRO Disk 2 into drive A, and press ENTER.

The computer will say, "Please insert Disk #3". Insert FOXPRO Disk 3 into drive A, and press ENTER three times.

The computer will say, "Programs To Install". Using the mouse, click the "Check All" button, then click the "Install" button.

The computer will say, "Please insert Disk #4". Insert FOXPRO Disk 4 into drive A, and press ENTER.

The computer will say, "Installation Complete". Press ENTER.

Turn off the computer so you can start fresh.

Start DBASE

To start using DBASE 4, turn on the computer without any floppy in drive A.

If you've put the DO.BAT file onto your hard disk (as I recommended in the MS-DOS chapter), type "do dbase". If you have *not* put DO.BAT onto your hard disk, you must type "cd dbase" and then "dbase".

(If you're using DBASE 4 version 1.0 or 1.1, the computer will say "This software is licensed". Press ENTER.)

The computer will say "DBASE 4 CONTROL CENTER". Press the Esc key. The computer will ask, "Are you sure?" Press the Y key.

At the screen's lower left corner, you'll see a period, which is called the **dot prompt**. After the dot prompt, you can type any DBASE command you wish.

Press the CAPS LOCK key, so any commands you type will be capitalized.

Old versions Here's how to start using DBASE 3 and 3+.

Without putting any DBASE floppies into the drives, turn on the computer. Wait for a DOS prompt to appear.

Put DBASE System Disk 1 in drive A.

Make sure you see an A prompt. (If you're using a hard disk, do that by typing "a:" after the C prompt.)

Peculiarity: if you're using DBASE 3+ version 1.1 and nobody's ever used your System Disk 1 before, you must give it an "ID" by following the instructions in the "Getting Started" booklet that came with the disk.

Regardless of which version of DBASE 3+ you're using, your next step is to type "dbase" after the A prompt.

If the bottom of the screen says "Press ENTER to assent to the License Agreement", press ENTER. If the computer says "Insert System Disk 2", do so and press ENTER. If the bottom right corner of the screen says "Exit — Esc", press the Esc key.

At the screen's lower left corner, you'll see a period, which is the dot prompt. Press the CAPS LOCK key, so any commands you type will be capitalized.

If you have a hard disk, type "SET DEFAULT TO C". If you lack a hard disk, put a blank formatted disk in drive B and type "SET DEFAULT TO B".

FOXPRO 2 Here's how to start using FOXPRO 2.

Turn on the computer without any floppy in drive A.

When you see the C prompt, type "cd foxpro2". When you see the FOXPRO2 prompt, type "foxprox". (If you don't have enough RAM to run "foxprox", type "fox" instead.)

In the middle of the screen, you'll see a rectangle that has the word "Command" at the top of it. That rectangle is called the "Command Window". To move that rectangle to a different part of the screen, use the mouse: point at the word "Command", and drag it. To change the rectangle's size, point at the dot in the rectangle's bottom right corner, and drag it.

For best results, drag until the rectangle consumes most of the top third of the screen.

Press the CAPS LOCK key, so any commands you type will be capitalized.

Arithmetic

If you want the computer to print the answer to 5+2, say "? 5+2" after the dot prompt, so your screen looks like this:

```
. ? 5+2
```

The computer will print:

```
       7
```

Notice that DBASE, like BASIC, uses a question mark to mean print. So "? 5+2" means: print 5+2. In DBASE, you *must* use the question mark; do *not* type the word PRINT.

DBASE, like BASIC, uses the symbols +, -, *, /, ^, E, and parentheses.

Unfortunately, DBASE gives the wrong answer to -5^2. According to mathematicians, -5^2 means "the negative of 5^2", which is "the negative of 25", which is -25. DBASE mistakenly thinks that -5^2 means "the square of -5" and therefore prints 25.

```
FOXPRO 2 You don't see a dot prompt. Just type:
? 5+2
   Your typing will appear in the Command Window. At the end of your typing,
when you press the ENTER key, the computer will print this answer at the
screen's bottom:
7
```

Strings

DBASE, like BASIC, lets you use quotation marks to create strings. So if you say —

```
. ? "I LOVE YOU"
```

the computer will print:

```
I LOVE YOU
```

Multiple computations

You can print several computations on the same line. For example, if you say —

```
. ? 2+3,2-3,2*3,2/3
```

the computer will print:

```
        5        -1         6      0.67
```

QUIT

When you finish using DBASE, do *not* turn off the computer's power. Turning off the power will wreck the data files you've been working on.

Instead of turning off the power, say QUIT, so your screen looks like this:

```
. QUIT
```

That QUIT command makes the computer put the finishing touches on all your data files. Then the computer will stop using DBASE, and will say:

```
C:\>
```

After the "C:\>", you can give any DOS command, or turn off the power.

Create a data file

Let's create a data file about families in your neighborhood. Begin by saying:

```
. CREATE FAMILIES
```

That makes the computer create, on your disk, a data file named "FAMILIES.DBF". (The ".DBF" stands for "Data Base File".)

Complete the chart

Let's store each family's NAME, annual INCOME, and POPULATION (number of people in the family). Suppose the longest family NAME is Anagnostopoulos, the highest INCOME is 125000.00, and the largest POPULATION is 13 (because the family includes a mother, father, and 11 kids).

To prepare the computer to handle such data, feed the computer this chart:

Num	Field Name	Field Type	Width	Dec	Index
1	NAME	Character	15		N
2	INCOME	Numeric	9	2	N
3	POPULATION	Numeric	2	0	N

The second column says that for each family we're storing these **fields**: the family's NAME, INCOME, and POPULATION. The left column numbers those fields: 1, 2, and 3. The third column says that each family's NAME is a string of characters, and that each family's INCOME and POPULATION are numbers. The remaining columns say that each NAME can be up to 15 characters long (such as "Anagnostopoulos"), each INCOME can be up to 9 symbols long (such as 125000.00) and has 2 digits after the decimal point, each POPULATION can be up to 2 digits long (such as 13) and has no decimals, and No field is indexed.

As soon as you say CREATE FAMILIES (and press the ENTER key at the end of that line), the computer asks you to feed it that chart. To help you start, the computer puts this on the screen:

Num	Field Name	Field Type	Width	Dec	Index
1		Character			N

Just fill in all the other entries in the chart — and press the ENTER key after each entry. Here are the details:

Begin by typing NAME (by pressing the N key, then A, then M, then E). Press the ENTER key at the end of that entry.

Since the computer's already typed the next entry for you (Character), press the ENTER key again.

Type the next entry (15). Press ENTER.

Since the computer's already typed the next entry for you (N), press the ENTER key again.

Type the next entry (INCOME). Press ENTER.

Start typing the next entry (Numeric). As soon as you type the N of Numeric, the computer automatically types the "umeric" for you and presses the ENTER key for you.

Type the next entry (9); press ENTER. Type the next entry (2); press ENTER. Accept the N, by pressing ENTER again.

Type the next entry (POPULATION). Since POPULATION is so long, when you finish typing it the computer will automatically beep (to warn you not to make it even longer!) and press ENTER for you.

Type the next entry (N) and the next entry (2); press ENTER. Type the final entry (0). Since you've finished typing the entire table, tap the END key *while holding down the CONTROL key.*

FOXPRO 2 Feed the computer this chart:

Name	Type	Width	Dec
NAME	Character	15	
INCOME	Numeric	9	2
POPULATION	Numeric	2	0

Begin by typing NAME. Press the TAB key at the end of that entry.

Since the computer's already typed the next entry for you (Character), press the TAB key again.

Type the next entry (15). Press TAB.

Type the next entry (INCOME). Press TAB.

Start typing the next entry (Numeric). As soon as you type the N of Numeric, the computer automatically types the "umeric" for you and presses the TAB key for you.

Type the next entry (9); press TAB. Type the next entry (2); press TAB. Type the next entry (POPULATION); press TAB. Type the next entry (N) and the next entry (2). The computer will automatically type the final 0.

Using the mouse, click the word "OK".

Input the data

The computer will ask:

```
Input data records now? (Y/N)
```

Tap the Y key, which means Yes.

On the screen, you'll see this:

```
NAME
INCOME            .
POPULATION
```

Notice that the NAME box is wide enough to hold 15 characters, the INCOME box already includes the decimal point, and the POPULATION box is wide enough to hold a 2-digit number.

Fill in the boxes. Here's how:

Type the first family's name (SMITH). As you type SMITH, you'll see it appear in the first box. When you finish typing SMITH, press ENTER.

Type family's income (24100.19). As you type 24100.19, you'll see it appear in the second box. When you type the decimal point, the number will automatically slide toward the right edge of the box, so that the decimal point you typed is at the same place as the decimal point that was already in the box. When you finish typing the number, the computer will automatically beep and move you to the third box.

Type the family's population (4). You'll see it appear in the third box.

When you press the ENTER key afterwards, the computer will record what you typed. Then the boxes will become blank again, so that you can enter a second family's data.

After entering the second family's data (and pressing the ENTER key if necessary), the screen will go blank again, so you can enter a third family's data.

Enter data for as many families as you wish.

When you've typed the data for the last family, and you're still looking at that data on the screen, tap the END key while holding down the CONTROL key.

The computer will display the dot prompt, so that you can give another DBASE command.

FOXPRO 2 When you finish typing an entry (such as SMITH), you can press either the ENTER key or the TAB key.

In a numeric field (such as INCOME), you don't see the decimal point until you type it.

When you finish typing the first family's data, that data does NOT disappear from the screen; instead, the computer lets you type the second family's data underneath the first family's.

When you finish typing the last family's data, click the close box (which is the yellow square in the window's top left corner).

See your data

After you've created a data file, you can say:

```
. LIST
```

That makes the computer list your file's information onto the screen, so the screen will look like this:

```
Record#  NAME              INCOME POPULATION
      1  SMITH           24100.19          4
      2  ANAGNOSTOPOULOS 65143.26          5
      3  SANCHEZ         50000.00         13
      4  JONES            9873.00          2
      5  SZCZEPANKIEWICZ 125000.00         4
      6  SANTINI         -4130.15          4
      7  WONG            15691.18          3
```

Notice that the Sanchez family has a high income (50000.00) but must split it among 13 people (mother, father, and 11 kids). The Jones family's population is just 2: a single mother and her baby. The Santini family's income is a negative number this year, because the family invested big money in the stock market and lost.

Choose your columns

You can make the computer omit some of the columns. If you say —

```
. LIST NAME,POPULATION
```

the computer will list the NAME and POPULATION columns but not the INCOME column; it will list this:

```
Record#  NAME            POPULATION
      1  SMITH                    4
      2  ANAGNOSTOPOULOS          5
      3  SANCHEZ                 13
      4  JONES                    2
      5  SZCZEPANKIEWICZ          4
      6  SANTINI                  4
      7  WONG                     3
```

If you say —

```
. LIST POPULATION,NAME
```

the computer will list the POPULATION column before the NAME column, like this:

```
Record#  POPULATION NAME
      1           4 SMITH
      2           5 ANAGNOSTOPOULOS
      3          13 SANCHEZ
      4           2 JONES
      5           4 SZCZEPANKIEWICZ
      6           4 SANTINI
      7           3 WONG
```

If you say —

```
. LIST OFF POPULATION,NAME
```

the computer will turn off the "Record#" column; it will list just this:

```
POPULATION NAME
         4 SMITH
         5 ANAGNOSTOPOULOS
        13 SANCHEZ
         2 JONES
         4 SZCZEPANKIEWICZ
         4 SANTINI
         3 WONG
```

For each family, let's compute the income *per person*. To do that, divide the family's income by the family's population. To display the income per person, and everything else, say —

```
. LIST NAME,INCOME,POPULATION,INCOME/POPULATION
```

The computer will list this:

```
Record#  NAME                 INCOME POPULATION INCOME/POPULATION
    1    SMITH              24100.19      4            6025.05
    2    ANAGNOSTOPOULOS    65143.26      5           13028.65
    3    SANCHEZ            50000.00     13            3846.15
    4    JONES               9873.00      2            4936.50
    5    SZCZEPANKIEWICZ   125000.00      4           31250.00
    6    SANTINI            -4130.15      4           -1032.54
    7    WONG               15691.18      3            5230.39
```

LIST FOR

To list just the low-income families (earning under $10,000), say:

```
. LIST FOR INCOME<10000
```

The computer will list:

```
Record#  NAME             INCOME POPULATION
    4    JONES           9873.00      2
    6    SANTINI        -4130.15      4
```

To list just the high-income families (earning at least $50,000), say:

```
. LIST FOR INCOME>=50000
```

That means: list for INCOME greater than or equal to $50,000.

When you're comparing strings, an equal sign means "begins with".
So to list every family whose NAME *begins with* "SAN", say:

```
. LIST FOR NAME="SAN"
```

The computer will list all data about SANCHEZ and SANTINI.

To list every family whose NAME does *not* begin with "SAN", say —

```
. LIST FOR NAME<>"SAN"
```

or, if you prefer, say:

```
. LIST FOR NAME#"SAN"
```

To list just the "SAN" families whose incomes are high, say:

```
. LIST FOR NAME="SAN" .AND. INCOME>=50000
```

That makes the computer list the data for SANCHEZ (whose income is 50000) but not SANTINI (whose income is -4130.15). Notice you must put periods around the word AND.

DBASE also understands the word OR, which you must surround with periods.

If you want to change DBASE, so that an equal sign between strings means "exactly equals" instead of "begins with", say:

```
. SET EXACT ON
```

The SET EXACT ON command remains in effect until you say QUIT or SET EXACT OFF.

> **FOXPRO 2** You can omit the periods around AND and OR. For example, you can say either ".AND." or "AND"; the computer doesn't care.

LIST STRUCTURE

If you say —

```
. LIST STRUCTURE
```

the computer will say:

```
Field  Field name   Type       Width   Dec   Index
   1   NAME         Character     15            N
   2   INCOME       Numeric        9     2      N
   3   POPULATION   Numeric        2            N
** Total **                       26
```

The computer will also say that the file contains 7 records, and it will say the date the file was last changed.

Compute the statistics
The computer can do statistics.

COUNT If you say —

```
. COUNT
```

the computer will count how many records are in the file. It will say:

```
    7 records
```

SUM If you say —

```
. SUM
```

the computer will sum all the numbers in the file. It will say:

```
    7 records summed
    INCOME POPULATION
  285677.48       35
```

That means: the sum of all the incomes is $285,677.48, and the sum of all the populations is 35. So altogether, your entire neighborhood earns a total of $285,677.48, and the neighborhood's total population is 35.

AVERAGE If you say —

```
. AVERAGE
```

the computer will average all the numbers in the file. It will say:

```
    7 records averaged
    INCOME POPULATION
   40811.07        5
```

That means the average family INCOME is $40,811.07, and the average family POPULATION is 5. (The average family population would be much lower if the Sanchez family didn't have 13 members.)

Restrictions After the word
COUNT, SUM, or AVERAGE, you can add restrictions.

For example, if you want to find the average of just the SANCHEZ and SANTINI families, say:

```
. AVERAGE FOR NAME="SAN"
```

The computer will say:

```
    2 records averaged
    INCOME      POPULATION
   22934.93         8.50
```

If you want to average just the incomes, and don't want to bother averaging the populations, say:

```
. AVERAGE INCOME FOR NAME="SAN"
```

> **Old versions** When you say AVERAGE FOR NAME="SAN", the average population is exactly 8.5, but DBASE 3 and 3+ make the computer shorten the answer and say just 8.

> **FOXPRO 2** When you say AVERAGE FOR NAME="SAN", the average population is exactly 8.5, but the computer rounds the answer and says 9.

Print on paper

To print on paper, you can use several tricks.

The simplest is to tap the PRINT SCREEN key. (If your keyboard doesn't have a PRINT SCREEN key, press the PrtSc key while holding down the SHIFT key.) That makes the printer print a snapshot of what's on the screen.

Another way is to type:

```
. SET PRINT ON
```

Afterwards, anything that will appear on the screen will also appear on paper simultaneously. The SET PRINT ON command remains in effect until you say SET PRINT OFF.

To LIST on paper, you can say:

```
. SET PRINT ON
. LIST
. SET PRINT OFF
```

A faster way to LIST onto paper is to say:

```
. LIST TO PRINT
```

Old versions If you say LIST TO PRINT while using DBASE 3+, the last line of the listing gets temporarily lost, in a part of RAM called the "buffer". That last line won't get transferred to paper until afterwards, when you give your next print-to-paper command, or when you say SET PRINT ON.

FOXPRO 2 If you say SET PRINT ON, anything that will appear on the screen's bottom line will appear on paper simultaneously. (Saying SET PRINT ON will NOT make the paper show what's in the Command Window.)

Interrupt the computer

If the computer is doing something you don't like, and you want to stop the computer, press the ESCAPE key (which says "Esc" on it). That makes the computer abort what it was doing.

For example, suppose you say LIST, and the computer starts printing a long listing. If you get impatient and don't want to see the rest of the listing, press the ESCAPE key.

In some situations, when you press the ESCAPE key, the computer asks:

```
Cancel  Ignore  Suspend
```

Confirm that you want to cancel: press the C key.

After the computer aborts, it displays the dot prompt, so you can give another DBASE command.

In DBASE, as in IBM's BASIC and PC-DOS, you can make the computer pause by pressing the PAUSE key. (If your keyboard doesn't have a PAUSE key, tap the NUM LOCK key while holding down the CONTROL key.) To make the computer continue where it left off, press the SPACE bar.

If you say DISPLAY ALL instead of LIST, the computer will list the file but will automatically pause at the end of each screenful. At the end of each screenful, it will say, "Press any key to continue". When you press ENTER, the computer will continue on to the next screenful.

Short-cut: instead of saying DISPLAY ALL FOR NAME="SAN", you can say DISPLAY FOR NAME="SAN". Here's the rule: before the word FOR, you can omit ALL.

Old versions Instead of saying "Cancel Ignore Suspend", DBASE 3+ says "Cancel, Ignore, or Suspend? (C, I, or S)"; DBASE 3 says "Terminate command file?", to which you respond by tapping the Y key.

Grab a particular record

To list just the 3rd record say:

```
. LIST RECORD 3
```

The computer will say:

Record#	NAME	INCOME	POPULATION
3	SANCHEZ	50000.00	13

Instead of saying LIST RECORD 3, you can say:

```
. GO 3
. DISPLAY
```

That makes the computer GO to record #3 and DISPLAY it. That pair of lines (GO 3 and DISPLAY) has exactly the same effect as saying LIST RECORD 3.

After you've gotten the record, you can use that record's NAME, INCOME, and POPULATION for further computations. For example, if you say —

```
. ? INCOME/20
```

the computer will print that record's INCOME divided by 20, which is:

```
2500
```

To go to record #1, which is the top record, you can say either GO 1 or GO TOP. If your file contains 7 records, and you want to go to record #7, which is the bottom record, you can say either GO 7 or GO BOTTOM. (After giving a GO command, remember to say DISPLAY.)

If you're lazy, you can usually omit the word GO. Instead of saying —

```
. GO 3
```

you can say just:

```
. 3
```

But you can*not* omit the GO from "GO TOP" and "GO BOTTOM".

SKIP SKIP means "go to the next record".

For example, suppose you've been looking at record #3 (because you said GO 3 and DISPLAY), and you want to go to the next record, which is record #4. Just say:

```
. SKIP
. DISPLAY
```

If you say SKIP 2, the computer will skip ahead 2 records. For example, if you've been looking at record #4 and then say SKIP 2, the computer will go to record #6.

If you say SKIP -1, the computer will skip back to the previous record. For example, if you've been looking at record #6 and then say SKIP -1, the computer will go back to record #5.

LOCATE If you say —

```
. LOCATE FOR NAME="SAN"
. DISPLAY
```

the computer will start at the first record, and keep hunting until it finds a record whose NAME begins with "SAN". Then it will DISPLAY that record:

Record#	NAME	INCOME	POPULATION
3	SANCHEZ	50000.00	13

To find the next "SAN", say:

```
. CONTINUE
. DISPLAY
```

The computer will display:

Record#	NAME	INCOME	POPULATION
6	SANTINI	-4130.15	13

If you say CONTINUE again, the computer will continue hunting for SAN's. If the computer reaches the end of the file and still hasn't found another SAN, it will give up, and say:

```
End of LOCATE scope
```

Old versions DBASE 3 and 3+ say just "End of LOCATE"; they omit the word "scope".

Attach fancy restrictions

If you say:

```
. GO 3
. DISPLAY
```

the computer will display just the 3rd record. If you say —

```
. GO 3
. DISPLAY NEXT 2
```

the computer will display 2 records (the 3rd and the 4th). If you say —

```
. GO 3
. DISPLAY NEXT 4
```

the computer will display 4 records (the 3rd, 4th, 5th, and 6th). If you say —

```
. GO 3
. DISPLAY REST
```

the computer will display the 3rd record and all the records that come after it. For example, if the data file contains 7 records, the computer will display the 3rd, 4th, 5th, 6th, and 7th records. (If your data file is long, the computer will pause at the end of each screenful, and wait for you to tell it to continue. If you don't want such pauses, say LIST instead of DISPLAY.)

If you say —

```
. GO 3
. DISPLAY WHILE INCOME<100000
```

the computer will start with the 3rd record, and continue displaying records as long as INCOME <100000. Here are the details....

The computer starts with the 3rd record, sees that its INCOME is less than 100000, and displays that record. Then the computer checks the 4th record, sees its INCOME is less than 100000, and displays that record. Then the computer checks the 5th record, sees its INCOME is *not* less than 100000, and refuses to display the 5th record. The computer stops there, and refuses to look at any more records. so the only records it displays are the 3rd and 4th.

Those four commands — DISPLAY and DISPLAY NEXT and DISPLAY REST and DISPLAY WHILE — are all affected by where you said to GO. Three different commands — DISPLAY ALL and DISPLAY RECORD and DISPLAY FOR — are unaffected by GO. Even if you said GO 3, a DISPLAY ALL will display the entire file, DISPLAY RECORD 2 will display record #2, and DISPLAY FOR INCOME<100000 will display *all* the records whose INCOMEs are less than 100000.

The words NEXT, REST, WHILE, ALL, RECORD, and FOR are called **restrictions**. You can attach a restriction to any DBASE command that scans data records. For example, you can add a restriction to DISPLAY, LIST, COUNT, SUM, AVERAGE, and LOCATE.

Old versions DBASE 3 doesn't understand the word REST.

Revise your data

To revise your data, you can say EDIT, BROWSE, REPLACE, APPEND, INSERT, DELETE, or ZAP.

EDIT

To edit record #3, say —

```
. EDIT RECORD 3
```

or say —

```
. EDIT 3
```

or say:

```
. GO 3
. EDIT
```

The computer will display the 3rd record on the screen and let you edit it. While you edit, you can use the four arrow keys (to move around the screen), the BACKSPACE key (to erase the previous character), the DELETE key (to delete the current character), and the INSERT key (to switch from "replacing" to "inserting" and back to "replacing" again). DBASE handles those keys the same way as good word processors (such as Word Perfect, Q&A's word processor, and DOS 5's EDIT).

To erase all the data in a field, just move to that field (by using the arrow keys); then tap the Y key while holding down the CONTROL key.

After editing the 3rd record, if you press the PAGE DOWN key, the computer will let you edit the 4th record. If you press the PAGE DOWN key again, the computer will let you edit the 5th record. (Exception: if a record is too long to fit on the screen, pressing the PAGE DOWN key will get you to the next screenful of the same record.)

By pressing the PAGE UP key, you can return to earlier records. For example, if you've been editing the 5th record and then press the PAGE UP key, the computer will let you re-edit the 4th record.

When you've finished editing all the records you wish, tap the END key while holding down the CONTROL key. Then the computer will display the dot prompt, so you can type another DBASE command.

FOXPRO 2 While you're editing the 3rd record, the screen also shows the 4th and 5th records. When you finishing editing the 3rd record, you can move to the 4th record by either pressing the PAGE DOWN key once or by pressing the down-arrow key several times.

When you finish editing all the records you wish, you can either press CONTROL with END or click the close box (the yellow square in the window's top left corner).

BROWSE

To see several records on the screen simultaneously, so you can edit them all at once, say:

```
. GO 1
. BROWSE
```

That makes the computer LIST the first several records in your file. The computer will let you use the arrow keys to move through the list and edit your data. To hop right to the next field, press the TAB key; to hop left to the previous field, press the TAB key *while holding down the SHIFT key*.

The computer will list as many records as can fit on the screen; to see the next screenful of records, press the PAGE DOWN key. The computer will list as many fields as can fit across the screen; to see other fields, tap the right-arrow key while holding down the CONTROL key.

When you've finished editing the data, tap the END key while holding down the CONTROL key.

> **Old versions** In DBASE 3 and 3+, the TAB key doesn't work. Instead, hop to the next field by pressing END; hop back to the previous field by pressing HOME.
>
> **FOXPRO 2** The computer will list as many fields as fit across the window. To see other fields, press the TAB key several times.
>   The computer will list as many records as fit in the window. To see other records, press the PAGE DOWN key once or twice (or press the down-arrow key several times).
>   When you've finished editing the data, click the close box (or press CONTROL with END).

REPLACE

A more literary way to edit records is to type a sentence that begins with the word REPLACE.

For example, to change record #3's INCOME to $60,000, say:

```
. GO 3
. REPLACE INCOME WITH 60000
```

To increase record #5's INCOME by $700, say:

```
. GO 5
. REPLACE INCOME WITH INCOME+700
```

To increase *everybody's* INCOME by $700, say:

```
. REPLACE ALL INCOME WITH INCOME+700
```

To increase the INCOME of just families whose NAME begins with "SAN", say:

```
. REPLACE FOR NAME="SAN" INCOME WITH INCOME+700
```

APPEND

To add extra records, say:

```
. APPEND
```

The computer will display a blank record on the screen, and let you fill it in.

For example, if your data file contains 7 records, and you say APPEND, the computer will let you type record #8. When you finish typing it (and press the ENTER key at the end of the last field), the computer will let you type record #9, then record #10, etc.

When you've finished typing all the records you want to add, tap the END key while holding down the CONTROL key. Then the computer will display the dot prompt, so you can type another DBASE command.

> **FOXPRO 2** When you've finished typing all the records you want to add, click the close box (or press CONTROL with END).

INSERT

To insert an extra record between record #3 and record #4, say:

```
. GO 3
. INSERT
```

The computer will display a blank record on your screen, and let you fill it in. When you finish filling it in, tap the END key while holding down the CONTROL key. The new record that you typed will become record #4; the old record #4 will become record #5; the old record #5 will become record #6; etc.

The computer will then display the dot prompt, so you can type another DBASE command.

> **FOXPRO 2** When you finish filling in the record, click the close box (or press CONTROL with END).

DELETE

To delete records 3, 5, and 6, say:

```
. DELETE RECORD 3
. DELETE RECORD 5
. DELETE RECORD 6
. PACK
```

Here's why. When you give the DELETE commands, the computer makes notes about which records you want to delete. But it doesn't actually delete those records, until you say PACK.

When you say PACK, the computer finally deletes those records. It also renumbers all the other records, to fill the gaps left by the records you deleted.

Renumbering all the records takes a long time; so while the computer's doing a PACK, you should take your coffee break or lunch break. If you don't want to take a break yet, delay saying PACK until later. Say PACK at the end of the day, or when it's time to QUIT or to switch to a different file.

DELETE without PACK If you say to DELETE some records, but you haven't said PACK yet, what happens when you try to LIST the file? The listing will show an asterisk next to each record you said to delete. The asterisked records will disappear later, when you say PACK.

If you say —

```
. SET DELETED ON
```

the computer hides the asterisked records, so they don't appear in listings and don't affect the COUNT or SUM or AVERAGE. But although the asterisked records are hidden, they're still in the file, until you say PACK.

SET DELETED ON remains in effect until you say QUIT or SET DELETED OFF.

RECALL If you say DELETE RECORD 3 and then change your mind, you can get the record back by saying RECALL RECORD 3. But RECALL works only if you haven't said PACK yet.

Short cuts Instead of saying DELETE RECORD 3, you can say:

```
. GO 3
. DELETE
```

Here's another way to delete record 3: get that record onto your screen (by saying EDIT or BROWSE, and playing with the PAGE UP and PAGE DOWN keys); and while you're looking at that record, tap the U key while holding down the CONTROL key. (The U stands for Undo.)

To delete everybody whose name begins with "SAN", say:

```
. DELETE FOR NAME="SAN"
. PACK
```

ZAP

To delete *all* the records, instead of saying DELETE ALL and PACK, just say:

```
. ZAP
```

Then the computer asks whether you're sure; tap the Y key. Then the computer ZAPs the file, so that all the records are gone. But the computer will still remember how wide you wanted each field, so you can add new records without having to say CREATE.

Switch files

You can switch to a different file. Here's how....

USE

Suppose you create a DBASE file called FAMILIES.DBF, then create a DBASE file called FOODS.DBF. If you say LIST, the computer will assume you want to list the newest file (FOODS.DBF). If you want to list FAMILIES.DBF instead, say:

```
. USE FAMILIES
. LIST
```

Saying USE FAMILIES makes the computer switch its attention to FAMILIES.DBF, so that any future command you give (such as LIST or GO or DISPLAY) applies to FAMILIES.DBF. To switch to FOODS.DBF again, say USE FOODS.

If you QUIT using DBASE but return to DBASE later, the computer forgets which file you were using. Before saying LIST, say USE FAMILIES or USE FOODS.

DIR

To see a directory of all the files in your hard disk's DBASE folder, say:

```
. DIR *.*
```

To see a special directory of just your DBASE data files (which end in .DBF), say just:

```
. DIR
```

That makes the computer print a special directory showing each data file's name, *how many records it contains*, how many bytes it contains, and the date it was last changed.

COPY

Suppose you're using the FAMILIES.DBF file, and want to make a backup copy of it.

If you want the backup copy to be called FRED.DBF, say:

```
. COPY TO FRED
```

That makes FRED.DBF be an exact copy of the whole file.

If you want FRED.DBF to include just the records of families whose names begin with "SAN", say:

```
. COPY TO FRED FOR NAME="SAN"
```

If you want FRED.DBF to include every family's NAME and POPULATION but not the INCOME, say:

```
. COPY TO FRED FIELDS NAME,POPULATION
```

If you want FRED.DBF to include no records at all, but just have the same structure (the same lengths for all the fields), say:

```
. COPY STRUCTURE TO FRED
```

If you want FRED.DBF to contain all the records, but rearranged so that the NAMEs are in alphabetical order, say —

```
. SORT ON NAME TO FRED
```

If you want FRED.DBF to contain all the records, but rearranged so that the INCOMEs are in increasing order, say —

```
. SORT ON INCOME TO FRED
```

If you want FRED.DBF to contain all the records, but rearranged so that the INCOMEs are in decreasing order (from the largest to the smallest), say —

```
. SORT ON INCOME/D TO FRED
```

ERASE

If you ever want to erase FAMILIES.DBF, say:

```
. ERASE FAMILIES.DBF
```

> **Hassle** While you're in the middle of using FAMILIES.DBF, the computer will refuse to erase it. To stop using it (so you can erase it), tell the computer to use a different file instead (by giving a command such as USE FOODS), or just say —
> ```
> . USE
> ```
> which makes the computer use no file at all. Then you can say ERASE FAMILIES.DBF.

MODIFY STRUCTURE

When you said CREATE, you filled in a chart: for each field you chose a name (such as INCOME), type (such as Numeric), and width (such as 9).

If you later want to modify that chart, say:

```
. MODIFY STRUCTURE
```

The screen will again show the chart that you created. By using the arrow keys, you can move through the chart and modify it. You can change a field's name, type, width, or number of decimal places.

To delete a field altogether, move to that field, then tap the U key while holding down the CONTROL key. (The U stands for Undo.)

To insert an extra field, move to where you want the field to be, then tap the N key while holding down the CONTROL key. (The N stands for iNsert New.)

Change as many fields as you like.

When you've finished modifying the chart, tap the END key while holding down the CONTROL key. If the computer asks "Should data be COPIED from backup for all fields?", tap the Y key.

The computer will ask, "Are you sure you want to save these changes?" Tap the Y key.

The computer will revise your entire data file, so that the file matches the chart. For example, if you said to make a field wider, the computer will do so by adding extra spaces to your data; if you said to make a field narrower, the computer will do so by abridging your data.

To see what the computer did to your data file, say LIST.

> **Hassle** If you make the computer change names of fields, the computer can't reliably change anything else at the same time. So to make lots of changes, say MODIFY STRUCTURE and change names of fields; afterwards say MODIFY STRUCTURE *again* and make all the other changes you wish (widths, decimal places, types, deleted fields, and extra fields).
>
> **Old versions** After giving the MODIFY STRUCTURE command, DBASE 3 and 3+ make your disk contain *two* versions of your data file. For example, if you've been dealing with FAMILIES.DBF, your disk will contain a file called FAMILIES.DBF (which is the new, modified version), and your disk will also contain a file called FAMILIES.BAK (which is the previous unmodified version). FAMILIES.BAK is called the ``backup'': use it only if you accidentally made a mistake when giving the MODIFY STRUCTURE command. To use FAMILIES.BAK, say:
> ```
> . USE
> . ERASE FAMILIES.DBF
> . RENAME FAMILIES.BAK TO FAMILIES.DBF
> . USE FAMILIES
> ```
>
> **FOXPRO 2** To move through the chart quickly, use the mouse: click the part of the chart that interests you. To delete a field altogether, click that field then click the word "Delete". To insert an extra field, click where you want the field to be then click the word "Insert". When you finish modifying the chart, click the word "OK" then click the word "Yes". Like DBASE 3 and 3+, FOXPRO 2 creates a .BAK file; for details, read the paragraph above (entitled "Old versions").

Index files

Suppose you're using a file called FAMILIES.DBF. Let's play a trick, so that every time you say LIST or DISPLAY the NAMEs will appear in alphabetical order, to help you find a particular NAME very quickly.

Say:

```
. INDEX ON NAME TO FAMNAME
```

That makes the computer create a file called FAMNAME.NDX, which is an iNDeX file that helps the computer find each family's NAME.

Then if you say LIST, the computer will list the families in alphabetical order:

Record#	NAME	INCOME	POPULATION
2	ANAGNOSTOPOULOS	65143.26	5
4	JONES	9873.00	2
3	SANCHEZ	50000.00	13
6	SANTINI	-4130.15	4
1	SMITH	24100.19	4
5	SZCZEPANKIEWICZ	125000.00	4
7	WONG	15691.18	3

In that file, the TOP is record #2: ANAGNOSTOPOULOS. So if you say —

```
. GO TOP
. DISPLAY
```

the computer will display:

Record#	NAME	INCOME	POPULATION
2	ANAGNOSTOPOULOS	65143.26	5

Then if you say —

```
. SKIP
. DISPLAY
```

the computer will skip the next record in the alphabetized list, and display:

Record#	NAME	INCOME	POPULATION
4	JONES	9873.00	2

In that alphabetized file, saying GO TOP has a different effect from saying GO 1. If you say GO TOP, you're going to the TOP record, which is ANAGNOSTOPOULOS; if you say GO 1, you're going to the record #1, which is SMITH.

If you want to add more records to the alphabetized list, say APPEND. As you type the extra records, the computer will automatically update the index file, so when you say LIST you'll see the entire data file — including even the new records — in alphabetical order.

> **FOXPRO 2** When you say INDEX ON NAME TO FAMNAME, FOXPRO 2 creates an index file called FAMNAME.IDX (instead of FAMNAME.NDX).

How to find

To display the first record whose NAME begins with SAN, you can say:

```
. LOCATE FOR NAME="SAN"
. DISPLAY
```

To find that record faster, say this instead —

```
. SEEK "SAN"
. DISPLAY
```

or say:

```
. FIND SAN
. DISPLAY
```

The only difference between SEEK and FIND is that SEEK must be followed by quotation marks (or a variable), whereas FIND lets you omit the quotation marks.

SEEK and FIND tell the computer to find the record *immediately*, by using the index file.

By contrast, the word LOCATE makes the computer locate the record slowly, by searching through all the records in the whole data file, from beginning to end. If your data file is very long, you'll have to wait a long time for the computer to LOCATE the record! For example, if your data file contains 2,000 records, the LOCATE command takes about 25 times as long as the SEEK and FIND commands. **The main reason for creating an index file is so that you can use the words SEEK and FIND.**

Since the index file makes the computer list all the names in alphabetical order, all the SAN names are listed near each other. So after you've found the first SAN (by saying FIND SAN and DISPLAY), you can display the next one immediately, by saying:

```
. SKIP
. DISPLAY
```

Hassles

If you QUIT or switch to a different data file, and later try to return to FAMILIES.DBF by saying USE FAMILIES, you must remind the computer to look at the index file. Instead of saying just USE FAMILIES, say:

```
. USE FAMILIES INDEX FAMNAME
```

If you accidentally forget to say INDEX FAMNAME, the computer will forget to look at the index. If you then APPEND or DELETE some records, the computer won't update the index, and the index will be wrong. If you get into that jam, get out of it by saying —

```
. USE FAMILIES INDEX FAMNAME
. REINDEX
```

That makes the computer create the index all over again, correctly.

To see the names of all your index files (such as FAMNAME.NDX), say:

```
. DIR *.NDX
```

> **FOXPRO 2** To see the names of all your index files (such as FAMNAME.IDX), say "DIR *.IDX".

Programs

Let's write a program so that whenever you say DO STATS, the computer will automatically print the SUM and AVERAGE of all the numbers in your data file. Here's how.

Begin by saying —

```
. MODIFY COMMAND STATS
```

That tells the computer you want to write a program called STATS.PRG.

Next, say what you want STATS to stand for. If you want STATS to stand for "the SUM followed by the AVERAGE", type:

```
SUM
AVERAGE
```

That pair of instructions (SUM and AVERAGE) is called the **program**. The computer does *not* put a dot prompt in front of the program lines.

While you're typing the program, you can edit it by using the arrow keys and all the other word-processing keys (DELETE, INSERT, PAGE UP, and PAGE DOWN).

To hop to the left margin, press the HOME key. To hop to the end of a line, press the END key.

To delete a line, move to that line, then tap the Y key while holding down the CONTROL key. (The Y stands for "Yank it out".) To insert an extra line between two other lines, move to where you want the extra line to begin, then tap the N key while holding down the CONTROL key. (The N stands for "iNsert New".)

When you've finished typing and editing the program, tap the END key while holding down the CONTROL key. That makes the computer put the entire program onto the disk. Then the screen will show a dot prompt.

If you want the computer to DO the STATS program you typed, say:

```
. DO STATS
```

Then the computer will print the SUM and AVERAGE of all the numbers in the current data file. For example, if you've been using the FAMILIES data file, the computer will print the SUM of the INCOMEs, SUM of the POPULATIONs, AVERAGE of the INCOMEs, and AVERAGE of the POPULATIONs. (If you haven't been using a data file, the computer will ask you which file to USE. If your data file doesn't contain any Numeric fields, the computer will gripe.)

If you ever want to revise that program, just say MODIFY COMMAND STATS again. The screen will show your program again and let you edit it. When you've finished editing it, tap the END key while holding down the CONTROL key. The new version of your program will be called STATS.PRG; the previous version of your program will still be on the disk but will be called STATS.BAK.

For another example, let's program the computer so that when you say DO SUPERDIR, the computer will print a superdirectory. Let's make the superdirectory include a directory of all your data files, followed by a directory of all your index files, followed by a directory of all your program files.

To make DO SUPERDIR accomplish all that, say:

```
. MODIFY COMMAND SUPERDIR
```

Then type this program —

```
DIR
DIR *.NDX
DIR *.PRG
```

End the program by tapping the END key while holding down the CONTROL key. From then on, whenever you say DO SUPERDIR, the computer will print a superdirectory.

Into a program, you can put any DBASE commands you wish. For example, your program can include a USE command (to switch to a different data file), an APPEND command (to let the user add extra records to the file), and a BROWSE command (to let the user browse through the entire file and edit it).

One of the lines in your program can even say DO a second program. When the computer encounters that line, the computer will DO the second program, then finish the original program.

Your program's bottom line can even say QUIT, so that when the computer finishes the program it will stop using DBASE.

> **Old versions** In DBASE 3 and 3+, here's how to hop to the left margin: tap the left-arrow key while holding down the CONTROL key. Here's how to hop to the end of the line: tap the right arrow key while holding down the CONTROL key.

> **FOXPRO 2** Saying "MODIFY COMMAND STATS" makes the computer create a window called "STATS.PRG". In that window, type your program, like this:
> SUM
> AVERAGE
> To insert an extra line, move to where you want the extra line to begin, then press ENTER. To delete a line, move to the beginning of that line, press SHIFT with down-arrow (so the line becomes brown), then press DELETE.
> When you've finished typing and editing the program, click the close box then click "Yes".
> In the SUPERDIR program, say "DIR *.IDX" instead of "DIR *.NDX".

TEXT

Let's program the computer so that whenever you say DO POEM, the computer will print this poem:

```
YOUR DATA FILES
ALL GIVE ME SMILES.
I FEEL SO LOW,
WHEN THEY MUST GO.
PLEASE DON'T ERASE
YOUR DATABASE!
        LOVE,
        YOUR COMPUTER
```

Here's how:

```
. MODIFY COMMAND POEM
? "YOUR DATA FILES"
? "ALL GIVE ME SMILES."
? "I FEEL SO LOW,"
? "WHEN THEY MUST GO."
? "PLEASE DON'T ERASE"
? "YOUR DATABASE!"
? "        LOVE,"
? "        YOUR COMPUTER"
```

But typing all those question marks and quotation marks is ridiculous! For a short-cut, type this instead:

```
. MODIFY COMMAND POEM
TEXT
YOUR DATA FILES
ALL GIVE ME SMILES.
I FEEL SO LOW,
WHEN THEY MUST GO.
PLEASE DON'T ERASE
YOUR DATABASE!
        LOVE,
        YOUR COMPUTER
ENDTEXT
```

The words TEXT and ENDTEXT tell the computer that everything between them should be printed as strings. To begin an indented passage (such as LOVE and YOUR COMPUTER), press the TAB key. Pressing the TAB key makes the computer indent the current line and all lines underneath, until you tell the computer to stop indenting (by pressing SHIFT with TAB).

Tricky output

Here are some commands you can put in your program, to produce tricky output.

To erase the screen, say:

```
CLEAR
```

If you say —

```
? "FAT"
?? "HER"
```

the double question mark makes the computer print HER on the same line as FAT. The computer will print:

```
FATHER
```

When using DBASE, the screen's top line is called *line 0*. Then come lines 1, 2, etc. In each line, the leftmost character is at *position 0*. Then come positions 1, 2, etc. To print the word DROWN beginning at line 3's 7th position, type this:

```
@3,7 SAY "DROWN"
```

SET HEADING OFF When you say LIST, DISPLAY, SUM, or AVERAGE, the computer prints data in columns and puts a heading at the top of each column. If you want the computer to omit the headings, say:

```
SET HEADING OFF
```

That command remains in effect until you say SET HEADING ON (or QUIT).

To invent your own customized heading, first get rid of the traditional headings (by saying SET HEADING OFF) and then print your own headings (by giving the "?" or "@SAY" commands).

SET TALK OFF While running your program, the computer prints messages telling you which records and numbers it's manipulating.

For example, if you say GO 3 and then SKIP 2, the computer prints a message saying it's skipping to record #5. If you say to COPY a file, the computer prints messages telling you how many records it's copied so far, until all the records are copied.

Those messages help DBASE programmers but confuse business executives who don't understand the messages' jargon. To stop the computer from printing those messages, say:

```
SET TALK OFF
```

That command remains in effect until you say SET TALK ON.

If you say SET TALK OFF, you'll have a hard time doing statistics: the simple COUNT, SUM, and AVERAGE commands don't work until you say SET TALK ON.

Variables

Like BASIC, DBASE lets you use variables easily. For example, if you say —

```
X=7-1
? X+3
```

the computer will print 9.

(While the computer performs X=7-1, the computer will also print a little message saying that X is 6, unless you say SET TALK OFF.)

A variable's name can be short (such as X) or longer. It can be up to 10 characters long (such as POPULATION). It can include underlines and digits (such as LOST_IN_86). It must begin with a letter. It cannot include blank spaces.

A variable can stand for either a number or a string. For example, if you say —

```
HUSBAND="TOM"
? HUSBAND
```

the computer will print TOM.

The computer handles two kinds of variables. A **field variable** stands for a field in a data file. For example, while you're using FAMILIES.DBF, you're using field variables called NAME, INCOME, and POPULATION. A **memory variable** is any variable that does *not* stand for a field. For example, if you say X=7-1, the X is a memory variable.

Suppose you're using FAMILIES.DBF, so INCOME is a field variable. to change a family's INCOME to 20000, do *not* say INCOME=20000. Instead, say:

```
REPLACE INCOME WITH 20000
```

Here's the rule: **to change the value of a memory variable, say "="; to change the value of a field variable, say "REPLACE".**

The computer will remember all your variables until you say CLEAR MEMORY (which erases the memory variables) or say to USE a different data file (which affects the field variables) or say CLEAR ALL (which erases *all* the variables and also makes the computer forget which file you were USEing).

The typical DBASE program begins by saying CLEAR ALL and ends by saying CLEAR ALL again, to make sure the variables from different programs don't interfere with each other.

STORE Instead of saying X=7-1, you can say STORE 7-1 TO X. Saying "STORE 7-1 TO X" has exactly the same effect as saying "X=7-1".

To make X, Y, and Z all be zero, say:

```
STORE 0 TO X,Y,Z
```

Statistics To make X be the SUM of all the INCOMEs in your data file, say:

```
SUM INCOME TO X
```

To make X be the SUM of all the INCOMEs and also make Y be the sum of all the POPULATIONs, say:

```
SUM INCOME, POPULATION TO X,Y
```

Similar commands work for COUNT and AVERAGE also. They all work even if you SET TALK OFF.

INPUT

Like BASIC, DBASE understands the word INPUT. If you say —

```
INPUT "HOW OLD ARE YOU? " TO AGE
```

the computer will ask —

```
HOW OLD ARE YOU?
```

and then wait for you to type a number. Whatever number you type will become the AGE.

The INPUT statement's variable must be a memory variable, not a field variable. For example, if you're using FAMILIES.DBF and want the person to input an INCOME (which is a field variable), you must *not* say INPUT "WHAT IS YOUR INCOME?" TO INCOME. Instead, input a memory variable called MINCOME, then copy it to a field by saying REPLACE, like this:

```
INPUT "WHAT IS YOUR INCOME? " TO MINCOME
REPLACE INCOME WITH MINCOME
```

ACCEPT

To input a string instead of a number, say ACCEPT instead of INPUT:

```
ACCEPT "WHAT IS YOUR FAVORITE FOOD? " TO FOOD
```

Underneath that ACCEPT statement, you might want to add this line:

```
FOOD=UPPER(FOOD)
```

It makes the computer convert the human's input to capital (upper-case) letters, in case the human forgot to press the CAPS LOCK key.

Like the INPUT statement, the ACCEPT statement takes a memory variable but *not* a field variable.

WAIT

This example says WAIT instead of ACCEPT:

```
WAIT "WHAT'S YOUR MIDDLE INITIAL? " TO INITIAL
? "CONGRATULATIONS!"
? "ACCORDING TO ASTROLOGY, THE FORCES OF THE UNIVERSE"
? "SHALL CAUSE WONDROUS JOYS TO BEFALL"
? "THOSE LUCKY PERSONS WHOSE EARTH-GIVEN NAMES ARE CENTERED"
? "AROUND THE LETTER",INITIAL
```

WAIT resembles ACCEPT. In that program, the first line makes the computer ask "WHAT'S YOUR MIDDLE INITIAL?" then wait for you to type a character. Whatever character you type will become the INITIAL. For example, if you type a Q, the Q will become the INITIAL.

If the line had said ACCEPT, the computer would have required you to press the ENTER key after the Q. But since the line said WAIT instead of ACCEPT, you do *not* have to press ENTER: as soon as you type the Q, the computer will know Q is the INITIAL (without waiting for ENTER) and will make the screen show this:

```
WHAT'S YOUR MIDDLE INITIAL? Q
CONGRATULATIONS!
ACCORDING TO ASTROLOGY, THE FORCES OF THE UNIVERSE
SHALL CAUSE WONDROUS JOYS TO BEFALL
THOSE LUCKY PERSONS WHOSE EARTH-GIVEN NAMES ARE CENTERED
AROUND THE LETTER Q
```

WAIT is nicer than ACCEPT, because WAIT doesn't force you to press the ENTER key after answering the question. But alas, WAIT restricts you to typing just one character: you can use WAIT for a middle initial, but not for a whole name.

GET

Suppose you live in San Francisco with most of your friends, but a *few* of your friends live elsewhere. Run this program:

```
CLEAR ALL
CLEAR
SET TALK OFF
CITY="SAN FRANCISCO"
STATE="CA"
@10,25 SAY "WHAT IS YOUR CITY?" GET CITY
@11,25 SAY "WHAT IS YOUR STATE?" GET STATE
READ
? "I AM GLAD TO HEAR YOU LIVE IN THE KOOKY CITY OF",CITY
? "IN THE SEDUCTIVE STATE OF",STATE
SET TALK ON
CLEAR ALL
```

Like most DBASE programs, that program begins by saying CLEAR ALL (to avoid interference from other programs), CLEAR (to erase the screen), and SET TALK OFF (to avoid excessive messages).

The next pair of lines make CITY be "SAN FRANCISCO" and make STATE be "CA".

The next pair of lines put this message in the middle of your screen:

```
                    WHAT IS YOUR CITY? SAN FRANCISCO
                    WHAT IS YOUR STATE? CA
```

The READ statement lets you edit the data in the boxes, by using the arrow keys, ENTER key, and other word-processing keys. (If you want to erase an entire box, move to that box, then tap the Y key while holding down the CONTROL key.) You can edit the boxes however you like — for example, change SAN FRANCISCO to RENO, and change CA to NV — or do no editing at all, so that you still have SAN FRANCISCO and CA. When you've finished doing all the editing you wish, tap the END key while holding down the CONTROL key, or just move to the bottom box and tap the ENTER key.

If you changed SAN FRANCISCO to RENO and changed CA to NV, the next two lines in the program will print this, at the bottom of the screen:

```
I AM GLAD TO HEAR YOU LIVE IN THE KOOKY CITY OF RENO
IN THE SEDUCTIVE STATE OF NV
```

Like most DBASE programs, that program ends by putting the computer back to its normal state (SET TALK ON and CLEAR ALL).

To use the word GET, you should put it in an @ SAY command. Underneath the @ SAY GET commands, say READ.

If you forget to include the SAY "WHAT IS YOUR CITY?", and instead type just @10,25 GET CITY, the computer will omit the question but will still show the CITY box. If you forget to say READ, you'll still see boxes full of data, but you won't get a chance to edit what's in them.

By using GET and READ, you can edit any kind of variable. The variable can be a number or a string; it can be a memory variable or a field variable.

If it's a field variable, the computer automatically makes the box wide enough to hold the entire field; and when you edit the data in the box, the computer automatically updates your data file. (You do *not* have to say REPLACE.)

If it's a memory variable instead, your program must include a statement such as CITY="SAN FRANCISCO", which tells the computer how wide to make the box. To make the box even wider, put extra spaces after SAN FRANCISCO, like this:

```
CITY="SAN FRANCISCO            "
```

If the memory variable stands for a number instead of a string, the computer automatically makes the box wide enough to hold 10 digits before the decimal point — or even wider.

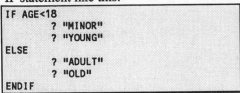

Control the flow

You can control the order in which the computer does your program's statements. Here's how....

IF

Like BASIC and PASCAL, DBASE lets you use the words IF and ELSE. Write the IF statement like this:

```
IF AGE<18
        ? "MINOR"
        ? "YOUNG"
ELSE
        ? "ADULT"
        ? "OLD"
ENDIF
```

Whenever you say IF, you must also say ENDIF. To indent the lines in between, tap the TAB key. (The indentation is optional.)

Here's how to say, "If the NAME begins with SAN and the INCOME is at least 50000":

```
IF NAME="SAN" .AND. INCOME>=50000
```

Remember to put periods around the word AND. For strings, the symbol "=" means "begins with", unless you said SET EXACT ON.

DO WHILE

To create a loop, say DO WHILE. If you want the loop to be infinite, say DO WHILE .T., like this:

```
DO WHILE .T.
        ? "CAT"
        ? "DOG"
ENDDO
```

The computer will print CAT and DOG repeatedly, like this:

```
CAT
DOG
CAT
DOG
CAT
DOG
etc.
```

To abort the program, tap the Esc key (which stands for "Escape") and then the C key (which stands for "Cancel").

Any program that says DO WHILE must also say ENDDO. The computer will repeat all the lines between DO WHILE and ENDDO, to form a loop.

This program makes the computer print all the numbers from 1 to 10 and then print "WOW":

```
SET TALK OFF
X=1
DO WHILE X<=10
        ? X
        X=X+1
ENDDO
? "WOW"
SET TALK ON
```

The top line prevents the computer from printing excessive messages. The next line says X starts at 1. The lines between DO WHILE and ENDDO are done repeatedly, as long as X<=10. If X gets past 10, the computer refuses to do the loop again, and instead proceeds to the line underneath ENDDO, which makes the computer say WOW. The bottom of the program says SET TALK ON, to put the computer back to normal. Altogether, the computer prints:

```
1
2
3
4
5
6
7
8
9
10
WOW
```

In BASIC, you can create loops by giving commands such as "GO TO 10" and "FOR I = 1 TO 10...NEXT". Unfortunately, DBASE doesn't understand how to GO TO line 10 or how to do a FOR...NEXT loop. In DBASE, the only way to create a loop is to say DO WHILE...ENDDO.

In the middle of a WHILE loop, you can put a line saying LOOP or EXIT. If the computer encounters a line saying LOOP, the computer loops back (by jumping back to the WHILE loop's top line). If the computer encounters a line saying EXIT, the computer exits from the loop (by jumping ahead to the line underneath ENDDO).

RETURN

Instead of using the BASIC word END, DBASE uses the word RETURN.

While the computer is DOing your program, if the computer encounters a line that says RETURN, the computer will skip the rest of the program.

The ULTIMATE program

Congratulations! Now you know enough about DBASE so that you're ready to create the ULTIMATE program. This program lets you store and retrieve *any* information about *any* topic! Moreover, the program is so nicely designed that even a novice who knows nothing about DBASE can run the program and use its full power.

How the program acts After you've written the program, you can start using it by just typing:

```
. DO ULTIMATE
```

Then the computer starts running the ULTIMATE program, which makes the computer ask:

```
What topic interests you? (If unsure, type a question mark. To end, type an x.)
```

If you type just an x or a capital X, the computer stops running the program and displays the dot prompt.

If you type a question mark instead, the computer displays a list of all the topics it was fed previously. For example, those topics might include SHRUB, BUSH, QUAIL, BIRDBRAIN, MANHATTAN, SEX, THE MEANING OF LIFE, and STRANGE JOKES. Then the computer says:

```
Pick one of those topics, or teach me a new one.

What topic interests you? (If unsure, type a question mark. To end, type an x.)
```

If you type anything other than an x or an X or a question mark, the computer searches through its file, to see whether it's been fed that topic. If it finds the topic in the file, it reveals all it knows about the topic, and then lets you edit that data. If it does *not* find the topic in the file, it says so, and gives you an opportunity to teach it about the topic.

How to invent the program To make the computer do all that, so a novice can store and retrieve data easily, a professional (such as yourself!) must previously put three things onto the disk: the program itself (which is called ULTIMATE.PRG), a data file (called INFO.DBF), and an index file (called INFOTOP.NDX). Here's how....

Data file Start by putting the data file INFO.DBF onto the disk. To do that, say:

```
. CREATE INFO
```

Then complete this chart:

Num	Field Name	Field Type	Width	Dec	Index
1	TOPIC	Character	25		N
2	DATA	Character	79		N

That allows each TOPIC to be 25 characters long, and the DATA about the topic to be 79 characters long.

After typing the chart, tap the END key while holding down the CONTROL key. Then tap the ENTER key. The computer will ask, "Input data records now?" Tap the N key.

Index file Next, put the index file INFOTOP.NDX onto the disk, by typing:

```
. INDEX ON TOPIC TO INFOTOP
```

That creates an index file called INFOTOP.NDX, which lets the computer find each TOPIC quickly.

The program itself Finally, put the program ULTIMATE.PRG onto the disk. To do that, begin by saying:

```
. MODIFY COMMAND ULTIMATE
```

Then type the program's introduction:

```
CLEAR ALL
CLEAR
SET TALK OFF
SET HEADING OFF
SET EXACT ON
SET DELETED ON
USE INFO INDEX INFOTOP
```

That introduction says to CLEAR ALL influences from previous programs, CLEAR the screen, SET the DBASE program so you have complete control over everything, and USE the INFO data file INDEXed by INFOTOP.

Then type the program's loop:

```
DO WHILE .T.
        ?
        ?"What topic interests you? "
        ?? "(If unsure, type a question mark. To end, type an x.)"
        ACCEPT TO DESIRE
        DESIRE=UPPER(DESIRE)
        CLEAR
        DO CASE
        CASE DESIRE="X"
                EXIT
        CASE DESIRE="?"
                GO TOP
                IF EOF()
                        ? "I don't know any topics yet. My mind is blank. "
                        ?? "Please teach me a new topic."
                ELSE
                        ? "I know about these topics:"
                        DISPLAY ALL OFF TOPIC
                        ? "Pick one of those topics, or teach me a new one."
                ENDIF
```

```
        CASE DESIRE=""
        OTHERWISE
                SEEK DESIRE
                IF FOUND()
                        ? "Here's what I know about",DESIRE+":"
                        @2,0 GET DATA
                        ? "You can edit that info now."
                        ? "(If you want me to forget about",DESIRE
                        ?? ", tap Y while holding down the CTRL key.)"
                        ? "When you're done, tap the ENTER key."
                        READ
                        CLEAR
                        IF DATA=""
                                DELETE
                        ENDIF
                ELSE
                        ? "I don't know anything about",DESIRE+"."
                        ? "Tell me about",DESIRE+"."
                        ? "(If you don't want to tell me, type an x.)"
                        ACCEPT TO NEWDATA
                        IF UPPER(NEWDATA)#"X"
                                APPEND BLANK
                                REPLACE TOPIC WITH DESIRE
                                REPLACE DATA WITH NEWDATA
                        ENDIF
                ENDIF
        ENDCASE
ENDDO
```

In that loop, each print statement uses small letters instead of capitals, so that the printing will look more sophisticated. (To create the small letters, just turn off the CAPS LOCK key, by tapping it.)

After saying ACCEPT TO DESIRE, the next statement says DESIRE=UPPER(DESIRE), which converts the user's desired topic to capital letters. That saves the user from worrying about whether to type REAGAN or Reagan or reagan: whichever of those the user types, the computer will convert it to REAGAN.

The DESIRE can be four kinds of things: it can be an X (which means the user wants to exit), a question mark (which means the user is confused and would like to see a list of topics), nothing at all (which means the user accidentally pressed the ENTER key an extra time), or a topic. The DO CASE statement tells the computer to handle those four cases: DESIRE="X", DESIRE="?", DESIRE="", and DESIRE=otherwise. Let's look at those four cases in more detail.

In the CASE where DESIRE="X", the computer lets the user EXIT from the DO WHILE loop.

In the CASE where DESIRE="?", the computer begins by checking whether the file contains any undeleted topics. Here's how. The lines GO TOP and IF EOF() tell the computer to GO to the TOP of the file and see if the TOP of the file is also the End Of the File. If the TOP of the file is also the End Of the File, the file doesn't contain any records yet (or all its records have been DELETED), so the computer will print "I don't know any topics yet. My mind is blank." If the computer's mind is *not* blank, the computer will say "I know about these topics" and will DISPLAY ALL of the TOPICS. The computer will display the topics themselves but will *not* display their record numbers, since the DISPLAY statement says to turn the record numbers OFF.

In the CASE where DESIRE="", the computer does nothing at all.

In the case where DESIRE is OTHERWISE, the computer will hunt through all the topics in the file, to SEEK the user's DESIRE.

If the user's DESIRE is FOUND in the file, the computer is commanded to print "Here's what I know about",DESIRE+":". In that command, the word DESIRE is followed by a plus sign instead of a comma, to prevent the computer from leaving a blank space after DESIRE.

If the user's DESIRE is *not* FOUND in the file, the computer is commanded to print "I don't know anything about",DESIRE+".". Then the computer asks the user to type some NEWDATA about the topic. If the user does indeed type some useful NEWDATA (instead of just an X), the computer appends the NEWDATA to the end of the file. To do that, the computer first APPENDs a BLANK record, then puts the NEWDATA into that record by using REPLACE.

The remaining lines say ENDIF twice (to end the two IF statements) and ENDCASE (to end the DO CASE statement) and ENDDO (to end the DO WHILE statement).

At the bottom of the program, add these lines:

```
SET DELETED OFF
COUNT FOR DELETED() TO DELCOUNT
IF DELCOUNT>RECCOUNT()/4
        ? "Please wait, "
        ?? "while I compress your data."
        PACK
        ? "The compression is done."
ENDIF
SET EXACT OFF
SET HEADING ON
SET TALK ON
CLEAR ALL
```

The computer reaches those lines when the user chooses to EXIT from the DO WHILE loop (by saying the DESIRE is "X"). Those lines say to SET the computer back to normal and to CLEAR ALL interference from later programs.

One of those lines says to PACK the file. But if fewer than a quarter of the records have been marked for deletion, the program tells the computer not to bother PACKing.

Here's how the computer figures out whether to bother PACKing. The program says to COUNT how many records have been marked to be DELETED, and call that the DELCOUNT. The program says that IF the DELCOUNT is greater than the RECord COUNT divided by 4, then PACK.

After you've typed that entire program, tap the END key while holding down the CONTROL key. Then you're done: you've created the ULTIMATE data-management program!

Consequences Some parts of that program were hard to invent, but the program is super-easy to use. Try it!

Then challenge yourself: think of further improvements to the ULTIMATE program, to make the program even easier to use and even more powerful!

Such programs would be much harder to develop, if we were using BASIC, LOGO, PASCAL, C, COBOL or any other major computer language. That's why programmers love DBASE!

Old versions DBASE 3 doesn't understand RECCOUNT(); instead of saying IF DELCOUNT>RECCOUNT()/4, say COUNT TO RECCOUNT and then IF DELCOUNT>RECCOUNT/4.

DBASE 3 doesn't understand the word FOUND. DBASE 3+ version 1.0 handles FOUND incorrectly if you deleted some records. For those versions of DBASE, instead of saying IF FOUND(), say IF .NOT. EOF().

LOGO

Turtle graphics

Like BASIC, **LOGO** is a computer language. LOGO is better than BASIC in three ways: by using LOGO, you can more easily create graphics, build "lists of lists", and design your own computer language (by adding your own words to LOGO). Let's see how!

I'll explain the best version of LOGO, then explain how other versions differ.

To start using LOGO, put the LOGO disk into the computer, then turn the computer on. The computer will say:

```
WELCOME TO LOGO
```

Differences Some versions of LOGO come on tapes or ROM cartridges instead of disks. Some versions use a mouse and require you to point at a LOGO icon.

Most versions of LOGO don't understand small letters; they understand just capitals. If your computer has a CAPS LOCK key, make sure it's pressed down.

To start Commodore LOGO, say:
```
LOAD "LOGO",8
RUN
```

To start the disk version of Radio Shack Color LOGO, say:
```
LOADM "LOGO"
EXEC
```

After Radio Shack Color LOGO says "LOGO:", tap the R key.

To use a version of LOGO called "LOGO Writer", use the student disk that your teacher created from the master disk, or use the TRY ME disk. Before using the TRY ME disk on an IBM PC; do the following: insert the PC-DOS disk, turn on the computer, type the date and time, insert the TRY ME disk, then type —
```
A>logowrit
```

When you start using LOGO Writer, the top of the screen will say CONTENTS. To continue beyond that point, press the ENTER key.

Show the turtle

To draw pictures, you move a turtle across the screen. To see the turtle, say **SHOWTURTLE**, like this:

```
SHOWTURTLE
```

SHOWTURTLE is all one word. Do *not* put a space between SHOW and TURTLE.

LOGO lets you abbreviate most words. The abbreviation for SHOWTURTLE is ST; so instead of typing SHOWTURTLE you can type just ST, like this:

```
ST
```

After you say SHOWTURTLE (or ST), you'll see a turtle in the center of your screen.

You can make the turtle either visible or invisible. To make it invisible, say **HIDETURTLE** (or HT). To make it visible again, say **SHOWTURTLE** (or ST) again.

Differences Many versions of LOGO put a question mark on the screen and expect you to type a command after the question mark. For example, to say SHOWTURTLE, type SHOWTURTLE after the question mark, so your screen looks like this:
`?SHOWTURTLE`

Atari 800 LOGO shows a good picture of a turtle (including the turtle's head, feet, tail, and shell), but most other versions of LOGO show just the turtle's nose, which looks like an arrowhead.

LOGO Writer and Atari 800 LOGO require you to abbreviate. For example, they require you to say ST instead of SHOWTURTLE.

Rotate the turtle

The screen acts as a map of the turtle's desert. Since the desert's only occupant is the turtle, the turtle's the only thing you see on the screen.

Like most maps, the screen's a rectangle whose top edge is called north, bottom edge is south, right edge is east, and left edge is west.

When you start using LOGO, the turtle's at the screen's center. The turtle faces north and stares at the screen's top edge.

As on a compass, north is called 0 degrees, east is 90 degrees, south is 180 degrees, and west is 270 degrees. To make the turtle face east, say **SETHEADING 90** (or SETH 90).

When typing that command, you must press the SPACE bar before you type the 90. That command makes the turtle rotate, so that it faces east.

The turtle can rotate to any angle you wish. For example, to make the turtle face northeast, say SETHEADING 45.

You can choose any angle from 0 to 360. You can even choose decimals and negative numbers. Experiment!

Rotate to the right
In LOGO, rotating clockwise is called "rotating to the right". To make the turtle rotate to the right, 90 degrees, say **RIGHT 90** (or RT 90).

For example, if the turtle is facing north, and you say RIGHT 90, the turtle will face east. Then if you say RIGHT 90 again, the turtle will turn clockwise 90 degrees more, so that the turtle will face south. If you say RIGHT 90 again, the turtle will face west. If you say RIGHT 90 again, the turtle will face north again.

Rotate to the left
Rotating counterclockwise is called "rotating to the left". To make the turtle rotate to the left, 90 degrees, say **LEFT 90** (or LT 90).

Differences The computer's RAM accurately handles decimals (such as 4.1 degrees), but the screen shows just an approximation of what's in the RAM. For most versions of LOGO, the screen shows the turtle's angle rounded to the nearest 15 degrees; Radio Shack Color LOGO shows the angle rounded to the nearest 45 degrees.

Move the turtle

To make the turtle walk 50 steps in the direction it faces, say **FORWARD 50** (or FD 50).

For example, if the turtle faces east, and you say FORWARD 50, the turtle will walk 50 steps east. If you then say FORWARD 50 again, the turtle will walk 50 steps farther east.

To make the turtle retreat 50 steps *backwards*, say **BACK 50** (or BK 50). For example, if the turtle faces east and you say BACK 50, the turtle will retreat 50 steps backwards: the turtle will retreat to the west while still facing east.

The point at the screen's center is called **home**. That's where the turtle's life began. To make the turtle return to its home and its original heading (facing north), say **HOME**.

Set the position
To make the turtle hop to the point whose coordinates are [30 70], say **SETPOS [30 70]**.

That makes the turtle hop to the point that's 30 steps east and 70 steps north of home. The turtle hops there regardless of where the turtle was before.

Hopping does *not* change the direction the turtle faces. For example, if the turtle faced south before hopping, the turtle still faces south after the hop, even if it's hopped north of where it started.

Instead of saying SETPOS [30 70], you can say **SETX 30** and then **SETY 70**, like this:

```
SETX 30
SETY 70
```

The SETX 30 makes the turtle hop across the screen horizontally east-west, until it reaches a point that's 30 steps further east than home was. The SETY 70 makes the turtle hop vertically north-south, until it reaches a point that's 70 steps further north than home was.

The screen's edge When you try to move the turtle past the screen's edge, what happens? The answer depends on which kind of universe you create. You have three choices.

If you say **FENCE**, the computer erects a fence around the desert, so that the turtle can't move past the screen's edge. If you give the turtle a command that requires the turtle to go past the fence, the turtle gripes, refuses to do the command at all, and doesn't even walk up to the fence.

If you say **WINDOW** instead of FENCE, the computer lets the turtle wander off the screen, to locations you can't see. Your screen acts as a window, through which you see just part of the turtle's universe.

If you say **WRAP** (instead of WINDOW or FENCE), moving the turtle past the screen's edge makes the turtle take a quick trip around the world. For example, if the turtle travels west, past the screen's west edge, the turtle quickly travels around the world and returns from the east. If the turtle travels north, past the screen's top edge, the turtle quickly travels around the world (past the north and south poles) and returns from the south.

When you start using LOGO, you automatically begin with a WRAPped universe, but you can switch to a FENCE or WINDOW.

Leisure-time jog When the turtle isn't busy obeying your commands, how does it spend its leisure time? Normally, the turtle just sits still. But if you say **SETSP 30**, the turtle will spend all its leisure time jogging at speed 30, in whatever direction the turtle is facing.

For example, suppose the turtle is facing north, and you say SETSP 30. The turtle will jog north, at speed 30. The turtle will keep jogging north, until you give it another command. If you don't give another command soon, it will reach the edge of the screen, and its further fate depends on whether you said FENCE or WINDOW or WRAP.

While the turtle jogs, if you tell it to change direction (by saying SETHEADING or RIGHT or LEFT), it will continue jogging but in the new direction.

While the turtle jogs, if you tell it to walk (by saying FORWARD, BACK, SETPOS, SETX, or SETY), the turtle will walk where you said and then continue jogging from that new location.

To stop the jogging, say SETSP 0 (which sets the jogging speed to 0) or HOME (which makes the turtle go home and rest there).

> **Differences** Atari 800 LOGO understands SETSP, but most other versions of LOGO don't. Some versions of LOGO don't understand FENCE. LOGO Writer lacks SETSP, FENCE, WINDOW, WRAP, SETX, and SETY.
>
> For MIT versions of LOGO (such as Krell LOGO, Terrapin Apple LOGO, and Commodore LOGO), change FENCE to NOWRAP, don't say WINDOW, and change SETPOS [30 70] to SETXY 30 70; if the second number in the SETXY command is negative, put that number in parentheses. Radio Shack Color LOGO resembles MIT versions but lacks some commands, such as SETXY.

Change the pen

The turtle's belly has a ball-point pen sticking out of it. While the turtle moves, the pen scrapes along the ground and draws a line on the ground. That line's called the turtle's **trail**. It appears on your screen, since your screen's a map of what's on the ground. Even if you make the turtle invisible (by saying HIDETURTLE), you'll still see the turtle's trail.

If you say **PENUP** (or PU), the turtle lifts its pen from the ground, so that the pen stops drawing a trail. To put the pen back down on the ground again, say **PENDOWN** (or PD).

Create colors You can change the pen's ink to a different color. To switch to color #2, say **SETPC 2**. That makes the computer set the pencolor to 2.

Erase You can replace the pen by an eraser. To do that, say **PENERASE** (or PE). Then as the turtle moves, it erases any ink on the ground. For example, if you turn the turtle around and make it walk back along the trail it created, it will erase the trail.

The eraser scrapes across the ground until you lift it (by saying PENUP) or insert a pen instead (by saying PENDOWN).

Reverse colors You can replace the pen by a reverser. To do that, say **PENREVERSE** (or PX). When you draw with the reverser on black ground, the ground becomes white, when you draw on white ground, the ground becomes black; when you draw on colored ground, the ground changes to the opposite color.

The reverser works until you lift it (by saying PENUP) or switch to a pen or eraser (by saying PENDOWN or PENERASE).

Fill in the middle After you draw a polygon (such as a triangle, rectangle, or octagon), you can fill in the middle. To do so, lift the pen (by saying PENUP), then move the turtle to somewhere in the middle of the polygon, then say PENDOWN, then say **FILL**. The FILL command makes the pen leak, until the ink fills the entire polygon.

> **Differences** Instead of saying SETPC, LOGO Writer and Atari 800 LOGO say SETC; MIT versions say PC.
>
> Instead of PENERASE, Commodore LOGO says PC -1; Krell and Terrapin Apple LOGO say PC 0; Radio Shack Color LOGO says PC 3.
>
> Instead of PENREVERSE, Krell and Terrapin Apple LOGO say PC 6. Commodore LOGO and Radio Shack Color LOGO lack the concept.
>
> Apple's colors are numbered from 0 to 5, IBM's and the Color Computer's from 0 to 3, Commodore's and the Atari ST's from 0 to 15, and the Atari 800's from 0 to 127.
>
> LOGO Writer, IBM LOGO, DR LOGO, and Atari ST LOGO understand FILL, but most other versions don't.

Change background

The desert sand is called the turtle's **background**. The sand appears a different color if you shine colored light at it. To make the sand appear to have color #1, say **SETBG 1**. That makes the computer set the background color to 1.

If you say **CLEAN**, a gust of wind blows all the sand around, so that the sand covers all the trails that the turtle made, and the screen is clean again: all that remains on the screen is the turtle itself.

To erase everything you did and "start over", you could say HOME (which makes the turtle return home and face north) and CLEAN (which erases the turtle's trails). But instead of saying HOME and then CLEAN, you can combine those two commands into this single command: **CLEARSCREEN** (or CS).

If you say **DOT [20 50]**, a drop of ink will fall from the sky and land on the point whose coordinates are [20 50], so that you see a dot of ink at that point.

> **Differences** For LOGO Writer, change CLEARSCREEN to CG (which means "Clear the Graphics"); to clear the graphics and the rest of the screen and make everything "fresh", say CT RG (which means "Clear the Text and Reset the Graphics"). For MIT versions of LOGO, change CLEARSCREEN to DRAW, change CLEAN to CLEARSCREEN, and change SETBG to BG. LOGO Writer, MIT versions, and Atari 800 LOGO don't understand DOT.

Extra turtles

You can create several turtles, called turtle 0, turtle 1, turtle 2, turtle 3, etc. Normally, your commands are obeyed by just turtle 0.

To talk to turtle 1 instead, say **TELL 1**. That makes turtle 1 appear on the screen, and all your future commands will be obeyed by turtle 1 instead of turtle 0.

While turtle 1 obeys your commands and prances around, turtle 0 will sit quietly (unless you told it to jog, by saying SETSP 30).

To start talking to turtle 0 again, say TELL 0. To talk to turtle 2, say TELL 2. To talk to turtle 3, say TELL 3.

If you say TELL [0 1 2 3], you'll be talking to turtles 0, 1, 2, and 3 simultaneously. Any commands you give will be obeyed by all those turtles.

Differences LOGO Writer, Commodore LOGO, and Atari 800 LOGO understand TELL, but most other versions of LOGO don't. LOGO Writer and Commodore LOGO hide turtles 1, 2, and 3, until you make them appear by typing ST.

In Commodore LOGO, TELL must be followed by a single number, not a list of numbers; and before saying TELL, you must feed the computer TELL's definition, by putting the Utilities Disk in the drive and typing:
```
READ "SPRITES
```
Put the quotation mark before SPRITES but not afterwards.

Graphics versus text

Usually, the top of the screen shows the map of the turtle's desert, and the bottom of the screen shows the commands you've been typing. For example, if you say SHOWTURTLE, the top of the screen shows the turtle, and the bottom of the screen shows what you typed: the word SHOWTURTLE.

If you want to devote the *entire* screen to the map, say **FULLSCREEN** (or FS). Then the map fills the entire screen, so that you see a larger portion of the desert. Since the entire screen shows the map instead of your typing, what you type will be invisible, until you return to the normal setup (by typing **MIXEDSCREEN** or MS) or devote the entire screen to your typing instead of a map (by saying **TEXTSCREEN** or TS).

Differences For MIT versions, change MIXEDSCREEN to SPLITSCREEN, and don't use the abbreviations FS, MS, and TS. LOGO Writer always gives you a mixed screen and won't let you change to fullscreen or textscreen.

Math

To make the computer print the answer to 5+2, say **PRINT 5+2** (or PR 5+2). The computer will print the answer:
```
7
```
Like BASIC, LOGO lets you use arithmetic symbols (+, -, *, and /), negative numbers, decimals, E notation, and parentheses.

Differences For Apple LOGO 2, put a blank space before and after the symbol /. LOGO Writer puts its answers at the top of the screen and lacks E notation.

Square roots

SQRT 9 means "the square root of 9". So to print the square root of 9, type this:
```
PR SQRT 9
```
The computer will print the answer:
```
3
```
If you say —
```
PR SQRT 9+7
```
the computer will print the square root of 16, which is 4. If you leave extra spaces, like this —
```
PR SQRT 9 + 7
```
the computer will ignore the extra spaces: it will still print the square root of 16, which is 4. If you say —
```
PR (SQRT 9)+7
```
the computer will find the square root of 9, which is 3, and then add 7, so it will print 10.

Differences LOGO Writer lacks SQRT.

Turtle numbers

To find out where the turtle is, say PR XCOR (which prints the X coordinate) and PR YCOR (which prints the Y coordinate).

To slide the turtle 20 steps farther east, say SETX XCOR+20. That says to increase the X coordinate by 20.

To slide the turtle 20 steps farther west instead, say SETX XCOR-20. To slide the turtle 20 steps north, say SETY YCOR+20. To slide the turtle 20 steps south, say SETY YCOR-20.

If you say PR HEADING, the computer will tell you which direction the turtle's facing. For example, if the turtle's facing east, the computer will print 90. The HEADING will always be a number between 0 and 360.

If you say PR TOWARDS [30 70], the computer will tell you which direction to turn the turtle, to make the turtle face the point [30 70]. The direction will be a number between 0 and 360. To actually turn the turtle in that direction, so that the turtle faces the point [30 70], say SETHEADING TOWARDS [30 70]. So to make the turtle "walk 10 steps towards the point [30 70]", say this:
```
SETHEADING TOWARDS [30 70]
FORWARD 10
```
To find out the color of the ink in the turtle's pen, say PR PENCOLOR (or PR PC); the computer will print the color's number. To find out the color of the background sand, say PR BACKGROUND (or PR BG).

To find out which turtle you're talking to, say PR WHO. The computer will print the turtle's number.

Differences For MIT versions, change PENCOLOR to LAST TS, change BACKGROUND to ITEM 3 TS, and omit the brackets after TOWARDS. For LOGO Writer, change PENCOLOR to COLOR, change XCOR to FIRST POS, change YCOR to LAST POS, and don't say TOWARDS.

Random numbers

If you say PR RANDOM 5, the computer randomly chooses one of these 5 integers: 0, 1, 2, 3, 4. The computer prints the integer it chooses.

Rounding

If you say PR INT 3.9, the computer will convert 3.9 to an INTeger by omitting everything after the decimal point. The computer will print just 3.

If you say PR ROUND 3.9, the computer will ROUND 3.9 to the nearest integer, which is 4. The computer will print 4.

Differences For MIT versions, change INT to INTEGER. LOGO Writer lacks INT and ROUND.

Fancy division

If you say PR 11/4, the computer will divide 11 by 4 and print the answer, which is 2.75.

If you say PR QUOTIENT 11 4, the computer will divide 11 by 4 but ignore what comes after the decimal point. The computer will print just 2.

If you say PR REMAINDER 11 4, the computer will divide 11 by 4, and realize that 4 goes into 11 "2 times, with a remainder of 3". The computer will print the remainder, 3.

Differences LOGO Writer lacks QUOTIENT.

Trigonometry

To print the sine of 30 degrees, say PR SIN 30. To print the cosine of 30 degrees, say PR COS 30.

Since the tangent is "the sine divided by the cosine", you can print the tangent of 30 degrees by saying PR (SIN 30)/COS 30.

The opposite of tangent is arctangent. To print the arctangent of .58, say PR ARCTAN .58. That makes the computer print how many degrees are in the angle whose tangent is .58.

Differences LOGO Writer and Atari 800 LOGO lack ARCTAN. For MIT versions, change ARCTAN .58 to ARCTAN .58 1.

Structures

To make the computer print the word LOVE, type this:

```
PR "LOVE
```

In LOGO, a quotation mark means: the word. So that whole line means: PRint the word LOVE.

Make sure you put the quotation mark before LOVE, but do not put a quotation mark afterwards! That line is pronounced: P R quotes LOVE.

When you press the ENTER key at the end of that line, the computer will print:

```
LOVE
```

Lists

To print a list of words, put the list in brackets, like this:

```
PR [MA CAN'T LOOK]
```

That tells the computer to print a list of three words. The first word is MA; the second is CAN'T; the third is LOOK.

The computer will print the list but won't bother to print the brackets. The computer will print just:

MA CAN'T LOOK

If you say **SHOW** instead of PR, the computer will print the brackets also, like this:

[MA CAN'T LOOK]

The computer understands FIRST, LAST, and similar concepts:

Function	Meaning	Result
FIRST [MA CAN'T LOOK]	the list's first item	MA
LAST [MA CAN'T LOOK]	the list's last item	LOOK
ITEM 2 [MA CAN'T LOOK]	the list's 2nd item	CAN'T
COUNT [MA CAN'T LOOK]	how many items	3
BUTFIRST [MA CAN'T LOOK]	all but the first item	[CAN'T LOOK]
BUTLAST [MA CAN'T LOOK]	all but the last item	[MA CAN'T]
FPUT "WOW [MA CAN'T LOOK]	put WOW first	[WOW MA CAN'T LOOK]
LPUT "WOW [MA CAN'T LOOK]	put WOW last	[MA CAN'T LOOK WOW]
WORD "WOW "MA	combine words into long word	WOWMA
LIST "MA "CAN'T	combine words to form a list	[MA CAN'T]
SENTENCE [WOW MA] [CAN'T LOOK]	combine lists	[WOW MA CAN'T LOOK]

When you type those examples, begin each line by saying PR or SHOW. For example, if you say —

```
SHOW BUTFIRST [MA CAN'T LOOK]
```

the computer will say:

```
[CAN'T LOOK]
```

You can abbreviate BUTFIRST to BF, BUTLAST to BL, and SENTENCE to SE.

A word's a list of characters. For example, the word FUN is a list of three characters (F, U, and N). So all the list concepts (such as FIRST, LAST, ITEM, and COUNT) apply to words also. For example, if you say —

```
SHOW BUTFIRST "FUN
```

or —

```
PR BUTFIRST "FUN
```

the computer will say:

```
UN
```

Since FIRST [MA CAN'T LOOK] is MA, whose last character is A, the computer knows that LAST FIRST [MA CAN'T LOOK] is A.

You can put lists inside lists. For example, since FIRST [[MA PA] CAN'T LOOK] is [MA PA], whose last item is PA, the computer knows that LAST FIRST [[MA PA] CAN'T LOOK] is PA.

Differences MIT versions don't understand SHOW. For Commodore LOGO, change SHOW to FPRINT.

Atari 800 LOGO doesn't understand ITEM. Version 1 of Terrapin Apple LOGO didn't understand ITEM and COUNT. Version 1 of Apple LOGO could find an ITEM within a list of words but not within a single word.

Multiple commands

You can put several LOGO commands on the same line. For example, you can say:

```
FD 50 RT 90
```

When you press the ENTER key at the end of that line, the turtle will go forward 50 and then turn right 90 degrees.

If you say —

```
PR 5+2 PR 30+9.1
```

the computer will print the answers on separate lines:

```
7
39.1
```

If you say —

```
PR [SKY IS BLUE] PR [SO ARE YOU]
```

the computer will print this poem:

```
SKY IS BLUE
SO ARE YOU
```

REPEAT

Let's make the turtle draw a square, so that each side is 50 steps long.

To do that, first make sure the turtle's pen is down, so that the turtle will draw as it moves. To make sure the pen's down, you can say PENDOWN (or PD).

To make the turtle draw the first side, say FORWARD 50 (or FD 50). Then tell the turtle to turn right 90 degrees, by saying RIGHT 90 or RT 90. Draw the second side, by saying FD 50 again. Then tell the turtle to turn right 90 degrees again, etc.

Altogether, these commands make the turtle draw all four sides of the square:

```
FD 50 RT 90 FD 50 RT 90 FD 50 RT 90 FD 50 RT 90
```

But instead of typing all that, you can type this short cut:

```
REPEAT 4 [FD 50 RT 90]
```

That makes the computer **REPEAT**, 4 times, the act of going forward 50 and turning right 90 degrees.

Let's make the computer print the word WOW, twenty times. Here's how:

```
REPEAT 20 [PR "WOW]
```

The computer will print the words on separate lines, like this:

```
WOW
WOW
WOW
etc.
```

Here's how to make the computer say FRANCE IS FUNNY, twenty times:

```
REPEAT 20 [PR [FRANCE IS FUNNY]]
```

Variables

You can **MAKE** a word stand for something. To make the word DRINKINGAGE stand for 21, type this:

```
MAKE "DRINKINGAGE 21
```

In that line, DRINKINGAGE is called the **variable** or the **name**; 21 is called **DRINKINGAGE's value** or **the thing that DRINKINGAGE stands for**.

After you type that line, you can say:

```
PR THING "DRINKINGAGE
```

That makes the computer print the THING that DRINKINGAGE stands for. The computer will print:

```
21
```

Instead of typing THING and then a quotation mark, you can type just a colon, like this:

```
PR :DRINKINGAGE
```

That means: PRint the thing that DRINKINGAGE stands for. It means: PRINT the value of DRINKINGAGE. The computer will print:

```
21
```

LOGO programmers have a nickname for the colon: they call it dots. So the statement —

```
PR :DRINKINGAGE
```

is pronounced: P R dots DRINKINGAGE.

Here's another example:

```
MAKE "MAGICNUMBER 7
PR :MAGICNUMBER+2
```

The first line makes the word MAGICNUMBER stand for 7. The next line says to print the value of the MAGICNUMBER, plus 2. The computer will print 9.

A word can stand for anything; it can even stand for a list. For example, you can say:

```
MAKE "STOOGES [MOE LARRY CURLEY]
PR COUNT :STOOGES
```

The first line says the word STOOGES stands for the list [MOE LARRY CURLEY]. The next line makes the computer print the COUNT of how many items are in that list; the computer will print:

```
3
```

Here's the rule: to *define* a word, say MAKE and type a quotation mark; to *use* the word's value, type a colon instead.

Programs

To teach the computer what the word SQUARE means, type this:

```
TO SQUARE
REPEAT 4 [FD 50 RT 90]
END
```

The first line means: here's how **TO** do a SQUARE. The next line gives the definition itself: repeat 4 times the act of going forward 50 steps and turning right 90 degrees. The bottom line of every definition says **END**.

Those three lines form the **definition** of SQUARE. They're also called the **program** for square, and the **procedure** for how to do a SQUARE.

After you type those three lines, the computer will know the meaning of SQUARE. So in the future, whenever you say —

```
SQUARE
```

the turtle will draw a square.

Differences Before you type the word TO, LOGO Writer requires you to tap the F key while holding down the CONTROL key (on the IBM) or Open Apple key (on the Apple); Radio Shack Color LOGO requires you to tap the BREAK key, then tap the CLEAR key while holding down the SHIFT key, then tap the E key.

Many versions of LOGO automatically put the symbol ">" at the beginning of each line of the definition.

After you type the word END, some versions of LOGO require you to tap an extra key or two: for LOGO Writer, tap the F key while holding down the CONTROL key (IBM) or Open Apple key (Apple); for Commodore LOGO, tap the RUN STOP key; for Krell and Terrapin Apple LOGO, tap the C key while holding down the CONTROL key; for Radio Shack Color LOGO, tap the BREAK key then the R key.

Pinwheel

If you draw a square, then rotate 10 degrees, then draw another square, you get this:

Suppose you continue that process: draw a square, then rotate 10 degrees, then draw another square, then rotate 10 degrees again, then draw another square, then rotate 10 degrees again, etc. You'll get this pinwheel:

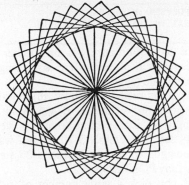

Let's define PINWHEEL to be that shape. Here's how:

```
TO PINWHEEL
REPEAT 36 [SQUARE RT 10]
END
```

Rebuke

Let's define REBUKE to be this message:

```
YOU LOOK TERRIF!
YOU DRESS SO SPIFF!
YOU ACT SO COOL!
YOU MAKE ME DROOL!

BUT YOU'RE A FOOL!
YOU'RE FAILING SCHOOL!
YOU'RE REALLY DUMB!
A FIRST - CLASS BUM!

SO GET YOUR MIND
OFF ITS BEHIND,
AND YOU WILL FIND
YOU'RE ONE - OF - A - KIND!
```

Here's how:

```
TO REBUKE
PR [YOU LOOK TERRIF!]
PR [YOU DRESS SO SPIFF!]
PR [YOU ACT SO COOL!]
PR [YOU MAKE ME DROOL!]
PR []
PR [BUT YOU'RE A FOOL!]
PR [YOU'RE FAILING SCHOOL!]
PR [YOU'RE REALLY DUMB!]
PR [A FIRST - CLASS BUM!]
PR []
PR [SO GET YOUR MIND]
PR [OFF ITS BEHIND,]
PR [AND YOU WILL FIND]
PR [YOU'RE ONE - OF - A - KIND!]
END
```

Then whenever you say —

```
REBUKE
```

the computer will print the poem. (To see the whole poem on the screen at once, say TEXTSCREEN before saying REBUKE.)

To have fun, say that poem out loud in a jive rap style, and clap your hands twice at the end of each line.

EDIT

After you've defined a word (such as REBUKE), you can **EDIT** that definition by saying —

```
EDIT "REBUKE
```

The computer will put your definition on the screen and let you edit that definition, by using the arrow keys and the other edit keys. When you've finished editing the definition, tap the ESCAPE key.

If you say EDIT [REBUKE PINWHEEL], the computer will put both definitions on the screen simultaneously and let you edit them both. When you've finished editing them, tap the ESCAPE key.

If you say just EDIT, the screen will show what you edited last time, so you can edit it again.

The abbreviation for EDIT is ED.

Differences While editing, experiment! Try tapping the arrow keys, ENTER key, RETURN key, BACKSPACE key, DELETE key, INSERT key, CONTROL key, and any other edit keys on your keyboard. When using LOGO, those keys act the same as when using most word processors.

On old Apples that lack up-arrow, down-arrow, and DELETE keys, do this: to move up to the Previous line, tap the P key while holding down the CONTROL key; to delete the Next line, tap the N key while holding down the CONTROL key; to delete the character left of the cursor, tap the ESCAPE key; if you have Apple LOGO 1 and want to move Back to the left, tap the B key while holding down the CONTROL key.

For MIT versions, omit the quotation mark after EDIT.

Instead of tapping the ESCAPE key, do the following: for MIT versions and Apple LOGO 1, tap the C key while holding down the CONTROL key; for Apple LOGO 2, tap the A key while holding down the open-Apple key.

For LOGO Writer and Radio Shack Color LOGO, instead of saying EDIT, follow the procedure for saying TO.

Flexible definitions

Let's change the definition of SQUARE, to make it more flexible. Let's define SQUARE so that SQUARE 50 will be a square that's 50 steps long on each side, and SQUARE 100 will be a square that's 100 steps long on each side, and SQUARE 6 will be a square that's 6 steps long on each side, etc.

To do all that, edit the definition of SQUARE by saying:

```
EDIT "SQUARE
```

The computer will show our old definition of SQUARE:

```
TO SQUARE
REPEAT 4 [FD 50 RT 90]
END
```

Using the arrow keys, insert :SIDE after SQUARE, and change the 50 to :SIDE, so that the definition looks like this:

```
TO SQUARE
REPEAT 4 [FD :SIDE RT 90]
END
```

When you've finished the editing, press the ESCAPE key.

Then if you say —

```
SQUARE 100
```

the computer will look at the new definition of SQUARE, realize that :SIDE is 100, and do REPEAT 4 [FD 100 RT 90], which draws a square having 100 steps on each side.

After changing the definition of SQUARE in that way, you must always put a number after the word SQUARE. If you say SQUARE 100, the computer will draw a square whose side is 100; if you say SQUARE 6, the computer will draw a square whose side is 6; but if you say just SQUARE, the computer won't know how long to make the side and will gripe, by saying NOT ENOUGH INPUTS TO SQUARE.

After changing the definition of SQUARE, you must update the definition of PINWHEEL, so that it uses the new definition of SQUARE. Edit PINWHEEL so that it becomes:

```
TO PINWHEEL :SIDE
REPEAT 36 [SQUARE :SIDE RT 10]
END
```

Then if you say PINWHEEL 50, the computer will draw a normal pinwheel; if you say PINWHEEL 100, the computer will draw a pinwheel that's twice as long in each direction; if you say PINWHEEL 30, the computer will draw a pinwheel that's small.

Polygon

Let's define POLYGON so that POLYGON 5 40 will be a regular polygon having 5 sides, and each side will be 40 steps long.

Here's how:

```
TO POLYGON :N :SIDE
REPEAT :N [FD :SIDE RT 360/:N]
END
```

In that definition, :N is the number of sides (such as 5), and :SIDE is the length of each side (such as 40).

That definition will draw *any* regular polygon. For example, if you want a triangle so that each side is 60 steps long, say POLYGON 3 70. If you want an octagon so that each side is 20 steps long, say POLYGON 8 20.

If you pick a large number of sides (such as 36), the polygon will look almost like a circle. That's how you can make LOGO imitate a circle!

Star

Let's define STAR so that STAR 5 40 will be a 5-pointed star, and each side will be 40 steps long.

The definition is almost the same as POLYGON's:

```
TO STAR :N :SIDE
REPEAT :N [FD :SIDE RT 360/:N FD :SIDE
LT 720/:N]
END
```

That definition makes the turtle start drawing a polygon, by drawing a polygon's first side (FD :SIDE), then turning right by the polygon's angle (RT 360/:N), then drawing the polygon's second side (FD :SIDE). But then the turtle veers sharply to the left (LT 720/:N). Repeating that procedure :N times produces a star:

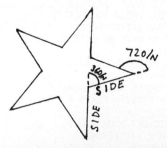

Choose as many points as you wish. For a 5-pointed star, say STAR 5 40. For a 6-pointed star (a "Jewish star"), say STAR 6 40. For an 8-pointed star that's smaller and has just 20 steps per side, say STAR 8 20.

Recursion

Here's a poem about LOGO lovers:

```
LOGO LOVERS LOOK LOVELY!
LINGERING LINES, LONGINGLY LEFT!
```

Let's program the computer so that when you say LOVERS, the computer will print that poem again and again, forever, like this:

```
LOGO LOVERS LOOK LOVELY!
LINGERING LINES, LONGINGLY LEFT!

LOGO LOVERS LOOK LOVELY!
LINGERING LINES, LONGINGLY LEFT!

LOGO LOVERS LOOK LOVELY!
LINGERING LINES, LONGINGLY LEFT!

etc.
```

Type this:

```
TO LOVERS
PR [LOGO LOVERS LOOK LOVELY!]
PR [LINGERING LINES, LONGINGLY LEFT!]
PR []
LOVERS
END
```

The three PR statements make the computer print the poem and a blank line underneath. The bottom line says END; but above the word END, I inserted the word LOVERS, which makes the computer do LOVERS again, so the computer again prints the poem and blank line and comes to the LOVERS line again, so the computer *again* prints the poem and blank line and comes to the LOVERS line again, etc. The program's an infinite loop.

After you type that definition of LOVERS, you can activate it by saying just LOVERS or — better yet — say TEXTSCREEN and then LOVERS.

To abort the program, press the BREAK key.

Notice I inserted the word LOVERS into the definition of LOVERS, so that LOVERS is defined in terms of itself. That's called a **self-referent** definition or **circular** definition or **recursive** definition. Using recursive definitions is called **recursion**. In LOGO, recursion's the usual way to create loops.

> **Differences** Atari 800 LOGO and Radio Shack Color LOGO let you abort by tapping the BREAK key, but most other versions of LOGO abort differently. For IBM LOGO, tap the BREAK key while holding down the CONTROL key. For LOGO Writer, tap the ESCAPE key. For Apple LOGO 2, tap the ESCAPE key while holding down the Open Apple key. For Apple LOGO 1, Atari ST LOGO, DR LOGO, and MIT versions, tap the G key while holding down the CONTROL key.

Countdown

Let's program the computer so that COUNTDOWN 10 will make the computer count down from 10, like this:

```
10
9
8
7
etc.
```

Here's the definition:

```
TO COUNTDOWN :N
PR :N
COUNTDOWN :N-1
END
```

To count down from a number N, that definition tells the computer to print the number N and then count down from N-1.

Unfortunately, that definition's an infinite loop! For example, if you say COUNTDOWN 10, that definition will make the computer print 10, 9, 8, 7, 6, 5, 4, 3, 2, 1, 0, -1, -2, -3, -4, etc., forever!

Let's edit that definition, to **STOP** the computer from printing negative numbers. Say:

```
EDIT "COUNTDOWN
```

Then use the arrow keys, to change the definition of COUNTDOWN to this:

```
TO COUNTDOWN :N
IF :N<0 [STOP]
PR :N
COUNTDOWN :N-1
END
```

Differences For MIT versions, omit the brackets around STOP.

Squiral

Let's make the computer draw the first side of a square (by saying FD :SIDE), then turn right 90 degrees (by saying RT 90), then draw the second side — but make the second side shorter than the first! Then make the third side even shorter! Then make the fourth side even shorter!

The result will be a "shrinking square" whose fourth side doesn't meet the first side. It looks something like a square, but it spirals inward, becoming smaller. It's called a **squiral**.

To create an amazing squiral, feed the computer this definition:

```
TO SQUIRAL :SIDE
FD :SIDE
RT 90
SQUIRAL :SIDE-3
END
```

That program's an infinite loop. The side becomes smaller and smaller (decreasing by 3 each time), until finally the side becomes a negative number, which makes the turtle go wild and draw fascinating weird graphics on the screen.

Feed the computer that definition. Then for the most dramatic results, feed the computer this definition —

```
TO DRAMATICSQUIRAL
WRAP
PENREVERSE
FULLSCREEN
SQUIRAL 100
END
```

and type:

```
DRAMATICSQUIRAL
```

When you invent a definition, the computer puts it into a part of the RAM called the **workspace**. The workspace holds your definitions of names (such as MAKE "DRINKINGAGE 21) and your definitions of procedures (such as TO SQUARE do REPEAT 4 [FD 50 RT 90] then END).

Printouts

To see *all* those definitions on your screen, say TEXTSCREEN, so that the computer can use the entire screen for text; then say **POALL**, which means Print Out ALL. The computer will print out all the definitions. For example, if you defined the name DRINKINGAGE and then MAGICNUMBER, and then defined the procedure SQUARE :SIDE and then PINWHEEL :SIDE, the computer will print all those definitions, like this:

```
TO PINWHEEL :SIDE
REPEAT 36 [SQUARE :SIDE RT 10]
SQUARE
END

TO SQUARE :SIDE
REPEAT 4 [FD :SIDE RT 90]
END

MAKE "MAGICNUMBER 7
MAKE "DRINKINGAGE 21
```

The computer begins with the newest procedure (PINWHEEL), then any other procedures (such as SQUARE), then the newest name (MAGICNUMBER), then any other names (such as DRINKINGAGE).

If you don't want to see all that, you can ask for an abridgment. To see definitions of just the procedures (PINWHEEL and SQUARE), say **POPS**, which means Print Out ProcedureS. To see definitions of just the names (MAGICNUMBER and DRINKINGAGE), say **PONS**, which means Print Out NameS.

To see just the top line of each procedure, say **POTS**, which means Print out TopS or Print Out TitleS; the computer will print:

```
TO PINWHEEL :SIDE
TO SQUARE :SIDE
```

To see the definition of just the SQUARE procedure, say **PO "SQUARE**. That makes the computer print the definition of SQUARE :SIDE. To see that definition first, then the definition of PINWHEEL, say PO [SQUARE PINWHEEL].

Differences LOGO Writer doesn't understand any of those commands; instead, tap the F key

while holding down the CONTROL or Open Apple key, then browse through all the procedures you created, by pressing the up-arrow and down-arrow keys.

For MIT versions, change POALL to PO ALL, change POPS to PO PROCEDURES, change PONS to PO NAMES, change POTS to PO TITLES, and change PO "SQUARE to PO SQUARE.

Erase the definitions

If you no longer need the definitions you invented, you can erase them.

To ERase ALL the definitions, say **ERALL**. To ERase just the definitions of ProcedureS (such as PINWHEEL and SQUARE), say **ERPS**. To ERase just the definitions of NameS (such as MAGICNUMBER and DRINKINGAGE), say **ERNS**.

To **ERASE** just the definition of the PINWHEEL procedure, say:

```
ERASE "PINWHEEL
```

The abbreviation for ERASE is ER.

To ERase just the definition of the Name MAGICNUMBER, say **ERN "MAGICNUMBER**.

Differences LOGO Writer doesn't understand any of those commands; instead, get onto the screen the procedures you want to erase, then erase them by holding down the DELETE or BACKSPACE key.

For MIT versions, change ERALL to ER ALL, change ERPS to ER PROCEDURES, change ERNS to ER NAMES, change ERASE "PINWHEEL to ERASE PINWHEEL, and change ERN to ERNAME.

Save to disk

After you've *formatted* a blank disk (by using DOS or BASIC or some other method), you can put that disk into the drive and copy all your definitions onto the disk. Here's how.

Invent a filename (such as FRED) and say **SAVE "FRED**. On the disk, the computer will create a new file called FRED and copy all your definitions to FRED.

Later, whenever you want to use FRED, just say **LOAD "FRED**. The computer will go to the disk, find FRED, and copy FRED's definitions to the RAM, so you can use them.

To see a list of all the LOGO files on your disk, say **CATALOG**.

To delete FRED from the disk, say **ERASEFILE "FRED**.

Differences For MIT versions, change LOAD to READ. For IBM LOGO, DR LOGO, and Atari ST LOGO, change CATALOG to DIR. For LOGO Writer, change ERASEFILE to ERPAGE, change LOAD to GETPAGE (or GP), change CATALOG to PR PAGELIST, and change SAVE "FRED to NAMEPAGE "FRED NEWPAGE (or NP "FRED NEWPAGE). For the Atari 800, change ERASEFILE to ERF, change "FRED to "D:FRED, and change CATALOG to CATALOG "D:.

FORTRAN

Fun

The most popular computer language is BASIC, which I explained earlier. Now you'll learn a different computer language, called **FORTRAN**.

Most maxicomputers and minicomputers understand both BASIC and FORTRAN. Some ideas are easier to express in BASIC; others are easier in FORTRAN. **Most scientists and engineers on large computers use FORTRAN, not BASIC.**

IBM invented the first version of FORTRAN in 1957. Then came improvements, called **FORTRAN II**, **FORTRAN III**, and **FORTRAN IV**. The next version was called **FORTRAN 77** because it was invented in 1977. The newest version is called **FORTRAN 90** because it was invented in 1990.

Some computers use FORTRAN 77 or FORTRAN 90. Others still use FORTRAN IV or a slightly souped-up version of it (called **FORTRAN IV-EXTENDED** or **FORTRAN V** or **WATFOR** or **WATFIV** or **FORTRAN 10**).

This chapter explains the popular FORTRAN features that work on practically all computers.

Simple programs

Here's a FORTRAN program:

```
      PRINT 10
10    FORMAT (1X,'CHIPMUNKS ARE CHUBBY')
      PRINT 20
20    FORMAT (1X,'GOLDFISH GIGGLE')
      PRINT 10
      END
```

The top line says to print what's in line 10, so the computer will print CHIPMUNKS ARE CHUBBY. The next line says to print what's in line 20, so the computer will print GOLDFISH GIGGLE. The next line says to print what's in line 10, so the computer will print CHIPMUNKS ARE CHUBBY again. Altogether, the program makes the computer print:

```
CHIPMUNKS ARE CHUBBY
GOLDFISH GIGGLE
CHIPMUNKS ARE CHUBBY
```

Notice:

```
Each program line is indented 6 spaces, so it begins in the 7th position.
Each FORMAT begins with 1X.
Each string is enclosed in apostrophes.
```

You must number every line that's referred to. For example, you must number the FORMAT lines, since the PRINT lines refer to them. You don't have to number the PRINT lines.

The bottom line of every FORTRAN program must be END.

Different versions On PDP computers, say TYPE instead of PRINT. On CDC computers using TS FORTRAN, replace each apostrophe by an asterisk. On IBM computers, put STOP above END, so the bottom two lines of your program are:

```
      STOP
      END
```

How to type the program Ask the people in your computer center how to feed a FORTRAN program into the computer. On some computers, you must put an edit number in front of each line:

```
00100         PRINT 10
00110    10   FORMAT (1X,'CHIPMUNKS ARE CHUBBY')
00120         PRINT 20
00130    20   FORMAT (1X,'GOLDFISH GIGGLE')
00140         PRINT 10
00150         END
```

Some computers don't require you to indent each line. To indent quickly on PDP computers, hold down the CONTROL key, while you type the letter I.

Be brief Each line of your program must be brief: no more than 72 characters, including the spaces at the beginning of the line.

Carriage controls

The 1X at the beginning of each FORMAT is called the **carriage control**. It means: print the format normally.

For weirder printing, replace the 1X by '0' or '1' or '+':

```
      PRINT 10
10    FORMAT (1X,'NIFTY')
      PRINT 20
20    FORMAT ('0','SAL')
      END
```

In line 10, the 1X makes the computer print NIFTY normally. **In line 20, the zero-in-apostrophes make the computer leave a blank line, then print SAL.**

The computer will print:

```
NIFTY

SAL
```

Suppose you change the carriage control to '1':

```
      PRINT 10
10    FORMAT (1X,'NIFTY')
      PRINT 20
20    FORMAT ('1','SAL')
      END
```

If your terminal uses paper, **the '1' makes the computer print SAL on a new page**. If your terminal uses a screen instead of paper, the '1' makes the computer erase the screen before printing SAL.

Suppose you change the carriage control to '+':

```
      PRINT 10
10    FORMAT (1X,'NIFTY')
      PRINT 20
20    FORMAT ('+','SAL')
      END
```

If your terminal uses paper, **the '+' makes the computer print SAL in the same place as NIFTY**, like this:

```
SALTY
```

If your terminal uses a screen instead, the computer will print NIFTY, but then the NIF will suddenly disappear, and you'll see SALTY.

To print the symbol θ, print 0 in the same place as -. To print the symbol ≠, print = in the same place as /. To print θ≠A, print 0=A in the same place as -/. If your terminal uses paper, this program prints θ≠A:

```
      PRINT 10
10    FORMAT (1X,'0=A')
      PRINT 20
20    FORMAT ('+','-/')
      END
```

Different versions If you're using a Hazeltine terminal or CDC TS FORTRAN, the carriage controls won't work.

Fancy formats

In the format line, you can play fancy tricks.

Multiple fields Examine this program:

```
      PRINT 10
10    FORMAT (1X,'JOHN','NY')
      END
```

The FORMAT consists of three **fields**: the first is the carriage control 1X, the second is `JOHN`, and the third is `NY`. The computer will print JOHN and NY on the same line:

```
JOHNNY
```

Another example:

```
      PRINT
10    FORMAT (1X,'EAT A',8X,'MEATBALL')
      END
```

The computer will print EAT A, then 8 blank spaces, then MEATBALL:

```
EAT A        MEATBALL
```

This program does the same thing:

```
      PRINT 10
10    FORMAT (1X,'EAT A',T15,'MEATBALL')
      END
```

It makes the computer print EAT A, then Tab over to the 15th position on the line, and print MEATBALL. When the computer tabs to the 15th position, **it considers the carriage control to be the first "position"**; the E in EAT is the first character the computer will print, and the computer considers it to be the second "position"; the A in EAT is the second character the computer will print, and the computer considers it to be the third "position"; the M in MEATBALL is the 14th character the computer will print, since the T15 says it is the 15th "position".

Here's another program for meatball lovers:

```
      PRINT 10
10    FORMAT (1X,'EAT A',1X,'MEATBALL')
```

The computer will print EAT A, then 1 blank space, then MEATBALL:

```
EAT A MEATBALL
```

If you say X instead of 1X, the computer will gripe.

Multiple records This program quotes Julius Caesar:

```
      PRINT 10
10    FORMAT (1X,'I CAME')
      PRINT 20
20    FORMAT (1X,'I SAW')
      PRINT 30
30    FORMAT (1X,'I CONQUERED')
      END
```

The computer will print:

```
I CAME
I SAW
I CONQUERED
```

This program does the same thing:

```
      PRINT 10
10    FORMAT (1X,'I CAME'/1X,'I SAW'/1X,'I CONQUERED')
      END
```

Line 10 consists of 3 **records**: the first is 1X,`I CAME`; the second is 1X,`I SAW`; the third is 1X,`I CONQUERED`. Each record begins with a carriage control; the records are separated by slashes. The computer will print each record on a separate line.

Example:

```
      PRINT 10
10    FORMAT (1X,'PLEASE'/1X,'NIBBLE'//1X,'MY'/////1X,'CHEESE')
      END
```

Line 10 makes the computer print several lines. The first line will say PLEASE. The next line will say NIBBLE. The next line will be blank. The next line will say MY. The next 4 lines will be blank. The last line will say CHEESE. So altogether, the computer will print:

```
PLEASE
NIBBLE

MY




CHEESE
```

Repeated formats The computer can feel very depressed:

```
      PRINT 10
10    FORMAT (1X,'I FEEL ',3('DOWN'))
      END
```

Line 10 is an abbreviation for this format:

```
      1X,'I FEEL ','DOWN','DOWN','DOWN'
```

The computer will print:

```
I FEEL DOWNDOWNDOWN
```

Let's burp and pray:

```
      PRINT 10
10    FORMAT (1X,'JACK ',2('BURPS'/1X,'MARY '),'ALSO PRAYS')
      END
```

Line 10 is an abbreviation for this format:

```
      1X,'JACK ','BURPS'/1X,'MARY ','BURPS'/1X,'MARY ','ALSO PRAYS'
```

The computer will print:

```
JACK BURPS
MARY BURPS
MARY ALSO PRAYS
```

Double apostrophe To make the computer print an apostrophe, use two apostrophes next to each other.

```
      PRINT 10
10    FORMAT (1X,'MOMMY ISN''T HERE')
      END
```

The computer will print:

```
MOMMY ISN'T HERE
```

Continuation

Some computers look at only the first 72 characters of each line of your program: if your line contains more than 72 characters, it won't work.

If you want to type a long statement, type just the first 72 characters. On the line below, type the remaining characters, beginning in the 7th print position; and in the 6th print position type a 6:

```
      PRINT 10
10    FORMAT (1X,'I LIKE ROSES IN MY TEA.'/1X,'THEY MAKE IT GLOW RED, LI
6KE HOT BLOOD.')
      END
```

The computer will print:

```
I LIKE ROSES IN MY TEA.
THEY MAKE IT GLOW RED, LIKE HOT BLOOD.
```

A line that has a 6 in column 6 is called a **continuation line**, because it's a continuation of the line above it.

(I suggest you put a 6 in column 6, or a * in column 6, or a $ in column 6. In fact, you can put *any character* in column 6, except a zero. Choose your favorite character; the computer doesn't care.)

Different versions On PDP computers, put the 6 immediately after a controlled I, instead of in column 6:

```
10        FORMAT (1X,'I LIKE ROSES IN MY TEA.'/1X,'THEY MAKE IT GLOW RED, LI
          6KE HOT BLOOD.')
```

(I suggest you put a 6 after the controlled I. But you can put in *any non-zero digit*, instead of a 6.)

On CDC computers using TS FORTRAN, type a + instead of a 6, and put it immediately after the edit number, with no intervening spaces:

```
00120 10 FORMAT (1X,'I LIKE ROSES IN MY TEA.'/1X,'THEY MAKE IT GLOW RED, LI
00130+KE HOT BLOOD.')
```

GO TO

You can say GO TO:

```
10    PRINT 20
20    FORMAT (1X,'CAT')
      PRINT 30
30    FORMAT (1X,'DOG')
      GO TO 10
      END
```

The top line says to print what's in line 20, so the computer will print:

```
CAT
```

The next line says to print what's in line 30, so the computer will print:

```
DOG
```

The next line makes the computer go back to line 10. The computer will print CAT again, then DOG again, then jump back to line 10 again…. The computer will try to print the words CAT and DOG again and again, forever.

STOP

The computer understands the word STOP:

```
      PRINT 10
10    FORMAT (1X,'BUBBLE GUM')
      PRINT 20
20    FORMAT (1X,'SHAKESPEARE')
      STOP
      PRINT 30
30    FORMAT (1X,'DADA')
      END
```

The top line says to print what's in line 10, so the computer will print BUBBLE GUM. The next line says to print what's in line 20, so the computer will print SHAKESPEARE. The next line says STOP, so the computer will stop. It will never print DADA.

Math

FORTRAN handles math rather well.

Integers versus real numbers

FORTRAN distinguishes between **integers** and **real numbers**. Here's how FORTRAN defines them....

An **integer** contains no decimal point and no exponent.

Integer	Not an integer	Comment
-27	-27.0	An integer contains no decimal point.
50000	5E4	An integer contains no exponents.

A **real number** contains either a decimal point or the letter E.

Real number	Not a real number
-27.0	-27
2.35E8	235000000
5E4	50000

The largest permissible integer is different from the largest permissible real:

Computer	Largest integer	Largest real	Tiniest real
PDP-11 using Fortran IV	32767	1.7E38	2.9E-39
PDP-11 using Fortran IV-Plus	2147483647	1.7E38	2.9E-39
PDP-10 or Honeywell	34359738367	1.7E38	2.9E-39
IBM mainframe	2147483647	7.2E75	5.4E-79
CDC	281474976710655	2.5E322	3.1E-294

Integers are also called **fixed-point numbers**. Real numbers are called **floating-point numbers**.

Variables

In BASIC, X can stand for a number, such as 3.7. The same is true in FORTRAN. A variable can be a letter (such as X) or a letter-followed-by-a-combination-of-letters-and-digits (such as FUN4U2).

The variable must be short: no more than 6 characters. AVERAGE is too long: say AVERAG instead.

If the variable begins with I, J, K, L, M, or N, it stands for an integer. If it begins with some other letter, it stands for a real number.

Using integer variables

Here's a simple example:

```
    JUNKY=-47
    PRINT 10, JUNKY
10  FORMAT (1X,I3)
    END
```

Since JUNKY begins with J, it stands for an integer. The first line says JUNKY stands for the integer -47. The second line says to print JUNKY, using line 10. Line 10 explains how to print JUNKY. **The I3 means: print it as an Integer having 3 characters.** The computer will print:

```
-47
```

If you change the I3 to I4, the computer will print JUNKY as an Integer having 4 characters. To print a total of 4 characters, the computer will print a blank space in front of -47, like this:

```
 -47
```

If you change to I5, the computer will print JUNKY as an Integer having 5 characters, by printing two blank spaces in front of -47:

```
  -47
```

If you change to I2, the computer will try to print JUNKY as an integer having 2 characters. But it's impossible to express -47 by using only 2 characters. The computer will obey the format and print 2 characters, but will make them asterisks:

```
**
```

Another example:

```
    NUM=31.9
    PRINT 10, NUM
10  FORMAT (1X,I4)
    END
```

Since NUM begins with N, it stands for an integer. The program's top line tries to make NUM stand for 31.9; but that's impossible, since 31.9 isn't an integer. The computer will omit the .9 and make NUM stand for the integer 31. The computer will print 31, using an I4 format:

```
  31
```

Example:

```
    JOE=-5.8
    PRINT 10, JOE
10  FORMAT (1X,I4)
    END
```

The computer will set JOE equal to the integer -5 and print it:

```
  -5
```

Example:

```
    JAIL=74
    KRIMNL=829
    PRINT 10, JAIL,KRIMNL
10  FORMAT (1X,I2,I3)
    END
```

Since JAIL begins with J, and KRIMNL begins with K, they're both integers. The computer will print JAIL and KRIMNL, using the format in line 10. The format says to print a 2-character integer, then a 3-character integer. The computer will print:

```
74829
```

If you change the format to (1X,I2,4X,I3), the computer will print a 2-character integer, then 4 blanks, then a 3-character integer:

```
74    829
```

If you change the format to —

```
10    FORMAT (1X,'JAIL NUMBER',1X,I2,1X,'CONTAINS CRIMINAL',1X,I3)
```

the computer will print JAIL NUMBER, then a blank, then a 2-character integer, then a blank, then CONTAINS CRIMINAL, then a blank, then a 3-character integer:

```
JAIL NUMBER 74 CONTAINS CRIMINAL 829
```

Example:

```
      J=43
      K=75
      L=96
      M=81
      N=24
      PRINT 10, J,K,L,M,N
10    FORMAT (1X,I2,I2,I2,I2,I2)
      END
```

The computer will print 43, then 75, then 96, then 81, then 24:

```
4375968124
```

You can write that format more briefly:

```
10    FORMAT (1X,5I2)
```

If you change the format to (1X,5I3), the computer will print each integer as 3 characters — a blank followed by two digits:

```
 43 75 96 81 24
```

If you change the format to (1X,I3), the computer will print only one integer per line:

```
 43
 75
 96
 81
 24
```

If you change the format to (1X,2I3), the computer will print 2 integers per line:

```
 43 75
 96 81
 24
```

If you change the format to (1X,'GOSH',I3,1X,'SUPERB',I3,1X,'JEE PERS'), the computer will print 2 integers per line:

```
GOSH 43 SUPERB 75 JEEPERS
GOSH 96 SUPERB 81 JEEPERS
GOSH 24 SUPERB
```

To be safe, use I14 format for integers. On most computers, I14 handles even the largest integers, and prints blank spaces between them.

Using real variables

The I format is only for integers. **For real numbers, use F or G format** instead.

F format The F format is easy to understand:

```
      RADIUS=-586.39
      PRINT 10, RADIUS
10    FORMAT (1X,F7.2)
      END
```

Since RADIUS doesn't begin with I, J, K, L, M, or N, it stands for a real number. The first line says RADIUS stands for the real number -586.39. The second line says to print RADIUS, using the format in line 10. **The F7.2 means: print it as a floating-point number having 7 characters, 2 of them after the decimal point.** The computer will print:

```
-586.39
```

If you change the F7.2 to a different format, the following chart shows what happens; in the chart, each ▓ represents a blank space:

Format	What the computer prints	Comment
F8.2	▓-586.39	To print 8 characters instead of 7, it prints a blank space at the beginning.
F8.3	-586.390	To print 3 characters after the decimal point instead of 2, it prints a zero at the end.
F8.1	▓▓-586.4	To print 1 character after the decimal point instead of 2, it rounds the .39 to 4.
F8.4	********	To print 4 characters after the decimal point, the computer would have to print -586.3900. Since that requires more than 8 characters, the computer complains by printing asterisks.

G format **To print a real number, the safest format is G14.6**, because G14.6 can handle *any* real number well, even if the number is very large or very tiny.

G14.6 prints 14 characters altogether, 6 of which are significant digits. Here are examples of numbers printed in G14.6 format:

```
▓-0.283941E-29
▓▓0.293027▓▓▓▓
▓▓5.34523▓▓▓▓
▓▓39.4539▓▓▓▓
▓▓47802.3▓▓▓▓
▓▓986327.▓▓▓▓
▓▓0.288341E+24
```

Example:

```
      PRUNES=17
      PRINT 10, PRUNES
10    FORMAT (1X,G14.6)
      END
```

Since PRUNES doesn't begin with I, J, K, L, M, or N, it stands for a real number. When the computer encounters the first line of the program, it will set PRUNES equal to the real number 17.0. It will print:

```
17.0000
```

The program will run faster if you change the top line to this:

```
      PRUNES=17.0
```

E format For real numbers, the usual formats are F and G, but another option is E.

If you say E14.6 instead of G14.6, the computer will print an E in the answer. Here are examples:

Using G14.6 format	Using E14.6 format
▓-0.283941E-29	▓-0.283941E-29
▓▓0.293027▓▓▓▓	▓0.293027E+00
▓▓5.34523▓▓▓▓	▓0.534523E+01
▓▓39.4539▓▓▓▓	▓0.394539E+02
▓▓47802.3▓▓▓▓	▓0.478023E+05
▓▓986327.▓▓▓▓	▓0.986327E+06
▓0.288341E+24	▓0.288341E+24

The G14.6 format is easier for a human to read than E14.6. But most programmers are stupid, don't know about G14.6, and use E14.6 instead.

P format FORTRAN's notation differs from BASIC.

If you ask the computer to print 288341000000000000000000.0 in FORTRAN by using G14.6 (or E14.6), the computer will normally print a 0 before the decimal point, like this: 0.288341E+24. In BASIC, the computer will print a non-zero digit before the decimal point, like this: 2.88341E+23.

If you're writing a program in FORTRAN, but you prefer BASIC's notation, ask for 1PG14.6 (or 1PE14.6). The 1P makes the computer imitate BASIC. But if a FORMAT contains 1PG, it must not contain F afterwards; this will print a wrong answer:

```
FORMAT (1X,1PG14.6,F8.2)
```
(Here is P.) (The F afterwards prints a wrong answer!)

Operations

For addition, subtraction, multiplication, and division, FORTRAN uses the same symbols as BASIC.

```
      N=2*(3+1)
      S=7.3+2.1
      PRINT 10, N,S
10    FORMAT (1X,I14,G14.6)
      END
```

Since N is 8, and S is 9.4, the computer will print:

```
      8    9.40000
```

Exponents
For exponents, FORTRAN uses a double star:

```
      J=7**2
      P=.5**3
      PRINT 10, J,P
10    FORMAT (1X,I14,G14.6)
      END
```

Since J is 7² (which is 49), and P is .5³ (which is .125), the computer will print:

```
      49    0.125000
```

For negative exponents, you need parentheses. You must say 6.1**(-2), not 6.1**-2.

What type of answer?
When you combine integers, the answer's an integer:

2+3	is 5
8-8	is 0
2*4	is 8
399/100	is 3 (not 3.99)
11/4	is 2 (not 2.75)
3/4	is 0 (not 0.75)
10**(-2)	is 0 (not 0.01)

When you combine real numbers, the answer is real:

4.1+2.9	is 7.0 (not 7)
8.0-8.0	is 0.0 (not 0)
399.0/100.0	is 3.99
11.0/4.0	is 2.75
3.0/4.0	is .75
10.0**(-2.0)	is .01

When you combine an integer with a real number, the answer is real:

3+2.0	is 5.0
399/100.0	is 3.99
11/4.0	is 2.75
3/4.0	is .75
10.0**(-2)	is .01

Compare these:

7/10*10	is 0	(because 7/10 is 0)
7/10*10.0	is 0.0	(because 0*10.0 is 0.0)
7/10.0*10	is 7.0	(because 7/10.0 is .7)

Example:

```
      JERK=20.0+30.9
      PRINT 10, JERK
10    FORMAT (1X,I14)
      END
```

Since JERK begins with J, it stands for an integer. Since 20.9+30.9 is 51.8, JERK stands for the integer 51. The computer will print:

```
      51
```

Another example:

```
      APPLE=37/10
      PRINT 10, APPLE
10    FORMAT (1X,G14.6)
      END
```

Since APPLE begins with A, it stands for a real number. Since 37/10 is 3, APPLE stands for the real number 3.0. The computer will print:

```
      3.00000
```

Crimes that slow down the computer cop
If you commit one of these crimes, the computer will work slowly....

Little crime:	use a real number
Medium crime:	mix reals with integers
Big crime:	use a real exponent

For example, the computer handles 2.0+2.0 slower than 2+2, because 2.0+2.0 is a little crime.

The bigger the crime, the slower the computer works. For example, the computer handles 2.1+7 (which is a medium crime) slower than 2.1+7.0 (which is just a *little* crime). Likewise, X=0 (a medium crime) gets handled slower than X=0.0 (a little crime).

5.1**2.0 is a big crime, since its exponent (2.0) is real. The computer handles it slower than 5.1**2, which is just a medium crime.

5**3.1 is a gigantic crime, since it's a medium crime and a big crime simultaneously. Because the crime's so gigantic, some computers refuse to handle it. Say 5.0**3.1 instead.

Advice about variables

FORTRAN, like BASIC, distinguishes variables, constants, and expressions:

X	is a variable
2.7	is not a variable; it's a **numeric constant**
'LOVE'	is not a variable; it's a **string constant**
X+Y	is not a variable; it's an **expression**

In a PRINT statement, some computers allow only variables....

allowed:	PRINT 10, X	
not allowed:	PRINT 10, 2.7	instead, say X=2.7 and PRINT 10, X
not allowed:	PRINT 10, 'LOVE'	instead, say PRINT 10 and 10 FORMAT (1X,'LOVE')
not allowed:	PRINT 10, X+Y	instead, say Z=X+Y and PRINT 10, Z

Other computers are more generous and allow anything. Find out about yours.

To help other humans understand your program, **use long variable names throughout your program**. Say RADIUS, not R; say AREA, not A; say VOLUME, not V; say SUM, not S; say TOTAL, not T. Because FORTRAN's variables are restricted to six characters, you might have to omit the last few syllables (*revolutions* becomes REVOLU) or the last few vowels (RVLTNS).

If you want a variable to be real, but its English name begins with I, J, K, L, M, or N, begin its FORTRAN name with an A (*mass* becomes AMAS; *length* becomes ALENGT or ALNGTH). If you want a variable to be an integer, but its English name doesn't begin with I, J, K, L, M, or N, begin its FORTRAN name with an I (*population* becomes IPOPUL) or misspell it (*count* becomes KOUNT) or choose a synonym (instead of *position*, say *location*, which is LOCATN).

Pleasant I/O

You learned how to make the computer PRINT by using a FORMAT. Now you'll learn about PRINT's opposite (READ) and how to omit FORMATs altogether.

READ

The computer can READ.

```
      PRINT 10
10    FORMAT (1X,'TYPE SOME DIGITS')
      READ 20, N
20    FORMAT (I4)
      PRINT 30, N
30    FORMAT (1X,I4)
      END
```

When you run the program, here's what happens....
The top two lines make the computer print:

```
TYPE SOME DIGITS
```

The word READ makes the computer wait for you to type something; it's like the BASIC word INPUT. The computer will wait for you to type the value of N, but line 20's FORMAT makes the computer read just the first 4 characters. For example, if you type —

```
-75198622
```

the computer will read just the first 4 characters, which are -751; it will ignore the 98622; so N will be -751. Line 30's FORMAT makes the computer print:

```
-751
```

Altogether, the run looks like this:

The computer says:	TYPE SOME DIGITS
You say:	-75198622
The computer replies:	-751

Hassles Line 30's FORMAT contains a carriage control 1X, but line 20's FORMAT omits the carriage control. **Put a carriage control in formats that PRINT, but not in formats that READ.**

On PDP computers, say ACCEPT instead of READ.

Blank spaces **If you input a blank space, the computer treats it as a zero.**

For example, suppose you input:

```
-3 28219
```

Because of the I4 format, the computer will read just the first 4 characters, which are -3 2; the blank space between the 3 and the 2 is treated as a zero, so N will be -302.

Suppose you input:

```
57
```

Because of the I4 format, the computer will read the 5, the 7, and two blanks. Since the blanks are treated as zeros, N will be 5700.

Suppose you input:

```
▪▪▪9527
```

Because of the I4 format, the computer will read the three beginning blanks and the 9. Since the blanks are treated as zeros, N will be 0009, which is 9. Line 30 makes the computer print:

```
9
```

Multiple variables Suppose you write a program containing these lines:

```
      READ 20, L,M,N
20    FORMAT (I3,I4,2X,I2)
```

When you run that program, suppose you input:

```
58194138972824
```

The I3 format makes the first 3 characters (581) be L. The I4 format makes the next 4 characters (9413) be M. The 2X format makes the next 2 characters (89) be skipped over. The I2 format makes the next two characters (72) be N. The remaining characters (824) are ignored. So the line is split like this....

Line you input:	581	9413	89	72	824
Fields in the FORMAT statement:	I3	I4	2X	I2	
Variables in the READ statement:	L	M		N	

Suppose you write a program containing these lines:

```
      READ 20, J,K,L,M,N
20    FORMAT (2I3)
```

The format says to read two 3-character integers on each line. Suppose you input:

```
78345692
85431684
46185327
```

J will be 783, and K will be 456. L will be 854, and M will be 316. N will be 461.

Real variables Here's how to input a real number:

```
      PRINT 10
10    FORMAT (1X,'TYPE SOME DIGITS')
      READ 20, P
20    FORMAT (F6.2)
      PRINT 30, P
30    FORMAT (1X,G14.6)
      END
```

The F6.2 format means: read 6 characters; if they don't contain the decimal point, insert it before the last 2 digits.

For example, suppose you input:

```
327514968
```

The computer reads the first 6 characters (327514). Since they don't contain the decimal point, the computer inserts it before the last 2 digits, so P is 3275.14. Line 30 prints:

```
  3275.14
```

Suppose you input:

```
7.5423967
```

The computer reads the first 6 characters (7.5423). Since they already contain the decimal point, P is 7.5423. Line 30 says to print that number by using 6 significant digits, so the computer prints:

```
  7.54230
```

Suppose you input:

```
497E3
```

The computer reads 6 characters (497E3, followed by a blank). Since blanks are treated as zeros, the computer gets 497E30. Since 497E30 doesn't contain the decimal point, the computer inserts it before the last 2 digits, so P is 4.97E30. Line 30 prints:

```
  0.497000E+31
```

Omitting formats

Most computers let you omit numeric formats. This program works on most modern computers (such as computers having FORTRAN 77, PDP-20 computers, PDP-10 computers using FORTRAN 10, PDP-11 computers using FORTRAN IV-PLUS, CDC computers using FORTRAN IV-EXTENDED, and IBM computers using FORTRAN H-EXTENDED):

```
      PRINT 10
10    FORMAT (1X,'TYPE TWO INTEGERS')
      READ *, M,N
      ISUM=M+N
      PRINT *, ISUM
      END
```

(On PDP computers, say TYPE instead of PRINT, and ACCEPT instead of READ.)

The word READ is followed by an asterisk, instead of a FORMAT number. The last PRINT is followed by an asterisk also. **The asterisk makes the computer invent its own FORMAT.** To make the program add 241 and 82976, **input the numbers, separated by a comma**:

```
241,82976
```

The computer will notice the comma's location and automatically use an I3 format for 241, a 1X format to skip over the comma, and an I5 format for 82976. To print ISUM, the computer will use a safe format, such as I14 or I15.

By omitting formats, you gain two advantages:

```
1. You can write FORTRAN programs faster.

2. The person who inputs needn't worry whether his
spacing matches the format. The computer invents a
format matching his input.
```

Different versions
On CDC computers using TS FORTRAN and on Honeywell computers, omit the asterisk after READ and PRINT:

```
      PRINT 10
10    FORMAT (1X,'TYPE THE NUMBERS')
      READ, M,N
      ISUM=M+N
      PRINT, ISUM
      END
```

On PDP-10 computers using F40 FORTRAN, and on PDP-11 computers using regular FORTRAN IV, you need FORMATs, but omit the number in the I format:

```
      TYPE 10
10    FORMAT (1X,'TYPE THE NUMBERS')
      ACCEPT 20, M,N
20    FORMAT (1X,2I)
      ISUM=M+N
      TYPE 30, ISUM
30    FORMAT (1X,I)
      END
```

Real numbers
You can use similar shortcuts for real numbers.

Logic

You learned how to say GO TO and STOP. Taking those concepts further, let's see how to say IF and DO and give a *computed* GO TO.

IF

FORTRAN uses these clauses:

Clause	Meaning
IF (I .LT. 5)	If I is Less Than 5
IF (I .GT. 5)	If I is Greater Than 5
IF (I .LE. 5)	If I is Less than or Equal to 5
IF (I .GE. 5)	If I is Greater than or Equal to 5
IF (I .EQ. 5)	If I is EQual to 5
IF (I .NE. 5)	If I is Not Equal to 5

Notice that each **relational operator** (such as LT) must be enclosed in periods, and each **condition** (such as I .LT. 5) must be enclosed in parentheses.

By using those clauses, you can build statements:

Statement	Meaning
IF (I .LT. 5) J=3	If I is Less Than 5, let J=3
IF (I .LT. 5) GO TO 80	If I is Less Than 5, go to line 80
IF (I .LT. 5) STOP	If I is Less Than 5, stop
IF (I .LT. 5) PRINT 10, J	If I is Less Than 5, print J using line 10's FORMAT

You can use the words AND and OR:

Idea	How to say it in FORTRAN
If I is 2 or 9 or 13	IF (I .EQ. 2 .OR. I .EQ. 9 .OR. I .EQ. 13)
If I is an integer from 1 to 8	IF (I .GE. 1 .AND. I .LE. 8)
If X<Y<Z	IF (X .LT. Y .AND. Y .LT. Z)
If A is less than both B and C	IF (A .LT. B .AND. A .LT. C)
If X negative or between 5 & 9	IF (X .LT. 0.0 .OR. X .GE. 5.0 .AND. X .LE. 9.0)

Take this test: cover the column that says "How to say it in FORTRAN". Try to translate each "Idea" into FORTRAN, then check your answers. If one of your answers is shorter than the correct answer, take the test again! For example, the following answer to the first idea is *wrong*:

```
IF (I .EQ. 2 .OR. 9 .OR. 13)
```

END IF FORTRAN 77 lets you say "END IF".

For example, here's how FORTRAN 77 lets you say, "If I is greater than 5, let J be 80 and let K be 90":

```
      IF (I .GT. 5) THEN
         J=80
         K=90
      END IF
```

Here's how FORTRAN 77 lets you say, "If I is greater than 5, let J be 80 and let K be 90; but if I is *not* greater than 5, let J be 30 and let K be 50":

```
      IF (I .GT. 5) THEN
         J=80
         K=90
      ELSE
         J=30
         K=50
      END IF
```

Here's how FORTRAN 77 lets you say, "If I is greater than 5, let J be 80 and let K be 90; if I is *not* greater than 5, but I is greater than 2, let J be 81 and let K be 92; if I is not greater than 2, let J be 30 and let K be 50":

```
      IF (I .GT. 5) THEN
         J=80
         K=90
      ELSE IF (I .GT. 2) THEN
         J=81
         K=92
      ELSE
         J=30
         K=50
      END IF
```

Warning: to say "END IF", you must get FORTRAN 77. If you use FORTRAN IV instead, "END IF" doesn't work. I recommend that you get FORTRAN 77.

Three-way IF
Here's a different kind of IF statement:

```
IF (X) 20,50,90
```

It means:

```
If X is a negative number, go to line 20.
If X is zero, go to line 50.
If X is a positive number, go to line 90.
```

That kind of IF statement is called a **three-way IF**, or an **arithmetic IF**. (To pronounce "arith*metic*", put the accent on *met*.) The other kind of IF is called a **logical IF**.

Computed GO TO

In your program, you can say:

```
GO TO (80,100,20,350), I
```

That means: go to either 80, 100, 20, or 350, depending on what I is. More specifically, it means:

```
Go to line  80, if I is 1.
Go to line 100, if I is 2.
Go to line  20, if I is 3.
Go to line 350, if I is 4.
Proceed to the line underneath, if I is a different integer.
```

That FORTRAN statement is called a **computed GO TO**.

DO

This program prints the square of every number from 80 to 95, and then prints GET LOST:

```
BASIC                    FORTRAN
FOR I = 85 TO 100            DO 20 I=80,95
   PRINT I ^ 2               J=I**2
                             PRINT 10, J
                        10   FORMAT (1X,I14)
NEXT                    20   CONTINUE
PRINT "GET LOST"             PRINT 30
                        30   FORMAT (1X,'GET LOST')
                             END
```

If you compare the BASIC with the FORTRAN, you'll notice FORTRAN uses the word DO instead of FOR, uses a comma instead of TO, and uses CONTINUE instead of NEXT. The statement **DO 20 I=5,9** means: DO every line up through line 20, repeatedly, as I goes from 5 to 9. In BASIC, programmers indent every line between FOR and NEXT; in FORTRAN, programmers indent every line between DO and CONTINUE. In BASIC, the indented lines are called a **FOR...NEXT loop**; in FORTRAN, they're called a **DO loop**.

If you want the computer to print the square of every *fifth* number from 80 to 95, change the program's top line:

```
BASIC                     FORTRAN
FOR I = 80 TO 95 STEP 5   DO 20 I=80,95,5
```

Restrictions
In a DO statement, some computers allow only positive integer variables and constants:

Not allowed	Why	Say this instead
DO 10 X=1.0,5.0	reals are not allowed	DO 10 I=1,5
DO 10 X=17.3,98.5	reals are not allowed	DO 10 I=173,985 X=I/10.0
DO 10 I=0,5	0 is not positive	DO 10 J=1,6 I=J-1
DO 10 I=-3,5	-3 is not positive	DO 10 J=1,9 I=J-4
DO 10 I=100,7,-1	-1 is not positive	DO 10 J=7,100 I=107-J
DO 10 I=5,J+K	+ is not allowed	L=J+K DO 10 I=5,L

Other computers are more generous and allow anything. Find out about yours.

In the middle of a DO loop, don't change the value of the index. For example, if your DO loop begins with —

```
DO 10 I=1,100
```

don't insert this line in the middle of your loop:

```
I=14
```

It will confuse the computer.

Zero-trip DO loops
If you say —

```
DO 10 I=1,N
```

the computer will do up through line 10, N times. For example, if N is 73, the computer will do up through line 10, 73 times. If N is 2, the computer will do up through line 10, twice. If N is 1, the computer will do up through line 10, once.

What happens if N is less than 1? The answer depends on which version of FORTRAN you're using.

If you're using FORTRAN 77, the computer will skip the loop, and proceed to the line below line 10. But if you're using FORTRAN IV, the computer will do the loop once, as if N were 1.

FORTRAN 77 makes more sense; but alas, many computers still use FORTRAN IV.

A DO loop that FORTRAN 77 skips (because N is less than 1) is called a **zero-trip DO loop**, because the computer takes "zero trips through the loop" (instead of 1 trip or 2 trips or many trips).

Find out whether *your* computer's version of FORTRAN resembles FORTRAN 77 and permits zero-trip DO loops.

Lists

To handle lists, use these tricks....

Subscripts

Like BASIC, FORTRAN permits subscripts:

```
     DIMENSION X(4)
     X(1)=.21
     X(2)=.3
     X(3)=1.08
     X(4)=5.0
     SUM=X(1)+X(2)+X(3)+X(4)
     PRINT 10, X,SUM
10   FORMAT (1X,G14.6)
     END
```

The top line says X will be a list of 4 numbers, called X(1), X(2), X(3), and X(4). Since X doesn't begin with I, J, K, L, M, or N, the 4 numbers will be real.

The PRINT statement makes the computer print the list and the SUM, like this:

```
0.210000
0.300000
1.08000
5.00000
6.59000
```

If you change the format to (1X,5G14.6), the computer will print all 5 numbers on the same line:

```
0.210000      0.300000      1.08000      5.00000      6.59000
```

You must say DIMENSION if your program uses subscripts, even if the subscripts are small. **Say DIMENSION at the very top of the program**. Make sure you say DIMENSION, not DIM or DIMENSIONS. The computer assumes all subscripts will be positive, so don't say X(0). If a subscript is zero or negative or larger than the DIMENSION statement says, the computer might not notice your error, and will print wrong answers without warning you.

If your program begins like this —

```
      DIMENSION A(6)
      READ 10, A
```

the computer will begin by reading 6 real numbers, which will become A(1), A(2), A(3), A(4), A(5), and A(6).

Double subscripts
If you want T to be a table of numbers, and you want T to have 4 rows and 2 columns, begin your program by saying:

```
      DIMENSION T(4,2)
```

To print T, say:

```
      PRINT 10, T(1,1), T(1,2)
      PRINT 10, T(2,1), T(2,2)
      PRINT 10, T(3,1), T(3,2)
      PRINT 10, T(4,1), T(4,2)
10    FORMAT (1X,2G14.6)
```

If you say —

```
      PRINT 10, T
```

the computer will print the entire table T, but in an undesirable order: it will print T(1,1), T(2,1), T(3,1), and T(4,1), then T(1,2), T(2,2), T(3,2), and T(4,2). Similarly, "READ 5, T" makes the computer read T in an undesirable order.

Implied DO

This statement —

```
      PRINT 10, X(3),X(4),X(5),X(6),X(7)
```

can be written more briefly, like this:

```
      PRINT 10, (X(I), I=3,7)
```

It means: using line 10's format, print the value of X(I), for I = 3 to 7. The construction (X(I), I=3,7) is called an **implied DO loop**. Notice the parenthesis at the beginning, the parenthesis at the end, and the commas.

Here are other examples of implied DO loops:

Implied DO loop	Meaning
(X(I), I=100,120,5)	X(100),X(105),X(110),X(115),X(120)
(X(I),Y(I), I=3,7)	X(3),Y(3), X(4),Y(4), X(5),Y(5), X(6),Y(6), X(7),Y(7)

Calendar
Here's a calendar:

```
 1  2  3  4  5  6  7
 8  9 10 11 12 13 14
15 16 17 18 19 20 21
22 23 24 25 26 27 28
29 30 31
```

This program prints it:

```
      PRINT 10, (I, I=1,31)
10    FORMAT (1X,I2,1X,I2,1X,I2,1X,I2,1X,I2,1X,I2,1X,I2)
      END
```

The program's top statement says to print every value of I, for I = 1 to 31. The FORMAT says to print 7 integers on each line, and separate the integers by spaces.

Since 1X followed by I2 is about the same as I3, you can write the FORMAT more briefly:

```
10    FORMAT (I3,I3,I3,I3,I3,I3,I3)
```

You can be even briefer:

```
10    FORMAT (7I3)
```

Tables
If T is a table having 3 rows and 5 columns, these lines will print it in the correct order:

```
      PRINT 20, T(1,1), T(1,2), T(1,3), T(1,4), T(1,5)
      PRINT 20, T(2,1), T(2,2), T(2,3), T(2,4), T(2,5)
      PRINT 20, T(3,1), T(3,2), T(3,3), T(3,4), T(3,5)
20    FORMAT (1X,5G14.6)
```

This shortcut does the same thing:

```
      PRINT 20, (T(1,J), J=1,5)
      PRINT 20, (T(2,J), J=1,5)
      PRINT 20, (T(3,J), J=1,5)
20    FORMAT (1X,5G14.6)
```

Here's a shorter cut:

```
      PRINT 20, ((T(I,J), J=1,5), I=1,3)
20    FORMAT (1X,5G14.6)
```

To read the table, say:

```
      READ 10, ((T(I,J), J=1,5), I=1,3)
```

DATA

This program shows FORTRAN's DATA statement, which differs from BASIC's:

```
      DATA X/8.7/, Y/1.4/, Z/9.0/
      X=100.6
      PRINT 10, X,Y,Z
10    FORMAT (1X,3G14.6)
      END
```

That DATA statement says X is 8.7, Y is 1.4, and Z is 9.0. The next line changes X to 100.6. The computer will print:

```
100.600      1.40000      9.00000
```

In that DATA statement, you must write 9.0, not 9: the number must be real, since Z is real.

The DATA statement resembles these three statements —

```
      X=8.7
      Y=1.4
      Z=9.0
```

but is faster.

Here's another way to type the DATA statement:

```
      DATA X,Y,Z/8.7,1.4,9.0/
```

It says X, Y, and Z are 8.7, 1.4, and 9.0 respectively.

Like the DIMENSION statement, the DATA statement belongs at the very top of the program. If you want both a DIMENSION statement and a DATA statement, put the DIMENSION statement first.

This DATA statement says A, B, C, D, and E are all 1.7, and X, Y, and Z are all 9.6:

```
        DATA A,B,C,D,E,X,Y,Z/1.7,1.7,1.7,1.7,1.7,9.6,9.6,9.6/
```

Since the first 5 numbers are 1.7, and the next 3 numbers are 9.6, you can write more briefly:

```
        DATA A,B,C,D,E,X,Y,Z/5*1.7,3*9.6/
```

Subscripted DATA
To make A be this list —

```
81.7
92.6
25.3
49.8
72.1
68.8
```

begin your program with these lines:

```
        DIMENSION A(6)
        DATA A/81.7,92.6,25.3,49.8,72.1,68.8/
```

To make T be this table —

```
8.4 9.7
5.1 6.8
2.5 7.2
6.3 9.8
```

begin your program with these lines:

```
        DIMENSION T(4,2)
        DATA T/8.4,5.1,2.5,6.3,9.7,6.8,7.2,9.8/
```

Notice you must list the entire first column, then the second.

String variables

This program works on most computers:

```
        N='UP'
        PRINT 10, N
10      FORMAT (1X,A2)
        END
```

The top line says N is the string 'UP'. The next line says to print N, using the format in line 10. **The A2 format means a 2-character string.** (The A is derived from the word Alphabet.) The computer will print:

```
UP
```

Different versions Some computers allow apostrophes only in FORMAT, DATA, and CALL statements. (You'll learn about CALL statements later.) On such computers, the statement N='UP' is illegal. Instead say:

```
        DATA N/'UP'/
```

Restrictions A string statement should look like an integer: it should begin with the letter I, J, K, L, M, or N. You can say N='UP' but shouldn't say X= 'UP'.

The string a variable stands for must be short. You can say N='UP' but not N= 'SUPERCALIFRAGILISTICEXPIALIDOCIOUS'. The longest permissible string depends on your computer:

Computer	Longest string allowed
PDP-11 (using FORTRAN IV)	2 characters
PDP-11 (using FORTRAN IV-PLUS), IBM	4 characters
PDP-10, PDP-20, Honeywell	5 characters
CDC	10 characters

Fancy examples Examine this program:

```
        PRINT 10
10      FORMAT (1X,'DO YOU LIKE ME?')
        READ 20, IREPLY
20      FORMAT (A1)
        IF (IREPLY .EQ. 'Y') PRINT 30
30      FORMAT (1X,'I LIKE YOU TOO!')
        PRINT 40
40      FORMAT (1X,'SO LONG, BUSTER.')
        END
```

The first pair of lines make the computer print DO YOU LIKE ME? The next pair set IREPLY equal to the first letter the human types. If the human types YESIREE, the computer will set IREPLY equal to 'Y' and will therefore print:

```
I LIKE YOU TOO!
SO LONG, BUSTER.
```

But if the human types NOT AT ALL, the computer will set IREPLY equal to 'N' and will therefore print just:

```
SO LONG, BUSTER.
```

In that program, the string is called IREPLY instead of REPLY, to make it an integer.

Advanced example:

```
        DIMENSION NAME(25)
        PRINT 10
10      FORMAT (1X,'WHAT IS YOUR NAME?')
        READ 20, NAME
20      FORMAT (25A2)
        PRINT 30, NAME
30      FORMAT (1X,'I HATE ANYONE NAMED ',25A2)
        END
```

The top line says NAME will be a list of 25 elements. The next pair of lines print WHAT IS YOUR NAME? If the human answers —

```
BARTHOLOMEW HIERONYMOUS MCGILLICUDDY, M.D.
```

the format in line 20 sets NAME equal to 25 two-character strings:

NAME(1) is 'BA'	NAME(14) is 'GI'
NAME(2) is 'RT'	NAME(15) is 'LL'
NAME(3) is 'HO'	NAME(16) is 'IC'
NAME(4) is 'LO'	NAME(17) is 'UD'
NAME(5) is 'ME'	NAME(18) is 'DY'
NAME(6) is 'W '	NAME(19) is ', '
NAME(7) is 'HI'	NAME(20) is 'M.'
NAME(8) is 'ER'	NAME(21) is 'D.'
NAME(9) is 'ON'	NAME(22) is ' '
NAME(10) is 'YM'	NAME(23) is ' '
NAME(11) is 'OU'	NAME(24) is ' '
NAME(12) is 'S '	NAME(25) is ' '
NAME(13) is 'MC'	

Format 30 prints:

```
I HATE ANYONE NAMED BARTHOLOMEW HIERONYMOUS MCGILLICUDDY, M.D.
```

To make that program run faster, use fewer strings. For example, if you have a CDC computer, each string can be as long as 10 characters, so you need only 5 strings to make 50 characters:

```
        DIMENSION NAME(5)
        PRINT 10
10      FORMAT (1X,'WHAT IS YOUR NAME?')
        READ 20, NAME
20      FORMAT (5A10)
        PRINT 30, NAME
30      FORMAT (1X,'I HATE ANYONE NAMED ',5A10)
        END
```

FORTRAN 77 strings On computer having FORTRAN 77, and on IBM computers using WATFIV, you can request super-long strings:

```
        CHARACTER*50 NAME
        PRINT 10
10      FORMAT (1X,'WHAT IS YOUR NAME?')
        READ 20, NAME
20      FORMAT (A50)
        PRINT 30, NAME
30      FORMAT (1X,'I HATE ANYONE NAMED ',A50)
        END
```

The top line requests that NAME be a 50-character string. Like the DIMENSION statement, the CHARACTER statement must be put at the very top of the program, above even the DATA statements.

Functions

To do advanced math, use FORTRAN's functions.

Square root

This program finds the square root of 9:

```
      A=SQRT(9.0)
      PRINT 10, A
10    FORMAT (1X,G14.6)
      END
```

The computer will print:

```
3.00000
```

In that program, you must say SQRT(9.0), not SQRT(9). If you say SQRT(9), the computer will either gripe or print a wrong answer.

The number in parentheses must be real. That's why you can say SQRT(9.0) but not SQRT(9). You can say SQRT(8.0+1.0) but not SQRT(8+1). You can say SQRT(X) but not SQRT(J).

Be careful when you translate from BASIC to FORTRAN: in BASIC, you say SQR; in FORTRAN, you say SQRT instead.

This program prints a table, showing the square root of 2.0, the square root of 3.0, the square root of 4.0, the square root of 5.0, etc.:

```
      X=2.0
10    Y=SQRT(X)
      PRINT 20, X,Y
20    FORMAT (1X,2G14.6)
      X=X+1.0
      GO TO 10
      END
```

The computer will print:

```
2.00000        1.41421
3.00000        1.73205
4.00000        2.00000
5.00000        2.23607
6.00000        2.44949
7.00000        2.64575
8.00000        2.82843
9.00000        3.00000
10.0000        3.16228
etc.
```

FLOAT

If you say FLOAT, the computer will create a FLOATing-point number (in other words, a real number), by using an integer. For example, FLOAT(3) is 3.0. If J is 7, then FLOAT(J) is 7.0.

The word FLOAT can help you solve the following problems....

Find the square root of an integer J

Unfortunately, you aren't allowed to say SQRT(J), because what you take the square root of must be a real number. You can say SQRT(X) but not SQRT(J). *Solution:* say X=J, and then say SQRT(X). *Shorter solution:* say SQRT(FLOAT(J)).

Divide J by K accurately

Unfortunately, saying J/K gives an inaccurate answer, because when the computer divides integers it gives an integer answer, instead of an accurate real answer. *Solution:* say X=J, then Y=K, then X/Y. *Shorter solution:* say FLOAT(J)/FLOAT(K).

Random numbers

Here's how to set R equal to a random decimal between 0 and 1:

Computer	What to say
CDC	R=RANF(0)
PDP-10, PDP-20	R=RAN(0)
PDP-11	R=RAN(ISEED,ISEED2)

To randomize the random numbers on PDP-10 and PDP-20 computers, put these lines near the top of your program:

```
      CALL TIME(ISEED,ISEED2)
      CALL SETRAN(MOD(ISEED/2+ISEED2/2, 2147483648))
```

On other computers, randomizing is even more complicated; ask the people who run your computer center.

Maxima and minima

To find the maximum real number in a list, ask for AMAX1.

For example, AMAX1(4.7, 2.8, 41.6, 9.2, 82.3, 9.7) is 82.3. And AMIN1(4.7, 2.8, 41.6, 9.2, 82.3, 9.7) is the minimum, which is 2.8.

If the numbers in the list are integers, say MAX0 instead of AMAX1, and say MIN0 instead of AMIN1. When you type "MAX0" and "MIN0", make sure you end with a zero, not the letter "oh".

Absolute value

ABS(X) means the ABSolute value of X; in other words, X without its minus sign. For example:

```
ABS(-5.2) is 5.2
ABS(-7.0) is 7.0
ABS(9.3)  is 9.3
```

For integers, say IABS instead of ABS. For example, IABS(-7) is 7.

Remainder

When you divide 11 by 4, the remainder is 3:

```
        2
    4 ) 11
       -8
        3  is the remainder
```

If you ask for MOD(11,4) the computer will divide 11 by 4 and get the remainder, which is 3; so MOD(11,4) is 3.

Use MOD for integers; use AMOD for reals. For example, AMOD(11.0, 4.0) is 3.0.

Trigonometry

If your computer has FORTRAN 77, or your computer is an IBM having FORTRAN H-EXTENDED, or your computer is a PDP-11 having FORTRAN IV-PLUS, you can use these trigonometric functions:

Symbol	Meaning
SIN(X)	the SINe of X radians
COS(X)	the COSine of X radians
TAN(X)	the TANgent of X radians
ASIN(X)	the ArcSINe of X in radians; the number whose sine is X
ACOS(X)	the ArcCOSine of X in radians; the number whose cosine is X
ATAN(X)	the ArcTANgent of X in radians; the number whose tangent is X
SINH(X)	the SINe Hyperbolic of X
COSH(X)	the COSine Hyperbolic of X
TANH(X)	the TANgent Hyperbolic of X

If your computer is old-fashioned, it restricts you:

Old-fashioned system	Restriction
PDP-10, PDP-20	You can't say TAN(X).
CDC	You can't say SINH(X) or COSH(X).
other IBM computers	Say ARSIN(X) instead of ASIN(X). Say ARCOS(X) instead of ACOS(X).
FORTRAN IV computers	You can't say TAN(X), ASIN(X), or ACOS(X). You can't say SINH(X) or COSH(X).

You can replace X by any *real* number. For example, you can say SIN(4.0) but not SIN(4); you can say SIN(Y) but not SIN(J).

Be careful when you translate from BASIC to FORTRAN: in BASIC, you say ATN; in FORTRAN, you say ATAN instead.

You've seen that SIN(X) is the sine of X *radians*. But what's the sine of X *degrees*? On PDP-10 and PDP-20 computers, you can find the sine of X degrees by asking for SIND(X); and you can find the cosine of X degrees by asking for COSD(X).

ATAN2(Y,X) is about the same as ATAN(Y/X), but is faster, more accurate, and gives a useful answer even when X is zero or negative. ATAN2(Y,X) is the angle (in radians) of the line that goes through the origin and the point (X,Y).

Calculus

You can use these functions:

Function	Meaning
EXP(X)	e^x
ALOG(X)	$\log_e X$
ALOG10(X)	$\log_{10} X$

You can replace X by any real number, but not by an integer. Each of those functions produces a *real* answer, since none of them begins with I, J, K, L, M, or N.

The logarithm function is called ALOG instead of LOG, to avoid beginning with L. Be careful when you translate from BASIC to FORTRAN: in BASIC, you say LOG; in FORTRAN, you say ALOG instead.

Exotic features

Let's take off our handcuffs and go wild!

Let's go beyond integers and reals, to other kinds of numbers that are wilder: **double precision** and **complex**.

Let's go beyond standard functions and invent our *own* functions. Let's go beyond standard statements and invent our *own* statements, by using subroutines and comments. Let's go beyond the DATA statement and invent data *files*.

Here we go....

Comments

If you type C instead of a line number, the computer will ignore the line.

```
    N=50+13
C I HATE COMPUTERS!
    PRINT 10, N
10  FORMAT (1X,I14)
    END
```

The computer will ignore the Comment. The computer will print 63.

The C in FORTRAN is like the REMARK in BASIC: use it to document your program.

DOUBLE PRECISION

Some computers are more accurate than others:

Computer	Accuracy for real numbers
PDP-11, IBM	7 digits
PDP-10, PDP-20, Honeywell	8 digits
CDC	14 digits

For example, suppose you feed this program to a PDP-11 or IBM:

```
    A=5398.1642376236
    PRINT 10, A
10  FORMAT (1X,F15.10)
    END
```

Expect the first 7 digits the computer prints to be correct (5398.164), but the remaining digits it prints to be wrong: they arise from round-off error inside the computer.

A PDP-11 or IBM prints *some* numbers to an accuracy of 8 digits and others to an accuracy of just 6 digits, but 7 digits is typical.

For real numbers, I recommend you use a G14.6 format, because it's safe: it prints just the first 6 digits. If you want to see further digits that are probably correct, use these formats instead:

Computer	Format	What the format does
PDP-11, IBM	G15.7	prints the first 7 digits
PDP-10, PDP-20, Honeywell	G16.8	prints the first 8 digits
CDC	G22.14	prints the first 14 digits

You can get extra accuracy by requesting **double precision**:

Computer	Accuracy for double precision	Format
PDP-11	14 digits	D22.14
PDP-10 (using KA), Honeywell	16 digits	D24.16
IBM	17 digits	D25.17
PDP-10 (using KI or KL), PDP-20	18 digits	D26.18
CDC	29 digits	D37.29

Each of these programs computes the square root of 6.3x108 on a PDP-11 computer:

Using reals	Using double precision
	DOUBLE PRECISION A
A=SQRT(6.3E8)	A=DSQRT(6.3D8)
PRINT 10, A	PRINT 10, A
10 FORMAT (1X,G15.7)	10 FORMAT (1X,D22.14)
END	END

The program on the left computes 7 digits. The program on the right computes 14. Comparing the programs, you'll notice four differences:

1. For double precision you must use **double precision numbers**. Instead of saying 6.3E8, say 6.3D8. The D means Double precision.

Real number	Double precision
6.3E8	6.3D8
29.6	29.6D0
	↑
	this is a zero

2. For double precision, you must use **double precision functions**. Instead of saying SQRT, say DSQRT.

Real function	Double precision		Real function	Double precision
SQRTD	SQRT		SIN	DSIN
AMAX1	DMAX1		COS	DCOS
AMIN1	DMIN1		TAN	DTAN
ABS	DABS		ASIN	DASIN
AMOD	DMOD		ACOS	DACOS
EXP	DEXP		ATAN	DATAN
ALOG	DLOG		ATAN2	DATAN2
ALOG10	DLOG10		SINH	DSINH
SIN	DSIN		COSH	DCOSH
COS	DCOS		TANH	DTANH

3. For double precision, you must use **double precision variables**. Normally, the variable A would be real; to make it double precision instead, say:

```
DOUBLE PRECISION A
```

Normally, the variables LENGTH and MASS would be integers, and SPEED would be real; to make them all double precision, say:

```
DOUBLE PRECISION LENGTH,MASS,SPEED
```

Like the DIMENSION and CHARACTER statements, the DOUBLE PRECISION statement must be put at the very top of the program, above even the DATA statements. If you say —

```
IMPLICIT DOUBLE PRECISION(D)
```

every variable whose first letter is D will automatically be double precision; for example, DISTAN and DIAMET and DSIZE will automatically be double precision.

4. For double precision you must use **double precision formats**. Instead of a G format, use D22.14, or whichever D format is appropriate for your computer.

<u>Expense</u> Although double precision arithmetic is more precise than real arithmetic, it's also more expensive: it consumes more of the computer's time, and the numbers consume more of the computer's memory.

<u>Combinations</u> If you combine an integer or a real number with a double precision number, the answer will be double precision.

COMPLEX

In mathematics, the square root of -1 is called i. So i^2 is -1. The number i obeys most of the rules of algebra:

```
 i+ i is 2i
2i+3i is 5i
(8+2i) + (7+3i) is 15+5i
(8+2i) * (7+3i) is 8*7 + 8*3i + 2i*7 + 2i*3i,
        which is 56 + 24i + 14i + 6i²,
        which is 56 + 24i + 14i + -6,
        which is 50 + 38i
```

The number i is neither positive nor negative nor zero; it's pictured instead as being above the real number line:

```
                   i
-5 -4 -3 -2 -1  0  1  2  3  4  5
```

2i is further above the real number line: it's 2 units above 0. Another example: 5+2i is 2 units above 5.

A number that involves i is called **complex**. So 5+2i is complex. Its **real part** is 5, its **imaginary part** is 2, and its **conjugate** is 5-2i.

This program multiplies 8+2i by 7+3i and prints the correct answer, 50+38i:

```
      COMPLEX B
      B=(8.0, 2.0) * (7.0, 3.0)
      PRINT 10, B
10    FORMAT (1X,2G14.6)
      END
```

FORTRAN says (8.0, 2.0) instead of 8+2i. The decimal points and parentheses are required.

To make B complex instead of real, say COMPLEX B. Like the DIMENSION and CHARACTER and DOUBLE PRECISION statements, the COMPLEX statement must be put at the very top of the program, above even the DATA statements.

To print B, use the G14.6 format twice (once for the real part, and once for the imaginary part). The computer will print:

```
 50.0000        38.0000
```

If you say IMPLICIT COMPLEX(C), every variable whose first letter is C will automatically be complex.

Although you can write 8+2i as (8.0, 2.0), you cannot write X+Yi as (X, Y); instead write CMPLX(X, Y).

Here's the rule: to build a complex number from variables instead of from constants, say CMPLX. The variables that the complex number is built from must be real.

If B is complex, you can use these functions:

Function	Meaning
CSQRT(B)	the complex number that's the square root of B
CSIN(B)	the complex number that's the sine of B
CCOS(B)	the complex number that's the cosine of B
CEXP(B)	the complex number that's e^B
CLOG(B)	the complex number that's log B
CABS(B)	the real number that's the absolute value of B
REAL(B)	the real number that's the real part of B
AIMAG(B)	the real number that's the imaginary part of B
CONJG(B)	the complex number that's the conjugate of B

This program finds the square root of -9 and prints the correct answer, 3i:

```
      COMPLEX B,Z
      B=-9
      Z=CSQRT(B)
      PRINT 10, Z
10    FORMAT (1X,2G14.6)
      END
```

Since the top line says B is complex, the second line makes B the complex number -9+0i. The next line makes Z the square root of -9+0i, which is 0+3i. The computer will print the 0 and the 3:

```
 0.000000        3.00000
```

Since that program sets B equal to -9+0i, which FORTRAN writes as (-9.0, 0.0), you can shorten the program to this:

```
      COMPLEX Z
      Z=CSQRT( (-9.0, 0.0) )
      PRINT 10, Z
10    FORMAT (1X,2G14.6)
      END
```

Make sure the number inside CSQRT's parentheses is complex: you need the decimal points, comma, and parentheses.

When the computer combines a complex number with an integer, a real, or a double precision number, the result is complex.

Some computers limit your use of complex numbers, by restrictions such as:

```
"Don't say a complex number equals a double precision number."
"Don't combine a complex number with a double precision number."
"Don't raise a number to a complex power."
"Don't raise a complex number to a power, unless the power is an integer."
```

Find out whether *your* computer has those restrictions.

Subroutines

This program is a combination of two **routines**:

```
      PRINT 10
10    FORMAT (1X,'KIDS')
      CALL YUMMY
      PRINT 20
20    FORMAT (1X,'LOLLIPOPS')
      END

      SUBROUTINE YUMMY
      PRINT 10
10    FORMAT (1X,'SUCK')
      RETURN
      END
```

Each routine ends with the word END.

The first routine is called the **main routine**.

The second routine is called the **subroutine**, and begins with the word SUBROUTINE. I decided to name it YUMMY, so its top line says SUBROUTINE YUMMY.

Above the word SUBROUTINE, I put a blank line. That blank line is optional; it helps humans find where the subroutine begins.

In the main routine, the top pair of lines makes the computer print:

```
KIDS
```

The next line says CALL YUMMY, which makes the computer skip down to subroutine YUMMY. Subroutine YUMMY makes the computer print —

```
SUCK
```

and then RETURN to the main routine, which finishes by printing:

```
LOLLIPOPS
```

Altogether, the program prints:

```
KIDS
SUCK
LOLLIPOPS
```

Notice that line 10 in the main routine is different from line 10 in the subroutine. Similarly, an X in the main routine is different from one in the subroutine:

```
      X=3.4
      CALL FUNNY
      PRINT 10,X
10    FORMAT (1X,G14.6)
      END

      SUBROUTINE FUNNY
      X=925.1
      Y=X+1.0
      PRINT 10, Y
10    FORMAT (1X,G14.6)
      RETURN
      END
```

The computer will set the main routine's X equal to 3.4. Then it will call FUNNY. The X in FUNNY is 925.1, so Y is 926.1, and the computer will print:

```
 926.100
```

When the computer returns to the main routine, it will print the main routine's X, which is still:

```
 3.40000
```

Pass information between routines

To pass information from one routine to another, put the information in parentheses:

```
      A=5.2
      CALL LEMON(A)
      PRINT 10, A
10    FORMAT (1X,G14.6)
      END

      SUBROUTINE LEMON(X)
      PRINT 100, X
100   FORMAT (1X,G14.6)
      X=7.1
      RETURN
      END
```

The computer sets A equal to 5.2. Then it calls LEMON. **The A and X in parentheses mean: the main routine's A is the subroutine's X**, so the subroutine's X is 5.2. Line 100 prints:

```
 5.20000
```

The next line changes X to 7.1. When the computer returns to the main routine, the main routine's A is the subroutine's X, so the main routine's A is 7.1. Line 10 prints:

```
 7.10000
```

A harder example:

```
      P=2.1
      CALL JUNK(P)
      PRINT 10, P
10    FORMAT (1X,G14.6)
      END

      SUBROUTINE JUNK(P)
      P=3.0*P
      RETURN
      END
```

The computer sets P equal to 2.1 and then calls JUNK. **The P in parentheses means: the main routine's P is the subroutine's P**. The subroutine triples P, so P becomes 6.3. When the computer returns to the main routine, line 10 prints:

```
 6.30000
```

Another example:

```
      Q=1.4
      CALL FAT(5.0, Q+.3, R)
      PRINT 10, R
10    FORMAT (1X,G14.6)
      END

      SUBROUTINE FAT(X, Y, Z)
      Z=X+Y
      RETURN
      END
```

When the main routine calls FAT, the subroutine's X is 5.0; Y is Q+.3, which is 1.7; and Z is R, which is undefined. The subroutine sets Z equal to X+Y, which is 6.7. When the computer returns to the main routine, the main routine's R is the subroutine's Z, which is 6.7. Line 10 prints:

```
 6.70000
```

In that CALL, you must say 5.0, not 5, since X must be real. Saying 5 will confuse the computer and make it print a wrong answer.

Sum & average of a trio

This subroutine finds the sum and average of three real numbers — X, Y, and Z:

```
      SUBROUTINE STAT(X, Y, Z, SUM, AVERAG)
      SUM=X+Y+Z
      AVERAG=SUM/3.0
      RETURN
      END
```

This main routine uses STAT to find the sum and average of 8.1, 2.6, and 9.3:

```
      CALL STAT(8.1, 2.6, 9.3, SUM, AVERAG)
      PRINT 10, SUM,AVERAG
10    FORMAT (1X,2G14.6)
      END
```

This subroutine finds the sum and average of three *double precision* numbers:

```
      SUBROUTINE DSTAT(X, Y, Z, SUM, AVERAG)
      DOUBLE PRECISION X, Y, Z, SUM, AVERAG
      SUM=X+Y+Z
      AVERAG=SUM/3D0
      RETURN
      END
```

This main routine uses DSTAT to find the sum and average of π, e, and my phone number (6666644):

```
      DOUBLE PRECISION SUM, AVERAG
      CALL DSTAT(3.1415926535898D0, 2.7182818284590D0, 6666644D0, SUM,
     6AVERAG)
      PRINT 10, SUM, AVERAG
10    FORMAT (1X,2D22.14)
      END
```

You must say DOUBLE PRECISION in both the main routine and the subroutine.

Sum & average of a long list

This subroutine finds the sum and average of X1, X2, X3, ..., XN:

```
      SUBROUTINE STAT2(X, N, SUM, AVERAG)
      DIMENSION X(N)
      SUM=0.0
      DO 10 I=1,N
         SUM=SUM+X(I)
10    CONTINUE
      AVERAG=SUM/N
      RETURN
      END
```

This main routine uses STAT2 to find the sum and average of 8.4, 9.6, 20.1, 7.2, 91.5, and 3.6:

```
      DIMENSION X(6)
      DATA X/8.4,9.6,20.1,7.2,91.5,3.6/
      CALL STAT2(X, 6, SUM, AVERAG)
      PRINT 10, SUM,AVERAG
10    FORMAT (1X,2G14.6)
      END
```

You must put the DIMENSION statement in both the main routine and the subroutine. In the main routine, the DIMENSION must be a constant (6); in the subroutine, the DIMENSION can be a variable (N).

This main routine asks you to input some numbers, then prints their sum and average by using STAT2:

```
       DIMENSION X(100)
       PRINT 10
10     FORMAT (1X,'HOW MANY NUMBERS WOULD YOU LIKE TO GIVE ME?')
       READ *, N
       PRINT 20
20     FORMAT (1X,'TYPE THE NUMBERS')
       READ *, (X(I), I=1,N)
       CALL STAT2(X, N, SUM, AVERAG)
       PRINT 30, SUM,AVERAG
30     FORMAT (1X,'THE SUM IS',G14.6,' AND THE AVERAGE IS',G14.6)
       END
```

That DIMENSION statement lets you input up to 100 numbers.

If a main routine says DIMENSION X(100), and X is passed between the main routine and the subroutine, the subroutine's DIMENSION statement must say no more than X(100): if the subroutine's DIMENSION statement says X(N), the N must be no more than 100.

Pass double subscripts For *double* subscripts, the main routine's DIMENSION statement must be *exactly* the same as the subroutine's.

For example, suppose the main routine says DIMENSION X(25,4). Then the subroutine must say DIMENSION X(25,4) also. The subroutine must not say DIMENSION X(20,3). If the subroutine says DIMENSION X(M,N), the M must be exactly 25.

Famous subroutines The **Scientific Subroutine Package (SSP)** is a collection of subroutines written by IBM that do statistics, calculus, equation-solving, and advanced math. The **Calcomp subroutines** make the computer operate a Calcomp plotter (a device that draws fancy shapes on paper, by using a felt-tip or ballpoint pen).

Most big computers store the SSP and Calcomp subroutines on disk permanently. Ask the people in your computer center how to combine your own main routines with those subroutines, and how to put your *own* library of subroutines onto the disk.

How to write a big program If you and your friends want to write a big program together, divide the problem into a main routine and several subroutines. Have each person write one routine.

Although you'll need a group conference to decide what the SUBROUTINE and CALL statements will be, you don't have to agree on the names of variables, since the names of subroutine variables have nothing to do with the names of main-routine variables.

Your own functions

Instead of using functions such as SQRT and ABS, you can invent your *own* functions. Here's how to invent a function called F, and how to use the function you've invented:

```
       A=F(5.2)+1.0
       PRINT 10, A
10     FORMAT (1X,G14.6)
       END

       FUNCTION F(X)
       F=2.0*X
       RETURN
       END
```

The program consists of two routines. The first routine is the *main* routine. The second routine is the definition of the FUNCTION F. Each routine ends with the word END.

The main routine's top line requires the computer to find F(5.2), so the computer hunts for the definition of FUNCTION F. The definition says F is twice 5.2, which is 10.4. So A is 11.4. The computer will print:

```
 11.40000
```

Like a subroutine, a function definition can be very long and have many variables in parentheses.

Naming your function You can give your function the name F or G or any other name, such as MASS. If the function's name begins with I, J, K, L, M, or N, the computer will assume its value is an integer.

If you want the function MASS(X) to be double precision instead of an integer, begin your main routine by saying —

```
       DOUBLE PRECISION MASS
```

and begin your function definition with this line:

```
       DOUBLE PRECISION FUNCTION MASS(X)
```

Files

The computer can write its answers onto a data file:

```
       A=14.6+75.2
       WRITE(3,10) A
10     FORMAT (1X,G14.6)
       WRITE(7,20)
20     FORMAT (1X,'TINA, PLEASE TICKLE MY TUBA')
       END
```

Since A is 89.8, the second line makes the computer write 89.8 onto "file 3", using line 10's format. The next pair of lines make the computer write onto "file 7", using line 20's format; so the computer will write TINA, PLEASE TICKLE MY TUBA onto file 7.

Before running that program, tell the computer where to put files 3 and 7. You can make the computer put them on a disk, line printer, tape, terminal, or wherever else you please. Ask the people in your computer center how to tell the computer where to put the files.

If your program has many statements saying to write onto file 3, the computer will write many lines onto file 3, so the file will become long.

Use carriage controls only if the file is on a line printer or terminal.

If you say —

```
       READ(4,30) X
```

the computer will read the value of X from file 4, using line 30's format. If you say file 4 is the card reader, the computer will wait for you to feed in a card; it you say file 4 is your terminal, the computer will wait for you to type on the terminal; if you say file 4 is on a tape or disk, the computer will assume you created the file before running the program.

For handling files, the word READ works even on PDP computers.

For PDP-10 and PDP-20 computers, here's how to make file 3 be on disk and named JOE.... Near the beginning of your program, say:

```
       OPEN(UNIT=3, DEVICE='DSK', FILE='JOE.')
```

Near the end of your program, say:

```
       CLOSE(UNIT=3)
```

COBOL

Like BASIC and PASCAL, **COBOL** is a computer language. "COBOL" is pronounced "koe ball" and stands for "COmmon Business Oriented Language".

COBOL solves *business* problems that involve *large* files of data, so COBOL's used mainly by *businesses* having *maxicomputers*. But today, you can use COBOL even on minicomputers and microcomputers.

In the "help wanted" section of your local newspaper, many ads that say "programmer wanted" are placed by businesses that have maxicomputers and use COBOL. To get a job through the "help wanted" section, a knowledge of COBOL will help you more than PASCAL or FORTRAN.

The first version of COBOL was called **COBOL 60**, because it was invented in 1960. Then came **COBOL 61**, **COBOL 65**, **COBOL 68**, **COBOL 74**, and **COBOL 85**. Today, most computers still use COBOL 74 or a variation of it. This chapter explains how to write COBOL programs that work on most computers.

During the 1960's and early 1970's, COBOL programmers used a style called "easy programming". Today, most COBOL programmers use a more sophisticated style, called **structured programming**. This chapter explains structured programming. Though it's harder to learn than easy programming, it will make your boss kiss you.

Simple programs

Every COBOL program is written as an outline. Here's a short outline; to turn it into a COBOL program, just fill in the blanks:

```
IDENTIFICATION DIVISION.
PROGRAM-ID.
        The program's name.
AUTHOR.
        Your name.

ENVIRONMENT DIVISION.
CONFIGURATION SECTION.
SOURCE-COMPUTER.
        The computer's name.
OBJECT-COMPUTER.
        The computer's name again.

DATA DIVISION.

PROCEDURE DIVISION.
MAIN-ROUTINE.
        What you want the computer to do.
        STOP RUN.
```

For example, here's a COBOL program I wrote:

Program	Reason
IDENTIFICATION DIVISION.	
PROGRAM-ID.	
HARRY.	The program's name is HARRY.
AUTHOR.	
RUSS WALTER.	My name is Russ Walter.
ENVIRONMENT DIVISION.	
CONFIGURATION SECTION.	
SOURCE-COMPUTER.	
DECSYSTEM-20.	My computer's a DECsystem-20.
OBJECT-COMPUTER.	
DECSYSTEM-20.	
DATA DIVISION.	
PROCEDURE DIVISION.	
MAIN-ROUTINE.	
DISPLAY "LIFE STINKS."	I want the computer to gripe.
STOP RUN.	

When I run that program, the computer will print:

```
LIFE STINKS
```

Every COBOL program consists of four parts.

> The first part of the program is called the IDENTIFICATION DIVISION. It includes the program's name and the programmer's name.
>
> The second part of the program is called the ENVIRONMENT DIVISION. It includes the computer's name.
>
> The third part of the program is called the DATA DIVISION. For a simple program, the DATA DIVISION is blank.
>
> The fourth part of the program is the PROCEDURE DIVISION. It says what you want the computer to do.

The order is important: the IDENTIFICATION DIVISION must come *first*, then the ENVIRONMENT DIVISION, then the DATA DIVISION, and finally the PROCEDURE DIVISION. So to become an expert COBOL programmer, you must memorize: "IDENTIFICATION, ENVIRONMENT, DATA, PROCEDURE".

To memorize that easily, memorize this easy sentence: "I enjoy data processing". In that sentence, the words begin with the letters "I E D P" — and so do the four COBOL divisions.

In the program, each blank that you fill is called a **paragraph**.

> In the first paragraph, write the program's name. In the next paragraph, write your *own* name. In the next two paragraphs, write the computer's name. In the last paragraph, write what you want the computer to do.
>
> The first paragraph is called the PROGRAM-ID. The next paragraph is called the AUTHOR. The next two paragraphs are the SOURCE-COMPUTER and the OBJECT-COMPUTER. The last paragraph is called the MAIN-ROUTINE.

Each paragraph is indented. To indent on PDP and Eclipse computers, type a controlled I.

In COBOL, the only important punctuation mark is the period. When writing a simple program, **put a period at the end of each line**. COBOL never requires commas or semicolons.

Don't forget the hyphens! Put a hyphen in PROGRAM-ID, SOURCE-COMPUTER, OBJECT-COMPUTER, and MAIN-ROUTINE.

Use correct spacing.

Right:	DISPLAY "BURP".
Wrong:	DIS PLAY "BURP".
Wrong:	DISPLAY"BURP".
Wrong:	DISPLAY "BURP" .

In the paragraphs that are called SOURCE-COMPUTER and OBJECT-COMPUTER, you must type the computer's name correctly. Here are the correct names for some famous computers:

```
IBM-360.
IBM-370.
PDP-11.
DECSYSTEM-10.   (It means you have a PDP-10.)
DECSYSTEM-20.   (It means you have a PDP-20.)
ECLIPSE C300.
6600.           (It means you have a CDC 6600.)
```

Don't forget the hyphens!

Go ahead: try writing your *own* COBOL program. In the PROCEDURE DIVISION, remember to say DISPLAY:

```
BASIC:    PRINT "LIFE STINKS"
PASCAL:   WRITELN('LIFE STINKS');
COBOL:    DISPLAY "LIFE STINKS".
```

Old-fashioned computers On IBM computers, instead of using quotation marks, you must use apostrophes.

```
Most computers:   DISPLAY "LIFE STINKS".
IBM computers:    DISPLAY 'LIFE STINKS'.
```

On IBM and CDC computers, you must indent the entire program, like this (each ▓ represents a blank space):

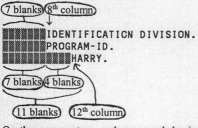

On those computers, each paragraph begins in column 12, and must not go farther to the right than column 72. (The computer ignores everything in columns 73-80.)

Abridgments

If you're lazy, you can omit the AUTHOR paragraph:

Complete IDENTIFICATION DIVISION	Abridged version

IDENTIFICATION DIVISION.
PROGRAM-ID.
    HARRY.
AUTHOR.
    RUSS WALTER.
	IDENTIFICATION DIVISION.
	PROGRAM-ID.
	    HARRY.

If you're lazy, *and you're using a PDP-10, PDP-20, Eclipse, or IBM computer*, you can omit the CONFIGURATION SECTION, SOURCE-COMPUTER, and OBJECT-COMPUTER:

Complete ENVIRONMENT DIVISION	Abridged version

ENVIRONMENT DIVISION.
CONFIGURATION SECTION.
SOURCE-COMPUTER.
    The computer's name.
OBJECT-COMPUTER.
    The computer's name.
	ENVIRONMENT DIVISION.

If you're *very* lazy, and you're using a PDP-10 or PDP-20 computer, you can abridge the program even further, so that the entire program looks like this:

```
IDENTIFICATION DIVISION.
PROCEDURE DIVISION.
      DISPLAY "LIFE STINKS".
      STOP RUN.
```

But if you're working for a big company, your employer will expect you *not* to be lazy: if you're lazy, you get fired!

Fancy displays

You've seen that every COBOL program consists of four divisions: IDENTIFICATION, ENVIRONMENT, DATA, and PROCEDURE. The most important division is the PROCEDURE DIVISION. Let's look at it more closely.

Here's a cute PROCEDURE DIVISION:

```
PROCEDURE DIVISION.
MAIN-ROUTINE.
      DISPLAY "BILLIE AND BONNIE".
      DISPLAY "BURP".
      STOP RUN.
```

It makes the computer display:

```
BILLIE AND BONNIE
BURP
```

Another example:

```
PROCEDURE DIVISION.
MAIN-ROUTINE.
      DISPLAY "FLU" "SHED".
      STOP RUN.
```

The computer will display FLU and SHED on the same line:

```
FLUSHED
```

PERFORM

Let's make the computer display "I LOVE YOU", then display "I HATE YOU" six times, then display "I AM CONFUSED", like this:

```
I LOVE YOU
I HATE YOU
I HATE YOU
I HATE YOU
I HATE YOU
I HATE YOU
I HATE YOU
I AM CONFUSED
```

Here's the PROCEDURE DIVISION:

```
PROCEDURE DIVISION.
MAIN-ROUTINE.
      DISPLAY "I LOVE YOU".
      PERFORM EXPRESS-THE-HATRED 6 TIMES.
      DISPLAY "I AM CONFUSED".
      STOP RUN.
EXPRESS-THE-HATRED.
      DISPLAY "I HATE YOU".
```

That PROCEDURE DIVISION consists of two paragraphs. The first paragraph is called the MAIN-ROUTINE. The second paragraph is called EXPRESS-THE-HATRED.

The computer obeys the first paragraph: it displays "I LOVE YOU", then performs the EXPRESS-THE-HATRED 6 times, then displays "I AM CONFUSED", and finally stops.

When you invent your own PROCEDURE DIVISION, the first paragraph should be called the MAIN-ROUTINE; for the other paragraphs underneath, invent whatever names you like (such as EXPRESS-THE-HATRED). A paragraph's name should be hyphenated, and should contain no more than 30 characters. (EXPRESS-THE-HATRED contains 18 characters, so it's okay.) The first paragraph is the main routine, the paragraphs underneath are subroutines. The bottom line of the main routine should say STOP RUN. In the middle of the main routine, you should say to PERFORM the subroutines.

In the example above, the main routine says to PERFORM the EXPRESS-THE-HATRED subroutine 6 times. If you'd like to see more hatred, say 100 times instead of 6:

```
      PERFORM EXPRESS-THE-HATRED 100 TIMES.
```

If you'd rather see just a *little* hatred, say just —

```
      PERFORM EXPRESS-THE-HATRED 1 TIMES.
```

or say just:

```
      PERFORM EXPRESS-THE-HATRED.
```

Let's make the computer display:

```
I KNOW THAT
YOU ARE DRIVING
ME CRAZY
YOU ARE DRIVING
ME CRAZY
YOU ARE DRIVING
ME CRAZY
YOU ARE DRIVING
ME CRAZY
AND YET I LOVE YOU
```

Here's the PROCEDURE DIVISION:

```
PROCEDURE DIVISION.
MAIN-ROUTINE.
        DISPLAY "I KNOW THAT".
        PERFORM ACT-AS-IF-GOING-INSANE 4 TIMES.
        DISPLAY "AND YET I LOVE YOU".
        STOP RUN.
ACT-AS-IF-GOING-INSANE.
        DISPLAY "YOU ARE DRIVING".
        DISPLAY "ME CRAZY".
```

Let's make the computer display:

```
THE ASTRONAUTS GO
UP
UP
UP
UP
UP
AND THEN THEY COME
DOWN
DOWN
DOWN
DOWN
DOWN
```

Here's the PROCEDURE DIVISION:

```
PROCEDURE DIVISION.
MAIN-ROUTINE.
        DISPLAY "THE ASTRONAUTS GO".
        PERFORM SHOW-THE-ASTRONAUTS-RISING 5 TIMES.
        DISPLAY "AND THEN THEY COME".
        PERFORM SHOW-THE-ASTRONAUTS-FALLING 5 TIMES.
        STOP RUN.
SHOW-THE-ASTRONAUTS-RISING.
        DISPLAY "UP".
SHOW-THE-ASTRONAUTS-FALLING.
        DISPLAY "DOWN".
```

Let's make the computer display:

```
YOU ARE VERY SWEET
HA-HA-HA!
HO-HO-HO!
YOU CANNOT BE BEAT
HA-HA-HA!
HO-HO-HO!
YOUR LIPS ARE LIKE WINE
HA-HA-HA!
HO-HO-HO!
BUT YOU SMELL LIKE TURPENTINE
HA-HA-HA!
HO-HO-HO!
YOU STINK!
```

Here's the PROCEDURE DIVISION:

```
PROCEDURE DIVISION.
MAIN-ROUTINE.
        DISPLAY "YOU ARE VERY SWEET".
        PERFORM LAUGH-A-LOT.
        DISPLAY "YOU CANNOT BE BEAT".
        PERFORM LAUGH-A-LOT.
        DISPLAY "YOUR LIPS ARE LIKE WINE".
        PERFORM LAUGH-A-LOT.
        DISPLAY "BUT YOU SMELL LIKE TURPENTINE".
        PERFORM LAUGH-A-LOT.
        DISPLAY "YOU STINK!".
        STOP RUN.
LAUGH-A-LOT.
        DISPLAY "HA-HA-HA!".
        DISPLAY "HO-HO-HO!".
```

Variables

Like other languages, COBOL lets you use variables. The name of a variable can be a letter (like X or Y) or a hyphenated phrase (like NUMBER-OF-BULLIES-I-SQUIRTED). A hyphenated phrase can have up to 30 characters.

To use a variable, you must describe it in the data division, as in this example:

```
IDENTIFICATION DIVISION.
PROGRAM-ID.
        JUNK.
AUTHOR.
        RUSS WALTER.

ENVIRONMENT DIVISION.
CONFIGURATION SECTION.
SOURCE-COMPUTER.
        DECSYSTEM-20.
OBJECT-COMPUTER.
        DECSYSTEM-20.

DATA DIVISION.
WORKING-STORAGE SECTION.
01      K PICTURE IS XXX.

PROCEDURE DIVISION.
MAIN-ROUTINE.
        MOVE "HER" TO K.
        DISPLAY "PUS" K "S".
        STOP RUN.
```

Instead of "RUSS WALTER", write your own name. Instead of "DECSYSTEM-20", write your own computer's name.

In the DATA DIVISION's WORKING-STORAGE SECTION, the "01   K" says K is a variable. The PICTURE IS XXX says K is a string that has three characters; each X stands for a character. In the PROCEDURE DIVISION, the first sentence makes K become this 3-character string: "HER". The next sentence makes the computer display:

```
PUSHERS
```

When you type that program, make sure you **put a hyphen between WORKING and STORAGE**. If you forget the hyphen, the computer will act crazy, and will say that your program contains many, many errors.

Suppose you change the picture from XXX to XX, so that the DATA DIVISION and PROCEDURE DIVISION look like this:

```
DATA DIVISION
WORKING-STORAGE SECTION
01      K PICTURE IS XX.

PROCEDURE DIVISION.
MAIN-ROUTINE.
        MOVE "HER" TO K.
        DISPLAY "PUS" K "S".
        STOP RUN.
```

K will be a string having only two characters. When the computer tries to move "HER" to K, only the first two characters of "HER" will fit, so K will be "HE". The computer will display:

```
PUSHES
```

Suppose you change the picture to XXXX. K will have four characters. When the computer tries to move "HER" to K, it needs to move a fourth character also, so it moves a blank space at the end, which makes K be "HER ". The computer will display:

```
PUSHER S
```

This program shows how revolutionary politics lead to revolutionary clothing:

```
DATA DIVISION.
WORKING-STORAGE SECTION.
01     FIRST-PRESIDENT PICTURE IS XXXXXXXXXX.
01     CLEANING-METHOD PICTURE IS XXXX.

PROCEDURE DIVISION.
MAIN-ROUTINE.
       MOVE "WASHINGTON" TO FIRST-PRESIDENT.
       MOVE FIRST-PRESIDENT TO CLEANING-METHOD.
       DISPLAY CLEANING-METHOD " MY BLUE JEANS".
       STOP RUN.
```

Above the DATA DIVISION, write your own IDENTIFICATION DIVISION and ENVIRONMENT DIVISION. The DATA DIVISION says FIRST-PRESIDENT will be a string having ten characters, and CLEANING-METHOD will be a string having four. The first sentence of the MAIN-ROUTINE makes FIRST-PRESIDENT be "WASHINGTON". The next sentence tries to move "WASHINGTON" to CLEANING-METHOD; but because of CLEANING-METHOD's picture, the computer moves "WASH" instead. The computer will display:

```
WASH MY BLUE JEANS
```

To make sure you understand the word MOVE, examine this example:

```
DATA DIVISION.
WORKING-STORAGE SECTION.
01     C PICTURE IS XXX.
01     D PICTURE IS XXX.

PROCEDURE DIVISION.
MAIN-ROUTINE.
       MOVE "CAT" TO C.       C becomes "CAT".
       MOVE C TO D.           D becomes "CAT".
       DISPLAY C.             The computer displays "CAT".
       MOVE "HE" TO C.        C becomes "HE ".
       DISPLAY C "BLED".      The computer displays "HE BLED".
       STOP RUN.
```

COBOL allows abbreviations. You can say PIC instead of PICTURE IS, and X(7) instead of XXXXXXX.

Numeric variables

Let's make the computer add 53 and 4, and display the sum, 57. Here's how:

```
DATA DIVISION.
WORKING-STORAGE SECTION.
01     K PIC 99.

PROCEDURE DIVISION.
MAIN-ROUTINE.
       COMPUTE K = 53 + 4.
       DISPLAY K.
       STOP RUN.
```

The PIC 99 says K is a number having two digits. (Each 9 stands for a digit.) The MAIN-ROUTINE sets K equal to 53 + 4, which is 57. The computer will display:

```
57
```

In the COMPUTE statement, the equal sign and the plus sign must be surrounded by spaces.

Right:	COMPUTE K = 53 + 4.
Wrong:	COMPUTE K=53+4.
Wrong:	COMPUTE K = 53+4.

If you change the picture to 999, K will be a number having three digits. It will be 057 instead of 57. The computer will display:

```
057
```

(Exception: PDP-10 and PDP-20 computers are lazy; they don't bother to display the 0 at the left; they display just 57.)

If you change the picture to 9, K will be a number having only one digit. so K will not be 57. The computer will not display the correct sum.

Like FORTRAN, COBOL uses these operators:

Operator	Meaning
+	plus
-	minus
*	times
/	divided by
**	exponent

You must put a blank space before and after each operator:

Right	Wrong
53 + 4	53+4
7 ** 2	7**2
- J + 3	-J + 3

Like other computer languages, COBOL lets you use parentheses. Do *not* put a space after a left parenthesis:

Right
```
COMPUTE K = I * (- J + 3)
                ↑↑  ↑  ↑
            no space  spaces
```

You can use these shortcuts:

Sentence	Shortcut
COMPUTE A = A + 7.	ADD 7 TO A.
COMPUTE B = B - 4.	SUBTRACT 4 FROM B.

Operators are allowed only in sentences that say COMPUTE, IF, UNTIL, or WHEN.

Allowed:	COMPUTE A = 2 * 3.
Not allowed:	DISPLAY 2 * 3.
Not allowed:	MOVE 2 * 3 TO A.
Not allowed:	ADD 2 * 3 TO A.

Decimals

You can use decimals:

```
DATA DIVISION.
WORKING-STORAGE SECTION.
01     K PIC 9999V99.

PROCEDURE DIVISION.
MAIN-ROUTINE.
       COMPUTE K = 2.208 + 4.109.
       DISPLAY K.
       STOP RUN.
```

The PIC 9999V99 says K is a number having four digits, followed by a decimal point, followed by two digits. (The V stands for the decimal point.) The MAIN-ROUTINE tries to set K equal to 2.208 + 4.109, which is 6.317; but because of K's picture, I will be 0006.31 instead. So the computer should display 0006.31.

PDP-10 and PDP-20 computers don't bother to display the zeros: they display 6.31. PDP-11, IBM, CDC, and Eclipse computers don't bother to display the decimal point: they display 000631.

You can change that program by saying ROUNDED:

```
       COMPUTE K ROUNDED = 2.208 + 4.109.
```

The computer will find the sum (6.317), and round it so K is 0006.32 instead of 0006.31.

If J's picture is 99, saying "COMPUTE J = 200 / 3" makes J be 66. Saying "COMPUTE J ROUNDED = 200 / 3" makes J be 67.

Which is better: saying "COMPUTE X = 4.9" or "MOVE 4.9 TO X"? You should usually say "MOVE 4.9 TO X", because the computer handles it more quickly. But MOVE cannot round; so if you want to round, say COMPUTE.

MOVE can do strange things:

```
DATA DIVISION.
WORKING-STORAGE SECTION.
01      L PIC 999V99.

PROCEDURE DIVISION.
MAIN-ROUTINE.
        MOVE 16725.048 TO L.
        DISPLAY L.
        STOP RUN.
```

L's picture makes the computer move the three digits just left of the decimal point and the two digits just right of it. L will be 725.04.

Negatives

You can use negative numbers:

```
DATA DIVISION.
WORKING-STORAGE SECTION.
01      K PIC S9999.

PROCEDURE DIVISION.
MAIN-ROUTINE.
        COMPUTE K = 100 - 367.
        DISPLAY K.
        STOP RUN.
```

In K's picture, the S stands for a sign (which can be plus or minus). K will be -0267. The computer should display -0267.

PDP-10 and PDP-20 computers don't bother to display the zero: they display -267. Some other computers display the minus sign on top of the right digit, like this: 026̄7. On many computers, the minus combines with the 7 and forms a P, like this: 026P.

If you omit the S from K's picture, K will be 0267 instead of -0267.

To find the negative of a power, use parentheses:

```
        COMPUTE A = - (3 ** 2).
```

If you omit the parentheses, the computer will get the wrong answer.

ACCEPT

Here's how to translate the BASIC word **INPUT** into PASCAL and COBOL.

```
BASIC:  INPUT K
PASCAL: READ(K);
COBOL:  ACCEPT K.
```

Let's look at a COBOL example:

```
DATA DIVISION.
WORKING-STORAGE SECTION.
01      K PIC XXX.

PROCEDURE DIVISION.
MAIN-ROUTINE.
        DISPLAY "THIS PROGRAM WANTS YOU TO TYPE SOMETHING".
        ACCEPT K.
        DISPLAY K.
        STOP RUN.
```

The computer displays:

```
THIS PROGRAM WANTS YOU TO TYPE SOMETHING
```

The statement ACCEPT K makes the computer wait for you to type something. If you type —

```
FIGHT
```

the computer will try to move "FIGHT" to K; but since K's picture is XXX, K will be "FIG". The computer will display:

```
FIG
```

If you type —

```
ME
```

the computer will try to move "ME" to K; since K's picture is XXX, K will be "ME ". The computer will display:

```
ME
```

Suppose a program says L PIC 999 and ACCEPT L. If you input —

```
4
```

a PDP-10 or PDP-20 computer will make L be 004, but an IBM or CDC computer will make L be 400.

Suppose a program says M PIC S9999V99 and ACCEPT M. If you want M to be -0034.27, here's what to input....

```
On PDP-10 & PDP-20 computers:    -0034.27 or -34.27
On IBM and CDC computers:        003427̄
```

Editing

The computer can edit the output:

```
DATA DIVISION.
WORKING-STORAGE SECTION.
01      K PIC XXXBXXX.

PROCEDURE DIVISION.
MAIN-ROUTINE.
        MOVE "HITHER" TO K.
        DISPLAY K.
        STOP RUN.
```

In K's picture, **B means a blank space**. So when the computer moves "HITHER", K becomes "HIT HER". The computer will display:

```
HIT HER
```

This program displays the Boston Computer Society's phone number:

```
DATA DIVISION.
WORKING-STORAGE SECTION.
01      PHONE-NUMBER PIC 999B9999.

PROCEDURE DIVISION.
MAIN-ROUTINE.
        MOVE 3678080 TO PHONE-NUMBER.
        DISPLAY PHONE-NUMBER.
        STOP RUN.
```

When the computer moves 3678080, PHONE-NUMBER becomes "367 8080". The computer will display:

```
367 8080
```

This program is of historical importance:

```
DATA DIVISION.
WORKING-STORAGE SECTION.
01      K PIC 9B9B9999.

PROCEDURE DIVISION.
MAIN-ROUTINE.
        COMPUTE K = 741775 + 1.
        DISPLAY "THE DECLARATION OF INDEPENDENCE WAS SIGNED
ON " K.
        STOP RUN.
```

The computer will display:

```
THE DECLARATION OF INDEPENDENCE WAS SIGNED ON 7 4 1776
```

Using B to insert a blank is called **editing**. You've learned four kinds of variables:

Kind of variable	Symbols in picture
string	X
edited string	X B
number	9 V S
edited number	9 B Z , $ * . + - DB CR

You can use these pictures for editing numbers:

K's picture	Meaning	What K will be if you move 50320 to K	What K will be if you move 0 to K
B99999999	a blank then eight digits	" 00050320"	" 00000000"
ZZZZZZZZZ	blanks then digits	" 50320"	" "
$,$$$,$$$	put $ before the digits	" $50,320"	" "
*,***,***	stars instead of blanks	"***50,320"	"*********"

To edit decimals, put a decimal point in the picture.

K's picture	If you move 50320.6 to K	If you move .04 to K	If you move 0 to K
Z,ZZZ,ZZZ.ZZ	" 50,320.60"	" .04"	" "
$,$$$,$$$.$$	" $50,320.60"	" $.04"	" "
*,***,***.**	"***50,320.60"	"*********.04"	"*********.**"

With those pictures, if you move 0 to K the computer doesn't put any digits in K. To guarantee that K contains a digit, put 9 in the picture:

K's picture	If you move 50320.6 to K	If you move .04 to K	If you move 0 to K
Z,ZZZ,ZZ9.99	" 50,320.60"	" 0.04"	" 0.00"
$,$$$,$$9.99	" $50,320.60"	" $0.04"	" $0.00"
*,***,**9.99	"***50,320.60"	"*********0.04"	"*********0.00"

To edit negative numbers, use +, -, DB, or CR.

K's picture	Meaning	If you move -2.6 to K	If you move 2.6 to K
ZZZ.ZZ+	put - or + afterwards	" 2.60-"	" 2.60+"
ZZZ.ZZ-	put - or blank afterwards	" 2.60-"	" 2.60 "
ZZZ.ZZDB	if negative, put DB (for debit)	" 2.60DB"	" 2.60 "
ZZZ.ZZCR	if negative, put CR (for credit)	" 2.60CR"	" 2.60 "

For fancier pictures, replace the Z by $, *, or 9.

Here's how to put the sign before the digits:

K's picture	Meaning	If you move -2.6 to K	If you move 2.6 to K
+++.++	put - or + before digits	" -2.60"	" +2.60"
---.--	- or blank before digits	" -2.60"	" 2.60"

Here are the differences between numbers and edited numbers:

	Number	Edited number
how to put decimal point in the picture	V	.
how to put a sign in the picture	S	+, -, DB, or CR
how to fill up most of the picture	9	9, Z, $, *, +, or -
what the value should be	intermediate result in long calculation	the final answer to be displayed
If the value's called K, can you say ACCEPT K?	yes	no
If the value's called K, can you use K in further computations (such as COMPUTE L = K + 1)?	yes	no
What happens if you try to DISPLAY the value?	"0", ".", and "-" might look wrong	displays correctly

DECIMAL-POINT IS COMMA

Some Europeans write commas instead of decimal points, and write decimal points instead of commas.

United States and England:	5,243,794.95
France and Italy:	5.243.794,95
Germany:	5 243 794,95

To write a COBOL program for a Frenchman, an Italian, or a German, make three changes....

Change #1 Insert this line:

```
DECIMAL-POINT IS COMMA.
```

Put that line in a SPECIAL-NAMES paragraph, at the end of the ENVIRONMENT DIVISION's CONFIGURATION SECTION:

```
CONFIGURATION SECTION.
SOURCE-COMPUTER.
     The computer's name.
OBJECT-COMPUTER.
     The computer's name again.
SPECIAL-NAMES.
     DECIMAL-POINT IS COMMA.
```

Change #2 Type all numbers in French-Italian-German notation. So instead of typing —

```
MOVE 5243794.95 TO K
```

type:

```
MOVE 5243794,95 TO K
```

Change #3 Use French-Italian-German notation in pictures for *edited* numbers.

For a Frenchman or Italian:	K PIC Z.ZZZ.ZZ,ZZ
For a German:	K PIC ZBZZZBZZZ,ZZ

Those are the only changes Europeans make. They still put a period at the end of every sentence, and still use English COBOL words such as MOVE and DISPLAY.

American COBOL:	DISPLAY "HELLO, STUPID".
French COBOL:	DISPLAY "BONJOUR, BETE".

Logic

COBOL lets you do logic.

IF

Like other computer languages, COBOL uses the word IF:

```
BASIC              COBOL
INPUT i            ACCEPT I.
IF i > 5 THEN      IF I > 5
  j = 80                      MOVE 80 TO J
  k = 90                      MOVE 90 TO K.
END IF
```

COBOL also lets you say ELSE:

```
BASIC              COBOL
INPUT i            ACCEPT I.
IF I > 5 THEN      IF I > 5
  j = 80                      MOVE 80 TO J
  k = 90                      MOVE 90 TO K
ELSE               ELSE
  j = 30                      MOVE 30 TO J
  k = 50                      MOVE 50 TO K.
END IF
```

In COBOL, **when you write the IF statement, do not put a period at the end of every line; instead, put the period just at the end of the entire IF idea**.

Notice that I indented the word MOVE. The indentation is optional, but is a good habit. To indent on PDP and Eclipse computers, type a controlled I; to indent on IBM and CDC computers, press the space bar several times.

COBOL uses these IF lines:

IF line	Meaning
IF I = 5	If I is equal to 5
IF I NOT = 5	If I is not equal to 5
IF I > 5	If I is greater than 5
IF I NOT > 5	If I is not greater than 5
IF I < 5	If I is less than 5
IF I NOT < 5	IF I is not less than 5

You can use the words AND and OR and abbreviate:

```
IF line:        IF J > 1 AND J < 100
Abbreviation:   IF J > 1 AND < 100

IF line:        IF K < -3 OR K = 6 OR K = 9 OR K = 12 OR K > 50
Abbreviation:   IF K < -3 OR = 6 OR 9 OR 12 OR > 50
```

You can say this:

```
        IF AGE < 13
                DISPLAY "CHILD"
        ELSE IF AGE < 20
                DISPLAY "TEENAGER"
        ELSE IF AGE < 40
                DISPLAY "YOUNG ADULT"
        ELSE IF AGE < 60
                DISPLAY "MIDDLE-AGED"
        ELSE
                DISPLAY "SENIOR CITIZEN".
```

It means, "If AGE is less than 13, display the word CHILD; if not less than 13, do the following: if AGE is less than 20, display the word TEENAGER; if not less than 20, do the following: if AGE is less than 40,…" and so on. The computer will display just one phrase, to describe the person's AGE.

UNTIL

You can say UNTIL:

```
DATA DIVISION.
WORKING-STORAGE SECTION.
01      I PIC 999.

PROCEDURE DIVISION.
MAIN-ROUTINE.
        MOVE 5 TO I.
        PERFORM FIDDLE-WITH-I UNTIL I > 100.
        STOP RUN.
FIDDLE-WITH-I.
        DISPLAY I.
        COMPUTE I = I * 2.
```

The computer will perform FIDDLE-WITH-I repeatedly, until I > 100. The computer will display 5, 10, 20, 40, and 80. It will not display 160.

Here are the details. When the computer encounters PERFORM FIDDLE-WITH-I UNTIL I > 100, it checks whether I > 100. If I > 100, the computer proceeds to the next statement (the STOP RUN); but if I is *not* greater than 100, the computer performs FIDDLE-WITH-I and then re-executes the statement PERFORM FIDDLE-WITH-I UNTIL I > 100.

To translate a BASIC "FOR...NEXT loop" into COBOL, say "PERFORM":

```
BASIC                     COBOL
FOR i = 5 TO 17           PROCEDURE DIVISION.
  PRINT i                 MAIN-ROUTINE.
NEXT                              PERFORM DISPLAY-IT
                                          VARYING I FROM 5 BY 1 UNTIL I > 17.
                                  STOP RUN.
                          DISPLAY-IT.
                                  DISPLAY I.



FOR i = 5 TO 17 STEP 3    PROCEDURE DIVISION.
  PRINT i                 MAIN-ROUTINE.
NEXT                              PERFORM DISPLAY-IT
                                          VARYING I FROM 5 BY 3 UNTIL I > 17.
                                  STOP RUN.
                          DISPLAY-IT.
                                  DISPLAY I.



FOR i = 5 TO 17           PROCEDURE DIVISION.
  FOR j = 1 TO 3          MAIN-ROUTINE.
    PRINT i, j                    PERFORM DISPLAY-IT
  NEXT                                    VARYING I FROM 5 BY 1 UNTIL I > 17
NEXT                                      AFTER J FROM 1 BY 1 UNTIL J > 3.
                                  STOP RUN.
                          DISPLAY-IT.
                                  DISPLAY I J.
```

GO TO

Like other computer languages, COBOL lets you say GO TO. In COBOL, **put a space between GO and TO**. (In PASCAL, you do *not* put a space between GO and TO.)

For example, instead of saying STOP RUN, you can say GO TO MAIN-ROUTINE:

```
PROCEDURE DIVISION.
MAIN-ROUTINE.
        DISPLAY "WHEATIES".
        DISPLAY "ARE WONDERFUL".
        GO TO MAIN-ROUTINE.
```

The computer will display "WHEATIES" and "ARE WONDERFUL", repeatedly:

```
WHEATIES
ARE WONDERFUL
WHEATIES
ARE WONDERFUL
WHEATIES
ARE WONDERFUL
etc.
```

The main routine can consist of *two* paragraphs, called MAIN-ROUTINE-BEGINNING and MAIN-ROUTINE-LOOP:

```
PROCEDURE DIVISION.
MAIN-ROUTINE-BEGINNING.
        DISPLAY "PLEASE".
MAIN-ROUTINE-LOOP.
        DISPLAY "KISS".
        DISPLAY "ME".
        GO TO MAIN-ROUTINE-LOOP.
```

The computer will display PLEASE, then repeatedly display KISS and ME:

```
PLEASE
KISS
ME
KISS
ME
KISS
ME
etc.
```

The main routine can consist of *three* paragraphs, called MAIN-ROUTINE-BEGINNING, MAIN-ROUTINE-LOOP, and MAIN-ROUTINE-ENDING:

```
DATA DIVISION.
WORKING-STORAGE SECTION.
01      HUMAN-RESPONSE PIC XXX.

PROCEDURE DIVISION.
MAIN-ROUTINE-BEGINNING.
        DISPLAY "I WILL RECITE A SHORT POEM".
MAIN-ROUTINE-LOOP.
        DISPLAY " ".
        DISPLAY "YOUR NOSE".
        DISPLAY "BLOWS".
        DISPLAY " ".
        DISPLAY "WOULD YOU LIKE TO HEAR THE POEM AGAIN?".
        ACCEPT HUMAN-RESPONSE.
        IF HUMAN-RESPONSE = "YES"
                GO TO MAIN-ROUTINE-LOOP.
MAIN-ROUTINE-ENDING.
        DISPLAY "YOU HAVE BEEN A GREAT AUDIENCE".
        STOP RUN.
```

When you run that program, the computer says:

```
I WILL RECITE A SHORT POEM
```

Then it recites the poem:

```
YOUR NOSE
BLOWS
```

Then it asks:

```
WOULD YOU LIKE TO HEAR THE POEM AGAIN?
```

If you answer YES, the computer repeats the poem, then asks whether you'd like to hear it a third time. If you answer YES again, the computer recites the poem a third time, then asks whether you'd like to hear it a *fourth* time. The computer recites the poem repeatedly, until you finally stop answering YES. Then the computer says —

```
YOU HAVE BEEN A GREAT AUDIENCE
```

and stops.

In that program, if you don't answer YES, the computer doesn't repeat the poem. So if you don't answer YES, the computer acts as if you said NO. The following version is an improvement; if you don't answer YES, and you don't say NO, the computer asks the question again:

```
DATA DIVISION.
WORKING-STORAGE SECTION.
01      HUMAN-RESPONSE PIC XXX.

PROCEDURE DIVISION.
MAIN-ROUTINE-BEGINNING.
        DISPLAY "I WILL RECITE A SHORT POEM".
MAIN-ROUTINE-LOOP.
        DISPLAY " ".
        DISPLAY "YOUR NOSE".
        DISPLAY "BLOWS".
        DISPLAY " ".
        PERFORM GET-HUMAN-RESPONSE.
        IF HUMAN-RESPONSE = "YES"
                GO TO MAIN-ROUTINE-LOOP.
MAIN-ROUTINE-ENDING.
        DISPLAY "YOU HAVE BEEN A GREAT AUDIENCE".
        STOP RUN.
GET-HUMAN-RESPONSE.
        DISPLAY "WOULD YOU LIKE TO HEAR THE POEM AGAIN?".
        ACCEPT HUMAN-RESPONSE.
        IF HUMAN-RESPONSE NOT = "YES" AND NOT = "NO"
                DISPLAY "PLEASE SAY YES OR NO!"
                GO TO GET-HUMAN-RESPONSE.
```

GO TO resembles PERFORM. Here's the difference between GO TO and PERFORM....

> To go to a *different routine*, say PERFORM.
> To go to a different paragraph in the *same routine*, say GO TO.

For example, suppose you want to go from MAIN-ROUTINE-BEGINNING to FUNNY-SUBROUTINE; since you're going to a *different routine*, say PERFORM.

Suppose you want to go from MAIN-ROUTINE-BEGINNING to MAIN-ROUTINE-ENDING; since you're going to a different paragraph in the *same* routine, say GO TO.

THRU

Like the main routine, a subroutine can consist of several paragraphs. For example, subroutine FUNNY-FACE can consist of three paragraphs, called FUNNY-FACE-BEGINNING, FUNNY-FACE-LOOP, and FUNNY-FACE-ENDING. To make the computer do the entire subroutine, say:

```
PERFORM FUNNY-FACE-BEGINNING THRU FUNNY-FACE-ENDING.
```

Data files

To manipulate a data file whose name is POEM, fill in the blanks:

```
IDENTIFICATION DIVISION.
PROGRAM-ID.
        The program's name.
AUTHOR
        Your name.

ENVIRONMENT DIVISION.
CONFIGURATION SECTION.
SOURCE-COMPUTER.
        The computer's name.
OBJECT-COMPUTER.
        The computer's name again.
INPUT-OUTPUT SECTION.
FILE-CONTROL.
        SELECT POEM-FILE ASSIGN TO the file's location.

DATA DIVISION.
FILE SECTION.
FD      POEM-FILE how the file is labeled.
01      POEM-LINE PIC a picture of a line of the file.
WORKING-STORAGE SECTION.
A description of each variable that's not in the file.

PROCEDURE DIVISION.
MAIN-ROUTINE.
        OPEN output or input POEM-FILE.
        What you want to do to the file.
        CLOSE POEM-FILE.
        STOP RUN.
```

The four divisions

Like every COBOL program, that outline consists of four divisions: the IDENTIFICATION DIVISION, the ENVIRONMENT DIVISION, the DATA DIVISION, and the PROCEDURE DIVISION. Let's look at each division.

IDENTIFICATION DIVISION The IDENTIFICATION DIVISION consists of two paragraphs: the PROGRAM-ID and the AUTHOR. For the PROGRAM-ID, fill in the program's name, *which must be different from the name of the file*. Since the name of the file is POEM, the name of the program must *not* be POEM. If you're lazy, you can omit the AUTHOR.

ENVIRONMENT DIVISION The ENVIRONMENT DIVISION consists of two sections: the CONFIGURATION SECTION and the INPUT-OUTPUT SECTION.

The CONFIGURATION SECTION consists of two paragraphs: the SOURCE-COMPUTER and the OBJECT-COMPUTER. On CDC and PDP-11 computers, the CONFIGURATION SECTION is required; but on IBM, Eclipse, PDP-10, and PDP-20 computers, the entire CONFIGURATION SECTION is optional, so you can abridge the ENVIRONMENT DIVISION:

```
ENVIRONMENT DIVISION.
INPUT-OUTPUT SECTION.
FILE-CONTROL.
        SELECT POEM-FILE ASSIGN TO the file's location.
```

The INPUT-OUTPUT SECTION consists of just one paragraph, which is the FILE-CONTROL. The FILE-CONTROL paragraph consists of a sentence that says SELECT, then the file's name (POEM-FILE), then ASSIGN TO, and finally a blank (which you must fill in, and which tells the file's location).

What do you put in that blank? The answer depends on the file's location. Is the file on a disk? On punched cards? Or on paper produced by the printer? **Here's what to put in the blank, for various computers:**

	Printer	Card reader	Disk
Eclipse	PRINTER	"$CDR"	"POEM"
CDC	OUTPUT	INPUT	POEM
PDP-11	"LP:"	"CR:"	"DK:"
PDP-10, PDP-20	LPT	CDR	DSK RECORDING MODE ASCII
IBM using OS	UT-S-POEM	UT-S-POEM	UT-S-POEM

DATA DIVISION The DATA DIVISION consists of two sections: the FILE SECTION and the WORKING-STORAGE SECTION.

At the beginning of the FILE SECTION, say FD (which means "File Description"). To the right of the FD, say POEM-FILE, and then **fill in the blank, which tells how the file is labeled:**

Hardware	What to put in the blank
CDC	LABEL RECORDS ARE OMITTED
PDP-11 disk	LABEL RECORDS ARE STANDARD VALUE OF ID "POEM"
PDP-11 printer	LABEL RECORDS ARE OMITTED
PDP-11 card reader	LABEL RECORDS ARE OMITTED
PDP-10, PDP-20	VALUE ID "POEM▨▨▨"
IBM using OS	LABEL RECORDS ARE STANDARD

On PDP-10 and PDP-20 computers, put enough blank spaces (▨) after POEM so that the string has 9 characters. On Eclipse computers, do *not* fill in the blank; just say:

```
FD      POEM-FILE.
```

Underneath the line that says FD, you must say 01. The 01 line includes a picture of a line of the file. For example, if a line of the file is an 80-character string, the 01 line should say:

```
01      POEM-LINE PIC X(80).
```

The WORKING-STORAGE SECTION describes each variable that's not in the file.

PROCEDURE DIVISION The PROCEDURE DIVISION's MAIN-ROUTINE should begin with the word OPEN, and end with the words CLOSE and STOP RUN.

In the OPEN statement, you can say either —

```
        OPEN OUTPUT POEM-FILE.
```

or:

```
        OPEN INPUT POEM-FILE.
```

If you say OPEN OUTPUT POEM-FILE, the computer will output to the POEM-FILE; so it will copy information from the RAM to the POEM-FILE. If you say OPEN INPUT POEM-FILE, the computer will input from the POEM-FILE; so it will copy information from the POEM-FILE to the RAM.

In the PROCEDURE DIVISION, when you fill in the blank about "what you want to do to the file", you must say either WRITE POEM-LINE or READ POEM-FILE. If the file is OPEN OUTPUT (which means you're copying from the RAM to the file), say WRITE POEM-LINE; if the file is OPEN INPUT (which means you're copying from the file to the RAM), say READ POEM-FILE.

Writing

Here's a poetic masterpiece:

```
CANDY IS DANDY
BUT LIKKER IS QUIKKER
```

It was composed by the famous poet Ogden Nash.

This program makes the computer write that masterpiece onto a disk, and make the masterpiece become a file named POEM:

Program	Meaning
IDENTIFICATION DIVISION.	
PROGRAM-ID.	
CANDY.	This program is named CANDY.
ENVIRONMENT DIVISION.	
CONFIGURATION SECTION.	
SOURCE-COMPUTER.	
<u>The computer's name</u>.	
OBJECT-COMPUTER.	
<u>The computer's name again</u>.	
INPUT-OUTPUT SECTION.	
FILE-CONTROL.	
SELECT POEM-FILE ASSIGN TO <u>the file's location</u>.	This program uses a file called POEM.
DATA DIVISION.	
FILE SECTION.	
FD POEM-FILE how the file is labeled.	
01 POEM-LINE PIC X(21).	Make each line have 21 characters, like this:
	CANDY IS DANDY▓▓▓▓▓▓▓
PROCEDURE DIVISION.	BUT LIKKER IS QUIKKER
MAIN-ROUTINE.	
OPEN OUTPUT POEM-FILE.	Prepare to output to POEM-FILE.
MOVE "CANDY IS DANDY" TO POEM-LINE.	Make POEM-LINE be "CANDY IS DANDY▓▓▓▓▓▓▓".
WRITE POEM-LINE.	Copy that POEM-LINE to the file.
MOVE "BUT LIKKER IS QUIKKER" TO POEM-LINE.	Make POEM-LINE become this new string: "BUT LIKKER IS QUIKKER".
WRITE POEM-LINE.	Copy that new POEM-LINE to the file.
CLOSE POEM-FILE.	Finish using POEM-FILE.
STOP RUN.	Stop running this program.

That program doesn't require a WORKING-STORAGE SECTION, so I omitted it. Since I was lazy, I also omitted the AUTHOR paragraph.

When you run that program, the computer will create a file on disk. The file will be called POEM. It will contain this message:

```
CANDY IS DANDY▓▓▓▓▓▓▓
BUT LIKKER IS QUIKKER
```

Reading

This program reads the file named POEM and displays it on your screen:

IDENTIFICATION DIVISION.	
PROGRAM-ID.	
READER.	
The ENVIRONMENT DIVISION and DATA DIVISION are the same as the previous program's.	
PROCEDURE DIVISION.	
MAIN-ROUTINE-BEGINNING.	
OPEN INPUT POEM-FILE.	Find the POEM file on the disk, and prepare to input from it.
MAIN-ROUTINE-LOOP.	
READ POEM-FILE AT END GO TO MAIN-ROUTINE-ENDING.	Read a line from POEM-FILE; if there are no more lines, go to the next paragraph.
DISPLAY POEM-LINE.	Display that line, so you see it on your screen.
GO TO MAIN-ROUTINE-LOOP.	Go back to read another line.
MAIN-ROUTINE-ENDING.	
DISPLAY "THAT WAS THE WHOLE POEM".	Display "THAT WAS THE WHOLE POEM" on your screen.
CLOSE POEM-FILE.	Finish using POEM-FILE.
STOP RUN.	Stop running this program.

In the MAIN-ROUTINE-LOOP, the first line means: try to READ a line from POEM-FILE; but if a line can*not* be read (because the file has ended), go to MAIN-ROUTINE-ENDING instead.

The READ statement differs from the WRITE statement in two ways:

```
A WRITE statement mentions a LINE, but a READ statement mentions a FILE.
A READ statement must contain the words AT END.
```

Counting

This program reads a file called POEM, counts how many lines are in it, and displays the count:

```
IDENTIFICATION DIVISION.
PROGRAM-ID.
      COUNTS.

The ENVIRONMENT DIVISION is same as previous program's.

DATA DIVISION.
FILE SECTION.
FD    POEM-FILE how the file is labeled.
01    POEM-LINE PIC X(21).                    Assume each POEM-LINE has 21 characters.
WORKING-STORAGE SECTION.
01    COUNT-OF-HOW-MANY-LINES PIC 99.         Assume the count is a two-digit number,
                                              so assume POEM has less than 100 lines.
PROCEDURE DIVISION.
MAIN-ROUTINE-BEGINNING.
      OPEN INPUT POEM-FILE.                   Find the POEM file on the disk.
      MOVE 0 TO COUNT-OF-HOW-MANY-LINES.      Start the count at 0.
MAIN-ROUTINE-LOOP.
      READ POEM-FILE AT END GO TO MAIN-ROUTINE-ENDING. Read a line from POEM-FILE.
      ADD 1 TO COUNT-OF-HOW-MANY-LINES.       Add 1 to the count.
      GO TO MAIN-ROUTINE-LOOP.                Go read another line.
MAIN-ROUTINE-ENDING.                          When all lines have been read,
      DISPLAY COUNT-OF-HOW-MANY-LINES.        display the count,
      CLOSE POEM-FILE.                        finish using POEM-FILE,
      STOP RUN.                               and stop running this program.
```

Copying

This program reads a file called POEM, and creates a copy of it; the copy is a file called POEM2:

```
IDENTIFICATION DIVISION.
PROGRAM-ID.
      COPIER.

ENVIRONMENT DIVISION.
CONFIGURATION SECTION.
SOURCE-COMPUTER.
      The computer's name.
OBJECT-COMPUTER.
      The computer's name again.
INPUT-OUTPUT SECTION.
FILE-CONTROL.
      SELECT POEM-FILE ASSIGN TO the location of POEM.
      SELECT POEM2-FILE ASSIGN TO the location of POEM-2.

DATA DIVISION.
FILE SECTION.
FD    POEM-FILE the labeling for POEM.
01    POEM-LINE PIC X(21).
FD    POEM2-FILE the labeling for POEM2.
01    POEM2-LINE PIC X(21).

PROCEDURE DIVISION.
MAIN-ROUTINE-BEGINNING.
      OPEN INPUT POEM-FILE.                    Prepare to input from POEM-FILE,
      OPEN OUTPUT POEM2-FILE.                  and output to POEM2-FILE.
MAIN-ROUTINE-LOOP.                             Do the following repeatedly:
      READ POEM-FILE AT END GO TO MAIN-ROUTINE-ENDING. read a line from POEM-FILE,
      MOVE POEM-LINE TO POEM2-LINE.            copy that line to POEM2-LINE,
      WRITE POEM2-LINE.                        and write POEM2-LINE to POEM2-FILE.
      GO TO MAIN-ROUTINE-LOOP.
MAIN-ROUTINE-ENDING.                           At the end,
      DISPLAY "THE FILE HAS BEEN COPIED".      display "THE FILE HAS BEEN COPIED",
      CLOSE POEM-FILE POEM2-FILE.              finish using the files,
      STOP RUN.                                and stop running this program.
```

Pictures

Suppose you're dealing with a file named JOE, and each line of JOE-FILE is a three-digit number. Should the line's picture be edited (JOE-LINE PIC ZZZ) or unedited (JOE-LINE PIC 999)?

When you read a file, the line's picture must be unedited and match the picture in the program that wrote the file.

When you write a file, ask yourself, "What will read it?" If the answer is "a COBOL program", the picture must be unedited. If the answer is "only a human", edit the picture.

Remember: if one program writes a file, and another program reads it, both programs must use the same picture. For example, if a program writes JACK-FILE and says JACK-LINE PIC S9999V99, the program that reads JACK-FILE must also say JACK-LINE PIC S9999V99.

Peculiarities

To write and read unedited numbers, the computer takes a short-cut: it omits decimal points, and locates the negative sign on top of the last digit. For example, instead of writing -0034.27 in JACK-FILE, the computer writes just 003427. When another program reads 003427 from the file, the S9999V99 picture tells the computer the 003427 means -0034.27.

After you WRITE a line, you cannot use the line again in the program. For example, after you say WRITE POEM-LINE, you should not say MOVE POEM-LINE TO K; it won't work.

Multiple widths

Let's make the computer compute the square of 12 and the square of 13 and write this file:

```
HERE ARE THE SQUARES:
144
169
THEY WERE REAL GROOVY
```

The top and bottom lines are long strings whose pictures are X(21). The other two lines are short numbers whose pictures are 999.

Here's the program:

```
IDENTIFICATION DIVISION.
PROGRAM-ID.
        SQUARE.

ENVIRONMENT DIVISION.
CONFIGURATION SECTION.
SOURCE-COMPUTER.
        The computer's name.
OBJECT-COMPUTER.
        The computer's name again.
INPUT-OUTPUT SECTION.
FILE-CONTROL.
        SELECT REPORT-FILE ASSIGN TO location of REPORT.    This program uses a file called REPORT.

DATA DIVISION.
FILE SECTION.
FD      REPORT-FILE the labeling for REPORT.
01      REPORT-LINE PIC X(21).                              REPORT-LINE is a 21-character string.
01      REPORT-LINE2 PIC 999.                               REPORT-LINE2 is a 3-digit number.

PROCEDURE DIVISION.
MAIN-ROUTINE.
        OPEN OUTPUT REPORT-FILE.                            Create a file called REPORT.
        MOVE "HERE ARE THE SQUARES:" TO REPORT-LINE.        REPORT-LINE is "HERE ARE THE SQUARES:".
        WRITE REPORT-LINE.                                  Write "HERE ARE THE SQUARES:".
        COMPUTE REPORT-LINE2 = 12 * 12.                     REPORT-LINE2 is 144.
        WRITE REPORT-LINE2.                                 Write 144.
        COMPUTE REPORT-LINE2 = 13 * 13.                     REPORT-LINE2 is 169.
        WRITE REPORT-LINE2.                                 Write 169.
        MOVE "THEY WERE REAL GROOVY" TO REPORT-LINE.        REPORT-LINE is "THEY WERE REAL GROOVY".
        WRITE REPORT-LINE.                                  Write "THEY WERE REAL GROOVY".
        CLOSE REPORT-FILE.                                  Finish using REPORT.
        STOP RUN.                                           Stop running this program.
```

Advanced structures

COBOL lets you create and manipulate advanced structures.

Group items

In the data division, you can say:

```
01      K.
        02      L PIC 999.
        02      M PIC 9.
        02      N PIC 99.
```

That means K is a combination of L, M, and N. If the procedure division says —

```
        MOVE 427 TO L.
        MOVE 8 TO M.
        MOVE 31 TO N.
```

then K will be "427831".

Since K is a combination of other variables, K is called a **group variable** or **group item**. L, M, and N are **elementary items**. Notice that K is the string "427831", not the number 427831. **A group item is always a string.** Since K is a string, not a number, you cannot say ADD 1 TO K, although you can say ADD 1 TO L or ADD 1 TO M or ADD 1 TO N.

Here's a group item, for a weight-reducing studio:

```
01      PERSONAL-INFO-ABOUT-CLIENT.
        02      CLIENT-NAME.
                03      FIRST-NAME PIC X(15).
                03      MIDDLE-INITIAL PIC X.
                03      LAST-NAME PIC X(20).
        02      CLIENT-SEX PIC X.    A person's sex is "M" or "F".
        02      CLIENT-AGE PIC 99.
        02      WEIGHT-PROGRESS.
                03      WEIGHT-WHEN-ENTERED-PROGRAM PIC 999.
                03      WEIGHT-THIS-WEEK PIC 999.
                03      NUMBER-OF-WEEKS-SO-FAR PIC 999.
```

PERSONAL-INFO-ABOUT-CLIENT is composed of CLIENT-NAME (which is composed of FIRST-NAME, MIDDLE-INITIAL, and LAST-NAME), CLIENT-SEX, and WEIGHT-PROGRESS (which is composed of WEIGHT-WHEN-ENTERED-PROGRAM, WEIGHT-THIS-WEEK, and NUMBER-OF-WEEKS-SO-FAR). So PERSONAL-INFO-ABOUT-CLIENT is composed of numbers and strings.

Altogether, PERSONAL-INFO-ABOUT-CLIENT contains 48 characters (15 + 1 + 20 + 1 + 2 + 3 + 3 + 3). The computer considers PERSONAL-INFO-ABOUT-CLIENT to be a string whose picture is X(48).

If you say L PIC X(48), you can move all the PERSONAL-INFO-ABOUT-CLIENT to L by saying:

```
        MOVE PERSONAL-INFO-ABOUT-CLIENT TO L.
```

To move the CLIENT-NAME to M, without moving the CLIENT-SEX, CLIENT-AGE, and WEIGHT-PROGRESS, say:

```
        MOVE CLIENT-NAME TO M.
```

To write lots of information to a file, make the file's LINE be a group item.

How to extract from a file Suppose you've already created a file whose name is EMPLOY; it's on disk or cards. Suppose the file contains information about employees. Suppose each line of the file contains 80 characters, as follows. Characters 1-40 are the employee's name. Characters 61-70 are the employee's home phone number, including the area code. The other characters (41-60 and 71-80) are miscellaneous information (such as the employee's age, sex, address, salary, kind of job, and number of years with the company).

Let's create a new file, called REPORT, on disk or on the printer's paper. Let's make REPORT contain just the employees' names and phone numbers, and omit the "miscellaneous information". Here's how:

```
IDENTIFICATION DIVISION.
PROGRAM-ID.
       PHONES.


ENVIRONMENT DIVISION.
CONFIGURATION SECTION.
SOURCE-COMPUTER.
       The computer's name.
OBJECT-COMPUTER.
       The computer's name again.
INPUT-OUTPUT SECTION.
FILE-CONTROL.
       SELECT EMPLOY-FILE ASSIGN TO location of EMPLOY.
       SELECT REPORT-FILE ASSIGN TO location of REPORT.


DATA DIVISION.
FILE SECTION.
FD     EMPLOY-FILE the labeling for EMPLOY.
01     EMPLOY-LINE.
       02     EMPLOYEE-NAME PIC X(40).
       02     FILLER PIC X(20).
       02     HOME-PHONE.
              03     AREA-CODE PIC 999.
              03     PHONE-EXCHANGE PIC 999.
              03     REST-OF-PHONE-NUMBER PIC 9999.
       02     FILLER PIC X(10).
FD     REPORT-FILE the labeling for REPORT.
01     REPORT-LINE.
       02     EMPLOYEE-NAME-REPORTED PIC X(40).
       02     HOME-PHONE-REPORTED.
              03     LEFT-PARENTHESIS PIC X.
              03     AREA-CODE-REPORTED PIC 999.
              03     RIGHT-PARENTHESIS PIC X.
              03     PHONE-EXCHANGE-REPORTED PIC B999.
              03     THE-DASH PIC X.
              03     REST-OF-PHONE-NUMBER-REPORTED PIC 9999.


PROCEDURE DIVISION.
MAIN-ROUTINE-BEGINNING.
       OPEN INPUT EMPLOY-FILE.
       OPEN OUTPUT REPORT-FILE.
MAIN-ROUTINE-LOOP.
       READ EMPLOY-FILE AT END GO TO MAIN-ROUTINE-ENDING.
       MOVE EMPLOYEE-NAME TO EMPLOYEE-NAME-REPORTED.
       MOVE "(" TO LEFT-PARENTHESIS.
       MOVE AREA-CODE TO AREA-CODE-REPORTED.
       MOVE ")" TO RIGHT-PARENTHESIS.
       MOVE PHONE-EXCHANGE TO PHONE-EXCHANGE-REPORTED.
       MOVE "-" TO THE-DASH.
       MOVE REST-OF-PHONE-NUMBER TO REST-OF-PHONE-NUMBER-REPORTED.
       WRITE REPORT-LINE.
       GO TO MAIN-ROUTINE-LOOP.
MAIN-ROUTINE-ENDING.
       CLOSE EMPLOY-FILE REPORT-FILE.
       STOP RUN.
```

Throughout the DATA DIVISION, the special word "FILLER" stands for data the program won't use.

Characters 1-40 are EMPLOYEE-NAME.
Characters 41-60 are irrelevant.

Characters 61-63 are AREA-CODE.
Characters 64-66 are PHONE-EXCHANGE.
Characters 67-70 are REST-OF-PHONE-NUMBER.
Characters 71-80 are irrelevant.

The PICs say HOME-PHONE looks like this —
6036666644
but make HOME-PHONE-REPORTED look like this:
(603) 666-6644

The MAIN-ROUTINE-LOOP
reads a line from EMPLOY-FILE,
copies data into each part of REPORT-LINE,

and then writes REPORT-LINE.

SORT

Suppose CUSTOM is a disk file that contains information about your customers. Suppose each line of the file contains 80 characters, as follows....

> Characters 1-20: the customer's last name
> Characters 21-80: other information about the customer

Alphabetical order Here's how to put the file in alphabetical order, according to the customer's name:

```
IDENTIFICATION DIVISION.
PROGRAM-ID.
        ALPHA.

ENVIRONMENT DIVISION.
CONFIGURATION SECTION.
SOURCE-COMPUTER.
        The computer's name.
OBJECT-COMPUTER.
        The computer's name again.
INPUT-OUTPUT SECTION.
FILE-CONTROL.
        SELECT CUSTOM-FILE ASSIGN TO the location of CUSTOM.
        SELECT SORT-FILE ASSIGN TO the location of SORT.

DATA DIVISION.
FILE SECTION.
FD      CUSTOM-FILE the labeling for CUSTOM.
01      CUSTOM-LINE PIC X(80).
SD      SORT-FILE.
01      SORT-LINE.
        02      LAST-NAME PIC X(20).
        02      FILLER PIC X(60).

PROCEDURE DIVISION.
MAIN-ROUTINE.
        SORT SORT-FILE
                ASCENDING KEY LAST-NAME
                USING CUSTOM-FILE
                GIVING CUSTOM-FILE.
        STOP RUN.
```

Putting a file in order, by alphabetizing or any other method, is called **sorting**. To sort the CUSTOM-FILE, the computer has to create a temporary disk file called a SORT-FILE.

In the sentence that says SELECT SORT-FILE, here's what to put for "the location of SORT":

Computer	The location of SORT
Eclipse	"SORT"
CDC	SORT
PDP-10, PDP-20	DSK DSK DSK RECORDING MODE ASCII
IBM using OS	UT-S-POEM
IBM using DOS	SYS001-UT-3330-S-SORTWK1

In the DATA DIVISION's FILE SECTION, the SD means a Sort-file Description. In the PROCEDURE DIVISION, the SORT sentence makes the computer automatically open the CUSTOM-FILE, sort it, and close it.

In the SORT sentence, if you replace ASCENDING by DESCENDING, the computer will sort the file in reverse order, so the Z's come first and the A's come last.

You can make the program fancier, by inserting extra statements before and after the SORT statement. But since the SORT statement automatically tells the computer to open CUSTOM-FILE, the CUSTOM-FILE must not be open already. If you already said OPEN CUSTOM-FILE, you must say CLOSE CUSTOM-FILE before you give the SORT statement.

If you replace GIVING CUSTOM-FILE by GIVING REPORT-FILE, the computer won't change CUSTOM-FILE, but will create a REPORT-FILE containing the information sorted. For REPORT-FILE, you must type an FD and SELECT it. The computer will automatically open it, so it must not be open already.

Who bought the most? Within each line of CUSTOM-FILE, suppose characters 51-57 tell how much the customer bought from you during the past year. Let's find out which customers bought the most.

Let's make the computer print the customer that bought the most, then the customer that bought the next most, etc. If two customers bought exactly the same amount, let's make the computer print their names in alphabetical order.

This program does it:

```
IDENTIFICATION DIVISION.
PROGRAM-ID.
        BIGBUY.

The ENVIRONMENT DIVISION is same as the previous program's.

DATA DIVISION.
FILE SECTION.
FD      CUSTOM-FILE the labeling for CUSTOM.
01      CUSTOM-LINE PIC X(80).
SD      SORT-FILE.
01      SORT-LINE.
        02      LAST-NAME PIC X(20).          characters 1-20
        02      FILLER PIC X(30).             characters 21-50
        02      AMOUNT-BOUGHT-DURING-YEAR PIC 99999V99.
        02      FILLER PIC X(23).

PROCEDURE DIVISION.
MAIN-ROUTINE.
        SORT SORT-FILE
                DESCENDING KEY AMOUNT-BOUGHT-DURING-YEAR
                ASCENDING KEY LAST-NAME
                USING CUSTOM-FILE
                GIVING CUSTOM-FILE.
        STOP RUN.
```

The SORT sentence says: sort the file so that AMOUNT-BOUGHT-DURING-YEAR is in DESCENDING order; in case of a tie, put LAST-NAME in ASCENDING order.

MERGE

Suppose OLDCUS and NEWCUS are files: OLDCUS describes your old customers, and NEWCUS describes your newer customers. In those files, each line contains 80 characters; characters 1-20 contain the customer's last name. Each file's already in alphabetical order, by customer's last name.

Let's combine the two files. In other words, let's create a "combination" file (on disk or printer paper), called ALLCUS, that contains *all* the customers; and let's make ALLCUS be in alphabetical order also. Here's how:

```
IDENTIFICATION DIVISION.
PROGRAM-ID.
        MERGER.

ENVIRONMENT DIVISION.
CONFIGURATION SECTION.
SOURCE-COMPUTER.
        The computer's name.
OBJECT-COMPUTER.
        The computer's name again.
INPUT-OUTPUT SECTION.
FILE-CONTROL.
        SELECT OLDCUS-FILE ASSIGN TO the location of OLDCUS.
        SELECT NEWCUS-FILE ASSIGN TO the location of NEWCUS.
        SELECT ALLCUS-FILE ASSIGN TO the location of ALLCUS.
        SELECT SORT-FILE ASSIGN TO the location of SORT.

DATA DIVISION.
FILE SECTION.
FD      OLDCUS-FILE the labeling for OLDCUS.
01      OLDCUS-LINE PIC X(80).
FD      NEWCUS-FILE the labeling for NEWCUS.
01      NEWCUS-LINE PIC X(80).
FD      ALLCUS-FILE the labeling for ALLCUS.
01      ALLCUS-LINE PIC X(80).
SD      SORT-FILE.
01      SORT-LINE.
        02      LAST-NAME PIC X(20).
        02      FILLER PIC X(60).

PROCEDURE DIVISION.
MAIN-ROUTINE.
        MERGE SORT-FILE
                ASCENDING KEY LAST-NAME
                USING OLDCUS-FILE NEWCUS-FILE
                GIVING ALLCUS-FILE.
        STOP RUN.
```

That program creates ALLCUS, which is a combination of OLDCUS and NEWCUS. To do that, the computer must create a SORT-FILE.

The word MERGE automatically opens and closes all the files involved. so do *not* say OPEN or CLOSE.

Warning: the word MERGE is in COBOL 74 but not in COBOL 68. So if your computer is old-fashioned and understands just COBOL 68, it doesn't understand the word MERGE.

If your computer understands the word MERGE, you can merge as many files as you like. For example, if you have files called CUS1, CUS2, and CUS3, you can say:

```
MERGE SORT-FILE
        ASCENDING KEY LAST-NAME
        USING CUS1-FILE CUS2-FILE CUS3-FILE
        GIVING ALLCUS-FILE.
```

Before you MERGE, make sure that the files you're USING are already in alphabetical order.

Subscripts

Like other computer languages, COBOL lets you use subscripts.

For example, suppose your 4 favorite friends are SUE, JOE, TOM, and ANN. Let's make FAVORITE-FRIEND (1) be "SUE", FAVORITE-FRIEND (2) be "JOE", FAVORITE-FRIEND (3) be "TOM", and FAVORITE-FRIEND (4) be "ANN". Here's how:

```
DATA DIVISION.
WORKING-STORAGE SECTION.
01      FAVORITE-FRIEND-TABLE.
        02      FAVORITE-FRIEND OCCURS 4 TIMES PIC XXX.

PROCEDURE DIVISION.
MAIN-ROUTINE.
        MOVE "SUE" TO FAVORITE-FRIEND (1).
        MOVE "JOE" TO FAVORITE-FRIEND (2).
        MOVE "TOM" TO FAVORITE-FRIEND (3).
        MOVE "ANN" TO FAVORITE-FRIEND (4).
        DISPLAY FAVORITE-FRIEND (1).
        DISPLAY FAVORITE-FRIEND (2).
        DISPLAY FAVORITE-FRIEND (3).
        DISPLAY FAVORITE-FRIEND (4).
        STOP RUN.
```

Line 02 says you have 4 FAVORITE-FRIENDS; each has PC XXX.

The computer will display:

```
SUE
JOE
TOM
ANN
```

When typing the program, remember to put a blank space before the subscript:

```
FAVORITE-FRIEND (1)
```
blank space

In COBOL, you say "OCCURS" instead of "DIMENSION":

```
BASIC:    DIM F(4)
FORTRAN:  DIMENSION F(4)
PASCAL:   F: ARRAY [1..4]
COBOL:    F OCCURS 4 TIMES
```

The subscript can be a variable. For example, instead of saying —

```
DISPLAY FAVORITE-FRIEND (1).
DISPLAY FAVORITE-FRIEND (2).
DISPLAY FAVORITE-FRIEND (3).
DISPLAY FAVORITE-FRIEND (4).
```

you can say:

```
DISPLAY FAVORITE-FRIEND (I).
```

To do that, you must tell the computer that the I goes from 1 to 4. Here's how:

```
DATA DIVISION.
WORKING-STORAGE SECTION.
01      FAVORITE-FRIEND-TABLE.
        02      FAVORITE-FRIEND OCCURS 4 TIMES PIC XXX.
01      I PIC 9.                                        I is a one-digit number.

PROCEDURE DIVISION.
MAIN-ROUTINE.
        MOVE "SUE" TO FAVORITE-FRIEND (1).
        MOVE "JOE" TO FAVORITE-FRIEND (2).
        MOVE "TOM" TO FAVORITE-FRIEND (3).
        MOVE "ANN" TO FAVORITE-FRIEND (4).
        PERFORM SHOW-FRIENDSHIP
                VARYING I FROM 1 BY 1 UNTIL I > 4.      I will be 1, 2, 3, 4.
        STOP RUN.
SHOW-FRIENDSHIP.
        DISPLAY FAVORITE-FRIEND (I).                    I is the subscript.
```

To make the program run faster, say "COMP" at the end of the subscript's picture:

Computer	What to say
PDP, Eclipse	01 I PIC 9 COMP.
CDC	01 I PIC 9 COMP-1.
IBM	01 I PIC 9 COMP SYNC.

COMP stands for the word COMPUTATIONAL; SYNC stands for the word SYNCHRONIZED.

A subscript cannot contain an operation:

Okay:	FAVORITE-FRIEND (3)	
Wrong:	FAVORITE-FRIEND (2 + 1)	The + is not allowed.

Here's how to make Y-TABLE be a table that has 4 rows and 6 columns:

```
01      Y-TABLE.
        02      Y-ROW OCCURS 4 TIMES.
                03      Y OCCURS 6 TIMES PIC XXX.
```

The entire table is called:

```
Y-TABLE
```

The first row of Y-TABLE is called:

```
Y-ROW (1)
```

The second row of Y-TABLE is called:

```
Y-ROW (2)
```

The entry in the 2nd row and 5th column of Y-TABLE is called:

```
Y (2, 5)
  ↑    ↑
  spaces
```

Test scores Suppose you teach 25 students, you've given each student 4 tests, and you want to put the scores in a table.

You want the table to contain 25 rows (a row for each student). In each row, you want the student's first name, middle initial, last name, and 4 scores.

Here's how:

```
01      STUDENT-INFORMATION-TABLE.
        02      STUDENT-INFORMATION-ROW OCCURS 25 TIMES.
                03      FIRST-NAME PIC X(15).
                03      MIDDLE-INITIAL PIC X.
                03      LAST-NAME PIC X(20).
                03      TEST-SCORE OCCURS 4 TIMES PIC 999.
```

The entire table is called:

```
STUDENT-INFORMATION-TABLE
```

The table contains 25 rows. The first row is called:

```
STUDENT-INFORMATION-ROW (1)
```

The twelfth row is called:

```
STUDENT-INFORMATION-ROW (12)
```

The information in the twelfth row is called:

```
FIRST-NAME (12)
MIDDLE-INITIAL (12)
LAST-NAME (12)
TEST-SCORE (12, 1)
TEST-SCORE (12, 2)
TEST-SCORE (12, 3)
TEST-SCORE (12, 4)
```

Extra comments

Put extra comments in your program, to help your colleagues understand how the program works.

IDENTIFICATION DIVISION

The IDENTIFICATION DIVISION can include these paragraphs:

```
PROGRAM-ID.
AUTHOR.
INSTALLATION.
DATE-WRITTEN.
DATE-COMPILED.
SECURITY.
```

In each paragraph after the PROGRAM-ID, put whatever garbage you please. The computer ignores everything the IDENTIFICATION DIVISION says.

The IDENTIFICATION DIVISION helps the computer center's librarian classify your program. The librarian wants the INSTALLATION paragraph to contain the computer center's name and address, the DATE-WRITTEN paragraph to tell when you finished debugging the program, the DATE-COMPILED paragraph to tell when the computer translated the program from COBOL into machine language, and the SECURITY paragraph to tell who may look at the program and who must not.

If you put the wrong date in the date-compiled paragraph, don't worry: when you ask the computer to produce a **COBOL listing** of your program, the listing will automatically show the correct date instead.

Asterisks

The computer ignores any line that begins with an asterisk. So if you put this line in your program —

```
*THIS IS A LOUSY PROGRAM
```

— the computer will ignore the comment.

Create comments that explain how your program works. Put the comments near the bottom of the IDENTIFICATION DIVISION, near the top of the PROCEDURE DIVISION, and wherever your program looks confusing.

On PDP and Eclipse computers, put the asterisk at the far left; don't put any blank spaces before the asterisk. On IBM and CDC computers, put six blank spaces before the asterisk, so that the asterisk is in column 7.

Charts

You've already learned the most popular computer languages: BASIC, PASCAL, C, C++, JAVA, DBASE, LOGO, FORTRAN, and COBOL.

But those 9 languages are just the tip of the iceberg. Programmers have invented *thousands* of others.

Here's a multilingual dictionary that lets you translate 17 languages. For example, it shows that BASIC says "DIM x(4)" but FORTRAN says "DIMENSION X(4)" instead.

```
BASIC    DIM x(4)                    FOR i = 5 TO 17                              fred         GOTO 50
FORTRAN  DIMENSION X(4)              DO 10 I=5,17                                 CALL FRED    GO TO 50
PL/I     DECLARE X(4)                DO I = 5 TO 17                               CALL FRED    GO TO GAIL

ALGOL    REAL ARRAY X[1:4]           FOR I := 5 STEP 1 UNTIL 17 DO                FRED         GO TO GAIL
PASCAL   X: ARRAY[1..4] OF REAL      FOR I := 5 TO 17 DO                          FRED         GOTO 50
MODULA   X: ARRAY[1..4] OF REAL      FOR I := 5 TO 17 DO                          FRED         not available
ADA      X: ARRAY(1..4) OF FLOAT     FOR I IN 5..17 LOOP                          FRED         GO TO GAIL

C        float x[4]                  for (i=5; i<=17; ++i)                        fred()       goto gail
C++      float x[4]                  for (int i=5; i<=17; ++i)                    fred()       goto gail
JAVA     float [] x=new float x[4]   for (int i=5; i<=17; ++i)                    fred()       not available

EASY     PREPARE X(4)                LOOP I FROM 5 TO 17                          FRED         SKIP TO GAIL
DBASE    DECLARE X[4]                not available                               DO FRED      not available
COBOL    X OCCURS 4 TIMES            PERFORM SAM VARYING I FROM 5 BY 1 UNTIL I > 17  PERFORM FRED  GO TO GAIL

LOGO     DEFAR "X 4 1                not available                               FRED         GO "GAIL
LISP     (ARRAY ((X (4) LIST)))      not available                               (FRED)       (GO GAIL)
SNOBOL   X = ARRAY(4)                not available                               FRED()       :(GAIL)
PILOT    DIM:#X(4)                   not available                               U:FRED       J:*GAIL
```

```
BASIC    IF x = 4.3 THEN       INPUT k                j = k + 2         PRINT k                   'silly stuff
FORTRAN  IF (X .EQ. 4.3)       READ *, K              J=K+2            PRINT *, K                C  SILLY STUFF */
PL/I     IF X=4.3 THEN         GET LIST(K)            J=K+2            PUT LIST(K)               /* SILLY STUFF */

ALGOL    IF X=4.3 THEN         READ(K)                J:=K+2           PRINT(K)                  COMMENT  SILLY STUFF
PASCAL   IF X=4.3 THEN         READ(K)                J:=K+2           WRITELN(K)                {SILLY STUFF}
MODULA   IF X=4.3 THEN         READINTEGER(K)         J:=K+2           WRITEINTEGER(K,6)         (*SILLY STUFF*)
ADA      IF X=4.3 THEN         GET(K)                 J:=K+2           PUT(K)                    --SILLY STUFF

C        if (x==4.3)           scanf("%d",&k)         j=k+2           printf("%d",k)            /* silly stuff */
C++      if (x==4.3)           cin >>k                j=k+2           cout <<k                  //silly stuff
JAVA     if (x==4.3)           k=Integer.parseInt(s)  j=k+2           System.out.println(k)     //silly stuff

EASY     IF X=4.3              GET K                  LET J=K+2        SAY K                     'SILLY STUFF
DBASE    IF X=4.3              INPUT TO K             J=K+2           ? K                       &&SILLY STUFF
COBOL    IF X = 4.3            ACCEPT K               COMPUTE J = K + 2  DISPLAY K               *SILLY STUFF

LOGO     IF :X=4.3             MAKE "K READWORD       MAKE "J :K+2     PRINT :K                  !SILLY STUFF
LISP     (COND ((EQUAL X 4.3)  (SETQ K (READ))        (SETQ J (PLUS K 2))  K                    ;SILLY STUFF
SNOBOL   EQ(X,4.3) :S(         K = INPUT              J = K + 2        OUTPUT = K                *SILLY STUFF
PILOT    (#X=4.3)              A:#K                   C:#J=#K+2        T:#K                      R:SILLY STUFF
```

The dictionary clumps the languages into groups. For example, look at the languages in the second group: ALGOL, PASCAL, MODULA, and ADA. Those 4 languages are almost identical to each other. For example, in each of them you say "J:=K+2".

The bottom group (LOGO, LISP, SNOBOL, and PILOT) differs wildly from the others. For example, look at how those 4 languages translate "IF x = 4.3 THEN" and "j = k + 2". They're called **radical languages**; the other 13 languages are called **mainstream**.

Two other radical languages are APL and FORTH. They're so weird that they won't fit in that chart!

Here's how to make the computer do 2+2 and print the answer (4), using each of those languages:

```
BASIC            LOGO            EASY          DBASE          APL          LISP             FORTH
PRINT 2 + 2      PRINT 2+2       SAY 2+2       ? 2+2          2+2          (PLUS 2 2)       2 2 + .

SNOBOL           PILOT      ALGOL          PASCAL          FORTRAN       PL/I                              ADA
 OUTPUT = 2 + 2  C:#N=2+2   BEGIN          BEGIN           N=2+2         HARRY:  PROCEDURE OPTIONS(MAIN);  PROCEDURE HARRY IS
END              T:#N         PRINT(2+2);    WRITELN(2+2);   PRINT *, N              PUT LIST(2+2);        BEGIN
                              END            END.            END                     END;                  PUT(2+2);
                                                                                                           END;

C++                     C                    MODULA                JAVA                        COBOL
#include <iostream.h>   #include <stdio.h>   MODULE HARRY;         public class Class1         IDENTIFICATION DIVISION.
void main()             void main()            FROM INOUT          {                           DATA DIVISION.
{                       {                        IMPORT WRITEINTEGER;  public static void main (String[] args)  WORKING-STORAGE SECTION.
  cout <<2+2;             printf("%d",2+2);  BEGIN                 {                           01    N PIC 9.
}                       }                    WRITEINTEGER(2+2,6);    System.out.println(2+2);  PROCEDURE DIVISION.
                                             END HARRY.            }                           MAIN-ROUTINE.
                                                                   }                                 ADD 2 2 GIVING N.
                                                                                                     DISPLAY N.
                                                                                                     STOP RUN.
```

Notice that APL's the briefest (just say 2+2), and COBOL's the most verbose (it requires 9 lines of typing).

Each of those 19 languages is flexible enough to program anything. Which language you choose is mainly a matter of personal taste.

Other languages are more specialized. For example, a language called "GPSS" is designed specifically to analyze how many employees to hire, to save your customers from waiting in long lines for service. DYNAMO analyzes social interactions inside your company and city and throughout the world; then it graphs your future. SPSS analyzes tables of numbers, by computing their averages, maxima, minima, standard deviations, and *hundreds* of other measurements used by statisticians. APT helps you run a factory by controlling "robots" that cut metal. PROLOG lets you store answers to your questions and act as an **expert system**. RPG spits out long business reports for executives who don't have enough time to program in COBOL.

The following table reveals more details about all those languages. Within each category ("mainstream", "radical", and "specialized"), the table lists the languages in chronological order.

Name	What the name stands for	Original use	Version 1 arose at	When	Names of new versions
Mainstream languages					
FORTRAN	FORmula TRANslating	sciences	IBM	1954-1957	FORTRAN 90, Lahey FORTRAN
ALGOL	ALGOrithmic Language	sciences	international	1957-1958	ALGOL W, ALGOL 68, BALGOL
COBOL	COmmon Business-Oriented Language	business	Defense Department	1959-1960	COBOL 85
BASIC	Beginners All-purp. Symbolic Instruc. Code	sciences	Dartmouth College	1963-1964	QBASIC, Visual BASIC
PL/I	Programming Language One	general	IBM	1963-1966	PL/I Optimizer, PL/C, ANSI PL/I
PASCAL	Blaise PASCAL	general	Switzerland	1968-1970	Turbo PASCAL, DELPHI
MODULA	MODULAr programming	systems programming	Switzerland	1975	MODULA-2, OBERON
C	beyond B	systems programming	Bell Labs	1971-1973	ANSI C
ADA	ADA Lovelace	military equipment	France	1977-1980	ADA final version
DBASE	Data BASE	database management	Jet Prop'n Lab & Ashton-T.	1978-1980	Visual DBASE 7.5, Visual FOXPRO 6
EASY	EASY	general	Secret Guide	1972-1982	EASY
C++	C increased	systems programming	Bell Labs	1979-1983	Visual C++, Borland C++, ISO C++, C#
JAVA	as stimulating as JAVA coffee	Web-page animation	Sun Microsystems	1990-1995	JAVA 2, Visual J++, JBuilder
Radical languages					
LISP	LISt Processing	artificial intelligence	MIT	1958-1960	Common LISP
SNOBOL	StriNg-Oriented symBOlic Language	string processing	Bell Labs	1962-1963	SNOBOL 4B
APL	A Programming Language	sciences	Harvard & IBM	1956-1966	APLSV, APL PLUS, APL 2, J
LOGO	LOGO	general	Bolt Beranek Newman	1967	Terrapin LOGO, LCSI MicroWorlds Pro
FORTH	FOuRTH-generation language	business & astronomy	Stanford Univ. & Mohasco	1963-1968	FORTH 83, FIG-FORTH, MMS FORTH
PILOT	Programmed Inquiry, Learning, Or Teaching	tutoring kids	U. of Cal. at San Francisco	1968	Atari PILOT
Specialized languages					
APT	Automatically Programmed Tools	cutting metal	MIT	1952-1957	APT 77
DYNAMO	DYNAmic Models	simulation	MIT	1959	DYNAMO 3, STELLA
GPSS	General-Purpose Simulation System	simulation	IBM	1961	GPSS 5
RPG	Report Program Generator	business	IBM	1964	RPG 3
SPSS	Statistical Package for the Social Sciences	statistics	Stanford University	1965-1967	SPSS 10
PROLOG	PROgramming in LOGic	artificial intelligence	France	1972	Arity PROLOG, Turbo PROLOG

Of those 25 languages, 5 were invented in Europe (ALGOL, PASCAL, MODULA, ADA, and PROLOG). The others were invented in the United States.

5 were invented at IBM's research facilities (FORTRAN, PL/I, APL, GPSS, and RPG), 3 at MIT (LISP, APT, and DYNAMO), 3 at Bell Labs (C, C++, and SNOBOL), 2 at Stanford University (FORTH and SPSS), and 2 by Professor Niklaus Wirth in Switzerland (PASCAL and MODULA). The others were invented by geniuses elsewhere.

Mainstream languages

The first mainstream languages were **FORTRAN**, **ALGOL**, and **COBOL**. They were the **big 3**.

> FORTRAN appealed to engineers, ALGOL to logicians, and COBOL to business managers & government bureaucrats. FORTRAN was invented by IBM, ALGOL by an international committee, and COBOL by a committee based at the Pentagon.

Beyond the big 3

Other mainstream languages came after the big 3 and were just slight improvements of the big 3. This family tree shows how the mainstream languages influenced each other:

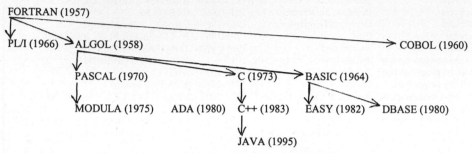

In that tree, a vertical line means "a direct influence" (like a parent); a slanted line means "an indirect influence" (like an aunt or uncle). For each language, I show the year when the language's first version was complete. As each language grew, it stole features from other languages (just like English stole the word "restaurant" from French); the tree shows just history's main thrust. Now let's dig into the details....

Why BASIC? Two professors at Dartmouth College combined FORTRAN with ALGOL, to form **BASIC**. It was designed for students, not professionals: it included just the *easiest* parts of FORTRAN and ALGOL. Students liked it because it was easy to learn, but professionals complained it lacked advanced features.

Why PL/I? After inventing FORTRAN and further improvements (called FORTRAN II, FORTRAN III, FORTRAN IV, and FORTRAN V), IBM decided to invent the "ultimate" improvement: a language that would include all the important words of FORTRAN V and **ALGOL** and **COBOL**. At first, IBM called it "FORTRAN VI"; but since it included the best of everything and was the first *complete* language ever invented, IBM changed its name to **Programming Language One** (written as **PL/I**). IBM bragged about how PL/I was so eclectic, but most programmers considered it a confusing mishmash and continued using the original three languages (FORTRAN, ALGOL, and COBOL), which were pure and simple.

Why PASCAL and MODULA? Among the folks who disliked PL/I was Niklaus Wirth, who preferred ALGOL. At a Swiss university, he invented an improved ALGOL and called it **PASCAL**. Then he invented a further improvement, called **MODULA**. ALGOL, PASCAL, and MODULA are all very similar to each other. He thinks MODULA's the best of the trio, but critics disagree. Today, PASCAL is still the most popular of that trio; hardly anybody uses the original ALGOL anymore, and MODULA is considered a controversial experiment.

While Wirth was developing and improving MODULA, other researchers were developing four competitors: C, ADA, DBASE, and EASY. Here's why....

Why C? Fancy languages, such as PL/I and MODULA, require lots of RAM. At Bell Labs, researchers needed a language small enough to fit in the tiny RAM of a minicomputer or microcomputer. They developed the ideal tiny language and called it **C**. Like PL/I, it borrows from FORTRAN, ALGOL, and COBOL; but it lacks PL/I's frills. It's "lean and mean" and runs very quickly. Later, Bell Telephone Labs invented an improved C, called **C++**, which includes extra commands. Then Sun invented a C++ variant, called **JAVA**, to handle animation on Web pages.

Why ADA? The Department of Defense, which was happily using COBOL to run the military's bureaucracy, needed to invent a second kind of language, to control missiles and other military equipment. The Department held a contest to develop such a language and said it wanted the language to resemble PL/I, ALGOL, and PASCAL. (It didn't know about MODULA, which was still being developed.) The winner was a French company. The Department adopted that company's language and called it

ADA. It resembled MODULA but included more commands — and therefore consumed more RAM and was more expensive. Critics complain that ADA, like PL/I, is too large and complex.

Why DBASE? Inspired by languages such as BASIC and PL/I, Wayne Ratliff invented **DBASE**. Like BASIC, DBASE is easy; like PL/I and PASCAL, DBASE creates loops by saying WHILE instead of GO TO. What makes DBASE unique is its new commands for manipulating databases.

Why EASY? My own attempt to create the ideal language is called **EASY**. It's even easier to learn than BASIC, yet includes the power of languages such as PASCAL. But since I don't have the time to put EASY onto a computer, EASY's remained just an idea whose time should have come.

Dig in! Here are the inside secrets about all those mainstream languages....

FORTRAN

During the early 1950's, the only available computer languages were specialized or awkward. FORTRAN was the first computer language good enough to be considered mainstream. ALGOL and COBOL came shortly afterwards. FORTRAN, ALGOL, and COBOL were so good that they made all earlier languages obsolete.

How FORTRAN developed

In 1954, an IBM committee said it was planning a new computer language that would help engineers make the computer handle math formulas. The committee called the language **FORTRAN**, to emphasize that the language would be particularly good for TRANslating FORmulas into computer notation.

Those original plans for FORTRAN were modest:

> They did *not* allow long variable names, subroutines, long function definitions, double precision, complex numbers, or apostrophes. A variable's name had to be short: just two letters. A function's definition had to fit on a single line. Instead of using apostrophes and writing 'PLEASE KISS ME', the programmers had to write 14HPLEASE KISS ME; the 14H meant a 14-character string.

Then came improvements:

> The first working version of FORTRAN (1957) allowed longer variable names: up to 6 characters.
>
> FORTRAN II (1958) allowed subroutines and long function definitions.
>
> IBM experimented with FORTRAN III but never released it to the public.
>
> FORTRAN IV (1962) allowed double precision and complex numbers.
>
> Apostrophes around strings weren't allowed until later.

The original plans said you'd be able to add an integer to a real. That didn't work in FORTRAN I, FORTRAN II, and FORTRAN IV, but it works today.

The original plans said an IF statement would compare any two numbers. FORTRAN I and FORTRAN II required the second number to be zero, but FORTRAN IV removed that restriction.

IBM waged a campaign to convince everyone that FORTRAN was easier than previous methods of programming. IBM succeeded: FORTRAN became immediately popular. FORTRAN was easy enough so that, for the first time, engineers who weren't computer specialists could write programs.

Other manufacturers sold imitations of IBM's FORTRAN, but with modifications. The variety of modifications from all the manufacturers annoyed engineers, who wished manufacturers would all use a single, common version of FORTRAN. So the engineers turned to the **American National Standards Institute (ANSI)**, which is a non-profit group of engineers that sets standards.

"ANSI" is pronounced "an see". It sets standards for practically all equipment in your life. For example, ANSI sets the standard for screws: to tighten a screw, you turn it clockwise, not counterclockwise.

In 1966, ANSI decided on a single version of FORTRAN IV to be used by all manufacturers. Thereafter, each manufacturer adhered to the ANSI standard but also added extra commands, to try to outclass the other manufacturers.

After several years had gone by, enough extra commands had been added by manufacturers so engineers asked ANSI to meet again and develop a common standard for those extras. ANSI finished developing the standard in 1977 and called it **FORTRAN 77**.

Now each major manufacturer adheres to the standard for FORTRAN 77, so you can run FORTRAN 77 programs on most maxicomputers, minicomputers, and microcomputers. Each manufacturer adds extra commands beyond FORTRAN 77.

In 1984, an ANSI committee developed a "FORTRAN 88". 40 members of the committee approved it, but the other 2 members — IBM and DEC — refused to endorse it. In 1991, a variant called **FORTRAN 90** was finally approved by all.

FORTRAN's popularity
FORTRAN became popular immediately because it didn't have any serious competitors. Throughout the 1960's and 1970's, FORTRAN remained the most popular computer language among engineers, scientists, mathematicians, and college students. Colleges required all freshman computer-science majors to take FORTRAN.

But at the end of the 1970's, FORTRAN's popularity began to drop.

Engineers switched to newer languages, such as BASIC (which is easier), PASCAL (more logical), and C (faster and more economical of RAM). Although FORTRAN 77 included extra commands to make FORTRAN resemble BASIC and PASCAL, those commands were "too little, too late": FORTRAN's new string commands weren't quite as good as BASIC's, and FORTRAN's new IF command wasn't quite as good as PASCAL's.

Now high-school kids are required to study BASIC or PASCAL, college kids are required to study C++, and hardly anybody studies FORTRAN. People who still program in FORTRAN are called "old-fashioned" by their colleagues.

But in some ways, FORTRAN's still better for engineering that BASIC, PASCAL, or C++. Here's why:

FORTRAN includes more commands for handling "complex numbers".

FORTRAN programmers have developed libraries containing *thousands* of FORTRAN subroutines, which you can use in your own FORTRAN programs. Such large libraries haven't been developed for BASIC, PASCAL, or C yet.

Though BASIC, PASCAL, and C++ work well on microcomputers and minicomputers, no *good* versions of those languages have been invented for IBM maxicomputers yet. The only language that lets you unleash an IBM maxicomputer's full power to solve engineering problems is FORTRAN.

ALGOL
In 1955, a committee in Germany began inventing a computer language. Though the committee spoke German, it decided the computer language should use English words instead, since English was the international language for science.

In 1957 those Germans invited Americans to join them. In 1958 other European countries joined also, to form an international committee, which proposed a new computer language, called "IAL" (International Algebraic Language).

The committee eventually changed the language's name to **ALGOL 58** (the ALGOrithmic Language invented in 1958), then created an improved version called **ALGOL 60**, then created a further revision called **ALGOL 60 Revised**, and disbanded. Today, programmers who mention "ALGOL" usually mean the committee's last report, ALGOL 60 Revised.

ALGOL differs from FORTRAN in many little ways....

How to end a statement
At the end of each statement, FORTRAN requires you to press the ENTER key. ALGOL requires you to type a semicolon instead.

ALGOL's advantage: you can type many statements on the same line, by putting semicolons between the statements. ALGOL's disadvantage: those ugly semicolons are a nuisance to type and make your program look cluttered.

Integer variables
To tell the computer that a person's AGE is an integer (instead of a real number), FORTRAN requires you to put the letter I, J, K, L, M, or N before the variable's name, like this: IAGE. ALGOL requires you to insert a note saying "INTEGER AGE" at the top of your program instead.

ALGOL's advantage: you don't have to write unpronounceable gobbledygook such as "IAGE". ALGOL's disadvantage: whenever you create a new variable, ALGOL forces you to go back up to the top of your program and insert a line saying "INTEGER" or "REAL".

Assignment statements
In FORTRAN, you can say J=7. In ALGOL, you must insert a colon and say J:=7 instead. To increase K by 1 in FORTRAN, you say K=K+1. In ALGOL, you say K:=K+1.

ALGOL's disadvantage: the colon is a nuisance to type. FORTRAN's disadvantage: according to the rules of algebra, it's impossible for K to equal K+1, and so the FORTRAN command K=K+1 looks like an impossibility.

ALGOL's beauty
Here's how ALGOL avoids FORTRAN's ugliness:

In ALGOL, a variable's name can be practically as long as you like. In FORTRAN, a variable's name must be short: no more than 6 characters.

ALGOL lets you write 2 instead of 2.0, without affecting the computer's answer. In FORTRAN, if you write 1/2 instead of 1/2.0, you get 0 instead of .5; and if you write SQRT (9) instead of SQRT (9.0), you get nonsense.

ALGOL's IF statement is very flexible: it can include the words ELSE, BEGIN, and END, and it lets you insert as many statements as you want between BEGIN and END. ALGOL even lets you put an IF statement in the middle of an equation, like this: X:=2+(IF Y<5 THEN 8 ELSE 9). The IF statement in FORTRAN I, II, III, and IV was very limited; the IF statement in FORTRAN 77 copies some of ALGOL's power, but not yet all.

ALGOL's FOR statement is very flexible. To make X be 3.7, then be Y+6.2, then go from SQRT(Z) down to 5 in steps of .3, you can say "FOR X:=3.7, Y+6.2, SQRT(Z) STEP -.3 UNTIL 5 DO". FORTRAN's DO is more restrictive; some versions of FORTRAN even insist that the DO statement contain no reals, no negatives, and no arithmetic operations.

At the beginning of a FORTRAN program, you can say DIMENSION X(20) but not DIMENSION X(N). ALGOL permits the "DIMENSION X(N)" concept; in ALGOL you say ARRAY X[1:N].

ALGOL's popularity When ALGOL was invented, programmers loved it. Europeans began using ALGOL more than FORTRAN. The American computer association (called the **Association for Computing Machinery, ACM**) said all programs in its magazine would be in ALGOL.

But IBM refused to put ALGOL on its computers. Since most American programmers used IBM computers, most American programmers couldn't use ALGOL.

> That created a ridiculous situation: American programmers programmed in FORTRAN instead, but submitted ALGOL translations to the ACM's magazine, which published the programs in ALGOL, which the magazine's readers had to translate back to FORTRAN in order to run on IBM computers.
>
> IBM computers eventually swept over Europe, so that even Europeans had to use FORTRAN instead of ALGOL.
>
> In 1966 the ACM gave in and agreed to publish programs in FORTRAN. But since ALGOL was prettier, everybody continued to submit ALGOL versions anyway.
>
> IBM gave in also and put ALGOL on its computers. But IBM's version of ALGOL was so limited and awkward that nobody took it seriously, and IBM stopped selling it and supporting it.
>
> In 1972 Stanford University created **ALGOL W**, a better version that ran on IBM computers. But ALGOL W came too late: universities and businessmen had already grown tired of waiting for a good IBM ALGOL and had committed themselves to FORTRAN.

Critics blamed IBM for ALGOL's demise. But here's IBM's side of the story:

> IBM had invested 25 man-years to develop the first version of FORTRAN. By the time the ALGOL committee finished the report on ALGOL 60 Revised, IBM had also developed FORTRAN II and FORTRAN III and made plans for FORTRAN IV. IBM was proud of its FORTRANs and wanted to elaborate on them. Moreover, IBM realized that **computers run FORTRAN programs more quickly than ALGOL**.

When asked why it didn't support ALGOL, IBM replied that the committee's description of ALGOL was incomplete. IBM was right; the ALGOL 60 Revised Report has three loopholes:

> 1. **The report doesn't say what words to use for input and output,** because the committee couldn't agree. So computers differ. If you want to transfer an ALGOL program from one computer to another, you must change all the input and output instructions.
>
> 2. **The report uses symbols such as ÷ and ∧, which most keyboards lack.** The report underlines keywords; most keyboards can't underline. To type ALGOL programs on a typical keyboard, you must substitute other symbols for ÷, ∧, and underlining. Here again, manufacturers differ. To transfer an ALGOL program to another manufacturer, you must change symbols.
>
> 3. **Some features of ALGOL are hard to teach to a computer.** Even today, no computer understands all of ALGOL. When a manufacturer says its computer "understands ALGOL", you must ask, "*Which* features of ALGOL?"

Attempts to improve ALGOL

Long after the original ALGOL committee wrote the ALGOL 60 Revised Report, two other ALGOL committees were formed.

One committee developed suggestions on how to do input and output, but its suggestions were largely ignored.

The other committee tried to invent a much fancier ALGOL. That committee wrote its preliminary report in 1968 and revised it in 1975. Called **ALGOL 68 Revised**, that weird report requires you to spell words backwards: to mark the end of the IF statement, you say FI; to mark the end of the DO statement, you say OD. The committee's decision was far from unanimous: several members refused to endorse the report.

ALGOL today

Few programmers still use ALGOL, but many use PASCAL (which is very similar to ALGOL 60 Revised) and BASIC (which is a compromise between ALGOL and FORTRAN).

COBOL

During the 1950's, several organizations developed languages to solve problems in business. The most popular business languages were IBM's COMMERCIAL TRANSLATOR (developed from 1957-1959), Honeywell's FACT (1959-1960), Sperry Rand's FLOW-MATIC (1954-1958), and the Air Force's AIMACO (1958).

In April 1959, a group of programmers and manufacturers met at the University of Pennsylvania and decided to develop a *single* business language for *all* computers. The group asked the Department of Defense to help sponsor the research.

The Department agreed. At a follow-up meeting held at the Pentagon in May. At that meeting, the group tentatively decided to call the new language "CBL" (for "Common Business Language") and created three committees.

> The Short-Range Committee would meet immediately to develop a temporary language. A Medium-Range Committee would meet later to develop a more thoroughly thought-out language. Then a Long-Range Committee would develop the ultimate language.

The Short-Range Committee met immediately and created a language nice enough so that the Medium-Range and Long-Range Committees never bothered to meet.

The Short-Range Committee wanted a more pronounceable name for the language than "CBL". At a meeting in September 1969, the committee members proposed six names:

> "BUSY" (BUsiness SYstem)
> "BUSYL" (BUsiness SYstem Language)
> "INFOSYL" (INFOrmation SYstem Language)
> "DATASYL" (DATA SYstem Language)
> "COSYL" (COmmon SYstem Language)
> "COCOSYL" (COmmon COmputer SYstem Language)

The next day, a member of the committee suggested "COBOL" (COmmon Business-Oriented Language), and the rest of the committee agreed.

I wish they'd have kept the name "BUSY", because it's easier to pronounce and remember than "COBOL". Today, COBOL programmers are still known as "BUSY bodies".

From Sperry Rand's FLOW-MATIC, the new language (called "COBOL") borrowed two rules:

> Begin each statement with an English verb.
> Put data descriptions in a different program division than procedures.

From IBM's COMMERCIAL TRANSLATOR, COBOL borrowed group items (01 and 02), PICTURE symbols, fancy IF statements, and COMPUTE formulas.

Compromises

On some issues, the members of the committee couldn't agree, so they compromised.

For example, some members wanted COBOL to let the programmers construct mathematical formulas by using these symbols:

> + - * / = ( )

But other members of the committee disagreed: they argued that since COBOL is supposed to be for stupid businessmen who fear formulas, COBOL ought to use the words ADD, SUBTRACT, MULTIPLY, and DIVIDE instead. The committee compromised: when you write a COBOL program, you can use the words ADD, SUBTRACT, MULTIPLY, and DIVIDE; if you prefer, you can use a formula instead, but you must warn the computer by putting the word COMPUTE in front of the formula.

Can COBOL handle long numbers? How long? The committee decided that COBOL would handle any number up to 18 digits long. The committee also decided that COBOL would handle any variable name up to 30 characters long. So the limits of COBOL are "18 and 30".

> Why did the committee pick those two numbers — "18 and 30" — instead of "16 and 32"? Answer: some manufacturers wanted "16 and 32" (because their computers were based on the numbers 16 and 32), but other manufacturers wanted other combinations (such as "24 and 36"); the committee, hunting for a compromise, chose "18 and 30", because *nobody* wanted it, and so it would give no manufacturer an unfair advantage over competitors. In other words, COBOL was designed to be equally terrible for everybody! That's politics!

COBOL's popularity In 1960, the Defense Department announced it would buy just computers that understand COBOL, unless a manufacturer can demonstrate why COBOL isn't helpful. In 1961, Westinghouse Electric Corp. made a similar announcement. Other companies followed. COBOL became the most popular computer language. Today it's still the most popular computer language for maxicomputers, though programmers on minicomputers and microcomputers have switched to newer languages.

Improvements The original version of COBOL was finished in 1960 and called **COBOL 60**. Then came an improvement, called **COBOL 61**. The verb SORT and a "Report Writer" feature were added in 1962. Then came **COBOL 65**, **COBOL 68**, **COBOL 74**, and **COBOL 85**.

COBOL's most obvious flaw To write a COBOL program, you must put info about file labeling into the data division's FD command. Since file labeling describes the **environment**, not the **data**, COBOL should have been changed, to put the labeling in the environment division instead.

Jean Sammet, who headed some of the Short-Term Committee's subcommittees, admits her group goofed when it decided to put labeling in the data division. But COBOL's too old to change now.

BASIC

The first version of BASIC was developed in 1963 and 1964 by a genius (John Kemeny) and his friend (Tom Kurtz).

How the genius grew up John Kemeny was a Jew born in Hungary in 1926. In 1940 he and his parents fled from the Nazis and came to America. Although he knew hardly any English when he began high school in New York, he learned enough so he graduated as the top student in the class. Four years later, he graduated from Princeton **summa cum laude** even though he had to spend 1½ of those years in the Army, where he helped solve equations for the atomic bomb.

Two years after his B.A., Princeton gave him a Ph.D. in mathematics *and* philosophy, because his thesis on symbolic logic combined both fields.

While working for the Ph.D., he was also Einstein's youngest assistant. He told Einstein he wanted to quit math and instead hand out leaflets for world peace. Einstein replied: handing out leaflets would waste his talents; the best way for him to help world peace would be to become a famous mathematician, so people would *listen* to him, as they had to Einstein. He took Einstein's advice and stayed with math.

After getting his Ph.D., he taught symbolic logic in Princeton's philosophy department. In 1953, most of Dartmouth College's math professors were retiring, so Dartmouth asked Kemeny to come to Dartmouth, chair the department, and "bring all your friends". He accepted the offer and brought his friends. That's how Dartmouth stole Princeton's math department.

At Dartmouth, Kemeny invented several new branches of math. Then Kemeny's department got General Electric to sell Dartmouth a computer at 90% discount, in return for which his department had to invent programs for it and let General Electric use them. To write the programs, Kemeny invented his own little computer language in 1963 and showed it to his colleague Thomas Kurtz, who knew less about philosophy but more about computers. Kurtz added features from ALGOL and FORTRAN and called the combination "BASIC".

After inventing BASIC, Kemeny became bored and thought of quitting Dartmouth. Then Dartmouth asked him to become president of the college. He accepted.

Later, when the Three-Mile Island nuclear power plant almost exploded, President Jimmy Carter told Kemeny to head the investigation, because of Kemeny's reputation for profound philosophical and scientific impartiality. Kemeny's report was impartial — and sharply critical of the nuclear industry.

BASIC versus ALGOL & FORTRAN BASIC is simpler than both ALGOL and FORTRAN in two ways:

> 1. In ALGOL and FORTRAN, you must tell the computer which variables are integers and which are reals. In ALGOL, you do that by saying INTEGER or REAL. In FORTRAN, you do that by choosing an appropriate first letter for the variable's name. **In BASIC, the computer assumes all variables are real**, unless you specifically say otherwise.
>
> 2. In ALGOL and FORTRAN, output is a hassle. In FORTRAN, you have to worry about FORMATs. In ALGOL, each computer handles output differently — and in most cases strangely. **BASIC's PRINT statement automatically invents a good format.**

Is BASIC closer to ALGOL than to FORTRAN? On the one hand, BASIC uses the ALGOL words FOR, STEP, and THEN and the ALGOL symbol ↑ (or ^). On the other hand, BASIC, uses the FORTRAN words RETURN and DIMENSION (abbreviated DIM); and BASIC's "FOR I = 1 TO 9 STEP 2" puts the step size at the *end* of the statement, like FORTRAN's "DO 30 I = 1,9,2" and unlike ALGOL's "FOR I:=1 STEP 2 UNTIL 9".

BASIC versus JOSS BASIC is *not* the simplest computer language. **JOSS**, which was developed a year earlier by the RAND Corporation, is simpler to learn. But JOSS doesn't have string variables and doesn't name programs (you must give each program a number instead, and remember what the number was). Also, programs written in JOSS run more slowly and require more of the computer's memory than if written in BASIC.

A few programmers still use JOSS and three of its variants, which are called **AID**, **FOCAL**, and **MUMPS**. They all run on computers built by DEC. AID is used by high-school kids on PDP-8 computers, FOCAL by scientists on PDP-10 computers, and MUMPS by doctors designing databases of patient records on PDP-11 computers. Though MUMPS *does* have string variables and other modern features, it's gradually being replaced by newer database languages such as DBASE.

Six versions Kemeny and Kurtz finished **the original version** of BASIC in May 1964. It included just these statements:

> PRINT, GO TO, IF...THEN, FOR...NEXT, DATA...READ, GOSUB...RETURN, DIM, LET (for commands such as LET X=3), REM (for REMarks and comments), DEF (to DEFine your own functions), and END

In that version, the only punctuation allowed in the PRINT statement was the comma. **The second version** of BASIC (October 1964) added the semicolon.

The third version (1966) added the words INPUT, RESTORE, and MAT. (The word MAT helps you manipulate a "MATrix", which means an "array". Today, most versions of BASIC omit the word MAT, because its definition consumes too much RAM.)

In all those versions, you could use variables. For example, you could say LET X=3. A variable was a letter that stood for a number. **The fourth version** (1967) added a new concept: string variables (such as A$). That version also added TAB (to improve the printing), RANDOMIZE (to improve RND), and ON...GO TO.

The fifth version (1970) added data files (sequential access and random access).

The sixth version (1971) added PRINT USING and a sophisticated way to handle subroutines — a way so sophisticated that most microcomputers don't have it yet!

How BASIC became popular

During the 1960's and 1970's, Kemeny & Kurtz worked on BASIC with a fervor that was almost religious.

> They believed *every* college graduate should know how to program a computer, and be as literate in BASIC as in English.
>
> They convinced Dartmouth to spend as much on its computer as on the college library. They put computer terminals in practically every college building (even in the dorms), and let all the kids who lived in the town come onto the campus and join the fun. Altogether, the campus had about 300 terminals. Over 90% of all Dartmouth students used BASIC before they graduated.
>
> Dartmouth trained high-school teachers how to use BASIC. Soon many colleges, high schools, and prep schools throughout New England had terminals connected to Dartmouth's computer by phone.

General Electric, which built Dartmouth's computer, quit making computers and sold its computer factory to Honeywell. So now Dartmouth's computer is called a "Honeywell".

Since Dartmouth's research on BASIC was partially funded by the National Science Foundation, BASIC was in the public domain. Other computer manufacturers could use it without having to worry about copyrights or patents.

DEC

The first company to copy Dartmouth's ideas was Digital Equipment Corporation (DEC).

> DEC put BASIC and FOCAL on DEC's first popular minicomputer, the PDP-8. When DEC saw that programmers preferred BASIC, DEC stopped developing FOCAL and devoted all its energies to improving BASIC further.
>
> DEC invented fancier minicomputers (the PDP-11 and Vax) and maxicomputers (the Decsystem-10 and Decsystem-20) and put BASIC on all of them. DEC's versions of BASIC were similar to Dartmouth's. Though the versions put on the PDP-8 were quite primitive (almost as bad as Dartmouth's first edition), the versions put on DEC's fancier computers were more sophisticated. Eventually, DEC put decent versions of BASIC even on the PDP-8.
>
> DEC's best version of BASIC is **VAX BASIC**, which works just on VAX computers. DEC's second-best version of BASIC is **BASIC-PLUS-2**, which works on the VAX, the PDP-11, and the Decsystem-20. DEC's third-best version of BASIC is **BASIC-PLUS**, which works only on the PDP-11. DEC's other versions of BASIC aren't as fancy.

HP

Soon after DEC started putting BASIC on its computers, Hewlett-Packard (HP) decided to do likewise.

> HP put BASIC on the HP-2000 computer, and then put a better version of BASIC on the HP-300 computer.
>
> Unfortunately, HP's BASIC was more difficult to use than DEC's. On Hewlett-Packard computers, each time you used a string you had to write a "DIM statement" that warned the computer how long the string would be: the DIM statement had to say how many characters the string would contain.

Other major manufacturers

Most other manufacturers imitate the versions of BASIC invented by Dartmouth and DEC. Unfortunately, Data General, Wang, and IBM made the mistake of copying Hewlett-Packard instead.

That's how BASIC developed on maxicomputers and minicomputers.

How Microsoft BASIC arose

The first popular *micro*computer was the Altair 8800, which used a version of BASIC invented by a 20-year-old kid named Bill Gates. His version imitated DEC's.

The Altair computer was manufactured by a company called **Mits**. When Mits didn't treat Bill Gates fairly, he broke away from Mits and formed his own company, called **Microsoft**.

Bill Gates and his company, Microsoft, invented many versions of BASIC.

> The first was called **4K BASIC**, because it consumed only 4K of memory chips (RAM or ROM). Then came **8K BASIC**, which included a larger vocabulary. Then came **Extended BASIC**, which included an even larger vocabulary and consumed 14K. All those versions were intended for primitive microcomputers that used tapes instead of disks. Finally came **Disk BASIC**, which came on a disk and included all the commands for handling disks. His **Disk BASIC version 4** was further improved, to form **Disk BASIC version 5**, which is the version of BASIC still used on CP/M computers and on the Radio Shack model 4. It's also called **MBASIC** and **BASIC-80**.

All those versions of BASIC were written for computers that contained an 8080 or Z-80 CPU. Simultaneously, he wrote

6502 BASIC, for Apple 2 and Commodore computers.

> The Apple 2 version of 6502 BASIC is called **Applesoft BASIC**. Commodore's version of 6502 BASIC is called **Commodore BASIC**.

Unfortunately, 6502 BASIC is rather primitive: it resembles his 8K BASIC. So if you're trying to learn advanced BASIC programming, you should *not* get an Apple 2e or 2c or Commodore 64!

After writing 6502 BASIC, Bill wrote an improved version of it, called **6809 BASIC**, which is available only for Radio Shack's Color Computer. Radio Shack calls it **Extended Color BASIC**.

Texas Instruments (TI) asked Bill to write a version of BASIC for TI computers. Bill said "yes". Then TI told Bill what kind of BASIC it wanted. Bill's company — Microsoft — found 90 ways in which TI's desires would contradict Microsoft's traditions. Microsoft convinced TI to change its mind and remove 80 of those 90 contradictions, but TI stood firm on the other 10.

> So TI BASIC (which is on the TI-990 and TI-99/4A computers) contradicts all other versions of Microsoft BASIC in 10 ways. For example, in TI BASIC, the INPUT statement uses a colon instead of a semicolon, and a multi-statement line uses a double colon (::) instead of a single colon.

Because of those differences, TI's computers became unpopular, and TI stopped making them. Moral: if you contradict Bill, you'll die!

Bill later invented an amazingly wonderful version of BASIC, better than all the other versions that had been invented. He called it **GW BASIC** (which stands for "Gee-Whiz BASIC"). It runs only on the IBM PC and clones.

When you buy PC-DOS from IBM, you typically get GW BASIC at no extra charge. (IBM calls it **BASICA**.) When you buy MS-DOS for an IBM clone, the typical dealer includes GW BASIC at no extra charge, but ask!

Beyond GW BASIC

GW BASIC was the last version of BASIC that Bill developed personally. All further improvements & variants were done by his assistants at Microsoft.

Microsoft's newest variations are **Microsoft BASIC for the Mac**, **Amiga Microsoft BASIC** (for the Commodore's Amiga computer), **Quick BASIC** (for the IBM PC and clones), **QBASIC** (which you get instead of GWBASIC when you buy MS-DOS version 5 or 6), and **Visual BASIC** (which lets you easily create Windows-style programs that let the human use a mouse and pull-down menus). Those BASICs are slightly harder to learn how to use than GW BASIC; but once you understand them, you'll prefer them because they run faster and include a better editor, more words from ALGOL and PASCAL, and fancier output.

While developing those versions of BASIC, Microsoft added three new commands that are particularly exciting: SAY, END IF, and SUB.

The SAY command makes the computer talk, by using a voice synthesizer. for example, to make the computer's voice say "I love you", type this command:

```
SAY TRANSLATE$("I LOVE YOU")
```

That makes the computer translate "I love you" into phonetics and then say the phonetics. That command works on the Amiga, and I hope Microsoft will put it on other computers also.

The END IF and SUB commands give BASIC some of PASCAL's power. By using the END IF command, you can make the IF statement include many lines, like this:

```
IF AGE<18 THEN
      PRINT "YOU ARE STILL A MINOR."
      PRINT "AH, THE JOYS OF YOUTH!"
      PRINT "I WISH I COULD BE AS YOUNG AS YOU!"
END IF
```

By using the SUB command, you can give a subroutine a name.

Borland

Microsoft's main competitor for languages is **Borland**, which made **Turbo PASCAL**, **Turbo C**, and **Turbo BASIC**.

Turbo BASIC version 1.1 runs faster than Quick BASIC, is easier to understand, and includes almost as many commands. But Borland has stopped marketing Turbo BASIC, so that Borland can devote its energies to other Borland products that are more profitable (such as Turbo PASCAL, Turbo C, Quattro, and Paradox).

Divergences

GW BASIC, Microsoft BASIC for the Macintosh, Amiga Microsoft BASIC, Quick BASIC, and Turbo BASIC are all wonderful.

Over the years, several microcomputer manufacturers tried to invent their own versions of BASIC, to avoid paying royalties to Bill Gates. They were sorry!

For example, **Radio Shack** tried hiring somebody else to write Radio Shack's BASIC. That person quit in the middle of the job; Radio Shack's original BASIC was never completed. Nicknamed "Level 1 BASIC", it was a half-done mess. Radio Shack, like an obedient puppy dog, then went to Bill, who finally wrote a decent version of BASIC for Radio Shack; Bill's version was called "Level 2". Today, Radio Shack uses further improvements on Bill's Level 2 BASIC.

Apple's original attempt at BASIC was called "Apple Integer BASIC". It was written by Steve Wozniak and was terrible: it couldn't handle decimals, and it made the mistake of imitating Hewlett-Packard instead of DEC (because Steve had worked at Hewlett-Packard). Eventually, Steve wised up and hired Bill, who wrote Apple's better BASIC, called **Applesoft** (which means "Apple BASIC by Microsoft"). Applesoft was intended for tapes, not disks. Later, when Steve Wozniak wanted to add disks to the Apple computer, he made the mistake of not rehiring Bill — which is why Apple's disk system is worse than Radio Shack's.

At **Atari**, an executive who didn't want to hire Bill made the mistake of hiring the inventor of Apple's disastrous DOS. That guy's BASIC, which is called **Atari BASIC**, resembles Hewlett-Packard's BASIC. Like Apple's DOS, it looks pleasant at first glance but turns into a nightmare when you try to do any advanced programming. As a result, Atari's computers didn't become as popular as Atari hoped, and the executive who "didn't want to hire Bill" was fired. Atari finally hired Bill's company, which wrote **Atari Microsoft BASIC version 2**.

Two other microcomputer manufacturers — **North Star Computers** and **APF** — tried developing their own versions of BASIC, to avoid paying royalties to Bill. Since their versions of BASIC were lousy, they went out of business.

While DEC, Hewlett-Packard, Microsoft, and other companies were developing their own versions of BASIC, professors back at Dartmouth College were still tinkering with Dartmouth BASIC version 6. In 1976, Professor Steve Garland added more commands from ALGOL, PL/I, and PASCAL to Dartmouth BASIC. He called his version "Structured BASIC" or **SBASIC**.

One of BASIC's inventors, Professor Tom Kurtz, became chairman of an ANSI committee to standardize BASIC. His committee published two reports.

The 1977 report defined **ANSI Standard Minimal BASIC**, a minimal standard that all advertised versions of "BASIC" should live up to. That report was quite reasonable, and everybody agreed to abide by it. (Microsoft's old versions of BASIC were written before that report came out. Microsoft Disk BASIC version 5 was Microsoft's first version to obey that standard.)

In 1985, ANSI created a more ambitious report, to standardize the most advanced aspects of BASIC.

The report said that the advanced aspects of BASIC should closely follow SBASIC and the other versions developed at Dartmouth. But Bill Gates, who invented Microsoft BASIC and was also one of the members of the committee, disliked some aspects of Dartmouth's BASIC and quit the committee. (He was particularly annoyed by the committee's desire to include Dartmouth's MAT commands, which consume lots of RAM and which hardly anybody uses.) He refused to follow the committee's recommendations.

That left two standards for advanced BASIC: the "official" standard, defined by the ANSI committee; and the "de facto" standard, which is Bill Gates' GW BASIC, the version of BASIC that most people use.

The two standards are quite different from each other. For example, in GW BASIC you say:

```
10 INPUT "WHAT IS YOUR NAME"; A$
```

In ANSI BASIC, you say this instead:

```
10 INPUT PROMPT "WHAT IS YOUR NAME? ": A$
```

Notice that in ANSI BASIC, you must insert the word PROMPT after INPUT, insert a questions mark and blank space before the second quotation mark, and type a colon instead of a semicolon.

Tom Kurtz (who chaired the ANSI committee) and John Kemeny (who invented BASIC with Tom Kurtz) put ANSI BASIC onto Dartmouth's computer. So ANSI BASIC became Dartmouth's seventh official version of BASIC.

Then Kurtz and Kemeny left Dartmouth and formed their own company, which invented **True BASIC**. It's a version of ANSI BASIC that runs on the IBM PC and the Apple Macintosh.

In some ways, True BASIC is slightly better than Microsoft's GW BASIC and Quick BASIC. In other ways, True BASIC is slightly worse. Since Microsoft's BASIC versions have become the de facto standard, and since True BASIC isn't *significantly* better, hardly anybody is switching from Microsoft BASIC to True BASIC.

Comparison chart This chart compares the most popular versions of BASIC for microcomputers today:

	Video			Audio			Logic		
	USING	LINE	CIRCLE	SOUND	PLAY	SAY	ELSE	END IF	SUB
IBM PC color with Visual BASIC (2 or later) or QBASIC Commodore Amiga with Microsoft BASIC	√ √	√ √	√ √	√ √	√	√	√ √	√ √	√ √
Apple Macintosh with Quick BASIC	√	√	√	√			√	√	√
IBM PC color GW BASIC, Commodore 128, or TRS-80 Color	√	√	√	√	√		√		
Atari ST	√	√	√	√			√		
IBM PC monochrome with GW BASIC Atari XE (or XL) with Microsoft BASIC	√ √	√		√	√		√	√	
TRS-80 Model 3, 4, 4P, or 4D	√						√		
Apple 2, 2+, 2e, 2c, 2c+, or 2GS		√							
Commodore 64 or Vic-20									

It shows which versions of BASIC understand these 9 words: USING, LINE, CIRCLE, SOUND, PLAY, SAY, ELSE, END IF, and SUB.

The versions of BASIC at the top of the chart (Amiga BASIC, Visual BASIC, and QBASIC) are the best: they understand 8 of the 9 words. The versions of BASIC at the bottom of the chart (Commodore 64 BASIC & Vic-20 BASIC) are the worst: they understand none of the words.

Here's what those 9 words accomplish:

The word USING (which you put immediately after the word PRINT) lets you control how many digits the computer will print after the decimal point.

LINE makes the computer draw a diagonal line across the screen.
CIRCLE makes the computer draw a circle as big as you wish.
SOUND and PLAY make the computer create music.
SAY makes the computer talk.
ELSE and END IF let you create fancy IF statements.
SUB lets you name subroutines.

Although the Commodore 128 and Radio Shack TRS-80 Color Computer are cheap, the chart shows their versions of BASIC are better than the Apple 2c's. If schools would have bought Commodore 128 and Radio Shack TRS-80 Color Computers instead of Apple 2c's, students would be better programmers!

PL/I

During the early 1960's, IBM sold two kinds of computers. One kind was for use by scientists; the other kind was for use by business bookkeepers. For the scientific kind of computer, the most popular language was FORTRAN. For the business kind of computer, the most popular language was COBOL.

In 1962, IBM secretly began working on a project to create a single, large computer that could be used by everybody: scientists and businesses. IBM called it the **IBM 360**, because it could handle the full circle of applications. What language should the IBM 360 be programmed in? IBM decided to invent a single language that could be used for both science and business.

IBM's first attempt at such a language was "FORTRAN V". It ran all the FORTRAN IV programs but also included commands for handling strings and fields in data files. But IBM never announced FORTRAN V to the public; instead, in 1963 IBM began working on a dramatically more powerful language called "FORTRAN VI", which would resemble FORTRAN but be much more powerful and modern (and hence incompatible). It would also include *all* the important features of COBOL and ALGOL.

As work on FORTRAN VI progressed, IBM realized it would be so different from traditional FORTRAN that it should have a different name. In 1964, IBM changed the name to "NPL" (New Programming Language), since the language was intended to go with the IBM 360 and the rest of IBM's New Product Line.

When IBM discovered that the letters "NPL" already stood for the National Physics Laboratory in England, IBM changed the language's name to **Programming Language One (PL/I)**, to brag it was the first good programming language and all its predecessors were worth zero by comparison.

Troublesome timing
The committee that invented PL/I had a hard time.

> The committee consisted of just 6 official members (3 from IBM and 3 from a FORTRAN user group). A few friends of the committee attended also. The committee could meet only on weekends, and only in hotel rooms in New York State and California. The first meeting was in October 1963 (at the Motel-on-the-Mountain on the New York Thruway), and IBM insisted that the entire language design be finished by December. It was a rush job!
>
> The committee didn't meet the deadline. It finished two months late, in February.

After the design was finished, the language still had to be put onto the computer. Since that took 2½ more years of programming and polishing, the language wasn't available for sale to IBM's customers until August 1966.

That was too late. It was *after* IBM had already begun shipping the IBM 360. The 360's customers continued using FORTRAN and COBOL, since PL/I wasn't available initially. After those customers bought, installed, and learned how to use FORTRAN and COBOL on the 360, they weren't willing to switch to PL/I. Switching was too much trouble.

Other troubles
PL/I was expensive to run. It required twice as much RAM as COBOL, four times as much RAM as FORTRAN. It ran slowly: it took 1½ times as long to compile as COBOL, twice as long as FORTRAN.

Another obstacle to PL/I's acceptance was lethargy: most programmers already knew FORTRAN and COBOL, were satisfied with those languages, and weren't willing to spend the time to learn something new.

Some programmers praise PL/I for being amazingly powerful. Others call it just a scheme by IBM to get people to buy more RAM. Others call it a disorganized mess, an "ugly kitchen sink of a language", thrown together by a committee that was in too much of a rush.

Since PL/I is such a large language, hardly anybody understands it all. As a typical harried PL/I programmer, you study just the part of the language you intend to use. But if you make a mistake, the computer might not gripe: instead, it might think you're trying to give a different PL/I command from a different part of the language that you never studied. So instead of griping, the computer will perform an instruction that wasn't what you meant.

Universities
Universities debated which language to teach freshman. For a while, the choice was between FORTRAN (the "standard"), ALGOL (the "pure and simple"), and PL/I (the "powerful").

In 1972, Cornell University developed a stripped-down version of PL/I for students. That version, called **PL/C**, is a compromise between PL/I's power and ALGOL's pure simplicity.

In 1975, The University of Toronto developed an even *more* stripped-down version of PL/I, and called it **SP/k**. Although it allows fewer statements than PL/C, it runs faster and prints messages that are even more helpful. SP/k comes in several sizes: the tiniest is SP/1; the largest is SP/8.

Stripped-down versions of PL/I remained popular in universities until about 1980, when they began to be replaced by PASCAL.

Microcomputers
Digital Research invented a tiny version of PL/I for microcomputers, and called it **PL/M**. Unfortunately, PL/M can't handle decimals. PL/M was popular during the late 1970's and early 1980's, but most PL/M programmers eventually switched to C.

Maxicomputers
PL/I is still used on large IBM computers, because it's the only language that includes enough commands to let programmers unleash IBM's full power.

Statements PL/I uses many statements for input and output. The statement's meaning depends mainly on the statement's first word:

First word	What the computer will do
GET	input from a terminal or simple file
PUT	print on a terminal or simple file
OPEN	start using a file
CLOSE	stop using a file
READ	input from a file whose picture is unedited
WRITE	print on a file whose picture is unedited
DELETE	delete an item from a file
REWRITE	replace an item in a file
LOCATE	print a "based" variable onto a file
UNLOCK	let other programs use the file
FORMAT	use a certain form for spacing the input and output
DISPLAY	chat with operator who sits at computer's main terminal

These statements interrupt:

First word	What the computer will do
STOP	stop the program
EXIT	stop a task (in a program that involves several tasks)
HALT	interrupt the program; free the terminal to do other tasks
DELAY	pause for a certain number of milliseconds
WAIT	pause until other simultaneous routines finish their tasks

These statements handle conditions:

First word	What the computer will do
IF	if a certain condition occurs now, do certain statements
ON	if a certain condition occurs later, do certain statements
SIGNAL	pretend a condition such as OVERFLOW occurs
REVERT	cancel the ON statements

These statements handle variables:

First word	What the computer will do
DECLARE	make some variables be integers, other be reals, etc.
DEFAULT	assume all variables are integers, or a similar assumption
ALLOCATE	create a temporary variable
FREE	destroy a temporary variable and use its RAM otherwise

These statements handle general logic:

First word	What the computer will do
GO	go to a different line
CALL	go to a subroutine
RETURN	return from a subroutine to the main routine
ENTRY	skip the subroutine's previous lines; begin here instead
PROCEDURE	begin a program or subprogram
DO	begin a loop or compound statement
BEGIN	begin a block of statements
END	end program, subprogram., loop, compound statement, or block

Half of those statements are borrowed from FORTRAN, ALGOL, and COBOL.

from FORTRAN:	FORMAT, STOP, CALL, RETURN, DO
from ALGOL:	IF, GO, PROCEDURE, BEGIN, END
from COBOL:	OPEN, CLOSE, READ, WRITE, DISPLAY, EXIT

Like ALGOL, PL/I requires a semicolon at the end of each statement. Besides the statements listed above, you can also give an **assignment statement** (such as "N=5;"), a **null statement** (which consists of just a semicolon), and a **preprocessor statement** (which tells the computer how to create its own program).

PASCAL

In 1968, a European committee tried to invent an improved version of ALGOL. The majority of the committee agreed on a version called "ALGOL 68". It was strange: it even required you to spell some commands backwards.

A few members of the committee were dissidents who disagreed with the majority and thought ALGOL 68 was nuts. One of the dissidents, Niklaus Wirth, quit the committee and created his own version of ALGOL. He called his version

PASCAL. Today, most computerists feel he was right and the majority of the committee was wrong, PASCAL is better than ALGOL 68.

He wrote PASCAL in Switzerland, for a CDC maxicomputer that used punched cards. His version of PASCAL couldn't handle video screens, couldn't handle random-access data files, and couldn't handle strings well. Those three limitations were corrected in later versions of PASCAL — especially the version invented at the University of California at San Diego (UCSD), which even includes LOGO-style commands that move a turtle.

Apple's PASCAL Apple Computer Company got permission to sell an Apple version of UCSD PASCAL. Apple ran full-page advertisements, bragging that the Apple 2 was the only popular microcomputer that could handle PASCAL.

For $495, Apple Computer Company sold the "Apple Language System", which included 4 disks containing PASCAL, 2 disks containing souped-up BASIC, and a card containing 16K of extra RAM. Many people spent the $495 for PASCAL but were disappointed. They expected that by spending $495, they'd be able to write programs more easily, but they discovered that PASCAL is *harder* to learn than BASIC.

PASCAL is helpful only if the program you're writing is very long. PASCAL helps you organize and dissect long programs more easily than BASIC. But the average Apple owner never writes long programs and never needs PASCAL.

Many customers felt "ripped off", since they had spent $495 and received no benefit in return. But maybe that's what "marketing" is all about.

PASCAL's popularity Many programmers who've been writing large FORTRAN programs for large computers are switching to PASCAL, because PASCAL helps organize large programs better, and because FORTRAN is archaic. Many programmers who've been using PL/I are switching to PASCAL, because PASCAL consumes less RAM than PL/I and fits in smaller computers.

Most colleges require freshman computer-science majors to take PASCAL.

Most high-school seniors applying to attend college take tests given by the College Entrance Examination Board. The most famous such test is the Scholastic Aptitude Test (SAT), but the board offers many others. One of the board's newest tests is the **Advanced Placement Test in Computer Science**; a high-school senior who scores high on that test can skip the first year of college computer-science courses and go immediately into college-sophomore courses. Since that test requires a knowledge of PASCAL, many high-school seniors are studying PASCAL.

Best versions The most powerful PASCAL for microcomputers is **Turbo PASCAL**, published by Borland. It's available for the IBM PC, Mac, and CP/M computers.

If you have a Mac, get either the Mac version of Turbo PASCAL or **Think PASCAL**. If you have an Apple 2e or 2c, get **Instant PASCAL** (which is much easier to use than the UCSD PASCAL that was sold under the name "Apple PASCAL").

MODULA

After Niklaus Wirth invented PASCAL, he began designing a more ambitious language, called **MODULA**.

He designed the first version of MODULA in 1975. In 1979 he designed an improvement called **MODULA-2**. When today's programmers discuss "MODULA", they mean MODULA-2.

MODULA-2 is very similar to PASCAL. Like PASCAL, MODULA-2 requires each program's main routing to begin with the word BEGIN; but MODULA-2 does *not* require you to say BEGIN after DO WHILE or IF THEN:

```
PASCAL                              MODULA-2
IF AGE<18 THEN                      IF AGE<18 THEN
  BEGIN                               WRITESTRING("YOU ARE STILL A MINOR");
  WRITELN('YOU ARE STILL A MINOR');   WRITESTRING("AH, THE JOYS OF YOUTH");
  WRITELN('AH, THE JOYS OF YOUTH');  ELSE
  END                                 WRITESTRING("GLAD YOU ARE AN ADULT");
ELSE                                  WRITESTRING("WE CAN HAVE ADULT FUN")
  BEGIN                             END;
  WRITELN('GLAD YOU ARE AN ADULT');
  WRITELN('WE CAN HAVE ADULT FUN');
  END;
```

That example shows four ways that MODULA-2 differs from PASCAL: MODULA-2 says WRITESTRING instead of WRITELN, uses regular quotation marks (") instead of apostrophes, lets you omit the word BEGIN after IF ELSE (and WHILE DO), and lets you omit the word END before ELSE.

Advanced programmers like MODULA-2 better than PASCAL because MODULA-2 includes extra commands for handling subroutines.

C

Many programmers use **C**.

How C arose In 1963 at England's Cambridge University and the University of London, researchers developed a "practical" version of ALGOL and called it the **Combined Programming Language (CPL)**. In 1967 at Cambridge University, Martin Richards invented a simpler, stripped-down version of CPL and called it **Basic CPL (BCPL)**. In 1970 at Bell Labs, Ken Thompson developed a version that was even more stripped-down and simpler; since it included just the most critical part of BCPL, he called it **B**.

Ken had stripped down the language *too* much. It no longer contained enough commands to do practical programming. In 1971, his colleague Dennis Ritchie added a few commands to B, to form a more extensive language, which he called **New B**. Then he added even more commands and called the result **C**, because it came after B. Most of C was invented in 1972. In 1973, it was improved enough so that it was used for something practical: developing a new version of the **Unix** operating system. (Unix was invented at Bell Labs. The original version of Unix was created by using B. Beginning in 1973, Unix versions were created by using C.)

So C is a souped-up version of New B, which is a souped-up version of B, which is a stripped-down version of BCPL, which is a stripped-down version of CPL, which is a "practical" version of ALGOL.

C's peculiarities Like B, C is a tiny language.

C doesn't even include any words for input or output. When you buy C, you also get a **library** of routines that can be added to C. The library includes words for output (such as printf), input (such as scanf), math functions (such as sqrt), and other goodies. When you write a program in C, you can choose whichever parts of the library you need: the other parts of the library don't bother to stay in RAM. So if your program uses just a *few* of the library's functions, running it will consume very little RAM. It will consume less RAM than if the program were written in BASIC or PASCAL.

In BASIC, if you reserve 20 RAM locations for X (by saying DIM X(20)) and then say X(21)=3.7, the computer will gripe, because you haven't reserved a RAM location of X(21). If you use C instead, the computer will *not* gripe about that kind of error; instead, the computer will store the number 3.7 in the RAM location immediately after X(20), even if that location's already being used by another variable, such as Y. As a result, Y will get messed up. Moral: **C programs run quickly and dangerously, because in C the computer never bothers to check your program's reasonableness.**

In your program, which variables are integers, and which are real?

BASIC assumes all variables are real. FORTRAN and PL/I assume all variables beginning with I, J, K, L, M, and N are integers and the rest are real. ALGOL and PASCAL make no assumptions at all; they require you to write a declaration saying "integer" or "real" for each variable. C, by contrast, assumes all variables are integers, unless you specifically say otherwise.

ADA

In 1975, the U.S. Department of Defense decided it wanted a new kind of computer language, so the Department wrote a list of requirements the language would have to meet.

The original list of requirements was called the Strawman Requirements (1975). Then came improved versions, called Woodenman (1975), Tinman (1976), Ironman (1978), and finally Steelman (1979).

While the Department was moving from Strawman to Steelman, it also checked whether any existing computer language could meet such requirements. The Department concluded that no existing computer language came even close to meeting the requirements, and so a new language would indeed have to be invented. The Department also concluded that the new language would have to resemble PASCAL, ALGOL 68, or PL/I, but be better.

Contest In 1977, the Department held a contest, to see which software company could invent a language meeting such specifications (which were in the process of changing from Tinman to Ironman).

16 companies entered the contest.

The Department selected 4 semifinalists and paid them to continue their research for six more months. The semifinalists were CII-Honeywell-Bull (which is French and owned partly by Honeywell), Intermetrics (in Cambridge, Massachusetts), SRI International, and Softech.

In 1978, the semifinalists submitted improved designs, which were all souped-up versions of PASCAL (instead of ALGOL 68 or PL/I). To make the contest fair and prevent bribery, the judges weren't told which design belonged to which company. The 4 designs were called "Green", "Red", "Yellow", and "Blue".

Yellow and Blue lost. The winning designs were Green (designed by CII-Honeywell-Bull) and Red (designed by Intermetrics).

The Department paid the two winning companies to continue their research for one more year. In 1979, the winning companies submitted their improved versions.

The winner was the Green language, designed by CII-Honeywell-Bull.

The Department decided that the Green language would be called **ADA** to honor Ada Lovelace, the woman who was the world's first programmer.

So ADA is a PASCAL-like language developed by a French company (CII-Honeywell-Bull) under contract to the U.S. Department of Defense.

Popularity Will ADA become popular? Wait and see.

Many researchers are trying to make computers understand ADA. So far, the results are incomplete: you can buy disks containing *parts* of ADA, but the full version isn't on disk yet.

When full versions of ADA become available and programmers try using them, we'll know whether the language is a pleasure or a pain.

DBASE

DBASE was invented by Wayne Ratliff because he wanted to bet on which football teams would win the 1978 season. To bet wisely, he had to know how each team had scored in previous games, so every Monday he clipped pages of football scores from newspapers. Soon his whole room was covered with newspaper clippings. To reduce the clutter, he decided to write a data-management program to keep track of all the statistics.

He worked at the Jet Propulsion Laboratory (JPL). His coworkers had invented a data-management system called the **JPL Display and Information System (JPLDIS)**, which imitated IBM's **RETRIEVE**.

Unfortunately, RETRIEVE and JPLDIS both required maxicomputers. Working at home, he invented **VULCAN**, a stripped-down version of JPLDIS that was small enough to run on the CP/M microcomputer in his house. It was even good enough to let him compile football statistics — though by then he'd lost interest in football and was more interested in the theory of data management and business applications.

In 1979, he advertised his VULCAN data-management system in Byte Magazine. The mailman delivered so many orders to his house that he didn't have time to fill them all — especially since he still had a full-time job at JPL. He stopped advertising, to give himself a chance to catch up on filling the orders.

In 1980, the owners of Discount Software phoned him, visited his home, examined VULCAN, and offered to market it for him. He agreed.

Since "Discount Software" was the wrong name to market VULCAN under, Discount Software's owners — Hal Lashlee and George Tate — thought of marketing VULCAN under the name "Lashlee-Tate Software". But since the "Lashlee" part sounded too wimpy, they changed the name to *Ashton*-Tate Software.

Instead of selling the original version of VULCAN, Ashton-Tate Software decided to sell Wayne's further improvement, called **DBASE 2**. It ran faster, looked prettier on the screen, and was easier to use.

At Ashton-Tate, George Tate did most of the managing. Hal Lashlee was a silent partner who just contributed capital.

Advertisement George Tate hired Hal Pawluck to write an ad for DBASE 2. Hal's ad was ingenious. It showed a photograph of a bilge pump (the kind of pump that removes water from a ship's bilge). The ad's headline said: "DBASE versus the Bilge Pump". The ad went on to say that most database systems are like bilge pumps: they suck!

That explicit ad appeared in *Infoworld*, which was a popular, concise weekly newspaper read by all computer experts. Suddenly, all experts knew that DBASE was the database-management system that claimed not to suck.

The ad generated just one serious complaint — from the company that manufactured the bilge pump!

George Tate offered to add a footnote, saying "*This* bilge pump does *not* suck". The pump manufacturer didn't like that either but stopped complaining.

Beyond DBASE 2 The original DBASE 2 ran on computers using the CP/M operating system. It worked well. When IBM began selling the IBM PC, Wayne invented an IBM PC version of DBASE 2, but it was buggy.

He created those early versions of DBASE by using assembly language. By using C instead, he finally created an IBM PC version that worked reliably and included extra commands. He called it **DBASE 3**.

DBASE 2 and DBASE 3 were sold as programming languages, but many people who wanted to use databases didn't want to learn programming and didn't want to hire a programmer. So Ashton-Tate created a new version, called **DBASE 3 PLUS**, which you can control by using menus instead of typing programming commands; but those menus are hard to learn how to use and incomplete: they don't let you tap DBASE 3 PLUS's full power, which requires that you learn programming.

In 1988, Ashton-Tate began shipping **DBASE 4**, which includes extra programming commands.

> Some of DBASE 4's commands were copied from a database language called **Structured Query Language (SQL)**, which IBM invented for mainframes. DBASE 4 also boasted better menus than DBASE 3 PLUS. Unfortunately, Ashton-Tate priced DBASE 4 high: $795 for the plain version, $1295 for the "developer's" version.

Over the years, Ashton-Tate became a stodgy bureaucracy. George Tate died, Wayne Ratliff quit, the company's list price for DBASE grew ridiculously high, and the company was callous to DBASE users.

In 1991, Borland bought Ashton-Tate. In 1994, Borland began selling **DBASE 5**, then further improvements. In 1999, Borland gave up trying to sell DBASE; Borland transferred all DBASE rights to **KSoft**, which sells **VISUAL DBASE 7.5** and is trying to develop **DBASE 2000 (DB2K)**.

Dramatic improvements to DBASE have been created by other companies, who make clones of DBASE that outshine DBASE itself! The most popular clone is **VISUAL FOXPRO 6**, which runs faster than DBASE, includes extra commands, and is marketed by Microsoft.

EASY

EASY is a language I developed several years ago. It combines the best features of all other languages. It's easy to learn, because it uses just these twelve keywords:

```
SAY & GET
LET

REPEAT & SKIP
HERE

IF & PICK
LOOP

PREPARE & DATA
HOW
```

Here's how to use them....

SAY EASY uses the word SAY instead of BASIC's word PRINT, because SAY is briefer. If you want the computer to say the answer to 2+2, give this command:

```
SAY 2+2
```

The computer will say the answer:

```
4
```

Whenever the computer prints, it automatically prints a blank space afterwards but does *not* press the ENTER key. So if you run this program —

```
SAY "LOVE"
SAY "HATE"
```

the computer will say:

```
LOVE HATE
```

Here's a fancier example:

```
SAY "LOVE" AS 3 AT 20 15 TRIM !
```

The "AS 3" is a format: it makes the computer print just the first 3 letters of LOVE. The "AT 20 15" makes the computer begin printing LOVE at the screen's pixel whose X coordinate is 20 and whose Y coordinate is 15. The computer usually prints a blank space after everything, but the word TRIM suppresses that blank space. The exclamation point makes the computer press the ENTER key afterwards.

Here's another example:

```
SAY TO SCREEN PRINTER HARRY
```

It means that henceforth, whenever you give a SAY command, the computer will print the answer simultaneously onto your screen, onto your printer, and onto a disk file named HARRY. If you ever want to cancel that "SAY TO" command, give a "SAY TO" command that contradicts it.

GET EASY uses the word GET instead of BASIC's word INPUT, because GET is briefer. The command GET X makes the computer wait for you to input the value of X. Above the GET command, you typically put a SAY command that makes the computer ask a question.

You can make the GET command fancy, like this:

```
GET X AS 3 AT 20 15 WAIT 5
```

The "AS 3" tells the computer that X will be just 3 characters; the computer waits for you to type just 3 characters and doesn't require you to press the ENTER key afterwards. The "AT 20 15" makes the computer move to pixel 20 15 before your typing begins, so your input appears at that part of the screen. The "WAIT 5" makes the computer wait just 5 seconds for your response. If you reply within 5 seconds, the computer sets TIME equal to how many seconds you took. If you do *not* reply within the 5 seconds, the computer sets TIME equal to -1.

LET The LET statement resembles BASIC's. For example, you can say:

```
LET R=4
```

To let R be a random decimal, type:

```
LET R=RANDOM
```

To let R be a random integer from 1 to 6, type:

```
LET R=RANDOM TO 6
```

To let R be a random integer from -3 to 5, type:

```
LET R=RANDOM FROM -3 TO 5
```

REPEAT If you put the word REPEAT at the bottom of your program, the computer will repeat the entire program again and again, forming an infinite loop.

SKIP If you put the word SKIP in the middle of your program, the computer will skip the bottom part of the program. SKIP is like BASIC's END or STOP.

HERE In the middle of your program, you can say:

```
HERE IS FRED
```

An earlier line can say SKIP TO FRED. A later line can say REPEAT FROM FRED. The SKIP TO and REPEAT FROM are like BASIC's GO TO.

IF In your program, a line can say:

```
IF X<3
```

Underneath that line, you must put some indented lines, which the computer will do if X<3.

Suppose you give a student a test on which the score can be between 0 and 100. If the student's score is 100, let's make the computer say "PERFECT"; if the score is below 100 but at least 70,

let's make the computer say the score and also say "OKAY THOUGH NOT PERFECT"; if the score is below 70, let's make the computer say "YOU FAILED". Here's how:

```
IF SCORE=100
  SAY "PERFECT"
IF SCORE<100 AND SCORE>=70
  SAY SCORE
  SAY "OKAY THOUGH NOT PERFECT"
IF SCORE<70
  SAY "YOU FAILED"
```

To shorten the program, use the words NOT and BUT:

```
IF SCORE=100
  SAY "PERFECT"
IF NOT BUT SCORE>=70
  SAY SCORE
  SAY "OKAY THOUGH NOT PERFECT"
IF NOT
  SAY "YOU FAILED"
```

The phrase "IF NOT" is like BASIC's ELSE. The phrase "IF NOT BUT" is like BASIC's ELSE IF.

PICK You can shorten that example even further, by telling the computer to pick just the first IF that's true:

```
PICK SCORE
  IF 100
    SAY "PERFECT"
  IF >=70
    SAY SCORE
    SAY "OKAY THOUGH NOT PERFECT"
  IF NOT
    SAY "YOU FAILED"
```

LOOP If you put the word LOOP above indented lines, the computer will do those lines repeatedly. For example, this program makes the computer say the words CAT and DOG repeatedly:

```
LOOP
  SAY "CAT"
  SAY "DOG"
```

This program makes the computer say 5, 8, 11, 14, and 17:

```
LOOP I FROM 5 BY 3 TO 17
  SAY I
```

That LOOP statement is like BASIC's "FOR I = 5 TO 17 STEP 3". If you omit the "BY 3", the computer will assume "BY 1". If you omit the "FROM 5", the computer will assume "FROM 1". If you omit the "TO 17", the computer will assume "to infinity".

To make the computer count down instead of up, insert the word DOWN, like this:

```
LOOP I FROM 17 DOWN BY 3 TO 5
```

PREPARE To do an unusual activity, you should PREPARE the computer for it. For example, if you want to use subscripted variables such as X(100), you should tell the computer:

```
PREPARE X(100)
```

In that example, PREPARE is like BASIC's DIM.

DATA EASY's DATA statement resembles BASIC's. But instead of saying READ X, say:

```
LET X=NEXT
```

HOW In EASY, you can give any command you wish, such as:

```
PRETEND YOU ARE HUMAN
```

If you give that command, you must also give an explanation that begins with the words:

```
HOW TO PRETEND YOU ARE HUMAN
```

Interrelated features In the middle of a loop, you can abort the loop. To skip out of the loop (and progress to the rest of the program), say SKIP LOOP. To hop back to the beginning of the loop (to do the next iteration of loop), say REPEAT LOOP.

Similarly, you can say SKIP IF (which makes the computer skip out of an IF) and REPEAT IF (which makes the computer repeat the IF statement, and thereby imitate PASCAL's WHILE).

Apostrophe Like BASIC, EASY uses an apostrophe to begin a comment. The computer ignores everything to the right of an apostrophe, unless the apostrophe is between quotation marks or in a DATA statement.

Comma If two statements begin with the same word, you can combine them into a single statement, by using a comma. For example, instead of saying —

```
LET X=4
LET Y=7
```

you can say:

```
LET X=4, Y=7
```

Instead of saying —

```
PRETEND YOU ARE HUMAN
PRETEND GOD IS DEAD
```

you can say:

```
PRETEND YOU ARE HUMAN, GOD IS DEAD
```

More info I stopped working on EASY in 1982 but expect to continue development again. To get on my mailing list of people who want details and updated info about EASY, phone me at 603-666-6644 or send me a postcard.

C++

Most C programmers have switched to an improved C, called **C++**.

JAVA

JAVA is a variant of C++ that runs slower but can be easier to learn.

While you're using the Internet's World Wide Web, you often see ads that are animated cartoons. Those ads are created by using JAVA. That's JAVA's main purpose: to create ads that are annoyingly eye-catching.

Radicals

Let's examine the radical languages, beginning with the oldest radical — the oldest hippie — LISP.

LISP

LISP is the only language made specifically to handle lists of concepts. It's the most popular language for research into artificial intelligence.

It's the father of LOGO, which is "oversimplified LISP" and the most popular language for young children. It inspired PROLOG, which is a LISP-like language that lets you make the computer imitate a wise expert and become an **expert system**.

Beginners in artificial intelligence love to play with LOGO and PROLOG, which are easier and more fun than LISP. But most professionals continue to use LISP because it's more powerful than its children.

The original version of LISP was called **LISP 1**. Then came an improvement, called **LISP 1.5** (because it wasn't different enough from LISP 1 to rate the title "LISP 2"). Then came a slight improvement on LISP 1.5, called **LISP 1.6**. The newest version of LISP is called **Common LISP**; it runs on maxicomputers, minicomputers, and microcomputers.

I'll explain "typical" LISP, which is halfway between LISP 1.6 and Common LISP.

Typical LISP uses these symbols:

BASIC LISP	
5+2	(PLUS 5 2)
5-2	(DIFFERENCE 5 2)
5*2	(TIMES 5 2)
5/2	(QUOTIENT 5 2)
5^2	(EXPT 5 2)
"LOVE"	'LOVE old versions say (QUOTE LOVE)

If you want the computer to add 5 and 2, just type:

```
(PLUS 5 2)
```

When you press the ENTER key at the end of that line, the computer will print the answer. (You do *not* have to say PRINT or any other special word.) The computer will print:

```
7
```

If you type —

```
(PLUS 1 3 1 1)
```

the computer will add 1, 3, 1, and 1 and print:

```
6
```

If you type —

```
(DIFFERENCE 7 (TIMES 2 3))
```

the computer will find the difference between 7 and 2*3 and print:

```
1
```

If you type —

```
'LOVE
```

the computer will print:

```
LOVE
```

Notice that you must type an apostrophe before LOVE but must *not* type an apostrophe afterwards. The apostrophe is called a **single quotation mark** (or a **quote**).

You can put a quote in front of a word (such as 'LOVE) or in front of a parenthesized list of words, such as:

```
'(LAUGH LOUDLY)
```

That makes the computer print:

```
(LAUGH LOUDLY)
```

LISP 1, LISP 1.5, and LISP 1.6 don't understand the apostrophe. On those old versions of LISP, say (QUOTE LOVE) instead of 'LOVE, and say (QUOTE (LAUGH LOUDLY)) instead of '(LAUGH LOUDLY).

The theory of lists LISP can handle lists. Each list must begin and end with a parenthesis.

Here's a list of numbers: (5 7 4 2). Here's a list of words: (LOVE HATE WAR PEACE DEATH).

Here's a list of numbers and words: (2 WOMEN KISS 7 MEN). That list has five items: 2, WOMEN, KISS, 7, and MEN.

Here's a list of four items: (HARRY LEMON (TICKLE MY TUBA TOMORROW AT TEN) RUSSIA). The first item is HARRY; the second is LEMON; the third is a list; the fourth is RUSSIA.

In a list, **the first item is called the CAR, and the remainder of the list is called the CDR** (pronounced "could er" or "cudder" or "coo der"). For example, the CAR of (SAILORS DRINK WHISKEY) is SAILORS, and the CDR is (DRINK WHISKEY).

To make the computer find the CAR of (SAILORS DRINK WHISKEY), type this:

```
(CAR '(SAILORS DRINK WHISKEY))
```

The computer will print:

```
SAILORS
```

If you type —

```
(CDR '(SAILORS DRINK WHISKEY))
```

the computer will print:

```
(DRINK WHISKEY)
```

If you type —

```
(CAR (CDR '(SAILORS DRINK WHISKEY)))
```

the computer will find the CAR of the CDR of (SAILORS DRINK WHISKEY). Since the CDR of (SAILORS DRINK WHISKEY) is (DRINK WHISKEY), whose CAR is DRINK, the computer will print:

```
DRINK
```

You can insert an extra item at the beginning of a list, to form a longer list. For example, you can insert MANY at the beginning of (SAILORS DRINK WHISKEY), to form (MANY SAILORS DRINK WHISKEY). To do that, tell the computer to CONStruct the longer list, by typing:

```
(CONS 'MANY '(SAILORS DRINK WHISKEY))
```

The computer will print:

```
(MANY SAILORS DRINK WHISKEY)
```

Notice that CONS is the opposite of CAR and CDR. The CONS combines MANY with (SAILORS DRINK WHISKEY) to form (MANY SAILORS DRINK WHISKEY). The CAR and CDR break down (MANY SAILORS DRINK WHISKEY), to form MANY and (SAILORS DRINK WHISKEY).

Variables To make X stand for the number 7, say:

```
(SETQ X 7)
```

Then if you say —

```
(PLUS X 2)
```

the computer will print 9.

To make Y stand for the word LOVE, say:

```
(SETQ Y 'LOVE)
```

Then if you say —

```
Y
```

the computer will say:

```
LOVE
```

To make STOOGES stand for the list (MOE LARRY CURLEY), say:

```
(SETQ STOOGES '(MOE LARRY CURLEY))
```

Then if you say —

```
STOOGES
```

the computer will say:

```
(MOE LARRY CURLEY)
```

To find the first of the STOOGES, say:

```
(CAR STOOGES)
```

The computer will say:

```
MOE
```

Your own functions You can define your own functions. For example, you can define (DOUBLE X) to be 2*X, by typing this:

```
(DEFUN DOUBLE (X)
      (TIMES 2 X)
)
```

Then if you say —

```
(DOUBLE 3)
```

the computer will print:

```
6
```

REPEAT Let's define REPEAT to be a function, so that (REPEAT 'LOVE 5) is (LOVE LOVE LOVE LOVE LOVE), and (REPEAT 'KISS 3) is (KISS KISS KISS), and (REPEAT 'KISS 0) is ().

If N is 0, we want (REPEAT X N) to be ().

If N is larger than 0, we want (REPEAT X N) to be a list of N X's.

> That's X followed by N-1 more X's.
> That's the CONS of X with a list of N-1 more X's.
> That's the CONS of X with (REPEAT X (DIFFERENCE N 1)).
> That's (CONS X (REPEAT X (DIFFERENCE N 1))).
> That's (CONS X (REPEAT X (SUB1 N))), since (SUB1 N) means N-1 in LISP.

You can define the answer to (REPEAT X N) as follows: if N is 0, the answer is (); if N is *not* 0, the answer is (CONS X (REPEAT X (SUB 1 N))). Here's how to type that definition:

```
(DEFUN REPEAT (X N)
    (COND
        ((ZEROP N) ())
        (T (CONS X (REPEAT X (SUB1 N))))
    )
)
```

The top line says you're going to DEfine a FUNction called REPEAT (X N). The next line says the answer depends on CONDitions. The next line gives one of those conditions: *if N is ZERO*, the answer is (). The next line says: *otherwise*, the value is (CONS X (REPEAT X (SUB1 N))). The next line closes the parentheses opened in the second line. The bottom line closes the parentheses opened in the top line.

Then if you type —

```
(REPEAT 'LOVE 5)
```

the computer will print:

```
(LOVE LOVE LOVE LOVE LOVE)
```

The definition is almost circular: the definition of REPEAT assumes you already know what REPEAT is. For example:

> (REPEAT 'KISS 3) is defined as the CONS of KISS with the following:
> (REPEAT 'KISS 2), which is defined as the CONS of KISS with the following:
> (REPEAT 'KISS 1), which is defined as the CONS of KISS with the following:
> (REPEAT 'KISS 1), which is defined as the CONS of KISS with the following:
> (REPEAT 'KISS 0), which is defined as ().

That kind of definition, which is almost circular, is called **recursive**.

> You can say "The definition of REPEAT is **recursive**", or "REPEAT is **defined recursively**", or "REPEAT is **defined by recursion**", or "REPEAT is **defined by induction**", or "REPEAT is a **recursive function**".

LISP was the first popular language that allowed recursive definitions.

When the computer uses a recursive definition, the computer refers to the definition *repeatedly* before getting out of the circle. Since the computer repeats, it's performing a loop. In traditional BASIC and FORTRAN, the only way to make the computer perform a loop is to say GO TO or FOR or DO. Although LISP contains a go-to command, LISP programmers avoid it and write recursive definitions instead.

ITEM As another example of recursion, let's define the function ITEM so that (ITEM N X) is the Nth item in list X, and so that (ITEM 3 '(MANY SAILORS DRINK WHISKEY)) is the 3rd item of (MANY SAILORS DRINK WHISKEY), which is DRINK.

If N is 1, (ITEM N X) is the first item in X, which is the CAR of X, which is (CAR X).

If N is larger than 1, (ITEM N X) is the Nth item in X. That's the (N-1)th item in the CDR of X. That's (ITEM (SUB1 N) (CDR X)).

So define (ITEM N X) as follows: if N is 1, the answer is (CAR X); if N is not 1, the answer is (ITEM (SUB 1 N) (CDR X)). Here's what to type:

```
(DEFUN ITEM (N X)
    (COND
        ((ONEP N) (CAR X))
        (T (ITEM (SUB1 N) (CDR X)))
    )
)
```

If your computer doesn't understand (ONEP N), say (EQUAL 1 N) instead.

SNOBOL

SNOBOL lets you analyze strings more easily than any other language. It can handle numbers also.

Simple example Here's a simple SNOBOL program:

```
    A = -2
    B = A + 10.6
    C = "BODY TEMPERATURE IS 9" B
    OUTPUT = "MY " C
END
```

When you type the program, indent each line except END. Indent *at least* one space; you can indent more spaces if you wish. Put spaces around the symbol =, the symbol +, and other operations.

The first line says A is the integer -2. The next line says B is the real number 8.6. The next line says C is the string "BODY TEMPERATURE IS 98.6". The next line makes the computer print:

```
BODY TEMPERATURE IS 98.6
```

In SNOBOL, a variable's name can be short (like A or B or C) or as long as you wish. The variable's name can even contain periods, like this:

```
NUMBER.OF.BULLIES.I.SQUIRTED
```

Looping This program's a loop:

```
FRED    OUTPUT = "CAT"
        OUTPUT = "DOG" :(FRED)
END
```

The first line (whose name is FRED) makes the computer print:

```
CAT
```

The next line makes the computer print —

```
DOG
```

and then go to FRED. Altogether the computer will print:

```
CAT
DOG
CAT
DOG
CAT
DOG
etc.
```

Replacing

SNOBOL lets you easily replace one phrase by another.

```
        X = "SIN ON A PIN WITH A DIN"
        X "IN" = "UCK"
        OUTPUT = X
END
```

The first line says X is the string "SIN ON A PIN WITH A DIN". The next line says: in X, replace the first "IN" by "UCK". So X becomes "SUCK ON A PIN WITH A DIN". The next line says the output is X, so the computer will print:

```
SUCK ON A PIN WITH A DIN
```

That program changed the *first* "IN" to "UCK". Here's how to change *every* "IN" to "UCK":

```
        X = "SIN ON A PIN WITH A DIN"
        X "IN" = "UCK"
        X "IN" = "UCK"
        X "IN" = "UCK"
        OUTPUT = X
END
```

The first line says X is "SIN ON A PIN WITH A DIN". The second line replaces an "IN" by "UCK", so X becomes "SUCK ON A PIN WITH A DIN". The next line replaces another "IN" by "UCK", so X becomes "SUCK ON A PUCK WITH A DIN". The next line replaces another "IN", so X becomes "SUCK ON A PUCK WITH A DUCK", which the next line prints.

This program does the same thing:

```
        X = "SIN ON A PIN WITH A DIN"
LOOP    X "IN" = "UCK" :S(LOOP)
        OUTPUT = X
END
```

The first line says X is "SIN ON A PIN WITH A DIN". The next line replaces "IN" successfully, so X becomes "SUCK ON A PIN WITH A DIN". At the end of the line, the :S(LOOP) means: if Successful, go to LOOP. So the computer goes back to LOOP. The computer replaces "IN" successfully again, so X becomes "SUCK ON A PUCK WITH A DIN", and the computer goes back to LOOP. The computer replaces "IN" successfully again, so X becomes "SUCK ON A PUCK WITH A DUCK", and the computer goes back to LOOP. The computer does not succeed. So the computer ignores the :S(LOOP) and proceeds instead to the next line, which prints:

```
SUCK ON A PUCK WITH A DUCK
```

Deleting

This program deletes the first "IN":

```
        X = "SIN ON A PIN WITH A DIN"
        X "IN" =
        OUTPUT = X
END
```

The second line says to replace an "IN" by nothing, so the "IN" gets deleted. X becomes "S ON A PIN WITH A DIN", which the computer will print.

This program deletes *every* "IN":

```
        X = "SIN ON A PIN WITH A DIN"
LOOP    X "IN" = :S(LOOP)
        OUTPUT = X
END
```

The computer will print:

```
S ON A P WITH A D
```

Counting

Let's count how often "IN" appears in "SIN ON A PIN WITH A DIN". To do that, delete each "IN"; but each time you delete one, increase the COUNT by 1:

```
        X = "SIN ON A PIN WITH A DIN"
        COUNT = 0
LOOP    X "IN" = :F(ENDING)
        COUNT = COUNT + 1 :(LOOP)
ENDING  OUTPUT = COUNT
END
```

The third line tries to delete an "IN": *if successful*, the computer proceeds to the next line, which increases the COUNT and goes back to LOOP; *if failing* (because no "IN" remains), the computer goes to ENDING, which prints the COUNT. The computer will print:

```
3
```

How SNOBOL developed

At MIT during the 1950's, Noam Chomsky invented a notation called **transformational-generative grammar**, which helps linguists analyze English and translate between English and other languages. His notation was nicknamed "linguist's algebra", because it helped linguists just as algebra helped scientists. (A decade later, he became famous for also starting the rebellion against the Vietnam War.)

Chomsky's notation was for pencil and paper. In 1957 and 1958, his colleague Victor Yngve developed a computerized version of Chomsky's notation: the computerized version was a language called **COMIT**. It was nicknamed "linguist's FORTRAN", because it helped linguists just as FORTRAN helped engineers.

COMIT manipulated strings of *words*. In 1962 at Bell Telephone Laboratories (Bell Labs), Chester Lee invented a variant called the **Symbolic Communication Language (SCL)**, which manipulated strings of *mathematical symbols* instead of words and helped mathematicians do abstract mathematics.

A team at Bell Labs decided to invent a language similar to SCL, but easier to learn and including features from COMIT. At first, they called their new language "SCL7", because it resembled SCL. Then they changed its name to "SEXI" (which stands for String EXpression Interpreter), but the management of Bell Labs didn't like sex. Then, as a joke, they named it SNOBOL, using the flimsy excuse that SNOBOL stands for StriNg-Oriented symBOlic Language.

Cynics jeered that SNOBOL didn't have "a snowball's chance in Hell". But the cynics were wrong, and SNOBOL became popular. It was used mainly for writing programs that translate between computer languages. (For example, you could write a SNOBOL program that translates FORTRAN into BASIC.)

Which is better: COMIT or SNOBOL?

> People who like Chomsky's notation (such as linguists) prefer COMIT. People who like algebra (such as scientists) prefer SNOBOL.
>
> SNOBOL's supporters were more active than COMIT's: they produced SNOBOL 2, SNOBOL 3, SNOBOL 4, and SNOBOL 4B, taught SNOBOL to the newest computers, wrote many books about SNOBOL, and emphasized that SNOBOL can solve *any* problem about strings, even if the problem had nothing to do with linguistics. They won: most people use SNOBOL instead of COMIT, though COMIT might still make a comeback.

Today, most versions of SNOBOL are named after baseball pitching methods — such as FASBOL, SLOBOL, and SPITBOL. (SPITBOL stands for SPeedy ImplemenTation of snoBOL.)

APL

APL lets you manipulate lists of numbers more easily than any other language. APL uses special characters that aren't on a normal keyboard.

To compute 8+9, type this:

```
    8+9
```

Notice the line is indented. Whenever it's your turn to type, the computer automatically indents the line for you.

When you press the RETURN key at the end of that line, the computer will print the answer. (You don't have to say PRINT or any other special word.) The computer will print:

```
17
```

Scalar operators APL uses these **scalar operators**:

APL name	Symbol	Meaning
PLUS	A+B	add
identity	+B	same as just B
MINUS	A-B	subtract
negative	-B	negative
TIMES	A×B	multiply
signum	×B	1 if B>0; ¯1 if B<0; 0 if B=0
DIVIDE	A÷B	divide
reciprocal	÷B	1 divided by B
POWER	A*B	A raised to the Bth power; A^B
exponential	*B	e raised to the Bth power, where e is 2.718281828459045
LOG	A⍟B	logarithm, base A, of B
natural log	⍟B	logarithm, base e, of B
CEILING	⌈B	B rounded up to an integer
maximum	A⌈B	A or B, whichever is larger
FLOOR	⌊B	B rounded down to an integer
minimum	A⌊B	A or B, whichever is smaller
MAGNITUDE	∣B	the absolute value of B
residue	A∣B	the remainder when you divide A into B; so 4∣19 is 3
FACTORIAL	!B	1 times 2 times 3 times 4 times… times B
combinations	A!B	how many A-element subsets you can form from a set of B
ROLL	?B	a random integer from 1 to B
deal	A?B	list of A random integers, each from 1 to B, no duplicates
PI TIMES	○B	π times B
circular	A○B	sin B if A=1 arcsin B if A=¯1 square root of $1+B^2$ if A=4
		cos B if A=2 arccos B if A=¯2 square root of $1-B^2$ if A=0
		tan B if A=3 arctan B if A=¯3 square root of B^2-1 if A=¯4
		sinh B if A=5 arcsinh B if A=¯5
		cosh B if A=6 arccosh B if A=¯6
		tanh B if A=7 arctanh B if A=¯7
EQUAL	A=B	1 if A equals B; otherwise 0
not equal	A≠B	1 if A is not equal to B; otherwise 0
LESS	A<B	1 if A is less than B; otherwise 0
less or equal	A≤B	1 if A is less than or equal to B; otherwise 0
GREATER	A>B	1 if A is greater than B; otherwise 0
greater or equal	A≥B	1 if A is greater than or equal to B; otherwise 0
AND	A∧B	1 if A and B are both 1; otherwise 0
nand	A⍲B	1 if A and B are not both 1; otherwise 0
OR	A∨B	1 if A or B is 1; otherwise 0
nor	A⍱B	1 if neither A nor B is 1; otherwise 0
NOT	~B	1 if B is 0; otherwise 0

To make the symbol ⍟, type the symbol *, then press the BACKSPACE key, then type the symbol ○.

Order of operations
Unlike all other popular languages, APL makes the computer do all calculations *from right to left*. For example, if you type —

```
    2×3+5
```

the computer will start with 5, add 3 (to get 8), and then multiply by 2 (to get 16). The computer will print:

```
16
```

In BASIC and most other languages, the answer would be 11 instead.

If you type —

```
    9-4-3
```

the computer will start with 3, subtract it from 4 (to get 1), and then subtract from 9 (to get 8). The computer will print:

```
8
```

In most other languages, the answer would be 2 instead.

You can use parentheses. Although 9-4-3 is 8, (9-4)-3 is 2.

Compare these examples:

```
    -4+6  is ¯10
```
```
    ¯4+6  is 2
```

In both examples, the 4 is preceded by a negative sign; but in the second example, the negative sign is raised, to be as high as the 4. (To make the raised negative, tap the 2 key while holding down the SHIFT key. To make a regular negative, tap the + key while holding down the SHIFT key.) The first example makes the computer start with 6, add 4 (to get 10), and then negate it (to get ¯10). The second example makes the computer start with 6 and add ¯4, to get 2.

Double precision
APL is super-accurate. It does all calculations by using double precision.

Variables
You can use variables:

```
    X←3
    X+2
```

The first line says X is 3. The second line makes the computer print X+2. The computer will print:

```
5
```

A variable's name can be long: up to 77 letters and digits. The name must begin with a letter.

Vectors

Vectors A variable can stand for a list of numbers:

```
Y←5 2 8
Y+1
```

The first line says Y is the **vector** 5 2 8. The next line makes the computer add 1 to each item and print:

```
6 3 9
```

This program prints the same answer:

```
5 2 8+1
```

The computer will print:

```
6 3 9
```

This program prints the same answer:

```
1+5 2 8
```

You can add a vector to another vector:

```
A←5 2.1 6
B←3 2.8 ̄7
A+B
```

The computer will add 5 to 3, and 2.1 to 2.8, and 6 to ̄7, and print:

```
8 4.9 ̄1
```

This program prints the same answer:

```
5 2.1 6+3 2.8 ̄7
```

This program prints the same answer:

```
A←5 2.1 6
B←3 2.8 ̄7
C←A+B
C
```

Here's something different:

```
X←4 2 3
+/X
```

The first line says X is the vector 4 2 3. The next line makes the computer print the sum, 9.

This program prints the same answer:

```
Y←+/4 2 3
Y
```

You can combine many ideas on the same line, but remember that the computer goes from right to left:

```
219-1 4 3+6×+/5 1 3×2 4 7
```

The computer will start with 2 4 7, multiply it by 5 1 3 (to get 10 4 21), find the sum (which is 35), multiply by 6 (to get 210), add 1 4 3 (to get 211 214 213), and then subtract from 219 (to get 8 5 6). The computer will print:

```
8 5 6
```

Each of APL's scalar operators works like addition. Here are examples:

```
2 4 10×3 7 9      is 6 28 90
÷2 4 10           is .5 .25 .1
-2 4 10           is ̄2 ̄4 ̄10
×/2 4 10          is 2×4×10, which is 80
-/9 5 3           is 9-5-3, which is 7 (since the computer works from right to left)
⌊/6.1 2.7 4.9     is 6.1⌊2.7⌊4.9, which is 2.7 (since ⌊ means minimum)
⌊6.1 2.7 4.9      is ⌊6.1 then ⌊2.7 then ⌊4.9, which is 6 2 4 (since ⌊ means floor)
```

Vector operators Here are **vector operators**; the examples assume V is 8 5 6:

APL name	Symbol	Value	Reason
SHAPE	ρV	3	V has 3 items
reshape	7ρV	8 5 6 8 5 6 8	make 7 items from V
REVERSE	⌽V	6 5 8	reverse V
rotate	1⌽V	5 6 8	rotate V, by beginning after the 1st item
GENERATE	⍳3	1 2 3	count up to 3
index of	V⍳5	2	in V, find 5; it's the 2nd item
TAKE	2↑V	8 5	the first 2 items from V
drop	2↓V	6	omit the first two items from V
SUBSCRIPT	V[2]	5	V's 2nd item
catenate	V,9 4	8 5 6 9 4	V followed by 9 4
COMPRESS	1 0 1/V	8 6	take part of V, using this pattern: take, omit, take
expand	1 0 0 1 1\V	8 0 0 5 6	insert zeros into V, using this pattern: item, 0, 0, item, item
GRADE UP	⍋V	2 3 1	here are V's numbers in increasing order: 5 (V's 2nd number), 6 (V's 3rd), 8 (V's 1st)
grade down	⍒V	1 3 2	here are V's numbers in decreasing order: 8 (V's 1st number), 6 (V's 3rd), 5 (V's 2nd)
DECODE	10⊥V	856	8, times 10, plus 5, times 10, plus 6
encode	10⊤856	8 5 6	opposite of decode
MEMBER	5∊V	1	search for 5 in V (1=found, 0=missing)

Love or hate? Some programmers love APL, because its notation is brief. Other programmers hate it, because its notation is hard for a human to read. The haters are winning, and the percentage of programmers using APL is decreasing.

LOGO

LOGO began in 1967, during an evening at Dan Bobrow's home in Belmont, Massachusetts.

Dan had gotten his Ph.D. from MIT and was working for a company called **Bolt, Beranek, and Newman (BBN)**. In his living room were three of his colleagues from BBN (Wally Feurzeig, Cynthia Solomon, and Dick Grant) and an MIT professor: Seymour Papert.

BBN had tried to teach young kids how to program by using BBN's own language (TELCOMP), which was a variation of JOSS. BBN had asked Professor Seymour Papert for his opinion. The group was all gathered in Dan's house to hear Seymour's opinion.

Seymour chatted with the group, and the entire group agreed with Seymour on several points:

First, TELCOMP was *not* a great language for kids. It placed too much emphasis on mathematical formulas. The group agreed that instead of struggling with math, the kids ought to have more fun by programming the computer to handle strings instead.

The group also agreed that the most sophisticated language for handling strings was LISP, but that LISP was too complex for kids. The group concluded that a new, simplified LISP should be invented for kids, and that it should be called "LOGO".

That's how LOGO began. Professor Seymour Papert was the guiding light, and all the other members of the group gave helpful input during the conversation.

That night, after his guests left, Dan went to the terminal in his bedroom and started programming the computer to understand LOGO. Specifically, he wrote a LISP program that explained to the computer how to handle LOGO. That's how LOGO was born.

Work on LOGO continued. The three main researchers who continued improving LOGO were Seymour (the MIT guru), Wally (from BBN), and Cynthia (also from BBN). LOGO resembled LISP but required fewer parentheses.

After helping BBN for a year, Seymour returned to MIT. Cynthia and several other BBN folks worked with him at MIT's Artificial Intelligence Laboratory to improve LOGO.

Turtles At first, LOGO was as abstract and boring as most other computer languages. But in the spring of 1970, a strange creature walked into the LOGO lab. It was a big yellow mechanical turtle. It looked like "half a grapefruit on wheels" and had a pen in its belly:

wheel pen wheel

It also had a horn, feelers, and several other fancy attachments. To use it, you put paper all over the floor and then programmed it to roll across the paper. As it rolled, the pen in its belly drew pictures on the paper. The turtle was controlled remotely by a big computer programmed in LOGO.

Suddenly, LOGO became a fun language whose main purpose was to control the turtle. Kids watching the turtle screamed with delight and wanted to learn how to program it. LOGO became a favorite programming game for kids. Even kids who were just 7 years old started programming in LOGO. Those kids were barely old enough to read, but reading and writing were *not* prerequisites for learning how to program in LOGO. All the kids had to know was that "FD 3" made the turtle go forward 3 steps, and "RT 30" made the turtle turn to the right 30 degrees.

As for the rest of LOGO — all that abstract stuff about strings and numbers and LISP-like lists — the kids ignored it. They wanted to use just the commands "FD" and "RT" that moved the turtle.

The U.S. Government's National Science Foundation donated money, to help MIT improve LOGO further. Many kids came into the LOGO lab to play with the turtles.

The turtles were expensive, and so were the big computers that controlled them. To let more kids use LOGO, the first problem was to reduce the cost of the turtle and its controlling computer.

During the early 1970's, computer screens got dramatically cheaper. To save money, MIT stopped building mechanical turtles and instead bought cheap computer screens that showed pictures of turtles. Those pictures were called "mock turtles".

Cheaper computers The original version of LOGO was done on BBN's expensive weird computer (the MTS 940). Later versions were done on the PDP-1 (in 1968), the PDP-10 (in 1970), and finally on a cheaper computer: the PDP-11 minicomputer (in 1972).

At the end of the 1970's, companies such as Apple and Radio Shack began selling microcomputers, which were even cheaper. MIT wanted to put LOGO on microcomputers but ran out of money to pay for the research.

Texas Instruments (TI) came to the rescue....

TI LOGO TI agreed to pay MIT to research how to put LOGO on TI's microcomputers (the TI-99/4 and the TI-99/4A).

TI and MIT thought the job would be easy, since MIT had already written a PASCAL program that made the computer understand LOGO, and since TI had already written a version of PASCAL for the CPU chip inside the TI-99/4. Initially, MIT was worried because the PASCAL program running on MIT's PDP-10 computer handled LOGO too slowly; but TI claimed TI's PASCAL was faster than the PDP-10's and that LOGO would therefore run fast enough on the TI.

TI was wrong. TI's PASCAL couldn't make LOGO run fast enough, and TI's PASCAL also required too much RAM. So TI had to take MIT's research (on the PDP-10) and laboriously translate it into TI's assembly language, by hand.

The hand translation went slower that TI expected. TI became impatient and took a short-cut: it omitted parts of LOGO, such as decimals. TI began selling its version of LOGO, which understood just integers.

MIT Apple LOGO After TI started selling its LOGO, the MIT group invented a version of LOGO for the Apple. The Apple version included decimals. But alas, the Apple version omitted "sprites" (which are animated creatures that carry objects across the screen) because Apple's hardware couldn't handle sprites fast enough. (TI's hardware was fancier and *did* handle sprites.)

MIT wanted to sell the Apple version to schools since more schools owned Apples than TI computers. But if MIT were to make lots of money from selling the Apple version, MIT might get into legal trouble, since MIT was supposed to be non-profit. And anyway, who "owned" LOGO? Possible contenders were:

> MIT, which did most of the research
> BBN, which trademarked the name "LOGO" and did the early research
> Uncle Sam, whose National Science Foundation paid for much research
> TI, which also paid for much research

Eventually, MIT solved the legal problems and sold the rights for "MIT Apple LOGO" to two companies: Krell and Terrapin.

Krell was strictly a marketing company. It sold MIT Apple LOGO to schools but made no attempt to improve LOGO further.

Terrapin, on the other hand, was a research organization that had built mechanical turtles for several years. Terrapin hired some MIT graduates to improve LOGO further.

LCSI versus competitors Back when MIT was asking its lawyers to determine who owned Apple LOGO, a group of MIT's faculty and students became impatient. The group, headed by Cynthia Solomon (one of the original inventors of LOGO), left MIT and formed a company called **LOGO Computer Systems Incorporated (LCSI)**. That company invented its own version of LOGO for the Apple.

LCSI became quite successful. Apple, IBM, Atari, and Microsoft all hired LCSI to write versions of LOGO. Commodore hired Terrapin instead.

If you have an Apple 2c (or 2e or 2+), you can buy either the official Apple LOGO (sold by Apple Computer Inc. and created by LCSI), or "Terrapin LOGO for the Apple" (sold by Terrapin), or the original "MIT LOGO for the Apple" (sold by Krell).

Krell has become less popular. That leaves just two major players: Terrapin and LCSI. Generally speaking, LCSI's versions of LOGO are daring — LCSI tried wild experiments — while Terrapin's versions of LOGO are conservative — closer to the MIT original.

The two companies have different styles. Terrapin is small and friendly and charges very little. LCSI is large, charges more, and is often rude. Terrapin gives more help to customers on the phone than LCSI.

The original owners of Terrapin had financial difficulties, moved to Maine, then sold the company to **Harvard Associates** (a Massachusetts company that had invented a LOGO version called "PC LOGO").

> So now Terrapin is part of Harvard Associates, which is run by Bill Glass, a friendly guy. To find out about his Terrapin LOGO, look at his Web site (www.terrapinlogo.com) then phone him at 800-774-Logo (or 617-547-Logo) or write to 10 Holworthy St., Cambridge MA 02138.

LCSI's newest, daring version of LOGO is **MicroWorlds Pro**.

> To find out about it, look at LCSI's Web site (www.lcsi.ca) then phone LCSI at 800-321-5646. LCSI is based in Montreal, Canada, but accepts US mail at PO Box 162, Highgate Springs VT 05460.

LOGO versus BASIC

Most of LOGO's designers *hate* BASIC. They believe BASIC should be eliminated from schools altogether.

They believe LOGO is easier to learn than BASIC, and that LOGO encourages a kid to be more creative. They also believe that LOGO leads the kid to think in a more organized fashion than BASIC. They also argue that since LOGO is best for little kids, and since switching languages is difficult, the kids should continue using LOGO until they graduate from high school and should never use BASIC.

That argument is wrong. It ignores the fact that a knowledge of BASIC is *essential* to surviving in our computerized society. Today, most programs are still written in BASIC, not LOGO, because BASIC consumes less RAM and because BASIC's newest versions contain many practical features for business and science and graphics that LOGO lacks.

Another advantage of BASIC over LOGO is that LOGO suffers from awkward notation. For example, in BASIC you can type a formula such as —

```
A=B+C
```

but in LOGO you must type:

```
MAKE "A :B+:C
```

Notice how ugly the LOGO command looks! Notice you must put a quotation mark before the A but must *not* but a quotation mark afterwards! And look at those frightful colons! Anybody who thinks such notation is great for kids is a fool.

Extensible One of the nicest things about LOGO is that you can change it and turn it into your *own* language! That's because LOGO lets you invent your own commands and add them to the LOGO language. A language (such as LOGO) that lets you invent your own commands is called an **extensible language**. Although some earlier languages (such as LISP) were extensible also, LOGO is *more* extensible and more pleasant.

FORTH

Like LOGO, FORTH is extensible. But FORTH has two advantages over LOGO:

```
1. FORTH consumes less memory. You can easily run FORTH on a computer having just 8K of RAM.
2. FORTH runs faster. The computer handles FORTH almost as fast as assembly language.
```

Since FORTH is extensible and consumes so little of the computer's memory and time, professional programmers use it often. Famous programs written in FORTH include Easywriter (which is a word-processing program for the Apple and the IBM Personal Computer), Valdocs (which is the operating system for Epson's first computer), and Rapid File (an easy-to-learn data-management system developed by Miller Microcomputer Systems and sold by Ashton-Tate).

Unfortunately, the original versions of Easywriter and Valdocs contained many bugs, but that's because their programmers were careless.

In FORTH, if you want to add 2 and 3 (to get 5) you do *not* type 2+3. Instead, you must type:

```
2 3 +
```

The idea of putting the plus sign afterwards (instead of in the middle) is called **postfix notation**. The postfix notation (2 3 +) has two advantages over infix notation (2+3): the computer handles postfix notation faster, and you never need to use parentheses for "order of operations". On the other hand, postfix notation seems inhuman: it's hard for a human to read.

Like FORTH, Hewlett-Packard pocket calculators use postfix notation. So if you've already had experience with a Hewlett-Packard calculator, you'll find FORTH easy.

Postfix notation is the reverse of **prefix notation** (+ 2 3), which was invented around 1926 by the Polish mathematician Lukasiewicz. So postfix notation is often called **reverse Polish notation**.

Since FORTH is so difficult for a human to read, cynics call it "an inhuman Polish joke".

FORTH was invented by Chuck Moore, during his spare time while he worked at many schools and companies. He wanted to name it "FOURTH", because he considered it to be an ultra-modern "fourth-generation" language. Since he was using an old IBM 1130 minicomputer, which couldn't handle a name as long as "FOURTH", he omitted the letter "U".

PILOT

PILOT was invented at the San Francisco branch of the University of California, by John Starkweather in 1968. It's easier to learn than BASIC, but it's intended to be used by teachers instead of students. Teachers using PILOT can easily make the computer tutor students about history, geography, math, French, and other schoolbook subjects.

For example, suppose you're a teacher and want to make the computer chat with your students. Here's how to do it in BASIC, and more easily in PILOT:

```
BASIC program
10 CLS
20 PRINT "I AM A COMPUTER"
30 INPUT "DO YOU LIKE COMPUTERS";A$
40 IF A$="YES" OR A$="YEAH" OR A$="YEP" OR A$="SURE" OR A$="SURELY" OR A$="I SUR
E DO" THEN PRINT "I LIKE YOU TOO" ELSE PRINT "TOUGH LUCK"
```

PILOT program	What the computer will do
T:I AM A COMPUTER	Type "I AM A COMPUTER".
T:DO YOU LIKE COMPUTERS?	Type "DO YOU LIKE COMPUTERS?"
A:	Accept the human's answer.
M:YE,SURE	Match. (See whether answer contains "YE" or "SURE".)
TY:I LIKE YOU TOO	If there was a match, type "I LIKE YOU TOO".
TN:TOUGH LUCK	If no match, type "TOUGH LUCK".

Notice that the PILOT program is briefer than BASIC.

Atari, Apple, and Radio Shack all sell versions of PILOT that include commands to handle graphics. Atari's version is the best, since it includes the fanciest graphics and music and even a LOGO-like turtle, and since it's also the easiest version to learn how to use.

Although PILOT is easier than BASIC, most teachers prefer to learn BASIC because BASIC is available on more computers, costs less, and accomplishes a greater variety of tasks. Hardly anybody uses PILOT.

Specialists

For specialized applications, use a special language.

APT

If you use APT, the computer will help you cut metal.

Type an APT program that says how you want the metal cut. When you run the program, the computer will create a special instruction tape. If you feed that tape into a metal-cutting machine, the machine will cut metal as you said.

Let's write an APT program that makes the machine cut out the shaded area:

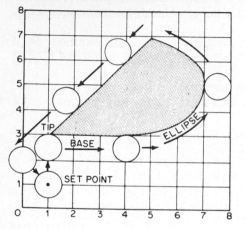

We'll make the machine move the cutter where the circles are.

Here's the program:

Program	What the computer will do
CUTTER/1	Use a cutter whose diameter is 1".
TOLER/.005	The tolerance of the cut is .005".
FEDRAT/80	Use a feedrate of 80" per minute.
HEAD/1	Use head 1.
MODE/1	Operate the tool in mode 1.
SPINDL/2400	Turn the spindle on, at 2400 rpm.
COOLNT/FLOOD	Turn the coolant on, at flood setting.
PT1=POINT/4,5	PT1 = the point whose coordinates are (4,5).
FROM/(SETPT=POINT/1,1)	SETPT = point (1,1). Start tool from SETPT.
INDIRP/(TIP=PIONT/1,3)	TIP = (1,3). Aim tool in direction of TIP.
BASE=LINE/TIP, AT ANGL, 0	BASE = line going through TIP at 0 degrees.
GOTO/BASE	Make the tool go to BASE.
TL RGT, GO RGT/BASE	With tool on right, go right along BASE.
GO FWD/(ELLIPS/CENTER, PT1, 3,2,0)	Go forward along ellipse whose center is PT1, semi-major axis is 3", semi-minor axis is 2", and major axis slants 0 degrees.
GO LFT/(LINE/2,4,1,3,), PAST, BASE	Go left along the line that joins (2,4) and (1,3), until you get past BASE.
GOTO/SETPT	Make the tool go to SETPT.
COOLNT/OFF	Turn the coolant off.
SPINDL/OFF	Turn the spindle off.
END	End use of the machine.
FINI	The program is finished.

DYNAMO

DYNAMO uses these symbols:

Symbol	Meaning
.J	a moment ago
.K	now
.JK	during the past moment
.KL	during the next moment
DT	how long "a moment" is

For example, suppose you want to explain to the computer how population depends on birth rate. If you let P be the population, BR be the birth rate, and DR be the death rate, here's what to say in DYNAMO:

```
P.K=P.J+DT*(BR.JK-DR.JK)
```

The equation says: Population now = Population before + (how long "a moment" is) times (Birth Rate during the past moment - Death Rate during the past moment).

World Dynamics The most famous DYNAMO program is the **World Dynamics Model**, which Jay Forrester programmed at MIT in 1970. His program has 117 equations that describe 112 variables about our world.

Here's how the program begins:

```
* WORLD DYNAMICS
L P.K=P.J+DT*(BR.JK-DR.JK)
N P=PI
C PI=1.65E9
R BR.KL=P.K*FIFGE(BRN,BRN1,SWT1,TIME.K)*BRFM.K*BRMM.K*BRCM.K*BRPM.K
etc.
```

The first line gives the program's title. The next line defines the Level of Population, in terms of Birth Rate and Death Rate.

The second equation defines the iNitial Population to be PI (Population Initial). The next equation defines the Constant PI to be 1.65e9, because the world's population was 1.65 billion in 1900.

The next equation says the Rate BR.KL (the Birth Rate during the next moment) is determined by the Population now and several other factors, such as the BRFM (Birth-Rate-from-Food Multiplier), the BRMM (Birth-Rate-from-Material Multiplier), the BRCM (Birth-Rate-from-Crowding Multiplier), and the BRPM (Birth-Rate-from-Pollution Multiplier). Each of those factors is defined in later equations.

When you run the program, the computer automatically solves all the equations simultaneously and draws graphs that show how the population, birth rate, etc. will change during this century and the next. Here are some of the results:

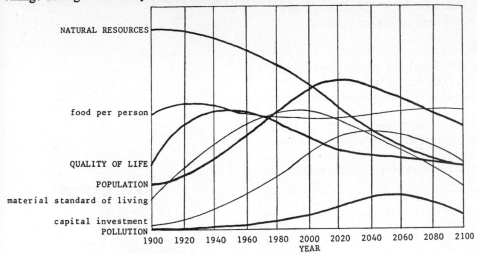

The graph shows the quality of life will decrease because of the overpopulation, pollution, and dwindling natural resources. Although the material standard of living will improve for a while, it too will eventually decrease, as will industrialization (capital investment).

Dwindling natural resources are the main problem. Suppose scientists suddenly make a new discovery that lets us reduce our usage of natural resources by 75%. Will our lives be better?

Here's what the computer predicted would happen, if the "new discovery" were made in 1970:

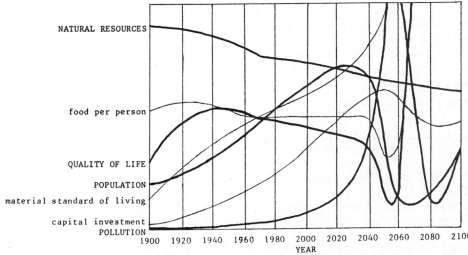

In that picture, you see the graph of natural resources changing sharply in 1970, because of the new scientific discovery. As a result, people live well, so that in 2030 the population is almost 4 times what it was in 1970. But the large population generates too much pollution; in 2030, the pollution is being created faster than it can dissipate. From 2040 to 2060, a pollution crisis occurs: the pollution increases until it is 40 times as great as in 1970; then most people on earth die, so that the world population in 2060 is a sixth of what it was in 2040. After the crisis, the few survivors create little pollution and enjoy a very high quality of life.

Forrester tried other experiments on the computer. To improve the quality of life, he tested the effect of requiring birth control, reducing pollution, and adopting other strategies. Each of them backfired. The graphs showed that the only way to maintain a high quality of life throughout the next century is to adopt a *combination* strategy now:

reduce natural resource usage by 75%
reduce pollution generation by 50%
reduce the birth rate by 30%
reduce capital-investment generation by 40%
reduce food production by 20%

Other popular applications

Although the World Dynamics Model is DYNAMO's most famous program, DYNAMO has also been applied to many other problems.

The first DYNAMO programs ever written were aimed at helping managers run companies. Just plug your policies about buying, selling, hiring, and firing into the program's equations; when you run the program, the computer draws a graph showing what will happen to your company during the coming months and years. If you don't like the computer's prediction, change your policies, put them into the equations, and see whether the computer's graphs are more optimistic.

How DYNAMO developed

DYNAMO developed from research at MIT.

At MIT in 1958, Richard Bennett invented a language called **SIMPLE**, which stood for "Simulation of Industrial Management Problems with Lots of Equations". In 1959, Phyllis Fox and Alexander Pugh III invented DYNAMO as an improvement on SIMPLE. At MIT in 1961, Jay Forrester wrote a book called *Industrial Dynamics*, which explained how DYNAMO can help you manage a company.

MIT is near Boston, whose mayor from 1960 to 1967 was John Collins. When his term as mayor ended, he became a visiting professor at MIT. His office happened to be next to Forrester's. He asked Forrester whether DYNAMO could solve the problems of managing a city. Forrester organized a conference of urban experts and got them to turn urban problems into 330 DYNAMO equations involving 310 variables.

Forrester ran the program and made the computer graph the consequences. The results were surprising:

The graph showed that if you try to help the underemployed by giving them low-cost housing, job-training programs, and artificially-created jobs, here's what happens: as the city becomes better for the underemployed, more underemployed people move to the city. Then the percentage of the city that is underemployed increases, and the city is worse than before the reforms were begun. In other words, socialist reform just backfires.

Another example: free public transportation creates *more* traffic, because it encourages people to live farther from their jobs.

Instead, the graphs show the only long-term solution to the city's problems is to knock down slums, fund new "labor-intensive export" businesses (businesses that will hire many workers, occupy little land, and produce goods that can be sold outside the city), and let the underemployed fend for themselves in this new environment.

Another surprise: any city-funded housing program makes matters *worse* — regardless of whether the housing is for the underemployed, the workers, or the rich — because additional housing means less space for industry and hence fewer jobs.

If you ever become a mayor or President, use the computer's recommendations cautiously: they'll improve the cities, but only by driving the underemployed out to the suburbs, which will worsen.

In 1970 Forrester created the World Dynamics Model to help "The Club of Rome", a private club of 75 people who try to save the world from ecological calamity.

GPSS

A **queue** is a line of people who are waiting. GPSS analyzes queues. For example, let's use GPSS to analyze the customers waiting in "Quickie Joe's Barbershop".

Joe's the only barber in the shop, and he spends exactly 7 minutes on each haircut. (That's why he's called "Quickie Joe".)

About once every 10 minutes, a new customer enters the barbershop. More precisely, the number of minutes before another customer enters is a random number between 5 and 15.

To make the computer imitate the barbershop and analyze what happens to the first 100 customers, type this program:

```
       SIMULATE
       GENERATE   10,5    A new customer comes every 10 minutes ± 5 minutes.
       QUEUE      JOEQ    He waits in the queue, called JOEQ.
       SEIZE      JOE     When his turn comes, he seizes JOE,
       DEPART     JOEQ      which means he leaves the JOEQ.
       ADVANCE    7       After 7 minutes go by,
       RELEASE    JOE       he releases JOE (so someone else can use JOE)
       TERMINATE  1         and leaves the shop.
       START      100     Do all that 100 times.
       END
```

Indent so that the word SIMULATE begins in column 8 (preceeded by 7 spaces) and the "10,5" begins in column 19.

When you run the program, the computer will tell you the following....

Joe was working 68.5% of the time. The rest of the time, his shop was empty and he was waiting for customers.

There was never more than 1 customer waiting. "On the average", .04 customers were waiting.

There were 101 customers. (The 101st customer stopped the experiment.) 79 of them (78.2% of them) obtained Joe immediately and didn't have to wait.

The "average customer" had to wait in line .405 minutes. The "average not-immediately-served customer" had to wait in line 1.863 minutes.

How to make the program fancier
Below the RELEASE statement and above the TERMINATE statement, you can insert two extra statements:

```
       TABULATE   1
1      TABLE      M1,0,1,26
```

(Indent so that the 1 before TABLE is in column 2.) Those two statements make the computer add the following comments.

Of the 100 analyzed customers, the "average customer" spent 7.369 minutes in the shop (from when he walked in to when he walked out).

More precisely, 79 customers spend 7 minutes each, 9 customers spend 8 minutes each, 9 customers spend 9 minutes each, 2 customers spend 10 minutes each, and 1 customer had to spend 11 minutes.

The computer also prints the "standard deviation", "cumulative tables", and other statistical claptrap.

On your own computer, the numbers might be slightly different, depending on how the random numbers came out. To have more faith in the computer's averages, try 1000 customers instead of 100.

Alternative languages
For most problems about queues, GPSS is the easiest language to use. But if your problem is complex, you might have to use **SIMSCRIPT** (based on FORTRAN) or **SIMULA** (an elaboration of ALGOL) or **SIMPL/I** (an elaboration of PL/I).

RPG

RPG is the most popular language for IBM minicomputers, such as the IBM system/3, System/32, System/34, and System/36.

For example, suppose you have a file called MANHOURS, containing one punched card per employee:

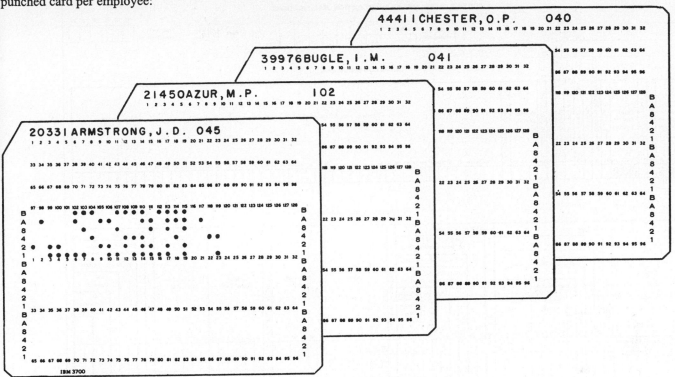

On each card, column 1-5 contain the employee's identification number, columns 6-20 contain his name, and columns 21-23 tell how many hours he worked. Let's make an IBM System/3 minicomputer print the whole file on the line printer, with extra spacing, and also print the total number of man-hours in the company, like this:

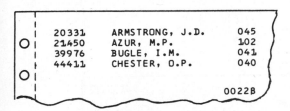

```
    20331      ARMSTRONG, J.D.      045
    21450      AZUR, M.P.           102
    39976      BUGLE, I.M.          041
    44411      CHESTER, O.P.        040

                                   0022B
```

To write the program, fill out four forms.

The first form describes the controls and files, like COBOL's environment division. Here's how to fill it out:

IBM — International Business Machines Corporation — Form X21-9092, Printed in U.S.A.

RPG CONTROL CARD AND FILE DESCRIPTION SPECIFICATIONS

Page 01

Control Card Specifications

Line 01: `H 008   008`

File Description Specifications

Line	Form Type	Filename	File Type	Record Length	Device
02	F	MANHOURS	IP	96	MFCU1
03	F	ADDLIST	O	96	PRINTER
04	F				

Line 01 says "008 008". That makes the computer reserve 8 kilobytes of memory for the program.

Line 02 describes the file MANHOURS. The "IP" means the file is for Input and is the Primary file. The "96" means each card in the file has 96 columns. The "MFCU1" means card reader #1.

Line 03 says "ADDLIST" will be the name of the Output file, which has 96 columns and will appear on the PRINTER.

The second form describes the input:

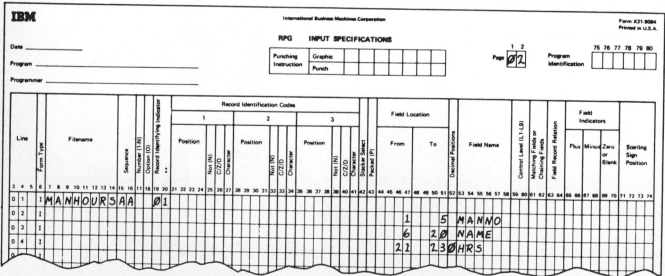

IBM — International Business Machines Corporation — Form X21-9094, Printed in U.S.A.

RPG INPUT SPECIFICATIONS

Page 02

Line	Form Type	Filename	Sequence	Number (1-N)	Option (O)	Record Identifying Indicator	From	To	Decimal Positions	Field Name
01	I	MANHOURS	AA			01				
02	I						1	5		MANNO
03	I						6	20		NAME
04	I						21	23	0	HRS

Line 01 says the file MANHOURS is unorganized ("AA"), reading a card from the file is called "activity #01". The remaining lines say that on each card, columns 1-5 contain MANNO, columns 6-20 contain NAME, and columns 21-23 contain HRS, which is a number having 0 digits after the decimal point.

The third form describes the calculations:

International Business Machines Corporation

Form X21-9093
Printed in U.S.A.

RPG   CALCULATION SPECIFICATIONS

Date _____
Program _____
Programmer _____

Line	Form Type	Control Level (L0-L9, LR, SR)	Indicators (And / And / Not)	Factor 1	Operation	Factor 2	Result Field	Field Length	Decimal Positions	Half Adjust (H)	Resulting Indicators	Comments
0 1	C		01	HRS	ADD	TOTAL	TOTAL	50				
0 2	C											

That form says: after each occurrence of activity #01, let HRS + TOTAL be the new TOTAL, which is a 5-digit number having 0 digits after the decimal point.

The fourth form describes the output:

International Business Machines Corporation

Form X21-9090
Printed in U.S.A.

RPG   OUTPUT - FORMAT SPECIFICATIONS

Date _____
Program _____
Programmer _____

Line	Form Type	Filename	Type (H/D/T/E)	Stacker Select/Fetch Overflow (F)	Space Before/After	Skip Before/After	Output Indicators (And/And/Not)	Field Name	Edit Codes	Blank After (B)	End Position in Output Record	Packed Field (P)	Constant or Edit Word	Sterling Sign Position
0 1	O	ADDLIST	D			10	01							
0 2	O							MANNO			5			
0 3	O							NAME			23			
0 4	O							HRS			29			
0 5	O		T			30	LR							
0 6	O							TOTAL			29			
0 7	O													

Edit Codes:

	Commas	Zero Balances to Print	No Sign	CR	-	
	Yes	Yes		A	J	X = Remove Plus Sign
	Yes	No	1	B	K	Y = Date Field Edit
	No	Yes	2	C	L	Z = Zero Suppress
	No	No	3	D	M	
			4			

That form explains how to print the file ADDLIST.

In line 01, the "D" means "here's how to print each line of Details". The "10 01" means "press the carriage return 1 time before you print the line, press it 0 times after you print the line, and do the printing after each occurrence of activity #01".

Line 02 says to print MANNO so it ends in column 5.

Line 03 says to print NAME so it ends in column 23. Since the second form said NAME requires 15 columns, the computer will print NAME in columns 9-23.

Line 04 says to print HRS so it ends in column 29. Since the second form said HRS requires 3 columns, the computer will print HRS in columns 27-29.

In line 05, the "T" means "here's how to print the Total". The "30" means "press the carriage return 3 times before you print the line, and 0 times after". The "LR" means "print it only after the last card's been read (Last Record)".

Line 06 says to print TOTAL so it ends in column 29. Since the third form said TOTAL requires 5 columns, the computer will print TOTAL in columns 25-29.

After you've filled out the four forms in longhand, type what you wrote. Here's the RPG program:

```
0101 H008  008
0102 FMANHOURSIP      96              MFCU1         ⎫ from the first form
0103 FADDLIST O        96              PRINTER       ⎭
0201 IMANHOURSAA  01                                ⎫
0202 I                            1   5 MANNO       ⎪ from the second form
0203 I                            6  20 NAME        ⎬
0204 I                           21  230HRS         ⎭
0301 C   01      HRS     ADD  TOTAL     TOTAL    50 ⎬ from the third form
0401 OADDLIST D 10      01                          ⎫
0402 O                        MANNO       5         ⎪
0403 O                        NAME       23         ⎬ from the fourth form
0404 O                        HRS        29         ⎪
0405 O        T 30      LR                          ⎪
0406 O                        TOTAL      29         ⎭
```

To do that in BASIC, FORTRAN, or traditional COBOL, you'd have to write a loop; you'd have to say GO TO, DO, or PERFORM. RPG makes the computer do loops automatically, without forcing you to specify how. The order in which you write statements is less important in RPG than in those other languages; you're less likely to err; RPG is more reliable.

But today, RPG is considered old-fashioned, since newer languages (such as DBASE) let you generate loops, totals, and reports even more easily than RPG. Moreover, DBASE costs less than RPG and can run on cheaper computers.

SPSS

The most popular computer language for statistics is **SPSS**, which stands for **Statistical Package for the Social Sciences**.

Simple example Suppose you survey 10 of your friends and ask each of them two questions:

> 1. In the next election, will you probably vote Republican or Democrat?
> 2. Are you male or female?

Maybe you can guess the answer to the second question by just looking at the person; but to be sure, you'd better ask.

Suppose nobody gives an unusual answer (such as Prohibitionist or Communist or Transsexual or Undecided). You think it would be cool to feed all the data into the computer. For example, if a person said "Republican Female", you'd feed the computer this line:

```
RF
```

If a person said "Democrat Male", you'd feed the computer this line:

```
DM
```

This SPSS program makes the computer analyze the data:

Program		Meaning
VARIABLE LIST	PARTY,SEX	Read each person's PARTY and SEX,
INPUT FORMAT	FIXED (2A1)	using this FORTRAN FORMAT: "2A1".
N OF CASES	10	There are 10 people.
INPUT MEDIUM	CARD	The data to read is on the "cards" below.
PRINT FORMATS	PARTY,SEX (A)	To print the PARTY and SEX, use "A" format.
CROSSTABS	TABLES=SEX BY PARTY	Print table showing how SEX relates to PARTY.
READ INPUT DATA		The data to read is on the following lines.
RF		
DM		
RM		
RM		
DF		— the "data cards"
DM		
DF		
DF		
RM		
DF		
FINISH		The program is finished.

In the top line, the word PARTY begins in column 16. Most SPSS statements consist of a **control field** (columns 1-15) followed by a **specification field** (columns 16-80).

When you run the program, the computer will print this kind of table:

```
                    ROW
        R     D    TOTAL
M       3     2     5
     60.0% 40.0%  50.0%
     75.0% 33.3%
     30.0% 20.0%

F       1     4     5
     20.0% 80.0%  50.0%
     25.0% 66.7%
     10.0% 40.0%

COLUMN  4     6     10
TOTAL 40.0% 60.0% 100.0%
```

Look at the top number in each box. Those numbers say there were 3 male Republicans, 2 male Democrats, 1 female Republican, and 4 female Democrats. The first box says: the 3 male Republicans were 60% of the males, 75% of the Republicans, and 30% of the total population.

The computer prints the table in reverse-alphabetical order: "M" before "F", and "R" before "D". Each row is a SEX, and each column is a PARTY. In the program, if you change "SEX BY PARTY" to "PARTY BY SEX", each row will be a PARTY, and each column will be a SEX.

Fancy features The CROSSTABS statement has **options**. Here are some of them.

> option 3: don't print the row percentages (the 60.0%, 40.0%, 20.0%, and 80.0%)
> option 4: don't print the column percentages (75.0%, 33.3%, 25.0%, and 66.7%)
> option 5: don't print the total percentages (30.0%, 20.0%, 10.0% and 40.0%)

If you want options 3 and 5, insert this statement underneath the CROSSTABS statement:

```
OPTIONS      3,5
```

The CROSSTABS statement has **statistics**. Here are some of them:

> 1. chi-square, its degrees of freedom, level of significance
> 2. phi or Cramer's V
> 3. contingency coefficient
> 4. lambda, symmetric and asymmetric
> 5. uncertainty coefficient, symmetric and asymmetric
> 6. Kendall's tau b and its level of significance
> 7. Kendall's tau c and its level of significance
> 8. gamma
> 9. Somer's D

Those statistics are numbers that help you analyze the crosstab table. If you want statistics 1 and 8, insert this statement underneath the CROSSTABS and OPTIONS statements:

```
STATISTICS      1,8
```

It makes the computer print statistics 1 and 8 underneath the table. If you want the computer to print all 9 statistics, say:

```
STATISTICS      ALL
```

The CROSSTABS statement is called a **procedure**. Here are other procedures SPSS can handle:

```
AGGREGATE  ANOVA  BREAKDOWN  CANCORR
CONDESCRIPTIVE  DISCRIMINANT  FACTOR
FREQUENCIES  GUTTMAN SCALE
NONPAR CORR  ONEWAY  PARTIAL CORR
PEARSON CORR  REGRESSION  SCATTERGRAM
T-TEST  WRITE CASES
```

Each procedure has its own OPTIONS and STATISTICS.

SPSS includes many other kinds of statements:

```
ADD CASES    ADD DATA LIST    ADD SUBFILES
ADD VARIABLES    ALLOCATE
ASSIGN MISSING    COMMENT    COMPUTE
COUNT    DATA LIST    DELETE SUBFILES
DELETE VARS    DO REPEAT    DOCUMENT
EDIT    END REPEAT    FILE NAME
GET ARCHIVE    GET FILE    IF    KEEP VARS
LIST ARCHINFO    LIST CASES
LIST FILEINFO    MERGE FILES
MISSING VALUES    NUMBERED    PAGESIZE
PRINT BACK    RAW OUTPUT UNIT
READ MATRIX    RECODE    REORDER VARS
RUN NAME    RUN SUBFILES    SAMPLE
SAVE ARCHIVE    SAVE FILE    SELECT IF
SORT CASES    SUBFILE LIST    TASK NAME
VALUE LABELS    WEIGHT    WRITE FILEINFO
```

SPSS contains more statistical features than any other language. If you don't need quite so many features, use an easier language, such as STATPAK or DATATEXT.

PROLOG

In 1972, PROLOG was invented in France at the **University of Marseilles**. In 1981, a different version of PROLOG arose in Scotland at the **University of Edinburgh**. In 1986, **Turbo PROLOG** was created in California by Borland International (which also created Turbo PASCAL).

Those versions of PROLOG are called **Marseilles PROLOG**, **Edinburgh PROLOG**, and **Turbo PROLOG**.

Today, PROLOG programmers call Marseilles PROLOG the "old classic", Edinburgh PROLOG the "current standard", and Turbo PROLOG the "radical departure".

Turbo PROLOG has two advantages over its predecessors: it runs programs extra-fast, and it uses English words instead of weird symbols. On the other hand, it requires extra lines at the beginning of your program, to tell the computer which variables are strings.

The ideal PROLOG would be a compromise, incorporating the best features of Marseilles, Edinburgh, and Turbo. Here's how to use the ideal PROLOG, and how the various versions differ from it....

Creating the database

PROLOG analyzes relationships. Suppose Alice loves tennis and sailing, Tom loves everything that Alice loves, and Tom also loves football (which Alice does *not* love). To feed all those facts to the computer, give these PROLOG commands:

```
loves(alice,tennis).
loves(alice,sailing).
loves(tom,X) if loves(alice,X).
loves(tom,football).
```

The top two lines say Alice loves tennis and sailing. In the third line, the "X" means "something", so that line says: Tom loves something if Alice loves it. The bottom line says Tom loves football.

When you type those lines, be careful about capitalization.

> You must capitalize variables (such as X). You must *not* capitalize specifics (such as tennis, sailing, football, alice, tom, and love).

At the end of each sentence, put a period.

That's how to program by using ideal PROLOG. Here's how other versions of PROLOG differ....

For Edinburgh PROLOG, type the symbol ":-" instead of the word "if".

For Marseilles PROLOG, replace the period by a semicolon, and replace the word "if" by an arrow (->), which you must put in every line:

```
loves(alice,tennis)->;
loves(alice,sailing)->;
loves(tom,X) -> loves(alice,X);
loves(tom,football)->;
```

For Turbo PROLOG, you must add extra lines at the top of your program, to warn the computer that the person and sport are strings ("symbols"), and the word "loves" is a verb ("predicate") that relates a person to a sport:

```
domains
        person,sport=symbol
predicates
        loves(person,sport)
clauses
        loves(alice,tennis).
        loves(alice,sailing).
        loves(tom,X) if loves (alice,X).
        loves(tom,football).
```

(To indent, press the TAB key. To stop indenting, press the left-arrow key.) When you've typed all that, press the ESCape key and then the R key (which means Run).

Simple questions

After you've fed the database to the computer, you can ask the computer questions about it.

Does Alice love tennis? To ask the computer that question, type this:

```
loves(alice,tennis)?
```

The computer will answer:

```
yes
```

Does Alice love football? Ask this:

```
loves(alice,football)?
```

The computer will answer:

```
no
```

That's how the ideal PROLOG works. Other versions differ. *Marseilles PROLOG* is similar to the ideal PROLOG. *Turbo PROLOG* omits the question mark, says "true" instead of "yes", and says "false" instead of "no". *Edinburgh PROLOG* puts the question mark at the beginning of the sentence instead of the end, like this:

```
?-loves(alice,tennis).
```

Advanced questions

What does Alice love? Does Alice love something? Ask this:

```
loves(alice,X)?
```

The computer will answer:

```
X=tennis
X=sailing
2 solutions
```

What does Tom love? Does Tom love something? Ask:

```
loves(tom,X)?
```

The computer will answer:

```
X=tennis
X=sailing
X=football
3 solutions
```

Who loves tennis? Ask:

```
loves(X,tennis)?
```

The computer will answer:

```
X=alice
X=tom
2 solutions
```

Does anybody love hockey? Ask:

```
loves(X,hockey)?
```

The computer doesn't know of anybody who loves hockey, so the computer will answer:

```
no solution
```

Does Tom love something that Alice doesn't? Ask:

```
loves(tom,X) and not (loves(alice,X))?
```

The computer will answer:

```
X=football
1 solution
```

That's ideal PROLOG.

Turbo PROLOG is similar to ideal PROLOG. For *Marseilles PROLOG,* replace the word "and" by a blank space.

For *Edinburgh PROLOG,* replace the word "and" by a comma. After the computer finds a solution, type a semicolon, which tells the computer to find others; when the computer can't find any more solutions, it says "no" (which means "no more solutions") instead of printing a summary message such as "2 solutions".

PROLOG's popularity

After being invented in France, PROLOG quickly became popular throughout Europe.

Its main competitor was LISP, which was invented in the United States before PROLOG. Long after PROLOG's debut, Americans continued to use LISP and ignored PROLOG.

In the 1980's, the Japanese launched the **Fifth Generation Project**, which was an attempt to develop a more intelligent kind of computer. To develop that computer's software, the Japanese decided to use PROLOG instead of LISP, because PROLOG was non-American and therefore furthered the project's purpose, which was to one-up the Americans.

When American researchers heard that the Japanese chose PROLOG as a software weapon, the Americans got scared and launched a counter-attack by learning PROLOG also.

When Borland — an American company — developed Turbo PROLOG, American researchers were thrilled, since Turbo PROLOG ran faster than any other PROLOG. It ran faster on a cheap IBM PC than Japan's PROLOG ran on Japan's expensive maxicomputers! The money that Japan had spent on maxicomputers was wasted! The Americans giggled with glee.

Moral: though the Japanese can beat us in making hardware, we're still way ahead in software. But wouldn't it be great if our countries could work together and *share* talents?

ASSEMBLER

Number systems

Most humans use the **decimal system**, which consists of ten digits (0, 1, 2, 3, 4, 5, 6, 7, 8, 9), because humans have ten fingers. The computer does not have fingers, so it prefers other number systems instead. Here they are....

Binary

Look at these powers of 2:

$$2^0 = 1$$
$$2^1 = 2$$
$$2^2 = 4$$
$$2^3 = 8$$
$$2^4 = 16$$
$$2^5 = 32$$
$$2^6 = 64$$

Now try an experiment. Pick your favorite positive integer, and try to write it as a sum of powers of 2.

For example, suppose you pick 45; you can write it as 32+8+4+1. Suppose you pick 74; you can write it as 64+8+2. Suppose you pick 77. You can write it as 64+8+4+1. *Every* positive integer can be written as a sum of powers of 2.

Let's put those examples in a table:

Original number	Written as sum of powers of 2	Does the sum contain...						
		64?	32?	16?	8?	4?	2?	1?
45	32+8+4+1	no	yes	no	yes	yes	no	yes
74	64+8+2	yes	no	no	yes	no	yes	no
77	64+8+4+1	yes	no	no	yes	yes	no	yes

To write those numbers in the **binary system**, replace "no" by 0 and "yes" by 1:

Decimal system	Binary system
45	0101101 (or simply 101101)
74	1001010
77	1001101

The **decimal system** uses the digits 0, 1, 2, 3, 4, 5, 6, 7, 8, and 9 and uses these columns:

thousands	hundreds	tens	units

For example, the decimal number 7105 means "7 thousands + 1 hundred + 0 tens + 5 units".

The **binary system** uses just the digits 0 and 1, and uses these columns:

sixty-fours	thirty-twos	sixteens	eights	fours	twos	units

For example, the binary number 1001101 means "1 sixty-four + 0 thirty-twos + 0 sixteens + 1 eight + 1 four + 0 twos + 1 unit". In other words, it means seventy-seven.

In elementary school, you were taught how to do arithmetic in the decimal system. You had to memorize the addition and multiplication tables:

DECIMAL ADDITION

	0	1	2	3	4	5	6	7	8	9
0	0	1	2	3	4	5	6	7	8	9
1	1	2	3	4	5	6	7	8	9	10
2	2	3	4	5	6	7	8	9	10	11
3	3	4	5	6	7	8	9	10	11	12
4	4	5	6	7	8	9	10	11	12	13
5	5	6	7	8	9	10	11	12	13	14
6	6	7	8	9	10	11	12	13	14	15
7	7	8	9	10	11	12	13	14	15	16
8	8	9	10	11	12	13	14	15	16	17
9	9	10	11	12	13	14	15	16	17	18

DECIMAL MULTIPLICATION

	0	1	2	3	4	5	6	7	8	9
0	0	0	0	0	0	0	0	0	0	0
1	0	1	2	3	4	5	6	7	8	9
2	0	2	4	6	8	10	12	14	16	18
3	0	3	6	9	12	15	18	21	24	27
4	0	4	8	12	16	20	24	28	32	36
5	0	5	10	15	20	25	30	35	40	45
6	0	6	12	18	24	30	36	42	48	54
7	0	7	14	21	28	35	42	49	56	63
8	0	8	16	24	32	40	48	56	64	72
9	0	9	18	27	36	45	54	63	72	81

In the binary system, the only digits are 0 and 1, so the tables are briefer:

BINARY ADDITION

	0	1
0	0	1
1	1	10 because two is written "10" in binary

BINARY MULTIPLICATION

	0	1
0	0	0
1	0	1

If society had adopted the binary system instead of the decimal system, you'd have been spared many hours of memorizing!

Usually, when you ask the computer to perform a computation, it converts your numbers from the decimal system to the binary system, performs the computation by using the binary addition and multiplication tables, and then converts the answer from the binary system to the decimal system, so you can read it. For example, if you ask the computer to print 45+74, it will do this:

```
  45   converted to binary is     101101
 +74   converted to binary is    +1001010
                                  1110111   converted to decimal is   119
                                     ↑
                            because 1+1=10
```

The conversion from decimal to binary and then back to decimal is slow. But the computation itself (in this case, addition) is quick, since the binary addition table is so simple. The only times the computer must convert is during input (decimal to binary) and output (binary to decimal). The rest of the execution is performed quickly, entirely in binary.

You know fractions can be written in the decimal system, by using these columns:

units	point	tenths	hundredths	thousandths

For example, $1\frac{5}{8}$ can be written as 1.625, which means "1 unit + 6 tenths + 2 hundredths + 5 thousandths".

To write fractions in the binary system, use these columns instead:

units	point	halves	fourths	eighths

For example, $1\frac{5}{8}$ is written in binary as 1.101, which means "1 unit + 1 half + 0 fourths + 1 eighth".

You know $\frac{1}{3}$ is written in the decimal system as 0.3333333..., which unfortunately never terminates. In the binary system, the situation is no better: $\frac{1}{3}$ is written as 0.010101.... Since the computer stores just a finite number of digits, it can't store $\frac{1}{3}$ accurately — it stores just an approximation.

A more distressing example is $\frac{1}{5}$. In the decimal system, it's .2, but in the binary system it's .0011001100110011.... So the computer can't handle $\frac{1}{5}$ accurately, even though a human can.

Most of today's microcomputers and minicomputers are inspired by a famous maxicomputer built by DEC and called the DECsystem-10 (or PDP-10). Though DEC doesn't sell the DECsystem-10 anymore, its influence lives on!

Suppose you run this BASIC program on a DECsystem-10 computer:

```
10 PRINT "MY FAVORITE NUMBER IS";4.001-4
20 END
```

The computer will try to convert 4.001 to binary. Unfortunately, it can't be converted exactly; the computer's binary approximation of it is slightly too small. The computer's final answer to 4.001-4 is therefore slightly less than the correct answer. Instead of printing MY FAVORITE NUMBER IS .001, the computer will print MY FAVORITE NUMBER IS .000999987.

If your computer isn't a DECsystem-10, its approximation will be slightly different. To test your computer's accuracy, try 4.0001-4, and 4.00001-4, and 4.000001-4, etc. You might be surprised at its answers.

Let's see how the DECsystem-10 handles this:

```
10 FOR X = 7 TO 193 STEP .1
20    PRINT X
30 NEXT X
40 END
```

The computer will convert 7 and 193 to binary accurately, but will convert .1 to binary just approximately; the approximation is slightly too large. The last few numbers it should print are 192.8, 192.9, and 193, but because of the approximation it will print slightly more than 192.8, then slightly more than 192.9, and then stop (since it is not allowed to print anything over 193).

There are only two binary digits: 0 and 1. A **binary digit** is called a **bit**. For example, .001100110011 is a binary approximation of $\frac{1}{5}$ that consists of twelve bits. A sixteen-bit approximation of $\frac{1}{5}$ would be .0011001100110011. A bit that is 1 is called **turned on**; a bit that is 0 is **turned off**. For example, in the expression 11001, three bits are turned on and two are off. We also say that three of the bits are **set** and two are **cleared**.

All information inside the computer is coded, in the form of bits:

Part of the computer	What a 1 bit is	What a 0 bit is
electric wire	high voltage	low voltage
punched paper tape	a hole in the tape	no hole in the tape
punched IBM card	a hole in the card	no hole in the card
magnetic drum	a magnetized area	a non-magnetized area
core memory	core magnetized clockwise	core magnetized counterclockwise
flashing light	the light is on	the light is off

For example, to represent 11 on part of a punched paper tape, the computer punches two holes close together. To represent 1101, the computer punches two holes close together, and then another hole farther away.

Octal

Octal is a shorthand notation for binary:

Octal	Meaning
0	000
1	001
2	010
3	011
4	100
5	101
6	110
7	111

Each octal digit stands for three bits. For example, the octal number 72 is short for this:

To convert a binary integer to octal, divide the number into chunks of three bits, starting at the right. For example, here's how to convert 11110101 to octal:

To convert a binary real number to octal, divide the number into chunks of three bits, starting at the decimal point and working in both directions:

Hexadecimal

Hexadecimal is another short-hand notation for binary:

Hexadecimal	Meaning
0	0000
1	0001
2	0010
3	0011
4	0100
5	0101
6	0110
7	0111
8	1000
9	1001
A	1010
B	1011
C	1100
D	1101
E	1110
F	1111

For example, the hexadecimal number 4F is short for this:

```
01001111
  4    F
```

To convert a binary number to hexadecimal, divide the number into chunks of 4 bits, starting at the decimal point and working in both directions:

```
11010110100.1111111
  6  B  4 . F  E
```

To store a character in a string, the computer uses a code.

ASCII

The most famous code is the **American Standard Code for Information Interchange (ASCII)**, which has 7 bits for each character. Here are examples:

Character	ASCII code	ASCII code in hexadecimal
space	0100000	20
!	0100001	21
"	0100010	22
#	0100011	23
$	0100100	24
%	0100101	25
&	0100110	26
'	0100111	27
(	0101000	28
)	0101001	29
*	0101010	2A
+	0101011	2B
,	0101100	2C
-	0101101	2D
.	0101110	2E
/	0101111	2F
0	0110000	30
1	0110001	31
2	0110010	32
etc.		
9	0111001	39
:	0111010	3A
;	0111011	3B
<	0111100	3C
=	0111101	3D
>	0111110	3E
?	0111111	3F
@	1000000	40
A	1000001	41
B	1000010	42
C	1000011	43
etc.		
Z	1011010	5A
[	1011011	5B
\	1011100	5C
]	1011101	5D
^	1011110	5E
_	1011111	5F

"ASCII" is pronounced "ass key".

Most terminals use 7-bit ASCII. Most microcomputers and the PDP-11 use an "8-bit ASCII" formed by putting a 0 before 7-bit ASCII.

PDP-8 computers use mainly a "6-bit ASCII" formed by eliminating 7-bit ASCII's leftmost bit, but they can also handle an "8-bit ASCII" formed by putting a 1 before 7-bit ASCII.

PDP-10 computers use mainly 7-bit ASCII but can also handle a "6-bit ASCII" formed by eliminating ASCII's second bit. For example, the 6-bit ASCII code for the symbol $ is 0 00100.

CDC computers use a special CDC 6-bit code.

EBCDIC

Instead of using ASCII, IBM mainframes use the **Extended Binary-Coded-Decimal Interchange Code (EBCDIC)**, which has 8 bits for each character. Here are examples:

Character	EBCDIC code in hexadecimal	Character	EBCDIC code in hexadecimal
space	40	A	C1
¢	4A	B	C2
<	4C	C	C3
(	4D	D	C4
+	4E	E	C5
|	4F	F	C6
&	50	G	C7
!	5A	H	C8
$	5B	I	C9
*	5C	J	D1
)	5D	K	D2
;	5E	L	D3
¬	5F	M	D4
-	60	N	D5
/	61	O	D6
,	6B	P	D7
%	6C	Q	D8
_	6D	R	D9
>	6E	S	E2
?	6F	T	E3
:	7A	U	E4
#	7B	V	E5
@	7C	W	E6
'	7D	X	E7
=	7E	Y	E8
"	7F	Z	E9
		0	F0
		1	F1
		2	F2
		etc.	
		9	F9

"EBCDIC" is pronounced "ebb sih Dick".

IBM 360 computers can also handle an "8-bit ASCII", formed by copying ASCII's first bit after the second bit. For example, the 8-bit ASCII code for the symbol $ is 01000100. But IBM 370 computers (which are newer than IBM 360 computers) don't bother with ASCII: they stick strictly with EBCDIC.

80-column IBM cards use **Hollerith code**, which resembles EBCDIC but has 12 bits instead of 8. 96-column IBM cards use a 6-bit code that's an abridgement of the Hollerith code.

Here's a program in BASIC:

```
10 IF "9"<"A" THEN 100
20 PRINT "CAT"
30 STOP
100 PRINT "DOG"
110 END
```

Which will the computer print: CAT or DOG? The answer depends on whether the computer uses ASCII or EBCDIC.

Suppose the computer uses 7-bit ASCII. Then the code for "9" is hexadecimal 39, and the code for "A" is hexadecimal 41. Since 39 is less than 41, the computer considers "9" to be less than "A", so the computer prints DOG.

But if the computer uses EBCDIC instead of ASCII, the code for "9" is hexadecimal F9, and the code for "A" is hexadecimal C1; since F9 is greater than C1, the computer considers "9" to be greater than "A", so the computer prints CAT.

Bytes

A **byte** usually means: eight bits. For example, here's a byte: 10001011.

For computers that use 7-bit ASCII, programmers sometimes define a byte to be 7 bits instead of 8. For computers that use 6-bit ASCII, programmers sometimes define a byte to be 6 bits. So if someone tries to sell you a computer whose memory can hold "16,000 bytes", he probably means 16,000 8-bit bytes, but might mean 7-bit bytes or 6-bit bytes.

Nibbles

A **nibble** is 4 bits. It's half of an 8-bit byte. Since a hexadecimal digit stands for 4 bits, **a hexadecimal digit stands for a nibble**.

Sexy assembler

In this chapter, you'll learn the fundamental concepts of assembly language, quickly and easily.

Unfortunately, different CPU's have different assembly languages.

I've invented an assembly language that combines the best features of all the other assembly languages. My assembly language is called **SEXY ASS**, because it's a Simple, EXcellent, Yummy ASSembler.

After you study the mysteries of the SEXY ASS, you can easily get your rear in gear and become the dominant master of the assemblers sold for Apple, Radio Shack, IBM, DEC, etc. Mastering them will become so easy that you'll say, "Assembly language is a piece of cheesecake!"

Bytes in my ASS

Let's get a close-up view of the SEXY ASS....

CPU registers The computer's guts consist of two main parts: the brain (which is called the **CPU**) and the **main memory** (which consists of RAM and ROM).

Inside the CPU are many electronic boxes, called **registers**. Each register holds several electrical signals; each signal is called a **bit**; so each register holds several bits. Each bit is either 1 or 0. A "1" represents a high voltage; a "0" represents a low voltage. If the bit is 1, the bit is said to be **high** or **on** or **set** or **true**; if the bit is 0, the bit is said to be **low** or **off** or **cleared** or **false**.

The CPU's most important register is called the **accumulator** (or A). In the SEXY ASS system, the accumulator consists of 8 bits, which is 1 byte. (Later, I'll explain how to make the CPU handle several bytes simultaneously; but the accumulator itself holds just 1 byte.)

Memory locations Like the CPU, the main memory consists of electronic boxes. The electronic boxes *in the CPU* are called **registers**, but the electronic boxes *in the main memory* are called **memory locations** instead. Because the main memory acts like a gigantic post office, the memory locations are also called **addresses**. In the SEXY ASS system, each memory location holds 1 byte. There are many *thousands* of memory locations; they're numbered 0, 1, 2, 3, etc.

Number systems When using SEXY ASS, you can type numbers in decimal, binary, or hexadecimal. (For SEXY ASS, octal isn't useful.) For example, the number "twelve" is written "12" in decimal, "1100" in binary, and "C" in hexadecimal. To indicate which number system you're using, **put a percent sign in front of each binary number, and put a dollar sign in front of each hexadecimal number.** For example, in SEXY ASS you can write the number "twelve" as either 12 or %1100 or $C. (In that respect, SEXY ASS copies the 6502 assembly language, which also uses the percent sign and the dollar sign.)

Most of the time, we'll be using hexadecimal, so let's quickly review what hexadecimal is all about. **To count in hexadecimal, just start counting as you learned in elementary school** ($1, $2, $3, $4, $5, $6, $7, $8, $9); **but after $9, you continue counting by using the letters of the alphabet ($A, $B, $C, $D, $E, and $F). After $F (which is fifteen), you say $10** (which means sixteen), then say $11 (which means seventeen), then $12, then $13, then $14, etc., until you reach $19; then come $1A, $1B, $1C, $1D, $1E, and $1F. Then come $20, $21, $22, etc., up to $29, then $2A, $2B, $2C, $2D, $2E, and $2F. Then comes $30. Eventually, you get up to $99, then $9A, $9B, $9C, $9D, $9E, and $9F. Then come $A0, $A1, $A2, etc., up to $AF. Then come $B0, $B1, $B2, etc., up to $BF. You continue that pattern, until you reach $FF. Get together with your friends, and try counting up to $FF. (Don't bother pronouncing the dollar signs.) Yes, you too can count like a pro!

Each hexadecimal digit represents 4 bits. Therefore, an 8-bit byte requires *two* hexadecimal digits. So a byte can be anything from $00 to $FF.

Main segment I said that the main memory consists of *thousands* of memory locations, numbered 0, 1, 2, etc. The most important part of the main memory is called the **main memory bank** or **main segment**: that part consists of 65,536 memory locations (64K), which are numbered from 0 to 65,535. Programmers usually number them in hexadecimal; the hexadecimal numbers go from $0000 from $FFFF. ($FFFF in hexadecimal is the same as 65,535 in decimal.) Later, I'll explain how to use other parts of the memory; but for now, let's restrict our attention to just 64K main segment.

How to copy a byte Here's a simple, one-line program, written in the SEXY ASS assembly language:

```
LOAD    $7000
```

It makes the computer copy one byte, from memory location $7000 to the accumulator. So after the computer obeys that instruction, the accumulator will contain the same data as the memory location. For example, if the memory location contains the byte %01001111 (which can also be written as $4F), so will the accumulator.

Notice the wide space before and after the word LOAD. To make the wide space, press the TAB key.

The word LOAD tells the computer to copy from a memory location to the accumulator. The opposite of the word LOAD is the word STORE: it tells the computer to copy from the accumulator to a memory location. For example, if you type —

```
STORE    $7000
```

the computer will copy a byte from the accumulator to memory location $7000.

Problem: write an assembly-language program that copies a byte from memory location $7000 to memory location $7001. Solution: you must do it in two steps. First, copy from memory location $7000 to the accumulator (by using the word LOAD); then copy from the accumulator to memory location $7001 (by using the word STORE). Here's the program:

```
LOAD    $7000
STORE   $7001
```

Arithmetic

If you say —

```
INC
```

the computer will **increment** (increase) the number in the accumulator, by adding 1 to it. For example, if the accumulator contains the number $25, and you then say INC, the accumulator will contain the number $26. For another example, if the accumulator contains the number $39, and you say INC, the accumulator will contain the number $3A (because, in hexadecimal, after 9 comes A).

Problem: write a program that increments the number that's in location $7000; for example, if location $7000 contains $25, the program should change that data, so that location $7000 contains $26 instead. Solution: copy the number from location $7000 to the accumulator, then increment the number, then copy it back to location $7000....

```
        LOAD    $7000
        INC
        STORE   $7000
```

That example illustrates the fundamental rule of assembly-language programming, which is: **to manipulate a memory location's data, copy the data to the accumulator, manipulate the accumulator, and then copy the revised data from the accumulator to memory.**

The opposite of INC is DEC: it **decrements** (decreases) the number in the accumulator, by subtracting 1 from it.

If you say —

```
ADD     $7000
```

the computer will change the number in the accumulator, by adding to it the number that was in memory location $7000. For example, if the accumulator had contained the number $16, and memory location $7000 had contained the number $43, the number in the accumulator will change and become the sum, $59. The number in memory location $7000 will remain unchanged: it will still be $43.

Problem: find the sum of the numbers in memory locations $7000, $7001, and $7002, and put that sum into memory location $7003. Solution: copy the number from memory location $7000 to the accumulator, then add to the accumulator the numbers from memory locations $7001 and $7002, so that the accumulator to memory location $7003....

```
        LOAD    $7000
        ADD     $7001
        ADD     $7002
        STORE   $7003
```

The opposite of ADD is SUB, which means SUBtract. If you say SUB $7000, the computer will change the number in the accumulator, by subtracting from it the number in memory location $7000.

Immediate addressing

If you say —

```
LOAD    #$25
```

the computer will put the number $25 into the accumulator. The $25 is the data. In the instruction "LOAD #$25", the symbol "#" tells the computer that the $25 is the data instead of being a memory location.

If you were to omit the #, the computer would assume the $25 meant memory location $0025, and so the computer would copy data from memory location $0025 to the accumulator.

An instruction that contains the symbol # is said to be an **immediate** instruction; it is said to use **immediate** addressing. Such instructions are unusual.

The more usual kind of instruction, which does *not* use the symbol #, is called a **direct** instruction.

Problem: change the number in the accumulator, by adding $12 to it. Solution:

```
ADD     #$12
```

Problem: change the number in memory location $7000, by adding $12 to that number. Solution: copy the number from memory location $7000 to the accumulator, add $12 to it, and then copy the sum back to the memory location....

```
        LOAD    $7000
        ADD     #$12
        STORE   $7000
```

Problem: make the computer find the sum of $16 and $43, and put the sum into memory location $7000. Solution: put $16 into the accumulator, add $43 to it, and then copy from the accumulator to memory location $7000....

```
        LOAD    #$16
        ADD     #$43
        STORE   $7000
```

Video RAM

The video RAM is part of the computer's RAM and holds a copy of what's on the screen.

For example, suppose you're running a program that analyzes taxicabs, and the screen (of your TV or monitor) shows information about various cabs. If the upper-left corner of the screen shows the word CAB, the video RAM contains the ASCII code numbers for the letters C, A, and B. Since the ASCII code number for C is 67 (which is $43), and the ASCII code number for A is 65 (which is $41), and the ASCII code number for B is 66 (which is $42), the video RAM contains $43, $41, and $42. The $43, $41, and $42 represent the word CAB.

Suppose that the video RAM begins at memory location $6000. If the screen's upper-left corner shows the word CAB, memory location $6000 contains the code for C (which is $43); the next memory location ($6001) contains the code for A (which is $41); and the next memory location ($6002) contains the code for B (which is $42).

Problem: assuming that the video RAM begins at location $6000, make the computer write the word CAB onto the screen's upper-left corner. Solution: write $43 into memory location $6000, write $41 into memory location $6001, and write $42 into memory location $6002....

```
        LOAD    #$43
        STORE   $6000
        LOAD    #$41
        STORE   $6001
        LOAD    #$42
        STORE   $6002
```

The computer knows that $43 is the code number for "C". When you're writing that program, if you're too lazy to figure out the $43, you can simply write "C"; the computer will understand. So you can write the program like this:

```
        LOAD    #"C"
        STORE   $6000
        LOAD    #"A"
        STORE   $6001
        LOAD    #"B"
        STORE   $6002
```

That's the solution if the video RAM begins at memory location $6000. On *your* computer, the video RAM might begin at a different memory location instead. To find out about *your* computer's video RAM, look at the back of the technical manual that came with your computer. There you'll find a **memory map**: it shows which memory locations are used by the video RAM, which memory locations are used by other RAM, and which memory locations are used by the ROM.

Flags

The CPU contains **flags**. Here's how they work.

Carry flag A byte consists of 8 bits. The smallest number you can put into a byte is %00000000. The largest number you can put into a byte is %11111111, which in hexadecimal is $FF; in decimal, it's 255.

What happens if you try to go higher than %11111111? To find out, examine this program:

```
LOAD    #%10000001
ADD     #%10000010
```

In that program, the top line puts the binary number %10000001 into the accumulator. The next line tries to add %10000010 to the accumulator. But **the sum, which is %100000011, contains 9 bits instead of 8, and therefore can't fit into the accumulator.**

The computer splits that sum into two parts: the left bit (1) and the remaining bits (00000011). The left bit (1) is called the <u>carry bit</u>; the remaining bits (00000011) are called the **tail**. Since the tail contains 8 bits, it fits nicely into the accumulator; so the computer puts it into the accumulator. **The carry bit is put into a special place inside the CPU; that special place is called the <u>carry flag</u>.**

So that program makes the accumulator become 00000011, and makes the carry flag become 1.

Here's an easier program:

```
LOAD    #%1
ADD     #%10
```

The top line puts %1 into the accumulator; so the accumulator's 8 bits are %00000001. The bottom line adds %10 to the number in the accumulator; so the accumulator's 8 bits become %00000011. Since the numbers involved in that addition were so small, there was no need for a 9th bit — no need for a carry bit. To emphasize that no carry bit was required, the carry flag automatically becomes 0.

Here's the rule: if an arithmetic operation (such as ADD, SUB, INC, or DEC) gives a result that's too long to fit into 8 bits, the carry flag becomes 1; otherwise, the carry flag becomes 0.

Negatives The largest number you can fit into a byte %11111111, which in decimal is 255. Suppose you try to add 1 to it. The sum is %100000000, which in decimal is 256. But since %100000000 contains 9 bits, it's too long to fit into a byte. So the computer sends the leftmost bit (the 1) to the carry flag, and puts the tail (the 00000000) into the accumulator. As a result, the accumulator contains 0.

So in assembly language, if you tell the computer to do %11111111+1 (which is 255+1), the accumulator says the answer is 0 (instead of 256).

In assembly language, %11111111+1 is 0. In other words, %11111111 solves the equation x+1=0.

According to high school algebra, the equation x+1=0 has this solution: x=-1. But we've seen that in the assembly language, the equation x+1=0 has the solution x=%11111111. Conclusion: in assembly language, -1 is the same as %11111111.

Now you know that -1 is the same as %11111111, which is 255. Yes, -1 is the same as 255. Similarly, -2 is the same as 254; -3 is the same as 253; -4 is the same as 252. Here's the general formula: -n is the same as 256-n. (That's because 256 is the same as 0.)

%11111111 is 255 and is also -1. Since -1 is a shorter name than 255, we say that %11111111 is *interpreted as* -1. Similarly, %11111110 is 254 and also -2; since -2 is a shorter name than 254, we say that %11111110 is interpreted as -2. At the other extreme, %00000010 is 2 and is also -254; since 2 is a shorter name than -254, we say that %11111110 is interpreted as 2. Here's the rule: if a number is "almost" 256, it's interpreted as a negative number; otherwise, it's interpreted as a positive number.

How high must a number be, in order to be "almost" 256, and therefore to be interpreted as a negative number? The answer is: if the number is at least 128, it's interpreted as a negative number. Putting it another way, if the number's leftmost bit is 1, it's interpreted as a negative number.

That strange train of reasoning leads to the following definition: **a negative number is a byte whose leftmost bit is 1**.

A byte's leftmost bit is therefore called the **negative bit** or the **sign bit**.

Flag register You've seen that the CPU contains a register called the **accumulator**. The CPU also contains a second register, called the **flag register**. In the SEXY ASS system, the flag register contains 8 bits (one byte). Each of the 8 bits in the flag register is called a **flag**; so the flag register contains 8 flags.

Each flag is a bit: it's either 1 or 0. If the flag is 1, the flag is said to be **up** or **raised** or **set**. If the flag is 0, the flag is said to be **down** or **lowered** or **cleared**.

One of the 8 flags is the carry flag: it's raised (becomes 1) whenever an arithmetic operation requires a 9th bit. (It's lowered whenever an arithmetic operation does *not* require a 9th bit.)

Another one of the flags is **the <u>negative flag</u>: it's raised whenever the number in the accumulator becomes negative**. For example, if the accumulator becomes %11111110 (which is -2), the negative flag is raised (i.e. the negative flag becomes 1). It's lowered whenever the number in the accumulator becomes *non*-negative.

Another one of the flags is **the <u>zero flag</u>: it's raised whenever the number in the accumulator becomes zero**. (It's lowered whenever the number in the accumulator becomes *non*-zero.)

Jumps

You can give each line of your program a name. For example, you can give a line the name FRED. To do so, put the name FRED at the beginning of the line, like this:

```
FRED    LOAD    $7000
```

The line's name (FRED) is at the left margin. The command itself (LOAD $7000) is indented by pressing the TAB key. In that line, FRED is called the **label**, LOAD is called the **operation** or **mnemonic**, and $7000 is called the **address**.

Languages such as BASIC let you say "GO TO". **In assembly language, you say "JUMP" instead of "GO TO".** For example, to make the computer GO TO the line named FRED, say:

```
JUMP    FRED
```

The computer will obey: it will JUMP to the line named FRED.

You can say —

```
JUMPN    FRED
```

That means: JUMP to FRED, if the Negative flag is raised. So the computer will JUMP to FRED if a negative number was recently put into the accumulator. (If a *non*-negative number was recently put into the accumulator, the computer will *not* jump to FRED.)

JUMPN means "JUMP if the Negative flag is raised." JUMPC means "JUMP if the Carry flag is raised." JUMPZ means "JUMP if the Zero flag is raised."

JUMPNL means "JUMP if the Negative flag is Lowered." JUMPCL means "JUMP if the Carry flag is Lowered." JUMPZL means "JUMP if the Zero flag is Lowered."

Problem: make the computer look at memory location $7000; if the number in that memory location is negative, make the computer jump to a line named FRED. Solution: copy the number from memory location $7000 to the accumulator, to influence the Negative flag; then JUMP if Negative....

```
LOAD    $7000
JUMPN   FRED
```

Problem: make the computer look at memory location $7000. If the number in that memory location is negative, make the computer print a minus sign in the upper-left corner of the screen; if the number is positive instead, make the computer print a plus sign instead; if the number is zero, make the computer print a zero. Solution: copy the number from memory location $7000 to the accumulator (by saying LOAD); then analyze that number (by using JUMPN and JUMPZ); then LOAD the ASCII code number for either "+" or "-" or "0" into the accumulator (whichever is appropriate); finally copy that ASCII code number from the accumulator to the video RAM (by saying STORE)....

```
        LOAD    $7000
        JUMPN   NEGAT
        JUMPZ   ZERO
        LOAD    #"+"
        JUMP    DISPLAY
NEGAT   LOAD    #"-"
        JUMP    DISPLAY
ZERO    LOAD    #"0"
DISPLAY STORE   $6000
```

Machine language

I've been explaining assembly language. **Machine language** resembles assembly language; what's the difference?

To find out, let's look at a machine language called **SEXY MACHO** (because it's a Simple, EXcellent, Yummy MACHine language Original).

SEXY MACHO resembles SEXY ASS; here are the major differences....

In SEXY ASS assembly language, you use words such as LOAD, STORE, INC, DEC, ADD, SUB, and JUMP. Those words are called *operations* or *mnemonics*. In SEXY MACHO machine language, you replace those words by code numbers: the code number for LOAD is 1; the code number for STORE is 2; INC is 3; DEC is 4; ADD is 5; SUB is 6; and JUMP is 7. The code numbers are called the **operation codes** or **op codes**.

In SEXY ASS assembly language, the symbol "#" indicates immediate addressing; a lack of the symbol "#" indicates direct addressing instead. In SEXY MACHO machine language, you replace the symbol "#" by the code number 1; if you want direct addressing instead, you must use the code number 0.

In SEXY MACHO, all code numbers are hexadecimal.

For example, look at this SEXY ASS instruction:

```
ADD    #$43
```

To translate that instruction into SEXY MACHO machine language, just replace each symbol by its code number. Since the code number for ADD is 5, and the code number for # is 1, the SEXY MACHO version of that line is:

```
5143
```

Let's translate STORE $7003 into SEXY MACHO machine language. Since the code for STORE is 2, and the code for direct addressing is 0, the SEXY MACHO version of that command is:

```
207003
```

In machine language, you can't use any words or symbols: you must use their code numbers instead. To translate a program from assembly language to machine language, you must look up the code number of each word or symbol.

An **assembler** is a program that makes the computer translate from assembly language to machine language.

The CPU understands just machine language: it understands just numbers. It does *not* understand assembly language: it does not understand words and symbols. **If you write a program in assembly language, you must buy an assembler, which translates your program from assembly language to machine language**, so that the computer can understand it.

Since assembly language uses English words (such as LOAD), assembly language seems more "human" than machine language (which uses code numbers). Since programmers are humans, programmers prefer assembly language over machine language. Therefore, the typical programmer writes in assembly language, and then uses an assembler to translate the program to machine language, which is the language that the CPU ultimately requires.

Here's how the typical assembly-language programmer works. First, the programmer types the assembly-language program and uses a word processor to help edit it. The word processor automatically puts the assembly-language program onto a disk. Next, the programmer uses the assembler to translate the assembly-language program into machine language. The assembler puts the machine-language version of the program onto the disk. So now the disk contains *two* versions of the program: the disk contains the original version (in assembly language) and also contains the translated version (in machine language). The original version (in assembly language) is called the **source code**; the translated version (in machine language) is called the **object code**. Finally, the programmer gives a command that makes the computer copy the machine-language version (the object code) from the disk to the RAM and run it.

Here's a tough question: how does the assembler translate "JUMP FRED" into machine language? Here's the answer....

The assembler realizes that FRED is the name for a line in your program. The assembler hunts through your program, to find out which line is labeled FRED. When the assembler finds that line, it analyzes that line, to figure out where that line will be in the RAM after the program is translated into machine language and running. For example, suppose the line that's labeled FRED will become a machine-language line which, when the program is running, will be in the RAM at memory location $2053. Then "JUMP FRED" must be translated into this command: "jump to the machine-language line that's in the RAM at memory location $2053". So "JUMP FRED" really means:

```
JUMP    $2053
```

Since the code number for JUMP is 7, and the addressing isn't immediate (and therefore has code 0 instead of 1), the machine-language version of JUMP FRED is:

```
702053
```

System software

The computer's main memory consists of RAM and ROM. In a typical computer, the first few memory locations ($0000, $0001, $0002, etc.) are ROM: they permanently contain a program called the **bootstrap**, which is written in machine language.

When you turn on the computer's power switch, the computer automatically runs the bootstrap program. If your computer uses disks, the bootstrap program makes the computer start reading information from the disk in the main drive. In fact, it makes the computer copy a machine-language program from the disk to the RAM. The machine-language program that it copies is called the **DOS**.

After the DOS has been copied to the RAM, the computer starts running the DOS program. The DOS program makes the computer print a message on the screen (such as "Welcome to CP/M" or "Welcome to MS-DOS") and print a symbol on the screen (such as "A>") and then wait for you to type a command.

That whole procedure is called **bootstrapping** (or **booting up**), because of the phrase "pull yourself up by your own bootstraps". By using the bootstrap program, the computer pulls itself up to new intellectual heights: it becomes a CP/M machine or an MS-DOS machine or an Apple DOS machine or a TRSDOS machine.

After booting up, you can start writing programs in BASIC. But how does the computer understand the BASIC words, such as PRINT, INPUT, IF, THEN, and GO TO? Here's how:

While you're using BASIC, the computer is running a machine-language program, that makes the computer *seem* to understand BASIC. That machine-language program, which is in the computer's ROM or RAM, is called the **BASIC language processor** or **BASIC interpreter**. If your computer uses **Microsoft** BASIC, the BASIC interpreter is a machine-language program that was written by Microsoft Incorporated (a "corporation" that consists of Bill Gates and his pals).

How assemblers differ

In a microcomputer, the CPU is a single chip, called the **microprocessor**. The most popular microprocessors are the **8088**, the **68000**, and the **6502**.

The **8088**, designed by Intel, hides in the IBM PC and clones. (The plain version is called the 8088; a souped-up version, called the **80286**, is in the IBM PC AT.)

The **68000**, designed by Motorola, hides in the computers that rely on mice: the Apple Mac, Commodore Amiga, and Atari ST. (The plain version is called the 68000; a souped-up version, called the **68020**, is in the Mac 2; an even fancier version, called the **68030**, is in fancier Macs.)

The **6502**, designed by MOS Technology (which has become part of Commodore), hides in old-fashioned cheap computers: the Apple 2 family, the Commodore 64 & 128, and the Atari XL & XE.

Let's see how their assemblers differ from SEXY ASS.

Number systems SEXY ASS assumes all numbers are written in the decimal system, unless preceded by a dollar sign (which means hexadecimal) or percent sign (which means binary).

68000 and 6502 assemblers resemble SEXY ASS, except that they don't understand percent signs and binary notation. Some stripped-down 6502 assemblers don't understand the decimal system either: they require all numbers to be in hexadecimal.

The 8088 assembler comes in two versions:

> The full version of the 8088 assembler is called the **Microsoft Macro ASseMbler (MASM)**. It lists for $150, but discount dealers sell it for just $83. It assumes all numbers are written in the decimal system, unless followed by an H (which means hexadecimal) or B (which means binary). For example, the number twelve can be written as 12 or as 0CH or as 1100B. It requires each number to begin with a digit: so to say twelve in hexadecimal, instead of saying CH you must say 0CH.
>
> A stripped-down 8088 assembler, called the **DEBUG mini-assembler**, is part of DOS; so you get it at no extra charge when you buy DOS. It requires all numbers to be written in hexadecimal. For example, it requires the number twelve to be written as C. Do *not* put a dollar sign or H next to the C.

Accumulator Each microprocessor contains *several* accumulators, so you must say *which* accumulator to use. The main 8-bit accumulator is called "A" in the 6502, "AL" in the 8088, and "D0.B" in the 68000.

Labels SEXY ASS and the other full assemblers let you begin a line with a label, such as FRED. For the 8088 full assembler (MASM), add a colon after FRED. Mini-assemblers (such as 8088 DEBUG) don't understand labels.

Commands Here's how to translate from SEXY ASS to the popular assemblers:

Computer's action	SEXY ASS	6502	68000	8088 MASM
put 25 in accumulator	LOAD #$25	LDA #$25	MOVE.B #$25,D0	MOV AL,25H
copy location 7000 to accumulator	LOAD $7000	LDA $7000	MOVE.B $7000,D0	MOV AL,[7000H]
copy accumulator to location 7000	STORE $7000	STA $7000	MOVE.B D0,$7000	MOV [7000H],AL
add location 7000 to accumulator	ADD $7000	ADC $7000	ADD.B $7000,D0	ADD AL,[7000H]
subtract location 7000 from acc.	SUB $7000	SBC $7000	SUB.B $7000,D0	SUB AL,[7000H]
increment accumulator	INC	ADC #$1	ADDQ.B #1,D0	INC AL
decrement accumulator	DEC	SBC #$1	SUBQ.B #1,D0	DEC AL
put character C in accumulator	LOAD #"C"	LDA #'C	MOVE.B #'C',D0	MOV AL,"C"
jump to FRED	JUMP FRED	JMP FRED	JMP FRED	JMP FRED
jump, if negative, to FRED	JUMPN FRED	BMI FRED	BMI FRED	JS FRED
jump, if carry, to FRED	JUMPC FRED	BCS FRED	BCS FRED	JC FRED
jump, if zero, to FRED	JUMPZ FRED	BEQ FRED	BEQ FRED	JZ FRED
jump, if neg. lowered, to FRED	JUMPNL FRED	BPL FRED	BPL FRED	JNS FRED
jump, if carry lowered, to FRED	JUMPCL FRED	BCC FRED	BCC FRED	JNC FRED
jump, if zero lowered, to FRED	JUMPZL FRED	BNE FRED	BNE FRED	JNZ FRED

Notice that in 6502 assembler, each mnemonic (such as LDA) is three characters long.

To refer to an ASCII character, SEXY ASS and 8088 MASM put the character in quotes, like this: "C". 68000 assembler uses apostrophes instead, like this: 'C'. 6502 assembler uses just a single apostrophe, like this: 'C.

Instead of saying "jump if", 6502 and 68000 programmers say "branch if" and use mnemonics that start with B instead of J. For example, they use mnemonics such as BMI (which means "Branch if MInus"), BCS ("Branch if Carry Set"), and BEQ ("Branch if EQual to zero").

To make the 68000 manipulate a byte, put ".B" after the mnemonic. (If you say ".W" instead, the computer will manipulate a 16-bit word instead of a byte. If you say ".L" instead, the computer will manipulate long data containing 32 bits. If you don't specify ".B" or ".W" or ".L", the assembler assumes you mean ".W".)

8088 assemblers require you to put each memory location in brackets. So whenever you refer to location 7000 hexadecimal, you put the 7000H in brackets, like this: [7000H].

Debug

When you buy PC-DOS for your IBM PC (or MS-DOS for your clone), you get a disk that contains many DOS files. One of the DOS files is called **DEBUG**. It helps you debug your software and hardware.

It lets you type special debugger commands. It also lets you type commands in assembly language.

How to start

Press the CAPS LOCK key, so that everything you type will be capitalized. At the C prompt, type the word DEBUG, so your screen looks like this:

```
C:\>DEBUG
```

When you press the ENTER key after DEBUG, the computer will print a hyphen, like this:

```
-
```

After the hyphen, you can give any DEBUG command.

Registers

To see what's in the CPU registers, type an R after the hyphen, so your screen looks like this:

```
-R
```

When you press the ENTER key after the R, the computer will print:

```
AX=0000  BX=0000  CX=0000  DX=0000
```

That means the main registers (which are called AX, BX, CX, and DX) each contain hexadecimal 0000. Then the computer will tell you what's in the other registers, which are called SP, BP, SI, DI, DS, ES, SS, CS, IP, and FLAGS. Finally, the computer will print a hyphen, after which you can type another command.

Editing the registers

To change what's in register BX, type RBX after the hyphen, so your screen looks like this:

```
-RBX
```

The computer will remind you of what's in register BX, by saying:

```
BX 0000
:
```

To change BX to hexadecimal 7251, type 7251 after the colon, so your screen looks like this:

```
:7251
```

That makes the computer put 7251 into register BX.

To see that the computer put 7251 into register BX, say:

```
-R
```

That makes the computer tell you what's in all the registers. It will begin by saying:

```
AX=0000  BX=7251  CX=0000  DX=0000
```

Experiment! Try putting different hexadecimal numbers into the registers! To be safe, use just the registers AX, BX, CX, and DX.

Segment registers

The computer's RAM is divided into **segments**. The **segment registers** (DS, ES, SS, and CS) tell the computer which segments to use.

Do *not* change the numbers in the segment registers! Changing them will make the computer use the wrong segments of the RAM and wreck your DOS and disks.

The CS register is called the **code segment** register. It tells the computer which RAM segment to put your programs in. For example, if the CS register contains the hexadecimal number 0AD2, the computer will put your programs in segment number 0AD2.

Mini-assembler

To use assembly language, type A100 after the hyphen, so your screen looks like this:

```
-A100
```

The computer will print the code segment number, then a colon, then 0100. For example, if the code segment register contains the hexadecimal number 0AD2, the computer will print:

```
0AD2:0100
```

Now you can type an assembly-language program!

For example, suppose you want to move the hexadecimal number 2794 to register AX and move 8156 to BX. Here's the assembly-language program:

```
MOV AX,2794
MOV BX,8156
```

Type that program. As you type it, the computer will automatically put a segment number and memory location in front of each line, so your screen will look like this:

```
0AD2:0100 MOV AX,2794
0AD2:0103 MOV BX,8156
0AD2:0106
```

After the 0AD2:0106, press the ENTER key. The computer will stop using assembly language and will print a hyphen.

After the hyphen, type G=100 106, so your screen looks like this:

```
-G=100 106
```

That tells the computer to run your assembly-language program, going from location 100 to location 106, so the computer will start at location 100 and stop when it reaches memory location number 106.

After running the program, the computer will tell you what's in the registers. It will print:

```
AX=2794  BX=8156  CX=0000  DX=0000
```

It will also print the numbers in all the other registers.

Listing your program

To list your program, type U100 after the hyphen, so your screen looks like this:

```
-U100
```

The U stands for "Unassemble", which means "list". The computer will list your program, beginning at line 100. The computer will begin by saying:

```
0AD2:0100 B89427    MOV    AX,2794
0AD2:0103 BB5681    MOV    BX,8156
```

The top line consists of three parts. The left part (0AD2:0100) is the address in memory. The right part (MOV AX, 2794) is the assembly-language instruction beginning at that address.

The middle part (B89427) is the machine-language translation of MOV AX,2794. That middle part begins with B8, which is the machine-language translation of MOV AX. Then comes 9427, which is the machine-language translation of 2794; notice how machine language puts the digits in a different order than assembly language.

The machine-language version, B89427, occupies three bytes of RAM. The first byte (address 0100) contains the hexadecimal number B8; the next byte (address 0101) contains the hexadecimal number 94; the final byte (address 0102) contains the hexadecimal number 27.

So altogether, the machine-language version of MOV AX,2794 occupies addresses 0100, 0101, and 0102. That's why the next instruction (MOV BX,8156) begins at address 0103.

After the computer prints that analysis of your program, the computer will continue by printing an analysis of the next several bytes of memory also. Altogether, the computer will print an analysis of addresses up through 011F. What's in those addresses depends on which program your computer was running before you ran this one.

Editing your program

To edit line 0103, type:

```
-A103
```

Then type the assembly-language command you want for location 103.

When you finish the command and press the ENTER key, the computer will give you an opportunity to edit the next line (106). If you don't want to edit or create a line 106, press the ENTER key again.

After editing your program, list it (by typing U100), to make sure you edited correctly.

Arithmetic

This assembly-language program does arithmetic:

```
MOV AX,7
ADD AX,5
```

To feed that program to the computer, say A100 after the hyphen, then type the program, then press the ENTER key an extra time, then say G=100 106.

That program's top line moves the number 7 into the AX register. The next line adds 5 to the AX register, so the number in the AX register becomes twelve. In hexadecimal, twelve is written as C, so the computer will say:

```
AX=000C
```

The computer will also say what's in the other registers.

The opposite of ADD is SUB, which means subtract. For example, if you say —

```
SUB AX,3
```

the computer will subtract 3 from the number in the AX register, so the number in the AX register becomes smaller.

To add 1 to the number in the AX register, you can say:

```
ADD AX,1
```

For a short cut, say this instead:

```
INC AX
```

That tells the computer to INCrement the AX register, by adding 1.

To subtract 1 from the number in the AX register, you can say:

```
SUB AX,1
```

For a short cut, say this instead —

```
DEC AX
```

which means "DECrement the AX register".

Half registers

A register's left half is called the **high part**. The register's right half is called the **low part**.

For example, if the AX register contains 9273, the register's high part is 92, and the low part is 73.

The AX register's high part is called "A high" or AH. The AX register's low part is called "A low" or AL.

Suppose the AX register contains 9273 and you say:

```
MOV AH,41
```

The computer will make AX's high part be 41, so AX becomes 4173.

Copying to memory

Let's program the computer to put the hexadecimal number 52 into memory location 7000.

This command *almost* works:

```
MOV [7000],52
```

In that command, the brackets around the 7000 mean "memory location". That command says to move, into location 7000, the number 52.

Unfortunately, if you type that command, the computer will gripe, because the computer can't handle two numbers simultaneously (7000 and 52).

Instead, you split that complicated command into two simpler commands, each involving just one number. Instead of trying to move 52 directly into location 7000, first move 52 into a register (such as AL), then copy that register into location 7000, like this:

```
MOV AL,52
MOV [7000],AL
```

After running that program, you can prove the 52 got into location 7000, by typing:

```
-E7000
```

That makes the computer examine location 7000. The computer will find 52 there and print:

```
0AD2:7000 52.
```

That means: segment 0AD2's 7000th location contains 52.

If you change your mind and want it to contain 53 instead, type 53 after the period.

Next, press the ENTER key, which makes the computer print a hyphen, so you can give your next DEBUG command.

Interrupt 21

Here's how to write an assembly-language program that prints the letter C on the screen.

The ASCII code number for "C" is hexadecimal 43. Put 43 into the DL register:

```
0AD2:0100 MOV DL,43
```

The DOS code number for "screen output" is 2. Put 2 into the AH register:

```
0AD2:0102 MOV AH,2
```

To make the computer use the code numbers you put into the DL and AH registers, tell the computer to do DOS interrupt subroutine #21:

```
0AD2:0104 INT 21
```

So altogether, the program looks like this:

```
0AD2:0100 MOV DL,43
0AD2:0102 MOV AH,2
0AD2:0104 INT 21
0AD2:0106
```

To make the computer do that program, say G=100 106. The computer will obey the program, so your screen will say:

```
C
```

After running the program, the computer will tell you what's in all the registers. You'll see that DL has become 43 (because of line 100), AH has become 02 (because of line 102), and AL has become 43 (because INT 21 automatically makes the computer copy DL to AL). Then the computer will print a hyphen, so you can give another DEBUG command.

Instead of printing just C, let's make the computer print CCC. Here's how. Put the code numbers for "C" and "screen output" into the registers:

```
0AD2:0100 MOV DL,43
0AD2:0102 MOV AH,02
```

Then tell DOS to use those code numbers, three times:

```
0AD2:0104 INT 21
0AD2:0106 INT 21
0AD2:0108 INT 21
0AD2:010A
```

To run that program, say G=100 10A. The computer will print:

```
CCC
```

Jumps

Here's how to make the computer print C repeatedly, so that the entire screen gets filled with C's.

Put the code numbers for "C" and "screen output" into the registers:

```
0AD2:0100 MOV DL,43
0AD2:0102 MOV AH,02
```

In line 104, tell DOS to use those code numbers:

```
0AD2:0104 INT 21
```

To create a loop, jump back to line 104:

```
0AD2:0106 JMP 104
```

Altogether, the program looks like this:

```
0AD2:0100 MOV DL,43
0AD2:0102 MOV AH,03
0AD2:0104 INT 21
0AD2:0106 JMP 104
0AD2:0108
```

To run that program, say G=100 108. The computer will print C repeatedly, so the whole screen gets filled with C's. To abort the program, tap the BREAK key while holding down the CONTROL key.

Interrupt 20

I showed you this program, which makes the computer print the letter C:

```
0AD2:0100 MOV DL,43
0AD2:0102 MOV AH,2
0AD2:0104 INT 21
0AD2:0106
```

If you run that program by saying G=100 106, the computer will print C and then tell you what's in all the registers.

Instead of making the computer tell you what's in all the registers, let's make the computer say:

```
Program terminated normally
```

To do that, make the bottom line of your program say INT 20, like this:

```
0AD2:0100 MOV DL,43
0AD2:0102 MOV AH,2
0AD2:0104 INT 21
0AD2:0106 INT 20
0AD2:0108
```

The INT 20 makes the computer print "Program terminated normally" and then end, without printing a message about the registers.

To run the program, just say G=100. You do *not* have to say G=100 108, since the INT 20 ends the program before the computer reaches 108 anyway. The program makes the computer print:

```
C
Program terminated normally
```

Strings

This program makes the computer print the string "I LOVE YOU":

```
0AD2:0100 MOV DX,109
0AD2:0103 MOV AH,9
0AD2:0105 INT 21
0AD2:0107 INT 20
0AD2:0109 DB "I LOVE YOU$"
0AD2:0114
```

The bottom line contains the string to be printed: "I LOVE YOU$". Notice you must end the string with a dollar sign. In that line, the DB stands for Define Bytes.

Here's how the program works. The top line puts the string's line number (109) into DX. The next line puts 9, which is the code number for "string printing", into AH. The next line (INT 21) makes the computer use the line number and code number to do the printing. The next line (INT 20) makes the program print "Program terminated normally" and end.

When you run the program (by typing G=100), the computer will print:

```
I LOVE YOU
Program terminated normally
```

If you try to list the program by saying U100, the listing will look strange, because the computer can't list the DB line correctly. But even though the listing will look strange, the program will still run fine.

Saving your program

After you've created an assembly-language program, you can copy it onto your hard disk. Here's how.

First, make sure the program ends by saying INT 20, so that the program terminates normally.

Next, invent a name for the program. The name should end in .COM. For example, to give your program the name LOVER.COM, type this:

```
-NLOVER.COM
```

Put 0 into register BX (by typing -RBX and then :0).

Put the program's length into register CS. For example, since the program above starts at line 0100 and ends at line 0114 (which is blank), the program's length is "0114 minus 0100", which is 14; so put 14 into register CX (by typing -RCX and then :14).

Finally, say -W, which makes the computer write the program onto the hard disk. The computer will say:

```
Writing 0014 bytes
```

Quitting

When you finish using DEBUG, tell the computer to quit, by typing a Q after the hyphen. When you press the ENTER key after the Q, the computer will quit using DEBUG and say:

```
C:\>
```

Then give any DOS command you wish.

If you used assembly language to create a program called LOVER.COM, you can run it by just typing:

```
C:\>LOVER
```

The computer will run the program and say:

```
I LOVE YOU
```

Then the computer will print "C:\>" again, so you can give another DOS command.

Notice that the computer doesn't bother to print a message saying "Program terminated normally". (It prints that message just when you're in the middle of using DEBUG.)

Now you know how to write assembly-language programs. Dive in! Write your own programs!

Inside the CPU

Let's peek inside the CPU and see what lurks within!

Program counter

Each CPU contains a special register called the **program counter**.

The program counter tells the CPU which line of your program to do next. For example, if the program counter contains the number 6 (written in binary), the CPU will do the line of your program that's stored in the 6th memory location.

More precisely, here's what happens if the program counter contains the number 6....

A. The CPU moves the content of the 6th memory location to the CPU's **instruction register**. (That's called **fetching** the instruction.)

B. The CPU checks whether the instruction register contains a complete instruction written in machine language. If not — if the instruction register contains just *part* of a machine-language instruction — the CPU fetches the content of the 7th memory location also. (The instruction register is large enough to hold the content of memory locations 6 and 7 simultaneously.) If the instruction register still doesn't contain a complete instruction, the CPU fetches the content of the 8th memory location also. If the instruction register still doesn't contain a complete instruction, the CPU fetches the content of the 9th memory location also.

C. The CPU changes the number in the program counter. For example, if the CPU has fetched from the 6th and 7th memory locations, it makes the number in the program counter be 8; if the CPU has fetched from the 6th, 7th, and 8th memory locations, it makes the number in the program counter be 9. (That's called **updating the program counter**.)

D. The CPU figures out what the instruction means. (That's called **decoding** the instruction.)

E. The CPU obeys the instruction. (That's called **executing** the instruction.) If it's a "GO TO" type of instruction, the CPU makes the program counter contain the address of the memory location you want to go to.

After the CPU completes steps A, B, C, D, and E, it looks at the program counter and moves on to the next instruction. For example, if the program counter contains the number 9 now, the CPU does steps A, B, C, D, and E again, but by fetching, decoding, and executing the 9th memory location instead of the 6th.

The CPU repeats steps A, B, C, D, and E again and again; each time, the number in the program counter changes. Those five steps form a loop, called the **instruction cycle**.

Arithmetic/logic unit

The CPU contains two parts: the **control unit** (which is the boss) and the **arithmetic/logic unit (ALU)**. When the control unit comes to step D of the instruction cycle, and decides some arithmetic or logic needs to be done, it sends the problem to the ALU, which sends back the answer.

Here's what the ALU can do:

Name of operation	Example	Explanation
plus, added to, +	10001010 +10001001 100010011	add, but remember that 1+1 is 10 in binary
minus, subtract, -	10001010 -10001001 00000001	subtract, but remember that 10-1 is 1 in binary
negative, -, the two's complement of	-10001010 01110110	*left of the rightmost 1,* do this: replace each 0 by 1, and each 1 by 0
not, ~, the complement of, the one's complement of	~10001010 01110101	replace each 0 by 1, and each 1 by 0
and, &, ∧	10001010 ∧10001001 10001000	put 1 wherever both original numbers had 1
or, inclusive or, ∨	10001010 ∨10001001 10001011	put 1 wherever some original number had 1
eXclusive OR, XOR, ⩛	10001010 ⩛10001001 00000011	put 1 wherever the original numbers differ

Also, the ALU can shift a register's bits. For example, suppose a register contains 10111001. The ALU can shift the bits toward the right:

```
before  10111001
after   01011100
```

It can shift the bits toward the left:

```
before  10111001
after   01110010
```

It can rotate the bits toward the right:

```
before  10111001
after   11011100
```

It can rotate the bits toward the left:

```
before  10111001
after   01110011
```

It can shift the bits toward the right **arithmetically**:

```
before  10111001
after   11011100
```

It can shift the bits toward the left arithmetically:

```
before  10111001
after   11110010
```

Doubling a number is the same as shifting it left arithmetically. For example, doubling six (to get twelve) is the same as shifting six left arithmetically:

```
six     00000110
twelve  00001100
```

Halving a number is the same as shifting it right arithmetically. For example, halving six (to get three) is the same as shifting six right arithmetically:

```
six     00000110
three   00000011
```

Halving negative six (to get negative three) is the same as shifting negative six right arithmetically:

```
negative six    11111010
negative three  11111101
```

Using the ALU, the control unit can do operations such as:

A. Find the number in the 6th memory location, and move its negative to a register.
B. Change the number in a register, by adding to it the number in the 6th memory location.
C. Change the number in a register, by subtracting from it the number in the 6th memory location.

Most computers require each operation to have one source and one destination. In operations A, B, and C, the source is the 6th memory location; the destination is the register.

The control unit can*not* do a command such as "add together the number in the 6th memory location and the number in the 7th memory location, and put the sum in a register", because that operation would require two sources. Instead, you must give two shorter commands:

1. Move the number in the 6th memory location to the register.
2. Then add to that register the number in the 7th memory location.

Flags

The CPU contains a **flag register**, which comments on what the CPU is doing. In a typical CPU, the flag register has six bits, named as follows:

> the Negative bit
> the Zero bit
> the Carry bit
> the Overflow bit
> the Priority bit
> the Privilege bit

When the CPU performs an operation (such as addition, subtraction, shifting, rotating, or moving), the operation has a source and a destination. The number that goes into the destination is the operation's **result**. The CPU automatically analyzes that result.

Negative bit If the result is a negative number, the CPU turns on the **Negative bit**. In other words, it makes the Negative bit be 1. (If the result is a number that's *not* negative, the CPU makes the Negative bit be 0.)

Zero bit If the result is zero, the CPU turns on the **Zero bit**. In other words, it makes the Zero bit be 1.

Carry bit When the ALU computes the result, it also computes an extra bit, which becomes the **Carry bit**.

For example, here's how the ALU adds 7 and -4:

```
7 is                    00000111
-4 is                   11111100
binary addition gives  100000011
                       (Carry)(result)
```

So the result is 3, and the Carry bit becomes 1.

Overflow bit If the ALU can't compute a result correctly, it turns on the **Overflow bit**.

For example, in elementary school you learned that 98+33 is 131; so in binary, the computation should look like this:

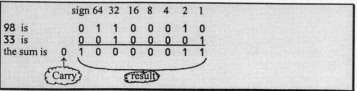

	128	64	32	16	8	4	2	1
98 is		1	1	0	0	0	1	0
33 is			1	0	0	0	0	1
the sum is	1	0	0	0	0	0	1	1, which is **131**

But here's what an 8-bit ALU will do:

	sign	64	32	16	8	4	2	1
98 is	0	1	1	0	0	0	1	0
33 is	0	0	1	0	0	0	0	1
the sum is	0	1	0	0	0	0	1	1

Carry   result

Unfortunately, the result's leftmost 1 is in the position marked **sign**, instead of the position marked 128; so the result looks like a negative number.

To warn you that the result is incorrect, the ALU turns on the Overflow bit. If you're programming in a language such as BASIC, the interpreter or compiler keeps checking whether the Overflow bit is on; when it finds that the bit's on, it prints the word OVERFLOW.

Priority bit While your program's running, it might be interrupted. Peripherals might interrupt, in order to input or output the data; the **real-time clock** might interrupt, to prevent you from hogging too much time, and to give another program a chance to run; and the computer's sensors might interrupt, when they sense that the computer is malfunctioning.

When something wants to interrupt your program, the CPU checks whether your program has priority, by checking the **Priority bit**. If the Priority bit is on, your program has priority and cannot be interrupted.

Privilege bit On a computer that's handling several programs at the same time, some operations are dangerous: if your program makes the computer do those operations, the other programs might be destroyed. Dangerous operations are called **privileged instructions**; to use them, you must be a **privileged user**.

When you walk up to a terminal attached to a large computer, and type HELLO or LOGIN, and type your user number, the operating system examines your user number to find out whether you are a privileged user. If you are, the operating system turns on the Privilege bit. When the CPU starts running your programs, **it refuses to do privileged instructions unless the Privilege bit is on**.

Microcomputers omit the Privilege bit, and can't prevent you from giving dangerous commands. But since the typical microcomputer has just one terminal, the only person your dangerous command can hurt is yourself.

Levels of priority & privilege Some computers have *several* levels of priority and privilege.

If your priority level is "moderately high", your program is immune from most interruptions, but not from all of them. If your privilege level is "moderately high", you can order the CPU to do most of the privileged instructions, but not all of them.

To allow those fine distinctions, large computers devote *several* bits to explaining the priority level, and *several* bits to explaining the privilege level.

Where are the flags? The bits in the flag register are called the **flags**. To emphasize that the flags comment on your program's status, people sometimes call them **status flags**.

In the CPU, the program counter is next to the flag register. Instead of viewing them as separate registers, some programmers consider them to be parts of a single big register, called the **program status word**.

Tests You can give a command such as, "Test the 3rd memory location". The CPU will examine the number in the 3rd memory location. If that number is negative, the CPU will turn on the Negative bit; if that number is zero, the CPU will turn on the Zero bit.

You can give a command such as, "Test the difference between the number in the 3rd register and the number in the 4th. The CPU will adjust the flags according to whether the difference is negative or zero or carries or overflows.

Saying "if" The CPU uses the flags when you give a command such as, "If the Negative bit is on, go do the instruction in memory location 6".

Speed

Computers are fast. To describe computer speeds, programmers use these words:

Word	Abbreviation	Meaning
millisecond	msec or ms	thousandth of a second; 10^{-3} seconds
microsecond	μsec or μs	millionth of a second; 10^{-6} seconds
nanosecond	nsec or ns	billionth of a second; 10^{-9} seconds
picosecond	psec or ps	trillionth of a second; 10^{-12} seconds

1000 picoseconds is a nanosecond; 1000 nanoseconds is a microsecond; 1000 microseconds is a millisecond; 1000 milliseconds is a second.

Earlier, I explained that the **instruction cycle** has five steps:

A. Fetch the instruction.
B. Fetch additional parts for the instruction.
C. Update the program counter.
D. Decode the instruction.
E. Execute the instruction.

The total time to complete the instruction cycle is about a microsecond. The exact time depends on the quality of the CPU, the quality of the main memory, and the difficulty of the instruction, but usually lies between .1 microseconds and 10 microseconds.

Here are 5 ways to make the computer act more quickly:

Method	Meaning
multiprocessing	The computer holds more than one CPU. (All the CPUs work simultaneously. They share the same main memory. The operating system decides which CPU works on which program. The collection of CPUs is called a **multiprocessor**.)
instruction lookahead	While the CPU is finishing an instruction cycle (by doing steps D and E), it simultaneously begins working on the next instruction cycle (steps A and B).
array processing	The CPU holds at least 16 ALUs. (All the ALUs work simultaneously. For example, when the control unit wants to solve 16 multiplication problems, it sends each problem to a separate ALU; the ALUs compute the products simultaneously. The collection of ALUs is called an **array processor**.)
parallel functional units	The ALU is divided into several functional units: an addition unit, a multiplication unit, a division unit, a shift unit, etc. All the units work simultaneously; while one unit is working on one problem, another unit is working on another.
pipeline architecture	The ALU (or each ALU functional unit) consists of a "first stage" and a "second stage". When the control unit sends a problem to the ALU, the problem enters the first stage, then leaves the first stage and enters the second stage. But while the problem is going through the second stage, a new problem starts going through the first stage. (Such an ALU is called a **pipeline processor**.)

Parity

Most large computers put an extra bit at the end of each memory location. For example, a memory location in the PDP-10 holds 36 bits, but the PDP-10 puts an extra bit at the end, making 37 bits altogether. The extra bit is called the **parity bit**.

If the number of ones in the memory location is even, the CPU turns the parity bit on. If the number of ones in the memory location is odd, the CPU turns the parity bit off.

For example, if the memory location contains these 36 bits —

```
000000000100010000001100000000000000
```

there are 4 ones, so the number of ones is even, so the CPU turns the parity bit on:

If the memory location contains these 36 bits instead —

```
000000000100010000000100000000000000
```

there are 3 ones, so the number of ones is odd, so the CPU turns the parity bit off:

Whenever the CPU puts data into the main memory, it also puts in the parity bit. Whenever the CPU grabs data from the main memory, it checks whether the parity bit still matches the content.

If the parity bit doesn't match, the CPU knows there was an error, and tries once again to grab the content and the parity bit. If the parity bit disagrees with the content again, the CPU decides that the memory is broken, refuses to run your program, prints a message saying PARITY ERROR, and then sweeps through the whole memory, checking the parity bit of every location; if the CPU finds another parity error (in your program or anyone else's), the CPU shuts off the whole computer.

Cheap microcomputers (such as the Apple 2c and Commodore 64) lack parity bits, but the IBM PC has them.

UAL

Universal Assembly Language (UAL) is a notation I invented that makes programming in assembly language easier.

UAL uses these symbols:

Symbol	Meaning
M5	the number in the 5th memory location
R2	the number in the 2nd register
P	the number in the program counter
N	the Negative bit
Z	the Zero bit
C	the Carry bit
V	the oVerflow bit
PRIORITY	the PRIORITY bits
PRIVILEGE	the PRIVILEGE bits
F	the content of the entire flag register
F[5]	the 5th bit in the flag register
R2[5]	the 5th bit in R2
R2[LEFT]	the left half of R2; in other words, the left half of the data in the 2nd register
R2[RIGHT]	the right half of R2
M5 M6	long number whose left half is in 5th memory location, right half is in 6th location

Here are the UAL statements:

Statement	Meaning
R2=7	Let number in the 2nd register be 7 (by moving 7 into the 2nd register).
R2=M5	Copy the 5th memory location's contents into the 2nd register.
R2= = M5	Exchange R2 with M5. (Put 5th location's content into 2nd register and vice versa.)
R2=R2+M5	Change the integer in 2nd register, by adding to it the integer in 5th location.
R2=R2-M5	Change the integer in 2nd register, by subtracting the integer in 5th location.
R2=R2*M5	Change the integer in 2nd register, by multiplying it by integer in 5th location.
R2 REM R3=R2/M5	Change R2, by dividing it by the integer M5. Put division's remainder into R3.
R2=-M5	Let R2 be the negative of M5.
R2=NOT M5	Let R2 be the one's complement of M5.
R2=R2 AND M5	Change R2, by performing the AND operation.
R2=R2 OR M5	Change R2, by performing the OR operation.
R2=R2 XOR M5	Change R2, by performing the XOR operation.
SHIFTL R2	Shift left.
SHIFTR R2	Shift right.
SHIFTRA R2	Shift right arithmetically.
SHIFTR3 R2	Shift right, 3 times.
SHIFTR (R7) R2	Shift right, R7 times.
ROTATEL R2	Rotate left.
ROTATER R2	Rotate right.
TEST R2	Examine number in 2nd register, and adjust flag register's Negative and Zero bits.
TEST R2-R4	Examine the difference between R2 and R4, and adjust the flag register.
CONTINUE	No operation. Just continue on to the next instruction.
WAIT	Wait until an interrupt occurs.
IF R2<0, P=7	If the number in the 2nd register is negative, put 7 into the program counter.
IF R2<0, M5=3, P=7	If R2<0, do both of the following: let M5 be 3, and P be 7.

M5 can be written as M(5) or M(2+3). It can be written as M(R7), if R7 is 5 — in other words, if register 7 contains 5.

Addressing modes

Suppose you want the 2nd register to contain the number 6. You can accomplish that goal in one step, like this:

```
R2=6
```

Or you can accomplish it in two steps, like this:

```
M5=6
R2=M5
```

Or you can accomplish it in three steps, like this:

```
M5=6
M3=5
R2=M(M3)
```

Or you can accomplish it in an even weirder way:

```
M5=6
R3=1
R2=M(4+R3)
```

Each of those methods has a name. The first method (R2=6), which is the simplest, is called **immediate addressing**. The second method (R2=M5), which contains the letter M, is called **direct addressing**. The third method (R5=M(M3)), which contains the letter M twice, is called **indirect addressing**. The fourth method (R5=M(4+R3)), which contains the letter M and a plus sign, is called **indexed addressing**.

In each method, the 2nd register is the destination. In the last three methods, the 5th memory location is the source. In the fourth method, which involves R3, the 3rd register is called the **index register**, and R3 itself is called the **index**.

Each of those methods is called an **addressing mode**. So you've seen four addressing modes: immediate, direct, indirect, and indexed.

Program counter

To handle the program counter, the computer uses other addressing modes instead.

For example, suppose P (the number in the program counter) is 2073, and you want to change it to 2077. You can accomplish that goal simply, like this:

```
P=2077
```

Or you can accomplish it in a weirder way, like this:

```
P=P+4
```

Or you can accomplish it in an even weirder way, like this:

```
R3=20
P=R3 77
```

The first method (P=2077), which is the simplest, is called **absolute addressing**.

The second method (P=P+4), which involves addition, is called **relative addressing**. The "+4" is the **offset**.

The third method (P=R3 77) is called **base-page addressing**. R3 (which is 20) is called the **page number** or **segment number**, and so the 3rd register is called the **page register** or **segment register**.

The first **microprocessor** (CPU on a chip) was invented by Intel in 1971 and called the **Intel 4004**. Its accumulator was so short that it held just 4 bits! Later that year, Intel invented an improvement called the **Intel 8008**, whose accumulator held 8 bits. In 1973 Intel invented a further improvement, called the **Intel 8080**, which understood more op codes, contained more registers, handled more RAM (64K instead of 16K), and ran faster. Drunk on the glories of that 8080, Microsoft adopted the phone number VAT-8080, and the Boston Computer Society adopted the soberer phone number DOS-8080.

In 1978 Intel invented a further improvement, called the **8086**, which had a 16-bit accumulator and handled even more RAM & ROM (totalling 1 megabyte). Out of the 8086 came 16 wires (called the **data bus**), which transmitted 16 bits simultaneously from the accumulator to other computerized devices, such as RAM and disks. Since the 8086 had a 16-bit accumulator and 16-bit data bus, Intel called it a **16-bit CPU**.

But computerists complained that the 8086 was impractical, since nobody had developed RAM, disks, or other devices for the 16-bit data bus yet. So in 1979 Intel invented the **8088**, which understands the same machine language as the 8086 but has an 8-bit data bus. To transmit 16-bit data through the 8-bit bus, the 8088 sends 8 of the bits first, then sends the other 8 bits shortly afterwards. That technique of using a few wires (8) to imitate many (16) is called **multiplexing**.

When 16-bit data buses later became popular, Intel invented a slightly souped-up 8086, called the **80286** (nicknamed the **286**).

Then Intel invented a 32-bit version called the **80386** (nicknamed **386**). Intel also invented a multiplexed version called the **386SX**, which understands the same machine language as the 386 but transmits 32-bit data through a 16-bit bus (by sending 16 of the bits first, then sending the other 16). The letters "SX" mean "SiXteen-bit bus". The original 386, which has a 32-bit bus, is called the **386DX**; the letters "DX" mean "Double the siXteen-bit bus".

Then Intel invented a slightly souped-up 386DX, called the **486**. It comes in two versions: the fancy version (called the **486DX**) includes a **math coprocessor**, which is circuitry that understands commands about advanced math; the stripped-down version (called the **486SX**) lacks a math coprocessor.

Finally, Intel invented a souped-up 486DX, called a **Pentium**.

Here's how to use the 8088 and 8086. (The 286, 386, 486, and Pentium include the same features plus more.)

Registers

The CPU contains fourteen 16-bit registers: the **accumulator (AX)**, **base register (BX)**, **count register (CX)**, **data register (DX)**, **stack pointer** (which UAL calls **S** but Intel calls **SP**), **base pointer (BP)**, **source index (SI)**, **destination index (DI)**, **program counter** (which UAL calls **P** but Intel calls the **instruction pointer** or **IP**), **flag register** (which UAL calls **F**), **code segment (CS)**, **data segment (DS)**, **stack segment (SS)**, and **extra segment (ES)**.

In each of those registers, the sixteen bits are numbered from right to left, so the rightmost bit is called **bit 0** and the leftmost bit is called **bit fifteen**.

The AX register's low-numbered half (bits 0 through 7) is called **A low** (or **AL**). The AX register's high half (bits 8 through fifteen) is called **A high (AH)**.

In the flag register, bit 0 is the carry flag (which UAL calls **C**), bit 2 is for parity, bit 6 is the zero flag (**Z**), bit 7 is the negative flag (which UAL calls **N** but Intel calls **sign** or **S**), bit eleven is the overflow flag (**V**), bits 4, 8, 9, and ten are special (**auxiliary carry**, **trap**, **interrupts**, and **direction**), and the remaining bits are unused.

Memory locations

Each memory location contains a byte. In UAL, the 6th memory location is called **M6** or **M(6)**. The pair of bytes M7 M6 is called **memory word 6**, which UAL writes as **MW(6)**.

Instruction set

The next page shows the set of instructions that the 8088 understands. For each instruction, I've given the assembly-language mnemonic and its translation to UAL, where all numbers are hexadecimal.

The first line says that INC (which stands for INCrement) is the assembly-language mnemonic that means x=x+1. For example, INC AL means AL=AL+1.

The eighth line says that IMUL (which stands for Integer Multiply) is the assembly-language mnemonic that means x=x*y. For example, IMUL AX,BX means AX=AX*BX.

In most equations, you can replace the x and y by registers, half-registers, memory locations, numbers, or more exotic entities. To find out what you can replace x and y by, experiment!

For more details, read the manuals from Intel and Microsoft. They also explain how to modify an instruction's behavior by using flags, segment registers, other registers, and three **prefixes**: REPeat, SEGment, and LOCK.

Math

INCrement	x=x+1
DECrement	x=x-1
ADD	x=x+y
ADd Carry	x=x+y+C
SUBtract	x=x-y
SuBtract Borrow	x=x-y-C
MULtiply	x=x*y UNSIGNED
Integer MULtiply	x=x*y
DIVide	AX=AX/x UNSIGNED
Integer DIVide	AX=AX/x
NEGate	x=-x
Decimal Adjust Add	IF AL[RIGHT]>9, AL=AL+6
	IF AL[LEFT]>9, AL=AL+60
Decimal Adjust Subtr	IF AL[RIGHT]>9, AL=AL-6
	IF AL[LEFT]>9, AL=AL-60
Ascii Adjust Add	IF AL[RIGHT]>9, AL=AL+6, AH=AH+1
	AL[LEFT]=0
Ascii Adjust Subtract	IF AL[RIGHT]>9, AL=AL-6, AH=AH-1
	AL[LEFT]=0
Ascii Adjust Multiply	AH REM AL=AL/0A
Ascii Adjust Divide	AL=AL+(0A*AH)
	AH=0

Logic

AND	x=x AND y
OR	x=x OR y
XOR	x=x XOR y
CoMplement Carry	C=NOT C
SHift Left	SHIFTL(y) x
SHift Right	SHIFTR(y) x
Shift Arithmetic Right	SHIFTRA(y) x
ROtate Left	ROTATEL(y) x
ROtate Right	ROTATER(y) x
Rotate Carry Left	ROTATEL(y) C x
Rotate Carry Right	ROTATER(y) C x
CLear Carry	C=0
CLear Direction	DIRECTION=0

CLear Interrupts	INTERRUPTS=0
SeT Carry	C=1
SeT Direction	DIRECTION=1
SeT Interrupts	INTERRUPTS=1
TEST	TEST x AND y
CoMPare	TEST x-y
SCAn String Byte	TEST AL-M(DI); DI=DI+1-(2*DIRECTION)
SCAn String Word	TEST AX-MW(DI); DI=DI+2-(4*DIRECTION)
CoMPare String Byte	TEST M(SI)-M(DI)
	SI=SI+1-(2*DIRECTION)
	DI=DI+1-(2*DIRECTION)
CoMPare String Word	TEST MW(SI)-MW(DI)
	SI=SI+2-(4*DIRECTION)
	DI=DI+2-(4*DIRECTION)

Moving bytes

MOVe	x=y
Load AH from F	AH=F[RIGHT]
Store AH to F	F[RIGHT]=AH
Load register and DS	x=MW(y); DS=MW(y+2)
Load register and ES	x=MW(y); ES=MW(y+2)
LOaD String Byte	AL=M(SI); SI=SI+1-(2*DIRECTION)
LOaD String Word	AX=MW(SI); SI=SI+2-(4*DIRECTION)
STOre String Byte	M(DI)=AL; DI=DI+1-(2*DIRECTION)
STOre String Word	MW(DI)=AX; DI=DI+2-(4*DIRECTION)
MOVe String Byte	M(DI)=M(SI);
	DI=DI+1-(2*DIRECTION)
	SI=SI+1-(2*DIRECTION)
MOVe String Word	MW(DI)=MW(SI)
	DI=DI+2-(4*DIRECTION)
	SI=SI+2-(4*DIRECTION)
Convert Byte to Word	AH=-AL[7]
Convert Word to Dbl	DX=-AX[0F]
PUSH	S=S-2; MW(S)=x
PUSH F	S=S-2; MW(S)=F
POP	x=MW(S); S=S+2
POP F	F=MW(S); S=S+2
IN	x=PORT(y)
OUT	PORT(x)=y
ESCape	BUS=x
eXCHanGe	x= =y
XLATe	AL=M(BX+AL)
Load Effective Address	x=ADDRESS(y)

Program counter

JuMP	P=x
Jump if Zero	IF Z=1, P=x
Jump if Not Zero	IF Z=0, P=x
Jump if Sign	IF N=1, P=x
Jump if No Sign	IF N=0, P=x
Jump if Overflow	IF V=1, P=x
Jump if Not Overflow	IF V=0, P=x
Jump if Parity	IF PARITY=1, P=x
Jump if No Parity	IF PARITY=0, P=x
Jump if Below	IF C=1, P=x
Jump if Above or Eq	IF C=0, P=x
Jump if Below or Eq	IF C=1 OR Z=1, P=x
Jump if Above	IF C=0 AND Z=0, P=x
Jump if Greater or Eq	IF N=V, P=x
Jump if Less	IF N<>V, P=x
Jump if Greater	IF N=V AND Z=0, P=x
Jump if Less or Equal	IF N<>V OR Z=1, P=x
Jump if CX Zero	IF CX=0, P=x
LOOP	CX=CX-1; IF CX<>0, P=x
LOOP if Zero	CX=CX-1; IF CX<>0 AND Z=1, P=x
LOOP if Not Zero	CX=CX-1; IF CX<>0 AND Z=0, P=x
CALL	S=S-2; MW(S)=P; P=x
RETurn	P=MW(S); S=S+2
INTerrupt	S=S-6; MW(S)=P; MW(S+2)=CS; MW(S+4)=F
	P=MW(4*x); CS=MW(4*x+2)
	INTERRUPTS=0; TRAP=0
INTerrupt if Overflow	IF V=1, S=S-6, MW(S)=P, MW(S+2)=CS,
	MW(S+4)=F, P=MW(10), CS=MW(12),
	INTERRUPTS=0, TRAP=0
Interrupt RETurn	P=MW(S); CS=MW(S+2); F=MW(S+4); S=S+6
No Operation	CONTINUE
HaLT	WAIT
WAIT	WAIT FOR COPROCESSOR

ENDNOTES

Background

Computer experts know that when reading a computer book, the really interesting stuff is usually hidden in the back of the book, buried in the appendices, which are secret vaults full of fascinating treasures, hidden from the view of casual readers duped into assuming that the appendices contain "nothing important".

In this book, too, some of the most brilliant jewels are hidden in the appendices.

Here are the appendices. I hope you enjoy them. I was afraid to move them to the front of the book because some of them are tough, controversial. But so are computers!

Enjoy the final leg of your adventure.

MAINTENANCE

Prevent problems

These tips will help keep your computer in good shape, so you'll have fewer problems and need fewer repairs.

Hot weather

If possible, avoid using the computer in hot weather.

When the room's temperature rises above 93 degrees, the fan inside the computer has trouble cooling the computer sufficiently. Wait until the weather is cooler (such as late at night), or buy an air conditioner, or buy a window fan to put on your desk and aim at the computer, or use the computer for just an hour at a time (so that the computer doesn't have a chance to overheat).

Another problem in the summer is electrical brownouts, where air conditioners in your house or community consume so much electricity that not enough voltage gets to your computer.

Transporting your computer

Some parts inside the computer are delicate. Don't bang or shake the computer! If you need to move the computer to a different location, be gentle!

Before moving the computer, make backups: copy everything important from the computer's hard disk onto floppy disks. For example, copy all the documents, spreadsheets, and database files you created, and also copy AUTOEXEC.BAT, CONFIG.SYS, and COMMAND.COM.

Transporting by hand If you must move the computer to a different desk or building, be *very gentle* when you pick up the computer, carry it, and plop it down. Be especially gentle when walking on stairs and through doorways.

Transporting by car If you're transporting your computer by car, put the computer in the *front* seat, put a blanket underneath the computer, and drive slowly (especially around curves and over bumps).

Do *not* put the computer in the trunk, since the trunk has the least protection against bumps. If you have the original padded box that the computer came in, put the computer in it, since the box's padding is professionally designed to protect against bumps.

Transporting by air If you're transporting your computer by air, avoid checking the computer through the baggage department.

The baggage handlers will treat the computer as if it were a football, and their "forward pass" will make you pissed.

Instead, try to carry the computer with you on the plane, if the computer's small enough to fit under your seat or in the overhead bin. If the whole computer won't fit, carry as much of the computer as *will* fit (the keyboard, monitor, or system unit?) and check the rest as baggage. If you *must* check the computer as baggage, use the original padded box that the computer came in, or else find a giant box and put a *lot* of padding material in it.

When going through airport security, it's okay to let the security guards X-ray your computer and disks. Do *not* carry the computer and floppy disks in your hands as you go through the metal detector, since the magnetic field might erase your disks.

For best results, just tell the guards you have a computer and disks, Instead of running the computer and disks through detection equipment, the guards will inspect your stuff personally.

To make sure your computer doesn't contain a bomb, the guards might ask you to unscrew the computer or prove that it actually works. If your computer's a laptop and you need to prove it works, make sure you brought your batteries — and make sure the batteries are fully charged!

Since airport rules about baggage and security continually change, ask your airport for details before taking a trip.

Beware of theft. Crooks have used this trick:

A crook waits for you to put your laptop on the X-ray conveyor belt. Then the crook cuts in front of you and purposely gives himself trouble going through the metal detector (by having keys in his pocket). While he delays you and distracts security guards, his partner grabs your laptop off the conveyor belt and walks away with it.

Transporting by mail Computer companies have discovered that FedEx handles computers more carefully — and causes less damage — than the post office and UPS.

Parking the head If your computer is ancient (an 8088 or an early-vintage 286), it might have come with a program called **SHIPDISK** or **PARK**.

That program is *not* part of DOS; instead, the program comes on a floppy disk called "Utilities" or "Diagnostics".

That program does an activity called **parking the head**: it moves the hard drive's head to the disk's innermost track, where there's no data. Then if the head accidentally bangs against the disk, it won't scrape off any data.

If your computer came with a SHIPDISK or PARK program, run it before you transport the computer. After your journey, when you turn the computer back on, the head automatically unparks itself and reads whatever data you wish.

If your computer did *not* come with a SHIPDISK or PARK program, don't worry about it.

Modern disk drives park the head automatically whenever you turn the power off. For older disk drives, handling the computer gently is more important than parking the head. In any case, do *not* borrow a SHIPDISK or PARK program from a friend, since somebody else's program might assume the hard drive has a different number of tracks.

Repair shops use an extra-fancy PARK program: it tests the hard drive, determines how many tracks are on it, and then moves the head to the correct innermost track.

Save your work

When you're typing lots of info into a word-processing program or spreadsheet, the stuff you've typed is in the computer's RAM. Every ten minutes, copy that info onto the hard disk, by giving the Save command. (To learn how to give the Save command, read my word-processing and spreadsheet chapters.)

That way, if the computer breaks down (or you make a boo-boo), the hard disk will contain a copy of most of your work, and you'll need to retype at most ten minutes worth.

Don't trust automatic backups If your word-processor is modern, it has a feature called "automatic timed backup", which makes the computer automatically save your document every 10 minutes. Don't trust that automatic feature! It might be saving your latest error instead of what you want.

For example, if you accidentally wreck part of your document and then automatic timed backup kicks in, you've just replaced your good, saved document by a wrecked one, and the good one is gone forever. Give the Save command *manually*, so that *you*, not the computer, will decide when and what to save.

Split into chapters If you're using a word-processing program to type a book, split the book into chapters. Make each chapter be a separate file. That way, if something goes wrong with the file, you've lost just one chapter instead of the whole book.

Create disk space

Make sure your hard disk isn't full.

If you're running just DOS without Windows, make sure your hard disk has at least 2 megabytes of unused space. If you're running Windows 3 or 3.1 or 3.11, make sure your hard disk has at least 10 megabytes of unused space. If you're running Windows 95 or 98, make sure your hard disk has at least 30 megabytes of unused space.

If your hard disk is too full, some of your programs might act unreliably, because the programmers who wrote those programs were too lazy to check whether the programs would work on a hard disk that's so full. Some of those programs try to create temporary files on your hard disk; but if your hard disk is nearly full, the temporary files won't fit, and so the computer will gripe at you, act nuts, and seem broken.

Overly fancy software

Avoid buying and using software that adds many lines to your CONFIG.SYS and AUTOEXEC.BAT files.

The longer and more complicated your CONFIG.SYS and AUTOEXEC.BAT files are, the greater the chance that something will go wrong with them, and your computer will refuse to boot up.

To squeeze more data onto your hard disk, you can use a **compression program**, which stores your data as a compressed code that consumes less space.

The most famous compression programs are **Double Space** (which is part of DOS 6 & 6.2), **Drive Space** (which is part of DOS 6.22 and Windows 95 & 98), and **Stacker** (which inspired the others). Those programs are dangerous: if you accidentally erase them (or erase or modify the CONFIG.SYS file that mentions them), you won't be able to use *any* of the data on your hard disk! Avoid using them.

DOS 6, 6.2, 6.21, and 6.22 include two other dangerous routines: **Mem Maker** and **Smart Drive**. Avoid using them.

Mem Maker modifies your CONFIG.SYS and AUTOEXEC.BAT files so specific programs get put into specific places in RAM. It's supposed to make your computer run better but causes this headache: each time you buy another program that modifies CONFIG.SYS or AUTOEXEC.BAT, you must warn Mem Maker; if you forget to warn Mem Maker, the computer has a memory conflict and screws up.

Smart Drive tries to make your hard disk seem faster, by making part of your RAM be a **disk cache**, which holds a copy of your hard disk's recently-used sectors. When you tell the computer to deal with your hard disk, Smart Drive makes the computer try to use the disk cache instead of the hard disk, since the disk cache is faster. If you try to write to the hard disk, Smart Drive makes the computer write to the disk cache instead; later, when you seem to be pausing from using the computer (and scratching your head wondering what to do next), Smart Drive copies the disk cache's contents to the hard disk; but before Smart Drive copies to the hard disk, what if you turn off the computer, or the computer's hardware or software malfunctions? Then the hard disk's contents are incomplete and inconsistent. The entire hard disk can become unusable, especially if you've been using compression software, which renders your hard drive useless at the first sign of trouble. If you ignore my advice and decide to use Smart Drive anyway, wait 10 seconds before turning off your computer, to give Smart Drive a chance to copy the disk cache's contents to the hard disk.

Clean your hardware

Eventually, your computer will get covered with dust, dirt, cigarette smoke, pollen, spilled drink, spilled food, dead insects, dandruff, and other unmentionable body parts.

Once a month, clean the computer, to increase the happiness of the computer and the people who see it (you, colleagues, customers, and visitors). To make cleaning easier, many companies prohibit employees from smoking, drinking, or eating near the computer.

Easy cleaning

Before cleaning the computer, turn its power off.

Just take a paper towel, dampen it with plain water, and wipe grime off the keyboard, the monitor's screen, the monitor's case, and the system unit's case.

Do *not* dribble water into the electronics. That would cause a short circuit and corrosion. Put water just onto the paper towel, *not* directly onto the hardware.

Do *not* open the monitor, since it contains high voltages even when "off".

Don't use the computer until the water has dried.

Inside the system unit

If you wish to open the system unit's case, to remove dust from inside it, be careful not to give your computer a shock of static electricity. The computer's chips are delicate and can get destroyed by even the smallest spark. To avoid shocks, do this:

Avoid working on the computer in the winter, when the air is cold and the humidity is low. Wait until summer, when the air is warm and the humidity is high.

Avoid shuffling across the carpet in rubber-soled shoes. Remove your shoes and socks (so you look like a beach bum or hippie). Remove the carpet, or cover it with a plastic mat (or newspaper), or put anti-static spray on the carpet.

While working on the computer, keep it turned off but still plugged into a 3-prong grounded socket. Keep touching the outside of the computer's case, which will be grounded. You can also keep touching other big metal objects in the room — so you'll shock them instead of your computer.

Avoid directly touching the chips.

When fiddling inside the computer's case, make sure you don't loosen any of the cables inside, since if a cable gets loose you might forget which socket it belongs in and which direction it should be twisted in.

To remove dust, wipe it off — or just take a deep breath and blow, but try to avoid blowing spit.

Professional cleaning

That's how to clean your computer for free. Professional repair shops usually spend extra money:

Instead of using water, they use **isopropyl alcohol**, which dries faster.

Instead of using a paper towel, they use a **soft lint-free cloth**.

Instead of blowing from their mouths, they blow from a **can of compressed air**, bought at Radio Shack.

Instead of touching objects to dissipate static electricity, they wear an **electrostatic-discharge wrist strap (ESD wrist strap)**, which is a wrist strap that comes with a wire you can run from your wrist to a grounded metal object (such as the outside of a grounded computer case).

When cleaning a monitor's screen, do *not* use alcohol or traditional "glass cleaners", since they can harm the screen's anti-glare coating.

Clean your mouse

Here's how to clean the mouse's bottom and innards:

Turn the mouse upside down. Using your fingernail, scrape off any gunk you see. (Gunk tends to accumulate on the mouse's rubber strips or rubber feet.)

In the mouse's belly, you typically see a rubber ball, whose purpose is to roll on your desktop (or on your mouse pad). Remove the ball's circular cover (by turning the cover counterclockwise or sliding it toward you). Remove the ball.

On the ball, you'll probably see a little dust, dirt, hair, or food. Clean the ball by rubbing it against your clothes. (Oooooh! That felt Gooooo!) If you prefer, you can clean the ball by using water, but do *not* use alcohol, which can shrink the ball and make it lopsided.

Look inside the mouse, in the hole where the ball was. On the sides of that hole, you'll see two rollers (looking like rolling pins) that the ball is supposed to rub against. One of those rollers is for motion in the X direction (horizontal); the other roller is for motion in the Y direction (vertical). Dust and dirt are probably caked onto the middle of each roller. Scrape the dust and dirt off, by using your fingernail.

Then put the ball back into the mouse and put its cover back on (by turning the cover clockwise or sliding it away from you).

Clean your software

For about 20 years, I've been giving free help to folks whose computers got messed up. That extensive experience has taught me most computer problems can be solved by **software cleaning**: just remove any software routines that distract the computer from what you want to accomplish! If you remove those distractions, the computer can concentrate on accomplishing your goal. The computer's headaches — and yours — will disappear. The computer will run reliably — and faster.

Here's how to do software cleaning in the three most common operating-system environments: Windows 95&98, Windows 3.1, and DOS 6.2. (Windows Me is very similar to Windows 98; if you're using Windows Me, start following my instructions for Windows 98.)

Windows 95&98 cleaning

To make Windows 95&98 run better, you can use many methods. I'll start with the methods that are the simplest and most foolproof, then progress to methods that are more advanced and risky. To get free help using these methods and my other tricks (which are more bizarre), phone me anytime at 603-666-6644.

Shut down If the computer is on, try to shut it down properly: try to click Start, then Shut Down, then Yes, then turn the power off. (If you can't do that shut-down procedure properly, give up and just turn the power off.)

Wait for the computer to quiet down.

Start the computer again Turn the computer on. Wait for the Windows main screen to appear, so you see the Start button.

If the computer refuses to show you the Start button, go into **safe mode** by doing this procedure:

> Turn the computer on. *If you're using Windows 98*, immediately hold down the Ctrl key, and keep holding it down. (*If you're using Windows 95*, do this instead: immediately put your finger near the F8 key and watch carefully for the words "Starting Windows 95" to appear; they appear in white letters, on a black background, just *before* you see the clouds; when the words "Starting Windows 95" appear, press the F8 key immediately.)
>
> The computer will say "Microsoft Windows Startup Menu". From that menu, choose "Safe mode" (by pressing 3 and then pressing the ENTER key).
>
> After several minutes (be patient!), the computer should eventually say "Windows is running in safe mode". (If the computer refuses to say that, skip ahead to the section called "get to the C:\WINDOWS prompt".)
>
> Press the ENTER key. Now you see the "Start" button, but all four corners of the screen say "Safe mode". While you're in Safe mode, you can repair your computer's software but cannot use fancy features: you cannot use the CD-ROM, printer, sound, fancy colors, or tiny icons (you see big icons instead).

Close whatever is open Get out of any programs you're in (by clicking their X boxes). Close any windows that are open (by clicking their X boxes).

At the screen's bottom, to the right of the Start button, you might see some other buttons.

> **Narrow buttons** (narrower than the Start button) **are okay** (and commonly occur in Windows 98).
>
> If you see **a button that's very wide** (over twice as wide as the Start button), get rid of that button (by clicking it then clicking the X button that comes up).

Simplify the display Find a spot in the screen's middle where there's no icon yet. *Right*-click there (by using the mouse's *right*-hand button). From the pull-down menu that appears, left-click the bottom choice (which is "Properties"). You'll see the Display Properties window.

For Wallpaper, choose "None". Here's how:

> Look under the word "Wallpaper". You see a list of choices. Click the top choice, which should be "None". If you don't see "None" as a choice, make that choice appear by clicking the "▲", then click "None".

For Pattern, choose "None". Here's how:

> (If you're using Windows 98, begin by clicking "Pattern".) Look under the word "Pattern". You see a list of choices. Click the top choice, which should be "None". If you don't see "None" as a choice, make that choice appear by clicking the "▲", then click "None". (If you're using Windows 98, then click "OK".)

Click the "Screen Saver" tab (which is at the top of the window). Then **for Screen Saver, choose "None"**; here's how:

> Click the "▼", then click "None", which should be the top choice. If you don't see "None" as a choice, make that choice appear by clicking the "▲", then click "None".

Although patterns, wallpaper, and screensavers are cute fun, you should delete them (by choosing "none") because they consume RAM, slow down the computer, distract the computer, distract you, and are unnecessary (since all modern monitors are built well and don't need to be protected by screensavers).

Click the "Appearance" tab. Then **for Scheme, choose "Windows Standard"**; here's how:

> Click the "▼", then click "Windows Standard", which should be the third-from-bottom choice. If you don't see "Windows Standard" as a choice, make that choice appear by clicking the "▼", then click "Windows Standard".

Click the "Settings" tab. Then **for Color palette, choose "High Color 16-bit"** (for Windows 98) **or "256 Colors"** (for Windows 95). To do so, click the "▼". You see this list of choices:

Choice	Meaning	
16 Colors	2^4 colors	(= 16 colors)
256 Colors	2^8 colors	(= 256 colors)
High Color (16 bit)	2^{16} colors	(= 65,536 colors)
True Color (24 bit)	2^{24} colors	(= 16,777,216 colors)
True Color (32 bit)	2^{32} colors	(= 4,294,967,296 colors)

Click the choice you want.

> **"High Color 16-bit"** or **"256 Colors"** are the choices preferred by most programs. "High Color 16-bit" produces more colors than "256 Colors" but requires more hardware: more main RAM, more RAM on the video card, and a faster CPU chip. Since the typical Windows 95 computer is old and lacks that hardware, Windows 95 is typically used with just "256 Colors". The typical Windows 98 computer is advanced enough to handle "High Color", which is required for viewing fancy artwork and fancy video clips.
>
> "True Color 24-bit" and "True Color 32-bit" produce even more colors but run too slowly and consume too much RAM, so hardly any RAM is left to run the programs you want, and those programs stop working. Photographers and advanced artists occasionally try experimenting with them.
>
> "16 Color" uses the least RAM, works with even the worst video cards, works even if you have no video driver loaded, and runs the fastest, but 16 colors aren't enough to handle modern graphical programs.

For Desktop area, the safest choice is "640 by 480 pixels". That's the choice that's most likely to work. It's also the most pleasant choice if your screen is small (14-inch) or your eyesight is poor, since it makes all the characters appear as big as possible. To choose it, drag the slider to the left (by using the mouse).

Instead of choosing "640 by 480", you can choose higher numbers if your eyes are good and your screen is big and your video card has a reasonably large amount of RAM and your video drivers are correctly installed.

> **For a 15" screen, the most appropriate choice is " 800 by 600".**
> **For a 17" screen, the most appropriate choice is "1024 by 768".**
> **For a 19" screen, the most appropriate choice is "1280 by 1024".**

But if you have a 15", 17", or 19" screen and the "appropriate choice" doesn't work, drop down to 640 by 480, which always works though it's less pleasant.

Click "OK". If the computer says "The computer will now resize your desktop", do this:

> Press ENTER. Wait for the screen to look different, then immediately click "Yes" (before the image goes away).

Right-click in the screen's middle (where there are no icons). **Click "Arrange Icons"**, then click "by Name".

Check your total RAM
Windows 95 needs 4M of RAM to run at all, 8M of RAM to run reasonably, and 16M of RAM to run fast. Windows 98 need 16M of RAM to run at all, 32M of RAM to run reasonably, and 64M of RAM to run fast. If your RAM is less than the quantity needed for "fast", the main way you can make Windows run better is to buy more RAM.

To discover your total amount of RAM, right-click the "My Computer" icon, then click "Properties" and read the message on the screen. (When you finish reading it, click its X box.)

Clean up your hard disk
Double-click the Recycle Bin icon. You see the Recycle Bin window, which shows a list of what's in the Recycle Bin. To see the list better, maximize the window (by clicking the box next to its X box).

That's the list of files you said to get rid of. Those files are still on your hard disk and consuming the hard disk's space, until you **empty the Recycle Bin**.

If you're sharing the computer with friends, ask their permission before emptying the Recycle Bin.

If you're sure you don't need any of those files anymore, empty the entire Recycle Bin (by clicking "File" then "Empty Recycle Bin"). If you want to erase just *some* of those files, click the first file you want to erase, then (while holding down the Ctrl key) click each additional file you want to erase, then press the DELETE key then ENTER.

Then close the Recycle Bin window (by clicking its X box).

Next, **find out how full your hard disk is**. To find out, double-click the "My Computer" icon, then right-click the hard drive's icon (which says "C:"), then click "Properties". You see a pie chart. **Make sure the amount of free space (colored red) is at least 30,000,000 bytes and is at least 10% of the disk's total capacity.** If your free space is less, you're in danger of having the computer gradually slow down or quit functioning, so you should delete some files. Later, I'll explain the best way to delete unused programs.

Now remove any defects from your hard disk's directories. Here's how:

> While you're looking at the pie chart, click "Tools" then "Check Now". Click "Standard" (unless you have the patience to choose "Thorough", which will make you wait about an hour), then click "Start". That makes the computer **run the ScanDisk program**, which analyzes your hard disk. While the computer analyzes, choose "Discard" whenever the computer lets you. That makes the computer discard useless files. At the end of the ScanDisk process, the computer will say "ScanDisk Results". Press ENTER twice.

Next, **run the Defrag program**, by clicking "Defragment Now" then "Start". That makes the computer rearrange your hard disk's files, so you can access them faster.

Then press ENTER and close all windows (by clicking their X boxes).

Delete unused programs. Here's how:

> Click "Start" then "Settings" then "Control Panel". Double-click "Add/Remove Programs".
>
> You see a list of all programs that are on your hard disk and "designed for Windows 95 or 98". (You see the list's beginning; to see the rest of the list, use the scroll arrows at the list's right side.)
>
> In that list, if you find a program that you're sure you'll never use again (such as a lousy game), delete it as follows: click the program's name, then "Add/Remove", then follow the instructions on the screen. Then the computer will try to delete the program completely: the computer will deletes the program's folder, the program's icons, and (hopefully) all references to the program.
>
> Find and delete all other programs that you're sure you'll never use again. Then close all windows (by clicking their X boxes).

Examine the task list
Here's how to analyze what Windows is doing at any moment: **while holding down the Ctrl and Alt keys, tap the DELETE key** (just once, not twice).

You'll see the Close Program window. In it you see the **task list**. That's a list of all tasks that the computer is running at the moment.

If your computer is "clean" (not distracted by any extraneous tasks), the only tasks that should be on that task list are Explorer and maybe Systray. (If you're running in "Safe mode", the only task on the task list is Explorer.)

Explorer is needed because it gives you the desktop picture. Systray is optional: it creates the sound-volume icon at the screen's bottom-right corner, if your sound card is good enough to have its volume changed by software.

If your task list contains more than just Explorer and Systray, your computer should be pitied, since right now your computer is trying to run all the programs on the task list simultaneously! I've seen too many computers where the task list contains a dozen items: the poor computer is trying to run all those tasks simultaneously and it's amazing the computer hasn't **crashed** already! ("**Crashed**" means "stopped working".) The more tasks you have on the list, the more likely that your computer will crash, because each task consumes RAM and confuses the computer by interrupting its attention from the task you wanted to focus on.

Giving a computer a long task list is like giving a juggler too many knives to juggle: he might quit or die.

That's one of the many reasons **I hate companies such as Compaq, Packard Bell, and Dell: they put too many routines on the task list.** Their customers eventually complain that the computers don't run well and phone me to bail them out. **I prefer companies such as Quantex**, which keeps the task list short.

I also get annoyed by magazines who tell readers to buy all sorts of fancy routines that are supposed to make your computer "better". Though each routine is fine by itself, when you try to run them all simultaneously they interfere with each other and create crashes.

Although you can end a task by clicking the task's name and then the "End Task" button, that ends the task just *temporarily*. To end the task *permanently*, so it won't resurface the next time you boot up the computer, follow some of the strategies listed below....

Empty your StartUp folder
If you click on Start, then Programs, then StartUp (yeah, it's there, keep looking), you'll see what's in the StartUp folder. Each time you start running Windows, the computer automatically runs all the programs in the StartUp folder. (That folder is the Windows equivalent of DOS's AUTOEXEC.BAT file.)

On a clean machine (such as mine), the StartUp folder should be empty (so your task list stays short). Microsoft Office tends to put two items into the StartUp folder ("Microsoft Office Fast Start" and "Microsoft Office Find Fast Indexer"), but if you eliminate those two items Microsoft Office will still run fine.

Here's how to remove items from the StartUp folder....

> *Right*-click the Start button (by using the mouse's *right*-hand button), then click "Open", then double-click "Programs". You see a list of all folders that are in your Programs menu. (To see the list better, maximize its window.) Double-click "StartUp". You'll see icons for all the programs in the StartUp folder.
>
> To remove a program from the StartUp folder, click that program's icon then press the DELETE key then ENTER. (To remove *all* programs from the StartUp folder, do this: tap the A key while holding down the Ctrl key, then press the DELETE key then ENTER.)

If you're not sure whether to remove a program from the StartUp folder, go ahead and try it (after consulting with any friends who share your computer). Trying to remove a program from the StartUp folder is an experiment that's safe for three reasons:

> "Removing" an icon from the StartUp folder just sends the icon to the Recycle Bin, so you can restore the icon later if you change your mind. (To be extra-safe, tell your friends not to empty the Recycle Bin for several weeks, until you're sure your newly emptied StartUp folder makes you happy.)
>
> The icon you're sending to the Recycle Bin is just a *shortcut* icon (since it has a bent arrow on it) rather than the program itself.
>
> No items in the StartUp folder are ever needed to start Windows. In fact, Windows starts itself up before it bothers to look at the StartUp folder.

When you've finished, close all windows (by clicking their X boxes).

Remove unwanted networking

Click "Start" then "Settings" then "Control Panel". Double-click "Network". (If the computer says "Your network is not complete", press ENTER.)

You see a list of network components. Remove any components you don't need.

The typical computer communicates with other computers by using just an ordinary phone cord and an ordinary Internet Service Provider. Such a computer needs just two network components:

> **Dial-Up Adapter** (which teaches the computer how to use the phone cord)
> **TCP/IP** (which teaches the computer how to communicate with the Internet)

So for such a computer, keep just those two components and remove any others. (To remove a component, click the component's name and then click "Remove".)

If your computer is fancier, it needs more network components. For example, if your computer communicates with the Internet by using **America OnLine** (which is a non-standard Internet Service Provider), you must also keep a network component about **AOL**. If your computer communicates with the Internet by using a **cable modem** (which attaches to a cable-TV wire instead of a phone wire) or communicates with other computers by using an **Ethernet card and a local-area network (LAN)**, you must keep network components that teach the computer about those features.

Here's why you should remove components you're not using: your computer will run faster, stop asking for passwords to unused networks, and stop complaining about half-completed networks.

When you finish saying which components to remove, click "OK". (If the computer says "Your network is not complete", press ENTER. If the computer asks you to restart, let it restart.)

Get to the C:\WINDOWS prompt

To do more software cleaning, make the computer say "C:\WINDOWS>". Here's how.

If you started the computer normally (without having to use "safe mode"), do this:

> Click "Start" then "Programs" then "MS-DOS Prompt".
>
> If you see a black window, make it fill the whole screen by doing this: while holding down the Alt key, tap the ENTER key. (If you mess up, press Alt with ENTER again.)
>
> Now the whole screen is black (except for white writing on it). The screen says:
> `C:\WINDOWS>`

If you had to start the computer by using "safe mode" (or your computer was so messed up that even "safe mode" didn't work), do this instead:

> Try to shut down the computer properly: try to click Start, then Shut Down, then Yes, then turn the power off. (If you can't do that shut-down procedure properly, just be mean and turn the power off.) Wait for the computer to quiet down.
>
> Turn the computer back on. *If you're using Windows 98*, immediately hold down the Ctrl key, and keep holding it down. (*If you're using Windows 95*, do this instead: immediately put your finger near the F8 key and watch carefully for the words "Starting Windows 95" to appear; they appear in white letters, on a black background, just *before* you see the clouds; when the words "Starting Windows 95" appear, press the F8 key immediately.)
>
> The computer will say "Microsoft Windows Startup Menu". Near the menu's bottom, you'll see a choice called "Safe mode command prompt only". Choose that (by pressing that choice's number, which is usually 6 or 7, and then pressing the ENTER key).
>
> The computer will say:
> `C:\>`
> Type "cd windows", so your screen looks like this:
> `C:\>cd windows`
> At the end of that line, press the ENTER key. Then the screen looks like this:
> `C:\WINDOWS>`

Empty the TEMP folder

Your computer contains a WINDOWS folder. In that folder, you'll find a TEMP folder. It's supposed to hold "temporary" files.

Some programs temporarily put files into that TEMP folder. Those files are supposed to self-destruct when you finish running the program that created them, but sometimes the computer gets amnesia and forgets to help those files self-destruct. For example, suppose while you're using a program that created temporary files, the electricity suddenly goes out (or the computer crashes for some other reason); then the computer will forget to destroy those files.

After several months of using the computer, you'll discover that the TEMP folder still contains many files that the computer forgot to delete. Those old TEMP files waste space on your hard disk. They also make your computer slower, because whenever the computer needs to create a new TEMP file it must skip past all the TEMP files that are still there, to find free space.

You should delete those old TEMP files. Here's how....

After the "C:\WINDOWS", type "deltree temp" (which stands for "delete the tree of TEMP"), so your screen looks like this:

> `C:\WINDOWS>deltree temp`

Type that very carefully: after typing the word "deltree", make sure you press the SPACE bar and then the word "temp". (If you forget to type the word "temp", you'll delete all of Windows!) At the end of typing that line, press the ENTER key.

The computer will ask whether you're sure. Press the Y key, then the ENTER key. Then the computer will delete the TEMP folder.

Next, type "md temp", so your screen looks like this:

> `C:\WINDOWS>md temp`

At the end of typing that line, press the ENTER key. That causes the computer to "make a directory called TEMP", so the computer creates an empty folder called TEMP.

You see "C:\WINDOWS>" again.

Get to the C:\ prompt

Type "cd \" (and press ENTER afterwards). Now the screen says:

> `C:\>`

Delete CHK files

Type "del *.chk", so the screen looks like this:

```
C:\>del *.chk
```

That makes the computer delete any files that end in ".CHK". Here's why:

> Any file that ends in ".CHK" was created by using "chkdsk" or "scandisk". That file is just a "lost chain" (fragment of a discarded file). It's useless. It just wastes space on your hard disk. It should be deleted.

Strip CONFIG.SYS and AUTOEXEC.BAT

Windows 95 and 98 don't need a CONFIG.SYS or AUTOEXEC.BAT file.

On too many computers, the CONFIG.SYS and AUTOEXEC.BAT files are lengthy messes that waste RAM, make the computer sluggish, and cause memory conflicts. I'll explain how to strip them down. This stripping process usually takes just a few minutes, but beware: it can go haywire, so **try this procedure just if you have a few hours to experiment....**

Type "ren autoexec.bat *.a", so your screen looks like this:

```
C:\>ren autoexec.bat *.a
```

That makes the computer **rename AUTOEXEC.BAT to AUTOEXEC.A**, so you no longer have a file named "AUTOEXEC.BAT". (If you change your mind later, you can reverse the renaming by saying "copy autoexec.a *.bat".)

Type "ren config.sys *.a", like this:

```
C:\>ren config.sys *.a
```

That makes the computer **rename CONFIG.SYS to CONFIG.A**, so you no longer have a file named "CONFIG.SYS". (If you change your mind later, you can reverse the renaming by saying "copy config.a *.sys".)

After you've renamed CONFIG.SYS to CONFIG.A, you can make one further improvement, if you have the patience.

> The improvement consists of typing this:
>
> ```
> C:\>copy con config.sys
> device=windows\himem.sys /testmem:off
> device=windows\emm386.exe ram d=64
> dos=high,umb
> ```
>
> At the end of each line, press the ENTER key. At the end of the last line, press the ENTER key, then the F6 key (which creates the symbol "^Z"), then the ENTER key again. That creates a 3-line CONFIG.SYS file, which is *slightly* better than having no CONFIG.SYS at all. The 3-liner increases the available RAM and also creates expanded memory.

You see "C:\>" again.

Shut down your computer

If you started your computer normally (and therefore did software cleaning by clicking "MS-DOS prompt"), do this:

> Type "exit" (and press ENTER). You see the Windows desktop screen again (with the Start button and the My Computer icon). Click "Start" then "Shut Down" then "Yes".

Finally, regardless of how you started your computer, turn the power off.

Test your computer

When the computer has quieted down, turn it back on and watch what happens.

Probably Windows will start fine (faster and better!) because of the software cleaning you did, such as changes you made to CONFIG.SYS and AUTOEXEC.BAT.

Probably **your DOS programs will work fine (even your DOS games!) if you start them the way Microsoft recommends:** click "Start" then "Programs" then "MS-DOS Prompt"; then if you see just a small black window, enlarge it by pressing Alt with ENTER. If you start DOS that way, the mouse & CD-ROM will work even while you're running DOS software.

Though stripping CONFIG.SYS and AUTOEXEC.BAT improves the performance of most computers, *your* computer might have "special needs". (In the old days, computers having "special needs" were called "handicapped", but I guess that's not politically correct anymore.) For example, most Compaq computers have "special needs". (Here we go again, another slam at Compaq. But Compaq deserves it!) Such computers require some "special needs" lines in CONFIG.SYS and AUTOEXEC.BAT.

If Windows refuses to start properly after you've fiddled with CONFIG.SYS and AUTOEXEC.BAT, change them back. Here's how:

> Shut down the computer. (If possible, shut it down gracefully by using the Shut Down menu. If you can't get to the Shut Down menu or it doesn't react properly, just turn the power off.)
>
> Then turn the computer back on. *If you're using Windows 98,* immediately hold down the Ctrl key, and keep holding it down. (*If you're using Windows 95,* do this instead: immediately put your finger near the F8 key and watch carefully for the words "Starting Windows 95" to appear; they appear in white letters, on a black background, just *before* you see the clouds; when the words "Starting Windows 95" appear, press the F8 key immediately.)
>
> **The computer will say "Microsoft Windows Startup Menu". From that menu, choose "Safe mode command prompt only"** (by pressing a number such as 6 or 7 and then pressing ENTER).
>
> The computer will say "C:\>". Then you can restore your original CONFIG.SYS and AUTOEXEC.BAT files by saying:
>
> ```
> C:\>copy config.a *.sys
> C:\>copy autoexec.a *.bat
> ```
>
> Finally, turn the power off, wait for the computer to quiet down, turn the computer back on, and you should be back where you were before you tried this experiment.
>
> Then if you're ambitious, edit CONFIG.SYS and AUTOEXEC.BAT more carefully, trying to figure out which lines to keep and which to discard. Read my DOS chapter for further details. You can phone me for help at 603-666-6644.

Strip WIN.INI

Another file that affects how Windows boots is WIN.INI. Like CONFIG.SYS and AUTOEXEC.BAT, this file is slightly dangerous to play with, so **try this procedure just if you have a few hours to experiment....**

Click "Start" then "Run". Then type "win.ini" (and press ENTER). You see a window showing you the many equations that comprise WIN.INI.

Two of those equations should say:

```
load=
run=
```

In those "load=" and "run=" equations, typically nothing should come after the equal sign.

Any program mentioned after the equal sign will be loaded and run automatically every time you start Windows. A program should be mentioned after the equal sign just if you really *do* want to run that program every time you start Windows.

After scribbling a careful note on a sheet of paper about what junk came after the equal sign, delete the unwanted junk (by clicking just after the equal sign and then pressing the DELETE key several times). Or deactivate the entire line by putting a semicolon at the line's beginning, so the two lines begin by saying ";load=" and ";run=".

Then exit from the editor (by clicking its X box and then pressing ENTER).

Shut down the computer completely (by clicking "Start" then "Shut Down" then "Yes" then turning the power off). When the computer has quieted down, turn it back on and watch what happens.

Probably Windows will start fine (faster and better!) because of the changes you made to WIN.INI. If not, revert the WIN.INI file back to its original state. (Phone me at 603-666-6644 if you need any help reverting.)

Windows 3.1 & 3.11 cleaning

The following comments apply to Windows 3.1 and 3.11.

The best way to make Windows 3.1 (or 3.11) work better is to upgrade to Windows 95 (or 98).

> Microsoft tried hard to make Windows 95 fix all of Windows 3.1's problems — and on the whole, Microsoft succeeded! Also, the newest versions of all popular programs *require* you to buy Windows 95 (or 98). Internet access is faster, simpler, and more reliable if you buy Windows 95 (or 98). Windows 95&98 are technically superior: they do a better job of handling multitasking (many tasks in the RAM simultaneously), new devices (they automatically detects any new hardware you buy), and repairs (they try to automatically fix themselves when anything goes wrong). Many Windows 3.1 headaches arise from incorrect CONFIG.SYS and AUTOEXEC.BAT files, but Windows 95&98 don't need those files at all!
>
> Windows 95 needs 8M of RAM to run acceptably (16M of RAM to run well). Windows 98 needs 16M of RAM to run acceptably (32M of RAM to run well). If you have enough RAM, the only disadvantage of Windows 95&98 is that they take longer to boot up and shut down. So if possible, upgrade to Windows 95 or 98.

If you refuse to upgrade (because you're an old fuddy-duddy), the following tricks will make your old Windows run as well as possible. They're similar to the tricks for making Windows 95&98 run well. I'll start with the tricks that are the simplest and most foolproof, then progress to the tricks that are more advanced and risky. To get free help using these tricks and others that are more bizarre, phone me anytime at 603-666-6644.

Close whatever is open
Go to Windows 3.1's main screen. **Make sure the very top of the screen says "Program Manager" and no other windows or programs are open or running.**

Here's how:

> If another window is open, close it by double-clicking its control box (the white horizontal bar in the window's top left corner).
>
> If a program is running, exit from it by choosing "Exit" from its File menu.
>
> If the words "Program Manager" appear at the top of a window but not at the top of your screen, maximize the window by clicking the "▲" (which is in the window's top right corner).
>
> If the words "Program Manager" appear under an icon, click the icon and then click "Maximize".

Make sure the computer takes you seriously. To do that, click "Options" (which is at the top of the screen, next to the word "File"). You see the Options menu. **Make sure a check mark is in front of "Save Settings on Exit"** and no check marks are elsewhere in the Options menu. (To add or remove a check mark, click where you want the check mark to be created or destroyed; then click "Options" again to see whether you succeeded. If you forgot to put a check mark in front of "Save Settings on Exit", the computer does *not* save what you're doing, does *not* take you seriously, and does *not* let your fooling around affect future sessions of Windows.)

Make the Options menu go away (by pressing the Esc key).

Simplify the display
Double-click "Main" (which is an icon) then "Control Panel" (so you see the Control Panel window) then "Desktop".

Make the Pattern, Screen Saver, and Wallpaper each be "None". If one of them isn't "None", click the down-arrow at its right, so you see a menu; click "None", which is the menu's top choice, which you might have to scroll up to see.

When Pattern, Screen Saver, and Wallpaper are each "None", click "OK".

Turn off the Print Manager
While you're looking at the Control Panel window, double-click the Printers icon. **You'll see the Printers window. At its bottom left corner, you'll see a box labeled "Use Print Manager". If that box has an X in it, eliminate the X** (by clicking it), so the computer will *not* use Print Manager.

Here's why:

> Print Manager is well-intentioned software that unfortunately screws up. It tries to help you by playing this trick: whenever you tell the computer to print on paper, Print Manager diverts the request: instead of printing the output directly onto paper, Print Manager prints the output onto your disk instead, then later copies that output from the disk to your printer. So it's a two-step process: output to be printed is sent first to the hard disk, then copied from the hard disk to the printer. As soon as the first part of the process has finished (all the output has reached the hard disk), Print Manager lets you use your keyboard and mouse again, so you can accomplish whatever further computerized tasks you wish, while output is being sent from the disk to the printer. The result is that you can start working on a second task before the first task has finished printing.
>
> But Print Manager screws up, for two reasons....
>
> First, you must have enough room on the disk to hold the output. If your disk is almost full and you then try to print long output (such as a 20-page report or a high-resolution picture containing millions of dots), Print Manager has trouble sending the output to the disk and gives up: your computer **crashes** (ignores all your keystrokes and mouse strokes) and you must reboot.
>
> The second reason why Print Manager screws up is that your computer probably doesn't have enough RAM to run Print Manager at the same time as other software.
>
> That's why I recommend *not* using Print Manager in Windows 3.1.
>
> In Windows 95, Print Manager is usually okay, since Windows 95 manages RAM problems better and since most folks using Windows 95 have bought lots of RAM and a huge hard disk.

When you finish eliminating the X from the Use Print Manager box, click "Close".

Then close the Control Panel window. Close the Main window.

Empty your StartUp folder
Double click "StartUp" (which is an icon). You'll see what's in the StartUp folder. Each time you start running Windows, the computer automatically runs all the programs in the StartUp folder.

Typically, the StartUp folder should be empty, so your computer won't be distracted by having to run junk. If your StartUp folder is *not* empty, you see icons in it. You should probably delete all those icons. Before deleting an icon, try to figure out each icon's purpose, and figure out whether you have a copy of it in another folder besides StartUp. If you have another copy of the icon, or if the icon is for software that you never use, do this:

> Click on the icon (just once, not twice), so its name appears in a blue box.
>
> From the File menu, choose Properties. (To do that, click the word "File" at the screen's top left corner, then click the word "Properties".) You'll see info about the file's properties. Onto a sheet of paper, copy that info (the file's Description, Command Line, and Working Directory), so if you change your mind and want the file back, you'll have an easier time reconstructing the file. Then click OK.
>
> From the File menu, choose Delete. Then press ENTER. The icon will vanish.

If you're not sure whether to delete an icon from the StartUp folder, the safest procedure is to drag the icon temporarily into another folder instead. (To do that, get both folders opened at the same time, drag the folders away from each other to minimize the overlap, then drag the icon from the StartUp folder to the other folder.) A quicker alternative is to just be brave and delete the icon by using the procedure I explained in the box; but make sure you include the step about File Properties so you can reconstruct the icon if you change your mind. (Here's how to reconstruct a StartUp icon: click anywhere in the StartUp folder, then choose New from the File menu, then press ENTER, then fill in the blanks by using the notes you'd written on the sheet of paper, then press ENTER).

When you've finished examining and fiddling with the StartUp folder, close it.

Do DOS cleaning If you're using Windows 3.1 or 3.11, the next step is to do DOS cleaning, which I explain in the next section. (Go ahead, peek at the "DOS cleaning" section, do what it says, then return here.)

Strip WIN.INI After you've done DOS cleaning, the next thing to do to improve Windows is to strip WIN.INI. Here's how.

At the C prompt, say "edit windows\win.ini", so your screen looks like this:

```
C:\>edit windows\win.ini
```

When you press the ENTER key at the end of that line, your screen will turn blue. (If it doesn't turn blue, recheck your typing, or try saying "dos\edit" instead of "edit".)

On the blue screen, you'll see the many equations that comprise WIN.INI. Two of those equations should say:

```
load=
run=
```

In those "load=" and "run=" equations, typically nothing should come after the equal sign.

Any program mentioned after the equal sign will be loaded and run automatically every time you start Windows. A program should be mentioned after the equal sign just if you really *do* want to run that program every time you start Windows.

After scribbling a careful note on a sheet of paper about what junk came after the equal sign, delete the unwanted junk (by clicking just after the equal sign and then pressing the DELETE key several times). Or deactivate the entire line by putting a semicolon at the line's beginning, so the two lines begin by saying ";load=" and ";run=".

Then exit from the editor (by pressing the Alt key, then the F key, then the X key). The computer will say "Loaded file is not saved." Press the ENTER key (which saves the file).

Turn off the computer. When the computer has quieted down, turn it back on and watch what happens.

Probably Windows will start fine (faster and better!) because of the changes you made to WIN.INI. If not, revert the WIN.INI file back to its original state. (Phone me at 603-666-6644 if you need any help reverting.)

Why Windows 3.1 screws up The main reason why Windows 3.1 (or 3.11) screws up is insufficient conventional RAM.

Windows 3.1 needs at least 565K of conventional RAM free, in order to run well. Unfortunately, companies such as Gateway and Dell have shipped computers having *less* than 565K of conventional RAM free. To find out how much conventional RAM you have free, say "mem".

To increase the amount of conventional free RAM, follow my suggestions on page 588, in the section called "insufficient memory". You should also get rid of screen savers.

Windows wants 8M of RAM altogether. If your computer's total RAM is much less than 8M (for example, if you bought just 4M), get rid of the AUTOEXEC.BAT line that mentions SMARTDRV.EXE and change the number of buffers in CONFIG.SYS to 40. Exception: if you compressed your hard drive, you must keep SMARTDRV.EXE, in order to prevent your hard drive from seeming too slow.

Another source of Windows 3.1 headaches is a full hard drive.

Make sure your hard drive has at least 10M free. To check that, say "chkdsk" and look at the number of "bytes available on disk". If you have less than 10M free, erase the files you don't use.

DOS cleaning

The following comments apply to MS-DOS 6.2 (or 6.21 or 6.22) on a computer having at least a 386 CPU and at least 2M of RAM.

If you're using an earlier version of MS-DOS, you should upgrade to one of those versions. The upgrade usually costs $50. If you're using MS-DOS 6.0, you can get use a cheaper upgrade called the "MS-DOS 6.2 Step-Up", which costs just $10 from the repair departments of most computer stores. If you refuse to upgrade, read my CONFIG.SYS and AUTOEXEC.BAT advice on pages 132-137 to find out how old DOS versions differ.

If you're using a later version of MS-DOS, you must be using Windows 95 or 98, so read the "Windows 95&98 cleaning" section instead.

If your computer is less than a 386 or has less than 2M of RAM, read my CONFIG.SYS and AUTOEXEC.BAT advice on pages 132-137 to find out what to do differently.

Get a standard C prompt Get to a standard C prompt, so your screen looks like this:

```
C:\>
```

If you're in Windows instead, get to the C prompt by choosing "Exit Windows" from the File menu. If you're in DOS shell, get to the C prompt by pressing the F3 key.

If your C prompt is too short and says just "C>", make it longer by saying "prompt pg". If your C prompt is too long and has extra words in it, get rid of the extra words by saying "cd \".

Delete CHK files At the C prompt, type this:

```
C:\>del *.chk
```

That makes the computer delete any files that end in ".CHK". Here's why:

Any file that ends in ".CHK" was created by using "chkdsk" or "scandisk". That file is just a "lost chain" (fragment of a discarded file). It's useless. It just wastes space on your hard disk. It should be deleted.

Delete temporary files Type the word "set", like this:

```
C:\>set
```

You'll see several equations. One of the equations probably begins by saying "TEMP=C:\". That equation tells which directory contains your temporary files.

All temporarily files should have been deleted by the computer; but sometimes the computer forgets to delete them. Delete them yourself, manually. Here's how:

What the TEMP equation says	What to type
TEMP=C:\temp	C:\>del temp
TEMP=C:\windows\temp	C:\>del windows\temp
TEMP=C:\pbtools\wintemp	C:\>del pbtools\wintemp
TEMP=C:\dos	C:\>del dos*.tmp
	C:\>del dos\~*.*
	C:\>md temp
TEMP=C:\windows	C:\>del windows*.tmp
	C:\>del windows\~*.*
	C:\>md temp

When typing those lines, type carefully. If you make a mistake, you'll delete files that are important.

To type the symbol "~", hold down the SHIFT key while tapping the key that's typically next to the number 1. If you have questions about how to type, phone me at 603-666-6644 for help.

If the computer asks "Are you sure?", press the Y key then ENTER. If the computer says "file not found", there were no temporarily files to delete.

Make copies Make copies of CONFIG.SYS and AUTOEXEC.BAT (to protect yourself in case you screw up), by typing this:

```
C:\>copy config.sys *.a
C:\>copy autoexec.bat *.a
```

While typing those lines, make sure you put the spaces, asterisks, and periods in the right places, and make sure you type the "c" at the end of "autoexec".

Those lines make copies of CONFIG.SYS and AUTOEXEC.BAT. The copies are called CONFIG.A and AUTOEXEC.A and are stored on your hard disk.

Edit CONFIG.SYS Edit CONFIG.SYS by typing this:

```
C:\>edit config.sys
```

The screen should turn blue. (If it remains black and says "bad command or file name", the computer doesn't understand "edit". To get around that problem, try typing "dos\edit" instead of just "edit".)

On the blue screen, you'll see your current version of CONFIG.SYS. **A standard CONFIG.SYS looks like this:**

```
device=dos\himem.sys /testmem:off
device=dos\emm386.exe ram d=64
dos=high,umb
stacks=0,0
buffers=40
files=50
```

If you have a CD-ROM drive, you need an extra line at the bottom. The extra line should begin by saying "devicehigh=" and should also have a "/d:" in it. It usually also has the letters "cd" buried in it somewhere, perhaps as part of an longer word. The line's exact details depend on which brand of CD-ROM drive you have — and also on what kind of motherboard and sound card you're attaching it to. If the line begins with "device=", change it to "devicehigh=".

Some CD-ROM drives require you to put one or two extra "helper" lines before the CD-ROM drive line. Those "helper" lines mention the same subdirectory (folder) as the CD-ROM drive line. Those lines should begin by saying "devicehigh=". (If they say "device=" instead, change them to "devicehigh=".)

Except for the line about the CD-ROM drive, your CONFIG.SYS file should typically consist of just the 6 lines I listed above.

For example, **if you have a line saying "stacks=9,256", change it to "stacks=0,0".** Making that change will gain you $2\frac{1}{8}$K of conventional RAM.

In the line about "files", the number should be at least 50. A few programs require more than 50. If the number is less than 50, raise it to 50. If the number is *more* than 50, leave it alone; don't bother fiddling with it.

If you have a line saying "dos=high" and a line saying "dos=umb", combine them into a line saying "dos=high,umb".

Typically, the buffers line should say "buffers=40". If you're using a program called "smartdrv" (which is pronounced "smart drive"), buffers should be 15 instead. Normally I recommend avoiding smartdrv (because it consumes too much RAM and occasionally destroys your files); but if your drive is compressed (a dangerous activity that I don't recommend), you must use smartdrv (to help it run fast) and set buffers to 15.

The only lines that should begin with "device=" are typically the lines about himem.sys and emm386.exe. (Some hard drives need a third "device=" line to handle the "disk manager".) **Any other "device=" line should typically be changed to "devicehigh="** (to make sure the device driver is loaded into upper memory, to free up your conventional memory.)

If a line begins with "devicehigh", make sure nothing comes between that word and the equal sign. **Delete anything coming between "devicehigh" and the equal sign.** For example, if a line's start is "devicehigh /L:1,30; 3:30=", shorten that start to "devicehigh=". (The "/L" and other numbers between the "devicehigh" and the equal sign were put there by the memmaker program, which tries to improve RAM usage by forcing the computer to load software into specific addresses; but those specific addresses usually conflict with other addresses and make your software crash. Never use memmaker: it's the most counterproductive utility that Microsoft ever created. If you do what I say, your RAM usage will be better than memmaker's attempt.)

If a line mentions "qemm", you should typically delete the line (since "qemm" is a memmaker competitor that causes as many conflicts as memmaker). **But if the qemm line mentions "c:" twice, keep the second "c:" reference** (and delete the first "c:" reference, which mentions "qemm"). Make the line begin by saying "devicehigh=c:"

More comments about CONFIG.SYS are on pages 132-134. Advice about using the editor is on pages 128-129.

When you finish editing CONFIG.SYS, exit from the editor (by pressing the Alt key, then the F key, then the X key). The computer will say "Loaded file is not saved." Press the ENTER key (which saves the file).

Edit AUTOEXEC.BAT Edit AUTOEXEC.BAT by typing this:

```
C:\edit autoexec.bat
```

The screen should turn blue. (If it remains black and says "bad command or file name", the computer doesn't understand "edit". To get around that problem, try typing "dos\edit" instead of just "edit".)

On the blue screen, you'll see your current version of AUTOEXEC.BAT.

AUTOEXEC.BAT's top line should say:

```
@echo off
```

If that line is elsewhere, move it to the top. Here's how: move to that line by using the down-arrow key, then press Ctrl with Y (which yanks the line from its old position), then move up the beginning of the first line, then press Shift with INSERT (which inserts the line where desired).

Fix the other lines in AUTOEXEC.BAT by reading the info on pages 135-137. Just as you did in CONFIG.SYS, remove any junk that was inserted by memmaker or qemm.

When you've finished editing AUTOEXEC.BAT, exit from the editor (by pressing Alt then F then X then ENTER).

Reboot After you've edited CONFIG.SYS and AUTOEXEC.BAT, your changes don't take effect until you reboot. So to find out whether your editing was successful, reboot! (To do that, turn off the computer, then wait for it to become quiet, then turn the computer back on again.)

If you have any trouble rebooting, use this trick to reboot:

Reboot the computer again, but when the computer says "Starting MS-DOS" immediately press the F5 key. You'll be at a C prompt. Then try again to edit CONFIG.SYS and AUTOEXEC.BAT. If you wish to return to your original CONFIG.SYS and AUTOEXEC.BAT, type this:
```
C:\>copy config.a *.sys
C:\>copy autoexec.a *.bat
```
After making CONFIG.SYS and AUTOEXEC.BAT the way you wish, reboot again.

After you've rebooted successfully, try running your favorite programs, to make sure they still work okay.

Probably, they'll work better! If they have trouble working, edit again or phone me at 603-666-6644 for advanced tricks.

Strategies for repair

To repair a computer, follow these general principles....

Ask

Ask for help. Instead of wasting many hours scratching your head about a computer problem, get help from your dealer, your computer's manufacturer, your software's publisher, your colleagues, your teachers, your friends, and me. You can phone me day or night, 24 hours, at 603-666-6644; I'm almost always in, and I sleep only lightly.

Most computers come with a one-year warranty. If your computer gives you trouble during that first year, make use of the warranty: get the free help you're entitled to from your dealer. If your "dealer" is a general-purpose department store that doesn't specialize in computers, the store might tell you to phone the computer's manufacturer. For tough software questions, the dealer might tell you to phone the software's publisher.

Most computers come with a 30-day money-back guarantee. If the computer is giving you lots of headaches during the first 30 days, just return it!

Clean

Most repair problems can be solved by cleaning your software (as I explained on pages 575-581). Many other repair problems can be solved by cleaning your hardware (as I explained on page 574) or by getting rid of viruses (which I'll explain in the next chapter).

Chuck

If the broken part is cheap, don't fix it: chuck it! For example, if one of the keys on your keyboard stops working, don't bother trying to fix that key; instead, buy a new keyboard. A new keyboard costs about $25. Fixing one key on a keyboard costs many hours of labor and is silly.

If a 2-gigabyte hard disk stops working, and you can't fix the problem in an hour or so, just give up and buy a new hard disk, since 2-gigabyte hard disks are obsolete anyway. Today, 2 gigabytes aren't worth much; the price difference between an 8-gigabyte drive and a 10-megabyte drive is about $5.

Observe

Read the screen. Often, the screen will display an error message that tells you what the problem is.

If the message flashes on the screen too briefly for you to read, try pressing the computer's PAUSE key as soon as the message appears. The PAUSE key makes the message stay on the screen for you to read. When you finish reading the message, press the ENTER key.

If you're having trouble with your printer, and your printer is modern enough to have a built-in screen, read the messages on that screen too.

Check the lights. Look at the blinking lights on the front of the computer and the front of the printer; see if the correct ones are glowing. Also notice whether the monitor's POWER light is glowing.

Check the switches. Check the ON-OFF switches for the computer, monitor, and printer: make sure they're all flipped on. If your computer equipment is plugged into a power strip, make sure the strip's ON-OFF switch is turned on.

Check the monitor's brightness and contrast knobs, to make sure they're turned to the normal (middle) position.

If you have a dot-matrix printer, make sure the paper is feeding correctly, and make sure you've put into the correct position the lever that lets you choose between tractor feed and friction feed.

Check the cables that run out of the computer. They run to the monitor, printer, keyboard, mouse, and wall. Make sure they're all plugged tightly into their sockets. To make *sure* they're plugged in tight, unplug them and then plug them back in again. (To be safe, turn the computer equipment off before fiddling with the cables.) Many monitor and printer problems are caused just by loose cables.

Make sure each cable is plugged into the correct socket. Examine the back of your computer, printer, monitor, and modem: if you see two sockets that look identical, try plugging the cable into the other socket. For example, the cable from your printer might fit into *two* identical sockets at the back of the computer (LPT1 and LPT2); the cable from your phone system might fit into *two* identical sockets at the back of your modem (LINE and PHONE).

Strip

When analyzing a hardware problem, run no software except the operating system and diagnostics. For example, if you're experiencing a problem while using a word-processing program, spreadsheet, database, game, or some other software, exit from whatever software you're in. Turn off your printer, computer, and all your other equipment, so the RAM chips inside each device get erased and forget that software.

Then turn the computer back on.

> If writing appears on your screen, and you can read it, your screen is working fine.
>
> If you can make the hard disk show you what's on it (by by double-clicking "My Computer" then "C:" in Windows 95 & 98, or by typing "dir" in DOS), your hard disk is working fine.
>
> If you can print something simple on paper (by typing "I love you" in WordPad and then printing that 3-word document, or by typing " "dir>prn" in DOS), your printer is working fine. (On some laser printers, such as the Hewlett Packard Laserjet 2, you need to manually eject the paper: press the printer's ON LINE button, then the FORM FEED button, then the ON LINE button again.)

If your computer, monitor, hard drive, and printer pass all those tests, your hardware is basically fine; and so the problem you were having was probably caused by software rather than hardware. For example, maybe you forgot to tell your software what kind of printer and monitor you bought.

Relax

Don't get upset! Just relax. Stay, calm, cool, and collected while you analyze the problem. Have the attitude of Sherlock Holmes!

Perhaps you'd react to error messages more calmly if they were written as meditative poetry. In February 1998, an online magazine called **Salon.com** held a contest to turn each error message into a **haiku** (a Japanese meditative poem that has 5 syllables on the first line, 7 syllables on the second line, and 5 syllables on the third line). Here are the winning entries (as edited by me).

Missing Web pages
The Web site you seek
Cannot be located, but
Countless more exist.

You step in the stream,
But the water has moved on.
This **page is not here**.

Site moved, now secret.
We'd tell you where, but then we'd
Have to delete you.

Crashing
A **crash** reduces
Your expensive computer
To a simple stone.

Serious error.
All shortcuts have disappeared.
Screen. Mind. Both are **blank**.

Yesterday it worked.
Today it is **not working**.
Windows is like that.

The ten thousand things,
How long do any persist?
Windows, too, has gone.

Stay the patient course.
Of little worth is your ire.
The **network is down**.

Windows NT crashed.
I am the **Blue Screen of Death**.
No one hears your screams.

Lost data
Three things are certain:
Death, taxes, and **lost data**.
Guess which has occurred.

With searching comes loss
And the presence of absence:
"My Novel" **not found**.

Rather than a beep
Or a rude error message,
These words: **"File not found."**

Having been **erased**,
The document you're seeking
Must now be retyped.

A file that's so big?
It might be very useful.
But now it is **gone**.

Everything is gone.
Your life's work has been destroyed.
Squeeze trigger (yes/no)?

Starting over
Chaos reigns within.
Reflect, repent, and **reboot**.
Order shall return.

Seeing my great fault
Through darkening blue windows,
I **begin again**.

Aborted effort.
Close all that you have worked on.
You ask far too much.

Login incorrect.
Only perfect spellers may
Enter this system.

Server's poor response
Not quick enough for browser.
Timed out, plum blossom.

Errors have occurred.
We won't tell you where or why.
Lazy programmers.

To have no **errors**
Would be life without meaning:
No struggle, no joy.

Inadequate hardware
Printer not ready.
Could be a fatal error.
Have a pen handy?

The Tao that is seen
Is not the true Tao — until
You bring fresh **toner**.

No **keyboard** present.
Hit F1 to continue.
Zen engineering?

First snow, then silence.
This thousand-dollar **screen dies**
So beautifully.

Out of memory.
We wish to hold the whole sky,
But we never will.

I'm sorry, there's…um…
Insufficient…what's-it-called?
The term eludes me.

The code was willing.
It considered your request.
But the **chips** were weak.

You've reached a chasm
Of carbon and **silicon**
No software can bridge.

Here's who wrote them:

Missing Web pages:	Joy Rothke, Cass Whittington, Charles Matthews
Crashing:	James Lopez, Ian Hughes, Margaret Segall, Jason Willoughby, David Ansel, Peter Rothman
Lost data:	David Dixon, Howard Korder, Len Dvorkin, Judy Birmingham, David Liszewski, David Carlson
Starting over:	Suzie Wagner, Chirs Walsh, Mike Hagler, Jason Axley, Rik Jespersen, Charlie Gibbs, Brian Porter
Inadequate hardware:	Pat Davis, Bill Torcaso, Jim Griffith, Simon Firth, Francis Heaney, Owen Mathews, Barry Brumitt, Rahul Sonnad

Common problems

Here are the most common computer problems and how to solve them.

Booting problems
Turning the computer on is called **booting**. When you turn the computer on, you might immediately experience one of these problems.

Unusual beeping When you turn the computer on, you're supposed to hear a single short beep. If **you hear unusual beeping** (such as *several* short beeps or a long beep), your computer's fundamental circuitry isn't working right.

If you hear *many* short beeps or a *very long* beep, your computer is having an electrical problem, so do this:

Turn the computer off immediately. Perhaps the electrical problem was caused by a loose power cord: make sure the power cord is plugged in tight to the back of the computer and to the wall's outlet (or surge protector), not dangling loose. If the computer got damp recently (from a rainstorm or a spilled drink or dew caused by bringing the computer in from the cold), wait for the computer to dry thoroughly before turning it back on. If you moved the computer recently, perhaps a part got loose in shipment; if you wish, open the computer and make sure nothing major is loose; for example, make sure the PC cards and chips are firmly in their sockets (but before you touch any chips, reduce any static electricity in your fingers by grounding yourself, such as by touching a big metal object or the computer's power supply while it's still plugged into a grounded wall socket).

By listening to the computer's beeps, you can tell which part of the computer is ill. For example if the motherboard's BIOS chip is designed by **American Megatrends Incorporated (AMI)**, you'll hear these short beeps:

Beeps	Which part of the computer is ill
no beeps	speaker, power supply, power cable, or motherboard
1 beep	no illness; everything is fine
2 beeps	RAM's parity bit (probably because the RAM chips are loose)
3 beeps	first 64K of RAM (probably because those RAM chips are loose)
4 beeps	timer chip (or loose RAM chips)
5 beeps	CPU chip (or loose RAM chips)
6 beeps	keyboard (or its controller chip or its fuse)
7 beeps	motherboard (or CPU chip)
8 beeps	video card (probably the card is loose or the RAM chips on it are)
9 beeps	ROM BIOS chip
10 beeps	CMOS chips (so you'll probably buy a new motherboard)
11 beeps	RAM cache

If the motherboard's BIOS chip is designed by **IBM**, you'll hear these beeps:

Beeps	Which part of the computer is ill
no beeps	speaker, power supply, power cable, or motherboard
1 short beep	no illness; everything is fine
2 short beeps	CMOS setup (probably because dead battery)
many short beeps	power supply
unending beep	keyboard (a key is stuck down) or power supply
1 long then 1 short beep	motherboard
1 long then 2 short beeps	video card
1 long then 3 short beeps	EGA video card
1 long then 4 short beeps	laptop battery (low voltage, needs to be recharged)

If the motherboard's BIOS chip is designed by **Award**, you'll hear these beeps:

Beeps	Which part of the computer is ill
no beeps	speaker, power supply, power cable, or motherboard
1 short beep	no illness; everything is fine
1 long beep	the first 64K of RAM
1 long then 2 short beeps	video card (or cable to the monitor)
1 long then 3 short beeps	keyboard controller chip (or keyboard)
many beeps	RAM (or video card)
2 short beeps	any less-important computer part (non-fatal error)

If the motherboard's BIOS chip is designed by **Phoenix**, you'll hear groups of short beeps:

Beeps	Which part of the computer is ill
no beeps	speaker, power supply, power cable, or motherboard
1 beep	no illness; everything is fine
1 beep then 1 then 2	CPU chip
1 beep then 1 then 3	CMOS chips
1 beep then 1 then 4	ROM BIOS chip
1 beep then 2 then 1	timer chip
1 beep then 2 then 2	DMA controller chip
1 beep then 2 then 3	DMA controller chip or RAM
1 beep then 3 then some	the first 64K of RAM (or motherboard)
1 beep then 4 then some	the first 64K of RAM (or motherboard)
2 beeps then some	the first 64K of RAM
3 beeps then 1 then some	motherboard
3 beeps then 2 then 2	motherboard
3 beeps then 2 then 4	keyboard controller chip (or keyboard)
3 beeps then 3 then 1	CMOS (because the CMOS chips or battery is bad)
3 beeps then 3 then 2	CMOS setup (probably because dead battery)
3 beeps then 3 then 4	video RAM chips (or the video card that they're on)
3 beeps then 4 then 1	video card
4 beeps then 2 then 1	timer chip
4 beeps then 2 then 2	CMOS chips
4 beeps then 2 then 3	keyboard controller chip (or keyboard)
4 beeps then 2 then 4	CPU chip
4 beeps then 3 then 1	motherboard's circuitry that controls the RAM
4 beeps then 3 then 3	timer chip
4 beeps then 3 then 4	time-of-day clock chip (or CMOS chips or battery)
4 beeps then 4 then 1	serial port
4 beeps then 4 then 2	parallel port
4 beeps then 4 then 3	math coprocessor chip

Signal missing

If the **screen says "signal missing" or "no signal"**, the monitor is not receiving any electrical signal from the computer. The monitor is complaining.

Look at the two cables coming out of the monitor's rear. One of those cables is a power cord that plugs into the wall (or into a surge protector). The other cable is the **video cable**, which is supposed to plug into the back of the computer, so the computer can send signals to the monitor. Probably, that video cable is loose. Tighten it. To make sure it's tight, unplug it from the back of the computer and then shove it into the computer's backside again, firmly.

If tightening the video cable doesn't solve the problem, maybe the computer is turned off. Make sure the computer is turned on:

If the computer is turned on, lights should be glowing on the front of the computer and on the keyboard, and you should hear the fan inside the computer whir. If you don't see and hear those things, the computer is turned off. Try turning the computer on, by pressing its ON switch or by turning on the surge protector that the computer's plugged into.

Another possibility is that the video card (which is inside the computer) is loose (because you recently moved the computer) or got fried (from a power surge caused by a thunderstorm) or got damaged (because you were fiddling with the computer's innards and you caused a shock or short or break). Make sure the video card is in tight; if a tight video card doesn't solve the problem, borrow a video card from a friend; if that still doesn't give you any video, maybe your whole motherboard is damaged, so give up and take your computer to a repair shop.

No video

When you turn the computer on, the screen is supposed to show you words, pictures, or marks, or at least a cursor (little line). If the **screen stays completely black**, probably your monitor is getting no electricity or no electrical signals.

Make sure the monitor is turned on. Make sure its two cables (to the power and to the computer's video card) are both plugged in tight (since they can easily come loose.) Make sure the monitor's contrast and brightness are turned up (by fiddling with the knobs or buttons on the monitor's front, back, or sides).

If the monitor has a power-on light, check whether that light is glowing. (If the monitor doesn't have a power-on light, peek through the monitor's air vents and check whether anything inside glows). If you don't see any glow, the monitor isn't getting any power (because the on-off button is in the wrong position, or the power cable is loose, or the monitor is broken). If the monitor is indeed broken, do *not* open the monitor, which contains high voltages even when turned off; instead, return the monitor to your dealer.

If you've fiddled with the knobs and cables, and the power-on light (or inside light) is glowing but the screen is still blank, boot up the computer again, and look at the screen carefully: maybe a message *did* flash on the screen quickly?

If a message did appear, fix whatever problem the message talks about. (If the message was too fast for you to read, boot up again and quickly hit the PAUSE key as soon as the message appears, then press ENTER when you finish reading the message.) If the message appears but does not mention a problem, you're in the middle of a program that has crashed (stopped working), so the fault lies in software mentioned in CONFIG.SYS or AUTOEXEC.BAT or COMMAND.COM or some other software involved in booting; to explore further, put to drive A your DOS disk (or Windows 95/98 emergency recovery start-up boot disk) and reboot.

If absolutely no message appears on the screen during the booting process, so that the screen is entirely blank, check the lights on the computer (maybe the computer is turned off or broken) and recheck the cables that go to the monitor. If you still have no luck, the fault is probably in the video card inside the computer, though it might be on the motherboard or in the middle of the video cable that goes from the video card to the monitor. At this point, before you run out and buy new hardware, try swapping with a friend whose computer has the same kind of video as yours (for example, you both have VGA): try swapping monitors, then video cables, then video cards, while making notes about which combinations work, until you finally discover which piece of hardware is causing the failure. Then replace that hardware, and you're done!

SETUP

Each modern computer (286, 386, 486, or Pentium) contains CMOS RAM, which tries to remember the date, time, how many megabytes of RAM you've bought, how you want the RAM used, what kind of video you bought, and what kind of disk drives you bought. A battery feeds power to the CMOS RAM, so that the CMOS RAM keeps remembering the answers even while the main power switch is off. If the **computer says "Invalid configuration specification: run SETUP"** (or a similar error message), your computer's CMOS RAM contains wrong info — probably because the battery died and needs to be replaced or recharged. In most computers, the battery is rechargeable; it recharges itself automatically if you leave the computer turned on for several hours.

To react to the error message, try running the CMOS SETUP program, which asks you questions and then stores your answers to the CMOS RAM.

If your computer's CPU is an old 286, the CMOS SETUP program comes on a floppy disk. That disk is *not* in the set of MS-DOS disks; instead, the CMOS SETUP program comes on a separate utility disk. You probably got that disk when you bought the computer. If you lost that disk, borrow one from a friend that has a similar old computer, or get it from your dealer or at any computer store's repair department.

If your computer is a newer 286 or a 386 or 486, the CMOS SETUP program does *not* come on a floppy disk. Instead, the CMOS SETUP program hides in a ROM chip inside your computer and is run when you hit a "special key" during the bootup's RAM test. That "special key" is usually either the DELETE key or the Esc key or the F1 key; to find out what the "special key" is on *your* computer, read your computer's manual or ask your dealer.

Once the CMOS SETUP program starts running, it asks you lots of questions. For each question, it also shows you what it guesses the answer is. (The computer's guesses are based on what information the computer was fed before.)

On a sheet of paper, jot down what the computer's guesses are. That sheet of paper will turn out to be *very* useful!

Some of those questions are easy to answer (such as the date and time).

A harder question is when the computer asks you to input your **hard-drive type number**. If your BIOS chip is modern and your hard drive is modern (IDE), you can make the computer automatically figure out the hard-drive type number: just choose "auto-detect hard drive" from a menu. Otherwise, you must type the hard-drive type number, as follows:

> The answer is a code number from 1 to 47. If your hard drive is modern (IDE), choose 47 or "user"; if your hard drive is older, you must choose a lower number, which you must get from your dealer. (If your dealer doesn't know the answer, phone the computer's manufacturer. If the manufacturer doesn't know the answer, look inside the computer at the hard drive; stamped on the drive, you'll see the drive's manufacturer and model number; then phone the drive's manufacturer, tell the manufacturer which model number you bought, and ask for the corresponding hard-drive type number.)
>
> If you say 47 or "user", the computer will ask you technical questions about your drive. Get the answers from your dealer (or drive's manufacturer or by looking at what's stamped on the drive).

If you don't know how to answer a question and can't reach your dealer for help, just move ahead to the next question. Leave intact the answer that the computer guessed.

After you've finished the questionnaire, the computer will automatically reboot. If the computer gripes again, either you answered the questions wrong or else the battery ran out — so that the computer forgot your answers!

In fact, the most popular reason why the computer asks you to run the CMOS SETUP program is that the battery ran out. (The battery usually lasts 1-4 years.)

> To solve the problem, first make sure you've jotted down the computer's guesses, then replace the battery, which is usually just to the left of the big power supply inside the computer. If you're lucky, the "battery" is actually a bunch of four AA flashlight batteries that you can buy in any hardware store. If you're unlucky, the battery is a round silver disk, made of lithium, like the battery in a digital watch: to get a replacement, see your dealer.
>
> After replacing the battery, run the CMOS SETUP program again, and feed it the data that you jotted down.

That's the procedure. If you're ambitious, try it. If you're a beginner, save yourself the agony by just taking the whole computer to your dealer: let the dealer diddle with the CMOS SETUP program and batteries for you.

Whenever you upgrade your computer with a better disk drive or video card or extra RAM, you must run the CMOS SETUP program again to tell the computer what you bought.

In many computers, the ROM BIOS chip is designed by **American Megatrends Inc. (AMI)**. AMI's design is called the **AMIBIOS** (pronounced "Amy buy us"). Here's how to use the 4/4/93 version of AMIBIOS. (Other versions are similar.)

When you turn the computer on, the screen briefly shows this message:

```
AMIBIOS (C)1993 American Megatrends Inc.
000000 KB OK
Hit <DEL> if you want to run SETUP
```

Then the number "000000 KB" increases, as the computer checks your RAM chips. While that number increases, try pressing your keyboard's DEL or DELETE key.

That makes the computer run the AMIBIOS CMOS SETUP program. The top of the screen will say:

```
AMIBIOS SETUP PROGRAM - BIOS SETUP UTILITIES
```

Underneath, you'll see this **main menu**:

```
STANDARD CMOS SETUP
ADVANCED CMOS SETUP
ADVANCED CHIPSET SETUP
AUTO CONFIGURATION WITH BIOS DEFAULTS
AUTO CONFIGURATION WITH POWER-ON DEFAULTS
CHANGE PASSWORD
AUTO DETECT HARD DISK
HARD DISK UTILITY
WRITE TO CMOS AND EXIT
DO NOT WRITE TO CMOS AND EXIT
```

The first and most popular choice, "STANDARD CMOS SETUP", is highlighted. Choose it (by pressing ENTER).

The computer will warn you by saying:

```
Improper use of Setup may cause problems!!!
```

Press ENTER again.

The computer will show you the info stored in the CMOS about the date, time, base memory, extended memory, hard drives, floppy drives, video card, and keyboard.

If that stored info is wrong, fix it! Here's how:

> By using the arrow keys on the keyboard, move the white box to the info that you want to fix. (Exception: you can't move the white box to the "base memory" or "extended memory".) Then change that info, by pressing the keyboard's PAGE UP or PAGE DOWN key several times, until the info is what you wish.

When you've finished examining and fixing that info, press the Esc key. You'll see the main menu again.

If you're having trouble with a modern (IDE) hard drive, choose "AUTO DETECT HARD DISK" from the main menu (by pressing the down-arrow key six times, then pressing ENTER). The computer will try to detect what kind of drive C you have, then it will say:

```
Accept Parameters for C: (Y/N) ?
```

Press the Y key then ENTER. Then the computer will try to detect what kind of drive D you have and say:

```
Accept Parameters for D: (Y/N) ?
```

Press Y again then ENTER. You'll see the main menu again.

When you've finished using the main menu, you have two choices:

> If you're *unsure* of yourself and wish you hadn't fiddled with the SETUP program, just turn off the computer's power! All your fiddling will be ignored, and the computer will act the same as before you fiddled.
>
> On the other hand, if you're *sure* of yourself and want the computer to take your fiddling seriously, press the F10 key then Y then ENTER. The computer will copy your desires to the CMOS and reboot.

Non-system disk If the **computer says "Non-system disk or disk error"**, the computer is having trouble finding the hidden system files. (In MS-DOS and Windows 95 & 98, the hidden system files are called IO.SYS and MSDOS.SYS. In PC-DOS, the hidden system files are called IBMIO.COM and IBMDOS.COM.)

Those hidden system files are supposed to be on your hard disk. You can get that error message if those hidden system files are missing from your hard disk — because you accidentally erased those files, or a virus erased them, or your hard disk is new and not yet formatted, or when you formatted the disk you forgot to put "/s" at the end of DOS's format command (or forgot to put a check mark in Windows format's "Copy system files" box).

A more common reason for getting that error message is: you accidentally put a floppy disk into drive A! When the computer boots, it looks at that floppy disk instead of your hard disk, and gripes because it can't find those system files on your floppy disk.

Cure:

> Remove any disk from drive A. Turn the computer off, wait until the computer quiets down, then turn the computer back on. If the computer still says "Non-system disk or disk error", find the floppy disks that DOS or Windows came on and try again to install DOS or Windows onto your hard disk.

Command interpreter If the **computer says "Bad or missing command interpreter"**, the computer is having trouble finding and using your COMMAND.COM file. That file is supposed to be in your hard disk's root directory — unless your CONFIG.SYS file contains a "shell=" line that tells the computer to look elsewhere.

Probably you accidentally erased COMMAND.COM, or a virus erased it, or you tried to edit it, or your COMMAND.COM file came from a different version of DOS or Windows than your hidden files, or you accidentally put a floppy disk in drive A (which makes the computer look for COMMAND.COM on your floppy disk instead of your hard disk).

Cure:

> Remove any disk from drive A then try again to boot. If you get the same error, put into drive A the main floppy disk that DOS or Windows came on, and reboot again. (Make sure you use the original floppy, not a copy. Make sure you use the same version of DOS or Windows as before; don't switch versions. For DOS 4, insert the disk labeled "install"; for DOS 5 or 6, insert the disk labeled "setup"; for Windows 95 or 98, use whatever combination of floppy disks and CD-ROM disks your manufacturer gave you for "recovery" or "setup" or "boot"; if a disk says "upgrade", that disk isn't bootable and you must find a different disk instead.)
>
> Then try to copy DOS or Windows onto your hard disk again.
>
> If you accidentally erased COMMAND.COM from your hard disk, you might have also erased CONFIG.SYS & AUTOEXEC.BAT and need to reconstruct them.

SHARE

If the **computer says "Warning — SHARE should be loaded for large media"**, you're using DOS 4, and it's installed wrong.

> Your best bet is to upgrade to DOS 5 or 6 (or Windows 95 or 98). Then the message will go away.
>
> If you refuse to upgrade, here's how to make sure the error disappears: put the SHARE.EXE program into your hard disk's root directory and also your hard disk's DOS directory. (The SHARE.EXE program came on the original DOS 4 floppy disks and is probably already in your hard disk's DOS directory. To copy it to the root directory, just give the copy command.)

Slow

If the **computer acts slower than before**, it's clogged with too many programs or too much data. Here are three possible reasons:

> 1. The hard disk is nearly full.
> 2. You have too many programs running in the RAM simultaneously.
> 3. You've left the computer on for too many hours, so fragments of programs you ran and abandoned are still in the RAM (because Windows and DOS are imperfect at erasing them from RAM).

Cure:

> Shut down the computer, then turn it back on. That usually makes the computer faster (since you've eliminated cause #3). If the computer is still too slow, do the software-cleaning procedure (on pages 575-580), which helps eliminate causes #1 and #2.

Windows 95 & 98 problems

If you're using Windows 95 or 98, you might experience the following problems. (Comments about Windows 98 also apply to Windows Me, which is similar.)

Windows doesn't finish loading

When the computer starts going into Windows, if the **Windows logo & clouds appear on the screen but never go away** (so the computer seems stuck and you never see the Start button or icons), the computer is encountering a software conflict. Cure:

> Turn the computer's power off. Go into safe mode, by following the instructions in the big gray box in page 575's column 1. Finish the software-cleaning procedure, by reading from that gray box up through page 578.

Useless password request

When the computer starts going into Windows, if the **computer unexpectedly asks you for a password**, you probably told the computer you're on a network (which requests passwords) or your computer is being shared by several people.

> If you don't know any password, press ENTER or the Esc key.
>
> To prevent the computer from asking for passwords, follow the procedure to "Remove unwanted networking" (on page 577, column 1). If that doesn't get rid of the password requests, look in the Control Panel window, at the "Passwords" icon (and, if you're using Windows 98, the "Users" icon).

Illegal operation

If the **computer says "This program has performed an illegal operation and will be shut down"**, a program is trying to use a RAM section it's not allowed to. That RAM section is being used by a different program, with which your program is having a memory conflict. Cure:

> Press ENTER. Then do the software-cleaning procedure (on pages 575-578), which makes memory conflicts less likely to occur.

Start button in wrong corner

The Start button is supposed to be in the screen's bottom left corner. If **your Start button is in a different corner**, you accidentally moved the Start button.

To move the Start button back, use one of these methods....

Method 1: just "drag the taskbar to where you want it." Here's how:

> One corner of your screen contains the Start button. Another corner contains the time. Running from the Start button to the time is a gray bar, called the **taskbar**.
>
> Point at the taskbar's middle, in a blank area where there are no buttons. While pressing the mouse's left button; drag to where you want the taskbar's middle to go: the middle of the screen's bottom. While you drag, you won't see the taskbar move; but eventually, you'll see a gray (or red or yellow) line where you want to taskbar to be. Then take your finger off the mouse's button.

Method 2: just "restart in safe mode, then restart in normal mode". Here's how:

> Click "Start" then "Shut Down" then "Restart" then "OK". If you're using Windows 98, immediately hold down the Ctrl key, and keep holding it down; if you're using Windows 95, press the F8 key as soon as the computer says "Starting Windows 95" (in white letters on the black background).
>
> The computer will say "Microsoft Windows Startup Menu". From that menu, choose "Safe mode" (by pressing 3 then ENTER). After several minutes, the computer will say "Windows is running in safe mode". Press ENTER.
>
> Click "Start" then "Shut Down" then "Restart" then "OK".

Start button missing

If the **Start button is missing and so is the time** (although the rest of the screen looks normal), you accidentally shrunk them.

The Start button and time are part of a gray bar, called the **taskbar**, that's suppose to stretch across the bottom of the screen and be about half an inch tall. You accidentally shrunk the taskbar.

To solve the problem, first close all windows (by clicking their X buttons).

If doing that makes the taskbar reappear, your problem is just that you accidentally set your taskbar to "Auto hide". Stop hiding the taskbar, by doing this:

> Click "Start" then "Settings" then "Taskbar" (which in Windows 98 is called "Taskbar & Start Menu"). Remove any checkmark from "Auto hide" (by clicking). Click "OK".

If closing all windows does *not* make the taskbar reappear, look at the screen's bottom.

If you see a gray line running across the screen's bottom, that gray line is your shrunken taskbar; make it taller by doing this:

> Point at that gray line's top edge, so the mouse pointer becomes a black arrow (which has white edges and points upward). When pressing the mouse's left button, drag up about half an inch. Suddenly there, you'll see a gray (or red or yellow) line stretch across the screen. Then take your finger off the mouse's button.

If you *don't* see a gray line running across the screen's bottom, the gray line is running along some other edge and is too messed up to deal with, so just "restart in safe mode, then restart in normal mode", by doing this:

> If your keyboard has a flying-Windows key, press it. If your keyboard lacks such a key, do this instead: while holding down the Ctrl key, press the Esc key. You'll see the Start menu. Click "Shut Down" then "Restart" then "OK".
>
> If you're using Windows 98, immediately hold down the Ctrl key, and keep holding it down; if you're using Windows 95, press the F8 key as soon as the computer says "Starting Windows 95" (in white letters on the black background).
>
> The computer will say "Microsoft Windows Startup Menu". From that menu, choose "Safe mode" (by pressing 3 then ENTER). After several minutes, the computer will say "Windows is running in safe mode". Press ENTER.
>
> Click "Start" then "Shut Down" then "Restart" then "OK".

Icons missing If **some icons are missing from the desktop screen** (the main screen), they're probably they're just hiding behind other icons or past the screen's edge. To see them again, do this:

> Close any windows (by clicking their X buttons). Right-click in the screen's middle, where there is nothing. Click "Arrange Icons" then "By Name".

If that doesn't make the icons reappear, the icons might be in the Recycle Bin, so do this:

> Double-click the "Recycle Bin" icon. If the Recycle Bin window shows one of the missing icons, right-click that icon then click "Restore".

Dialog box too big For the screen's resolution, you can choose "640 by 480" or "800 by 600" or "1024 by 768", by using a settings dialog box. If the **settings dialog box is too big to fit on the screen** (so the box's "OK" button hides below the screen's bottom), the computer is confused about what resolution you want. Instead of trying to click "OK", press ENTER. If pressing ENTER doesn't work, do this:

> Close the dialog box (by clicking its X button), then recreate the dialog box again, then choose a resolution again, then try pressing ENTER again.

Unwanted document on menu If you click "Start" then "Documents", you see the Document menu, which is a list of the last 15 documents you used. That list might annoy you, for two reasons:

> One of the documents might be embarrassing (perhaps because it's pornographic or a private letter), and you want to hide it from your colleagues and family.
>
> Even after you've deleted a document, that document's name might still be in the Document menu.

If the **Document menu annoys you**, here's how to delete documents from it:

> The Document menu shows just the names of *the last 15* documents you mentioned. Go use other documents; they'll go onto the Document-menu list and bump off the older documents.
>
> Another way to get a document off the Document menu is to erase the entire Document menu; here's how: click "Start" then "Settings" then "Taskbar" (which Windows 98 calls "Taskbar & Start Menu") then "Start Menu Programs" then "Clear".

Windows 3.1 & 3.11 problems

If you're using Windows 3.1 (or 3.11), you might experience the following problems.

Window too tall If a **window is too high to fit on the screen**, the computer is confused about how tall the window and screen are.

Since the window's top line is higher than the screen and can't be seen, you can't use the mouse to move the window down. To move the window down, use the keyboard instead of the mouse, by doing this procedure:

> Press Alt then the SPACE bar then M (which means "move"). You should see a four-headed white arrow. Press the keyboard's down-arrow key a few times, until the window is low enough to fit on the screen. Then press ENTER.

If that procedure doesn't work (and you don't see the four-headed arrow), it's probably because you accidentally pressed the Alt key twice instead of once, so try the procedure again.

File Manager icon missing In the Main window, you're supposed to see a File Manager icon. If the **File Manager icon is missing**, you accidentally deleted it. Here's how to recreate it:

> Open the Main window. Click "File" then "New" then "OK". Type "File Manager" then press the TAB key. Type "WINFILE.EXE" then press ENTER.

Major icons missing If **some icons are missing from the Program Manager window**, they're probably they're just hiding behind other icons or past the screen's edge. Cure:

> Get the Program Manager window onto the screen, and close all other windows. Maximize the Program Manager window, so it consumes the whole screen. Click the word "Window" (which is near the screen's top) then "Arrange Icons". If that doesn't make the icons reappear, reinstall the software.

Insufficient memory If the **computer says "Insufficient memory"**, the computer is claiming you don't have enough RAM chips.

> You might have to buy more RAM chips (Windows wants you to have at least 8 megabytes), or run fewer programs simultaneously (run just one program at a time!), or edit your CONFIG.SYS and AUTOEXEC.BAT files to make more conventional RAM (the conventional RAM is the first 640K of RAM, and at least 600K of it ought to be free, a goal you can accomplish by doing the "Windows 3.1 cleaning" procedure on pages 579-580), or create more free space on your hard disk (since a full hard disk makes Windows get so confused that it thinks you don't have enough RAM chips).

Microsoft Word problems

While using Microsoft Word (which is a word-processing program), you might experience the following problems.

Toolbar missing Near the screen's top, you're supposed to see the standard toolbar (which includes buttons for New, Open, Save, Print, etc.) and the formatting toolbar (which includes buttons for bold, italic, underline, etc.). If a **toolbar disappears**, you accidentally deleted it. Cure:

> Click "View" then "Toolbars". You'll see a list of toolbars; make sure "Standard" and "Formatting" have check marks in front of them (by clicking). For details, read about "Toolbars" in page 175's column 2.

Document disappears While you're typing a document, if the whole **document suddenly disappears**, you accidentally deleted it. Here's why:

> You tried to type a capital A, but instead of pressing the SHIFT key you accidentally pressed the Ctrl key. "Ctrl with A" tells the computer to "select the whole document", so the whole document becomes highlighted. The next character you type replaces the highlighted text, so the highlighted text is all lost.

Cure:

> Immediately say "undo". (The easiest way to do that is to press Ctrl with Z. Another way is to click the Undo button. Another way is to choose Undo from the Edit menu.) That undoes your last action. Say "undo" several times, until you've undone enough of your actions to undo the calamity.

Unwanted document on list At the bottom of Microsoft Word's file menu, you see a list of Microsoft Word documents you recently used. That list might annoy you, for two reasons:

> One of the documents might be embarrassing (perhaps because it's pornographic or a private letter), and you want to hide it from your colleagues and family.
>
> Even after you've deleted a document, that document's name might still be in the File menu.

If the **document list annoys you**, delete documents from it, as follows....

> The File menu shows just the names of *the last few* Microsoft Word documents you mentioned. Go use other Microsoft Word documents; they'll go onto File menu and bump off the older documents.
>
> Another way to get a document off the File menu is to erase the entire list of documents from the File menu. Here's how. Click "Tools" then "Options" then "General". Remove the check mark from the "Recently used file list" square (by clicking). Click "OK". That erases the entire document list from the File menu. Afterward, let the computer create a *new* document list in the File menu, as follows: click "Tools" then "Options", then put a check mark back into the "Recently used file list" square (by clicking), then click "OK".

Mouse problems

Mice can cause problems.

Mouse pointer lurches When you move the mouse, the mouse pointer (on the screen) is supposed to move also. **If the mouse pointer lurches erratically** (sometimes going fast, sometimes going too slow or not at all) **or moves in just one direction** (just horizontally, or just vertically, but not both), the mouse is dirty. Clean it by using the procedure on page 575; then the mouse will probably work well.

If the mouse doesn't work well yet, try this experiment:

> Take the ball out again. Rub your finger against the X and Y mouse rollers, and see if the mouse pointer moves also. If the mouse pointer works fine using your fingers but not by using the ball, the ball isn't touching the rollers, probably because the ball's cover isn't locking the ball into the proper position. Reposition the ball and its cover.

If the mouse *still* doesn't work well, just buy a new mouse. You can buy a plain mouse for under $10.

Mouse pointer hard to see While moving the mouse fast, you might have **difficulty seeing where the mouse pointer went**, because the mouse pointer seems to become temporarily invisible.

That means your screen, video card, or eyes are too slow to keep up with you. That's probably because you're using a notebook computer that has the slowest kind of screen (passive-matrix). It could also be because your eyesight is poor or you're a beginner who feels lost. Like a magician, your hand is quicker than the eye or your screen.

To make the mouse pointer easier to see, create "long mouse trails" (by following the Windows 95&98 procedure in page 106's column 2) or buy a bigger monitor or a better notebook computer (having an active-matrix screen, which is faster than a passive screen).

Dead mouse If nothing happens on screen when you move the mouse, try these strategies....:

Perhaps you're just in the middle of a routine that doesn't use the mouse. Try these ways to get out of a routine:

> Press the Esc key twice (which might exit from a routine).
> If the mouse doesn't work yet, press Ctrl with C.
> If the mouse doesn't work yet, press the Alt key.
> If the mouse doesn't work yet, press the Alt key again.

If the mouse still doesn't work yet, maybe the task you've been performing has crashed, so end that task by doing this:

> While holding down the Ctrl and Alt keys, tap the Delete key. (If you're using Windows 95 or 98, then press ENTER.)

If the mouse still doesn't work, maybe the mouse's cord is loose (tighten it!) or the mouse is dirty (clean it by following the procedure for "mouse pointer lurches") or the computer forgot what kind of mouse you have (reinstall the mouse-driver software that came with your mouse, or reinstall Windows) or just buy a new mouse.

Keyboard problems

Your keyboard might seem broken. Here's what to do.

Wet keyboard If **your keyboard got wet** (because you spilled water, coffee, soda, or some other drink), turn the computer off immediately (because water can cause a short circuit that can shock & burn the keyboard and computer and you). Unplug the keyboard from the computer.

Turn the keyboard upside-down for a few minutes, in the hope that some of the liquid drips out. Then let the keyboard rest a few hours, until the remaining liquid in it dries.

Try again to use the keyboard. It will probably work fine. If the keyboard doesn't work yet, do this:

> Unplug the keyboard again. Submerge and wash the keyboard in warm water (you can even put the keyboard into a dishwasher!) but use no soap. Dry off the keyboard. Wait a day for the keyboard to dry thoroughly. If still no luck, the keyboard has been permanently damaged, so buy another.

Dead keyboard If **pressing the keyboard's letters has no effect**, either the keyboard is improperly hooked up or the computer is overheating or you're running a frustrated program (which is ignoring what you type or waiting until a special event happens). For example, the program might be waiting for the printer to print, or the disk drive to manipulate a file, or the CPU to finish a computation, or your finger to hit a special key or give a special command.

Try getting out of any program you've been running. Here's how:

> Press the Esc key (which might let you escape from the program) or the F1 key (which might display a helpful message) or ENTER (which might move on to the next screenful of info) or Ctrl with C (which might abort the program) or Ctrl with Break. If the screen is unchanged and the computer still ignores your typing, reboot the computer; then watch the screen for error messages such as "301" (which means a defective keyboard), "201" (which means defective RAM chips), or "1701" (which means a defective hard drive).

If the keyboard seems to be "defective", it might just be unplugged from the computer.

> Make sure the cable from the keyboard is plugged *tightly* into the computer. To make sure it's tight, unplug it and then plug it back in again.
> If you stand behind the original IBM PC (instead of a newer computer), you'll see two sockets that look identical. The left one (which usually has the word "Keyboard" and a "K" next to it) is for the keyboard cable; the other is for a cassette tape recorder (which nobody uses).

Underneath a keyboard built by a clone company, you might see a switch marked "XT - AT" (or simply "X - A").

> Put that switch in the XT (or X) position if your computer is an IBM XT (or an original IBM PC or any computer containing an 8088 CPU). Put the switch in the AT (or A) position if your computer is an IBM AT (or any computer containing a 286, 386, or 486 CPU). If you don't see such a switch, make sure your keyboard was designed to work with your computer.

If fiddling with the cable and the XT-AT switch doesn't solve your problem, reboot the computer and see what happens. Maybe you'll get lucky.

Maybe some part of the computer is overheating. Here's how to find out:

> Turn the computer off. Leave it off for at least an hour, so it cools down.
> Then turn the computer back on. Try to get to a C prompt.
> After the C prompt, type a letter (such as x) and notice whether the x appears on the screen.
> If the x appears, don't bother pressing the ENTER key afterwards. Instead, walk away from the computer for two hours — leave the computer turned on — then come back two hours later and try typing another letter (such as y). If the y doesn't appear, you know that the computer "died" sometime after you typed x but before you typed y. Since during that time the computer was just sitting there doing nothing except being turned on and getting warmer, you know the problem was caused by overheating: some part inside the computer is failing as the internal temperature rises. That part could be a RAM chip, BIOS chip, or otherwise.
> Since that part isn't tolerant enough of heat, it must be replaced: take the computer in for repair.

That kind of test — where you leave the computer on for several hours to see what happens as the computer warms up — is called **letting the computer cook**.

> During the cooking, if smoke comes out of one of the computer's parts, that part is said to have **fried**. That same applies to humans: when a programmer's been working hard on a project for many hours and become too exhausted to think straight, the programmer says, "I'm **burnt out**. My brain is **fried**." Common solutions are sleep and pizza ("getting some z's & 'za").
> When computers are manufactured, the last step in the assembly line is to leave the computer turned on a long time, to let the computer cook and make sure it still works when hot. A top-notch manufacturer leaves the computer on for 2 days (48 hours) or even 3 days (72 hours), while continually testing the computer to make sure no parts fail. That part of the assembly line is called **burning in** the computer; many top-notch manufacturers do **72-hour burn in**.

Sluggish key After pressing one a keys, if the **key doesn't pop back up fast enough**, probably there's dirt under the key. The "dirt" is probably dust or coagulated drinks (such as Coke or coffee).

If *many* keys are sluggish, don't bother trying to fix them all. Just buy a new keyboard (for about $20).

If just one or two keys are sluggish, here's how to try fixing a sluggish key:

> Take a paper clip, partly unravel it so it becomes a hook, then use that hook to pry up the key, until the keycap pops off. Clean the part of the keyboard that was under that keycap: blow away the dust, and wipe away grime (such as coagulated drinks). With the keycap still off, turn on the computer, and try pressing the plunger that was under the keycap. If the plunger is still sluggish, you haven't cleaned it enough. (Don't try too hard: remember that a new keyboard costs just about $20.) When the plunger works fine, turn off the computer, put the keycap back on, and the key should work fine.

Caps While you're typing, **if each capital letter unexpectedly becomes small, and each small letter becomes capitalized**, the SHIFT key or CAPS LOCK key is activated.

The culprit is usually the CAPS LOCK key. Probably you pressing it accidentally when you meant to press a nearby key instead. The CAPS LOCK key stays activated until you deactivate it by pressing it again.

Cure:

> Press the CAPS LOCK key (again), then try typing some more, to see whether the problem has gone away.
>
> If your keyboard is modern, its top right corner has a CAPS LOCK light. That light glows when the CAPS LOCK key is activated; the light stops glowing when the CAPS LOCK key is deactivated.
>
> If pressing the CAPS LOCK key doesn't solve the problem, try jiggling the left and right SHIFT keys. (Maybe one of those SHIFT keys was accidentally stuck in the down position, because you spilled some soda that got into the keyboard and coagulated and made the SHIFT key too sticky to pop all the way back up.)
>
> If playing with the CAPS LOCK and SHIFT keys doesn't immediately solve your problem, try typing a comma and notice what happens. If the screen shows the symbol "<" instead of a comma, your SHIFT key is activated. (The CAPS LOCK key has no effect on the comma key, since the CAPS LOCK key affects just letters, not punctuation.) If pressing the comma key makes the screen show a comma, your SHIFT key is *not* activated, and any problems you have must therefore be caused by the CAPS LOCK key instead.
>
> Perhaps the CAPS LOCK key is being activated automatically by the program you're using. (For example, some programs automatically activate the CAPS LOCK key because they want your input to be capitalized.) To find out, exit from the program, reboot the computer, get to a C prompt (in DOS) or WordPad (in Windows 95 or 98), and try again to type. If the typing is displayed fine, the "problem" was probably caused by just the program you were using — perhaps on purpose.
>
> In some old Leading Edge Model D computers, the ROM has a defect that occasionally misinterprets the signals from the CAPS LOCK and SHIFT keys. When that happens, tap those keys until the display returns to normal.

Printer problems

You might have trouble printing, for several reasons.

First, many modern printers work just while using Windows. They won't work while you're using MS-DOS.

Also, many printers sold today require an expensive cable, called an **IEEE 1284 cable**. It looks like a plain cable or a bidirectional cable but contains fancier circuitry.

If you're having trouble printing, try the following experiment. Shut down the computer and the printer (so you can start fresh). When the computer's become quiet, turn it back on; then turn the printer back on. If you're using Windows 95 or 98, do this:

> Go into WordPad (by clicking "Start" then "Programs" then "Accessories" then "WordPad". Type a document that contains three words (such as "I love you") and also the word "abcdefghijklmnopqrstuvwxyz". Click "File" then "Print". Make sure the Name box contains the name of your printer; if it doesn't, click that box's down-arrow, then choose your printer from the list. Click "OK."

If you're using DOS (or Windows 3.1 or 3.11), do this instead:

> Get out of Windows and any other software you're in, so you have a C prompt, like this:
> ```
> C:\>
> ```
> Then say "dir>prn" like this:
> ```
> C:\>dir>prn
> ```
> That's supposed to make the printer print a copy of your directory. Another experiment to try is this:
> ```
> C:\>echo abcdefghijklmnopqrstuvwxyz>prn
> ```
> That's supposed to make the printer print the alphabet.

If that experimenting works fine, all your hardware is okay. Any remaining problem is probably just software: for example, you forgot to tell your program or Windows what kind of printer you bought, or you told it incorrectly.

If the experiments do *not* work fine, you're having a hardware problem: the problem lies in your printer, your computer, or the cable connecting them. Here are further details....

Incomplete characters When you look at the printed paper, you might see that **part of each character is missing**. For example, for the letter "A" you see just the top part of the "A", or just the bottom part, or everything except the middle. That means you're using an ink-jet or dot-matrix printer, and some of the ink jets or pins aren't successfully putting ink onto the paper.

If you're using a dot-matrix printer and the bottom part of each character is missing, your ribbon is too high, so that the bottom pins miss hitting it.

> Push the ribbon down lower. Read the instructions that came with your printer and ribbon, to find out the correct way to thread the ribbon through your printer. If you're using a daisy-wheel printer, also check whether the daisy-wheel is inserted correctly: try removing it and then reinserting it.

If you're using a dot-matrix printer and some other part of each character is missing, probably one of the pins broke or is stuck.

> Look at the print head, where the pins are. See if one of the pins is missing or broken. If so, consider buying a new print head, but beware: since print heads are *not* available from discount dealers, you must pay full list price for the print head, and pay almost as much for it as discount dealers charge for a whole new printer!

If you're using an ink-jet printer, probably one of the jets is clogged and needs to be cleaned.

> Follow the manufacturer's instructions on how to test and clean the ink jets. If cleaning doesn't solve the problem, try buying a new ink cartridge.

Substitute characters When you tell the printer to print a word, the printer might print the correct number of characters but **print wrong letters of the alphabet**. For example, instead of printing an "A", the printer might print a "B" or "C".

That's probably because the cable going from the computer to the printer is loose, so do this:

> Turn off the printer. Grab the cable that goes from the computer to the printer, unplug both ends of the cable, then plug both ends in again *tightly*. Try again to print. If you succeed, the cable was just loose: congratulations, you tightened it!

If tightening the cable does *not* solve the problem, the cable is probably defective.

> To *prove* it's defective, borrow a cable from a friend and try again. If your friend's cable works with your computer and printer, your original cable was definitely the culprit.
>
> Once you've convinced yourself that the problem is the cable, go to a store and buy a new cable. It's cheaper to buy a new cable than to fix the old one. Make sure you buy the right kind: your printer might require an IEEE 1284 cable.
>
> If the new cable doesn't solve your problem, try a *third* cable, since many cables are defective!

If buying a new cable doesn't solve your problem, you have defective circuitry in your printer or in your computer's parallel-printer port.

> Get together with a friend and try swapping printers, computers, and cables: make notes about which combinations work and which don't. You'll soon discover which computers, cables, and printers work correctly and which ones are defective.

Extra characters When using a program (such as a word-processing program), the printer might **print a few extra characters at the top of each page**.

Those extra characters are special codes that the printer should *not* print. Those codes are supposed to tell the printer *how* to print. Your printer is misinterpreting those codes, because those codes were intended for a different kind of printer — or your printer cable is loose.

First, make sure the printer cable is tight.

Then try again to tell your software which printer you bought. Here's how. If you're using Windows 95 or 98, do this:

> Click "Start" then "Settings" then "Printers". Double-click "Add Printer". Follow the prompts on the screen.

If you're using Windows 3.1, do this:

> Go to the program manager. Double-click the Main icon then the Control Panel icon then the Printers icon. Follow the prompts on the screen.

To tell a non-Windows program which printer you bought, read the program's manual: look for the part of the manual that explains "printer installation & selection & setup".

Misaligned columns

When printing a table of numbers or words, the columns might wiggle: some of the words and numbers might be printed slightly too far left or right, even though they looked perfectly aligned on the screen.

That's because you're trying to print by using a proportionally spaced font that doesn't match the screen's font.

The simplest way to solve the problem is to **switch to a monospaced font**, such as Courier or Prestige Elite or Gothic or Lineprinter.

> Since those fonts are monospaced (each character is the same width as every other character), there are no surprises. To switch fonts while using Windows, use your mouse: drag across all the text whose font you wish to switch, then say which font you wish to switch to.

Unfortunately, monospaced fonts are ugly. If you insist on using proportionally spaced fonts, which are prettier, remember that when moving from column to column you should **press the TAB key, not the SPACE bar**.

> In proportionally spaced fonts, the SPACE bar creates a printed space that's too narrow: it's narrower than the space created by the typical digit or letter.
>
> If the TAB key doesn't make the columns your favorite width, customize how the TAB key works by adjusting the TAB stops. (In most word-processing programs, you adjust the TAB stops by sliding them on the layout ruler.)

Normally, the computer tries to *justify* your text: it tries to make the right margin straight by inserting extra spaces between the words. But when you're printing a table, those extra spaces can wreck your column alignment. So when typing a table of numbers, do *not* tell the computer to justify your text: **turn justification OFF**.

Touching characters

The printer might **bump some characters into each other**, that "cat" looks like "cat". That means the computer fed the printer wrong info about how wide to make the characters and how much space to leave between them. That's because you told the computer wrong info about which printer you're going to use.

Tell the computer again which printer to use.

> For example, suppose you plan to type a document by using your home computer's word-processing program, then copy the document onto a floppy disk, take the floppy disk to your office, and print a final draft on the *office's* printer. Since you'll be printing the final draft on the office's printer, tell your home computer that you'll be using the *office's* printer.
>
> If you're using Windows 95 or 98, here's how: click "Start" then "Settings" then "Printers" then double-click "Add Printer", then follow the prompts on the screen.
>
> If you're using Windows 3.1, do this instead: double-click the Main icon then the Control Panel icon then the Printer icon, then click the Add button, then double-click the printer's name.

Margins On a sheet of paper, all the printing might be too far to the left, or too far to the right, or too far up, or too far down. That shows you forgot to tell the computer about the paper's size, margins, and feed, or you misfed the paper into the printer.

Software makes assumptions:

> Most computer software assumes the paper is 11 inches tall and 8½ inches wide (or slightly wider, if the paper has holes in its sides). The software also assumes you want 1-inch margins on all four sides (top, bottom, left, and right).
>
> If you told the software you have a dot-matrix printer, the software usually assumes you're using **pin-feed paper** (which has holes in the side); it's also called **continuous-feed paper**. For ink-jet and laser printers, the software typically assumes you're using **friction-feed paper** instead (which has no holes).
>
> If those assumptions are not correct, tell the software. For example, give a "margin", "page size", or "feed" command to your word-processing software.

If you make a mistake about how tall the sheet of paper is, the computer will try to print too many or too few lines per page. The result is **creep**: on the first page, the printing begins correctly; but on the second page the printing is slightly too low or too high, and on the third page the printing is even more off.

> To solve a creep problem, revise slightly what you tell the software about how tall the sheet of paper is. For example, **if the printing is fine on the first page but an inch too low on the second page, tell the software that each sheet of paper is an inch shorter**.
>
> On pin-feed paper, the printer can print all the way from the very top of the paper to the very bottom. On friction-feed paper, the printer can*not* print at the sheet's very top or very bottom (since the rollers can't grab the paper securely enough while printing there). So on friction-feed paper, the printable area is smaller, as if the paper were shorter. Telling the software wrong info about feed has the same effect as telling the software wrong info about the paper's height: you get creep.
>
> So **to fix creep, revise what you tell the software about the paper's height or feed**. If the software doesn't let you talk about the paper's feed, kill the creep by revising what you say about the paper's height.
>
> If you're using a dot-matrix printer that can handle both kinds of paper (pin-feed and friction-feed), **you'll solve most creep problems by choosing pin-feed paper**.

If all printing is too far to the left (or right), adjust what you tell the software about the left and right margins; or if you're using pin-feed paper in a dot-matrix printer with movable tractors, slide the tractors to the left or right (after loosening them by flipping their levers). For example, **if the printing is an inch too far to the right, slide the tractors an inch toward the right**.

Other hardware problems

If you try to install extra hardware, it might not work — and installing it might make your other hardware stop working also.

One reason is a **hardware conflict**: your new hardware might conflict with the old hardware. For example, if your new hardware tries to use the same **Interrupt ReQuest (IRQ)** as other hardware, neither hardware will work correctly; that's called an **IRQ conflict**. Your computer handles just 16 Interrupt Requests, which are numbered from 0 to 15:

IRQ	hardware usually assigned to it
0	system timer
1	keyboard (and the keyboard's controller chip)
2	programmable interrupt controller (which helps handle IRQ #8-#15)
3	modem (or other device attached to COM2 or COM4)
4	serial mouse (or other device attached to COM1 or COM3)
5	speakers & their sound card (or LPT2, which controls a secondary printer)
6	floppy-disk controller (which controls floppy disk drives A & B)
7	main printer (or other device attached to LPT1)
8	real-time clock (which keeps track of the date & time)
9	network interface card
10	(available for new hardware)
11	PCMCIA card (for notebook computer) or SCSI card or PCI video card
12	PS/2 bus mouse
13	math coprocessor (which is part of the CPU chip or a separate chip)
14	primary IDE adapter (which controls your first two IDE hard drives)
15	secondary IDE adapter (which controls your next two IDE hard drives)

For example, if you have a modem on COM2 and a device on COM4, they'll conflict with each other, since they're both trying to use IRQ 3. If you have a traditional sound card and two printers, the sound card will conflict with your second printer, since they're both trying to use IRQ 5.

Here's how to find out which IRQs are being used in your computer:

> **Windows 95 & 98:** right-click "My Computer", click "Properties", click "Device Manager", double-click "Computer"; you'll see the list of IRQs.
>
> **MS-DOS 6 & 6.22:** at the C prompt, type "msd" (and press ENTER), then press the Q key; you'll see the list of IRQs, in which "reserved" means unused; when you finish examining the list, press ENTER then the F3 key.

If two devices are trying to use the same IRQ number as each other and aren't working, remove one of those devices or change the IRQ number of one of those devices (by following the instructions that came with the device).

Here are more details about specific devices....

Floppy-drive light If the **floppy-drive light stays on**, the data cable from the floppy drive is plugged into the motherboard (or floppy-drive controller card) upside-down.

> Shut the computer down. Then flip that cable upside-down, so its red wire is at the computer's front (and attaches to the part of the motherboard (or floppy-drive controller card marked "pin 1").

No sound If **you don't hear sounds** (such as beeps and music), the problem could be caused by hardware or software.

Make sure the speakers are plugged into the computer. Make sure they're plugged into the computer's speaker jack tightly, not the microphone jack. If the speakers contain batteries, make sure the batteries are working. If the speakers need to be plugged into a wall socket or power strip, make sure they are. If the speakers have an ON button, make sure it's in the ON position.

Make sure all volume knobs are turned up:

> There's probably a volume knob on the front of the speakers. On the back of the computer, where the speakers plug into the computer, you might find a volume dial.

If you're still not hearing sounds, do software cleaning (by following pages 575-581), which reduces memory conflicts, because when the computer is faced with a memory conflict it gives up trying to produce sounds.

If you're *not* using Windows 95 or 98, you must put lines in your AUTOEXEC.BAT file that tell the computer what kind of sound card you bought and how to handle it:

> Look for old versions of AUTOEXEC.BAT by giving this command:
> `C:\>dir autoexec.*`
> That command makes the computer show you a list of AUTOEXEC files, with the dates they were changed. Find an AUTOEXEC file dated shortly before the sound problem occurred, and the use the sound lines in it, by putting those lines into your current AUTOEXEC.BAT file or by copying the entire old AUTOEXEC file to AUTOEXEC.BAT. For more info about AUTOEXEC.BAT, read pages 135-137. Phone me at 603-666-6644 if you want further help.

If you *are* using Windows 95 or 98, do the following instead....

At the screen's bottom right corner, next to the time, you might find a Volume icon (which looks like a blaring loudspeaker). If so, do this:

> Click the Volume icon. You see a Mute box; make sure it's unchecked. You see a slider; drag it up to the top. Try clicking the slider; you should hear a bell sound, at the volume level you requested.
> Click "Start" then "Accessories" then "Multimedia" (which Windows 98 calls "Entertainment") then "Volume Control". You'll see many sliders. Make sure each volume slider is dragged to the top, make sure each balance slider is centered, and make sure each Mute box is unchecked. Then close the window (by clicking its X button).

Click "Start" then "Settings" then "Control Panel". Double-click "Sounds". Make sure the Schemes box says "Windows Default". (If it doesn't, click that box's down-arrow, then choose "Windows Default" from the list.) Then do this test:

> In the big white box, scroll down to "Start Windows". Make sure the Name box says "The Microsoft Sound". Make sure the Preview box has a loudspeaker in it, instead of being blank. Make sure the triangle to its right is black, instead of being grayed out. If the Preview box is empty and the triangle is grayed out, the computer thinks you have no sound card. If you're lucky, and the triangle is black, click it: you should hear a long loud chord, accompanied by a background of synthesized outer-space new-age sounds. If you don't hear that chord, the computer thinks everything is fine, but everything isn't.

If you're still not having any luck, you can try having Windows redetect your hardware (click "Start" then "Settings" then "Control Panel" then double-click "Add New Hardware" then press ENTER), but that's typically useless. An approach that's slightly more likely to succeed, if you have the patience, is to reinstall Windows. Phone me at 603-666-6644 if you want further help.

CD-ROM not working If the **CD-ROM drive stops working**, the cause is probably dust, bad disks, a loose cable, or CD-ROM driver software.

First, get rid of dust. Dust off the CD-ROM disks and tray. Take a deep breathe and blow air into the CD-ROM drive, but avoid spit. If you wish, buy a CD-ROM head cleaner at Radio Shack; it's a fake CD-ROM disk that has brushes on it, to brush dust off the CD-ROM lens.

If a CD-ROM disk has scratches on it, that disk might be damaged and never work. Try other disks instead.

If you're using a "homemade" CD-R or CD-RW disk created on another computer, the signals on that disk might be too weak to be detected by an old CD-ROM drive. Try disks created in other ways instead, or try using a different CD-ROM drive.

Open the computer and check the cable that runs out of the CD-ROM drive. Probably one end of that cable is loose and flimsy. Try to plug it in more snugly.

If you're using Windows 95 or 98, and the four corners of your screen say "Safe mode", you can't use the CD-ROM drive while your computer is in that mode: you must shut down the computer and restart in "Normal mode".

You must teach the computer what kind of CD-ROM drive you have. Here's the general strategy (but if you want help with the details, phone me at 603-666-6644):

> If your computer came with Windows 95 or 98, it should have come with a floppy disk called an "Emergency Recovery Start-Up Multimedia CD-ROM Boot Disk" (or some abridgment of that name). Put that disk into the computer, then reboot the computer. That disk usually makes the CD-ROM drive work, at least temporarily. While the CD-ROM drive is working, reinstall Windows.
>
> If you're *not* using Windows 95 or 98, you must put lines in your CONFIG.SYS and AUTOEXEC.BAT files about the CD-ROM drive. The line in AUTOEXEC.BAT should typically be "Lh mscdex /d:mscd000 /m:12 /e", but the line in CONFIG.SYS depends on which CD-ROM drive you bought and how you installed other devices that might conflict with it. Comments about AUTOEXEC.BAT and CONFIG.SYS files are on pages 134-137; but before you try to edit those files, check whether your hard disk or floppy disk still has old but workable versions of those files. For example, the old version of CONFIG.SYS might be called CONFIG.OLD or CONFIG.000 or something similar. To find out whether you have such a file, say:
> `C:\>dir config.*`
> That makes the computer print a list of all CONFIGs in your hard disk's root directory. In that list, notice the date of each file; try reusing a CONFIG that has a date slightly before when your CD-ROM drive stopped working. Try using that old CONFIG.SYS and old AUTOEXEC.BAT by renaming them to CONFIG.SYS and AUTOEXEC.BAT, after making backup copies of your current (non-working) CONFIG.SYS and AUTOEXEC.BAT.

VIRUSES

Virus secrets

A **computer virus** is a program that purposely does mischief and manages to copy itself to other computers, so the mischief spreads. Since computer viruses are **malicious malevolent software**, they're called **malware**.

People create viruses for several reasons.

> **Some people think it's funny** to create mischief, by creating viruses. They're the same kind of people who like to play "practical jokes" and, as kids, pulled fire alarms.
>
> **Some people are angry** (at dictatorships, at the military, at big impersonal corporations, at clients who don't pay bills, at lovers who rejected them, and at homosexuals). To get revenge, they create viruses to destroy their enemy's computers.
>
> **Some people are intellectuals who want the challenge** of trying to create a program that replicates itself. Too often, the program replicates itself too well and too fast and accidentally does more harm that the programmer intended.
>
> **Some people want to become famous** (or infamous or influential) by inventing viruses. They're the same kinds of people who, as kids, wrote graffiti on school walls and in bathrooms.

People who create viruses tend to be immature. Many are teenagers or disgruntled college students.

Different viruses perform different kinds of mischief.

> Some viruses **print nasty messages**, containing four-letter words or threats or warnings, to make you worry and waste lots of your time and prevent you from getting work done.
>
> Some viruses **erase some files**, or even your entire hard disk.
>
> Some viruses **screw up your computer** so it prints wrong answers or stops functioning.
>
> Some viruses **clog your computer**, by giving the computer more commands than the computer can handle, so the computer has no time left to handle other tasks, and all useful computer tasks remain undone.

The damage done by a virus is called the virus's **payload**. Some viruses are "benign": they do very little damage; their payload is small. Other viruses do big damage; they have a **big payload**. If a virus destroys your files, it's said to have a **destructive payload**.

Propagation tricks

To propagate, viruses use two main tricks.

Trojan horse Homer's epic poem, *The Iliad*, describes how the Greeks destroyed Troy by a trick: they persuaded the Trojans to accept a "gift" — a gigantic wooden horse that secretly contained Greek warriors, who then destroyed Troy.

Some computer viruses use that trick: they look like a pleasant gift program, but the program secretly contains destructive warriors that destroy your computer. A pleasant-seeming program that secretly contains a virus is called a **Trojan horse**.

Time bomb If a virus damages your computer immediately (as soon as you receive it), you'll easily figure out who sent the virus, and you can stop the perpetrator. To prevent such detection, clever viruses are **time bombs**: they purposely delay damaging your computer until you've accidentally transmitted the virus to other computers; then, several weeks or months after you've been secretly infected and have secretly infected others, they suddenly destroy your computer system, and you don't know why. You don't know whom to blame.

How viruses arose

The first computer virus was invented in 1983 by Fred Cohen as an innocent experiment in computer security. He didn't harm anybody: his virus stayed in his lab.

In 1986, a different person invented the first virus that ran on a PC. That virus was called **Brain**. Unfortunately, it accidentally escaped from its lab; it was found next year at the University of Delaware. (A virus that escapes from its lab is said to be found **in the wild**.)

Most early viruses harmed nobody, but eventually bad kids started invented destructive viruses. The first destructive virus that spread fast was called the **Jerusalem virus** because it was first noticed at the Hebrew University of Israel in 1987. It's believed to have been invented by a programmer in Tel Aviv or Italy.

Most people still thought "computer viruses" were just myths; but in 1988, magazines began running articles saying computer viruses really exist. Then researchers began to invent **anti-virus programs** to protect against viruses and destroy them. In 1989, anti-virus programs started being distributed to the general public, to protect against the 30 viruses that had been invented so far.

Unfortunately, the nasty programmers writing viruses began protecting their viruses against the anti-virus programs. Now there are over 50,000 viruses, though many are just **copycat viruses** that are slight variants of others.

Companies writing anti-virus software are working as hard as the villains writing the viruses. Most anti-virus companies release updates (quarterly, or monthly, or immediately by downloading from the Internet), sometimes for free.

Popular anti-virus programs

MS-DOS 6 & 6.2 come with an anti-virus program called **msav** (which stands for **MicroSoft Anti-Virus**). But msav is rather useless, since most viruses were invented after it and outsmart it.

The best anti-virus program is **Norton AntiVirus**, which is published by **Symantec** and costs just $40.

> You can also get Norton AntiVirus 2000 as part of **Norton SystemWorks**, which costs $60 and includes other utilities. Buy AntiVirus or SystemWorks from any computer store or mail-order dealer. The most convenient mail-order dealer is PC Connection (at 800-800-0003), which charges just $5 for overnight shipping. (You can order late at night and still receive it in the morning!)

The second-best anti-virus program is **McAfee VirusScan**, which is published by **Network Associates** and costs just $20 for the plain version, $30 for the Deluxe version.

> You can also get it as part of **McAfee Office**, which costs $45 for the plain version, $60 for the Pro version. A stripped-down version of McAfee VirusScan is often included free when you buy a computer.

You can get a free anti-virus checkup, called **HouseCall**, from an Internet Web site called "housecall.antivirus.com". That Web site is run by **Trend Micro**, which also sells an anti-virus program called **PC-cillin**.

If you have Windows 95 (or 98), make sure you get anti-virus software that's designed for Windows 95 (or 98). Older anti-virus software thinks Windows 95 is one big virus and tries to erase all of Windows 95.

Alas, using virus-scanning software can make your computer run slower, since virus-scanning can take a long time and consume RAM.

Who gets viruses

The most common place to find traditional viruses is at schools.

That's partly because most viruses were invented at schools (by bright, mischievous students) but mainly **because many students share the school's computers**. If one student has an infected floppy disk (purposely or accidentally) and puts it into one of the school's computers, that computer's hard disk will probably get infected. Then it will infect all the other students who use that computer. As disks are passed from that computer to the school's other computers, the rest of the school's computers become infected.

Then the school's **students, unaware of the infection, take the disks home** with them and infect their families' home computers. Then the **parents bring infected disks to their offices** (so they can transfer work between home and office) and infect their companies. Then company employees take infected disks home and infect their home computers, which infect any disks used by the kids, who, unaware of the infection, then take infected disks to school and start the cycle all over again.

Anybody who shares programs with other people can get a virus. Most programs are copyrighted and illegal to share. People who share programs illegally are called **pirates**. Pirates spread viruses. For example, many kids spread viruses when they try to share their games with their friends.

Another source of viruses is computer stores, in their computer-repair departments.

While trying to analyze and fix broken computers, the repair staff often shoves diagnostic disks into the computers, to find out what's wrong. If one of the broken computers has a virus, the diagnostic disks accidentally get viruses from the broken computers and then pass the viruses on to other computers. So if you bring your computer to a store for repairs, don't be surprised if your computer gets fixed but also gets a virus.

Occasionally, a major software company will screw up, accidentally get infected by a virus, and unknowingly distribute it to all folks buying the software. Even companies as big as Microsoft have accidentally distributed viruses.

The newest viruses are spread by Internet communications, such as e-mail, instead of by floppy disks. Internet-oriented viruses spread quickly all over the world: they're an international disaster!

7 kinds of viruses

Viruses fall into 7 categories: you can get infected by a **file virus**, a **boot-sector virus**, a **multipartite virus**, a **macro virus**, an **e-mail worm**, a **denial-of-service attack**, or a **hoax**.

Here are the details....

File viruses

A **file virus** (also called a **parasitic virus**) secretly attaches itself to an innocent program, so the innocent program becomes infected. Whenever you run the infected innocent program, you're running the virus too!

Here are the file viruses that are most common. For each virus, I begin by showing its name, the country it came from, and the month it was first discovered in the wild. Let's start with the oldest....

Yankee Doodle

(From Bulgaria in September 1989) Every day at 5 PM, this virus **plays part of the song Yankee Doodle** on the computer's built-in speaker.

This virus is also called **Old Yankee** and **TP44VIR**. It infects .COM & .EXE files, so they become 2899 bytes longer.

Die Hard 2

(From South Africa in July 1994) This virus infects .COM & .EXE files and makes them become exactly 4000 bytes bigger.

The virus also overwrites .ASM files (programs written in assembler) with a short program. When you try to compile the .ASM program, the computer hangs.

It's also called **DH2**.

Chernobyl

(From Taiwan in June 1998) Back on April 26, 1986, radioactive gas escaped from a nuclear reactor in Chernobyl in the Soviet Union. The Chernobyl virus commemorates that event by **erasing your hard disk on April 26th every year**. (A variant, called **version 1.4**, erases your hard disk on **the 26th of every month**.)

If you get infected by this virus, you won't notice it until the 26th; then suddenly your hard disk gets erased — and so do the hard disks of all your friends to whom you'd accidentally sent the virus!

The virus was written in Taiwan by a 24-year old guy named Chen Ing-Hau. Since his initials are CIH, the virus is also called the **CIH virus**.

The virus was first noticed in June 1998. It did its first damage on April 26, 1999. Computers all over the world lost their data on that day. Most American corporations were forewarned and forearmed with anti-virus programs; but **in Korea a million computers lost their data, at a cost of 250 million dollars**, because Koreans don't use anti-virus programs but do use a lot of pirated software.

Here's how the virus erases your hard disk:

It starts at the disk's beginning and writes random info onto every sector (beginning at sector 0), until your computer stops working. The data that was previously on those overwritten sectors is gone forever and cannot be recovered.

The virus also tries to attack your computer's Flash BIOS chips, by writing wrong info into them. If the virus succeeds, your computer will be permanently unable to display anything on the screen and also have trouble communicating with the keyboard, ports, and other devices, unless you bring your computer into a repair shop.

The virus destroys data just if you're using Windows 95 or 98 (not Windows 3.1, not Windows NT).

Here's how the virus spreads:

Whenever you run an infected program, the virus in the program copies itself into the RAM memory chips, stays there (until you turn the computer off), and infects every other program you try to run or copy. To infect a program, the virus looks for unused spaces in the program's file, then breaks itself up and puts pieces of itself into unused spaces, so the file's total length is the same as before and the virus is undetected.

Before you attack the virus by using an anti-virus program, boot by using an uninfected floppy. If instead you just boot normally from your hard disk, your hard disk's infected files copy the virus into RAM; then when you tell the anti-virus program to "scan all programs to remove the virus", the anti-virus program accidentally *copies* the virus onto all those programs and infects them all. Yes, the virus tricks your anti-virus program into becoming a *pro*-virus program!

Boot-sector viruses

On a floppy disk or hard disk, the first sector is called the disk's **boot sector** or, more longwindedly, the disk's **master boot record (MBR)**. A virus that hides in the boot sector is called a **boot-sector virus**. Whenever the computer tries to boot from a drive containing an infected disk, the virus copies itself into RAM memory chips (even if the booting is unfinished because the disk is considered "unbootable").

Before hiding in the boot sector, the typical boot-sector virus makes room for itself by moving data from the boot sector to a "second place" on the disk. Unfortunately, whatever data had been in the "second place" gets overwritten and cannot be recovered.

The typical boot-sector virus makes the computer eventually **hang** (stop reacting to your keystrokes and mouse strokes).

Here are the boot-sector viruses that are most common....

Stoned

(From New Zealand in December 1987) Of all the viruses common today, this is the oldest. It was invented in 1987 by a student at the University of Wellington, New Zealand.

If you boot from a disk (floppy or hard) infected with this virus, there's a 1-in-8 chance your computer will beep and display this message: "Your PC is now Stoned".

It was intended to be harmless, but it assumes your floppy disk is 360K and **accidentally erases important parts of the directory** on higher-capacity floppy disks (such as 1.44M disks). It also **makes your computer run slower** — as if your computer were stoned.

It doesn't infect files and can't infect other computers over a network. In its most common form, it reduces your total conventional RAM memory by 4K, so you have 636K instead of 640K. It also contains this message, which doesn't get displayed: "Legalise Marijuana". This virus is also called **Marijuana**, **Hemp**, and **New Zealand**. Many other virus writers have created imitations & variants, called **strains**. Some strains reduce your total conventional RAM memory by 1K or 2K instead of 4K.

Form

(From Switzerland in June 1990) This virus is supposed to just play a harmless prank: **on the 18th day of each month, the computer beeps whenever a key is pressed**. But this virus is badly written and accidentally causes problems. For example, **if your hard disk ever becomes full, the virus makes the hard disk become unbootable**. And if the computer ever fails to read from a disk, the virus can make the system hang.

It reduces your total conventional RAM memory by 2K, so you have 638K instead of 640K. The virus's second sector contains this message, which never gets displayed: "The FORM-Virus send greetings to everyone who's reading this text. FORM doesn't destroy data! Don't panic! Fuckings go to Corinne."

Michelangelo

(From Sweden in April 1991) Inspired by the Stoned virus (and sometimes called **Stoned Michelangelo**), this virus sits quietly on your hard disk until Michelangelo's birthday, March 6th. Each year, **on March 6th, the virus tries to destroy all data on your hard drive**, by writing **garbage** (random meaningless bytes) everywhere.

This virus was invented before big hard drives became popular, so it assumes your hard drive is small: it writes the garbage onto just the first 17 sectors of each of the first 256 tracks of each of the first 2 platters, both sides. The overwritten data cannot be recovered. The virus reduces your total conventional RAM memory by 1K, so you have 639K instead of 640K. The simplest way to avoid damage from the virus is to adopt this trick: on March 5th, before you turn off the computer, change the computer's date to March 7th, skipping March 6th.

Monkey

(From the USA in October 1992) Inspired by the Stoned virus (and sometimes called **Stoned Empire Monkey**), this virus **encrypts the hard drive's partition table**, so **the hard drive is accessible just while the virus is in memory**. If you boot the system from a clean (uninfected) floppy disk, the hard drive is unusable. This virus is tough to remove successfully, since **removing the virus will also remove your ability to access the data**.

It reduces your total conventional RAM by 1K, so you have 639K instead of 640K.

Parity Boot

(From Germany in September 1993) Every hour, this virus checks whether it's infected a floppy disk. If it hasn't infected a disk in the last hour, it says "PARITY CHECK" and **hangs the computer**.

This virus consumes 1K of your RAM, so your conventional RAM is 639K instead of 640K. The virus stays in RAM even if you press Ctrl with Alt with Del: to unload the virus from RAM, you must turn off the computer's power or press the Reset button.

Ripper

(From Norway in November 1993) This virus **randomly corrupts data being written to disk**.

The chance of a particular write being corrupted is just 1 out of 1024, so the corruption occurs just occasionally and to just a few bytes at a time. You typically don't notice the problem until several weeks have gone by and the infection has spread to many files and your backups, too! Then it's too late to recover your data! Yes, Ripper has the characteristic of a successful virus: its effects are so subtle that you don't notice it until you've infected your hard disk, your backups, and your friends! Then ya wanna die! It's also called **Jack Ripper**, because it contains this message which is never displayed: "(c)1992 Jack Ripper". It contains another undisplayed message: "FUCK 'EM UP !"

Anti-EXE

(From Russia in December 1993) This virus monitors disk activity and waits for you to run a certain important .EXE program. (Virus researchers haven't yet discovered which .EXE program is involved.) When you run that important .EXE program (so that program's in your RAM), the virus corrupts the copy that's in the RAM (but not the copy that's on disk). While you run that corrupted copy, **errors occur, and the computer usually hangs**.

Anti-CMOS

(From the USA in February 1994) **This virus changes your system's CMOS settings**, as follows:

Your hard drive becomes "not installed".
Your 1.44M floppy drive becomes "1.2M".
A 1.2M floppy drive becomes "not installed".
A 360K floppy drive becomes "720K", and vice-versa.

To evade detection and give itself time to spread to other computers, it waits awhile before doing that damage: it waits until you've accessed the floppy drive many times; on the average, it waits for 256 accesses.

It's spread just when someone tries to boot the system from an infected floppy disk. It reduces your total conventional RAM memory by 2K, so you have 638K instead of 640K. After it's damaged your CMOS settings, here's how to recover: run your computer's CMOS setup program, which lets you reset the CMOS to the correct settings.

A variant virus, **Anti-CMOS.B**, generates sounds from the computer's built-in speaker instead of changing the CMOS.

New York Boot

(From the USA in July 1994) This virus's only function is to spread itself. But it spreads itself fast and often. It's also called **NYB**.

Multipartite viruses

You've learned that some viruses, (called **boot-sector viruses**) infect the disk's boot sector, while other viruses (called **file viruses**) infect the disk's file system. If a virus is smart enough to infect the disk's boot sector and file system simultaneously, it's called a **multipartite virus**.

Yes, a multipartite virus hides in *two* places: the boot sector and also the file system. If you remove the virus from just the boot sector (or from just files), you still haven't completely removed the virus, which can regenerate itself from the place you missed.

If a virus is very smart, it's called a **stealth polymorphic armored multipartite virus (SPAM virus)**:

> A **stealth virus** makes special efforts to hide itself from anti-virus software. For example, it tricks anti-virus software into inspecting a clean copy of a file instead of letting it read the actual (infected) file.
>
> A **polymorphic virus** changes its own appearance each time it infects a file, so no two copies of the virus look alike to anti-virus programs.
>
> An **armored virus** protects itself against anti-virus disassembly.
>
> A **multipartite virus** hides in *two* places: the boot sector and also the file system.

One Half

(From Austria in October 1994) The most common multipartite virus is **One Half**. It slowly **encrypts the hard drive**. Each time you turn on the computer, the virus encrypts two more cylinders (starting with the innermost 2 tracks and working toward the outer tracks). The encrypting is done by using a random code. You can use the encrypted cylinders as long as the virus remains in memory. When about half of the hard drive's cylinders are encrypted, the computer says: "Dis is one half Press any key to continue......"

This virus is tough to remove successfully, since **removing the virus will also remove your ability to access the data**.

It infects the hard disk's MBR, each floppy disk's boot sector, and .EXE and .COM files. It scans filenames for text relating to anti-virus programs (such as MSAV, NOD, SCAN, CLEAN, and FINDVIRU): it won't infect anti-virus programs! It's hard to detect, since it's polymorphic and uses stealth. It reduces your total conventional RAM memory by 4K, so you have 636K instead of 640K. It's also called **Dis**, **Slovak Bomber**, **Explosion 2**, and **Free Love**.

Macro viruses

A **macro virus** hides in **macros**, which are little programs embedded in Microsoft Word documents and Excel spreadsheets. The virus spreads to another computer when you give somebody an infected document (on a floppy disk or through a local-area network or as an e-mail attachment). During the past few years, e-mail has become prevalent, and so have macro viruses: they're more prevalent than all other viruses combined.

Here are the most prevalent macro viruses....

Concept

(From the USA in July 1995) This virus infects Microsoft Word documents and templates. When you load an infected document for the first time, you see a dialog box that says "1", with an OK button. Once you click OK, the virus takes over. It forces all documents to be saved as templates, which in turn affect new documents.

It consists of 5 macros: **AutoOpen**, **PayLoad**, **FileSaveAs**, **AAAZAO**, and **AAAZFS**. You can see those macros in an infected Word document by choosing "Macro" from the Tools menu.

Invented in 1995, it was historic:

> It was the first macro virus. It was the first virus that infects documents instead of programs or boot sectors. It was the first virus that can infect *both* kinds of computers: IBM and Mac!

Old anti-virus programs can't detect it.

It was intended as just a harmless prank demonstration of what a macro virus could do (and is therefore also called the **Prank Macro virus**), but it spread fast.

> In 1995, it became more prevalent than any other virus. Microsoft Word's newest versions (Word 97 and Word 2000) protect themselves against the virus, but their predecessor (Word 7) is vulnerable unless you buy an anti-virus program that includes anti-Concept.

Wazzu

(From the USA in June 1996) Inspired by the Concept virus, this virus consists of a macro called **AutoOpen** that forces Microsoft Word documents to be saved as templates. Whenever you open a document, the virus also **rearranges up to 3 words and inserts the word "Wazzu" at random**.

Laroux

(From the USA in July 1996) This virus was first discovered in July 1996 in Africa and Alaska. It was the first macro virus that infected Excel spreadsheets (instead of Word documents). It does no harm except copy itself. It works just in Windows, not on Macs.

Tristate

(From the USA in March 1998) This macro virus is called "Tristate" because it's smart enough to infect *three* things: Microsoft Word documents, Excel spreadsheets, and PowerPoint slides.

Class

(From the USA in October 1998) This macro virus infects Microsoft Word documents. It just displays a stupid message on your screen occasionally.

> The original version (called **Class.A**) says "This is Class" on your screen, on the 31st day of each month. The most prevalent version (called **Class.D**) displays this message on the 14th day of each month after May: "I think", then your name, then "is a big stupid jerk!" The craziest version (called **Class.E**) says "Monica Blows Clinton! -=News@11=-" occasionally (at random, 1% of the time); and on the 17th day of each month after August, it says "Today is Clinton & Monica Fuck-Fest Day!"

Ethan

(From the USA in January 1999) When you use Microsoft Word, if you click "File" then "Properties" then "Summary", you see a window where you can type a document's title, author, keywords, and other items. When you close a document infected by the Ethan virus, this virus has a 30% chance of **changing the document's title to "Ethan Frome", the author to "EW/LN/CB", and the keywords to "Ethan"**.

That's to honor *Ethan Frome*, a novel written by Edith Wharton in 1911, about a frustrated man — the kind of man who would now write viruses.

Melissa

(From the USA in March 1999) This macro virus infects Microsoft Word documents. When you look at (open) a document, if the document is infected, the virus tries to e-mail copies of the infected document to the first 50 people mentioned in Microsoft Outlook's address book (which is called the **Contacts folder**), unless the virus e-mailed to those people previously. Yes, **your document gets secretly e-mailed to 50 people**, without you knowing!

Each of those 50 people get an e-mail from you. The e-mail's subject says "Important message from" and your name. The e-mail's body says "Here is that document you asked for ... don't show anyone else ;-)". Attached to that e-mail is your document, infected by the virus.

This virus spreads fast just if your computer has Microsoft Outlook.

The typical large corporation *does* have Microsoft Outlook on each computer (since Microsoft Outlook is part of Microsoft Office), so the virus e-mails itself to 50 people automatically, and each of those people e-mails to 50 other people, etc., so the virus spreads fast.

The FBI hunted for the perpetrator and concluded that the Melissa virus was invented by David L. Smith in New Jersey.

He called it "Melissa" to honor a Florida topless dancer. Her name is hidden in the virus program. The virus spread all over the world suddenly, on March 26, 1999, when he put it in a message in the alt.sex newsgroup. His infected document, called LIST.DOC, contained a list of porno Web sites. In just a few days, 10% of all computers connected to the Internet contained the virus. It spread faster than any other virus ever invented. Since it created so much e-mail (from infected documents and from confused people denying they meant to send the e-mail), many Internet computers handling e-mail had to be shut down.

On April 2, 1999, the FBI had New Jersey police arrest David, who was 31. At first, he denied he distributed the virus; but on December 13, 1999, he finally pleaded guilty, apologized, and faced fines and jail.

A TV cartoon show called "The Simpsons" has an episode called "The Genius", where Bart Simpson abruptly ends a Scrabble game by claiming he won with the word "Kwyjibo". The virus can put into your document this quote from him: "Twenty-two points, plus triple-word-score, plus fifty points for using all my letters. Game's over. I'm outta here."

The virus inserts that quotation just if you open or close the document at the precise minute when, on the computer's clock, the number of minutes equals the date. For example, on May 27th it will insert that quotation if the time is 1:27, 2:27, 3:27, 4:27, 5:27, 6:27, 7:27, 8:27, 9:27, 10:27, 11:27, or 12:27.

The virus runs just if you have Microsoft Word 97 or 2000.

The virus is harmless if you have Microsoft Word 7 or earlier. Microsoft Word 97 & 2000 are supposed to protect you against macro viruses, but the Melissa virus is smart enough to disable that protection. The virus spreads quickly just if you have Microsoft Outlook; the virus uses just the address book in Microsoft Outlook, *not* the address book in Microsoft Outlook Express.

Although the original virus's e-mail subject line said "Important message from", a new variant of the virus has a blank subject line, making the virus harder to notice.

Marker

(From the USA in April 1999) This macro virus infects Microsoft Word documents. On the first day of each month, it **tries to invade your privacy by copying your name (and your company's name and your address) to an Internet site** run by codebreakers.org. (If it successfully uploads your info, it doesn't bother redoing it in future months.)

It uses whatever name and address you gave when you installed Microsoft Word. To see what name and address would be copied, go into Microsoft Word and then click "Tools" then "Options" then "User Information".

Thus

(From the USA in August 1999) This macro virus infects Microsoft Word documents. It lurks there until December 13th, when **it erases drive C**. It's called "Thus" because its macro program begins with the word "thus".

Prilissa

(From the USA in November 1999) Here's how this variant of Melissa differs from Melissa:

The e-mail's subject says "Message from" and your name. The e-mail's body says "This document is very Important and you've GOT to read this !!!". Instead of printing a quotation from Bart Simpson, the virus waits until Christmas then does this:

1. It says "©1999 - CyberNET Vine...Vide...Vice...Moslem Power Never End... You Dare Rise Against Me... The Human Era is Over, The CyberNET Era Has Come!"

2. It draws several colored shapes onto the currently opened document.

3. It changes your AUTOEXEC.BAT file so that the next time you boot, **the entire C drive will be erased** (by reformatting) and you'll see this message: "Vine...Vide...Vice...Moslem Power Never End... Your Computer Have Just Been Terminated By -= CyberNET =- Virus !!!".

E-mail worms

An **e-mail worm** is a malicious program that comes as an e-mail attachment and pretends to be innocent fun.

The following e-mail worms are the most prevalent....

Happy 99

(From the USA in January 1999) This program, called HAPPY99.EXE, comes as an e-mail attachment. If you open it, you see a window titled "Happy New Year 1999 !!". In that window, you see a pretty firework display.

But **while you enjoy watching the fireworks, the HAPPY99.EXE program secretly makes 3 changes to your SYSTEM folder** (which is in your WINDOWS folder):

1. In that folder, it puts a copy of itself, and calls the copy SKA.EXE (which is why the Happy 99 worm is also called the **SKA worm**).

2. In that folder, it puts a file called SKA.DLL (by extracting SKA.DLL from HAPPY99.EXE).

3. It modifies that folder's WSOCK32.DLL file, after saving that file's original version as WSOCK32.SKA.

The modified WSOCK32.DLL file **forces your computer to attach the Happy 99 worm to every e-mail you send**. So in the future, whenever you send an e-mail, the person who receives your e-mail will also receive an attachment called HAPPY99.EXE. When the person double-clicks the attachment, the person will see the pretty firework display, think you sent it on purpose, and not realize you sent an e-mail worm virus.

To brag about itself, the virus keeps a list of everybody you sent the virus to. That list of e-mail addresses is in your SYSTEM folder and called LISTE.SKA.

Here's how to get rid of the virus:

Disconnect from the Internet. (If you're attached to the Internet by using a cable modem or local-area network instead of a simple phone line, disconnect by clicking "Start" then "Shut down" then "Restart in MS-DOS mode".) Delete SKA.EXE and SKA.DLL from the SYSTEM folder (which is in the WINDOWS folder). In the SYSTEM folder, rename WSOCK32.DLL to WSOCK32.BAK and rename WSOCK32.SKA to WSOCK32.DLL. Delete the downloaded file, HAPPY99.EXE, from whatever folder you put it in. Look at the list of people in LISTE.SKA (which is an ASCII text file in the SYSTEM folder) and warn them that you sent them the Happy99 virus.

An updated version, called **Happy 00**, comes as a file called HAPPY00.EXE. It says "Happy New Year 2000!!" instead of "Happy New Year 1999 !!".

Pretty Park

(From France in May 1999) This virus comes in an e-mail. The e-mail's subject line, instead of saying "Important message", says just "C:\CoolPrograms\Pretty Park.exe". The e-mail's body, instead of containing sentences, says just "Test: Pretty Park.exe :)" and **shows a drawing of a boy wearing a hat**. The boy is Kyle, from the "South Park" TV cartoon show. The icon is labeled "Pretty Park.exe". If you double-click it, you'll be opening an attachment called PrettyPark.exe, which is a virus.

Then you might see the 3D Pipes screensaver (which is one of the screensavers that you get free as part of Windows 98). But secretly, **every 30 minutes, the virus peeks in Microsoft Outlook's address book and sends copies of itself to your friends listed there**. Every 30 seconds, it also tries to connect your computer to an Internet Relay Chat server computer, so the virus can invade your privacy by sending info about you and your computer to the virus's author or distributor, though there's no evidence that any private info about anyone has actually been transmitted yet.

This virus was first distributed in May 1999 by an e-mail spammer from France.

Explore ZIP

(From the USA in June 1999) **This virus destroys all your Microsoft Word documents** (and all other file that end in .doc), **all your Excel spreadsheets** (and all other files that end in .xls), **all your PowerPoint presentations** (and all other files that end in .ppt), all your assembly-language programs (and all other files that end in .asm), and all files that end in .h, .c, or .cpp.

It destroys the files by replacing them with files that have 0 length.

> Since the file names still exist, you won't immediately notice that their contents are destroyed, and backup software won't notice which files are gone.
> It destroys those files on drives C, D, E, etc. For example, if your computer is part of a network, the virus destroys those files on your hard drive and also on the network server's hard drive.

It also **looks in your e-mail's Inbox** (created by Outlook Express or Outlook or Exchange), **notices any messages you haven't replied to yet, and replies to them itself!**

> For example, if an e-mail from Joan with a subject line saying "Buy soap" hasn't been replied to yet, the virus sends a reply who subject is "Re: Buy soap" and whose body says: "Hi Joan! I received your email and I shall send you a reply ASAP. Till then, take a look at the attached zipped docs. Bye."

The reply comes with an attachment called zipped_files.exe.

> If the recipient opens that attachment, zipped_files.exe starts running. To fool the victim, it displays a fake error message (which begins by saying "Cannot open file"). Then it puts a copy of itself into the SYSTEM folder (which is in the WINDOWS folder); the copy is called "Explore.exe" or "_setup.exe". It also modifies the "run" line in your computer's WIN.INI file so the program will run each time Windows starts.

Here's how to get rid of the virus:

> Remove the "run=" line from your computer's WIN.INI file (which is in the WINDOWS folder). While holding down the Ctrl and Alt keys, tap the Delete key; cick any task named "Explore" or "_setup" (but *not* "Explorer"), then click the "End Task" button. Delete the file Explore.exe (or _setup.exe) from your SYSTEM folder (which is in the WINDOWS folder).

Free Link

(From the USA in July 1999) This virus sends, to people in Microsoft Outlook's address book, an e-mail whose subject line says "Check this" and whose body says "Have fun with these links. Bye." Clicking the e-mail's attachment makes the virus infect the recipient's computer and then tell the recipient, "This will add a shortcut to free XXX links on your desktop. Do you want to continue?"

If the recipient clicks "Yes", **the virus creates a shortcut icon pointing to an adult-sex Web site**. But even if the recipient clicks "No", the virus has already infected the computer and will use that computer to send e-mails, which will **embarrass the computer's owner when those e-mails reach the owner's friends**.

Kak

(From France in December 1999) **Of all the viruses ever invented, the Kak virus is now the most prevalent.**

If your computer gets infected by this virus, every e-mail you send by using Microsoft Outlook Express gets infected (unless you have Microsoft's correction to this security hole). The virus infects by acting as an e-mail signature instead of an attachment, so **everybody reading your e-mail will get infected, even if the recipients don't look at any attachments**.

> If your computer is infected, it will do this at 5PM on the first day of each month: it will protest against Microsoft by saying "Kagou-Anti-Kro$oft says not today!" and then the computer will shut itself down (as if you had clicked "Start" then "Shut Down" then "OK").

The virus is called **Kagou-Anti-Krosoft**, which is abbreviated as **Kak**. Its main file is KAK.HTM, which is put into your Windows folder. It temporarily puts a file called KAK.HTA into your Startup folder but erases that file when you reboot.

Here are 5 signs that you've been infected by the virus:

> 1. Your Windows folder contains KAK.HTM.
> 2. If you click "Start" then "Programs" then "Startup", you see a reference to "kak".
> 3. If you click "Start" then "Programs" then "Find" then "Files or Folders" then type "kak" (and press ENTER), you see a reference to "kak" (besides any references to "kakworm", which are harmless documents from anti-virus sites). If you see a reference to "kak", delete it by clicking it (just once) then pressing SHIFT with DELETE then pressing ENTER.
> 4. Your AUTOEXEC.BAT file mentions "kak.hta".
> 5. While using Outlook Express (Internet Explorer 5's e-mail system), if you click "Tools" then "Options" then "Signatures", the File box is white (instead of gray) and says "C:\WINDOWS\kak.htm".

Love Bug

(From Philippines in May 2000) This virus comes in an e-mail whose subject line says "ILOVEYOU". The e-mail's body says "kindly check the attached LOVELETTER coming from me." and comes with an attachment called LOVE-LETTER-FOR-YOU.TXT.vbs. That attachment is the virus. When you activate it (by clicking the attachment), the virus infects your computer and does 3 dastardly deeds:

> **It sends a copy of itself to everybody in your Microsoft Outlook address book.** This will embarrass you, when everybody in your address book gets an e-mail that says "ILOVEYOU". Your boss, assistant, colleagues, customers, friends, and ex-friends will all be surprised to get an e-mail saying that you love them and sent them a love letter. (They'll be upset later when they discover the "love letter" is a virus you gave them!)
> **It wrecks graphics files and some programs.** Specifically, it wrecks all files whose names end in .jpg, .jpeg, .vbs, .vbe, .js, .jse, .css, .wsh, .sct, and .hta. It wrecks them by renaming the files and inserting copies of itself into the files. Also, it hides music files (all files that end in .mp3 or .mp2), so you can't use those files until you "unhide" them. When looking for files to wreck or hide, it looks at your computer's hard drive and also the hard drives of any network server computers you're attached to.
> It tries makes your computer download, from an Internet Web site in the Philippines, a program misleadingly called WIN-BUGSFIX.EXE. That program **tries to steal your passwords** by e-mailing them to a Philippines e-mail address called MAILME@SUPER.NET.PH. To that address, tries to secretly send your Internet passwords, network passwords, your own name, your computer's name, and your Internet settings, so the virus inventor's computer can imitate yours and have all your Internet and network privileges.

This virus spread faster than all other viruses.

> It began in the Philippines on May 4, 2000, and spread across the whole world in one day (traveling from Hong Kong to Europe to the United States), infecting 10% of all computers connected to the Internet and causing about 7 billion dollars in damage. Most of the "damage" was the labor of getting rid of the virus and explaining to recipients that the sender didn't mean to say "I love you". The Pentagon, CIA, and British Parliament all had to shut down their e-mail systems to get rid of the virus — and so did most big corporations. It did less damage in India (where employees are conservative and don't believe "I love you" messages) and the Philippines (where few people use the Internet because it's so expensive).

An international manhunt for the perpetrator finally led to a 23-year-old computer student in the Philippines city of Manila.

> On May 11th (one week after the virus spread), he held a news conference. Accompanied by his lawyer and sister, he said his name was Onel de Guzman and didn't mean to do so much harm.
> In the Philippines, Internet access normally costs 100 pesos ($2.41) per hour, and 100 pesos is a half day's wages! For his graduation thesis in computer science, he created a program that would help low-income Filipinos get free access to the Internet by stealing passwords from rich people. The university rejected his thesis because it was illegal, so he couldn't graduate. Helped by a group of friends called the Grammersoft Group (which was in the business of illegally selling theses to other students), he made his virus be fancy and distributed it the day before the school held its graduation ceremony.
> The middle of the virus's program says the virus is copyright by "Grammersoft Group, Manila, Philippines" and mentions his college. The authorities found him by checking (and shutting down) the Philippine Web sites and e-mail addresses that the virus uses (to steal passwords), chatting with the college's computer-science department, looking for the Grammersoft Group in Manila, and comparing the virus with earlier viruses written by his friends.
> But charges against him were finally dropped, since the Philippines had no laws yet against creating viruses.

It's called the **Love Bug** because it's a virus (bug) transmitted by a love letter. It's also called the **Love Letter virus** and the **Killer from Manila**.

Copycats have edited the virus's program and created 28 variants. The original version is called **version A**. Here are examples of other versions:

> **Version A (the original version)** says "ILOVEYOU" then "kindly check the attached LOVELETTER coming from me." It attaches "LOVE-LETTER-FOR-YOU.TXT.vbs".
>
> **Version C ("Very Funny")** says "fwd: Joke" then has a blank body. It attaches "Very Funny.vbs".
>
> **Version E ("Mother's Day")** says "Mothers Day Order Confirmation" then "We have proceeded to charge your credit card for the amount of $326.92 for the mothers day diamond special. We have attached a detailed invoice to this email. Please print out the attachment and keep it in a safe place. Thanks Again and Have a Happy Mothers Day! mothersday@subdimension.com". It attaches mothersday.vbs.
>
> **Version M ("Arab Air")** says "Thank You For Flying With Arab Airlines" then "Please check if the bill is correct, by opening the attached file". It attaches ArabAir.TXT.vbs.
>
> **Version Q ("LOOK!")** says "LOOK!" then "hehe…check this out." It attaches LOOK.vbs.

The following variants pretend to cure the virus but actually are viruses themselves:

> **Version F** says "Dangerous Virus Warning" then "There is a dangerous virus circulating. Please click attached picture to view it and learn to avoid it." It attaches virus_warning.jpg.vbs.
>
> **Version G** says "Virus Alert!!!" then a long message. This version also wrecks .bat and .com files.
>
> **Version K** says " "How to protect yourself from the ILOVEYOU bug!" then "Here's the easy way to fix the love virus." It attaches Virus-Protection-Instructions.vbs.
>
> **Version T** says "Recent Virus Attacks — Fix" then "Attached is a copy of a script that will reverse the effects of the LOVE-LETTER-TO-YOU.TXT.vbs as well as the FW:JOKE, Mother's Day and Lithuanian siblings." It attaches BAND-AID.DOC.VBS. This version also wrecks many other files, and it totally deletes .mp3 and .mp2 files.
>
> **Version W** says "IMPORTANT: Official virus and bug fix" then "This is an official virus and bug fix. I got it from our system admin. It may take a short while to update your system files after you run the attachment." It attaches "Bug and virus fix.vbs".
>
> **Version AC** says "New Variation on LOVEBUG Update Anti-Virus!!" then "There is now a newer variant of love bug. It was released at 8:37 PM Saturday Night. Please Download the following patch. We are trying to isolate the virus. Thanks Symantec." It attaches antivirusupdate.vbs.

Life Stages

(From USA in May 2000) Here's a famous comment about life stages:

The male stages of life:	
Age	**Seduction line**
17	"My parents are away for the weekend."
25	"My girlfriend is away for the weekend."
35	"My fiancée is away for the weekend."
48	"My wife is away for the weekend."
66	"My second wife is dead."

Age	**Favorite sport**
17	sex
25	sex
35	sex
48	sex
66	napping

Age	**Definition of a successful date**
17	"Tongue!"
25	"Breakfast!'
35	"She didn't set back my therapy."
48	"I didn't have to meet her kids."
66	"Got home alive!"

The female stages of life:

Age	**Favorite fantasy**
17	tall, dark, and handsome
25	tall, dark, and handsome, with money
35	tall, dark, and handsome, with money and a brain
48	a man with hair
66	a man

Age	**Ideal date**
17	He offers to pay.
25	He pays.
35	He cooks breakfast next morning.
48	He cooks breakfast next morning for the kids.
66	He can chew his breakfast.

The Life Stages virus tries to e-mail that comment, but the transmission is imperfect: the virus misspells "handsome" as "hansome" and makes other errors in spelling and punctuation.

The e-mail's subject is "Life stages" or "Funny" or "Jokes", with maybe the word "text" afterwards, and maybe "Fw:" beforehand.

> So there are 12 possible subjects, such as this: "Fw: Life stages text". (The computer chooses among the 12 at random.) By having 12 possible subjects instead of 1, the virus is harder for anti-virus programs to stop.

The e-mail's body says "The male and female stages of life". Attached to it is a file that pretends to be just a simple text document called LIFE_STAGES.TXT, but actually it's a virus program called LIFE_STAGES.TXT.SHS.

> The **.SHS** means it's a **SH**ell **S**crap object program. When you open it, you see the comment about the stages of life. (You see it in a Notepad window.) While you read that comment, the virus secretly infects your computer, so your computer transmits the virus to 100 randomly-chosen people in your Outlook address book and to Internet chat groups.

After e-mailing the virus to your friends, the computer erases those e-mails from your Sent folder, so you don't know the e-mails were sent. To stop you from eradicating the virus by editing the registry, the virus changes the name of the computer's REGEDIT.EXE program to "RECYCLED.VXD", then moves it to the Recycle Bin and makes it a hidden file so you can't see it.

The virus is called **Life Stages** (or just **Stages**). You can remove it by using the Internet to go to www.symantec.com/avcenter/venc/data/fix.vbs.stages.html.

DoS attacks

Your computer can attack an Internet Web-site server computer (called the **target**) by sending so many strange requests to the target computer that the target computer can't figure out how to respond to them all. The target computer gets confused and becomes so preoccupied worrying about your requests that it ignores all other work it's supposed to be doing, so nobody else can access it. Everybody who tries to access it is denied service because it's too busy. That's called a **denial-of-service attack (DoS attack)**.

In the attack, the "strange request" asks the target computer to reply to a message; but when the target computer tries to reply, it gets flummoxed because the return address is a **spoof** (a fake address that doesn't exist). The target computer tries to transmit to the fake address and waits hopelessly for acknowledgement that the reply was received. While the target computer waits for the acknowledgement, the attacking computer keeps sending more such requests, until the target computer gets overloaded, gives up, and dies.

Denial-of-service attacks were invented in 1997. In March 1998, denial-of-service attacks successfully shut down Internet computers run by the Navy, the US space agency (NASA), and many universities.

Distributed DoS attacks

In the summer of 1999, an extra-powerful denial-of-service attack was invented. It's called a **distributed denial-of-service attack (DDoS attack)**. Here's how it works:

> A virus spreads by e-mail to thousands of innocent computers (which are then called **zombie agents** or **drones**). The virus waits in those computers until a preset moment, then forces all those computers to simultaneously attack a single Internet target computer by sending strange requests to that computer, thereby overloading that computer and forcing it to deny service to other customers.

The first DDoS attack viruses were **Trin00** and **Tribe Flood Network (TFN)**. Shortly afterwards came versions that were more sophisticated: **Tribe Flood Network 2000 (TFN 2K)** and **Stacheldraht** (which is the German word for "barbed wire").

> Those viruses are flexible: you can teach them to attack any target. Though the inventors of those viruses said they were just "experiments", other folks used those viruses to attack Yahoo and many other Web sites in February 2000. The attacks were successful: they shut down Yahoo, CNN.com, Amazon.com, eBay.com, eTrade.com, Buy.com, Datek.com, and the FBI's Web site.

Hoaxes

A **hoax** is just an e-mail message that contains a scary incorrect rumor and warns you to "pass the message to all your friends".

The hoax is *not* a program; it's just a document.

Though it theoretically does "no harm", actually it's as harmful as traditional viruses, since it wastes your time, waste your friends' time, embarrasses you (when you later discover the rumor is a lie and should be retracted), and creates a worldwide clogging of e-mail systems forced to transmit the rumor and retractions to millions of people.

Good Times

(From the USA in May 1994) Beginning in 1994, people began sending each other e-mails spreading **a rumor that if you receive a file called "Good Times", don't download it**, because downloading it will erase your hard disk. The rumor was false: there is no "Good Times" virus.

The person who started the rumor knew it was false and started it as a prank. The rumor traveled fast and clogged e-mail systems all across the country, so the rumor *itself* became as annoying as a traditional virus.

The rumor gradually got wilder, and said that "Good Times" was an e-mail message, and just reading the message would erase your hard disk.

The rumor eventually became even more bizarre. Here's an abridgement of the rumor's current version:

"The FCC released a warning, last Wednesday, of major importance to any regular user of the Internet. A new computer virus has been engineered that's unparalleled in its destructive capability. Other viruses pale in comparison to this newest creation by a warped mentality.

"What makes this virus so terrifying, said the FCC, is that no disk need be inserted to infect a computer. The virus can be spread through Internet e-mail. Once a computer is infected, its hard drive will most likely be destroyed. If the program is not stopped, it will create a loop that can severely damage the processor if left running too long. Unfortunately, most novice users will not realize what's happening until far too late.

"Luckily, there's a way to detect what's now know as the 'Good Times' virus: the virus always travels to new computers in an e-mail message whose subject line says 'Good Times'. Avoiding infection is easy once the file has been received: don't read it.

"The program is highly intelligent: it will send copies of itself to everyone whose e-mail address is in a received-mail file or a sent-mail file. It will then trash the computer it is running on.

"So if you receive a file with the subject line 'Good Times', delete it immediately! Do not read it!

"Warn your friends about this newest threat to the Internet! It could save them a lot of time and money."

Again, there is no Good Times virus, but the *rumor* of the virus is itself a kind of virus!

Personal viruses

(From the USA in July 1997) By July 1997, jokers began collecting fake reports of personal viruses. Afterwards, the collection grew bigger, so now it includes these:

The **Jack Kevorkian** virus deletes all old files. The **Joey Buttafuoco** virus attacks just minor files. The **Woody Allen** virus bypasses the motherboard and turns on a daughter card. The **Lorena Bobbitt** virus reformats your hard drive into a 3½-inch floppy then discards it through Windows. The **Tonya Harding** virus turns your .BAT files into lethal weapons. The **Jeffrey Dahmer** virus eats away at your system resources, piece by piece. The **Mike Tyson** virus quits after two bytes. The **Arnold Schwarzenegger** virus terminates and stays resident; it'll be back. The **Monica Lewinsky** virus sucks all data out of your computer, then e-mails everyone about what it did. The **Ross Perot** virus activates every component in your system, just before the whole thing quits. The **Adam & Eve** virus takes a couple of bytes out of your Apple. The **Oprah Winfrey** virus makes your 300M hard drive shrink to 80M then gradually expand to 200M. The **Martha Stewart** virus sorts all your files and folds them into cute little doilies, displayed on your desktop. The **Spice Girl** virus has no real function but makes a pretty desktop.

The **Titanic** virus makes your whole system go down. The **Star Trek** virus invades your system in places no virus has gone before. The **Disney** virus makes everything in the computer go Goofy. The **AT&T** virus tells you, every 3 minutes, what a great service you're getting. The **MCI** virus tells you, every 3 minutes, that you're paying too much for the AT&T virus. The **PBS** virus makes your PC stop what it's doing every few minutes to ask for money. The **LAPD** virus claims it feels threatened by other files and erases them in self-defense. The **Prozac** virus totally screws up your RAM, but your processor doesn't care.

The **Congressional** virus freezes the screen; then each half of the screen blames the other half for the problem. The **Healthcare** virus tests your system for a day, finds nothing wrong, then sends you a bill for $4500. The **Airline** virus: you're in Dallas, but your data is in Singapore. The **Gallup** virus makes 60% of infected PCs lose 38% of their data 14% of the time. The **Right To Life** virus won't let you delete any files until you see a counselor about alternatives. The **Politically Correct** virus never calls itself a "virus" but instead an "electronic micro-organism".

Bad Times

(From the USA in December 1997) In 1997, inspired by the Good Times virus hoax, Joe Garrick (and later others) published a rumor about a "Bad Times" virus. Here's the rumor's newest version (abridged):

"If you receive an email entitled "Badtimes", delete it immediately. Don't open it.

"This one is pretty nasty. It will erase everything on your hard drive, delete anything on disks within 20 feet of your computer, demagnetize the stripes on all your credit cards, reprogram your ATM access code, screw up the tracking on your VCR, and scratch any CD you try to play.

"It will recalibrate your refrigerator so your ice cream melts and milk curdles, give your ex-lover your new phone number, mix antifreeze into your fish tank, drink all your beer, and leave dirty socks on the coffee table when company's coming over.

"It will hide your car keys, move your car randomly around parking lots so you can't find it, make you fall in love with a hardened pedophile, give you nightmares about circus midgets, and make you run with scissors.

"It will give you Dutch Elm Disease and Psittacosis. It will rewrite your backup files, changing all active verbs to passive and incorporating misspellings that grossly change the meaning.

"It will leave the toilet seat up and your hair dryer plugged in dangerously close to a full bathtub. It will molecularly rearrange your cologne, making it smell like dill pickles.

"It is insidious, subtle, dangerous, terrifying to behold, and an interesting shade of mauve.

"Please forward this message to everyone you know!!! Everyone deserves a good laugh."

E-mail tax

(From Canada in April 1999) In April 1999, a rumor swept across Canada, by e-mail, saying the Canadian government would start charging 5¢ for each e-mail ever sent, to reimburse the Canadian postal service, which was losing money because people were sending e-mails instead of regular letters. The rumor was false, a prank.

The next month, a U.S. variant began, which said "U.S." instead of "Canada".

Here's an abridgement of the rumor. [Brackets show where the Canadian and US versions differ.]

"Please read the following carefully if you intend to stay online and continue using e-mail.

"The Government of [Canada, the United States] is attempting to quietly push through legislation that will affect your use of the Internet. Under proposed legislation, [Canada Post, the U.S. Postal Service] will bill e-mail users.

"Bill 602P will permit the government to charge a 5-cent surcharge on every e-mail, by billing Internet Service Providers. The consumer would be billed in turn by the ISP. [Toronto, Washington DC] lawyer Richard Stepp is working to prevent this legislation from becoming law.

"The [Canada Post Corporation, US Postal Service] says e-mail proliferation costs nearly [$23,000,000, $230,000,000] in lost revenue per year. Since the average citizen receives about 10 e-mails per day, the cost to the typical individual would be an extra 50 cents per day, or over $180 dollars per year, beyond regular Internet costs.

"Note that this money would be paid directly to [Canada Post, the US Postal Service] for a service they don't even provide. The whole point of the Internet is democracy and non-interference.

"One [back-bencher, congressman], Tony Schnell, has even suggested a '20-to-40-dollar-per-month surcharge on all Internet service' beyond the government's proposed e-mail charges. Most major newspapers have ignored the story, the only exception being the [Toronto Star, Washingtonian], which called the idea of an e-mail surcharge 'a useful concept whose time has come'.

"Don't sit by and watch your freedoms erode away! Send this e-mail to all [Canadians, Americans] on your list. Tell your friends and relatives to write to their [MP, congressman] and say 'No!' to Bill 602P. — Kate Turner, Assistant to Richard Stepp"

That rumor is entirely fiction. There is no "Bill 602P", no "Tony Schnell", no "Richard Stepp", and no desire by postal authorities or newspapers for a surcharge.

Ancient history

The first programmable computers were invented in the 1940's. Before then, people were stuck with the abacus, adding machine, and slide rule.

During the 1950's, 1960's, and 1970's, most computers used punched cards — whose history is weird. The cards were first used for *weaving tapestries*. Where the cards had holes, rods could move through the cards; those moving rods in turn made other rods move, which caused the threads to weave pictures. That machine was called the **Jacquard loom**.

Charles Babbage

Charles Babbage was a wild-eyed English mathematician who, in the 1800's, believed he could build a fancy computing machine. He convinced the British government to give him lots of money, then bilked the government for more. Many years later — and many British pounds later — he still hadn't finished his machine. So he dropped the idea and — can you believe this? — tried to build an even fancier machine. He didn't finish that one either. You might say his life was a failure that was expensive for the British government.

But Charlie (as I'll call him) is admired by all us computerniks (in spite of his face, which was even sterner than Beethoven's), because **he was the first person to realize that a computing machine must consist of 4 parts:**

an input device (he used a card reader)
a memory (which he called "The Store")
a central processing unit (which he called "The Mill")
an output device (he used a printer)

Lady Lovelace

Feminists will kill me if I don't mention Charlie's side-kick, Lady Lovelace. (No, she's not related to Linda.) She was one of Charlie's great admirers, but he never noticed her until she translated his stuff. And boy, it was impossible for him not to notice her translations. Her "footnotes" to the translation were three times as long as what she was translating!

She got very intense. She wrote to Charlie, "I am working very hard for you — like the Devil in fact (which perhaps I am)."

The two became love-birds, although he was old enough to be her father. (By the way, her father was Lord Byron, the poet. She was Lord Byron's only "official" daughter. His other daughters were illegitimate.) Some people argue that she was actually brighter than Charlie, despite Charlie's fame. She was better at explaining Charlie's machines and their implications than Charlie was. **Some people have dubbed her "the world's first programmer".**

Stunning She stunned all the men she met. She was so bright and... a woman! Here's how the editor of The Examiner described her (note the pre-Women's-Lib language!):

"She was thoroughly original. Her genius, for genius she possessed, was not poetic, but metaphysical and mathematical. With an understanding thoroughly masculine in solidity, grasp, and firmness, Lady Lovelace had all the delicacies of the most refined female character. Her manners, tastes, and accomplishments were feminine in the nicest sense of the word; and the superficial observer would never have divined the strength and knowledge that lay hidden under the womanly graces. Proportionate to her distaste for the frivolous and commonplace was her enjoyment of true intellectual society. Eagerly she sought the acquaintance of all who were distinguished in science, art, and literature."

Mad Eventually, she went mad. Mattresses lined her room to prevent her from banging her head. Nevertheless, she died gruesomely, at the ripe young age of 36, the same age that her father croaked. (I guess premature death was popular in her Devilish family.)

Who's the heroine? I wish feminists would pick a different heroine than Lady Lovelace. She was not the most important woman in the history of computing.

Far more important were Grace Hopper and Jean Sammet. In the 1950's Grace Hopper invented the first programming languages, and she inspired many of us programmers until her recent death. Jean Sammet headed the main committee that invented COBOL; she's the world's top expert on the history of programming languages, and she's been president of the computer industry's main professional society, the ACM.

Lady Lovelace was second-string to Babbage. Grace Hopper and Jean Sammet were second-string to nobody.

But since Hopper and Sammet led less racy lives, journalists ignore them; and since Hopper was an Admiral in the Navy (bet you didn't know the Navy had lady Admirals!), she irked some of us doves. Nevertheless, whenever she stepped in front of an audience she got a standing ovation because all of us realize how crucial she was to the computer industry.

But I'm straying from my story....

Herman Hollerith

The U.S. Bureau of the Census takes its census every ten years. To tabulate the results of the 1880 census, the Bureau took *7 years*: they didn't finish until 1887. When they contemplated the upcoming 1890 census, they got scared; at the rate America was growing, they figured that tallying the 1890 census would take 12 years. In other words, the results of the 1890 census wouldn't be ready until 1902. So they held a contest to see whether anyone could invent a faster way to tabulate the data.

The winner was Herman Hollerith. **He was the first person to successfully use punched cards to process data.**

Hermie (as I'll call him) was modest. When people asked him how he got the idea of using punched cards, he had two answers. One was, "Trains": he had watched a train's conductor punch the tickets. His other, more interesting answer was, "Chicken salad". After saying "Chicken salad", he'd pause for you to ask the obvious question, "Why chicken salad?" Then he'd tell his tale:

One day, a girl saw him gulping down chicken salad. She said, "Oh, you like chicken salad? Come to my house. My mother makes excellent chicken salad." So he did. And her father was a head of the Census. (And he married the girl.)

By the way, Herman Hollerith hated one thing: spelling. In elementary school, he jumped out a second-story window, to avoid a spelling test.

In some versions of FORTRAN, every string must be preceded by the letter H. For example, instead of saying ___

'DOG'

you must say:

3HDOG

The H is to honor Herman Hollerith.

The Census used Hollerith's punched-card system in 1890 and again in 1900.

In 1910 the Census switched to a fancier system created by a Census Bureau employee, James Powers, who later quit his job and started his own company, which merged into **Remington-Rand-Sperry-Univac**. Meanwhile, Herman Hollerith's own company merged into **IBM**. That's how the first two computer companies began doing data processing.

World War II

The first programmable computers were invented in the 1940's because of World War II. They could have been invented sooner — most of the know-how was available several decades earlier — but you can't invent a computer unless you have big bucks for research. And the only organization that had big enough bucks was the Defense Department (which in those days was more honestly called the "War Department"). And the only event that was big enough to make the War Department spend that kind of money was World War II.

Of course, the Germans did the same thing. A German fellow, Konrad Zuse, built computers which in some ways surpassed the American ones. But since the Germans lost the war, you don't hear much about old Konrad anymore. Fortunately, throughout World War II the German military ignored what he was doing.

During the 1940's, most computers were invented at universities, usually funded by the War-Defense Department. Some of the most famous computers were the **Mark I** (at Harvard with help from IBM), the **ENIAC** and the **EDVAC** (both at the University of Pennsylvania), the **Whirlwind** (at the Massachusetts Institute of Technology, M.I.T.), and the **Ferranti Mark I** (at the University of Manchester, in England). Which of those computers deserves to be called "the first programmable computer"? The answer's up for grabs. Each of those machines had its own peculiar hang-ups and required years of debugging before working well.

Each of those computers was, as they say in the art world, a "signed original". No two of those computers were alike.

1st generation (1951-1958)

The first computer to be mass-produced was the UNIVAC I, in 1951. It was made by the same two guys (Eckert & Mauchly) who'd built the ENIAC and EDVAC at the University of Pennsylvania. (Mauchly was an instructor there, and Eckert was the graduate student who did the dirty work.) While others at the school were helping build the EDVAC, Eckert and Mauchly left and formed their own company, which invented and started building the UNIVAC. While building the UNIVAC, the Eckert-Mauchly company merged into Remington Rand (which later merged into Sperry-Rand, which later merged into Unisys).

The UNIVAC I was so important that historians call it the beginning of the "first generation". As for computers before UNIVAC — historians disparagingly call them the "zeroth generation".

So the first generation began in 1951. It lasted through 1958. Altogether, from 1951 to 1958, 46 of those UNIVACs were sold.

46 might not sound like many. But remember: in those days, computers were very expensive, and could do very little. Another reason why just 46 were sold is that newer models came out, such as the UNIVAC 1103, the UNIVAC 80, and the UNIVAC 90. But the biggest reason why only 46 of the UNIVAC I were sold is IBM.

The rise of IBM Although IBM didn't begin mass-marketing computers until 1953 — two years after UNIVAC — the IBM guys were much better salesmen, and soon practically everybody was buying from IBM. During the first generation, the hottest seller was the **IBM 650**. IBM sold hundreds and hundreds of them.

There were many smaller manufacturers too. People summarized the whole computer industry in one phrase: **IBM and the Seven Dwarfs**.

Who were the dwarfs? They kept changing. Companies rapidly entered the field — and rapidly left when they realized IBM had the upper hand. By the end of the first generation, IBM was getting 70% of the sales.

Primitive input and output During the first generation, there were no terminals. To program the UNIVAC I, you had to put the program onto magnetic tape (by using a non-computerized machine), feed that tape to the computer, and wait for the computer to vomit another magnetic tape, which you had to run through another machine to find out what the tape said.

One reason why the IBM 650 became more popular was that it could read cards instead of tapes. It really liked cards. In fact, the answers came out on cards. To transfer the answers from cards to paper, you had to run the cards through a separate non-computerized machine.

Memory At the beginning of the first generation, there were no RAM chips, no ROM chips, and no "core memory". Instead, the UNIVAC's main memory was banks of liquid mercury, in which the bits were stored as ultrasonic sound waves. It worked slowly and serially, so the access time ranged from 40 to 400 microseconds per bit.

UNIVAC's manufacturer and IBM started playing around with a different kind of memory, called the Williams tube, which was faster (10 to 50 microseconds); but since it was less reliable, it didn't sell well.

In 1953, several manufacturers started selling computers that were much cheaper, because they used super-slow memory: it was a drum that rotated at 3600 rpm, giving an average access time of 17000 microseconds (17 milliseconds). (During the 1970's, some computers still used drums, but for *auxiliary* memory, not for *main* memory.) The most popular first generation computer, the IBM 650, was one of those cheap drum computers.

Eventually, computer manufacturers switched to a much better scheme, called **core memory**. It consists of tiny iron donuts strung on a grid of wires, whose electrical current magnetizes the donuts. Each donut is one bit and called a **core**. The donuts are strung onto the wire grid by hand, by women knitting.

> Core memory was first conceived in 1950. The first working models were built in 1953 at M.I.T. and RCA, which argued with each other about who owned the patent. The courts decided in favor of M.I.T., so both RCA *and* IBM came out with core-memory computers. Core memory proved so popular that most computers used it through the 1970's, though in the 1980's RAM chips finally overshadowed it, since RAM chips don't require hiring knitters.

Languages During the first generation, computer programming improved a lot. During the early 1950's, all programs had to be written in **machine language**. In the middle 1950's, **assembly language** became available. By 1958, the end of the first generation, three major high-level languages had become available: **FORTRAN**, **ALGOL**, and **APT**.

Fancy programs Programmers tried to make computers play a decent game of chess. All the attempts failed. But at IBM, Arthur Samuel had some luck with checkers:

> He got his first checkers program working in 1952 and then continually improved it, to make it more and more sophisticated. In 1955, he rewrote it so that it learned from its own mistakes. In 1956, he demonstrated it on national TV. He kept working on it. Though it hadn't reached championship level yet, it was starting to look impressive.

Computer music scored its first big success in 1956, on the University of Illinois' ILLIAC computer:

> Hiller & Isaacson made the ILLIAC compose its own music in a style that sounded pre-Bach. In 1957, they made the program more flexible, so that it produced many styles of more modern music. The resulting mishmash composition was dubbed "The ILLIAC Suite" and put on a phonograph record.

In 1954, IBM wrote a program that translated simple sentences from Russian to English. Work on tackling harder sentences continued — with too much optimism.

2nd generation (1959-1963)

Throughout the first generation, each CPU was composed of vacuum tubes. Back in 1948, Bell Telephone had invented the transistor, and everybody realized that transistors would be better than vacuum tubes; but putting transistors into computers posed many practical problems that weren't solved for many years.

Finally, **in 1959, computer companies started delivering transistorized computers. That year marked the beginning of the second generation.** Sales of vacuum-tube computers immediately stopped.

All second-generation computers used core memory.

IBM The *first* company to make transistors for computers was Philco, but the most *popular* second-generation computer turned out to be the **IBM 1401**, because it was business-oriented and cheap.

> IBM announced it in 1959 and began shipping it to customers in 1960. Its core memory required 11½ microseconds per character. Each character consisted of 6 bits. The number of characters in the memory could range from 1.4K up to 16K. Most people rented the 1401 for about $8,000 per month, but you could spend anywhere from $4,000 to $12,000 per month, depending on how much memory you wanted, etc.

Altogether, IBM installed 14,000 of those machines.

IBM also installed 1,000 of a faster version, called the **1410**.

> It required just 4½ microseconds per character, had 10K to 80K, and rented for $8,000 to $18,000 per month, typically $11,000.

Altogether, IBM produced six kinds of computers....

small business computers:	the 1401, 1410, 1440, and 1460
small scientific computers:	the 1620
medium-sized business computers:	the 7010
medium-sized scientific computers:	the 7040 and 7044
large business computers:	the 7070, 7074, and 7080
large scientific computers:	the 7090 and 7094

CDC Several employees left Remington-Rand-Sperry-Univac and formed their own company, called the **Control Data Corporation (CDC)**. During the second generation, CDC produced popular scientific computers: the 1604, the 3600, and the 3800.

Software During the second generation, software improved tremendously.

The three major programming languages that had been invented during the first generation (FORTRAN, ALGOL, and APT) were significantly improved. Six new programming languages were invented: **COBOL**, **RPG**, **LISP**, **SNOBOL**, **DYNAMO**, and **GPSS**.

Programmers wrote advanced programs that answered questions about baseball, wrote poetry, tutored medical students, imitated three-person social interaction, controlled a mechanical hand, proved theorems in geometry, and solved indefinite integrals. The three most popular sorting methods were invented: the Shuffle Sort, the Shell Sort, and Quicksort.

Dawn of 3rd generation (1964-1967)

The third generation began with a big bang, in 1964. Here's what happened in 1964, 1965, 1966, and 1967....

Families The first modern computer families were shipped. They were the **CDC 6600**, the **IBM 360**, and DEC's families (the **PDP-6**, **PDP-8**, and **PDP-10**).

> Of those families, the CDC 6600 ran the fastest. The IBM 360 was the most flexible and was the only one that used integrated circuits (chips). The PDP-6 and PDP-10 were the best for timesharing. The PDP-8 was the cheapest.

Here are the dates:

> CDC began shipping the CDC 6600 in 1964. IBM announced the IBM 360 in 1964 but didn't ship it until 1966. DEC began shipping the PDP-6 maxicomputer in 1964, the PDP-8 minicomputer in 1965, and the PDP-10 maxicomputer (a souped-up PDP-6) in 1967.

New languages IBM announced it would create **PL/I**, a new computer language combining FORTRAN, COBOL, ALGOL, and all other popular languages. It was designed especially for IBM's new computer, the 360. In 1966, IBM began delivering PL/I to customers.

Programmers invented the first successful languages for *beginners* using *terminals*. Those languages were **BASIC**, **JOSS**, and **APL**.

> Dartmouth College invented the first version of **BASIC** in 1964, and significantly improved it in 1966 and 1967.
>
> The RAND Corporation invented **JOSS** in 1964 for the JOHNNIAC computer, and put an improved version (JOSS II) on the PDP-6 in 1965. In the 1970's, three popular variants of JOSS arose: a souped-up version (called AID), a stripped-down version (FOCAL), and a business-oriented version (MUMPS).
>
> IBM completed the first version of **APL** in 1965 and put it on an IBM 7090. IBM wrote a better version of APL in 1966 and put it on an IBM 360. IBM began shipping APL to customers in 1967.

Stanford University invented the most popular language for statistics: **SPSS**.

Artificial intelligence Researchers calling themselves "experts in artificial intelligence" taught the computer to chat in ordinary English.

> For example, Bertram Raphael made the computer learn from conversations, Daniel Bobrow made it use algebra to solve "story problems", The Systems Development Corporation made it know everything in an encyclopedia, General Electric made it answer military questions, Ross Quillian made it find underlying concepts, and Joe Weizenbaum made it act as a psychotherapist.

Also, Richard Greenblatt wrote the first decent chess program. It was good enough to play in championship tournaments against humans.

Era of boredom (1968-1974)

As you can see, the first three generations — up through 1967 — were exciting, full of action. But then, from 1968 to 1974, *nothing newsworthy happened.* That was the era of boredom.

During that era, progress was made, but it was gradual and predictable. Nothing dramatic happened.

Of course, nobody actually came out and said, "Life is boring." People phrased it more genteelly. For example, in September 1971 Robert Fenichel and Joe Weizenbaum wrote this introduction to *Scientific American*'s computer anthology:

> "Partly because of the recent recession in the American economy, but more for reasons internal to the field, computer science has recently relaxed its pace. Work has not stopped, but that the current mood is one of consolidation can scarcely be doubted. Just a few years ago, computer science was moving so swiftly that even the professional journals were more archival than informative. This book could not then have been produced without great risk of misfocus. Today it's much easier to put the articles that constitute this book — even the most recent ones — into context."

Since the first generation had lasted eight years (1951-1958), and the second generation had lasted four years (1959-1963), people were expecting the third generation to last at most four years (1964-1967) and some kind of "fourth generation" to begin about 1968. But it never happened.

The only "major" announcement around then came in 1970, when IBM announced it would produce a new line of computers, called the **IBM 370**, which would make the IBM 360 obsolete. But to IBM's dismay, many computer centers decided to hang onto the old 360 instead of switching to the 370.

> Since the 370's advantage over the 360 was small, not even IBM claimed the 370 marked a fourth generation. Computer historians, desperate for something positive to say about the 370, called it the beginning of the "late third generation", as opposed to the 360, which belonged to the "early third generation".

Unfortunately, in the entire history of computers, there was just one year all computer manufacturers acted together to produce something new. That year was 1959, when all manufacturers switched from vacuum tubes to transistors. Since 1959, we haven't had any consistency.

Although the third generation began with a "big bang" in 1964, each manufacturer was banging on a different drum. IBM was proclaiming how great the IBM 360 would be because it would contain integrated circuits; but other manufacturers decided to ignore integrated circuits for several years, and concentrated on improving other aspects of the computer instead. For many years after the beginning of the third generation, CDC and DEC continued to use discrete transistors (a sign of the second generation) instead of integrated circuits.

Why? The era of boredom happened for three reasons:

1. The preceding years, 1964-1967, had been so successful that they were hard to improve on.
2. When the Vietnam War ended, the American economy had a recession, especially the computer industry, because it had depended on contracts from the Defense Department. In 1969, the recession hit bottom, and computer companies had to lay off many workers. In that year, General Electric gave up and sold its computer division to Honeywell. In 1971, RCA gave up too and sold its computer division to Remington-Rand-Sperry-Univac.
3. The world wasn't ready yet for "the era of personal computing", which began in 1975.

Quiet changes During the era of boredom, these changes occurred — quietly....

In 1970, DEC began shipping the **PDP-11**.

The PDP-8 and PDP-11 became the most popular minicomputers — far more popular than IBM's minicomputers. So in the field of minicomputers, IBM no longer had the upper hand.

BASIC became the most popular language for the PDP-8 and PDP-11 and most other minicomputers (except IBM's, which emphasized RPG). In high schools and business schools, most of the introductory courses used BASIC, instead of FORTRAN or COBOL.

Many businesses and high schools bought their own minicomputers, instead of renting time on neighbors' maxicomputers. The typical high-school computer class used a PDP-8. The richest high schools bought PDP-11's.

In universities, **the social sciences started using computers** — and heavily — to analyze statistics.

All new computer families used 8-bit bytes, so the each word's length was a multiple of 8 (such as 8, 16, 32, or 64).

Most older computer families, invented before the era of boredom, had used 6-bit bytes, so the length of each word had been a multiple of 6: for example, the PDP-8 had a word of 12 bits; the PDP-10 , UNIVAC 1100, and General Electric-Honeywell computers had a word of 36 bits; and the CDC 6600 had a word of 60 bits. The IBM 360 was the first computer to use 8-bit bytes instead of 6-bit; during the era of boredom, all manufacturers copied that feature from IBM.

CRT terminals (TV-like screens attached to keyboards) got cheaper, until they finally became as cheap as hard-copy terminals (which use paper).

Most computer centers switched from hard-copy terminals to CRT terminals, because CRT terminals were quicker, quieter, and could do fancy editing. Also, many computer centers switched from "punched cards and keypunch machines" to CRT terminals.

Interest in new computer languages died. Most computer managers decided to stick with the old classics (FORTRAN and COBOL), because switching to a progressive language (such as PL/I) would require too much time to retrain the programmers and rewrite all the old programs.

Programmers made two last-ditch attempts to improve ALGOL. The first attempt, called **ALGOL 68**, was too complicated to win popular appeal. The second attempt, called **PASCAL**, eventually gained more support.

Maxicomputers were given **virtual core** — disks that pretend to be core, in case you're trying to run a program that's too large to fit into core.

Memory chips got cheaper, until they were finally cheaper than core. Most manufacturers switched from core to memory chips.

In 1971, **Intel** began shipping **the first microprocessor** (complete CPU on a chip).

It was called the **4004** and had a word of just 4 bits. In 1972, Intel began shipping an improved version, the **8008**, whose word had 8 bits. In 1973, Intel began shipping an even better version, the **8080**.

Micro history

In 1975, the first popular microcomputer was shipped. It was called the **Altair** and was built by a company called **MITS**. It cost just $395.

It was just a box that contained a CPU and very little RAM: just ¼ of a K!

It included no printer, no disk, no tape, no ROM, no screen, and not even a keyboard! The only way to communicate with the computer was to throw 25 switches and watch 36 blinking lights.

It didn't understand BASIC or any other high-level computer language. To learn how to throw the switches and watch the blinking lights, you had to take a course in "machine language".

You also had to take a course in electronics — because the $395 got you just a kit that you had to assemble yourself by using a soldering iron and reading electronics diagrams. Moreover, when you finished building the kit, you noticed some of the parts were missing or defective, so that you had to contact MITS for new parts.

That computer contained several empty slots to hold PC cards. Eventually, many companies invented PC cards to put into those slots. Those PC cards, which were expensive, let you insert extra RAM and attach a printer, tape recorder, disk drives, TV, and terminal (keyboard with either a screen or paper).

Bill Gates invented a way to make the Altair handle BASIC. He called his method **Microsoft BASIC**. He patterned it after DEC's BASIC; but he included extra features that exploited the Altair's ability to be "personal", and he eliminated features that would require too much RAM.

Gary Kildall invented a disk operating system that the Altair could use. He called that operating system **CP/M**.

Many companies built computers that imitated the Altair. Those imitations became more popular than the Altair itself. Eventually, the Altair's manufacturer (MITS) went out of business.

The computers that imitated the Altair were called **S-100 bus computers**, because they each used a Standard cable containing 100 wires.

In those days, the microcomputer industry was standardized. Each popular microcomputer used Microsoft BASIC, CP/M, and the S-100 bus. The microcomputer was just a box containing PC cards; it had no keyboard, no screen, and no disk drive. A cable went from the microcomputer to a terminal, which was priced separately. Another cable went from the microcomputer to a disk drive, which was also priced separately.

Built-in keyboards

In 1977, four companies began selling microcomputers that had built-in keyboards, so you didn't have to buy a terminal. Their computers became popular immediately. The four companies were **Processor Technology**, **Apple**, **Commodore**, and **Radio Shack**.

Processor Technology's computer was called the **Sol 20**, to honor Solomon Libes, an editor of Popular Electronics.

Apple's computer was called the **Apple 2**, because it improved on the Apple 1, which had lacked a built-in keyboard.

Commodore's computer was called the **Pet** (inspired by Pet Rocks).

Radio Shack's computer was called the **TRS-80**, because it was manufactured by Tandy's Radio Shack and contained a Z-80 CPU.

For a fully assembled computer, Processor Technology charged $1850, Apple charged $970, Commodore charged $595 (but quickly raised the price to $795), and Radio Shack charged $599 (but soon lowered the price to $499).

Notice that Commodore and Radio Shack had the lowest prices. Also, the low prices from Commodore and Radio Shack *included* a monitor, whereas the prices from Processor Technology and Apple didn't. So Commodore and Radio Shack were the real "bargains".

In those days, "the lower the price, the more popular the computer".

> The cheapest and most popular computer was Radio Shack's. The second cheapest and second most popular was Commodore's Pet. The third cheapest and third most popular was the Apple 2. Processor Technology, after a brief fling of popularity, went bankrupt. The most expensive kind of microcomputer was the CP/M S-100 bus system, which was the oldest kind and therefore had accumulated the greatest quantity of business software.

Improvements

In 1978 and 1979, the three main companies (Apple, Commodore, and Radio Shack) improved their computers.

The improved Apple 2 was called the **Apple 2-plus**. The improved Commodore Pet was called the **Commodore Business Machine (CBM)**. The improved Radio Shack TRS-80 was called the **TRS-80 model 2**.

After announcing the Apple 2-plus, Apple Computer Company stopped selling the plain Apple 2.

Commodore continued selling its old computer (the Pet) to customers who couldn't afford the new version (the CBM), which cost more. Likewise, Radio Shack continued selling its model 1 to customers who couldn't afford the model 2.

Texas Instruments & Atari

In 1979, Texas Instruments (TI) and Atari entered the microcomputer marketplace and began selling low-priced computers.

TI's microcomputer was called the **TI 99/4**. Atari offered *two* microcomputers: the **Atari 400** and the **Atari 800**.

> TI charged $1150. Atari charged $1000 for the regular model (the Atari 800) and $550 for the stripped-down model (the Atari 400).
>
> TI's price included a color monitor. Atari's prices did *not* include a screen; you were to attach Atari's computers to your home's TV.
>
> TI's computer was terrible, especially its keyboard. The Atari 800 computer was wonderful; reviewers were amazed at its easy-to-use keyboard, easy-to-use built-in editor, gorgeous color output on your TV, child-proofing (safe for little kids), and dazzling games, all at a wonderfully low price! It was cheaper than an Apple (whose price had by then risen to $1195) and yet was much *better* than an Apple.

From that description, you'd expect Atari 800 to become the world's best-selling computer, and the TI 99/4 to become an immediate flop. Indeed, that's what most computer experts hoped. And so did the TI 99/4's product manager: when he saw what a mess the TI 99/4 had become, he quit TI and went to work for Atari, where he became the product manager for the Atari 400 & 800!

But even though computer experts realized that TI's computer was junk, TI decided to market it aggressively:

> TI coaxed Milton Bradley and Scott Foresman to write lots of programs for the 99/4. TI paid researchers at MIT to make the 99/4 understand LOGO (a computer language used by young children and very popular in elementary schools). TI improved the keyboard just enough so that people would stop laughing at it; the version with the new keyboard was named the **99/4A**. TI paid Bill Cosby to praise the 99/4A and ran hundreds of TV ads showing Bill Cosby saying "wow". TI dramatically slashed the $1150 price to $650, then $150, and then finally to just $99.50! (To bring the price that low, TI had to exclude the color monitor from the price; instead, TI included a hookup to your home's color TV.)

By contrast, Atari did hardly anything to market or further improve the Atari 400 & 800.

> Atari concentrated on its other products: the big Atari game machines (which you find in video arcades) and the Atari VCS machine (which plays video games on your home TV).

The TI 99/4A therefore became more popular than the Atari 400 & 800 — even though the TI 99/4A was inherently worse.

Sinclair, Osborne, backlash

In 1980 and 1981, two important companies entered the microcomputer marketplace: Timex Sinclair (1980) and Osborne (1981).

The first complete computer selling for less than $200 was invented by a British chap named Clive Sinclair and manufactured by Timex.

> The original version was called the **ZX-80** (because it was invented in 1980, contained a Z-80 CPU, and was claimed to be "Xellent"); it sold for $199.95. In 1981, Clive Sinclair invented an improved version, called the **ZX-81**. Later, he and Timex invented further improvements, called the **ZX Spectrum** and the **Timex Sinclair 1000**. When TI dropped the price of the TI 99/4A to $99.50, Timex retaliated by dropping the list price of the Timex Sinclair 1000 to $49.95, so the Timex Sinclair 1000 remained the cheapest complete computer.

In April 1981, Adam Osborne began the Osborne Computer Corp. and began selling the **Osborne 1** computer, designed by Lee Felsenstein (who'd invented Processor Technology's Sol 20 computer).

> The Osborne 1 computer included practically everything a business executive needed: its $1795 price included a keyboard, a monitor, a Z-80A CPU, a 64K RAM, two disk drives, CP/M, Microsoft BASIC, a second version of BASIC, the Wordstar word processor, and the Supercalc spreadsheet program. Moreover, it was the world's first portable business computer: the entire computer system (including even the monitor and disk drives) was collapsible and turned itself into an easy-to-carry attaché case. (Many years later, Compaq copied Osborne's idea.)

While Timex Sinclair and Osborne were entering the marketplace, Radio Shack, Apple, and Commodore were introducing new computers of their own:

> In 1980, Radio Shack began selling three new computers. The **TRS-80 model 3** replaced Radio Shack's cheapest computer (the model 1) and was almost as good as Radio Shack's fanciest computer (the model 2). The **TRS-80 Color Computer** drew pictures in color and cost less than the model 3. The **TRS-80 Pocket Computer** fit into your pocket, looked like a pocket calculator, and was built for Radio Shack by Sharp Electronics in Japan.
>
> In 1980, Apple began selling the **Apple 3**. It was overpriced; and to make matters worse, the first Apple 3's that rolled off the assembly line were defective. Apple eventually lowered the price and fixed the defects; but since the Apple 3 had gotten off to such a bad start, computer consultants didn't trust it and told everybody to avoid it.
>
> In 1981, Commodore began selling the **Vic-20**, which drew pictures in color and cost less than Radio Shack's Color Computer. In fact, the Vic-20 was the first computer that drew pictures in color for less than $300.
>
> The Vic-20 originally sold for $299.95. When TI lowered the price of the TI 99/4A to $99.95, Commodore lowered the price of the Vic-20. At discount department stores (such as K Mart, Toys R Us, and Child World), you could buy the Vic-20 for just $85: it was still the cheapest computer that could handle color. (The Timex Sinclair 1000 was cheaper but handled just black-and-white.)
>
> Moreover, the Vic-20 had standard Microsoft BASIC, whereas the Timex Sinclair 1000 and TI 99/4A did not; so the Vic-20 was the cheapest computer that had standard Microsoft BASIC. It was the cheapest computer that was pleasant to program.
>
> Also, the Vic-20 had a nice keyboard, whereas the keyboards on the Timex Sinclair 1000 and TI 99/4A were pathetic.
>
> The Vic-20 became immediately popular.

IBM PC

On August 12, 1981, IBM announced a new microcomputer, called the **IBM Personal Computer (IBM PC)**.

Although IBM had previously invented other microcomputers (the IBM 5100 and the IBM System 23 Datamaster), they'd been overpriced and nobody took them seriously — not even IBM. The IBM Personal Computer was IBM's first *serious* attempt to sell a microcomputer.

The IBM Personal Computer was a smashing success, because of its amazingly high quality and amazingly low price. It became the standard against which the rest of the microcomputer industry was judged.

Cycles

Every 8 years, the country's mood about computers has changed. After 8 years of dramatic revolution, we switched to 8 years of subtle evolution, then back again.

Pivotal years

The pivotal years were 1943 (beginning the first revolution), 1951 (beginning the first period of *evolution*), 1959 (revolution), 1967 (evolution), 1975 (revolution), 1983 (evolution), 1991 (revolution), and 1999 (evolution). Here are the details....

Revolution From 1943 to 1950, researchers at universities were building the first true computers, which were big monsters. Each was custom-built; no two were alike.

Evolution In 1951, Sperry began selling the first mass-produced computer: the **UNIVAC I**. Sperry built 46 of them. During the 8-year era from 1951 to 1958, computers gradually became smaller and cheaper and acquired more software. That evolutionary era was called the **first generation**.

Revolution The next computer revolution began in 1959, when IBM began selling the **IBM 1401**, the first IBM computer to use transistors instead of vacuum tubes. During that eight-year revolution from 1959 to 1966, computerists polished FORTRAN and ALGOL (which had been begun earlier), invented 9 other major computer languages (COBOL, BASIC, PL/I, LISP, SNOBOL, APL, DYNAMO, GPSS, and RPG), and began developing FORTH and SPSS. They created many amazing programs for artificial intelligence, such as Weizenbaum's Eliza program, which made the computer imitate a therapist. During that same eight-year period, IBM invented the **IBM 360**: it was the first popular computer that used integrated circuits, and all of IBM's modern mainframes are based on it.

Evolution The years from 1967 to 1974 showed a gradual evolution. Computer prices continued to drop and quality continued to improve. DEC began selling PDP-10 and PDP-11 computers, which became the favorite computers among researchers in universities.

Revolution In 1975, MITS shipped the first popular microcomputer, the **Altair**, which launched the personal computer revolution. Soon Apple, Commodore, Tandy, and IBM began selling microcomputers also. Programmers developed lots of useful, fun software for them. The revolution climaxed at the end of 1982, when many Americans bought microcomputers as Christmas presents.

Evolution In January 1983, the cover of *Time* magazine declared that the 1982 "man of the year" was the personal computer. But consumers quickly tired of the personal-computer fad, chucked their Commodore Vic and Timex Sinclair computers into the closet, and shifted attention to less intellectual pursuits. Many computer companies went bankrupt. In 1983, Lotus announced **1-2-3**, but that was the computer industry's last major successful new product. After that, prices continued to fall and quality gradually increased, but no dramatic breakthroughs occurred. The computer industry became boring. During that time, if you were to ask "What fantastically great happened in the computer industry during the past year?" the answer was: "Not much".

Revolution In 1991, the computer industry became exciting again. Here's why:

Part of that excitement came from revolutionary influences of the previous two years: in 1989 & 1990 the Berlin Wall fell, the Cold War ended, a new decade began, Microsoft finally invented a version of Windows that worked well (version 3.0), and Apple invented a color Mac that was affordable (the LC). In 1991, Microsoft put the finishing touches on Windows (version 3.1) and DOS (version 5).

In 1991 and 1992, a series of price wars made the cost of computers drop 45% per year instead of the customary 30%. Those lower prices made people spend *more* money on computers, because the ridiculously low prices for fancy stuff encouraged people to buy fancier computers: 486 instead of 286, Super VGA instead of plain VGA, 8M RAM instead of 1M, 200M hard drives instead of 40M.

The sudden popularity of Windows whetted the public's hunger for those muscle machines, since Windows requires lots of muscle to run well. That growing American muscle (bigger and bigger!) then made Windows practical enough to become desirable. All big software companies hastily converted their DOS and Mac software to Windows.

The challenge of doing that conversion forced them to rethink the twin questions of software wisdom: "What makes software easy to use?" and "What kinds of software power do users want?" Many creative solutions were invented to answer those questions.

During the 1992 Christmas season, fast CD-ROM drives finally became cheap enough to create a mass market: many American bought them, and CD-ROMs became the new standard way to distribute encyclopedias, directories, other major reference works, and software libraries (full of fonts and shareware). The attention given to CD-ROMs made customers think about the importance of sound, and many customers bought sound cards such as the Sound Blaster.

In 1995, Windows 95 was invented, Netscape Navigator 2.0 was invented, and the Internet began to become popular. During the next few years, the Internet's popularity grew wildly.

Evolution In 1999, interest in the Internet peaked, then declined, as Internet companies began running out of clever ideas. Microsoft stopped coming out with major new products, partly because Microsoft got distracted by lawsuits against it. In the fall of 1999, RAM prices shot up. In November 1999, Packard Bell went out of business. In December 1999, many companies selling on the Internet developed bad reputations by not shipping goods in time for Christmas. Companies prepared for computer problems that the year 2000 might cause.

The year 2000 began boringly, a disappointing way to begin a new millennium. In January 2000, IBM and Acer stopped selling desktop computers through retail stores. In March 2000, the Internet part of the stock market crashed. In June 2000, a judge ruled that Microsoft should be split into two companies. Will the computer industry continue to disintegrate? What does this "evolution" accomplish? Stay tuned!

Presidential politics

The 8-year computer cycle coincides with the American cycle of switching political parties. After years of Roosevelt & Truman, the presidential election of 1952 ushered in eight years of a Republican (Eisenhower); 1960 brought eight years of Democrats (Kennedy & Johnson); 1968, eight years of Republicans (Nixon & Ford).

1976 began another 16-year experience of "Democrat followed by Republicans"; but alas, the Democrat (Carter) got just 4 of those years, and the Republicans (Reagan and Bush) got the remaining 12. (Carter got just 4 of those years instead of 8 because he lost face in the middle of the Iran hostage crisis, oil crisis, and recession.)

1992 began another experience of "Democrat followed by Republicans". The Democrat was Clinton (8 years). The Republican will probably be Bush's son, but as I write this book I'm waiting for the election.

When Americans love liberals and revolution, they vote for Democrats; when Americans prefer conservative evolution, they vote for Republicans. As historian Krigsman remarked, "An excitable mood in the country causes a computer revolution, and the next year the Democrats grab power."

Events

Nine events dramatically changed the public's perception of what a computer is.

Powerful computers

In the **1940's**, universities built the first powerful computers, to help World War II Allies calculate ballistics (trajectories of bullets and bombs). Before then, "powerful computers" were just science fiction; suddenly they'd become reality!

Mass-produced computers

The first computer to be mass-produced was the UNIVAC I, in **1951**. Before then, computers were just military research projects; suddenly they'd become practical commercial tools!

Forty-six UNIVAC I computers were built, and competitors such as IBM began building computers in much bigger quantities.

Transistors & high-level languages

In **1959**, computer manufacturers began using transistors (instead of vacuum tubes), so that computers became much smaller, cheaper, more reliable, and more powerful. About the same time, the first reasonable computer languages were invented: FORTRAN, COBOL, and ALGOL.

For the first time, computers became cheap enough and easy enough to program so that colleges could encourage students to take computer courses.

Chips & BASIC

The first computer to contain integrated circuits (chips) weas the IBM 360, which IBM began selling in **1966**. Chips had been invented by other companies earlier, but chips weren't used in complete computer systems until 1966. Afterwards, other computer brands began using chips also. The chips made computers even smaller, cheaper, more reliable, and more powerful. About the same time, the first easy full-featured computer language was invented: BASIC.

For the first time, computers became cheap enough and easy enough so that high schools could encourage students to take computer courses.

Personal computers

In **1975**, MITS began selling the first popular personal computer, the Altair, for $395. Before then, computers were too expensive for individuals to afford.

Unfortunately, the Altair came as a kit that was hard to assemble, and it contained inadequate hardware and software. But soon afterwards, in 1977, came personal computers that were easy to set up and contained reasonable hardware, built by Apple, Commodore, and Radio Shack.

For the first time, computers became easy enough and cheap enough to be put into the typical American home.

IBM PC

In **1981**, IBM began selling the IBM PC. It was slightly better than earlier personal computers and set the standard for all future personal computers.

Mouse & graphical interfaces

In **1984**, Apple began selling the Macintosh computer. Priced at $2495, it was the first affordable computer to use a mouse. It was a stripped-down version of Apple's Lisa computer and Xerox's Alto computer, which had been invented earlier but were too expensive.

The Macintosh became immediately popular and led Microsoft to create Windows, which made the IBM PC try to act like a Mac. Versions 1 and 2 of Windows worked terribly, but Windows 3 (which came out in 1990) worked well. Then came Windows 3.1, Windows 3.11, Windows 95, and Windows 98, which worked better.

Now every desktop personal computer comes with a mouse, and every notebook computer comes with a mouse or an imitation (such as a Touchpad).

CD-ROMs & multimedia

During the Christmas season of **1992**, many folks bought CD-ROM drives. The drives were available before then, but the public had to wait until 1992 for the drives to become cheap enough and the disks to become plentiful enough.

Now most software comes on CD-ROM disks instead of floppy disks. CD-ROM disks hold enough info to make the storage of music possible, so now most computers come with nice sound cards and speakers, and entertainment software produces nice music. CD-ROM disks can also hold short video clips; longer video clips are available on souped-up CD-ROM disks called DVD.

Internet

In **1995**, the Internet suddenly became popular, as Netscape 2 came out. (Earlier browsers and e-mail systems were awkward and less powerful.) Also in 1995, Windows 95 came out, which was the first version of Windows that could attach to the Internet well. That year, Americans took crash courses in how to use the Internet.

Now most computers come with modems or other ways to connect to the Internet, and the Internet continues to expand.

Become an expert

To become a computer expert, you need a computer, literature, and friends.

A computer to practice on

If possible, buy an IBM PC or clone. You can buy a nice one for about $1000, a plain one for about $500. If you can't afford even $500, get a used computer. Ask your computer friends whether they want to get rid of any "used junky obsolete computers" for under $100, or ask them whether they can lend you a computer for a weekend. Swap: if they lend you an Apple for a weekend, bake them an apple pie.

Another way to save money is to join your friends for a group purchase. For example, if 9 of you each chip in $10, you can buy a $90 computer. Divide the 9 of you into 3 trios, and rotate the computer from trio to trio every day, so that you get to use the computer every third day.

Literature to read

Begin by reading *The Secret Guide to Computers*. Then read the manuals that came with your computer.

Find out what's new by subscribing to computer magazines or reading them in your town's library.

You can get computer books and magazines from the bookstore at your local college. You can also try your local branch of **Waldenbooks** or **B. Dalton Booksellers**, which are nationwide chains. A cheerier chain is **Borders**, whose salespeople are more knowledgeable. If you live near Denver, visit **Tattered Cover**, which is America's largest independent bookstore (303-322-7727).

To pay less, shop at discount chains such as **Staples** (which has a 15% discount on the few books it stocks) and **Comp USA** (which has big discounts on magazines and a 20% discount on all books). If you live near Boston, go to Harvard Square in Cambridge to visit **Words Worth** (10% discount on all paperbacks, 617-354-5201).

The following big stores specialize in computer & technical books, and most are willing to ship all over the world. They usually charge full price:

```
Opamp Bookstore (Los Angeles, 213-464-4322)
Computer Literacy Bookshops (San Jose CA, 408-592-5775)
Stacey's Bookstore (San Francisco 415-421-4687, Palo Alto CA 415-326-0681)
Computer Book Works (New York City, 212-385-1616)
McGraw-Hill Bookstore (New York City, 212-997-1221)
Quantum Books (Cambridge MA, 617-494-5042)
Calgary Computer Books (Calgary Alberta Canada, 403-270-0952)
```

Since *The Secret Guide to Computers* is an underground book, you won't find it in stores that are "overground". To find out which nifty bookstores, computer stores, and consultants near you carry the *Secret Guide*, phone me at 603-666-6644, and I'll look up your ZIP code in my computer.

Friends to chat with

When you have a computer question, phone me at 603-666-6644. Another way to get help is to join a computer club.

The biggest and best computer club was the **Boston Computer Society (BCS)**, which had about 30,000 members, held over 1,000 meetings per year, published many magazines and newsletters, and had hundreds of volunteers who gave free phone help on technical topics. It began in 1977 but shut down in 1996. Its founder and first president was a 13-year-old kid. I hope some other 13-year-old kid starts something equally wonderful someday!

If you live near New York City, join a computer club called **New York Personal Computer (NY PC)**. Membership costs $45 for 1 year, $80 for 2 years, $30 per year for students. The best way to find out about the club is to look at its Web site, www.nypc.org, which also includes info about other clubs in New York, New Jersey, and Connecticut. Some info is also available by phoning 212-643-NYPC for a recorded message.

If you live near Philadelphia, join a computer club called the **Philadelphia Area Computer Society (PACS)**. Membership costs $37 per year ($32 per year for senior citizens). The best way to find out about the club is to look at its Web site, www.pacsnet.org. The club's phone number, 215-842-9600, usually gives you just a recorded message telling you to visit the Web site.

Americans living in Tokyo have started the **Tokyo PC Users Group (TPC)**. Their newsletter, written in English, is top-notch! The best way to find out about the club is to look at its Web site, www.tokyopc.org. If you're in Japan, phone 03-5956-7228 (for a recorded message about membership) or write to Tokyo PC Club, PO Box 103, Shibuya-Ku, Tokyo 150-8691 Japan.

The biggest and best computer clubs are in retirement communities in Arizona (near Mesa) and Florida.

To find computer clubs near *you*, ask employees at your local computer stores, high schools, and colleges. You can also check the list put out by the **Association of PC User Groups (APCUG)** at http://database.apcug.org/database/loclist.asp.

The biggest and best club for Macintosh computers was the **Berkeley Macintosh User Group (BMUG)**, but it is shutting down. Its remnants are at www.bmug.org.

If you take a computer course, get personal help by chatting with your teacher and classmates. To save money, sign up for the cheap courses given by your high school's "adult education" evening program and your local community college.

I occasionally travel around the world and give courses inexpensively or for free. Heads of the computer industry got their training from my courses. To join us, use the coupon on the back page.

Land a computer job

To become a lawyer, you must graduate from law school and pass the Bar Exam. But to become a computer expert, there's no particular program you must graduate from, no particular exam to pass, and no particular piece of paper that "proves" you're an expert or even competent.

You can get a job in the computer industry even if you've never had any training. Your job will be sweeping the floor.

To become a top computer expert, you must study hard, day and night. Read lots of computer manuals, textbooks, guidebooks, magazines, newspapers, and newsletters. Practice using many kinds of computers, operating systems, languages, word-processing programs, spreadsheets, database systems, graphics packages, and telecommunications programs. Also explore the many educational programs for kids. Use many kinds of printers, disk drives, and modems. Study the human problems of dealing with computers. No matter how much you already know, learn more!

When I surveyed computer experts, I found that the average expert spends two hours per day reading about computers, to fill holes in the expert's background and learn what happened in the computer industry that day! In addition to those two hours, the expert spends many more hours practicing what was read and swapping ideas by chatting with other computerists.

As a computer expert, you can choose your own hours, but they must be numerous: if your interest in computers lasts just from 9 AM to 5 PM, you'll never become a computer expert.

To break into the computer field, you can use six tools: college, home consulting, home programming, salesmanship, job expansion, and on-the-job training.

College

The most traditional way to get a computer job is to go to college and get a Ph.D. or M.A. in computer science. Unfortunately, that takes a lot of time.

Home consulting

The fastest way to break into the field is to keep your current job but spend your weekends and evenings helping your neighbors, friends, and colleagues learn about computers. Help them buy hardware and software. Then customize the software to meet their own personal needs. Then train them in how to use it all. Lots of folks want training in how to use DOS, Word Perfect, and other popular software.

At first, do it all for free. After you've become an experienced expert and developed a list of happy clients who will vouch for your brilliance, start requesting money from new clients. Start cheaply, at about $10 per hour, then gradually raise your rates over the next few years. Most computer consultants charge about $50 per hour, and some charge much more than that; but I suggest that you be gentler on your clients' pocketbooks! By charging little, you'll get more clients, they'll rack up more hours with you, and you won't need to spend lots of time and money on "advertising". For example, at $20 per hour you'll be very popular!

Home programming

You can write computer programs at home to sell to friends and software publishers, but make sure your programs serve a real need and don't duplicate what's already on the market. Be creative!

Salesmanship

For a quicker career path, learn enough about microcomputers to get a job selling them in a store. As a salesperson, you'll be helping people decide which hardware and software to buy; you'll be acting as a consultant.

The store will probably give you permission to take hardware, software, and literature home with you, so you can study and practice new computer techniques every evening and become brilliant. If you wish, you can even moonlight by helping your customers use the software they bought and designing your own customized programs for them.

After working in the store several months, you'll have the knowledge, experience, contacts, and reputation to establish yourself as an independent consultant. You can call your former customers and become their advisor, trainer, and programmer — or even set up your *own* store.

Job expansion

Another way to break into the field is to take a non-computer job and gradually enlarge its responsibilities, so that it involves computers.

For example, if you're a typist, urge your boss to let you use a word processor. If you're a clerk, ask permission to use spreadsheet and data-management programs to manage your work more efficiently. If you're a math teacher, ask the principal to let you teach a computer course or help run the school's computer club.

Keep your current job, but expand it to include new skills so you gradually become a computer expert.

On-the-job training

The final way to break into the field is to get a job in a computer company, as a janitor or clerk, and gradually move up by using the company's policy of free training for employees.

Phone me

Many companies phone me when they're looking for computer experts. If you think you're an expert and can demonstrate your expertise, I'll be glad to pass your name along to employers.

Occasionally, I even have job openings here at The Secret Guide to Computers. Feel free to ask. Although some of the jobs here are mundane, a nice fringe benefit is that you get to play with my 40 computers and oodles of software packages and take them home with you. You can also choose your own hours: work whenever you please! After you work here a few months and do your job well, I'll gladly give you an excellent reference that will help you get an even nicer job elsewhere.

If somebody's interested in hiring you to be a programmer or consultant, you must decide what rate to charge.

If this is your *first* such job, be humble and charge very little because your first job's main goal should *not* be money. Instead, your goal should be to gain experience, enhance your reputation, and find somebody you can use as a reference and who'll give you a good recommendation. Convince your first employer that you're the best bargain he ever got, so that he'll be wildly enthusiastic about you and give you a totally glowing recommendation when you go seek your second job.

If you can't find anyone willing to pay you, work for free, just so that you can put on your résumé that you "helped computerize a company". After such an experience, you should easily find a second job that pays better.

Although your first computer job might pay little or nothing at all, it gets your foot in the computer industry's door. After your first job, your salary will rise rapidly because the most valuable attribute you can have in this field is *experience*.

Since experienced experts are in short supply, they get astronomical salaries. On the other hand, there's a *surplus* of "kids fresh out of college" who know nothing. So consider your first job to be an extremely valuable way to gain experience, even if the initial salary is low. When applying for your first job, remember that you're still unproven, and be thankful that your first employer is willing to take a risk on you.

Asking for a raise

After several months on the job, when you've thoroughly proved that you're worth much more than you're being paid, and your employer is thoroughly thrilled with your performance, gently ask your employer for a slight raise. If he declines, continue working at that job, but also keep your eyes open for a better alternative.

Negotiating a contract

The fundamental rule of contract negotiation is: never make a large commitment.

For example, suppose somebody offers to pay you $10,000 if you write a fancy program. Don't accept the offer; the commitment is too large. Instead, request $1,000 for writing a stripped-down version of the program.

After writing the stripped-down version, wait and see whether you get the $1,000; if you get it without any hassles, then agree to make the version slightly fancier, for a few thousand dollars more. That way, if you have an argument with your employer (which is common), you've lost only $1,000 of effort instead of $10,000.

Contract headaches

Arguments between programmers and employers are common, for six reasons:

1. As a programmer, you'll probably make the mistake of **underestimating the time** for debugging the program, because you'll tend to be too optimistic about your own abilities.

2. Your employer **won't be precise enough** when he tells you what kind of program to write. You'll write a program that you *think* satisfies the employer's request and then discover that the employer really wanted something slightly different.

3. Your employer will forget to tell you about the various "**strange cases**" that the company must handle. They'll require extra "IF" statements in your program.

4. When the employer finally sees your program working, he'll suddenly think of **extra** things he'd like the program to do, and which will require extra programming effort from you.

5. When the program finally does everything that the employer expects, he'll want you to **teach** his staff how to use the program and the computer. If his staff has never dealt with computers before, the training period could be quite lengthy. He'll also want you to write a manual about the program, and to put the manual into the company's library.

6. **After the company begins using the program, the employer will want you to make additional changes**, and might even expect you to make them at no charge.

To minimize those six kinds of conflicts, be honest and kind to your employer. Explain to him that you're worried about those six kinds of conflicts, and that you'd like to chat about them *now*, before either you or he makes any commitments. Then make a small commitment for a small payment for a short time, and make sure that both you and the employer are happy with the way that small commitment worked out before attempting any larger commitments.

Here are further tricks for developing your career.

Programmer

A **programmer** is a teacher: the programmer teaches the computer new tricks. For example, the programmer might teach the computer how to do the payroll. To do that, the programmer feeds the computer a list of instructions, that explain to the computer how to do the payroll. The list of instructions is called a **program**.

Languages The program is written by using the very limited vocabulary that the computer understands already. Earlier in *The Secret Guide to Computers*, I explained a vocabulary called BASIC, which consists of words such as PRINT, INPUT, GO TO, IF, THEN, and STOP. That vocabulary — BASIC — is called a **computer language**. It's a small part of English. No computer understands the whole English language. The programmer's job is to translate an English sentence (such as "do the payroll") into language the computer understands (such as BASIC). So *the programmer is a translator*.

Some computers understand BASIC. Other computers understand a different vocabulary, called COBOL. For example, COBOL uses the words DISPLAY and WRITE instead of PRINT.

Before programming a computer, you must find out which language the computer understands.

Does it understand BASIC? Or does it understand COBOL instead? Or does it understand a yet different language? The most popular languages are BASIC, COBOL, C++, and JAVA; but there are also *thousands* of others. Your computer understands at least one of those languages; if you're lucky, your computer understands *several* of those languages.

When you apply for a programming job, the first question to ask the interviewer is: which languages does the company's computer understand? Or better yet, ask, "Which language do you want me to program in?" The interviewer will say "BASIC" or "COBOL" or "C++" or "JAVA" or some similar answer and then ask you, "Do you know that language?"

Of those popular languages, BASIC is the easiest and the most fun. To become a programmer, begin by studying BASIC, then move on to the other languages, which are yuckier.

Since BASIC's so easy, saying you know BASIC is less prestigious than saying you know languages such as C++. To get lots of prestige, learn *many* languages. To convince the interviewer you're brilliant, say that you know many languages well even if the job you're applying for needs just one language.

The most prestigious languages to know are assembly and machine languages, because they're the hardest.

> If you can convince the interviewer that you know assembly and machine languages, the interviewer will assume you're God and offer you a very high salary, even if the job doesn't require a knowledge of those languages.

Specific computers
Before going to the interview, learn about the specific computer the company uses.

> For example, if the company's computer is an IBM maxicomputer, study the IBM maxi's details. Study its operating system and its languages. If the job requires COBOL, study the particular dialect of COBOL used on the IBM maxi. Each computer has its own dialect of COBOL, its own dialect of BASIC, etc. Usually, the differences between dialects are small, but you must know them. For assembly and machine languages, the differences between dialects are much greater: the assembly language on an IBM PC is almost entirely different from the assembly language on an IBM maxi.

Analysis versus coding
The act of programming consists of two stages.

In the first stage, analyze the problem to make it more specific.

> For example, suppose the problem is, "Program the computer to do the payroll". The first stage is to decide exactly how the company wants the payroll to be done. Should it be done weekly, bi-weekly, semi-monthly, or monthly? While computing the payroll checks, what other reports do you want the computer to generate? For example, do you want the computer to also print a report about the employees' attendance, and about how much money each department of the company is spending on salaries? Maybe one of the departments is over-budgeting. And what kind of paychecks do you want the computer to *refuse* to print? For example, if somebody in the company tries to make the computer print a paycheck for a ridiculous amount (such as $1,000,000 or ½¢), you want the computer to refuse (and perhaps signal an alarm).

That stage — analyzing a vague problem (such as "do the payroll") to make it more specific — is called **analysis**. A person who analyzes is called an **analyst** or, more prestigiously, a **systems analyst**.

After analyzing the vague problem and transforming it into a series of smaller, more specific tasks, the analyst turns the problem over to a team of **coders**. Each coder takes one of the tasks and translates it into BASIC or COBOL or some other language.

If you're hired to be a "programmer", your first assignment will probably be as a coder. After you gain experience, you'll be promoted to a systems analyst.

The ideal systems analyst knows how to analyze a problem but also has prior experience as a coder. A systems analyst who knows how to both code and analyze is called a **programmer/analyst**. An analyst who doesn't know how to code — who doesn't know BASIC or COBOL — who merely knows how to break a big problem into a series of little ones — is paid less.

Three kinds of programming
Programming falls into three categories: **development**, **testing**, and **maintenance**.

> **Development** means inventing a new program.
>
> **Testing** means making sure the program works.
>
> **Maintenance** means making minor improvements to programs that were written long ago. The "improvements" consist of eliminating errors that were discovered recently, or making the program conform to changed government regulations, or adding extra features so that the program produces extra reports or handles extra-special cases.

Development is more exciting than testing, which is more exciting than maintenance. So if you're a new programmer, the other programmers will probably "stick you" in the maintenance department, where you'll be part of the maintenance crew. Since your job will consist of "cleaning up" old programs, cruel programmers will call you a "computer janitor".

"Application program" versus "system program"
Programs fall into two categories.

The usual kinds of program is called an **application program**. It handles a specific application (such as "payroll" or "chess" or "send rocket to moon").

The other kind of program is called a **system program**; its only purpose is to help programmers write applications programs.

> For example, hidden inside the computer is a program that makes the computer understand BASIC. That program explains to the computer what the words PRINT, INPUT, and IF mean. That program (which is called the **BASIC language processor**) is an example of a system program.
>
> Another system program is called the **operating system**. It tells the computer how to control the disks and printer and terminals. If the operating system is fancy, it even tells the computer how to handle many programmers at once.
>
> Another system program is the **editor**. It lets you edit files and programs. For example, on big old computers, the editor lets you edit programs written in old languages such as COBOL and FORTRAN.
>
> So system programs are tools, which help programmers write application programs. When you buy a computer, buy some system programs so you can create applications programs easily.

A person who invents system programs is called a **systems programmer**. To become a systems programmer, learn assembly language and machine language.

Creating a system program is very difficult; so a systems programmer usually gets paid more than an applications programmer.

The word "systems" is prestigious: it's used in the phrase "systems analyst" and in "systems programmer". In some companies, if your boss wants to praise you, the boss will put the word "systems" in front of your title even if your job has nothing to do with "systems".

How to learn programming
To be a good programmer, you need experience. You can't become a good programmer by just reading books and listening to lectures; you must **get your hands on a computer and practice**.

If you take a computer course, the books and lectures are much less valuable than the experience of using the school's computer. Spend lots of time in the computer center. Think of the course as just an excuse to get permission to use the school's computer. The quality of the lecture is less important than the quality of the school's computer center. The ideal computer center:

> has a computer that can understand many languages
> gives you *unlimited* use of the computer (no "extra charges")
> is open 24 hours a day
> has enough terminals so you don't have to wait for somebody else to finish
> has a staff of "teaching assistants" who'll answer your questions
> has a rack full of easy-to-read manuals that explain how to use the computer
> lets you borrow books and manuals, to take home with you
> has *several* kinds of computers, so that you get a broad range of experience.

Before you enroll in a computer course, find out whether the school's computer center has those features.

Many computer schools are unnecessarily expensive. To save money, take fewer courses, and buy more books and magazines instead. Better yet, buy a computer yourself and keep it at home!

> You can buy a used 486 computer for about $300. Keep the computer a few months, practice writing BASIC programs on it and using some Windows applications, then sell it to a friend for $100 less than you paid — so that using it cost you just $100 and gave you several *months* of education. That's a much better investment of your money than spending many hundreds of dollars on a computer course.

Another cheap way to get an education is to phone your town's board of education, and ask whether the town offers any adult-education courses in computers. Some towns offer adult-education computer courses for under $100.

For an even better deal, phone your town's board of education — or high school — and ask whether you can sit in the back of a high-school computer class.

> If you're an adult resident of the town, you might be able to sit in the back of the class for free. Your only "expense" will be the embarrassment of sitting in the same room as youngsters. After a day or two of feeling strange, you'll get used to it, and you'll get an excellent free education.

Community colleges offer low-cost courses that are decent. Explore the community colleges before sinking money into more expensive institutions that are over-priced.

Starting salary

For your first programming job, your salary will be somewhere between $20,000 and $30,000. The exact amount depends on which languages you know, how many programs you wrote previously, whether you have a college degree, whether you've had experience on the particular kind of computer the company uses, and whether you know the application area. (For example, if you're a programmer for an insurance company, it's helpful to know something about insurance.)

Degrees

A college degree ain't needed, but wow can it make you look smart! Try to get a degree in "computer science" or "management information systems".

"Computer science" emphasizes the underlying theory, systems programming, assembly language, C++, and applications to science. "Management information systems" emphasizes BASIC, COBOL, DBASE, and applications to business.

A major in "mathematics" that emphasizes computers is also acceptable.

Discrimination

If you're a woman or non-white or physically handicapped, you'll be pleased to know that the computer industry discriminates less than in other occupations. Being a woman or non-white or physically handicapped actually works to your *advantage*, since many companies have affirmative-action programs.

But discrimination *does* exist against older people. If you're over 40 and trying to get a job as an entry-level programmer, you'll have a tough time since the stereotypical programmer is "young, bright, and a fast thinker". If you're old, they'll assume you're "slow and sluggish".

Because of that unfair discrimination, if you're old you should probably try entering the computer industry through a different door: as a consultant, or a computer salesperson, or a computer-center manager, or a computer teacher. For those positions, your age works to your *advantage*, since those jobs require *wisdom*, and people will assume that since you're old, you're wise.

Shifting careers

If you're older, the best way to enter the computer field is to combine your knowledge of computers with other topics you knew previously.

> If you already knew a lot about how to sell merchandise, get a job selling computers. If you already knew a lot about teaching, get a job teaching about computers — or helping teachers deal with computers. If you already knew a lot about real estate, computerize your real estate office.

In other words, do *not* try to "hop" careers; instead, gradually *shift* your responsibilities so that they deal more with computers.

To get into the computer field safely, keep your current job but computerize it.

> For example, if you're already a math teacher, keep teaching math but convince your school to also let you teach a computer course, or at least incorporate computers into the math curriculum or help run the school's computer center. If you already work for a big company and your job bores you, try to transfer to a department that puts you in closer contact with the computer. After a year in such a transitional state, you can break into the computer field more easily since you can put the word "computer" somewhere on your résumé as "job experience".

If you're a college kid, write programs that help the professors, or help others during your summer vacations.

> Agree to write the programs for little or no pay. Your goal is *not* money: your goal is to put "experienced programmer" on your résumé.

Interviews

When applying for your first computer job, try to avoid the "personnel" office. The bureaucrats in that office will look at your résumé, see it includes too little experience, and trash it.

Instead, play the who-you-know game. Contact somebody who actually works with computers. Convince that person you're brighter than your résumé indicates. Prove you've learned so much (from reading, courses, and practice) that you can *quickly* conquer any task laid before you. If you impress that person enough, you might get the job even though your paper qualifications look too brief.

When you get an interview, be assertive.

> Ask the interviewer more questions than the interviewer asks you. Ask the interviewer about the company's computer, and about why the company doesn't have a different one instead. Ask the interviewer how the other people in the company feel about the computer center. Ask the same kinds of questions a data-processing manager would ask. That way, the interviewer will assume you have the potential to become a data-processing manager, and will hire you immediately. You'll also be showing you *care* enough about the company to ask questions. And you'll be showing you have a vibrant personality, and are not just "another vegetable who came through the door".

One of the strange things about applying for a programming job is that the interviewer will *not* ask to see a sample of your work. The interviewer doesn't have time to read your program. Even if the interviewer *did* have time to read your program, he couldn't be sure you wrote it yourself. Instead, the interviewer will just *chat* with you about your accomplishments. You must "talk smart". The best way is to know all the buzzwords of the computer industry — even if they don't really help you write programs. For example, during the interview you'll probably be asked whether you know **structured programming**.

> A **structured program** is a program that's well-organized. It consists of a short main routine and many subroutines. (In some languages, the "routines" are called **procedures**.) To write a structured program, avoid the words GO TO; instead, use words that involve subroutines (procedures).

Later joys

In your first job, your salary will be low, but don't worry about it. During your first job, you'll receive lots of training: you're getting a free education. After your training period is over, your salary will rise rapidly — especially if you do extra studying during evenings and weekends. Your *real* job is: to become brilliant.

After you've become brilliant and experienced, other companies will eagerly want to hire you. Your best strategy is to leave your current company and work elsewhere to gain new experiences. **Whenever you feel you're "coasting" and not learning anything new, it's time to move to a different job.** The "different job" can be in a new company — or in a different department of the same company.

By moving around — by gaining a wide variety of experiences — you can eventually become a qualified, wise consultant. And you'll feel like God.

Social contacts Being a programmer is not always glamorous. You'll spend many long hours staring at your screen and wondering why your program doesn't work. The job is intellectual, not social. But after you've become an expert coder, you get into "systems analysis" and "consulting" and "teaching" and "management", and interact with people more.

Software publishing To be a programmer, you do *not* have to work for a large company. Instead, you can sit home, write programs on your personal microcomputer, and sell them to software publishers, for a royalty.

> If the software publisher sells many copies of your program, you become rich. On the other hand, if your program is *not* a "smash hit", you remain poor.
>
> Since your program might not become popular, do *not* rely on software publishing as a steady source of income. Instead, view it as a part-time activity which, if successful, will put some extra money in your pocket.
>
> The most famous software publishers are Microsoft, Corel, Symantec, Electronic Arts, and Softkey. There are many others. Browse through the ads in microcomputer magazines.

Software houses A company whose only goal is to produce software is called a **software house**. Software houses dealing with large computers typically hire full-time programmers and pay them fixed salaries. Software houses dealing with microcomputers sometimes pay royalties instead.

Management

Programming is fun for young kids. But as you get older, you'll tire of machines and want to deal with people instead. As you approach retirement, you'll want to help the younger generation relate to the computers you've mastered.

To be a successful manager, you need three skills: you must be **technically competent**; you must be **wise**; and you must **know how to handle people**.

You should know how to program. Know the strengths and weaknesses of each computer company, and be able to compare their products. Develop a philosophy about what makes a "good" computer center. Understand people's motives and channel them into constructive avenues.

Keep up to date. Read the latest books and periodicals about computers. Chat with other computer experts by phone, at conventions, and at computer clubs.

Here are hints about how to manage a computer center:

> Many computer centers put four-foot-high partitions between their programmers, to give the programmers "privacy". Unfortunately, the partitions are counter-productive: they're too low to block noise, and too high to permit helpful conversation with your neighbor. Knock the partitions down!
>
> When putting a computer center into a school, you must develop a *cadre* of hot-shot students who are bright, friendly, and outgoing, and who will help and encourage the other students to use the computer. If the hot-shots are *not* outgoing — if they become an elitist, snobbish club — the rest of the school will avoid the computer.
>
> If you've hired "programming assistants" who help the programmers, don't let the programming assistants hide in an office or behind a desk. The programming assistants should walk up to the programmers at the computer keyboards and offer help.
>
> In too many organizations, computers are locked in the offices of prestigious people and aren't used. Let *everybody* share the computers.
>
> Too often, managers judge their own worth by the size of the computer center's budget: the bigger the budget, the more prestigious the manager. Remember that the sign of being a good manager is *not* having a big budget; the sign of a good manager is the ability to meet the company's needs on a *small* budget.

Too often, the head of the computer center decides who can use the computer. So the head of the computer center becomes powerful — and evil. To avoid concentrating so much power in the hands of one bureaucrat, use **distributed processing**: get several small computers instead of one big monster, and give each department its own small computer.

If you're a "microcomputer consultant" and honest, you'll tell your client to buy low-cost popular programs, instead of telling him to pay you to invent "customized" programs.

Sales

You can find three kinds of salesmen:

> The "slick" kind knows "how to sell", but doesn't know any technical details about the computer he's selling. He doesn't know how to program, and doesn't know much about the computers sold by his competitors. All he knows is the "line" that his boss told him to give the customers. That kind of salesman usually resorts to off-color tactics, such as claiming that all computers sold by competitors are "toys".
>
> The opposite kind of salesman is technical: he knows every detail about every computer manufactured, but can't give you any *practical* advice about which computer best meets *your* needs.
>
> **The best kind of salesman is a consultant.** He asks a lot of questions about your particular needs, tells you which of his computers meets your needs best, and even tells you the *limitations* of his computer and why another, more expensive computer sold by a competitor might be better. He's an "honest Joe". He clinches the sale because you trust him, and because you know you won't have any unpleasant surprises after the sale. While selling you a computer, he teaches you a lot. He's a true friend.

A woman can sell computers more easily than a man. That's because most computer customers are men, and men are more attracted to women. It's also because, in our society, women are more "trusted" than men. But if you're a woman, say some technical buzzwords to convince the customer that you're technically competent. Otherwise, the customer will assume that since you're a woman, you must be a "dumb secretary".

Be an entrepreneur

How about starting a rental service, where people can rent microcomputers? How about starting a camp, where kids can spend the summer playing with computers? How about starting a computer set-up service, where you teach businesses how to start using microcomputers? How about writing easy manuals explaining the most popular software? Each of those ideas has been tried successfully; join the fun!

Learn to spell

If you don't spel gud, yur coleegs wil thinc yure an idiut.

Be especially careful with these words, which beginners often misspell:

Wrong	Right	Comments
computor	computer	"Computer" is a machine or person that computes. "Computor" is a snobbish computer.
softwear	software	"Software" is the opposite of "hardware". "Softwear" is a negligée.
imput	input	"Input" is what the computer takes "in". "Imput" is said only by "im"beciles.
silicone	silicon	"Silicon" is what you put in an integrated circuit. "Silicone" is what you put in your breast.
hexidecimal	hexadecimal	"Hexadecimal" means "six and ten", or "sixteen". "Hexidecimal" is icky.
hobbiest	hobbyist	A "computer hobbyist" likes computers. A "computer hobbiest" is even more hobbier.
Epsom	Epson	"Epson" provides printers. "Epsom" provides salt.
COBAL	COBOL	"COBOL" is "COmmon Business-Oriented Language". "COBAL" is a co-ed who likes sex.
TSR-80	TRS-80	"TRS-80" stands for "Tandy's Radio Shack". "TSR-80" is a nut who says the alphabet backwards.

For the following words, choose your favorite spelling:

> Most computer experts write "disk", but some write "disc".
>
> For "half a byte",
> humble programmers write "nibble", but snobbish programmers write "nybble".

Change your personality

As you spend time with computers, your personality will change. You'll gradually become a **hacker** (a person skilled at fiddling with the internal workings of computer hardware and software). I hope you become a **helpful hacker** instead of a **cracker** (a hacker who creates mischief by screwing up the internal workings of computer hardware and software, such as by writing a virus or by using password-evasion tricks to secretly spy at private files).

Back in 1993, 100 hackers in an Internet newsgroup got together and wrote a description of a hacker's personality. Here's the description, as edited by Eric Raymond (in his *New Hacker's Dictionary*) and then further edited by me. Not all hackers fit this description — but most do!

If you hang around computers a long time, this description will probably start applying to you too! Watch yourself!

As America and the world become more computerized, the hacker personality will gradually dominate our planet. If you don't like the "hacker personality", see what you can do to alter it.

Hacker intelligence

The hacker mind is intelligent but strange.

College intelligence Most hackers past their teens have a college degree or are self-taught to a similar level. Before becoming a full-fledged hacker, the typical hacker majored in computer science or electrical engineering or math or physics or linguistics (since studying human languages is a good stepping stone to studying computer languages) or philosophy (since philosophy analyzes the meaning of language and "life forms").

Read a lot Hackers read a lot, and read a wide variety, though with extra emphasis on science facts and science fiction. A hacker's home includes a big library, with many shelves full of books that the hacker has read. A hacker spends more spare time reading books & magazines than watching TV. A hacker spends as much spare time reading as the average non-hacker spends watching TV.

Bad handwriting Hackers have bad handwriting — their script is hard to read — so they usually write in simple capital block letters (LIKE THIS), as if they were junior draftsmen writing on a blueprint. The capital block letters make sense, especially when writing math equations or programming instructions that contain lots of symbols; script would be no faster.

Inhuman communication Since programming requires good organization and precise use of language, hackers are good at composing sentences, paragraphs, and compositions. But though hackers are good writers, they're bad talkers, since they don't get much practice chatting with humans. They're not skilled at arguing with humans, confronting them, and negotiating with them; they're better at communicating with computers, which don't argue.

Good at memorizing Hackers are good at memorizing details, such as computer codes.

Neat just in output Hackers produce programs, writings, and thinking that are very neat and well-organized; but a hacker is too busy to make the hacker's environment equally neat, so a hacker's desk and office floor are typically piled high with a disorganized mess of resources.

Hacker bodies

Here's what a hacker looks like, and where to find one.

Near universities Half of the USA's best hackers live within 100 miles of Boston or San Francisco. That's because, during the 1950's and 1960's, the top researchers in artificial intelligence were at two universities: the **Massachusetts Institute of Technology** (**MIT**, in Cambridge, Massachusetts, near Boston) and **Stanford University** (in Silicon Valley's Palo Alto, near San Francisco). Those researchers spawned proteges, who want to keep living near the master researchers even after graduation, to stay connected to the intellectual community.

Mostly male Most hackers are male, but females are more common in hackerdom than in other technical professions.

Mostly Caucasian In the USA, most hackers are Caucasian. On the West Coast, many hackers are Asian; on the East Coast, many hackers are Jewish.

Relatively unbigoted Hackers are less bigoted than other Americans, since hackers care more about what a person wrote than the person's appearance. Hackers believe computers can act like humans and therefore believe in the humane treatment of all computers and all people.

Casual dresser Hackers dislike "business attire". The typical hacker would quit a job if it required wearing a suit.

Hackers like to wear clothes that are casual, easy to take care of, post-hippie: T-shirts (with slogans on them), jeans, running shoes (or barefoot), and backpacks.

Scruffy appearance Hackers look scruffy. Many hackers have long hair. Men hackers often have beards and moustaches. Women hackers try to look "natural" by wearing little or no makeup.

Since hackers love computers, which are mostly indoors, hackers don't get tans.

Night owls Hackers often stay up all night, to finish work on excitingly frustrating programming challenges. Then they sleep late in the morning.

Extreme food For dinner, hackers prefer spicy ethnic food instead of "American" food. The most popular is spicy Chinese (Szechuan or Hunan style, rather than Cantonese, which is too bland). Alternatives, popular occasionally, are Thai food and Mexican food.

For a change, hackers like high-quality Jewish-deli food, when available.

For midnight snacks while in the middle of marathon programming sessions, hackers prefer pizza and microwave burritos. Back in the 1970's, hackers used to eat a lot of junk food, but modern hackers are more into "health food".

Hackers tend to be extreme: either too skinny or too fat. More hackers are too skinny than too fat.

Nearly drug-free Hackers need to protect their heads from drugs, so they don't do drugs. They don't smoke. Most hackers don't drink alcohol, though a few hackers experiment with fancy wines and exotic beers.

Since hackers favor experimentation, they tolerate folks who use non-addictive drugs such as pot and LSD. But hackers criticize people who take "downers" and opiates, since those drugs make you act stupid.

To help stay up late at night programming, hackers often take mild "uppers" such as caffeine (in coffee and Jolt cola) and sugar (in soft drinks and junk food).

Experimental sex Hackers are more likely than "normal" folks to experiment sexually. Many hackers openly have multiple boyfriends or girlfriends, or live in communes or group houses, or practice open marriage (where both partners agree that extra-marital relationships are okay), or are gay or lesbian.

Hacker beliefs

Here's how to make a hacker happy.

Toys better than money Hackers don't care about earning lots of money or social approval. Instead, hackers just want the intellectual pleasure of inventing beautiful programs and products — and exploring the beautiful products invented by others. So to bribe a hacker, don't offer money or a fancy title; instead, offer a lab full of computer hardware and software for the hacker to play with, and permission for the hacker to spend time playing with and inventing fantastic technology.

Non-religious Since hackers don't like to be told what to do, they don't like organized religion: Since hackers are into facts, not beliefs, they tend not to believe in God. When asked "What religion are you?", many hackers reply by calling themselves "atheist" or "agnostic" or "non-observant Jewish". Some hackers join "parody" religions, such as Discordianism and the Church of the SubGenius. Some hackers have fun participating in "mystical" religions such as Zen Buddhism and neo-paganism.

Libertarian politics Hackers like freedom to explore computers. They don't like restrictions. They don't like being told what to do. They dislike authoritarians, managers, MBA's, and big government. They tend to be Libertarian. They dislike the dogmatic insistence of the far left and far right. If asked to choose between Democrats and Republicans, they tend to choose Democrats because Democrats permit more social freedoms, so hackers are classified as "left of center".

Cat lovers Hackers are more likely to have cats than dogs, because cats are like hackers: clever rather than belligerent.

No team sports Hackers don't like to watch sports. Hackers don't watch sports on TV and don't go to sports stadiums.

Hackers would rather participate than watch. Though half of all hackers don't make time to participate, the other half *do* participate, but mainly in individual sports rather than team sports. The only team sport they like is volleyball, because it's non-contact and friendly.

They prefer individual sports that involve dexterity, concentration, and stamina, rather than brute force. Their favorite sports are bicycling, hiking, rock climbing, caving, kite-flying, juggling, martial arts, roller skating, ice skating, skiing, target shooting, and auto racing, and aviation.

Strange cars Hackers don't wash their cars. Hackers drive extreme cars: either beat-up heaps (unwashed because they're junk) or (if the hackers are rich) luxury sports cars (unwashed anyway).

Brainy hobbies Hackers like to play music, play board games (such as chess and Go), dabble in ham radio, learn about linguistics & foreign languages, and do "theater teching" (give technical support to theater productions).

Hate stupidity Hackers like active intelligent freedom, so they dislike dishonesty, boredom, business suits, stupid incompetent people (especially stupid incompetent managers who wear business suits), stupid music (such as "easy listening music"), and stupid culture (such as TV, except for TV's cleverly cynical cartoons & movies & the old Star Trek).

Computerize your home

Back in 1970, computerists tried to predict what life would be like in 1990. Let's look at their predictions and see which ones came true. The predictions appeared in:

Martin & Norman's *The Computerized Society* (published by Prentice-Hall in 1970)
John Kemeny's *Man and the Computer* (published by Scribner's in 1972)
G. Cuttle's prize-winning essay (published in 1969)

Work at home

Cuttle said:

"It may be more economical for companies to subsidize home 'communications rooms' for their employees than renting expensive office space to commute to. Some establishments are already starting to provide computer terminals for the homes of senior staff. This is sensible when one considers the tendency for great ideas to materialize in the bath. Many of the better characteristics of the cottage industry may return, particularly in terms of personal freedom."

Martin & Norman said:

"The first widespread use of home terminals will probably be sponsored by employers. Mothers who participate may be relieved of the boredom they feel when they are unable to leave their children."

Kemeny said:

"Executives complain they rush into their offices then spend half their time talking on the phone, which they could have done as well at home. Office files will be kept in national computer networks, accessible from home. If we remove the need for millions of people to rush in and out of the city daily, we'd be on our way to solving urban problems. Perhaps the central city will become truly an info center where the machines are but not the humans who use them. Since cities still would have a central location, they might expand their roles as entertainment centers and places to live for those who insist on seeing a play or sports event in person rather than on TV."

What happened instead Personal computers have become so cheap that most homes contain them instead of terminals attached to timesharing services. Personal computers can communicate with national computer networks by using the Internet. Many executives work at home on personal computers during evenings and weekends but still prefer to meet face-to-face with other employees during the day.

Electronic shopping

Martin & Norman said:

"Instead of going to a store, the consumer could scan a list of available goods and prices at different shops on the home terminal, then use the terminal to order."

Kemeny said:

"For items costing over a dollar, cash transactions will totally disappear."

What happened instead Since banks charge merchants big fees to handle charge cards and fund transfers, some merchants discourage cash for purchases under $10. Some attempts to develop computerized shopping failed because consumers want to see photos of goods before buying. On TV, infomercials succeed by letting consumers view before buying.

Appliances

Cuttle said:

"Anyone doubting a computer's ability to cook breakfast has only to remember the average housewife's state of mind at 7AM to realize that preparing breakfast is a very mechanical task. Many other household tasks are equally suitable for computers to invade. At present each appliance needing a computer has its own small one built in, but the logical development is to have a bigger household computer tucked under the stairs. Circuits could be wired through the house so each individual gadget could be plugged in."

Martin & Norman said:

"A family driving home after a few days away will phone home and key some digits on the phone to switch on the heat or air conditioner. A woman before leaving for work will preprogram her kitchen equipment to cook a meal; she'll then phone at the appropriate time and have the meal prepared."

What happened instead Now that we have microwave ovens and gourmet frozen dinners, housewives (and househusbands!) can create dinner in less than 5 minutes without using a computer. Instead of being linked to a big household computer, each appliance contains its own fancy microprocessor (which controls the timing, temperature, etc.), since microprocessors have become so cheap.

Government

Cuttle said:

"The householder could ask the computer whether any legislation in progress affects his neighborhood or interests. He could have easier access to his congressman. Conversely, he could be asked questions, and this might be a better way to keep congressmen in touch with the feelings of constituents."

What happened instead Rich citizens can send e-mail messages to politicians by using the Internet. Low-income citizens haven't bought modems yet.

Newspapers

Kemeny said:

"Consider a system under which The New York Times, instead of publishing hundreds of thousands of copies, would store the same info in a computer tied to a national network, from which each reader could retrieve the items he wanted, in as much detail as he desired. Sitting at home, he could dial the computer network and ask for his personalized New York Times. The computer would remember which topics he normally reads and present stories on them a frame at a time. He could ask for more details. He'd have available at any moment, day or night, completely up-to-date info. The system would make sure he doesn't miss any news that concerns him. If The New York Times adopts this suggestion, it should change its motto to 'All the news that you see fit to read.'"

What happened instead On-line services, such as America OnLine and the Internet, provide the complete text of daily newspapers around the country. Few people use those services, since they work just while the reader sits by a phone jack, and since the computer screen is too small to display the contents of a full newspaper page pleasantly.

Medicine

Cuttle said:

"Automatic diagnosis by computer could be a useful aid. Interrogation through a home terminal could pinpoint some everyday ailments. Much treatment can be carried out at home that today might need hospital treatment. It may be far cheaper and pleasanter for the patient to have monitoring equipment brought home and connected through the terminal to a hospital computer."

What happened instead Many doctors and pharmacists use computers to double-check diagnoses and also warn of interactions between drugs. Diagnosis by computer-assisted tomography is widespread in hospitals. Many invalids stuck at home use beepers to call help when needed. Most patients trust neither computers nor doctors.

The whole family

Kemeny said:

"Father, if he brings his work home from the office, can use the terminal in place of a sizable office staff. Mother can do most of her shopping through a computer terminal. If by 1990 the roles of men and women have been completely reversed, the computer terminal will be equally happy to work out business problems for mother and to help father with his shopping and housework; Children will find the home terminal an immeasurable asset in doing homework; indeed the child of 1990 will find it impossible to conceive how the older generation managed to get through school without the help of a computer."

What happened instead The feminist revolution has encouraged role reversal. Kids use computers mainly to play games, practice programming, do word processing, print greeting cards & posters, send e-mail, and access the Internet.

Teach your kids

Here's how to introduce kids to computers.

Curriculum

Here's how to develop the curriculum.

When should kids start learning about computers? Programs have been developed even for kids in nursery school! You can get "alphabet fun" programs: when the kid presses the A key, pictures of apples appear all over the screen; when the kid presses B, the screen is filled with bears; C generates cats, etc. To make the program fun, the pictures on the screen are **animated**; they dance!

Kids should start writing simple programs in BASIC when they're in the third grade. (The brightest kids can start even younger!) Before the third grade, the typical kid should learn how to run other people's programs and maybe learn LOGO (a language that's easier than BASIC for beginners).

Which kids should take computer courses? Expose *all* kids to a computer. Give them the opportunity to press the buttons, run programs, and do other fun things.

Let all kids deal with the computer *before* entering high school. The intro instruction should be broad: dip into BASIC programming, hardware jargon, applications (such as word processing), and social effects.

The intro is important for *all* kids, regardless of math ability. Most computer programming requires hardly any math.

Include even the kids who are "slow" or "hate school", since the computer often helps them "turn on" to school. LOGO's been particularly effective at that.

If your school lacks enough computers to start an extensive program, wheel the computers from classroom to classroom so each kid gets to spend at least a few minutes with the computer each semester. Let kids who want to go further join an after-school computer club.

Which language should kids learn to program in? More programs have been written in BASIC than any other computer language. A person who doesn't understand BASIC is "out of touch" with reality and a computer illiterate. Every kid should learn BASIC before graduating from high school.

The youngest kids might also want to try LOGO, which lets you draw pictures more easily than BASIC. The oldest kids might also want to try PASCAL, C++, or JAVA, which are more "sophisticated" than BASIC. But BASIC's the most "practical" language to learn, since it can handle a wider variety of applications easily. Another advantage of BASIC is that it comes free with most computers; the other languages cost extra (except for free versions that are unreasonably awkward).

What should a computer course emphasize? The course should emphasize hands-on programming with a wide variety of amusing applications.

The course should *not* be restricted to math and science. In fact, less than half the programming examples should involve math or science. Most examples should involve the arts, business, word processing, etc.

If the computer course is taught by a math teacher, the school's principal should make sure the teacher doesn't spend too much time talking about math.

In the "computer curriculum", how important are music & graphics? Any computer for kids should play music and draw color graphics, because music & graphics create fun and maintain the kids' interest.

Any course on computer programming should discuss how to program music and graphics. Besides being fun, such a discussion emphasizes that computers are not "just for numbers", and also illustrates visually the effects of programming concepts such as FOR … NEXT loops.

What homework should a computer course assign? The homework should including writing a computer program. To make that practical, the school must have enough computers to handle all the kids. Though the

teacher should assign some standard exercises, the kids should also be encouraged to invent their *own* programming projects.

In what order should computer topics be taught? The course should begin with hands-on experience. The kids should write elementary programs (in BASIC or LOGO) and also run programs that others wrote. As the course progresses and programming examples become more complex, give the kids a breather by inserting light-hearted topics such as video games, computer graphics, word processing, the Internet, business software, kinds of hardware, computer companies, effects on society, and careers.

Educational applications

The computer can help teach many topics.

English While trying to write a program, the kid learns the importance of punctuation: the kid learns to distinguish colons, semicolons, commas, periods, parentheses, and brackets. The kid also learns the importance of spelling: if the kid misspells the word PRINT or INPUT, the computer gripes. The kid learns to handle long words, while wading through computer manuals.

Some kids "hate to write English compositions". The computer can change that attitude!

> If you let a kid use a word-processing program, the kid suddenly discovers that writing an English composition can be fun! The composition suddenly becomes "electronic"; it appears on screen! Revising the composition can be even *more* fun since the kid gets to use the computer's nifty editing tools. The whole experience becomes as much fun as a video game. The typical word processor can correct spelling without forcing the kid to endlessly thumb through the dictionary; it even corrects grammar and style. Watching the computer correct spelling, grammar, and style is educational and fun.

To make the kid understand why parts of speech (such as "nouns", "verbs", and "adjectives") are important, give the kid a computer program that writes sentences by choosing random nouns, random verbs, and random adjectives. Then tell the kid to invent his *own* nouns, verbs, and adjectives, feed them into the program, and watch what kind of sentences the program produces now.

Young kids enjoy a program called **Story Machine**.

> It gives you a list of nouns, verbs, adjectives, and other parts of speech that you can use to build a story. You type the story using any words on the list. As you type the story, the computer will *automatically illustrates it!* For example, if you type, "The boy eats the apple," your screen will automatically show a picture of a boy eating an apple! If you type *several* sentences, to form a longer story, the computer will automatically illustrate the entire story and produce an animated cartoon of it! The program will also criticize your story's structure. For example, if you say "The boy eats the apple" but the boy isn't near the apple yet, the program will recommend that you insert a sentence such as "The boy runs to the apple" beforehand. The program comes on a $25 disk from Softkey (1 Kendall Square, Cambridge, MA 02139, phone 617-494-1200). To run the program, you need an Apple 2 computer.

History The computer can make history come "alive" by throwing the student into an historical situation.

For example, a graduate of my teacher-training institute wrote a program that says, "It's 1910. You're **Kaiser Wilhelm**. What are you going to do?" Then it gives you several choices.

> For example, it asks "Would you like to make a treaty with Russia?" If you answer "yes", the computer replies, "Russia breaks the treaty. *Now* what are you going to do?" No matter how you answer the questions, there are only two ways the program can end: either "You've plunged Europe into a World War" or "You've turned Germany into a second-rate country". After running that program several times, you get a real feeling for the terrible jam that the Kaiser was in, and you begin to pity him. Running the program is more dramatic than reading a book about the Kaiser's problems, because the program forces you to step into the Kaiser's shoes and react to his surroundings: you are there. When you finish running the program, you feel you've lived another life — the life of a 1910 Kaiser.

Such a program is called an historical **simulation**, since it makes the computer **simulate** (imitate) an historical event.

Current events The best way to teach current events is through simulation.

For example, when California's Governor Brown had trouble controlling **medflies**, teachers wrote programs that began by saying, "You're Governor Brown. What are you going to do?" (One of the programs was even called "Medfly Mania".)

The best way to encourage the student to analyze the conflict between **Israel and the Arabs** is have the student run a program that begins by saying "You're Israel's Prime Minister" then run a program that says "You're the PLO's leader, Yassir Arafat".

> By running both programs, the student learns to take both sides of the argument and understands the emotions of both leaders. Such programs could help warring nations understand each other enough to bring peace!

When **Three-Mile Island** almost exploded, teachers wrote a program saying "You're in the control room at Three-Mile Island".

> Your computer's screen shows a picture of the control room. Your goal: make as much money as possible for the electric company without blowing the place up. You can buy two versions of the program: one's called just "Three-Mile Island"; the other's called "Scram". To teach kids about Three-Mile Island, it's easier to buy the program than to get permission from parents to "take the kids on a field trip to Three-Mile Island" (which also requires that you sit on a bus while listening to 100 choruses of "100 bottles of beer on the wall" and worrying about kids who get lost at Three-Mile Island).

The best way to teach **economics and politics** is to give the student a program that says "You're running the country" and then asks the student to input an economic and political strategy. At the end of the program, the computer tells how many years the student lasted in office, how well the country fared, and how many people want to assassinate him.

The best way to learn anything is "by experience". Computer simulations let the student learn by "simulated experience", which condenses into a few minutes what would otherwise require many *years* of "natural experience".

Biology The computer can do **genetics** calculations: it can compute the probabilities of having various kinds of offspring and predict how the characteristics of the population will shift over time.

The computer can handle **taxonomy**: it can classify different kinds of animals and plants.

> The computer asks you a series of questions about an organism and finally tells you the organism's name. One of the most popular programs is a game called "Animals", which lets the student teach the computer which questions to ask.

To teach **ecology**, a graduate of my teacher-training institute wrote a simulation program that begins by saying, "You're the game warden of New Jersey. What are you going to do?"

> It asks how many weeks you want the deer-hunting season to last. If you make the hunting season too long, hunters kill all the deer, and deer-loving environmentalists hate you. On the other hand, if you make the deer-hunting season too short, hunters hate you; moreover, the deer overpopulate, can't find enough to eat, then die of starvation, whereupon *everybody* hates you. Your goal is to stay in office as long as possible.

Sex education When Dartmouth College (which for centuries had been all-male and rowdy) suddenly became coed in 1971, its biology department realized the importance of teaching about **birth control**. The professors wrote a program that asks how old you are and which birth control method you wish to use this year.

> You have 9 choices, such as pill, diaphragm, IUD, condom, rhythm method, and "Providence". After you type your choice, the computer computes the probability of having children and may print (if you're unlucky) ***BOY*** or ***GIRL***. The computation is based, as in nature, on a combination of science and chance (random numbers). Then the computer asks your strategy for the next year. The program continues until the computer finally prints ***MENOPAUSE***. The program lets you explore how different strategies yield different numbers of children. It's safer to experiment with the program than to experiment on your body. It's also faster, but maybe not as fun.

How can programs that tutor, drill, and test students be made exciting? Let the

programs use the same techniques that make video games exciting.

> Let the programs include animated graphics and require the student to answer quickly. Display a running total of the student's points, so whenever the student answers correctly the screen shows the score increase immediately.
>
> At the end of the educational game, the computer shouldn't say "excellent" or "fair" or "poor". Instead, it should just state the total number of points accumulated and ask whether the student wants to try again, to increase the score.
>
> If the student's score is high, the computer should reward the student by giving praise and storing the student's name on the disk. If the student's score is low, no criticism should be given other than asking "Would you like to try again?"

Management

Here's advice on how to manage the school's computers.

Should kids play games on the computers?

Give each kid the experience of briefly playing high-speed computer games.

> They're fun, encourage speed and agility, reward self-improvement, create a positive attitude towards computers and technology, lead the kid to thinking about strategies and programming methods, and provide examples of the best programs ever invented.

But discourage kids from spending *excessive* time on games.

> Give game-players lower priority than other kids who want to use the computers. To do that, you can restrict game-playing to just a few of the computers or a few times of day, or require game-players to leave when non-game-players want to use their computers.

By charging a small fee for game-playing, you can collect enough money to buy more computers.

Which rooms should contain computers?

The safest place to put computers is in the **library**.

> That reduces the chance of theft, encourages disks to be checked out like books, and makes sure the computer lab is run by a humanities-oriented librarian instead of a narrow-minded mathematician.
>
> Most librarians know how to run audio-visual equipment and access big databases, so they don't fear technology. Since librarians enjoy humanities (especially reading) but can also deal with scientific technology, librarians are the ideal choice for running a computer center that meets the needs of the *whole* school. The library's the only place in the school where all students and faculty can feel comfortable — except for the cafeteria.

Try moving some cheap computers into the **cafeteria** for students to use during lunch and study breaks.

> That will increase the computers' visibility and turn lunch into an intellectual affair. With adequate supervision, you can overcome the cafeteria's dangers (theft, food fights, and spilled drinks).

How can you supervise computers cheaply? Get parents to volunteer. Many parents would

love the opportunity to work in a computer environment, in the hope of entering a full-blown computer career later.

Turn your school's computer club into a "Computer Service Organization" that helps teach the rest of the school about computers. The club's members can mention such service on their résumés, which will help them get into college.

Give a speech to all students: tell them to help each other at the computers. Encourage teamwork.

How can you pay less for software? If

you're a teacher, **tell your hot-shot students to write software for you**.

> Your students will love the opportunity to work on a project that's useful. Tell the students that if their software is good you'll write them glowing recommendations saying that they computerized the school.

Many software publishers give **educational discounts**. Some publishers offer **"site licenses"**, where you pay a big fee but then can make as many copies of the software as you wish. The nicest publishers of business software offer **"trial size" versions** (for $10 or even free), which let you practice the software but require you to keep your documents and files brief.

How could computers change human society? The many good ways are obvious. Here are the bad ones.

Errors

Although the computer can have a mechanical breakdown, the usual reason for computer errors is *mental* breakdown — on the part of the people who run it. The usual computer blooper is caused by a programmer who writes a wrong program, or a user who inputs a wrong number. If you want the computer to write a check for $10.00 but you forget to type the decimal point, the computer will nonchalantly write a check for $1000.

The biggest computer blooper ever made occurred at Cape Kennedy:

> A rocket rose majestically from its launch pad and headed toward Venus. Suddenly it began to wobble. It had to be destroyed after less than 5 minutes of flight. The loss was put at $18,500,000. What went wrong? After much head-scratching, the answer was finally found. In one of the lines of one of the programs, a programmer omitted a hyphen.

In one city's computer center, every inhabitant's vital statistics were put on cards. One lady in the town was 107, but the number 107 wouldn't fit on the card properly, because the space allotted for AGE was only two digits.

> The computer just examined the last two digits, which were 07, and assumed she was 7 years old. Since she was 7 and not going to school, the computer printed a truant notice. So city officials visited the home of the 107-year-old lady and demanded to see her mom.

A man in Germany received a bill from a computer requesting the payment of "zero deutschmark".

> He ignored it, but two weeks later the machine sent him a letter reminding him that he had not paid the sum of "zero deutschmark". Two weeks after that another and more strongly worded letter arrived. He still took no action other than photocopying the letters and gleefully showing them to his friends. But the computer persisted and eventually announced that it was referring his failure to pay to the company lawyers. So he telephoned the company. They explained to him there was a minor oversight in the program, assured him it was being corrected, but requested him to send a check for "zero deutschmark" to simplify the reconciliation. He duly made out a check for "0.0 DM." and mailed it. Two days later the check was returned to him from the bank with a polite (nonautomated) letter stating that the bank's computer was unable to process the check.

That last anecdote was from Martin and Norman's *The Computerized Society*. This is from *Time Magazine*:

> Rex Reed, writer and sometime actor, ordered a bed from a Manhattan department store. Three months passed. Then came the long anticipated announcement: the bed will be delivered on Friday.
>
> Reed waited all day. No bed. Having disposed of his other bed, he slept on the floor.
>
> Next day deliverers brought the bed but couldn't put it up. No screws.
>
> On Monday, men appeared with the screws. But they couldn't put in the mattresses. No slats. "That's not our department."
>
> Reed hired a carpenter to build them. The department store's slats finally arrived 15 weeks later.
>
> Undaunted, Reed went to the store to buy sheets. Two men came up and declared: "You're under arrest." Why? "You're using a stolen credit card. Rex Reed is dead." Great confusion. Reed flashed all his identity cards. The detectives apologized — and then tore up his store charge card. Why? "Our computer has been told that you are dead. And we cannot change this."

On a less humorous note, a woman died from freezing because an errant computer thought she hadn't paid her utility bill.

At the end of 1999, people were nervous about the **year 2000 problem** (which is also called the **Y2K problem** and the **millennium bug**). Here's what those people said:

> "Many people still use old computer programs that store each year as a 2-digit number. For example, the year 1983 is stored as 83. When the year 2000 comes, some of those old programs will still assume the first two digits of the year will be 19. So they'll store the year 2000 as 00 and assume it means 1900. They'll think the clock has been turned back to the year 1900, think bills that

were due are being paid at the wrong time, and think machines haven't been repaired at the right time, so they'll shut down all the machines they control, including cars, elevators (which will plunge), airplanes (which will crash), hospital life-support systems (which will shut down and kill all their patients), utility companies (which will shut off your electricity, water, and phones), and bank machines (which will give customers no more cash)."

Programmers worked to solve that problem. January 1, 2000, came and went without major disasters.

Unemployment

Since the computer's a labor-saving device, it may make laborers unemployed. Clerks and other low-echelon white-collar workers might find themselves jobless and penniless.

> Newspaper companies in New York City realized they'd save money by hiring fewer printers and using computers instead. But the printers union, upset, cried "Breach of contract!" The companies and printers finally agreed to get the computers, hire no new printers, but retain the current ones until retirement.

The advent of computers doesn't have to mean fewer jobs. In fact, new ones are created.

> Not all computer-related jobs require abstract thinking: there's a need for mechanics, typists, secretaries, salespeople, editors, librarians, etc. There's a need for people to tell the programmers what kind of things to program. Running a computer center is a business, and there's a need for business executives.

When computers do human work, will there be *enough* work left for us humans to do? Don't worry: when no work is necessary, humans have an amazing talent for inventing it.

> That's the purpose of Madison Avenue — to create new longings. Instead of significantly shortening the work week, Americans have always opted for a work week of nearly equal length but devoted to more luxurious ends. That's the gung-ho Protestant work ethic we're so famous for. Computers will change but not reduce our work.

…That's what will happen in the long run. But for the next decade or two, as society shifts to computers, many folks will be temporarily out of a job.

Quantification

Since the computer handles numbers easily, it encourages people to reduce problems to numbers. That's both good and bad:

> It's good because it forces people to be precise. It's bad because some people are starting to make quantification a goal in itself, forgetting that it's but a tool to other ends. Counting the words that Shakespeare wrote is of no value in itself: it must be put to some use. In both the humanities and the social sciences, I'm afraid the motto of the future will be, "If you can't think, count." Some cynics have remarked, "The problem with computers is that they make meaningless research possible."

Since only quantifiable problems can be computerized, there's a danger that, in a burst of computer enthusiasm, people will decide that unquantifiable problems aren't worth investigating, or that unquantifiable aspects of an otherwise quantifiable problem should be ignored. John Kemeny gives this example:

> At an open hearing about designing a new Los Angeles freeway, some voters complained bitterly that the freeway would go right through the midst of a part of the city heavily populated by blacks and destroy the community spirit they'd slowly and painfully built up. The voters' arguments were defeated by the simple statement that, according to an excellent computer, the proposed route was the best possible.
> Apparently nobody knew enough to ask how the computer had been instructed to evaluate the routes. Was it asked just to consider the costs of building & acquiring property (in which case it would have found routing through a ghetto area highly advantageous), or was it also asked to take into account human suffering a route would cause?
> Perhaps the voters would have agreed it's not possible to measure human suffering in terms of dollars. But if we omit consideration of human suffering, then we're equating its cost to zero, which is certainly the worst of all procedures!

People are being reduced to numbers: telephone numbers, social security numbers, zip codes, etc. When you start treating another human as just a wrong telephone number and hang up in his face, something is wrong.

Asocial behavior

The computer's a seductive toy that can wreck your social life.

> When you walk up to the computer, you expect to spend just a few minutes but wind up spending hours instead. Whether catching bugs or playing Pac-Man, you'll probably while away lots of time. You may find yourself spending more time with the computer than with people. That can be dangerous. For the average American child, his mother's a TV set. **Will the computer replace TV as the national fixation?**
> Getting along with the computer is easy — perhaps *too* easy. Though it can gripe at you, it can't yell. If you don't like its behavior, you can turn it off. You can't do the same thing to people. Excessive time spent with the computer can leave you unprepared for the ambiguities and tensions of real life.
> **The computer replaces warmth by precision.** Excessive time spent with it might inhibit your development as a loving individual.

Irresponsibility

Computerization is part of the coming technological bureaucracy. Like all bureaucracy, it encourages the individual to say, "Don't blame me — I can't change the bureaucracy." But now the words read, **"Don't blame me — the computer did it."**

> When John Kemeny's sister asked a saleswoman whether a certain item was in stock, the woman said she couldn't answer, because the info was kept by a computer. The woman hadn't been able to answer questions about stock even before the computer came in; the computer was just a new scapegoat.

Computers will run governments and wars. The thought of someone saying, "I can't change that — that's the way the computer does it" is frightening.

Concentrated power

As computers amass more info about people, computers will become centers of knowledge. The people who control them — the programmers, sociologists, generals, and politicians — will gain lots of power. The thought of so much power being concentrated in the hands of a few is frightening. A handful of people, pressing the wrong buttons, could atom-bomb the earth.

Nobody should have complete control over a computer center. The power should be diversified. Sensitive data and programs should be protected by passwords and other devices, so no single individual can access all of it.

Crime

The computer's the biggest tool in the kit of the white-collar criminal. All he has to do is insert a zero, and the computer will send him a paycheck for ten times the correct amount.

> To catch computer criminals, computers are programmed to do lots of double-checking; but if the criminal evades the double-checks, he won't get caught. Police have a hard time finding computer criminals, because fingerprints and other traditional forms of evidence are irrelevant. Most computers have passwords to try to stop people from fooling around with sensitive data, but a bright programmer can devise tricks to get around the passwords.
> The crudest is to bug the wires that go to the terminals. The cleverest is to slip extra lines into an innocent program and get someone else to run it; the extra lines transfer money to the programmer's account.

Since you must be smart to be a computer criminal, if you're caught you'll be admired. Instead of saying "What a terrible thing you've done!" folks say "Gee, you must be smart. Tell me how you did it." A bright button-down computer criminal who steals $100,000 electronically gets a lighter sentence than the dude who must resort to a gun to get $1000. Is that justice?

Invaded privacy

Of all the harm computers can do, "invaded privacy" worries people the most. George Orwell, in his book *1984*, warned that someday "Big Brother will be watching you" via a computer. His prediction's already a reality: your whereabouts are constantly checked by computers owned by the FBI, the IRS, the military, credit-card companies, and mail-order houses.

My brother once wrote an innocent letter asking for stamps. Instead of using his own name, he used the name of our dog, Rusty. Since then, we've received letters from many organizations, all addressed to "Mr. Rusty". Our dog's name sits in computers all across the country.

The info computers have stored about you may be misleading. If you never find out about the error, the consequences can haunt you the rest of your life. Examples:

A teacher saw one of the little boys in her class kiss another boy. She entered on his computerized school records, "displays homosexual tendencies".

According to computer records, a certain man had "three lawsuits against him". In fact, the first was a scare suit 30 years before, over a magazine subscription he never ordered; the second had been withdrawn after a compromise over a disputed fee; the third case had been settled in his favor.

You've a right to see what info is stored about you, and change it if it's wrong. For example, if a teacher or employer writes a "confidential recommendation" about you, you've a right to examine it, to prevent misleading statements from haunting you for life.

Even if the info stored about you is accurate, you've a right to prevent its dissemination to the general public. No organization should store or disseminate info unjustifiably.

What's "justifiable"? Fearing "Big Brother", people don't want politicians to access personal info. On the other hand, fearing criminals, people want the police to have a free hand in sleuthing. How to give info to the police without giving it to politicians can be puzzling.

Outdated info should be obliterated. An individual shouldn't be haunted by his distant past; he should be given a chance to turn over a new leaf. Moreover, info 50 years old may be couched in words that have been redefined. To be a "leftist", for example, means something different in each decade.

Only facts should be stored, not opinions. It's okay to store that someone lives on Fifth Avenue, but not that he lives in a "nice neighborhood".

It's unfortunate that people feel a need for privacy. If the info stored about you is correct, why argue? But many people feel a need to be secretive, and I suppose people have that right. It's called the right to be "let alone".

People don't want to feel their whole lives are on stage, recorded by a computer. It inhibits them from acting free and natural.

Even if the computer doesn't store any damaging info about you, the mere *thought* that all your actions are being recorded is damaging, because it makes you act more conservatively. You may be afraid to adopt a good but unusual lifestyle, because anything "different" about you will look bad on the computerized records used by banks, credit-card companies, insurance companies, and other conservative institutions. The harmful thing is not that Big Brother is watching, but that you *feel* he's watching. You are subjugated.

Read good books

Begin by reading *The Secret Guide to Computers*.

Then read the hardware and software manuals that came with your computer. Although a beginner can't understand those manuals, *you'll* understand them — after you've mastered *The Secret Guide to Computers*!

Then read some of these books:

software:	*PCs for Busy People* by Einstein (Osborne/McGraw-Hill, $23)
	Office 2000 for Busy People by Weverka (Osborne/McGraw-Hill, $20)
hardware:	*How Computers Work* by White (Ziff-Davis, $40)
	The Winn L. Rosch Hardware Bible by Rosch (Que, $40)
repairs:	*A+ Certification for Dummies* by Gilster (IDG, $30)
	The Complete PC Upgrade & Maintenance Guide by Minasi (Sybex, $40)
Windows 98:	*Windows 98 for Dummies* by Rathbone (IDG, $20)
	Windows 98 Secrets by Livingston & Straub (IDG, $50)
Windows 3.1 & 3.11:	*More Windows for Dummies* by Rathbone (IDG, $20)
	Windows 3.1 Secrets by Livingston (IDG, $40)
MS-DOS:	*DOS for Dummies* by Gookin (IDG, $17)
	Running MS-DOS by Wolverton (Microsoft, $20)
Mac:	*Macs for Dummies* by Pogue (IDG, $20)
	The Macintosh Bible by Judson (Peachpit, $30)
hacker subculture:	*Hackers* by Levy (Delta, $13)
	The New Hacker's Dictionary by Raymond (MIT Press, $23)
Bill Gates' life:	*Hard Drive* by Wallace & Erickson (Harper-Collins, $14)
	Gates by Manes & Andrews (Touchstone, $14)
Internet survey:	*The Internet for Dummies* by Levine & Baroudi & Young (IDG, $20)
	Microsoft Internet Explorer Book by Pfaffenberger (Microsoft, $25)
Internet Netscape:	*Netscape and the World Wide Web for Dummies* by Hoffman (IDG, $20)
	Netscape Navigator 3.0 Book by James (Netscape/Ventana, $40)
Internet sites:	*The Internet Yellow Pages* by Hahn & Stout (Osborne/McGraw-Hill, $30)
	Internet Insider by Prevost (Oracle & Osborne/McGraw-Hill, $15)
classic BASIC:	*BASIC & the Personal Computer* by Dwyer & Critchfield (Addison-Wesley, OP)
	Guide to Structured Programming in BASIC by Presley (Lawrenceville, $35)
Visual BASIC:	*Visual BASIC 4 for Windows for Dummies* by Wang (IDG, $20)
	The Beginner's Guide to Visual BASIC 4 by Wright (Wrox, $35)
DBASE:	*Everyman's Database Primer* by Byers & Prague (Prentice-Hall, $20)
	DBASE 2 for the Programmer by Dinerstein (Scott Foresman, $18)
PASCAL:	*Introduction to PASCAL* by Zaks (Sybex, OP)
	Oh! Pascal! by Cooper & Clancy (Norton, $47)
C:	*The C Programming Language* by Kernighan & Ritchie (Prentice-Hall, $38)
	The C Primer by Hancock & Krieger (McGraw-Hill, $30)
LOGO:	*LOGO for the Apple II* by Abelson (McGraw-Hill, $30)
	Mindstorms by Papert (Basic Books & International Soc. for Technology, $14)
FORTRAN:	*FORTRAN 77 for Humans* by Page & Didday (West, $43)
	The Elements of FORTRAN Style by Kreitzberg & Shneiderman (Harcourt, OP)
COBOL:	A Simplified Guide to Structured COBOL Programming by McCracken (Wiley, OP)
	Structured ANS COBOL by Murach & Noll (Mike Murach, 2 volumes, $33 each)
language survey:	*Introduction to Programming Languages* by Peterson (Prentice-Hall, $49)
	Programming Languages by Tucker (McGraw-Hill, OP)
numeric languages:	*SPSS Primer* by Klecka & Nie & Hadlai (SPSS & McGraw-Hill, $16)
	APL an Interactive Approach by Gilman & Rose (Krieger, $48)
stack languages:	*Starting FORTH* by Brodie (Prentice-Hall, $35)
	LISP by Winston & Horn (Addison-Wesley, $40)
assembly language:	*Ass. Lang. Primer for the IBM PC&XT* by Lafore (New American Library, OP)
	Assembly Language for the PC by Socha & Norton (Brady/Prentice-Hall, OP)

For each topic, I've shown the two best books. If you read both books about the topic, you'll become an expert.

For each book, I've shown the title, author, and publisher. I've also shown the list price (rounded to the nearest dollar) or said "OP" (which means "Out of Print"). If a book is OP, try to find it at your local library.

Thank you for reading *The Secret Guide to Computers*. If you have any questions about what you've read, phone me at 603-666-6644, day or night.

Editions

You've been reading the 27th edition. I've been revising the *Guide* for over 27 years:

Edition	Published	Format	Total pages & price		How typed	What it praised	New tutorials it included
edition 0	1972 spring	pamphlet	17 pages	free	typewriter	HP-2000	BASIC
edition 1	1972 fall	pamphlet	12 pages	free	typewriter	DEC-10	DEC computers
edition 2	1972 fall	pamphlet	20 pages	free	typewriter	DEC-10	FORTRAN
edition 3	1972 fall	pamphlet	32 pages	$1	typewriter	DEC-10	data files
edition 4	1973 January	2 pamphlets	63 pages	$2	typewriter	DEC-10	ALGOL
edition 5	1973 September	booklet	73 pages	$2	typewriter	DEC-10	graphics
edition 6	1974 July	3 booklets	260 pages	$5.20	typewriter	DEC-10	artificial intelligence, numerical analysis
editions 7-9	1976-1979	6 booklets	410 pages	$16.25	typewriter	TRS-80 model 1	hardware, micros, COBOL, language survey
edition 10	1980-1982	8 booklets	696 pages	$29.60	typewriter	TRS-80 model 3	discount dealers, video graphics, PASCAL
edition 11	1983-1984	2 books	750 pages	$28	TRS-80 model 3	IBM PC	IBM PC, word processing
edition 12	1986-1987	3 books	909 pages	$24	TRS-80 model 3	clones by LeadingEdge	DOS, WordPerfect, spreadsheets, DBASE, C, LOGO
edition 13	1988 Sept.-Oct.	3 books	909 pages	$24	TRS-80 model 3	clones by Swan	Q&A
edition 14	1990 June	reference	607 2-column	$15	Word Perfect 5.0	clones by Gateway	Mac, Excel, Quattro
edition 15	1991 September	reference	607 2-column	$15	Word Perfect 5.1	clones by Gateway	Windows, advanced WordPerfect
edition 16	1992 May	reference	607 2-column	$15	Word Perfect 5.1	clones by Micro Express	DOS 5, Quattro Pro
edition 17	1993 April	reference	607 2-column	$15	Word Perfect 5.1	clones by Vtech	Mac System 7, Microsoft Word, Excel 4, repairs
edition 18	1993 August	reference	607 2-column	$15	Word Perfect 5.1	clones by Vtech	DOS 6
edition 19	1994 August	reference	639 2-column	$15	Word Perfect 5.1	clones by Vtech	Pentium, multimedia computers, DOS 6.2
edition 20	1995 March	reference	639 2-column	$15	Word Perfect 5.1	clones by Quantex	Microsoft Word 6, Terminal, AMIBIOS
edition 21	1995 November	reference	639 2-column	$15	Word Perfect 5.1	clones by Quantex	Windows 95, QBASIC
edition 22	1996 June	reference	639 2-column	$15	Word Perfect 5.1	clones by Quantex	Internet, advanced Windows 95
edition 23	1997 May	reference	639 2-column	$15	Microsoft Word 7	clones by Quantex	Visual BASIC, viruses, advanced Internet
edition 24	1997 December	reference	639 2-column	$15	Microsoft Word 7	clones by Quantex	Pentium 2, AMD K-6, backup-storage devices
edition 25	1998 December	reference	639 2-column	$15	Microsoft Word 7	clones by NuTrend	Windows 98, iMac, Microsoft Word 97, Excel 97, Works
edition 26	1999 September	reference	639 2-column	$16.50	Microsoft Word 7	clones by NuTrend	Microsoft Word 2000, Excel 2000, create Web pages
edition 27	2000 October	reference	639 2-column	$16.50	Microsoft Word 7	clones by NuTrend	FileMaker, Access, PowerPoint, Publisher, C++, JAVA

To get on the mailing list for a *free* brochure about the 28th edition, use the coupon on page 639, or just send me a postcard with your name, address, and the words "send 28th edition info".

Let's meet

I hope to meet you someday. If you ever visit New Hampshire, drop in! Say hello and browse through my computer library. My heavy workload prevents me from chatting long, but at least we can grin.

If you like, join one of my blitz courses, where we cover everything worth knowing about computers in one intensive weekend. I give the course in many cities and charge just $2.50 per hour.

I can also visit your home town and give a course to you and your friends privately. If you have lots of friends, the cost per person can get quite cheap.

For more information about what I can do for you at little or no charge, phone me at 603-666-6644 or mail the coupon on the back page.

How to give a course

After you practice using computers and become a computer expert, why not give your *own* courses? You too can become a guru. Here are some suggestions.

When giving a course, you won't have enough time to cover every detail, so don't even try. Tell the students that the details can be found in *The Secret Guide to Computers* and the manuals that come with their computers.

Instead of grinding through details, have fun! **Demonstrate** hardware and software that the audience hasn't seen, **argue cheerily** about computer hassles, **let the audience ask lots of questions**, and give the audience **hands-on experience aided by tutors**.

Here are some of the lines I use to liven up my classes and loosen up my students. Feel free to copy them.

> "Hi, I'm Russ. I'm supposed to turn all of you into computer experts by five o'clock. I'll try."
>
> "In this course, I'm your slave. Anything you want, you get."
>
> "If you're a boring group, we'll follow the curriculum. If you're interesting, you'll ask lots of questions and we'll dig into the good stuff."
>
> "Don't bother taking notes. If God wanted you to be a Xerox machine, He would have made you look like that way. So just relax. If you forget what I say, phone me anytime, and I'll repeat it all back to you."
>
> "There's no attendance requirement. Leave whenever you wish. If we hit a topic that bores you, that's a good time to go to the bathroom, get some munchies, or take a walk in the fresh air. Better yet, play with the computers at the back of the room, so you become super-smart. The tutors will get you any software you wish."

When you're planning to teach a course, phone me for free help with curriculum, dramatics, and tricks of the trade.

Your first course might have some rough edges, because you haven't had experience yet in giving demonstrations, fielding audience questions, and dramatically varying the pace so that your audience stays awake. So for your first course, play safe: charge as little as possible, so everybody in the audience feels the course was a "good deal" and a "wonderful bargain" and nobody feels "ripped off". For that first course your goal should *not* be money: instead, your goal should be to gain experience and a good reputation.

No matter how great you think you are, your audience will tire of you eventually. To keep your audience awake, offer variety by including your friends as part of your act.

Good luck. Try hard. You can cast a spell over the audience. Courses change lives.

Your source of free help, at your service, your computer butler, Russ Walter, 603-666-6644

NUMERICAL ANALYSIS

Errors

Computers make mathematical errors. Here's why.

Twin problems that confuse the computer

Look at this pair of problems.

Problem 1: solve the equation $x^2-4x+4 = 0$.
Problem 2: solve the equation $x^2-4x+3.9999999 = 0$.

Those two problems resemble each other. The only difference is that where the second problem says 3.9999999, the first problem says 4. But the correct solutions to the problems are quite different from each other:

The correct solution to problem 1 is "$x = 2$".
The correct solution to problem 2 is "$x = 1.9996838$ or $x = 2.0003162$".

Unfortunately, problem 1 looks so similar to problem 2 that the computer can hardly tell the difference. **Some computers treat 3.9999999 as if it were 4.** If you ask such a computer to solve problem 2, it will solve problem 1 instead, and its answer to problem 2 will therefore be wrong.

Here's another pair of problems.

Problem 3: solve the equation $(x-1)*(x-2)*(x-3)*(x-4)*...*(x-20) = 0$.
Problem 4: solve the equation $(x-1)*(x-2)*(x-3)*(x-4)*...*(x-20) -2^{-23}*x^{19} = 0$.

Those two problems resemble each other. In fact, if you "expand the polynomial", you'll see that problem 3 can be rewritten like this:

$x^{20} - 210x^{19} + ... = 0$.

Problem 4 can be rewritten like this:

$x^{20} - (210+2^{-23})x^{19} + ... = 0$.

So problem 4 differs from problem 3 just by saying $210+2^{-23}$ instead of 210. Since 2^{-23} is a tiny number (approximately .0000001), some computers can't tell the difference between 210 and $210+2^{-23}$, can't distinguish problem 4 from problem 3, and say the same answer to problem 4 as to problem 3. But the *correct* solutions to the two problems are different:

The correct solution to problem 3 is "$x=1$ or $x=2$ or $x=3$ or $x=4$ or ... or $x=20$".

The correct solution to problem 4 is "$x=1.000$ or $x=2.000$ or $x=3.000$ or $x=4.000$ or $x=5.000$ or $x=6.000$ or $x=7.000$ or $x=8.007$ or $x=8.917$ or $x=10.095\pm.644i$ or $x=11.794\pm1.652i$ or $x=13.992\pm1.519i$ or $x=16.731\pm2.813i$ or $x=19.502\pm1.940i$ or $x=20.847$". (i denotes the square root of -1.)

Here's one more case.

Problem 5: solve the simultaneous equations "$913x+659y=254$ and $780x+563y=217$".
Problem 6: solve the simultaneous equations "$913x+659y=254$ and $780x+563y=216.999$".

Although the problems are almost identical (so that some computers can't distinguish them from each other), the correct solutions are quite different:

The correct solution to problem 5 is "$x=1$ and $y=-1$".
The correct solution to problem 6 is "$x=.341$ and $y=-.087$".

That last case of "confusing twins" leads to this fascinating paradox.... Suppose you tell your friendly computer to "guess" an x and y to solve problem 5:

$913x + 659y = 254$
$780x + 563y = 217$

If the computer guesses "$x=.999$ and $y=-1.001$", it finds:

$913x + 659y = 252.428$
$780x + 563y = 215.757$

But if the computer guesses "$x=.341$ and $y=-.087$" instead, it finds:

$913x + 659y = 254$
$780x + 563y = 216.999$, which is about 217

The computer therefore deduces that its second guess is almost perfect and much better than its first guess. But — here's the paradox — the second guess is *not* better than the first guess; the *first* guess is better, because the correct solution is "$x=1$ and $y=-1$", which is closer to the *first* guess.

Reduce round-off error

By the laws of mathematics, $5+.14+.14+.14$ should be the same as $.14+.14+.14+5$. But a calculator that holds just two significant digits gives different answers:

5+.14+.14+.14	.14+.14+.14+5
5.0	.14
+.14	+.14
5.1	.28
+.14	+.14
5.2	.42
+.14	+5.0
5.3	5.4

Since the correct answer is 5.42, the calculation on the right is more accurate. The general rule is: **when adding a list of numbers, you'll get more accuracy if you begin with the numbers closest to 0**. The rule is valid even on a top-quality computer, although the computer's inaccuracies are not so obvious.

By the laws of mathematics, $(3^1/_5 - 3^1/_7)*70$ is 4:

$$3\frac{1}{5} = 3\frac{7}{35}$$
$$-3\frac{1}{7} = 3\frac{5}{35}$$
$$\frac{2}{35} * 70 = 4$$

But if we try that calculation on our two-digit calculator, we get a totally different answer:

$$3\frac{1}{5} = 3+.2 = 3.2$$
$$-3\frac{1}{7} = 3+.14 = 3.1$$
$$.1 * 70 = 7.0$$

The general warning is: **when you subtract two numbers that are almost equal (like $3^1/_5$ and $3^1/_7$), few of the digits in your answer will be correct**. The warning is valid even on a top-quality computer, although the computer's inaccuracies are not so obvious.

Estimates

The computer can estimate an answer.

Connecting the dots

Suppose you're given the value of y when x is 1, 2, 3, 4, and 5:

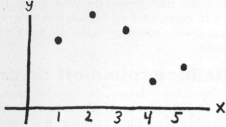

Suppose you'd like to make an "intelligent guess" as to the value of y when x is 1.5, 3.01, 100, -400, and other values. Guessing y for an in-between x (such as 1.5 and 3.01) is called **interpolation**; guessing y for a very large x or a very small x (such as 100 and -400) is called **extrapolation**.

One way to guess is to connect the points with line segments:

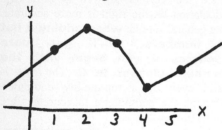

That's called **piecewise linear** estimation.

You get a much smoother picture by using a **cubic spline**:

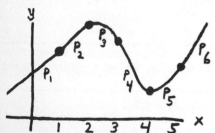

P_1 and P_6 are parts of straight lines. P_2, P_3, P_4, and P_5 are parts of four different cubics (third-degree polynomials), chosen so that, at the point where P_i meets P_{i+1}, P_i has the same **derivative** and **second derivative** as P_{i+1}. (The term "derivative" is defined by calculus.)

Least-square line

Suppose you're given these **approximate** values of y:

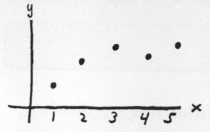

To estimate y for other values of x, you could use piecewise linear estimation or a cubic spline. But notice the points lie almost on a straight line:

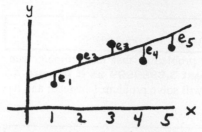

The points aren't exactly on that line; the errors in the y values are e_1, e_2, e_3, e_4, and e_5. The line's **squared error** is $e_1^2 + e_2^2 + e_3^2 + e_4^2 + e_5^2$. This line has a larger squared error:

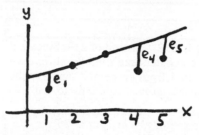

The line having the smallest squared error is called the **least-square line**, and is considered to be the line that best approximates the data.

Solve equations

The computer can solve equations.

Single equations

Suppose you want to solve a tough equation, such as $2^x+x^3=20$. Rewrite it to make the right side be 0:

$$2^x+x^3-20=0$$

Let f(x) denote the left side of the equation:

$$f(x) \text{ is } 2^x+x^3-20$$

So the equation you want to solve is f(x)=0. Here's a way to solve it — called the **secant method**....

Let x_1 and x_2 be your favorite numbers. Graph $f(x_1)$ and $f(x_2)$:

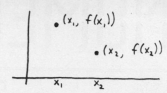

Let x_3 be where the line connecting those points hits the x axis:

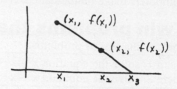

Graph $f(x_3)$; it's probably close to 0:

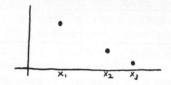

Connect the x_2 point to the x_3 point, to find x_4:

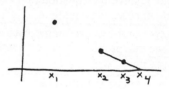

Connect the x_3 point to the x_4 point, to find x_5:

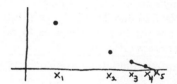

Probably you'll get closer and closer to the point where f(x) is 0.

A different method, called **Muller's method**, uses parabolas instead of straight lines....

Let x_1, x_2, and x_3 be your three favorite numbers. A common choice is -.5, .5, and 0. Graph $f(x_1)$, $f(x_2)$, and $f(x_3)$:

Draw the parabola that passes through those points:

The parabola hits the x axis at two points (although the points might be what mathematicians call "imaginary"). Let x_4 be at one of those points. For best results, choose the point that's closer to the origin:

Graph $f(x_4)$:

Draw a parabola through the x_2, x_3, and x_4 points, to find x_5:

Probably you'll get closer to the place where $f(x)$ is 0.

Usually, Muller's method moves toward the solution more rapidly than the secant method. It can even find complex, "non-real" solutions, since the x value where the parabola hits the x axis might be of the form $a+bi$, where i denotes the square root of -1. (If you're interested in just solutions that are real, pretend b is 0.)

Using either the secant method or Muller's, suppose you finally find a solution of the equation $2^x+x^3-20=0$. Let s_1 denote that solution. To hunt for additional solutions, try solving this equation:

$$\frac{2^x+x^3-20}{x-s_1} = 0$$

If you find a solution of that new equation, call it s_2, and solve this equation:

$$\frac{2^x+x^3-20}{(x-s_1)(x-s_2)} = 0$$

If that produces a solution s_3, solve

$$\frac{2^x+x^3-20}{(x-s_1)(x-s_2)(x-s_3)} = 0$$

to find s_4. The solutions s_1, s_2, s_3, s_4, etc., are all solutions of the original equation.

The round-off error will be less if $|s_1| < |s_2| < |s_3| < |s_4| < \dots$. So when you hunt for solutions, begin by trying to find the solutions closest to zero. That's why, when Muller's parabola hits the x axis in two points, you should pick the point that's closer to zero. And that's why a common choice for x_1, x_2, and x_3 is numbers near zero.

Simultaneous equations

Try to solve these simultaneous linear equations:

$$8x + y - z = 8$$
$$2x + y + 9z = 12$$
$$x - 7y + 2z = -4$$

An obvious way is **Gauss-Jordan elimination**. Eliminate the first coefficient:

$$x + \tfrac{1}{8}y - \tfrac{1}{8}z = 1 \quad \text{multiplied by 1/8}$$
$$2x + y + 9z = 12$$
$$x - 7y + 2z = -4$$

Eliminate everything below it:

$$x + \tfrac{1}{8}y - \tfrac{1}{8}z = 1$$
$$\tfrac{3}{4}y + \tfrac{37}{4}z = 10 \quad \text{subtracted twice row 1}$$
$$-\tfrac{57}{8}y + \tfrac{17}{8}z = -5 \quad \text{subtracted row 1}$$

Eliminate the first coefficient in row 2:

$$x + \tfrac{1}{8}y - \tfrac{1}{8}z = 1$$
$$y + \tfrac{37}{3}z = \tfrac{40}{3} \quad \text{multiplied by 4/3}$$
$$-\tfrac{57}{8}y + \tfrac{17}{8}z = -5$$

Eliminate everything above and below it:

$$x \quad - \tfrac{5}{3}z = -\tfrac{2}{3} \quad \text{subtracted 1/8 times row 2}$$
$$y + \tfrac{37}{3}z = \tfrac{40}{3}$$
$$90z = 90 \quad \text{added 57/8 times row 2}$$

Eliminate the first coefficient in row 3:

$$x \quad - \tfrac{5}{3}z = -\tfrac{2}{3}$$
$$y + \tfrac{37}{3}z = \tfrac{40}{3}$$
$$z = 1 \quad \text{multiplied by 1/90}$$

Eliminate everything above it:

$$x \quad = 1 \quad \text{added 5/3 times row 3}$$
$$y \quad = 1 \quad \text{subtracted 37/3 times row 3}$$
$$z = 1$$

That's the solution. (It's depressing that so much computation was needed, to get such a simple solution!)

In that example, I pivoted on the first coefficient of the row 1, then the first coefficient of the row 2, and finally the first coefficient of the row 3. To reduce the computer's round-off error, it's better at each stage to pivot on the coefficient that has the biggest absolute value, relative to the coefficients in its row. For example, at this stage —

$$x + \tfrac{1}{8}y - \tfrac{1}{8}z = 1$$
$$\tfrac{3}{4}y + \tfrac{37}{4}z = 10 \quad \text{subtracted twice row 1}$$
$$-\tfrac{57}{8}y + \tfrac{17}{8}z = -5 \quad \text{subtracted row 1}$$

it would have been better to pivot on $-\tfrac{57}{8}$ than on $\tfrac{3}{4}$, since $\tfrac{57}{8}$ divided by $\tfrac{17}{8}$ is bigger than $\tfrac{3}{4}$ divided by $\tfrac{37}{4}$.

Now let's go back to the original equations —

$$8x + y - z = 8$$
$$2x + y + 9z = 12$$
$$x - 7y + 2z = -4$$

and solve them by a different method, called **Gauss-Seidel iteration**. In each equation, find the variable whose coefficient has the largest absolute value, and put that variable on one side:

$$x = -\tfrac{1}{8}y + \tfrac{1}{8}z + 1$$
$$z = -\tfrac{2}{9}x - \tfrac{1}{9}y + \tfrac{4}{3}$$
$$y = \tfrac{1}{7}x + \tfrac{2}{7}z + \tfrac{4}{7}$$

Begin by guessing that x, y, and z are all 0, then improve the guesses by using those equations. Here are the calculations, to three decimal places:

$$x = 0$$
$$y = 0$$
$$z = 0$$

$$x = -\tfrac{1}{8}y + \tfrac{1}{8}z + 1 = 1.000$$
$$y = \tfrac{1}{7}x + \tfrac{2}{7}z + \tfrac{4}{7} = .714$$
$$z = -\tfrac{2}{9}x - \tfrac{1}{9}y + \tfrac{4}{3} = 1.032$$
$$x = -\tfrac{1}{8}y + \tfrac{1}{8}z + 1 = 1.041$$
$$y = \tfrac{1}{7}x + \tfrac{2}{7}z + \tfrac{4}{7} = 1.014$$
$$z = -\tfrac{2}{9}x - \tfrac{1}{9}y + \tfrac{4}{3} = .990$$
$$x = -\tfrac{1}{8}y + \tfrac{1}{8}z + 1 = .997$$
$$y = \tfrac{1}{7}x + \tfrac{2}{7}z + \tfrac{4}{7} = .996$$
$$z = -\tfrac{2}{9}x - \tfrac{1}{9}y + \tfrac{4}{3} = 1.002$$
$$x = -\tfrac{1}{8}y + \tfrac{1}{8}z + 1 = 1.001$$
$$y = \tfrac{1}{7}x + \tfrac{2}{7}z + \tfrac{4}{7} = 1.000$$
$$z = -\tfrac{2}{9}x - \tfrac{1}{9}y + \tfrac{4}{3} = 1.000$$
$$x = -\tfrac{1}{8}y + \tfrac{1}{8}z + 1 = 1.000$$
$$y = \tfrac{1}{7}x + \tfrac{2}{7}z + \tfrac{4}{7} = 1.000$$
$$z = -\tfrac{2}{9}x - \tfrac{1}{9}y + \tfrac{4}{3} = 1.000$$

In the example, x and y and z gradually approach the correct solutions.

Is Gauss-Seidel iteration better or worse than Gauss-Jordan elimination?

A disadvantage of Gauss-Seidel iteration is: it doesn't guarantee you'll approach the correct solution. If you follow the advice about pivoting on the coefficient that has the largest relative absolute value, you stand a better chance of approaching the correct solution, but there's no guarantee.

On the other hand, if Gauss-Seidel iteration *does* approach a solution, the solution will have less round-off error than with Gauss-Jordan elimination.

INDEX

Vendor phone book

For the typical company, I give:

the company's **name** (in bold)
the company's **purpose**
the **main toll-free phone number** (which begins with 800 or 888)
other general phone number
the **technical-support phone number** (to call if you have technical questions)
Internet World Wide Web address (which begins with "www" or "http://")
Internet Usenet newsgroup (begins with "news:", exists if company is huge)
street address (in parentheses)
Secret Guide pages analyzing the company

A+ Memory Express sells chips: 800-877-8188, 626-333-6389, www.memexpress.com (15140 Valley Blvd., City of Industry CA 91744), page 24

ABS Computer Technologies sells computers cheap: 800-876-8088, 562-695-8823, tech 800-685-3471, www.abscomputer.com (9997 Rose Hills Rd., Whittier CA 90601), pages 12&73

Acer sells computers: 408-432-6200, tech 800-445-6495, www.acer.com, news:alt.sys.pc-clone.acer (2641 Orchard Parkway, San Jose CA 95134), page 81

ACP sells chips: 800-fone-ACP (1310 E. Edinger, Santa Ana CA 92705), page 24

Adobe Systems publishes desktop publishing software (PageMaker, FrameMaker, Acrobat), graphics (Adobe Illustrator), and fonts (Adobe Type Manager): 800-272-3623, 408-536-6000, tech 206-628-5728, www.adobe.com (345 Park Ave., San Jose CA 95110), pages 65&289

America OnLine (AOL) is an online service: 800-827-6364, tech 888-265-8006, pages 65&205&210

Apple Computer makes computers (Apple II, Macintosh): 800-my-Apple, tech 800-sos-Apple, www.apple.com (1 Infinite Loop, Cupertino CA 95014), pages 12&14&82&150

BlueLight is a free Internet service funded by K-Mart, Yahoo, Spinway, and SoftBank: 888-945-9255, tech 979-776-6515, www.bluelight.com, page 209

Borland, which is part of Inprise, publishes programming languages (Turbo Pascal, Borland C++, a version of JAVA called "J Builder", Turbo Assembler, and database languages called "Delphi" and "Paradox"): 800-336-6464, 408-461-9000, tech 800-523-7070, www.borland.com (4585 Scotts Valley Dr., Scotts Valley CA 95066), pages 64&472

Broadax Systems Inc. (BSI) sells notebook computers cheap: 800-872-4547, 626-442-0020 (9440 Telstar Ave. #4, El Monte CA 91731), page 79

Brøderbund Software, which is owned by The Learning Company, publishes easy graphics programs (Kid Pix, Print Shop) and games (Myst, Riven, Where in the World is Carmen Sandiego): 415-382-4400, tech 415-382-4700, www.broderbund.com (500 Redwood Blvd., Novato CA 94947), pages 65&276

Canon is a Japanese company that makes printers: 516-488-6700, tech 800-423-2366, www.ccsi.canon.com (1 Canon Plaza, Lake Success NY 11042), page 48

Chip Merchant sells chips: 800-426-6375, 619-268-4774 (9541 Ridgehaven Ct., San Diego CA 92123), page 24

Comp USA is a chain of computer superstores: 800-Comp-USA, 214-702-0055, www.compusa.com (3750 Realty Rd., Dallas TX 75244), pages 12&22

Compaq Computer makes computers: 800-888-0344, 713-370-0670, tech 800-ok-Compaq (free if under warranty, $20 on your credit card if out of warranty) or 900-RED-HELP ($2 per minute or $20 total, whichever is less, on your phone bill), www.compaq.com (PO Box 692000, Houston TX 77269), pages 12&14&78&576

Compaq Factory Outlet Store, which is owned by Compaq, sells refurbished Compaq computers cheap: 888-202-4368, 281-927-6700, www.compaq.com (10251 N. Freeway, Houston TX 77037), page 79

Compuserve is an online service owned by America Online: 800-848-8990, www.compuserve.com, pages 74&205

Computer Associates International publishes office software (CA-SuperProject, CA-Simply Tax, CA-Simply Accounting, CA-Simply Money): 516-342-5224, www.cai.com (1 Computer Associates Plaza, Islandia NY 11788), page 65

Corel Systems is a Canadian company that publishes graphics (CorelDraw) and word processing software (WordPerfect): 800-77-Corel, 613-728-0826, www.corel.com, www.wordperfect.com (1600 Carling Ave., Ottawa ON K1Z 8R7 Canada), pages 60&63&64&194&277&289

Dell Computer makes computers: 800-BUY-DELL, 512-338-4400, tech 800-624-9896, www.dell.com, news:alt.sys.pc-clone.dell (9505 Arboretum Blvd., Austin TX 78759), pages 12&79&576

Dirt Cheap Drives sells hard drives & CD-ROM drives cheap: 800-473-0960, 281-534-4140, tech 281-534-6292, www.dirtcheapdrives.com (3716 Timber Dr., Dickinson TX 77539) pages 38&40

Diskettes Unlimited sells diskettes: 800-dog-disk, 713-643-9939 (6206 Long Dr., Houston TX 77087), page 35

EarthLink is an Internet service provider: 888-EARTHLI, 800-395-8425, 404-815-0770, tech 800-890-5128, www.earthlink.net (1430 W. Peachtree St. NW #400, Atlanta GA 30309), page 209

Egghead was a chain of software stores but now sells just on the Internet: 800-EGGHEAD, 650-470-2400, www.egghead.com (1350 Willow Rd., Menlo Park CA 94025), page 21

Emachines makes computers that cost under $500 and distributes them through chains of superstores: 714-505-5001, tech 877-566-e4me, www.e4me.com (14350 Myford Rd., Irvine CA 92606-1002), page 74

Epson is a Japanese company that makes printers: 800-go-Epson, 562-981-3840, www.epson.com (3840 Kilroy Airport Way, Long Beach CA 90806), pages 46&48

Fractal Design, which is part of Meta Creations, publishes graphics programs (Painter, Dabbler, Sketcher, Expression, Ray Dream Studio): 800-846-0111, 408-688-8800, www.fractal.com (335 Spreckels Dr., Aptos CA 95003), page 276

Galaxy Internet Services is an Internet service provider that offers low prices: 888-334-2529, 617-558-0900, tech 617-558-0909 (188 Needham St. #230, Newton MA 02164), page 209

Gateway is a big mail-order clone maker: 800-555-2068, 605-232-2000, tech 800-846-2301, www.gateway.com, news:alt.sys.pc-clone.gateway2000 (610 Gateway Dr., N. Sioux City SD 57049), pages 12&74&90&210

Harmony Computers & Electronics sells computers, software, and printers: 800-441-1144, 718-692-3232, tech 718-692-2828, www.hramonycomputers.com (1801 Flatbush Ave., Brooklyn NY 11210), pages 22&45&58

Hewlett-Packard (HP) makes printers and computers: 800-752-0900, 719-531-4000, printer tech 208-323-2551, www.hp.com (8020 Foothills, Roseville CA 95678), pages 12&14&48&59&80

HyperData sells notebook computers cheap: 800-786-3343, 909-468-2960, tech 909-468-2950, www.hyperdatadirect.com (809 S. Lemon Ave., Walnut CA 91789), pages 14&79&80

IBM makes computers, publishes software (OS/2, IBM Antivirus), and bought a software publisher called Lotus: 800-IBM-4-you, 914-765-1900, tech 800-772-2227, www.ibm.com (Old Orchard Rd., Armonk NY 10504), pages 11&64&67&209

Insight sells hard drives and other hardware at low prices: 800-INSIGHT, 602-902-1176, tech 800-377-3000, www.insight.com (1912 W. Fourth St., Tempe AZ 85281), pages 21&38

Intel makes chips: 800-538-3373, 503-264-7354, tech 800-628-8686 www.intel.com (2200 Mission College Boulevard, Santa Clara CA 95051), pages 15&24

Intuit publishes financial and accounting software (Quicken, QuickBooks, TurboTax): 800-781-6999, tech 800-624-8742, www.intuit.com (155 Linfield Dr., Menlo Park CA 94025), pages 65&298

Jargon dictionary

For each common computer term, here's a **quick definition** and the **page number** where you'll find more details. (I edited these definitions from research done by my assistant, Len Pallazola.) For computer terms that are more bizarre, see the master index on pages 632-637.

access denied This error message means you're not allowed to do what you tried. For example, you can't delete a file marked "read-only". *144*

access time The amount of time (usually measured in milliseconds) required to read data from a disk. *37*

active-matrix screen The most expensive type of notebook-computer screen. *44,72*

archives Stored or compressed files that you plan to use seldom, if ever. *59*

artificial intelligence This kind of program lets the computer try to learn and think for itself. *324*

ASCII American Standard Code for Information Interchange. A coding convention that lets different types of computers share text. *98,139,398,558*

AT bus The most common type of bus. Also called an ISA bus. *68*

AT computer IBM PC with Advanced Technology. At the time, it was advanced. AT computers are now considered slow and obsolete. *12,24,68*

AUTOEXEC.BAT A batch file of commands automatically performed when the computer is turned on. *135,139,578,581,587*

backslash A slash descending to the right. Example: \. *54,119,121*

backup A separate copy of your data, which you'll keep in a safe place if you know what's good for you. A backup can consist of disks or tapes. *36,38,59,145,148,273,573*

bad command This error means you typed a command the computer doesn't recognize. Make sure you spelled the command correctly. *123,135*

bad or missing command interpreter This error happens when COMMAND.COM is missing. *585*

bad sectors Unusable or damaged spots on a disk. *123*

batch file A text file containing a series of DOS commands (and identified by the extension .BAT). The operating system processes all commands in the batch file, one after the other. *130*

baud The number of bits of data transferred per second. Used for measuring the speed of a modem or network. *57,205*

binary A number system in which the only digits are ones and zeros. For example, 1001010 is the binary way to write the number seventy-four. *24,556*

BIOS Basic input/output system. The part of the operating system that teaches the computer how to handles the keyboard, disk drives, and other fundamentals. In most computers, the BIOS is in a CMOS ROM chip on the motherboard. *31,585*

bipolar chip An old type of chip that's extra-fast but too expensive. Lots of bipolar chips were used in old, expensive computers. Modern computers use mainly MOS chips instead to reduce costs, but still use a few bipolar chips in the RAM cache, which is a tiny, high-speed part of the RAM. *24*

bit Binary digit. The smallest unit for measuring data size. A bit can hold a value of either 1 or 0. *24,557*

boldface Text displayed **darker** for emphasis **(like this)**. *46,99,156,165*

boot the computer Turn the computer on. *131,137*

bootable disk A disk containing the "system files", which are needed when you turn the computer on. The system files tell the computer how to start running. A bootable disk is also called a "boot disk" or "boot floppy". *138*

bps Bits per second. Used for measuring the speed of a modem or network. Sometimes called "baud". *24,57*

buffer Memory set aside to temporarily store data being transferred from one device to another. *133,581*

bug In a program, a mistake that makes the program malfunction. *374*

bus On the motherboard, the wires that transfer data from the motherboard to the computer's expansion slots. *67*

byte Used for measuring data's size, a "byte" is the amount of memory consumed by a letter of the alphabet or any other character. One byte equals eight bits. *29,558*

cache Faster memory that holds an extra copy of info you've been recently using, so you can access that info faster. Web pages you've recently viewed are stored in a cache on your disk. Disk info you've recently worked on is stored in a cache made of RAM. The RAM info you've recently worked on is stored in a cache made of higher-speed RAM, called "bipolar RAM". *31,38,70,215*

CAD Computer-Aided Design. A type of program used by architects and engineers to create blueprints. *62,277*

case The casing which holds the "guts" of your computer, including the power supply, motherboard, CPU, RAM, adapter cards, and drives. Cases come in two popular styles: "desktop" and "tower". *59,70*

CD-ROM drive A component that lets your computer read compact disks (CDs). Compact disks can store a large amount of data and have become the preferred way to distribute software. *15,32,39,63,70,297*

CGA video Color Graphics Adapter. The oldest (and worst) kind of IBM-compatible color monitor. It produces few colors and just low resolution. *42,67,383*

character A letter of the alphabet, a number, or any other symbol you can type. *29,98,139,163*

chip A tiny square on which is etched a miniaturized electronic circuit. *15,23*

clip art Bitmaps or other graphics that can easily be added to word processing documents. *277, 290,292*

clock cycle An electrical pulse that instructs the computer to perform the next step in whatever process it is running. The typical computer generates millions of clock cycles each second. *25*

CMOS Complimentary metal-oxide semiconductor. A type of computer chip that consumes very little electricity, so it can run on batteries. *24,30,68,584,594*

CMOS SETUP program A program usually found on a ROM chip inside the computer. This program lets you teach the computer which monitor, disk drives, and chips are installed. *68,584*

cold boot Here's how to "do a cold boot": restart the computer by flipping its power switch. If the computer's already on, here's how to cold boot: flip the power switch off, then wait for the computer to quiet down, then flip the power switch back on. *137*

COM port Communication port. An outlet, in the computer's back wall, to which you can attach devices. A typical computer has a mouse attached to COM1 and a modem attached to COM2. Also called a "serial port". *205*

command interpreter A system file that teaches the computer to understand DOS commands typed at a prompt. Usually called "COMMAND.COM". *585*

competitive upgrade This type of software will install just if you already have either the previous version or a product that competes with the program being installed. Companies use this technique to steal customers from the competition. *63,65,66*

computer Any machine that can seem to do useful thinking. *10,16*

CONFIG.SYS An ASCII file containing equations that teach the computer how to manage attached devices. *132,139,578,581,587*

Control Panel A Microsoft Windows component that lets you set options affecting how Windows runs. *106,113*

conventional memory The first 640 kilobytes of RAM. Also called "base memory". *30*

coprocessor A supplementary chip that helps a primitive CPU handle advanced math problems fast. Also called a "math chip". If your CPU is modern (486DX, Pentium, or Pentium Pro), it already includes built-in math coprocessor circuitry, so you don't need to buy a separate coprocessor chip. *27*

copy protection Any method that prevents disks or programs from being copied or pirated. *36,66,125*

cpi Characters per inch. Used for measuring fonts. *51*

cps Characters per second. Used for measuring the speed of printers, modems, and networks. *53*

CPU Central processing unit. The computer's brain, where thinking occurs. In most computers, the CPU is a single chip, called "the microprocessor". In computers that are very old or very big, the CPU is a *set* of chips or circuits working together. Sometimes simply called "the processor". *15,24,70*

crippled software A program that's just partly functional, usually distributed as a free demo for you to try. The idea is that if you like the demo, you'll eventually buy the uncrippled "full" version. *66*

CRT Cathode Ray Tube. The picture tube that's in your computer's monitor. *41*

cursor A small blinking line (or block) on your screen. In most software, the cursor's position shows where new text will appear when typed. *202*

data Info stored in the computer's RAM, ROM, or disks. The data can then flow into the CPU or through modems. Sometimes the word "data" is used in a narrower sense, to refer just to info consisting of documents and database lists, rather than programs. *16,63*

database A list of names and addresses, or any other large mass of stored info, or the program that lets you store it. *62,254*

debugging Fixing bugs or mistakes in a program. *374*

Defrag A program that corrects disk fragmentation. The Defrag program is included as part of DOS 6.2 and Windows 95. *105,141,576*

demo disk A disk containing a sample of a program, so you can see the program in action before buying the program's full version. The demo disk is usually free or costs under $10, but lacks advanced features and comes with just an abridged instruction manual, if any. *66*

desktop computer A computer designed to be put on your desk (instead of on your lap). A traditional desktop computer's case is wide, not tall, and rests on the desk; the computer's monitor sits atop the case; but the term "desktop computer" is also used loosely to include tower computers that are small enough to fit on your desk or under your desk. *13*

desktop-publishing program A program that lets you combine graphics with text to create posters, ads, and newsletters. Pagemaker, Frame Maker, Venture Publisher, and Quark Xpress are fancy desktop-publishing programs. Microsoft Publisher is easier to learn but does less. *62,277,289*

device driver A program that teaches your computer how to handle a specific device. For example, a mouse driver teaches your computer to handle your mouse; a CD-ROM driver teaches your computer to handle your CD-ROM drive. When you buy a mouse or CD-ROM drive, it usually comes with a floppy disk containing the device driver. *132*

diagnostic software Programs that check a computer for problems. *105,140*

dialog box A big box that appears on your screen and waits for you to fill in its blanks or click "OK" or otherwise feed it info. *109*

disk A round device that rotates, holds computer data, and makes all its data accessible fast. Three kinds of disks are popular. A "CD-ROM disk" looks like a music CD but holds computer data instead of music. A "floppy disk" is made of magnetic material; though round, it's permanently sealed in a square jacket, so it looks square. Inside the typical computer, a stack of "hard disks" hide permanently and are never seen. *15,32,114*

disk drive A device that can hold a disk, rotate the disk, and read the info that's on the disk. *15,32,70*

document A computer file that contains text, such as a word processor file. *97,111,154,161*

documentation The manual, online help text, and other printed matter that comes with a program. *419*

DOS Disk Operating System. A primitive program that teaches your computer how to use disks and run other programs. *60,114*

dot pitch The distance between adjacent same-color dots on a monitor's screen. Most monitors have a dot pitch of either .26mm (excellent), .28mm (good), .39mm (bad), or higher (even worse). *43,69*

dot-matrix printer A type of printer that sticks some pins at an inked ribbon. The pins press the ribbon against the paper, to form the letters of the alphabet and low-quality graphics. *13,45,46,52*

double-click Position the mouse pointer over an item and then quickly press the mouse's button twice. On a two-button or three-button mouse, this is usually done using the left button. *101,153*

double-sided disk A type of floppy disk that can store data on both sides. It's more modern and more popular than single-sided disks. *33*

Double Space A program that comes with MS-DOS 6 and can compress a hard drive, so more disk space becomes available. But it decreases your free RAM and creates many software conflicts. Stacker, SuperStor, and Drive Space are similar programs. *114,574*

download Copy a file or program to your computer (from a bigger computer) electronically, by using a network or modem or special cable. *205*

draft quality A printing option that makes the printer print faster and consume less ink by generating a lower-quality printout, appropriate for a rough draft. *51*

drag Move an item that's on your screen, by using the mouse. To do so, first point at the item you want to move; then while holding down the mouse's button, move the item to the desired new location. Finally, release the mouse's button. *110,151*

DRAM Dynamic random access memory. The most common type of RAM chip. *31,70*

drive A device that makes a disk or tape rotate. To use a disk or tape, you must put it into a drive. *32,39,70,121*

dual-scan color screen An improved passive-matrix screen used in notebook computers. *44,72*

EGA video Enhanced Graphics Adapter. A type of color monitor having slightly better resolution than CGA monitors. *42,68,383*

EIDE Enhanced Integrated Drive Electronics An even faster type of hard drive than IDE. EIDE can handle drive sizes larger than 528 megabytes. *37*

e-mail Electronic mail. Messages sent from one person to another by using a network. For example, to send e-mail you can use a network such as the Internet or America Online or a bulletin-board service or a local-area network. *205,217,218*

EMM Expanded memory manager. A device driver that manages upper memory and lets XMS memory be used as EMS memory. The most common EMM is EMM386.EXE, which comes with DOS and Windows. *133,140*

Ethernet A type of hardware that uses special wires and adapter cards to connect computers, creating a local-area network (LAN). *13,209,232,233*

expanded memory (EMS memory) RAM memory that's above the first 1024 kilobytes and managed in an old-fashioned way, which is slower than XMS but required by some old DOS programs. *133,140*

extended memory (XMS memory) RAM memory above the first 1024 kilobytes. For example, if your computer has 4 megabytes of RAM, it has three megabytes of extended memory. *30,132,140*

FAT File Allocation Table. This index stores the locations and sizes of all files stored on a disk. *118*

fax/modem A modem that also lets you use your computer as a fax machine. *58,70,231*

floppy disk A small disk contained inside a square dust jacket. Also called a "diskette". Floppy disks usually come in two sizes: 3½-inch and 5¼-inch. Though 3½-inch disks each come in a hard plastic jacket, they're called "floppy disks", not "hard disks". *15,32,36,70,159*

font A set of characters of a certain style. Also called a "typeface". *46,49,51,100,166,179,185,195,290*

format a disk To prepare a disk for use, or to erase the disk. "IBM format" means that the disk can be used by IBM compatible computers. "Mac format" means that the disk can be used on a Macintosh. *34,103,138*

forward slash A slash rising to the right. Example: /. *54*

fragmented file On a disk, a file that's unfortunately been split into several parts, on several parts of the disk, so you can't retrieve all of it at once, and accessing its data is slow. This can be corrected by using Defrag, which is a program that's part of DOS 6.2 and Windows 95. *105,141*

freeware A program that costs no money, so it's free. *66*

gigabyte Used for measuring the size of data, "gigabyte" unfortunately has two definitions: a "small" gigabyte is 1,000,000,000 bytes; a "big" gigabyte is "1024 times 1024 times 1024 bytes." *29*

hard drive A computer component that can store many files or programs by using magnetic material. For a typical computer, the hard drive hides permanently inside the computer's main box (system-unit case) and never comes out. *15,32,36,70*

Hayes-compatible modem A modem that's standard and therefore compatible with most software. *58*

help A program's built-in documentation, usually found in a menu labeled "Help". Some Windows software includes more info in the Help system than in the printed manual. *106,143,144,160,182,193*

Hercules video A type of video card that can generate graphics on monochrome monitors. *68,383*

hertz (Hz) One cycle per second. The smallest unit for measuring computer speed. *25*

hexadecimal A number system based on 16 digits instead of ten. The 6 extra "digits" are called A, B, C, D, E, and F. Here's how you count in hexadecimal: 0, 1, 2, 3, 4, 5, 6, 7, 8, 9, A, B, C, D, E, F, 10, 11, 12, etc. Hexadecimal is used as a shorthand notation for binary numbers. *557,559*

hidden file A file hidden from file lists and directories. Important operating system files are usually hidden, so novices won't see them, won't try to manipulate them, and won't wreck them. *120,132,145*

high memory The first 640K of RAM is called the "base memory". The next 384K of RAM is called the "upper memory". Together, those kinds of RAM consume 1 megabyte. The remaining RAM, which is beyond the first megabyte, is sometimes all called "high memory", though the term "high-memory area" often means just the first 64K of that remaining RAM. *133,134*

high-density disk A type of floppy disk that can store more than one megabyte of data. *33*

home page The first page that your Internet browser shows you, or the first page of a company's Web site, or a Web page created for personal use. *212,217*

http HyperText Transport Protocol. An Internet Web-page address. *211*

I/O devices Input/output devices. Devices to let your computer communicate with humans & other computers. Examples: the keyboard & mouse (input); printer & monitor (output); and modem & network adapter (both input & output). *15*

icon On your screen, a tiny picture that represents a command or file. If you click on the icon by using your mouse, the computer will perform the command or open the file. *82,93,109,150*

IDE Integrated Drive Electronics. A fast type of disk drive. An IDE drive can't hold more than 528 megabytes; to hold more, get an Extended IDE drive instead. *37*

iMac The most popular kind of Mac computer because it's the cheapest. It has a built-in 15" monitor, comes in wild colors, and is shaped like an airplane's nose cone. *11,28,85,86*

infinite loop In a program, a routine that continuously repeats itself and never stops repeating. *343*

ink-jet printer A printer that squirts ink onto the paper, through tiny nozzles. If the printer is made by Canon, it's called a "Bubble Jet"; if made by Hewlett-Packard, it's called a "DeskJet". *45,48*

input device Any device that sends info into the computer, from a human or another source. The most popular input devices are the keyboard, mouse, joystick, microphone, and scanner. *15*

power supply A computer component that converts line voltage from a wall electrical outlet to the voltages needed by the computer components. Also called an "AC/DC power transformer". *16,67*

ppm Pages per minute. Used for measuring a laser printer's speed. *53*

prompt Any message that appears on your screen and waits for you to reply. For example, when you're giving MS-DOS commands you see a prompt that says "C:\>". *116,135,349,420*

proportional font A typestyle in which some characters are wider than others. For example, in a proportional font, the letter "m" is wider than the letter "i". It's the opposite of "monospaced font". *51*

pull-down menu A menu where you usually see just the menu's title. When you click that title, the rest of the menu appears. *84,109,151*

RAM Random-access memory. Memory chips that store info just temporarily and erase the info when the computer's turned off. *15,29,69,70,95,131,267,580,587*

read-only file A file that the computer refuses to change or delete, because the file was marked "read-only" by DOS's ATTRIB command. *144*

reboot the computer Restart the computer. To do that, flip the computer's power switch off then on, or press the restart button, or simultaneously press three weird keys (Ctrl, Alt, and DELETE). *137*

registered user A software owner who, being the responsible type who gives the paperboy a nice tip each holiday, mailed in the registration card after installing the program. *66*

relational database A type of database that lets more than one data file be open at once, letting data in one file be linked to data in another. *255*

resolution How many dots ("pixels") are shown on the screen. For example, the resolution can be 640-by-480 or 1024-by-768 pixels. Used for measuring a monitor's quality based on its sharpness & clarity. *42,383,575*

right-click Position the mouse pointer on an item and click the mouse's rightmost button. *102*

ROM Read-only memory. Memory chips that contain permanent info which can't be modified. *15,31*

root directory A disk's main directory, which contains all the other directories and files. *120*

save Copy the current file to a disk (hard or floppy), so you can use the file again later. *100,155,170,185,198,246*

scanner A device that copies printed info or photographs into the computer. The info is then stored as a graphics file. *13,56,277*

screen dump A printed copy of the current display, usually generated by pressing the Print Screen key. *143*

SCSI Small Computer System Interface. A fast type of disk drive (or disk-controller card). *37*

sector A section of a disk. *33,123*

seek time How long you must wait for the disk drive's head to move to the track containing your data. *37*

server A network's main computer. The files on its hard disk can be accessed by the other networked computers. It runs the network software. Typically it has a bigger hard drive and more RAM than the other networked computers. *11,232*

shareware A program you can use free for a while (typically 2 or 3 months). When the free period ends, you're supposed to mail the program's author a donation or stop using the program. *66*

shift-click Hold down the shift key while clicking the mouse's button. *155,158*

SIMM Single In-line Memory Module. The most common type of RAM memory card. *15,30*

site license A contract between a firm and a software company that lets the firm install the same program on many computers. *66*

sneaker net The cheapest type of network. To share info, copy it onto a floppy disk and walk it over to the other computer. Also called "Nike Net". *235*

software In a narrow sense, "software" means "programs" (including application programs and also the operating system). The word "software" is often used more broadly, to include *all* info that the computer handles: programs and also the data. *16,60,71*

Sound Blaster The most popular sound card. Most games and programs require that your sound card be "Sound Blaster compatible". *40,56*

sound card An expansion card that lets you attach stereo speakers to your computer. Most games require a sound card. *15,56,70*

sound driver Software that makes your sound card work. *135*

source code The original version of a program, in the original programming language. *562*

Start menu Windows 95's main menu, shown when you click the Start button. *95,105*

surge suppressor A device to protect your computer from power surges. One end of it has an electric cord (which you plug into your office's wall); the other end has several electrical outlets, into which you plug the computer, printer, and monitor. *59*

SVGA video Super Video Graphics Array. A type of monitor that can handle a resolution of 800 by 600 pixels. The best SVGA monitors can handle resolutions that are even higher. *42,69*

system files Program files that are fundamental parts of the operating system and required before the computer can run other programs. On a computer using MS-DOS, the main system files are MSDOS.SYS, IO.SYS, and COMMAND.COM. *132*

tape drive A drive that stores data on tape. *58*

telecommunication Using a modem and telephone lines to communicate with other computers. *57,205*

terminal A device (usually a keyboard with a monitor) to communicate with a main computer elsewhere by modem or network. Also, "Terminal" is the name of a communication program included with Windows. *43,205*

toolbar In a program, a strip of buttons that perform frequently-used commands. *165,170,175,184,587*

touch screen An input device that lets you touch the screen to run commands, instead of using the keyboard or mouse. *56*

touchpad An input device consisting of a small (usually 2-inch) pad and 1 or 2 buttons. Modern notebook computers use it instead of a mouse. Glide your finger along the pad to move the pointer on your screen. Use the buttons or tap the pad to "click" on an icon on your screen. *14,56*

tower computer A computer case built to stand on the floor. Tower computers typically contain more room than desktop computers (to hold extra drives) and come in three general sizes "mini tower" (18 inches tall), "mid tower" (24 inches), and "full tower" (32 inches). *13,70*

trackball An input device consisting of a ball set in a cage and 1 or 2 buttons. Some notebook computers use it instead of a mouse. Roll the ball within its cage to move the pointer on your screen. *56*

tractor-feed paper Paper that comes in a long, continuous sheet and has holes in its left and right margins. When it's fed into a "tractor-feed printer", the printer's tractors clamp down on the paper and pull it through. When the printing is finished, the user tears off the output, using perforations in the paper. *52*

True Type font The standard type of font used by Windows. It's also available for the Mac. Each True Type font can be resized and prints the same size on paper as on the screen, so the screen provides an accurate mock-up of what you'll see on paper. *100,167*

upgrade An upgrade (noun) is something purchased to improve what's already there. For example, a CPU upgrade makes your computer faster. An upgrade to your word-processing program adds new features. To upgrade (verb) is to add the new equipment or software. *63,65*

upload Send a file or program from your computer to a bigger computer that runs a network or bulletin board or Web site, by using network commands or a modem. *205,229*

upper memory The first 384 kilobytes of RAM after the base (conventional) memory. *30,133*

VESA local bus (VLB) Video Electronics Standards Association local bus. A fast type of bus that was popular because it could handle fast video. The newest computers use the PCI bus instead, which works even faster. *69*

VGA video Video Graphics Array. A type of monitor that can handle a resolution of 640 by 480 pixels. The best VGA monitors can handle resolutions that are even higher. *42,69,383*

video RAM The RAM on a computer's video card. *69,560*

virus Evil computer programs that hide inside other programs so they can sneak inside your computer and screw it up. Mean people write viruses. *63,120,142,592*

volume label An eleven character "name" for a disk. It's used by installation programs to determine which disk is in the drive. *124*

warm boot Restart your computer without turning the power off and on, by pressing the Control, Alt, and Delete keys simultaneously. Also called the "three-finger salute". *137*

wave-table sound The best kind of sound card, with built-in pre-recorded sounds. *70*

Web browser A program that lets you access the Internet's World Wide Web. The most popular Web browsers are Netscape Navigator and Internet Explorer. *210*

wildcard A character (such as "?" or "*") that lets you select many items matching particular criteria, while you're running a program or giving a command. *120*

Windows The most popular operating system. It lets you use a mouse, and it can run several programs simultaneously. It runs on IBM-compatible computers and makes them act somewhat like a Macintosh. *60,95,102,205,575*

World Wide Web (WWW) The most popular Internet feature. A collection of "Web pages" (containing text, graphics, and sound) that link to other Web pages. To use the World Wide Web, you need a Web browser (such as Internet Explorer or Netscape Navigator). *207,210*

Menus & icons

Languages

C & C++

Command	Page
char grade;	464
cin >>age;	460
cout <<"I love you";	457
cout.precision(15);	459
cout.setf(ios::showpoint);	459
double mortgage_rate;	460
else	461
for (int i=20; i<=29; ++i)	462
goto yummy;	462
if (age<18)	461
#include <iostream.h>	457
#include <math.h>	459
#include <stdio.h>	465
#include <string.h>	464
int n;	460
int n=3;	460
main()	465
printf("I love you");	465
putchar('A');	465
puts("I love you");	465
return (a+b)/2	463
scanf("%d",&age);	465
strcpy(y,x)	464
void main()	457
void x()	462
while (1)	461
x=3;	460
x[0]=3;	461
x();	462
++x;	460
--x;	460
// Zoo program is fishy	462
/* Zoo program is fishy */	465

JAVA

Command	Page
BufferedReader br=new etc.	469
char grade;	468
double mortgage_rate;	468
else	470
for (int i=20; i<=29; ++i)	471
if (age<18)	470
import com.ms.wfc.util.*	469
import java.io.*;	469
InputStreamReader is=etc.	469
int n;	468
int n=3;	468
public class Class1	466
public static void etc.	466
String x;	469
System.out.print("x");	466
System.out.println("x");	466
while (i<30)	471
while (true)	471
while (true);	466
x=3;	468
x[0]=3;	468
++x;	468
--x;	468
// Zoo program is fishy	471

PASCAL

Command	Page
BEGIN;	449
ELSE	452
END.	450
FOR I := 6 TO 10 DO	453
GOTO 10;	454
IF AGE<18 THEN	452
LABEL 10;	454
PROCEDURE INSULT;	455
PROGRAM WINE;	450
READLN(X);	452
REPEAT	453
UNTIL GUESS=6;	453
VAR	451
WHILE I<1000 DO	453
WRITELN('I WOULD KISS');	449
X: ARRAY [1..5] OF REAL;	455
X: CHAR;	455
X: INTEGER;	453
X: REAL;	453
X: STRING;	455
X:=2;	453
X[1]:=2;	455
{ZELDA HATES COMPUTERS}	454

FORTRAN

Command	Page
CALL YUMMY	509
CHARACTER*50 NAME	506
CLOSE(UNIT=3)	511
COMPLEX B	509
CONTINUE	504
DATA X/8.7/, Y/1.4/	505
DIMENSION X(4)	504
DO 30 I=80,100	504
DOUBLE PRECISION A	508
ELSE	503
END	496
END IF	501
FORMAT (1X,'CHIPMUNKS')	496
FUNCTION F(X)	511
GO TO 10	498
GO TO (10,100,20,350), I	504
IF (I .LT. 5) J=3	503
IF (I .LT. 5) THEN	503
IF (X) 20,50,90	504
IMPLICIT DOUBLE etc.	508
JUNKY=-47	499
JUNKY(1)=-47	504
OPEN(UNIT=3, DEVICE=etc.	511
PRINT 10	496
READ 20, N	502
RETURN	509
STOP	498
SUBROUTINE YUMMY	509
WRITE(3,10) A	511

BASIC

BASIC index is on pp. 333-334.

DBASE

DBASE index is on page 472.

COBOL

Command	Page
ACCEPT K.	516
ADD 7 TO A.	515
CLOSE POEM-FILE.	520
COMPUTE K = 53 + 4.	515
DISPLAY "LIFE STINKS".	512
GO TO MAIN-ROUTINE.	519
IF I > 5 etc.	518
MERGE SORT-FILE etc.	526
MOVE "HER" TO K.	514
OPEN OUTPUT POEM-FILE.	520
PERFORM HATE-IT 6 TIMES.	513
READ P-FILE AT END etc.	521
SORT SORT-FILE etc.	525
STOP RUN.	512
SUBTRACT 4 FROM B.	515
WRITE POEM-LINE.	521

Outline	Page
IDENTIFICATION DIVISION.	512
PROGRAM-ID.	512
AUTHOR.	512
INSTALLATION.	527
DATE-WRITTEN.	527
DATE-COMPILED.	527
SECURITY.	527
ENVIRONMENT DIVISION.	512
CONFIGURATION SECTION.	512
SOURCE-COMPUTER.	512
OBJECT-COMPUTER.	512
SPECIAL-NAMES.	517
INPUT-OUTPUT SECTION.	520
FILE-CONTROL.	520
DATA DIVISION.	512
FILE SECTION.	520
FD	520
SD	525
WORKING-STORAGE SECTION.	514
PROCEDURE DIVISION.	512

EASY

Command	Page
DATA MEAT	540
GET X	540
HERE IS FRED	540
HOW TO PRETEND	540
IF X<3	540
LET R=4	540
LOOP	540
PICK SCORE	540
PREPARE X(100)	540
REPEAT	540
SAY 2+2	539
SKIP	540

8088 Assembler

Command	Page
ADD AX,5	565
DB "I LOVE YOU$"	566
DEC AX	565
INC AX	565
INT 20	566
INT 21	565
JMP 104	565
MOV AX,2794	564
SUB AX,3	565

LOGO

Command & abbrev.		Page
BACK 50	BK	488
CATALOG		495
CLEAN		489
CLEARSCREEN	CS	489
DOT [20 50]		489
EDIT "REBUKE	ED	493
END		493
ERALL		495
ERASE "PINWHEEL	ER	495
ERASEFILE "FRED		495
ERN "MAGICNUMBER		495
ERNS		495
ERPS		495
FENCE		489
FILL		489
FORWARD 50	FD	488
FULLSCREEN	FS	490
HIDETURTLE	HT	488
HOME		488
IF :N<0 [STOP]		495
LEFT 90	LT	488
LOAD "FRED		495
MAKE "AGE 21		492
MIXEDSCREEN	MS	490
PENDOWN	PD	489
PENERASE	PE	489
PENREVERSE	PX	489
PENUP	PU	489
PO "SQUARE		495
POALL		495
PONS		495
POPS		495
POTS		495
PRINT 5+2	PR	490
REPEAT 4 [FD 50]		492
RIGHT 90	RT	488
SAVE "FRED		495
SETHEADING 90	SETH	488
SETBG 1		489
SETPC 2		489
SETPOS [30 70]		488
SETSP 30		489
SETX 30		488
SETY 70		488
SHOW [MA CAN'T]		491
SHOWTURTLE	ST	488
STOP		495
TELL 1		490
TEXTSCREEN	TS	490
TO SQUARE		493
WINDOW		489
WRAP		489

LISP

Command	Page
(CAR '(WE EAT HAM))	541
(CDR '(WE EAT HAM))	541
(COND	542
(CONS 'M '(WE EAT))	541
(DEFUN (DOUBLE (X)	541
(DIFFERENCE 5 2)	541
(EXPT 5 2)	541
(PLUS 5 2)	541
(QUOTE LOVE)	541
(QUOTIENT 5 2)	541
(SETQ X 7)	541
(SUB1 N)	542
(TIMES 5 2)	541

Master index

Get more copies

You'll want more copies of *The Secret Guide to Computers* for yourself and your friends. You get quantity discounts. The books make great presents for Christmas, birthdays, graduations, and celebrations. To get books or free brochures, you can use this page's coupon. Photocopy it for your friends.

Money-back guarantee

If you're not sure whether to order a book, go ahead: you can return unused books anytime for a 100% refund.

Many ways to order

The simplest way to order is to mail this page's coupon, along with a check, money order, credit-card info, or cash. Here are other ways to order….

You can **visit** us in New Hampshire to pick up the books personally: phone 603-666-6644 for directions and a pickup time.

To order by **credit card**, mail this coupon or phone 603-666-6644 or send e-mail to russ@secretfun.com (if you don't mind sending e-mail that's not "secure"). Give your credit-card number, expiration date, and name printed on the card. We take Master Card, Visa, American Express and Discover.

We can **bill** you, and make the bill be due in 30 days, if you bought at least 10 books from us before or you're employed by (or retired from) one of these organizations: an established computer company, bookstore, school, government agency, or public utility. Mail us this coupon or phone 603-666-6644 or send e-mail to russ@secretfun.com.

Other countries

We accept 4 forms of payment from other countries:

international postal money order (written in U.S. dollars)

credit-card number (Master Card, Visa, American Express, or Discover, with expiration date and the name printed on the card)

check (written in U.S. dollars and having a U.S. or Canadian city printed somewhere on the check)

cash (we convert foreign currency & send you change)

Review copies

If you write reviews for magazines, run a big computer department, teach many computer students, or plan to introduce the book to at least 100 people, phone 603-666-6644 to request a complimentary book for review.

Special services

To discover our special services, read page 9 of *The Secret Guide to Computers*.

CUT OUT THIS COUPON

Books with discounts

The Secret Guide to Computers lists for **$16.50**. To pay less, team up with your friends.

20% discount if you order at least 2 books: pay just	$13.20 per book.
40% discount if you order at least 4 books: pay just	$9.90 per book.
60% discount if you order at least 60 books: pay just	$6.60 per book.

Because of those discounts, don't order 3 books (order 4 instead); don't order 40-59 books (order 60 instead).

How many books do you want? _____

Free brochures & bulletins

Peek at the **Secret Brochure** about our books and services! How many **free** copies of it do you want, for yourself and friends? _____

To get **Secret Bulletins**, **free**, revealing the next edition of *The Secret Guide to Computers*, *Secret Guide to Tricky Living*, courses, & videos, put × in this box: ❑

Address

Print the name and address where you want the goods sent.

Optional: your phone numbers will help us if we have questions about your order; your e-mail address will get you our free e-mail newsletter. If you want goods sent to *several* addresses, write a note; for example, if you want 2 books *but sent to 2 separate addresses*, you get a 20% discount *but pay 2 shipping charges.*

Shipping (typically just $1 total)

For shipping to the USA, we offer 3 methods:

Method	Usual time to ship the books from us to you		Shipping charge to an address
standard	1 week to ZIP codes under 27000	1½ weeks elsewhere	just **$1** total, even if order is huge
UPS	2 days to ZIP codes under 27000	1 week elsewhere	just **$5** total, even if order is huge
air	2 days to ZIP codes under 27000	3 days elsewhere	multiply number of books by **$3**

The UPS method is available just if you order at least 2 books, stay in the original 48 states or DC (not in AK, HI, PR, APO, FPO), and give a street address (not a PO Box).

For shipping to other countries, we offer 2 methods:

Method	Usual time to ship the books from us to you	Shipping charge
standard	2½ weeks to Canada, 4 weeks to Britain, 6 weeks elsewhere	multiply number of books by **$2**
air	1 week to Canada/Britain/Japan/Australia, 2 weeks elsewhere	multiply number of books by **$9**

Circle the shipping method you want.

Final steps

Multiply the number of books by the price per book, then add the shipping charge, and write the sum here: $_____.

Which payment method do you prefer? Put × in the box:

❑ **check or money order** (made out to *The Secret Guide to Computers*; we ship *immediately*)
❑ **credit card** (MasterCard/Visa/AmEx/Discover; at bottom write your number, expiration date, signature)
❑ **cash** (we ship *immediately*; we accept cash from all countries, convert foreign currency, and send change)
❑ **bill** (available just if you bought at least 10 books from us before or belong to organizations listed at left)

If the books are a gift to a friend, include a greeting card or note for us to give your friend. On the back of this coupon, please write comments (pro or con) about the *Guide*.

Mail to *The Secret Guide to Computers*, 196 Tiffany Lane, Manchester NH 03104-4782.

Get more copies

You'll want more copies of *The Secret Guide to Computers* for yourself and your friends. You get quantity discounts. The books make great presents for Christmas, birthdays, graduations, and celebrations. To get books or free brochures, you can use this page's coupon. Photocopy it for your friends.

Money-back guarantee

If you're not sure whether to order a book, go ahead: you can return unused books anytime for a 100% refund.

Many ways to order

The simplest way to order is to mail this page's coupon, along with a check, money order, credit-card info, or cash. Here are other ways to order....

> You can **visit** us in New Hampshire to pick up the books personally: phone 603-666-6644 for directions and a pickup time.
>
> To order by **credit card**, mail this coupon or phone 603-666-6644 or send e-mail to russ@secretfun.com (if you don't mind sending e-mail that's not "secure"). Give your credit-card number, expiration date, and name printed on the card. We take Master Card, Visa, American Express and Discover.
>
> We can **bill** you, and make the bill be due in 30 days, if you bought at least 10 books from us before or you're employed by (or retired from) one of these organizations: an established computer company, bookstore, school, government agency, or public utility. Mail us this coupon or phone 603-666-6644 or send e-mail to russ@secretfun.com.

Other countries

We accept 4 forms of payment from other countries:

> **international postal money order** (written in U.S. dollars)
>
> **credit-card number** (Master Card, Visa, American Express, or Discover, with expiration date and the name printed on the card)
>
> **check** (written in U.S. dollars and having a U.S. or Canadian city printed somewhere on the check)
>
> **cash** (we convert foreign currency & send you change)

Review copies

If you write reviews for magazines, run a big computer department, teach many computer students, or plan to introduce the book to at least 100 people, phone 603-666-6644 to request a complimentary book for review.

Special services

To discover our special services, read page 9 of *The Secret Guide to Computers*.

CUT OUT THIS COUPON

Books with discounts

The Secret Guide to Computers lists for **$16.50**. To pay less, team up with your friends.

> **20% discount if you order at least   2 books: pay just $13.20 per book.**
> **40% discount if you order at least   4 books: pay just $9.90 per book.**
> **60% discount if you order at least 60 books: pay just $6.60 per book.**

Because of those discounts, don't order 3 books (order 4 instead); don't order 40-59 books (order 60 instead).

How many books do you want? _____

Free brochures & bulletins

Peek at the **Secret Brochure** about our books and services!
How many **free** copies of it do you want, for yourself and friends? _____

To get **Secret Bulletins, free**, revealing the next edition of *The Secret Guide to Computers*, *Secret Guide to Tricky Living*, courses, & videos, put × in this box: ❑

Address

Print the name and address where you want the goods sent.

> Optional: your phone numbers will help us if we have questions about your order; your e-mail address will get you our free e-mail newsletter. If you want goods sent to *several* addresses, write a note; for example, if you want 2 books *but sent to 2 separate addresses*, you get a 20% discount *but pay 2 shipping charges*.

Shipping (typically just $1 total)

For shipping to the USA, we offer 3 methods:

Method	Usual time to ship the books from us to you		Shipping charge to an address
standard	1 week to ZIP codes under 27000	1½ weeks elsewhere	just **$1** total, even if order is huge
UPS	2 days to ZIP codes under 27000	1 week elsewhere	just **$5** total, even if order is huge
air	2 days to ZIP codes under 27000	3 days elsewhere	multiply number of books by **$3**

The UPS method is available just if you order at least 2 books, stay in the original 48 states or DC (not in AK, HI, PR, APO, FPO), and give a street address (not a PO Box).

For shipping to other countries, we offer 2 methods:

Method	Usual time to ship the books from us to you	Shipping charge
standard	2½ weeks to Canada, 4 weeks to Britain, 6 weeks elsewhere	multiply number of books by **$2**
air	1 week to Canada/Britain/Japan/Australia, 2 weeks elsewhere	multiply number of books by **$9**

Circle the shipping method you want.

Final steps

Multiply the number of books by the price per book, then add the shipping charge, and write the sum here: $_____.

Which payment method do you prefer? Put × in the box:

> ❑ **check or money order** (made out to *The Secret Guide to Computers*; we ship *immediately*)
> ❑ **credit card** (MasterCard/Visa/AmEx/Discover; at bottom write your number, expiration date, signature)
> ❑ **cash** (we ship *immediately*; we accept cash from all countries, convert foreign currency, and send change)
> ❑ **bill** (available just if you bought at least 10 books from us before or belong to organizations listed at left)

If the books are a gift to a friend, include a greeting card or note for us to give your friend. On the back of this coupon, please write comments (pro or con) about the *Guide*.

Mail to *The Secret Guide to Computers*, 196 Tiffany Lane, Manchester NH 03104-4782.